The New York Times
20th Century in Review

THE VIETNAM WAR

VOLUME II: 1969–2000

Other Titles in
The New York Times 20th Century in Review

The Balkans
The Cold War
The Gay Rights Movement
Political Censorship
The Rise of the Global Economy

The New York Times
20th Century in Review

THE VIETNAM WAR

VOLUME II: 1969–2000

Editor
Mark Lawrence

Introduction by David K. Shipler

Series Editor
David Morrow

FITZROY DEARBORN PUBLISHERS
CHICAGO   LONDON

For information write to:

FITZROY DEARBORN PUBLISHERS
919 North Michigan Avenue, Suite 760
Chicago IL 60611
USA

or

FITZROY DEARBORN PUBLISHERS
310 Regent Street
London W1B 3AX
England

British Library and Library of Congress Cataloging in Publication Data are available.

ISBN 1-57958-368-7

First published in the USA and UK 2001

Interior Design and Typeset by Print Means Inc., New York, New York

Printed by Edwards Brothers, Ann Arbor, Michigan

Cover Design by Peter Aristedes, Chicago Advertising and Design, Chicago, Illinois

CONTENTS
VOLUME I: 1945–1969

Preface by Mark Lawrence vii

Introduction by David K. Shipler xiii

Part I The First Indochina War, 1945–1954 1
- The Nationalist Surge 1
- The Franco-U.S. Partnership 13
- Dienbienphu and Geneva 36

Part II The Nation-Building Years 1954–1961 61
- The Two Vietnams 61
- Toward a Second Indochina War 89

Part III Kennedy and the Mounting Commitment, 1961–1963 99
- Neutralization in Laos, New Commitments in Vietnam 99
- The End of the Diem Regime 136

Part IV Going to War, 1963–1965 169
- To the Brink 169
- The Bombing Campaign 198
- Launching the Ground War 222

Part V America at War, 1965–1968 257
- Waging Limited War 257
- Crisis in the South 289
- Intensifying the War, Probing for Peace 304
- Opposition and Optimism: The Year Before Tet 344

Part VI Tet and After, 1968–1969 393
- The Tet Offensive 393
- Months of Crisis 434
- Fighting and Negotiating 474

VOLUME II: 1969–2000

Part VII Nixon and the Expanded War, 1969–1971 499
- New Departures, Old Problems 499
- Cambodia and Laos 567
- The Pentagon Papers 623

Part VIII The End of the American War, 1971–1975 639
- The War for the South 639
- Making Peace 676
- The War After the War 728

Part IX The Aftermath of War, 1975–2000 773
Nations in Torment 773
Contested Legacies 809
Beyond the Cold War 857

General Index 903

Byline Index 921

PART VII

NIXON AND THE EXPANDED WAR, 1969–1971

NEW DEPARTURES, OLD PROBLEMS

January 20, 1969

THOUSANDS OF WAR FOES STAGE COUNTER-INAUGURAL MARCH DOWN PENNSYLVANIA AVE.

PROTEST MARRED BY ROCK THROWING

3 Policemen Hurt—

Young Militants Mostly Stick to Banners and Chants

By BEN A. FRANKLIN

Special to The New York Times

WASHINGTON, Jan. 19—The antiwar and anti-Nixon Left sent thousands of militant—but for the most part genial—young marchers down Pennsylvania Avenue today. Symbolically they marched in reverse, from west to east, in a counter-inaugural parade. About 18 persons were arrested.

The nonviolent performance of most of the demonstrators was marred as night fell by sporadic incidents of rock throwing at the police. About a dozen youths were arrested outside a reception for Vice President-elect Spiro T. Agnew at the Smithsonian Institution as the march broke up. Three policemen, including a deputy chief of the United States Park Police, were reported injured when a handful of demonstrators ripped planks from outdoor trash bins and used them as clubs against the police.

The protest march of the National Mobilization Committee to End the War in Vietnam came just 24 hours before President-elect Richard M. Nixon rides the other way—from his swearing in at the United States Capitol on the east to take up residence in the White House on the west. The marchers' mood appeared dampened by the prospect of Mr. Nixon's presiding over the liquidation of the war.

Muddy at Rallying Point

A rainy morning and an afternoon of overcast skies with a raw wind and temperatures in the mid-40's also seemed to cool potential confrontations. The ground at the demonstrators' rallying point on the Mall, a 100 by 300-foot circus tent, was churned into a cold, sticky expanse of mud.

The marchers carried banners and chanted slogans that might have shocked some Republicans. One youth wearing a Nixon mask marched the entire 20-block distance in a mime of picking his nose. Another group chanted. "Two, four six, eight—Organize and smash the state!"

One of the hundreds of placards carried by marchers, in a play on Mr. Nixon's 1968 campaign slogan, "Nixon's the One," called the President-elect "The No. 1 War Criminal." Another, a 15 foot banner carried by a group called "the revolutionary contingent," proclaimed "Victory for the Vietcong." The group chanted "Ho, Ho, Ho Chi Minh, the N.L.F. is going to win."

But there were other signs that said "We miss Bobby," a reference to the late Senator Robert F. Kennedy, and "Freedom and Peace party—Coney Island."

Theme of Banners

The marchers were estimated by the police to number no more than 5,000, and by the demonstration leaders, 10,000 to 12,000.

Their banners included everything from American "racism" and "fascism" to "liberation for women" and "freedom for Greece." But the main themes of the banners were "peace now" and "join us." The parade was led by four men described as "active duty G.I.'s" to illustrate what demonstration leaders said was antiwar activity in the armed forces.

The downtown Government offices area, usually nearly deserted on Sunday in January, was full of inaugural traffic. The parade permit gave the marchers a route that included only the four eastbound lanes of Pennsylvania Avenue, south of the central dividing line. Automobiles in the westbound lanes and on cross streets were jammed for the 15 minutes it took the six-block-long parade to pass.

Some of the arrests for disorderly conduct were made at the end of the demonstration after a dispute between activists and more restrained elements of the march over whether to haul down the United States flag in front of the Department of Health, Education and Welfare at Third Street and Independence Avenue, Northwest. There was a scuffle there, too, as some marchers sought to cross the police lines and move toward the Capitol.

Tonight, so many young marchers and Washington-area teen-agers tried to attend the counter inaugural ball in the tent by the Tidal Basin that hundreds had to mill around outside.

The mud was so thick that it pulled shoes from feet. Inside, rock music was provided by the Fugs and a number of local bands. The program was to include the "inhoguration" of a pig as a symbol of contempt of the events in Washington.

At a rally before the march in the rented tent of the National Mobilization Committee—called "the Mob" by the marchers—the rhetoric was fierce but there were repeated calls for "responsibility."

The New York Times

ANTI-PARADE: The protest march moving toward the Capitol along Pennsylvania Avenue in Washington. Banners proclaimed opposition to new Administration and Vietnam War.

Phil Ochs, the folk singer, was cheered when he observed that it was necessary "to have a sense of dignity along with militancy."

"The country is degenerating," he said, that there no sense in our joining them."

Mr. Ochs appeared to hold the attention of those at the rally far more easily than a long list of other speakers who excoriated "racism" in the United States, "the imperialism of the United Fruit Company in Guatemala," the "capitalist, war-profit system."

The speakers included David Dellinger, chairman of the National Mobilization Committee, and three present or former Army enlisted men, but not—as stated earlier—Kathleen Cleaver, the wife of Eldridge Cleaver, the Black Panther leader now a fugitive from a parole violation charge in California. There were few Negroes in the march.

* * *

January 26, 1969

FIRM BUFFER ZONE IS URGED BY LODGE AT VIETNAM TALKS

He Terms a Demilitarized Area the 'First Practical Move Toward Peace'

FOE COOL TO PROPOSAL

Session Lasts 6½ Hours— U. S. Delegate Calls for Goodwill of All Parties

By HENRY TANNER
Special to The New York Times

PARIS, Jan. 25—Henry Cabot Lodge, in his first appearance as chief United States delegate to the Vietnam peace talks, called today for the immediate restoration of a genuine demilitarized zone astride the border between South and North Vietnam as a first "practical move toward peace."

Although they spoke critically of Mr. Lodge's presentation, spokesmen for North Vietnam and the National Liberation Front, or Vietcong, seemed to take care in briefings after the meeting to avoid an outright rejection of the American's proposal.

Mr. Lodge appealed in the first plenary session of the expanded talks to the goodwill of all the delegates. "Let us—together—take up the task of peace," he said.

Emphasizes the Future

The United States delegate added: "No purpose is served by repeating the list of familiar charges to recite once more the chronology which brought us here. Our responsibility is to the future, not the past."

Marking the Nixon Administration's first venture into public diplomacy, he quoted from the President's inaugural address the following words, among others: "We cannot learn from one another unless we stop shouting at one another—until we speak quietly enough so that our words can be heard as well as our voices."

Supervision Proposed

Mr. Lodge, in submitting his proposal for restoration of a genuine demilitarized zone, also proposed more effective international supervision.

He said that the nations of the area, which had "the most crucial interest in peace and stability in the region," should be involved in controlling any agreement that might eventually be reached.

He urged that the restoration be immediate and that all negotiating partners commit themselves publicly to the project. He also called for a mutual withdrawal of "external" military forces and for an early release of prisoners.

At his briefing after the meeting, Tran Hoai Nam, spokesman for the Front, confined himself to criticizing "the manner" in which Mr. Lodge had made his proposals and added that the Front's answer would be "made at the coming meetings."

Nguyen Thanh Le, spokesman for the Hanoi delegation, said that the chief North Vietnamese negotiator, Mr. Thuy, in "preliminary remarks" to the plenary meeting had termed Mr. Lodge's proposal "a maneuver to camouflage the American aggression" but had reserved the right to comment at future meetings on the American initiative.

Mr. Lodge was cautiously optimistic as he returned to the United States Embassy on Place de la Concorde for another meeting with his staff.

"The fact that we all sit together in a room for six-and-a-half hours and talk in a correct, courteous tone is in itself a gain—that is good," he said. He added: "It is a very good sign when you are through for the day and everyone agrees unanimously to the next meeting at a certain time."

This, Mr. Lodge said, should be the spirit of the conference.

60 Delegates Participate

Sixty delegates took part in today's session—15 each for the Americans, the South Vietnamese, the North Vietnamese and the National Liberation front. They were sitting around a round table, 27 feet in diameter, with two gaps marked by small secretarial tables separating the Communist teams from the American and South Vietnamese teams.

A lower-level meeting of fewer delegates around a smaller round table last Saturday was devoted to procedural questions and paved the way for today's meeting.

The next plenary session will be held Thursday. A proposal to this effect, made by Pham Dang Lam, the South Vietnamese representative, was adopted without discussion in a short exchange that followed the formal statements by the four chief negotiators.

Mr. Lodge's was the shortest of the four statements made today at the Center for International Conferences, formerly the Majestic Hotel.

Pham Dang Lam, the representative of the Saigon Government, and Tran Buu Kiem, the representative of the National Liberation Front, made long, bitter speeches, stating their

United Press International

PEACE TALKS OPEN IN PARIS: U.S. delegation is at front, with Henry Cabot Lodge turning to face camera. Opposite U.S. are North Vietnamese delegates, with aides at the rear. National Liberation Front is represented at left, and South Vietnam at right. Out of range at top right and bottom left there are small tables for clerical aides.

respective positions in great detail and hurling charges of crime and aggression at "the other side."

Xuan Thuy, the North Vietnamese delegate, using far milder language than Mr. Kiem, appeared to be at pains to leave the center of the stage to the Front.

Timing Held Significant

William J. Jorden, the spokesman for the United States delegation, said later that the significance of Mr. Lodge's proposal for immediate restoration of the demilitarized zone lay in its timing rather than its substance.

W. Averell Harriman, Mr. Lodge's predecessor, had also made this suggestion, Mr. Jorden said. But he added that at that time the North Vietnamese were refusing to talk about anything but cessation of American bombing.

"We took them seriously," Mr. Jorden said. "Now the bombing has stopped and substantitive talks have started. [the North Vietnamese] have been saying they would talk about anything once the bombing stopped."

Mr. Jorden added that he was "not hopeful" for an early acceptance by the Communist delegations of Mr. Lodge's proposal.

He said that Mr. Thuy, in a brief statement at the end of today's meeting, said that "in the past" the North Vietnamese had rejected American proposals on the demilitarized zone. Mr. Jorden added that the American delegation did not regard this as a definite rejection. According to Mr. Jorden, the meeting was held in an atmosphere of courtesy. "The language sounded harsh but the tone was restrained and serious," he said of the statements made by Mr. Kiem and Mr. Thuy.

The harshness in Mr. Kiem's declaration included charges that the United States was pursuing "criminal objectives" and "extremely perfidious and cruel" policies in Vietnam and that the Saigon Government was "tyrannical and blood-thirsty."

His statement included a history of United States intervention in Vietnam, as the Communists see it, as well as a restatement of the program of the Front—unity of the Vietnamese people, victory, the overthrow of the Saigon "puppet regime," creation of a national coalition government and rebuilding of a "democratic, peaceful, neutral and prosperous South Vietnam, which will move toward a peaceful reunification" of the country.

Mr. Kiem is a slim, craggy-faced man of 48 who has been one of the key organizers of the Liberation Front and as chairman of the Front's External Relations committee is its "foreign minister."

Organized Youth Front

A native of the Mekong Delta in the South, he was graduated from the University of Hanoi and became a North Vietnamese citizen. Before slipping back into the South, he organized the "Communist Youth Front" in the North and held posts in President Ho Chi Minh's Administration.

Mr. Thuy, round-faced and white-haired, made some of the standard references to American "aggression" as "the deep root of the trouble" of Vietnam. He repeated a phrase that had also been used by Mr. Kiem: "If the Government of the United States has any real desire to seek a political solution to the problem of Vietnam, it must enter serious conversations with the National Liberation Front of South Vietnam."

The Communists have long held that the Front is the only "authentic representative of the population of South Vietnam."

Ambassador Lam, the South Vietnamese, spoke for two and a half hours, including translation from Vietnamese, far longer than any other speaker. Mr. Kiem spoke an hour and a half, Mr. Thuy just over an hour and Mr. Lodge 25 minutes.

Mr. Lam, a career diplomat and two-time Foreign Minister of the Saigon Government gave a historical survey of events since the 1954 Geneva Conference on Indochina, accusing the Communists of having been "traitors" to the country's independence. He denounced the front as the "political instrument of aggression" by the North.

He likened Vietnam to "the two other divided countries—Korea and Germany"—and insisted that "allied troops" could be withdrawn only after the "Communists have put an end to their armed aggression." "You will never be able to annex the south," he told the North Vietnamese.

* * *

January 29, 1969

VIETCONG REJECT NIXON PROPOSALS

Insist on Political Terms—Set 7-Day Tet Truce

By PAUL HOFMANN
Special to The New York Times

PARIS, Jan. 28—The Vietcong delegation at the peace talks here rejected today President Nixon's remarks on Vietnam yesterday, and reaffirmed that the United States must accept the political demands of the guerrilla movement and North Vietnam.

At his news conference, Mr. Nixon reiterated allied proposals for a restoration of the demilitarized zone, a guaranteed mutual withdrawal of external forces in South Vietnam and an exchange of prisoners as a basis on which progress could be made in Paris. The proposals were put before the peace talks on Saturday by Ambassador Henry Cabot Lodge, the chief United States representative at the talks.

[In a broadcast monitored Wednesday in Saigon, the Vietcong proclaimed a ceasefire Feb. 15 to Feb. 22 for Tet, the Lunar New Year, according to The Associated Press.]

The Vietcong—or, formally, National Liberation Front—expressed its reaction to Mr. Nixon's views in a statement issued in Paris. The North Vietnamese also issued a statement here, rebuffing an overture for private contacts between the Saigon regime and "the other side." That overture was made yesterday by South Vietnam's Vice President, Nguyen Cao Ky.

Mr. Ky, who is coordinator of the South Vietnamese delegation, mentioned possible confidential talks with the Hanoi Vietcong side in an impromptu news conference yesterday.

The Vietcong statement asserted by implication that President Nixon had attempted to "mask the aggressive designs of the United States" in Vietnam.

The phrase was taken from a rebuttal that the Vietcong's chief negotiator here, Tran Buu Kiem, was said to have made after declarations by Ambassador Lodge Saturday, when the first plenary meeting of the broadened peace talks took place.

The Vietcong statement asserted that President Nixon had spoken about Vietnam's problems in exactly the same way as Mr. Lodge had on Saturday, and that Mr. Kiem's comment needed no elaboration.

The statement added that acceptance by the United States of North Vietnam's four-point program and of the Vietcong's five points were the only "correct basis for a political settlement of the Vietnam problem."

The four points and five points, which were formally introduced in the talks by the North Vietnamese and Vietcong chief delegates Saturday, differ only slightly. They call for an end to "American aggression," withdrawal of United States and non-Vietnamese allied troops from South Vietnam, a settlement of South Vietnam's internal affairs without foreign interference, gradual and peaceful reunification between North and South Vietnam, and a policy of neutrality for South Vietnam.

The United States and South Vietnamese delegations held consultations today preparatory to the next plenary four-way meeting on Thursday.

A special representative of President Nguyen Van Thieu of South Vietnam, Nguyen Phu Duc, arrived earlier today, and participated this afternoon in a working session at the United States Embassy.

Conference observers noted today that despite the enemy's insistence on a political settlement, the Vietcong negotiating team had recently been reinforced by a military expert. He is Dang Van Thu, described as a "superior cadre of the Popular Liberation Armed Forces of South Vietnam." "Cadre" is Communist parlance for officer or organization leader. The Liberation Army is the official name of the guerrillas.

* * *

March 7, 1969

MR. NIXON AND THE VIETNAM CASUALTIES

By JAMES RESTON

In a few weeks, at the present casualty rate, more Americans will have been killed in Vietnam than in any other conflict in U.S. history except the Civil War and the two World Wars.

Last week, 453 Americans were killed in Vietnam and 2,593 wounded. This brought the total U.S. combat dead to 32,376—very close to the 33,629 total for the entire Korean War.

In the face of this terrible waste and killing, the urgent need for a new and creative effort to end the fighting is manifest. The negotiators are stuck in Paris. The new government in Washington is following the same old policies. The language of the war is lower but the cost is higher.

The Death Talks

In fact, 9,425 Americans have been killed in Vietnam since the preliminary peace talks began in Paris last May 13, and 2,319 of these have died since South Vietnam joined the enlarged talks last Dec. 7.

The carnage among the Vietnamese meanwhile is almost beyond comprehension. On the enemy side alone, according to the official U.S. command in Saigon, at least 457,132 Vietcong and North Vietnamese soldiers have been killed since the beginning of 1961 when the United States entered the war, and nobody has the heart to estimate the dead among the civilian population, North and South.

The reaction to all this is remarkably casual. Even expressions of pity are now seldom heard. The enemy continues his rocket attacks on Saigon. Ambassador Henry Cabot Lodge says in Paris that "the consequences of these attacks" are the enemy's responsibility. President Nixon says that if the attacks go on, he will make "some response that is appropriate." And Secretary of Defense Laird says in Saigon: "We will not tolerate continued enemy escalation of the war."

There is not even any agreement on the terms of the Paris peace talks or on whether the enemy was first to step up the military pressure, or vice versa. Washington says it had an "understanding" that there would be no enemy attacks on the cities if it stopped the bombing of North Vietnam. Hanoi holds there was no such understanding. Hanoi says the U.S. kept up the bombing pressure and the search-and-destroy raids early this year; Washington says it did so in response to the enemy's increasing pressure.

Meanwhile, despite all the recent expressions of mutual understanding between President Nixon and officials of the Soviet Union and the Western European countries, the efforts of London, Paris, Moscow and even the United Nations to bring about a cease-fire have virtually ceased.

The Critical Point

In this situation, it is fairly clear that President Nixon is not going to get a settlement without a shift in policy. He has apparently been hoping that by sounding reasonable toward both Saigon and Hanoi, the enemy will come forward with the compromise President Johnson could not get, but this is not forthcoming.

The sticking point for the enemy is his doubt that the United States intends to withdraw from that peninsula. Hanoi simply cannot believe that the United States would sacrifice over 32,000 lives and spend over $30 billion a year in defense of a principle, then make peace and take its men back home.

In actual fact, there is reason for believing that if Mr. Nixon could get a negotiated peace, he would be willing to do precisely that, but he has not made the point clear, and so long as the enemy is in doubt about this critical point, the chances are that the war will go on indefinitely.

If this intention were emphatically stated instead of merely being discussed around the White House as a likely objective of U.S. policy, then it might be possible to bring the influence of the world community, including the Soviet Union, to bear on the Paris talks.

The Wishful Waiting

But the President hesitates. He is still hoping the old policy will work simply because it is in new hands and is being expressed in different language. He is back on the brink again of one more military response to the enemy's attacks, though there is no evidence that the enemy, having lost over 450,000 men, will hesitate to keep on sacrificing until it is sure American power will definitely be removed as part of any settlement.

Sooner or later, Mr. Nixon will probably have to come to this decision, and the longer he waits, the harder it will be to make the switch, the greater the danger of one more round, of escalation, and the higher the death tolls.

* * *

March 9, 1969

THE PRESIDENT'S VIETNAM TEST

The challenge confronting President Nixon in the current Vietcong offensive is to resist the Lyndon Johnson tendency to react, in the words of one high official of the old Administration, "as if his manhood were at stake."

The sudden doubling of American casualties in South Vietnam is a bitter new indication of the high price of this dismal war, one that makes clearer than ever the necessity for ending it with maximum speed. That endeavor will not be aided by another rash of self-defeating responses dictated by frustration and anger.

In his foreign policy news conference last week, President Nixon confirmed that the Communist attacks in South Vietnam have been "primarily directed toward military targets." Only "technically," in his phrase, do they contravene the American warning that attacks against major cities would make it impossible to maintain the bombing halt.

Several factors need consideration before an Administration decision on what to do about the present attacks. The first is that experience at all stages of the war indicate that Communist offensives soon run out of supplies and that their duration is not significantly affected by bombing North Vietnam.

Before President Johnson ordered the halt last Nov. 1, it had become abundantly clear that attempts at aerial interdiction of supply routes through North Vietnam were incapable of stopping the tortuous flow of arms and equipment into the South. Nor has the punishment and economic damage inflicted on the North ever visibly shaken Hanoi's will to fight.

The most predictable effect of precipitate resumption of the bombing would be to alienate world opinion again and hamper negotiations on Vietnam and other critical issues with the Russians. It certainly would halt the Paris talks, prolong the war and escalate the fighting, thus increasing instead of reducing the ultimate cost in American casualties.

Moreover, as former Ambassador Harriman last week told James A. Wechsler of The New York Post, the present Vietcong offensive is "essentially a response to our actions rather than a deliberate, reckless attempt to dictate the peace terms or torpedo the talks." General Abrams after the Nov. 1 bombing halt was instructed by Washington to maintain "all-out pressure on the enemy" in South Vietnam.

Pentagon figures show that from November to January the number of allied battalion-sized operations increased more than one-third, from 800 to 1,077. Of these 919 were South Vietnamese, 84 American and 74 combined. Meanwhile, the North Vietnamese pulled all but three of their 25 regiments in the northern sections of South Vietnam back across the borders. This freed more than a full division of American troops to join in maximum military pressure further south as a means of maintaining morale there and encouraging Saigon to get into the Paris talks.

American spokesmen have heralded successes on the battlefield and in renewed pacification efforts as improving both the allied bargaining position in Paris and the Saigon Government's chances for surviving a peace settlement. There have even been repeated claims that an allied military victory was ripe for the taking.

The United States simply cannot have it both ways. It cannot demand the right to press the fighting with increased vigor itself while charging doublecross whenever the Communists do the same. The sad fact is that the Paris talks have been left on dead center while Ambassador Lodge awaits a White House go-ahead for making new peace proposals or for engaging in private talks out of which the only real progress is likely to come. Everything has been stalled while the Nixon Administration completes its military and diplomatic review.

Now that the Communists have responded with a new military offensive in South Vietnam, the United States will simply have to grit its teeth and see the battle through. Hanoi as well as Washington and Saigon must once again learn the hard way that military victory is an impossibility for both sides, that the sole real hope lies in ending the drift in the peace talks. Anything either side does to retard progress there simply condemns more life and treasure to destruction in the bottomless pit that is the Vietnam war.

* * *

March 13, 1969

FIELD CHECKS IN VIETNAM SHOW ALLIES UNDERSTATED FOE'S GAINS

By CHARLES MOHR

Special to The New York Times

SAIGON, South Vietnam, March 10—Investigations in the field have indicated in case after case that the intensity and results of the current enemy offensive were understated in communiqués and by official allied spokesmen.

To longtime observers of events in Vietnam, it appeared that an effort had been made to deny the enemy a "psychological victory" by omitting important details about the attacks from official accounts—or even by denying them.

In each case, the enemy was finally driven out, and often he suffered serious losses. The contention of officials in Saigon that the attacks had essentially failed seemed justified, even after fuller details became known. One example involved Songbe, an isolated little town in the jungles about 70 miles north of Saigon. Songbe was one of more than 100 targets struck by the enemy before dawn on Feb. 23, the first day of the offensive.

That evening, the news that the senior American adviser in Songbe—a lieutenant colonel—and one of his majors had been killed reached Saigon through the informal network of concerned friends.

An American military spokesman confirmed the deaths in a telephone inquiry that night but no effort was made to disclose the news at the regular news briefing in Saigon on Monday. The information was given then only in response to a question.

On two occasions an official spokesman denied that Songbe had been "overrun" or partly occupied by enemy forces. No attempt has been made publicly or privately to correct this statement.

However, American military men on the scene have said since then that much of the town, including the American military compound, was over-run and that the two advisers were killed—possibly with satchel explosive charges—by enemy troops who found them in a mortar bunker. Other Americans fled to a South Vietnamese Army compound, which held out successfully.

Strong units of the United States First Cavalry Division (Airmobile) were later sent to Songbe to "retake it," informants said.

Another example was the attack at Dautieng, where the Third Brigade of the United States 25th Infantry Division has its headquarters on the Michelin rubber plantation, northwest of Saigon.

A communiqué said that Vietcong forces had "briefly penetrated the perimeter" at Dautieng.

Witness Tells of Attack

Witnesses said that the attack had begun about 3 A. M. and that 100 to 150 enemy sappers had overrun five bunkers to gain a breach in the defenses. The enemy was not killed or driven out until daylight, sources said.

The sappers spread through the spacious plantation and got within a short distance of the important Tactical Operations Center of the brigade before they were contained. One witness said that some South Vietnamese Special Forces troops—who would not normally be present—had been the first to engage the infiltrators and helped to blunt the attack, in which 21 Americans were killed.

Meanwhile, other Vietcong had infiltrated much of Dautieng town and serious damage was done to some houses, which American troops had to shell because the Vietcong were firing from them. In addition, the Vietnamese resident manager of the rubber plantation was assassinated with a shot through the head in a nearby village.

At Mytho, a provincial capital 40 miles south of Saigon, a visitor learned that about 100 Vietcong had captured the helicopter landing pad, which borders a lake in the heart of the city. All seven of the militiaman guarding the landing pad were killed.

Enemy Force Fled

The enemy force later fled, and three battalions of Vietcong failed to reach their targets in town. This exploit, more embarrassing than important, was never reported in Saigon.

In Quangngai, in the northern part of South Vietnam, an enemy force penetrated the provincial capital and left behind 25 dead soldiers and such bulky weapons as a 57-mm recoilless rifle. The enemy killed an American official in his home, blew up a Canadian hospital and inflicted more than 20 casualties on Government troops when they counterattacked.

The penetration of the town was not mentioned, either in communiqués or oral briefings, and was brought out only in response to questioning.

Newspapermen who had witnessed the attack were solely responsible for the revelation that sappers had penetrated an American division headquarters a Cuchi, northwest of Saigon, and destroyed nine large transport helicopters.

The United States Command never revealed that at another American division base camp seven Cobra armed helicopters—which cost $350,000 each—had also been destroyed during the offensive.

* * *

March 18, 1969

M'GOVERN SCORES NIXON ON VIETNAM

Says He Holds to Johnson's 'Tragic Course,' but Other Doves Call for Patience

By JOHN W. FINNEY
Special to The New York Times

WASHINGTON, March 17—The first significant rumblings of discontent with the Administration's Vietnam policy were heard in the Senate today as Senator George S. McGovern criticized President Nixon for continuing the "tragic course" of the Johnson Administration.

In a Senate speech, Mr. McGovern, one of the more outspoken Senate doves, castigated the Administration for what he called its lack of "strength and courage to genuinely reverse our course in Vietnam."

Rather than seeking military disengagement and a settlement of the war, the South Dakota Democrat said, the Nixon Administration seems intent on pursuing the past "policy of military attrition and moral disaster in Vietnam."

Misgivings Grow

Mr. McGovern's speech represented the first open attack by the restive doves on the Nixon Administration's Vietnam policy. The speech reflected the growing misgivings of the doves but apparently did not herald a full-scale attack on the new Administration.

As one Republican dove remarked after the speech, "George is just a little premature."

For the moment, the prevailing mood among the Senate doves and the Democratic leadership is that President Nixon should be given a little more time to disengage himself from the Johnson Administration's policies and to work out a program for settling the Vietnam war.

This was reflected in the comments to reporters of the Senate Democratic leader, Mike Mansfield, and Senator Edward M. Kennedy, the Democratic whip.

No Words of Support

Both sat on the near vacant Senate floor and followed the text of Mr. McGovern's speech, but neither uttered words of support or concurrence.

In an apparent snub to Senator McGovern, who had circulated his speech in advance, the Republicans stayed away except for Senator George D. Aiken of Vermont, who in the past has criticized Vietnam policy.

The Senate Republican leader. Everett McKinley Dirksen, stood briefly in the Republican aisle to listen to Senator McGovern, then turned his back and strode off to the cloakroom.

Asked by reporters about Mr. McGovern's speech, Senator Dirksen said: "I would just politely like to know what they [the doves] are going to do about the war."

Senator Mansfield, one of the prominent critics of the Johnson Administration's Vietnam policy, said that he would also "like to see the President put into effect his own policies rather than continue policies he inherited."

But the Montana Democrat took the position that "we should give him a further chance" to work out a settlement of the war before the criticism was reviewed.

"My belief is that the President still wants a reasonable peace." Senator Mansfield said in an interview. "But he doesn't have too much time, and I see no sense in shaving that time any closer."

'Act-React Syndrome'

Noting that the President has told Congressional leaders that he has a "peace plan" for Vietnam, Senator Kennedy said to reporters, "We ought to give him the opportunity for the plan to be tested."

But on one major point, Senator Mansfield joined in Mr. McGovern's criticism, namely, the continuation of search-and-destroy missions after the bombing of North Vietnam was halted last October.

Senator Mansfield said that it was his understanding that after the bombing halt, orders had been given to the American military commanders in South Vietnam "to keep the Communist forces off balance."

The result, he said, was to "set off the act-react syndrome in the Vietnam war despite the fact that North Vietnam withdrew three divisions into Cambodia and Laos."

In much more acerbic terms, Senator McGovern suggested that the United States, by its intensified military activities, bore much of the blame for the stepped-up level of hostilities in recent weeks.

Noting that the President at his news conference last week maintained that the current escalation of hostilities was the responsibility of the Communist side, Senator McGovern said, "The president's assignment of blame for the escalation of the war is too one-sided."

Instead of seeking "a military disengagement" after the Paris talks began, he said, "we have pursued the opposite course."

"While the North Vietnamese responded to our bombing halt by withdrawing 22 full regiments from South Vietnam," he said, "we were preparing a great extension of our own offensive operations in the south. Air, Marine and ground engagements increased in number an intensity."

This winter, for example, he said, the total number of battalion-size operations undertaken by South Vietnamese and American troops has climbed from 820 in November to 1,077 in January.

"Let us be honest about the present military activities in South Vietnam," Senator McGovern said, "Are the current attacks by the Vietcong in the south a calculated offensive ordered by Hanoi and designed to trigger a general escalation of hostilities by all combatants?

"Or is this Vietcong drive a response to our own offensives over the last five months—a response determined more by our own aggressive combat operations than by any design of Hanoi's?"

* * *

March 20, 1969

THE OLD MERRY-GO-ROUND

By TOM WICKER

WASHINGTON, March 19—President Nixon has elaborated a sort of chicken-or-egg argument that, for a number of months past, American forces have not been conducting an offensive in Vietnam—just spoiling operations to blunt a Communist offensive they knew was coming. The Communist offensive came anyway, and now the allies have mounted a counter-offensive. This is the same old game of lethal leap-frog.

Mr. Nixon has also said that "in view of the current offensive on the part of the North Vietnamese and the Vietcong," there was no prospect of a reduction of American forces in South Vietnam. Secretary Laird, testifying before Congress, said that more money was necessary to prepare South Vietnamese to take over the fighting from Americans so that Americans could come home. This is the same old merry-go-round.

As for the Paris negotiations, the best information available here is that the kind of private talks that might produce substantive progress are not yet going on, although such talks may soon begin, and Mr. Nixon said Friday that "significant progress" was being made toward such a beginning.

This is a familiar and melancholy story; it is almost as if nothing had happened—no elections had been held last year, no change of Administrations had taken place, no profound public decision had been registered to take this country out of a dispiriting and divisive war that can neither be won nor justified—no more today than in November.

Like Graven Commitments

So, it seems, the fighting must go on—although, to his credit, Mr. Nixon has not made the slightest move to renew the attack on North Vietnam itself. There is no prospect of withdrawing American troops; there has been no political initiative, and apparently none is being prepared; and the new Administration like the old stands by the Saigon Government and all the past American "commitments" as if they had been carved in stone and handed down from Mount Sinai.

Where are the fresh ideas and the new start—let alone any "plan" to end the war—so many Americans believed they were voting for? What has happened to the opportunities and maneuverability of new men unsullied by the conflicts and policies of the past? The answer from the high councils of this Administration is that it does not wish to give away the game. It is "locked in" to many positions. It has "commitments."

The reasons for this are not entirely ideological and geopolitical—although Mr. Nixon's fifteen-year record on Indo-China clearly shows him to be intellectually comfortable with the current stance of his Administration; nor are they all to be found in the pressures of the military-diplomatic bureaucracy which has so great a vested interest in vindicating its long, fruitless prosecution of this war.

The Pressure Is Off

In fact, these influences and whatever others are at work within the Administration are having their effect only because Mr. Nixon and his associates have decided that they are under no domestic political pressure to settle the war swiftly. They believe that President Johnson's withdrawal, the opening of the Paris talks, the suspension of the bombing of the North, the change of Administrations—that all of these pacified the great outpouring of public unrest and dissent that was the most striking phenomenon of 1968.

Mr. Nixon and other high officials are known to believe that not before the end of summer or perhaps even longer will domestic peace pressures become significant; and that in the interim they are free of any political necessity to take unilateral action to end the war, or to launch major new initiatives to that end.

So far, this estimate has no doubt been accurate. How long it will remain so is another question. Congressional doves are already restive. But whether it is next week or next autumn before the rallies and the demonstrations begin all over, before the picket lines form again wherever the President goes, before the whole angry and dangerous business of public confrontation is renewed, the Administration will wait that long only at great cost.

And that cost will include not only the lives, money and energies cruelly wasted in Vietnam; it will include also another corrosive demonstration of how dubiously, if at all, the American "democratic" process works on questions of high policy. Even after voting twice in four years for Presidents who promised peace, must Americans once again go into the streets to get it?

* * *

April 6, 1969

NIXON HAS BEGUN PROGRAM TO END WAR IN VIETNAM

Secret Talks and Increased South Vietnamese Effort Called Parts of Plan

'VICTORY' DOWNGRADED

Shift in Tactics Would Cut U.S. Casualties and Allow Pullout of Some Troops

By MAX FRANKEL
Special to The New York Times

WASHINGTON, April 5—The Nixon Administration has set in motion an essentially secret program of diplomatic and military measures designed to extricate the United States from Vietnam.

Officials here confirm the adoption of a new approach to the war but refuse to discuss its details. They predict, however, that their approach will become evident by the end of 1969, presumably through a decline in the rate of American casualties and the recall of some American troops.

The current and partly known efforts to arrange secret talks in Paris and to turn over more combat assignments to South Vietnamese units in the war zone are said to be part of the Administration's program, but only a part.

Speak of Gradual Change

Informed officials here also talk about a gradual change of military tactics to reduce casualties while providing greater security for some of South Vietnam's major population centers.

As described here, this change would confirm Washington's readiness to settle for something less than military victory, but it would also buy time for negotiations and the evolution of new political processes in South Vietnam before the final American pullout.

It is still not clear here how much progress has been made in recent days to arrange secret talks, both between Washington and Hanoi and between the Saigon Government and the National Liberation. Front, or Vietcong.

All Parts of Maneuvering

However, senior officials contend that every conversation in Paris, many consultations with Moscow and the course of the battle itself are now an essential part of the maneuvering by both sides.

They also contend that American military measures are now geared to diplomatic objectives and that "negotiations" in the largest sense are therefore under way.

It is not clear either whether the announced 10 per cent cutback in B-52 bombing raids in South Vietnam had a clear diplomatic purpose as a part of this program. Defense Secretary Melvin R. Laird represented the cutback as an economy measure. Some officials have encouraged speculation that it was a signal to Hanoi, but others say the cutback was only a budget measure that was mistakenly announced at an awkward moment.

Yet despite the secrecy here surrounding some of the specific diplomatic and military gestures toward the North Vietnamese, senior officials have been saying enough both in public and private to reveal their basic assumption and objectives at this stage.

They start with the assumption that Hanoi is seriously interested in a settlement that would yield it something less than a takeover of South Vietnam by force. But in pressing the search for such a settlement, the Administration's planners also wish to prepare a fallback position, that is, a tenable alternative in case negotiation fails.

Hanoi's interest in negotiation is thought to flow from a combination of pressures: a degree of military and economic exhaustion; fear of a loss of Soviet support because of other crises, particularly Moscow's conflict with Peking, and realization that American forces cannot be defeated or forced to withdraw from South Vietnam if Mr. Nixon succeeds in appeasing domestic public opinion.

Moreover, officials here still count on some marginal, though secret Soviet support in arranging a settlement. They think that Moscow would favor a compromise that vindicates neither American intervention in Vietnam nor the guerrilla warfare habitually endorsed by Communist China.

Seek Mutual Withdrawal

If they can get substantial negotiations, Administration officials would want to arrange for a schedule of mutual troop withdrawals by North Vietnam and the United States while the political future of South Vietnam is left to the talks between the Saigon Government and the National Liberation Front.

Indirect diplomatic exchanges appear to have left officials here with the impression that the Front is prepared to deal with the Saigon Government, at least long enough to work out some new political processes.

And the attitude of the Saigon Government is said to have changed remarkably in recent weeks as the Nixon Administration privately made plain its determination to move toward disengagement. American officials do not now expect the Saigon regime to obstruct agreements for the withdrawal of outside forces.

The Saigon leaders also are said now to understand the need to strengthen their political and military position against the day when they must cope alone with their rivals.

Public pressure on Saigon is thought here to be self-defeating, because it helps Hanoi's campaign to undermine the existing South Vietnamese Government. But the private prodding has continued; President Nixon is said to have remarked that it may be difficult to make peace with Saigon but it will be impossible to make peace without Saigon.

Behind that comment, and behind the entire Nixon approach to the war as described here, lies the Administration's judgment that the United States cannot simply withdraw and let Saigon fall to armed insurgence or invaders.

The Administration is not unalterably committed to the existing Saigon Government, but it has concluded that the investment of more than 500,000 American troops and of solemn American commitments must be redeemed in some minimal way regardless of the merits of the initial involvement.

It is not know whether the President has tried to define his minimum terms. But some of his senior officials say that they have concluded that there must be some genuine "self-determination" in South Vietnam and not merely some arrangement that camouflages a Vietcong victory by force of arms.

Therefore, the Administration appears to be seeking a phased withdrawal of American and North Vietnamese troops over a period of time long enough to let new political processes develop in South Vietnam. Simultaneously, it is contemplating the possible need for an even slower pace of American withdrawal if negotiations are unproductive.

Officials refused to discuss the numbers of troops that they might recall even if negotiations fail. Some estimates have ranged from 50,000 to 100,000 over the next 18 months; some estimates have been even greater. Officials say they will not talk about these numbers because they do not wish to undermine the talks with Hanoi about mutual withdrawal.

But it is clear that the Administration is definitely thinking of unilateral withdrawals of some magnitude as an alternative to a negotiated settlement.

Either way, therefore, the American military deployments in South Vietnam will henceforth be designed to hasten the day of South Vietnam's self-sufficiency, to give American public opinion a sense of progress and diminishing cost and thus to reinforce the interest of Hanoi and the National Liberation Front in a negotiated settlement.

Officials here say they see no major difficulty with various parts of their plan—that is, in the separate policies it implies for dealing with Hanoi, Moscow, Saigon and American opinion. The main difficulty at the moment, they say, is moving simultaneously on several fronts and making certain that each step in different directions supports the long-range objective.

* * *

April 28, 1969

ANTIWAR G.I.'S AND ARMY HEAD FOR CLASH OVER VIETNAM

Officials Concerned but 'Think We Can Hold Our Ground'

By BEN A. FRANKLIN
Special to The New York Times

WASHINGTON, April 27—"The new action army" that is proclaimed these days in recruiting posters is approaching a collision over the war in Vietnam with the young dissenters and militant New Leftists who have been filling its ranks through the draft.

The young activists in uniform are declaring that their growing display of assertedly "legal" harassment and frankly illegal resistance is the decisive Battle of Vietnam, which will not only help to end the war but may also rebuke "militarism" in the United States.

Although it may be too early to make such sweeping claims, there is no question that the G.I. dissenters, despite their small number among 1.4 million soldiers, are causing serious concern within the Army's leadership.

Personnel and legal officers in Washington and base commanders in the field report that they are feeling more and more the same frustrations and worries about young Americans that have plagued embattled college presidents, mayors and police chiefs in civilian life.

The Pentagon acknowledges that "we do not have everything under control."

Motivation Unzipped

"Certainly, you can't fight an army whose motivation is coming unzipped," is the way one Pentagon spokesman put it, "but we think we can probably hold our ground."

The conflicts within the Army may merely reflect the unrest in civilian society, as seen on campuses and in slums across the country. But in the Army there is a difference, for there dissent and protest are not merely defiant gestures. They are often treated as serious military crimes.

And the Army acknowledges punishment of dissent is in turn creating resentment in many of the young Army men who had not been politically "turned on" about Vietnam or apparently any other national issue when they were inducted.

In recent months, the Army has convened conferences in Washington of base commanders to prepare them for the G.I.

movement's growth. Army headquarters has issued guidelines setting forth early warning symptoms of G.I. unrest. But since last summer the phenomenon has spread.

Major Cases Listed

A catalogue of the major cases illustrates the trend:

What civilian defense lawyers call "the classic case" involves the so-called Fort Jackson eight.

Authorities at the big South Carolina infantry training center are seeking to court-martial eight alleged members of an interracial activist group called G.I.'s United Against the War in Vietnam for speaking against the war during off-duty hours outside a barracks building last March 20.

The Fort Jackson soldiers have filed a civil suit in the Federal courts seeking to overthrow as an unconstitutional bar to free speech the Army's regulations forbidding public antiwar discussion and distribution of antiwar literature.

Two Negro marines, Pfc. George Daniels and Lance Cpl. William L. Harvey of Queens, are appealing prison sentences of 10 and six years at hard labor, respectively, given them by courts-martial for having urged other Negro marines at Camp Pendelton, Calif., to report to superior officers their feeling that Vietnam was "a white man's war" and that Negroes should not be required to fight in it.

Unable to bring actionable court-martial charges against many well-behaved activists, the Army has resorted to administrative methods by giving them undesirable or unsuitability discharges.

Twenty-seven stockade prisoners at the Presidio in San Francisco were given stiff sentences for "mutiny" after they had staged a sit-down demonstration to protest their prison conditions and the death of a G.I. prisoner shot by a stockade guard.

Specialist 4 Allen Myers, who published an antiwar newspaper at Fort Dix, believes that the in-uniform resistance has "solidified under President Nixon."

"The level of opposition is still small compared to what it may grow to be, but it has risen since the Paris negotiations on the war began to fail," the 26-year-old soldier said recently.

"Morale is gone. Eventually, it's going to get so bad in the Army that they can no longer fight this war."

Officers Perplexed

Dozens of officers on bases from New Jersey to Texas and the West Coast told an interviewer this month that they were perplexed or angered by the feelings among enlisted men that appear to run much deeper than the usual "gripes" about military life.

Hard facts about the size and effect of the militant G.I. movement are hard to come by. It is reported, however, that a rash of conscientious objector applications—the number is believed in the G.I. movement to total many thousands—has been filed by men facing Vietnam duty.

The Pentagon reports receiving only 239 objector applications from Army ranks so far this year, compared to 282 for the full year of 1968.

But this total does not include applications that cases now on appeal in civilian courts have disclosed. Commanders in the field have been accused of not forwarding applications to the Department of the Army, as regulations require.

Soldiers with a college background are also said to be making application for Officers Candidate School to delay embarkation for Vietnam, then decline to enroll.

'The Explosive Truth'

There are also scattered incidents of group "disrespect for military authority" and reluctance or refusal to obey orders. According to the Army, each such incident erodes discipline and morale and encourages the "cowardice" that most troop commanders feel is at the root of the problem. There is no doubt that the incidents and the Army's reaction to them are giving encouragement to the G.I. resistance.

The movement's morale, compared with that of the Army's generally, seems high, with little evidence of radical or conspiratorial discipline.

"The reason we're going to win, and the reason the right is on our side, is that we've got the explosive truth with us," said Fred Gardner, a curly-haired, boyish-looking 1963 Harvard graduate.

He has led and largely financed, with $10,000 of his own money, the opening of the three off-base G.I. coffee houses now in operation in this country.

The coffee houses are centers of antiwar activity at Columbia, S.C. near Fort Jackson: Killeen, Tex., near Fort Hood, and Tacorsa, Wash., at Fort Lewis.

Their appeal to soldiers is designed to be "cultural" rather than aggressively political, to offer a haven of what is called "the life-style of today's youth" amid the clutter of cheap bars and prostitutes lining the streets of many Army base towns.

But antiwar politics is served with the coffee and folk-rock music.

"The mind-blowing truth, and the Army knows it," Mr. Gardner said in an interview in California, "is that there is not a guy in his right mind in America who wants to interrupt his life to go 10,000 miles and run through the jungle to kill some farm kid. For what? They should have asked themselves that before they asked us to do this."

Mr. Gardner, 26, a former member of The Harvard Crimson and an editor in New York of The Scientific American before he became a free-lance and motion picture writer in San Francisco, is an Army reservist.

Reporting that two new coffee houses were to be opened this summer at undisclosed sites, he talked about the guiding policy of the G.I. movement.

'Something New'

"We see coffee houses run by young civilians as a way to give substance to the idea that civilians who are against the war are not against the soldiers required by a crazy system to fight it," he said. "That is something new. The civilian movement used to think of soldiers as fascists.

"The army is a very lonely place. They don't let you do things together, and guys in the army have been too cowed to act. We are showing them that they are not alone.

"The guys are discovering that there are other G.I.'s in the same boat who are good guys and good soldiers but who are fed up, disgusted and demanding some control over their lives."

In this assessment, Mr. Gardner is not alone.

"The army is simply an anachronism," says Brian Drolet, a 26-year-old "seminary dropout." He said that he turned in his draft card a year ago this month as a protest and has been counseling antiwar and runaway soldiers in the San Francisco area since then.

While waiting for the Government to react to his refusal to carry a draft card he has been working in a San Francisco church office for a New York-based antiwar group. Clergy and Layman Concerned About Vietnam.

Desertion Rate Rising

"People will no longer do things simply because they are told to," Mr. Drolet said. "They have to see a reason for it, and the G.I. antiwar movement is coming up with better reasons for not doing it than the Army—or the country, really—has for this absurd war."

Army officials in Washington are concerned about the rising rate of desertion, which has just passed the Korean war peak of 28 for each 1,000 men in uniform and is expected to go on rising.

But after studying extensive psychiatric reports of returned and apprehended deserters and A.W.O.L.'s, the Army believes that dropping out in the military is "probably the most subjective of all inservice violations"—an act of single-minded desperation rarely shared with others.

There is little disposition, accordingly, to ascribe A.W.O.L.'s or desertions to the militants.

Army officers who must explain the growth of militancy among the troops to superiors and to Congress are not happy about it. They say that their real concern is over the soldiers' growing links to the civilian antiwar militants and radicals who are supporting them.

"We have a varied number of responses to keep them off balance," one Pentagon official said. Without much confidence, he added, "We hope it keeps them off balance as much as they keep us off balance"

* * *

May 9, 1969

VIETCONG PRESENT 10-POINT PROGRAM AT PEACE TALKS

Proposal Calls for Coalition Government in Saigon and Free Elections

U.S. PULLOUT DEMANDED

Hanoi's Withdrawal Vague—Desire for Negotiations Appears to Be Indicated

By DREW MIDDLETON
Special to The New York Times

PARIS, May 8—The Vietcong presented a 10-point program today for an "over-all solution" of the war in Vietnam.

The program, offered at the peace talks here after months in which the enemy side appeared to be more interested in propaganda than in serious bargaining, seemed to indicate a desire for negotiations on the basis of the principles outlined in the document.

It renewed the enemy demand for the unilateral, unconditional withdrawal of United States forces and the liquidation of military bases, coupled with free elections, the drafting of a new constitution and ultimately a coalition government in Saigon.

A Vietnamese Resolution

There was no reference to the withdrawal of North Vietnamese forces in South Vietnam. The document said only that the question "shall be resolved by the Vietnamese parties among themselves."

"On the basis of these principles," the proposal said, an understanding could be reached "with a view to ending the war in South Vietnam and contributing to restore peace in Vietnam."

Ambassador Henry Cabot Lodge and the rest of the United States delegation apparently were surprised by the Vietcong's presentation of a program. Beyond saying that it would be given "careful study," Harold Kaplan, the American spokesman, made no substantive comment.

'Commentary' Offered

Mr. Lodge offered what Mr. Kaplan called a "commentary" on the program toward the close of the session, the 16th of the peace talks. Begun Jan. 25, they are held in the International Conference Center near the Arc de Triomphe.

The United States, the chief delegate said, would not accept the Vietcong's demand for unilateral withdrawal "without any mutual action" on the part of North Vietnam.

The use of the phrase "mutual action" rather than "mutual withdrawal" encouraged speculation that the Nixon Administration might be prepared to accept some action other than the withdrawal of North Vietnamese forces, such as an appreciable reduction in ground operations.

Mr. Lodge also emphasized in his commentary that the United States considered the political future of South Vietnam, on which the fourth and fifth points of the program

United Press International

ARRIVE TO PRESENT PROGRAM: Tran Buu Kiem, right, representative of National Liberation Front, in Paris yesterday with Mrs. Nguyen Thi Binh, who said she brought with her from Vietnam a 10-point program for "solution" to war. At center is interpreter.

focus, as an issue to be decided by the people without outside interference.

As presented by Tran Buu Kiem, the Vietcong program says this too. The difference lies in each side's interpretation of outside interference.

Nguyen Trieu Dan, the South Vietnamese spokesman, said he could not tell whether the program was a hopeful sign. Everything depends, he emphasized, on "what happens in the next few weeks" at the conference.

Among diplomats, opinion differed over whether the importance of the program lay in its exact wording or in the promise, however faint, it gave of movement toward negotiation.

There is a growing belief among diplomats that North Vietnam and the National Liberation Front, the Vietcong, are eager to promise four-power talks in secret and that the program could be regarded as an inducement to the allies to open such discussions.

The future government of South Vietnam, as envisaged in the program, would be the result of political forces representing the "various social strata and political tendencies" of South Vietnam. These forces were identified as those standing for "peace, independence and neutrality."

The coalition Government that will rest on this base will have five chief tasks, the program said. The most important of these, in the context of the present peace talks, will be to "implement the agreements" to be concluded on the withdrawal of American forces.

Timing Is Uncertain

Nothing was said about the relationship between the timing of a coalition government's formation and this withdrawal. Nor did the program indicate whether other points would take effect after a partial American troop withdrawal or after complete withdrawal.

The program was categoric in saying that all troops "must" be withdrawn without the United States' opposing any conditions whatsoever."

The Liberation Front's presentation of the program, conference sources and neutral diplomats agreed, had won it stature. From the outset, the Front has striven to establish a position as a political entity, in its own right and not simply an appendage of the North Vietnamese.

Mrs. Nguyen Thi Binh, the deputy negotiator, announced that she had returned from Vietnam with the program.

Under persistent questioning at a news conference, Mrs. Binh refused to give any clear indication of the timing of steps in the program or of the identity of the "Vietnamese armed forces" whose presence in South Vietnam would be decided by "the Vietnamese parties." Nor would she identify these parties.

The program includes the pledge of "broad democratic freedoms" and the promise of "free and democratic general elections" at an unspecified date.

The military demarcation line between North and South Vietnam provided by the 1954 Geneva agreements was termed by the program provisional and not constituting "in any way" a political or territorial boundary.

The program also proposed that the United States "bear full responsibility" for the "losses and devastation" in both North and South Vietnam.

* * *

May 9, 1969

RAIDS IN CAMBODIA BY U.S. UNPROTESTED

By WILLIAM BEECHER

Special to The New York Times

WASHINGTON, May 8—American B-52 bombers in recent weeks have raided several Vietcong and North Vietnamese supply dumps and base camps in Cambodia for the first time, according to Nixon Administration sources, but Cambodia has not made any protest.

In fact, Cambodian authorities have increasingly been cooperating with American and South Vietnamese military men at the border, often giving them information on Vietcong and North Vietnamese movements into South Vietnam.

Information from knowledgeable sources indicates that three principal factors underlie the air strikes just inside the Cambodian border, west and northwest of Saigon:

- Rising concern by military men that most of the rockets and other heavy weapons and ammunition being used by North Vietnamese and Vietcong forces in the southern half of South Vietnam now come by sea to Cambodia and never have to run any sort of bombing gantlet before they enter South Vietnam.

- A desire by high Washington officials to signal Hanoi that the Nixon Administration, while pressing for peace in Paris, is willing to take some military risks avoided by the previous Administration.
- Apparent increasing worry on the part of Prince Norodom Sihanouk, Cambodia's Chief of State, that the North Vietnamese and Vietcong now effectively control several of Cambodia's northern provinces and that he lacks sufficient power to disrupt or dislodge them.

No Desire to Extend War

Officials say that there is no Administration interest at this time in extending the ground war into Cambodia, or Laos either.

Discussing the on-again, off-again statements of Prince Sihanouk on the re-establishment of relations with the United States, one official said: "Although the Prince has made various statements in recent speeches questioning the sincerity of our recognition of his frontiers, he has made none of these protestations to us. It may be that he's simply demonstrating to his people that any new deal he makes will be on his own terms."

The Prince has made United States recognition of Cambodia's "present frontiers" a condition for the re-establishment of relations.

Some American ground commanders have long urged that battalion-size forces occasionally be allowed to sweep into sanctuaries in Laos and Cambodia to follow up air strikes. This plea has been rejected by President Nixon as it was by President Johnson.

But sources here say that to assure that accurate information can be obtained to provide "lucrative" targets for the bombers, small teams of men are permitted to slip across both the Cambodian and Laotian borders to locate enemy concentrations of men and matériel.

Coincided With Other Raids

The sources report, for instance, that to try to reduce losses in B-52 raids the enemy has dug in and dispersed supply caches in such a way that it is unlikely that all supplies in any one area would be hit by the linear pattern of bombs dropped by a B-52. Each plane, which normally carries about 30 tons of bombs, lays out a pattern that is 1,000 feet wide and 4 miles long.

The raids into Cambodia, the sources say, coincided with heavy B-52 raids on the Vietnamese side of the border 50 to 75 miles northwest of Saigon.

Over the last two weeks more than 5,000 tons of bombs have been dropped by B-52's in this area, according to one estimate.

There are reported to be three enemy divisions operating back and forth across the border in this area: the First and Seventh North Vietnamese Divisions and the Ninth Vietcong Division. Another division, the Fifth Vietcong, is now operating south and southeast of Saigon.

The decision to demonstrate to Hanoi that the Nixon Administration is different and "tougher" than the previous Administration was reached in January, well-placed sources say, as part of a strategy for ending the war.

Hints by Sihanouk Noted

Limited, selective bombing strikes into Cambodia, the sources say, were considered feasible because Prince Sihanouk had dropped hints that he would not oppose such actions and because they seemed to offer relatively little risk of either expanding the war or disrupting the Paris peace talks.

In the past, American and South Vietnamese forces had occasionally fired across the border and even called in fighters or helicopter gunships to counter fire they received from enemy units there. But there had been no bombing of supply stockpiles or base camps in Cambodia, military men say.

Over the last several weeks the military sources say, Cambodian Army officers in border posts have held secret meetings with Americans and South Vietnamese to "coordinate" some actions against enemy forces.

The South Vietnamese have provided them with radios and in some instances the Cambodians have radioed information on enemy units moving into South Vietnam. At other times, the Cambodians have fired colored flares—for example, red to mark an enemy unit and blue to mark their own—so that allied forces would not fire at the wrong unit.

"This cooperation is only starting to get off the ground," said one officer. "It's too early to tell how important this will turn out to be."

* * *

May 15, 1969

NIXON ASKS TROOP PULLOUT IN A YEAR AND WOULD JOIN VIETNAM POLITICAL TALKS

SPEAKS TO NATION

Hints Partial Cutback of U.S. Forces Will Come in Any Case

By ROBERT B. SEMPLE Jr.
Special to The New York Times

WASHINGTON, May 14—President Nixon proposed tonight a phased, mutual withdrawal of the major portions of United States, allied and North Vietnamese forces from South Vietnam over a 12-month period.

Then, according to Mr. Nixon's proposal, the remaining non-South Vietnamese forces would withdraw to enclaves, abide by a cease-fire and complete their withdrawals.

The President made the proposal in a nationwide television address in which he gave his first full-length report to the country on the war in Vietnam.

Although the President indicated that such full-scale withdrawals would probably require lengthy negotiations, he hinted strongly that "the time is approaching" when some partial reductions of combat troops could be accomplished regardless of what happens in the negotiations in Paris.

Prepared to Negotiate

Mr. Nixon said further that the United States was prepared to participate in negotiations leading to a political settlement, rather than continue to insist that Saigon and the Vietcong conduct political negotiations while Hanoi and Washington dealt only with military issues.

White House sources sought to contrast Mr. Nixon's offer of a "simultaneous start on withdrawal" with the last formal United States proposal.

That proposal, offered at the Manila conference of the United States and its allies in Vietnam in October, 1966, said that American withdrawals would be completed within six months after North Vietnamese withdrawals. The implication of the Manila proposal was that there would be some American troops left in the country after all of Hanoi's forces had withdrawn.

Supervised Elections Offered

The President also offered, for the first time, internationally supervised elections to insure "each significant group in South Vietnam a real opportunity to participate in the political life of the nation."

The proposal for internationally supervised elections was regarded as reflecting a concession by Saigon to the extent that such outside supervision would infringe on the sovereignty of the Saigon regime.

The President said that the proposals were made on the basis of full consultation with President Nguyen Van Thieu of South Vietnam, and White House sources said that President Thieu had agreed to them.

The President delivered the speech from a small theater in the east wing of the White House. His demeanor was solemn, as he hurried through his complicated, 3,000-word text.

Much of Mr. Nixon's address was familiar, carrying echoes of his own campaign and of President Johnson's speeches on Vietnam. He declared that the right of the South Vietnamese people to determine their own destiny remained a nonnegotiable point at the bargaining table and he ruled out any settlement that could be construed as a disguised defeat.

Wants to End War

"I want to end this war," Mr. Nixon declared. "The American people want to end this war. The people of South Vietnam want to end this war. But we want to end it permanently so that the younger brothers of our soldiers in Vietnam will not have to fight in the future in another Vietnam someplace in the world."

The President rejected the idea of a one-sided pullout of American troops as demanded by Hanoi and the National Liberation Front, or Vietcong. In its 10-point peace proposal offered last week, the Vietcong called for the unconditional withdrawal of American forces.

At the same time, however, he held out the promise of an early, partial reduction in allied forces because of what he described as Saigon's increasing military strength. He emphasized that this might be accomplished quite apart, from what occurred in the negotiations in Paris.

"The time is approaching," the President declared, "when South Vietnamese forces will be able to take, over some of the fighting fronts now being manned by Americans."

White House sources said that such withdrawals, when they occurred, would very definitely involve combat troops and would not be confined to supply forces behind the lines.

The President offered Hanoi a face-saving method of removing its troops, by dropping the Johnson Administration's insistence that Hanoi admit it had regular troops fighting in South Vietnam.

In a paragraph dropped, possibly inadvertently, from his prepared text, but which the White House said the President stood by, he declared:

"If North Vietnam wants to insist that it has no forces in South Vietnam, we will no longer debate the point—provided that its forces cease to be there, and that we have reliable assurances that they will not return," he declared.

This was one of several places in the speech where the President offered a flexible negotiating technique, or ambiguous language, that could be developed in future secret bargaining.

Two Tones Are Noted

He emphasized that none of the American proposals was being put forward on a "take-it-or-leave-it basis," and that he was "quite willing to consider other approaches," including Hanoi's or the Vietcong's.

On the subject of withdrawals, Mr. Nixon insisted on one point. If North Vietnam agreed to withdraw its forces on the basis of a phased time-table, he said, it would be required to withdraw them not only from South Vietnam but from Cambodia and Laos as well. The Cambodian border is only 35 miles from Saigon, the Laotian border only 25 miles from Hue, and the allies would not accept withdrawals that left those two major South Vietnamese centers exposed to renewed war.

The speech sounded to some observers as if it had been written in two parts and by two hands. Observers found the flexibility of Mr. Nixon's specific proposals in decided contrast to his rather stern rhetoric.

He asserted that the credibility of the United States would be badly damaged if Saigon were abandoned, and added:

"If Hanoi were to succeed in taking over South Vietnam by force—even after the power of the United States had been engaged—it would greatly strengthen those leaders who scorn negotiation, who advocate aggression and who minimize the risks of confrontation with the United States. It would bring peace now, but it would enormously increase the danger of a bigger war later.

"If we are to move successfully from an era of confrontation to an era of negotiation, then we have to demonstrate—at the point at which confrontation is being tested—that confrontation with the United States is costly and unrewarding."

An Apparent Warning

At another point the President appeared to be warning the enemy that these proposals represented genuine concessions, a conciliatory position that could be ignored or repudiated only at some risk.

"I must also make it clear, in all candor, that if the needless suffering continues, this will affect other decisions. Nobody has anything to gain by delaying," Mr. Nixon declared.

Pressed for an explanation of this sentence, White House sources, said simply that it ought to be self-explanatory.

White House officials refused to characterize the address as another element in the Administration's accelerating effort to, assure the American public that progress was being made and, thus to purchase additional time in which to carry out negotiations free of heavy public pressure.

At the same time, however, the President made what appeared to be a direct bid for continued patience. He conceded that he could not legitimately demand "unlimited patience from a people whose hopes for peace have too often been raised and cruelly dashed over the past four years," but added:

"Tonight, all I ask is that you consider these facts and, whatever our differences, that you support a program which can lead to a peace we can live with and a peace we can be proud of.

"Nothing could have a greater effect in convincing the enemy he should negotiate in good faith than to see the American people united behind a generous and reasonable peace offer."

The White House also rejected speculation that the speech had been scheduled as a response to the Vietcong's 10-point plan. The White House explanation for the timing was that quite apart from recent developments it was a "propitious moment" for "developing momentum" in the Paris peace talks.

* * *

May 22, 1969

U.S. AIDES DEFEND APBIA PEAK BATTLE

By B. DRUMMOND AYRES Jr.
Special to The New York Times

SAIGON, South Vietnam, Thursday, May 22—The United States command said this morning that the fight for Apbia Mountain in the northwest part of South Vietnam "may well have been another battle of Hue," the old imperial capital, some 30 miles to the east.

The spokesman's comment came after the battle, which ended Tuesday in an allied victory, had stirred adverse comment in the United States. Senator Edward M. Kennedy, Democrat of Massachusetts, termed the fight "senseless and irresponsible" and asserted that "American lives are too valuable to be sacrificed for military pride."

Forty-five Americans were killed and 269 were wounded in the struggle to take the 3,074-foot mountain, situated in an uninhabited area a few miles from the Laotian border.

The American spokesman here refused to comment directly on Senator Kennedy's charges, but in what seemed to be an indirect comment, he said:

"We were not fighting for terrain as such. We did not attack the hill for the purpose of taking a hill. We were going after the enemy.

"The operation may well have been another battle of Hue. The enemy has often massed in the mountains before moving on the city. When such a battle can be fought near the border rather than in and around the city, enormous civilian casualties and damage can be avoided."

In concluding that the operation had been "real fine," the spokesman asserted that relative casualties were one way to measure success.

He noted that enemy losses had been put at 502 killed.

The fight for the peak was the most sustained and difficult combat in South Vietnam in several months. The fighting was so bloody that allied troops began referring to the mountain as "Hamberger Hill." Some infantrymen complained about being sent up its slopes time after time in the face of extremely heavy small-arms fire.

An American colonel familiar with allied strategy and tactics noted here yesterday that the Apbia Mountain was in an area that United States and South Vietnamese troops had been sweeping through for several weeks.

"Our job," the colonel said, "was—and is—to push through that area in search of enemy base camps, supply depots and infiltration routes. A good offense is always the best defense.

"Sweeping is the way we fight this war. Just because an area is isolated and the enemy troops there haven't been bothering anybody lately is no reason for us to stay away.

"We have no guarantee the Charlies around that mountain suddenly are thinking peace and should be left alone. In the past, they've always roared out of those hills, sooner or later."

Another American colonel agreed with the sweeping offense theory but expressed reservation about whether Apbia should have been taken by infantrymen.

"I've fought in that area," he said, "and it seems to me we might have assaulted more with planes than with men. Why not a few B-52 strikes?

"We can get ourselves into another Korean war situation if we keep loosing men on hills that don't have to be taken today or tomorrow. What's wrong with cordoning off a place and pounding the hell out of it?"

A Korean-war situation would require that the enemy strongly resist every time allied units attack. The reverse has been the case in recent weeks, except for the Apbia battle.

United Press International

CASUALTIES: Wounded paratroopers of 101st Airborne Division are helped down Apbia Mountain after the battle.

During the last 24 hours allied units made numerous contacts but in almost every instance the enemy faded away. Thus, most of the skirmishes left fewer than a dozen men dead.

* * *

June 1, 1969

THE GRIM AND INACCURATE CASUALTY NUMBERS GAME

SAIGON—Continuing American and enemy casualties in Vietnam while peace talks are going on in Paris are at the heart of the controversy in the United States over strategy for the war.

The current aim of both allied and enemy strategy is not so much to seize territory as to inflict heavy losses in the hope that the other side will consider the punishment too harsh to continue fighting. Thus the "body counts" and "kill ratios" become all-important.

No one knows how many Vietnamese have been killed in the fighting that has swept their country over the past quarter of a century—first against the French and then in the current conflict. The combat has been so vicious and destructive at times that many men—and women and children, too—literally have been blown away.

The North Vietnamese and the Vietcong do not report their losses, not even to mothers and wives.

Doubtful Figures

On the other hand, the South Vietnamese and the Americans regularly offer statistics on losses by both sides. But the allied statisticians have been caught off base so often that their figures are greeted with considerable skepticism.

Last week, for example, the statisticians calculated that the total number of enemy killed in South Vietnam since January, 1961, had passed the half-million mark and stood at 500,509.

At the same time, the allied command was telling newsmen in Saigon that 45 Americans had been killed in the bloody and controversial struggle for Apbia Mountain west of Hue, although correspondents on the scene were reporting at least 60 dead.

The discrepancy illustrated the difficulty in determining the exact number of people killed. If there could be wide disagreement in a single battle involving fewer than a hundred

Americans dead, how far off was the figure of half a million for eight and a half years?

There are American and South Vietnamese commanders who, like the statisticians, put great stock in the "body count" and therefore urge their units to compete for "kills."

"How many did you get?" is a question heard frequently over field radios. Some units keep elaborate kill charts. During morning and evening briefings, they are displayed with considerable pride.

Some helicopter gunships are decorated with neat rows of tiny figures in conical hats, a practice reminscent of World War II when fighter planes sported swastikas or rising suns to show the number of enemy aircraft shot down.

What does it all mean?

Perhaps more than anything, body counts and kill ratios are symptomatic of the never-ending effort to qualify progress in a war that has no frontlines. The statistics replace the frontlines.

There are people in Saigon who sit all day in clean, air-conditioned comfort and ponder the data and developments in an effort to determine what the phrase "unacceptable losses" means to Hanoi. They are frankly confused.

They have fresh reports that Ho Chi Minh has called on his battlefield commanders to "economize human and material resources." They have his Defense Minister, Vo Nguyen Giap, "casually" telling Oriana Fallaci, a correspondent for the Milanese magazine L'Europeo, that half a million North Vietnamese have been killed.

Enemy Manpower

North Vietnam has a population of about 20 million that produces perhaps 500,000 draft-age youths every year. Indications are that about 130,000 of them are inducted and the remainder are either deferred or found physically or mentally unqualified.

Of the 181,146 enemy soldiers reported killed last year, perhaps half were North Vietnamese. This does not mean, however, that Hanoi's armed forces ended up with a net gain of about 40,000 men for 1968.

Into the equation must be cranked the number of wounded who died and were not found, the number of bodies that were never counted or counted twice, and the number of men discharged. These figures are not available, of course. So the meaning of "unacceptable losses" remains illusive.

As for the Vietcong, they too obviously have suffered great losses; but, again the lack of precise figures prohibits any solid conclusions.

Finally, there is one extremely important non-statistical element that must be taken into consideration in judging enemy strength and weakness. It is that the enemy leaders do not have to worry about popularity polls.

B. Drummond Ayres Jr.

* * *

June 9, 1969

NIXON TO REDUCE VIETNAM FORCE, PULLING OUT 25,000 G.I.'S BY AUG. 31; HE AND THIEU STRESS THEIR UNITY

A MIDWAY ACCORD

Leaders Agree First Cutbacks Will Begin Within 30 Days

By HEDRICK SMITH

Special to The New York Times

MIDWAY ISLAND, June 8—President Nixon met with President Nguyen Van Thieu of South Vietnam today and announced that 25,000 American soldiers would be withdrawn from Vietnam before the end of August.

After the first two hours of five hours of talks on this Pacific island, Mr. Nixon emerged to declare that the Presidents had agreed that troop withdrawals would begin within 30 days.

And with Mr. Thieu standing at his side, Mr. Nixon held out the hope of further reductions in the 540,000-man American force when this first phase was completed.

Replacements Available

He said that the equivalent of a combat division could leave Vietnam because of progress in the training and equipping of South Vietnam's Army.

Both President Nixon and President Thieu underscored the point that the American forces being withdrawn would be replaced in the field by South Vietnamese forces.

Mr. Nixon termed the withdrawal a "significant step forward" toward a lasting peace in Vietnam. At the end of the five-hour conference, Mr. Thieu said that the step was "good news for the American people that Vietnamese forces replace United States combat forces."

Both in announcing the troop withdrawal and in presenting a joint statement to the press at the end of their meeting, the two leaders sought to emphasize their solidarity.

Differences Not Mentioned

Their joint communiqué made no allusion to differences in approach to the Paris negotiations, and President Thieu remarked afterward that it was "not true" that he had come to Midway to thresh out differences with the new American Administration. But little was noted in the public statements of either man that might quiet Saigon's fears about the ultimate intentions of the United States leadership.

Although the announcement of the troop withdrawal was aimed at placating domestic critics of the war and putting pressure on North Vietnam and the Vietcong to negotiate more seriously in Paris by seeking to demonstrate South Vietnam's growing strength, Mr. Nixon mentioned neither American war critics nor the enemy.

As if pleading for more patience from the American public, President Thieu said at a news conference: "We will do our best from now on to alleviate the burden of the United

Associated Press

REVIEW HONOR GUARD: Mr. Nixon and South Vietnam's President, Nguyen Van Thieu, at Midway Airport yesterday.

States people." Minutes later, at 4:20 P.M. (10:20 P.M. New York time), he departed for Saigon. Mr. Nixon left for Hawaii about 20 minutes later.

Whatever private differences the two leaders may have talked out in their first encounter since Mr. Nixon's election, the public emphasis here was on harmony.

President Thieu did not obtain from Mr. Nixon a clear pledge to support the present government in Saigon. But he did win a declaration that both Presidents reject the enemy effort to "impose" any form of government "such as a coalition without regard to the will of the people of South Vietnam."

Room Left for Saigon

This stopped short of an unequivocal requirement that nationwide elections precede any coalition with the Vietcong, but left room for Saigon to agree eventually to a negotiated coalition. President Thieu is adamantly opposed to this concept now and there was no evidence that President Nixon tried to persuade him at Midway to accept it.

The communiqué did not contain any new negotiating proposals, but merely referred to the previous plans put forward by the two Presidents and avoided detail on the delicate questions of special elections, demanded by the Vietcong.

The major outcome of the meeting at this Navy base was the decision to start pulling out the equivalent of an American combat division. In announcing this step, President Nixon sought to forestall concern that this might weaken the allied military position.

"As replacement of United States forces begins," he asserted, "I want to emphasize two fundamental principles: No actions will be taken which threaten the safety of our troops, and the troops of our allies, and second, no action will be taken which endangers the attainment of our objective, the right of self-determination for the people of South Vietnam."

Plan Backed by Abrams

Mr. Nixon said troop withdrawal had been recommended by President Thieu and by Gen. Creighton W. Abrams, the American commander in Vietnam.

"I have decided to order the immediate redeployment from Vietnam of the divisional equivalent of approximately 25,000 men," Mr. Nixon said. "This troop replacement will begin within the next 30 days and it will be completed by the end of August."

"I will announce plans for further redeployment as decisions are made," Mr. Nixon added.

Mr. Nixon and Mr. Thieu met with reporters under the palm trees outside the home of Capt. Albert S. Yesensky, the naval commander of Midway. The Presidents conferred at the home.

Mr. Nixon, his hands clasped in front of him, was calm and relaxed as he reported on the morning's private talk and announced the troop decision. President Thieu, who spoke in English, appeared a bit nervous and read from a prepared statement.

The announcement was made after the two Presidents met privately for two hours accompanied only by their personal aides—Henry A. Kissinger, Mr. Nixon's adviser for national security, and Nguyen Phu Duc of Mr. Thieu's staff. The Cabinet-level advisers of the Presidents met separately.

After the announcement of the troop withdrawal, the Presidents went to a private lunch, where they continued their discussions. Later they met with all their advisers before issuing the communiqué.

President Nixon arrived here from his overnight stop in Honolulu at 10 A.M. (4 P.M., New York time). When Mr. Thieu landed 20 minutes later, Mr. Nixon greeted him with a long, vigorous handshake but did not offer the kind of lavish personal reception that had typified President Lyndon B. Johnson's five Pacific meetings with South Vietnamese leaders.

Nonetheless, President Thieu's prestige at home was likely to be bolstered by his opportunity to meet with Mr. Nixon in a show of solidarity. Saigon would have liked the meeting to be longer than the six hours the two Presidents spent here and would have preferred more ceremony.

The differences that the two leaders brought here concerned the details of their approach to the Paris negotiations on a political settlement in Vietnam and reflected the conflicting domestic pressures in their two countries.

President Thieu arrived concerned with right-wing pressures against approving too many concessions to the National Liberation Front, or Vietcong. President Nixon arrived with critics of the war calling on him to show maximum flexibility on his terms for ending it.

Neither man gave any public indication of these pressures. The arrival ceremonies were brief and formal. In a break with the procedure at President Johnson's meetings, there were no welcoming remarks by either man.

Cloudy skies that hovered over this chip of sand 1,304 miles northwest of Honolulu cleared just before the two Presidents flew into Midway.

President Nixon's arrival on this flat, sandy island was five minutes ahead of schedule. When President Thieu's chartered Pan American airliner landed 20 minutes later, the two men met at the foot of the ramp from Mr. Thieu's plane.

The South Vietnamese fell into easy banter with Mr. Nixon as they strode across the blue-black runway. The South Vietnamese delegation went through a receiving line of senior American officials and then the two Presidents were given a 21-gun salute by an honor guard flown in from Honolulu.

Immediately afterward, the two leaders began their conference at Captain Yesensky's home.

Senior members of the American and South Vietnamese delegations met at the same time at the squat, single-story officers' club about a quarter of a mile away, near a beach.

The American officials with the President were Secretary of State William P. Rogers, Secretary of Defense Melvin R. Laird, Mr. Kissinger, Gen. Earle G. Wheeler, chairman of the Joint Chiefs of Staff, Ambassador Henry Cabot Lodge, Ambassador Ellsworth Bunker, General Abrams and Adm. John S. McCain Jr., commander of American forces in the Pacific.

The South Vietnamese delegation was considerably smaller. President Thieu had with him Foreign Minister Tran Chanh Thanh, Defense Minister Nguyen Van Vy, Gen. Cao Van Vien, chairman of the Joint General Staff, Mr. Duc and Bui Diem, South Vietnam's Ambassador to the United States.

A report on the negotiations in Paris was given to the full conference by Mr. Lodge, the chief American delegate.

* * *

July 11, 1969

GIRLS, BANDS AND TICKER TAPE GREET TROOPS FROM VIETNAM IN SEATTLE

By STEVEN V. ROBERTS
Special to The New York Times

SEATTLE, July 10—Rain, martial music, pretty girls, ticker tape, public speeches and the shouts of about 50 antiwar demonstrators today greeted the first G.I.'s pulled out of

Associated Press

AND GOOD LUCK: Helmet of a member of the Ninth Marine Regiment speaks for him as he boards a plane at Quangtri. He was in group sent from South Vietnam to Okinawa.

United Press International

A soldier accepting a rose from one of a number of girls distributing them yesterday as the troops marched in Seattle.

Vietnam in President Nixon's effort to de-escalate the war. The 814 members of the Third Battalion, 60th Infantry, Ninth Infantry Division landed yesterday at McChord Air Force Base 30 miles away. Today they marched through the wind-whipped streets of Seattle and heard Army Secretary Stanley R. Resor tell them that their presence was "tangible evidence of the progress we have made" in Vietnam. Fewer than 200 of the men actually fought with the Third Battalion in the Mekong Delta area of Vietnam. When the transfer order came, those with time left to serve in Vietnam were moved to other units and the battalion was filled with men ready to rotate home. The men will not be specifically replaced in Vietnam. But the day they landed at McChord, more than 1,000 fresh troops left the base for a year's tour in the war zone. This month, more than 10,000 others will follow them to Vietnam.

As the returning troops lined up in front of the reviewing stand, young girls threw red roses to them, flags waved, and bands played "When Johnny Comes Marching Home."

Across the street, antiwar demonstrators shouted, "Bring them all home now." And to some people in the crowd, the chant appeared to express their private feelings as they watched the tanned, young soldiers in green fatigues and camouflaged helmets stand at attention.

"I'm just grateful our boy is home," said Mrs. Kenneth Spence of Portland, Ore., whose son, Specialist 5 Gary Spence, was in the marching group. "He looks great, and he feels great—except he's got a cold.

"But he was due home anyway. I hope the war ends shortly and all the boys come home where they belong. We have another boy coming along and we don't want him to go. We've had too many good-by's."

"I have two very good friends over there now and wish they'd come home," added 18-year-old Carol Bacon, as she grasped a bunch of flowers for the soldiers. "World War II only took four years and here's this little country and we can't seem to win. They'll probably send twice as many troops over to replace these."

Some felt the day was a chance to display their patriotism. "I came out to counter-balance all the kooks who are out today," said Reginald Kees, a Navy veteran who watched the parade with his wife and two children.

An elderly lady in a pink coat said she had been a member of the Ladies Auxiliary of the Veterans of Foreign Wars since

1922. "I'm a fighter," she said. "We should have let General Pershing clean up the Germans after World War I and we should do the same in Vietnam."

* * *

July 26, 1969

NIXON PLANS CUT IN MILITARY ROLE FOR U.S. IN ASIA

Starting Tour, He Promises Respect for Commitments, but Under New Forms

ARRIVES IN PHILIPPINES

President, at Guam, Asserts Nation Won't Be Drawn Into More Vietnams

By ROBERT B. SEMPLE Jr.
Special to The New York Times

MANILA, Saturday, July 26—President Nixon declared yesterday that the United States would not be enticed into future wars like the one in Vietnam and would redesign and reduce its military commitments throughout non-Communist Asia.

Mr. Nixon promised, however, that the United States would continue to play a sizable role in the Pacific and would not forsake its treaty commitments.

This was the essence of views put forward by the President in an informal news conference before he set forth from Guam on the diplomatic leg of his global journey.

President Exhilarated

The President, who seemed exhilarated by the successful moon venture of Apollo 11, arrived here today for the first foreign stop of a tour taking him to Indonesia, Thailand, India, Pakistan, Rumania and, briefly, Britain.

During his short stop in Guam, Mr. Nixon set forth in considerable detail the purposes of his week-and-a-half trip and disclosed major points he would be making to the Asian leaders. He spoke for publication but asked that his words not be directly quoted.

The President defined his Asian policy in more specific and forceful terms than at any time since taking office. Some of his views had been expressed earlier in articles and in the political campaign last fall, but he went further today in emphasizing his intention of limiting United States commitments.

New Aid Is Hinted

Specifically, he said he might order a reduction of military operations in South Vietnam if that would help the negotiations to end the war.

The President also hinted that new forms of economic aid to the Asian nations might soon be forthcoming, but—perhaps mindful of growing ill will toward foreign aid at home and the constraints that inflation has placed on new Government spending—he carefully avoided promising an increase in aid.

The President spent the major part of his news conference, held at the naval officers' club in Guam, on questions relating to Vietnam and Asia, demonstrating that despite all the early publicity devoted to visit he will pay to Rumania Aug. 2, he himself was placing highest priority on the Asian part of the journey. Yet in the course of his unusually relaxed and unusually long session—it last 52 minutes, compared with his average news-conference length of 30 minutes—Mr. Nixon also made these points:

He remains willing to participate in a top-level meeting with the Soviet Union to talk about the Vietnam war, the Middle Eastern crisis and the arms race, but only if such a meeting were to be preceded by lower-level consultations and held out some promise of success.

While he most wishes for a summit meeting to enlist the Soviet Union in the search for an end of the war, he doubts that Moscow would work for a settlement, even if it wants one, in so public and highly visible a forum.

There is no basis for what he called speculation that his visit to Rumania would be an affront to either the Soviet Union or Communist China; instead, it is designed to develop communication with Eastern European nations.

Recent charges by some Senators that the United States had struck a secret defense agreement with Thailand are without foundation.

Mr. Nixon acknowledged at the outset his consuming interest in the future of Asia after the end of the war in Vietnam. He said further that the Asians were equally interested in whether the United States would continue to play a significant role in their area or whether, like the French, British and Dutch, it would withdraw from the Pacific and play a minor part.

He conceded that many Americans were extremely frustrated by the Vietnam war and, in their frustration, wished for a substantial reduction of America's Pacific commitments. He indicated by his tone that he understood these frustrations and to a certain extent sympathized with them.

But he argued that the United States could not withdraw from its Asian commitments, first because withdrawal might well pave the way for other wars; and second, because the United States itself is a Pacific power with a major stake in Asian stability.

In answering subsequent questions, however, Mr. Nixon sought more clearly to define the future dimensions of that commitment. He asserted, for example, that except when Asian nations were threatened by a nuclear power such as Communist China, the United States would insist that both internal subversion and external aggression be dealt with increasingly by the Asians themselves.

Collective Security Urged

He said it was foolish to believe that the non-Communist Asian nations could soon devise collective security arrangements enabling them to defend themselves against Communism. Collective security now is a weak reed to lean on, he said, and it will take five to 10 years for the non-Communist Asian nations to devise adequate collective security arrangements among themselves.

This blunt assessment of the prospects for collective security prompted a question on what the United States would do in the event of another Vietnam situation in the five to 10 years in which the Asian nations would be struggling to devise mechanisms for self-protection. The President replied that such incidents would have to be judged case by case.

But he will consider each case very carefully, he asserted, with an eye to avoiding what he called creeping involvements that eventually submerge a great nation, as, he said, the Vietnam conflict has submerged the United States in emotional discord and economic strain.

To illustrate his point, the President recalled a line from his election campaign that he said he had used in every speech, drawing loud applause each time. He said the statement had been made to him by Mohammad Ayub Khan, former President of Pakistan, in 1964.

"The role of the United States in Vietnam or the Philippines, or Thailand, or any of these other countries which have internal subversion," the statement went, "is to help them fight the war but not fight the war for them."

Mr. Nixon then declared, in answer to a question, that military assistance of all kinds, including the commitment of United States troops, would be reduced. He did not say how large such reductions would be, or how soon they would be carried out.

To compensate in part for the reduced military assistance, Mr. Nixon indicated that the United States would soon be suggesting initiatives on the economic side designed to add fresh momentum to what he said was the developing economic strength of non-Communist Asia. He promised that United States aid would be adequate to meet the challenge of Asian economic problems.

The President professed to see several hopeful signs that non-Communist Asia had recently become stronger, including rapid economic development. He rattled off an impressive list of statistics showing the economic growth of South Korea, Japan, Thailand, Indonesia, India and Pakistan.

Another sign, he said, was the dwindling capacity of Communist China to foment internal insurgencies in other countries. Early in the news conference, Mr. Nixon declared that China was the single biggest threat to stability in Asia, but later he expressed a conviction that the appeal of the Communist philosophy had dwindled in some Asian countries in the last 16 years. He cited Pakistan, India, Indonesia and Japan as examples.

The President returned to the same themes on his arrival at the Manila International Airport, where he was greeted by President and Mrs. Ferdinand E. Marcos and a large delegation of Filipino officials.

"I want to convey throughout the trip," he said, "the great sense of respect and affection which the people of the United States feel for their Asian neighbors and the readiness of my country to support the efforts of Asian nations to improve the life of their peoples. I will also offer the view that peace and progress in Asia must be shaped and protected primarily by Asian hands and that the contribution which my country can make to that process should come as a supplement to Asian energies and in response to Asian leadership."

* * *

July 31, 1969

NIXON SEES THIEU, TALKS TO TROOPS IN VIETNAM VISIT

Says Allies Have Gone as Far as They Can or Should to Open 'Door to Peace'

BIDS ENEMY RESPOND

President Tells G.I.'s They Fight in a Worthy Cause—He Arrives in India

By ROBERT B. SEMPLE Jr.
Special to The New York Times

BANGKOK, Thailand, July 30—President Nixon made a quick trip to South Vietnam today that combined public displays of loyalty to the South Vietnamese with intense private deliberations over future American troop withdrawals and possible changes in military tactics.

After conferring with President Nguyen Van Thieu, Mr. Nixon declared:

"We have gone as far now as we can or should go in opening the door to peace, and now it is time for the other side to respond."

[President Nixon arrived in India Thursday after a flight from Bangkok and was greeted by Prime Minister Indira Gandhi, The Associated Press reported.]

Mr. Nixon's visit to Saigon, accompanied by Mrs. Nixon, marked the first time an American President had gone to the South Vietnamese capital. He also paid a call on American troops of the First Infantry Division at Dian, a relatively secure base 12 miles north of Saigon.

Says Vietnamese Can Choose

There he told the troops that the war had been fought in a worthy cause—to allow the South Vietnamese "to choose their own way" and to "reduce the chances of more wars in the future."

Disregarding the heat, dust and mud, the President plunged among the troops, shaking hands, chatting in folksy tones about their favorite baseball and football teams, and commending them for their heroism and sacrifice in a difficult war that he described as "one of America's finest hours."

What seemed to buoy Mr. Nixon's aides most of all was the simple fact that he had risked a visit to the war zone and carried it off. Not incidentally, however, he managed to squeeze in two hours of talk with Mr. Thieu, and, on the plane that bore him from Bangkok early this morning to an airfield near

Saigon, an hour or so with Gen. Creighton W. Abrams, commander of United States troops in South Vietnam.

In the course of these sessions, according to usually well informed sources, Mr. Nixon was said to have done these things:

Discussed with President Thieu the rate and magnitude of future troop withdrawals. About 25,000 United States troops are now being withdrawn and, according to officials here, a firm decision on further cuts will be made in two weeks to a month.

Expressed deep interest in the possible meanings of the current lull in the fighting, despite the obvious efforts of his military commanders to dismiss it as having little or no diplomatic significance.

Reviewed with General Abrams possible changes in military tactics to diminish casualties, shore up his public support at home, and strengthen his hand in the Paris peace negotiations.

'The Record Is Clear'

Publicly, Mr. Nixon's posture was one of resolution and firmness. Although the allied position here is obviously precarious in some respects, he suggested over and over again that it was not so bad that the North Vietnamese should expect further concessions.

"I believe the record is clear," he said in remarks following his meeting with Mr. Thieu at the Presidential Palace in Saigon, "as to which side has gone the extra mile in behalf of peace.

"We have stopped the bombing of North Vietnam. We have withdrawn 25,000 American troops. They have been replaced by South Vietnamese. We have made, and you [Mr. Thieu] have made, a peace offer which is as generous as any ever made in the history of warfare.

"It is a peace of reconciliation that is offered, a peace in which the people will decide, a peace that is just for both sides, a peace which is fair to both sides, a peace which offers an equal chance to both sides.

"We have gone as far now as we can or should go in opening the door to peace, and now it is time for the other side to respond."

And when he visited the troops, he expressed in somewhat more colloquial but no less resolute terms his stated belief that the war had been fought in a worthy cause—to allow the South Vietnamese "to choose their own way"—and should therefore be concluded on honorable terms that would "discourage aggression and reduce the chances of more wars in the future."

Moon Landing Cited

Addressing two companies in full battle dress, both of which were preparing to go out on missions in the surrounding countryside, he declared:

"I suppose out here, as is always the case, you perhaps get tired of lectures. I don't mean to lecture now.

"But I want you to know that we are going to record some time the history of this time, and in that history it is going to be one of the most exciting periods in all the history of man—the landing on the moon, those three brave men who landed there.

United Press International

SOUTH VIETNAM: President Nixon with First Infantry Division troops in Dian yesterday.

"But also out here in this dreary difficult war, I think history will record that this may have been one of America's finest hours, because we took a difficult task and we succeeded."

"You are doing your job," he concluded, adding with emphasis:

"I can assure you we are going to try to do ours to see that you didn't fight in vain."

As if to demonstrate his faith in military progress, Mr. Nixon allowed his wife to accompany him to the war zone. Mrs. Nixon also visited Vietnamese orphanages in Saigon and a field hospital near Toansonnhut airfield near Saigon.

Secret Service Objected

White House sources disclosed that Mr. Nixon had planned for several weeks to make a side trip to South Vietnam despite what they said were strenuous objections from the Secret Service.

The security precautions were exceptionally tight. In Saigon, streets were cleared for six blocks around the Presidential palace. All communications were blocked so that no one could get word of Mr. Nixon's presence out of the city. Reporters were told last night that they would be going to

Saigon with the President, but the visit to the Dian base was not revealed ahead of time.

Helicopters swarmed in circular fashion around the palace in Saigon like horses on a carousel throughout the Presidential visit. There were armed vehicles and heavily-manned bunkers everywhere.

The route to Dian was carefully plotted in advance to conform with Secret Service specifications. Although there have been no known incidents of ground fire at airplanes near Dian in over a year, the Presidential helicopter nevertheless flew at a higher altitude than usual. Mr. Nixon's aircraft was also accompanied by several armed helicopters equipped to respond quickly to trouble on the ground or in the air.

Mr. Nixon proceeded without incident from point to point; so smooth was his tour that it was difficult to believe that a war was going on.

Yet for all Mr. Nixon's public expressions of confidence, some observers professed to find an inconsistency between his bold rhetoric and his displays of unbending resolution, and the fact that he devoted most of his private talks to troop withdrawals and the possibility of softening the "maximum pressure" strategy that has prevailed on the battlefields of South Vietnam for many months.

To these observers, it was difficult to reconcile Mr. Nixon's assertion that "we have gone as far now as we can or should go" with the prospect of modifications in either troop levels or battlefield tactics, which might only encourage the enemy to hold out for further concessions and avoid serious bargaining in Paris.

Looking to Public

The President's top diplomatic advisers asserted that there was no such contradiction. They suggested that while a "maximum pressure" might well be the proper course in a conventional war, the war in Vietnam was anything but conventional and involved the important diplomatic and psychological considerations.

The clear implication was that revised battlefield tactics, leading to lower casualties might soften public opposition to the war and purchase for Mr. Nixon the time he feels he needs to negotiate a satisfactory solution in Paris.

As for the lull, Presidential aides said it might wall represent a decision on the part of the enemy to de-escalate the war. They said the evidence was that enemy troops had not been withdrawn to North Vietnam, as Mr. Nixon wants, but had instead retreated into Laos and Cambodia.

Even so, officials said they were studying the lull very carefully to see whether it would yield evidence that Hanoi was beginning to take reciprocal steps to de-escalate the fighting.

Gen. Earl G. Wheeler, chairman of the Joint Chiefs of Staff, has said publicly that the enemy lull has no diplomatic significance and is merely a staging period for new offensives. The American military commanders in South Vietnam have made no secret of their desire to keep up the pressure at a time when they think the enemy has been badly hurt.

Mr. Nixon apparently enjoyed his excursion among the troops and showed direct, open enthusiasm.

Took Copter to Dian

After his two hours in private meetings at the palace in Saigon, he boarded a helicopter for the eight-minute flight to Dian.

When his helicopter landed Mr. Nixon jumped out, walked briskly to a waiting Jeep and got in. Then, almost surreptitiously, he brushed the side of the Jeep with his right forefinger, looking for dust, as he must have seen countless officers do in his Navy days 25 years ago. When he saw reporters watching him, he smiled sheepishly, and said: "I feel right at home."

The motorcade, consisting of 11 Jeeps, two trucks for photographers, several staff cars and two press buses, roared off down the road, coming to a halt about 300 yards away where two rifle companies had assembled in battle gear.

Mr. Nixon presented four Distinguished Service Crosses, and made a five-minute speech in which he did not seek to minimize the ambiguities of the war.

"This war is the most difficult war any army has ever fought," he said, noting that "this is the first time in our history when we have had a lack of understanding of why we are here, what the war is all about."

"What happens in Vietnam, how this war is ended, may well determine what happens to peace and freedom in the world," he said.

When he finished, he moved among the troops to shake hands with them and be photographed with them. Then, he stepped backward into a mud puddle.

Mr. Nixon laughed at his misfortune and went on.

"Vietnam, is the only place in the world where you can be blinded by a dust storm while sinking in the mud," a nearby observer said. But Mr. Nixon gamely brushed the dust from his eyes, kicked the mud from his shoes, and moved on through the men around him.

"Where are you from, soldier?" he asked.

"Riverside," was the reply.

"Riverside? That's where my wife and I were married; 1940, it was. Probably before you were born."

"Yes sir."

"And where are you from?"

"Texas."

"Texas? I'll be darned. Think the Cowboys can beat the Packers this year?"

"I hope so, sir."

"They've lost their quarterback, you know," the President said knowledgeably.

Mr. Nixon has often said that he reads the sports pages first every morning.

"And where are you from?"

"Chicago."

"Chicago! Have you seen the Cubs this year? They might take it all. Are you a Cub or a White Sox fan?"

"I'm a Yankee fan, sir."

This brought laughter.

"That World Series is going to be tough for the Yankees to make," the President said with a frown. Then, brightening. "They're not the best team, but they're moving along. Got a lot of speed. Stick with the Yankees, our daughter is a Yankee fan."

The President obviously enjoyed himself, the men, the tour and the idea that he had successfully managed a visit to a combat area, which, in his view, Lyndon Johnson had not done when he visited the remote and tranquil fortress at Camranh Bay.

Some of this sense of one-upmanship emerged during the flight from Bangkok this morning. Mr. Nixon was asking reporters about their own experience in Vietnam—this was his eighth visit—and when one of them replied that he had covered Mr. Johnson during his two visits to Camranh Bay, Mr. Nixon said:

"That doesn't count, that isn't Vietnam."

* * *

August 29, 1969

G.I.'S IN BATTLE AREA SHRUG OFF THE STORY OF BALKY COMPANY A

By JAMES P. STERBA
Special to The New York Times

IN THE HIETDUC VALLEY, South Vietnam, Aug. 28—When 900 American soldiers began moving along the valley floor south of Danang at 5:30 A.M. today, the temperature stood at 84 degrees. By noon it was 118 degrees and enemy fire had killed at least a dozen of the Americans.

Several hundred men have been fighting here for more than a week. Today some of them shrugged when they heard of an incident that occurred early on Sunday when a company commander, ordered to move forward, told his superior, "My men refuse to go."

Several of the marines and infantrymen here said they had seen incidents in which soldiers—like those on Sunday in Company A of the Third Battalion, 21st Infantry—temporarily refused to continue. Generally, they said, the reluctant troops, again like those of Company A, go back into battle after pep talks.

Sometimes, they added, combat-toughened men liked to test new commanders by grumbling.

Why the men of Company A refused to fight seemed simple to those interviewed. None of the explanations concerned fighting in lost causes, fighting for no apparent reason, antiwar sentiment, troop withdrawals or the Paris peace talks.

The elephant grass here cuts arms and faces, sometimes drawing blood that mixes with sweat and forms itchy scabs that become infected after a few days. There are no showers in this valley, and few shaves. Water is for drinking only.

The soldiers here zigzag through the shoulder-high grass wearing sweaty jungle boots, inch-thick flak jackets, three to five canteens and steel helmets and carrying 30 to 70 pounds of ammunition and gear.

Sleep is precious. Lapses into slumber compete with thoughts of enemy ambushes and mortar attacks. The two do not mix well.

The enemy, fresh and heavily armed, chose to stand and fight in this valley, 18 miles west of the coastal city of Tamky. It had been enemy territory for years until March, when the village of Hietduc was retaken for the first time since the Vietcong overran it in 1965.

With 3,900 civilians there, the village pacification program was going strong, officials reported. According to military commanders, captured prisoners and documents, the enemy target was to overrun the village again. It was estimated that 2,000 to 5,000 enemy troops had been committed to the effort.

The Americans caught them and began a "pre-emptive drive" before the town was hit. The incident involving Company A was being portrayed by commanders here as trivial. Except for the company commander, Lieut. Eugene Shurtz Jr. who is being reassigned to a headquarters position in the 196th Light Infantry Brigade, no further action is planned against the men involved, spokesmen in Chulai said.

"It is over and forgotten as far as I am concerned," a top commander said.

Soldiers in the field supported his judgment.

"Everybody gripes," said a Marine private, Larry Cuellar, a 21-year-old member of Company M, which lost 4 men killed and 12 wounded in 10 hours of fighting today.

"When guys don't want to go; they just make them go, and once you're out there it's O.K.," he said. "There's too much to think about."

Another soldier said of the Company A affair:

"A lot of guys don't want to go back in there and they say so. But they do it anyway. They complain all the while, until the shooting starts. A good company commander will take care of you out there. Word never gets out. He'll give you hell and then plead with headquarters to get you some relief. That C.O. must have been new. He didn't know the ropes. And word got out and now there's a big stink. But it's all a lot of bull—it really is."

General Gives Views

SAIGON, South Vietnam, Aug. 28 (UPI)—A United States Army general said today that the case of the American infantrymen who temporarily refused to go into battle was an insignificant incident that detracted from the bravery shown by thousands of other G. I.'s in scoring a major victory in the Vietnam war.

"When you focus on this very small, insignificant incident involving the five men," Maj. Gen. Lloyd B. Ramsey said, "It detracts from the outstanding contributions and accomplishments of more than 3,000 troops who did their jobs as professionals." General Ramsey, commander of the Americal Divison, gave his view by telephone from his headquarters at Chulai.

* * *

August 31, 1969

RETURN TO QUAGMIRE

From the beginning of the American involvement in Vietnam, the United States repeatedly has been drawn in more deeply than the country realized or its President intended.

Neither Dwight D. Eisenhower nor John F. Kennedy would have favored policies they knew would commit a half-million American troops to major land warfare in Southeast Asia; yet that is the unhappy end point of the programs they initiated. Even Lyndon B. Johnson, who made the most fatal errors, undoubtedly believed at the start—as he pledged in his 1964 campaign—that he would never send large American combat forces to take principal responsibility for fighting South Vietnam's war.

And now Richard M. Nixon finds himself trapped—in defiance of both will and reason—on a road that can only lead to fresh disasters.

Mr. Nixon's commitment to disengagement, not only from Vietnam but from future Asian military adventures, is unmistakable. His Guam doctrine of a reduced American defense role in Asia after Vietnam is being set in motion even before the Vietnam war has ended. The negotiations the Administration is conducting with Thailand and Japan and the study mission in Southeast Asia that Senator Mansfield undertook at the President's request demonstrate the genuineness of the Nixon objective. Yet, on the crucial pre-condition—ending the war in Vietnam—Mr. Nixon increasingly seems to be slipping toward the same quagmire that seized and finally submerged President Johnson.

Mr. Nixon's fundamental error from the first has been the assumption that he has time for intricate maneuvers in diplomacy, psychological warfare and military tactics—maneuvers that might enable him to gain at the conference table what American military power has been unable to wrest away from the Communists on the ground. Thus, instead of a dramatic initiative to prove that policies as well as Administrations had changed, his negotiators in Paris started with instructions to play hard to get. They were not directed to open secret talks nor were they provided with new substantive proposals they could explore.

While Ambassador Lodge waited for the other side to make the first move, General Abrams in Saigon was confirmed in his orders to maintain "maximum pressure" militarily. This obvious effort to influence the Paris outcome by attempting to increase Saigon's area of control on the ground may not have represented a revival in Washington of the delusive idea that the war could be "won" by either side; but it did play into the hands of those in Saigon, both Americans and Vietnamese, who preferred to fight on rather than accept a compromise settlement.

Even before Mr. Nixon took office, the top North Vietnamese delegates in Paris had warned the American representatives that there "could be no progress" in the negotiations as long as stepped-up military efforts were being made to alter the territorial *status quo* in South Vietnam. The Communists also pointed out, as Ambassador Harriman reported in last Sunday's New York Times Magazine, that their military offensives were criticized as hampering negotiations, yet when they de-escalated, American and Saigon military leaders swung to the misconception that victory was in sight.

Despite this lugubrious history, the long lull in Communist military initiatives this summer was first ignored, then met with a minimum response. Worse still, after a brief two-day upsurge in Communist operations occurred Aug. 11 and 12—and in the face of a swift acknowledgment by Secretary of State Rogers that "activity is back to what it was prior to that time"—Mr. Nixon decided to delay the major American troop withdrawal he had been scheduled to announce.

The whole Nixon strategy for ending the war, if strategy there is, could be vitiated by this maneuver. The threat to halt American troop withdrawals will not lead Hanoi to absorb allied offensives without striking back. But Mr. Nixon could rob himself indefinitely of his main instrument for pressing President Thieu to broaden his government and to seek an accommodation with the Vietcong. As long as Saigon believes United States forces will go on fighting its war, it will have little reason to negotiate a settlement.

Valuable time and invaluable lives are being lost purposelessly, for sooner or later American troop withdrawals must resume, if only to ease the pressure of outraged American opinion. With student antiwar protests again being organized on a nationwide basis and with battlefield war weariness reflecting itself in the refusal of a company of troops to go into action in South Vietnam, time clearly is running out on diplomatic stalling tactics as a device for extracting concessions from the other side.

What is needed now is rapid resumption of American troop cuts, linked with proposals for a standstill cease-fire. North Vietnam has gone far to disengage itself from dependence on Communist China by sending home the Chinese labor battalions that were repairing bomb damage. The Vietcong representatives in Paris have offered to de-escalate the war if the United States takes the lead.

A proposal for a cease-fire in place that would freeze the territorial *status quo,* while opening negotiations for a federal system and elections in South Vietnam, offers the only hope for a compromise settlement both sides could accept.

* * *

September 4, 1969

HO CHI MINH DEAD AT 79; NORTH VIETNAM EXPECTED TO HOLD TO WAR POLICIES

NO EFFECT IS SEEN ON TALKS IN PARIS

U. S. Officials Say Death of Mystical Leader Won't Alter Peace Outlook

By RICHARD HALLORAN
Special to The New York Times

WASHINGTON, Sept. 3—United States officials said here tonight that the death of Ho Chi Minh meant the loss of an almost mystical leader but that it was not likely to change the course of the war in South Vietnam or to affect the prospects of reaching a settlement in the peace negotiations in Paris.

Sources close to the Vietnam situation said here that the most immediate impact would be the loss of leadership that has been embodied in Ho Chi Minh, the nationalist, the fighter for Vietnamese independence and the poetic revolutionary.

He has been such a figure for many of the Vietnamese for a half-century since he appeared at the Versailles Peace Conference in 1919 to seek more rights for his countrymen, who were then living under French colonial rule.

No Outstanding Figure

In the North, no other member of the inner circle of Communist leaders, some of whom have served with him for more than 30 years, enjoys anything like the stature of President Ho.

His quality of leadership cannot be passed on, it is thought here, and thus the future cohesion of North Vietnamese leadership is in some doubt. It is thought probable that a collective leadership, as in the Soviet Union after the death of Stalin, will emerge.

In the South, it is thought, the National Liberation Front, or Vietcong, may well have lost their most effective means of appeal for the allegiance—or at least the nonresistance—of the peasantry. "Uncle Ho," as he was widely known, was regarded by friend and foe alike as a symbol of Vietnamese aspirations.

Some officials here are not so sure that President Ho's death will be a great loss for the Vietcong in the South. They argued that the new leaders in Hanoi could be expected to invoke the memory of President Ho and continue to use his name as the symbol of their cause.

In the uncertainty following Mr. Ho's death, they said, the leaders in Hanoi will most likely hold fast, continuing the war along present lines and maintaining the unbending policy that has been followed in Paris. Not until there has been an internal political shakeout in Hanoi will they expect much change in the guerrilla fighting or at the negotiating table, they said.

The legal procedure for succession calls for the North Vietnamese Vice President to assume the office of President until an election has been held. But the current Vice President, a contemporary of President Ho, is so obscure and so politically unimportant a figure that American officials who

Camera Press Pix

Ho Chi Minh

work on Vietnamese questions every day could not recall his name today without referring to their files.

He is Ton Duc Thang, and it is taken for granted that he will be a figurehead at the most.

Four Leading Contenders

Officials here expect that the real jockeying for position will involve four men: Premier Pham Van Dong; Defense Minister Vo Nguyen Giap; Le Duan, First Secretary of the Vietnam Workers (Communist) party; and Truong Chinh, a leading theoretician.

These men may incline variously toward the Soviet or Chinese brands of Communism, but officials here consider them all to be essentially Vietnamese nationalists who will act in what they think is their own and their nation's best interests.

The likeliest to succeed, in the view here, is Pham Van Dong, who has gradually taken a more prominent role in Hanoi in recent years, evidently with the approval of President Ho. But the sources said Mr. Dong would not automatically rise to the top nor would he be likely to have the complete command that President Ho had.

Premier Dong, who is 62 years old, is considered here to favor the Soviet Union over Communist China as an ally.

Le Duan, the party secretary, also 62, was not among the early leaders of the group, but he has been on the rise since taking part in guerrilla wars against the French from 1950 to 1954.

Truong Chinh, who is 61, is chairman of the standing committee of the National Assembly but is not regarded as being in high standing. He has been ill and was reported to have returned recently from Eastern Europe, where he had gone for medical treatment.

General Giap, the hero of the victory over the French at Dienbienphu in 1954, is probably the most pragmatic of the group and is respected by professional soldiers almost universally as a military genius.

General Giap, who is 60, lost some prestige, however, after the all-out Lunar New Year offensive of 1968, which he is reported to have conceived and carried out. Sources here said the North Vietnamese, now considered that offensive to have been a failure.

* * *

September 4, 1969

HO CHI MINH WAS NOTED FOR SUCCESS IN BLENDING NATIONALISM AND COMMUNISM

From Youth He Pursued A Goal of Independence

By ALDEN WHITMAN

Among 20th-century statesmen, Ho Chi Minh was remarkable both for the tenacity and patience with which he pursued his goal of Vietnamese independence and for his success in blending Communism with nationalism.

From his youth Ho espoused freedom for the French colony of Vietnam. He persevered through years when his chances of attaining his objective were so minuscule as to seem ridiculous. Ultimately, he organized the defeat of the French in 1954 in the historic battle of Dienbienphu. This battle, a triumph of guerrilla strategy, came nine years after he was named President of the Democratic Republic of Vietnam.

After the supposed temporary division of Vietnam at the 17th parallel by the Geneva Agreement of 1954 and after that division became hardened by United States support of Ngo Dinh Diem in the South, Ho led his countrymen in the North against the onslaughts of American military might. In the war, Ho's capital of Hanoi, among other cities, was repeatedly bombed by American planes.

At the same time Ho was an inspiration for the National Liberation Front, or Vietcong, which operated in South Vietnam in the long, bloody and costly conflict against the Saigon regime and its American allies.

In the war, in which the United States became increasingly involved, especially after 1964, Ho maintained an exquisite balance in his relations with the Soviet Union and the People's Republic of China. These Communist countries, at ideological sword's points, were Ho's principal suppliers of food-stuffs and war goods. It was a measure of his diplomacy that he kept on friendly terms with each.

Small and Frail

To the 19 million people north of the 17th parallel and to other millions below it, the small, frail, ivorylike figure of Ho, with its long ascetic face, straggly goatee, sunken cheeks and luminous eyes, was that of a patriarch, the George Washington of his nation. Although his name was not attached to public squares, buildings, factories, airports or monuments, his magnetism was undoubted, as was the affection that the average citizen had for him.

He was universally called "Uncle Ho," a sobriquet also used in the North Vietnamese press. Before the exigencies of war confined him to official duties, Ho regularly visited villages and towns. Simply clad, he was especially fond of dropping into schools and chatting with the children. Westerners who knew him were convinced that, whatever his guile in larger political matters, there was no pose in his expressions of feeling for the common people.

Indeed, Ho's personal popularity was such that it was generally conceded, even by many of his political foes, that Vietnam would have been unified under his leadership had the countrywide elections pledged at Geneva taken place. As it was, major segments of South Vietnam were effectively controlled by the National Liberation Front despite the presence of hundreds of thousands of American troops.

Intelligent, resourceful and dedicated, though ruthless, Ho created a favorable impression on many of those who dealt with him. One such was Harry Ashmore of the Center for the Study of Democratic Institutions and former editor of The Arkansas Gazette.

Mr. Ashmore and the late William C. Baggs, editor of The Miami News, were among the last Americans to talk with Ho at length when they visited Hanoi in early 1967.

"Ho was a courtly, urbane, highly sophisticated man with a gentle manner and without personal venom," Mr. Ashmore recalled in a recent interview. At the meeting Ho was dressed in his characteristic high-necked white pajama type of garment, called a cu-nao, and he wore open-toed rubber sandals. He chain-smoked cigarettes, American-made Salems.

Adept in English

Their hour-long conversation started out in Vietnamese with an interpreter, Mr. Ashmore said, but soon shifted to English. Ho astonished Mr. Ashmore by his adeptness in English, which was one of several languages—the principal others were Chinese, French, German and Russian—in which he was fluent.

At one point Ho reminded Mr. Ashmore and Mr. Baggs that he had once been in the United States. "I think I know the American people," Ho said, "and I don't understand how they can support their involvement in this war. Is the Statue of Liberty standing on her head?"

This was a rhetorical question that Ho also posed to other Americans in an effort to point up what to his mind was an inconsistency: a colonial people who had gained independence in a revolution were fighting to suppress the independence of another colonial people.

Ho's knowledge of American history was keen, and he put it to advantage in the summer of 1945 when he was writing the Declaration of Independence of the Democratic Republic of

Vietnam. He remembered the contents of the American Declaration of Independence, but not its precise wording. From an American military mission then working with him he tried in vain to obtain a copy of the document, and when none could supply it Ho paraphrased it out of his recollections.

Thus his Declaration begins, "All men are created equal; they are endowed by their Creator with certain inalienable Rights; among these are Life, Liberty, and the pursuit of Happiness." After explaining that this meant that "all the peoples on the earth are equal from birth, all the peoples have a right to live, to be happy and free," Ho went on to enumerate, in the manner of the American Declaration, the grievances of his people and to proclaim their independence.

'Likable and Friendly'

Apart from Americans, Ho struck a spark with many others who came in contact with him over the years. "Extraordinarily likable and friendly" was the description of Jawaharlal Nehru, the Indian leader. Paul Mus, the French Orientalist who conducted delicate talks with Ho in 1946 and 1947, found him an "intransigent and incorruptible revolutionary, a la Saint Just."

A French naval commander who observed the slender Vietnamese for the three weeks he was a ship's passenger concluded that Ho was an "intelligent and charming man who is also a passionate idealist entirely devoted to the cause he has espoused" and a person with "naive faith in the politico-social slogans of our times and, generally, in everything that is printed."

Ho was an enormously pragmatic Communist, a doer rather than a theoretician. His speeches and articles were brought together in a four-volume "Selected Works of Ho Chi Minh" issued in Hanoi between 1960 and 1962. The late Bernard B. Fall, an American authority on Vietnam, published a collection of these in English in 1967 under the title "Ho Chi Minh on Revolution." They are simply and clearly worded documents, most of them agitational or polemical in nature and hardly likely to add to the body of Marxist doctrine.

Like Mao Tse-tung, a fellow Communist leader, Ho composed poetry, some of it considered quite affecting. One of his poems, written when he was a prisoner of the Chinese Nationalists in 1942–43, is called "Autumn Night" and reads in translation by Aileen Palmer:

In front of the gate, the guard stands with his rifle.
Above, untidy clouds are carrying away the moon.
The bedbugs are swarming around like army tanks on maneuvers,
While the mosquitoes form squadrons, attacking like fighter planes.
My heart travels a thousand li toward my native land.
My dream intertwines with sadness like a skein of a thousand threads.
Innocent, I have now endured a whole year in prison.
Using my tears for ink, I turn my thoughts into verses.

Ho's rise to power and world eminence was not a fully documented story. On the contrary, its details at some crucial points are imprecise. This led at one time to the suspicion that there were two Hos, a notion that was discounted by the French Sureté when it compared photographs of the early and the late Ho.

One explanation for the confusion is that Ho used about a dozen aliases, of which Ho Chi Minh (which can be translated as Ho, the Shedder of Light) was but one. Another was Ho's own reluctance to disclose biographical information. "You know, I am an old man, and an old man likes to hold on to his little mysteries," he told Mr. Fall. With a twinkle, he continued, "Wait until I'm dead. Then you can write about me all you want."

Nonetheless, Mr. Fall reported, before he left Hanoi he received a brief, unsigned summary of Ho's life "obviously delivered on the old man's instructions."

Despite Ho's apparent self-effacement, he did have a touch of personal vanity. Mr. Fall recalled having shown the Vietnamese leader a sketch of him by Mrs. Fall. "Yes, that is very good. That looks very much like me," Ho exclaimed. He took a bouquet of flowers from a nearby table and, handing it to Mr. Fall, said:

"Tell her for me that the drawing is very good and give her the bouquet and kiss her on both cheeks for me."

Although there is some uncertainty over Ho's birth date, the most reliable evidence indicates he was born May 19, 1890, in Kimlien, a village in Nghe-An Province in central Vietnam. Many sources give his true name as Nguyen Ai Quoc, or Nguyen the Patriot. However, Wilfred Burchett, an Australian-born correspondent who knew Ho well, believes (and it is now generally accepted) that Ho's birth name was Nguyen Tat Thanh.

He was said to be the youngest of three children. His father was only slightly better off than the rice peasants of the area, but he was apparently a man of some determination, for by rote learning he passed examinations that gave him a job in the imperial administration just when the French rule was beginning.

An ardent nationalist, Ho's father refused to learn French, the language of the conquerors of his country, and joined anti-French secret societies. Young Ho got his first underground experience as his father's messenger in the anti-French network. Shortly, the father lost his Government job and became a healer, dispensing traditional Oriental potions.

Ho's mother was believed to have been of peasant origin, but he never spoke of her.

Attended Lycée

Ho received his basic education from his father and from the village school, going on to a few years of high school at the Lycée Quoc-Hoc in the old imperial capital of Hue. This institution, founded by the father of Ngo Dinh Diem, was designed to perpetuate Vietnamese national traditions. It had a distinguished roster of graduates that included Vo Nguyen

Giap, the brilliant guerrilla general, and Pham Van Dong, the current Premier of North Vietnam.

Ho left the school in 1910 without a diploma and taught briefly at a private institution in a South Annam fishing town. It was while he was there, according to now accepted sources, that he decided to go to Europe. As a step toward that goal, he went to a trade school in Saigon in the summer of 1911 where he learned the duties of a kitchen boy and pastry cook's helper, skills in demand by Europeans of that day.

His training gave Ho a gourmet's palate, which he liked to indulge, and an ability to whip up a tasty dish, which he delighted to do when he could.

For the immediate moment, though, his training enabled him to sign aboard the Latouche-Treville as a kitchen boy, a job so menial that he worked under the alias Ba. In his travels, he visited Marseilles and ports in Africa and North America. Explaining the crucial significance of these voyages for Ho's education as a revolutionary, Mr. Fall wrote in "The Two Vietnams":

"His contacts with the white colonizers on their home grounds shattered any of his illusions as to their 'superiority', and his association with sailors from Brittany, Cornwall and the Frisian Islands—as illiterate and superstitious as the most backward Vietnamese rice farmer—did the rest.

"Ho still likes to tell the story of the arrival of his ship at an African port where, he claims, natives were compelled to jump into the shark-infested waters to secure the moorings of the vessel and were killed by the sharks under the indifferent eyes of passengers and crew.

"But his contacts with Europe also brought him the revelation of his own personal worth and dignity, when he went ashore in Europe in a Western suit, whites for the first time in his life, addressed him as 'monsieur,' instead of using the deprecating 'tu,' reserved in France for children but used in Indochina by Frenchmen when addressing natives, no matter how educated."

In his years at sea, Ho read widely—Shakespeare, Tolstoy, Marx, Zola. He was even then, according to later accounts, an ascetic and something of a puritan, who was offended when prostitutes clambered aboard his ship in Marseilles. "Why don't the French civilize their own people before they pretend to civilize us?" he is said to have remarked.

(Ho, incidentally, is believed to have been a bachelor, although the record on this point is far from clear.)

With the advent of World War I, Ho went to live in London, where he worked as a snow shoveler and as a cook's helper under Escoffier, the master chef, at the Carlton Hotel. Escoffier, it is said, promoted Ho to a job in the pastry kitchen and wanted to teach him the art of cuisine. However that may be, the 24-year-old Vietnamese was more interested in politics. He joined the Overseas Workers Association, composed mostly of Asians, and agitated, among other things, for Irish independence.

Sometime during the war, Ho gave up the Carlton's kitchen for the sea and journeyed to the United States. He is believed to have lived in Harlem for a while. Ho himself often referred to his American visit, although he was hazy about the details. According to his close associate, Pham Van Dong, what impressed Ho in the United States were "the barbarities and ugliness of American capitalism, the Ku Klux Klan mobs, the lynching of Negroes."

Out of Ho's American experiences came a pamphlet, issued in Moscow in 1924, called "La Race Noire" ("The Black Race"), which assailed racial practices in America and Europe.

About 1918 Ho returned to France and lived in a tiny flat in the Montmartre section of Paris, eking out a living by retouching photos under the name of Nguyen Ai Quoc.

At the Versailles Peace Conference of 1919 Ho emerged as a self-appointed spokesman for his native land. Seeing in Woodrow Wilson's proposal for self-determination of the peoples the possibility of Vietnam's independence, Ho, dressed in a hired black suit and bowler hat, traveled to the Palace of Versailles to present his case. He was, of course, not received, although he offered a program for Vietnam. Its proposals did not include independence, but basic freedoms and equality between the French rulers and the native population.

Whatever hopes Ho may have held for French liberation of Vietnam were destroyed in his mind by the failure of the Versailles Conference to settle colonial issues. His faith was now transferred to Socialist action. Indeed, his first recorded speech was at a congress of the French Socialist party in 1920, and it was a plea not for world revolution but "against the imperialists who have committed abhorrent crimes on my native land." He bid the party "act practically to support the oppressed natives."

Immediately afterward Ho became, fatefully, a founding member of the French Communist party because he considered that the Socialists were equivocating on the colonial issue whereas the Communists were willing to promote national liberation.

"I don't understand a thing about strategy, tactics and all the other big words you use," he told the delegates, "but I understand well one single thing: The Third International concerns itself a great deal with the colonial question. Its delegates promise to help the oppressed colonial peoples to regain their liberty and independence. The adherents of the Second International have not said a word about the fate of the colonial areas."

Edited Weekly Paper

With his decision to join the Communists, Ho's career took a marked turn. For one thing, he became the French party's resident expert on colonial affairs and edited Le Paria (The Outcast), the weekly paper of the Intercolonial Union, which he was instrumental in founding in 1921. This group was a conglomeration of restless Algerian, Senegalese, West Indian and Asian exiles in Paris who were united by a fervid nationalism and, to a lesser extent, by a common commitment to Communism.

For another thing, the fragile-looking Ho became an orator of sorts, traveling about France to speak to throngs of Vietnamese soldiers and war workers who were awaiting repatriation.

In addition, Ho gravitated to Moscow, then the nerve center of world Communism. He went there first in 1922 for the Fourth Comintern Congress, where he met Lenin and became a member of the Comintern's Southeast Asia Bureau. By all accounts, Ho was vocal and energetic, meeting all the reigning Communists and helping to organize the Krestintern, or Peasant International, for revolutionary work among colonial peoples.

After a brief sojourn in France, Ho was back in Moscow, his base for many years thereafter. He attended the University of the Toilers of the East, receiving formal training in Marxism and the techniques of agitation and propaganda.

Following his studies in Moscow, Ho was dispatched to Canton, China, in 1925 as an interpreter for Michael Borodin, one of the leaders of the Soviet mission to help Chiang Kai-shek, then in Communist favor as an heir of Sun Yat-sen. Once in Canton, Ho set about to spread the spirit of revolution in the Far East He organized Vietnamese refugees into the Vietnam Revolutionary Youth Association and set up the League of Oppressed Peoples of Asia, which soon became the South Seas Communist party, the fore-runner of various national Communist groups, including Ho's own Indochinese Communist party of 1930.

For two years, until July, 1927, when Chiang turned on his Communist allies, Ho sent apt Vietnamese to Chiang's military school at Whampoa while conducting a crash training course in political agitation for his compatriots.

Fled to Moscow

After the Chiang-Communist break, Ho fled to Moscow by way of the Gobi. His life immediately thereafter is not clear, but it is believed that he lived in Berlin for a time and traveled in Belgium, Switzerland and Italy, using a variety of aliases and passports.

After 1928 Ho turned up in eastern Thailand, disguised as a shaven-headed Buddhist monk. He traveled among Vietnamese exiles and organized political groups and published newspapers that were smuggled over the border into Vietnam.

In 1930, on advice from the Comintern, Ho was instrumental in settling the vexatious disputes that had arisen among Communists in Indochina and in organizing the Indochinese Communist party, which later became the Vietnamese Communist party and, still later, the Vietnamese Workers party.

In that same year a peasant rebellion erupted in Vietnam, which the Communists backed. On its suppression by the French, Ho was sentenced to death in absentia. At the time he was in a British jail in Hong Kong, having been arrested there in 1931 for subversive activities.

The French sought his extradition, but Ho argued that he was a political refugee and not subject to extradition. The case, which was handled in London by Sir. Stafford Cripps in a plea to the Privy Council, was decided for Ho. He was released, and fled Hong Kong in disguise (this time as a Chinese merchant) and made his way back to Moscow.

There he attended Communist schools—the Institute for National and Colonial Questions and the celebrated Lenin School. He was, however, back in China in 1938, now as a communications operator with Mao Tse-tung's renowned Eighth Route Army. Subsequently, he found his way south and entered Vietnam in 1940 for the first time in 30 years.

A Master Stroke

The timing was a master stroke, for the Japanese, virtually unopposed, had taken effective control of the Indochinese Peninsula and the French administrators, most of them Vichy adherents, agreed to cooperate with the Japanese. With great daring and imagination, Ho took advantage of World War II to piece together a coalition of Vietnamese nationalists and Communists into what was called the Vietminh, or Independence Front.

The Vietminh created a 10,000-man guerrilla force, "Men in Black," that battled the Japanese in the jungles with notable success.

Ho's actions projected him onto the world scene as the leading Vietnamese nationalist and as an ally of the United States against the Japanese. "I was a Communist," he said then, "but I am no longer one. I am a member of the Vietnamese family, nothing else."

In 1942 Ho was sent to Kunming, reportedly at the request of his American military aides. He was arrested there by Chi-ang Kai-shek's men and jailed until September 1943, when he was released, it has been said, by American request.

On his release, according to Mr. Fall, Ho cooperated with a Chinese Nationalist general in forming a wide Vietnamese freedom group. One result of this was that in 1944 Ho accepted a portfolio in the Provisional Republican Government of Vietnam. That Government was largely a paper affair, but it permitted Ho to court vigorously the American Office of Strategic Services. Thus when Ho's Vietminh took over Hanoi in 1945, senior American military officials were in his entourage. It was in this period that he took the name of Ho Chi Minh.

Independence Proclaimed

With the end of World War II, Ho proclaimed the independence of Vietnam, but it took nine years for his declaration to become an effective fact. First, under the Big Three Agreement at Potsdam, the Chinese Nationalists occupied Hanoi and the northern sector of Vietnam. Second, the French (in British ships) arrived to reclaim Saigon and the southern segment of the country. And third, Ho's nationalist coalition was strained under pressure of these events.

Forming a new guerrilla force around the Vietminh, Ho and his colleagues, according to most accounts, dealt summarily with dissidents unwilling to fight in Ho's fashion for independence. Assassinations were frequently reported. Meantime, as the Chinese withdrew from the north and the French advanced from the south, Ho negotiated with the French to save his nationalist regime.

In a compromise that Ho worked out in Paris in 1946, he agreed to let the Democratic Republic of Vietnam become a part of the French Union as a free state within the Indochina federation. The French recognized Ho as chief of state and promised a plebiscite in the South on the question of a unified Vietnam under Ho.

By the start of 1947, the agreement had broken down, and Ho's men were fighting the French Army. The Vietminh guerrillas held the jungles and the villages, the French the cities. For seven years the war raged as Ho's forces gathered strength, squeezing the French more and more. For most of this time, Ho was diplomatically isolated, for he was not recognized by Communist China or the Soviet Union until his victory over the French was virtually assured.

In an effort to shore up their political forces, the French resurrected Bao Dai, the puppet of the Japanese who held title as Emperor. Corrupt and pleasure-loving, he soon moved with his mistresses to France, leaving a weak and splintered regime in Saigon.

This, of course, proved no support for the French Army, which was also sapped by General Giap's guerrilla tactics. Finally, on May 8, 1954, the French forces were decisively defeated at Dienblenphu. The Indochina war ended officially in July at a cost to the French of 172,000 casualties and to the Vietminh of perhaps three times that many.

The cease-fire accord was signed in Geneva July 21, 1954, and it represented far less than Ho's hopes. But by that time the United States was involved in Vietnam on the French side through $800-million a year in economic aid. Fear of Communist expansion in Asia dominated Washington, with Vice President Richard M. Nixon saying, "If, to avoid further Communist expansion in Asia, we must take the risk of putting our boys in, I think the Executive Branch has to do it."

The Geneva Accord, however, divided Vietnam at the 17th parallel, creating a North and a South Vietnam. It removed the French administration from the peninsula and provided for all Vietnam elections in 1956 as a means of unifying the country.

Although a party to the Geneva Accord, the United States declined to sign it. South Vietnam, also a nonsignatory, refused to hold the elections. Meantime, the United States built up its military mission in Saigon and its support of the regime of President Ngo Dinh Diem as a counter to continued guerrilla activity of the National Liberation Front, which became pronounced after 1956.

The front, technically independent of Ho Chi Minh in the North, increased its sway into the nineteen-sixties. It supplied itself from captured American arms and from materiel that came through from the North. Beginning in 1964, thousands of American troops were poured into South Vietnam to battle the Vietcong and then to bomb North Vietnam.

The halt of American bombing in 1968 finally led to the peace negotiations in Paris, but in the meantime the fighting in South Vietnam continued.

Confident of Victory

Throughout, Ho was confident of victory. In 1962, when the war was still a localized conflict between the South Vietnamese forces and 11,000 American advisers on the one hand and a smaller guerrilla force on the other, he told a French visitor:

"It took us eight years of bitter fighting to defeat you French, and you knew the country and had some old friendships here. Now the South Vietnamese regime is well-armed and helped by the Americans.

"The Americans are much stronger than the French, though they know us less well. So it perhaps may take 10 years to do it, but our heroic compatriots in the South will defeat them in the end.

Ho was still confident in early 1967, when he talked with Mr. Ashmore and Mr. Baggs. "We have been fighting for our independence for more than 25 years, he told them, and of course we cherish peace, but we will never surrender our independence to purchase a peace with the United States or any party."

At the close of his conversation, he clenched his right fist and said emotionally, "You must know of our resolution. Not even your nuclear weapons would force us to surrender after so long and violent a struggle for the independence of our country."

Of his own death he appeared unemotional. He had been urged to give up cigarettes, but, he persisted in smoking. "When you are as old as I am," he remarked, "you do not worry about the harm of cigarettes."

* * *

September 21, 1969

U.S. MILITARY SPURS CAMPAIGN TO CURB MARIJUANA IN VIETNAM

Helicopters and Television in Suppression Drive

By B. DRUMMOND AYRES Jr.
Special to The New York Times

SAIGON, South Vietnam, Sept. 20—So many United States soldiers in South Vietnam are smoking marijuana that it has become a cash crop for farmers and a major worry for military commanders.

American authorities are fighting back with a campaign of suppression that involves Federal agents, helicopters, police dogs and spot television announcements.

Scores of soldiers have been reprimanded for smoking marijuana. Dozens more have been docked pay and reduced in rank for possessing several packets of cigarettes. A few men have been dishonorably discharged and imprisoned for making sales.

The suppression effort, which coincides with a similar antimarijuana drive in the United States, also has resulted in the seizure and destruction of more than three tons of "grass," enough to make perhaps five million cigarettes.

"The squeeze is on and it's beginning to tell," says Col. W. H. Metzner, who is Provost Marshal for the American command and thus is the top United States military lawman in Vietnam.

Still, marijuana remains readily available on just about every busy street corner in the country. Shoeshine boys and trinket hawkers will quietly and quickly hand over ten "happy" cigarettes for a dollar, about a fifth of the average price in the United States.

The South Vietnamese Government has ordered its police to help the American authorities by clamping down on both hawkers and marijuana growers. Agents from the United States Bureau of Narcotics and Dangerous Drugs have been brought in to train Vietnamese law officers in detection techniques.

But the South Vietnamese effort is lagging. Government policemen already have their hands full with security problems and they find it difficult to concentrate on suppression of marijuana, which has never been widely used by Vietnamese youths.

3 Harvests a Year

Most Vietnamese consider marijuana nothing more than a weed. However, a number of farmers have discovered otherwise and they now raise it as a crop, particularly in the Mekong Delta, where the fertile soil produces three harvests a year.

United States and South Vietnamese authorities have begun using helicopters to spot the fields. On a recent flight, a pilot was wounded by an enemy soldier who thought he was the object of the low-level mission.

American officials have stepped up searches of barracks and base areas. Sometimes the search teams are accompanied by dogs specially trained to sniff out the distinctive grassy odor of marijuana.

Besides marijuana, the United States Command in Saigon also is worried about an increase in the use of so-called hard narcotics and drugs among American soldiers. But this problem apparently involves only a few hundred of the half-million servicemen in Vietnam, whereas the marijuana problem involves thousands, probably tens of thousands.

"One reason for the less serious use of narcotics and drugs," explains Colonel Metzner, "is that such things as opium and pep pills are much harder to come by than marijuana."

No Exact Figures

Precise figures on marijuana use by American soldiers in Vietnam are not available. As with civilian youth in the United States, the difficulty arises in pinpointing how many persons smoke undetected. Then it is important to determine how many of the undetected smoke only once or twice and how many smoke more or less regularly.

Interviews with military officers and with troops in the field indicate that very few marijuana users are caught, although violations obviously number in the many thousands and are increasing.

A chaplain in the 101st Airborne Division, based near Hue, estimated that one of every two soldiers in the average company smoked in varying degrees. Yet only a few were apprehended, according to reports by division officers.

Similarly, a military police investigator who spends most of his time in the Saigon area working on what he calls "the pot problem" said:

"We can safely assume that usage among G.I.'s in Vietnam is at least as high as usage among young civilians back in the States. It's rising there so it's surely rising here, since marijuana is considerably easier to come by in Saigon or some tiny hamlet than in, say, Seattle."

'We Wander Off and Turn On'

A machinegunner from the First Cavalry Division (Airmobile), operating out of an isolated firebase about 60 miles north of Saigon, said:

"We often have pot parties when we stand down for a few days after a month or so of bumping in the boonies. Usually one of the guys has a little bag of stuff and so a dozen or so of us will wander off to some quiet spot and turn on."

Compounding the problem of determining exactly how many servicemen in Vietnam use marijuana is the fact that military regulations permit unit commanders to punish minor violators and not report the punishment so long as it is only a reprimand, a transfer or a loss of pay and rank.

Much to the relief of the United States command in Saigon, most cases involve only minor violations, such as a soldier caught smoking a single cigarette.

The few major cases that occur are tried by military courts of record. For a violator charged with selling marijuana or smoking it while on a combat mission, judges can hand down a dishonorable discharge and five years in prison.

Actually, there is almost no evidence of the use of marijuana by men under fire. But the possibility that large numbers of combat troops might begin smoking in the front lines obviously worries United States officials.

'Pot Is Number 10'

They have ordered unit commanders and sergeants to give periodic lectures on the dangers of marijuana. They also have arranged for the distribution of millions of pamphlets, thousands of posters and dozens of films radio announcements and television spots that denounce marijuana.

One of the most striking posters is a black and white conglomeration of psychedelic scratchings, including a peace symbol. The message at the top reads: "Pot is Number 10".

In soldier slang, anything that is bad is "Number 10." Conversely, anything that is good is "Number 1."

More than one barracks artist has blacked out the zero on the poster.

The television and radio spots, which are broadcast over the Armed Forces Network, are considered particularly effective by military authorities. One especially dramatic TV production portrays a marijuana user dreamily going about guard duty.

"Don't bring me down, man, I'm enjoying the world," he tells a fellow trooper who urges him to put out "that stuff." Then the screen dissolves into a mass of psychedelic whorls, finally evolving into a scene that shows both men sprawled in grotesque death. An enemy soldier, rifle in hand, stands in the foreground.

* * *

October 12, 1969

THE ARVN IS BIGGER AND BETTER, BUT—

By TOM BUCKLEY

SAIGON—Can an army that since its founding has lost many more battles than it has won, that has been scorned even by its allies as cowardly and corrupt and relegated to the rear areas, redeem itself after nearly 10 years of increasingly savage warfare? On the answer to this question hinges the success of President Nixon's evolving strategy of disengagement, in which, over the next few years, a Vietnamese soldier, burning with aggressiveness and armed to the teeth, will leap into the breach left by every departing American.

A correspondent returning to Vietnam after an absence of 15 months is assured on every side that the reformation of the Vietnamese armed forces and the eventual "Vietnamization" of the war is moving along ahead of schedule.

President Nguyen Van Thieu said recently that his men were ready to take over the fighting right now, requiring only American air, artillery and supply support. Privately, everyone is far more cautious, particularly the American command. It is clear that Gen. Creighton W. Abrams and his staff are in no hurry to get home.

"Improvement is painfully slow," a senior American officer said recently, making a face like a man having a tooth pulled. "It takes a tremendous amount of effort. If you want to be discouraged, this is the place to settle down. But if you really dig in, roll up your sleeves and get on with the program, you'll find the product we're dealing with has the potential."

While the South Vietnamese are becoming stronger, he went on, exhaustion is overcoming the Vietcong and the North Vietnamese. "In comparison with the North Vietnamese coming into the country now, I would put my bets on the South Vietnamese soldier anytime," he said.

Supporting such assertions are a stream of reports from every corner of this sprawling land, analyzed, collated and fed into computers, which produce neatly crosshatched maps and diagrams on any subject. The product is impressive, but there has always been the suspicion that the basic statistics of the war—the body count, the kill ratio, the infiltration rate, the security rating of hamlets, even the data revealed in captured documents—often fit rather too neatly into the military thesis of the moment.[1]

At the moment, the thesis seems to be that a negotiated peace of almost any sort would be a disaster, and that if only something close to the present number of American troops can be kept here for the next year or two, fighting alongside the resurgent Vietnamese, a clear-cut victory—or at least a technical knockout—can still be achieved.

Beyond these considerations, there can be sensed an almost desperate desire to correct past errors and to remove the tarnish from American military prestige that would make the Pentagon willing to place one last plunger's bet. It was a civilian who put it best. "Everybody out here wants to win," he said. "My God, look how many dead Americans there have been—nearly 40,000. Have you ever seen the coffins being loaded aboard the planes at Tansonnhut? Well, I have. I go over there to watch every so often. It helps to remind me what's at stake here."

In assessing the state of the Vietnamese armed forces, only two major points seem indisputable. The first is that

---

1. The toll of American and Vietnamese dead, a far more reliable indicator, tells a different story. On the basis of figures for the first eight months of this year, 15,000 South Vietnamese and 10,000 Americans will have died in combat here in 1969. This is considerably lower than the total of 39,000 for 1968, and a reduction of American fatalities by a third, but higher than the combined toll of 22,000 for 1967. One can reasonably ask: Who is doing all this killing?

they are now about a third larger than they were at the time of the Tet offensive. The second is that their armaments, communications and transport are being sharply improved.

The Vietnamese Army (ARVN) now numbers 345,000. In addition, there are a total of 46,000 men in the all-volunteer Airborne Division, Marines and Rangers. The largest increases have been made in the Regional and Popular Forces, which are used mainly as village security forces, and now total 391,000. The Air Force and Navy number 21,000 each. Paramilitary forces—the National Police and Police Field Force, revolutionary development teams, Montagnard mercenaries and armed Vietcong defectors—total 185,000. In all, just over a million men are under arms, and a further increase of 90,000 is scheduled next year.

These, at any rate, are the official figures. Actual strengths are probably considerably lower. An average of 350 Vietnamese troops, nearly double American losses, are being killed each week. The desertion rate remains high, probably averaging between 20 per cent and 25 per cent a year.

Even so, they are impressive figures. Add the 500,000 American and 50,000 other allied troops now in Vietnam, and the total comes to about 1.6 million, an eight-to-one margin of superiority over the estimated 100,000 North Vietnamese and 100,000 Vietcong who oppose them.

A third line of defense has been created in the past 18 months. Called the People's Self-Defense Force, it is composed of women, youths of predraft age and those over 40 and thus beyond the reach of conscription. This unsalaried agglomeration, which has been equipped with hand-me-down weapons, is now said to number about a million members. It is probably less useful as a combat force than as a means of involving large numbers of people in the war.

After the bitter fighting of the first half of last year, the American command realized—belatedly, as is admitted now—that the enemy forces, which had been equipped with excellent automatic rifles, machine guns and rockets from Russian and Chinese arsenals, outgunned the Saigon troops, who were still using World War II weapons. A Vietnamese division had only a third of the artillery of an American division, a quarter of the machine guns, a tenth of the trucks and armored vehicles. The Vietnamese Air Force had only a handful of jet fighter-bombers and 100 worn-out helicopters.

A three-year $1-billion program to make up these deficiencies was begun in mid-1968. The issuing of M-16 automatic rifles, M-60 light machine guns and M-79 grenade launchers to the ARVN and the Regional and Popular Forces is scheduled to be completed by the end of this year. Forty UH-21 helicopters have already been delivered. Forty more will be delivered by the end of next year. Thereafter, they will be handed over as quickly as men are trained to fly and maintain them. Sixty A-37 jets are also on order.

Thousands of vehicles of all sorts are being turned over to the Vietnamese. The number of armored personnel carriers will rise from 600 at the beginning of 1968 to 1,500 at the end of this year. So many jeeps have been ordered that Representative Robert L. F. Sikes of Florida recently told the House that it looked as though it was the Pentagon's goal to put every Vietnamese soldier behind the wheel.

Many younger American officers question the wisdom of giving so much intricate equipment to the Vietnamese. "They will have to divert thousands of men from combat units to keep it in repair, which they won't be able to do in the long run, anyhow," said an adviser.

"Another thing is that conventional equipment dictates conventional tactics. The French couldn't win that way; the Vietnamese, fighting the same way, were nearly beaten in 1965, although they outnumbered and heavily outgunned the VC. When we stepped in with combat troops, we couldn't win a clear-cut victory, despite our enormous superiority of firepower. Now it looks like we're repeating the mistake all over again."

It is a military axiom that, unless it is a matter of slingshots vs. machine guns, manpower and equipment are of far less importance than training, tactics, leadership and morale. On the basis of visits to Vietnamese training camps, headquarters and combat units, and conversations with scores of officers, enlisted men and American advisers, it appears that in these areas little or no progress has been made.

The Quangtrung basic training center outside Saigon is the largest in the country. Twelve thousand men are assigned to spend the first nine weeks of their army service there. It is a pleasant place, built by the French, with tree-shaded barracks and open-air classrooms, neatly clipped parade grounds and rifle ranges.

However, the training the men receive is based on American Army practice of the Korean war period. It bears slight relation to the realities of combat in Vietnam. Although the recruits will soon be slogging hip-deep through flooded paddy fields, twisting through jungle and climbing rugged hills, their marching is done along paved roads and their maneuvering on flat and open ground. On the infiltration course, the recruits, their rifles cradled in their arms, crawl 100 yards or so, sliding under barbed-wire barriers, while a machine gun, held in brackets, fires live rounds a couple of feet over their heads. They are apparently being taught to infiltrate their own outposts, since the Vietcong and North Vietnamese seldom, if ever, string barbed wire.

The enemy fights and moves at night for the most part, but at Quangtrung daylight is preferred. An officer told me proudly that his men spent "many nights" out of their barracks. What that turned out to mean was that they slept in pup tents pitched nearby, an adventure comparable to an American youngster's getting his parents' permission to camp out in the back yard.

All over Vietnam, officers and enlisted men have wormed their way into safe and comfortable jobs—often, it is said, through personal influence or the payment of bribes. Quangtrung is no exception. By and large, the recruits are trained by men who have been assigned there for five years or more. Many of them have never been in combat.

The psychological-warfare officer, who said he had been assigned to the camp for eight years, almost the entire period of the war, proved to be the most ferocious character I have encountered in Vietnam. "You know the way to win the war," he said, "the only way. You must kill the Vietcong to the last man."

The continuous presence of officers and noncoms makes it difficult for recruits to speak freely at Quangtrung, but soldiers who have passed through the camp recently report that the food is poor in quality and inadequate in quantity. The concessionaires who run the food PX are said to charge whatever the hungry trainees are willing to pay to supplement their diet. Privileges, such as weekend passes and excusals from drill and kitchen police, they say, are sold openly. For $500 and up, I was told, it is possible to arrange a transfer to a safe assignment or even a medical discharge.

Combat is the final test, and here only one of the 10 Vietnamese divisions, the First, based at Hue, is rated as excellent by the American headquarters. "With equal support, it's as good as any American division," a general told me. Aside from the Paratroopers, Marines and Rangers, who are generally dependable, the other divisions are graded from mediocre to terrible. Such judgments are impossible for an individual correspondent to confirm or contradict, but visits to several units around the country provide some clues as to overall performance.

The First Battalion of the 42d Independent Infantry Regiment was hacking its way through the tangled jungle and thickly wooded hills 20 miles north of Pleiku in the central highlands on the third day of a five-day sweep one day recently when my interpreter and I flew in by helicopter to join them.

"This—patrol," my interpreter heard one soldier say. "Five days without a bath."

A corporal said, "I've been in this unit for a year, and I haven't had a day off yet."

"This is easy country," another said. "The last time, the hills went straight up."

The objective of the operation was the North Vietnamese 24th Regiment and a hospital it was supposed to have established somewhere in the vicinity. The battalion—about 400 men—had been divided into two parallel columns that were moving northeastward toward a company of troops of the American Fourth Infantry Division who occupied a blocking position, ready to intercept any enemy forces that were flushed.

As jungle sweeps go in Vietnam, this one was well-conducted. The Vietnamese battalion moved carefully and fairly quietly, and it was only the American visitor who tripped on the "wait-a-minute" vines that curled across the jungle floor.

But if there was little chance of being surprised by the enemy, there was equally little chance of achieving surprise. Helicopters and observation planes circled in the clear sky, and when the other column reported that it was being sniped at, artillery fire from a base five miles away was called for, and it echoed in the valley that separated the parallel ridges on which the columns were then advancing.

The men in the battalion, half of them draftees and the other half volunteers, were carrying their new M-16 rifles, machine guns and grenade launchers. "We are now equal to the North Vietnamese," one soldier told my interpreter. The men took good care of their weapons—better than many American troops do.

At 11 A.M., the column halted, established a perimeter defense, and began cooking the first of the two meals a day that are eaten during operations. My interpreter told me that the men covered their cooking pots when he walked by. "I ask them why they do that," he said, "and they tell me they are ashamed of how poor their food is."

In the Vietnamese Army, each battalion buys its own rations. The cash allowance is 39 piasters daily for each man. It provides 750 grams (not quite four cups) of rice a day, but little else.

Wages were raised by a third in July, but hardly kept pace with inflation, and worked out to about $20 a month at the free-market rate of exchange, a fairly accurate index of purchasing power. For a single man, this sum will scarcely buy minimum comforts—cigarettes, toilet articles, an occasional bottle of beer and a restaurant meal. A man with a family gets an additional $5 a month for his wife and each child. It is not enough.

"I make less than a garbage collector in Saigon," one soldier said. "My pay lasts my wife only 20 days each month. After that, she has to borrow." Many wives go to work, some doing heavy manual labor, others finding an easier income as bar girls or prostitutes.

If a Vietnamese soldier is killed, and more than 100,000 have been since 1960, the Government provides a death benefit of a year's salary. The sum is hardly more than a token, but a bribe is often necessary to collect it, I was told. If the soldier is crippled, he is likely to end up as a beggar, since his pension will be hardly more than $5 a month.

No one tells the troops what is going on around the country or tries to buck them up when things are going badly. The Vietcong and the North Vietnamese have become abstractions. "They are good fighters," is all that anyone would say about them. Rumor, called *tin vit,* or "duck talk," takes the place of fact. A trooper in another units asked my interpreter if it was true that the head of the Vietcong delegation in Paris had visited the United States.

Some soldiers in the battalion I was with had been able to move their families to the shantytowns, called euphemistically "dependents' housing areas," that encircle Pleiku, and saw them during the one week in four that the battalion spent in its base camp. The others had to depend on mail, slow and uncertain, for information from home. A Vietnamese soldier is entitled to 15 days of leave a year, but men I talked to all over the country said that it was almost impossible to get.

When they returned to their base camp, a stocky soldier said, with their boots worn out and their fatigues torn, they couldn't get new ones. "It's not so bad being out in the forest," he said. "At least, you don't have to feel inferior to the rich people in the town."

The troops discussed these matters, my interpreter said, with an undertone of "What's to be done?" that might well be described as Oriental fatalism. And yet it seems certain that for such a family-centered people, these worries must affect morale, if not on a sunny day with no enemies in sight, then very likely at the moment of collision, when each man must decide whether to stand and fight or keep his head down and look for the way out.

And yet every Vietnamese serviceman I talked with said that although he wanted peace—wanted it with an intensity that Americans scarcely begin to imagine—he did not want a Vietcong government. It is impossible to know whether they were saying what they believed an American wanted to hear, but the country has been so bitterly divided by the heightened combat of the past three years that I suspect most of them meant what they said. (On the other hand, surveys of the rural population, which bears the brunt of the war, indicate that the desire for peace is uppermost.)

The man who holds the battalion together is its commander. Maj. Bui Van Lim. a slim, weather-beaten figure, who stands very straight, says little and marches along with his men. His troops are convinced that Major Lim does his best for them. More important, he treats them with respect. "He never calls us *may,* like the Dalat officers do," a stocky, smiling grenadier said. My interpreter explained that the word, pronounced "my," and meaning "you," has strong connotations of superiority and contempt.

Instead, the soldier went on, the major addressed them as *anh,* a formal but friendly term meaning "brother," or as *chu,* a warm greeting, meaning "little uncle."

When I mentioned to him what his men had said, the major replied, through the interpreter: "Yes, I know how much it means. I began my own military career as a private." That was in 1943, he said, when he enlisted in a French colonial regiment in Hoabinh Province in North Vietnam.

"My older brother was a sergeant," he said, "and I liked the military life. In those days, even as a private, the pay was good—more than a Vietnamese civil servant got. In 1950, I was sent to officers' school. I fought at Dienbienphu before the siege began. When the war ended, I went south, because I knew about their terrorism, and as an officer in the French Army I knew I could expect to be killed."

In the new Vietnamese Army, in which promotion from the ranks was—and still is—all but unknown, his humble beginnings and the fact that he had only a primary education undoubtedly slowed his progress, although he did not say so.

He had spent all but one year since 1954 assigned to units in the Central Highlands, the most difficult, dangerous and remote area in the country. Without emotion, he noted that many officers who were junior to him were already lieutenant colonels or colonels, and that, although thousands of Vietnamese officers have been sent to the United States to attend the Infantry School or the Command and General Staff College, he had not been selected. (Such pleasant assignments are often given on the basis of personal connections rather than ability.)

"Let's go," the major said, putting on his helmet. The men of the column, who had already packed their mess gear and were catching a brief sleep, shook themselves awake and quickly formed up. When radio messages told him that the flank patrols were in position, the column began silently to push forward.

Late in the afternoon, waiting in a valley clearing where Montagnard tribesmen had planted cucumbers, a private squatted and ran the loamy red soil through his fingers. "This land is more fertile than my home village," he said. "When peace comes, if the Government would clear the land and provide seeds and money to me and my comrades, we could have a good life here."

When I returned to Pleiku, I learned that while more than 600 men had been maneuvering fruitlessly through the jungle, a Vietcong platoon had attacked a Popular Forces outpost on a hilltop 10 miles from the city on the previous night. Five militiamen had been killed. No enemy bodies had been found.

There are thousands of Popular Forces outposts like the one near Pleiku all over Vietnam—at bridges, at road junctions, along the canals in the Delta, on the fringes of hamlets, overlooking the paddy fields in which the pale green young rice sways and the sheets of shallow water reflect the rose and blue sky.

By day, only one or two men are on duty at such outposts. The others—15 or 20 men—sleep, work around their own homes or lounge at the nearest cafe. The great attraction for enlisting in the Popular Forces for a Vietnamese is the certainty of being stationed in his own village. For the home-loving Vietnamese—who dislike being separated from their families, their land (if they own any) and the graves of their ancestors—it is a consideration that outweighs the poor pay, the sketchy training and the danger.

But as the afternoon wears on and the sun begins to set, a Popular Forces outpost becomes a lonely place. Patrolling army units return to their bases. The Regional Forces—better-armed and better-trained than the Popular Forces, and usually quartered in the district and province capitals—are supposed to be on call if an attack should come, but seldom, in fact, take the risk of mines or an ambush on a dark road.

Just as in the days of the first Indochina war, described by Graham Green in "The Quiet American," Popular Forces outposts are attacked and overrun somewhere in the country every night. Until 1968, the militia—predominately the Popular Forces—although smaller than the army, suffered more than 50 per cent of the combat deaths. Even now, the rate is about 45 per cent.

In districts where the enemy is strong, it is not surprising that many Popular Forces units make private treaties with the guerrillas: "You don't bother us, and we won't bother you when you come into the village at night to collect taxes and make propaganda." The members of a P.F. platoon know that the refusal to cooperate may well mean not only their deaths, but also the deaths of their families—and help is far away.

"We know it's going on," an American civilian official in the Delta told me, "but what can we do about it? No one admits these accommodations, and it's almost impossible to prove. But when the guerrillas keep by-passing this or that village or hamlet, you have a right to be suspicious."

On the night of Jan. 31, 1968, Vietcong troops trotted south on Highway 1, not bothering to conceal themselves, as they moved into position to attack the enormous American base area at Longbinh and the city of Bienhoa, about 20 miles north of Saigon. Whatever Popular Forces units saw them were either eliminated or frightened into silence.

Since then, the Government has established many new posts on the highway, and an interpreter and I visit one of these. The main blockhouses stand at either end of a 100-foot bridge that crosses a deep gully. They are built of dark green sandbags, filled with earth, that deteriorate quickly in the heavy rain, producing their own crop of weeds.

Convoys of army trucks speed by, carrying troops, dirty and muddy, returning from an operation a few miles to the north. Tractor-trailer combinations, air horns blaring and plumes of black diesel smoke trailing, rush boxes of shells in the opposite direction. Market women returning from Saigon, carrying empty baskets, crowd seven and eight together in three-wheeled motorcycle jitneys and American military police jeeps, each carrying three men wearing helmets and flak jackets, and mounting machine guns on a post in the back seat, roll by slowly.

One of the guards has gone off to awaken the sergeant in charge of the detachment. He turns up, his boot laces untied and his dark green shirt unbuttoned, sleepy, but his gold inlays bright as he smiles a welcome.

He points down the gully to the west. "We put out ambush patrols and listening posts every night," he says. "This is a Catholic village. I have been in the militia ever since we came from North Vietnam in 1954."

Turning to the hand-me-down carbines lying on the roof of the blockhouse, the sergeant says: "I hope we get our M-16's. We'll need them if the Communists attack us some night."

For 15 years now, American advisers have tried to improve the combat performance of the Vietnamese Army. In the past year, the objectives of the program have been changed. The number of advisers assigned to army units has been halved, and they have been redesignated "combat assistance teams," a title that more accurately reflects their function.

"Hell's bells, I can't advise this man," said a downy-cheeked second lieutenant, four months out of Officers' Candidate School, at Firebase Mahone, 20 miles north of Saigon. The Vietnamese captain sitting next to him, smoking a pipe, nodded. He had been commanding his battery for five years.

"What I can do is get him things that he doesn't have," said the lieutenant. "A chronograph, for example. It measures the speed of the shell leaving the tube. From that, you can tell the wear of the tube, and compensate for it in your settings and improve your accuracy."

In effect, the advisers have become liaison officers. Only they can call for American air strikes, helicopters, artillery and the like. This power can be used as a form of blackmail to prevent a Vietnamese commander from doing something of which the adviser strongly disapproves.

Of course, such actions merely underscore the image of the Americans as the rich kids who think they can be the captains of all the teams because they own the bats, balls and gloves. For the Vietnamese, even the humblest American private is a figure of opulence.

Any Vietnamese division base camp is a military ghetto. Chickens peck and dogs bark. The advisory compound is, by comparison, a resort area—airy, brightly painted barracks, dozens of local women to do the cleaning, a mess hall that dispenses more calories in a day than a Vietnamese soldier probably gets in a week, and even a swimming pool.

Beyond these points of tension is the language barrier. Few advisers have even a rudimentary knowledge of Vietnamese. Many Vietnamese officers speak a little English, but few are fluent. Vietnamese interpreters are assigned to each battalion, but their English is limited and, worse, inaccurate. Since it is clearly impossible to offer or accept advice, particularly when decisions affecting many lives must be made in minutes, the adviser and his counterpart often simply go their own ways.

For American officers, there is little chance to make a glowing record as an adviser. Most try to make the best of a bad deal, avoiding friction with their Vietnamese counterparts, and counting the minutes until the one-year tour is over and they can look forward to a better assignment. (Many Vietnamese battalion commanders, like Major Lim, have seen a half-dozen or more advisers come and go.)

Meanwhile, they tell head-quarters what they think it wants to hear—which at the moment is that the Vietnamese armed forces are rapidly improving. A senior officer admitted to me that this was often the case. "There's a natural feeling among advisers that they're being rated on performance of their units," he said. "This is recognized and steps are being taken to combat it. Some of the reports we get are brutally critical. More and more, we're taking these up with the Vietnamese, and we note an improved receptiveness on their side to this professional effort to call a spade a spade."

Nearly every adviser I spoke to agreed that the reasons that "our" Vietnamese did not yet fight as well as the Vietcong and the North Vietnamese could be summed up in two words: "Leadership" and "motivation."[2]

It is difficult to find a single improvement in these areas since the Tet offensive supposedly led the Saigon Government "to realize that we weren't going to win the war for it

---

2. One school of thought holds that the North Vietnamese, by virtue of their more difficult living conditions, simply are tougher than the Southerners, whose rice grows better with less effort, and who can pluck—like South Sea islanders—bananas, pineapples and papayas from every bush. Under this theory, the excellence of the South Vietnamese First Division is explained by the fact that most of its men are drawn from the northernmost provinces. The southerners *do* seem to be gayer, less amenable to discipline and less inclined to political fanaticism. North Vietnamese officials have complained from time to time, according to captured documents, of a relative lack of seriousness among the Vietcong.

and finally pull up its socks," to quote the official American cheering section, for whom patriotism and optimism have always been synonymous in Vietnam.

By general agreement, President Thieu has failed to increase his popularity since taking office in November, 1967. He has proved to be adept, however, at consolidating his power—mainly at the expense of Vice President Nguyen Cao Ky, rather than in rallying his cynical and war-weary countrymen. The second-place finisher in the election, Truong Dinh Dzu, is now confined at Conson Prison, the Devil's Island of Vietnam, allegedly for urging negotiations with the Vietcong, an offense of which Secretary of State Rogers, among others, also appears to be guilty. The third-place finisher, the widely respected Tran Van Huong, appointed Premier at American urging, but given no real powers, has now been dismissed.

His replacement by Gen. Tran Thien Kheim, the Minister of Interior and a central figure in military intrigues for 10 years, put the military in every position of importance in the country. The Senate and the House, dominated by right-wing elements, have turned out to be ineffective. Every province and every district is run by an officer. It appears that even the recent village elections were dominated by commanders of militia units and security officials.

By all accounts, corruption and favoritism still flourish in the armed forces and the Government. The price for being chosen as the chief of a rich province is said to be 10 million piasters—or $50,000, at the free-market rate of exchange. The approved method of pay-off, I am told, is for the wife of the nominee to "lose" the money to the wife of the collector at poker or mah-jongg, which Vietnamese ladies of leisure play with a skill and ferocity—and for stakes, even when the game is on the level—that would dazzle the sisterhoods of the Rockaways.

Even if Thieu showed an inclination to halt these practices—and he has not—it is doubtful whether he could accomplish much. The system is pervasive and long-established. An effort to destroy it would be more likely to lead to his downfall than almost any other action he could take. Beneath their veneer of Western organization and equipment the Vietnamese armed forces and Government operate in the traditional Oriental way. Family loyalties, shifting personal alliances, graft and the payoff count for more than abstract notions of national welfare.

Because of the system, incompetence and dishonesty are not necessarily punishable offenses, nor is merit often rewarded for its own sake. Not long ago, the commander of the Second Division was accused of renting out his trucks, and pocketing the proceeds, to carry a cinnamon crop to market. Before being cleared of the charge, the general was promoted. The intrepid officer of the Army Inspectorate who submitted the report was urged to recheck his findings, and nothing further has been heard of the matter.

During the months of good resolutions that followed the enemy offensives in 1968—which are, incidentally, described by American officials as a "great victory" or a "salutary shock," depending on the point they are trying to make—relentless American pressure brought about the dismissal of two inept and reportedly unusually corrupt Vietnamese corps commanders, Lieut. Gen. Prince Vinh Loc, a nephew of the deposed Emperor Bao Dai, and Lieut. Gen. Dang Van Quang. The two have now been restored to favor as, respectively, the Army's Director of Training and the personal assistant and confidante of the President.

More recently, the American command was congratulating itself on having secured the ouster of the commander of the 25th Division, which had been criticized openly as being not just the worst division in the Vietnamese Army—which covers a lot of ground—but the worst division in *any* army *anywhere.* The cheers turned to tears when he was promoted and appointed deputy commander of the Third Corps—probably the most important of the four into which the country is divided, since it encompasses the provinces that encircle Saigon to the north.

In August, two other divisional generals, relieved after what their superior, Lieut. Gen. Do Cao Tri, the Third Corps commander, told me was a year of effort, were then named to soft and pleasant assignments as the commandants of the infantry officers' candidate school at Thuduc in the Saigon suburbs and of the noncommissioned officers' academy at the seaside city of Nhatrang. When I visited Thuduc one rainy day recently, the only activity that seemed to be taking place was the erecting of a barbed wire barricade around the new commandant's tree-shaded white stucco villa.

On the other hand, the vigorous and incorruptible Lieut. Gen. Nguyen Duc Thang, a great favorite of the American command, who succeeded the infamous Quang as the commander of the Fourth Corps in the Delta during the heady days of rededication after Tet, 1968, lasted just four months before his offenses against the system led to his dismissal. He currently has the nominal assignment of Special Assistant to the Chairman of the Joint General Staff, but he has no duties and he spends his time *o nha*—or "at home"—studying mathematics for his own amusement.

So the stately saraband of intrigue continues, quietly, with Oriental dignity and finesse. The 40-odd generals, admirals and air marshals of the Vietnamese armed forces form an exclusive club, to which new members are seldom admitted, since that would require a further sharing of the power and profit.

As a result, rumbles of discontent are being heard from the officers just below them in rank. Some are followers of Vice President Ky who failed to change sides quickly enough after his fall. Others, no doubt, simply want a larger share of the takings. There are also those, especially in combat units, who may be motivated by the notion that winning the war ought to come first. But with no strong civilian government to force reforms on the military, it may be a revolt of the colonels that will bring about changes—possibly for the better.

"The command of the ARVNAF [Armed Forces of the Republic of Vietnam] is in the hands of a bunch of tired old cronies," a knowledgeable American said, "but there's the beginning of a ferment, and we're well aware of it."

Agreement came from General Tri—who, like virtually all the generals on active duty, is less than 45 years old, but who says he feels older after more than 20 years of almost continuous warfare. "This is our weakness," he says. "Unless we change our organization and stress leadership, we can't expect to have a good army. We have two kinds of military leaders. Most of them achieved high rank through politics; only a few by fighting."

Every general or man of equivalent rank in the Vietnamese armed forces—certainly, the overwhelming majority of the colonels and lieutenant colonels—served with the French forces during the first Indochina war. For the most part, they seem to have forgotten about the casual gallantry of the French. Men like Major Lim are rare exceptions in leading their men in combat operations.

What has been retained is the swagger and snobbery. Not so strange, since the origins of these officers are in the main middle-class or lower. Thieu's father was a fisherman; Ky is the son of a village schoolteacher Mandarin families tended to shun the military—or even civil service—with the French, because of strong nationalist feelings or, perhaps more important, because in the traditional ranking of Vietnamese society—*si, nong, cong, thuong, binh*—the "soldier" comes last, after the "scholar," "farmer," "merchant" and "artisan."

This élitist spirit has led to serious weaknesses in the ranks of new lieutenants, the platoon leaders and—later—company commanders who have the most direct influence on success or failure in battle. Only youths who have passed their second baccalaureate examinations—which, under the French system that is still in force here, are usually given after 12 years of school—are sent to officers' candidate school. Those with the first baccalaureate, taken after 10 years, are sent to a noncommissioned officers' school. The rest are marked off as permanent privates.

Since education after the first three or four years is costly and not widely available outside the cities and major towns, the average lieutenant is a slim, pampered young dandy, a member of a well-to-do urban family—more at home on his Honda, buzzing along the boulevards of Saigon than inching through the hostile wilderness.

Thus, countless small units are commanded by young men without any measurably offensive spirit, while the tough, unlettered peasant boys who would, in time, make excellent sergeants, lieutenants, colonels—as, first, the Vietminh and, now, the Vietcong have been demonstrating for 20 years—are given no chance to advance.

The Vietnamization of the war has hardly begun, and its effects cannot yet be felt. It will be impossible to tell whether the Vietnamese can carry the burden of combat until they begin to do so. Even then, it may be many months before an assessment can be made, since enemy forces may well keep the level of combat low to speed up the American departure. The Vietcong and the North Vietnamese still have the advantage of sanctuaries safe from ground and air attack. Even inside Vietnam, they have repeatedly shown that they are able to mass and move without discovery.

If the history of Vietnam for the past quarter of a century shows anything at all, it is that these developments cannot be halted by military means alone. The better weapons and greater size of the Vietnamese armed forces can hardly be significant without a cause to fight for—and men the people respect to lead the fight.

A young lieutenant in the First Battalion of the 42d Infantry Regiment put it this way: "What we need is not peace, but a social revolution. If we won—if peace came tomorrow—the troubles would happen again, because the majority of the people would still be poor. Diem, Khanh, Ky, Thieu—they all talk about a social revolution, but nothing has happened. Thieu, Ky, Khiem—they are young men with stars on their collars. They aren't experienced in politics. How can they cope with a political-military war?"

Tom Buckley is a member of The New York Times Magazine staff.

* * *

October 16, 1969

VIETNAM MORATORIUM OBSERVED NATIONWIDE BY FOES OF THE WAR

OPPONENTS REACT

Many Show Support for Nixon by Flying Flags Full-Staff

By JOHN HERBERS

Protests ranging from noisy street rallies to silent prayer vigils and involving a broad spectrum of the population were held across the nation yesterday in an effort to demonstrate the growing public opposition to the war in Vietnam.

Only scattered incidents of violence marred the outpourings of small and vast crowds in which the black armband was the standard symbol.

The Vietnam Moratorium—which began as a national protest by college students and spilled over to include such groups as the United Automobile Workers union and the Pittsburgh City Council—was termed an overwhelming success by its planners, the youthful members of the Vietnam Moratorium Committee.

But it also demonstrated the great divisions in American society created by the prolonged American involvement in Southeast Asia. The demonstrations generated counter protests in some areas, and some supporters of the war who had been quiet for months spoke out in anger.

Largest Protest So Far

It was the largest public protest of the many that have been held against the Vietnam war. Historians in the Library of Congress said that as a nationally coordinated antiwar demonstration it was unique.

There was no way to estimate immediately the total numbers involved, but counting the demonstrators, the children who stayed out of school, the workers who did not report for their jobs, those who did and wore armbands and those who prayed in homes and churches, possibly millions were involved.

The demonstrations drew largely on students and other youths, the middle class and professional groups. Blue-collar workers and Negroes did not participate in great numbers, even though unions such as the United Auto Workers and the United Shoeworkers of American endorsed the moratorium. In a number of communities blue-collar workers made up the active opposition to the moratorium.

The Pentagon's civil disturbance command post-termed the national situation "generally quiet" but said that, as a precaution, troops had been made available in Boston, at Fort Dix, N. J., and near Rock Island, Ill. National Guardsmen were placed on alert by Gov. Marvin Mandel of Maryland and Gov. William G. Milliken of Michigan.

Regionally, the biggest and most enthusiastic demonstrations occurred in the Northeast and the West Coast although in Northern California heavy rains reduced the expected turnout. For example, the police in Boston estimated that close to 100,000 had jammed Boston Common. The demonstrations tended to be somewhat subdued in the South and Middle West.

Although some communities were cool or hostile to the moratorium, it reached unexpected places with unexpected impact such as conservative, prowar Orange County, Calif., the birthplace of President Nixon. The concrete campus of California State College, which had never yet seen a demonstration, echoed with chants of "Peace now" and "hell no we won't go."

The demonstration was organized by Edward Whetmore, a 23-year-old senior, whose father, State Senator James E. Whetmore, is supported by the John Birch Society. "I guess each of us marches by a different drummer," the young man said with a shy smile under his mustache.

Across the nation, the moratorium took this general form:

As expected, the protests pre-empted all other business on hundreds of college campuses, ranging from poetry reading, folk singing and teach-ins at the University of Kansas to a bizarre ceremony at Monmouth College in New Jersey in which students buried a coffin in the athletic field containing the names of New Jersey war dead.

Great numbers of high school students joined in the demonstrations and boycotted classes. In White Plains, for example, about three-quarters of the crowd of 4,000 that marched for two hours were high school students, some accompanied by their parents. It was a strange mixture of black arm bands and a holiday mood.

Church bells tolled at regular intervals in a number of communities as ministers and priests took prominent roles in the demonstrations. In Washington, priests in the National Cathedral offered prayers for peace every hour, and in Worcester, Mass., both clergy and laymen read the names of known American war dead from the Chestnut Street Congregational church from midnight Tuesday to midnight Wednesday.

In view of the numbers involved in the demonstrations, violence was minor, as indicated in these three incidents: In Detroit's Kennedy Square, demonstrators and hecklers threw stones, bottles and insults at one another. In Washington, a band of young black militants carrying black crosses, a coffin and a Vietcong flag tried to storm the White House grounds and were forced back by the police. And at the University of Indiana, Clark Kerr, the former president of the University of California was hit square in the face with a custard pie but wiped his glasses and continued his lecture.

Opposition to the moratorium emerged in various ways. In the upstate village of Glen Aubrey, there was outspoken opposition by citizens. In Ontonagon, Mich., scores of flags flew at full staff in support of President Nixon's position. And across the country motorists drove with their headlights on during the day, as suggested by the pro-war Committee for Responsible Patriotism. On a trip from Maine to Connecticut, a motorist counted 110 cars with headlights burning, perhaps 10 per cent of those on the road.

In several communities the division of sentiment was shown by the flag, which was flown half-staff for the moratorium and full-staff in support of President Nixon. In Atlanta, for example, Gov. Lester G. Maddox drove to work with his headlights on and an American flag flying, full-staff, from his radio antenna.

At the state Capitol, the Georgia Governor ordered the flag flown at full staff over the gold-domed building. A block away, Mayor Ivan Allen Jr. ordered the flag over City Hall lowered to half-staff "in honor of those who have died in Vietnam."

Goals Defined Broadly

There was no clear understanding among the participants of specifically what they would have the American Government do to end the war.

The moratorium committee had defined the protest in general terms as an effort "to maximize public pressure to end the war by encouraging a broad section of Americans to work against the war."

Originally, the committee had planned to extend the moratorium to two days during November, three days in December and so on until the war was brought to an end. But when the protest spread outside the colleges, the sponsors said they had postponed deciding any strategy for the future.

At the committee headquarters in Washington yesterday, David Hawk, one of the coordinators, said: "We are a success in the fact that we've brought public attention to the issue once more. Hopefully, today's events will show there is a political constituency for immediate withdrawal of the troops."

If the moratorium strengthened the "dove" position on the war, it also seemed to have polarized even further the "hawkish" position of some conservatives.

In the House of Representatives, for example, a group of conservatives led by Sam Steiger, Republican of Arizona, and including Rogers C. B. Morton of Maryland, national Republican chairman, urged a sudden, major escalation of the war as a means of ending it.

This group had been silent on the war as President Nixon pressed his policy of reaching a negotiated settlement in Paris.

"We, as concerned Americans who represent constituents, are fed up with half-way measures and talk of cowardly retreat," the group said in a letter, to the President.

On both sides of the issue, there were unexpected developments. In Paterson, N. J., 100 employes of Lite Industries, Inc., members of Local 404 of the United Electrical Workers, called for an end to the war—even though such a development would put them out of work. The company makes bullet-proof vests and body bags used in the war.

At Cape Kennedy, Fla., on the other hand, thousands of space workers signified their backing of President Nixon's conduct of the war by driving to work with their headlights on.

And in Philadelphia, Merritt H. Taylor Jr., president of the Philadelphia Suburban Transportation Company, draped the city's buses and trolleys with American flags to express "a feeling of patriotism."

In Chicago, where the extreme positions on the war have culminated in the trial of the "Chicago eight" conspiracy defendants, all eight appeared in court yesterday wearing black armbands and carrying a large Vietcong flag.

One of them, Abbie Hoffman, engaged in a brief tug of war with a Federal marshal over the flag, which he tried to drape over the defense table along with a smaller American flag. The marshals took both flags away.

David Dellinger, another defendant, then began to read the names of Illinois men killed in the war. Deputy marshals pounded their gavels, but Mr. Dellinger read 10 names before Judge Julius Hoffman entered the room. As the jury filed in, Mr. Dellinger rose and asked for a moment of silence.

Judge Hoffman ordered the jury from the room. The defense attorney. William Kunstler, then rose to object and the United States Attorney, Thomas Foran, jumped to his feet and said in anger:

"That is outrageous. This man is the mouthpiece for these defendants. The Government protests this man's attitude and I'd like to note that he is wearing a black arm band like the defendants."

This angered Mr. Kunstler, who said: "I want this man admonished. The word 'mouth-piece' is contemptible."

Judge Hoffman said: "Mr. Foran was properly defending his client, the United States of America. To hoist the flag of an enemy country on the table of this courtroom with your approval is improper."

There were scenes reminiscent of past protests against the war. In Charlotte. N. C. the widow of a young Quaker who burned himself to death on the steps of the Pentagon almost four years ago marched quietly in one of the parades.

Mrs. William Beidler, the former Mrs. Norman Morrison, is now married to the head of the philosophy department—at Queens College, a small women's institution.

There were moments of drama, as in Lexington, Mass. at the site of the first skirmish of the American Revolution where American colonists "fired the shot heard 'round the world."

Gov. Francis W. Sargent, a World War II combat veteran, was interrupted by a small group of youthful hecklers, who were opposing the Moratorium.

"I know the war and you never will know war," the Governor said to the youths. "so you listen to me. This war is costing America its soul."

The youths became quiet.

* * *

October 16, 1969

PACIFICATION IN RURAL VIETNAM MAKING BIG BUT FRAGILE GAINS

By TERENCE SMITH

Special to The New York Times

SAIGON, South Vietnam, Oct. 15—The road that runs south from Saigon to Cantho is clogged these days with trucks and cars that rattle along with careless abandon.

Sixteen months ago, in the wake of the Lunar New Year offensive, a drive along the stretch between Mytho and Cantho was a perilous adventure. Vietcong guerrillas regularly planted mines under the pavement and floated explosives under the bridges. In the evening and early morning snipers fired at passing cars from the trees lining the road.

Today, as an extensive auto trip has confirmed, the only danger along Route 4 is the traffic, which is dreadful, and the potholes, which can shatter an axle.

The improved security along the road is one of the more visible examples of the progress achieved over the last year by the allied pacification program. While the enemy has concentrated his attacks on military targets, the $600-million-a-year effort to secure and develop the South Vietnamese countryside has proceeded almost without opposition.

The gains during the period have been striking. Rural security has been greatly increased—although American officials concede that it is still fragile—and the Saigon Government's control now reaches deeper into the countryside than it has for at least two years.

The expanded security in the countryside is a result of a combination of the pacification program and the enemy's decision during the last 10 months to concentrate on military targets.

With an eye toward escalating American casualties, the North Vietnamese and Vietcong have directed their principal efforts this year against Allied military installations rather than civilian targets. As a result, the forces assigned to the pacification program have encountered little opposition as they have pushed deeper into the countryside.

They have been operating in a sort of military vacuum, and the American officials in charge of the program are quick to concede that the progress that has been made would not have been possible had the enemy been determined to frustrate it.

Nonetheless, the officials, capitalizing on the opportunity, have redoubled their efforts during the widespread lull that has descended over the battle-field since the middle of August. They are attempting to make the most of it because they realize that it cannot last indefinitely. They acknowledge that the major test lies ahead, when the enemy turns his attention to the fruits of the program.

Tet Offensive Recalled

The officials well remember the Tet offensive of 1968, which delivered a severe setback to the gains achieved by the pacification program in 1967 and shattered the boundless optimism that characterized the official American attitude at the time.

"There has been a steady expansion of security and Government control throughout the year," William E. Colby, who directs the pacification effort, said in a recent interview. "But we realize its limits. We know it is still thin in many areas. It is thin at night and in the rural areas away from the towns."

To test the security, this reporter set off with two others on a five-day, 400 mile drive through the heart of the Mekong Delta. Unarmed and in a Volkswagen sedan, we drove the length of Route 4 from Saigon to Cantho, then up the bank of the Mekong River to Chaudoc, a lovely province capital on the Cambodian border, and back through Sadec and Mytho to Saigon.

No Sound of Gunfire

We passed through towns, villages and hamlets and through miles of lush, green paddy fields without hearing a shot. Men and women are working the fields without visible concern for their safety, and in the towns the restaurants were busy until the curfew forced them to close.

A handful of mining incidents were reported during the week on some of the roads we used, but we encountered none of them.

The areas toured seemed prosperous as well as secure. Television antennas poked up from innumerable thatched roofs, and in the towns gleaming new Japanese motorcycles crowded the sidewalks.

As another example of the improved security, Jim Clare, a reporter for Stars and Stripes, the Army newspaper, recently hitchhiked the length of Route 1—the late Bernard Fall's "Street Without Joy"—from the demilitarized zone to Saigon. He made the trip in 13 days without incident, arriving here last week.

In January, 1967, Michele Ray, a French free-lance journalist was kidnapped by the Vietcong when she attempted the same trip. She was released after three weeks in captivity. No one else had tried it since.

Gerold Hickey, the anthropologist who first came to Vietnam in 1962, recently compared the present security to the conditions that prevailed in the summer of 1964, before the vast American build-up was under way.

Still Many Risky Areas

"We used to drive up and down the coast and all through the delta in those days," he said. "Now people are doing it again. You can drive from Danang to Dongha now. A year or 18 months ago it would have been suicide."

None of this is to say that there are not areas that the Vietcong dominate either wholly or in part. There are still many districts in the delta and in the north where an American driving in anything less substantial than a tank is risking his life.

And there are still many areas that the Vietcong can rely on for sanctuary, support and supplies. Even in many of the regions where the Government presence has recently been established, the Vietcong still conduct their business at night and collect taxes on a regular basis.

But the pendulum has swung in the direction of the Government during the last year, and the shift is reflected in the much-maligned computerized analyses prepared each month by the experts on pacification. In the past their findings have been sharply challenged, by members of Congress among others.

According to official American figures, 89 per cent of the South Vietnamese people were living under "relatively secure" control of the Saigon Government as of Aug. 31—15.3 million of a population of 17.3 million. In the rural areas the figures are lower but still high; 84 per cent of those outside the cities enjoy "relative security."

A Definition by Thieu

In some cases that security is very relative—particularly at night, when the Vietcong are most active. In a recent speech President Nguyen Van Thieu came up with a definition of a relatively secure area that most people agree with. It means, he said, an area that "Government representatives can visit without military escort in the daytime."

Even President Thieu would readily acknowledge that the situation can easily change at night or from one day to another.

The generally improved security is mainly a result of the enlarging and equipping of the regional and popular forces, nicknamed the Ruff Puffs, which along with the regular army, have taken over a large share of the military side of pacification. As a result of relentless American prodding, and in the absence of significant enemy opposition, they have spread out into the countryside and taken up the front-line defense of much of the rural population.

In addition a home-grown militia composed of men too young or too old for the draft and of some women and girls has been developed over the last year and a half. There are about 1.5 million members of these people's self-defense forces who guard their own villages or hamlets at night. About a million of them have received some rudimentary military training, and they have some 300,000 arms.

Although their contribution to defense may not be great in purely military terms, their presence has provided a major boost to morale.

Shift From Vietcong Areas

The relative security, despite its thinness, is attracting people into the newly pacified communities. Increasing numbers of refugees are leaving the Communist-controlled areas and moving into those more or less under Government control. Politics is not usually involved; people are simply in search or an opportunity to live and work in peace—a rare luxury in Vietnam.

Few officials doubt that the tide would be running in the opposite direction if the people believed they had a better prospect in the Vietcong areas.

There has also been a stirring of political life in the villages during the last year, and this too is a by product of the pacification program. Elections have been held in about 1,900 of the 2,300 villages in South Vietnam, and though some difficulty was experienced in getting enough people who were both qualified and willing to run, the voting is said to have had a generally positive effect.

New village officials have been given substantial budgets to use for local development, and they now have administrative control over the rural-development workers sent by the central Government as part of the pacification effort.

As a result the officials are operating with greater autonomy than they have had since President Ngo Dinh Diem suspended village elections 14 years ago. Returned to their traditional role, they have a vested interest in continued Government control.

Government troops and pacification workers recently pushed into an area in Sadec Province, in the Mekong Delta, long held by the Vietcong and known as the Triangle. They secured three villages that had been abandoned for more than a year, and within a month refugees poured back into the area. The fields surrounding the villages have been planted for the first time in several seasons, village elections have been held and the Government presence appears to be firmly established.

"The elections have produced the beginnings of community awareness and responsibility in the villages," Mr. Colby said. "But let's not overdo it—it's just a beginning, and we know it."

"The important thing is whether the structure we have set up is strong enough to resist the shock of an enemy attack," he said. "We have been working for the past year in a relative vacuum, but now we have documents that indicate that the enemy feels he must do something about the situation. So it's up to us to prepare for it."

The pacification program is a massive assistance and advisory effort that employs 14,500 people, including 7,300 Americans. Its goal is to extend the Government's presence in the countryside and rejuvenate economic and political life in the rural areas that have been disrupted by the Vietcong. But its primary task is security, and that is how its success is measured.

Officials of the pacification program have been expecting some enemy response since early this year, and they acknowledge that they have been mystified by the lack of it.

Now, as the result of the capture of a command-level enemy document, they expect it shortly. The document, which American analysts believe to be authentic, calls for a concerted military and political campaign to reverse the gains achieved.

In its ominous way the document is a compliment to the program—the first clear indication that the enemy is sufficiently concerned to attempt to counteract it.

* * *

November 4, 1969

NIXON CALLS FOR PUBLIC SUPPORT AS HE PURSUES HIS VIETNAM PLAN ON A SECRET PULLOUT TIMETABLE

POLICY UNCHANGED

President Says Hasty Withdrawal Would Be a 'Disaster'

By MAX FRANKEL
Special to The New York Times

WASHINGTON, Nov. 3—President Nixon pleaded tonight for domestic support as he persisted in his effort to find peace in Vietnam and as he unfolded what he said was a plan to bring home all United States ground combat forces on an orderly but secret timetable.

It was the first time Mr. Nixon had spoken of a plan to recall "all" combat infantry units, though he set no deadline, and the first time he had referred to a private timetable, though he did not commit himself to a definite pace.

He made clear that his policies on Vietnam remained the same as the ones he outlined last May, the only difference being that a recent enemy restraint on the battlefield had rendered the withdrawal time-table "more optimistic."

Hasty Withdrawal Rejected

Delivering his long-awaited report on Vietnam policy by television and radio from the White House, Mr. Nixon rejected a "precipitate withdrawal," which he said would be a prescription for "a disaster of immense magnitude."

He said the enemy alone bore responsibility for the deadlock in the peace negotiations and offered in evidence some of his hitherto private diplomatic initiatives, including an exchange of letters with the late President of North Vietnam, Ho Chi Minh.

If a settlement cannot be negotiated, Mr. Nixon reiterated, then the nation's responsibility to its allies and to the peace of the world requires a measured pace of disengagement. That pace, the President said again, will be geared to the ability of the South Vietnamese forces to take over combat duties and to the level of combat imposed by the enemy.

Critics' Advice Resisted

Though the emphasis on a deliberate plan to find a lasting peace was clearly addressed to impatient critics of his tactics in Congress and around the country, the President resisted most of the critics' advice for a bold new initiative or announcement, such as a unilateral cease-fire or a public timetable for withdrawal.

In fact, the President placed some of the burden for success of his plan on the cooperation of his critics.

"I pledged in my campaign for the Presidency to end the war in a way that we could win the peace," he said. "I have initiated a plan of action which will enable me to keep that pledge.

"The more support I can have from the American people, the sooner that pledge can be redeemed, for the more divided we are at home, the less likely the enemy is to negotiate in Paris.

"Let us be united for peace. Let us also be united against defeat. Because let us understand: North Vietnam cannot defeat or humiliate the United States. Only Americans can do that."

Taking only oblique notice of the Oct. 15 moratorium and other massive demonstrations for peace. Mr. Nixon said he would be untrue to his oath and obligations if he allowed national policy "to be dictated by the minority" who he said counsel defeat in Vietnam and "who attempt to impose it on the nation by mounting demonstrations in the street."

As a White House aide remarked, in advising reporters that Mr. Nixon was holding to his deliberate course in Vietnam, the President had decided to try to do "what was right and not what was new."

The President began his speech by citing reasons why he had decided after assuming office not to end the war by withdrawing all forces from Vietnam, though he said it would have been easy to attribute the blame for military defeat to his predecessor, Lyndon B. Johnson.

He then cited some of his efforts to explore "every possible private avenue" to peace, including the letter to President Ho, which was sent in mid-July. Mr. Nixon said that President Ho's reply, received three days before the North Vietnamese leader died on Sept. 3, "flatly rejected" his initiative.

Future Course Described

Mr. Nixon cited the new orders to prepare the South Vietnamese to assume full responsibility for their own security, disclosed a 20 per cent reduction in air operations in South Vietnam—since August, aides said—noted the recent signs of enemy restraint and then described his future course in these words:

"We have adopted a plan that we have worked out in cooperation with the South Vietnamese for the complete withdrawal of all United States ground combat forces and their replacement by South Vietnamese forces on an orderly scheduled timetable.

"This withdrawal will be made from strength and not from weakness. As South Vietnamese forces become stronger, the rate of American withdrawal can become greater."

The President said he could not divulge the timetable because disclosure would deprive him of necessary flexibility and would also eliminate Hanoi's incentive to negotiate in good faith.

Other informed officials here have given as a further reason the feeling that a definite timetable ran the risk of either provoking domestic dissent or undermining the confidence and stability of the South Vietnamese, or both. But Mr. Nixon did not allude to this reasoning.

"We must retain the flexibility to base each withdrawal decision on the situation as it is at that time." Mr. Nixon said. He noted that he would be influenced not only by the capacities of the South Vietnamese forces but also by possible progress in the Paris talks and the level of enemy combat activity.

For example, the President explained, his timetable for the withdrawal of ground combat troops—which had been previously estimated to number about 250,000—is "more optimistic" now than it was in June because enemy infiltration into South Vietnam and the rate of American casualties have markedly decreased in recent months.

But if the infiltration or casualty rates should increase again, he added, this would reflect a "conscious decision" by the enemy and require an adjustment in his own policy.

Warning Given to Hanoi

Mr. Nixon asserted that Hanoi could make no greater mistake than to increase the violence again. An increase, he said, would not only affect his withdrawal timetable but, to the extent that it jeopardized the remaining American forces in Vietnam, would evoke "strong and effective measures" by the United States.

He cited efforts to enlist the help of the Soviet Union and other governments that maintain diplomatic relations with Hanoi, and the exchange of letters with President Ho Chi Minh through a personal friend of the North Vietnamese leader. Aides said the intermediary had refused to be identified.

Mr. Nixon's letter, dated July 15, reaffirmed a desire to work for a just peace and said there was nothing to be gained by delay. President Ho Chi Minh's reply, dated Aug. 25 but received in Paris on Aug. 30, only three days before his death, demanded a complete withdrawal of American troops.

"It has become clear that the obstacle in negotiating an end to the war is not the President of the United States," Mr. Nixon said. "And it is not the South Vietnamese Government."

Hanoi's intransigence would continue, the President predicted, as long as it is convinced "that all it has to do is to wait for our next concession and the next until it gets everything it wants."

In summarizing the choices available to him at this stage of the war. Mr. Nixon expressed the conviction that they were basically only two:

"I can order an immediate precipitate withdrawal of all Americans from Vietnam without regard to the effects of that action," he said, citing the risk of massacre in Vietnam, the risk of new threats to the peace in many parts of the world and the danger of "remorse and divisive recrimination" among the American people.

"Or we can persist in our search for a just peace through a negotiated settlement if possible," he said, "or through continued implementation of our plan for Vietnamization if necessary—a plan in which we will withdraw all of our forces from Vietnam on a schedule in accordance with our program, as the South Vietnamese become strong enough to defend their own freedom."

Contradiction Denied

This reference to "all of our forces" as opposed to an earlier reference to "all U.S. ground combat forces" represented no contradiction, aides explained. They said the first, and more concrete portion of the President's program dealt with combat troops whereas his reference to all troops covered a still longer time span.

The President's repeated use of the word "plan" appeared to be a semantic innovation, but it corresponded almost exactly to his use of the word "program" for peace in his first major Vietnam address. Mr. Nixon indicated at several points that his plan was a continuing policy, not a new one.

His first Vietnam report, on May 14, laid out a program to end the war that involved neither a "purely military" solution nor a "one-sided withdrawal." If offered negotiations for the mutual withdrawal of all non-South Vietnamese forces and for arrangements that would give the people of South Vietnam a "free choice" or political future.

Although Mr. Nixon's address tonight covered much of the same ground—often in strikingly similar phrases—as his first Vietnam policy address on May 14, he gave new emphasis to his hopes for "Vietnamization" of the war effort, spoke more critically of the policies of former President Johnson and stressed at length his disappointment over what he said was Hanoi's refusal to bargain for a settlement.

He cited "two private offers" for a rapid settlement that he said he had made even before his inauguration January 20 through a person who he said was in contact with the leaders of North Vietnam. To these, he said, Hanoi replied in effect with calls "for our surrender," Mr. Nixon said.

Mr. Nixon indicated in May that even without negotiation some American troops could begin to come home as the South Vietnamese forces proved themselves capable of assuming a larger combat burden. In June the President announced a first reduction of 25,000 men by Aug. 31. In September, after a month's delay due to disagreement in the Administration and the threat of enemy offensives, he scheduled a further reduction, of 35,000 men, to be completed by Dec. 15.

The whole approach had two distinct facets: either negotiation for a political solution and fairly swift withdrawal of most American troops or "Vietnamization" of the war to give the South Vietnamese an increasing share of the combat burden while the Americans withdrew gradually.

Double Disappointment

The President and his associates were disappointed in two respects.

First, their negotiating package failed to energize the Paris talks. They received hints that Hanoi and the Vietcong might be willing to deal separately with Washington, but the President refused to negotiate behind the back of the Saigon Government.

Second, the domestic support that had greeted the President's speech began to erode through the summer. Demands for a more rapid withdrawal were pressed on him by members of Congress, former officials of the Johnson Administration and commentators.

During this period of accelerating public pressure, and two days before Moratorium Day, Mr. Nixon took the unusual step of scheduling his address three weeks in advance.

The White House never explained why he left so much time for more debate and more pressure. His aides insisted that the timing was unrelated to elections tomorrow in several states and many municipalities.

The White House said that the South Vietnamese Government had been briefed on the speech through normal diplomatic channels. But Congressional leaders were given only a brief outline this evening. Reporters were unabled to write from a text only half an hour before the President went on the air, at 9:30 P.M.

* * *

November 4, 1969

MR. NIXON'S 'PLAN FOR PEACE'

President Nixon disappointed the nation's hope for a reordering of American priorities with a "plan for peace" that looks more like a formula for continued war. He proposed no new American initiative at Paris or in South Vietnam, preferring instead to reiterate the American position in terms reminiscent of those used by President Johnson and Secretary Rusk.

The President in effect committed this nation to defend the present Government of South Vietnam until it can defend itself. This is at best a remote prospect judging by the record of the past fifteen years. It also seems to contradict Mr. Nixon's own Asian doctrine under which, according to the President, the United States would leave with Asian governments the primary responsibility for their own defense.

There is justification for Mr. Nixon's impatience with Hanoi for its intransigence in the Paris talks and in private negotiations that have now been revealed for the first time. However, Mr. Nixon failed to mention even the possibility of such proposals as a cease-fire or a democratization and liberalization of the Saigon Government.

President Nixon has offered a plan for Vietnamizing the war. What is needed is a program for Vietnamizing the peace.

* * *

November 12, 1969

MANY IN U.S. BACK NIXON WAR STAND ON VETERANS DAY

President's 'Silent Majority' Holds Parades and Rallies Attended by Thousands

DISSENTERS CONDEMNED

Administration Will Permit Vietnam Critics to March on Pennsylvania Avenue

By WILLIAM BORDERS

Thousands of Americans who place themselves in what President Nixon has called "the great, silent majority" of the country used Veterans Day observances yesterday to demonstrate their support for his Vietnam policies.

From the Los Angeles Coliseum, where General of the Army Omar N. Bradley urged that America "keep the faith," to the Colonial streets of Manchester, N. H., where housewives in a Silent Majority Division marched beside veterans, the war dead of the past were linked to the war effort of the present.

"There's more feeling this year because a lot of people are just fed up with all the noisy dissenters," said a demonstrator named Richard Drew as he marched through downtown Denver in one of several parades around the country that were described as larger than those usually held on Veterans Day.

In Washington, a rally at the Washington Monument drew a crowd of several thousand, waving American flags.

'Keep Up the Fight'

"There are more of us patriotic Americans than those pro-Hanoi-crats," said Representative L. Mendel Rivers of South Carolina. "Keep up the fight."

In New York City, a parade down Fifth Avenue and a wreath-laying ceremony in Madison Square drew what was officially described as "the largest turnout in many years."

Many of the traditional Veterans Day ceremonies had a special tone and a new fervor this year as participants sought to counter the effect of the massive antiwar demonstrations planned for later this week in Washington.

In Washington, the Nixon Administration yesterday authorized an antiwar demonstrators' parade on Pennsylvania Avenue to within a block of the White House Saturday. It expressed confidence that the protest would be peaceful.

The holiday, the 51st anniversary of the armistice ending World War I, was also seen as an occasion to respond to President Nixon's speech on Vietnam Nov. 3, when he appealed for support, promising.

"The more support I can have from the American people, the sooner that pledge [to end the war] can be redeemed."

The speech by Mr. Rivers, which was cheered enthusiastically, typified the tone of a number of rallies around the country, which drew expressions of support for President Nixon that were considerably more militant than Mr. Nixon's own position.

At a wreath-laying ceremony in Buffalo, for example, Henry Vogt, county commander of the American Legion, said:

"There is a dangerous and vicious new type of thinking spreading over our land. Unless we, as good citizens, work as a patriotic team, we can rest assured that this pattern will ultimately open wide the door to anarchy."

In the parade through the Loop district of Chicago, some signs urged "Bomb Hanoi."

In Atlanta, Gov. Lester G. Maddox referred to dissenters as "moraforiumites" and said that their purpose was to "betray our boys in battle."

He spoke at a capitol rally after a march down Peachtree Street.

Around the country, motorists responded to appeals from veterans groups to keep their automobile lights on, as a gesture of support for the President, and flags were hung from many windows.

Pittsburgh's parade drew a crowd of 100,000—the largest the police superintendent could recall—and banners bore such legends as "Do Not Reason With Treason" and "Support Our Men in Vietnam."

Like the parades in several other cities, the march through Pittsburgh was opened to civilians for the first time this year. Five hundred of them took up positions in the rear, chanting "Hey, Hey, U.S.A."

As they reached the reviewing stand, many reached up to shake hands with Gen. William C. Westmoreland, United States Army Chief of Staff, who said in a luncheon speech that antiwar protests "tend to confuse Hanoi as to our national will."

'Old Glory Marathon'

The American Legion in Ashland, Ky, organized an "Old Glory Marathon" in which high school boys running one mile each passed four flags along 25-mile routes that converged at the Eternal Light in Ashland.

"It was a beautiful sight, as they laid those flags down in front of the flame," said David Smith, a high school principal in nearby Chesapeake, Ohio, from which one of the teams had started out.

The marathon, run this year for the first time, "wasn't particularly aimed at the demonstrators anywhere," Mr. Smith said, adding: "But it does show that at least here we're still patriotic."

* * *

November 14, 1969

AGNEW SAYS TV NETWORKS ARE DISTORTING THE NEWS

Accuses Some Commentators of Bias and Calls on Viewers to Complain—Criticizes Harriman's Paris Role

By E. W. KENWORTHY
Special to The New York Times

WASHINGTON, Nov. 13—Vice President Agnew accused the television networks tonight of permitting producers of news programs, newscasters and commentators to give the American people a highly selected and often biased presentation of the news.

In a speech released here and delivered in Des Moines, Iowa, before the Mid-West Regional Republican Committee, the Vice President called upon the American people to "let the networks know that they want their news straight and objective."

Mr. Agnew urged television viewers to register "their complaints" by writing to the networks and phoning to local stations.

Thousands of Americans immediately responded to the Vice President's invitation by calling the networks and many newspapers and venting their views on the media's handling of the news.

The Vice President's speech was vigorously defended and denounced. In some cities, such as Dallas, television stations reported that most callers supported Mr. Agnew's views. In other cities, such as New York, the reaction was more mixed.

In addition to attacking the networks, the Vice President also denounced the Johnson Administration and W. Averell Harriman, the former United States peace negotiator in Paris, for the "concessions" that he asserted had been made to the North Vietnamese.

During the 10 months that Mr. Harriman was chief negotiator, Mr. Agnew said, "the United States swapped some of the greatest military concessions in the history of warfare for an enemy agreement on the shape of a bargaining table."

Mr. Agnew did not say what the "concessions" were.

Negotiations over the shape of the table took place after the end of the bombings of North Vietnam, Nov. 1, 1968, and were completed in mid-January.

The Vice President's press secretary, Herbert Thompson, said that he did not know what concessions the Vice President had in mind. He contended that Mr. Agnew would not have made the statement without substantive information to back up his charges.

Mr. Agnew said that Mr. Harriman, who had commented on the President's Vietnam speech two weeks ago over the American Broadcasting Company's network, was apparently under "heavy compulsion to justify his failures to anyone who will listen," and "the networks have shown themselves willing to give him all the time he desires."

At the conclusion of his speech, Mr. Agnew seemed to challenge the networks to carry his speech nationally. He said that every elected leader depended on the television media and yet "whether what I have said to you tonight will be heard and seen at all by the nation is not my decision, it is not your decision, it is their decision."

The three networks accepted the challenge. They all carried the speech live. In New York their regular news programs moved up to clear time for Mr. Agnew's address.

In an interview in the current U.S. News & World Report, Mr. Agnew sharply criticized the press, saying that he sometimes thought those writing for the papers, especially the "big-city liberal media, were "about the most superficial thinkers I've ever seen."

In his Des Moines speech, Mr. Agnew said that the American people would be right in refusing to tolerate in Government the kind of concentration of power that had been allowed in the hands "of a tiny and closed fraternity of privileged men, elected by no one, and enjoying a monopoly sanctioned and licensed by Government."

As a particularly flagrant example of what he called the biased reporting of "self-appointed analysts," the Vice President cited the treatment of the President's speech on Vietnam two weeks ago.

Most of the commentators, he said, expressed "in one way or another, their hostility to what he had to say," and "it was obvious that their minds were made up in advance."

Expanding his criticism to cover also the producers of the programs, the Vice President said:

"To guarantee in advance that the President's plea for national unity would be challenged, one network trotted out Averell Harriman for the occasion."

"When the President concluded," Mr. Agnew went on, "Mr. Harriman recited perfectly. He attacked the Thieu Government as unrepresentative; he criticized the President's speech for various deficiencies; he twice issued a call for the Senate Foreign Relations Committee to debate Vietnam once again; he stated his belief that the Vietcong or North Vietnamese did not really want a military takeover of South Vietnam . . ."

"Every American," Mr. Agnew declared, "has a right to disagree with the President of the United States, and to express publicly that disagreement. But the President of the United States has a right to communicate directly with the people who elected him, and the people of this country have the right to make up their own minds and form their own opinions about a Presidential address without having the President's words and thoughts characterized through the prejudices of hostile critics before they can even be digested."

In recent weeks Mr. Agnew has drawn both criticism and praise for the pungency of his language as he has characterized Vietnam war critics as "an effete corps of impudent snobs" and demonstrations against the war as "a carnival in the streets."

There has been much speculation here on whether the President has encouraged; or at least not disapproved, the Vice President's recent speeches.

There were some who thought that the President was encouraging Mr. Agnew to play the "point of the spear," as Mr. Nixon did in the early years of the Eisenhower Administration.

There were others who believed that Mr. Agnew was acting on his own.

But there seemed little question that in his attack on the networks Mr. Agnew was expressing the resentments of the White House. Several White House officials have made no secret of their anger at the way at least one network handled the commentary after the President's speech.

Gerald Warren, the assistant White House press secretary, said that neither the President nor the press office had seen the text of Mr. Agnew's speech. Mr. Warren said that there would be no immediate comment from the White House.

Asked for comment tonight on Mr. Agnew's criticism of him, Mr. Harriman said:

"I don't think that the statement deserves serious comment. All can say is that I'm glad to be included with the television news media, which I feel, by and large are trying to do a conscientious job of keeping the American public informed on many subjects of national interest."

An examination of what Mr. Harriman said as a guest commentator for A.B.C. suggests that he was not explicitly critical of the President.

He began by saying, "I'm sure you know that I wouldn't be [so] presumptuous [as] to give a complete analysis of a very carefully thought-out speech by the President of the United States. I'm sure he wants to end this war and no one wishes him well any more than I do."

Not Seeking Censorship

Mr. Harriman went on to say that his approach to the problem differed in some ways from that of the President, and gave his reasons. But he concluded by saying: "There are so many things we've got to know about this, but I want to end this by saying I wish the President well, I hope he can lead us to peace. But this is not the whole story that we've heard tonight."

Mr. Agnew said that he was not asking for Government censorship of the networks. He was, he said, simply asking whether the commentators themselves were not censoring the news.

"The views of this fraternity," he said, "do not represent the views of America. That is why such a great gulf existed between how the nation received the President's address—and how the networks reviewed it."

While not proposing censorship of television commentary, Mr. Agnew seemed to suggest that the networks had not the same claim to First Amendment rights as the newspapers.

The situations were not identical, Mr. Agnew said, because television has more impact than the printed page, and because the networks have a near monopoly and the viewers have little selection, whereas a man who does not like a newspaper's views or news handling can switch to another paper.

* * *

November 16, 1969

250,000 WAR PROTESTERS STAGE PEACEFUL RALLY IN WASHINGTON; MILITANTS STIR CLASHES LATER

A RECORD THRONG

Young Marchers Ask Rapid Withdrawal From Vietnam

By JOHN HERBERS
Special to The New York Times

WASHINGTON, Nov. 15—A vast throng of Americans, predominantly youthful and constituting the largest mass march in the nation's capital, demonstrated peacefully in the heart of the city today, demanding a rapid withdrawal of United States troops from Vietnam.

The District of Columbia Police Chief, Jerry Wilson, said a "moderate" estimate was that 250,000 had paraded on Pennsylvania Avenue and had attended an antiwar rally at the Washington Monument. Other city officials said aerial photographs would later show that the crowd had exceeded 300,000.

Until today, the largest outpouring of demonstrators was the gentle civil rights march of 1963, which attracted 200,000. Observers of both marches said the throng that appeared today was clearly greater than the outpouring of 1963.

At dusk, after the mass demonstration had ended, a small segment of the crowd, members of radical splinter groups, moved across Constitution Avenue to the Labor and Justice Department buildings, where they burned United States flags, threw paint bombs and, other missiles and were repelled by tear gas released by the police.

There were a number of arrests and minor injuries, mostly the result of the tear gas.

Exodus Begins

At 8 P.M., most of the demonstrators, who had come from all parts of the country, were on buses, trains and cars leaving the city. By 11 P.M., the police said all was quiet in the city.

About 3,000 youths were unable to get to their buses, which were parked by the Tidal Basin, because of the tear gas and heavy traffic, so the city operated an emergency shuttle service of sightseeing buses.

The predominant event of the day was that of a great and peaceful army of dissent moving through the city.

At midday, under clear skies and in the face of a cold north wind, a solid moving carpet of humanity extended from the foot of the Capitol, 10 long blocks up Pennsylvania Avenue to the Treasury Building, four blocks down 15th Street and out across the grassy hill on which the Washington Monument stands.

The crowds brought to Washington a sense of urgency about a Vietnam peace and impatience with President Nixon's policy of gradual withdrawal. This theme, which was repeated throughout the day in various forms, was expressed at the beginning of the march by Senator Eugene J. McCarthy,

Democrat of Minnesota, who ran for President last year on an antiwar platform.

"The record of history, I think, is clear," Senator McCarthy told the demonstrators as they gathered on the Mall for the march early this morning, "the cases in which political leaders out of misjudgment or ambition in ancient time and in modern times basing their action on the loyalty of their people have done great harm to their own countries and to the world.

"The great loyalty of the Roman citizens moved the Caesars to war," he went on. "The great loyalty of the French moved Napoleon to actions which should never have been taken. Let us in the United States take warning from that experience."

Except for clusters of middle-aged marchers and a few in their latter years, the crowd in appearance could have been a merging of the college campuses across the nation. There was a small percentage of blacks.

Gathering of the Left

Overall, it was a mass gathering of the moderate and radical Left, including the 100 organizations that make up the New Mobilization Committee to End the War in Vietnam, sponsor of the demonstrations; old-style liberals; Communists and pacifists and a sprinkling of the violent New Left.

The outpouring was a climax to three days of antiwar demonstrations here and across the country. A 40-hour demonstration that the protesters called a "March Against Death," in which 40,000 filed past the White House bearing the names of the United States dead in Vietnam, ended at 7:30 A.M.

Shortly thereafter, the crowds began assembling at the foot of the Capitol for the mass march.

An eruption of violence last night—in which about 2,000 militants marched on the South Vietnamese Embassy and were turned back by the police with tear gas as they broke windows and damaged police cruisers—did not discourage the outpouring of peaceful demonstrators this morning.

By contrast with the incident last night, the tone of the march and the assembly at the Washington Monument was peaceful and subdued.

The temperature was in the low 30's, warming up to near 40 in the day.

The march, scheduled to begin at 10 A.M., got under way 25 minutes late. In the lead were three drummers, followed by youths carrying aloft 11 wooden coffins that contained placards bearing the names of the dead. The placards had been paraded past the White House. The coffin bearers were surrounded by a cordon of young, who were joining hands.

Next came a man bearing an immense wooden cross, followed by a large banner saying "Silent Majority for Peace" and then row after row of marchers 17 abreast shouting, "Peace now, peace now."

At 15th Street, there was a solid row of municipal buses parked along the curb between the marchers and the White House, which was only one-half block away. Before the march began, the police had cleared a 24 block area around the White House of everyone except those who lived or had business there, and the area looked virtually deserted.

At 2 P.M., the last stragglers reached the Monument.

The Pentagon and the District of Columbia government had prepared for the chance of major violence. More than 2,000 metropolitan policemen were on duty in the Capital today.

In each of the Federal buildings on or near the parade route, including the Justice, Labor and Commerce Department buildings, Army and Marine Corps troops were held in reserve.

But the real work of keeping order and containing the mäss of demonstrators along Pennsylvania Avenue and the Monument grounds and performed by the trained marshals of the Mobilization Committee.

Marshals Strict

The marshals, identified by blue and white arm bands, were strict and assertive. They were firm not only with restless demonstrators but also with accredited reporters and photographers, and they occasionally jostled even the "celebrities" of the peace movement, such as Arlo Guthrie the folk singer, when the first rank of marchers was being lined up this morning.

The march along Pennsylvania Avenue was contained by an impregnable, hand-to-hand line—at some points a double line—of marshals. One man observed sourly that the marshals were "more officious than the police," and at times there seemed to be as many marshals as marchers.

The inner courts of the Pentagon and the Justice Department looked like bristling fortresses as hundreds of rifle-carrying paratroopers stood in formation.

But the troops were never seen on the streets during the march and rally, and the policemen who were seen around the parade route were reduced to directing the scattered traffic or simply standing and shivering in the cold.

By midafternoon the only arrest clearly related to the demonstration was that of Dominic Angerame, 20 years old, of Buffalo, who was charged with disorderly conduct for painting a peace symbol on the Washington Monument.

Hundreds of Banners

There were hundreds of banners and posters on parade. Some of the legends were old. Many were humorous, with Vice President Agnew a special target.

Over-all, the slogans, like the sign. "We're here because we love our country," seemed to be asserting that the demand for withdrawal from Vietnam is now the only moderate course.

Among the signs: "Good trick, Dick, you brought us together again"; "A majority for a silent Agnew"; "Spiro for Apollo 13"; "Vietnam: Love it or leave it"; "Tyranny has always depended on a silent majority"; "I'm an effete intellectual snob for peace"; "Silent majority condoned Hitler"; "Support your local planet"; "What plan, Mr. President."

Only one of the slogans was threatening: "Nixon: This is our last march. The fire next time." Many of the marchers chanted, "One, two, three four Tricky Dick, stop the war."

By 3 P.M. the chilled demonstrators were building little bonfires with their placards to keep warm on the Monument grounds.

Counterdemonstrators provoked a number of shouting matches but no major confrontations.

Their principal weapon was signs: "America is worth saving"; "Put victory back into our vocabulary"; "Communism is the total enemy of freedom"; "Heroism is not Hanoism"; and "Support the Pentagon."

Ambrose P. Salmini, a manufacturer of marine equipment from 12 Park Hill Terrace, Yonkers, N. Y., had the most spectacular sign.

His "Will Vietnam satisfy the Reds?" trailed from a plane that flew over the capital at midday.

After the parade, the crowd, closely packed, covered most of the grassy acreage around the Monument. The outpouring was reminiscent of the crowd that gathered on the warm summer day of Aug. 28, 1963, at the Lincoln Memorial and heard the late Rev. Dr. Martin Luther King Jr. and other Negro leaders appeal for civil rights legislation.

There were famous faces in the crowd from both the Old and New Left, from Government and the arts. Black Americans were more heavily represented among the leaders and speakers than in the ranks of the demonstration.

Three United States Senators were there, Mr. McCarthy and George S. McGovern of South Dakota—both defeated candidates for the Democratic Presidential nomination last year—and Charles E. Goodell, Republican of New York. Paul O'Dwyer of New York, defeated for the Senate last year, marched among the Senators.

Black Leaders

Among the black leaders marching here today were Mrs. Coretta Scott King, widow of Dr. King; Phil Hutchings, a former officer of the Student Nonviolent Coordinating Committee, who is a columnist for The Guardian; George Wiley, head of the National Welfare Rights Organization, and Dick Gregory, the comedian-turned-activist.

Among the performing artists: Mary, of the Peter, Paul and Mary singing group; the actor-playwright Adolphe Green, and Leonard Bernstein, the composer and former conductor of the New York Philharmonic, who looked out at the crowd around the Monument this afternoon and said, "I'm with you. You're beautiful."

Senator Goodell, the only Republican officeholder who took an active part in the demonstration, said: "We are told that a United States pullout would result in a bloodbath in South Vietnam."

"This assumes," he said, "that one million South Vietnamese under arms will be slaughtered by a force of 200,000. And what in the world has been going on for the last six and a half years if not a blood-bath?"

"We are not here to break a President or even a Vice President," said Senator Goodell. "We are here to break the war and begin the peace."

* * *

November 17, 1969

VIETNAMESE SAY G.I.'S SLEW 567 IN TOWN

By HENRY KAMM

Special to The New York Times

TRUONGAN, South Vietnam, Nov. 16—A group of South Vietnamese villagers reported today that a small American infantry unit killed 567 unarmed men, women and children as it swept through their hamlet on March 16, 1968.

They survived, they said, because they had been buried under the bodies of their neighbors.

The villagers told their story in the presence of American officers at their new settlement, which lies in contested territory less than a mile from the ruins of their former home.

The officers refused to comment pending the outcome of an Army investigation into charges of murder against First Lieut. William Laws Calley Jr., 26 years old, of Miami.

A squad leader in the lieutenant's platoon. S. Sgt. David Mitchell, 29, of St. Francisville, La., has also been charged in the case, with assault with intent to murder.

[In Washington, a spokesman for the Army said that it would have no comment, in accordance with American Bar Association standards on pretrial discussion.

[Capt. James L. F. Bowdish, attorney for Sergeant Mitchell, said in Houston that estimates of 400 to 600 dead went "far beyond" any figures he had heard.

[George W. Latimer Lieutenant Calley's lawyer, said in San Antonio that he was "shocked" by the report, according to United Press International. "I only know what is in official records," he said. "My client had nothing to do with the killing of any civilians."]

A former soldier now studying at Claremont Men's College in California, Ronald L. Ridenhour, said yesterday that he had prompted the Army investigation by writing letters to Government officials after hearing several accounts of the alleged atrocity while stationed in Vietnam.

The site of the villagers' former home, about nine miles northeast of the provincial capital of Quangngai, is a desolate-looking place now.

Viewed from a helicopter, the ruins of houses along a well-used dirt road testify that a community once stood there.

The provincial Governor, Col. Ton That Khien, said today in an interview that the killings had occurred, but he added that the number of dead was perhaps exaggerated.

A responsible Vietnamese official close to the case said that those slain probably numbered between 450 and 500.

Villagers' Account

As told by one of the villagers, Do Hoai, in the presence and with the assent of a number of others, this is what happened:

A heavy artillery barrage awakened the villagers around 6 A.M. It lasted for an hour, then American soldiers entered the village, meeting no opposition. They ordered all inhabitants out of their homes.

Although the area had been largely under Vietcong control, the villagers had engaged in no hostile action against the Americans and bore no arms.

The Americans forced the villagers to gather in one place in each of the three clusters of houses that formed part of the village of Songmy. The settlements bore the names of Tucong, Dinhhong and Myhoi.

The three death sites were about 200 yards apart.

When the houses had been cleared, the troops dynamited those made of brick and set fire to the wooden structures. They did not speak to the villagers and were not accompanied by an interpreter who could have explained their actions.

Then the Vietnamese were gunned down where they stood. About 20 soldiers performed the executions at each of the three places, using their individual weapons, presumably M-16 rifles.

In the interview, Colonel Khien said that the killings had probably been carried out by fewer soldiers than Mr. Hoai reported, but said he did not know the exact number.

Mr. Hoai, 40, a rice farmer like most of the villagers in this green and marshy area between the central highlands and the South China Sea, said that those who escaped the slaughter, as he and his wife did, had hidden under the bodies of victims until the Americans left. The whole incident, he said, took about 15 minutes.

Mr. Hoai said that his mother, his older brother and the brother's three children had been killed.

A gaunt old woman, wearing the black pajamas and flat conic of Vietnamese peasants, interrupted to say that her 19-year-old son had also been killed.

A number of people in the crowd during the conversation at the edge of the new settlement said that Mr. Hoai's account was correct.

Witnesses Questioned

Mr. Hoai, informed that the United States Army might prosecute Lieutenant Calley for murder, said that he stood ready to go to the United States to testify at a court-martial.

Earlier today, an investigator of the Army's Criminal Investigation detachment visited the Americal Division, which conducted the operation during which the incident occurred. He questioned witnesses and left accompanied by two surviving village officials.

Mr. Hoai and the other villagers said that they had arrived at the death toll of 567 by subtracting the number of survivors—132 according to them—from the total known population of the hamlet.

They said they thought that all survivors had been found in three new locations.

The Provincial Governor said that the dead had been buried by survivors within three days of the killings and no body count had been made.

Another Vietnamese official said that the village chief had turned over to him a list of the dead, but the official refused to disclose their total number.

Colonel Khien, who is 40 years old and considered friendly to Americans, said that he had been notified of the killings within a week but at first had assumed that they had been the result of an artillery barrage and therefore a sad but unavoidable act of war.

The colonel said that the operation had taken place in the Americans' stipulated zone and that therefore no Vietnamese clearance had been required for the shelling and infantry advance.

Later, he said, the Vietcong distributed a propaganda leaflet about the incident. For that reason, he said, full silence was observed to avoid providing support for enemy propaganda.

When he realized three months later that the case was more serious, Colonel Khien said, the scene of action was no longer accessible because of Vietcong mortar fire and he could do no more than interrogate about 30 survivors. They gave him identical accounts of the killings, he said.

Praises Division's Work

The Provincial Governor said that as far as he knew President Thieu had not been informed of the slayings and no official complaint had been lodged with the American command. The senior province adviser for Quangngai, C. Edward Dillery, also declined comment on the accusation.

The Governor declared that he admired the pacification work done in this province by the American division and considered the killings an unfortunate exception. On the whole, he said, American troops were more solicitous of Vietnamese lives than his own troops are.

While declining to comment on what action the American Army should take to assertain Lieutenant Calley's role, Colonel Khien said that if one of his officers were suspected of killing women and children he would have to face a military court.

The colonel said that he doubted Mr. Hoai's assertion that all of the villagers had been unarmed. While most of those killed were probably not Communists, he said, there were Vietcong cadres in the village who may have used arms against the Americans.

Another responsible Vietnamese official, who declined to be identified because he feared the propaganda use that the enemy might make of the case, ruled out the possibility that the American soldiers might have killed the villagers because they had previously shown hostility to the Americans.

He said that the village had never before been entered by American troops.

Earlier, the village was identified mistakenly as Mylair, the name of six different hamlets in the vicinity.

Comments by Lawyer

Captain Bowdish, questioning estimates of the toll in the village, had this to say.

"There's a lot about this case that's unknown not only to me but to the people who are investigating it.

"I don't have many of the facts yet. I don't know how many people were killed or why.

"Sergeant Mitchell is charged with assaulting 30 people. I don't know what else went on in the village. From what I gather the platoon was pretty spread out as it went through the village and things may have taken place in one spot that were not seen in other parts."

* * *

November 25, 1969

MURDER TRIAL SET FOR ARMY OFFICER IN VILLAGE DEATHS

6 Counts Against Lieutenant Allege Slaying of 109— Earlier Inquiry Studied

By DOUGLAS ROBINSON
Special to The New York Times

FORT BENNING, Ga., Nov. 24—The Army announced today that a young officer accused of killing a large number of South Vietnamese civilians last year would be given a general court-martial on charges of premeditated murder.

Specifically the officer, First Lieut. William L. Calley Jr., is charged with the murders of at least 109 men, women and children on or about March 16, 1968, in the village of Songmy in Quangngai Province in South Vietnam.

The case, the Army said, will be tried as a capital offense, which means that if Lieutenant Calley is found guilty, he will face a penalty of death or life imprisonment.

Included in the six counts of premeditated murder against the 26-year-old officer is a charge of having shot and killed a 2-year-old child. All of the killings, the charges said, were carried out by Lieutenant Calley armed with a rifle.

Original Inquiry Studied

In Washington, the Army announced that it had appointed Lieut. Gen. William R. Peers to "explore the nature and scope" of the original Army investigation into the alleged killings. That investigation, conducted in April, 1968, concluded that no disciplinary action was appropriate.

The court-martial announcement was officially made by Maj. Gen. Orwin C. Talbott, commanding general of Fort Benning, but it was read at a news conference by Lieut. Col. Douglas B. Tucker, the Fort Benning information officer.

No date was set for the trial, which will be held here. "The date will be determined by the length of time needed by the defense and the prosecution to prepare for trial," Colonel Tucker said. "It is anticipated that this will require at least a month."

Open to Public

The trial, he continued, will be open to the public, although the military judge "is authorized to close portions of the trial to spectators to prevent the unauthorized disclosure of classified security information."

While awaiting court-martial, it was learned, Lieutenant Calley, who is now working in an administrative job in the office of the deputy post commander, will continue his duties. He will be free to leave the post to visit nearby Columbus. If he wants to leave the Fort Benning area, he would have to apply for permission as all soldiers do.

An officer denied that this was unusual treatment for a man facing a court-martial for a capital offense, saying that "incarceration is only used to protect a man or to make sure he's available for trial."

Since last September, when Lieutenant Calley was first charged with murder, he has been permitted to leave the post. On at least one occasion he visited his family in Miami.

There was no mention made today of a court-martial for Staff Sgt. David Mitchell of St. Francisville, La., a squad leader in Lieutenant Calley's platoon. Sergeant Mitchell has been charged with assault with intent to murder 30 Vietnamese civilians in the same incident. The sergeant is now stationed at Fort Hood, Tex.

"That investigation is continuing," an officer said.

The six specifications against Lieutenant Calley charge that he violated Article 118 of the Uniform Code of Military Justice. The article defines the crimes under which a person may be tried for "unlawfully" killing a human being "without justification or excuse."

The formal charges refer to the village as Mylai 4, the military designation for the village of Songmy, which is one of a cluster of hamlets. Americans in the Quangngai area nick-named the group of villages "Pinkville."

The first specification against Lieutenant Calley lists four murders, the second is for killing "not less than 30" civilians, the third is for three persons, the fifth charge is for one male and the sixth is for a 2-year-old child "whose name and sex is unknown."

70 in Fourth Count

The fourth specification reads as follows:

"In that First Lieut. William L. Calley Jr., U.S. Army, 40th Company, the Student Brigade, U.S. Infantry School, Fort Benning, Ga. (then a member of Company C, First Battalion, 20th Infantry) did, at Mylai 4, Quangngai Province, Republic of South Vietnam, on or about 16 March 1968, with premeditation, murder an unknown number of Oriental human beings, not less than 70, males and females of various ages, whose names are unknown, occupants of the village of Mylai 4 by means of shooting them with a rifle."

Lieutenant Calley's attorneys at the trial will be George W. Latimer of Salt Lake City, a former judge of the Court of Military Appeals, and Maj Kenneth A. Raby.

Major Raby, who is stationed at Fort Benning in the Judge Advocate General branch, had no comment when asked about the decision for a court-martial. Lieutenant Calley was unavailable for comment.

Last week, the Defense Department said that 26 men, including 15 who are now civilians, were under investigation in the South Vietnamese incident.

Survivors of the alleged massacre, who now live at a new settlement less than a mile from the ruins of their former homes, have told reporters that an American infantry unit killed 567 unarmed men, women and children.

The Army began the investigation of the shootings after a former soldier, Ronald Riden-hour of Claremont, Calif., wrote a three-page letter relating details of the incident that he had heard from a friend who had served in the unit.

An initial investigation was made in March, 1968, by the South Vietnamese and the United States 11th Infantry It apparently concluded that no massacre had occurred.

Lieutenant Calley was born and brought up in Miami. He spent a year at Palm Beach Junior College in Lake Worth, Fla. In 1964 he worked on the struck Florida East Coast Railway. Later he went west as an appraiser for an insurance concern.

As a railroad worker, he had been given a draft deferment. He lost it when he went into the insurance business. Anticipating being drafted, he enlisted in the Army in New Mexico in July, 1966, and went to officers' school in Fort Benning before his assignment to Vietnam in September, 1970. He served there about 22 months, having volunteered to stay past the usual one-year tour.

When Lieutenant Calley was first charged in September, he had been scheduled for discharge. For his service in Vietnam, the 5-foot 3-inch, 130 pound bachelor had been awarded a Bronze Star with oak leaf cluster and had been awarded the Purple Heart for a combat wound.

* * *

December 3, 1969

MUCH OF WORLD VIEWS SONGMY AFFAIR AS AN AMERICAN TRAGEDY

By HENRY TANNER
Special to The New York Times

UNITED NATIONS, N. Y., Dec. 2—In much of the world's press and for many ordinary citizens the village of Songmy has become the symbol of an American tragedy, even more than a Vietnamese tragedy.

Apart from the predictable exploitation by the Communists, the atrocities allegedly committed by American soldiers have moved the world to feelings of sorrow, shock, anger and a deep fear that the continuation of the war will have a corrosive, brutalizing effect on American youth and American society as a whole.

These feelings emerge as the main theme from reports by correspondents of The New York Times from some 30 countries.

Although comparisons with wartime Nazi crimes and with crimes committed by Communist forces in Vietnam were being drawn by some, the survey showed that the great majority in most countries do not see Americans in a similar light.

Judgments Vary

Most persons, the survey showed, apply one set of moral judgments to dictatorships, both Communist and Nazi, and another to the United States. Although an implied tribute, this only deepened the anger and the sorrow of those who have considered themselves the friends of Americans.

"What is happening to America, arbiter of the world, with its high moral standards." an Italian university professor asked. "Are you fighting the war by the standards of your enemies?"

The reports also showed that in Europe and Asia the Songmy affair has rekindled sharp public concern over Vietnam, reversing a trend toward growing indifference that an earlier survey had found a few days after President Nixon's speech on Vietnam of Nov. 3.

Threat to Americans Seen

Many people linked the alleged massacre in the settlement of Mylai No. 4, which is a part of Songmy, to what they saw as the inherent evil of the Vietnam war. They renewed their criticism of Mr. Nixon's Vietnam policies and renewed their appeals for the United States Government to end the war.

American withdrawal now is "both a necessary act of state and a human imperative," wrote The Spectator, the conservative-inclined London weekly, in a typical comment.

"Continued war now means a deadly threat not only to Vietnam but to the American people," an editorial in Dagens Nyheter, the respected Swedish daily said.

From Oslo a correspondent reported that the common theme of virtually all available comment was "the war has to stop" and one of the most urgent reasons for stopping it "is to save American youth from slow moral poisoning."

In several countries Songmy awakened memories of other wars and other atrocities—atrocities committed as well as atrocities suffered.

Other Villages Recalled

"The Americans have learned that the Americans in Vietnam have become the equal of the French in Indochina, Madagascar, Algeria and of the Germans at Oradour," wrote the Paris weekly L'Express, whose publisher, Jean Jacques Servan-Schreiber, first gained prominence abroad by writing a book about a young lieutenant—himself—being caught up in the "vicious circle of violence" in Algeria.

Oradour-sur-Glane was a village in central France that was razed and its entire male population killed by the Germans in reprisal against an attack by partisans in 1944.

In Germany too, newspaper editorialists recalled not only Oradour, but also Lidice, the Czechoslovak village, and Filetto di Camarda, a village in Italy, both of which suffered atrocities.

In Spain an official remarked: "Perhaps if American writers were dealing with the civil war now they would not be so quick to draw moral conclusions from the terrible things that happened then," referring to the Spanish Civil War of 1936 to 1939.

"I am shocked," a grocer in Athens said. If atrocities like this are tolerated by the United States Army and we are sim-

Associated Press

A workman removing a swastika Monday from a memorial to President Kennedy. Monument is in Runnymede, England.

ply told that the Reds are doing worse, one wonders what it is the Americans are fighting for in Vietnam."

Redeeming Aspects

"Almost every army has its killers, but these Americans have done away with the American dream of being different," said an official in Belgrade.

And in The Hague, an editorial in the Socialist daily Het Vrije Volk wrote: "The Americans have been killing the people they wanted to protect. This means the bankruptcy of United States Vietnam policy."

Many persons abroad noted that the American press had given detailed coverage to the eyewitness accounts. This public debate and the Administration's, promise to investigate and mete out justice are the only redeeming aspects of the tragedy, in the view of foreign public opinion, the survey showed.

Aldo Rizzo, an editorialist in the Bologna Daily Il Resto del Carlino condemned the alleged massacre and added:

"All this must be said explicitly and without mental reservation, but it is necessary to add that the war crime of Songmy is being examined, evalued and discussed in America today with a frankness and sincerity that has no precedent in the sad history of such things."

La Stampa, the respected Turin daily, wrote in a front-page editorial: "But the civilization of a people is judged above all by the courage and the severity with which it isolates certain individuals and denounces their crimes. The American press has done and is doing its duty."

Government officials in most countries have refrained from making statements. Among the exceptions were those in Britain, Sweden, Norway and West Germany.

Prime Minister Wilson, six days before the White House issued its statement, said that it would be a grave atrocity if the charges made thus far turned out to be only a quarter true.

Efforts are under way to bring the issue into the House of Commons for formal debate or at least before a meeting of the Parliamentary Labor party prior to Mr. Wilson's departure for Washington in January.

The British press, politicians and people were quicker than their American counterparts to sense the full horror of the affair, a correspondent wrote from London, adding:

"Why should this be so? Perhaps it is easier for outsiders to see horror. The British admire us so much, and still have so many illusions about the United. States, that our wounds make them bleed. And they are less inured to violence than Americans now."

Termed Horrifying Example

Foreign Minister Torsten Nelsson, of Sweden said in a speech in Malmoe last week "World opinion cannot be silent about the American war crimes in Vietnam. We must say clearly what we think."

In Norway, Songmy was described during a debate in the Storting, or Parliament, as a horrifying example of the atrocities of war. It was the main reason why Gunnar Garbo and Olaf Kortner, respectively chairman and vice chairman of the Liberal party, which is part of the Government coalition, came out for recognition of Hanoi.

Guttorm Hansen the spokesman for the Labor opposition, which is spearheading the move for recognition, said: "This war is a heavy weight on America's relations with its friends around the world, and from the dead end street this great nation has driven itself into, there is only one way out: the way back."

In Bonn, Chancellor Willy Brandt was asked about Songmy at his first news conference since taking over the Government, and refused to draw a parallel with Nazi war crimes. He replied:

"If I were still a private citizen or a newspaperman I know what I would say. I can see how heavily the burden weighs on the American people and I feel it inappropriate for me to comment as if to put two things in the same pot that do not belong together."

* * *

January 1, 1970

QUESTIONS ON SONGMY

G.I.'s Are Seen Facing Moral Dilemmas In Deciding Whether to Shoot and Kill

By WILLIAM BEECHER
Special to The New York Times

WASHINGTON, Dec. 31—Each soldier, as he arrives in Vietnam for a tour of duty, is handed a small white card that he is instructed to study and carry with him at all times.

It states, among other things. "Mistreatment of any captive is a criminal offense. Every soldier is personally responsible for the enemy in his hands." For reasons still unexplained, some members of Company C. 11th Brigade, Americal Division, allegedly forgot or chose to ignore these instructions on March 16, 1968, in Mylai-4 hamlet, part of Songmy village, in the province of Quangnai.

The result of that apparent lapse is what the press has labeled variously the Songmy or Mylai massacre, which if the allegations already lodged against one of the participants proves correct, will go down as one of the worst atrocities charged to American fighting men in any of the nation's wars.

Moral Dilemmas

In the Pentagon, no less than in living rooms and commercial offices around the nation, the question is asked, if this happened, why did it happen? Is the need for instant obedience to orders so inculcated into the average G.I. that, right or wrong, be does what he is told?

The career military man; even more than his civilian countryman, feels that charges of this sort besmirch the profession that is supposed to defend America's interests and ideals. Yet many military men, particularly those who have fought in Vietnam, feel that the public generally fails to grasp the awful moral dilemmas that soldiers are forced to face almost daily in a guerrilla war.

At the same time, some concede that the training stress on "follow orders, complain later" may contribute to a tragedy.

"Killing with a rifle, an artillery shell or a bomb, is not moral," says one colonel. "In war it can be justifiable or unjustifiable depending on the circumstances. The trouble is there are so many gray areas in a war with no fixed lines, where most of the time the enemy does not wear uniforms, and where he employs terror as a routine instrument of warfare."

No one would question that in combat an American soldier has the right to shoot and kill an armed enemy soldier facing him. The same would be true if, in driving along a rural road, the G.I. came upon a peasant in black pajamas who suddenly grabbed a rifle and aimed at him.

But is he justified in shooting a woman or a 14-year-old Vietnamese boy who is pointing a rifle or preparing to toss a grenade his way? Anyone who has seen such things in Vietnam would not hesitate to answer yes. The woman or boy can kill as surely as a battle-hardened enemy soldier and often do.

More Difficult Question

What about a boy or woman found setting up mines and booby traps, which account for a large share of American deaths and casualties in Vietnam?

There the moral question is more difficult. If the person can be apprehended without firing a shot, that is what the serviceman is told to do. But if a G.I. has recently seen a buddy, blown to pieces by a booby trap, and if he is afraid that if he lets the minelayer get away he might fall victim to his or her next hidden explosive, he might tend to be trigger-happy.

How should this same G.I. conduct himself in an area, like the Songmy complex of hamlets, which has traditionally served as home base for guerrilla forces, where its women and children are believed to set out booby traps regularly and where they probably provide intelligence on American troop movements so the guerrillas can set up ambushes?

The rules, emphasized in basic and advanced training at home and in indoctrination sessions provided each newcomer in Vietnam, are clear: Civilians and captured enemy soldiers are to be treated humanely.

Turning again to the little white card, it says: "All persons in your hands, whether suspects, civilians or combat captives, must be protected against violence, insults, curiosity and reprisals of any kind. Leave punishment to the courts and the judges. The soldier shows his strength by his fairness and humanity to the persons in his hands."

Whether G Company received any fire from Mylai-4 that day is still unclear.

One General's Viewpoint

This is important in the view of one general with extensive service in Vietnam.

"If my troops received fire from a hamlet, there was no question but that they were to go in with guns blazing," he said. "I'm afraid, when you add up all the villages, we've killed hundreds of civilians this way, along with enemy soldiers. In this kind of war you have no choice.

"But that's not the same as lining up civilians, after you've secured the hamlet, and cold-bloodedly killing them—if, indeed, that did happen in this case."

Until World War II, it was American Army doctrine, as in most armies, that enlisted men were required to follow the orders of their officers. If in doing so a law was violated, it was the officer who was subject to punishment.

But the Nuremberg war crimes trials supposedly changed that. Army regulations were modified to declare that a soldier is not duty bound to obey any unlawful order and is ultimately responsible for his own actions.

This is discussed during several hours of training in the states. But experienced troop commanders concede that the stress, in training and in promotion, is on following orders. If a man believes an order unlawful, he is told that he may request an immediate audience with the next higher officer, or follow the order and complain later, or refuse to obey and take the risk of court-martial.

At the court martial he would have to prove that the order was illegal. Thus the burden of proof would be on him.

Question of Balance

Commanders concede that this is a forbidding prospect for most G. I.'s, but they argue that if in combat a soldier could refuse to do the distasteful or dangerous by "pulling out the Geneva conventions," he could jeopardize the lives of his buddies and their mission.

How to achieve a balance between accomplishing the mission and minimizing the chances of a misguided command leading to the deaths of innocents is admittedly a difficult problem. Many suggest that training procedures be improved to make even clearer the responsibilities and rights of all those involved in combat.

Some officers, trying to find an explanation for what may have happened at Mylai-4, say that anyone who has fought in Vietnam has run across heart wrenching examples of the foe's use of terror and atrocity—such as the public disemboweling of a hamlet chief and his family, the remains being displayed on sharp stakes in the hamlet square.

"One tends not to want to be too compassionate in dealing with an enemy like that," one man said.

But another countered: "Maybe one of, the reasons we're fighting over there is to prevent the enemy's standards from being applied throughout the country. We don't gain an awful lot if, in the course of fighting, their standards and ours become indistinguishable."

* * *

February 2, 1970

WAR-POLICY BASIS IS CALLED DUBIOUS

Report for Senate Unit Isn't Sure South Vietnam Can Ever Assume Burden

By JOHN W. FINNEY
Special to The New York Times

WASHINGTON, Feb. 1—The Senate Foreign Relations Committee made public a report today suggesting that the Nixon Administration's policy of Vietnamization rests on dubious assumptions about the abilities of the Saigon Government and the military intentions of North Vietnam.

The study questioned whether the South Vietnamese Army, once American combat troops are withdrawn, would be capable of withstanding a heavy North Vietnamese attack.

Even if Vietnamization—the program of turning the combat burden over to South Vietnam—should succeed, the study contended, a substantial American involvement would still be required in South Vietnam.

War 'Far From Over'

While not directly criticizing Administration policy, the report said the underlying assumptions of the policy "seem to rest on far more ambiguous, confusing and contradictory evi-

The New York Times

PLANS HEARING ON WAR: Senator J.W. Fulbright, Arkansas Democrat, whose Foreign Relations Committee will hold hearings on Vietnamization of the war.

dence than pronouncements from Washington and Saigon indicate."

The war, it said, "appears to be not only far from won but far from over."

While the report does not bear a specific committee endorsement, it had an important effect on the views of committee members as they prepared to open hearings on Vietnam this week.

In making public the report, which he describes as "sober, dispassionate and revealing," Senator J. W. Fulbright, the committee chairman, said it "has given me some sense of the realities of the continuing American involvement in Vietnam."

Reflecting the conclusions that he has drawn from the report, Senator Fulbright said: "I can only hope that, in the future, the decisions we make in Vietnam will be guided by realities and not, as in the past, by well-intentioned hopes or unintentional rationalizations."

The 18-page study an abbreviated, censored version of a longer confidential report submitted to the committee, was drafted by James G. Lowenstein and Richard M. Moose, two former foreign service officers who are now staff consultants of the committee. They were sent to Vietnam last December by Senator Fulbright, an Arkansas Democrat, to study the progress of pacification, the prospects for turning over more of the war burden to the South Vietnamese, the domestic political situation and the outlook for negotiations.

The central question about turning over more of the fighting to the South Vietnamese, the report observed, is whether the South Vietnamese Army could now, or soon, defend against a large North Vietnamese attack.

It said the view of senior United States and Vietnamese military officers and civilian officials "reflects a strong belief that the North Vietnamese are no longer capable of mounting a sufficiently powerful attack to defeat the South Vietnamese army, at least as long as American firepower and airpower are available."

On the other hand, it said, "there are Vietnamese, American journalists and even United States military officers and officials at middle and lower levels who say that the South Vietnamese Army could not now defend the country against a massive North Vietnamese attack, even with United States artillery and air support. A number doubt that the army will ever be able to do so."

The staff report marks a new approach by the committee in its study of Vietnam policy. Long a focal point of congressional opposition to the war in Vietnam, the committee is now shifting from a critical to an analytical approach with the new Administration.

No longer is the committee broadly attacking basic policy as it did during the Johnson Administration. To an extent the committee has been neutralized in its criticism by Mr. Nixon's policy of shifting the combat burden to Saigon and with-drawing United States troops a policy that the committee members feel is moving in the right direction.

The question now being raised by the committee are whether this policy is workable and what it means in terms of American disengagement.

The long delayed hearings on Vietnam will not be on the scale that was contemplated last fall before President Nixon delivered his policy speech on Nov. 3.

Hearings on Resolution

The committee will begin with hearings on various Vietnam resolutions introduced during the last session of Congress.

Later in the session, probably in April, the committee plans further hearings on the extent of the American involvement in Vietnam with testimony from officials of various civilian agencies in South Vietnam.

The purpose of the second round or hearings will not be to determine why the United States is in Vietnam and whether it should withdraw, but to find out how the assumption of a greater combat role by the South Vietnamese will affect the United States role in Vietnam.

The staff study is designed to provide a framework for the new set of hearings.

The report noted that the success of present American policy in Vietnam depended upon these related factors:

- A progressively larger military effort by the South Vietnamese.
- The stability and cohesiveness of President Nguyen Van Thieu's government.
- The expectation that the enemy can and will do nothing to inhibit the transfer of a greater combat role to the South Vietnamese or disrupt the Thieu Government's stability.

The report observed that there is "an intimate relationship" among these three factors to the point that "all must succeed—or, perhaps more accurately, that none may fail—if present U.S. objectives in Vietnam are to be realized."

Yet, it said, all the evidence leads at least to "the inference that the prospects for a successful outcome" of any one of the three factors, much less all three, "must be regarded as, at best, uncertain."

Of the three factors, the report observed, the assumption of a greater combat role by the South Vietnamese is probably the most important "because the possibility of a continuing progressive American withdrawal obviously depends upon its success."

While acknowledging that there has been progress in turning over more of the fighting to the Saigon force, the report said it is "common knowledge that the quality of South Vietnam army units is uneven."

The report also said that the Vietnamese have apparently not been given a timetable for withdrawal of American combat troops and their estimates vary widely on when South Vietnamese troops will be able to take over the combat burden.

One American official, for example, told the Senate investigators that President Thieu wanted the bulk of United States combat forces removed during 1970, but a high Vietnamese official told them the American combat troops should not be withdrawn until "1972 or 1973 and 1974."

Enemy Intentions Unknown

The success of the program to make Saigon militarily self-sufficient, the report maintained, may well depend upon the actions of the enemy and whether North Vietnam is willing to permit a phased withdrawal of American troops while South Vietnamese forces assume the combat burden.

"It seemed clear to us, however," the report said, "that no one has the slightest idea whether the enemy will attack in force" during the American withdrawal, or wait until American forces are withdrawn before striking or, finally, concentrate on political subversion rather than an intensified military effort.

On the question of pacification, the report said there was general agreement that the so-called Revolutionary Development Program, which seeks to insure the security of rural areas and develop their economics, "is producing considerable evidence of progress."

However, it said "many Americans in the field believe that, despite statistical progress, the gains in pacification are fragile."

As for the stability of the present Saigon Government, the report said the most frequently heard criticism was that President Thieu was becoming "increasingly autocratic, secretive and isolated."

* * *

February 5, 1970

VIETNAMIZATION OR NEGOTIATION

The Vietnam hearings of the Senate Foreign Relations Committee are taking place in the wake of an on-the-spot staff study that emphasizes many previously expressed doubts about President Nixon's policy of Vietnamization.

Despite his recognition of the Paris talks as the preferable route to peace, Mr. Nixon seems to be shifting emphasis from negotiation toward Vietnamization as the preferred mechanism to achieve American disengagement. This approach raises many questions.

One is whether Vietnamization will end the war or merely perpetuate it while transferring a heavier share of the fighting to Saigon's troops. Another is whether it will terminate the American involvement or merely continue it, by cutbacks, at a level more politically bearable in the United States. A third is whether the Saigon Government and Army really can take over all or a major part of the combat and the innumerable other functions now performed by Americans. The final question is what, if anything, Hanoi and the Vietcong can do or will do to inhibit Vietnamization and, should the program be disrupted, whether a new escalation of the war and of American involvement will follow.

That these are not idle questions but serious dangers emerges repeatedly in the staff report. Despite optimistic briefings about the progress of pacification and the badly battered condition of the Communist military forces, the Senate investigators found enough indications of Communist strength and Saigon weakness to conclude that military and pacification gains are fragile and could be reversed.

Much of the apparent progress appears, in fact, to reflect a shift in Communist tactics from large-unit military offensives back to small-unit guerrilla activity and a strategy of "protracted war." This shift, and a concomitant diversion of North Vietnamese manpower and resources for the time being to internal economic development, is confirmed in the important speech a few days ago by the emerging successor to Ho Chi Minh, Communist First Secretary Le Duan, on the fortieth anniversary of the Vietnamese Communist movement.

The implication is that Hanoi is simply conserving force and biding its time until the United States either withdraws completely or halts its withdrawals after a significant rundown of its forces. In the latter event, the Senate investigators note, a massive North Vietnamese attack could face the United States with the "agonizing prospect" of reversing the process of withdrawal or effecting an accelerated, complete withdrawal "which would be interpreted at home, and probably abroad, as a military and political defeat."

The central issue that emerges is whether there is not a fundamental contradiction between Vietnamization as currently implemented, and bringing the war to a conclusion, which can only be accomplished with Hanoi's consent—which is to say through negotiation.

Initially, the concept of Vietnamization was that American troop withdrawals, by worrying Saigon about its future weakness and Hanoi about the prospect of protracted war, would lead both sides to negotiate. In practice, the reverse seems to have occurred. Hanoi seems prepared for protracted war and convinced of Saigon's ultimate weakness. Saigon—encouraged by the slow rate of American withdrawal, illusions of pacification successes, acquisition of advanced arms and American acquiescence in President Thieu's refusal to broaden his Government—feels no compulsion to seek a negotiated settlement.

Re-evaluation of the Vietnamization program and a new strategy to revitalize the Paris negotiations are clearly required.

* * *

March 15, 1970

U. S. SHOWS SIGNS OF CONCERN OVER EFFECT OF 9-YEAR DEFOLIATION PROGRAM IN VIETNAM

By RALPH BLUMENTHAL

Special to The New York Times

SAIGON, South Vietnam, March 14—Many South Vietnamese who live adjacent to areas that are being defoliated by spray from United States planes are convinced that any ailments or misfortunes that they suffer are related to the sprayings.

There is no proof that they are right about the effect of the chemical sprays on the human body, but neither is there any assurance that they are wrong.

The New York Times (by Ralph Blumenthal)

Palm trees in Binhtre, South Vietnam, after being sprayed with defoliants by U.S. planes.

Although the defoliation program, organized and run by the United States, has been in operation for nearly nine years the full effect of the chemicals on animal and human life remains largely undetermined

The United States military command says the program, which is designed to strip plant cover from areas occupied by the enemy and to destroy crops that might yield him food, has covered about 5,000 of South Vietnam's 66,350 square miles.

U.S. Terms It Valuable

The United States command says the program has proved its military worth. "It has contributed materially to the security of units operating in the field by increasing their visibility from the ground as well as the air," the command said.

About 13 per cent of the program has been directed against crops, presumably food grown by and for the enemy. Because of the drifting of defoliants and the difficulty of assessing the results on the ground, it is virtually impossible to say how much of the crop has been destroyed by the chemicals, but it would not appear to be a significant part of the country's capacity. It has brought hardships, however, to individual farmers.

After years of assuring the South Vietnamese that this extensive spraying was harmless to animals and humans, United States officials are showing signs of concern over recent reports that the chemical sprays may have some little understood and alarming effects.

Panel Studying Effects

In the last several months, reportedly on instruction from Washington, the United States military command and the United States Embassy have formed a special committee to review the effects of the defoliation program, especially on humans.

The sensitivity of the issue has foreclosed official comment, but according to informed sources the science advisory office of the command is responsible for gathering data in interviews and tests that embassy officials will then evaluate.

The South Vietnamese Government regards the entire subject as taboo. Vietnamese newspapers have been suspended for publishing articles about birth defects allegedly attributed to the defoliants, and the public Health Ministry declines to provide any statistics on normal and abnormal births.

However, the concern felt among the Americans is shared by many South Vietnamese scientists, physicians, health officials and villagers interviewed in a three-week survey of the effects of the program.

Officers of the United States command are aware of the allegations of birth defects but they generally discount the reports.

Responsible South Vietnamese scientists and officials say they know virtually nothing about the effects of the chemical sprays.

Saigon's leading maternity hospital, Tudu, from which rumors of an increase of abnormal births emanate periodically, has not even compiled annual reports of statistics for the last three years. Recent monthly figures show an average of about 140 miscarriages and 150 premature births among approximately 2,800 pregnancies, but the hospital is not prepared to say whether this represents an increase and, if so, what the cause might be.

A high Agriculture Ministry official said: "I don't think the Americans would use the chemicals if they were harmful."

He conceded that his ministry had made no tests and asserted that his experts had been unable to get any information about the defoliants from the Defense Ministry, which considers such data secret. The main defoliant compounds and some information about them are available in the United States.

Last Oct. 29, President Nixon's science adviser, Dr. Lee A. Du Bridge, announced that as a result of a study showing that one of the defoliants used, 2, 4, 5-T, had caused an unexpectedly high incidence of fetal deformities in mice and rats, the compound would henceforth be restricted to areas remote from population.

Defoliants Were Concealed

That directive appears to be ambiguous in South Vietnam for military spokesmen assert that 2, 4, 5-T continues to be used only in "enemy staging areas"—by definition populated regions.

Don That Trinh, Minister of Agriculture from November, 1967 to May, 1968, and for 10 years professor of agronomy at Saigon University, said that while he was minister, the Defense Ministry "would try to conceal the defoliant products from me."

"I did not believe in defoliation," he added.

According to one of the Vietnamese directors of a Government research laboratory in Saigon; "We didn't know anything before the United States started spraying. It was only when we received complaints from the livestock people that we started getting interested." But, he added, there are still no Vietnamese studies.

Even the village of Tanhiep, 20 miles north of Saigon, on which 1,000 gallons of defoliants were jettisoned on Dec. 1, 1968, has not been the object of attention or study.

An American C-123 flying out of Bienhoa air base, Northeast of Saigon, developed engine trouble shortly after takeoff. To lighten the craft, the pilot sprayed the full load of chemicals over Tanhiep and nearby Binhtri in 30 seconds instead of the usual 4 minutes 30 seconds, which spreads the defoliant at the rate of three gallons an acre in unpopulated areas.

The defoliant involved, according to the United States command, was a 50–50 mixture of 2, 4-Dichlorophenoxyacetate, or 2, 4-D, and 2, 4, 5-Trichlorophenoxyacetate, or 2, 4, 5-T, in an oil base. It is one of three compounds the military says it uses here, the others being a Dow chemical product called Tordon 101, a mixture of amine salts of 2, 4-D and Picloram, and an arsenic compound of cacodylic acid.

No physicians visited Tanhiep to examine the people after their exposure, which, like eight similar emergency dumpings since 1968—some over unpopulated forests—was not made public by the United States command.

A United States Air Force medical team visited Binhtri shortly after the spraying and, according to American district officials, found the villagers had suffered no ill effects. There was no later inquiry.

Mrs. Tran Thi Tien of Tanhiep, who says she has four normal children, is convinced that the malfunction of her son, who still looks like a newborn at 14 months of age, "must be due to the chemicals I breathed."

Her neighbors, Mrs. Nguyen Thi Hai and Mrs. Tong Thi An, blame the spraying for the fact that their children, one year and 20 months old respectively, still crawl instead of walk.

Nguyen Van Nhap, a farmer, complains of suffering bouts of fever, sneezing and weakness.

"I was working in the field when the spray came down," Mrs. Tien said through an interpreter. "I felt dizzy, like vomiting and had to stay in bed three or four days."

Many other villagers reported feeling the same sensations as Mrs. Tien, but, except for the two children described as retarded in learning to walk, no other abnormal children were described to visitors at the village of 1,200 residents.

Such complaints are not limited to Tanhiep and Binhtri, where villagers were admittedly exposed to concentrated doses of defoliant—though just how concentrated has not been established.

In Bienhoa city, 10 miles from Tanhiep, any defoliant in the air drifts down from the heavily sprayed battle areas to the north.

However, the manager of another clinic reported no increase in miscarriages over the last several years.

Any increase in miscarriages has many possible explanations: perhaps the deterioration of the daily diet, the cumulative effect of the hardships of war, population and economic movements that register statistics of only certain groups, or air pollution, of which the defoliant chemicals are a part.

Probably the most authoritative survey of the effect of defoliants on plant life in South Vietnam was made in 1968 for the Defense Department by Dr. Fred H. Tschirley, then assistant chief of the Crops Protection Research Branch of the United States Agriculture Department.

Dr. Tschirley concluded: "That defoliation has caused an ecologic change is undeniable. I do not feel the change is irreversible but recovery may take a long time."

He also said that he had little information on the effect of defoliation on animals and that, moreover, such effect was "truly unknown."

Whether the defoliants are hazardous to health or not, the people believe they are, and that in itself appears to be an obvious drawback in psychological warfare.

Against the psychological drawbacks of the program, United States officials have maintained that the tactical benefits—saving allied lives by denying cover and food to enemy guerrillas—outweighed the liabilities.

* * *

March 19, 1970

SIHANOUK REPORTED OUT IN A COUP BY HIS PREMIER; CAMBODIA AIRPORTS SHUT

PRINCE IS ABROAD

He Hints At Forming An Exile Regime—Reaches Peking

By HENRY KAMM
Special to The New York Times

BANGKOK, Thailand, March 18—Prince Norodom Sihanouk, Chief of State of Cambodia, was overthrown today in his absence, the Pnompenh radio announced.

The Southeast Asian country was cut off from the world, except for the broadcasts. The nation's two commercial airports were closed to all traffic.

Power has apparently been seized by Lieut. Gen. Lon Nol, the Premier and Defense Minister, and the First Deputy Premier, Prince Sisowath Sirik Matak, a cousin of Prince Sihanouk.

Cheng Heng, President of the National Assembly, has been designated as interim Chief of State, pending elections, the radio announced. Informed Pnompenh sources considered him a figure of negligible political stature.

Leaves Moscow

When the announcement of his overthrow was made Prince Sihanouk, who is 47, was in Moscow where he had arrived from Paris five days ago, and was preparing to depart for Peking.

[Prince Sihanouk arrived in Peking Thursday morning from Moscow. In the Soviet capital, the Prince acted as if he were still Chief of State but spoke of the possibility of forming a government in exile.]

The announcement came after a week of anti-Communist rioting, reportedly officially inspired, in which the embassies of North Vietnam and the Vietcong were sacked. These events moved Cambodia close to open hostility with the Vietnamese Communists, who are operating in large number on the Cambodian side of the long frontier with South Vietnam.

Last Friday, the Cambodian Government asked North Vietnamese and Vietcong troops to leave the country by dawn Sunday. Meetings on the demand have been held subsequently in Pnompenh, but no progress has been reported. [Reuters reported that, following the coup, the National Assembly had adjourned after failing to agree on measures to rid the country of Communist forces.]

Prince Sihanouk, a neutralist whose policies swerved often between right and left in an effort to strike a balance, is known to have struggled for a year against the hard anti-Communist position of General Lon Nol and Prince Sirik Matak.

According to informed sources, that struggle precipitated Prince Sihanouk's downfall, but was not its principal cause.

What brought him down, the sources said, was his cult of personality, his expensive striving for grandeur, the stagnation of Cambodia's economy, the corruption of leading personalities and the bureaucracy and widespread smuggling and trading in contraband goods.

No reports of violence attendant on today's events have reached the outside world.

The broadcasts are being received here imperfectly, on powerful monitoring equipment. Cable and telephone connections are not functioning.

Cambodia's two commercial airports, Pnompenh and Siemreap, were closed shortly after noon today without prior warning. The war in South Vietnam and Laos, and political strains with Cambodia's other neighbor, Thailand, have effectively cut off access to Cambodia by road.

Neighboring countries learned of the events in Pnompenh from a French-language broadcast that said:

"Following the political crisis provoked by Prince Norodom Sihanouk in the past days, the National Assembly and the Royal Council in joint session, in accordance with the constitution of the Kingdom, unanimously withdrew their confidence from Prince Norodom Sihanouk. From this day, 18 March 1970 at 1300 hours [1 A. M. Wednesday, New York time], Prince Norodom Sihanouk ceases to be the Chief of State of Cambodia and will be replaced by Cheng Heng, the President of the National Assembly, who will assume the function of the Chief of State until the election of a new Chief of State in accordance with the text of the nation's Constitution."

Prince Sihanouk had left Pnompenh on Jan. 6 for the announced purpose of taking a cure in Grasse, France, for obesity and a blood disorder. He set out on the return journey, with scheduled stops in Moscow and Peking, after the rioting broke out.

The first indication of events more serious than the rioting and the challenge last Friday by Cambodia to the Vietnamese Communists to withdraw their troops came today with the sudden closing of Pnompenh Airport.

Plane Turns Back

A Union of Burma Airways commercial flight left here for Pnompenh at 11:30 A.M. after receiving clearance for the 50-minute flight from the Saigon Control Tower, which directs traffic for the Cambodian capital. On board the stewardess could be heard to announce that the landing was imminent. But then the pilot's voice came over the public-address system to announce that Pnompenh Airport was closed and he was turning the jet back toward Bangkok.

No reason was given, the pilot said. The mystery persisted until shortly before 3 P.M. The Pnompenh station then came on the air to announce that a Cambodian Government communiqué was being read to a special session of the National Assembly.

In the statement, the Government accused the Vietnamese Communists of spreading false rumors, bribing Cambodian officials and distributing anti-Government leaflets, all in an effort to set Cambodians against Cambodians.

In view of this, and for reasons that were not stated the Government announced that it was relieving the Pnompenh police chief of his functions and would take "extreme measures" to restore calm.

Although the Pnompenh radio usually goes off the air at 3 o'clock, it stayed on after the announcement, broadcasting light music.

At 5:07 P.M., the music was interrupted for the communiqué containing the decisive announcement of Prince Sihanouk's overthrow.

Prince Sihanouk abdicated the throne of Cambodia in 1955, because, he said, the monarch was the prisoner of a rigid system and could not serve his people as effectively as he wished. He became Chief of State.

Throne Is Vacant

His father, King Norodom Suramarit, succeeded him. Since his death in 1960, his widow, Prince Sihanouk's mother, Queen Kossamak Nearireath, has represented the monarchy while the throne remains vacant.

Mr. Cheng Heng went on the air after Prince Sihanouk's ouster was announced to declare his acceptance of the title of Acting Chief of State.

He was elected President of the National Assembly in 1968 and re-elected last year. He is a wealthy lawyer and former Agriculture Minister.

In the view of the sources recently in Pnompenh Prince Sihanouk in his last year as Chief of State had shown a pronounced shift to the right toward the position of his political adversaries. He had become increasingly harder in his pronouncements against the Communists and had noticeably diminished his tendency to balance anti-Communist statements with strident attacks on "American imperialism."

Military Discontented

Nevertheless, the increasing pressure of the North Vietnamese and Vietcong largely because of their increasing need to find sanctuary in territory safer from American firepower than South Vietnam, heightened the political struggle in Cambodia by causing discontent with Prince Sihanouk's policies within the military, the sources said.

The soldiers were described as exasperated by apparent differences in the Chief of State's words and his actions. They charged that though the Prince condemned the Vietnamese Communists as the enemy in speeches, he forced the Cambodian military to release all Vietcong they captured.

They saw a contradiction between his complaints that the Vietcong were obtaining much of their food through illegal purchases from Cambodian farmers and his recognition last year of the Vietcong's so-called provisional revolutionary government and his subsequent signing of a trade agreement with it.

The military were said to resent what they considered Prince Sihanouk's ambiguous policy of ordering the armed forces to intervene against American attacks on Vietnamese Communist military targets on Cambodian soil. Cambodian gunfire was reported to have brought down an American fighter-bomber attacking a Vietnamese anti-aircraft position in Cambodia last November. The result was a heavy American attack on the Cambodian installation that killed 27 Cambodians.

These sentiments were said to have contributed to turning General Lon Nol from a loyal follower of the Prince into a determined opponent. The general's control of the small military forces—about 35,000 in a nation of 7 million—is said to be complete.

Investments Assailed

Prince Sirik Matak's opposition was said to have been rooted more in his disapproval of what he considered his cousin's flamboyant megalomania, Prince Sihanouk's insistence on nationalization of Cambodia's few industries, wastefullness in the use of limited investment capital and tolerance of widespread corruption.

Prince Sirik Matak, according to the sources, was leader of a body of opinion that believed that Prince Sihanouk was condemning Cambodia to economic disaster by ill-planned investments. Among these were his plan to build a port city named after himself—Sihanoukville—in which less than one ship a day docked in 1969, as well as plants for the manufacture of tires, jute sacks, textiles and distilleries that produced no revenues for the state but were said to enrich those whom Prince Sihanouk named as directors.

Other investments cited were large hotels in places that do not need them; state-run nightclubs with taxi-dancers, and two movie houses, one for the international film festivals in which the Prince's own productions have on both occasions won the first prize, and one for the showing of the Prince's films to the public.

Prince Sirik Matak and General Lon Nol were reported to have agreed by last summer that the only way to return Cambodia to order was to limit the Chief of State's exercise of power. The issue was at the center of the 27th Congress last June of the Sangkum, the political movement founded by Prince Sihanouk to group all political factions under one organization, with himself on top.

When, subsequently, Premier Pen Nouth stepped down because of long illness and General Lon Nol was asked by the Chief of State to form a cabinet, the general replied that he would form a government only as Premier and not as merely a secretary to Prince Sihanouk.

A special congress was name by Prince Sihanouk and instructed to form a government. General Lon Nol, the overwhelming choice, rejected the office at first and accepted only after the Chief of State met his conditions.

They were, principally, that he would have the right to choose his ministers and that they would report to him, not to Prince Sihanouk.

Almost A Coup

The Chief of State accepted and the Cabinet took office last Aug. 12. This acceptance by Prince Sihanouk of a government with powers not dependent on his whims was considered by some observers a bloodless coup. The Premier and Prince Sirik Matak issued decrees in the early days of their government to solidify this "coup."

The Premier ordered all Government communications and letters to be addressed to the Premier's office rather than to the Chief of State. The Deputy Premier, who made, the country's economy his special field, ended the practice of having certain taxes, such as those on motorcycles and scooters, paid into the Chief of State's treasury rather than the Government's.

During the 28th Congress of the Sangkum, in the last days of last year, Prince Sirik Matak weakened the Chief of State's position by forcing the closing of the Pnompenh Casino over Prince Sihanouk's opposition. A few days later, Prince Sihanouk, reportedly under heavy pressure, left for France, with Prince Sirik Matak, in all but in name, in charge of Cambodia.

Action Against Communists

Last month, General Lon Nol, who had been in France, returned, and open measures against the Vietnamese Communists in Cambodia followed.

The sources said that one of the most significant anti-Communist moves was cooperation between the South Vietnamese and Cambodian armed forces in fighting the Vietcong in the border areas. This is effected according to the sources, by Cambodian officers' intentionally discussing on "insecure" telephone lines known to be overheard by the South Vietnamese the disposition of enemy troops.

The sacking of the North Vietnamese and Vietcong embassies in Pnompenh last Wednesday followed, and, in the view of the sources, Prince Sihanouk's ouster was the goal that the Prince's opponents had pursued since last summer.

In Paris the day after the embassies were sacked, Prince Sihanouk said that he believed a coup against him was a possibility, and he suggested that General Lon Nol might lead it.

* * *

April 21, 1970

NIXON TO PULL OUT 150,000 FROM VIETNAM IN A YEAR; SAYS HANOI BLOCKS PEACE

APPEALS TO FOE

Average Withdrawals of 12,000 a Month Would Continue

By ROBERT B. SEMPLE Jr.
Special to The New York Times

SAN CLEMENTE, Calif., April 20—President Nixon pledged tonight to withdraw 150,000 more troops from Vietnam over the next year and once again appealed to the North Vietnamese to undertake serious negotiations.

In a 15-minute address televised from the Western White House, Mr. Nixon set forth a withdrawal plan that seemed designed to reassure his domestic critics that he intended to proceed with his withdrawal strategy yet leave himself and his military commanders wide latitude to determine the pace of disengagement.

On the diplomatic front Mr. Nixon reported no progress. He fixed the blame entirely on the intransigence of the enemy and its insistence on the removal of the Saigon Government of President Nguyen Van Thieu as a precondition to meaningful talks.

"It is Hanoi and Hanoi alone, the President declared, "that stands today blocking the path to a just peace for all the peoples of Southeast Asia."

Commitment to Nation

Mr. Nixon gave a commitment that between now and next April the authorized force in Vietnam—the present ceiling by 150,000, to a new ceiling of 284,000.

To his military advisers he gave implicit assurances that the rate of withdrawal could be adjusted to the level of enemy activity and other battlefield factors in South Vietnam.

Since Mr. Nixon announced the first round of withdrawals last June, American troops have been leaving Vietnam at a rate of about 12,000 men a month. The average monthly reductions under the plan announced tonight would remain roughly the same.

But officials here conceded that, while they hoped to undertake "significant" withdrawals in the early stages of the plan, it was entirely possible that more men would be withdrawn near the end of the timetable, especially if battle-field conditions took a sudden turn for the worse. And the President himself said:

"The timing and pace of these new withdrawals within the over-all schedule will be determined by our best judgment of the current military and diplomatic situation."

On balance, however, officials here portrayed the announcement as a vote of confidence in the President's so-called Vietnamization program—the effort to train and equip South Vietnamese forces to assume a larger share of the burden, and to bring ever-larger areas of the rural countryside under Government control. Mr. Nixon noted "significant advances" on both fronts.

But Mr. Nixon condemned in strong terms what he described as the adventurism of the North Vietnamese in Laos and Cambodia in recent months. Despite what he said was a decline in over-all enemy force levels in South Vietnam, leading to a reduction in American casualties, he expressed deep concern over Hanoi's "overt aggression" against Cambodia, its "new offensives" in neutral Laos, and continuing infiltration of South Vietnam down the Ho Chi Minh trail.

The President did not seek to explain or interpret the meaning of the accelerated enemy activity throughout Indochina. Other officials, however, in what they described to be a cheerful interpretation, said that Hanoi might have concluded that military victory in South Vietnam was out of the question and had thus determined to take out its frustrations in Laos and Cambodia.

'The Just Peace'

The President himself gave a similarly negative assessment of Hanoi's prospects in South Vietnam, announcing that the enemy had "failed to win the war in Vietnam" and declaring:

"The decision. I have announced tonight means that we finally have in sight the just peace we are seeking."

Mr. Nixon offered no new diplomatic initiatives of his own. The Administration's major ambition, he said, remained a "political solution that reflects the will of the South Vietnamese people."

In what could turn out to be a subtle but important change, however, Mr. Nixon did not insist on free elections as the preferred mechanism by which "the will of the South Vietnamese people" could be translated into a new political order. The White House has placed heavy emphasis on free elections in the past.

Holding out the possibility that the United States would be willing to accept other means of reaching a political settlement, the President said:

"A fair political solution should reflect the existing relationship of political forces. We recognize the complexity of shaping machinery that would fairly apportion political power in South Vietnam. We are flexible."

This could mean—as Administration sources have hinted in the past—that Mr. Nixon would accept a settlement in which both sides would be given political control over areas they now dominate militarily.

The President also "noted with interest" the recent statement by the chief Soviet delegate to the United Nations, Yakov A. Malik, favoring a conference on Indochina, and said that Washington would continue to "explore" the implications of the proposal.

Mr. Nixon did not take note, however, of a subsequent comment by Mr. Malik that such a conference is "unrealistic at the present time."

Mr. Nixon's withdrawal announcement was consistent with the latest speculation from Washington about what he would do. Most observers had predicted that he would continue to withdraw troops at a rate of 12,000 a month. What was unexpected in his announcement was his decision to adopt a long-range schedule of withdrawals and to commit himself to the removal of 150,000 men over that period.

The troop withdrawal announcement was Mr. Nixon's fourth since he assumed office on Jan. 20, when the authorized troop ceiling for Vietnam stood at 549,500 men. Mr. Nixon then proceeded to reduce this figure by 115,500 in three successive stages.

The first withdrawal, reducing the ceiling by more than 25,000 men, was announced following a conference between Mr. Nixon and President Nguyen Van Thieu of South Vietnam on Midway Island last June. The second and third reductions of 35,000 and 50,000 men, respectively, were announced in September and December, and as of this morning, the ceiling stood at 434,000 men.

Actual troop strength, according to official figures, is somewhat below authorized strength. The United States Military Command in Saigon announced today that there were 425,000 American troops in Vietnam last week.

Tonight's disclosures followed weeks of speculation and months of hard bargaining within the Administration that cast Mr. Nixon's civilian advisers, including Secretary Laird, against his military advisers on the Joint Chiefs of Staff.

It was disclosed ten days ago that the Joint Chiefs had pleaded with the Secretary of Defense, Melvin R. Laird, to intercede with the President and obtain a delay of as much as 60 days in any further announcements of withdrawals. Their basic argument was that recent enemy thrusts in Laos and Cambodia had introduced new elements of uncertainty into the war. They further contended that defensive positions in some areas of South Vietnam would become dangerously thin if two or more combat divisions were pulled out over the summer.

Mr. Laird rejected their pleas, although he was said to have agreed that the pace of the next round of withdrawals whatever their aggregate size—would not exceed the rate of reductions since last June, which has averaged about 12,000 men a month. Personally, however, Mr. Laird was said to have favored an increase to a rate of about 15,000 to 20,000 men a month.

Mr. Laird's long-range hope has been to reduce United States troop levels in Vietnam to 225,000 to 250,000 by mid-1971. This hope was a basic assumption written into the new defense budget for the fiscal year starting July 1. Mr. Laird felt that his position was strengthened by a three-week inspection trip by an Administration team of Vietnam planners last month. The survey resulted in generally favorable reports on the progress of the South Vietnamese military force and on the extension of Government control into the countryside.

Yesterday, there were reports in Washington that the Administration was considering a new troop-reduction formula that would serve as a compromise between Mr. Nixon's civilian and military planners.

According to the report, the compromise called for the President to announce withdrawals of 45,000 to 50,000 men over four months—consistent with the existing pull out rate of 12,000 men a month.

Private Instructions

At the same time, military commanders in Saigon would be given private instructions to increase that total by 10,000 to 20,000 men toward the end of the summer, if it then appeared that potential problems in Cambodia, Laos and South Vietnam were not materializing.

The President's speech tonight went through at least 10 drafts, and he was still working on its contents late this afternoon. The basic drafts were written by Raymond K Price Jr., a Presidential speech-writer.

Mr. Price was one of a handful of aides who accompanied the President on his trip to Houston and to Honolulu, where he awarded the Medal of Freedom to the three Apollo 13 astronauts.

The trip has given the President and his staff a visible lift. Beset as he has been with domestic political difficulties over the last several weeks—caused largely by the fight over the nomination to the Supreme Court of G. Harrold Carswell—Mr. Nixon seemed to relish the opportunity to take an active public role in the ceremonies marking the completion of the Apollo 13 mission and to return, as he did tonight, to the complexities of diplomacy and foreign affairs.

Difficult and trying as his diplomatic problems are, Mr. Nixon has always appeared to feel more at home with them than with his domestic difficulties.

* * *

April 27, 1970

THE NEW TEMPTATION: CAMBODIA

By ANTHONY LEWIS

LONDON—How familiar it all seems as the generals and the jingoes begin their pressure for American intervention in Cambodia. The situation, we read, gives us a great chance to win the Vietnam war—if only we expand it. We must send arms and encourage the South Vietnamese Army to cross the border. The opportunity to clean out the Communist sanctuary is almost too good to be true. Etcetera.

After the pain of the war and the effort to disentangle ourselves from it, Americans naturally may find it frustrating to see the Vietnamese Communist forces enlarge their operations in Cambodia. And so the President's press secretary, Ronald Ziegler, denounces them as aggressors, aggressors blatantly violating the Geneva agreement in Cambodia as in Laos. But it is not that simple.

Forces and Tactics

For one thing, why should we expect the other side to play by our rules? We have B-52's and helicopters and CS gas and weapons beyond imagination; they have guerrilla tactics and ruthlessness. We operate from bases in Thailand and thousands of miles away they slip into the other states of Indochina. There does not seem a great moral distinction.

Nor is it so clear that only the Communists are blatant violators of the Geneva accords. The evasions and lies of successive administrations about the American military presence in Laos have begun to be exposed by Senator Symington.

And in Cambodia it was the anti-Communists who upset the status quo, with the coup against Prince Sihanouk. The Vietcong and North Vietnamese could hardly have been expected to agree quietly to the cutting of their supply line through Cambodia. Their military activity may be intended primarily as pressure on Gen. Lon Nol to restore the status quo.

The character of the Lon Nol regime may also give us pause. After a week of bodies floating down the Mekong River—bodies of innocent Vietnamese residents of Cambodia evidently murdered because of their race—we now have had the Cambodian Army using unarmed Vietnamese civilians as an advance guard to draw enemy fire. Many were killed. The general on the scene attributed that "psychological warfare plan" to Lon Nol.

The underlying conflict here is not political but racial, and centuries old. The Lon Nol Government, to the extent that it does govern, seems to have chosen to play on those ancient animosities. Do we really want to become involved in the encrusted bitterness of the Khmers and the Vietnamese, along with our other alien burdens?

A Siren Appeal

President Nixon now faces a siren appeal like the one that lured his predecessors in 1965: win the war by escalation. It may be worth remembering what America has done in that search for victory, and to what effect.

We have bombed Vietnam, North and South, with more explosives than were used in World War II. The military will of the North and of the Vietcong has not been broken.

We have pioneered the use of defoliants on a massive scale. Just now, belatedly, after much outcry, we have officially admitted that one of these chemicals may not only kill plants but cause human birth defects.

We have invented the concept of free-fire zones. That clean-sounding name actually tells American soldiers that they may kill any living thing with a clear conscience.

We have massacred civilians, women and children, in substantial numbers. Or so official investigations have concluded and legal proceedings charged.

Corruption of ourselves is the price we have paid for trying to impose our ideas on a scene where we do not belong. That is what American history will record, not the undoubted sacrifices in a selfless cause that President Nixon mentioned last week. The plea of good intentions will not suffice.

No Easy Way Out

To know all this, as the President must, is not to know an easy way out. But whatever the contradictions of his language, with the rhetorical gestures to victory, Mr. Nixon's policy is to reduce American involvement in Vietnam. And this time, in contrast to 1965, the issue is out in the open. There is no excuse for the President or any of us accepting an enlargement of the war without anticipating the consequences.

CAMBODIA AND LAOS

May 1, 1970

NIXON SENDS COMBAT FORCES TO CAMBODIA TO DRIVE COMMUNISTS FROM STAGING ZONE

'NOT AN INVASION'

President Calls Step an Extension of War to Save G.I. Lives

By ROBERT B. SEMPLE Jr.
Special to The New York Times

WASHINGTON, April 30—In a sharp departure from the previous conduct of war in Southeast Asia, President Nixon announced tonight that he was sending United States combat troops into Cambodia for the first time.

Even as the President was addressing the nation on television, several thousand American soldiers were moving across the border from South Vietnam to Cambodia to attack what Mr. Nixon described as "the headquarters for the entire Communist military operation in South Vietnam."

The area was described by sources here as the Fishhook area of Cambodia, some 50 miles northwest of Saigon.

White House sources said they expected tonight's operation to be concluded in six to eight weeks. They said its primary objective was not to kill enemy soldiers but to destroy their supplies and drive then from their sanctuaries.

The President described the action as "not an invasion of Cambodia" but a necessary extension of the Vietnam war designed to eliminate a major Communist staging and communications area. Thus it is intended to protect the lives of American troops and shorten the war, he asserted.

The President further described the action as "indispensable" for the continued success of his program of Vietnamization—under which he has been withdrawing American ground combat troops as the burden of fighting is gradually shifted to the South Vietnamese.

The President's rhetoric was tough—probably the toughest of his tenure in office—and was reminiscent of some of the speeches of Lyndon B. Johnson during the last years of his term as President.

Nixon Appears Grim

The President appeared grim as he delivered his address while sitting at his desk in the Oval Office of the White House. Occasionally he used a nearby map to point out the Communist-held sanctuaries, which were shaded in red. But no gesture could match the solemnity of his words.

He portrayed his decision as a difficult one taken without regard to his political future, which he said was "nothing compared to the lives" of American soldiers.

Discussing this future, Mr. Nixon said: "I would rather be a one-term President and do what I believe is right than to be a two-term President at the cost of seeing America become a second-rate power and to see this nation accept the first defeat in its proud 190-year history."

He added that he regarded the recent actions of the North Vietnamese as a test of American credibility requiring firm response.

"This action puts the leaders of North Vietnam on notice," he said, "that we will be patient in working for peace, we will be conciliatory at the conference table, but, we will not be humiliated. We will not be defeated. We will not allow American men by the thousands to be killed by an enemy from privileged sanctuaries."

"We live in an age of anarchy, both abroad and at home," the President declared. "We see mindless attacks on all the great institutions which have been created by free civilizations in the last 500 years. Here in the United States, great universities have been systematically destroyed. Small nations all over the world find themselves under attack."

Aid Asked by Cambodians

Somewhat surprisingly, the President spoke hardly at all about the request made by the Cambodian Premier, Lieut. Gen. Lon Nol, for extensive arms and supplies—perhaps to reinforce his efforts to portray the new action in Cambodia as a tactical incident related to the Vietnam war rather than a full fledged act of support for the Cambodian Government.

Mr. Nixon said, however, that, with other nations, the United States would try to provide small arms and equipment to the Cambodian army.

Pentagon sources said tonight that shipments would include small arms and automatic weapons, but no artillery or aircraft.

The President did not set forth any legal basis for his action, except to say that "I shall meet my responsibility as Commander in Chief of our Armed Forces to take the action I consider necessary to defend the security of our American men."

Nor did he seek to explain how the introduction of American troops into Cambodia was consistent with the doctrine that he enunciated at Guam last July—that in future he would rely on Asians to fight their own wars.

Mr. Nixon placed the responsibility for the failure of the Paris peace talks squarely on the North Vietnamese. He said they had rejected every American overture, public and private.

White House sources expressed hope, however, that tonight's action—far from deterring future negotiations—might well convince Hanoi of the Administration's resolve to weaken the enemy militarily and thus hasten the beginning of serious negotiations.

The section of Cambodia to which the American units have been sent is a sparsely populated, heavily wooded area in which enemy troops have built numerous complexes of bunkers and storage pits. It is known to military men as the Fishhook because of the configuration of the border at that point.

Area Used for Many Years

North Vietnamese and Vietcong soldiers have been operating there for years, darting across the border for raids against allied positions, then falling back to recuperate, resupply and retrain. Major command headquarters are thought to be situated in the area.

Past allied operations against similar base areas on the South Vietnamese side of the border have not always been notably successful.

Mr. Nixon's speech was virtually certain to cause new turmoil on Capitol Hill and among critics of the war throughout the country. Many Senators had already expressed dismay at yesterday's announcement by the Defense Department that American advisers had accompanied South Vietnamese troops on attacks into the Parrot's Beak section of Cambodia, about 35 miles from Saigon.

The Administration has acknowledged in the past that American commanders have permission to fire across the border at retreating enemy troops, and South Vietnamese troops have crossed the line on a number of occasions in recent days.

But it has never been clear whether American combat troops have crossed the border on the ground. The American military command in Saigon has never admitted such crossings.

Faced with the situation posed by what he said were "stepped-up" enemy guerrilla actions over the last two weeks, and with the Cambodian capital, Pnompenh, under increasing threats from Vietnamese Communist forces, the President said he had considered three options.

Policy of Inaction Rejected

The first was to "do nothing." Mr. Nixon said this would have "gravely threatened" the lives of Americans remaining in Vietnam after the next troop withdrawal.

The second, he said, was to provide "massive" military aid to Cambodia. He said that large amounts of aid could not be rapidly and effectively used by the small Cambodian Army.

The third choice, he said, was to "go to the heart of the trouble"—to clean out the sanctuaries that serve as bases for attacks on both Cambodian and American and South Vietnamese forces in South Vietnam.

Mr. Nixon's address came as Washington was still trying to digest the Defense Department's announcement yesterday that the United States had agreed to provide combat advisers, tactical air support and other forms of assistance to South Vietnamese troops attacking Communist bases in Cambodia.

The South Vietnamese offensive, involving thousands of troops, began yesterday morning and provoked widespread surprise, anger and frustration on Capitol Hill, mixed with quick expressions of support from some of the President's Congressional allies.

Many legislators, particularly Senators with a long history of opposition to the Vietnam war, saw the Cambodian action as a dangerous expansion of the conflict.

Informed sources reported that more than 1,200 telegrams arrived at the White House last night after the announcement of the South Vietnamese push into Cambodia, with United States support—an unusually large number on an issue on which the President himself had not yet made a public statement.

There was no indication of the tenor of these message but a recent Gallup Poll indicated that public approval of

Associated Press

The President points to Fishhook area of Cambodia. Dark areas are enemy strongholds.

Mr. Nixon's Vietnam policies had dropped from a high of 65 per cent in January to 48 per cent in early April. Therefore tonight's address was regarded in the White House as having considerable political as well as diplomatic significance.

After the Defense Department announcement yesterday, Senator John Sherman Cooper, Republican of Kentucky, and Senator Frank Church, Democrat of Idaho, began drafting legislation that would preclude use of any funds appropriated by Congress for military assistance or operations in Cambodia. This would be attached as an amendment to a military sales bill now before the Senate Foreign Relations Committee.

Some of the critics of yesterday's move—including Senator Mike Mansfield of Montana, the Senate majority leader—were among a dozen or so Congressional leaders from both parties who gathered at the White House at 8 P.M., one hour before the President was scheduled to go on the air, for an advance briefing from Mr. Nixon in the Cabinet room adjacent to the Oval Room, the President's office. Members of the Cabinet also attended.

During the briefing, Mr. Nixon was said to have summarized the speech and to have set forth the Administration's rationale for the decision to authorize American participation in the South Vietnamese offensive against areas that have served as sanctuaries for Communist forces on the Cambodian side of the border.

The main justification for the move offered yesterday and again this morning, in public statements and private conversations, was that North Vietnamese and Vietcong troops operating from Cambodia had the lives of American servicemen in South Vietnam and, posed an "increasing threat" to more broadly, to the Vietnamization program.

The offensive, Daniel Z. Henkin, Assistant Secretary of Defense for Public Affairs, declared at a briefing yesterday, "is a necessary and effective measure to save American and other free-world lives and to strengthen the Vietnamization program."

Top Aides Visit Capitol

In private, officials conceded that Mr. Nixon had deliberately chosen to widen the conflict—temporarily, they said—in an effort to bring it to an end more quickly.

This was essentially the approach taken by Administration officials who circulated on Capitol Hill today explaining the Administration's point of view. Both the Under Secretary of State, Elliot L. Richardson, and the Deputy Secretary of Defense, David Packard, were dispatched to the Capitol to brief Republican Senators on Mr. Nixon's reasoning.

It was emphasized that the joint South Vietnamese-United States operation on Cambodian territory should not be construed as Mr. Nixon's answer to the request made by Premier Lon Nol of Cambodia for military aid.

This distinction has been drawn carefully and emphatically in nearly every utterance on the Cambodian situation by Ronald L. Ziegler, the White House press secretary. This apparently reflects an effort to persuade newsmen that the operation in Cambodia is no more than an extension of the Vietnam operation and does not represent a commitment of United States manpower to the Government of Cambodia.

* * *

May 2, 1970

ALLIES DRIVE AHEAD IN CAMBODIA

FOE'S BASE SOUGHT

10,000 Soldiers Begin a Pincer Movement in Fishhook Area

By TERENCE SMITH
Special to The New York Times

LANDING ZONE X-RAY, Cambodia, May 1—A huge allied task force including 5,000 American infantrymen swept into Cambodia today and formed an arc around the suspected headquarters of the Vietnamese Communist forces.

The sky over this forward command post three miles inside Cambodia was filled with helicopters as American and South Vietnamese soldiers—totaling some 10,000 men—moved out on the operation announced by President Nixon last night.

Their mission was to find and destroy the Communist base known as the Central Office for South Vietnam, or COSVN. The headquarters were thought to be in a bamboo forest in the Fishhook area, about five miles inside Cambodia and 70 miles northwest of Saigon.

Another Drive Under Way

Mr. Nixon approved the mission a day after he authorized American advisers and air support for a South Vietnamese thrust into a section of Cambodia known as the Parrot's Beak, 35 miles west of Saigon.

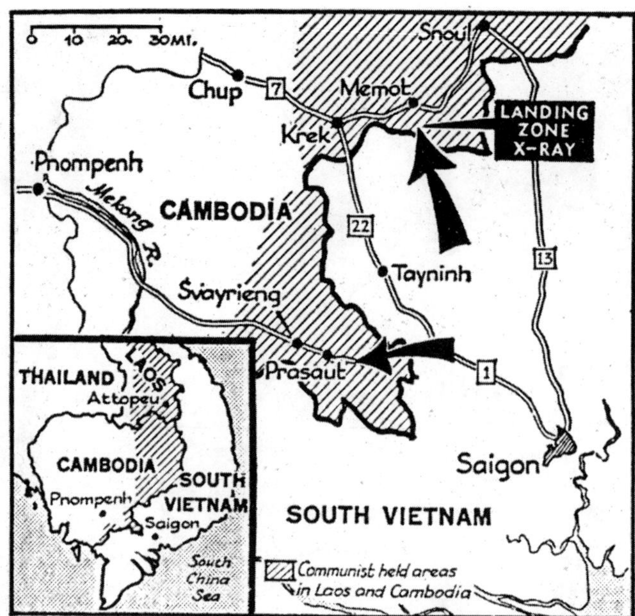

Allied task force swept into Cambodia to Landing Zone X-Ray while a South Vietnamese force reached Prasaut.

Reporting on the first day of the Fishhook operation, military, spokesmen said that 194 enemy soldiers had been killed, 161 by air strikes. United States casualties were put at six wounded, with no fatalities reported.

Hundreds of helicopters, planes, tanks and armored vehicles were involved in the operation, the largest allied war effort in the last two years. Three United States helicopters were brought down by ground fire, and one crewman was injured.

The allied troops met no substantial resistance during the first day, a fact that suggested the enemy might have slipped away, as he often has in the past, in advance of the attacking force.

Late tonight the enemy mounted small probes against American troops in night defensive positions. The United States command said that 10 enemy soldiers were killed during brief clashes. No American casualties were reported.

While the first American mechanized units crossed the border at 9:45 A.M. seven miles southeast of the Cambodian town of Memot, troops were still being brought in by helicopter late this afternoon. Two companies of the First Cavalry Division (Airmobile) were ferried into Landing Zone X-Ray shortly after 4 P.M.

After the helicopters came in at treetop level to an open field next to a rubber plantation about five miles southeast of Memot, the men broke into squads and cautiously began moving out to seek the enemy.

Little Difference in Terrain

"A week ago I never thought I'd be in Cambodia," Sgt. Carl Holzschub whispered as he moved through the knee-high underbrush between rows of rubber trees. "I suppose we're making history but as far as I can see, Cambodia is no different from Vietnam."

In the effort to trap the Communist command element in a pincer, three battalions of South Vietnamese airborne troops—nearly 2,000 men—were ferried by helicopter to positions north of the target and immediately began to sweep southward. Perhaps twice as many Americans drove north from the Vietnamese border atop tanks and armored personnel carriers.

"We think we have them in a bag," Maj. Gen. Elby B. Roberts, the commander of the First Cavalry Division, told reporters at a forward staging area on the border this afternoon. "In a day or two, we'll reach inside the bag and see what we have," he continued. "We can't be sure, but that's where our intelligence locates COSVN."

Hospital in Complex

The Central Office, described as the control center for all Communist military operations in South Vietnam, is thought to be a sizable but movable jungle headquarters.

It is believed to include a hospital, sleeping and working quarters for top commanders and an advanced communications network. It is protected by a regiment-sized security force, about 1,500 men.

Informed military sources said that the orders behind the planning for an invasion of the Fishook area were first received by the First Cavalry Division on April 24. The plans were completed by April 27, and two days later—Wednesday—the division was instructed to execute the plans at dawn today.

Elements of the task force assembled in northern Tayninh and Binhlong Provinces yesterday and during the night as waves of B-52 bombers pounded the target area. Heavy artillery began firing at the first light, and at 6:10 A.M. a 15,000-pound bomb was dropped 4 miles inside Cambodia.

The huge crater caused by the explosion became a forward artillery base, as large guns were dropped in by Chinook helicopters.

A few minutes before 7 o'clock the first of 148 air strikes, flown by American F-4 and F-100 fighter-bombers, began in the area.

The air strikes and the continuing artillery barrage were designed to prepare the way for the tanks and armored personnel carriers.

Eighty-two heavy artillery pieces have been positioned along and across the border. General Roberts said. He added that it had been the greatest massing of artillery he had seen in one area since World War II.

The noise of the big guns as they softened up the enemy territory had long ended as the First Cavalry Division squads moved through the rubber plantation southeast of Memot. The men talked softly as they listened for indications of the enemy's presence.

In the midst of the rubber trees, the soldiers encountered a frightened group of perhaps 15 Cambodian civilians, including several small children.

The men in the Cambodian group said that there had been many North Vietnamese troops in the area, but that they had all fled in the early morning after the heavy bombing. The men also reported that a number of Cambodian civilians in a nearby hamlet had been injured this morning when an American helicopter gunship strafed the town. There was no immediate way to confirm or deny their report.

About 6 P.M. the soldiers reached a clearing and established their temporary command post. Their orders were to hold the high ground in the area for an indefinite period—perhaps as long as 10 days.

None of the senior officers involved in the operation would speculate on how long the American units might remain in Cambodia.

"It depends on how much fighting we encounter" a major said. "It could last one week or six, depending on what happens."

* * *

May 2, 1970

NIXON PUTS 'BUMS' LABEL ON SOME COLLEGE RADICALS

By JUAN de ONIS

Special to The New York Times

WASHINGTON, May 1—President Nixon referred today to some campus radicals who violently oppose his Vietnam policies as "bums" and, in contrast, he said American soldiers were "the greatest."

The President's remarks on violence at universities and the war were made to a group of civilian employes who greeted him at the Pentagon, where he went for a briefing on the new United States military operations in Cambodia.

Mr. Nixon was cheered by public response to his television speech on Cambodia last night. Ronald L. Ziegler, White House press secretary, said telephone calls and telegrams received since Mr. Nixon spoke were "positive" in a ratio of six to one.

One such favorable comment came from a young woman in a group of Pentagon employes who told the President: "I loved your speech. It made me proud to be an American."

Smiling and obviously pleased, Mr. Nixon stopped and told how he had been thinking, as he wrote his speech, about "those kids out there."

"I have seen them. They are the greatest," he said. Then he contrasted them with antiwar activists on university campuses. According to a White House text of his remarks, he said:

"You see these bums, you know, blowing up the campuses. Listen, the boys that are on the college campuses today are the luckiest people in the world, going to the greatest universities, and here they are burning up the books, storming around about this issue. You name it. Get rid of the war there will be another one.

"Then out there we have kids who are just doing their duty. They stand tall and they are proud. I am sure they are scared. I was when I was there. But when it really comes down to it, they stand up and, boy, you have to talk up to those men. They are going to do fine and we have to stand in back of them."

The President's use of the term "bums" to refer to student radicals was the strongest language he has used publicly on the subject of campus violence, although he has been known to employ such terms in private.

Mr. Nixon's visit to the Pentagon this morning began a day that ended with his flying by helicopter to his Camp David retreat for a weekend of relaxation with his family and close friends.

Before departing from the capital, Mr. Nixon proclaimed Sunday a national day of prayer for all American prisoners and servicemen missing in action in Southeast Asia.

He was accompanied to the Pentagon by Henry A. Kissinger, his special assistant, and was briefed for one hour and 40 minutes by Secretary of Defense Melvin R. Laird and high military officials in the presence of the Joint Chiefs of Staff.

On leaving, Mr. Nixon commented:

"I did what I believed to be right. What really matters is whether it comes out right."

According to Mr. Ziegler, the information given the President indicated that the operations in Cambodia across the South Vietnam border "appear to be going well."

Mr. Ziegler said the President stayed up after his speech last night until about 1:30 A.M., receiving visitors and talking by telephone with "friends and officials around the country."

* * *

May 5, 1970

4 KENT STATE STUDENTS KILLED BY TROOPS

8 Hurt as Shooting Follows Reported Sniping at Rally

By JOHN KIFNER
Special to The New York Times

KENT, Ohio, May 4—Four students at Kent State University, two of them women, were shot to death this afternoon by a volley of National Guard gunfire. At least 8 other students were wounded.

The burst of gunfire came about 20 minutes after the guardsmen broke up a noon rally on the Commons, a grassy campus gathering spot, by lobbing tear gas at a crowd of about 1,000 young people.

In Washington, President Nixon deplored the deaths of the four students in the following statement:

"This should remind us all once again that when dissent turns to violence it invites tragedy. It is my hope that this tragic and unfortunate incident will strengthen the determination of all the nation's campuses, administrators, faculty and students alike to stand firmly for the right which exists in this country of peaceful dissent and just as strongly against the resort to violence as a means of such expression."

In Columbus, Sylvester Del Corso, Adjutant General of the Ohio National Guard, said in a statement that the guardsmen had been forced to shoot after a sniper opened fire against the troops from a nearby rooftop and the crowd began to move to encircle the guardsmen.

Frederick P. Wenger, the Assistant Adjutant General, said the troops had opened fire after they were shot at by a sniper.

"They were under standing orders to take cover and return any fire," he said.

This reporter, who was with the group of students, did not see any indication of sniper fire, nor was the sound of any gunfire audible before the Guard volley. Students, conceding that rocks had been thrown, heatedly denied that there was any sniper.

Gov. James A. Rhodes called on J. Edgar Hoover, director of the Federal Bureau of Investigation, to aid in looking into the campus violence. A Justice Department spokesman said no decision had been made to investigate.

At 2:10 this afternoon, after the shootings, the university president, Robert I. White, ordered the university closed for an indefinite time, and officials were making plans to evacuate the dormitories and bus out-of-state students to nearby cities.

Robinson Memorial Hospital identified the dead students as Allison Krause, 19 years old, of Pittsburgh: Sandra Lee Scheuer, 20, of Youngstown, Ohio, both coeds; Jeffrey Glenn Miller, 20, of 22 Diamond Drive, Plainview, L. I., and William K. Schroeder, 19, of Lorain, Ohio.

At 10:30 P.M. the hospital said that six students had been treated for gunshot wounds. Three were reported in critical condition and three in fair condition. Two others with superficial wounds were treated and released.

Students here, angered by the expansion of the war into Cambodia, have held demonstrations for the last three nights. On Saturday night, the Army Reserve Officers Training Corps building was burned to the ground and the Guard was called in and martial law was declared.

Today's rally, called after a night in which the police and guardsmen drove students into their dormitories and made 69 arrests, began as students rang the iron Victory Bell on the commons, normally used to herald football victories.

A National Guard jeep drove onto the Commons and an officer ordered the crowd to disperse. Then several canisters of tear gas were fired, and the students straggled up a hill that borders the area and retreated into buildings.

A platoon of guardsmen, armed—as they have been since they arrived here with loaded M-1 rifles and gas equipment—moved across the green and over the crest of the hill, chasing the main body of protesters.

The youths split into two groups, one heading farther downhill toward a dormitory complex, the other eddying around a parking lot and girls' dormitory just below Taylor Hall, the architecture building.

The guardsmen moved into a grassy area just below the parking lot and fired several canisters of tear gas from their short, stubby launchers.

Three or four youths ran to the smoking canisters and hurled them back. Most fell far short, but one landed near the troops and a cheer went up from the crowd, which was chanting "Pigs off campus" and cursing the war.

Tarentum Valley Daily News via Associated Press

A girl screams as fellow student lies dead after National Guardsmen opened fire at Kent State.

A few youths in the front of the crowd ran into the parking lot and hurled rocks or small chunks of pavement in the direction of the guardsmen. Then the troops began moving back up the hill in the direction of the college.

Students Cheer

The students in the parking lot area, numbering about 500, began to move toward the rear of the troops, cheering. Again, a few in front picked up stones from the edge of the parking lot and threw them at the guardsmen. Another group of several hundred students had gathered around the sides of Taylor Hall watching.

As the guardsmen, moving up the hill in single file, reached the crest, they suddenly turned, forming a skirmish line and opening fire.

The crackle of the rifle volley cut the suddenly still air. It appeared to go on, as a solid volley, for perhaps a full minute or a little longer.

Some of the students dived to the ground, crawling on the grass in terror. Others stood shocked or half crouched, apparently believing the troops were firing into the air. Some of the rifle barrels were pointed upward.

Near the top of the hill at the corner of Taylor Hall, a student crumpled over, spun sideways and fell to the ground, shot in the head.

When the firing stopped, a slim girl, wearing a cowboy shirt and faded jeans, was lying face down on the road at the edge of the parking lot, blood pouring out onto the macadam, about 10 feet from this reporter.

Too Shocked to React

The youths stood stunned, many of them clustered in small groups staring at the bodies. A young man cradled one of the bleeding forms in his arms. Several girls began to cry. But many of the students who rushed to the scene seemed almost too shocked to react. Several gathered around an abstract steel sculpture in front of the building and looked at a 30-caliber bullet hole drilled through one of the plates.

The hospital said that six young people were being treated for gunshot wounds, some in the intensive care unit. Three of the students who were killed were dead on arrival at the hospital.

One guardsman was treated and released at the hospital and another was admitted with heat prostration.

Associated Press

Ohio National Guardsmen advancing over the campus of Kent State University yesterday behind a screen of tear gas.

In early afternoon, students attempted to gather at various area of the Commons but were ordered away by guardsman and the Ohio Highway Patrol, which moved in as reinforcements.

There were no further clashes, as faculty members, graduate assistants and students leaders urged the crowd to go back to the dormitories.

But a bizarre atmosphere hung over the campus as a Guard helicopter hovered overhead, grim-faced officers maneuvered their men to safeguard the normally pastoral campus and students, dazed, fearful and angry, struggled to comprehend what had happened and to find something to do about it.

Students carrying suitcases and duffel bags began leaving the campus this afternoon. Early tonight the entire campus was sealed off and a court injunction was issued ordering all students to leave.

A 5 P.M. curfew was declared in Kent, and road blocks were set up around the town to prevent anyone from entering. A state of emergency was also declared in the nearby towns of Stow and Ravenna.

* * *

May 7, 1970

PROTESTS CLOSE OVER 80 COLLEGES

Two State Systems Shut

ILLINOIS DEPLOYS GUARD

By FRANK J. PRIAL

More than 80 colleges across the country closed their doors yesterday for periods ranging from a day to the remainder of the academic year as thousands of students joined the growing nationwide campus protest against the war in Southeast Asia.

In California, Gov. Ronald Reagan, citing "emotional turmoil," closed down the entire state university and college system from midnight last night until next Monday. More than 280,000 students at 19 colleges and nine university campuses are involved.

Pennsylvania State University, with 18 campuses, was closed for an indeterminate period.

In the New York metropolitan area about 15 colleges closed, some for a day, some for the week, and some for the rest of the term.

A spokesman for the National Student Association said that students had been staying away from classes at almost 300 campuses in the country.

Most, but not all, of the protesters eschewed violence. In Illinois, Gov. Richard Ogilvy ordered 5,000 National Guardsmen to duty at locations all over the state, with about 2,000 of them assigned to the Champaign-Urbana area, site of the downstate campus of the University of Illinois.

About 1,500 students clashed with the police there during the afternoon. One student and three policemen were reported injured. A similar clash was reported at Northwestern University, in Evanston, near Chicago.

Leaders on most campuses plan to organize participation Saturday in a national antiwar demonstration in Washington.

At American University in Washington, the police fired tear gas at 1,000 demonstrators last night. Four policemen were hurt by rocks, and 17 protesters were arrested.

Other student groups, notably at Columbia University, Harvard University and the University of Rochester, organized support for a recently proposed Congressional amendment that would cut off funds for the war in Southeast Asia.

A spokesman for Senator George S. McGovern, Democrat of South Dakota, one of five sponsors of the amendment, said the Senator's office had been in touch with "scores" of student leaders who voiced an interest in working for the amendment as an alternate to what they deemed less constructive forms of protest.

The amendment to the Defense Procurement Authorization bill is expected to reach the Senate floor in about 30 days.

At Brandeis University, in Waltham, Mass., a group called the National Student Strike Information Headquarters said it had counted 240 schools, mostly in the Northeast, where the students had voted to strike.

In Oberlin, Ohio, representatives of 15 northern Ohio colleges met and formed a coalition to combine student reaction to the Administration's Southeast Asian policies. The coalition called for a march Friday on Columbus and participation in the Saturday demonstration in Washington.

Similarly, representatives of 12 Eastern law schools met at New York University Law School to prepare for their participation in Saturday's demonstration in the Capital.

At least one government leader, New Jersey's Republican Governor, William T. Cahill, has responded to the student protests by criticizing the Administration's Southeast Asian policies.

Governor Cahill, a supporter of Mr. Nixon, said he was personally dissappointed by the President's decision to send troops into Cambodia, but added that he did not approve of student demonstrations as an effective way to protest that decision.

His statement came as 1,500 students from Rider and Trenton State Colleges, two New Jersey schools, marched on the New Jersey State House in Trenton to protest the war and the shooting to death of four students at Kent State University in Ohio.

Governor Cahill left the building as the students arrived, and an aide read his statement.

At the University of Kentucky, the state police and National Guardsmen "with mounted bayonets and live ammunition" were on hand in Lexington to enforce a dusk-to-dawn curfew.

Gov. Louie B. Nunn ordered the police and troops onto the campus when some 750 students ignored a 5 P.M. curfew.

At the University of Wisconsin in Madison, 3,500 students battled police all afternoon yesterday following a 1 P.M. rally. The university is officially open, but classrooms attendance was light and some classes had to be ended because tear gas from the fighting drifted through campus buildings.

In Austin, Tex., former Ambassador John Kenneth Galbraith pleaded with 5,000 University of Texas students and sympathizers at a campus rally to avoid violence. There had been threats yesterday to burn the Capitol in Austin.

"You are no longer an embattled minority," Mr. Galbraith said, as hundreds of policemen stood by, "but a majority and I ask you to maintain the discipline of a majority."

President Nixon was burned in effigy at least two campuses, the University of Cincinnati and Syracuse University. His impeachment was demanded by faculty members of five western Massachusetts colleges, including the ones attended by his daughter, Julie, and his son-in-law, David Eisenhower.

The schools were the University of Massachusetts, Amherst, Smith, Mount Holyoke and Hampshire Colleges. Julie Nixon Eisenhower attends Smith; her husband attends Amherst.

The same group also called for the impeachment of Vice President Agnew for "crossing state lines with the intent of inciting riots."

One of the most singular protests was planned by Haverford College, a Quaker school in Haverford, Pa. There, the entire faculty, administration and student body voted to go to Washington tomorrow for discussions with Congressional leaders and to join Saturday's protest rally.

College to Be Closed

The following is a partial list of colleges and universities that have announced they are closing:

All 19 state colleges and nine university campuses in California (through Sunday); Kent State University (indefinitely); all 18 campuses of Penn State University (indefinite); Boston University (end of term); Brown University (end of term); Tufts University (end of term); University of Notre Dame (end of week); Northwestern University (end of week); Bennington

College (indefinite); Massachusetts Institute of Technology (end of week).

Also, the University of Connecticut (indefinitely); Seton Hall University (end of term); Princeton University (end of term); Rutgers University (indefinite); Sarah Lawrence (indefinite); Finch College (through Sunday).

Also Ohio State University (indefinitely); Fairleigh Dickinson University (indefinitely); C. W. Post College (indefinitely); Hofstra University (indefinitely); Syracuse University (indefinitely); Brooklyn Polytechnic Institute (end of term).

Also University of New Mexico (through Sunday); Southampton College of Long Island University (until June 4); Manhattanville College (indefinite); Marymount College (indefinite).

Also Bronx Community College (indefinite); Hunter College (through Friday); City College of New York (through Friday).

Also, Adelphi University (end of week); Nassau Community College (end of week); Potsdam State University (undetermined); Queens College (through today); New School for Social, Research (end of week); Manhattan Community College (through today); Siena College (undetermined); Wells College (undetermined); Paterson State College (end of week); Montclair College (end of term); University of Akron (through Saturday).

* * *

May 9, 1970

WAR FOES HERE ATTACKED BY CONSTRUCTION WORKERS

City Hall Is Stormed

By HOMER BIGART

Helmeted construction workers broke up a student anti-war demonstration in Wall Street yesterday, chasing youths through the canyons of the financial district in a wild noontime melee that left about 70 persons injured.

The workers then stormed City Hall, cowing policemen and forcing officials to raise the American flag to full staff from half staff, where it had been placed in mourning for the four students killed at Kent State University on Monday.

At nearby Pace College a group of construction workers who said they had been pelted with missiles by students from the roof, twice invaded a building, smashing windows with clubs and crowbars and beating up students.

Earlier the workers ripped a Red Cross banner from the gates of Trinity Church and tried to tear down the flag of the Episcopal Church.

"This is senseless," said the Rev. Dr. John Vernon Butler, rector of Trinity Parish. "I suppose they thought it was a Vietcong flag."

Twice Father Butler ordered the gates closed against menacing construction workers.

Inside the church, doctors and nurses from the New York University Medical Center had set up a first-aid station, treating 40 to 60 youths who had been beaten by the workers.

The Mayor issued a statement saying that "a mob came perilously close to overwhelming the police guard at City Hall."

He added his "deep regrets" that the day of memory for the four students killed by Ohio National Guardsmen at Kent had been defiled by violence.

The police said that six persons had been arrested and that 19 persons, including four patrolmen, had been injured. However, Beekman-Downtown Hospital alone reported that 23 persons had been brought by ambulance from the Wall Street area suffering from cuts and bruises, none of them serious.

Fighting Erupts

It was about five minutes to noon when Wall Street suddenly erupted in a melee of fist-fighting that entrapped thousands of employes headed for lunch.

Starting at 7:30 A.M., hundreds of youths, mostly from New York University and others from Hunter College and city high schools gathered at Broad and Wall Streets in a demonstration demanding the immediate withdrawal of American troops from Vietnam and Cambodia, the immediate release of all "political prisoners in America" and the cessation of military-oriented work by the universities.

All accounts agree that the demonstration was without violence until the construction workers reached the scene.

The construction workers, most of them wearing brown overalls and orange and yellow hard hats, descended on Wall Street from four directions. A thin line of policemen had blocked off the steps of the Federal Hall National Memorial at Nassau and Wall Streets, from about a thousand students who were sitting on the side-walk and pavement listening to speakers denounce the war abroad and repression at home.

The morning was chilly, with a light rain. But toward noon the sky lightened and the day became warm and humid. The students were in good humor; they cheered a Broad Street lawyer, Charles F. Appel, 56 years old, who told the youths: "You brought down one President and you'll bring down another."

Then came the moment of confrontation. The construction workers, marching behind a cluster of American flags, swept the policemen aside and moved on the students. The youths scattered, seeking refuge in the lunch-hour crowds.

The workers sought them out, some selecting those youths with the most hair and swatting them with their helmets.

There did not seem to be more than 200 construction workers, but they were reinforced by hundreds of persons who had been drawn into the march by chants of "All the way, U.S.A." and "Love it or leave it."

On reaching the Federal Hall National Memorial, the workers at first pushed halfheartedly against the police line. "All we want to do is put our flag up on those steps," one worker said quietly to Inspector Harold Schryner. "If you try, there'll be blood to pay," the inspector replied.

The New York Times (by Carl T. Gossett, Jr.)

IN FINANCIAL AREA: Hard-hatted construction workers breaking up an antiwar rally at the Subtreasury Building.

But within two minutes the workers had surged over the memorial's steps, planting American flags on the statue of George Washington. Then they outflanked the police, driving demonstrators before them and hitting the youths with their helmets.

A Staged Assault?

From his 32d-floor office at 63 Wall Street, Edward Shufro of the brokerage firm of Shufro, Rose & Ehrman watched through binoculars two men in gray suits and gray hats who, he said, seemed to be directing the workers.

"These guys were directing the construction workers with hand motions," Mr. Shufro said.

At Exchange Place, Robert A. Bernhard, a partner at Lehman Brothers, tried to protect a youth from assault by a worker. The worker grabbed Mr. Bernhard and pushed him against a telephone pole.

A man who came to the aid of Mr. Bernhard was himself attacked by a worker and struck with a pair of pliers. Bleeding from a head wound the man was taken to Beekman-Downtown Hospital.

Near City Hall, a Wall Street lawyer, Michael Berknap, 29, a Democratic candidate for the State Senate, was beaten and kicked by a group of constructin workers yelling, "Kill the Commie bastards." He was treated at Beekman-Downtown Hospital with his right eye completely closed, a large welt on his head and five bootmarks on his back.

Mr. Berknap said the police had stood by and made no attempt to stop the assault.

"These people are rampaging and the police are not arresting them," he complained.

Among the student demonstrators taken to Trinity Church for first aid was Drew Lynch, a teacher in the Human Resources Administration's Brooklyn street program.

Mr. Lynch had both eyes blackened and was bleeding from the mouth. He said "at least four" workers had pummeled him to the street, then kicked him.

"A policeman finally grabbed me by the collar, dragged me away, and said: 'Get out of here,' " Mr. Lynch said.

The workers led a mob to City Hall, where an unidentified mailman went to the roof and raised the flag that Mayor Lindsay had ordered lowered to half staff for the slain students. The crowd cheered wildly.

But moments later an aide to Mayor Lindsay, Sid Davidoff, stalked out on the roof and lowered the flag again.

The mob reacted in fury. Workers vaulted the police barricades, surged across the tops of parked cars and past half a dozen mounted policemen. Fists flailing they stormed through the policemen guarding the barred front doors.

Uncertain whether they could contain the mob, the police asked city officials to raise the flag. Deputy Major Richard R. Aurelio, in charge during the absence of Mayor Lindsay, who was at Gracie Mansion, ordered the flag back to full staff.

Two plainclothes policemen, Pat Mascia and Bob Rudion, and the City Hall custodian, John Zissel, walked out on the roof and struggled with the flapping lanyard.

As the flag went up, the workers began singing. "The Star-Spangled Banner." A construction worker yelled to the police: "Get your helmets off."

Grinning sheepishly, about seven of 15 police who were on City Hall steps, removed their helmets.

Meanwhile, a group of workers had charged Pace College, across the street from City Hall Park, angered by a peace banner hanging from the roof. Some of them gained the roof of the modernistic four-story building, seized the banner and brought it down to the street, where it was burned. Others smashed windows in the lobby of the college and beat some students.

The scuffle over the flag at City Hall was accompanied by chants of "Lindsay's a Red."

"Stop being juveniles," a Lindsay aide, Donald Evans, admonished a construction worker.

"What do you mean, being juvenile?" he replied, punching Mr. Evans on the chin.

* * *

May 9, 1970

CHANGE OF HEART . . .

It has taken the awful toll of four young lives to create an atmosphere in Washington receptive at last to the voices of youthful protest. But the irony which should not be lost on the campuses of the nation is that it was not the fruitless violence of students that softened the Administration's attitude; it was the violence of authority itself—and the nationwide wave of revulsion it created.

In the wake of the appalling event at Kent State University the climate in the capital is undergoing a remarkable change, at least momentarily. President Nixon, in his news conference last night, emphasized his eagerness to have a dialogue with his youthful critics and has stressed his agreement with all their objectives for peace in Vietnam. His statement came after Secretary of the Interior Hickel had pleaded eloquently with Mr. Nixon for greater understanding of young Americans. The President has sympathetically received a Kent State delegation, conferred with the heads of eight universities and named one of them as his special adviser on student opinion. And, of most immediate importance, the Administration has made preparations to receive antiwar protesters arriving in the capital for today's demonstration in a cooperative, even sympathetic, spirit—a marked contrast to last November's protest parade, which Mr. Nixon ignored to watch a football game on television. This time the President has said he would be willing to meet personally with a delegation representing the demonstrators.

Now it is up to the students themselves to take full advantage of their improved position. They can retain their moral advantage best by keeping the demonstration free of all taint of violence. They have had no dearth of advice to that effect from those they most respect.

Kingman Brewster, president of Yale, has reminded them that the "clenched fist and 'shut-a-down' rhetoric" have served only to help the Administration "sterilize the political influence of the universities." Mayor Lindsay and numerous others have given similar good counsel. Even such radical leaders as David Dellinger and Rennie Davis of the Chicago Seven have pointed out, belatedly, that wild rampaging is "not the way to achieve revolutionary change."

Of more far reaching importance, campus activities are springing up that are more constructive than even peaceable demonstrations. Under Dr. Brewster's leadership some thousand Yale teachers and students will arrive in Washington Monday not to demonstrate at all but to meet and discuss issues with members of Congress who happen to be Yale alumni. Princeton faculty and students are putting together a Princeton Movement for a New Congress, pledged to work for candidates opposed to the war. Haverford's entire personnel—faculty, students, trustees and help—went *en masse* to Washington a few days ago to convey their opposition to the Cambodian adventure from office to office on Capitol Hill.

These departures from familiar and arid forms of protest—the student strike, the seizure of buildings, the chanting of obscenities—represent an impressive advance. But they make far greater demands on their practitioners. If students are to be heard, as the President himself now concedes they should be, it is surely desirable that they speak their minds coolly and persuasively, employing and receiving the courtesies of civilized discourse.

The extent to which this essential of democratic politics is now observed on both sides of the generation line is the extent to which even the infinitely sad deaths of the Kent State students will have advanced the cause of a free society.

* * *

May 10, 1970

NIXON, IN PRE-DAWN TOUR, TALKS TO WAR PROTESTERS

By ROBERT B. SEMPLE Jr.
Special to The New York Times

WASHINGTON, May 9—President Nixon left the White House shortly before dawn this morning, drove to the Lincoln Memorial and spent an hour chatting with young people who had come to protest his war policies.

The extraordinary visit, which caught his staff unawares and left the Secret Service "petrified," was Mr. Nixon's first

Associated Press

PROTEST: Demonstrators fill Ellipse, park near the White House. A ring of buses blocked of the Executive Mansion.

direct exchange with students massed here for a weekend of protest.

As he stood on the steps of the Memorial and talked, the crowd around him grew from eight to 30 to 50, and near the end of what appears to have been more monologue than dialogue, he asked the students "to try to understand what we are doing."

Breakfast at Hotel

Afterwards he drove to the Capitol, ate breakfast at the Mayflower Hotel—his first visit to a restaurant here since his inauguration—then returned to the White House. Then he spent the rest of the day with his family, protected from the demonstrators on the Ellipse but within earshot of their cheers, chants and taunts.

His excursion was brief, lasting three and one-half hours. But it provided a revealing glimpse of a man who has been under exceptional strain for the last few weeks, who has been forced to improvise rapidly to deal with the consequences of his own policies and the unexpected tragedy at Kent State, and who is said to have enjoyed few restful nights since he decided, on the evening of April 27, to send American troops into Cambodia.

Mr. Nixon was accompanied to the Lincoln Memorial only by his longtime valet, Manolo Sanchez, and several Secret Servicemen. The President gave an account of what happened to Garnett D. Horner, White House correspondent for The Washington Star, who arrived at the White House shortly after Mr. Nixon returned from his trip at 7:30 A.M.

As Mr. Nixon described the events, he remained awake until 2:30 this morning, accepting calls from old friends here and on the West Coast who telephoned him with comments about his appearance last night. He slept fitfully for an hour, rose, and called Mr. Sanchez and asked him whether he had ever seen the Lincoln Memorial at night. Mr. Sanchez never had, so the President said, "Let's go."

Before leaving, Mr. Nixon placed a telephone call to Helen Thomas, a White House reporter for United Press International. Miss Thomas was asleep at her apartment at the time. Only five hours earlier, the President had ended his news conference with a moment of silence for the late Merriman Smith, White House correspondent for U.P.I.

The President and Miss Thomas had what was described as a rambling conversation about Mr. Smith and other matters; and then Mr. Nixon summoned Mr. Sanchez.

The two men toured the Memorial, and when they emerged at about 5 A.M. they met about eight students on the steps.

They began talking about the war. "On the war thing," Mr. Nixon related to Mr. Horner, "I said I know you think we are a bunch of so and sos—I used a stronger word to them. I know how you feel—you want to get the war over.

"I told them that I know it is awfully hard to keep this in perspective. I told them that in 1939 I thought Neville Chamberlain was the greatest man living and Winston Churchill was a madman. It was not until years later that I realized Neville Chamberlain was a good man, but Winston Churchill was right.

"I doubt," he added, "if that got over."

Continuing his account, the President said:

"They were fine kids from all over the country and I told them, sure, you came here to demonstrate and shout your slogans on the Ellipse. That is all right. Just keep it peaceful. Remember, I felt just as deeply as you do about this."

Judging by the President's own account, he ranged over many subjects, including the race problem, the poverty of the Indians, the environment, the places he had seen and visited in his years as Representative, Senator and Vice President.

Mr. Nixon did not mention it in the account he gave Mr. Horner, but apparently he could not resist his penchant to talk about sports.

Joan Pelletier, a 20-year-old coed from Syracuse University who said she was among the 50 or so who eventually gathered to hear the President, told newsmen later:

"Here we come from a university that's completely upright, on strike, and when we told him where we were from, he talked about the football team, and when someone said he was from California, he talked about surfing."

When the conversation ended, the President drove to the Capitol, where the President showed Mr. Sanchez the House chamber, by then, three of his aides had caught up with him—Ronald L. Ziegler, the press secretary; Presidential assistant, H. R. Haldeman, and a special assistant, Dwight Chapman—and the five men then went to breakfast at the Rib Room of the Mayflower, where the President, in Mr. Ziegler's words, "had corned beef hash with an egg on it."

Mr. Nixon told Mr. Ziegler that it was his first corned beef hash with poached egg in five years.

* * *

May 21, 1970

FOR THE FLAG AND FOR COUNTRY, THEY MARCH

By FRANCIS X. CLINES

The rally and march in support of President Nixon's Indochina policy, held yesterday in lower Manhattan, included blue-collar workers, businessmen, secretaries and housewives, Here is a random sampling of some marchers and their views:

Richard Roeber, a crane operator from Queens:

"I think it's about time something like this has been done. Everybody grows up and everybody has somebody over them, and when the parents don't take over, things go wrong.

"And this is what's happening here: When your Congressmen and everybody else can't even stand up for America, what do they expect? And it can get worse and worse. The quicker Lindsay goes, the better . . . When your leader's wrong, what do you expect from the people?"

John Nash, 48, a printer at The Evening News of Newark and a veteran of World War II:

"We've got to beat these Communists somewhere. So we're fighting them. Let's win. Victory. No substitute for victory.

"I'm backing the President all the way. My boy goes into service Dec. 7. . . . I'm proud of him. It's a chance we all had to take. It's his turn. With small wars, there will be no big ones as long as we stand up like they're doing now . . . small compared with 100,000 a year like we did in World War II. It has to be paid. It's a sad thing, but it has to be realized, or else we'll be by ourselves in this whole world and we can't stand up."

Of those killed at Kent State University: "I have no sympathy for them. I'm not a college man, I'm not smart. But I know one thing: When a guy's got a gun, I don't throw rocks at him. I go the other way. . . . If I attacked that cop over there, I'd expect him to shoot me."

Of the flag: "Outside of God, it's the most important thing I know. I know a lot of good friends died under this. It stands for the greatest: America."

Robert Geary, 50, an office worker for the Colonial Hardware Corporation: "I'm very proud to be an American, and I know my boy that was killed in Vietnam would be here today if he was alive, marching with us. . . . I know he died for the right cause, because in his letters he wrote to me he knew what he was fighting for: to keep America free and to avoid any taking over by Communists—atheistic Communists, by the way.

"I think most of them [college dissenters] are influenced by a few vile people . . . I'll tell you one person who smudged the name of my son and that was Mayor Lindsay. When he stands up and says men who refuse to serve in the armed forces are heroic, then I presume by the same category that my son that was killed in Vietnam is a coward, the way he thinks.

"Eighty per cent of the people are behind America and the flag. . . . I believe that what we're fighting for is worth it, yes, but nobody likes war."

Of the flag: "It's me. It's part of me. I fought for it myself two or three years in the Second World War. . . . It's the greatest country in the world. All they [dissenters] have to do is move out."

Mrs. Allison Greaker, 411 100th Street, Brooklyn, marching with her children, Richard Nixon Greaker, 1, and Allison, 2:

"We're part of the silent majority that's finally speaking—and in answer to the creeps and the bums that have been hollering and marching against the President.

"I think he's doing everything he can to bring about an honorable peace. I think my kids are going to live better with Nixon in the White House.

"To stop Communist aggression [the war] has been worth it, yes. . . . If they had listened to Gen. Douglas MacArthur from the very beginning and gone into Manchuria, we wouldn't have had the problems we have. We would have put the Communists down back in 1952.

"I have a lot of faith in the college kids. . . . I think they're being heard enough, and we're answering them right now today. . . . They've tried to take over education, the Communists have, and I think this is where [the students are] getting their viewpoints from."

Robert Romano, 40, Princeton, N. J., general foreman for the Tishman Construction Company at World Trade Center site:

"I feel the children of today are getting carried away in their demonstrations. I don't think they're absolutely wrong. There are parts of things that they are right in, but most of the demonstration doesn't have to be violence."

"I feel they [college dissenters] have been with the silver spoon in their mouth too long and somebody has to take a hand in this to stop them, because if not, the country itself will come to ruins. My opinion is that protesting is a family deal. If children in college and high school have gripes, do it as a family group. . . . The parents have to participate."

And if parents and children disagree?

"Well let me tell you the old-fashioned way: Use your hand: My father didn't stop to hit me. If I said I didn't like something, he hit me. I learned to like it. That's the way it has to be."

James Tompkins, 50, World Trade Center excavation worker, veteran of World War II:

"I'm not against the war policies. I figure the big leaders should know what they're doing. I support the President. If he were not too right, I think the Congress would straighten him out."

Of young war dissenters: "I think they went too far in what they were trying to do. I don't like violence."

Of violence by construction workers: "The kids started to fight with them. If someone comes throwing stones and things at you, what are you going to do?. . . . That's what was happening, yes."

Of the Kent State deaths: "I think it was wrong to kill them, and the students could have been wrong on their part. . . . You have to work with them to understand how to deal with them."

Raymond Massaro, 25, electrician:

"This is my country, and I'm going to support it to the highest limits. I have a lot of friends that are over there being killed, and I don't go for this [war dissenting]

"I'm on the 1-A list right now. My union has been keeping me out because of school, but I should be called, any day. My local gets a deferment for training. I'll definitely serve this country 100 per cent. If America feels [the war] is right, it's right. There's a purpose for being over there, and I feel it's right.

"People [dissenters] have a right to feel the way they do, especially if they have brothers and friends [in the war]. But when you're over there, I'm sure there's a difference. I can't give you that feeling. But people who have been there say we have to be there.

"I'm for this country. These are my people, right here."

* * *

June 25, 1970

SENATORS, 81 TO 10, VOTE FOR REPEAL OF TONKIN ACTION

G.O.P. Seizes Initiative on Resolution Johnson Used as Basis for Wider War

HOUSE BACKING NEEDED

Doves Accuse Republicans of Indulging in Crude and Cynical Partisanship

By JOHN W. FINNEY
Special to The New York Times

WASHINGTON, June 24—The Senate voted today in favor of repeal of the 1964 Gulf of Tonkin resolution, once interpreted as the statutory equivalent of a declaration of war in Vietnam.

The legal effect of the action, by a vote of 81 to 10, is probably minimal since the Nixon Administration has stated that it is not relying on the resolution, enacted at the request of President Lyndon B. Johnson, as authority for current policies in Indochina. But the vote may have marked a turning point in the increasingly acerbic bickering in the Senate over the war.

Supporters of the Administration had seized the initiative from the Democratic leadership by moving yesterday to repeal the resolution and they threatened similar tactics against amendments on Vietnam offered by Senate doves.

1964 Passage Speedy

The doves responded by accusing the Republicans of indulging in crude and cynical partisanship.

The Tonkin Gulf resolution, which was often referred to by President Johnson as Congressional sanction for stepping up the war in Vietnam, was speedily passed in August, 1964, after two American destroyers reportedly had come under attack by North Vietnamese PT-boats.

The resolution gave Congressional support to the President's determination to "take all necessary measures" to prevent further aggression in Southeast Asia.

The action on the resolution, which had been adopted with two dissenting votes, was taken by the Senate with almost equal speed after two days of perfunctory debate.

Reasons Are Varied

Behind the decision, which must be concurred in by the House of Representatives, was a convergence of views between hawks and doves.

To some senators, particularly on the Republican side, the resolution had become meaningless. To others, particularly among the doves, the Senate was acting against a grant of warmaking power to the President. Still other senators were eager to vote for repeal of a resolution that had been used to justify an expansion of the war.

The repeal motion had been offered by Senator Robert J. Dole, a conservative Kansas Republican, as an amendment to the foreign military sales bill before the Senate. The Democratic leadership had planned a later measure separately repealing the Tonkin resolution.

It is likely that the House will balk at accepting the military sales bill—and thus also reject repeal—particularly if the bill contains the Cooper-Church amendment restricting future military operations in Cambodia.

In that case, the Democratic leadership would get another chance at repealing the resolution though a concurrent resolution, which does not require the President's signature.

The bipartisan Cooper-Church amendment to the military sales, bill would cut off all funds for American forces in Cambodia after July 1, the date set by President Nixon for termination of the operation there. The amendment has been the focus of protracted Senate debate on United States policy in Indochina, particularly in relation to the President's powers in wartime.

The vote in the Senate would probably have been virtually unanimous if there had not been objections to the tactics used by Senator Dole, one of the young Turks among the Republicans who are seeking a more conservative, pro-Administration stance.

Senator John Stennis of Mississippi, chairman of the Armed Services Committee, protested that it "bordered on the ridiculous" to attach such a major foreign-policy issue to a relatively minor bill. Senator J. W. Fulbright, whose Foreign Relations Committee had the separate measure to repeal the resolution, announced that he was voting no "to preserve the integrity of the procedures of the Senate."

The others voting against the amendment were James B. Allen, Democrat of Alabama; James O. Eastland of Mississippi, Allen J. Ellender of Louisiana, Ernest F. Hollings of South Carolina, Russell B. Long of Louisiana, John L. McClellan of Arkansas and Gale W. McGee of Wyoming, Democrats, and Henry Bellmon of Oklahoma, a Republican.

Senator George McGovern, Democrat of South Dakota, to require that all American forces be out of Vietnam by mid 1971, took the floor to assert that the Republicans were engaging in "crude and cynical partisanship" and were being contemptuous of the procedures of the Senate in proposing to call up the matter now with the purpose of defeating it, as Republicans have threatened to do.

By a 52–36 vote, the Senate rejected a proposal by Senator Jack Miller, Republican of Iowa, that would have eliminated from the military sales bill a Foreign Relations Committee provision requiring countries receiving American arms to put up 50 per cent of the value in local currencies. The money would be used to finance educational and cultural exchange programs.

* * *

July 1, 1970

SENATE PASSES WAR POWERS CURB

LONG DEBATE ENDS

Cooper-Church Limits on Cambodia Action Adopted, 58–37

By JOHN W. FINNEY
Special to The New York Times

WASHINGTON, June 30—The Senate, moving to reassert the war-making powers of Congress, today adopted the long-debated Cooper-Church amendment to limit Presidential action in Cambodia.

By a vote of 58 to 37, after 34 days of debate, the amendment was made part of the pending foreign military sales bill. The action was viewed as a victory for antiwar forces in the Senate, though it can take effect only if a similar measure passes the House, where the issue now goes. Considerable resistance is expected there.

Restrictions Are Detailed

The Senate's action represents the first time legislative restrictions on the President's powers as Commander in Chief have been voted during a shooting war. If it became law, the amendment—with an effective date of July 1—would bar the President from spending any funds without Congressional consent for the following purposes:

- To "retain" American forces in Cambodia.
- To send military advisers to instruct Cambodian forces.
- To provide air combat support to Cambodian forces.
- To provide financial assistance to advisers or troops of other countries that go to the assistance of Cambodia. This was known as the "anti-mercenary" provision designed to prevent the Administration, without the knowledge and consent of Congress, from following the example set in South Vietnam, where the United States has provided extra pay allowances for Thai, South Korean and Philippine troops supporting the Saigon Government's fight.

Military Sales Bill Approved

With the Cooper-Church amendment finally adopted after 288 speeches, the Senate went on to pass the foreign military sales bill by a 75 to 20 vote. The bill authorizes $300-million in credit sales of arms in the current and coming fiscal years and imposes new restrictions, opposed by the Pentagon, on the disposal of surplus weapons to other countries. The current fiscal year ends at midnight tonight.

The amendment was cosponsored by Senator John Sherman Cooper, Republican of Kentucky, and Senator Frank Church, Democrat of Idaho.

As the protracted, often slow-moving and confused debate drew to a climax, the Senate beat back an attempt to modify the amendment so that the United States could provide additional pay to foreign troops, such as those of Thailand, going to the military assistance of Cambodia. It took four roll-call votes, however, to defeat that modification, offered by Senator Robert P. Griffin of Michigan, the assistant Republican leader, at the specific request of the White House.

Senator Griffin proposed to alter the restrictions of the "anti-mercenary" provision so that it would rule out only the dispatch of "United States personnel" as advisers to the Cambodians. His argument was that restriction, as it stood, was so broadly phrased that it would interfere with the President's Guam Doctrine of helping Asians to defend themselves.

The Cooper-Church forces replied that nothing in the amendment would prevent the United States from supplying military assistance to other countries' forces going to the aid of Cambodia and that the restriction was designed only to prevent the United States from "hiring" troops to fight in Cambodia.

Initial Vote Reversed

The Griffin modification prevailed at first by a 47 to 46 vote in what appeared to be an Administration victory. But then through a series of parliamentary steps, the tide was turned as the Cooper-Church forces maneuvered for time and a reconsideration of the vote.

In the succeeding votes, Senator Stuart Symington, Democrat of Missouri, switched his position and voted against the Griffin modification after Senator J. W. Fulbright, chairman of the Senate Foreign Relations Committee, hurriedly conferred with him in the back of the Senate chamber.

Senator Symington's initial vote for the Griffin modification, after he had talked with Senator Henry M. Jackson, Democrat of Washington, a supporter of the Administration move caused gasps in the chamber. It was an investigation of "mercenary" arrangements in Vietnam and Laos by a Senate foreign relations subcommittee headed by Mr. Symington that had led to the prohibition in the Cooper Church amendment.

On the fourth vote the Griffin modification was defeated by 50 to 45.

Pending the outcome of the voting on the Cooper-Church amendment, the Nixon Administration has reportedly been holding up arrangements with the Bangkok Government for dispatch of Thai troops into Cambodia. The restrictions in the amendment would presumably not apply to South Vietnamese troops so long as the Saigon Government did not demand extra pay for its forces operating in Cambodia.

As had been their intent since the debate began on May 13, Republicans succeeded in preventing a vote on the Cooper-Church amendment until the President had announced the withdrawal of all American forces from Cambodia. With the troops withdrawn, Senator Griffin promptly declared the amendment to be legally meaningless—an opinion not shared by supporters of the Cooper-Church legislation, who have always maintained that the amendment was aimed at preventing a new military involvement in Cambodia.

The constitutional debate now shifts to a Senate-House conference committee—composed of members of the Senate Foreign Relations and the House Foreign Affairs Committees—to reconcile differences in the House and Senate versions of the military sales bill.

Whether the Senate Cambodian restrictions will be accepted by the House is problematical. From the start, the Administration has relied upon the more hawkish House to defeat the Cooper-Church amendment if it was adopted by the Senate.

But as Senator Church suggested, the Senate conferees will have one bargaining lever at their disposal—the desire of the Administration to obtain final approval of the foreign military sales bill. The clear implication in Senator Church's comments was that the Senate conferees might be prepared to see the entire bill die if the House members were unwilling to accept some variation of the Cooper-Church amendment.

During the debate, Hugh Scott of Pennsylvania, the Senate Republican leader, raised the possibility of a Presidential veto if the legislation reached Mr. Nixon with the Cooper-Church amendment intact. This suggestion came indirectly with Senator Scott's observation that the amendment would have been "acceptable" to the Administration if the Griffin modification had been accepted.

Under the amendment, as finally approved, the Administration, at least by implication, would be free to provide air support to Thai or South Vietnamese forces operating in Cambodia. But it would be prohibited under the amendment from providing air support to Cambodian forces, as both Administration and Cambodian officials have suggested was being contemplated in recent days.

The wording of the amendment would permit the Administration to carry out air raids against Communist supply lines and bases in Cambodia, such as President Nixon said were planned in his report today. Administration officials have pointed out that such "air interdiction" operations could legitimately, under a "dual purpose" concept, have the additional benefit of concurrently helping Cambodian forces.

During the debate, the preamble was revised to emphasize that the amendment was being offered "in concert" with the President's declared objectives of avoiding an involvement in Cambodia. A statement was also inserted affirming the constitutional powers of the President to protect the lives of American forces "wherever deployed."

* * *

July 1, 1970

FRUITS OF CAMBODIA

The most important result of the American "incursion" into Cambodia which ended yesterday is not the dubious military achievement claimed by the President in his lengthy report from San Clemente but the political reaction on Capitol Hill as reflected in Senate passage of the Cooper-Church amendment.

By adopting this amendment restricting future United States operations in Cambodia, the Senate moved at last to reassert the constitutional role of Congress in committing American forces to overseas military action. The Senate vote gives dramatic voice to widespread Congressional and public doubts about the wisdom of the Cambodian escalation which the President once again has defended with unpersuasive rhetoric.

Mr. Nixon asserts that the two-month operation in the border sanctuaries, which cost 339 American lives, has inflicted heavy losses in manpower and matériel on the enemy; has eliminated "an immediate threat" to allied forces; has diminished the enemy's capacity for offensive operations in southern South Vietnam, and will save American lives and assure the scheduled withdrawal of American troops from Vietnam. These claims may largely be justified, although the accuracy of most of them remains to be demonstrated.

Of greater significance are the dismal facts that the Communists now control far more of Cambodia than they did when the allied thrusts began: that the Lon Nol Government in Pnompenh is in a more precarious position than ever; that the Communists have secured new supply routes through which to infiltrate men and the additional supplies that have been promised by their friends in Moscow and Peking; that the American move has driven Indochinese Communists closer together and closer to Peking.

American forces, in short, are leaving Cambodia in far worse shape than it was when they entered. Mr. Nixon indicated he will try to meet this new situation by giving "encouragement and support" to intervention by Thai and South Vietnamese troops—traditional foes of the Cambodians—on behalf of the threatened Lon Nol regime. The Senate has prudently sought to foreclose this perilously unpromising gambit by retaining in the Cooper-Church amendment a ban on financial support for foreign troops in Cambodia. Even if the House fails to uphold the Senate action, as seems probable, the Administration has been put on notice that it faces powerful opposition to any such move.

The President came closer to the mood of Congress and of the country in those passages of his report in which he disavowed any faith in a military solution to the Indochinese conflict and promised renewed efforts to seek a negotiated settlement for the entire region. If he follows up these promising words with deeds—such as the prompt designation of a new top-level negotiator in Paris—he will find the new mood in Congress, which he has so stubbornly resisted, is really an asset that can help him and the nation out of an increasingly difficult predicament.

* * *

July 14, 1970

HAMLET, ITS MEN WITH VIETCONG, RESISTS PACIFICATION

By GLORIA EMERSON
Special in The New York Times

BINHSON HAMLET, South Vietnam, July 10—The trouble in Binhson hamlet is all the missing men. They left to join the Vietcong.

While statistics rarely give a realistic picture of the war in South Vietnam, there are figures that tell some of the history of Binhson. There are now 116 women between the ages of 16 and 30 living here. But, in the same age group, there are only 17 men. The population of the hamlet, once much larger, is now 918, or 621 females and 297 males. Eighty per cent are considered by military officials as Vietcong sympathizers. This leaves only the children unclassified.

It is a large, pretty hamlet that sprawls near a French-owned rubber plantation in the Longthanh district of Bienhoa Province, about 27 miles northeast of Saigon.

Binhson is a hard place to "pacify," perhaps an impossible one. Thai soldiers work at it, the Americans advise and pay for it, the South Vietnamese provide the police—and nothing seems to change. Perhaps the children are more nervous, and the adults more fearful, as some of them say they are. But the hoped-for transformation to a hamlet secure from the Vietcong has not taken place.

Three Killed in Forest

The Thais—who are anxious to improve Binhson, considered for so long to be a Vietcong supply depot and a trouble spot—say that they killed three members of the Vietcong on June 16. Some of the villagers feel that the three dead men may just have been unlucky civilians in the forest looking for mang, a bamboo plant they eat.

The Thai troops in South Vietnam—a division of more than 11,000 men—have not particularly distinguished themselves in the eyes of some Americans. The Thais have a small area of operations, most of which consists of the Longthanh district. They would like the security rating of Binhson to rise from the category of D to C or higher. In the American pacification program, hamlets are graded on a descending security scale from A to E. High-ranking Thais, however, do not always manage to conceal their weariness with the job.

"I do not know one from the other; it is so hard to tell them apart," said Col. Jetth Gongsakai, a deputy division commander who has been in the Thai Army for 35 years. He meant telling the difference between those Vietnamese who are Communists and those who are not.

Binhson hamlet is encircled by miles of barbed wire and there are mines placed near this rim. Villagers may not leave or enter from 7 P.M. to 6 A.M. The Thais are not allowed to search houses, so this is done, usually at a different time every day, by a platoon of South Vietnamese national policemen. A psychological-warfare team headed by an American tries to make amends to the villagers. The American flies out in a helicopter by 5 P.M. every day.

A Communications Problem

Lieut. Darrell Christensen, the genial and willing American, does not speak Vietnamese.

"Of course I think we should probably say we are sorry before people are disturbed by having their houses searched, not after it is done," he said. "But that's how it is. How do I communicate with the people? Sign language."

It is not certain how many Thai soldiers stay in the hamlet. One contingent mans a former American fire support base at the edge of the hamlet, where they fire the howitzers every night. The villagers hate the noise, but some of them accept it as part of a long, often strange punishment.

"Boom boom boom every night," a 14-year-old boy named Nguyen Van Tuyet said. He screwed up his face to describe to a Vietnamese visitor how loud the noise of the artillery is.

The Thais, under the direction of the American military personnel, have numerous charts listing what is being done in Binhson. There is a medical team, a public-health adviser, a psychological-warfare team, and a civic-action, or revolutionary-development, team, as it is now known. There is also a Vietnamese regional-forces platoon, and another platoon of the popular forces. Both are composed of trained soldiers who do their military service in their home towns, or home regions.

Villagers Restricted

The people of Binhson lead restricted lives. All of them have been photographed and questioned. They cannot leave the hamlet without passing through a strictly guarded checkpoint where the Vietnamese national police carry out their duties with a heavy hand.

Villagers, who often go to the district capital, Longthanh, to buy food, must not buy more than one can of fish, or any dried fish at all. It is feared that they may give it to the Vietcong. Fresh fish is not forbidden since it rots quickly.

There is less freedom, less food, less sleep and less work. At least 42 families have already left the hamlet. No one can explain whether the rubber plantation is partly closed because of military operations or because the monsoon has come. Both might account for the rise in unemployment. An estimated 50 per cent of the people of the hamlet were employed by the plantation, and the older men of Binhson grumble that their jobs have gone.

It is difficult for an outsider to find out much from the people here. They have learned to confide only in one another. It is not possible to ask them if it is their sons, their husbands, their fathers, who left to join the Vietcong. If the question were asked the expression "Vietcong" should not be used, for that is what the Saigon Government calls them. In Binhson the missing men are called brothers in the National Liberation Front.

* * *

September 12, 1970

MORE AMERICANS ARE MARRYING VIETNAMESE DESPITE THE OBSTACLES

By GLORIA EMERSON

Special to The New York Times

SAIGON, South Vietnam, Sept 11—"Hey honey, what is your name?" the 22-year-old lieutenant asked his Vietnamese fiancée at the United States Consulate here, where they were applying for a marriage affidavit.

The girl giggled. In wiggly letters she carefully wrote her name: Nguyen Thi Le. The lieutenant, looking surprised, tried to pronounce it but gave up.

"You're still Lee to me, honey," he said. The couple fell silent as they went on filling out forms.

It was not an unusual conversation in the crowded waiting room of the consulate, where an increasing number of Americans, military men and civilians, are applying for the papers needed to marry South Vietnamese.

There were 455 approvals by the military in 1969. In the first eight months of 1970 there have been 397. Whether the marriages took place is not known by the American military or the consulate, since the only records are in the districts concerned.

A rough analysis of marriages between Americans and Vietnamese is that a third of the men are military personnel on active duty, slightly fewer than a third are civilians employed here, and slightly more than a third are former servicemen returning to marry and take their wives home.

Since Americans can be legally married only in a Vietnamese civil ceremony, they must apply at the consulate for the papers that Vietnamese officials require of foreigners. Servicemen must have military permission—a process most of them find too long and confusing.

The consulate also handles applications for immigrant visas of the Vietnamese fiancées or wives of Americans, a routine procedure elsewhere. It is vastly complicated here because of the requirements of the South Vietnamese Ministry of the Interior, which must issue a passport and an exit permit before a United States visa can be granted.

Insulted by Red Tape

American enlisted men—and many younger officers—show that they feel insulted by the spate of Vietnamese and American civilian forms. Those required by the United States command exasperate most of them even more. Many soldiers start applying just before discharge and have to leave before marriage is possible.

Considerable resentment is caused by the need for a Vietnamese woman's birth certificate—a document that she may never have possessed or which may have been destroyed in the war—and a good-conduct certificate issued by the authorities in her district.

Analysis of the available information on American-Vietnamese marriage does not yield what would appear to be a typical case history. The brides are usually girls who worked on bases or in bars or nightclubs.

Many of them know in advance that they will miss their families, their friends and their traditions when they live in America. Few conceal their apprehensions when speaking with other Vietnamese.

A 19-year-old girl who did not want to give her name said that she was going to marry an American and live in Texas, but would not tell her parents.

"They are old people and they hardly understand this kind of marriage, which would cause them shame in our neighborhood," she said. "I don't hide my plans from my friends. It is necessary to be practical. My friends are practical."

She spoke in Vietnamese. The G.I. by her side at the consulate did not understand what she said.

Specialist 5 Frederick Black, a 23-year-old native of Stockton, Calif., hopes to marry 21-year-old Nguyen Thi Thieu, whom he met seven months ago in a United States Army supply depot in Danang, where he drives a truck and she works as a clerk-typist. She had not been outside her home town until the couple came to Saigon to begin filing their papers. She lives with her oldest brother and her mother, who is a 69-year-old laborer.

Discussing the obstacles, Specialist Black said: "I asked someone who gave me these forms, 'How come it's so difficult to get married?' and he couldn't explain."

The soldier, who hopes to become a highway patrolman after his discharge in November, has tried to explain to his fiancée that most Americans wear shoes and that there are indoor toilets and kitchens and big buildings. She has no idea of her new life.

He has not met her family. Miss Thieu, speaking in Vietnamese, which her fiancé does not understand, said that she had asked her mother and brother for permission to marry, but they refused it and she is afraid to admit her intentions.

"I am living in the home of my oldest brother, and the atmosphere is miserable." she said. "It is the wife of my brother who makes all of us suffer."

"Marrying an American and going away is better than staying home and marrying a Vietnamese," she said. "Excuse me, but I hate Vietnamese boys very much. They are lazy and most of them spend money like princes. They steal money from their mothers to spend on girls and on drinking. Even when they are married, they are not faithful to their wives."

"But I understand them—it is the war," she continued. "They do not know how long they will be alive. Sooner or later the army has them."

Her fiancé does not know much about her background or many of her opinions. Asked why he wanted to marry her, he said he could not explain it—and then did.

"She listens more, she's more understanding," he said. Many Americans give that as a reason for marrying Vietnamese.

"There might be problems back home for us, people making fun of us, other women giving her a hard time," he added. "They better not! I won't let anyone mess with me or my family."

* * *

October 8, 1970

NIXON URGES SUPERVISED TRUCE IN VIETNAM, CAMBODIA AND LAOS AND A WIDER PEACE CONFERENCE

STANDSTILL ASKED

President Says Offer Has No Conditions—Two Elements New

By ROBERT B. SEMPLE Jr.
Special to The New York Times

WASHINGTON, Oct. 7—President Nixon asked Hanoi and the Vietcong tonight to join the allies in a standstill cease-fire throughout Indochina. He also called for an Indochina peace conference to negotiate an end to the fighting in Laos and Cambodia as well as South Vietnam.

Addressing a nationwide television audience from his oval office in the White House, Mr. Nixon conceded that an internationally supervised cease-fire "in place" might be difficult to arrange and even harder to sustain.

He said, however, "An unconventional war may require an unconventional truce; our side is ready to stand still and cease firing."

He said that successful negotiations leading to such a cease-fire might well be a prelude to a large political and military settlement of the conflict and would at the very least bring "an end to the killing."

Allies Reportedly Approved

In his proposal for expanded talks, Mr. Nixon said that the Paris peace conference would remain "our primary forum" for reaching a settlement until such time as a broader arrangement began producing "serious negotiations." He added:

"This war in Indochina has proved to be of one piece; it cannot be cured by treating only one of its areas of outbreak."

The composition and location proposed by Mr. Nixon remained unclear, but Administration officials suggested that it might include not only the present parties in Paris—the United States, North Vietnam, the Vietcong, and South Vietnam—but also Laos, Cambodia, the Soviet Union and Communist China. These officals also said, as Mr. Nixon did yesterday, that Cambodia, Laos and South Vietnam had all approved the proposals.

Two New Elements

Administration officials portrayed the 12-minute speech as a fresh set of proposals designed to replace Mr. Nixon's original eight-point peace initiative of May 14, 1969. But they said the United States stood by some of the original proposals, such as its endorsement of internationally supervised free elections to determine the composition of a South Vietnamese government.

The only really new elements in tonight's initiative were the standstill cease-fire and the proposal for expanded peace talks. On two crucial questions that have been dividing both sides—troop withdrawals and the composition of the Saigon leadership—Mr. Nixon essentially restated earlier positions, which the North Vietnamese have routinely rejected.

On the subject of troops, Mr. Nixon proposed the eventual withdrawal of all United States forces on a timetable to be worked out in negotiations. He did not, for the first time, call for mutual withdrawals, but White House officials suggested that this was an oversight and that Mr. Nixon still insisted on matching troop reductions by the other side.

This is still a considerable distance from the position of the North Vietnamese, who have consistently demanded unilateral United States withdrawal as a precondition to any broader settlement of the military and political future of South Vietnam.

On the question of the composition of the Saigon government, the President once again stated his willingness to accept a solution "that reflects the will of the South Vietnamese people" and reflects as well "the existing relationship of political forces" in the South Vietnamese countryside.

By this, White, House officials implied, the Administration might be prepared to accept political control by the Vietcong over areas in which they now have military superiority.

However, a gulf appeared to remain between Mr. Nixon and the enemy negotiators in Paris. The President said he would not accept the dismantling of "organized non-Communist parties" in South Vietnam, where as the Vietcong and North Vietnamese have consistently demanded the ouster of the top leaders of the present Government as a condition to a broader settlement.

Proposal on P.O.W.'s.

Mr. Nixon also proposed the immediate and unconditional release of all prisoners of war held by both sides—including all journalists and other "innocent civilian victims of the conflict."

In his proposals of May 14, 1969, the President called for the release of prisoners of war at "the earliest possible time," but his inclusion of journalists and other civilians at this time represented a new element.

Of all the proposals, however, the President's call for a standstill cease-fire was clearly designed to attract the most attention at home as well as in Paris, where Ambassador David K. E. Bruce is expected to present the new package to the other side early tomorrow.

One significant aspect of the cease-fire proposal, in the view of observers here, was that it has the effect of separating the military and political dimensions of the conflict, offering an immediate halt in the fighting as a prelude to tough bargaining on the details of a political settlement. This is the first time that the United States cease fire might precede a comprehensive settlement. In his May 14 speech Mr. Nixon seemed to have tied a cease fire to mutual troop withdrawals negotiated in advance.

Mr. Nixon listed five general principles which, he said, must govern any cease-fire arrangement.

First, he said, a cease-fire must be effectively supervised not only by the contending parties but also by international observers. He did not set forth detailed arrangements for carrying this out, but White House officials said that if the other side was prepared to accept the idea in principle, the United States would be prepared to offer concrete recommendations.

In addition, the President said, a cease-fire should not be used by either side to improve its military position and it should embrace all kinds of warfare—including bombing and acts of terrorism. It should also embrace Cambodia and Laos as well as South Vietnam, he said.

Difficulties Acknowledged

Finally, he said, it should be part of a general move to end the war in Indochina. He presumably meant that the cease-fire should be regarded as the beginning of broader negotiations covering the political stability of the entire Indochina area.

"Let us consider for a moment what the acceptance of these proposals would mean," Mr. Nixon said. "Since the end of World War II, there has always been a war going on somewhere in the world. The guns have never stopped firing. By achieving a cease-fire in Indochina, and holding firmly to the cease-fire in the Middle East, we could hear the welcome sound of peace throughout the world for the first time in a generation."

Mr. Nixon did not try to conceal the difficulty of obtaining a cease-fire, and his aides said the consent of many contending forces would be required. In addition to the fighting in South Vietnam, Cambodia is torn by clashes between Government troops loyal to Premier Lon Nol and Vietcong and North Vietnamese troops and some indigenous Communist guerrillas. In Laos royal Laotian troops are fighting North Vietnamese troops and the pro-Communist Pathet Lao.

A White House official who briefed newsmen tonight before the speech was asked several times why the Administration had waited until now to offer a standstill cease-fire. The essence of his answer was that a cease-fire a year ago would have left the allied forces at a severe military disadvantage.

On another point, the same official said that captured enemy documents disclosed some internal discussion among the enemy on the subject of a cease-fire. But he said the United States had received no advance indication from enemy negotiators in Paris of their attitude toward such a proposal, and had no clear way of knowing whether they would accept it.

Under the ground rules governing background briefings, the identity of the official cannot be disclosed.

The President has been under pressure from various private and public groups to call for a standstill cease-fire. On Sept. 1, Senator Hugh Scott, the Senate Republican leader; Senator Henry A. Jackson, Democrat of Washington, and 28 other senators wrote and urged him to take this step. Accordingly, Congressional reaction tonight from both sides of the aisle was heavily favorable.

For example, Senator Frank Church, Democrat of Idaho and a persistent war critic, called the proposals "the most promising formula yet advanced for achieving a negotiated settlement."

But United Press International quoted another leading critic, Senator J. W. Fulbright, Democrat of Arkansas and chairman of the Senate Foreign Relations Committee, as having termed the overture as "better than nothing" but flawed by Mr. Nixon's apparent belief that "we will have to keep President Thieu and Vice President Ky in office."

Mr. Fulbright's sentiments were also shared by Senator John C. Stennis, the Mississippi Democrat who heads the Armed Services Committee and rarely agrees with Mr. Fulbright on the war. Despite seeing some grounds for hope, Mr. Stennis said, "I am afraid I cling to the idea that it does not offer North Vietnam so very much."

* * *

October 9, 1970

NIXON PEACE PLAN ASSAILED BY REDS AT TALKS IN PARIS

Hanoi and Vietcong Aides Criticize 'Maneuver' and Adhere to Demands

'REJECTION' IS AVOIDED

Private Discussions Viewed as Essential for Further Probes by 2 Sides

By HENRY GINIGER
Special to The New York Times

PARIS, Oct. 8—The Communist delegations to the Vietnam peace talks denounced President Nixon's five peace proposals today as "a maneuver to deceive world opinion" and held fast to their demands for unconditional and total American troop withdrawal and the overthrow of the "puppet" leaders in Saigon.

A whole string of epithets was used by Xuan Thuy, the North Vietnamese delegate, Mrs. Nguyen Thi Binh, the Vietcong delegate, and their press spokesmen to denounce Mr. Nixon and his "so-called" peace plan.

But neither of the two delegations would use the world "rejection" to characterize their attitude. They described their remarks as "preliminary" and reserved the right to return to the proposals in future negotiating sessions, although they made it clear it would be to criticize them.

[North Vietnam and the Vietcong, in statements broadcast Friday on the Hanoi radio, denounced but did not flatly reject Mr. Nixon's proposals.]

Private Talks Foreseen

It is generally assumed that if the two sides are to probe each other's meanings and intentions, the probing will not come in the regular Thursday negotiating sessions but in private talks. Nguyen Than Le, the North Vietnamese spokesman, said today that such talks had not yet taken place.

If they do, they will probably be held by David K. E. Bruce, the American delegate, and Mr. Thuy, since up to now the United States has refused to talk in private with the Vietcong without a representative of the Saigon Government present and both of the Communist delegations have refused to talk to the Saigon delegate.

Statement Read by Bruce

The Communist delegates evidently had already determined their response to Mr. Nixon's proposals before they entered the conference room in the former Majestic Hotel on the Avenue Kléber this morning and before Mr. Bruce had had a chance to lay Mr. Nixon's proposals on the table.

Mr. Bruce did little more than read what Mr. Nixon said in his speech last night, adding the hope that the proposals would receive "the most careful study and considered response by our side."

Mr. Le said his delegation had listened to Mr. Nixon as he spoke and had had eight hours to study what he said.

President Nixon, in his 12-minute speech, proposed a cease-fire covering all Indochina, negotiation for withdrawal of American forces, immediate release of all prisoners, an Indochina peace conference and a "fair political solution" in Vietnam.

Even though the first Communist judgment was hostile, the North Vietnamese and Vietcong delegations made it clear that they would pursue the matter. Their position has some similarity, although expressed in harsher terms to that adopted by Mr. Bruce three weeks ago when Mrs. Binh presented some clarification of standing Communist-peace proposals. The American delegate indicated then that he had not found Mrs. Binh's initiative very new but said he would continue to study it.

Mrs. Binh, on Sept. 17, proposed an American withdrawal by next June 30 in return for which, she said, her side was prepared to offer in effect a cease-fire for the withdrawing troops and immediate talks on the prisoner problem.

Joint Administration Proposed

Mrs. Binh also offered political talks with South Vietnamese persons favoring peace, neutrality, independence and democracy, and specifically excluded from such talks only President Nguyen Van Thieu, Vice President Nguyen Cao Ky and Premier Tran Thien Khiem. The talks could lead, she said, to a tripartite administration representing the Vietcong's provisional revolutionary government of South Vietnam, the Saigon administration and other persons outside the two groups. This government would then conduct elections, she said.

Mr. Le and Duong Dinh Thao, the Vietcong spokesman complained today that Mr. Nixon had not "seriously answered" Mrs. Binh's proposals. A "serious answer," they have made clear in the past, would have to be one virtually equivalent to acceptance.

In his statement during the meeting, Mr. Thuy declared:

"What can one say of the five points put forward last night by President Nixon? Only a gift certificate for the votes of the American electorate and a cover-up for misleading world public opinion, whereas new clarifications made by Mrs. Binh on

Sept. 17 constitute an important peace initiative to put an end to the war and settle the Vietnamese problem peacefully."

The updated Communist peace initiative and the counter-initiative taken by Mr. Nixon have given a new stimulus to the conference after months of dull routine. The press briefing hall was jammed and an expectancy akin to that attending the opening of the four sided talks in January of last year hung over the gathering.

At the end of the afternoon there was a feeling that little had happened to bring the conference out of its deadlock. The Communists' analysis of the war and their method of settling it appeared to have remained unshaken by Mr. Nixon's speech.

"As everyone knows." Mrs. Binh said "the war in Vietnam and in Indochina is a product of American aggression." A little later she declared:

"This is why, for peace to be re-established in Indochina, the United States must put an end to its aggression and withdraw completely from this zone."

The negotiating session and the press briefings that followed were full of statements directed to public opinion. Mr. Nixon was accused by the Communists of hypocrisy and his proposals were characterized as a false peace—a real war."

There was considerable interest shown here in the fact that Mr. Nixon did not specifically mention mutual withdrawals of all non-South Vietnamese forces in his speech, and did not speak of free elections in talking of "political processes" in South Vietnam.

But both Communist spokesmen agreed with their adversary, Nguyen Trieu Dan of the Saigon delegation, that the United States and Saigon were still demanding that North Vietnam withdraw its forces as the United States withdraws.

Such a demand was characterized by the Communists as "absurd" since, they said, it put the American "aggressors" on the same level as the Vietnamese who, they said, were defending themselves against aggression.

* * *

November 6, 1970

24 AMERICANS KILLED IN WEEK, LOWEST TOLL IN WAR SINCE '65

Special to The New York Times

SAIGON, South Vietnam, Nov. 5—The United States command reported today that 24 American soldiers were killed in combat in Indochina last week, the lowest weekly toll in five years.

The figure, 18 fewer than the previous week, is the lowest since the week ended Oct. 23, 1965, when 14 Americans were killed in action. It also is the fifth consecutive week that the American death toll in Indochina has been below 50.

In contrast, United States battle deaths averaged nearly 300 a week during 1968, the year of the enemy's Tet offensive.

The number of Americans wounded, however, rose sharply last week to 431, compared with 279 the week before. This increase reflects the fact that with the current low level of fighting, most American casualties were from booby traps, snipers and hit-and-run mortar attacks, which more often wound than kill.

The number of South Vietnamese battle deaths rose to 309 last week compared with 215 the week before, the South Vietnamese reported. Eight hundred Government troops were reported wounded last week, up from 625 the week before.

North Vietnamese and Vietcong combat deaths last week were put at 909, compared with 1,628 the week before. The figure, which is based partly on allied estimates and cannot be considered exact, is the lowest since the first week of January, 1967.

In a decade of fighting, 43,928 Americans have been killed, according to official figures, and 291,455 have been wounded. South Vietnamese casualties have risen to 115,396 killed and 245,311 wounded. The allies put the total enemy dead at 679,654.

* * *

February 8, 1971

SAIGON UNITS DRIVE INTO LAOS TO STRIKE ENEMY SUPPLY LINE

U.S. GIVES AIR HELP

Also Provides Artillery Support for 'Limited' Attack by Ally

By ALVIN SHUSTER
Special to The New York Times

SAIGON, South Vietnam, Monday, Feb. 8—Thousands of South Vietnamese troops, supported by American planes and artillery, crossed the border into Laos this morning to strike at the Ho Chi Minh Trail network in hopes of crippling Hanoi's main artery for supplying the Indochina war.

President Nguyen Van Thieu, announcing the operation in a statement this morning, called the attack an "act of legitimate self-defense" and added that it would be "limited in time as well as in space." He asserted that South Vietnam "does not have any territorial ambition whatsoever."

The United States military command emphasized in a statement that no United States ground combat troops and no United States advisers would go into Laos with the South Vietnamese forces. It said the United States would provide artillery support, fired from South Vietnam, and virtually unlimited air power—helicopter gunships, planes, logistics and medical evacuation missions.

U.S. Prepared Way

The attack was launched from South Vietnam's northern-most province of Quangtri and possibly other points at 7 A.M. today (6 P.M., Sunday, New York time).

American helicopters flew the South Vietnamese troops across the border while South Vietnamese armored columns and infantrymen moved across the border on Route 9, cleared last week up to the border by some of the 9,000 American troops involved in the operation along with about 20,000 South Vietnamese soldiers.

Correspondents attempting to cross the border with the South Vietnamese on Route 9 were stopped by American military policemen.

Since the operation moved into position in Quangtri in the early hours of Jan. 30, Americans have cleared roads, rebuilt bridges, set up forward command posts and artillery, and reoccupied the old Marine Corps base at Khesanh, 12 miles from the Laotian border. Thousands of South Vietnamese troops massed at the border waiting orders to strike.

It was understood here that President Theiu had given President Nixon the right to decide whether Saigon should go ahead with the ground strike against the supply network after the Americans had completed their initial operations in the north up to the border.

How long the South Vietnamese troops will remain in Laos, striking at roads and stockpiles of enemy war needs, was not disclosed, while President Thieu said the operation would be limited, some military sources expect an offensive that will continue at least many weeks.

When the operation is completed, President Thieu said today, his armed forces "will completely withdraw from the Laotian territory." He said his Government "always respects the independence, neutrality and sovereignty of the Royal Kingdom of Laos."

The attack against the enemy supply network represents a dramatic reversal of past policy. American military commanders and South Vietnamese officials had often proposed the operation in the past, but were repeatedly turned down by Washington, in large part out of fear of the political repercussions from moving into a country whose declared neutrality is protected by the Geneva accords of 1962.

New Enemy Attacks Seen

In his statement, President Thieu said that the North Vietnamese for many years have "blatantly violated" the accords against the presence of foreign troops in Laos. He cited the "great military and logistics bases" established by Hanoi in southern Laos to supply the war needs in South Vietnam, Cambodia and Laos. He said the Communists were "preparing themselves to launch fresh attacks in the forthcoming months."

"For these reasons," he went on "the attacks by our armed forces against the North Vietnamese Communist troops along the border within Laotian territory do not constitute an act of belligerence on our part, they are merely and solely a necessary act of legitimate self-defense on the part of the Republic of Vietnam against the North Vietnamese Communist aggressors.

"This is not an act of aggression of the Republic of Vietnam against the friendly nation of Laos. On the contrary, this is an action designed to stop the North Vietnamese Communists from expanding and perpetuating their aggressive potential.

"This is not an expansion of the war by the Republic of Vietnam, either. On the contrary, it is an action to help end soon the war in Vietnam and restore peace in this part of the world."

Long Talks With Bunker

President Thieu apparently argued successfully in long conversations with Ambassador Ellsworth Bunker and other American officials here that the time was running out for what he felt would be a decisive blow to the enemy war effort. The South Vietnamese army now was strong enough to take on the job with ground support from Americans, he reportedly believed. But he needed President Nixon's approval for the operation because of the vital role to be played by American air power.

With United States combat forces on their way out, the attack, in the view of its supporters, had to come now or never.

The military command justified the use of American air and logistics support for the operation as in line with "the objectives of helping to protect the lives of United States military personnel in South Vietnam and enhancing Vietnamization," which is the progressive turnover of the burden of the war to the South Vietnamese.

The command said that American ground troops in Military Region I, which includes Quangtri Province, continues in a "high state of alert in defensive and blocking positions."

The supply trail has been under intensive United States bombardment by giant B-52 and smaller fighters and bombers since October, when an enemy build-up was believed to be gathering speed after the monsoon season in eastern Laos.

Because the Cambodian port of Kompong Som, formerly Sihanoukville, is now closed to enemy war supplies, Hanoi is forced to limit its supply effort to the trail network, a maze of thousands of miles of dirt roads and jungle-covered trails.

* * *

February 11, 1971

THOUSANDS IN U.S. PROTEST ON LAOS

Students March in Several Cities and Stage Sit-Ins

By MARTIN ARNOLD

About 2,000 persons demonstrated here last evening against the Laos incursion and about 3,000 marched on the Boston Common.

But around the country, attendance at demonstrations was mostly slight. Nearly everywhere they were peaceful, with few arrests.

About 15 persons, however, were arrested after the Boston rally during a march from the Common to Northeastern University. There was sporadic stone-throwing and window-breaking, and several policemen and arrested persons were injured in clashes.

Fifteen were also arrested in similar incidents in Baltimore, where six policemen were reported hospitalized. And five persons were arrested in Washington, where 1,000 protested before the White House.

At the University of Wisconsin in Madison 1,000 demonstrators briefly took over a social science building. Gov. Patrick Lucey dispatched 100 Wisconsin state conservation officers and state traffic patrolmen to assist the local police in regaining control of the building.

Computer Center Occupied

Half a continent away, at Palo Alto, Calif., 70 students occupied a computer center at Stanford University to protest its use for war research. Five were arrested when they did not heed police orders to disperse.

In Berkeley, 1,500 anti-war protesters marched through the campus of the University of California. There was sporadic rock throwing and an automobile owned by the Atomic Energy Commission was set afire.

Twice the Berkeley police used tear gas to turn back protesters. Windows were smashed. One policeman was hurt and two persons were arrested.

In Albany, 100 university students chanted "Ho! Ho! Ho Chi Minh!" marched up the Capitol's main staircase to the third floor office of Assembly Speaker Perry B. Duryea, Suffolk County Republican, and started denouncing him for not appearing.

Suddenly the curtained door to his office opened, and Mr. Duryea emerged, silver-haired and smiling hesitantly.

"There's no reluctance, by any means, to discuss any problem," the Speaker said. He added that he favored American disengagement from the war, but that the place to protest was in Washington, not in Albany.

An epithet was shouted from the crowd and when this was followed by another, the Speaker withdrew saying, "If this is the tenor of the meeting, you don't need me any more."

Rally Here in Low Key

The demonstration here started out in low key, with about 300 persons, mostly students, gathering on the island between 43d and 44th Streets, which separates Seventh Avenue from Broadway in Times Square.

The crowd spilled off into the streets, causing the police to block the area to automobile traffic, and then as more students joined, the entire group marched off toward the National Broadcasting Company Building in Rockefeller Center to protest alleged mishandling of news about the Laos incursion. By this time the crowd had grown to several thousand.

It then moved to the Time-Life Building, where it dispersed shortly after 7 P.M. Two arrests were reported during the marches, one of a demonstrator who allegedly kicked a policeman and one of a man heckling the marchers.

Other demonstrations were smaller, partly because of the cold that settled over large sections of the country.

In Chicago, for instance, only about 300 people took part, and there was no violence. At Champaign, Ill., several hundred students of the University of Illinois burned an effigy of Secretary of Defense Melvin R. Laird.

About 100 persons took part in a protest in Detroit and about 1,000 at the University of Michigan in Ann Arbor. Mayor Robert Harris of Ann Arbor joined the marchers.

And in Cleveland only 75 persons showed up for a demonstration in front of the city's new Federal building.

* * *

February 15, 1971

NEWS OF WAR IN LAOS COMES IN BITS

By TILLMAN DURDIN
Special to The New York Times

VIENTIANE, Laos, Feb. 14—The war in Laos is still an out-of-bounds, largely secret war.

With occasional exceptions, journalists are rigorously barred from seeing it.

They must depend for news of the war on whatever Laotian and American officials choose to tell them and on scraps of often inaccurate information picked up from irregular sources.

The restrictions imposed on access to and information about the war and many related matters are jointly enforced by the United States Embassy and the Laotian authorities. Each passes the responsibility to the other with alacrity when pressed about the situation.

The reason for the restrictions is that there are many things in the combat zones that United States and Laotian officials do not want reporters to see—what, for example, United States individuals known to operate in advisory and liaison roles do at the fronts, what part bombing by American planes plays in support of Laotian forces and what there is to constant reports of special units from Thailand fighting with Laotian troops.

A Sensitive Matter

The nature of foreign participation on the Government's side in the war is clearly the most sensitive matter with United States and Laotian officials.

American spokesmen refuse to answer any questions in this sphere. Any formal query about how the Central Intelligence Agency is assisting Special Forces in Laos draws a quick "no comment."

Enforcing restrictions is simplicity itself. All transportation to war zones is officially controlled and journalists are kept away by being denied transportation.

Recent pleas by newsmen to be taken to the critical Sam Thong-Long Tieng combat zone have been categorically rebuffed. It is possible for civilians, including journalists, to travel by commercial plane to the few cities in the Mekong valley still held by the Government—Bon Houei, Sayaboury and Luang Prabang in the north, Savannakhet and Pakse in the south—and sometimes the fighting comes close enough to some of these centers to be seen.

Getting any further is just a fluke. But flukes have happened. An enterprising Japanese correspondent last year gave $100 to a Laotian fighter-plane pilot and was flown to Long Tieng. He spent a day there happily taking pictures, talking with the supposed-to-be uninterviewable Meo general of the supposed-to-be C.I.A.-supported Special Forces in the area, Vang Pao, and having a look at the supposed-to-be secret base.

The Japanese correspondent was thrown in jail by the Laotian authorities when he got back to Vientiane, but through intervention by the Japanese Embassy was out the next day and reportedly sold his pictures for $1,000.

An American correspondent here got into Long Tieng recently simply because he was invited to a wedding there by General Vang Pao. He went to Air America, the commercial airline hired by United States agencies to fly materials to combat and refugee areas of Laos, showed his invitation and was put aboard a plane for Long Tieng.

He said the "secret base" was so unexciting that he did not even write about it.

Roving enemy guerrilla patrols make practically all roads out of Vientiane and other cities and towns in Government-held areas unsafe for anyone as conspicuous as a foreigner. As a result, journalists are unable to take overland routes to combat zones.

* * *

February 18, 1971

AT BORDER CROSSING INTO LAOS, THE LITTER OF TROOPS AND HISTORY

By GLORIA EMERSON
Special to The New York Times

ON ROUTE 9, near the Laotian border, Feb. 15—Now there is only the garbage of war. Empty C-ration cans of fruit cocktail and turkey loaf, an empty Pall Mall cigarette package, a single khaki sock and two mounds of sandbags are strewn about at the border crossing into Laos on Route 9.

A week ago it was here that thousands of South Vietnamese troops, supported by American planes and artillery, marched into Laos, leaving the litter behind.

It hardly looks like a place where the history of Indochina has been dramatically changed.

No man stands guard. Stretched across the road are two long bamboo poles tied together with string to show where Laos begins and American soldiers must not go.

The sign "Warning! No U.S. Personnel Beyond This Point" has dozens of names scrawled on it. On the back, facing Laos, is a faintly scrawled message to the North Vietnamese Army: "Warning! No N.V.A. Beyond This Point."

No American Vehicles

There are no American trucks in this section of Route 9. A long, narrow roller coaster of a road, whose rising dust is white, then orange, sometimes dark brown, it cuts through elephant grass, bamboo trees and nine-foot stalks topped by ostrichlike plumes and is just wide enough for one truck to squeeze by another.

No supplies are moving into Laos on the road, for the South Vietnamese troops are being supplied by air. It is a lonely road and a bad one to walk on. There are snipers, there are North Vietnamese rockets coming in from positions in Laos as well as here in Vietnam. There is a silence even at noon that makes men with M-16 rifles uneasy.

The American soldiers are 300 yards from the border on a lump of a hill where seven tanks and armored personnel carriers form the defense perimeter of a miniature fire base. The men are soldiers from the Americal Division and from an infantry battalion of the First Brigade of the Fifth Infantry Division (Mechanized).

"Christ, we're defenseless here!" said Pvt. George Miller, a 22-year-old Newark man. "They could fire pot shots at us all day and all night long if they wanted to."

The Americans' job is to secure the road, search the area and stay alive.

Tribal Competitiveness

On the unnamed hill are a mixture of tankers—the men who drive the machines—the grunts, or infantryman, and the mortar squads. There is friendly friction, a tribal competitiveness, that provides their only entertainment.

Many of the Americans here, their faces sore from the dust and grime, their bodies covered with the small open boils that infest unwashed Westerners fighting in Vietnam, wish they could have gone into Laos.

"I'd love to go into Laos. If we did, we'd get everything organized right, see," Specialist 4 Anthony Hockman of Battletown, Ky., said.

Few of the men here think the South Vietnamese can seal off the Ho Chi Minh Trail network. There is still a deep suspicion that they will not do as well as Americans would; it is a conviction the G.I.'s like to voice.

"I saw them fight in Kontum—they got into contact and they ran out, they bugged out, and left two wounded behind," said Specialist 4 Harold Dingus of South Shore, Ky.

There are some men who feel that it is not doing any good to be here, who say they are outnumbered by the North Vietnamese in the surrounding highlands.

"You might say it's a case of the unwilling helping the ungrateful to kill the unwanted," Sgt. Kirk Coles said.

Less than a mile down from the border are South Vietnamese troops from the 11th Airborne Battalion. The paratroopers, who often trade their packages of precooked rice for C-rations, are not so sure that the Ho Chi Minh Trail can ever be cut.

Cpl. Le Ngu said in Vietnamese: "Do you think the N.V.A. are all fools? I can tell you the Ho Chi Minh Trail is very complicated—you attack here, you attack there, but they will get through in other places."

"When do we have peace, heh?" a Vietnamese paratrooper asked as he ate his lunch of rice and duck, using chopsticks made of bamboo.

'Write a Letter to Thieu'

Another soldier snorted. "Write a letter to Mr. Thieu and ask him," he said, referring to Nguyen Van Thieu, President of South Vietnam. Corporal Ngu shook his head, shoveled more rice into his mouth and replied: "Goddammit, Thieu never knows, Nixon never knows!"

Yesterday the South Vietnamese here suffered 20 wounded when two mortar rounds hit their camp, where there are nearly 150 men.

The Americans, who are closer to the border, were hit by a North Vietnamese rocket today. Every man jammed on his steel helmet.

Sitting on the sandbags around one of the two 81-mm mortars, Pvt. Richard Ferguson of Columbus, Ohio, told why he did not get married last year before he was drafted and sent to Vietnam.

"You read about all these guys getting shot up," he said. "I thought it was as bad as what it's getting to be." That struck half a dozen men as very witty.

'They Are Hard to Kill'

None of the G.I.'s here look upon the North Vietnamese forces as being on their last legs or as a ragtag army that has nothing to fight with and lacks the spirit to win.

"They are hard to kill—I once put six bullets in a gook and still he don't die," Specialist 4 Manuel R. Navarro of San Antonio, Tex., said. "He looked about 17."

At a few minutes before 2 P.M., an infantry platoon "got in real trouble," as one G.I. put it. The radio operator of the platoon, which believed it was surrounded, had the voice of a man trying hard to sound steady.

"Most of us had to retreat," he said. "I'll give you further word when I figure out what's going on around here."

No one seemed sleepy then. The small talk about favorite movies and much-loved cars, about girls with long blond hair and perfect legs, stopped.

Half a dozen men clustered around the field radio listening to the pilot of a gunship find his target, to the pilot of a helicopter removing wounded men through the triple canopy of jungle.

An hour later the site where the platoon had taken fire was mashed by 8-inch howitzer shells and burned by white phosphorus and blasted by 6,000 bullets a minute from the air.

"Goddam good show, and probably all for nothing, too," a soldier said. "The dinks have gone underground or scattered."

Specialist 4 Harry Crane of Steubenville, Ohio, began to cook dinner, as he does every night, in two steel helmets over an open fire.

"I use the same two pots for cooking every night," he said. "I just mix together a lot of C's and some rice and noodles that the Vietnamese trade us for cigarettes. You have to put in lots of hot sauce and garlic salt."

* * *

February 19, 1971

HANOI SAYS MOVES BY U.S. POSE THREAT TO RED CHINA

Special to The New York Times

PARIS, Feb. 18—North Vietnam charged at the peace talks here today that the United States was threatening to extend the war to North Vietnamese territory and by so doing was menacing Communist China as well.

Xuan Thuy, the chief North Vietnamese negotiator, asserted at the 103d session of the talks that the United States was threatening the two Communist countries by concentrating large land forces in the northern part of South Vietnam, reinforcing naval forces in the Gulf of Tonkin and extending operations in Laos.

He made no direct threat of reprisal, but his spokesman, Nguyen Thanh Le, said in response to questions at a briefing for newsmen that "China will not remain with its arms folded" before such a menace. The reason; he said, is that China has "common mountains, lakes and rivers" with North Vietnam and Laos.

[In Washington, Administration specialists on China expressed confidence that Communist China would not intervene in Indochina in a situation in which American troop withdrawals continue.]

Mr. Le's comment recalled a recent statement by the Chinese Communist Government that it "will not remain indifferent" to the operation being conducted in southern Laos by South Vietnamese troops with American support.

That statement, issued last Friday, said China would take "all effective measures" to aid the Communist forces in Indochina, but, like similar pledges made earlier, it also expressed confidence that the peoples of the area could handle the situation by themselves.

Mr. Thuy, in his accusations against the United States, was reacting to statements President Nixon made last night at a news conference, among them that he would put no limitation on the use of American air power anywhere in Indochina except to rule out the use of tactical nuclear weapons.

The Hanoi representative also expressed anger at the President's refusal to rule out a South Vietnamese thrust into North Vietnam and at Mr. Nixon's warning that time was running out for significant negotiation in Paris.

All these show, the North Vietnamese said, that the United States "does not want to settle the Vietnam problem peacefully."

Similar statements were made by Mrs. Nguyen Thi Binh, the Vietcong representative.

The chief United States negotiator, David K. E. Bruce, said to Mr. Thuy, "It is you, and no one else, who is responsible for the continued fighting and killing in Indochina."

Mr. Buce reported after the session that all the meeting produced was "false and useless propaganda that had nothing to do with the problem of negotiating an end to the war."

Also at today's session, a report on the South Vietnamese operation in Laos was made by Pham Dang Lam, Saigon's chief negotiator. He said that South Vietnamese forces had eliminated 600 regular North Vietnamese soldiers and had captured large quantities of supplies in a week of combat along the Communist supply trails. The operation began Feb. 8.

The supplies seized, he went on, include 10 pieces of heavy artillery, 6 antiaircraft batteries, more than 100 individual and crew-served weapons, more than 300 tons of rockets, mortars and ammunition, 70 tanks and trucks, 45,000 gallons of gasoline, 30 tons of foodstuffs, 3 tons of pharmaceutical products and 500 bales of uniforms of the North Vietnamese Army.

Mr. Lam also said that bunkers, training camps, communications centers and a network of supply and infiltration into South Vietnam and Cambodia has also been discovered.

* * *

February 19, 1971

NIXON'S TWO AUDIENCES: HANOI AND THE U.S.

By MAX FRANKEL
Special to The New York Times

WASHINGTON, Feb. 18—A President's public statements in wartime always represent a simultaneous play to different audiences. Notably the battlefield enemy and the restive folks at home.

For that reason, it is difficult to separate in President Nixon's latest discussion of Indochina the words that were uttered for their immediate effect in Hanoi and those that offer significant clues to his long-term strategy. Taken together, however, the President's responses at an informal news conference yesterday were plainly designed to convey an extraordinary degree of confidence in several respects:

He can now carry the war to the enemy physically and psychologically.

He does not have to bargain for a political compromise in South Vietnam as the price for American disengagement.

He is approaching the point where he can defend allied military positions and political interests in Indochina at a level that Americans will support.

He may, in the process, strike such an effective blow in Laos that he will wholly alter the complexion of the war and, in effect, win it.

Mr. Nixon left these impressions in very carefully chosen words, under a pattern of questioning that let him think through the subject and without the pressure of television cameras, which abhor hesitation or grimace. He was thus able to work at his objectives while the reporters could try to read his mind and intentions.

The President's short-range objectives relate directly to the current operation in Laos. As he explained, the allied purpose there is to cut or seriously disrupt Hanoi's "lifeline" to South Vietnam and Cambodia—the only significant supply route now that transshipment through Cambodian seaports is no longer feasible.

In a remarkably bold definition of the stakes, Mr. Nixon said the North Vietnamese "have to fight here"—in Laos—"or give up the struggle to conquer South Vietnam, Cambodia and their influence extending through other parts of Southeast Asia."

He then tried to offer some powerful reasons to deter them from fighting back in a major way. He said the allies were ready for a fight, with the South Vietnamese already performing in a superior way and American air power supporting them without restriction.

Invasion Not Ruled Out

Moreover, he left open the possibility that the South Vietnamese might have to invade North Vietnam itself—obviously hoping that this would keep the equivalent of three North Vietnamese divisions tied down inside their own borders and unavailable for the defense of the Laos rails.

And he threatened major bombing reprisals against North Vietnam if Hanoi should attempt an end run through the demilitarized zone into South Vietnam. In fact, he said Hanoi's foreknowledge of such a response "means that they are not going to take it."

All this amounted to a considered Presidential statement that Hanoi could either "give up" in Laos without a fight or risk further escalation in direct proportion to the extent of its resistance.

But this statement in psychological support of the current battlefield engagement, was clearly not the full expression of Mr. Nixon's thoughts about the course of the war. He said that the rains in May would end the fight for the Laos trails for this season and he acknowledged that Hanoi could mount a sizable challenge to South Vietnam next year.

The continuing American withdrawal from ground combat, he said, will make 1972 "the greatest point of danger." Since he also expects to be standing for re-election next year, Mr. Nixon is known to fear a major effort by Hanoi to inflict heavy casualties upon the declining American force, designed to compel him to make a total withdrawal or a quick bargain in Paris.

He is letting it be known that there is no real "time limit" on operations in Laos or Cambodia. In other words, the South Vietnamese will seek to keep the supply routes cut after the rains next fall.

And he is laying the ground-work for keeping a residual force of Americans in Indochina to support the Saigon forces—"enough Americans," as he put it, to give North Vietnam an incentive to trade their withdrawal for the release of American prisoners.

Quite apart from the chances of virtually winning the war in Laos in the next 90 days, therefore, the President is trying now to protect himself against serious setback next year. He is pleased to have drastically reduced the rate of American casualties in recent months.

He appears convinced that South Vietnamese and Cambodian soldiers, massively supported by American air and transport units, can keep the enemy forces off balance and undersupplied, at least for the foreseeable future.

And he seems to feel that such a level of engagement, combined with further American troop reductions, will make the war bearable politically within the United States.

So he is letting it be known that he will accept no limitations on the use of American air power, except the prohibition on nuclear weapons, either through pressure in Congress or the legacy of "so-called understandings" with Hanoi.

Mr. Nixon replied that the Paris talks no longer interested him except for the prisoner deal they might one day yield. Behind that suggestion lies the thought of many of his aides that the political risks of gradual disengagement, without negotiation, are now probably less than the risks of a political deal that would admit the Vietcong to a share of the power in Saigon.

The net impression left by these longer-term comments of the President as not so much that he is certain of winning the war soon as that he now feels confident he will not be defeated by it.

He has discounted any active intervention by Communist China. He thinks Saigon is "holding its own" in battle, and that, with luck and time, Cambodia too, will survive. To him, Hanoi seems hard-pressed while the home front seems reasonably well pacified.

It is clearly the most optimistic Presidential posture here in a long time, both on the surface and below.

* * *

February 23, 1971

CALLEY, ON STAND, TELLS OF HATRED

He Says Army Taught Him to Treat All Vietnamese as Potential Enemies

By HOMER BIGART
Special to The New York Times

FORT BENNING, Ga., Feb. 22—First Lieut. William L. Calley Jr., accused of killing 102 men, women and children during the alleged massacre of South Vietnamese civilians at Mylai, took the witness stand today and said that he had been indoctrinated by the Army to treat all Vietnamese, including children, as potential enemies.

He told how he had come to regard them all with deepening suspicion and hate.

The short, stocky 27-year-old officer, now the chief defendant in the Mylai case, said that although he had attended Army classes on the Geneva Convention, he could not recall anything he had been taught about the rules of war.

He was on the stand for 93 minutes reviewing his early background and his Army career up to the eve of the alleged massacre.

What did stick in his mind, he told the court-martial panel of six officers who will decide his guilt or innocence on four counts of premeditated murder, was the sickening horror of the conflict.

While still in Hawaii, he had read some action reports of the 25th Division, which had been in Vietnam for a year. From these reports, he said, he drew this conclusion: "It was essential that troops in Vietnam put out of their mind the World War II and Korean concept of giving candy and chewing gum and things to the children."

The children, he told the jury, were "even more dangerous" than men and women because, although they seemed so innocent, they threw grenades and were "very good at planting mines."

His fear and hatred of the Vietnamese was heightened, he said, during the enemy's Tet offensive of early 1968.

Shortly before Mylai, his men ran into a minefield and suffered heavy casualties, he went on. He was away on a rest-and-recreation leave when it happened, he said, but he got back in time to see a helicopter bring back the gear and the bodies of his buddies.

"I think the thing that really hit me hard were just the heavy boots," he said. "There must have been six boots there, with the feet still in them. Brains all over the place, and everything was just saturated with blood. Rifles just blown in half. I believe there was one arm and a piece of a man's face, half of a man's face, on the chopper with the gear."

Describes His Feelings

Q. (By the chief defense counsel, George W. Latimer) And what was your feeling when you saw this? A. I don't know if I can describe the feeling.

Q. Well, at least try. A. Anger, hate, fear, generally sick to your stomach, hurt.

Q. Did this have any impact on your future actions? A. I think [it] instilled an even deeper form of hatred towards the enemy, but I don't think I ever made up my mind or came to any conclusion what I'd do to the enemy.

Q. All right, now did you have any remorse or grief or anything? A. Yes, sir, I did.

Q. What was that? A. Remorse for losing my men in the minefield, remorse that those men ever had to go to Vietnam; remorse for being in that sort of a situation where you are completely helpless. I think I felt mainly remorse because I wasn't there. Although there was nothing I could do, I think there is a psychological factor of just not being there when everything is happening.

'Weren't Playing Games'

Lieutenant Calley told of the pervasive fear engendered by the Tet offensive and described an incident when "it dawned on me that we weren't playing games, that we weren't supposed to be a bunch of Boy Scouts out there playing."

He was on leave at a seashore village.

"I woke early in the morning, and there was about six mama-sans coming down the street with their choggie baskets and their wares to sell at the market. That is what I presumed. I don't know where they were going but just trying to get a head start so they could get a good place at the market.

"And on every corner the white mice [South Vietnam police] had a machine gun set up, and I'd say it was about a half an hour before twilight, and they cut them [the women] down. And that is how strict the war was becoming. At that time, you weren't supposed to move or be in an area. You'd best not be there, or you'd be dead."

"Rusty" Calley proved a taut witness. Although he holds a Bronze Medal and a Purple Heart, the only decoration he wore today was a Combat Infantryman's Badge. He was freshly barbered, and from his prematurely receding hairline a long brown lock was plastered to his forehead.

In the beginning, his heavy-lidded eyes, which give him a perpetually sleepy look, darted nervously from defense table to spectators, with only a few glances at the jury.

But under the gentle questioning of Mr. Latimer, the young officer relaxed slowly and turned more frequently to the somber-faced jurors, five of whom have had combat experience in Vietnam.

The small courtroom, with its patriotic decor of red carpet, white walls and blue curtains, was thronged. Mr. Latimer asked the judge to enforce the rule against any outbursts by spectators during Lieutenant Calley's testimony.

The lieutenant spoke of his early youth in Miami. He said that he came from a "stable" family, a family without friction and a reasonably prosperous family. The father ran his own heavy construction machinery business.

Was Claims Investigator

Lieutenant Calley said that he ran into some trouble in the seventh grade—"for cheating, basically, sir"—and got generally poor marks as he went on through military schools and a junior college. The family encountered hard times. Lieutenant Calley's father lost his business, and the family moved to North Carolina, where the mother died of cancer.

"Rusty," meanwhile, had a number of menial jobs—busboy, dishwasher, short order cook—"not that I knew how to cook," he told the court with a self-effacing chuckle—and a car drier in a minute car wash.

Then he was briefly a strikebreaking freight car conductor on the Florida East Coast Railway and finally an insurance claims investigator.

He was jobless in San Francisco when the draft notices caught up with him. He started East, but his car broke down in Albuquerque, where he went to a recruiting station and enlisted.

This morning, a psychiatrist, Dr. Wilbur M. Hannan of Alexandria, Va., testified that Lieutenant Calley had told him he had no intention of "destroying" all humans at Mylai but wanted to use some of them to clear minefields.

Lieutenant Calley never used the word "kill," Dr. Hannan said. The lieutenant told him that the military avoided that word because it caused "a very negative emotional reaction" among the men, who had been taught the commandment, "Thou shalt not kill."

Instead, Lieutenant Calley employed the word "destroy" or the phrase "waste 'em" which meant something quite different from kill, the psychiatrist said.

"Lieutenant Calley felt he was not killing human beings but destroying enemies, that he was carrying out legal orders," Dr. Hannan said.

The psychiatrist suggested that no American soldier—except psychopathic killers—could properly be tried for the Mylai incident or any similar action.

"It amounts to war," he said. "And if you're going to blame war on anyone, it might as well be God—you can't blame groups of individuals or nations."

He said that Lieutenant Calley had suffered no "diagnosable mental illness" but insisted that the young officer, because of personal background, training and combat stress, had been unable to commit premeditated murder at Mylai.

At the beginning of the afternoon session, the military judge, Col. Reid W. Kennedy, said that he had "intended no personal or professional harm" to Dr. Albert A. LaVerne, a psychiatrist on leave from Bellevue Hospital's psychiatric division in New York.

Dr. LaVerne was excused as a defense witness last Friday. Mr. Latimer said then that he had had "basic disagreements over strategy" with the psychiatrist, and Judge Kennedy expressed doubt as to the veracity of some of Dr. LaVerne's testimony, all of which was stricken from the record.

This morning, Dr. LaVerne came to the courthouse demanding vindication. Judge Kennedy said that Dr. LaVerne "explained what he meant by certain parts of his testimony" and ordered his own remarks about Dr. LaVerne stricken. Mr. Latimer praised Dr. LaVerne for "a terrific job of trying to help the accused."

* * *

February 25, 1971

LAOS AND THE OLD ILLUSIONS

By DAVID HALBERSTAM

So this time it is Laos.

On and on it goes: Who would have thought that instead of the light at the end of the tunnel we would have found a tunnel at the end of the tunnel. The rationalizations are familiar: shorten the war, bring the troops home quicker, protect American lives, improve the morale of the South Vietnamese Government, serve notice on Hanoi of the seriousness of our intent.

Yet one has a sense of microcosm about Laos; if it invokes all the old rationales it also reeks of all the old misconceptions and illusions.

The first is the belief that when we make a move the other side has no alternative, no counter-move. This is perhaps the most remarkable continuing illusion of the war. Its entire history going back to 1946 has been that the Vietnamese Communist forces possess the greater roots in society, the greater willingness to die for their ideas. (Thus the misconception of the Kennedy years when the idea of limited war was fashionable: you fight limited war, but the other side, small, under-developed, fights total war.)

The most neglected lesson of the war is that it is their country. Time is on their side. They can take all the time they want. (If the guerrilla is not defeated then he has won, once said the noted political scientist Henry A. Kissinger before he went from critic to second-stage architect of the war.) Whatever we do, they can match. We bomb the North; they send men down the trail. We send combat troops to the South; they send more men down the trail. We go after the Cambodian sanctuaries; they shift the war to Cambodia where once again they are stronger. So we move into Laos, South Vietnamese or American troops notwithstanding. Does anyone familiar with the painful history of the war really believe that they cannot move somewhere else where we are weak and they are strong?

The second illusion might be called the illusion of tangible structures. Trails, sanctuaries, main force units, depots, factories. Things to be seen, photographed, identified, and destroyed. This has always been a central problem. Do you see it as a war in which the tangible structures and the tangible force levels are the given? Or do you see it as a war in which these structures are the minor temporary reflection of the other side—the real factor being his ideas, his determination? Twenty-five years of war have proven that the latter view is the dominant one ("And how long do you Americans wish to fight?" Pham Van Dong asked four years ago in Hanoi. "One year? Two years? Twenty years? We will be glad to accommodate you."). Yet the instinct on the part of Westerners, particularly of Western military men, has always been to concentrate on structures and to overrate the results of temporary destruction of them.

There is a melancholy feeling to this. A feeling that we are back where we were a few years ago. The question is how and why we got here again. The earliest tipoff came during the silence of the 1968 campaign; had Nixon truly wanted to get out he would have surfaced with his thoughts then.

Then in early 1969 when there was still an official silence, when Mr. Kissinger went around Washington telling people that the greatest mistake of the Johnson Administration was Clifford and Harriman's attacks upon the Thieu Ky Government. And then Nixon's own attack on Clifford. Quickly after that the most important speech of the Administration, Nixon's Nov. 3, 1969, speech when he said we would get out, but get out with honor and where he bought the assumptions and the rhetoric of the war: that a viable non-Communist South Vietnam is vital to American interest.

That policy has of course become clearer ever since: The welcoming of hawkish labor leaders to the White House, the honoring of Joseph Alsop, the purging of a dovish Republican Senator, the unleashing of the Vice President upon the war's critics. And Cambodia and Laos. Last week Don Oberdorfer, the Washington Post White House correspondent, wrote a particularly incisive explanation of what had happened, noting "the cardinal point is that the President seems truly to believe that a non-Communist South Vietnam is extremely important to the interests of the United States. He appears to believe this may be achievable and he is prepared to take important risks and incur large costs to further this cause." In other words the President appears to believe that the United States can win the war, or if you prefer, can avoid losing it. He means by "peace" what other people think of as "victory."

So that is why we are where we are, making the same foolish mistakes and taking the same foolish risks.

It is all so futile; for years now the only question left on Vietnam is how much damage we will do to ourselves as a society. Eighteen months ago a group of foreigners went by Mr. Kissinger's office and talked about Vietnam with him.

Midway through Kissinger's explanation one of the foreigners said it sounded like they were repeating all the old mistakes. Kissinger, who is known and liked for his humor, stopped and answered, no. "We will make our own mistakes in our own way and they will be completely new mistakes." Very funny, very charming. Too bad he was wrong.

David Halberstam received the Pulitzer Prize for his Vietnam reporting while on The New York Times staff. He is a contributing editor of Harper's magazine.

* * *

March 5, 1971

PRESIDENT SAYS LAOS OPERATION AIDS U.S. PULLOUT

States at News Conference Drive Has Seriously Hurt Foe's Military Ability

REPORTS SUPPLIES DROP

He Calls Total Withdrawal Aim but Sets No Date for Last G.I.'s to Depart

By ROBERT B. SEMPLE Jr.
Special to The New York Times

WASHINGTON, March 4—President Nixon said tonight that the allied operation in Laos had "very seriously damaged" Hanoi's military ability and thus assured the continued withdrawal of American troops from South Vietnam this year and next.

In a televised news conference from the East Room of the White House, Mr. Nixon said that he would make another withdrawal announcement in April and that this would reduce American forces at least at the present rate of 12,500 men a month.

At the same time, however, and despite repeated opportunities to do so, Mr. Nixon refused to say when all Americans would be withdrawn. He said that his goal was total withdrawal but that this could not be reached until enemy forces withdrew from South Vietnam, Laos and Cambodia, and until Hanoi released American prisoners of war.

Only Foreign Policy

The questioning at the news conference was limited, by Presidential request, to foreign policy. In the course of the exchange, Mr. Nixon also made the following major points:

- He expressed hope that the cease-fire in the Middle East would be extended beyond the Sunday deadline, tacitly if not by agreement, and declined publicly to put pressure on Israel to make negotiating concessions even though the Arabs have indicated a willingness to sign a peace agreement with Israel.
- He repeated his suggestions in last week's report to the nation on foreign policy that he wished to "normalize" relations with Communist China, but not at the cost of expelling the Chinese Nationalists from the United Nations or otherwise threatening Taiwan's independent existence.
- He described as a "cheap shot" the suggestion by Senator Stuart Symington, Democrat of Missouri, that Secretary of State William P. Rogers had declined in influence and had been replaced by Henry A. Kissinger as the President's most influential adviser on foreign affairs.
- He described himself as still optimistic about what he termed the eventual success of arms limitation talks with the Soviet Union, although he seemed a shade less hopeful that an agreement could be reached soon. He also insisted that the United States would hold out for a settlement imposing limitation on both offensive and defensive nuclear weapons; the Soviet Union has sought to bar defensive missiles first.

Tries to Soften Comment

Mr. Nixon seemed in a relaxed mood in the early part of the news conference, but his reference to Mr. Symington's "cheap shot"—which he promptly tried to soften—brought a trace of perspiration to his upper lip. The question on the Middle East, which invited him to criticize the Israelis publicly, brought irritation to his voice, and on at least one occasion he indicated weariness with what he described as the "drumbeat" of press and television criticism of the operation in Laos.

On the whole, however, he answered questions quickly and smoothly, and while he did not provide much more information than he had at an informal news conference in his office Feb. 17, his aides thought it one of his best performances to date.

Saying he was somewhat surprised at the degree of skepticism about the value of the drive into Laos, Mr. Nixon sought to bolster his assertions by citing a report he said he received today from Gen. Creighton W. Abrams, the United States commander in South Vietnam.

He quoted General Abrams as having said that North Vietnamese supply traffic had already decreased 55 per cent along the Ho Chi Minh Trail of enemy lines—the first figure of this kind supplied by anyone in high authority since the beginning of the operation Feb. 8. He also quoted General Abrams as having commended the quality of the South Vietnamese troops—they "can hack it" by themselves—and he cited statistics suggesting that large numbers of enemy weapons and supplies had been seized.

In reporting the 55 per cent decrease in truck traffic down the trail, Mr. Nixon did not offer any elaboration. Apparently he meant to convey the impression that the decline had occurred since the beginning of the operation, but this was not clear.

Threats by Thieu

As he had at his informal news conference Feb. 17, Mr. Nixon pointedly let stand and indeed seemed to support threats of President Nguyen Van Thieu of a possible South Vietnamese attack against the North.

But he also repeated earlier restrictions on the use of American combat troops outside South Vietnam, and he said twice that "no plan" to use American air power in a South Vietnamese operation against the North "is under consideration" in Washington. He added that no such request for American air support had been received from President Thieu.

Given Three Opportunities

But once again Mr. Nixon refused to rule out completely the possibility of American support of an invasion of North Vietnam, in what was seen as a further apparent effort to keep the enemy off guard and pinned down in his own territory.

The President also repeated his position that he would not hesitate to use American air power against the North if enemy antiaircraft activity threatened American planes or if enemy infiltration seemed to "endanger our remaining forces in South Vietnam, particularly as we are withdrawing."

Mr. Nixon was given three opportunities to answer to speculation that he intended to keep a residual force in Vietnam after the main forces have left. He provided a summary in his first answer when he said in part:

"We are for a total withdrawal of all American forces on a mutual basis. I have stated, however, that as long as there are American P.O.W.'s—and there are 1,600 Americans in North Vietnam jails under very difficult circumstances at the present time—as long as there are American P.O.W.'s in North Vietnam, we will have to maintain a residual force in South Vietnam.

"That is the least that we can negotiate for. As far as our goal is concerned, our goal is to get all Americans out of Vietnam as soon as we can, by negotiation if possible and through our withdrawal program and Vietnamization program if necessary."

* * *

March 7, 1971

U.S. COPTER PILOTS IN LAOS INVASION QUESTION THE RISKS

By IVER PETERSON

Special to The New York Times

KHESANH, South Vietnam, March 6—Peter Hale, a 22-year-old warrant officer, climbed into his helicopter with the terrors of the previous day's mission still clear in his mind. Twelve miles west of here, beyond the Laotian border, the war's heaviest concentration of enemy antiaircraft guns was waiting.

"They are definitely good," said Mr. Hale's co-pilot of the waiting North Vietnamese gunners. "And they're getting better because of all the practice we've given them."

Despite their fear, the American pilots climb into their machines and fill the crude landing fields with the snap and rattle of their whirling rotor blades.

Reliance on Copters

The South Vietnamese sweep in Laos is an airborne operation and the American helicopter is its backbone. Every day for the past three weeks American "choppers" have flown over a thousand sorties a day, ferrying Government troops into Laos, keeping them supplied with "beans and bullets," protecting their base camps, and carrying their dead and wounded back to South Vietnam.

"This is supposed to be a South Vietnamese Army show," said the pilot of a rocket-firing gunship, "but we're still getting our tails shot off over there, and I'd like to know why."

Nearly 2,000 helicopter crewmen are assembled here and at other bases to fly support missions for the South Vietnamese attack on the Ho Chi Minh Trail in Laos.

Loaded with fuel and ammunition, their ungainly machines shudder off the ground in a cloud of red dust and small pebbles and struggle for altitude as they head westward.

The pilots, who are all volunteers, take a professionally courageous attitude toward the enemy groundfire. But they sometimes express resentment at being told to risk their lives for the South Vietnamese.

"Face it," said David Anderson, the 24-year-old pilot of a Slick, or troop-carrying chopper, "I'd rather hang it out for my own people—all of us would. The guys thought they were coming over here to work with Americans, and now we get blown away for people who don't even like us."

The United States command is sensitive about the toll of helicopters taken by the North Vietnamese guns. Officially, 38 have been shot down and destroyed in Laos, but the command refuses to disclose how many aircraft have been shot down and later recovered by American rescue teams. An operations officer has disclosed that as of March 1 the number of such planes was 219.

To achieve this toll, the North Vietnamese have lined the valley of the Se Pone, along which most American choppers fly into Laos, with a heavy concentration of weapons that are dangerous for swift jet fighter bombers and lethal against the slow-moving, delicate helicopters.

"I've brought aircraft back three days in a row with holes in them," said Warrant Officer Lynn Higgins, a 22-year-old helicopter pilot from Provo, Utah.

And like most other pilots, Mr. Higgins has seen his friends' aircraft take hits and falter, and has listened to the stricken planes' last radio messages—"I'm hit, I've lost my hydraulics, engine temp rising"—before they have been engulfed in sudden flames and fallen to the ground.

The mountainous terrain in Laos also helps the enemy, pilots say. "Down in the delta, I just jump over a treeline to get away from groundfire," said Capt. Wayne Baker of Duncan, Okla. "But up in those hills, they have 360-degree vision. They just sit there waiting for you, and when they open up, all you can do is break for the border while they follow you."

There are five basic types of choppers used in the Laotian war, and the pilots of each kind appear to have characters in keeping with their jobs.

The Loaches, the slang expression for light observation helicopters, flew the most dangerous missions until they were withdrawn from the campaign last week because of their vulnerability.

The Loaches depend on their swiftness and maneuverability. They skim along as close to the ground as possible to avoid being in the enemy's sights long enough for him to fire.

Their pilots call themselves "The Buckskin Scouts. "We get out ahead and look for the enemy," said one with the confident humor that is typical of proud men in dangerous jobs. "When we get shot we know we've found him."

The workhorses of the air calvalry are called "Slicks," the stripped down Huey choppers that ferry troops into the fight. "We're just the taxi drivers," said a Slick pilot. "We're not the heroes. We're so funky, no one talks to us, and our door-gunners are so freaky we won't even talk to them."

"There it is," agreed the pilot's scruffy, unshaven door-gunner.

The Slicks are often protected by older model Huey choppers called Charlie Models, which are equipped with rockets and heavy machineguns. Charlie Models are the slowest and most cumbersome of the helicopters and, despite their heavy armament, their crews appear to be the most morose about going into combat.

The aristocrats of helicopter warfare are the Cobra pilots because they undergo 10 months of flight training, instead of the 9 months that other pilots take, and must volunteer for an indefinite tour of duty to be accepted.

The wounded and dead are taken out on Medevas, or medical-evacuation helicopters, which are unarmed Hueys with large red crosses painted on their sides.

"I like it," said one Medevac pilot. "Our mission is to save human lives, and that's a good feeling. I guess I'm a romantic—you have to be to volunteer for over here."

* * *

March 9, 1971

DRAFT EXEMPTION BARRED TO CRITICS OF A SINGLE WAR

High Court Rules Objection Cannot Be Based on the Vietnam Action Alone

DECISION ON AN 8–1 VOTE

Douglas Calls Guarantee of Religious Freedom Shield Against 'Unjust' Conflict

By FRED P. GRAHAM
Special to The New York Times

WASHINGTON, March 8—The Supreme Court ruled today that young men were not entitled to draft exemptions as conscientious objectors if they objected only to the Vietnam conflict as an "unjust war" and did not oppose all wars.

In an 8-to-1 decision, the Court held that Congress had acted constitutionally when it ruled out "selective" conscientious objection by authorizing exemptions only for those men who were "conscientiously opposed to participation in war in any form."

The majority opinion, written by Justice Thurgood Marshall, said that this did not unconstitutionally favor religious denominations that teach total pacifism or did not infringe the freedom of religion of those who believe that only "unjust" wars must be opposed.

Rule Called Neutral

Justice Marshall declared that the rule against selective conscientious objection was essentially neutral in its treatment of various religious faiths and that any "incidental burdens" felt by particular draftees were justified by "the Government's interest in procuring the manpower necessary for military purposes."

The lone dissenter, Justice William O. Douglas, said: "I had assumed that the welfare of the single human soul was the ultimate test of the vitality of the First Amendment."

He argued that whether an individual's abhorrence of killing was the product of religious faith or individual conscience, the First Amendment's guarantee of freedom of religion should shield him from conscription into a war that he believed to be unjust.

In the two cases that were decided today, the Government conceded that each young man was sincere in his conscientious objection to the Vietnam war, but it insisted that they did not qualify for the C.O. exemption created by Congress because they did not oppose all wars.

Appellant From Yonkers

One appellant, Guy Porter Gillette of Yonkers, had told his draft board that his belief in the religion of humanism prevented him from serving in the military during the Vietnam war, which he considered unjust.

He was denied conscientious objector status because he conceded that he would fight in defense of the United States or in a peace-keeping effort by the United Nations. He was convicted of refusing to report for induction.

The other appellant was Louis A. Negre, a French-born Roman Catholic from California who had studied the writings of St. Thomas Aquinas and other Catholic theologians who taught that unjust wars should be opposed.

After being drafted, he applied for a C.O. discharge and was turned down, even though the Army conceded that his objections to the Vietnam conflict were sincere. The lower court supported the Army, and he was sent to Vietnam.

In affirming both actions, the Court dwelt at length on the Government's assertions that its military capacity might be paralyzed if selective conscientious objection were recognized as a constitutional right.

Justice Marshall said that draft boards would be saddled with the touchy task of deciding which draftees were sincere and which were having convenient attacks of conscience. Also, he said, the nature of an unpopular war might change so that those who once considered it unjust would change their minds.

Subordination of Views

He concluded that "the nature of conscription, much less war itself, requires the personal desires and perhaps the dissenting view of those who must serve to be subordinated in some degree to the pursuit of public purposes."

The legal provision under dispute was Section 6 (j), of the Military Selective Service Act of 1967. It provides that no person shall be subject to "service in the armed forces of the United States who, by reason of religious training and belief, is conscientiously opposed to participation in war in any form."

The two would-be C.O.'s had asserted that, by not honoring the "unjust war" doctrine, Congress had violated the First Amendment's prohibition against an official "establishment of religion" that favored certain denominations, as well as the Constitution's guarantee of "free exercise" of religion.

Justice Marshall said that First Amendment values must be weighed against other considerations and concluded that here the public considerations outweighed the individual's feelings.

A Justice Department spokesman said today that "quite a few" indictments against men who had refused induction as selective conscientious objectors would now be issued. The charges had been held pending today's decision.

The Selective Service System director, Curtis W. Tarr, was said by his office to be "relieved" by the decision because he believed that the draft system could not operate if selective conscientious objections were authorized. The spokesman said that Mr. Tarr also feared that Congress would eliminate the C.O. exemption entirely if the Supreme Court broadened it to include selective conscientious objectors.

The rise in the number of C.O. exemptions is expected to continue, however, because of earlier Supreme Court rulings that include any man whose opposition to warfare is "deeply felt." Since 1965 the rate of conscientious objector applications has doubled. From last August through Jan. 1 there were 56,700 applicants for C.O. and 18,700 were granted.

Conrad J. Lynn of New York argued for Mr. Gillette. Richard Harrington of San Francisco argued for Mr. Negre. Solicitor General Erwin N. Griswold argued for the United States.

* * *

March 28, 1971

SPIRIT OF SAIGON'S ARMY SHAKEN IN LAOS

By GLORIA EMERSON
Special to The New York Times

KHESANH, South Vietnam, March 27—The morale of many soldiers in South Vietnam's finest military units, who fought the North Vietnamese in Laos, is shattered.

Men in the crack First Infantry Division, in the marines and in the Airborne Division say that the Laos invasion was a nightmare for them and for other soldiers.

Through an interpreter they spoke of how the North Vietnamese outnumbered them and advanced in wave after wave, running over the bodies of comrades and never stopping.

In low, strained voices, the South Vietnamese spoke of what they termed the enemy's ability to survive American air strikes and B-52 bombings, which they themselves feared so much.

While these men did not say that they spoke for all the 20,000 South Vietnamese soldiers who took part in the Laos campaign, they asserted that the morale of their fellow soldiers was low. Those interviewed were in the state of dejected fatigue that is common to men coming out of a long retreat under heavy enemy fire, and perhaps their views will be less gloomy after some rest.

In Saigon, for example, a paratroop lieutenant who was wounded early in the campaign said that for the next six months his men would prefer to desert and risk jail rather than go into such a battle again, but that later, perhaps, they would be ready to face the enemy once more.

For many of the South Vietnamese soldiers, most of whom are in their twenties, the Laos campaign was their first fierce encounter with North Vietnamese ground forces: not for years has there been major fighting in South Vietnam to compare with the operation against enemy supply trails in Laos.

It was a test, and now most South Vietnamese veterans frankly admit that their forces failed. They had no chance, these men say.

Although it is not known whether the effects of the Laos operation will be permanent, some experienced South Vietnamese noncommissioned officers are wondering if their units will be able to fight well again and respect their officers.

What has dramatically demoralized many of the South Vietnamese troops is the large number of their own wounded who were left behind, begging for their friends to shoot them or to leave hand grenades so they could commit suicide before the North Vietnamese or the B-52 raids killed them.

Experienced in Cambodia

Some soldiers who had been in the drive into Cambodia last year said they had never dreamed that the Laos operation would not be as simple. Since there was no significant fighting in Cambodia, these South Vietnamese felt that the enemy was no longer a threat. They learned differently in Laos and they will not soon forget it.

"The best units were sent in and the best units got the worst beating in combat," Sgt. Nguyen Van Lac said. "Now you see the North Vietnamese chasing us out. We lost 59 artillery pieces—105-mm and 155-mm howitzers—or the equivalent of three artillery battalions."

The sergeant is an artillery liaison man at the forward command post here of an American unit, the First Brigade of the Fifth Infantry Division (Mechanized).

More chilling accounts of the Laos fighting came from the men who lived through it, the tired and shaken men who said they were not prepared for what had happened.

Without Packs or Helmets

In American helicopters they came out of Laos this week without their combat packs, their rations or their steel helmets—and sometimes without their weapons. Nothing mattered, they said, except getting out.

One of them was a 22-year-old marine who came back to South Vietnam on Wednesday after walking through the jungle for two nights and a day before the airlift.

His version of the fighting near a fire base called Delta on Hill 547, about eight miles inside Laos, told how the South Vietnamese troops ran for their lives, each man struggling for himself only.

"The last attack came at about 8 P.M.," Private Moc, the marine, said in Vietnamese. "They shelled us first and then came the tanks moving up into our positions. The whole brigade ran down the hill like ants. We jumped on each other to get out of that place. No man had time to look for his commanding officer. It was quick, quick, quick or we would die. Oh God, now I know for sure that I am really still alive."

Afraid of Punishment

Private Moc asked, as did other men, that his full name and unit be withheld for he was afraid that he would be punished for telling what happened to him.

"When I was far from the hill, with about 20 other marines, there was a first lieutenant with us," he continued. "We moved like ghosts, terrified of being ambushed by the North Vietnamese. We stopped many times when there was firing—not daring to breathe. How terrible those minutes were."

Private Moc came back to South Vietnam with the legs of his pants ripped off, and his thigh showing through the tatters. A small thin man, he had only his M-16 rifle left of his equipment. He continued his account of the action in Laos:

"Only last Tuesday our group bumped into a North Vietnamese unit, and we ran again like ants. And the Lieutenant, he whispered to us 'Disperse, disperse, don't stick together or we will all be killed.' After each firing, there were fewer and fewer of us. Nobody cared for anybody else at all."

The Scream to Attack

What made his blood run cold, Private Moc said, was how the North Vietnamese kept coming and coming, running over the bodies of their own men, and not stopping.

"They were everywhere and they were so daring," he said. "Their firepower was so enormous, and their shelling was so accurate, that what could we do except run for our lives."

Hearing the assault shout of the North Vietnamese, remembering how they screamed "Xung phong!" will long haunt one man, Sgt. Nguyen Minh. He fought with Brigade A of the Second Marine Artillery Battalion.

The entire brigade ran away, he said.

'Surrender, Brothers'

Its position in Laos was south of Route 9, the east west axis of the drive, about seven miles inside the border. The brigade arrived there March 5 and stayed for two weeks before it retreated.

"For days," he related "we had been made desperate by their constant shellings and assaults, by their strange attitude of ignoring death and always moving closer and closer to us. Never were the marines in such trouble, and we were never so afraid.

"They knew everything about us. They shouted to us, 'We know that you are Company One of Battalion Two, surrender brothers. We have hot meals and hot tea for you out here!'

"And then, hearing them shout for assault, knowing they were all around us, our fear was so great."

An infantry platoon leader who has been in the army for 18 years also discussed the terror he felt in Laos.

Sergeant Co, 38, is now AWOL. He does not care.

"All that counts is surviving the Laos operation," he said. "Being absent for a few days, getting some punishment, that is nothing to me."

There was no room on the American helicopters that came to pick up his battalion in Laos on March 6, so Sergeant Co clung to the skids of one craft.

"Each helicopter could have been the last one, so what choice was there for me?" he asked. "Only the madmen would stay and politely wait for the next helicopter."

During the last three days his battalion was in Laos, he said, 30 of the men were killed and 20 wounded. "Only about 100 men were still okay at the end out of 400," Sergeant Co said. "The North Vietnamese could have killed us all if they had wanted to do it."

A Corporal Remembers

A corporal in the marines who fought on Hill 547 in Laos on the night of March 22 said that many of his friends had killed themselves because they were wounded. No American helicopters could extract them because of heavy antiaircraft fire.

"The papers and the radio in Saigon kept on saying there was a Laos victory, I have learned now, but what a joke," Corporal Ti said. "We ran out like wounded dogs."

"The most heartbreaking thing," he continued, "was that we left behind our wounded friends. They lay there crying, knowing the B-52 bombs would fall on them. They asked buddies to shoot them but none of us could bring himself to do that. So the wounded cried out for grenades, first one man, then another, then more."

"I could not bear it," he said. "We ran out at 8 P.M. and about midnight we heard the bombs explode behind us. No more bodies! They all became dust. Some men who were wounded in the legs or arms tried to run out with us, but they could not make it."

As for the effect these experiences will have on the soldiers, a 38-year-old sergeant major who has seen combat with the infantry many times in the last 11 years is worried.

"I am afraid that we will have a lot of deserters," said the sergeant, who did not want to give his name. "When many of the men get back to the rear, and think back on what they have been through, and hear the other soldiers talk then their fear will get worse.

"It can happen. I know this kind of thing all too well."

* * *

March 28, 1971

SHOULD WE HAVE WAR CRIME TRIALS?

By NEIL SHEEHAN

The Book Review received the accompanying bibliography from Mr. Mark Sacharoff, assistant professor of English at Temple University, and sent the books to Neil Sheehan for review.

AGAINST THE CRIME OF SILENCE
Edited by John Duffet
672 pp. New York: Simon & Schuster-Clarion. Paper, $3.95.

AIR WAR—VIETNAM
By Frank Harvey
192 pp. New York: Bantam. Paper, 75 cents.

ATROCITIES IN VIETNAM
By Edward S. Herman
Illustrated. 104 pp. Philadelphia: Pilgrim Press. Paper, $1.95.

AT WAR WITH ASIA
By Noam Chomsky
314 pp. New York: Pantheon. Cloth, $7.95. Vintage. Paper, $1.95.

CASUALTIES OF WAR
By Daniel Lang
123 pp. New York: McGraw-Hill. Cloth, $4.50. Paper, $1.50.

CHEMICAL AND BIOLOGICAL WARFARE: Hearings of the U.S. Senate Committee on Foreign Relations.
Free from the Committee, U.S. Senate Office Building, Washington.

CHEMICAL AND BIOLOGICAL WARFARE
By Seymour M. Hersh
354 pp. Indianapolis and New York: Bobbs-Merrill. $7.50.

CHEMICAL AND BIOLOGICAL WARFARE
Edited by Steven Rose
209 pp. Boston: Beacon Press. Cloth, $7.50. Paper, $1.95.

CHEMICAL WARFARE
By Maj. Frederic J. Brown
355 pp. Princeton, N. J.: Princeton University Press. $11.

CONVERSATIONS WITH AMERICANS
By Mark Lane
248 pp. New York: Simon & Schuster. $6.95.

CRIMES OF WAR
Edited by Richard A. Falk, Gabriel Kolko and Robert J. Lifton.
608 pp. New York: Random House. Available late April.

DEFOLIATION
By Thomas Whiteside
168 pp. New York: Friends of the Earth-Ballantine.
Paper, 95 cents.

THE DESTRUCTION OF INDOCHINA
By The Stanford Biology Study Group
Box 3724, Stanford, Calif, 94305. Paper, 25 cents.

ECOCIDE IN INDOCHINA
By Barry Weisberg
Illustrated. 241 pp. New York: Canfield Press-Harper & Row.
Paper, $3.95.

EFFICIENCY IN DEATH
Sponsored by The Council On Economic Priorities
Illustrated. 233 pp. New York: Harper & Row. Paper, $1.50.

IN THE NAME OF AMERICA
Research Director, Seymour Melman
421 pp. New York: Clergy & Laymen Concerned About Vietnam, Room 547, 475 Riverside Drive, New York 10027. Cloth, $4.95.
Paper, $2.95.

THE INDOCHINA STORY
By The Committee of Concerned Asian Scholars
348 pp. New York: Pantheon. Cloth, $8.95. Bantam. Paper, $1.25.

MILITARISM, U.S.A.
By Col. James A. Donovan
265 pp. New York: Charles Scribner's Sons. Cloth, $6.95.
Paper, $2.95.

THE MILITARY HALF
By Jonathan Schell
224 pp. New York: Alfred A. Knopf. Cloth, $4.95. Vintage.
Paper, $1.65.

MY LAI 4
By Seymour M. Hersh
210 pp. New York: Random House. Cloth, $5.95.
Vintage. Paper, $1.95.

NUREMBERG AND VIETNAM
By Telford Taylor
A New York Times Book. 224 pp. Chicago: Quadrangle Books.
Cloth, $5.95. Paper, $1.95.

ONE MORNING IN THE WAR
By Richard Hammer
207 pp. New York: Coward, McCann & Geoghegan. Cloth, $5.95.
Paper, $3.95.

REFUGEE AND CIVILIAN WAR CASUALTY PROBLEMS IN INDOCHINA
Staff Report of the U. S. Senate Subcommittee on Refugees.
By Dale S. de Haan and Jerry Tinker. Free from the Subcommittee, U.S. Senate Office Building, Washington.

REFUGEE AND CIVILIAN WAR CASUALTY PROBLEMS IN LAOS AND CAMBODIA: Hearing of the U.S. Senate Subcommittee on Refugees.
Free from the Subcommittee, U.S. Senate Office Building, Washington.

REVOLUTIONARY NON VIOLENCE
By David Dellinger
390 pp. Indianapolis and New York: Bobbs-Merrill. Cloth, $7.50.
New York: Anchor. Paper, $2.50.

THE SILENT WEAPONS
By Robin Clarke
270 pp. New York: David McKay. $4.95.

THE SOCIAL RESPONSIBILITY OF THE SCIENTIST
Edited by Martin Brown
282 pp. New York: The Free Press. Cloth, $7.95.
Paper, $3.95.

THE ULTIMATE FOLLY
By Richard D. McCarthy
176 pp. New York: Alfred A. Knopf. Cloth, $5.95.
Vintage. Paper, $1.95.

VIETNAM AND ARMAGEDDON
By Robert F. Drinan, S.J.
210 pp. New York: Sheed & Ward.
$5.95.

THE VILLAGE OF BEN SUC
By Jonathan Schell
132 pp. New York: Alfred A. Knopf. Cloth, $4.95.
Vintage. Paper, $1.65.

WAR CRIMES AND THE AMERICAN CONSCIENCE
Edited by Erwin Knoll and Judith N. McFadden
208 pp. New York: Holt, Rinehart & Winston. Cloth, $5.95.
Paper, $2.95.

WEAPONS FOR COUNTERINSURGENCY
National Action/Research on the Military Industrial Complex
Illustrated
124 pp. Philadelphia: American Friends Service Committee. Paper, $1.

WHY ARE WE STILL IN VIETNAM?
Edited by Sam Brown and Len Ackland
144 pp. New York: Random House. Cloth, $5.95.
Vintage. Paper, $1.95.

"The tragic story of Vietnam is not, in truth, a tale of malevolent men bent upon conquest for personal gain or imperial glory. It is the story of an entire generation of leaders (and an entire generation of followers) so conditioned by the tensions of the cold war years that they were unable to perceive in 1965 (and later) that the Communist adversary was no longer a monolith . . . Lyndon Johnson, though disturbingly volatile, was not in his worst moments an evil man in the Hitlerian sense . . . Set against these facts, the easy designation of individuals as deliberate or imputed 'war criminals' is shockingly glib, even if one allows for the inexperience of the young."—Townsend Hoopes, the former Under Secretary of the Air Force, January, 1970.

Is the accusation glib? Or is it too unpleasant to think about? Do you have to be Hitlerian to be a war criminal? Or can you qualify as a well-intentioned President of the United States? Even when I saw those signs during the March on the Pentagon in 1967, "Hey, Hey L.B.J. How many kids did you kill today?" they didn't make me think that Lyndon Johnson, the President of the United States, might be a war criminal. A misguided man perhaps, an egomaniac at worst, but not a war criminal. That would have been just too much. Kids do get killed in war. Besides, I'd never read the laws governing the conduct of war, although I had watched the war for three years in Vietnam and had written about it for five. Apparently, a lot of the men in Saigon and Washington who were directing the war didn't read those laws either, or if they did, they interpreted them rather loosely.

Now a lot of other people are examining our behavior in Vietnam in the light of these laws. Mark Sacharoff, an assistant professor of English at Temple University, has gathered their work together into this bibliography. By this simple act he has significantly widened our consciousness. If you credit as factual only a fraction of the information assembled here about what happened in Vietnam, and if you apply the laws of war to American conduct there, then the leaders of the United States for the past six years at least, including the incumbent, President Richard Milhous Nixon, may well be guilty of war crimes.

There is the stuff of five Dreyfus affairs in that thought. This is what makes the growing literature on alleged war crimes in Vietnam so important. This bibliography represents the beginning of what promises to be a long and painful inquest into what we are doing in Southeast Asia. The more perspective we gain on our behavior, the uglier our conduct appears. At first it had seemed unfortunate and sad; we were caught in the quicksand of Indochina. Then our conduct had appeared stupid and brutal, the quagmire was of our own making, the Vietnamese were the victims and we were the executioners. Now we're finding out that we may have taken life, not merely as cruel and stubborn warriors, but as criminals. We are conditioned as a nation to believe that only our enemies commit war crimes. Certainly the enemy in Indochina has perpetrated crimes. The enemy's war crimes, however, will not wash us clean if we too are war criminals.

What are the laws of war? One learns that there is a whole body of such laws, ranging from specific military regulations like the Army's Field Manual 27–10, "The Law of Land Warfare," to the provisions of the Hague and Geneva Conventions, which are United States law by virtue of Senate ratification, to the broad principles laid down by the Nuremberg and Tokyo war crimes tribunals. These laws say that all is not fair in war, that there are limits to what belligerent man may do to mankind. As the Hague Convention of 1907 put it, "The right of belligerents to adopt means of injuring the enemy is not unlimited." In other words, some acts in war are illegal and they aren't all as obviously illegal as the massacre of several hundred Vietnamese villagers at Mylai.

Let's take a look at our conduct in Vietnam through the viewing glass of these laws. The Army Field Manual says that it is illegal to attack hospitals. We routinely bombed and shelled them. The destruction of Vietcong and North Vietnamese Army Hospitals in the South Vietnamese countryside was announced at the daily press briefings, the Five o'Clock Follies, by American military spokesmen in Saigon.

So somebody may have committed a war crime in attacking those hospitals. The Manual also says that a military commander acquires responsibility for war crimes if he knows they are being committed, "or should have knowledge, through reports received by him or through other means," and he fails to take action to stop them. President Johnson kept two wire-service teletypes in his office and he read the newspapers like a bear. There are thus grounds for believing that he may have known his Air Force and artillery were blowing up enemy hospitals. He was the Commander in Chief. Did his knowledge make him a war criminal? The Army Manual says that "every violation of the law of war is a war crime."

Let's proceed to one of the basic tactics the United States used to prosecute the war in South Vietnam—unrestricted air and artillery bombardments of peasant hamlets. Since 1965, a minimum of 150,000 Vietnamese civilians, an average of 68 men, women and children every day for the past six years, have been killed in the south by American military action or by weapons supplied to the Saigon forces by the United States. Another 350,000 Vietnamese civilians have been wounded or permanently maimed. This is a very conservative estimate. It is based on official figures assembled by Senator Edward M. Kennedy's Senate Subcommittee on Refugees and on a study for the Subcommittee by those eminent Government auditors, the General Accounting Office. The real toll may be much higher. This conservative attitude makes the documentation put together by the Senator and his staff aides, Jerry Tinker and Dale S. de Haan, among the most impressive in the bibliography. Many, perhaps the majority, of those half million civilian casualties were caused by the air and artillery bombardments of peasant hamlets authorized by the American military and civilian leaders in Saigon and Washington.

The United States Government tried and hanged in 1946 a Japanese general, Tomoyuki Yamashita, because he was held responsible for the deaths of more than 25,000 noncombatants killed by his troops in the Philippines.

Can a moral and legal distinction be drawn between those killings in World War II, for which General Yamashita paid with his life, and the civilian deaths ordered or condoned by American leaders during the Vietnam war? Again, if you accept only a portion of the evidence presented in this bibliography, and compare that evidence to the laws of war, the probable answer is, No. And President Nixon has spread this unrestricted bombing through Laos and Cambodia, killing and wounding unknown tens of thousands of civilians in those countries.

Looking back, one realizes that the war-crimes issue was always present. Our vision was so narrowly focused on the unfolding details of the war that we lacked the perspective to see it, or when the problem was held up to us, we paid no heed. This lesson becomes clear in reading the proceedings of the Russell Tribunal now published in "Against the Crime of Silence." The proceedings were widely dismissed in 1967 as a combination of kookery and leftist propaganda. They should not have been. Although the proceedings were one sided, the perspective was there.

One saw the substance all the time in Vietnam in the bombing and shelling of the peasant hamlets. In November, 1965, I found five fishing hamlets on the coast of Quangngai Province in central Vietnam, not far from Mylai, which had been ravaged over the previous two months by the five-inch guns of United States Navy destroyers and by American and South Vietnamese fighter-bombers. The local Vietnamese officials told me that at least 184 civilians had been killed. After a day of interviewing the survivors among the ruins, I concluded that a reasonable estimate might run as high as 600 dead. American Army officers working in the province told me that the most serious resistance the Vietcong guerrillas in the hamlets had offered was sniper fire. The hamlets and all their inhabitants had been attacked just because the Vietcong were present. I discovered that another 10 hamlets in the province had also been gutted and about 25 others severely damaged, all for like reasons.

Making the peasants pay so dearly for the presence of guerrillas in their hamlets, regardless of whether they sympathized with the Vietcong, seemed unnecessarily brutal and politically counter-productive to me, since this Hun-like treatment would alienate them from the Saigon authorities and the American forces. No common-sense military purpose seemed to be served. When I wrote my story describing the agony of the fisher folk, however, it did not occur to me that I had discovered a possible war crime. The thought also does not seem to have occurred to my editors or to most readers of The Times. None of the similar stories that I and other reporters wrote later on provoked any outrage, except among that minority with the field of vision to see what was happening. As Lieutenant Calley told the prosecutor at Fort Benning. "It wasn't any big deal, sir."

Reading through the news dispatches from 1965, 1966 and 1967 that Seymour Melman of Columbia and Richard Falk of Princeton assembled to document accusations of war crimes made by The Clergy and Laymen Concerned About Vietnam, "In the Name of America," is to view those scenes again in this new and disturbing perspective. Frank Harvey, in "Air War—Vietnam," recounts with the power of anecdotal narrative the casual destruction of peasant hamlets in the Mekong Delta by the United States Air Force. Usually the excuse was that a squad or so of guerrillas might be present in the hamlet or the mere location of the hamlet in guerrilla-dominated territory. Harvey is a convincing witness because he concludes with a defense of the war.

You might argue that this destruction, and concomitant loss of civilian life, were not deliberate, that they were among those haphazard horrors of war. The record says otherwise.

As early as the fall of 1965, the American Embassy in Saigon distributed to correspondents a Rand Corporation study on the air and artillery bombardments. The study concluded that the peasants blamed the Vietcong when their hamlets were blasted and their relatives killed; in effect, that shrapnel, white phosphorous and napalm were good political medicine. The study was dismissed by reporters as macabre proof that the Government could always find a think tank to tell it what it wanted to think.

In the summer of 1966, however, a lengthy secret study of the pacification program was done for the Embassy and military headquarters in Saigon by some of the most experienced Americans in the country. One of the study's recommendations was that this practice of unrestricted bombing and shelling should be carefully re-examined. According to the study there was evidence that the practice was driving hundreds of thousands of refugees into urban slums and squalid camps, causing unnecessary death and suffering, and angering the peasantry. The proposal for a re-examination was vetoed at the highest levels of American authority in Saigon.

By deciding not to reconsider, the American leadership in Saigon was deciding to ordain the practice, to establish a de facto policy. During those earlier years at least, the policy was not acknowledged in writing as far as I know, but neither can there be any doubt that this was the way things were to be done and that those American military and civilian leaders directing the war knew the grim cost of their decision not to look. Why did they establish the policy? Because devastation had become a fundamental element in their strategy to win the war.

I remember asking one of the most senior American generals in the late summer of 1966 if he was not worried by all the civilian casualties that the bombing and shelling were causing. "Yes, it is a problem," he said, "but it does deprive the enemy of the population, doesn't it?" A survey of refugees commissioned later that year by the Pentagon indicated that 54 per cent of those in Dinhtuong Province in the Mekong Delta were fleeing their hamlets in fear of bombing and shelling. So this was the game. The firepower that only American technology can muster, the General Motors of death we invented in World War II, was to defeat the Vietnamese Communists by outright military attrition, the body count, and by obliterating their strategic base, the rural population.

If you destroyed the rural society, you destroyed the resources the enemy needed to fight. You deprived him of recruits in the South, of the food and the intelligence the peasantry provide; you reversed Mao Tsetung's axiom by drying up the sea (the peasantry) in which the guerrillas swam.

All of those directives issued by the American military headquarters in Saigon about taking care to avoid civilian casualties, about protecting the livestock and the homes of the peasantry, were the sort of pharisaic prattle you hear from many American institutions. Whenever you say the institution is not behaving as it says it should, the institution can always point to a directive and say you must be mistaken. (General Electric had directives forbidding price fixing when some of its vice presidents were convicted of price fixing.) No one was fooling himself when he marked off those "free-fire zones," and ordered those "preplanned airstrikes" and that "harassing and interdiction fire" by the artillery. People and their homes were dehumanized into grid coordinates on a targeting map. Those other formalities, like obtaining clearance from the Vietnamese province chief before you bombed a hamlet, were stratagems to avoid responsibility, because he almost never refused permission. (Such legal fictions, by the way, are expressly forbidden by the laws of war.)

Out in the countryside the captains and majors did not disguise the design. One day in a heavily populated province in the Mekong Delta, a young Army captain swept his hand across the map over a couple of dozen hamlets in guerrilla-dominated territory near the provincial capital and remarked that the peasants were evacuating them and moving in near town. Why? I asked. "Because it's not healthy out there. We're shelling the hell out of them," he said.

By 1967, this policy of unrestricted air and artillery bombardments had been orchestrated with search and destroy operations by ground troops, B-52 strikes, and crop destruction with chemical herbicides into a strategy that was progressively laying waste much of the countryside. (The question of whether herbicides were dumped on the landscape to an extent that may constitute a separate war crime is treated at length in several of the books Mr. Sacharoff lists.) That year Jonathan Schell went to Quangnai to document the creeping destruction of the rural society in a two-part article that first appeared in The New Yorker magazine. It was later published with a title of understated irony, "The Military Half." Schell estimated that by this time about 70 per cent of the 450 hamlets in the province had been destroyed.

Did the military and civilian leaders directing the war from Washington know what was happening in Vietnam? How could they have avoided knowing? The newspapers, magazine articles like Schell's and the reports of the Kennedy Subcommittee indicated the extent of what was being done in their name. The statistics alone are enough to tell the tale: five million refugees, nearly a third of South Vietnam's population of 16 million people, and that conservative estimate of the civilian casualties from what is called "friendly" military action, of at least 150,000 dead and 350,000 wounded or maimed.

These peasant hamlets, one must bear in mind, were not being plowed under because American or South Vietnamese ground troops were attempting to seize them from the enemy in pitched battles. The hamlets were being bombarded in the absence of ground combat.

One might argue that though regrettable, though even immoral, the indiscriminate air and artillery bombardments of civilians in Vietnam were not a war crime. The Allies engaged in terror bombing of Japanese and German cities in World War II. Look at the incendiary raids on Dresden and Tokyo and the nuclear holocausts of Hiroshima and Nagasaki. None of the defendants at the Nuremberg and Tokyo trials were convicted of war crimes involving the bombing of civilian populations, because the prosecutors had done the same thing. By custom, therefore, one might argue, terror bombing is an accepted practice of war. Similarly, in the Korean War, the United States Air Force bombed Korean towns and cities.

But is Vietnam the same kind of war? There is good reason to think that it is not. In World War II opposing industrialized societies were fighting a war of survival. In this context of total war, the cities inevitably became targets to be destroyed. They contained the industries that fueled their opponent's war machine and the workers who manned the factories. The worker was as much a combatant as the uniformed soldier. Korea was also, more or less, a conventional conflict between uniformed armies, although bombing practices there would bear examination in the perspective of history.

In Vietnam, however, the most advanced technological nation in the world intervened in a civil war in a primitive, agricultural country. The Vietnamese Communists possess negligible industry, no air force of any size, and no intercontinental missiles that pose a threat to the survival of the United States. The intervention was, rather, undertaken for reasons of domestic politics and foreign policy, to avoid the repercussions at home of losing a war to Communists and to maintain a position of power and influence for the United States in Southeast Asia.

Moreover, as the literature in Sacharoff's bibliography amply documents, the use of the air weapon underwent a subtle and important change in South Vietnam from the previous two wars. Air power and artillery as a corollary weapon were directed by an occupying power, the United States, at the civilian population in the rural areas of the country under occupation. The targets of the bombs and shells were the noncombatants themselves, because it was believed that their existence was important to the enemy. Air power became a distinct weapon of terror to empty the countryside. Samuel P.

Huntington, of Harvard, has even coined a marvelously American euphemism for the technique—"forced-draft urbanization and modernization." Some of us prefer a quotation from Tacitus that the late Bernard Fall was fond of citing: "Where they make a desert they call it peace."

One key to understanding this use of airpower in South Vietnam is to compare the unrestricted bombing in the south with the elaborate restrictions that surrounded the air campaign against North Vietnam.

Although the North Vietnamese may not believe it, in the North a conscious effort was made to bomb only military, and what limited industrial targets were available, and to weigh probable civilian casualties against the military advantages to be gained from a particular airstrike. The ultimate objective of the air campaign against the North was to be sure, political rather than military. It sought to intimidate the North Vietnamese into withdrawing their forces from the South and taking the Vietcong guerrillas along with them. And undoubtedly the restrictions were also designed to escape the unfavorable publicity that would result from severe civilian casualties in the North.

The mere fact that an attempt was made to avoid them throws into sharp understanding the very different motives that lay behind the bombing in the south and the inherent acceptance of great civilian suffering. When Harrison Salisbury, an assistant managing editor of The New York Times, visited North Vietnam in December, 1966, to write his memorable series of articles on the destruction wrought by American air raids there (civilian homes, schools, hospitals and churches had been wrecked because the air campaign had never been the surgical operation Pentagon propaganda portrayed it as being), the most severe example of civilian deaths the North Vietnamese claimed was 89 in the town of Nandinh southeast of Hanoi, from six months of bombing, less than half the official South Vietnamese estimate of the number of civilians killed in the five hamlets I found on the coast of Quangngai Province in 1965.

Did the employment of the air weapon and the artillery in South Vietnam thus exceed the limits sanctioned by the laws of war?

The United States Army Field Manual says: "The law of war . . . requires that belligerents refrain from employing any kind or degree of violence which is not actually necessary for military purposes and that they conduct hostilities with regard for the principles of humanity and chivalry." The Manual goes on to explain what is meant by "actually necessary for military purposes," i.e. military necessity. "The prohibitory effect of the law of war is not minimized by 'military necessity' which has been defined as that principle which justifies those measures not forbidden by international law which are indispensable for securing the complete submission of the enemy as soon as possible. Military necessity has been rejected as a defense for acts forbidden by the customary or conventional laws of war inasmuch as the latter have been developed and framed with consideration for the concept of military necessity." In short, if you can demonstrate certain measures are required to defeat the enemy, and those measures are not specifically forbidden by the laws of war, you employ them.

Assuming that the use of air power in South Vietnam was not specifically forbidden by the laws of war, was this means necessary to defeat the enemy? He could have been deprived of the rural population by another, more humane method. This would have involved putting sufficient American ground troops in South Vietnam to occupy most of the countryside and thereby gain control over the rural hamlets. National mobilization and the dispatch of upwards of 600,000 troops to South Vietnam was proposed by the Joint Chiefs of Staff and rejected by President Johnson and his advisers, because this strategy would have meant higher draft calls, wage and price controls, and other measures that would have been unpopular with the American public. So there are grounds for believing that the use of the air weapon in the South was not a military necessity but a political convenience, a substitute for sufficient infantrymen to hold the countryside.

I am not saying that garrisoning South Vietnam with ground troops would have made the war a sensible enterprise. I am suggesting that the war's impact upon the Vietnamese might have been more merciful. The Marines, because of their pre-World-War-II experience with pacification in Central America and the Caribbean, did make an attempt to hold a good many of the hamlets in central Vietnamese provinces where they operated. Life for a Vietnamese farmer within these zones was safer than for his brethren in other regions.

In any case, to address the basic question of legal sanctions, it appears that the employment of air and artillery to terrorize the peasantry and raze the countryside was an act specifically forbidden by the laws of war. The Geneva Convention of 1949 Relative to the Protection of Civilian Persons in Time of War states:

"The High Contracting Parties specifically agree that each of them is prohibited from taking any measure of such a character as to cause the physical suffering or extermination of protected persons [civilians] in their hands. This prohibition applies not only to murder, torture, corporal punishment, mutilation and medical or scientific experiments not necessitated by the medical treatment of a protected person, but also to any other measures of brutality whether applied by civilian or military agents.

"No protected person may be punished for an offense he or she has not personally committed. Collective penalties and likewise all measures of intimidation or of terrorism are prohibited.

"Pillage is prohibited.

"Reprisals against protected persons and their property are prohibited."

The paragraphs seem to be a reasonably fair description of what was inflicted upon much of the South Vietnamese peasantry by the United States.

The Army Field Manual is more specific. "The measure of permissible devastation is found in the strict necessities of war," it says. "Devastation as an end in itself *or as a separate measure of war* [italics added] is not sanctioned by the law of war."

The adoption of devastation as a basic element of strategy also seems to have led American leaders into what may be related war crimes against South Vietnamese civilians. The Geneva Convention of 1949 states that a belligerent power has a duty, in so far as it is able, to care for the victims of war.

"The wounded and the sick, as well as the infirm, and expectant mothers, shall be the object of particular protection and respect. As far as military considerations allow, each party to the conflict shall facilitate the steps taken to search for the killed and wounded, to assist the ship-wrecked and other persons exposed to grave danger, and to protect them against pillage and ill-treatment."

The consignment of Vietnamese civilian war wounded to provincial hospitals that were little better than charnel houses has been a national scandal for the United States. The reports of the Kennedy Subcommittee describe the scenes of two wounded to a bed, no sheets or mattresses, no showers, filthy toilets, open sewers and swarms of flies spreading infection. In contrast, the United States military hospitals are models of medical science. Given the wide publicity the deplorable conditions in these Vietnamese civilian hospitals have received over the years, would it be possible for the responsible leaders of the United States to contend that the neglect was not deliberate?

A similar war crime may have been committed against civilians forcibly evacuated from their homes. These persons would appear to fall under the category of internees in the Geneva Convention of 1949. The Convention lays out in great detail the obligation of a belligerent power to provide such persons with adequate food, housing and medical care. Here is an excerpt from a report to the Kennedy Subcommittee by a team from the General Accounting Office which inspected so-called refugee camps in South Vietnam last summer. The excerpt describes a camp in Quangnam Province on the central coast:

"At this location, there were about 2,070 people. We were informed that only 883 were recognized as refugees and that they would receive temporary benefits. We were advised that these people were all Vietcong families and that they were relocated by force in February or March 1970. These people are under heavy guard by the Vietnamese military.

"During our inspection, we observed there were no latrines, no usable wells, no classrooms, and no medical facilities. The shelters were crudely constructed from a variety of waste material, such as empty ammunition boxes and cardboard. We observed that the number of shelters would not adequately house these people . . . The [American] refugee adviser stated that there were no plans to improve the living conditions at this site."

The fact that these persons are being held by the South Vietnamese authorities apparently does not absolve the United States of responsibility under the laws of war. Legally they remain our refugees. As the Army Field Manual explains:

"The restrictions placed upon the authority of a belligerent government cannot be avoided by a system of using a puppet government, central or local, to carry out acts which would be unlawful if performed directly by the occupant. Acts induced or compelled by the occupant are nonetheless its acts." The Saigon regime is not a puppet government, but it is a client regime whose existence is dependent upon the United States. A good argument could be made that because of this client relationship, the United States induces these acts. Telford Taylor, of Columbia, the former chief American prosecutor of Nuremberg, quantifies the neglect of the civilian war wounded and refugees. In "Nuremberg and Vietnam: An American Tragedy," he notes that the United States spent, at the most, a quarter-billion dollars to ease the civilian plight over the three years from 1965 through 1967. You will think this is a lot of money, until he tells you the amount was less than four per cent of the cost of air operations over the same period.

What about a relationship between the use of airpower and artillery in South Vietnam and the garden variety war crimes that many of the books in this bibliography allege—the individual acts of torture and murder of prisoners and civilians by American soldiers, the burning of peasant huts in "Zippo raids," the looting and the rape? Did the conduct of the war as approved at the highest levels create an atmosphere in which the lives of the Vietnamese were so cheapened that they became subhumans in the eyes of the soldier? If so, did this atmosphere help to incite these individual war crimes, given the traditional racism of Americans towards Asians—the dinks, the gooks, the slopeheads—and the psychological stress upon the soldier of fighting in a country where much of the population is hostile, where women and children do set mines and boobytraps and shoot at you?

The two accounts of the Mylai massacre mentioned in this bibliography, Richard Hammer's "One Morning in the War" and Seymour Hersh's "My Lai 4," as well as the testimony that has emerged at the court martial of Lieutenant Calley, of practices like driving civilians ahead of the troops to detonate mines with their bodies suggest that the general conduct of the war did contribute to these individual atrocities.

The word Lieutenant Calley used to describe the act of slaughtering the 102 men, women and children for whose deaths he is being held responsible evokes this atmosphere in uncanny fashion. He told the prosecutor that he was ordered "to waste the Vietnamese . . . waste, waste them, Sir." Were this just Lieutenant Calley speaking the word would not carry much meaning, but the word is from the argot of the American soldier in Vietnam. Human beings are "wasted" there, they are "blown away." Soldiers have a unique ability to find words to describe the reality of their wars.

Given such an atmosphere, the massacre at Mylai would be a departure from the norm only in that it consisted of the direct murder by rifle and machine gun fire of several hundred Vietnamese civilians at one time. The soldiers in Lieutenant Calley's platoon, whose moral sense led them to disregard his orders and not participate in the killings, do not appear to have been shocked by the lesser, individual atrocities that occurred prior to Mylai. Looked at coldly, Lieutenant Calley and the soldiers who did join him in the massacre were doing with their rifles what was done every day for reasons of strategy with bombs and artillery shells. There are Calleys in every army. What makes them dangerous is a set of circumstances in which their homicidal aberrations can run amok. The laws of war say that it is the responsibility of the highest leadership to do all in its power to prevent such circumstances from occurring.

Both the Army Field Manual and the Nuremberg Principles address this central issue in delineating when a claim of superior order can constitute a defense against a charge of war crimes. "The fact that a person acted pursuant to order of his Government or of a superior does not relieve him from responsibility under international law, *provided a moral choice was in fact possible for him*" [italics added], the Nuremberg Principles say. The Army Field Manual is a bit more elaborate. "In considering the question whether a superior order constitutes a valid defense, the court shall take into consideration the fact that obedience to lawful military orders is the duty of every member of the Armed Forces; that the latter cannot be expected, in condition of war discipline, to weigh scrupulously the legal merits of the orders received; that certain rules of warfare may be controversial; or that an act otherwise amounting to a war crime may be done in obedience to orders conceived as a measure of reprisal," the Manual says.

Curiously, Lieutenant Calley's lawyers have claimed that he has a robot-like personality incapable of resisting any orders from his superior, Capt. Ernest Medina, but they have not sought to defend Calley on the grounds that, given the general atmosphere in which the war was being conducted, and his interpretation of his orders that morning in Mylai, he may not have been capable of a moral choice. They may have hesitated to do so because they would have had to put the entire command structure from President Johnson on down in the witness chair. Telford Taylor notes in his book that a court martial at Fort Benning is too limited a forum for such a far-reaching inquiry.

Nevertheless, the question of higher responsibility hangs over Mylai. It hangs over the individual atrocities described in these books, it hangs over the use of airpower and artillery to lay waste the Vietnamese villages, if that, too, constitutes a war crime and the greatest one of all.

Many would contend, as Townsend Hoopes did in an exchange of articles with two reporters for the Village Voice who accused him and his colleagues of being war criminals, that raising the issue of war crimes in Vietnam is absurd and unwarranted in the context of a democracy like the United States. Worse, many would argue, it is vindictive, capable of perversion into a new McCarthysim. Hoopes was a Deputy Assistant Secretary of Defense and Under Secretary of the Air Force in the Johnson Administration. He wrote an admired account of the inside events behind the March 31, 1968, decision to restrict the bombing of North Vietnam and open peace negotiations. His view is important because it appears to be widely held.

Hoopes argued that since the President is elected, since the war was prosecuted from well-meaning if mistaken motives, since Congress voted the funds and there was broad public support at the outset, no official should acquire criminal liability. Judgment, he said, should be confined to voting the Government out of office. Attacking this position in his introduction to the Russell Tribunal proceedings, Noam Chomsky of M.I.T. states that Hoopes is claiming an immunity for American leaders which this country denied to the leaders of Japan and Germany. Marcus Raskin, co-director of the Institute for Policy Studies in Washington, the think-tank of the New Left, asserts that Congress cannot be held responsible as a body, because many Congressmen voted funds merely to ensure that American soldiers had the means to defend themselves. Telford Taylor, a mugwump Democrat, remarks that though good intentions may be mitigating circumstances, they do not negate the fact of a crime, if one occurred.

Taken to its logical end, the Hoopes argument also means that all Americans were responsible for the actual conduct of the war. If so, then the adult majorities of Japan and Germany should have been punished for war crimes. They applauded the beginning of World War II. And if everyone is responsible, of course no one is responsible. The Nuremberg and Tokyo tribunals rejected Hoopes's argument by making a distinction between those in the audience and those who held power, as do the laws of war. The Army Manual denies a collective copout: "The fact that a person who committed an act which constitutes a war crime acted as the head of a State or as a responsible government official does not relieve him from responsibility for his act."

(Hyperbole in describing what war crimes may have taken place in Vietnam seems just as unhelpful as the Hoopes argument. Chomsky in "At War With Asia," accuses the United States of intending genocide in Vietnam. So do Richard Falk, the international legal scholar, and Gabriel Kolko, the revisionist historian, both of whom have otherwise diamond-cutting minds, in "War Crimes and the American Conscience," the published proceedings of a Washington symposium on war crimes last year. Genocide does not appear to be an accurate characterization of American conduct in Vietnam. The story is more complicated and the facts do not support the charge. The population of the country has grown despite the war, from an estimated 15-million in 1962 to about 17-million now.)

But how is this country to determine whether war crimes were really committed in Vietnam and who is responsible for them?

Not even the wildest of anti-communist politicians has predicted the conquest of the United States by the Vietcong guerrillas and the North Vietnamese army. So it seems equally outlandish to imagine that a tribunal with the power of those at Tokyo and Nuremberg will ever sit in judgment on the leaders of this country.

The Army, the principal service involved in the Vietnam war, has shown that it will not enforce military law and judge itself. The dismissal of charges against Maj. Gen. Samuel W. Koster, the division commander of the troops at Mylai, demonstrated that the current leadership of the Army considers Lieutenant Calley and Captain Medina to be its only real war criminals. Barring unforeseen disclosures, no one more important than a few captains, a major and a colonel or two are likely to join Calley and Medina in the dock. For the Army had a good case against General Koster, who was in his helicopter over the Mylai area that morning. What the Army lacked was the will to prosecute.

Perhaps it is expecting too much of human nature to think that the Army would sit in judgment on its own conduct in Vietnam. A command structure so traumatized, so emotionally defensive because of its failure in Vietnam, is not, except under great outside duress, about to begin charging members of the inner circle with war crimes.

Indeed, the military services are in the greatest danger of becoming the scapegoats of a public witchhunt that could come from the left over the war crimes issue if responsible men do not prevail. Mark Lane's collection of purported eyewitness accounts of atrocities in Vietnam, "Conversations with Americans," is an example of the kind of scurrilous attack that is already being made. The military have few defenders in the current climate. Much of the intellectual community and many of the students are almost childishly indiscriminate in their assaults. A number of the former senior civilian officials of the country, who have changed their minds about the war they helped to prosecute, are now all to eager to blame everything on the generals.

Professional soldiers, whose frame of reference is almost by nature circumscribed, are being criticized for not having displayed the kind of broad wisdom and judgment self-proclaimed statesmen did not exhibit. If the generals did commit war crimes in Vietnam, they did so with the knowledge and consent of the civilians. If seeking to pacify with the fire and the sword of the 20th-century, airplanes and howitzers, constituted a war crime, then the civilians helped to induce this crime by denying the generals sufficient troops to garrison the countryside.

President Johnson and his closest advisers, Robert S. McNamara, Walt W. Rostow, and Dean Rusk, directed the unfolding of the conflict just as President Nixon and his senior advisers now do. The military almost always played a subordinate role. Mr. McNamara. for example, supervised the planning and the execution of the war for the President as the chief of a European General Staff would have done. In 1965 he often said: "We're going to trade firepower for men." He had no criminal intent, of course. What he meant was that he planned to expend ten bombs to kill five North Vietnamese soldiers, instead of trading the lives of five American infantrymen for the same job. But when the bombs were targeted on civilians, Mr. McNamara did not cry halt. This is not to say that the generals would be absolved of responsibility, only that the highest, and therefore the greatest, responsibility does not rest with them.

For precisely this reason, one cannot expect the Nixon Administration, of its own accord, to institute any meaningful inquiry into war crimes. Mr. Nixon is using the same air-power tactics in Laos and Cambodia that his predecessor employed in South Vietnam. His strategy of Vietnamization is even more dependent upon the unrestricted use of airpower than was Mr. Johnson's. Mr. Nixon has also sensed even more keenly the political convenience of this weapon. He has calculated correctly that the public will not worry much about the dead, or about their age or sex, so long as the bodies are far enough away that the photographers and the television crews can't get to them too often and so long as they are, most important of all, not American.

The Kennedy Subcommittee estimates that civilian casualties in Laos, which has a population of only three million, are now exceeding 30,000 a year, including more than 10,000 dead. Many of these casualties are attributable to American bombs. Classified military documents specifically talk about bombing villages in Communist-held areas "to deprive the enemy of the population resource." No one knows what the civilian casualty toll is in Cambodia, where the same kind of air attacks are taking place. The Kennedy Subcommittee guesses there are now about a million and a half refugees in Cambodia out of a population of 6.5 million and that civilian casualties are running in the tens of thousands a year.

When I asked a responsible official at the State Department about the refugees he said he didn't have an estimate. Why? I asked. "The Cambodians haven't really asked us for any assistance with refugees and until they do it's not our concern. Our staff in the Embassy is pretty small and they have a lot of other fish to fry." What about the civilian casualties? "The Cambodians haven't been compiling them," he said. "We're dependent on their statistics and they don't keep careful statistics on anything." Really, that's what he said. The new American aid program for Cambodia contains no funds specifically marked for civilian medical relief.

Yet the cleansing of the nation's conscience and the future conduct of the most powerful country in the world towards the weaker peoples of the globe, demand a national inquiry into the war crimes question. What is needed is not prison sentences and executions, but social judgments soberly arrived at, so that if these acts are war crimes, future American leaders will not dare to repeat them.

The sole hope for such a national inquiry would appear to rest with the Congress or a commission of responsible men, with military and judicial experience, appointed by Congress and empowered to subpoena witnesses and examine documents. They might try to answer one fundamental question that I have not attempted to deal with here because the arguments are still so tangled—whether the United States intervention in Vietnam was itself a violation of the Nuremberg Principles forbidding wars of aggression. There does not seem to be the stomach for such an inquiry in Congress now, but attitudes may change as the full import of the issue becomes known.

If Congress fails to undertake an inquiry that carries the authority of the nation, then hypocrisy will be added to our sins. The Nuremberg judgments upon such diabolical Nazi crimes as the extermination of the Jews will still stand as a monument to international justice. Even under the most critical scrutiny, nothing the United States has perpetrated approaches the satanic evil of Hitler and his followers. The Nazis were in a class by themselves.

But the other, lesser judgments at Nuremberg, and the verdicts at the Tokyo Tribunal, will become what many said they were at the time—the pronouncements of victors over vanquished. We ought to remember that at the Tokyo Tribunal, the United States went so far as to establish the legal precedent that any member of a Cabinet who learns of war crimes, and subsequently remains in that Government acquires responsibility for those crimes. Under our own criteria, therefore, Orville Freeman, the Secretary of Agriculture under President Johnson, could acquire responsibility for war crimes in Vietnam.

Recently, when I discussed with a Japanese friend the condemnation of General Yamashita for the death of more than 25,000 noncombatants in the Philippines, he remarked: "We Japanese have a saying. The victor is always right."

History shows that men who decide for war, as the Japanese militarists did, cannot demand mercy for themselves. The resort to force is the ultimate act. It is playing God. Those who try force cannot afford to fail. I do not mean to suggest that men should be free to attempt anything in war to ensure victory. Quite the opposite. The laws of war seek to mitigate the evil of war, to save what lives can be saved in the midst of great killing. War nonetheless remains an evil that imposes a unique burden upon those responsible. This will sound cynical to many, but if the Johnson Administration had won the war in Vietnam, few would be searching for war crimes among the physical and human ruins of Indochina. Evidence of murder and brutality on a grand scale would have been hushed in the shouts of success. The resort to force has failed, however, and that failure has helped to make the issue of war crimes in Vietnam a very real and a very fair one to be dealt with. Our failure presents an opportunity for humanity that should not be lost.

Neil Sheehan, who spent three years in Vietnam, is a correspondent in The Times Washington Bureau.

* * *

March 30, 1971

CALLEY GUILTY OF MURDER OF 22 CIVILIANS AT MYLAI; SENTENCE EXPECTED TODAY

APPEAL IS CERTAIN

Army Jury Must Set Penalty of Death or Life Imprisonment

By HOMER BIGART
Special to The New York Times

FORT BENNING, Ga., March 29—First Lieut. William L. Calley Jr. was found guilty today of the premeditated murder of at least 22 South Vietnamese civilians at Mylai three years ago.

He faces a mandatory sentence of death or life imprisonment. Arguments in mitigation will be heard tomorrow by the same jury of six officers that sentenced him today, and the punishment will probably be announced tomorrow afternoon.

An appeal is automatic within the military court system and could consume months.

The verdict in this protracted war crimes trial, the longest in the history of American military justice, was announced at 4:31 P.M. after 79 hours and 58 minutes of deliberation stretching over 13 days.

Courtroom Filled

The small, harshly lighted courtroom, with its red carpet, white walls and blue draperies, was only comfortably filled when the jury came in.

Lieutenant Calley, a short, stocky 27-year-old who led his platoon on a sweep through an undefended hamlet called Mylai 4 March 16, 1968, was escorted before the jury box. Silence fell in the courtroom.

He stiffly saluted the president of the jury, Col. Clifford H. Ford, a partly gray, 53-year-old veteran of World War II and Korea with three rows of ribbons on his chest. The colonel returned the salute and, in a gentle voice, began reading the verdict.

"Lieutenant Calley," he said, "it is my duty as president of this court to inform you that the court, in closed session, and upon secret, written ballot, two-thirds of the members present at the time the vote was taken concurring in each finding of guilty, finds you:

"Of specification one of the charge: guilty."

Four Specifications

The Government had charged Lieutenant Calley with four specifications of premeditated murder involving at least 102 men, women and children. The first specification charged that he killed at least 30 noncombatants along a trail at the south end of the village.

Colonel Ford announced that the jury had found Lieutenant Calley guilty of the premeditated murder of "an unknown number, no less than one."

The second specification charged Lieutenant Calley with the murder of at least 70 civilians in a ditch outside Mylai. Colonel Ford announced that the jury had found Lieutenant Calley guilty of the premeditated murder of "an unknown number, no less than 20" in this incident.

In the two remaining counts, the jury found Lieutenant Calley guilty of the premeditated murder of a South Vietnamese male in white robes, possibly a monk, and of assault with intent to commit the murder of a small child.

In the case of the child, the original charge was murder, but the judge told the jury, in his charge, that a verdict on the lesser charge was permissible.

One reason Lieutenant Calley was convicted of murdering 22 persons, rather than 102 as charged, was that witnesses

Associated Press

First Lieut. William L. Calley, Jr. being escorted by an Army sergeant yesterday from the courtroom where he heard the jury's verdict of guilty in the Mylai case. The lieutenant was taken to the stockade at Fort Benning, Ga.

disputed the number of dead at Mylai, some saying they had counted fewer than 100. The jury's finding, therefore, reflected its effort to reconcile the contradictions in the testimony.

As he heard the verdict, Lieutenant Calley stood ramrod stiff, his face flushed. His eyes, normally half-closed, were wide open as he stared at Colonel Ford.

He saluted again, this time rather crookedly, and walked stiffly back to the defense table.

There was no demonstration. The military judge, Col. Reid W. Kennedy, told the jury: "Gentlemen, we will go into the sentencing phase tomorrow."

Then Lieutenant Calley was led down a corridor to the office of his lawyers. Some 30 minutes passed before a confinement order, signed by Col. Frank L. Garrison, commanding officer of The Student Brigade, was produced.

A crowd of about 100 spectators stood outside the red brick courthouse. As Lieutenant Calley emerged, surrounded by military policemen, a woman yelled: "We're with you, Calley."

Calley Silent

Lieutenant Calley strode past the crowd and got into a military police car. He had orders from his chief counsel, George W. Latimer, not to talk until after the sentencing tomorrow.

But Mr. Latimer, a 70-year-old retired judge of the Court of Military Appeals, said of the verdict: "It was a horrendous decision for the United States, United States Army and for my client."

He said it was "much tougher than I anticipated" and said for his client: "Take my word for it, the boy is crushed."

Lieutenant Calley was not handcuffed when driven to the stockade.

He is expected to be flown to the Army Disciplinary Barracks at Fort Leavenworth, Kan., immediately after he is sentenced. Meanwhile, he is confined in a separate officers' cell at the stockade, rooms normally used by the chaplain as an office.

According to an Army news release distributed immediately after the verdict, the cell has two rooms.

The first room, the release said, is about 10 feet wide by seven and a half feet long and contains a desk with a straight chair.

The next room is about 10 feet wide by 12 feet long. The wall is green for the first five feet, then white. The room is furnished with a desk and a straight chair, a standard Army bunk with two sheets, two blankets and a pillow, an air conditioner and a radiator.

"This boy is a product of the system," Mr. Latimer said of the lieutenant today. "He was taken out of his own home, given automatic weapons, taught to kill. They ordered him to kill. And then the same Government tries him for killing and selects the judge, the court and the prosecutor."

Society is to blame, Mr. Latimer told reporters.

From now on, parents will be less willing than ever to send their boys to Vietnam, he said. And soldiers will be "less likely to obey orders in the field," he added.

Mr. Latimer said he would call no witnesses for tomorrow's hearing on mitigation and extenuation. He said he would appeal all the way through the military and civilian courts.

As for what he would say tomorrow in mitigation, he said: "Well, I'm not going to ask that they put him into the gallows and string him up by the neck."

The last time a soldier was executed was on April 13, 1961. He was Pvt. John Bennett, hanged for rape at Fort Leavenworth.

25 Men Charged

Lieutenant Calley was among the 25 officers and enlisted men originally charged by the Army with either participating in the atrocities at Mylai or attempting to "cover up" the tragedy.

Two of the 25 were tried and acquitted before today's verdict and charges against 19 have been dismissed.

Three await trial. They are Capt. Ernest L. Medina, charged with the over-all responsibility in the death of no fewer than 100 South Vietnamese, and two specific premeditated murders, one of a South Vietnamese woman and one of a small boy; Col. Oran K. Henderson, the former commander of the 11th Brigade, accused of dereliction of duty and failure to obey lawful regulations in suppressing information about the incident, and Capt. Eugene M. Kotouc, the intelligence officer of the 11th Brigade, accused of maiming a prisoner.

The Calley trial, which began last Nov. 12, was one of the longest and most sensational in the history of American military justice.

Testimony disclosed that the company in which Lieutenant Calley was a platoon leader committed acts that were outlawed by international conventions on the rules of war.

Unarmed civilians, including women, children and babies, were gunned down at point-blank range.

Orders were issued by Captain Medina to use captured Vietnamese as "guides" across suspected mine fields; they would become human mine detectors walking ahead of the troops.

Common Practice

(Lieutenant Calley testified that the prisoners were never so employed at Mylai because they moved too slowly and held up the advance. So, he said, he had them shot on Captain Medina's orders. Captain Medina acknowledged telling Lieutenant Calley to use the prisoners in the mine fields, but denied ordering them slain.)

It was a common practice among some American units to burn houses, kill all the animals and destroy the food and wells in villages suspected of harboring Vietcong.

Medical corpsmen joined in. Under the laws of war, medical personnel are noncombatants.

The trial also brought out that there were no provisions for the evacuation of civilians and for the treatment of wounded civilians. Following the Mylai assault, a prisoner was deliberately mutilated.

During the long trial, Lieutenant Calley said that his victims were not human but, in the words of his attorney, Mr. Latimer, "an enemy with whom one could not speak or reason."

Lieutenant Calley volunteered from the witness stand that he felt no remorse, that he had been following orders.

"They were all enemies," he said. "They were all to be destroyed."

This application of the "mere Gook rule"—that the natives are "mere Gooks"—brought the following reply from Capt. Aubrey M. Daniel 3d, the Government prosecutor, during the closing moments of the trial:

"They were human beings. Yet they were herded in the ditch like so many cattle. What can justify, gentlemen, the shooting in cold blood of an infant, a child, or any human being who is offering no resistance?

"Lieutenant Calley claims he did his duty. To make that assertion is to prostitute all the humanitarian principles for which this nation stands, to prostitute the true mission of the United States soldier.

"The defense would ask you to legalize murder."

"How could we as a nation ask for humane, treatment of our own prisoners while condoning inhumane treatment of theirs?"

Babies Not Trusted

Lieutenant Calley and another witness, Paul Meadlo, a rifleman in Calley's platoon and his alleged chief accomplice in the mass shootings, stressed that women and children were sometimes as dangerous as Vietcong soldiers. Neither could recall ever having been attacked by a child, but they said they had heard stories of children tossing grenades and planting mines and booby traps.

Even babies were not to be trusted, Mr. Meadlo testified.

"Any baby might have been loaded with grenades that the mother could have throwed," he explained.

The Geneva Convention says that persons suspected of violating the laws of war must be "treated with humanity" and not punished without trial.

Captain Daniel, who is 29 years old and only four years out of law school, said in his summation that Lieutenant Calley assumed at Mylai the self-appointed role of "judge, jury and high executioner" in mowing down women and children whose only crime, he said, was to be in the wrong place at the wrong time.

Lieutenant Calley was on the stand three days. He insisted he had acted on orders from Captain Medina. He said that on the eve of the attack, Captain Medina told members of Charlie Company that the unit had been cut down to half-strength by casualties inflicted in the area and "we would have to start treating them [the natives] as enemy."

To prevent the enemy from sifting through the assault line and attacking from the rear, Captain Medina ordered the men to destroy "everyone and everything" in Mylai, Lieutenant Calley said.

What Medina Said

Both the Government and the defense called witnesses to testify as to what Captain Medina told the soldiers on the eve of battle.

"Kill everything that breathes" was the recollection of defense witnesses.

But prosecution witnesses said that Captain Medina never gave orders to kill civilians. All agreed that Captain Medina, quoting intelligence reports, said that women and children would be at market in a nearby town at the time of the attack and that the troops would encounter only the enemy—the 48th Vietcong Battalion.

Finally Captain Medina took the stand as a witness for the court. Trim and soldierly, the 34-year-old company commander vehemently denied that he had given orders for indiscriminate killing.

With a hard, steady stare at Lieutenant Calley, Captain Medina said he told his men: "No, you do not kill women and children. You use common sense. If they have a weapon and they are trying to engage you, then you can shoot back, but you must use common sense."

It became a question of whether Captain Medina or Lieutenant Calley was telling the truth.

Captain Medina said it had taken him two and a half hours to realize that Mylai was undefended. It had taken him all day to discover the full extent of the civilian slaughter, he said. He said he had been disturbed early in the action by the sight of 20 to 28 dead villagers and that he had given repeated orders to the platoon leaders against killing "innocent civilians."

Two days later, he said, he called the platoon leaders together and asked if they were "aware of any atrocities." He said Lieutenant Calley had told him: "My God, I can still hear the screaming," a remark Judge Kennedy ordered stricken from the record.

Captain Medina acknowledged having tried to cover up the incident. He gave four reasons why.

"Number one," he said, "I realized exactly the disgrace that was brought upon the Army uniform that I am very proud to wear. Number two, I also realized the repercussions that it would have against the United States of America. Three, my family. And number four, lastly, myself, sir."

* * *

March 31, 1971

IMPACT OF CALLEY TRIAL

War Crimes Conviction Raises Series Of Legal Conflicts for Foot Soldiers

By FRED P. GRAHAM
Special to The New York Times

WASHINGTON, March 30—Historically, war crimes trials have been the business of victors. The United States has broken with the tradition by convicting in midwar one of its own men, First Lieut. William L. Calley Jr., of murdering Vietnamese civilians, and thus has confronted its foot soldiers and its commanders with News a series of legal Analysis conflicts. As so often happens, the pinch appears to be primarily upon the foot soldiers. Lieutenant Calley's conviction demonstrated, if there was any doubt, that the excuse that "I was just following orders" will not work. He contended that he had been ordered to "waste" the villagers at Mylai, but the Uniform Code of Military Justice says that this is no defense if "a man of ordinary sense and understanding would know [the order] to be illegal."

To anyone who has served in the infantry, the thought of a soldier in the field standing around pondering the legality of a superior's order is bizarre enough to demonstrate the unfairness of this rule.

This unfairness was academic so long as atrocity trials were mostly reserved for the losing side, but now that Lieutenant Calley has been convicted and cries of "scapegoat" are being heard, the legal plight of the soldier in Vietnam has been brought into sharp focus.

In the Calley case itself, the jury could either have disbelieved his contention that he had acted under orders when he shot women and children at close range, or decided that he should have realized that any such order was illegal and should be disobeyed.

But the case could have been much more difficult. Lieutenant Calley's immediate superior, Capt. Ernest L. Medina, denied issuing orders to shoot the civilians but acknowledged ordering the lieutenant to use the Vietnamese as "guides" across suspected mine fields.

There was also testimony that it was common practice in some United States units to burn the houses, kill all the animals and poison the fields and wells of villages suspected of harboring Vietcong.

These tactics and others ordered in Vietnam—the shelling of hospitals, the bombing of villages, the defoliation of forests—are arguably in violation of the laws of war.

Thus Lieutenant Calley and others could conceivably have been court-martialed for acts done under orders that were not palpably illegal. This has led many persons to insist that the scrutiny of Mylai must now range up the line of command, to include the generals and perhaps their civilian superiors.

Adrian S. Fisher, dean of Georgetown Law School and a technical adviser to the United States judges at the Nuremberg war crimes trial after World War II, has said that the American military high command must now "taste the cup" of guilt that it forced upon the Japanese after that war.

Appearing this morning on the National Broadcasting Company's "Today" show, Dean Fisher pointed out that the United States hanged Gen. Tomoyuki Yamashita, the Japanese commander in the Philippines, for atrocities committed by troops under his command.

General Yamashita's communications with the offending garrison at Manila were erratic. But the Supreme Court upheld a death sentence that was based on the theory that a commander must take steps to see that his men do not commit atrocities.

Thus the inquiry up the chain of command should question why the killings were not prevented, Dean Fisher said. In fact, the prosecution has concentrated on the troops in the field, and its focus has been narrowly on the events of Mylai and their aftermath.

Of the 25 enlisted men and officers originally charged with participating in the massacre or attempting to cover it up, two enlisted men have been tried and acquitted. Charges against 19 have been dropped, including those against the division commander, Maj. Gen. Samuel W. Koster, who had been accused of covering up the massacre.

Three officers are yet to be tried: Captain Medina, Col. Oran K. Henderson, the former brigade commander of the troops at Mylai, and Col. Ernest M. Kotouc, the brigade's intelligence officer. All are charged with crimes at the scene or attempting to cover them up.

The dismissal of the charges against General Koster—after he had been punished administratively—is a strong hint that the Pentagon has no stomach for a broadening of the Mylai question to include the "Yamashita" issue.

The obvious reason is to shield the high officers from the conflicting pressures inherent in ordering military operations that could later result in charges of war crimes.

But this leaves the foot soldier facing similar legal conflicts. He will almost surely be court-martialed for disobeying orders, and he could be court-martialed for following them.

It is the prospect of drafting young men and sending them into this quagmire of risks and duties that has produced the complaints that Lieutenant Calley was used as a scapegoat, while the generals protected their own.

As the lieutenant's lawyer put it yesterday, he was a victim of a system that "dragged him out of his home, taught him to kill, sent him overseas to kill, gave him automatic weapons to kill . . . then comes back and appoints the judge, the prosecutors, the jury and tries him."

* * *

April 7, 1971

PACIFICATION PUSH BEGUN IN VIETNAM

New Program, Most Costly Yet, Aimed at Vietcong's Political Apparatus

By TAD SZULC
Special to The New York Times

WASHINGTON, April 6—The most ambitious and costly pacification program yet planned for South Vietnam has been put into effect by Saigon and Washington.

Reportedly costing the United States considerably more than $1-billion and Saigon an undisclosed sum, the 1971 Community Defense and Local Development Plan would greatly expand pacification activities, which are aimed at destroying Communist subversive forces and widening self-government and development.

The 304-page plan, a copy of which was made available to The New York Times, lists as the "top priority" for the year the "neutralization" of the entrenched Vietcong political apparatus.

Authenticity Confirmed

The authenticity of the document was confirmed by Administration sources, who declined to discuss the contents because of the plan's confidential character.

In operation since March 1, and endorsed by the American command in Saigon, the new plan is reportedly the subject of wide controversy among United States officials, some of whom term it unrealistic and artificial.

Administration officials were unable to provide cost figures to the United States for previous pacification programs, but they said that the current plan, financed almost entirely in its military, security and civilian aspects by the Defense Department and the Central Intelligence Agency, was much more costly because of its increased scope.

Acknowledging for the first time that the activities of the Vietcong apparatus remain a major problem in 8 of South Vietnam's 44 provinces, including four in the allegedly pacified Mekong River Delta, and that South Vietnamese forces often prefer to "accommodate, rather than resist, the enemy," the plan provides for:

Expansion of the People's Self-Defense Force—the civilian antiguerrilla combat organization in rural areas—from 500,000 to four million. Women would be enlisted in combat units and children of both sexes over the age of 7 in supporting units.

Establishment of an elaborate "people's intelligence network" to inform on the enemy.

Elimination in the year starting last month, through killing or capture, of 14,400 Vietcong agents under expansion of the three-year-old Operation Phoenix, an intelligence-gathering program that is supported by the United States military.

Wider Social Benefits

The new pacification plan also seeks to complete the program of holding elections in all villages and hamlets; spur land reform by setting a goal of distributing nearly a million acres of land to farmers, and widen social benefits. This would be done by providing new assistance to 216,000 war veterans, and increasing aid to 43,002 disabled soldiers, 33,743 parents of dead servicemen, 71,005 war widows and 284,000 war orphans. In addition, the plan hopes to resettle 430,000 war refugees in new homes.

Other innovations in the 1971 pacification plan include programs for ethnic minorities and for cities where crime is rising.

Elaborated upon by the South Vietnamese Government, approved by President Nguyen Van Thieu and his Cabinet and fully endorsed by Gen. Creighton W. Abrams, the United States commander in Vietnam, the plan is designed to dovetail with the Nixon Administration's policy of Vietnamization, under which combat responsibilities are being gradually assumed by the South Vietnamese forces.

In transmitting the plan to Washington in January, General Abrams wrote in a covering memorandum that "while it is a Government of Vietnam document, it has been thoroughly coordinated" with the United States command and "I strongly endorse the 1971 Community Defense and Local Levelopment Plan and request your full support in its implementation."

"This document will be regarded as guidance, directive in nature, to advisory personnel at all echelons," he wrote.

While the Administration here and the Saigon Government report success for earlier pacification programs, some American experts question their effectiveness so far and are skeptical about the soundness of the new plan.

Their main criticism is that the whole pacification effort depends too much on the 8,000 United States officials and advisers in the Civil Operations and Rural Development Support program, an agency known as CORDS.

The agency, which supervises projects from Operation Phoenix to rural economic programs, is chiefly made up of Defense Department and Central Intelligence Agency employes, although it includes officials of the State Department, the Agency for International Development and the United States Information Agency.

Reports from the field indicate that CORDS officials are frequently not aware of the true state of affairs in districts and villages and that their colleagues in civilian government and the police fail to carry out their tasks.

Critics of the pacification program point to this statement in the 1971 plan:

"In some areas, the people are reluctant to associate with the Government of Vietnam for fear of retaliation by the enemy. Civil officials often become the target of enemy terrorism and assassination and thus are reluctant to perform their government tasks.

"Some police hesitate to conduct operations against the V.C. because they fear retaliation, and local security forces, under the threat of terrorism, often accommodate, rather than resist, the enemy."

The critics also raise the question of what will happen if CORDS is phased out and ask whether the agency may not have to be maintained in South Vietnam indefinitely.

Three Major Objectives

As expressed in the 1971 plan, the over-all concept of pacification consists of the three objectives of "local self-defense, local self government and local self-development."

The philosophy of the program is stated as follows in the plan:

"In his efforts to achieve political control of the Republic of Vietnam, the enemy attempts to demonstrate that the Government of Vietnam is not capable of governing the country or of providing credible security to the people. His offensive operations and the resultant reaction operations by friendly forces produce adverse effects on security of the people. The most effective way of assuring security of the Vietnamese people is to keep enemy forces away from them and by neutralizing the Vietcong infrastructure."

The plan emphasizes that the "strategic concept of national security" is not dependent on the presence of American forces and "paves the way for the transfer of the responsibility for security from military agencies to civilian ones."

To assist this proposed transfer and supervise the new police functions the South Vietnamese and United States Governments have turned to Sir Robert Thompson, the British counterinsurgency expert.

The pacification plan emphasized that among the 1971 targets is the reduction of "enemy terrorist incidents" to 6,010. The document did not report how many such incidents occurred in 1970, but said that the current target was to reduce them by 75 per cent in "secure areas" and by 50 per cent in areas "still undergoing pacification."

Statistics included in the plan showed that the military region that includes 15 provinces south of Saigon and in the Mekong Delta poses the most serious security problems.

The delta has been declared by the Saigon Government to be virtually pacified, except for the U Minh Forest area, and all American troops left the area in 1969. But the plan reports serious problems with an entrenched Vietcong apparatus in the provinces of Vinhlong, Dinhtuong, Kienhoa and Anxuyen. Similar problems are reported in Binhdinh province in the central part of the country and in Quangnam, Quangngai and Quangtin Provinces in the northern part.

The plan urges that special police units be assigned to these eight provinces.

To deal with the Vietcong apparatus the plan provides for 700,000 weapons to be issued this year to the People's Self-Defense Forces and for the establishment of the intelligence operation reaching into all of South Vietnam's villages and hamlets.

While the plan offers no over-all cost figures, informed officials here estimated the expense to the United States at $1-billion from Defense Department Funds and an unknown amount from the C.I.A. In the phasing out of CORDS operations, the Agency for International Development has programed $32-million in the 1972 fiscal year for pacification.

No figures are available here for the previous pacification plans but the costs were reported to have been below the 1971 program.

* * *

April 11, 1971

U.S. PILOTS FIND ENEMY TRAFFIC MOVING FREELY ON TRAIL IN LAOS

By HENRY KAMM

Special to The New York Times

DANANG, South Vietnam, April 7—American fighter and observation pilots who fly regularly over the Ho Chi Minh Trail report that traffic is moving freely along the enemy supply network now that the South Vietnamese have wound up their operation in Laos.

Pilots of the 130th Tactical Fighter Squadron at the air base here said in interviews that North Vietnamese trucks were driving northward and southward again along the supply trails that were cut by South Vietnamese troops during the incursion. It began Feb. 8 and ended late last month.

The pilots said also that antiaircraft fire, which had been diverted against troop-carrying helicopters taking part in the operation and so had given fighter pilots a period of respite, was "right back to where it was before."

During the operation they said, it had become "relatively safe" to approach such heavily defended regions as Tchepone at low angles, but Tchepone is again bristling with antiaircraft artillery, the pilots reported.

They said that reports that the South Vietnamese operations had been a failure were wrong as far as they were concerned. For the first time, they said, the enemy troops were massed and brought into the open to offer concentrated targets for bombing.

"During the operation we had some of the most enjoyable flying in a long time," Capt Bill Hohwiesner, a pilot, said.

Discussing the flow of enemy supplies, forward air controllers of the 20th Tactical Air Support Squadron reported that in the region immediately south of the trail-cutting operation traffic had, if anything, increased during the ground fighting.

This would indicate that the supply system was so well stocked in underground depots along the trail that it could have provided enough supplies for heavy traffic during the more than six weeks of fighting, which precluded resupplying of the depots from North Vietnam.

Appointed Rounds

Traffic on the Ho Chi Minh Trail does not move in the same truck straight from North Vietnam through Laos into South Vietnam or Cambodia. There are many depots along the trails, and each truck usually shuttles up and down the same short stretch of road.

Thus even during the fighting, supplies that were stocked south of the combat area—the east-west axis of Route 9—kept moving from the depots into South Vietnam. The only difference the forward observers noted was that during the fighting loaded trucks moved northward for the first time to supply North Vietnamese troops.

Lieut, Col. Edward Sullivan, a forward air controller, said that during the operation the enemy opened two new north-south roads on the western edge of the trail complex, the region farthest from the Vietnamese border with Laos.

The trail network has spread westward over the last year as a result of the enemy's loss of facilities at the Cambodian port of Sihanoukville—now Kompong Sam—and the need to supply enemy forces in Cambodia from North Vietnam.

New Roads on Ridges

Colonel Sullivan reported that the enemy was building new roads as much as possible on the ridges of the mountainous trail region. He said that this foiled the American bombing technique of making roads unusable by causing rockslides across them from adjacent hillsides.

The fliers added that in any event, even when the bombers succeeded in leaving craters in a road and causing rockslides to block it, the North Vietnamese consistently managed to remove the obstacles in hours and to fill the craters with crushed rock.

The trail region is cratered "like the backside of the moon," Colonel Cullivan said, but the roads are kept open. Fliers who operate over the trail are unanimous in their appreciation of the military engineering feat that the supply network represents.

* * *

April 23, 1971

ANGRY WAR VETERAN

JOHN FORBES KERRY

Special to The New York Times

WASHINGTON, April 22—Early in 1968, not long after his graduation from the Navy's officer candidate school, Lieut, j.g. John Forbes Kerry visited Vietnam for the first time when his ship stopped over in Danang after a brief tour in the Gulf of, Tonkin. "I went ashore and saw the barbed wire, the machine guns and a 'woodpile' of dead Vietcong bodies," Mr. Kerry recalls, "and it hit me all at once. This was my first contact with the land war, and at first it looked like something out of the movies. Then I realized—I said 'my God, what is going on here—this is really a war.' "

Mr. Kerry is here this week to protest that war as a leader of 1,000 or so veterans encamped on the grassy mall near the Capitol.

Last night, he stretched out his lean, 6-foot frame and recounted some of the experiences that turned him against American policy in Southeast Asia.

Mr. Kerry was born in Denver Dec. 11, 1943. He later lived in Washington and in France and Germany.

War Doubts at Yale

While still an undergraduate at Yale, Mr. Kerry developed some reservations about American foreign policy. This was reflected in the senior oration he delivered at his graduation in 1966 criticizing aspects of the draft and the war.

At Yale, Mr. Kerry won letters in soccer and lacrosse and belonged to the Skull and Bones Society. His plans to study abroad were quashed by a notice from his draft board that he would probably be called for service.

Neither jail nor self-exile appealed to him, he said, and "although I did have some doubts about the war in terms of policy, at that time I believed very strongly in the code of service to one's country." So, he added, "I enlisted in the Navy."

That first trip to Vietnam piqued his curiosity—"I wanted to go back and see for myself what was going on, but I didn't really want to get involved in the war." So, late in 1968 he volunteered for an assignment on "swift boats"—the short, fast aluminum craft that were then used for patrol duty off the Vietnam coast.

Two weeks before he arrived in Vietnam as a swift boat commander, he said, "they changed the policy on the use of the boats—decided to send them up the rivers to prove to the Vietcong that they didn't own the waters."

The river missions involved shooting at sampans and at huts along the banks and suddenly, Mr. Kerry recalls, "we said, 'hey, wait a minute—we don't know who these people are.' So we started to beach our boats to go ashore and find out what we had been shooting at."

Mr. Kerry, 27 years old, paused a moment, then remembered a time earlier in his life when his father, now a Massachusetts lawyer, was a Foreign Service officer stationed in Paris.

"My mother was born in France," he said, "and when we lived there, I used to play in the old German bunkers outside my grandmother's house. From listening to her stories, I got a vivid impression of what it was like to live in an occupied country, and when I went ashore in those villages, I realized that's exactly what I was in—an occupied country."

Because he had been wounded three times (in addition to the three Purple Hearts, he holds the Bronze and Silver Stars), he took advantage of a Navy regulation that allowed him to return to duty in the United States.

Mr. Kerry left Vietnam in March, 1969, and took a job as an admiral's aide in New York City. Shortly afterward he married. His wife, the former Julia Thorne, is 26. They have no children.

During this time, he says, "my opposition to the war was haunting me. The October moratorium came along and I did some work for it. It was just incredible, seeing all those people, and I said to myself, 'that's it.' "

He asked for, and was given, an early release from the Navy so he could run for Congress on an antiwar platform from his home district of Waltham, Mass. His campaign lasted a month, ending when he withdrew in favor of the Rev. Robert F. Drinan, the Jesuit who was elected to Congress last November.

While campaigning for Father Drinan, Mr. Kerry appeared on the Dick Cavett television program and was seen by members of the Vietnam Veterans Against the War, who asked him if he would work for their group. He has been a full-time organizer for them ever since.

During a veterans' meeting in Detroit last winter, Mr. Kerry said he became aware of increasing antiwar sentiment among returning veterans. "I saw guys there who couldn't talk about what they'd done in Vietnam without crying," he said. "That's when I realized that we had to take this thing to the Government."

Operation Dewey Canyon Three, the week-long veterans' protest now under way in the capital, is the result.

Mr. Kerry describes himself as "still a moderate—I'm not a radical in any sense of the word. I guess I'm just an angry young man."

He is not a pacifist—"if I have to pick up arms to defend something that is very real. If the shores of this country were threatened, I'd be the first to defend it."

* * *

April 24, 1971

VETERANS DISCARD MEDALS IN WAR PROTEST AT CAPITOL

Special to The New York Times

WASHINGTON, April 23—In twos and threes, the medals flew over a wire fence that had been hastily erected in front of the Capitol and landed at the feet of the statue of Chief Justice John Marshall at the building's west entrance. The men who had won the medals in Vietnam were throwing them away.

About 700 veterans discarded medals, before about 500 spectators. The capital police said tonight that the medals were still where they had been thrown.

"To President Nixon, I send you greetings," said one shaggy-haired young Army veteran, as he tossed a handful of service ribbons over the fence to join the Purple Hearts, Silver Stars, discharge papers and commendation medals piled there.

It was the last, and the most emotional, of the demonstrations this week by members of the Vietnam Veterans Against the War. About 1,000 members of the loosely organized group came to Washington last Monday to tell the Government and the nation about what many of them said had been the most profoundly shocking experience of their lives—the Vietnam war.

The White House, meanwhile, set a tone of official forbearance toward other antiwar demonstrators, expected to number 100,000 or more, who will gather tomorrow for the fourth mass protest here since Mr Nixon took office.

Ronald L. Ziegler, the White House press secretary, said there was no information to suggest violence. He added that the President had instructed his Administration "to proceed in a way that would not lead to possible violence of any sort and with the understanding that people have a right to express themselves."

At a special Senate hearing today a succession of the protesting veterans told an overflow audience in the new Senate Office Building about what they said was the previously unreported side of the war.

The session was attended by Senators George S. McGovern of South Dakota, Walter F. Mondale of Minnesota and Philip A. Hart of Michigan, all Democrats.

Representative Charles A. Vanik, Democrat of Ohio, was also present. The hearing was described by an aide to Mr. McGovern as a "special ad hoc" hearing to let the veterans present testimony.

Dale Grenada, 26 years old, a former quartermaster aboard the destroyer Richard B. Anderson, told of a mission in which he said his ship had been directed to "destroy a suspected Vietcong village."

After the shelling began, Mr. Grenada recalled, "the spotter planes reported people fleeing across the open fields, so we switched to fragmented shells and began to chop the people up. Then we began firing phosphorous shells, incendiaries, and burned what was left to the ground."

The only difference between himself and First Lieut. William L. Calley Jr., Mr. Grenada said, was, "Calley was guilty because he could see who he was killing—I couldn't, so I'm not guilty." Lieutenant Calley was convicted for murdering civilians at Mylai in South Vietnam.

Meanwhile, the national commander of the Veterans of Foreign Wars, Herbert Rainwater, said that "nothing could be further from the truth" than to suggest that the demonstrators typified Vietnam veterans, and some onlookers suggested that most of them were not even former servicemen.

There was no way to take an accurate count of the authentic veterans. Some showed their discharge papers to reporters and others rattled off serial numbers and military unit designations. Nobody questioned the authenticity of the amputees who frequently led the ragtag "search and destroy" mock marches in wheel chairs.

Yesterday, 106 of the veterans were arrested on the steps of the Supreme Court for conducting a noisy protest of the Court's decision, the night before, to uphold an injunction against sleeping on the Mall. Those arrested were originally charged with the serious offense of obstructing justice, but, at the request of the Justice Department, the charges were reduced to lesser ones of disorderly conduct. [The Government later dropped the disorderly conduct charges according to United Press International.]

United Press International

ANTIWAR GESTURE: A veteran tossing his war medals over a fence erected near the steps to the west entrance to the U.S. Capitol in final demonstration in week of protest.

Highlight of the Week

It was this morning's demonstration, though—the spectacle of the men stripping themselves of combat honors and medals given to them by parents of their dead buddies—that probably best exemplified the point the group had been trying to make for five days.

Joseph Bangert, a 22-year-old former Marine who, like most of the others, was dressed in parts of his jungle fatigue uniform, returned six medals including the Vietnamese Cross of Gallantry.

He said that he had first wanted to give them back while still in Vietnam "when I found out that the 'political force' we were fighting was the people. We were taught 'Don't trust the kids, don't trust the old women, they'll kill you.' It's the people's struggle against the aggressor, but we're the aggressor."

Joseph H. Triglio, 25, a former Air Force sergeant who threw back a plaque he received as an honor graduate of his basic training school, shook his longish hair. "It was three and a half years of wasted time," he said. "It was a disservice to my country. As far as I'm concerned, I'm now serving my country."

After several hundred of the veterans had filed past the statue, depositing along with the medals and citations a few uniform jackets, helmets and even a plastic submachine gun. Larry Rottman, a veterans' organizer from New Mexico, declared the week's protest "now formally concluded."

After the crowd had returned to the campsite, to clean the area before breaking camp, one of the remaining veterans was asked what would become of the medals.

"I guess somebody will sweep them up and throw them away," he said. "We sure as hell don't want them any more."

The veterans who protested today had suffered some setbacks. Their plan to hold a memorial service for Vietnam war dead inside the Arlington National Cemetery was blocked by locked gates. Their hopes of camping on the east end of the Capitol Mall, in clear view of Congress, seemed thwarted by a Federal Injunction, hastily obtained by worried officials, that prohibited sleeping on the Government's property.

But from these doubtful beginnings grew an antiwar protest that, judging by the reception this city ultimately gave it, had an impact far greater than its numbers.

The veterans heard their right to sleep on the Mall defended in the Senate and the House, and the Nixon Administration, which pursued the matter to the Supreme Court, where the order was upheld, finally backed down and allowed the injunction to be dissolved.

"It would not have served the purpose of cooling the country to have six minutes of film of television showing us arresting veterans," a White House official explained this morning.

Tonight thousands of long-haired youths and their conservatively dressed elders joined more than 600 active duty servicemen in a memorial service "for all Indochina war dead" at Washington Naval Cathedral.

They heard Representative Robert F. Drinan, Democrat of Massachusetts and a Jesuit, call for a $50-billion reparations fund to be paid over the next five years to "all peoples of Indochina."

* * *

May 16, 1971

G.I. HEROIN ADDICTION EPIDEMIC IN VIETNAM

By ALVIN M. SHUSTER
Special to The New York Times

SAIGON, South Vietnam, May 15—The use of heroin by American troops in Vietnam has reached epidemic proportions.

The United States military command, the American Embassy and the South Vietnamese Government have been slow to awaken to the crisis. Now they are intensifying their efforts to curtail the easy flow of heroin to the soldiers, punish the sellers and rehabilitate the soaring numbers of Americans who use what they and Vietnamese sellers call "scag."

So serious is the problem considered that Ambassador Ellsworth Bunker and Gen. Creighton W. Abrams, the military commander, recently met with President Nguyen Van Thieu on measures to be taken by the Saigon Government, including agreement on a special task force that will now report directly to Mr. Thieu.

John Ingersoll, the Director of the Bureau of Narcotics and Dangerous Drugs, also conferred with Mr. Thieu and other officials and returned to Washington, reportedly alarmed at the ease with which heroin circulates and fearful of the danger to American society when the addicted return craving a drug that costs many times more in the United States than it does here.

The epidemic is seen by many here as the Army's last great tragedy in Vietnam.

"Tens of thousands of soldiers are going back as walking time bombs," said a military officer in the drug field. "And the sad thing is that there is no real program under way, despite what my superiors say, to salvage these guys."

Most efforts so far, whether aimed at drying up the supplies or handling the addicted, are proving ineffective.

While moves to crack down on smuggling and improve police work are clearly important, there are experts here who argue that the pushers will merely counter by increasing their level of competence.

Accordingly, they say, the best hope lies in trying to save those young Americans who will continue to be exposed to the drug, readily at hand on Army bases, in the field, in hospitals and on the streets of every city and village near American installations.

Confusion and Uncertainty

Like a parent who has suddenly discovered that his son is a junkie, the United States command has reacted with confusion and uncertainty. Should the kid be punished and kicked out of the house? Or should he be encouraged to confess all and be helped to recover?

The answer of the command has been to try both, but with the heavier emphasis on punishment. Its officers are arguing the basic question of whether the military has a responsibility to go all-out to cure men they view as weak enough to use heroin. And the command does not want to make treatment of drug users "too attractive" out of fear that more men would turn to heroin just to get out of Vietnam.

Officially, the command says that it is "fully aware of the extent of the drug-use problem and is constantly developing new and innovative approaches." But it will not provide even estimates of the size of the problem, and the approaches it regards as "new and innovative" are viewed by many of its own officers as haphazard and unsure.

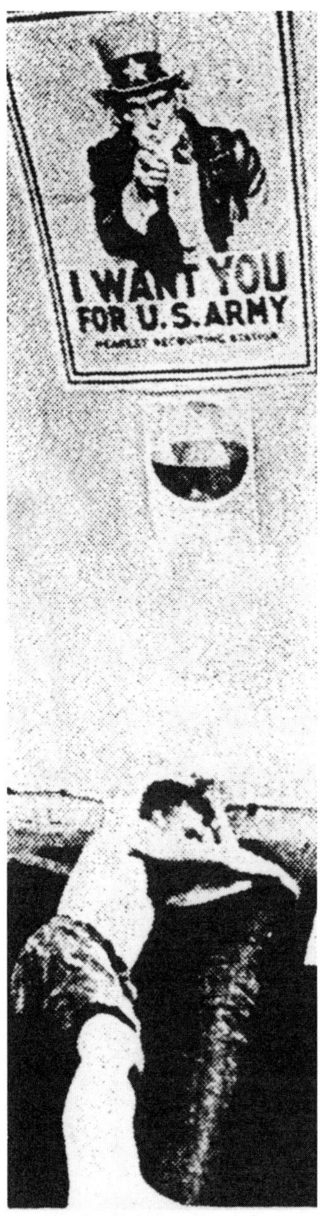

The New York Times/Dennis Cameron

American soldier going through drug withdrawal at a rehabilitation center in South Vietnam.

Overdose Deaths on Rise

The figure on heroin users most often heard here is about 10 to 15 per cent of the lower-ranking enlisted men. Since they make up about 245,000 of the 277,000 American soldiers here, this would represent as many as 37,000 men.

Some officers working in the drug-suppression field, however, say that their estimates go as high as 25 per cent, or more than 60,000 enlisted men, most of whom are draftees. They say that some field surveys have reported units with more than 50 per cent of the men on heroin.

The death toll from heroin overdose is expected to rise this year as well, despite the reduction in American troops. Thirty-five soldiers died from overdoses in the first three months of this year. Last year the quarterly average was 26 for a total of 103.

Reflecting the trend, almost as many have been reported arrested on heroin charges in the first three months of this year as in all of last year.

Through March, a total of 1,084 servicemen were charged with heroin use or possession, against 1,146 in all of 1970. In 1969, before heroin's wide-spread use here, there were 250 arrests.

In explaining why so many soldiers have turned to heroin, Maj. Richard Ratner, a psychiatrist from the Bronx working at a rehabilitation center called Crossroads at Longbinh, the sprawling American support base near Saigon, said the men were reacting to Vietnam much like the deprived in a ghetto.

"Vietnam in many ways is a ghetto for the enlisted man," he said. "The soldiers don't want to be here, their living conditions are bad, they are surrounded by privileged classes, namely officers; there is accepted use of violence, and there is promiscuous sex. They react the way they do in a ghetto. They take drugs and try to forget. What most of the men say when they come in to the center, however, is that they took to heroin because of the boredom and hassle of life here."

Rehabilitation Urged

A key reason that many think the military should concentrate on rehabilitation is the view that it is easier to get a soldier off the habit here than after he returns home as an addict, even though the strength of the heroin here is far greater.

In the United States, heroin of about 5 per cent purity is injected. Either by smoking or sniffing, soldiers here become addicted to heroin of about 95 per cent strength.

Some experts say that once addiction occurs it does not matter whether the user takes it intravenously or not because both types of users undergo severe withdrawal symptoms and hence crave the drug to avoid what the addicts here call the "jones", the pains of withdrawal. But not enough is known about smoking or sniffing the drug.

"We are taking the problem seriously because we think it is easier to get them off here, because they haven't been hooked as long as addicts in the States," said Brig. Gen. Robert Bernstein, the command's surgeon.

Despite the good intentions of many high-ranking officers and the length of the command's directives on drugs, many officers see the following faults in the present military program:

Rehabilitation is up to local commanders. The official directive says only that "rehabilitation centers are encouraged where feasible." Some commanders comply. Others leave the problem to medics at regular hospitals, to chaplains, to ex-addicts interested in curing others, or merely to the military police. A command spokesman defended this by saying that "we encourage individuality because we don't know the right patterns just as the solution escapes those in the States where many have long sought solutions."

Until today there has been no general policy on amnesty. The Army's program allows an addict to turn himself in for treatment in exchange for immunity from prosecution so long as he is not under investigation. The Air Force has a "limited program" that spokesmen say provides "a little immunity." The Navy finally announced an immunity program today.

The Army has only 10 rehabilitation centers, the largest able to handle about 30 men at a time. The men are kept five days to two weeks and then usually sent back to their units. In most instances, there is little continuing counseling.

Addicts are given no second chance. "The trouble is that once you go into that amnesty program you are a marked man back in your own unit," said one. "You can only do it once. The next time it's jail or a bad-conduct discharge that stays with you the rest of your life. Let's face it. I would have never been on the stuff if they hadn't sent me over here."

Because of the heavier reliance on punishment, drug cases are now clogging the military justice system. "Drug cases have become to the judicial system here what automobile accidents have become to the civil courts at home," said Henry Aronson of the Lawyers Military Defense Committee, which provides civilian counsel for accused soldiers.

In citing what they call a lack of interest in curing the addicts, some officers here are pointing to a study prepared by the Army for the establishment of a "security facility for drug abusers," an idea opposed by these officers who call it a "kind of drug concentration camp."

The report, called a "feasibility study," was signed by the deputy provost marshal. It suggests setting up the unit at Camp Frenzell Jones, near Saigon, for 125 soldiers facing charges of drug use or possession. The idea, one officer said, would be to speed up disciplinary action, with prosecutors, judges, and defense counsel on hand.

"They may get some medical attention, too," said an officer. "But the purpose is clearly to get the guys out of the service fast. I only wish the state of thought on rehabilitation was as advanced as that on punishment."

In dealing with the crisis and trying to persuade the young soldiers to avoid the temptations of heroin, the command has also been running into a credibility problem stemming from its earlier intense campaign against marijuana.

"My feeling is that the campaign against grass may have been counterproductive," said one Army doctor. "We kept telling them how dangerous that was. They tried it, probably tried at home first, and knew they weren't dying. We tell them how dangerous smoking scag is and they don't believe it. They find out soon enough, but too late."

Some addicts who may be exaggerating say that the crackdown and the arrests for smoking marijuana may have driven some soldiers to heroin. As one explained it.

"We smoke grass in the hootch and anybody can smell it and we're in trouble. We smoke scag and you have to be in the scag bag to detect it. We can smoke it in formation, in the orderly room, in the mess and nobody's going to bust you."

No one here is suggesting that a better rehabilitation program by the military is the ultimate solution. Not all addicts could be saved by it, but command spokesmen agree that much more in the way of psychiatric and medical counseling has to be done.

"Had to Shift Gears Fast'

"We had to shift gears fast from worry about marijuana to heroin and we're still shifting," one officer said. "It's just so new for us."

It was new, as well, for a 21-year-old from Georgia sitting this week in the Crossroads Center at Longbinh. A former military policeman who won the bronze star shortly after he arrived here, the soldier said he had never touched drugs in the United States.

"I moved in with this Vietnamese girl," he said. "I thought I'd try some scag. I never thought it would get to me. I got involved in the black market, selling stuff from the PX. The scag was everywhere, even in the hospital were I had to go for a time with a bad leg.

"I tell you it ruined my life. All it does is tear you up. All you think about is scag. I am going home soon and I don't want to go home strung out. I'm off and I'm staying off."

THE PENTAGON PAPERS

June 13, 1971

VIETNAM ARCHIVE: PENTAGON STUDY TRACES 3 DECADES OF GROWING U. S. INVOLVEMENT

By NEIL SHEEHAN

A massive study of how the United States went to war in Indochina, conducted by the Pentagon three years ago, demonstrates that four administrations progressively developed a sense of commitment to a non-Communist Vietnam, a readiness to fight the North to protect the South, and an ultimate frustration with this effort—to a much greater extent than their public statements acknowledged at the time.

The 3,000-page analysis, to which 4,000 pages of official documents are appended, was commissioned by Secretary of Defense Robert S. McNamara and covers the American involvement in Southeast Asia from World War II to mid-1968—the start of the peace talks in Paris after President Lyndon B. Johnson had set a limit on further military commitments and revealed his intention to retire. Most of the study and many of the appended documents have been obtained by The New York Times and will be described and presented in a series of articles beginning today.

Though far from a complete history, even at 2.5 million words, the study forms a great archive of government decision-making on Indochina over three decades. The study led its 30 to 40 authors and researchers to many broad conclusions and specific findings, including the following:

That the Truman Administration's decision to give military aid to France in her colonial war against the Communist-led Vietminh "directly involved" the United States in Vietnam and "set" the course of American policy.

That the Eisenhower Administration's decision to rescue a fledgling South Vietnam from a Communist takeover and attempt to undermine the new Communist regime of North Vietnam gave the Administration a "direct role in the ultimate breakdown of the Geneva settlement" for Indochina in 1954.

That the Kennedy Administration, though ultimately spared from major escalation decisions by the death of its leader, transformed a policy of "limited-risk gamble," which it inherited, into a "broad commitment" that left President Johnson with a choice between more war and withdrawal.

That the Johnson Administration, though the President was reluctant and hesitant to take the final decisions, intensified the covert warfare against North Vietnam and began planning in the spring of 1964 to wage overt war, a full year before it publicly revealed the depth of its involvement and its fear of defeat.

That this campaign of growing clandestine military pressure through 1964 and the expanding program of bombing North Vietnam in 1965 were begun despite the judgment of the Government's intelligence community that the measures would not cause Hanoi to cease its support of the Vietcong insurgency in the South, and that the bombing was deemed militarily ineffective within a few months.

That these four succeeding administrations built up the American political, military and psychological, stakes in Indochina, often more deeply than they realized at the time, with large-scale military equipment to the French in 1950; with acts of sabotage and terror warfare against North Vietnam beginning in 1954; with moves that encouraged and abetted the overthrow of President Ngo Dinh Diem of South Vietnam in 1963; with plans, pledges and threats of further action that sprang to life in the Tonkin Gulf clashes in August, 1964; with the careful preparation of public opinion for the years of open warfare that were to follow; and with the calculation in 1965, as the planes and troops were openly committed to sustained combat, that neither accommodation inside South Vietnam nor early negotiations with North Vietnam would achieve the desired result.

The Pentagon study also ranges beyond such historical judgments. It suggests that the predominant American interest was at first containment of Communism and later the defense of the power, influence and prestige of the United States, in both stages irrespective of conditions in Vietnam.

And it reveals a great deal about the ways in which several administrations conducted their business on a fateful course, with much new information about the roles of dozens of senior officials of both major political parties and a whole generation of military commanders.

The Pentagon study was divided into chronological and thematic chapters of narrative and analysis, each with its own documentation attached. The Times—which has obtained all but one of nearly 40 volumes—has collated these materials into major segments of varying chronological length, from one that broadly covers the two decades before 1960 to one that deals intensively with the agonizing debate in the weeks following the 1968 Tet offensive.

The months from the beginning of 1964 to the Tonkin Gulf incident in August were a pivotal period, the study makes clear, and The Times begins its series with this phase.

* * *

June 16, 1971

JUDGE, AT REQUEST OF U.S., HALTS TIMES VIETNAM SERIES FOUR DAYS PENDING HEARING ON INJUNCTION

ARGUMENT FRIDAY

Court Here Refuses to Order Return of Documents Now

By FRED P. GRAHAM

United States District Judge Murray I. Gurfein yesterday ordered The New York Times to halt publication of material from a secret Pentagon study of the Vietnam war for four days. Argument on publication thereafter will be heard Friday.

The judge granted a request by the Justice Department for temporary relief, but he gave no hint as to how he would eventually rule. He also refused to order The Times to return the massive report immediately to the Government.

Declaring that the case could be an important one in the history of relations between the Government and the press, Judge Gurfein said that any temporary harm done to The Times by his order "is far outweighed by the irreparable harm that could be done to the interests of the United States" if more articles and documents in the series were published while the case was in progress.

Times Says It Will Comply

The Times, in a statement issued after the hearing, said:

"The Times will comply with the restraining order issued by Judge Murray I. Gurfein. The Times will present its arguments against a permanent injunction at the hearing scheduled for Friday."

Lawyers for The Times and the Justice Department told the judge, at the proceedings in the Federal District Court House at Foley Square, that this appeared to be the first time in the nation's history that a newspaper was being restrained by a court from publishing an article.

Meanwhile, the Justice Department disclosed in Washington that the Federal Bureau of Investigation was investigating possible violations of federal criminal laws in connection with publication of the secret documents.

The bureau was known to be checking all who had access to the document, of which Justice Department sources said there were 15 copies.

Judge Gurfein, in his first day on the bench after having taken his oath of office last week, acted upon the Justice Department's argument that the publication of further articles by The Times would cause serious injury to the nation's international relations.

The 63-year-old judge deferred until Friday's hearing a decision on the Government's request that The Times be ordered immediately to return the voluminous documents from which its Vietnam series has been drawn.

Order Expires Saturday

The temporary restraining order issued by Judge Gurfein yesterday expires at 1 P.M. Saturday.

His action came a day after Attorney General John N. Mitchell had requested that The Times cease publishing the documents and The Times had refused to do so voluntarily.

Yesterday afternoon, the Justice Department filed a civil suit seeking to permanently enjoin The Times and 22 of its officers, editors and reporters from going ahead with the series of articles and documents on the origins of the Indochina war. Three installments had been published and The Times had said that the series was to continue.

Word filtered through the city's legal community yesterday that the Government had requested an afternoon hearing on a temporary restraining order against The Times, and the courtroom was packed—mostly with young lawyers and spectators—when the mustached judge took his seat in Room 605 of the United States Court House.

The arguments pitted a 30-year-old staff member of the United States Attorney's office, Michael D. Hess, against Prof. Alexander M. Bickel of the Yale Law School, a 46-year-old constitutional authority who has been mentioned as a possible Supreme Court nominee. Prof. Bickel represented The Times and its personnel.

The gist of the Government's argument was that The Times had violated a statute that makes it a crime for persons having "unauthorized possession" of Government documents to disclose their contents under circumstances that "could be used to the injury of the United States or to the advantage of any foreign nation."

In his argument, Mr. Hess asserted that "serious injuries are being inflicted on our foreign relations, to the benefit of other nations opposed to our form of government." He told the judge that Secretary of State William P. Rogers had said that several friendly nations had expressed concern over the disclosures in the articles.

With the Government facing the prospect of "irreparable injury" in its international relations, Mr. Hess said, The Times should be required to suffer a "slight delay" in its publication schedule until the case could be heard on Friday.

Otherwise, he said, the case would be mooted by publication of the material before a decision could be reached.

Professor Bickel, a tanned, dapper man in a brown suit and blue shirt, replied that this was a "classic case of censorship" that is forbidden by the First Amendment's free-press guarantee. He also insisted that the statute being invoked by the Government was an anti-espionage law that had never been intended by Congress to be used against the press.

The law, Title 18 of the United States Code, Section 793, provides for a maximum punishment of 10 years' imprisonment and a $10,000 fine against:

"Whoever having unauthorized possession of, access, to, or control over any document . . . relating to the national defense, or information relating to the national defense which information the possessor has reason to believe could be used to the injury of the United States or to the advantage of any foreign nation willfully communicates . . . the same to any person not entitled to receive it, or willfully retains the same and fails to deliver it to the officer or employe of the United States entitled to receive it."

Mr. Bickel contended that to rely upon this wording to bar a newspaper from publishing certain matter "for the first time in this history of the republic" would set an unfortunate precedent. "A newspaper exists to publish, not to submit its publishing schedule to the United States Government," he argued.

During a final discussion in his chambers, Judge Gurfein heard brief statements from two civil liberties groups that asked to be heard as friends of the court. Norman Dorsen, general counsel of the American Civil Liberties Union, and Kristin Booth Glen of the Emergency Civil Liberties Committee made the statements and asked to be heard again on Friday.

Judge Gurfein instructed them to file briefs and reserved judgment on their request to be heard.

He urged The Times to consent to a restraining order, but Mr. Bickel refused, saying that to do so would invite future Government efforts to curb news publications. The order was issued over Mr. Bickel's objections.

Order Not Appealed

The Times could have attempted to appeal the order to the United States Court of Appeals for the Second Circuit. However, such extraordinary appeals of temporary restraining orders are rarely granted, and The Times elected to have the issue tried on its merits before Judge Gurfein.

Mr. Bickel was accompanied in court by Floyd Abrams, a partner in the New York law firm of Cahill, Gordon, Sonnett, Reindel and Ohl.

The Justice Department named the following defendants in addition to The New York Times Company in today's injunction: Arthur Ochs Sulzberger, president and publisher, who will return today from a trip to London; Harding F. Bancroft and Ivan Veit, executive vice presidents; and Francis A. Cox, James C. Goodale, Sydney Gruson, Walter Mattson, John McCabe, John Mortimer and James Reston, vice presidents.

Also, John B. Oakes, editorial page editor; A. M. Rosenthal, managing editor; Daniel Schwarz, Sunday editor; Clifton Daniel and Tom Wicker, associate editors; Gerald Gold and Allan M. Siegal, assistant foreign editors; Neil Sheehan, Hedrick Smith, E. W. Kenworthy and Fox Butterfield, reporters; and Samuel Abt, a foreign desk copy editor.

* * *

June 21, 1971

THE VIETNAM PAPERS

On Nov. 25, 1964, some three weeks after President Johnson's election, The Times observed editorially that "another Vietnam reassessment is under way . . . [and] if there is to be a new policy now, if an Asian war is to be converted into an American war, the country has a right to insist that it be told what has changed so profoundly in the last two months to justify it." The country was not told.

Six months later, after repeated demands for "a straightforward explanation" of what was clearly becoming a major land war on the continent of Asia, this newspaper noted that "there is still no official explanation offered for a move that fundamentally alters the character of the American involvement in Vietnam" and pleaded "for the President to take the country into his confidence. . . ."

These comments illustrate how Congress and the American people were kept in the dark about fundamental policy decisions affecting the very life of this democracy during the most critical period of the war. The conviction even then that the Government was not being frank with the American people has been fully confirmed by the massive Pentagon history and documentation which The Times began to publish last week—until the Government undertook to censor it.

The running commentary and documents that did appear in this newspaper before the Government moved to block them throw a clear spotlight on the decision-making process during the period up to and including the major escalation of the Vietnam War in 1964 and 1965. The multi-volume study on which The Times' account was based shows beyond cavil how the decisions affecting American participation in and conduct of the war were planned and executed while their far-reaching political effect and profound significance, fully appreciated at the top reaches of government, were either deliberately distorted or withheld altogether from the public.

Even more important, the papers as published thus far suggest that almost no one in the upper ranks of the Administration during this crucial period six and seven years ago was probing into the basic political issue on which the military operation depended: Was the Saigon Government's control of South Vietnam of such vital, long-range interest to the United States that it warranted an open-ended American military involvement—or was this really an unexamined conclusion that had already become an article of faith? Nearly every official concerned was discussing the tactics and strategy of the war, how to handle it, how to win it, how to come out of it, what plans to make under various contingencies. These were important matters indeed and the officials in question would not have been doing their duty if they had failed to consider them. They should not be faulted for this; nor was it in any way improper to have planned for every conceivable military eventuality.

But the missing factor was discussion or argumentation the raison d'être of the war and the rationale for massive American involvement in it. It seems to have been accepted without question by virtually everyone in the top ranks, except Under Secretary of State George Ball, that the interests of the United States did indeed lie, at almost any cost and overriding almost any risk, in military victory for the South Vietnamese Government even to the point of major American participation in a war on the land mass of Southeast Asia.

This was the premise, this the context, and this the fateful error. If, as the principal officers of the Government saw the country being drawn into such a war, a full and frank debate and discussion in Congress and outside had been undertaken, it is quite possible that events would have moved in a different way. No one will ever know, for this "open covenant, openly arrived at" between American Government and American people never materialized.

This, then, is what the Vietnam Papers prove—not venality, not evil motivation, but rather an arrogant disregard for the Congress, for the public and for the inherent obligation of the responsibilities of leadership in a democratic society. The papers are not only part of the historical record; they are an essential part of that record. They are highly classified documents and so is the analytical study on which The Times' running commentary was based. But they carry the story of Vietnam no farther than 1968—now three years ago; they in no way affect current plans, operations or policy; and there seems no longer any justification for these papers—along with many others in governmental files—to bear the kind of classification that keeps them from general public access. Overclassification and misclassification of documents is at best a normal reflection of governmental inertia; but, as here, it is often used to conceal governmental error.

The material was not published by The Times for purposes of recrimination or to establish scapegoats or to heap blame on any individual in civilian or military ranks. It was published because the American public has a right to have it and because, when it came into the hands of The Times, it was its function as a free and uncensored medium of information to make it public. This same principle held for The Washington Post when it too obtained some of the papers. To have acted otherwise would have been to default on a newspaper's basic obligation to the American people under the First Amendment, which is precisely the point that Federal District Judge Murray Gurfein suggested in his memorable decision in this newspaper's favor last Saturday.

And yet the Government of the United States, in an action unprecedented in modern American history, sought and is continuing to seek to silence both The New York Times and The Washington Post, claiming that "irreparable injury" to the national security would be caused by publication of further chapters in the Vietnam study. The fact is that "irreparable injury" has been done to the Government itself, not because of anything that has been published but, quite the contrary, because of the extraordinary action the Government took to thwart and subvert in this manner the constitutional principle of freedom of the press which is the very essence of American democracy. Judge Gurfein's decision—whether or not it is sustained on appeal—surely represents a landmark in the endless struggle of free men and free institutions against the unwarranted exercise of governmental authority.

* * *

June 25, 1971

TIMES ASKS SUPREME COURT TO END RESTRAINTS ON ITS VIETNAM SERIES

ACTION TODAY SEEN

8 Justices Hold Closed Session on Appeal, Will Meet Again

By FRED P. GRAHAM
Special to The New York Times

WASHINGTON, June 24—The New York Times asked the Supreme Court today to permit it to resume publication of material from the Pentagon study of the Vietnam war.

Chief Justice Warren E. Burger and seven Associate Justices—Justice William O. Douglas was out of town—spent several hours in conference and then left for the day without acting on the appeal by The Times. They are expected to make a decision tomorrow.

Later today the Justice Department, turned down again by the Court of Appeals here, appealed to the Supreme Court in the effort to prevent The Washington Post from resuming publication of the same material.

Decisions in Conflict

The two appeals brought before the Supreme Court for the first time the question of any court's authority to restrain the press from publishing news that the Government says could seriously harm national security.

The prospects that the Supreme Court will hear the appeals are heightened because of the importance of the issues and also because lower courts' decisions are in conflict.

In New York, the United States Court of Appeals for the Second Circuit placed delays and restraints upon The Times's right to publish, while the Appellate Court here held that The Post could not be enjoined from publishing the material.

Closed Session Today

Although the Supreme Court is scheduled to recess for the summer—after holding a final public session Monday, it appears to have enough time to deal with the matter before then.

Tomorrow the Court will hold its usual closed Friday conference, and it is expected to decide then whether to review the two appeals. Under its rules it has complete discretion to hear the appeals or let the lower courts' decisions stand.

The rules favor review in important cases involving conflicting decisions below.

If review is granted the Justices could remain behind on Monday after they hand down their decisions and hear the case then or they could extend the term for a few days.

The action by the Justice Department came in the form of a motion by the Solicitor General, Erwin N. Griswold, to stay The Post from resuming publication pending a decision by the Supreme Court. The purpose, Mr. Griswold said, was to place The Times and The Post on an even footing.

He added that the Court could treat his application for a stay as a petition for review of the lower courts' proceedings.

Earlier in the day The Times brought the issue formally before the Court by asking it to lift the restraint on publication. The newspaper then asked in separate papers that the Court review and overturn the decision handed down yesterday by the Second Circuit Court of Appeals.

Today was the ninth day since Federal District Judge Murray I. Gurfein halted publication of The Times series. The series, which included documents accompanying the Pentagon study, appeared on June 13, 14 and 15, after which it was restrained.

The application by The Times for an immediate lifting of the restraint was addressed to Associate Justice John M. Harlan, who has jurisdiction over emergency petitions originating from the Second Judicial Circuit, which includes New York.

He referred the papers to the entire court because of the importance of the issues involved. Lawyers for The Times asked for oral arguments this afternoon on the sole question of lifting the restraint, but the request was not granted.

'News No Longer Current'

In the application The Times complained that the United States Court of Appeals here had refused to enjoin The Washington Post from printing materials from the Pentagon papers, so it would be free to resume publication in its Saturday editions. The articles, plus the material that has appeared in other newspapers would inflict "irreparable harm" on its interests, The Times argued. "News no longer current is stale and of severely diminished intrinsic value," it explained.

The Government, in a memorandum filed by Mr. Griswold, replied that for The Times to print the material now would render moot the very issue of restraint that it had asked the Justices to decide. Mr. Griswold strengthened his position later in the day when he asked the Court to place The Post on the same footing with The Times by forbidding it to publish more of the material until the issue was settled.

The Times, in its petition for certiorari (review) of the Second Circuit's decision, listed eight respects in which it said the Constitution was violated by the delays and restrictions on publication imposed by the Appellate Court.

The 5 to 3 ruling announced yesterday, held that The Times could resume publication of the series in its Saturday issue but could not use any material that the Government contended was dangerous to national security.

The court also instructed Judge Gurfein to hold secret hearings next week, as he did before handing down his decision last Saturday, and to determine by Saturday, July 3, which portions of those items cited by the Government posed "such grave and immediate danger to the security of the United States as to warrant their publication being enjoined."

Longer Delay Is Possible

The Times petition for review argued that the delay resulting from that procedure—which would total 18 days on July 3 and might extend far beyond that as a result of further appeals—violated the free-press guarantee of the First Amendment.

It also asserted that Congress had never given the Federal courts the power to impose "prior restraint" on newspaper publication and that the lower court's restraining orders violated the First Amendment and the separation-of-powers doctrine by doing so.

Further arguments were that the instruction by the Court of Appeals to Judge Gurfein were unconstitutionally vague and that the Government did not show that it was likely to win after all the evidence was in.

The Times maintained, furthermore, that a trial judge and an Appellate Court in the District of Columbia had held that the same material should not be enjoined and that any restraint of "articles relating to public affairs" might violate the First Amendment.

Both in the petition for review and in the application for an immediate lifting of the restraining order, The Times protested that the order for more hearings was based on assertions of fact made by the Government for the first time before the Court of Appeals. That amounts to offering testimony where cross-examination is impossible, The Times contended.

At issue was a secret "special appendix" given to the Court of Appeals Monday by the Justice Department. It is known to contain a 22-page typed inventory of portions of the 47-volume study that, according to the Government, would damage the nation's security if published.

The Court of Appeals gave the Government until tomorrow to add other items to the list if it wished, and Judge Gurfein was to hear secret testimony from Government officials as to how each item might affect security.

Today Mr. Griswold disclosed in his memorandum asking the Supreme Court not to lift the restrictions on The Times that the list took the form of sworn statements by Government officials. This bore out the assertions by counsel to The Times that the Court of Appeals relied on sworn "testimony" that had not been subjected to cross-examination.

* * *

June 29, 1971

ELLSBERG YIELDS, IS INDICTED; SAYS HE GAVE DATA TO PRESS

By ROBERT REINHOLD
Special to The New York Times

BOSTON, June 28—Dr. Daniel Ellsberg declared today that he had given the Pentagon study of the Vietnam war to the press. Moments later he surrendered to the United States Attorney here for arraignment on charges of unauthorized possession of secret documents.

Later in the day a Federal grand jury in Los Angeles returned a two-count indictment accusing Dr. Ellsberg of the theft of Government property and the unauthorized possession of "documents and writings related to the national defense."

The 40-year-old scholar and former Defense Department official had been described as the source of the Pentagon documents that The New York Times drew upon for its Vietnam series, the publication of which began on June 13 and was stopped on June 15 by Federal Court order.

Times Silent on Source

The Times refused again today to discuss the source of its documents.

After a one-hour hearing before United States Magistrate Peter W. Princi, Dr. Ellsberg was released on $50,000 bail. The Government had asked that bail be set at $100,000.

At almost exactly 10 o'clock this morning, as his lawyers promised Saturday, Dr. Ellsberg drove in a taxi to the Post Office Building, which houses the Federal courts.

Looking calm and confident and clutching his wife, Patricia, around the shoulders, he told the crushing throng of newsmen that in 1969 he gave the information contained in the documents to Senator J. W. Fulbright, chairman of the Senate Foreign Relations Committee.

"This spring, after two invasions and 9,000 more Americans deaths, I can only regret that at the same time I did not release them to the newspapers," he said. "I have now done so. I took this action solely at my own initiative.

"I did this clearly at my own jeopardy and I am prepared to answer to all the consequences of these decisions. That includes the personal consequences to me and my family, whatever these may be. Would not you go to prison to help end this war?"

In an interview later as he stood barefoot on the porch of his home in Cambridge, Dr. Ellsberg declined to discuss the details of how he gave the documents to the press. He would not confirm that The Times, the first newspaper to publish some of them, was the recipient of the 7,000-page study nor would he say whether he had a role in subsequent appearances of segments of it in other newspapers.

"I feel inhibited while there is litigation before the Supreme Court which turns in part on protection of sources," he said. "I don't want to say things that would make the case moot."

But, he added, "I was determined not to come forward without accepting responsibility."

First Appearance in 10 Days

It was Dr. Ellsberg's first public appearance in the 10 days since his name was mentioned publicly as The Times's source of the study, of which he was one of 30 or 40 authors. A warrant for his arrest was issued in Los Angeles late Friday, but his lawyers advised him to await a regular business day to surrender. Over the weekend he eluded an intensive search by Federal Bureau of Investigation agents.

The warrant charges Dr. Ellsberg, a former Marine Corps officer, who is now a research associate at the Massachusetts Institute of Technology, with possession and failure to return the secret papers, under Title 18, Section 793E, of the United States Code. He is not accused of transmitting documents to anyone else.

After pressing through an almost impenetrable crowd of newsmen and cheering well-wishers, Dr. Ellsberg and his lawyers, Leonard B. Boudin and Charles R. Nesson, both professors at the Harvard Law School, entered the 11th-floor offices of the United States Attorney, Herbert F. Travers Jr.

There he was placed under arrest by F.B.I. agents and taken to the United States Marshal's office for photographs and fingerprinting. About 30 minutes later, with two Federal marshals holding his arms he was taken to a 12th-floor courtroom.

There Dr. Ellsberg sat alone behind a brass rail and listened intently, his chin propped on his hand, as his lawyers and the Assistant United States Attorney, Lawrence P. Cohen, presented arguments over bail.

'Severity of the Crime'

Mr. Cohen argued for $100,000 bail because of the "severity of the crime as measured by the punishment"—up to 10 years in prison and a $10,000 fine, or both—and because Dr. Ellsberg did not turn himself in immediately upon issuance of the warrant, eluding the F.B.I. over the weekend. "This suggests the defendant has the resources to remain in hiding and frustrate this court," Mr. Cohen said.

In response Mr. Boudin asked that his client be released in his own recognizance. Magistrate Princi expressed some doubt, saying that if the defendant was proved guilty of being insensitive to laws protecting secret documents, then "might he not be also insensitive to his obligation to appear if he found things were not going as he anticipated."

Mr. Boudin sought to establish Dr. Ellsberg's reliability by reading a long list of his accomplishments and former positions—as special assistant to the Assistant Secretary of Defense and as a special assistant to the United States Ambassador to Vietnam. The lawyer added that the defendant waited until today to surrender to avoid the "Roman holiday" atmosphere that sometimes surrounds major F.B.I. arrests.

The United States Attorney replied that it was a matter of public notice that Dr. Ellsberg "has been in concealment for two weeks."

"I'd like something concrete," the Magistrate said. "He is here this morning. Is there any reason to believe he would not be here next week?"

Eventually Dr. Ellsberg, a slim, intense-looking man, asked that he be allowed to "make myself responsible to appear." After several more minutes, he rose again and said. "I do ask that my responsibility for my appearance be accepted."

At this the Magistrate said: "I am going to take you at your word. I am going to put you on $50,000 bail without surety. You're going to walk out and be free." He then scheduled a hearing on July 15 for the removal of Dr. Ellsberg to Los Angeles, where the case will presumably be tried.

At the conclusion of the hearing Dr. Ellsberg and his wife, both smiling, descended to the street and held an impromptu news conference under the bright sun in the middle of Post Office Square, which was thronged with cheering supporters.

He urged everyone to read the documents and expressed the hope that the disclosures would help "free ourselves from this war."

Asked if he had any regrets, Dr. Ellsberg replied, "Certainly not" and added that he was very pleased with the way the newspapers had defended the First Amendment.

"As a matter of fact, it's been a long time since I had as much hope for the institutions of this country," he continued. "When I see how the press and the courts have responded to their responsibilities to defend these rights, I am very happy about that as an American citizen."

Earlier he said that "as a responsible American I could no longer cooperate in concealing this information."

After having consented somewhat reluctantly to the interview, he discussed his motives for publicizing the documents.

The New York Times/Donal F. Holway

SAYS HE RELEASED PENTAGON PAPERS: Dr. Daniel Ellsberg at news conference outside Federal building in Boston with his wife after he surrendered himself yesterday.

Personal Responsibility

"I have wanted for about two years to try to raise the issue of personal responsibility and accountability of officials," he said, "not to punish but to make current officials conscious of their responsibility."

He took pains to dispute press reports that he was racked by guilt over his role in Vietnam, where he was connected with the pacification program.

"The simple fact is that I never felt tortured by guilt by anything I did in Vietnam," he asserted. "The kind of things I do blame myself for is not informing myself earlier than I did about the origins of the conflict."

He went on to say that his knowledge of the contents of the study was what drove him because it gave him a responsibility.

He maintained that not a single page of the documents he had disclosed "would do grave damage" to the country. He said he had not released documents that recounted direct negotiations between the Johnson Administration and foreign governments.

Dr. Ellsberg said he would expand on his comments tomorrow afternoon at a news conference at Faneuil Hall here.

* * *

July 1, 1971

SUPREME COURT, 6–3, UPHOLDS NEWSPAPERS ON PUBLICATION OF THE PENTAGON REPORT; TIMES RESUMES ITS SERIES, HALTED 15 DAYS

BURGER DISSENTS

First Amendment Rule Held to Block Most Prior Restraints

By FRED P. GRAHAM
Special to The New York Times

WASHINGTON, June 30—The Supreme Court freed The New York Times and The Washington Post today to resume immediate publication of articles based on the secret Pentagon papers on the origins of the Vietnam war.

By a vote of 6 to 3 the Court held that any attempt by the Government to block news articles prior to publication bears "a heavy burden of presumption against its constitutionality."

In a historic test of that principle—the first effort by the Government to enjoin publication on the ground of national security—the Court declared that "the Government has not met that burden."

The brief judgment was read to a hushed courtroom by Chief Justice Warren E. Burger at 2:30 P.M. at a special session called three hours before.

Old Tradition Observed

The Chief Justice was one of the dissenters, along with Associate Justices Harry A. Blackmun and John M. Harlan, but because the decision was rendered in an unsigned opinion, the Chief Justice read it in court in accordance with long-standing custom.

In New York Arthur Ochs Sulzberger, president and publisher of The Times, said at a news conference that he had "never really doubted that this day would come and that we'd win." His reaction, he said, was "complete joy and delight."

The case had been expected to produce a landmark ruling on the circumstances under which prior restraint could be imposed upon the press, but because no opinion by a single Justice commanded the support of a majority, only the unsigned decision will serve as precedent.

Uncertainty Over Outcome

Because it came on the 15th day after The Times had been restrained from publishing further articles in its series mined from the 7,000 pages of material—the first such restraint in the name of "national security" in the history of the United States—there was some uncertainty whether the press had scored a strong victory or whether a precedent for some degree of restraint had been set.

Alexander M. Bickel, the Yale law professor who had argued for The Times in the case, said in a telephone interview that the ruling placed the press in a "stronger position." He maintained that no Federal District Judge would henceforth temporarily restrain a newspaper on the Justice Department's complaint that "this is what they have printed and we don't like it" and that a direct threat of irreparable harm would have to be alleged.

However, the United States Solicitor General, Erwin N. Griswold, turned to another lawyer shortly after the Justices filed from the courtroom and remarked: "Maybe the newspapers will show a little restraint in the future." All nine Justices wrote opinions, in a judicial outpouring that was described by Supreme Court scholars as without precedent. They divided roughly into groups of three each.

The first group, composed of Hugo L. Black, William O. Douglas and Thurgood Marshall, took what is known as the absolutist view that the courts lack the power to suppress any press publication, no matter how grave a threat to security it might pose.

Justices Black and Douglas restated their long-held belief that the First Amendment's guarantee of a free press forbids any judicial restraint. Justice Marshall insisted that because Congress had twice considered and rejected such power for the courts, the Supreme Court would be "enacting" law if it imposed restraint.

The second group, which included William J. Brennan Jr., Potter Stewart and Byron R. White, said that the press could not be muzzled except to prevent direct, immediate and irreparable damage to the nation. They agreed that this material did not pose such a threat.

The Dissenters' Views

The third bloc, composed of the three dissenters, declared that the courts should not refuse to enforce the executive branch's conclusion that material should be kept confidential—so long as a Cabinet-level officer had decided that it should—on a matter affecting foreign relations.

They felt that the "frenzied train of events" in the cases before them had not given the courts enough time to determine those questions, so they concluded that the restaints upon publication should have been retained while both cases were sent back to the trial judges for more hearings.

The New York Times's series drawn from the secret Pentagon study was accompanied by supporting documents. Articles were published on June 13, 14 and 15 before they were halted by court order. A similar restraining order was imposed on June 19 against The Washington Post after it began to print articles based on the study.

Justice Black's opinion stated that just such publications as those were intended to be protected by the First Amendment's declaration that "Congress shall make no law . . . abridging the freedom of the press."

Paramount among the responsibilities of a free press, he said, "is the duty to prevent any part of the Government from deceiving the people and sending them off to distant lands to die of foreign fevers and foreign shot and shell.

"In my view, far from deserving condemnation for their courageous reporting. The New York Times, The Washington Post and other newspapers should be commended for serving the purpose that the Founding Fathers saw so clearly," he said. "In revealing the workings of government that led to the Vietnam war, the newspapers nobly did precisely that which the founders hoped and trusted they would do."

Justice Douglas joined the opinion by Justice Black and was joined by him in another opinion. The First Amendment's purpose, Justice Douglas argued, is to prohibit "governmental suppression of embarrassing information." He asserted that the temporary restraints in these cases "constitute a flouting of the principles of the First Amendment."

Justice Marshall's position was based primarily upon the separation-of-powers argument that Congress had never authorized prior restraints and that it refused to do so when bills were introduced in 1917 and 1957.

He concluded that the courts were without power to restrain publications. Justices Brennan, Stewart and White, who also based their conclusions on the separation-of-powers principle, assumed that under extreme circumstances the courts would act without such powers.

Justice Brennan focused on the temporary restraints, which had been issued to freeze the situation so that the material would not be made public before the courts could decide if it should be enjoined. He continued that no restraints should have been imposed because the Government alleged only in general terms that security breaches might occur.

Justices Stewart and White, who also joined each other's opinions, said that though they had read the documents they felt that publication would not be in the national interest.

But Justice Stewart, a former chairman of The Yale Daily News, insisted that "it is the duty of the executive" to protect state secrets through its own security measures and not the duty of the courts to do it by banning news articles.

He implied that if publication of the material would cause "direct, immediate, and irreparable damage to our nation or its people," he would uphold prior restraint, but because that situation was not present here, he said that the papers must be free to publish.

Justice White added that Congress had enacted criminal laws, including the espionage laws, that might apply to these papers. "The newspapers are presumably now on full notice," he said, that the Justice Department may bring prosecutions if the publications violate those laws. He added that he "would have no difficulty in sustaining convictions" under the laws, even if the breaches of security were not sufficient to justify prior restraint.

The Chief Justice and Justices Stewart and Blackmun echoed this caveat in their opinions—meaning that one less than a majority had lent their weight to the warning.

Chief Justice Burger blamed The Times "in large part" for the "frenetic haste" with which the case was handled. He said that The Times had studied the Pentagon archives for three or four months before beginning its series, yet it had breached "the duty of an honorable press by not asking the Government if any security violations were involved before it began publication.

He said he found it "hardly believable" that The Times would do this, and he concluded that it would not be harmed if the case were sent back for more testimony.

Justice Blackmun, also focusing his criticism on The Times, said there had been inadequate time to determine if the publications could result in "the death of soldiers, the destruction of alliances, the greatly increased difficulty of negotiation with our enemies, the inability of our diplomats to negotiate." He concluded that if the war was prolonged and a delay in the return of United States prisoners result from publication, "then the nation's people will know where the responsibility for these sad consequences rests."

In his own dissenting opinion, Justice Harlan said: "The judiciary must review the initial executive determination to the point of satisfying itself that the subject matter of the dispute does lie within the proper compass of the President's foreign policy relations power.

"The judiciary," he went on, "may properly insist that the determination that disclosure of that subject matter would irreparably impair the national security be made by the head of the executive department concerned—here the Secretary of State or the Secretary of Defense—after actual personal consideration.

"But in my judgment, the judiciary may not properly go beyond these two inquiries and redetermine for itself the probable impact of disclosure on the national security."

The Justice Department intially sought an injunction against The Times on June 15 from Federal District Judge Murray I. Gurfein in New York.

Judge Gurfein, who had issued the original temporary restraining order that was stayed until today, ruled that the material was basically historical matter that might be embarrassing to the Government but did not pose a threat to national security. Federal District Judge Gerhard A. Gesell of the District of Columbia came to the same conclusion in the Government's suit against The Washington Post.

The United States Coart of Appeals for the Second Circuit, voting 5 to 3, ordered more secret hearings before Judge Gurfein and The Times appealed. The United States Court of Appeals for the District of Columbia upheld Judge Gesell, 7 to 2, holding that no injunction should be imposed. Today the Supreme Court affirmed the Appeals Court here and reversed the Second Circuit.

The Supreme Court also issued a brief order disposing of a few other cases and adjourned until Oct. 4, as it had been scheduled to do Monday.

* * *

July 6, 1971

THE LESSONS OF VIETNAM

Pentagon's Study Uniquely Portrays The 'Greek Tragedy' of the U.S. Role

By MAX FRANKEL
Special to The New York Times

WASHINGTON, July 5—The Pentagon papers on how the United States went to war in Indochina probably mark the end of an era in American foreign policy—a quarter of a century of virtually unchallenged Presidential management and manipulation of the instruments of war and the diplomacy bearing on war. Yet the papers cannot be more than the beginning of reflection on that era and its climax, the nation's painful, disillusioning and still unresolved involvement in Vietnam.

Massive but incomplete, comprehensive but by no means exhaustive, remarkably honest but undoubtedly warped by perspective and experience, the papers are unlike any others ever composed in the midst of war and published within 3 to 10 years of the secret deliberations and calculations they describe.

They form a unique collection and they have been summarized under unique circumstances in nine installments in The New York Times—over the unique legal challenge of the United States Government. The very novelty of the papers and the contest over their publication have tended to divert attention from the essential tale they bear. There has already been dispute not only about what they mean but also about what they say.

From the perspective of 1971, they could be read as an anatomy of failure: the misapplication of an earlier day's theories and techniques for containing Communism and the misfire of the political wisdom of that day that the United States would pay any price and bear any burden to prevent the loss of one more acre of ground to Communists anywhere.

Yet, paradoxically, the Pentagon papers tell the story of the successful application of those theories and they demonstrate the great and still-surviving force of those political convictions and fears.

But they could also be read as a chronicle of success: the tenacious collaboration of four—and now perhaps five—administrations of both major parties in the preservation of a commitment to an ally, the demonstration of American fidelity to an enterprise once begun and the denial of victory to Communist adversaries.

Yet the Pentagon papers show that despite the sacrifices of life, treasure and serenity to the Vietnam war, the predominant American objective was not victory over the enemy but merely the avoidance of defeat and humiliation.

How Did the Agony Begin?

In sum, the papers and the discussion now swirling about them command at least a preliminary appraisal—of what they are and what they are not, of what they reveal and what they neglect. Who really deceived whom? And how did all this agony really arise?

Essentially the Pentagon papers are raw material for history—an insiders' study of the decision-making processes of four administrations that struggled with Vietnam from 1945 to 1968. The papers embody 3,000 pages of often overlapping analyses and 4,000 pages of supporting documents. They were commissioned by Secretary of Defense Robert S. McNamara, in a period of frustration with a war that critics sardonically gave his name to. But they were written and compiled by 36 analysts, civilian and military, most of them still anonymous, and they were finally printed and bound into fewer than 20 sets in the early months of the Nixon Administration, which paid them no heed until they began to appear in The Times.

The study drew primarily upon Pentagon files that are still sealed and upon some of the most important Presidential orders and diplomatic materials of the time under review. The analysts did not have access to the most private White House documents bearing on the moods and motives of the Presidents. And in the form obtained by The Times, the study also lacked several of the 47 volumes, among them four devoted to the diplomacy that surrounded the war.

Many Draft Proposals

But the Pentagon papers also offer more than the most polished of histories. They present not only the directives, conclusions and decisions of government in an era of prolonged crisis, but also many of the loose memorandums, speculations, draft proposals and contingency plans composed by influential individuals and groups inside that government.

Whatever is missing, for lack of access or perception, is more than recompensed by the sheer sweep and drama of this contemporaneous record.

Unlike diary, which can never escape the moment, and unlike history, which must distill at a remote future, the Pentagon study was able to re-enact a fateful progression of attitudes and decisions while simultaneously viewing them from a perspective greater than that of any of the participants.

So whatever its shortcomings, the study will stand as a vast trove of insights, hindsights and revelations about the plans and conceptions of small groups of men as they guided the nation into a distant but grievous venture, about how they talked and wrote to each other, to friend and foe, in public and in private. And the study is bound to stand as a new model for governmental analysis, raising questions normally reserved for literature: how powerful and sophisticated men take on commitments while they think themselves free, how they reach decisions while they see the mirage of choice, how they entrap themselves while they labor to induce or coerce others to do their will.

As the coordinator of the Pentagon study, Leslie H. Gelb, recently said of this story. "It was and is a Greek tragedy."

No Villains or Heroes

As written at the Pentagon and as recounted by The Times, the study found no villains or heroes. It made no historical value judgments. It argued no brief.

The portraits of the principal actors—especially those such as Secretary of State Dean Rusk, who were wary of betraying their views in interagency meetings and memorandums—are far from complete or satisfying. The portraits of the Presidents, even if their own files had been available, would remain inadequate until they were set against the political and international imperatives felt at the White House at every stage.

In the absence of a comparable study of the objectives and tactics of the Vietnam adversaries—notably the Government of North Vietnam and the coalition of insurgents in South Vietnam—the Pentagon papers could not presume to judge the morality or even the wisdom of the policies they record and describe.

And although many of the authors appear to have become disillusioned doves about the war, their study could stand almost as well as a brief for frustrated hawks; its central conclusion, that the nation simply pursued excessive aims with insufficient means, leaves entirely unresolved the central question of whether it would have been better to do more or to seek less.

Of all the revelations in the Pentagon papers, the most important deal with the patterns of thought and action that recur at almost every stage of the American involvement in Indochina:

This was a war not only decreed but closely managed by the civilian leaders of the United States. The military chiefs were in fact reluctant at the start, unimpressed by the strategic significance of Vietnam and worried throughout that they would never be allowed to expand the size and scope of the war to the point where they could achieve a clear advantage over the enemy.

This was not a war into which the United States stumbled blindly, step by step, on the basis of wrong intelligence or military advice that just a few more soldiers or a few more air raids would turn the tide. The nation's intelligence analysts were usually quite clear in their warnings that contemplated escalations of force and objective would probably fail.

Yet military considerations took precedence over political considerations at almost every stage. Since none of the Americans managing the Vietnam problem were prepared to walk away from it, they were forced to tolerate the petty political maneuvering in Saigon and Saigon's political and economic policies, even when Washington recognized them as harmful. As a result, even the military chiefs, and notably Gen. William C. Westmoreland, yielded to the temptation of seeking victory on the ground, although it was known that the enemy could always resupply just enough men to frustrate the American military machine.

The public claim that the United States was only assisting a beleaguered ally who really had to win his own battle was never more than a slogan. South Vietnam was essentially the creation of the United States. The American leaders, believing that they had to fight fire with fire to ward off a Communist success, hired agents, spies, generals and presidents where they could find them in Indochina. They thought and wrote of them in almost proprietary terms as instruments of American policy. Ineluctably, the fortunes of these distant, often petty men became in their minds indistinguishable from the fortunes of the United States.

The views of the world and the estimate of the Communist world that led the United States to take its stand in Indochina remained virtually static for the men who managed the Vietnam war. The "domino theory"—that all the other nations of Asia would topple if Indochina fell into Communist hands—moves robustly through the Pentagon papers, unshaken over two decades even by momentous events such as the split between the Soviet Union and Communist China, Peking's preoccupation with its Cultural Revolution and the bloody destruction of the Communist challenge in Indonesia.

The American objective in Vietnam, although variously defined over the years, remained equally fixed. Disengagement, no matter how artfully it might have been arranged or managed, was never seriously considered so long as a separate, pro-American and non-Communist government was not safely installed in Saigon.

The American Presidents, caught between the fear of a major war involving the Soviet Union or China and the fear of defeat and humiliation at the hands of a small band of insurgents, were hesitant about every major increase in military force. But they were unrestrained in both their public and private rhetorical commitments to "pay the price," to "stay the course" and to "do whatever is necessary."

The American military and civilian bureaucracies, therefore, viewed themselves as being on a fixed course. They took seriously and for the most part literally the proclaimed doctrines of successive National Security Council papers that Indochina was vital to the security interests of the nation. They thus regarded themselves as obligated to concentrate always on the questions of *what* to do next, not *whether* they should be doing it.

But the principal findings of the Pentagon papers cannot be fully understood without some recollection of the traditions, the training and the attitudes of the men who led the United States in the generation following World War II.

As The Economist of London has observed, these men were reared in the habits of the internationalist Presidents, notably Woodrow Wilson and Franklin D. Roosevelt, who also felt duty-bound to lead the nation into war after vowing to avoid it. The British weekly goes so far as to suggest that secret maneuver and public deception may be the only way to take great democracies to war.

Moreover, as Senator Frank Church of Idaho, one of the early Congressional critics of the war in Vietnam, remarked in Washington the other day, Presidents Truman, Eisenhower, Kennedy and Johnson were all reared to the conviction that only Presidents and their experts can have the perspective and knowledge needed to define the national interest in a hostile world.

They lived with the memory of Congress destroying Wilson's League of Nations and hampering Roosevelt's quest for safety in alliances against Germany and Japan.

They lived with the memory of two costly world wars, both of which they judged avoidable if, American power had been arrayed soon enough against distant aggression.

The Lesson of Munich

They lived with the nightmare that "appeasement" would only invite more aggression and lead directly to World War III, as the sacrifice of Czechoslovakia to Hitler at Munich led to World War II.

And they lived with the knowledge that another major war would be a nuclear war unless it were deterred with frequent demonstrations of American resolve and readiness to honor promises to friends and threats against adversaries.

These are the convictions that the men who made the Vietnam war carried into the post-world-war rivalry against the Soviet Union and against what they regarded for many years as a highly disciplined International Communist conspiracy, directed from Moscow and aimed at worldwide revolution and conquest.

After the "loss" of half of Europe to Communism, the American leaders set out to draw the line, wherever possible, to "contain" the Communists without major war.

They were imaginative and cold-blooded about the techniques they used in this effort. They broke the Berlin blockade without firing a shot. They poured $12-billion in economic aid into the revival of the economies of Western Europe. They led the United Nations into war in defense of South Korea. They sent military missions, military equipment, spies and agitators to all parts of the world. They sought to make and to destroy governments. They tried to "build" nations where none had existed before.

But they paid a profound psychological price. Their summons to sacrifice at home gave the contest an uncontrollable ideological fervor. The "loss" of China to Communism in 1949 and the further frustration of war in Korea in 1950 inspired a long hunt at home for knaves and traitors, in the White House and below, from which American politics is only beginning to recover.

Not Another Inch

Politicians and the politicians who became Presidents goaded each other to the conclusion that they could not "lose" another inch of territory to Communism, anywhere. The Republicans took after Democrats by saying they had been weak or treacherous about China and had accepted less than total victory in Korea. The Democrats took after Republicans by saying they had lost Cuba and dissipated American prestige and missile strength.

As President Eisenhower reached the end of his Administration, his greatest fear was the "loss" of Laos. And as President Kennedy assumed office, the Government's greatest ambition was the "liberation" of Cuba. No matter how small the nations or how marginal their threat to the United States, their "loss" came to be seen as an intolerable humiliation of American purpose and a dangerous invitation to aggression elsewhere.

Thus whenever aid and intrigue had failed, the cold war instinct was resort to overt force. And the failure of force in one place only magnified the temptation to use it elsewhere. The simultaneous fiasco at the Bay of Pigs in Cuba and dissolution of anti Communist forces in Laos in 1961 was uppermost in the minds of the Kennedy men who then proceeded to raise the stakes in Vietnam.

As the Pentagon papers show, they were motivated by the desire to contain China and what they considered to be the Asian branch of "international Communism," to protect the "dominoes" of non-Communist Asia, to discredit the Communist theories of guerrilla war and "wars of national liberation" and to demonstrate to allies everywhere that the United States would honor its pledges and make good on its threats no matter how difficult the task or insignificant the terrain.

These objectives were widely supported in the United States throughout the nineteen-fifties and long into the nineteen-sixties. But the Presidents who progressively decided on an ultimate test in Vietnam never shared with the Congress and the public what is now seen to have been their private knowledge of the remoteness of success.

As the Pentagon papers show, every President from Truman to Johnson passed down the problem of Vietnam in worse shape than he had received it. The study gives special point to President Johnson's recently disclosed remark to his wife in the spring of 1965, at the very start of his massive commitment of troops.

"I can't get out. I can't finish it with what I have got. So what the hell can I do?"

What he and his predecessors did not do was to inform the country of the dilemma and invite it to help make the choice.

The Pentagon papers reveal that all the difficulties of defining the Indochina problem date from the very earliest American experiences there, under Presidents Truman and Eisenhower. They show that Gen. George C. Marshall, a Secretary of State for Mr. Truman, recognized the Vietnamese Communists to be also the leaders of a legitimate Vietnamese anticolonialism. He thus recognized their challenge as different from any other Communist bid for power, but the distinction was soon lost.

The papers show that even after President Eisenhower reluctantly let the French go down to defeat in Indochina, his Administration refused to accept the compromise settlement of Geneva in 1954. It set out to supplant the French and to carry on the struggle, with hastily organized acts of sabotage, terror and psychological warfare against the new Communist Government in North Vietnam and with programs of aid and military training to establish a rival anti-Communist nation of South Vietnam.

A Complicating Factor

The stories now revealed make vastly more complicated the official American version of Vietnam history, in which the Hanoi Communists alone were charged with aggression and a ruthless refusal to leave "their neighbors" alone. Clearly, the American commitment to save at least half of Vietnam from Communism antedates the whole succession of Saigon governments to which it was nominally given.

Even in these early years of American involvement, the Governments of South Vietnam were perceived as mere instruments of larger American objectives. It was Gen. J. Lawton Collins, acting as President Eisenhower's personal representative in Indochina, who first proposed the ouster of Ngo Dinh Diem. The Vietnamese leader was saved at the time by agents of the Central Intelligence Agency, but several of those agents were still available to help arrange a coup against Mr. Diem eight years later.

Even in those early years, the Pentagon papers show, Washington's public optimism about the prospects for anti-Communists in Vietnam masked a private pessimism.

And even then the North Vietnamese Communists were being held responsible for the direction of the insurgency in the South, even though it was not for lack of trying that the Americans in the South failed to cause equal difficulty in the North.

In hindsight, with the benefit of the Pentagon papers, it is plain that the Kennedy years brought more, much more of the same.

The "domino theory" was now expanded to embrace concern about the fate of Indonesia, loosely regarded as also in Southeast Asia. The fiasco in Cuba and tension over Berlin made it seem even more imperative to take a stand somewhere, if only for demonstration purposes.

A Poor Place to Stand

Despite the Eisenhower warnings, Laos was deemed to be a poor place to make a stand. So it was partitioned among three rival factions, with the North Vietnamese gaining a convenient corridor for systematic infiltration into South Vietnam.

The deal had the effect of making the defense of South Vietnam vastly more difficult at the very moment when the American commitment to its defense was taking deeper root. The same paradoxical effect was achieved many times during the years of American involvement in Indochina.

The character of that involvement, it is now clear, also underwent a portentous though subtle change during the Kennedy years: American military and political activities came to be valued less for their intrinsic benefits than for the general encouragement they might give to the struggling South Vietnamese. They also came to be valued less for the damage they might inflict on the North Vietnamese than for the fear of still greater American involvement they were supposed to arouse.

Even though the Kennedy Administration knew the sad facts of instability, corruption and tyranny in South Vietnam, it consistently gave priority to military measures that would express its activism and bespeak its determination. Its vain but constant hope was that morale would improve in Saigon and that the threat of massive American intervention would somehow persuade Hanoi to relent.

Covert Operations Started

So for practical as well as domestic political reasons, private realism yielded even further to public expressions of optimism and confidence. Three weeks after the Bay of Pigs in April, 1961, Mr. Kennedy felt it necessary to order the start of new covert operations against the territory of North Vietnam and Communist regions in Laos.

Later in 1961, he heard so much debate about the growing need for American ground troops in Vietnam that the decision to send several thousand military "advisers" seemed a relatively modest and cautious move.

But the pressure built for a more direct American management of the entire war, an impulse that found its ultimate expression in Washington's complicity in the overthrow of President Diem. Once again, more than the President realized and perhaps more than he wanted, the obligation of the United States had been simultaneously deepened and made more difficult to redeem.

Along with the Kennedy term and the Kennedy men, President Johnson thus inherited a broad Kennedy commitment to South Vietnam. And twice in Mr. Johnson's first four months in office, Secretary McNamara returned from Saigon with the news that things were going from bad to miserable. Stable government now seemed impossible to achieve and the countryside was fast falling into Vietcong control.

Mr. McNamara and many other officials began to press for action, including new covert attacks against North Vietnam and at least urgent planning for open bombing and border patrols. They acknowledged privately that the real problems were in the South, but they could not yet conceive of any effective form of intervention.

So they built on the old formula of the Kennedy years—action for action's sake, not because it would achieve anything tangible but because it might help morale in Saigon and cause Hanoi to recognize that it could never "win" the war without confronting American power.

As the pentagon papers show, these "scenarios" for threat and escalation were written in the glib, cold but confident spirit of efficiency experts—the same experts whose careful plotting of moves and countermoves against the Soviet Union in the 1962 Cuban missile crisis had so gloriously vindicated the new political science of gamesmanship and probability theory.

Assistant Secretary of Defense John T. McNaughton, who eventually turned against the war with a pathetic confession of ignorance of the Vietnamese people, best typified this style of thought and planning at the upper levels of government.

In his memorandums, choices of more or less war were reduced to "options": "B—fast full squeeze. Present policies plus a systematic program of military pressures against the North . . ."; "C—progressive squeeze-and-talk. Present policies plus an orchestration of communications with Hanoi and a crescendo of additional military moves . . ."

Countries and peoples became "audiences": "The relevant audiences" of U.S. actions are the Communists (who must feel strong pressures), the South Vietnamese (whose morale must be buoyed), our allies (who must trust us as 'underwriters'), and the U.S. public (which must support our risk-taking with U.S. lives and prestige). . . . Because of the lack of 'rebuttal time' before election to justify particular actions which may be distorted to the U.S. public, we must act with special care—signaling to the D.R.V. that initiatives are being taken, to the GVN that we are behaving energetically despite the restraints of our political season, and to the U.S. public that we are behaving with good purpose and restraint."

Definition of Objectives

Many of these memorandums were only "contingency plans" that contemplated what else the United States might do in one or another eventuality. But there was nothing contingent in their definition of American purposes and objectives, in their analyses—in the crucial years of 1964–65—of the rapidly deteriorating situation in South Vietnam and in their revelation of the state of mind of the dozen or so top officials whose persistent clamor for action could be delayed but never ultimately denied by a President who shared their purpose.

And there was nothing "contingent" about the direct orders of the National Security Council and the Presidential messages that have turned up with the Pentagon papers. The lines of reasoning and decision from the action papers to the contingency papers are direct and unmistakable.

The Pentagon papers and The Times's reports on them confirm the judgment of contemporary observers that President Johnson was reluctant and hesitant to take the final decision at every fateful turn of his plunge into large-scale war.

Mr. Johnson and other officials were often evasive or coy with the press by creating the impression that plans for bombing were only "recommendations" without "decision" or that "requests" for more troops from the field were not "on my desk at this moment" because they lay formally elsewhere.

But these are not the most important deceptions revealed in the Pentagon papers.

There is, above all, much evidence that the four administrations that progressively deepened the American involvement in the war felt a private commitment to resist Communist advance, and then a private readiness to wage war against North Vietnam and finally a private sense of frustration with the entire effort much sooner and to a much greater extent than they ever acknowledged to the Congress and the nation.

There is evidence in the papers that the Congress was rushed into passing a resolution to sanction the use of force in Vietnam in 1964, ostensibly to justify retaliation for an "unprovoked" attack on American vessels, even though the Administration really intended to use the resolution as the equivalent of a declaration of war and withheld information that would have shown the North Vietnamese to have had ample reason for "retaliating" against the United States.

There is evidence that all the elaborately staged offers of negotiation and compromise with the Communist adversary were privately acknowledged in the Administration as demands for his virtual "surrender."

And there is evidence, scattered over the years, that the oft-proclaimed goal of achieving "self determination" for the South Vietnamese was in fact acceptable to the United States only as long as no South Vietnamese leader chose neutralism or any other form of nonalignment. As President Johnson put it in a cablegram to his ambassador in early 1964, "Your mission is precisely for the purpose of knocking down the idea of neutralization wherever it rears its ugly head."

The evidence for two very specific charges of deception that have been leveled against President Johnson since publication of the Pentagon papers is much less clear.

The Pentagon study itself did not make any charges and neither did The Times in its reports on the findings of the study. But many readers concluded that Mr. Johnson had lied to the country in 1964, when he denounced his Republican opponent, Senator Barry Goldwater, for advocating full-scale air attacks against North Vietnam, and again in April, 1965, when he secretly authorized the use of American troops in an offensive combat role.

The Pentagon study describes a "general consensus" among the President's advisers, two months before the 1964 election, that air attacks against North Vietnam would probably have to be launched. It reports an expectation among them that these would begin early in the new year. As The Times report added, the papers also showed the President "moving and being moved toward war, but reluctant and hesitant to act until the end."

Search Through the Files

Mr. Johnson and those who defend his public statements at the time are undoubtedly right in their contention that the President made no formal decision to authorize more bombing until there were additional attacks on American bases in February, 1965.

But the President also knew that most of his major advisers regarded such a decision as "inevitable"—because they thought South Vietnam to be in danger of imminent collapse, because the forces to conduct more air attacks were in place, because the target lists had long ago been prepared and because even sustained bombing was destined to be merely a stopgap measure until more troops could be rushed to South Vietnam.

In a search through his own dispatches from Washington at the time, this reporter has come upon three interesting accounts that help to explain the confusion but tend to support the much more thoroughly researched judgment of the Pentagon papers.

On Oct 9, 1964, The Times reported on a news conference question to Secretary Rusk about reports "here and in Saigon that the Administration was considering a 'major turn' in policy but deferring a decision until after Election Day, Nov. 3." Mr. Rusk refused to predict "future events" but said that domestic politics had no bearing on any such decisions.

On Feb. 13, 1965, after a new "retaliatory" raid on North Vietnam but before the start of sustained bombing, this reporter quoted two unidentified high officials as follows:

"There is no doubt that the President remains skeptical about a deeper involvement in Asia, but he is getting some very belligerent advice from very intimate quarters."

"History may determine that it was already too late, that the die is cast, but I am sure that the Government's strategy is not yet determined."

In other words, even high officials sensed that their President was still reserving final judgment and "decision," but they did not really know how much real choice remained.

After the Decision

Even after the decision had been made, however, there was no simple way to get a straight answer from the Johnson Administration in those days, as is evident in the opening lines of a dispatch on March 2, 1965:

"The Administration described today's air strikes against North Vietnam as part of a 'continuing' effort to resist aggression and made no effort, as in the past, to relate them to particular provocation. . . . The White House said only that there had been no change in policy. The State Department said nothing. . . ."

Some officials at the time, and Mr. Johnson on at least one occasion since then, suggested that such coyness after decision had been deemed necessary to avoid provoking intervention in the war by Soviet or Chinese Communist forces. They never explained, however, why either nation would make such a grave decision on the basis of announcements in Washington rather than on the facts of the bombing, which were well known to them.

A far more plausible explanation, one that sounds strange in matters of such weight but rings true to those who could observe Lyndon Johnson closely and sympathetically in those days, has been offered by Stewart Alsop in Newsweek: "President Johnson was trying to fool not the people but himself—and temporarily succeeding."

'The Awful Pressures'

What really emerges from the Pentagon papers, Mr. Alsop wrote approvingly, "is a picture of a desperately troubled man resisting the awful pressures to plunge deeper into the

Vietnam quagmire—resisting them as instinctively as an old horse resists being led to the knackers. The President bucks, whinnies and shies away, but always in the end the reins tighten—the pressures are too much for him."

As the Pentagon papers further show, Mr. Johnson was to make two or three other big decisions about troop commitments and carve them up into smaller, more digestible numbers, as if this could hide the magnitude of the American involvement. He knew that he was not winning the war and he knew that he was playing only for some unforeseeable stroke of good fortune, and it may be that his sense of statesmanship led him to conclude that the nation would be preserved longer if he minimized the task.

Whatever the motives, the methods for handling the awkwardness of Vietnam had then become almost traditional. But it was Mr. Johnson's misfortune to be President, as Mr. Gelb, the coordinator of the study has written, when the "minimum necessary became the functional equivalent of gradual escalation" and the "minimal necessity became the maximum" that international and domestic constraints would allow.

The overriding evidence in the Pentagon papers, quite apart from the timing of decisions or the candor with which they were disclosed, is that the United States Government involved itself deeply and consciously in a war that its leaders felt they probably could not win but that they also felt they could not afford to lose.

Gradually, some of the leading advocates of the war lost their enthusiasm for it, but even in disillusionment they felt a higher duty of loyalty to the President and his policy than to the public that had become deeply divided and tormented by the war.

As early as 1966, Mr. McNaughton perceived an "enormous miscalculation" and an "escalating military stalemate." By 1967, Mr. McNamara and probably others were recommending a reduction of objectives and perhaps a face-saving exit through the formation of a coalition government in Saigon.

But Mr. Johnson thought more unhappy Americans were hawks than doves and he was also forced, amid fears of noisy resignations, to negotiate with his military leaders, who were demanding more, rather than less, commitment.

Decisive Shock at Tet

Not until the shock of the enemy's Tet offensive in 1968, and the need to mobilize reserves if he was to meet the military's request for 206,000 additional men for the combat zone, did Mr. Johnson set a final limit on the American commitment, cut back the bombing of North Vietnam and announce his plan to retire without seeking a second term.

No one knows to this day whether by these moves the President intended to hurry out of the war in some face-saving manner or merely to buy still more time from the American voters for a final effort at vindication.

As the Pentagon papers disclose, his Administration did not expect much from the bombing limitation or the new offer to negotiate with Hanoi.

"We are not giving up anything really serious in this time frame" of four weeks, the State department informed its embassies, noting that poor weather would have curtailed the raids for that period in any case. It said that some of the air power would be switched to targets in Laos and South Vietnam and that in any case Hanoi was expected to reject the bid for talks and this would "free our hand after a short period."

Hanoi accepted the bid for talks, but has offered very little so far that interests Washington. Neither on the way in nor on the way out, it is now clear, was the American hand in Vietnam ever "free."

PART VIII

THE END OF THE AMERICAN WAR, 1971–1975

The War for the South

September 5, 1971

ARMY IS SHAKEN BY CRISIS IN MORALE AND DISCIPLINE

By B. DRUMMOND AYRES Jr.
Special to The New York Times

WASHINGTON, Sept. 4—The bitter Vietnam experience has left the United States Army with a crisis in morale and discipline as serious as any its oldest and toughest soldiers can remember.

At the fire bases around Saigon, in the guard towers at the Berlin Wall, on the parade ground at Fort Benning, Ga., there is concern that the men in the ranks no longer have the esprit necessary to make first-class fighters.

The men themselves are fed up with the war and the draft, questioning orders, deserting, subverting, smoking marijuana, shooting heroin, stealing from their buddies, hurling racial epithets and rocks at their brothers.

Their leaders, trained to handle a different sort of crisis, often seem as bewildered as the rawest recruits, compromising, innovating, ordering strategic retreats from tradition, tossing out the training manual—all with uncharacteristic pliability.

The desertion rate soars, so they do away with bed checks and permit psychedelic posters on barracks walls. The troops are bored, so they take them skiing and put beer machines in the day room. The troops refuse to advance, so they talk it over with them and try to find another way.

It is enough to tarnish an old soldier's brass. "I've got 18 in and I've never seen things so bad," says Sgt. Maj. Jerry Thompson, who plans to quit the Army after finishing a tour in the training command at Fort Leonard Wood, Mo. "If you're

The New York Times

A soldier gives the peace sign as his platoon moves along a dusty road during training hike at Fort Riley, Kansas.

going to have an Army, you've got to have discipline. If you've got rules, you've got to enforce them. Nobody is. I'm leaving."

While a few of the true professionals—the "lifer" non-coms and the "hardcore" colonels and generals—are quitting like Sergeant Thompson, most are sticking it out, gritting their teeth in frustration and digging in.

There is always a letdown when the worst of a war is past, they say, and as Vietnam is one of the most unpopular wars in the nation's history, it is not surprising that men compelled to take part in it are unhappy and recalcitrant. But the professionals are concerned just the same.

Challenge Is Discerned

"The challenge of putting it all back together again is certainly one of the greatest I've ever faced in 26 years in the service," said Maj. Gen. Hal Moore, the commanding officer of the basic recruit training facility at Fort Ord, Calif.

Publicly, General Moore's statement is about as far as men on active duty will go when talking about the Army's present troubles. The "system" does not encourage open discussion of problems.

Privately, the talk is much more candid. A brigadier general in the Pentagon waits until an aide has left his office, then leans forward and says:

"Okay, let's face it. We have units today that simply are not fit to go if the balloon goes up. It's going to take another year, at least, to get back in condition."

Retired officers speak even more bluntly and openly. Gen. Hamilton H. Howze, who retired several years ago after serving as commander of the elite 82d Airborne Division and the Eighth Army in Korea, wrote recently in Army magazine:

"The military forces of the United States face a disciplinary situation which, if not already critical, is at least one of rapidly growing proportions. Should senior commanders not be able to reverse the trend toward indiscipline, this country will, not long from now, lose its status as the world's first power and stand almost helpless against those who would humble it or destroy it."

Easing Is Expressed

It is not that the professionals have lost hope altogether. There is confidence that as the Vietnam fighting grinds down, as the Army cuts back from a wartime force of over 1.5 million men to a peacetime force of about 900,000, the problems will grind down, too.

This was the Marine Corp's experience when it left Southeast Asia, and there are a few tentative signs that it will be the Army's as well.

For example, the number of "underground" G.I. newspapers has dropped in the last year from a high of about 60 to a current low of 30.

These publications specialize in biting, often inflamatory criticism of military life. Their editors frequently slip onto military bases to counsel disgruntled soldiers.

But interest in such efforts seems to be declining. One of the surviving papers, F.T.A., printed in the Louisville area for 30,000 soldiers stationed at Fort Knox, sent the following note with its latest issue:

"We are sorry that you have not yet received the June and July issue of F.T.A. We have had and are still having some serious financial problems. . . . With only two men working on the project . . . we get on base about four times a week and are currently seeing two new people each week. This is not good."

While encouraged by the decline in the number of underground papers, the Army careful not to become overly optimistic. Two of the most important indices of morale and discipline—the desertion rate and the absenteeism rate—continue to climb rather than decline.

Over the last 12 months, 177 of every 1,000 American soldiers have been listed as "absent without leave," some three or four times. And 74 of every 1,000 men have stayed away a month or more and thus have been classified as deserters.

These rates represent roughly a three-fold increase over the desertion and absenteeism rates recorded five years or so ago when the Army was just beginning its buildup in Vietnam and the war was less a political issue.

For example, in 1966 only 57 of every 1,000 American soldiers were listed as absent without leave and only 15 of every 1,000 deserted.

Other indices of indiscipline and bad morale present an equally disturbing picture.

Medical tests given men leaving Vietnam indicate that about four of every hundred are drug users And military authorities in Saigon say they are making almost no progress in halting sales of the most troublesome narcotic—heroin.

"The Vietnam drug situation is extremely serious," says Brig. Gen. Robert G. Gard Jr., a Pentagon specialist in disciplinary problems. "The testing, thus far, has been spotty. And we even have cases of testers—they're mostly soldiers themselves—falsifying the test results for their buddies."

Drug abuse investigations are climbing rapidly everywhere. In 1969, for the Army as a whole, there were 12,000. Last year, this figure increased to 14,500. And this year the total is expected to approach 20,000.

No comprehensive figures are kept on resulting legal action, since some men are given only reprimands while others go to trial or enter the special "detoxification" clinics.

As for the amnesty program, still less than a year old, it has already attracted more than 15,000 men.

"In just the past few weeks, nine of my men have turned themselves in," says Col. Willard Lapham, commanding officer of the 197th Infantry Brigade, stationed at Fort Benning. "The problem has never actually affected unit performance and I think we're licking it. But if only one man is taking something, it's serious."

It is within units like the 197th that the problem shows up as something more than cold statistics.

Vehicles Locked Now

Posters plastered on barracks walls warn of the dangers of heroin and marijuana. Men are constantly attending lectures about addiction. Dogs trained to smell out narcotics prowl company areas.

On pay day, men are urged to be especially careful. The drug habit is expensive and addicts resort to crime to get cash.

Thus far this year, more than $5,500 in personal property has been stolen from the men of the 197th, $1,000 more than was taken in all of 1970. In July alone, there was almost one theft a day.

"Every one of my military vehicles now has a chain and lock attached to its steering wheel whenever it's parked," says Lieut. Col. Robert Faulkender, one of Colonel Lapham's battalion commanders.

At Fort Carson, Colo., home of the Fourth Mechanized Infantry Division, more than $22,000 in cash and goods was stolen last month in 173 thefts.

At Fort Leonard Wood, the picture is little changed. Men are warned repeatedly to lock up their personal possessions and urged not to venture into unlighted areas, where there have been some muggings.

And at Fort Ord, each unit has a special anti-crime guard team that patrols after hours. Members wear white helmets and carry heavy night sticks.

A brigade executive officer, Lieut. Col. James Gabriel, says: "I can remember when a military post was the safest place a man could be. Once inside the gates, you never had to worry about a thing. Not any more."

In fact, not even barracks rooms themselves are safe any longer in the United States Army.

Racial tensions have so polarized whites and blacks in many units that fights break out periodically in bunk areas and latrines. In mess halls, blacks and whites frequently sit down at separate tables, the blacks greeting each other with up-thrust black power salutes and elaborate "dap" hand shakes.

Outside bases in Vietnam, Korea and Germany, blacks and whites often frequent separate bars and brothels. Intruders are beaten.

"It's hard to believe, but what we've done is export our racism," says L. Howard Bennett, a Pentagon civil rights specialist. "That exporting includes 'black aggression,' too. There are far too many incidents overseas these days of four or five blacks ganging up one or two whites."

The Army keeps no statistics on minor racial incidents, such as verbal abuse and small fights. However, these almost certainly are increasing since major incidents, for which there are statistics, are increasing.

For example, between September, 1970, and August, 1971, the Army recorded 18 racial incidents—gang fights, protests, riots—that required "significant" police action. Only 10 such incidents occurred in the 12 months leading up to September, 1970.

To reduce tensions, the Pentagon has ordered four hours of instructions in race relations for every American soldier. Furthermore, many units have established racial harmony councils, which draw members from all ranks and all races.

"Our council really talks things out—very frankly—and I think we're beginning to take the steam out," says Maj. Gen. John Bennett, the commanding officer of the Fourth Division.

"At least we're communicating," says Specialist 5 William Manning, a black member of the Fort Carson council. "When I go back and tell the brothers that somebody is listening, that somebody is willing to talk about discrimination and harassing and fights and things like that, it seems to help."

General Bennett, who has tried many other morale building innovations, such as reducing the number of inspections, is optimistic about the Army's future. He says:

"I have to admit that some of the indicators still look bad, but I also have this feeling that we've touched bottom with the troublemakers and are heading up."

The troublemakers are primarily draftees, who must serve for two years, and draft-motivated volunteers, who must serve for three years but can choose their first duty station or their military occupation. Together, these two types of soldiers account for about half of the Army's over-all strength and perhaps four-fifths of its actual front-line strength.

To increase the number of true volunteers in its ranks and thus eliminate many of its troubles, the Army has begun implementing an ambitious program that includes not only the beer machines in the day rooms but also pay increases, a five-day work week, multi-million dollar recruiting campaigns and a renovation of the once hide-bound basic training course.

'Short Timers' Troublesome

But these steps take time. And meanwhile the rank and file at bases in this country and around the world continue to pose problems.

Perhaps the most serious of all the problems is the man just back in the states from Vietnam, the "short timer" with only a few months of service remaining, the combat veteran suddenly transferred from a world of misery-loves-company camaraderie and no saluting to a world of strangers and "lifer" discipline.

The Vietnam returnee is seldom in the mood for what he calls "Mickey Mouse." Training exercises do little to inspire him once he has experienced the real thing.

At Fort Riley, Kan., Specialist 5 John Ambrose waves his hand out toward the horizon, where men are going through various garrison drills, and says:

"Man, this is just so much hassling for us follows who've been up against Charlie. We're just barely going through the motions until we can go home."

An increasing number of returnees refuse even to go through the motions. Court-martial convictions for insubordination, mutiny and refusals to obey orders climbed from 230 in 1968 to 294 in 1969 to 331 last year. This year, convictions may exceed 450.

These figures represent only the extreme cases. No statistics are kept on the less serious incidents, which occur almost daily in many units.

"You hear guys giving the sergeants and lieutenants a hard time two or three times a week," says Specialist Ambrose.

"Mostly they manage to work it out or maybe a man gets some extra duty or loses a stripe."

"Working it out" first started in Vietnam, where the practice continues. The procedure is simple and has even been filmed by television news crews.

A unit or man refuses to advance or take an order. Everybody—including officers and sergeants—sits down and talks. A safer route or alternative job is agreed upon.

Officers and sergeants in Vietnam who refuse to participate in these discussions run the risk of being "fragged" by a hand grenade tossed into their bunk by one of their own men.

In 1969, there were 126 "actual" or "possible" fraggings. The count rose to 271 last year, and this year it probably will exceed 425. Seventy-eight men have been killed and more than 600 wounded.

Often, the lieutenants or sergeants sympathize with the men who do not want to advance or take part in training exercises. Many young officers are draft-motivated, one-tour reservists and many sergeants are draftees who have been promoted.

Retaining Careerists

Though the Army is holding onto most of its professionals despite its many problems, the retention of young career officers and enlisted men has reached a critical point. The squeeze comes not so much in loss of numbers—the Army can always induct more men or cut back its strength—as in loss of experience, attained at considerable training cost.

In the early nineteen-sixties, before antimilitary sentiment swept the nation's youth, one of every four volunteers was re-enlisting at the end of his first tour. Today, only one of every five is signing on for a second tour.

The re-enlistment figure for draftees, never very high, has fallen in 10 years from about 10 per cent to less than 5 per cent.

Among blacks, volunteers as well as draftees, re-enlistment has fallen in the last five years from three times the white rate to two times the white rate.

Enrollment in the Reserve Officers Training Corps, the college program that provides the Army with the majority of its commanders, has also declined sharply, from 165,000 men in 1961 to 74,000 this year. Some of the country's best schools, such as Harvard, Yale and Dartmouth, have dropped the course or made it an elective.

There has also been a decline in the number of R.O.T.C. graduates choosing to stay on in the service after their first tour. For example, in 1961 about one of every three re-enlisted. This year, only one in every five is staying on.

At the United States Military Academy, there are still more problems. Applications for appointments remain high, but the number of qualified applicants is falling.

And the number of academy alumni leaving the Army after five years of service—the minimum now required—is increasing. Only 15 per cent of the class of 1956 had resigned from active duty by the end of 1961. But with 1971 little more than half over, the class of 1966 already has lost 28 per cent of its members to civilian life.

There is, however, one bright spot in this rather gloomy picture.

On Army posts such as Fort Carson, where the "New Army" concepts are being tried—the beer machines, the five-day week, improved barracks and reduced inspections—re-enlistment rates are spurting.

In fact, they are already double the rates being achieved by posts still operating on the theory that the only kind of discipline is "lifer" discipline.

* * *

November 7, 1971

U.S. CUTS CIVILIAN ROLE, TOO, IN VIETNAM

By IVER PETERSON
Special to The New York Times

SAIGON, South Vietnam, Nov. 6—Along with the American combat role in Vietnam, the United States advisory program, with its separate army of soldiers and civilians, is winding down.

The principal advisory organization—known as Civilian Operations and Rural Development Support, or CORDS—has shrunk considerably since its peak period in January, when it had 7,650 military men and civilians working in the countryside.

It has about 4,600 today, and this figure, planners say, will be cut by almost half by next July. These advisers include about a thousand of the 1,387 civilian employes here of the United States Agency for International Development, the aid administering body. The others work in various Saigon headquarters. These civilians could be out of work Nov. 15 unless Congress revives the foreign aid program.

The other major aspect of the advisory program is the oldest one—that of advising the South Vietnamese armed forces, a role the Americans took over from the departing French in 1954.

In January, about 10,500 American military men were engaged in this program. There are 7,600 today, and further cuts are expected.

Officials concede that the program is being reduced partly because of budget cuts. But they also say that the progress achieved in rebuilding South Vietnam makes it unnecessary to keep the program going at the pace that was called for when the war was at its height and the rural economy was in wreckage.

Laird Ends 3-Day Visit

This may be the conclusion that Secretary of Defense Melvin R. Laird is taking back to Washington with him. Mr. Laird concluded a three-day visit to Saigon today, during which he reviewed the entire American involvement in South Vietnam. He is to report to President Nixon on Monday.

Officials here often describe the advisory system as a kind of shadow government.

The expression reflects the pervasiveness of American involvement in the daily functions of governing South-Vietnam.

There are American advisers in every Ministry and Government agency in Saigon, including the police force, customs, and public health. At the next lower level, Americans advise the officials and commanders of each of the four military regions into which the 44 South Vietnamese provinces are grouped.

At the province level, American teams work with the Saigon-appointed provincial government. And within the provinces, each district chief has a group of American advisers.

These advisers are the backbone of the American-supported pacification program.

They consult with local South Vietnamese officials, trying to share American methods with the country's fledging civil service.

Each provincial social-welfare officer or the local Ministry of Agriculture official, for example, has an American specialist who helps him in his daily round of chores, inspecting projects, pointing out problems, and suggesting solutions.

The American advisers are told not to work on problems directly with the South Vietnamese people. The object of the program, officials point out, is to build the competence of local governments—and the one in Saigon—and so increase the faith of the South Vietnamese in their officials.

Seek to Develop Economy

It is mainly these people—Army Engineer officers, nurses, chicken farmers and other agriculturalists, and some young Foreign Service officers—who try to develop the rural economy, raise the peasants' standard of living and so compete with the Communists while the South Vietnamese Army and American troops fight.

Describing his job, one district adviser, a United States Army major, said recently:

"I try to get these people to do things they should do and keep them from doing things they shouldn't do."

The task often involves frustration and ill will on both sides. The Americans, often seek to apply the principles of American local government to the isolated South Vietnamese hamlets, and these the South Vietnamese often do not understand.

When a district chief in the Mekong Delta, a South Vietnamese major, asked his American adviser how some Government building subsidies should be spent, the adviser replied.

"Well, back in America, people usually get together, call a P.T.A. meeting or something, and decide what they want to do."

The South Vietnamese "counterparts," as they are known, often point out that the Americans are unsuited to advise on matters affecting local people.

American officials reply that since the money and material being poured into rural development projects comes from the United States Government, Americans should have a hand in seeing that it is not wasted, or stolen.

The Americans' access to money and material characterizes much of the adviser's relations with his counterpart. When a district chief near Saigon came to his American adviser and invited him to inspect the progress in building a new school recently, the American said under his breath as he prepared to leave, "I was expecting this. He wants crushed rock for the schoolyard, I'll bet." The adviser was right.

Major Nguyen Xuan Bien chief of the Delta's Vungliem district, said:

"The adviser helps me in material support, in many ways. For example, when I need ammunition, it is easy for the adviser to give it to me, because the United States does not consider ammunition very precious.

"It is also easy for him to give me bricks and stone to build with, and medicine, so that I can provide medical help for the poor people."

Major Bien's adviser, Major Douglas MacLeod, and others like him, concede that the Americans' ability to get things faster through their own channels may have prevented the South Vietnamese Government from developing its own methods and increasing its efficiency.

Team to Be Disbanded

"Pull out of the advisory role?" Major MacLeod asked. "It may be a good thing—sometimes they use us as a crutch."

Accordingly, Major MacLeod's advisory team will be disbanded at the end of the year on the theory that he and his men have done just about all they can there. Similar cutbacks in district advisory teams have already taken place in the northern provinces. American planners in the Delta say that all district teams there will be gone by early 1973.

Despite the years of effort and some $3.3-billion spent on the pacification program, Americans are divided on the outcome of their efforts. The military advisers tend, on the whole, to be more optimistic about the South Vietnamese Government's ability to function on its own.

"Things will go slower when we're not around, that's for sure," an Army colonel who is a senior provincial adviser recently. "They'll start doing things more their own way, but they should do all right, if they want to. There's not much more we can teach them."

Another senior province adviser reflected the pessimistic view held by many other Americans: that the exertions of American advisers have stunted the development of local government in South Vietnam.

"I think they can continue like this as long as the Americans are here to keep up the pressure," this adviser, a civilian, said. "And when we go they'll just go back to their old corrupt ways and the Vietcong will come in and take over."

A motto on the wall of a district advisory team house just south of Saigon seemed to sum up the American attitude. It read:

"Better they do it imperfectly than you do it perfectly, for it is their country, their war, and your time is limited."

The quotation is from Lawrence of Arabia when he was an adviser to the Arabs in their war with the Turks at the time of World War I.

* * *

January 2 1972

VIETNAM: BOMBS TO SAVE THE NIXON POLICY

WASHINGTON—Why was so much of the country surprised last week when President Nixon ordered the bombing of North Vietnam? The President had said a year ago that he would do it.

Mr. Nixon is running a war in Indochina which the American public will not let him fight with United States ground troops, a war in which the armies of his Indochinese allies are falling back before an enemy offensive. So he turned to air power: American planes bombed North Vietnam for five straight days in the heaviest assaults against the North since Mr. Nixon's predecessor, Lyndon Baines Johnson, terminated his air war against the North a little over three years ago.

Many persons apparently had not believed Mr. Nixon when he made clear at a news conference in December, 1970 that he would accept no restrictions on the use of American air-power in Indochina, and that if Hanoi threatened his objective of preserving a non-Communist South Vietnam, he would bomb the North. The outcry last week by the President's critics, particularly Senator Edmund S. Muskie and the other leading Democratic contenders for the Presidential nomination, thus served as a kind of chorus to underscore the seriousness of Mr. Nixon's intent.

From last Sunday through Thursday Air Force and Navy jets flew about 1,000 attack sorties (a sortie is a single strike by one aircraft) against fuel and supply depots, antiaircraft gun, missile and radar sites, and MIG fighter airfields. The fighter-bombers ranged over the southern portion of North Vietnam below the 20th Parallel, about 200 miles north of the demilitarized zone and 70 miles south of Hanoi. Most of the raids, officially described as "reinforced protective reaction" or "limited duration" air strikes, were concentrated on fuel and supply dumps near the Banraving, Bankarai and Mugia mountain passes through which North Vietnamese troops and supply trucks travel on their way down the Ho Chi Minh Trail complex to South Vietnam and Cambodia.

The New York Times/Nancy Moran

These pictures depict a mission typical of the kind U.S. Planes carried out on North Vietnam and the Ho Chi Minh trail supply complex last week. Opposite page, top to bottom: an American crew is briefed aboard a carrier in the Tonkin Gulf; 500-pound bombs are loaded aboard an A-6 fighter bomber; the plane is signaled for take-off from the carrier deck. This page: the target area is left scorched and pocked by craters. The objective of the trail bombing is to interdict Communist troops and supplies.

The Administration offered varying official explanations for the bombing. Officials said that Hanoi had violated an understanding reached with President Johnson at the time of the bombing cessation in 1968, that Mr. Nixon was protecting the 158,000 American troops still in South Vietnam, that the North was seeking to embarrass the President with a military initiative on the eve of his visit to China, that the Administration was attempting to abort a planned enemy offensive in the South Vietnamese central high-lands.

Only the last reason was indicative of what well-placed Administration sources say is the central purpose of the air raids—the Administration is trying, with air power, to stave off a major military setback in Indochina, particularly during a sensitive election year. The fact is that the President's Vietnamization policy is once more endangered and, having progressively used up other means, he is now becoming more and more reliant on the air weapon to carry forward his strategy.

Under Vietnamization, President Nixon is seeking to strengthen the South Vietnamese army and administration to the point where it can—with help from United States air power and a residual force of about 40,000 to 50,000 American troops—hold the line against the Vietcong guerrillas and the North Vietnamese. He has gained time and political credit with the American public for Vietnamization by slowly drawing American troops down toward this residual force. The withdrawals have created a general public misimpression that the President is getting out of Vietnam entirely, a misimpression that explains much of the surprise at his bombing of the North.

The rub is that the Vietcong and the North Vietnamese, intent upon over-throwing the Saigon Government and forcing the United States out of the South, have sought to undermine Mr. Nixon's strategy. Each time the strategy has been threatened seriously he has taken action.

In May of 1970 when it appeared that the North Vietmanese might over-throw the pro-American regime of Gen. Lon Nol in Pnompenh and take over all of Cambodia along the southern border of South Vietman, Mr. Nixon sent American and South Vietnamese troops into that country. Had Mr. Nixon not sent in the troops, one senior general explained at the time, "we would have been outflanked and our strategy of Vietnamization would have had very little chance."

The Cambodian operation undoubtedly bought the President time through the destruction of enemy supplies, but the benefits have now largely worn off because the enemy today controls most of Cambodia.

Similarly, last February, Mr. Nixon sent a South Vietnamese force—backed by American air assaults—into southern Laos to cut the Ho Chi Minh Trail. The enemy counter-attacked and the South Vietnamese came out in what can most kindly be called a disorderly retreat. Again, the operation probably bought time at the cost of mauling some of the best units in the South Vietnamese army; but again the benefits have worn off. The North Vietnamese now control more of Laos than they ever did.

More importantly, Mr. Nixon cannot again send United States troops into Cambodia, because the American public would not tolerate the casualties, and the South Vietnamese have privately warned the Americans they are not about to repeat the Laos adventure.

Thus, when the military situation turned critical in Laos and Cambodia last month, with rapid enemy advances that threatened the pro-American Governments, Mr. Nixon resorted to the one major military tool left to him. The fighter-bombers went in to destroy the supplies before they could be trucked down the trail and to knock out the antiaircraft installations and MIG airfields that hamper the freedom of American planes to interdict the supply network and the advancing enemy forces in northeast Laos.

Were the Laotian and Cambodian Governments to collapse, the effect on the morale of the Saigon Government forces could be severe. And the President's critics at home would gain more powerful ammunition to attack his Vietnamization policy.

The Administration was also seeking to stave off, by crippling North Vietnam's offensive capability, a possible offensive in the South Vietnamese central highlands. The position of the Saigon Government troops may, according to reports from Vietnam, be weaker in the highlands than officially advertised.

The President apparently has concluded that the domestic political repercussions of renewed bombing of the North will be less than the political consequences of a major military defeat and the collapse of his Vietnamization policy in an election year.

Whether American air power will now prove sufficiently effective—despite the negative historical record—to stave off a serious setback in Indochina only the future can tell.

At a news conference in mid-December, Secretary of the Air Force Robert C. Seamans Jr. asserted that electronic sensors, rapid-fire gunships and other new techniques had destroyed all but 9,500 tons of the 68,500 tons of supplies the North Vietnamese started down the trail during the last dry season of 1970–71.

In Laos and Cambodia, however, the North Vietnamese and Vietcong troops have been operating as if they feared no ammunition shortage.

Much—perhaps Vietnamization, perhaps Mr. Nixon's political future—now rides with the American airmen in Southeast Asia.

Neil Sheehan

* * *

January 22, 1972

'GRUNTS' WONDER WHEN THEIR FIGHTING BECAME 'DEFENSIVE'

By GLORIA EMERSON
Special to The New York Times

NEAR FIRE BASE MELANIE, South Vietnam, Jan. 18—In the field—which means elephant grass, bamboo so thick and so tough a man must hack his way through it and heat that makes it punishing to walk a few hundred yards with an 80-pound pack—the infantrymen wait for a helicopter that links them to the outside world every three days.

The "dirty bird"—so named because the chopper whips up soil and soot that stings and dirties the men's faces—carries water, combat rations, hot lunches with ice cream, mail, cigarettes and reading matter.

In letters from home and in the newspapers, the "grunts" say, they are told that Americans are no longer fighting the war in Vietnam. It makes some men laugh: others shake their heads and curse.

At this outpost northeast of Saigon, Specialist 4 Gregory Langford is one of the soldiers angered and puzzled by the description of him—by the White House, the Secretary of Defense, the Secretary of the Army—as a soldier not in combat but in a "defensive" posture.

Sitting near a small cleared patch where helicopters can land, on earth and grass burned by recent fires caused by tracer bullets and by white phosphorus dropped by United States planes, Specialist Langford remarked that important people were using the wrong language.

He is not a man in revolt, only one who is suspicious and fed up. He wonders what he is doing carrying an M-16 rifle and looking for the enemy.

Closer to the Bases

The four battalions of the Third Brigade, whose rear area is Fire Base Melanie, have recently moved closer to the Longbinh and Bienhoa bases.

The reduction of United States forces has meant that those remaining are drawing in tighter around the American bases, especially with Tet, the Lunar New Year, coming next month. There have been predictions of a repetition of the Communist offensive launched throughout the country during the holiday period four years ago. The departure of Thai and Australian troops from Military Region III has also left gaps for Americans to fill.

As far as most of the men in Company A are concerned, the interpretations of whether they are on defensive or offensive duty change nothing.

"Look, we're in a combat role if we hit people," Specialist 4 Craig Roth said. "If we see them we hit them. We're not going to half-step."

Since Oct. 3, when 24 men were wounded at a landing zone, Company A's action has been limited to exchanges of fire with the enemy.

Few Take Seconds

The men in Company A lined up for their hot lunches, standing a few yards apart in case of incoming mortar fire. Though the menu was barbecued beef, cabbage, potatoes, soft drinks, milk and two kinds of ice cream, few went back for seconds. It was too hot and they were getting ready to move out.

The men are not complainers or whiners. Their officers say they are good soldiers.

"I am not sure Nixon is aware of what's going on here," said the 21-year-old soldier, who is married and has a son five months old.

"They told us we're in a defensive position—are we?" he continued. "Some colonel told us it's not really defensive, it's sort of offensive. Why don't people back home know what we're doing? On my last mission I was in the bush for 29 days. We had 24 guys wounded in October. I keep hearing that we're pulling out, but I keep seeing new people come in."

Specialist Langford, who has been in Vietnam for five months—"I was in the rear once for nine hours"—is in Company A of the Second Battalion, Eighth Cavalry, part of the Third Brigade of the First Cavalry Division (Airmobile).

The Cav, as it was called, officially withdrew last March, but the Third, formed as a separate brigade, stayed. Its primary mission is to cut enemy infiltration and supply routes and to be a quick reaction force against any enemy threat to United States bases in Military Region III—the Army's Longbinh base, the largest in South Vietnam, and the Bienhoa base, both of which are not far north of Saigon.

Company A, with its three platoons nicknamed Killer, Smokey and Plato—the names are borrowed from the Beetle Bailey comic strip—is in the jungle area 17 miles east of the Bienhoa base.

The draftees are resigned, except that they wish that people at home did not think "we are all in the rear standing guard duty or lying around on beaches," as one put it.

"I am a bush-beating grunt," Pvt. Gerald Scriven said, "but my wife, Bina, she supposes we're living good. Maybe Nixon's got to make a good impression before the election. Bina has the impression we're not doin' nothin'."

Specialist 4 Jeffrey Davis, a North Carolinian, did not try to guess why the President said the Army had ended its combat role. A machine-gunner, he was busy arranging his pack before moving out for three days and nights.

His M-60 weighs 60 pounds, the 100 rounds of ammunition he carries are nearly 6 pounds and he has 9 quarts of water, which weigh 18 pounds. Then there is the pack, which he figures at about 65 pounds.

He also has two onions, which he likes to mix in with his combat rations, and a paperback book.

There are lots of places where he would rather be than Vietnam, Specialist Davis remarked, but it could be worse. He has his onions and the other brothers and a good outfit. The enemy may be nearby, but things are quiet.

* * *

February 9, 1972

HOSTILITY TO AMERICANS GROWING IN SOUTH VIETNAM

By JOSEPH B. TREASTER

Special to The New York Times

HUE, South Vietnam, Feb. 6—The charred nameplate from a Ford truck was tacked above a neatly lettered sign saying, in Vietnamese, "Burn American cars to avenge the people."

Elsewhere in the room at the University of Hue, students had hung photographs of American soldiers and planes and slogans condemning American actions in Vietnam.

The exhibition of anti-American material; the centerpiece in a "cultural week" at the university, was one of the strongest statements so far in a growing climate of open South Vietnamese hostility to the American involvement here.

Embarrassed and Angry

Just how representative the exhibition is of South Vietnamese feelings is impossible to judge. But those who have studied the country carefully suspect that nowhere is the bitterness so great as in Hue, which has evolved as a center of extreme nationalism and radical politics.

Whatever the extent of the resentment against the United States among Vietnamese, there is profound xenophobia among them, bred through hundreds of years of foreign domination.

What began as aid from the United States led to dependence, and all too many South Vietnamese, many of them embarrassed and angry, know that they are at the mercy of the President of the United States and Congress.

So far, nonetheless, there has been only a relative handful of assaults on Americans in Hue and other cities.

There were several days of street demonstrations in Hue against the United States toward the end of the summer after American soldiers killed two students—one in a traffic accident, the other by rifle fire as he allegedly attempted to steal some PX goods. Some of the student opposition to President Nguyen Van Thieu's one-man election campaign also had strong anti-American overtones.

Since the Oct. 3 election the whitewashed walls of the two-story, block-long building that houses the schools of sciences and letters has been plastered with anti-American slogans and caricatures of President Nixon. There has been a running paintbrush battle between the students and the police. The students paint something like. "The people of Hue hate the American imperialists." With a few deft strokes policemen blot out "American imperialists" and substitute "Reds." At the weekend the students seemed to be slightly ahead.

For the moment officials in Hue do not appear to be prepared to force a confrontation with the students. They chose to ignore the exhibition, sponsored by the Hue Students Union, an influential group, even though it included some material critical of President Thieu and his troops as well as of the Americans.

Little Criticism of Vietcong

The principal objection to the Americans seemed to be that they were intruders in a Vietnamese problem. Some distaste for war was evident, but there was no criticism of the Vietcong in the exhibition and accompanying dramatic presentations or from most of the students interviewed.

Under a copy of a Pulitzer Prize-winning photograph showing a Vietnamese mother and her children struggling in flood waters up to their necks, the students had written, "Disaster by nature and disaster by Americans is the same."

Another shows a Vietcong soldier being dragged behind an American armored vehicle. The caption reads: "Millions of people will rise up to avenge you and burn this tank to ashes." "We consider the 32 million people living from the northern tip of Vietnam to the southern tip all to be Vietnamese," said Le Van Thuyen, chairman of the student union, speaking through an interpreter. "What we do to each other is an internal affair. Even though we commit condemnable crimes, we can still forgive each other. But it is unforgivable for foreigners to commit crimes in our country."

Red Infiltration Suspected

Such nationalistic talk has been a mainstay of the Communist radio. Some American military men in Hue maintain that the university has been heavily infiltrated by the Communists, but that is difficult to prove.

One display that attracted considerable attention featured reproductions of a photo taken during the Mylai massacre. The students crowding around the grisly scene had followed the disclosures of the atrocity in Vietnamese newspapers.

"Extremely cruel," said a young man who is studying to be a teacher. "The Americans are extremely cruel." Then, in the kind of balanced reflection that seems rare among Hue students, the young man, who would not give his name, shook his head sadly. "I believe the Vietcong did the same thing," he said.

"That's why I feel very desperate for the Vietnamese people," he added, "because Vietnam has been used as a testing area for the two blocs."

* * *

March 4, 1972

U.S. STAND IN CHINA ASSAILED BY HANOI

Reacting to Visit by Nixon, Paper Calls Him 'Tricky Imperialist Ringleader'

Special to The New York Times

HONG KONG, March 3—In its first official reaction to President Nixon's China trip, North Vietnam today denounced the American side of the joint Peking communiqué and accused the United States of "sowing discord" among Communist countries.

Even while issuing the denunciation in the official newspaper, Nhan Dan, Hanoi continued to keep from its people the fact that their ally China had received Mr. Nixon. It addressed its comments only to "a recent document."

Nhan Dan described Mr. Nixon as a "bellicose, ferocious, ruthless and tricky imperialist ringleader." It declared that the United States was the "enemy No. 1 of all nations in the world."

Cartoon of Nixon

Reporting this, North Vietnam's official press agency said Nhan Dan also published a cartoon showing a two-faced Nixon holding a bomb in one hand and an olive branch in the other.

Nhan Dan made the attack in an article signed with the byline "Commentator," a pen name used for reports written by senior officials.

Although its invective was directed against Mr. Nixon and the United States, the article appeared to be something of a rebuke to China for entertaining the American President.

Peking has repeatedly affirmed its support for Hanoi and the joint communiqué restated China's support of the Vietcong and North Vietnam, but there was more than a strong hint of disapproval of the visit in the Nhan Dan article.

Referring to the American statement on Vietnam in the communiqué, which recalled the eight point proposal of the United States and the Saigon Government, the Nhan Dan article said President Nixon "still insolently asked the Vietnamese people to pay a price for the complete withdrawal of American troops."

Terms Statement Ballyhoo

Dismissing his statements on the need to remove walls existing between nations and peoples and to relax tension in Asia and the world as "ballyhoo," Nhan Dan said that exactly at the same moment as he made the statements, the President ordered intensified air attacks on both North Vietnam and South Vietnam.

"This is how Nixon is working for peace and the self-determination of the Indochinese peoples," the article said.

Nhan Dan accused the United States of wrecking world peace, waging aggression, creating tension and "seeking hegemony in the Asia-Pacific region."

In the Peking communiqué, the two sides stated that neither should seek hegemony in the Asia-Pacific region.

Nhan Dan declared: "Listening to Nixon, one cannot help thinking of a gangster who, hiding his bloodstained hands behind his back, preaches morality."

'Most Dangerous Enemy'

The paper said: "It can be seen from Nixon's activities regarding the Vietnam question and other problems that this aggressive, bellicose, ferocious and obdurate nature of U.S. imperialism has not changed a bit, that U.S. imperialism is the most dangerous enemy, the enemy No. 1 of all nations in the world."

The Vietnamese people, Nhan Dan said, "resolutely expose the deceptive statements and acts of Nixon regarding the Vietnam problem" and firmly condemn his "savage war crimes."

The article said: "Our position is stronger and stronger our strength bigger and bigger and our road to complete victory is very clear. Our people and armed forces will not be deterred in this valiant advance by any barbarous act or any dark scheme of U.S. imperialism."

* * *

March 24, 1972

U.S. CALLS A HALT TO PARIS PARLEYS ON VIETNAM WAR

CHANGES AWAITED

Serious Effort Sought—Reds Say They Will Never Accept Terms

By JOHN L. HESS
Special to The New York Times

PARIS, March 23—The United States declared an indefinite suspension of the Paris peace conference on Vietnam today.

Ambassador William J. Porter told the Vietnamese Communists that there would be no further meetings until they showed willingness for "serious discussions" on concrete issues defined in advance. In reply the Communists charged that he was posing "conditions we can never accept."

[In Washington, the State Department said that the United States would take a "continuous assessment" each week to determine whether the Communists were prepared to negotiate seriously.]

The break, apparently the most serious of several interruptions in the three years of the negotiations, came at the 147th session of the conference in the former Hotel Majestic near the Arc de Triomphe. It was announced by Mr. Porter, head of the United States delegation, in an opening statement described by a spokesman as having been carefully prepared.

U.S. Voices Disappointment

In expectation that the Communists, who had first turn this time, would repeat previous positions, Mr. Porter's prepared remarks began: "I should not conceal from you the fact that our side is very disappointed by your presentations of today."

Finding no "give" in their position, Mr. Porter announced the suspension in these words:

"As you know, President Nixon, at the request of the Congress, has declared next week as a week of national concern for our men held prisoner by you and your associates. It would be a mockery of our concern for them were we to sit in this room with you and listen to more of your blackmail and distortions to the effect that the prisoner-of-war issue is an 'imaginary problem.' Therefore our side does not agree to a meeting next week.

"As for meetings in the weeks that follow we believe it would be preferable to await some sign from you that you are disposed to engage in meaningful exchanges on the various points raised in your and our proposals.

"Our side will be alert to signs of that nature which you may send through any convenient channel, including our liaison officers if you desire. If you do indicate a desire for 'serious discussion,' you will understand. I am sure, that we may need to explore your intentions rather fully prior to agreeing to meet."

P.O.W. Issued Stressed

Mr. Porter said that meetings on the treatment of prisoners would be particularly welcome, and that his side would "suggest meetings to discuss particular points or subjects whenever such discussions appear likely to be useful."

Each side has declined to attend meetings in the past for one or more weeks because of specific objections. The Communist side, for instance, has been absent in protest against American bombing of North Vietnam, and the United States recently canceled a meeting while a large conference of antiwar groups was being held in Versailles. However, this is the first time either side has announced an indefinite suspension.

Repeated efforts by reporters to obtain further clarification of the criteria for resuming the talks were vain. Ambassador Pham Dang Lam, head of the Saigon Government's delegation, did say as he left the conference that the American proposal "concerns concentrating each meeting on a concrete issue."

The American spokesman, Stephen Ledogar, clarified the United States position at a briefing later. "I am not Ambassador Lam's spokesman." Mr. Ledogar said, "but when he says 'concrete issues,' he meant all of them." Under a rain of questions, he declined to explain further or to acknowledge a breach or suspension of the talks.

Reds Visibly Angered

"I'm going to stick very closely to the language of our speech, which was very carefully drafted," he said.

The Communist spokesmen, usually serene, showed visible anger today, repeatedly denouncing the Porter declaration as "a maneuver of sabotage." Xuan Thuy, the North Vietnamese delegate, said at a curbside news conference that the Nixon Administration had had "many occasions to settle the Vietnamese problem" but instead had prolonged the war and was using Indochina as a "testing ground for new weapons."

Next week's session, he added, would be the sixth canceled by the United States "without a valid reason."

Ly Van Sau, spokesman for the Vietcong's provisional revolutionary government, said at a news conference: "The United States has undertaken today a new escalation in the sabotage of the conference. Mr. Porter has posed a whole series of conditions we can never accept."

'No Result Would Ensue'

"Who has given Mr. Porter the right to decide what is significant or not?" he demanded. "In these conditions, whatever we do, even if this conference were transferred to the moon, no result would ensue."

Similarly, Mr. Ledogar declared: "We can't be any worse off than we are now."

Neither side would comment on how exchanges on a possible solution might now proceed, or how, for example, a possible new proposal might be relayed by Mrs. Nguyen Thi Binh, the Vietcong foreign minister, who is due to return tomorrow after a long absence in Indochina. It appeared likely that such exchanges would not, in any case, occur on the stage of the Hotel Majestic.

Such a rupture had been the subject of wide speculation here since last fall, when Ambassador Porter, on his arrival, began taking a tough line.

* * *

April 1, 1972

TRUCK TRAFFIC IS HEAVY SOUTHWARD FROM HANOI

By SEYMOUR M. HERSH
Special to The New York Times

HANOI, North Vietnam, March 17—The Ho Chi Minh Trial starts in Hanoi. Every day hundreds of heavily laden trucks leave the capital to begin the drive of more than 300 miles through Laos and into South Vietnam.

A visitor, riding south in a jeep, was passed by more than 80 trucks during a four-hour, 100-mile drive along Highway 1, the main north-south road. The heavy-duty Soviet-built and Chinese-built trucks were driven fast, almost recklessly, along the highway, which was crowded as always with bicycles, water buffaloes, small lorries, other trucks, jeeps and swarms of people.

Officials said the vehicles were heading for Laos, and those going onto the trail were easy to identify, each had one headlight and was carefully camouflaged with branches and leaves piled on hood and roof. Perhaps one in four was loaded with 55-gallon oil drums. Many others were carrying wooden cases of what seemed to be small-arms ammunition.

The drivers were regular army men, and life along the road had some touches of uniformity. There were restaurant stops where dozens of soldiers could be seen eating meals—for which they had to pay—beside their vehicles. Only one passenger, a soldier, was visible on the trucks headed south. Most were tightly sealed.

Trains Laden With People

Only a few artillery pieces were being hauled, and no tanks or armored personnel carriers were sighted. Larger equipment may begin the journey south by railroad, but most of the trains that regularly rolled beside the highway were full of passengers. Only occasional freight trains were sighted; they invariably included half a dozen or more heavily camouflaged tank cars.

The other main road in North Vietnam, Highway 5, stretches about 60 miles from Hanoi to the harbor city of Haiphong. Although many trucks full of war matériel were seen on it, there were some distinct contrasts. None, not even those with one headlight, were camouflaged, and most of the drivers seemed to be civilians.

Both highways were heavily bombed during the air raids on the Hanoi-Haiphong area that ended in 1968; they have not been attacked in that region since.

Occasionally, large trucks carrying what the officials said were Soviet-made surface-to-air missiles could be seen parked along Highway 5. It was explained that the missile sites were regularly moved at night, after American reconnaissance flights were believed to be over for the day.

A Considerable Project

The missiles were covered but their unmistakable fins jutted out. The complex radar equipment used to guide the heat-seeking missiles was also being moved, a maneuver that—if conducted throughout the North every night—would involve a considerable number of vehicles, technicians and workers.

Military bases appear to be impossible for foreigners to find. None were encountered in more than 400 miles of travel, much of it along back roads. None of the Western diplomats stationed in Hanoi could recall seeing one. A North Vietnamese official said that the army bases were shifted regularly.

Soldiers could be seen constantly along the highways and in the cities. A group of sailors was conducting what seemed to be a forced march along a country road near Halong Bay, on the northeastern coast. The sailors, moving in crisp formation, had fresh uniforms, boots and back packs and shiny Chinese-made automatic rifles.

In the effort to counteract the air raids, dirt trails large enough to accommodate a truck were scratched out on each side of the highway wherever possible.

A Country Well Dug In

In general the country is well dug in. When factories were destroyed, the North Vietnamese simply picked up the pieces and moved them into nearby caves or grottoes.

An underground machine shop stands in a grotto in a small hill only a few miles from the much-bombed Hamrong Bridge in Thanhhoa Province, about 100 miles south of Hanoi. The plant, destroyed early in the air war, was reassembled in three sections by early 1967.

The section visited employed more than 30 workers in three around-the-clock shifts, turning out spare parts for tracks, generators and perhaps tanks. The employes lead an eerie subterranean life, with their work area lighted by less than a dozen weak bulbs. Most of the available power was being consumed by the seven lathes, presses and polishers.

Six of the heavy tools had been supplied by the Soviet Union and North Korea, the plant manager said, but he proudly pointed out a lathe manufactured in North Vietnam.

The plant, which, according to the manager, had to produce enough parts to repair 20 engines and 10 generators in January alone, consists of two narrow corridors, one about 30 feet and the other twice as long, crammed with raw materials, machine tools and workers.

* * *

April 2, 1972

FOE SWEEPS ACROSS DMZ; SAIGON TROOPS FALL BACK; CLOUDS BLOCK U.S. PLANES

ADVISERS UNEASY

See a Possible Threat to Hue and Danang if Push Continues

By CRAIG R. WHITNEY
Special to The New York Times

SAIGON, South Vietnam, Sunday, April 2—Thousands of North Vietnamese and Vietcong troops have driven past South Vietnam's northern line of defenses below the demilitarized zone and are pushing South Vietnamese forces in disarray toward their rear bases, United States military sources in Danang said yesterday.

The assault, reportedly by elements of one North Vietnamese main force division, the 304th, with additional artillery and other units equal to another division, followed three days of what was called the most intense enemy artillery and rocket bombardment of the war. A North Vietnamese division at full strength has about 10,000 men.

American sources said that they feared the enemy objective was to take Quangtri, the capital of South Vietnam's northernmost province, and hold it if they could, which would pose a serious threat to the city of Hue farther south and, eventually perhaps, to Danang, the largest city in the north.

Move Under Cloud Cover

The sources said that enemy troops were moving in the open, without their usual careful attempts to conceal themselves, under cover of cloudy skies that have made effective South Vietnamese and American air attacks impossible.

The clouds have also prevented retaliation against the long-range rockets and artillery pieces in and above the buffer zone that reportedly have rained more than 7,000 rounds on South Vietnamese positions since Thursday.

Lieut. Gen. Hoang Xuan Lam, the commander of Military Region I, covering the northern provinces, conferred at his headquarters in Danang with Gen. Frederick C. Weyand, the deputy commander of United States forces in Vietnam, and later General Lam issued a statement saying that "the Communist North Vietnamese are crossing the demilitarized zone to invade Quangtri Province."

His statement said that three artillery regiments and anti-aircraft units equipped with surface-to-air missiles, were taking part in the offensive.

American sources in Danang said that the third division General Lam referred to was the 308th, but that it was being held in reserve north of the demilitarized zone.

The North Vietnamese reportedly have moved more than 80 portable antiaircraft missile launchers to sites in the southern part of their country over the last two months. The missiles have been a source of concern to American commanders, who say the most effective way to counter the

North Vietnamese artillery fire is with fighter bombers, which are vulnerable to the missiles.

There is some evidence that United States air strength is being reinforced. The aircraft carrier Kitty Hawk was reportedly given orders to sail back to the Gulf of Tonkin from Subic Bay in the Philippines to join the two other carriers on station off the coast of North Vietnam, the Hancock and the Coral Sea.

So far, presumably because of the bad weather, there have been little American air strength in support of the retreating South Vietnamese forces. Only 31 strikes were flown between 6 A.M. Friday and 6 A.M. yesterday, and only two B-52 missions were reported in Quangtri Province, 13 and 19 miles northeast of Khesanh, against enemy troop concentrations and base camp areas.

The United States command said that between 6 A.M. yesterday and 6 A.M. today five B-52 missions were flown in Quangtri province, three of them just west of the abandoned Fire Base Fuller and two in the mountains southwest of Quantri city against North Vietnamese troop concentrations and antiaircraft artillery sites.

One other mission was flown, in Thuathien Province west of Hue, and five others attacked enemy staging areas and troop concentrations around Kontum, where there was a significant upsurge in fighting reported Friday, with 10 rocket and mortar attacks on Government infantry positions.

One ground assault was also repulsed and 87 North Vietnamese soldiers were killed at a fire base west of Kontum, according to the South Vietnamese command.

Other enemy artillery and rocket attacks were reported in Tayninh Province northwest of Saigon. A ground attack against one base camp near the Cambodian border was reportedly repulsed, and five South Vietnamese soldiers were killed and 27 were wounded while the North Vietnamese suffered 151 casualties, according to the Saigon command. These attacks were reported in Vietcong broadcasts, which took special pains to emphasize the attacks, leading some observers to believe that in all three areas a co-ordinated offensive was under way, most intensively in Quangtri Province.

The South Vietnamese base camps that reportedly fell under enemy attack today were Alfa 4, which when the United States Marines were there in 1968 was called Conthien, and Charlie 4, five miles to the south. Conthien is about two miles below the demilitarized zone, just to the east of the foothills of the Annamite Mountains.

Five miles to the east, a camp at Giolinh was abandoned Sunday under heavy attack, according to United States sources in Danang. The South Vietnamese command in Saigon described the withdrawal as an evacuation rather than an abandonment under attack.

The South Vietnamese Third Division's base at Camp Carroll, 12 miles west of Dongha, was reportedly under very heavy attack and bombardment late last night but was said to be "holding." Three bases on mountain-tops to the northwest and southwest of Camp Carroll, which lies on a knoll in a basin-like plain, have been abandoned by the South Vietnamese.

Another small South Vietnamese base three miles southeast of Camp Carroll, Mailoc, was also under siege.

All roads north of Dongha were said to be cut and thousands of refugees from the settlement at Camlo and Giolinh were streaming south, according to fragmentary American reports.

The Quangtri combat base, headquarters for the South Vietnamese Third Division, was reportedly hit by 40 122-mm rockets Friday night and by more during the day yesterday Dongha was also bombarded Friday, and 4 civilians were killed and 17 wounded, according to the Saigon command.

The South Vietnamese Third Division, a marine brigade, and of the local territorial forces of Quangtri Province were reported to be fighting hard as they pulled back, and they reported having killed more than 500 North Vietnamese soldiers.

American sources also reported casualties among American advisers with the South Vietnamese units, but the number was unknown. There are fewer than a thousand American military advisers in Quangtri Province. The American command is said to be considering a plan to evacuate these advisers from their compound in Quangtri proper, a few miles south of the combat base.

Late last night, an American officer in Danang said, "The question now is how well the Third Division is going to hang together, and we just don't know. If they fall apart the North Vietnamese will probably make a push on Hue with their 324th Division."

American officials in Saigon are also known to be concerned about the possibility that large-scale enemy attacks in the Central Highlands west of Kontum will follow smaller ones that began there Friday.

Nine B-52 missions dropped hundreds of tons of bombs on North Vietnamese troop concentration and storage areas in Kontum province in the 36 hours ending 6 A.M. today, the United States command said.

The only Americans stationed in the Central Highlands and the northern region below the demilitarized zone are advisers with South Vietnamese forces, plus support units of helicopters and observation planes. Three squadrons of United States jet fighter-bombers are based at Danang.

Also, according to the United States command in Saigon, an air cavalry troop of about 15 light observation helicopters and helicopter gunships has been sent to the area.

Elsewhere in South Vietnam, there are fewer than 100,000 American troops left. Ground troops consist of seven battalions or about a thousand men each. These are stationed west of Danang, with the 169th Infantry Brigade, at Camranh Bay, and east of Saigon, in the Third Brigade of the First Cavalry Division (air mobile). It is considered unlikely any of these would be sent to the north to reinforce the South Vietnamese there.

* * *

April 6, 1972

A BIG NEW PHASE OF WAR IS OPENING

By CRAIG R. WHITNEY
Special to The New York Times

SAIGON, South Vietnam, April 5—With the use of artillery, tanks and mobile antiaircraft defenses in their current drive across the demilitarized zone, the North Vietnamese, it is clear, have opened a large new phase of the war centering on conventional combat.

The South Vietnamese forces, which have been trained by the Americans in similar conventional tactics, have been caught at a serious disadvantage. It points up their dependence on American air power despite Vietnamization. The supersonic planes have not been able to fly because the North Vietnamese picked a week of heavy clouds and rain to begin their drive.

Intelligence analysts in Saigon have been impressed by what one of them called the very ambitious use of artillery—more than 10,000 Soviet-made shells and rockets fired from the demilitarized zone or the area above it. That shelling apparently persuaded the South Vietnamese to leave the 15 forward positions that have for years been their country's northern defenses rather than wait for North Vietnamese infantry assaults.

But the American pilots who have been able to get through the occasionally lifting clouds to strike at North Vietnamese tanks and trucks advancing openly along the main highway toward Dongha say there is something else that is new about the North Vietnamese tactics—the use of SAM-2 missiles to defend troops operating south of the border.

"It's a major factor for the first time ever inside South Vietnam," said Lieut. Col. John P. O'Gorman, commander of the 421st Tactical Fighter Squadron in Danang, in a telephone interview. "It's the first time in my experience that they've ever used SAM's to support an operation in country."

"In country" is the military phrase for "inside South Vietnam."

"They're towing antiaircraft guns, everything up to 37 mm, behind trucks right down the road," he added, "and then they fire SAM's at us to force us down into the antiaircraft fire."

The surface-to-air missiles are not effective at low altitudes; antiaircraft fire is. The pilots have retaliated by firing air-to-ground missiles across the zone 10 times in three days.

Colonel O'Gorman and other senior officers say that the North Vietnamese have not brought any SAM's south of the demilitarized zone but are firing just beyond it and from its northern sector at planes across the border.

The North Vietnamese have increased their SAM sites in the southern part of the demilitarized zone by about 25 per cent in the last year. The exact number is not known, but there are probably some 30 launchers. The missiles, which have a 21-mile range at 40,000 feet, can hit planes in most of Quangtri Province.

As for tanks, the enemy used them in 1968 in attacks on American outposts on the Laos border west of Khesanh and in 1970 against the Benhet Ranger camp in the Central Highlands, but never before have so many been used as in the current push toward Quangtri City.

Since bad weather has made it difficult to fly photo-reconnaissance missions, intelligence experts do not know exactly how many Soviet-built tanks the North Vietnamese are using. Estimates range from 50 to 100, manned by 300 to 400 men—a combination of amphibious 14-ton PT-76's and 30-ton T-54's or T-55's with 4-inch guns.

New Weapon Being Used

The attackers have relied most so far on heavy artillery, also provided by the Russians. The newest weapon, being used for the first time in the demilitarized zone and believed first used by the North Vietnamese in their attack on Long Tieng base in Laos in January, is the 130-mm gun. With a range of almost 19 miles, it can outshoot most South Vietnamese artillery. American-made 105-mm pieces fire 6 miles and 155-mm pieces fire less than 10; only the 175-mm gun, of which the South Vietnamese have few, has a longer range—20 miles.

The South Vietnamese say they "spiked" several 175-mm guns—made them useless as weapons—before they pulled out of Camp Carroll, one of the northern bases below the demilitarized zone and west of Dongha, Sunday night.

The South Vietnamese response is, of course, the critical factor in the battles taking place below the demilitarized zone and expected to follow soon in the Central Highlands and possibly in Tayninh and Binhlong Provinces, northwest of Saigon. Those are the fronts against which the biggest North Vietnamese main-force units are capable of moving.

American advisers in Hue have been critical of the defensive mentality the South Vietnamese have shown in the last week. They chose to pull out of their defense lines, abandon half of Quangtri Province to the enemy and improvise a defense line from Dongha and Quangtri to the coast.

The South Vietnamese also have heavy tanks, but they have not gone north of the defense line to challenge the enemy's armor. Instead the tanks have dueled back and forth across the Cua Viet, an estuary.

There were reports from Quangtri that the North Vietnamese had taken advantage of the 10 miles of terrain abandoned to them by the regrouping Government forces to move a few 130-mm guns below the demilitarized zone to points within easy range of Quangtri City.

Their attempts to get tanks through the South Vietnamese line of defense at the Cua Viet have been reported unsuccessful so far, although some military sources believe they may have succeeded in getting one or two across. The South Vietnamese say they have put 50 tanks out of action, mostly with slow-flying A-1 Skyraiders, which can go under the clouds to bomb.

In the meantime, the North Vietnamese are reported moving reinforcements east from the mountainous jungle and have driven Saigon's forces out of bases in the foothills west of Quangtri—Fire Base Anne fell yesterday and Fire Base Pedro, 10 miles south of Quangtri, today—and appear to be trying to encircle the city and cut Routel, linking it to Hue and the south.

A Prediction From Hanoi

So far, despite territorial gains by default, the North Vietnamese have not committed much of the 15,000-to-21,000-man force estimated to have infiltrated into Quangtri Province. Most are believed to be in the mountains of western Quangtri, where they are harder to detect and hit.

It appears unlikely that the North Vietnamese will apply large-unit conventional tactics in the same way in the two other likely battlegrounds, in the Central Highlands and near the Cambodian border northwest of Saigon, if only because they are believed to have no 130-mm guns or SAM missiles there.

Their most effective artillery in those areas consists of 122-mm rockets with a range of seven miles. They have also been used to good effect in Quangtri Province.

Earlier this year Hanoi emphasized the belief that the increasing withdrawal of American forces had prepared the way for "big, annihilating attacks" by regular forces. "These attacks are steel-like to annihilate the enemy in an important manner and rapidly change the balance of forces and the situation on the battlefield," said an editorial in December in Quan Doi Nhan Dan, the army newspaper.

That sounds like what happened in Quangtri Province last weekend. The recent infiltration of the 320th Division to the Central Highlands area and the eastward movement of elements of the Third, Fifth and Ninth Divisions from Cambodia toward the South Vietnamese border at Tayninh and Binhlong Provinces suggests that similar large actions may be planned there soon. The North Vietnamese are known to have some tanks and many mortars in both areas.

There were reports a few days ago, when Fire Base Pace just south of the Cambodian border on Highway 22 in Tayninh Province came under attack, that a second front was being opened in the area northwest of Saigon, but American officials said then that there was inconclusive evidence that the North Vietnamese had committed large forces to battle there.

Small-unit actions have played little part in the North Vietnamese strategy so far.

"It's forming up rapidly as a conventional war," an American officer said. "This is the kind of war we were accustomed to before the war in Vietnam started."

* * *

April 7, 1972

GIAP'S RISKY ADVENTURE

By JAMES RESTON

WASHINGTON, April 6—The Communists in Vietnam are now trying to win the war in one decisive stroke, as they defeated the French in the battle of Dienbienphu in 1954. It is a bold but puzzling strategy.

For while the enemy has thrown about 35,000 men into the battle just south of the demilitarized zone, and has had some initial success under cover of cloudy weather, there is little chance that they can corner and eliminate the main units of the South Vietnamese before the United States gets the full thump of its air power into the action.

This is not a Dienbienphu situation. The South Vietnamese now have over a million men under arms, and they are not concentrated and vulnerable as the French were in the bloody ending of the other Indochina war.

Also, the United States has over 500 attack planes in and around Southeast Asia, and these are being steadily reinforced and directed against the larger enemy units now invading South Vietnam, not in scattered guerrilla bands but in classic organized formations.

Apparently, Gen. Vo Nguyen Giap, who masterminded the Communist victory at Dienbienphu, hopes that dramatic victories in the north around Quangtri City, and in Binhlong Province, 75 miles north of Saigon, would stun and disorganize the entire South Vietnamese defense organization, but this is not likely with American planes dominating the air.

Moreover, the Communists have left themselves vulnerable at the rear. According to Pentagon estimates, twelve of North Vietnam's fourteen regular divisions are now operating outside of North Vietnam in Laos, Cambodia and South Vietnam.

In this recent operation, Hanoi has openly invaded South Vietnam across the DMZ and increased the risk of a counter-attack by air and sea in North Vietnam behind their advancing forces. Maybe Giap's swift organized blows, north and south at the same time, can split and paralyze the South, and provide a political capital for the National Liberation Front in South Vietnam, but it is a risky adventure.

The intriguing question is why Giap chose to move now. The weather favors the offense, and won't later on, but the United States expeditionary force will be down to 69,000 by May 1, and will be below the 50,000 mark a month later, with election pressure on the President to bring most of the remnant home before November.

The speculation in official quarters here is that Hanoi has already discounted the U.S. ground combat forces in Vietnam, now reduced to about 6,000, especially since President Nixon has ordered them to stay out of the ground fighting unless they are attacked, and that Giap believes he can defeat the South Vietnamese units, as he did in Laos.

Officials here are not assuming Giap's defeat, though they are reasonably confident the offensive can be contained, and they are even saying once again that if the enemy fails this time, Hanoi will finally agree to a negotiated settlement.

It has always been a mystery why the Nixon Administration thinks the enemy will negotiate a settlement with our forces winding down to 50,000, when Hanoi and the N.L.F. refused to negotiate and compromise when we had over 500,000 men in Vietnam; but even the highest officials here are still talking about Giap's "last gasp" and predicting a settlement if the invasion is stopped.

Giap always has the option, which he has taken many times before, of retreating across the Cambodian and Laotian frontiers if his invasion is stopped. He would obviously like to demonstrate that the Communists can defeat the South Vietnamese on the ground, even against American air power, and thus disrupt Washington's Vietnamization program and compel a settlement on Hanoi's terms.

But if he fails he can always break off the battle and regroup back home. He has not fought and waited for thirty years in order to settle just when the last of the American ground forces are packing up.

Maybe after the election, if he still finds President Nixon in the White House, free of political pressure to bring the Air Force home too, Giap might talk compromise rather than face four more years of punishment from the air. But to settle before the election, thus aiding Mr. Nixon's re-election, is scarcely plausible.

Meanwhile, the most serious military operation since the Tet offensive is under way, and the guess here is that, even if American air power is effective, the battle will last until mid-May. That is not a pleasant prospect here, for Mr. Nixon is due in Moscow on May 22, and if the invasion is not over by then, the atmosphere for the talks on critical world questions will not be very genial.

* * *

April 16, 1972

WAVES OF U.S. PLANES BOMB HAIPHONG AREA; HANOI ALSO RAIDED, ENEMY RADIO REPORTS

B-52'S TAKE PART

Foe Says F-4's Struck Capital—Claims 11 Planes Downed

By CRAIG R. WHITNEY
Special to The New York Times

SAIGON, Sunday, April 16—Waves of United States Air Force and Navy fighter-bombers and eight-engined B-52's last night bombed in the vicinity of the North Vietnamese port city of Haiphong, 60 miles east of Hanoi, for the first time since the end of March, 1968, the United States command announced this morning.

[Agence France-Presse reported from Hanoi that anti-aircraft guns had fired on a formation of American F-4 fighter-bombers early Sunday as the planes swept low over the North Vietnamese capital. The Hanoi radio said that American jets struck inside and outside Hanoi seven hours after the Haiphong raid, The Associated Press reported. The radio said that 11 American planes had been downed in the raids. A Pentagon spokesman refused to comment on the reports from Hanoi.]

It was the first systematic bombardment of military targets north of the 20th Parallel in four years, and was a dramatic reversal of the de-escalation of bombing in North Vietnam that began then. Some smaller bombing raids have been made north of the parallel in the last few years by American planes shooting back at antiaircraft and radar sites, but nothing as systematic as the bombing announced today.

The planes struck fuel dumps, warehouses, truck parks, "and other activities which are supporting the invasion of South Vietnam by the North Vietnamese forces," the United States command said in a terse statement, which did not say how many planes went on the raid.

Bombers Are Escorted

It said that escort planes had accompanied the bombers. Anti-aircraft fire was believed to have been intense and some planes may have been shot down by surface-to-air missiles and antiaircraft fire, but the command's announcement said only that "all B-52's returned safely."

"In response to the massive invasion across the demilitarized zone, previous B-52 strikes were conducted against military targets in the vicinity of Vinh and Baithuong," the announcement said.

Vinh and Baithuong are between the 20th Parallel and the demilitarized zone and are the sites of airfields used by North Vietnamese MIG-21 fighter-bombers.

The command's statement did not say what the effects of the bombings were.

The Haiphong area has never been struck before by B-52's, which fly at high altitudes more slowly than the speed of sound and drop hundreds of tons of bombs in long, rectangular patterns. Because of their vulnerability to ground fire, especially surface-to-air missiles, faster fighter-bombers must fly with them to draw away enemy fire.

Haiphong is the main port of North Vietnam and is the receiving point for most of the supplies the North Vietnamese get from the Russians—tanks, artillery pieces, surface-to-air missiles and ammunition—to pursue the war.

The command did not say where the targets that were hit were situated. The first raids against Haiphong were made on June 29, 1966, when petroleum storage areas were hit. North Vietnamese MIG's challenged the fighter-bombers on that mission, but it was unknown whether the MIG's challenged the B-52's and fighter-bombers in the latest raids.

American military commanders have expressed concern about the more aggressive use of the MIG's by the North Vietnamese since last fall. In December, MIG's flew across the border into Laos, shot down one American plane, and caused the loss of three others.

The North Vietnamese have also told Communist cadres in the South that they would get air support from the MIG's in the South this year. But so far no MIG's have been sighted on missions south of the demilitarized zone.

Attack on Hanoi Reported

HONG KONG, Sunday, April 16 (AP)—The Hanoi radio reported that waves of United States war planes bombed both Hanoi and Haiphong today.

The broadcast said the gunners in Hanoi and Haiphong had shot down 11 of the attacking planes, including one huge eight-jet B-52 bomber.

The radio said "waves of many bombers and fighter-bombers struck at areas both inside and just outside of Hanoi," the North Vietnamese capitol, beginning at 9:30 A.M. Hanoi time. This was seven and one-half hours after waves of planes bombed the port city of Haiphong, starting at 2 A.M.

Gunners in Hanoi shot down five jet fighter-bombers during the raids against the capital while Haiphong gunners and missile crews downed five jet fighter-bombers and one B-52, the Vietnamese language broad-cast bulletin monitored here said.

The broadcast did not say exactly what areas had been hit in either Hanoi or Haiphong. It gave no damage details. Nor did it disclose that fate of the crews of the planes it claimed had been downed.

* * *

April 19, 1972

THE STRATEGY OF FAILURE

President Nixon's decision to turn the clock back four years by escalating the bombing of North Vietnam from its southern panhandle to the Hanoi-Haiphong area is an exercise in folly and futility. It revives a strategy tried for three years and abandoned finally by President Johnson in 1968 because it was demonstrably a failure. The mystery is why it is being tried again.

Secretary Rogers and the White House in separate statements have indicated that the bombing was meant in part as a threat that Mr. Nixon will "take whatever action is necessary" to halt the North Vietnamese offensive in South Vietnam. The lull that has followed evidently is intended to underline this warning. Both statements ruled out the reintroduction of American ground forces into the war or, of course, the use of nuclear weapons. The threat then, directed presumably at Moscow as well as Hanoi, is that a continued Communist offensive will bring back large-scale bombing of North Vietnam as in 1965–68—extended, perhaps, to the mining or bombing of Haiphong harbor and other ports. But neither Hanoi nor Moscow is likely to be intimidated now by a threat they have already faced down.

Officials in Washington and Saigon acknowledge that the current North Vietnamese offensive is being fueled by supplies already in South Vietnam or nearby. Bombing Haiphong, the so called "top of the funnel," they assert, is aimed at the supplies that might reach the front during the summer or later and keep the battle going then—at a time even more embarrassing politically for President Nixon. If the Administration's objective is to prevent this, it is doomed in advance to fail.

As long ago as July 1966, the C.I.A. and the Pentagon's Defense Intelligence Agency reported that sixteen months of bombing North Vietnam "had had no measurable direct effect on Hanoi's ability to mount and support military operations in the South." Moreover, the intelligence estimate concluded that this situation was "not likely to be altered" by mining Haiphong and other harbors or adopting other military proposals then contemplated for expanding the air offensive.

A year later, after the air offensive had been expanded in most proposed ways except for hitting Haiphong harbor, Defense Secretary McNamara reported that "there continues to be no sign that the bombing has reduced Hanoi's will to resist, or her ability to ship the necessary supplies south."

The risk of conflict with the Soviet Union and China dissuaded President Johnson from attacking Haiphong harbor. He concluded that the Communist superpowers were more likely to increase their involvement than to back down if their supply ships were sunk. The damage reported by Moscow to four of its ships last weekend, although American planes had orders to avoid Haiphong harbor, emphasizes the danger.

President Nixon may be prepared to run this risk. He may be gambling that the Soviet Union will restrain Hanoi or restrict its supply flow rather than accept a confrontation that would endanger Mr. Nixon's May 22 visit to Moscow and, with it, such other Soviet objectives as a strategic arms agreement, increased trade with the United States and Bonn's ratification of the German-Soviet treaty and the European status quo.

But a SALT agreement and détente in Europe are as much Mr. Nixon's objectives as the Kremlin's, and they are important to his re-election campaign. Is he prepared to risk them and the peace of the world by going beyond implied threats of a naval-air blockade of Haiphong—which are unlikely to intimidate Moscow—to the reality? Does he dream of turning Soviet supply ships around in the Gulf of Tonkin the way President Kennedy turned them around during the Cuban missile crisis of 1962?

One danger is that the Soviet Union may feel that Mr. Nixon is bluffing and, calling him, find that he is not. Since the Cambodian invasion of 1970, the President's aides have boasted of Mr. Nixon's "unpredictability." The stakes are too high for the nation or the Congress any longer to accept such risks.

* * *

May 2, 1972

SOUTH VIETNAMESE QUIT QUANGTRI; 80 AMERICAN ADVISERS FLOWN OUT; ENEMY IS WITHIN 15 MILES OF HUE

PROVINCE IS LOST

Victory Foe's Biggest Since Month-Old Invasion Began

By SYDNEY H. SCHANBERG

Special to The New York Times

HUE, South Vietnam, Tuesday, May 2—The South Vietnamese abandoned Quangtri, their northernmost province

United Press International

U.S. advisors waiting yesterday in landing zone at Quangtri before copter flew them out.

capital, yesterday, giving the advancing North Vietnamese their biggest prize so far in their month-old invasion.

The city, the first province capital to be lost since the offensive began March 30, was abandoned by Government forces yesterday afternoon after three days of shelling during which the enemy moved troops and tanks to the edge of the city.

The loss of Quangtri city gave the North Vietnamese control of the entire northern province of the same name.

B-52's Covered Retreat

About 80 American advisers, the commander of the South Vietnamese Third Division and his staff were evacuated in the afternoon in four big rescue helicopters that flew through heavy enemy ground fire to get the men out.

United States B-52's reportedly bombed areas as close as one mile to the northeast of Quangtri city between noon yesterday and 6 A.M. today in efforts first to beat off the enemy attack and then to cover the retreat of the Government forces. One of the 14 missions was nine miles south of Quangtri.

Meanwhile, South Vietnamese units retreated southward toward the even more important city of Hue, Vietnam's ancient imperial capital, in Thuathien Province. They were accompanied by 10 American advisers who had decided to stay with them.

Steady Push by Foe

Hue, with a population that has swollen to more than 300,000 by fleeing refugees, is now directly threatened. The North Vietnamese have reportedly moved to within less than 15 miles of the city on the west and about 25 miles on the north.

[On other fronts, North Vietnamese troops reportedly continued their advance in northern Binhdinh Province on the central coast and tightened their siege of the province capital of Kontum to the west. On the front closer to Saigon, Anloc, the besieged province capital that has been nearly flattened by enemy fire, was subjected anew to intense artillery bombardment.]

Reports reaching Hue indicated that Quangtri had been abandoned without much of a fight by Government troops.

Describing the situation, Brig. Gen. Thomas W. Bowen, the deputy senior American adviser in the northern region, said here last night that the South Vietnamese forces "were being steadily pushed back.

"The situation is not desperate," he went on, "but there is certainly cause for serious concern. It's not a thing to be taken lightly."

Earlier in the day he said, "We have given up plans to defend Quangtri." He added that the troops left in the area would be "working their way out as best they can."

COURSE OF COMMUNIST OFFENSIVE

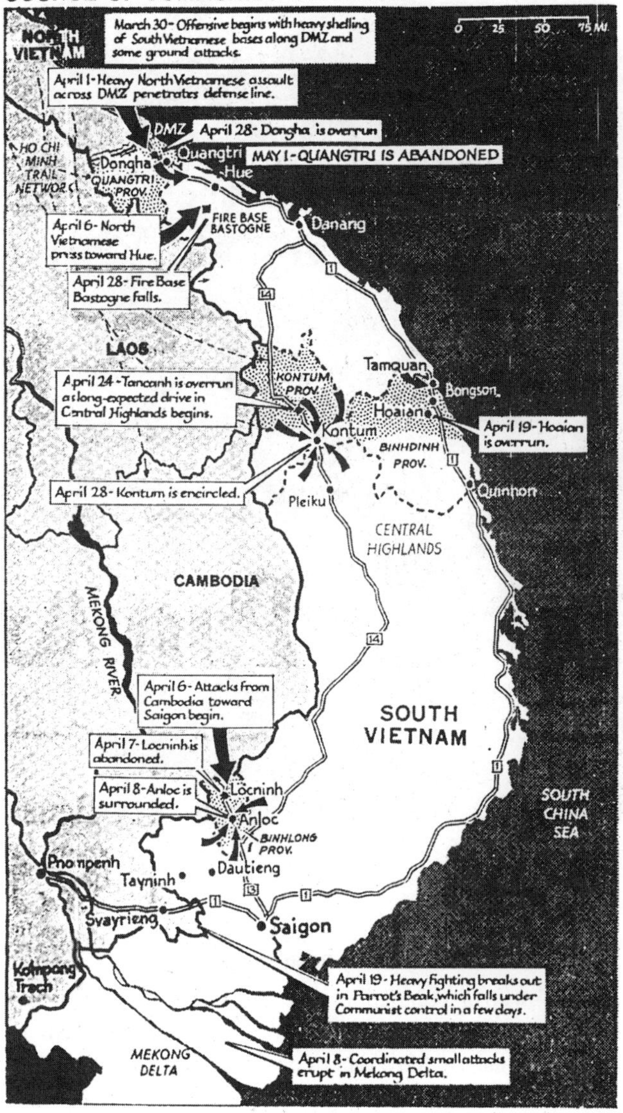

Quangtri City is the 1st provincial capital in South Vietnam lost as a result of the enemy offensive that began March 30. Quangtri Province and other areas similarly shaded are among the regions taken in recent weeks, but the North Vietnamese have also long operated in various parts of South Vietnam, along with the Vietcong.

Military advisers who flew over the scene said that no civilians were left in the town when the Government troops pulled out.

The civilians began fleeing the city, when intense shelling began three days ago. Yesterday the streets were filled with trucks and motorcycles and other vehicles abandoned by the residents. The vehicles had become useless because the enemy had cut the road to the south. Enemy soldiers had also knocked out some columns of trucks carrying refugees, killing and wounding many of them.

The North Vietnamese failed to take Quangtri in their first push from the north a month ago, but in a renewed offensive that began last Wednesday night they threw additional units and armor and artillery into the fight.

General Bowen said that the South Vietnamese division that was defending Quangtri had been badly mauled but added that the retreat had been fairly orderly. However, large numbers of Government troops on the northern front have reportedly been deserting in the last few days and many have made their way to Hue along with the civilian refugees.

Alarmed over the situation, the Government began a search for deserters in Hue and at least 500 were picked up by the military police and forced back into service.

Infiltrator Reported Seized

The military police set up checkpoints on the roads leading into Hue and also at the gates leading into the old walled section of the city to try to catch deserters. Infiltrators from the north are reportedly trying to organize students and others against the Saigon Government.

A reliable report said that at least one key leader has been picked up in the sweep. He was tentatively identified as Le Van Hao, a former instructor at Hue University who defected to the North Vietnamese during the Tet offensive of 1968 and reportedly slipped back into the Hue area during the current offensive. He is said to be a member of the cabinet of the Vietcong's provisional revolutionary government.

According to allied intelligence experts, the enemy wants to take Hue to establish a provisional government here.

Tensions continue to rise in Hue and the residents are beginning to evacuate to the south in increasingly large numbers. Tickets on Air Vietnam are virtually impossible to acquire and sea and river transport are also packed.

Foe Gains in Binhdinh

Special to The New York Times

QUINHON, South Vietnam, Tuesday, May 2—North Vietnamese troops continued their advances, in northern Binhdinh Province on the central coast yesterday, taking Tamquan District and tightening their siege of the Vietnamese 40th Regiment's headquarters at Landing Zone English, six miles north of Bongson.

All American advisers were withdrawn from both places today, according to senior Americans here.

The North Vietnamese are now effectively in control of the northern third of Binhdinh Province, where about 200,000 people live. The total population of the province is nearly a million.

North Vietnamese forces 60 miles to the west, reportedly continued to tighten their siege of the province capital of Konium after overrunning its northern defenses early last week.

The Government troops are heavily dependent on air support and United States planes dropped bombs close to Kontum between noon Sunday and noon yesterday.

The Pleiku airfield south of Kontum was the scene of intense military activity and near-panic among civilians trying frantically to board aircraft that would take them out of the battle area.

On the front closer to Saigon, enemy troops reportedly continued to attack the almost flattened province capital of

Anloc, 60 miles north of the capital, with intense artillery bombardments, but were not said to have made further advances on the ground. They have been attacking Anloc for more than three weeks.

* * *

May 2, 1972

ALLIED PROGRAM FAILS A KEY TEST

Vietnamization Hope Dashed in Coastal Province as Foe Overruns 3 Districts

By CRAIG R. WHITNEY
Special to The New York Times

QUINHON, South Vietnam, May 1—In Binhdinh Province, here on the coast of Central Vietnam, three county-size districts with a combined population of 200,000 have fallen to Communist attacks in two weeks with little real resistance.

Several years' work on pacification programs has been lost and Vietnamization has failed one of its most crucial tests. And the failure is readily conceded by both South Vietnamese and American officials in Quinhon, the provincial capital.

A regiment of South Vietnam's army, reduced to a quarter of its 3,000-man strength largely through desertions, is under attack near here. Few American advisers or South Vietnamese officials believe that it will pull through.

The unit—the 40th Regiment, fighting at a nearby landing zone named English—has reportedly failed every test it has faced in the last two weeks.

Since the fall of the Hoaian district on April 19, said a high-ranking South Vietnamese official who asked that his name not be disclosed, "the 40th Regiment has only 25 per cent of its strength—30 per cent were casualties and 40 per cent or so deserted."

"We lost Hoainhon after that because the local militia troops were demoralized," the official said.

"They thought the regular army had let them down," he went on. "We couldn't hold Hoainhon because the soldiers deserted, they left their posts during the night and didn't fight when the attacks came in the day." Bongson the capital of the Hoainhon district, fell last Saturday.

"The North Vietnamese are highly motivated—they know what they are doing," the official continued.

Priest Tells of Escape

What has been lost in Binhdinh Province? Perhaps the people of the province will tell. More than a fifth of them are now under Communist control, and local Vietcong agents are said to be preventing all the able-bodied young men from fleeing south and leaving as some of their women and children have done.

"I was stopped 10 times on the road between Bongson and Quinhon," said a young Roman Catholic priest who had walked 30 miles south. "The Communists told all the young men they must work to upset President Thieu and establish a new government of neutrality. I told them I was leading the people away because they did not want to be bombed by the Americans."

A few air strikes were called in on the northern part of Bongson and also in Hoaian after those places were abandoned, but American advisers say they took such action only in areas where they knew there would be few civilians left.

One of these advisers said that he had left Bongson after the 40th Regiment's commander and the Hoainhon district chief took their refrigerators, got in a jeep and fled, leaving their regular and militia troops behind to fend for themselves. Many of the soldiers gave up the fight and took to the hills.

"That whole district now is Communist-controlled," said the American. "If we were to sweep them out of there tomorrow, I doubt that we could get the people to tell us who among them had helped the other side. Those people will never feel safe with the Government again."

Many of the people of the captured districts—the third is Tamquan—have stayed there, or have gone back after fleeing the fighting. The region is on the coastal plain and the rice crop will soon be ready for harvest.

"There's usually a 25 per cent surplus of rice in Hoainhon," one of the advisers said. "You know who'll get it now."

Maj. George H. Watkins Jr., one of the Americans, was among the last to leave Bongson, a town of 40,000, before it fell Saturday afternoon.

He said that the morale of the militiamen and home guards had been "broken." They felt, he went on, that the 40th Regiment "had let them down by just not fighting at Hoaian district the week before."

The regiment did indeed give up Hoaian without a fight, according to the American advisers who were there, and they gave up Bongson with little resistance on Saturday, despite an abundance of American air power overhead.

"Hell, I had airplanes stacked up two and three rows high," said Major Watkins. "I couldn't use it as fast as it was coming in."

Air Power Alone Is Inadequate

Seldom before in all the analysis, claims and counter-claims in the rhetoric of Vietnamization has it been so clearly demonstrated that without effective fighting troops on the ground, air power is impotent. "The most effective weapon you have is the guy on the ground with his M-16 rifle," another adviser said.

A South Vietnamese official here, who may lose his job in the purge that is following on the heels of the Government debacle in Binhdinh, put it this way:

"The Americans were sincere, they tried to help the Vietnamese armed forces, and from A to Z they brought equipment here," he said "But one thing the Americans cannot bring here is leadership—they cannot bring that in from their arsenal."

"When the Communists were here before, from 1945 to 1954" he continued, "the people didn't have much to eat or good clothes on their backs but morally they were happy, because the Communists brought justice to this land for 10 years, not the corruption we have here now."

How the people of northern Binhdinh Province will react to the re-establishment of a Government presence depends on whether the 40th Regiment holds out. Its position, at Landing Zone English, was the headquarters of the American 173d Airborne Brigade before it pulled out last year. There are now rumors in the Vietnamese press that 2,000 United States Marines have landed in northern Binhdinh to pull the fat out of the fire as they did in 1965, when Communist control was also spreading in the province.

The rumor is not true and it does not seem likely that the Americans will come to the rescue this time. For the moment, the only sizable American installations are here in Quinhon in the southern and most populated part of the province. And the American advisers have been pulled out of landing Zone English.

* * *

May 3, 1972

RETREAT LEAVES SMALL UNIT OF MARINES FACING ENEMY

By SYDNEY H. SCHANBERG
Special to The New York Times

HUE, South Vietnam, May 2—Thousands of panicking South Vietnamese soldiers—most of whom did not appear to have made much contact with the advancing North Vietnamese—fled in confusion from Quangtri Province today, streaming south down Route 1 like a rabble out of control.

Commandeering civilian vehicles at rifle point, feigning nonexistent injuries, carrying away C rations but not their ammunition, and hurling rocks at Western news photographers taking pictures of their flight, the Government troops of the Third Infantry Division ran from the fighting in one of the biggest retreats of the war.

No one tried to stop them: their officers were running too.

The battlefront north of Hue was thus left solely to a brigade of a few thousand South Vietnamese marines.

The Third Division had fallen back before, at the beginning of the enemy offensive a month ago, but the commander, Brig. Gen. Vu Van Giai, had managed to scrape it together again and put it back on the line around Quangtri until yesterday.

But today, according to American advisers, virtually the entire division—about 10,000 infantrymen plus 1,000 rangers—was in rout, not even stopping at the checkpoints where military policemen were supposed to halt runaways and turn them around.

It was the force that was supposed to have defended the city of Quangtri, which was abandoned yesterday and which had been the northernmost town held by the Government.

There does not seem to be much now between the North Vietnamese and their next and more important objective, the city of Hue, whose residents are already packing up and fleeing farther south in large numbers.

Many of the retreating troops are not even stopping in Hue, which is about 40 miles, south of Quangtri, but are continuing on, taking their rifles, artillery pieces, tanks and armored cars with them.

The province chief went on the radio tonight, appealing to the people of Hue not to panic and flee and promising that the Government would defend them. As he spoke American advisers in Hue were calling Saigon to ask for every available aircraft to evacuate the thousands of refugees from the north who have flooded the city.

Bowling down Route 1 from Quangtri, the Government soldiers, their guns bristling at anyone who tried to interfere with them, clung to the sides and roofs and hoods and trunks of every available vehicle.

With horns blaring and headlights glowing in the midday sun, they raced down the center of the road, pushing other vehicles out of the way. They used trucks and tanks and they took over big buses and three-wheeled minibuses. They stole motorcycles, riding as many as four to the bike. There were also many on foot, particularly walking wounded.

Their anger at those who watched them running seemed born of their shame. Until the Third Division can be pulled together again, it hardly exists as a fighting force.

The South Vietnamese marines, the only units that have fought well on the northern front, are still holding three bridges on Route 1 between Quangtri and Hue. They are trying to slow the enemy advance, the first bridge being about 30 miles north of Hue and the last only 20 miles away.

No one expects that they can hold the positions very long. After those the only major defense before Hue is a large military base known as Camp Evans, or Hoa My, about 17 miles from the city. The new headquarters of the Third Division, it is packed with artillery pieces, which are constantly firing.

Rout Embarrasses Marines

At the southernmost of the bridges, at a village called Photrach, the South Vietnamese marines watched with pained faces as the army men fled. They would not talk about it, but their embarrassment was plain.

Their American advisers were not so inclined to silence. "This is really sickening," a Marine lance corporal said.

"It's unbelievable," said an American Marine major, Robert Sheridan, as he leaned on a jeep at the side of the road. "It's hard to comprehend. To stand here and watch this when you've seen the same people in your own units fight well because they have different leadership."

"You see the troops," he went on, waving his hand at the road. "But I don't blame them. Where are their officers? There's no one to tell them 'stop' and to pull them together."

The major said the Vietnamese marines in his unit were "very sad and very angry" at the army retreat. "They are embarrassed because I am standing here watching it," he added.

The marines stopped a thousand fleeing rangers last night as they tried to cross the northernmost bridge, he related. The

Associated Press

TATTERED AND MUDDY: South Vietnamese soldiers, many barefoot and in rags, reach South Vietnamese Marine lines north of Hue after escaping from Quangtri. Some who fled in confusion commandeered vehicles at gunpoint.

reason for blocking their flight, he said, was that "we couldn't tell if they were enemy." At daylight they were allowed to pass because the marines had no authority to stop them.

The marines fought "a hell of a battle" at the forward bridge this morning, the major said, knocking out 18 tanks with the help of artillery and air strikes.

The major said that last night, when the Communists started moving in the area, he wanted to call in naval gunfire from American vessels standing off the nearby coast, but that South Vietnamese officials held off the fire, apparently because they thought it might hit the retreating forces.

Many of those on foot had inexplicably thrown away their boots and were limping along barefoot. Some had bandaged their feet with rags. All were tattered and muddy. Even those who were riding had had to plod for 10 miles through the countryside during the night before they got to the first bridge held by the marines, where transport was available.

Whether riding or walking, the fleeing men had no time for anything but their own escape.

The body of a soldier lay on the road just outside Camp Evans under the baking sun, a victim, perhaps, of a road accident. His gear lay strewn about him. The troops passed without a glance.

Commandeering a Ride

As this correspondent turned back toward Hue today with three other correspondents, an interpreter and a driver in an old Citroën, South Vietnamese soldiers waving automatic rifles and pistols forced the car to halt. Fifteen pushed in and on blanketing the roof, hood and trunks. All appeared panic-stricken.

One was a major, Nguyen Van Niem, 45, commander of an ordinance company that had fled Quangtri. Laughing with embarrassment, he said he had no idea where his company was.

Like many of the fleeing men, Major Niem said that when he left Quangtri last night he had not seen any enemy troops, nor had he seen Government troops exchanging fire with the enemy. That apparently means that the Government force fled before it was attacked on the ground, although Quangtri had been under intense shelling by heavy artillery for three days.

Major Niem said he was going to Danang, 50 miles south of Hue, to join his parent unit. He said of the retreat: "We do not feel ashamed. The enemy fought very strongly and we have to withdraw and form a new front."

As the Citroën went on toward Hue, the driver craning out the window because the windshield was blocked, the soldiers brandished their weapons and uttered threats to keep others along the way from climbing on.

The ordnance major, who pushed his way into the car with great vigor, had developed a severe limp by the time the car reached Hue. He explained that he had been wounded by a rocket, and when he stepped out of the car he hobbled a few paces and collapsed into the arms of a military policeman, who carried him off.

Another soldier had a small neck wound that appeared to be healing nicely. Just before he got off in Hue he unwrapped his first-aid field bandage and asked that it be tied around his neck. A wounded man has a better chance of escaping shipment back to the battlefield.

Some of the retreating troops reached Hue early enough this morning to find time for relaxation and refreshment. A mud-spattered armored personnel carrier clanked through the gate of the main hotel at 9 A.M. and parked on the grass. A dozen soldiers and their captain clambered out, smiling, climbed the three flights to the terrace restaurant overlooking the Huong River and ordered an ample breakfast of omelets and French coffee.

* * *

May 9, 1972

NIXON ORDERS ENEMY'S PORTS MINED; SAYS MATÉRIEL WILL BE DENIED HANOI UNTIL IT FREES P.O.W.'S AND HALTS WAR

SPEAKS TO NATION

He Gives the Ships of Other Countries 3 Days to Leave

By ROBERT B. SEMPLE Jr.
Special to The New York Times

WASHINGTON, May 8—President Nixon announced tonight that he had ordered the mining of all North Vietnamese ports and other measures to prevent the flow of arms and other military supplies to the enemy.

Mr. Nixon told a nationwide television and radio audience that his orders were being executed as he spoke.

From the President's somber and stern speech and from explanations by other Administration officials, the following picture of the American action emerged:

- All major North Vietnamese ports would be mined, ships of other countries in the harbors, most of which are Russian, would have three "day-light periods" in which to leave. After that the mines will become active and ships coming or going will move at their own peril.
- United States naval vessels will not search or seize ships of other countries entering or leaving North Vietnamese ports, thus avoiding a direct confrontation with the Russians.
- American and South Vietnamese ships and planes would take "appropriate measures" to stop North Vietnam from unloading matériel on beaches from unmined waters.
- United States and South Vietnamese forces would interdict, presumably by bombing, the movement of material in North Vietnam over rail lines originating in China.

There was much confusion tonight about whether the United States and South Vietnam had proclaimed a blockade. The President did not use the word and Pentagon spokesmen denied that a blockade existed in the technical sense. But some observers felt that the practical effect on North Vietnam of the President's actions would be the same as a blockade.

[In Saigon, the United States command announced Tuesday that Navy planes had completed the initial phases of the mining operations in North Vietnamese harbors ordered by President Nixon.]

Two Basic Conditions

Mr. Nixon said the mining, the attacks on the rail lines within North Vietnam, and the efforts to interdict the movement of supplies by water would cease the moment the enemy agreed to two basic conditions: the return of American prisoners of war, and an internationally supervised cease-fire.

"Then," he said, "we will stop all acts of force throughout Indochina and proceed with the complete withdrawal of ali-forces within four months."

The White House would not say tonight whether, in these words, Mr. Nixon was in effect making the North Vietnamese a new peace proposal.

But observers here noted that he mentioned no political requirements for American withdrawal. Until now he has always insisted on some form of free presidential elections in South Vietnam to be organized under the terms of his proposal of Jan. 25 by an independent commission composed of all of South Vietnam's political elements.

Minutes after Mr. Nixon's speech, the State Department released the text of a letter from the United States representative at the United Nations, George Bush, to the Security Council, outlining the President's actions and the Administration's reasons for them. Mr. Bush's letter cited Article 51 of the United Nations Charter and called the President's actions "measures of collective self-defense" by the United States and South Vietnam.

The actions Mr. Nixon announced tonight seemed to stun much of official Washington, but reaction from the public was not clear, immediately after the speech, the White House switchboard was jammed with calls and it remained impenetrable for most of the evening.

Mr. Nixon seemed more pessimistic in his assessment of the military situation tonight than in any recent speech. He said the South Vietnamese had fought bravely, but conceded that "the Communist offensive has now reached the point where it gravely threatens the lives of 60,000 American troops who are still in Vietnam."

He did not, for once, talk about the progress of his program of Vietnamization, under which he hoped and presumably still hopes to turn over the fighting to the South Vietnamese. Accordingly, some here implied from his remarks a concession that the South Vietnamese were weaker, or the North Vietnamese stronger, than he had earlier suggested to the country.

In choosing to mine the harbors, Mr. Nixon adopted a course urged on the country by the Republican candidate, Barry Goldwater, in 1964, and rejected—despite the importunings of some of his military advisers—by Mr. Nixon's predecessor, Lyndon B. Johnson. Mr. Johnson felt that it would be unnecessarily provocative to the Soviet Union, the principal supplier of arms to the North Vietnamese.

Perhaps with this in mind, President Nixon aimed a major section at the end of his speech at the Soviet Union, although he addressed other audiences as well.

To the enemy leaders in Hanoi, he addressed a warning against compounding the plight of the Vietnamese people with "continued arrogance," calling upon them to "choose, instead, the path of peace that redeems your sacrifices."

To the South Vietnamese, he pledged continued support. But, in an apparent allusion to recent episodes in which South Vietnamese forces have retreated in panic, he said: "It is your spirit that will determine the outcome of the battle."

To the American people, he made a direct bid for support for his decisions and, apparently confident that he would get it, said that they, like him, wanted not just peace but peace with honor, "genuine peace, not a peace that is merely a prelude to another war."

Yet the audience to which he "particularly" wished to address himself, he said, was the Soviet Union. He asked the Russians to note that his actions did not directly threaten them, but that their continued efforts to resupply the North posed serious dangers to some 60,000 Americans remaining in the South.

"Let us not slide back toward the dark shadows of a previous age," he said. "We do not ask you to sacrifice your principles or your friends. But neither should you permit Hanoi's intransigence to blot out the prospects we together have so patiently prepared."

Mr. Nixon mentioned various major agreements on which, he said, the United States and the Soviet Union were near agreement, and in these and other ways he expressed the implicit hope that his forthcoming summit meeting in Moscow would not be endangered by his actions.

But some observers here wondered whether Mr. Nixon's plans to cap an election-year whirlwind of dramatic diplomacy with the Communist world could or would survive tonight's speech.

The Soviet Ambassador, Anatoly F. Dobrynin, visited Henry A Kissinger, Mr. Nixon's adviser on national security at the White House this afternoon, and was presumably informed of the contents of the speech. But it was not clear tonight whether Mr. Nixon had made other efforts to inform Moscow of his intentions.

One popular line of thought here was that Mr. Kissinger, who visited Moscow two weeks ago, set before the Russians in the most candid terms a wide range of actions Mr. Nixon might take if the North Vietnamese refused to engage in serious bargaining in Paris.

Mr. Kissinger returned from Moscow April 24 expressing hopes that the Russians would put pressure on Hanoi to participate in new and productive bargaining. But these hopes, by Nixon's account tonight, failed to bear fruit. Indeed, they were rudely shattered when North Vietnam continued its military pressure on the battlefield and proved unyielding at the bargaining table.

The President slowly led his audience to that point in the speech at which he announced his dramatic decisions, carefully listing the various options available to him.

He Cites Options

He said one option was "immediate withdrawal." This option, he said, might be "politically easy" but he called it repugnant because it would mean "turning 17 million South Vietnamese over to Communist tyranny and terror" and would deprive him of bargaining leverage in his efforts to win back American prisoners of war.

The second option, he said, was to continue to try to achieve a negotiated settlement. He said he would pursue such efforts, but insisted that to rely solely on negotiations would merely give "an intransigent enemy the time he needs to press his aggression on the battlefield."

Accordingly, he argued, he really had "no choice at all."

"There is only one way to stop the killing," he said, "that is to keep the weapons of war out of the hands of the international outlaws of North Vietnam."

The President's speech ended weeks of speculation about which course, if any, he would choose to shore up the South Vietnamese and halt the rapid deterioration of the allied position on the battlefield.

It also ended a day of intense activity at the White House, which began with a three hour meeting of the National Security Council, continued through the afternoon as Mr. Nixon, in the company of Secretary of the Treasury John B. Connally and other key aides, worked and reworked his speech, and ended with the address itself.

* * *

May 10, 1972

ANTIWAR PROTESTS ERUPT ACROSS U.S.

Columbia Rally Ends Again in Clash With the Police—2 Shot in New Mexico

By JOHN DARNTON

With mass marches, window-smashing sprees, silent vigils and traffic-blocking sit-ins, antiwar protesters by the thousands took to the streets yesterday in response to President Nixon's decision to mine North Vietnamese ports.

The coast-to-coast outburst of demonstrations was the most turbulent since May, 1970, when protests over the United States invasion of Cambodia closed universities across the country.

Most of the demonstrations yesterday began on college campuses, and many were peaceful. But some spilled over into city streets and turned into violent confrontations with the police.

For the second consecutive night, students from Columbia University met with violence when a rally that began on the Morningside campus in New York ended in a clash with the police on the city's Upper East Side.

United Press International

ALBUQUERQUE ANTIWAR PROTEST: Demonstrators who had been blockading Interstate 25 scattering as tear gas was fired by the police. Two students were shot during protest over decision to mine North Vietnamese ports.

At 10:30 P.M., about 300 orderly demonstrators found their path blocked by a cordon of policeman across Madison Avenue at 72d Street. The protesters turned west on 73d Street and were set upon from both sides by club-swinging members of the Tactical Patrol Force. At least five persons were clubbed to the ground but their injuries did not appear to be serious.

18 Are Arrested

Eighteen persons were eventually arrested, one for throwing a brick at a bank and 13 for vaulting over turnstiles without paying at the Columbus Circle subway station.

In Albuquerque, N. M., two students from the University of New Mexico were wounded by buckshot after the state police used tear gas to break up a crowd of 300 demonstrators blocking Interstate Highway 25.

One of those wounded, Mrs. Carolyn Babb Coburn, a 22-year-old first-year law student, was struck in the abdomen and chest and was listed in serious condition. The other was treated and released. The police, who carried shotguns, said there was no information "as to who fired the shot."

In Boulder, Colo., policemen fought 1,000 antiwar protesters with tear gas and clubs and arrested at least 70 persons last night in an effort to clear intersections and a highway bridge blocked with burning logs and automobiles.

It was the second time yesterday that the demonstrators, many of them University of Colorado students, had blocked the thoroughfares, including the main Boulder-Denver turnpike. At one point in the day, an angry driver who got out of his car with a shotgun was disarmed by the police.

In Oxford, Ohio, 2,000 Miami University students blocked the city's main street before dispersing.

At the University of Illinois in Champagne-Urbana, an 11:30 P.M. to 6 A.M. curfew was declared after thousands of students roamed the business section and campus; breaking windows in at least nine stores and looting at least six others. State troopers pushed the protesters back to the campus. There were at least two arrests, and three policemen and a student received minor injuries.

At Stanford University in Palo Alto, Calif., riot-equipped county sheriff's deputies moved in to break up sit-ins by 100 demonstrators who took over two campus buildings. The demonstrators were dispersed and street clashes between the police and students ensued. At least eight persons were arrested.

Near the University of Minnesota in Minneapolis, several hundred students threw eggs and rocks at the police, and several demonstrators were injured when the police broke up the demonstration.

About 1,500 protesters marched from the University of California campus at Santa Barbara to the city airport and closed it down shortly before 5 P.M. by occupying the runway. All incoming and outgoing flights were canceled, but the demonstrators were dispersed by the police ate last night.

Violence erupted for the second consecutive night at the University of California in Berkeley, where thousands of protesters moved off campus to the downtown business district, smashing windows and setting fires in trash cans. The police used night sticks and "ricochet" guns that fire hard rubber pellets in an attempt to disperse the crowd.

By nightfall, after a mass rally of 3,500 people that led to pitched battles with the police and the occupation of "People's Park," the scene of several disturbances in May, 1969, the situation verged on anarchy.

When the Berkeley City Council refused, by a vote of 5 to 4, to pass an ordinance that would have declared the city not at war with North Vietnam and provided reparations from city treasury, about 3,000 protesters rushed the stage and overturned tables. The crowd then moved to the City Hall, broke into the building and ignited huge bonfires outside.

At the University of Wisconsin in Madison, where disturbances also occurred Monday night, the police used tear gas to break a street blockage yesterday afternoon. At night, a peaceful torchlight procession of 8,000 to 10,000 persons to the state Capitol broke up into roving bands that vandalized a computer science building, firebombed a Navy R.O.T.C. building and smashed windows in other campus buildings and stores. At least two persons were arrested.

In Gainesville, Fla., about 3,000 students, mainly from the University of Florida, battled for three hours against a force of nearly 200 policemen who used tear gas, riot sticks and police dogs.

Highway Reoccupied

Earlier yesterday, the police used high pressure hoses to clear about 1,000 students from U.S. Route 441, a four-lane highway. The highway was reoccupied at 9 P.M., and at least 50 youths were arrested. It was not known how many persons were injured, but at least 12 ambulance trips were made.

Fifty-one persons, most of them students from the State University of New York, were arrested in Binghamton, N.Y., after sitting down to block the entrance to the Federal Building there.

About 50 persons were arrested in New Haven during a five-hour demonstration that involved mostly Yale University students.

A fire apparently set by arsonists destroyed an Army Reserve station in San Jose, Calif., causing damage estimated at $200,000.

Many protests involved the blocking of streets. This occurred across the country, from Westport, Conn., where 31 suburban residents were arrested for tying up traffic on the Boston Post Road, to Santa Barbara, Calif., where 1,500 students stopped motorists on U.S. Route 101 for more than an hour.

A group of protesters abandoned their cars on Chicago's Eisenhower Expressway during the morning rush hour, causing a massive traffic jam. Nine persons were arrested.

In New York, about 200 Vietnam Veterans Against the War attempted to storm the United Nations headquarters. Security guards locked the gates and clashed with a handful of protesters who fought their way inside the main building.

In St. Louis, seven men who said they were Vietnam veterans went to the top of the 630-foot Gateway Arch and "occupied" it for an hour. In Philadelphia, 200 activists blocked the entrance to the President's re-election headquarters.

About 30 protesters were ejected from the visitors gallery at the House of Representatives in Washington after shouting antiwar slogans.

Campus buildings were occupied by protesters at Rutgers University in New Brunswick, N.J., Syracuse University and the University of Rochester. The R.O.T.C. building at the University of Maryland was struck by a Molotov cocktail, but damage was reported to be slight.

In Davis, Calif., demonstrators sat on the railroad tracks and blocked the passage of five Southern Pacific trains for six hours, until they were dispersed by the police. Fifty-seven persons were arrested.

Two bridges in Amherst, Mass., were blocked by students for half an hour, and the New York Thruway was obstructed by students at the State University of New York in New Paltz for at least an hour.

* * *

May 22, 1972

DEATH IN PHUCLOC

By ANTHONY LEWIS

PHUCLOC, North Vietnam—At the southern boundary of the city of Haiphong the rice fields begin. The vista of watery green stretches out to the horizon, broken only by the occasional island of a tiny village.

About five miles out, down a dirt track in the middle of nowhere, is the village of Phucloc. In Vietnamese Phuc means peace and happiness; Loc means prosperity.

The houses in Phucloc, as in most villages of the Red River delta, are made of mud with straw roofs. Until April 16 the population was 611.

At 2:20 A.M. on Sunday, April 16, according to the North Vietnamese, American B-52's bombed Phucloc, killing 63 people and injuring 61. Of the 121 houses in the village, 78 were destroyed.

That is what the North Vietnamese say. After a visit to Phucloc one has no reason to doubt that such an attack occurred. The rubble and bomb craters are still there, a month after the attack, with some new houses built or going up amid the wreckage. But the physical evidence is less convincing than the emotional.

As we entered the village there was an old frail woman sitting on a pile of rubble, moaning and swaying. When she saw the foreigner she started to come over. My interpreter, embarrassed, took her gently by the arm to another mound where she stood, still wailing. The interpreter came back and explained: "Since the loss of her family she is mad."

Another woman, who refused to be kept away from me, was Mrs. Pham Thi Viet, 38 years old but looking much older. She said she was away the night of the bombing and came back to find four of her six children dead. So were her father, uncle, sister-in-law, niece and nephew.

"Why does Nixon send B-52's to kill our children while they are asleep?" she asked.

Often in North Vietnam people whom the authorities arrange for an American correspondent to meet say they know there are different kinds of Americans—some against the war. That did not happen in Phucloc.

The American strategists of the Vietnam war tend to think in large abstractions uncluttered by human beings. They say the war is necessary to preserve the prestige of the President, or to assure the sea routes to Australia—Walt Rostow wrote that recently. But would those objectives seem "so persuasive" if the cost in human terms were really understood?

Death is always less painful in the abstract. I was critical of the means used by the United States in this war before coming here. But tallying the numbers of bomb craters is not the same as seeing Phucloc.

The North Vietnamese believe that American bombing of such targets as villages and hospitals is done intentionally, to terrorize the population. I do not; I think it is a mistake. But that does not resolve the moral problem.

If Phucloc was hit by mistake, there is still the question of why it happened. Was American intelligence wrong? Were the pilots careless? Or is it simply impossible for men flying planes five miles above the earth in the middle of the night to know exactly what they are going to hit?

We cannot call back that early morning of April 16. But we can stop talking about precision bombing of military targets. We can avoid saving what others have after wars: We did not know.

* * *

June 9, 1972

SOUTH VIETNAMESE DROP NAPALM ON OWN TROOPS

By FOX BUITERFIELD

Special to The New York Times

TRANGBANG, South Vietnam, June 8—Standing in the company command post here today, Sgt. Nguyen Van Hai watched incredulously as a South Vietnamese plane mistakenly dropped flaming napalm right on his troops and a cluster of civilians.

In an instant five women and children and half a dozen South Vietnamese soldiers were badly burned, their skin peeling off in huge pink and black chunks.

"This is terrible, the worst I've ever seen!" said Sergeant Hai, a six-year veteran, as he tried to comfort a wounded man. "It is very bad for my soldiers—now they will not want to fight."

In fact, as the flames from the napalm flickered out, his soldiers ceased firing at the North Vietnamese soldiers entrenched nearby in this district town, 40 miles northwest of Saigon. The South Vietnamese, members of the 50th Regiment of the 25th Infantry Division, have been trying for three days to drive the enemy out of Trangbang's marketplace and reopen Highway 1 between Saigon and Tayninh, on the Cambodian border.

Major Drive Feared

Although overshadowed by the more spectacular battles at Hue in the North, Kontum in the Central and Anloc, farther north of Saigon, the recent fighting here at Trangbang and along nearby parts of Highway 1 in Haunghia Province is causing serious anxiety to allied officials in Saigon.

They fear that the North Vietnamese, who are operating in small company-size units, may be cutting the highway in preparation for a major drive on Saigon from the Parrot's Beak section of Cambodia, adjacent to Haunghia Province.

Over the last week, American intelligence analysts say, large numbers of North Vietnamese from the Fifth, Seventh and Ninth Divisions have been pulled back from Anloc and regrouped in the Parrot's Beak area.

Accidental bombing like today's is not a rare occurrence in Vietnam, but, such mistakes are seldom reported in the official United States or South Vietnamese daily military communiqués.

An Earlier Accident

Yesterday, for example South Vietnamese Air Force A-37 Dragonfly fighters mistakenly bombed South Vietnamese paratroopers seven miles southwest of Mychanh, on the northernmost defense line above Hue, according to a Saigon officer. Nine paratroopers were killed and 21 wounded, but the accident was not officially announced.

Sergeant Hai said that he could see little excuse for the incident at Trangbang, which began when a forward air controller, flying over the area in a small observation plane, marked the enemy positions with two white phosphorous rockets. From the ground it was unclear whether the air controller was American or South Vietnamese.

At the same time, the South Vietnamese troops identified their own lines by shooting off a purple smoke grenade. The opposing positions, judging by the two sets of smoke, lay about 150 yards apart, with a large pink pagoda marking the South Vietnamese soldiers' most forward area.

Two A-1E Skyraiders—single-engine, propeller-driven aircraft now flown only by the South Vietnamese—then began their bombing runs, diving in steep arcs until they almost touched the treetops. The first Skyraider dropped six bombs just to the left of the pagoda, more than a hundred yards off target. Then the second, with the napalm, swooped

Associated Press

ACCIDENTAL NAPALM ATTACK: South Vietnamese children and soldiers fleeing Trangbang on Route 1 after a South Vietnamese Skyraider dropped bomb. The girl at center has torn off burning clothes.

even farther over Government lines, unloading its deadly canisters beside a yellow masonry farmhouse serving as the South Vietnamese command post.

A South Vietnamese soldier who escaped without being burned said to an American visitor: "Vietnamese pilots Number 10"—which in soldiers' slang means the worst.

Back up the highway toward Saigon, a large crowd of travelers had gathered, blocked by the fighting from continuing on their way. A 10-year-old boy was selling ice-cream cones, and passengers on a bus had littered the road with the husks of fruit that another peddler had sold them.

Some of the passengers had made the trip up the highway for each of the last three days without getting through, a familiar experience for war-weary Vietnamese.

"This war has been going on longer than any war in history," remarked a man who was squatting on the highway with his family. "We Vietnamese have suffered terribly. Why is it we cannot get together and settle this war?"

Some of the napalm had hit a large blue signboard, leaving sticky grayish shreds on it. The sign read in Vietnamese and English: "The people and authorities of Trangbang welcome visitors."

* * *

June 9, 1972

B-52'S HIT NORTH VIETNAM FOR FIRST TIME IN 7 WEEKS

By JOSEPH B. TREASTER

Special to The New York Times

SAIGON, South Vietnam, Friday, June 9—For the first time in nearly seven weeks, United States B-52's have bombed North Vietnam, the American command in Saigon has announced.

The command-announced yesterday that the B-52's—which can carry up to 30 tons of bombs each—had struck twice Wednesday in the lower panhandle of North Vietnam and that the number of raids by fighter-bombers had been increased.

Eight raids were flown by the big bombers in the same areas yesterday, the command said today.

The targets of the raids were said to be units of a North Vietnamese division believed to be moving into South Vietnam to join in the Communist offensive.

One of the attacks yesterday was in the populous coastal plain about three miles south of the village of Chaple, the command said. Six of the raids reportedly were in the foothills 22 to 29 miles northeast of the northwest corner of the demilitarized zone. Another was said to have been in the mountains 16 miles north of the demilitarized zone.

[In Washington, favorable assessments of the progress of the air war over North Vietnam were presented at briefings by an admiral and an Air Force general, who noted that fewer targets were considered off limits now than in 1968.]

On Wednesday the B-52's had struck in the mountains and foothills 9 miles and 17 miles northeast of the northwest corner of the demilitarized zone.

There was no report last night on the damage done by the B-52's, which usually operate in flights of three planes.

But a command spokesman said that for the second day American fighter-bombers had hit the northeast rail line out of Hanoi about 20 miles from the Chinese border.

American pilots in Vietnam said that by using Bombs guided to their targets by either television cameras or laser beams, they had scored direct hits on the Lungtruong railroad tunnel, which is about 10 miles southwest of the town of Langson. Air Force officers said that reconnaissance photographs showed the bombs had collapsed the southwest end of the 600-foot-long tunnel.

Again using guided bombs, the pilots were said to have attacked a vehicle-maintenance area and vehicle-storage facility on the southwestern outskirts of Hanoi, destroying 2 buildings, damaging 16 and destroying or damaging 8 trucks.

The United States command, which reports air strikes 24 hours after they occur, said that throughout North Vietnam Wednesday there were more than 300 fighter-bomber strikes, as against the 260 to 270 reported in recent days. American military officers attributed the increase to improved weather over most of North Vietnam.

The officers said they believed the B-52's had been called into action for the first time since April 24 because the threat of surface-to-air missiles had diminished considerably in southern North Vietnam and because intelligence agencies had found what were regarded as good targets.

In contrast to the early days of the renewed bombing of North Vietnam, when scores of surface-to-air missiles were being fired, none were reported fired yesterday.

In the ground war, meanwhile, allied officers in the field reported that South Vietnamese troops had started two new drives in the northern provinces of South Vietnam. Both were aimed at further relieving North Vietnamese pressure on the old city of Hue.

In one of the operations, five battalions of about 2,500 marines were reported to be sweeping the coastal plain about five miles north of the southern boundary of Communist-held Quangtri Province. As night fell several elements were reported to be engaged in heavy fighting.

In the other operation, a major part of a regiment of the First South Vietnamese division, or about 3,500 men, was taken by helicopter to the high ground around Fire Base Veghle. The fire base, which fell to the North Vietnamese in April, is 17 miles southwest of Hue.

Meanwhile, a group of South Vietnamese paratroopers was lifted in helicopters to the southern edge of Anloc, the rubber-plantation town 60 miles northwest of Saigon that has been under siege for the last two months. The paratroopers linked up with other Government troops but, instead of trying to go into the town, began moving southward along Highway 13 toward Saigon.

Parts of the relief column that has been trying to reach Anloc on Highway 13 have been cut off by the enemy, and the road has been made unusable. A Government spokesman said the paratroopers would try to reunite the column and clear the road of enemy before an attempt to retake the town is made.

Scattered fighting continued along Highway 1 about 40 miles northwest of Saigon. The road, leading to Cambodia, remained cut by the North Vietnamese in at least two places and was impassable.

There were 235 attacks by fighter-bombers reported in South Vietnam along with 20 B-52 missions, seven of them northwest of Kontum. Bombardments from five destroyers and a destroyer escort were reported.

* * *

June 29, 1972

NIXON RULES OUT DUTY IN VIETNAM FOR NEW DRAFTEES

Only Volunteers Will Be Sent but Order Does Not Affect 4,000 Already There

NEW TROOP CUT IS SET

Reduction of 10,000 Will Leave 39,000 on Sept. 1—Pullback Rate Slowed

By ROBERT B. SEMPLE Jr.
Special to The New York Times

WASHINGTON, June 28—President Nixon ordered today that from now on, no draftees be sent to Vietnam unless they volunteer for duty there.

Mr. Nixon's decision was disclosed as part of an announcement from the White House that 10,000 more troops would be withdrawn from Vietnam by Sept. 1, reducing American military strength in South Vietnam to 39,000 men by that date but leaving sizable United States forces and fire power elsewhere in the Indochina theater.

The announcement does not affect the 4,000 draftees now serving in Vietnam or draftees already under orders to go to Vietnam.

Ground Forces Dwindling

However, it confirmed and will inevitably accelerate a trend that has seen professional soldiers assume an increasingly larger role in Vietnam as the number of ground combat forces—which consisted mainly of draftees—dwindled under Mr. Nixon's withdrawal program.

The President's latest decisions on troops were relayed to newsmen this morning by his press secretary, Ronald L. Ziegler. Mr. Ziegler said the President had made them "based on an assessment that the troops could be withdrawn without jeopardizing U. S. troops in Vietnam or the Vietnamization program"—the President's three-year effort to turn over a gradually growing share of the combat burden to South Vietnamese forces.

Mr. Ziegler also said that another announcement on troop strength in Vietnam would be made by Sept. 1, a time when the election contest between Mr. Nixon and his Democratic opponent is expected to begin in earnest.

Peace Terms Restated

In his brief announcement, and before television cameras later, Mr. Ziegler also restated the essence of the peace terms put forward by the President on May 8. The United States, he said, would withdraw all its troops four months after an agreement with Hanoi for an internationally supervised cease-fire throughout Indochina and the release of all American prisoners of war, including an accounting of those missing in action.

The announcement on troop withdrawals means that the present monthly rate of cutbacks would be halved, from about 10,000 men a month—the prevailing rate in May and June—to about 5,000 a month. This was not unexpected, given the reduction in the size of the American contingent in Vietnam and the belief among many American officials that some United States troops should remain there to impose leverage on the enemy to reach a settlement.

The announcement also dramatized two other characteristic trends of the President's Vietnamization policy. It meant, first that by Sept. 1 he will have removed some 510,000 troops from Vietnam since his inauguration in 1969. It also emphasized the extent to which, in pursuit of a solution he regards as honorable and in response to the recent enemy offensive, he has compensated for reduced American participation, on the ground with increased American participation in the air and on the sea.

45,000 Now in Thailand

According to statistics provided by the Defense Department, there are now 45,000 Americans in Thailand, compared with 32,000 when the North Vietnamese offensive began at the end of March. The Pentagon also estimated the present strength of naval forces offshore at 42,000 men, compared with 13,000 in January and 15,000 to 18,000 in March.

In addition, various support forces whose activities are related to the war in Vietnam have been increased at American installations in Guam, Okinawa, Japan and the Philippines. Some Pentagon sources have estimated that as many as 15,000 men may have been added to these forces since the beginning of the North Vietnamese offensive.

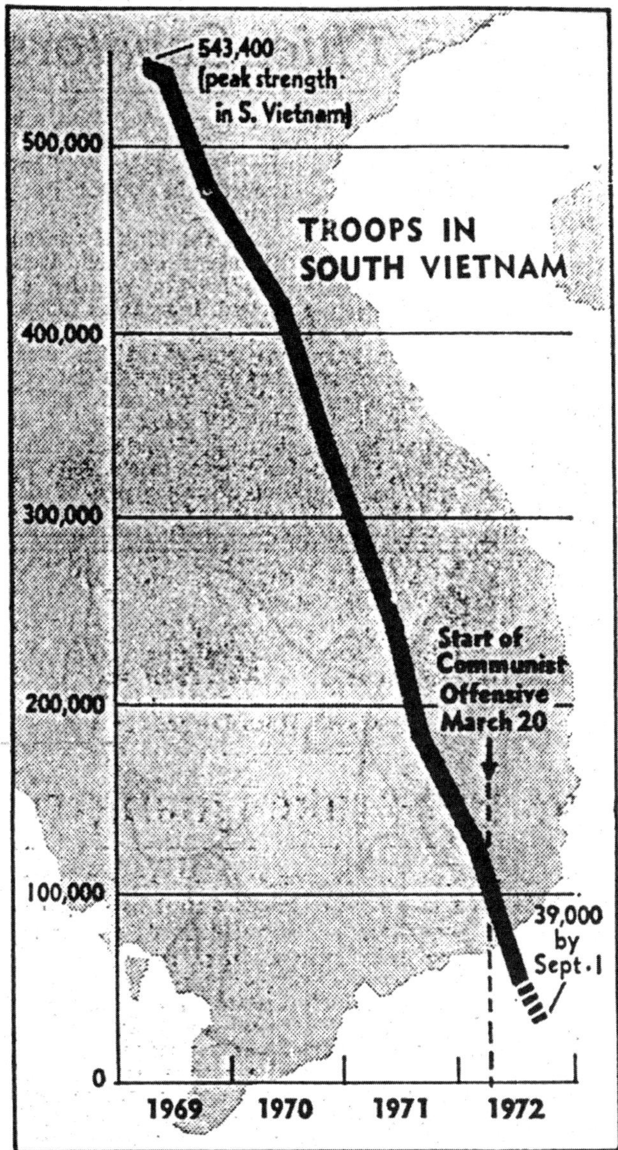

Taken together, the increases in Thailand, on ships offshore and at other American bases in the Pacific are estimated to total 50,000 to 60,000 men. This exceeds the reduction in troop strength in Vietnam during the same period.

By July 1, some 40,000 American troops will have left Vietnam since the beginning of the North Vietnamese offensive.

Most of the American troops now in Vietnam are helping the South Vietnamese with supply and logistical operations or providing combat support with helicopters; many of those in Thailand and on offshore carriers are involved in the expanded air war against North Vietnamese targets.

'Miniscule' Transfers Seen

On this point, Mr. Ziegler was asked at his morning briefing whether some of the 10,000 troops involved in today's announcement would simply, be transferred to Thailand or elsewhere in the war theater. He said such transfers would involve a "minuscule number."

The new ceiling of 39,000 men means that by, Sept. 1, the authorized troop strength in Vietnam will have been lowered to a figure not far from the size of the "residual force" envisioned by Secretary of Defense Melvin R. Laird and other officials as a form of permanent pressure on the North Vietnamese to release American prisoners and otherwise come to terms with the United States and its allies in South Vietnam.

* * *

July 3, 1972

RAINMAKING IS USED AS WEAPON BY U.S.

Cloud-Seeding in Indochina Is Said to Be Aimed at Hindering Troop Movements and Suppressing Antiaircraft Fire

By SEYMOUR M. HERSH
Special to The New York Times

WASHINGTON, July 2—The United States has been secretly seeding clouds over North Vietnam, Laos and South Vietnam to increase and control the rainfall for military purposes.

Government sources, both civilian and military, said during an extensive series of interviews that the Air Force cloud-seeding program has been aimed most recently at hindering movement of North Vietnamese troops and equipment and suppressing enemy antiaircraft missile fire.

The disclosure confirmed growing speculation in Congressional and scientific circles about the use of weather modification in Southeast Asia. Despite years of experiments with rainmaking in the United States and elsewhere, scientists are not sure they understand its long-term effect on the ecology of a region.

Some Opposed Program

The weather manipulation in Indochina, which was first tried in South Vietnam in 1963, is the first confirmed use of meteorological warfare. Although it is not prohibited by any international conventions on warfare, artificial rainmaking has been strenuously opposed by some State Department officials.

It could not be determined whether the operations were being conducted in connection with the current North Vietnamese offensive or the renewed American bombing of the North.

Effectiveness Doubted

Beginning in 1967, some State Department officials protested that the United States, by deliberately altering the natural rainfall in parts of Indochina, was taking environmental risks of unknown proportions. But many advocates of the operation have found little wrong with using weather modification as a military weapon.

"What's worse," one official asked, "dropping bombs or rain?"

All of the officials interviewed said that the United States did not have the capability to cause heavy floods during the summer in the northern parts of North Vietnam, where serious floods occurred last year.

Officially, the White House and State Department declined comment on the use of meteorological warfare. "This is one of those things where no one is going to say anything," one official said.

Most officials interviewed agreed that the seeding had accomplished one of its main objectives—muddying roads and flooding lines of communication. But there were also many military and Government officials who expressed doubt that the project had caused any dramatic results.

The sources, without providing details, also said that a method had been developed for treating clouds with a chemical that eventually produced an acidic rainfall capable of fouling the operation of North Vietnamese radar equipment used for directing surface-to-air missiles.

In addition to hampering SAM missiles and delaying North Vietnamese infiltration, the rainmaking program had the following purposes:

Providing rain and cloud cover for infiltration of South Vietnamese commando and intelligence teams into North Vietnam.

Serving as a "spoiler" for North Vietnamese attacks and raids in South Vietnam.

Altering or tailoring the rain patterns over North Vietnam and Laos to aid United States bombing missions.

Diverting North Vietnamese men and material from military operations to keep muddied roads and lines of communication in operation.

Keyed to Monsoon

The cloud-seeding operations necessarily were keyed to the two main monsoon seasons that affect Laos and Vietnam. "It was just trying to add on to something that you already got," one officer said.

Military sources said that one main goal was to increase the duration of the southwest monsoon, which spawns high-rising cumulus clouds—those most susceptible to cloud-seeding—over the panhandle areas of Laos and North Vietnam from May to early October. The longer rainy season thus would give the Air Force more opportunity to trigger rainstorms.

"We were trying to arrange the weather pattern to suit our convenience," said one former Government official who had detailed knowledge of the operation.

According to interviews, the Central Intelligence Agency initiated the use of cloud-seeding over Hue, in the northern part of South Vietnam. "We first used that stuff in about August of 1963," one former C.I.A. agent said, "when the Diem regime was having all that trouble with the Buddhists."

"They would just stand around during demonstrations when the police threw tear gas at them, but we noticed that when the rains came they wouldn't stay on," the former agent said.

"The agency got an Air America Beechcraft and had it rigged up with silver iodide," he said. "There was another demonstration and we seeded the area. It rained."

A similar cloud-seeding was carried out by C.I.A. aircraft in Saigon at least once during the summer of 1964, the former agent said.

Expanded to Trail

The intelligence agency expanded its cloud-seeding activities to the Ho Chi Minh supply trail in Laos sometime in the middle nineteen-sixties, a number of Government sources said. By 1967, the Air Force had become involved although, as one former Government official said, "the agency was calling all the shots."

"I always assumed the agency had a mandate from the White House to do it," he added.

A number of former CIA and high-ranking Johnson Administration officials depicted the operations along the trail as experimental.

The art had not yet advanced to the point where it was possible to predict the results of a seeding operation with any degree of confidence, one Government official said. "We used to go out flying around and looking for a certain cloud formation," the official said. "And we made a lot of mistakes. Once we dumped seven inches of rain in two hours on one of our Special Forces camps."

Despite the professed skepticism on the part of some members of the Johnson Administration military men apparently took the weather modification program much more seriously.

According to a document contained in the Pentagon papers, the Defense Department's secret history of the war, weather modification was one of seven basic options for stepping up the war that were presented on request by the Joint Chiefs of Staff to the White House in late February, 1967.

The document described the weather program over Laos—officially known as Operation Pop-Eye—as an attempt "to reduce trafficability along infiltration routes."

It said that Presidential authorization was "required to implement operational phase of weather modification process previously successfully tested and evaluated in same area." The brief summary concluded by stating that "risk of compromise is minimal."

A similar option was cited in another 1967 working document published in the Pentagon papers. Neither attracted any immediate public attention.

The Laos cloud-seeding operations did provoke, however, a lengthy and bitter, albeit secret, dispute inside the Johnson Administration in 1967. A team of State Department attorneys and officials protested that the use of cloud-seeding was a dangerous precedent for the United States.

"I felt that the military and agency hadn't analyzed it to determine if it was in our interest," one official who was involved in the dispute said. He also was concerned over the rigid secrecy of the project, he said, "although it might have been all right to keep it secret if you did it once and didn't want the precedent to become known."

The general feeling was summarized by one former State Department official who said he was concerned that the rainmaking "might violate what we considered the general rule of thumb for an illegal weapon of war—something that would cause unusual suffering or disproportionate damage." There was also concern he added, because of the unknown ecological risks.

A Nixon Administration official said that he believed the first use of weather modification over North Vietnam took place in late 1968 or early 1969 when rain was increased in an attempt to hamper the ability of antiaircraft missiles to hit American jets in the panhandle region near the Laotian border.

Over the next two years, this official added, "it seemed to get more important—the reports were coming more frequently."

It could not be learned how many specific missions were carried out in any year.

One well-informed source said that Navy scientists were responsible for developing a new kind of chemical agent effective in the warm stratus clouds that often shielded many key antiaircraft sites in northern parts of North Vietnam.

The chemical, he said, "produced a rain that had an acidic quality to it and it would foul up mechanical equipment—like radars, trucks and tanks."

"This wasn't originally in our planning," the official added, "it was a refinement."

Apparently, many Air Force cloud-seeding missions were conducted over North Vietnam and Laos simply to confuse or "attenuate"—a word used by many military men—the radar equipment that controls anti-aircraft missiles. The planes used for such operations, C-130's, must fly at relatively slow speeds and at altitudes no greater than 22,000 feet to disperse the rainmaking chemicals effectively.

A number of officials confirmed that cloud-seeding had been widely used in South Vietnam, particularly in the north along the Laos border. "We tried to use it in connection with air and ground operations," a military officer explained.

One Government official explained more explicitly that "if you were expecting a raid from their side, you would try to control the weather to make it more difficult." This official estimated that more than half of the actual cloud-seeding operations in 1969 and 1970 took place in South Vietnam.

Much of the basic research was provided by Navy scientists; and the seeding operations were flown by the Air Weather Service of the Air Force.

By 1967, or possibly earlier, the Air Force flights were originating from a special operations group at Udorn air base in Thailand. No more than four C-130's, and usually only two, were assigned in the highly restricted section of the base. Each plane was capable of carrying out more than one mission on one flight.

One former high-ranking official said in an interview that by the end of 1971 the program, which had been given at least three different code names since the middle nineteen-sixties, was under the direct control of the White House.

Interviews determined that many usually well-informed members of the Nixon Administration had been kept in the dark.

In the last year, there have been repeated inquiries and publicly posed questions by members of Congress about the weather modification programs in Southeast Asia, but no accurate information has been provided to them by the Department of Defense.

"This kind of thing was a bomb, and Henry restricted information about it to those who had to know," said one well-placed Government official, referring to Henry A. Kissinger, the President's adviser on national security.

Nonetheless the official said, "I understood it to be a spoiling action—that this was descriptive of what was going on north of the DMZ with the roads and the SAM sites."

Another source, said that most of the weather modification activities eventually were conducted with the aid and support of the South Vietnamese. "I think we were trying to teach the South Vietnamese how to fly the cloud-seeding missions," the source said.

It was impossible to learn where the staffing and research for the secret weather operation were carried out. Sources at the Air Force Cambridge Research Laboratories at Hanscomb Field in Bedford, Mass., and at the Air Weather Service headquarters, while acknowledging that they had heard of the secret operation, said they had no information about its research center.

One Government source did say that a group was "now evaluating the program to see how much additional rain was caused." He would not elaborate.

* * *

July 5, 1972

QUANGTRI VILLAGERS TELL OF FLEEING BOMBING

By SYDNEY H. SCHANBERG
Special to The New York Times

PHUDUONG, South Vietnam, June 29—They had lived for nearly two months under North Vietnamese occupation, but, they say, it was the constant pounding by American bombs and shells, not Communist rule, that finally drove them to desperation and to escape.

So the South Vietnamese rice farmers slipped out of the village at midnight, and, for 11 terror-ridden hours, walked and ran south along the coast until they found themselves in friendly hands.

They were shelled on the way by one of the American ships that roam along the coast in search of targets. One family was wiped out by the barrage—the husband and a child killed on the spot, and the mother and another child badly wounded and left behind.

"One hundred shells fell, there were explosions all around us," said Ho Ngu, whose family of six was part of the exodus. "We threw ourselves to the ground. Dirt and rocks fell all over us. We did not know if we were wounded until afterward, when we began to feel our backs and legs and found no blood. We were lucky."

Just Before Counterofffensive

Fifteen other families—a total of 70 people—were in the group that escaped from Communist-occupied Quangtri Province about a week ago. They fled just before a South Vietnamese force began a counteroffensive to try to recapture Quangtri, the country's northernmost province, which had fallen on May 1.

Mr. Ngu and others in his group recounted their life under the North Vietnamese and their night of escape to a visitor in this village about three miles northeast of Hue, where they are living with hundreds of others in a makeshift refugee camp in the compound of an elementary school.

The members of Mr. Ngu's group, which came from Haique Village in Quangtri, said they did not know that Government troops had abandoned the province until North Vietnamese troops appeared.

"No one gave us any warning," said Ho Vong, an old man with wispy chin whiskers and teeth lacquered black according to local custom, "so there was no way to run."

Some Were Vietcong

He shook his head in bewilderment as he related how the village officials fled without telling anyone of the collapse of the South Vietnamese troops—without even telling their own families, which they left to fend for themselves.

The refugees said that nearly all the Communist soldiers who entered their village were North Vietnamese—they could tell by their accent—but that a few were local Vietcong guerrillas "we had known before."

The Communists moved into the houses and the farmers moved into bunkers they dug in the paddy fields. Almost immediately bombing by B-52's and shelling began. The bombardment was so intense, the refugees related, that the Communists were too busy trying to stay alive to organize the village politically and give propaganda lectures.

"There was so much shelling and bombing that there was no time to do anything to us, good or bad," said another old man, Le San.

The one thing the North Vietnamese did do was ask the villagers to surrender their Government identification cards. Many got away with telling the Communists their cards had been lost or burned during the bombing, but others gave up the cards—and now face the bureaucratic struggle of getting new ones so they can qualify for refugee aid.

Youngsters Put in Militia

The lack of organizing by the North Vietnamese was apparently typical only in areas where the allied barrage was overwhelming. Refugees who have escaped from other areas or have been freed by the recent counteroffensive report that the Communists confiscated their rice, marshaled all boys and girls into an armed militia, made villagers work as forced laborers and held continual indoctrination sessions.

In Haique the peasants could stand it no longer after four or five days of the bombing and shelling and tried to flee, but the North Vietnamese told them it was safer to move to the next district north, Trieuphong, because the bombardment was less severe there.

Some of the villagers stayed, but most walked several miles north to Trieuphong, where they lived in a village about six miles east of Quangtri City, the province capital.

There they stayed in the houses of villagers who had been organized by the North Vietnamese and were frequently called out to indoctrination meetings at night. The Haique people, because they were not permanent residents, were not asked to attend the meetings and were generally ignored both by the local people and by the Communists.

"The people did not say anything about what went on at these meetings," Mr. Ngu reported, "and we did not ask any questions for fear they would suspect us as spies for the Government."

Trips Back for Rice

The group lived on rice they had brought with them. When that was gone some men trekked back to their village and cut more.

There was bombing and shelling, but it was not as fierce as that at Haique. The people dug bunkers again and spent much of their time in them, but several villagers were killed anyhow. They often heard tanks rumbling nearby but never saw them.

After nearly two months they decided that their only hope lay in escape to the south. "We knew that as long as we stayed," Mr. Vong related, "our lives could be counted in minutes, because wherever the North Vietnamese are, the Americans will bomb all the time."

They decided they would leave at the first pause in the bombardment on June 22. It came at midnight.

They started down the sand flats, carefully keeping between the shore, where they thought the Communists would have sentries, and the hamlets farther inland, which they felt were likely targets.

Only an hour after they left, they came under shelling. After that the fear of being detected kept them running or walking fast until first light, when a helicopter hovered over them and the pilot waved them south in a friendly way.

Four Families Joined Group

Their number had grown to about 90, for they had met four families escaping from other villages.

Late in the morning they came upon an advance element of about 100 South Vietnamese marines and began to feel safer. The marines gave them some dry rice, passed some money among the children to cheer them up and directed the group to Huongdien, a district town in South Vietnamese territory.

They reached the town after dark, having walked nearly 20 miles. They spent the night there and the next morning were carried by boat to a port near Hue and then by road to the refugee camp.

Living conditions here are poor. The rations are meager and many of the children have skin diseases and bronchial ailments. The most common sound is a deep, racking cough.

Stoicism is also common among these people who have been uprooted so many times by the war.

"Temporarily we just need food and lodging," said Mr. San, his wizened face showing nothing but dignity, "so we can live on until the day when we can go back to our village."

* * *

July 5, 1972

SAIGON INTELLECTUALS SEE MORALE COLLAPSE

By MALCOLM W. BROWNE
Special to The New York Times

SAIGON, South Vietnam, July 4—A feeling is growing within South Vietnam's small educated élite that national morale has so collapsed that only a total revolution in the whole social structure offers hope of redemption.

Such a revolution, some of them say privately, would be possible only under a strongly authoritarian government of the type in power in Hanoi. Harsh austerity, rigid enforcement of laws and compulsion to cooperate in rebuilding are viewed as vital.

Many contend that although world interest in South Vietnamese morale centers mainly on the war, the real importance of the national mood in its effect on future reconstruction of the country.

"Sociologically, China has a lot in common with Vietnam, including traditional loyalty to family with very little interest in communities larger than that," a teacher said.

"Before 1949," he pointed out, "the Chinese also had a mixture of wretched poverty and luxuriant corruption. Their warlords, whose power was like that of feudal princes, were something like our province chiefs.

"Now America has decided that the Chinese Communist system has worked in China, and yet they still throw up their arms in horror when it is suggested it might work here, too," he said.

The teacher, like most other South Vietnamese willing to discuss the subject, asked that care be taken not to identify him. A passing remark indicating any sympathy with Communist idea in this country is sufficient for summary deportation to the penal colony on Conson Island.

The views of educated Vietnamese, in common with those of the rest of the population, are unlikely to have any measurable effect on the administration of President Nguyen Van Thieu. There is general agreement that so long as the United States backs Mr. Thieu and the war effort, his political position is unassailable.

But traditionally, the leadership and administration of both North Vietnam and South Vietnam, in common with China, have been based on the ancient mandarin principle that the primary qualification for governing is education.

In South Vietnam, this has meant that leaders have generally emerged from the professional ranks of doctors, poets, archivists and so forth, and as a class, they have tended to dominate the national administration no matter what government is in power.

In a series of interviews, general agreement was expressed by scores of persons considering themselves members of South Vietnam's intelligentsia that their society is desperately sick.

"It's not simply a matter of paying the police a few hundred piasters to overlook a traffic violation, or even of the large-scale war profiteering and black-market operations," a leading Saigon journalist said. "There's corruption all over Asia and the rest of the backward world.

"With us its much more serious. Now we have reached the stage at which human pity has mostly left us. We steal some poor soldier's watch for a few extra piasters. Our commanders drive over their own troops in their desperation to escape battles. We are ready to sell our wives to afford a television set."

"We have come to despise ourselves and our nationality," he continued, "and the more revulsion we feel the more we excuse ourselves on ground that you cannot survive in such a system without participating in it."

A university professor looked contemptuously from the window of his drab office at a typical Saigon traffic jam and said:

"There you see Vietnamese society in microcosm. No police or stoplights, no one to tell them what to do, so they just try to jam their way ahead, making things even worse. No pedestrian could get past that—he would be run over without hesitation."

Sees Lack of Responsibility

"I have lived in London and Paris and New York," he continued, "so I know what traffic jams are in those cities. But even when they are bad, there remains a certain individual responsibility that tells drivers there that you must sometimes back up to let another car through if you ever want to move yourself. Here that never happens."

The lack of individual cooperation in any community enterprise larger than a family's is strikingly evident in the nation's politics, armed forces, and even business.

A Japanese businessman who left here recently after several years said:

"Our company is giving up on Vietnam to concentrate on Taiwan," he said. "We have never been able to solve the problem of organizing an effective Vietnamese middle level of management. Vietnamese just don't seem able to keep large groups organized, and in a factory that is essential."

Many South Vietnamese share this criticism.

Ton That Thien, a former Cabinet Minister and now head of the sociology department at Saigon's Van Hanh University, said:

"I'm afraid this country needs a taste of the whip. I don't mean it needs physical brutality, but it does need a strong hand to take absolute charge and make the Vietnamese people do the things they must to survive."

In common with many other South Vietnamese, Mr. Thien blames the Americans for many problems.

"The United States should have done one of two things," he said. "One would have been to really take charge of Vietnam and run it directly as a colony, at least for a time. They could have forced new skills and new attitudes on us that would have made-survival a possibility. The French at least built a civil service they left us."

"Failing that," he continued, "the United States should have left us to work out our own problems."

"But Washington did neither of those two things," he said. "They have preserved the fiction of Vietnamese sovereignty by avoiding taking direct control of anything. Instead, they run Vietnam more or less behind the scenes, tampering with every aspect of our national life. Worst of all, they send us amateurs instead of colonial professionals, and by the time they learn something here they are ready to leave and be replaced by a new batch."

Mr. Thien does not believe anti-American feeling in South Vietnam would have been any stronger than it is now if America had openly and completely taken over the administration.

In any case, he remains a committed anti-Communist, and believes that once America removes its advisers and "political manipulators" from South Vietnam the nation will regain the moral integrity required both to rebuild the society and defeat the Communists.

Other South Vietnamese believe that no matter what happens now, reconstruction will be possible only under Communism.

A former scholar from Hue, who said he and his family would probably be jailed or killed if the Communists come to power, said:

"We have no leaders worthy of the name at present, nor will there be any, as things stand now.

"Our childish political parties have no following and within them there is only petty bickering, never statesmanship. The public has no use for any of them, because every time some politician has shown signs of real strength, whatever Government in power has always managed to buy him off.

"Our impression is that a man becomes a politician solely to obtain leverage to force a way into the very Government he said he was opposing," he continued. "Too many of our best people refuse to try to become leaders, because they know that in the last analysis the American Embassy is the arbiter of all political events here."

"So now we are a social jungle, a vicious anarchy of indifference, greed and fear," he said.

"I hope the Communists win this war," he continued, "certainly not for myself, but for the nation. The Communists are Vietnamese too, and therefore subject to all our vices. The difference is that they are locked into a rigid system that extends from the top to the poorest farmer—a system that means no political freedom, but one in which crimes against society are punished by death.

"The Communists have both the strength and the will to restore Vietnam to the human condition."

Most educated South Vietnamese temper their criticism of the United States with expressions of gratitude for goodwill and expenditure of blood and treasure. They usually acknowledge that while the United States has made mistakes in South Vietnam, most of the social problems are of their own doing.

But a handful speak vengefully, even while denouncing the Communists.

One said: "You have exported the diseases of your own society to us, and now they are an epidemic here. It warms my heart to know, from what I read in the newspapers, that some of our diseases have infected you, too."

* * *

July 8, 1972

BOMBING IS TERMED MORE EFFECTIVE NOW

By JOSEPH B. TREASTER
Special to The New York Times

SAIGON, South Vietnam, July 6—Senior United States air officers say American pilots have inflicted more damage on North Vietnam since April than they did in a full year of President Johnson's heavy bombing campaign.

Rather than stepping up the air war gradually as President Johnson did, President Nixon has bombed with great force almost from the time he renewed regular air raids on the North in early April. He has tried to cripple North Vietnam's transportation and power systems and to destroy its fuel stores and its capacity to produce steel. He has also mined the seaports for the first time.

Senior officers here say they have been given more operational flexibility than they had from 1965 to 1968, when President Johnson was running the air war against North Vietnam under the code name Rolling Thunder.

"In two months we've destroyed more targets than we did in a whole year of Rolling Thunder," said one high-ranking Air Force officer in an assessment characteristic of those expressed by senior Air Force and Navy officers in a series of interviews here.

Another Air Force officer, referring to Mr. Nixon and the officials in Washington who control the air war, said: "Of course, they give you priorities and indicate things they consider important. You get plenty of guidance but they give you the flexibility so that you can get the job done."

"Back in the old days," the officer continued, "they'd select a couple of targets and say: 'O.K., these are the targets you're going to hit next week. Period. That's all you're permitted to hit.' And if those targets happened to be in an area where the weather was bad, that's too bad. No bombing was done.

"Now," the officer said, "they give us a whole shopping list of targets and let us decide when to hit them."

Destruction Is Greater

Senior officers say that with fewer limitations and more advanced equipment and weapons—especially the new "smart" bombs, which are guided to pinpoint accuracy by either laser beams or television—they are subjecting North Vietnam to "a whole new order of magnitude of war."

Fewer American planes are flying over North Vietnam now than at the height of the air war under President Johnson, they say, but more 2,000-pound bombs are being used and the total tonnage is about the same.

Because of the smart bombs, which Air Force efficiency experts say are 100 times more effective than nonguided bombs, the destruction is much greater.

As an illustration, senior officers point to the heavily defended Thanhhoa bridge, which pilots using smart bombs knocked out on their second try in early May.

When conventional bombs were used against the bridge during Operation Rolling Thunder, an Air Force officer recalled, "we put in over 1,000 sorties and never put it out of commission."

"We lost 30 aircraft and never damaged the superstructure," he added.

No aircraft were lost in the strikes on the bridge this time and over-all losses during the current campaign, called Operation Linebacker, have been lower than they were during Rolling Thunder, despite much heavier antiaircraft fire.

The officers attribute this to improvements in the principal attack planes—the Air Force F-4 Phantom and the Navy's A-7 Corsair—to advances in electronic gear that counters radar-controlled automatic weapons and surface-to-air missiles, and to the experience acquired by air commanders during Operation Rolling Thunder. Another factor, the officers say, is that the smart bombs can be dropped from higher altitudes, permitting pilots to stay out of range of some of the most effective antiaircraft guns.

A diplomat who studies North Vietnam from Saigon said that Hanoi seemed to be experiencing "a significantly higher level of problems"—since the resumption of the air war and added: "The North Vietnamese are clearly suspicious and uneasy about the effects of President Nixon's talking to Peking and Moscow."

At a news conference on June 29, Mr. Nixon said that the mining and bombing had caused a complete turnaround on the battlefield in South Vietnam, where in April and May it seemed that Saigon's troops might be overwhelmed.

Air Strength Increased

Senior officers here feel uncomfortable about disagreeing with the President, but they say it is too early for the campaign in the North to have had any significant impact on the battlefields in the South.

The North Vietnamese are still attacking with Soviet-made tanks that require enormous amounts of fuel and are still firing heavy 130-mm artillery shells.

One development that might diminish the effectiveness of the mining of the ports is the installation of a fuel pipeline from Hanoi to the Chinese border.

Many officers in the Army as well as the air services say that the South Vietnamese may have been saved from defeat by the extremely heavy direct air support—bombardment of advancing troops and tanks.

While Mr. Nixon has continued to withdraw American ground forces in South Vietnam during the Communist offensive, he has sharply increased American air strength in Southeast Asia. There are now nearly 900 fighter-bombers at seven bases in Thailand and on aircraft carriers offshore. In addition, there are about 200 B-52 Stratofortresses on Thailand and on Guam.

An average of about 270 American fighter-bombers strike in North Vietnam every day and there are rarely fewer than 300 operating in South Vietnam.

As the North Vietnamese menaced Hue again last week, the United States mounted attacks on some days with more than 90 B-52's, each carrying up to 30 tons of bombs.

When the commanders feel the B-52's can be spared from duty in the South and when there are targets that call for saturation bombing—a large camp or a sprawling storage complex—the planes are also used in North Vietnam.

None of the officers interviewed said they expected Operation Linebacker to stop the flow of men and supplies to the South completely. But some Army generals said they believed the bombing might cause the North Vietnamese to abandon the conventional war they have been conducting with heavy machinery and revert to guerrilla tactics.

"We've taken out virtually all of their power," said an Air Force officer as he went through a big loose-leaf album of glossy pictures of shattered buildings and bridges.

"We've taken out major warehouse storage areas, particularly those associated with trucking," he continued. "All the trains on the two main lines leading to China are stopped. We've got 15 bridges out on the northwest rail line and 14 out on the northeast line.

"Nothing is moving, starting with the Paul Doumer Bridge right in Hanoi itself. We've destroyed innumerable depots."

The officer, who had closely followed Operation Rolling Thunder, added: "It took us three years to get to the point where they were hurting for power. We were never able to really interdict the railroads. They were rebuilding the bridges faster than we could knock them out. Now it's no problem to stay well ahead of them."

Hanoi Tells of Damage

In a statement transmitted by the North Vietnamese news agency on June 30 and monitored in Hong Kong, the Mayor of Hanoi was quoted as saying that bombing in the North Vietnamese capital had destroyed "a large number of hospitals, ships and residential quarters of workers" and killed "hundreds of civilians."

The United States military command here, in keeping with its long-standing policy, refused to comment on the North Vietnamese charges. But senior officers and pilots say they carefully study targets and plan their strikes so as to minimize injury to civilians. They also deny accusations by Hanoi that dikes and dams have been bombed.

At his news conference, Mr. Nixon said that eyewitness reports that the dikes and dams had been damaged had been checked and "proved to be inaccurate."

"I do not intend to allow any orders to go out which would involve civilian casualties if it can be avoided," the President added.

In a discussion with newsmen last week, an Air Force colonel who commands a fighter-bomber wing based in Thailand made clear that in the kind of war the United States is conducting against North Vietnam civilian casualties cannot always be avoided.

A newsman asked about the bombing of the Thainguyen steel mill, 30 miles north of Hanoi, on June 23, saying that he presumed it had been full of civilian workmen.

The Air Force colonel replied. "Well, it would have to be but I think, you know, they were not the target. I mean that's just the unfortunate thing about war."

MAKING PEACE

August 2, 1972

KISSINGER MEETS PRIVATELY WITH HANOI AIDES AGAIN

By ROBERT B. SEMPLE Jr.
Special to The New York Times

WASHINGTON, Aug. 1—The White House disclosed this morning that Henry A. Kissinger, President Nixon's national security adviser, conferred privately today for the second time in less than two weeks with North Vietnamese negotiators in Paris.

[In Saigon, a United States Navy spokesman reported that American planes had bombed a shipyard at Haiphong that built and repaired shallow supply boats.]

According to Ronald L. Ziegler, the White House press secretary, Mr. Kissinger conferred during the day with Le Duc Tho, a member of the North Vietnamese Politburo, and Xuan Thuy, head of the North Vietnamese delegation to the peace talks.

Mr. Kissinger returned tonight to brief the President. No further details on the length or substance of the conversation were provided here and both the United States and North Vietnamese delegations in Paris kept complete silence.

The White House disclosure of the Kissinger trip came a day before another crucial and probably close Senate vote on an end-the-war amendment offered by Senator Edward W. Brooke, Republican of Massachusetts that would require withdrawal of all American forces from Indochina in four months, subject to the concurrent release of prisoners of war.

White House officials who have been lobbying to defeat the Brooke amendment had been hinting that Mr. Kissinger was about to engage in further secret negotiations with North Vietnamese representatives in Paris.

The meeting was Mr. Kissinger's 15th private talk with Hanoi's chief negotiators in the last two years. The most recent was on July 19, after Mr. Kissinger had flown to Paris from the summer White House in San Clemente.

In the absence of any further report from Mr. Kissinger or the White House, officials here preferred to reserve judgment on whether today's meeting had narrowed differences between the two sides. But they were not optimistic.

Publicly, they noted, both sides have recently seemed to harden their positions. There has been no indication that the North Vietnamese are willing to move toward Mr. Nixon's basic proposal for an internationally supervised cease-fire, an exchange of prisoners, and withdrawal of American troops four months after a settlement is reached.

On the contrary—at least in public—Hanoi has clung to its basic seven-point proposal, the key elements of which would involve an American withdrawal, the removal of support for President Nguyen Van Thieu, and the establishment of a three-part coalition government before a cease-fire or an exchange of prisoners.

Principal 'Hangup'

Mr. Nixon, at a news conference last Thursday, described Hanoi's insistence on a prior political settlement as the principal "hangup" in the negotiations, and said that he could not accede to any plan that would "impose a Communist government on South Vietnam."

This obstacle would also seem to threaten not only the achievement of a larger settlement but Mr. Nixon's hope of providing the voters with tangible evidence of diplomatic progress before the November election.

Some White House aides have been saying privately that, at a minimum, Mr. Nixon ought to obtain a cease-fire by November. But such an interim agreement would require a change in Hanoi's demands for a political settlement before a cease-fire and—despite a few hopeful hints—most officials here do not think the Communists are now prepared to make such a change.

Nixon Is Hopeful

At the same time, however, Mr. Nixon insisted that the chances for a peaceful settlement were better than ever and implored his critics in the Democratic party and on Capitol Hill to give him three months, unobstructed by competing proposals, to achieve a bargain.

He was particularly critical of various end-the-war resolutions that would, in effect, extract a prisoner exchange but not a cease-fire in return for withdrawal of American troops by a certain date.

Mr. Nixon said he thought the chances were better now because the enemy was suffering under heavy and continuous American bombing and was hurt on the battlefield. Other analysts here have derived hope from reports that North Vietnam's rice supply has dwindled badly and from hints in Paris that Hanoi might be willing to drop its insistence on the removal of Mr. Thieu as part of an initial settlement.

These hints gave rise to expectations here that the North Vietnamese might be prepared—as is Mr. Nixon—to work out a political solution after, and not before, an end to the fighting.

But these are frail reeds on which to base hopes for a major breakthrough, most analysts here acknowledge. Moreover, it is conceded among diplomats that Hanoi will be in no hurry to change its terms appreciably until it has a clearer picture of the outcome of the American election in November.

Hanoi has made no secret of its preference for the Democratic candidate, Senator George McGovern of South Dakota. Mr. McGovern has offered to end the bombing on Inauguration Day, withdraw all troops within three months and end support of the Saigon regime. He has said that the North Vietnamese would inevitably release American prisoners of war after these two steps were carried out, even though his plan does not meet Hanoi's demand for the creation of a coalition government acceptable to the Communists

* * *

August 11, 1972

END-WAR MEASURE BEATEN IN HOUSE BY 228–178 VOTE

Margin Is Said to Bar Any Action by Congress Now on a Pullout by U.S.

ADMINISTRATION VICTOR

House Goes On to Pass the $2.1-Billion Foreign Aid Bill by 221 to 172

By JOHN W. FINNEY
Special to The New York Times

WASHINGTON, Aug. 10—In a crucial setback for the anti-war movement in Congress, the House of Representatives rejected today an amendment demanding the withdrawal of all American forces from Indochina.

The vote of 228 to 178 was a major victory for the Administration, which had lobbied intensively to defeat the Vietnam troop withdrawal amendment that the House Foreign Affairs Committee had attached to a $2.1-billion foreign aid bill.

In view of the House action, it now seemed improbable that any "end-the-war" legislation would be passed in this session of Congress.

The House went on to pass the foreign aid bill by a vote of 221 to 172. The bill's authorization of $2.1-billion in military assistance in the current fiscal year is about $200-million less than the amount requested by the Administration. A similar foreign aid bill was killed in the Senate last month after an amendment on ending the war was attached.

Stand Seems Decisive

The Senate earlier this month attached an amendment to a military procurement bill that through a cut-off of funds would require withdrawal of all forces in four months, subject to concurrent release of prisoners of war, and it is likely that the Senate will add the same amendment to the foreign aid bill when it is received from the House.

With the decisive position taken by the House, however, all such Senate amendments are now likely to die in a Senate-House conference committee.

The 50-vote margin represented a loss of strength from last October for House critics of the Vietnam war policy. At that time in a procedural action the House voted 215 to 193 to instruct House conferees not to accept a troop-withdrawal amendment approved by the Senate. In advance of today's vote, a White House aide predicted, "if we win by 40 votes or more, end-the-war legislation is dead for this session."

House doves contributed to their own defeat because they were divided over what deadline to set for the withdrawal.

As approved by the House Foreign Affairs Committee, the amendment demanded a termination of all hostilities and withdrawal of all American forces by Oct. 1, subject to release of prisoners of war and a limited cease-fire with North Vietnam to assure the safe withdrawal of the troops.

The Oct. 1 deadline was set several months ago when the amendment was first being drafted by its co-sponsors—Representatives Lee H. Hamilton, Democrat of Indiana, and Charles W. Whalen Jr., Republican of Ohio.

Change in Deadline Sought

In an attempt to pick up added votes for the amendment. Representative Whalen moved on the floor to change the deadline to Dec. 31. Administration forces taunted supporters of the "end-the-war" amendment, saying they were proposing to "extend the war by another 90 days."

The change in the deadline was also opposed by some of the more outspoken doves, such as Representative Benjamin S. Rosenthal, Democrat of Queens, and Representative Ronald V. Dellums, Democrat of California.

In what was to be a critical test vote, some of the doves thus lined up with opponents of the amendment to reject an extension of the deadline by a vote of 304 to 109.

With that, the doves lost the support of Speaker Carl Albert and Representative Hale Boggs, the majority leader, both of whom had voted for extension of the deadline.

With the White House successful in holding the Republican ranks almost solid in opposition to the amendment, the votes of the two Democratic leaders had been regarded as crucial in swinging over some moderate Democrats.

As appraised by an official of Common Cause, the organization that mounted a nation-wide lobbying campaign for the amendment, the outcome depended in large measure upon some 50 Democrats, most of them committee chairmen or subcommittee chairmen and thus part of the Democratic Establishment, which has tended to support the President on foreign policy issues.

The two Democratic leaders were under intense political pressure from their own Democratic ranks to support the amendment, particularly in light of the action of the House Democratic caucus in April in calling for legislation providing a prompt termination of the war. It was the caucus action that influenced the once-hawkish House Foreign Affairs Committee to adopt the troop-withdrawal amendment.

Right up to the debate, the two Democratic leaders remained publicly uncommitted on how they would vote, an indecision that some doves felt was hurting their cause. Then with the decision not to extend the deadline, Representative Boggs came out publicly against the amendment.

Noting that it was unlikely that the foreign aid bill would be enacted before Oct. 1, Mr. Boggs roared from the well of the House:

"I am not going to stand here and do something that is a vain and useless thing and could be misinterpreted around the world."

Mr. Albert also then voted to strike the amendment from the bill. The only member of the Democratic leadership to vote for the amendment was Representative Thomas P. O'Neill Jr. of Massachusetts, the majority whip, who led the move to place the Democratic caucus on record in favor of legislation to end the war.

Among the doves, there also was some bitterness directed to Representative Thomas E. Morgan, the chairman of the House Foreign Affairs Committee, for insisting that the first vote come on whether to change the withdrawal deadline. The doves had felt they would be in a stronger position if there had been a vote first on the amendment, with a subsequent vote on changing the deadline.

Position Held Unclear

Mr. Morgan had supported the amendment in committee, but in the maneuvering on the floor, some doves felt he had worked to the advantage of the Administration.

The move to strike the amendment from the bill was led by Representative Richard Bolling. Democrat of Missouri, who argued that in a Government of divided powers "there is no way Congress can make the President accept terms he finds unacceptable" and "it is a cruelty to the American people to pretend otherwise."

By voice vote, the House accepted an amendment by Representative Ogden R. Reil, Democrat of Westchester, authorizing the President to suspend foreign aid to any nation that refuses to prosecute or extradite plane hijackers when requested to do so by the United States.

The House, by a vote of 253 to 140, also struck out a committee amendment restoring to the President authority to ban the importation of Rhodesian chrome in compliance with a United Nations embargo.

The President's authority to control the importation of strategic materials from Rhodesia was removed in legislation passed last year by Congress.

* * *

August 13, 1972

LAST G.I. COMBAT TROOPS LEAVE QUIETLY

By JOSEPH B. TREASTER
Special to The New York Times

SAIGON, South Vietnam, Aug. 12—In Danang this morning there were no flourishes, not even a parade, as the Third Battalion of the 21st Infantry and other components of what had been Task Force Gimlet said good-by to the war. Maj. Gen. H. H. Cooksey said a few words, pinned on some ribbons and then, for all practical purposes, the last American ground troops were gone.

Remaining in South Vietnam are about 43,500 men—mainly service personnel—in administrative and supply jobs, but also several hundred advisers and the pilots and crews of about 600 helicopters and 200 other combat planes.

As President Nixon has scaled down the American forces in South Vietnam itself, he has assembled an armada of more than 60 warships and 39,000 sailors and pilots off shore and has increased the American military strength in Thailand to about 50,000 men. All together, on three aircraft carriers and more than half a dozen bases in Thailand, there are more than 900 combat planes. Additional B-52's are based on Guam and other support troops are on Okinawa and elsewhere in the Pacific.

While it is sometimes possible for newsmen to arrange visits to the aircraft carriers, they are prohibited from entering the American bases in Thailand. Thus, a large part of the American military effort in Vietnam is in fact kept secret.

It is widely conceded that American air power saved the South Vietnamese Army from collapse under the pressure of the North Vietnamese offensive in April and May. Men close to President Nguyen Van Thieu say that he is trying to convince the United States that the only way to bring the war to a definite conclusion is to continue the heavy bombing for several more months.

For the moment, President Nixon and President Thieu seem to be in harmony. Air and naval air officers say they have been given much wider operational lattitude under Mr. Nixon than under President Johnson and that they have "more targets than we can hit."

When the Bombing Began

In early 1965, when the United States started bombing North Vietnam and sent the first of its marines to Danang, South Vietnam was coming apart at the seams politically and the military situation could hardly have been bleaker. The Vietcong said that they controlled three quarters of the country and more than half of the population.

Today the Communists control most of Quangtri Province, including the provincial capital, large portions of northern Binhdinh Province, the northern half of Binhlong Province and perhaps half of Chuongthien Province, in the heart of the Mekong delta. In addition, there are sweeping expanses of the delta, of the Central Highlands and of the northern provinces where non-Communists dare not venture.

Associated Press

Sgt. Maj. George R. Green of the 3d Battalion, 21st Infantry, furling the colors held by Lieut. Col. Rocco Negris, in stand down ceremony at Danang yesterday.

The price in lives to reach this point, according to the Department of Defense, has been 45,843 Americans, 173,696 South Vietnamese, 871,000 North Vietnamese and Vietcong soldiers, and tens of thousands of civilians.

The outlook for the war, as expressed by the highest-ranking American officers in South Vietnam, offers little encouragement. "This conflict could go on for quite a while without being resolved," said a senior Army officer, weariness in his tone.

Enemy Caches Cited

He said that while the North Vietnamese had suffered grave losses of men and equipment, they still seem to have supplies cached on the battlefields and that there were indications that enemy reinforcements were still being fed into the fighting, particularly at Quangtri. Highest-ranking Americans and South Vietnamese alike are convinced that either late August or early September will bring another surge in the fighting.

The officers expect a wave of terrorism, including rocket and demolition-team attacks on Saigon and other large cities and several large ground assaults. They say they expect the heaviest fighting to come in the two northern provinces, in Quangngai on the northern coast and in the Mekong River delta, where nearly 7 million people produce most of the nation's rice.

The American and South Vietnamese commanders say they doubt that the next attacks will be as severe as those mounted early in the North Vietnamese offensive. But they look for serious attempts to further grind down the South Vietnamese Army and expect the enemy forces to try to take whatever territory they can.

"We think he's shot off his major blow," said a senior officer privy to the thoughts of the American command "so now he'll lean more heavily on the political and psychological side."

* * *

August 21, 1972

POSTWAR SHOCK BESETS EX-G.I.'S

By JON NORDHEIMER

Special to The New York Times

SAN FRANCISCO, Aug. 20—The flights from Saigon and Danang reach California in 18 hours, telescoping night into day into night again, and the big jet transports drop out of the gloomy Pacific sky to land at Travis Air Force Base as another sunrise rims the high peaks of the Sierra Nevada range far to the east.

On board the planes are sleepy young soldiers, members of the dwindling force of American troops in Vietnam, coming home from a war in a strange land where they had served with gradations of comprehension and devotion.

They step out on the chilled Tarmac and stretch and shiver. The temperature is more than 30 degrees cooler here in northern California than it had been the day before in Vietnam.

It is the first shock of reentry for the Vietnam veteran. In the coming months, as the veterans fan out into America and try to pick up the threads of the life they had left behind, there will be more.

For it is now becoming clear, at a time when it is almost too late to do anything about it that a significant number of Vietnam veterans are encountering serious readjustment problems on return to civilian life that, for some at least, is as severe a test of emotional stability as any stress they encountered in the service.

The ailment has been called the post-Vietnam syndrome, or PVS, but the term is not sufficiently broad to encompass the wide range of emotional problems that some of the veterans are experiencing.

Hard to Define

Just what Vietnam service does to a young man emotionally—the post-Vietnam syndrome—is difficult to define, but it is clearly the effect of the shattering experience of war itself, with the added ingredient that this war, unlike others, does not give many of the men who wage it feelings of patriotism, heroism or even purpose.

The men who suffer post-Vietnam syndrome are not dramatically ill. They do not go berserk or totally withdraw. Instead they are bewildered, disillusioned, unable to cope. Their problems usually crop up after they leave the service and previous indications of trouble almost always went unnoticed by the military.

For the last two years, the Government has declared that the special circumstances of combat in Vietnam produced the lowest psychiatric casualty rate in the history of modern American warfare. The Defense Department contended that the rate of mental breakdowns was 12 per 1,000 troops; the corresponding rate for Korea was 37 per 1,000, and in World War II it was 101 per 1,000.

These figures are hotly disputed by private physicians who have made empirical studies of the PVS, and the debate has taken on political overtones that chilled the issue, with the Government digging in to defend its policies against what is perceived in Washington as an attack by critics of the war.

Essentially, the Government has viewed the problem as mild compared with the staggering number of combat-zone breakdowns that occurred among World War II servicemen. The critics have countered that what they describe as the Government's blindness and intransigence, produced by a desire to gain public support for the Nixon Administration's war policy, were contributing to a mental health disaster for the more than three million soldiers, sailors and airmen who had served in Vietnam.

Serious Social Problem

There is evidence that the problem is more pervasive than has been acknowledged by the Government, and may indeed be building to a social problem of serious magnitude.

Yet it is equally apparent from an extensive survey that the problem is slow to develop and difficult to identify and that its complexities defy easy explanations.

One interpretation advanced in some psychiatric quarters is that guilt over participation in a war many see as immoral is disturbing the veteran upon his return home.

Unquestionably, that is a source of dislocation for some of the better educated and more sensitive veterans as typified by the outcries of the Vietnam Veterans Against the War, and to some extent it may be detected in many others who have made no overt antiwar expression and may even support the country's Vietnam policies, the survey showed.

But for the majority of the emotionally distressed veterans it would appear that the restive nature of American society itself is a contributing factor, and the rapidly changing values the veteran finds at home, the hostility of his peers, the guilt of his parents and the disinterest of his community may combine with a poor job market to keep him off balance from the moment he takes off his uniform.

A psychiatrist compared the difficulty of the Vietnam veteran to a boy at an amusement park. "He has spent an exhausting day on the scariest, most dizzying thrill rides with apparent success, but he finds it impossible to step aboard a moving merry-go-round. His equilibrium has been upset, and he can't perform a simple task of balance. When he pukes, the people watching him can't figure out why such a simple exercise is so unsettling."

The survey made clear that in the majority of cases the emotional disorders of men who have served in Vietnam showed up not in the combat zone but, rather, after the return to the United States. This, unlike other wars, has been the chief psychiatric phenomenon of Vietnam for the American soldier.

An Unknown Factor

In some hospitals, more than 80 per cent of the mental patients suffered breakdowns after discharge from the military service. What is not known, when these figures are compared to past experience, is to what extent the greater sophistication about mental illness has contributed to a willingness among veterans to seek professional help than in the past.

Another finding was that the Government has been less than diligent in providing resources to investigate the nature of emotional illness that the veteran brings home from Vietnam and to deliver health care services to him.

Although the rate of full-blown psychosis among Vietnam servicemen has been low, and in line with what would be expected among this age group in the general population (for schizophrenia, about 8.5 per 1,000) the emotional problems in the greater number of cases have been characterized by anxiety, disillusionment, bewilderment, apathy and listlessness—fairly mild disorders that nonetheless can be as disabling in a social setting as schizophrenia.

Only infrequently does the ailment reach a point where the individual becomes a problem to society and is remanded for psychiatric care. Usually, because the Vietnam veteran tends to come from a low socioeconomic or minority group where his tensions and fears cannot find easy access to mental health care, his "odd" behavior or inactivity simply goes unnoticed or is dismissed as inconsequential to the community's safety.

This lack of access, it has been found, has led to the growing usage of drugs by the veteran back in the United States whether he had been addicted in Vietnam or not. The availability of drugs in this country, as it had been in Vietnam, can offer instant escape from tensions and anxiety, whether these fears have been created by the weapons of war or the more subtle hazards of civilian life.

Moreover, it was found that bureaucratic red tape and the lack of a focus of resources have cut psychiatric services to the veteran, should he seek help. The Veterans Administration has only in the last year officially recognized the scope of the problem and moved to adjust its program of care for the emotionally disturbed veteran. Yet a shortage of qualified psychiatric personnel still makes the V.A.'s 165 hospitals largely dependent on the dispensing of tranquilizers as the primary treatment schedule.

Staffs Are Strained

The best and most effective treatment of the PVS, when it is detected, would appear to be sympathetic counseling, which is what the V.A. has attempted to introduce in the last year, but the professional staffs have been strained by the rising number of veterans seeking help, particularly in the urban areas where they are doing more counseling work with drug addicts.

Another drain on manpower is the large number of neurological casualties coming home from Vietnam—men with damaged brains whose lives have been saved by the new technology of surgery and medicine but who have been deprived of the mental resources to care for themselves.

In 1967, only a small number of the V.A.'s 80,000 hospital beds were occupied by Vietnam veterans; by 1972, more than 50,000 psychiatric in-patients from Vietnam had been cared for and a larger number sought help in outpatient clinics, and admissions have grown each year.

Dr. Marc J. Musser, chief medical director of the Veterans Administration, who oversees the nation's largest total health care system, conceded in an interview that the veterans "usually have to get in pretty bad shape before they'll turn to an institution like ours for care."

He said that the V.A. was caught short by the differences in needs between the younger and older veterans, that the changes to provide care for "the new breed" were being implemented in hospitals around the country and that hospital directors had been encouraged to experiment with new programs. He remains unconvinced, however, that the differences have meaning beyond the generational approaches to life, he said, and added that the dire mental health development predicted by critics of the war had failed to materialize.

While V.A. administrators in Washington minimize the extent of the PVS, some experts on regional V.A. staffs, the men and women personally involved with veterans, are convinced that the figures used in Washington are more revealing of political pressures than reality. For the most part, these physicians were reluctant to express their views publicly for two reasons: They feared bureaucratic reprisals for challenging the views of superiors and they felt that the absence of hard research on the problem left them exposed to challenges that their conclusions could not be supported by documentation, which they concede.

At the same time, however, they point out that the V.A.'s own evidence is scanty and rests solely on research done with veterans whom it has made contact with and little or nothing is understood about the countless troubled veterans who shun V.A. assistance because the agency represents the system the veteran is reacting against at home.

"If you're all messed up inside," remarked one V.A. psychiatrist, "it's pretty hard to seek help in a Government hospital where the first thing you see is the picture of Richard Nixon on the wall, the guy who sent you to Vietnam in the first place."

More Candid Views

There were others with wide experience in the V.A. system who have become largely independent of it and consequently were more candid about the nature and scope of the problem.

"I'd say that 50 per cent of the men returning from Vietnam need some form of professional help to overcome the problems of adjustment," asserted Dr. Cherry Cedarleaf, a senior staff psychiatrist on a leave of absence from the V.A. Hospital in Minneapolis.

"That's not to say that one out of two veterans is crazy," she explained in an interview, "but that a sizable number of young men are returning to society as unmotivated, listless and apathetic individuals who would benefit from counseling."

Dr. George F. Solomon, an associate professor at Stanford University who has been attached for 10 years to the psychiatric research wing of the V.A. Hospital in Palo Alto, Calif., insisted that the Vietnam psychiatric casualty rate defended by the Government was "utterly misleading." He referred to the statistic that only 12 soldiers out of 1,000 broke down under stress in Vietnam.

"I've worked with lots of veterans outside the hospital and you see a lot of things that never come to the attention of the V.A.," Dr. Solomon said in an interview.

"I think the V.A. within the limitations of its bureaucracy and budgeting and the fact that it was designed for another era is trying," he went on. "But I don't think this problem should be perceived as just another problem for the V.A.—it should be a problem for society at large."

He said that the military services had failed to follow through on cases of emotional illness that become manifest in Vietnam. In most cases, he said, soldiers who break down there are returned to duty after a period of rest and the individual is regarded as normal unless the problem resurfaces or becomes exaggerated.

Moreover, he noted, soldiers displaying emotional symptoms are often given expeditious administrative discharges, branded as disciplinary problems instead of psychiatric. Military drug abuses are considered medical cases, he said, when they should be evaluated in relation to the stresses in Vietnam that led them to seek solace in drugs.

"I have strong feelings that drug-taking behavior prevented psychiatric casualties that otherwise would have been manifested in more traditional ways," Dr. Solomon said. "Heroin is a powerful tranquilizer."

Signaling for Help

No one knows how many of the veterans who experience re-entry problems had first signaled for help while still, in the military. The Defense Department has not published studies on the subject and, as far as could be determined, has not commissioned any.

There is no follow-up. If a soldier breaks down for one reason or another, he is considered cured if he starts acting rational after a reasonable period of rest.

An understanding of the mood of the returning Vietnam veteran is dependent on some knowledge of his Vietnam experience and the multiple pressures and frustrations he encounters on his return home. This is set forth here, based on scores of interviews across the country with veterans, physicians and Government officials. The italicized segments were based on conversations with Vietnam veterans who are psychiatric patients in V.A. hospitals or who have had serious adjustment problems.

Norman

"Why are they afraid of us? Family, friends and strangers? Why do they ask us questions about how many people we killed? I killed a few, but I don't want to talk about it. It was self-preservation. Why can't they understand that and let us alone?"

The one-year tour of duty in Vietnam has been cited as the chief asset in keeping psychiatric casualties low. From the day he entered the country, the American soldier knew the exact date of his departure, and all his efforts were directed toward surviving the next 365 days.

This knowledge was especially comforting if the individual, as was true in a great number of cases, did not support the cause he was asked to risk his life for, or if he felt the military was restrained from exercising its full might against an ambiguous enemy, further jeopardizing his personal safety. The result is that the soldier had no investment in the war and its outcome other than his own survival.

There were other advantages that militated against emotional trouble. The United States enjoyed superior fire power and controlled the skies over Vietnam. There were no enemy air or artillery bombardments, except at temporarily besieged outposts; that placed prolonged stress on the "grunt" in the field. There was also the awareness that, if wounded, the soldier could be evacuated within minutes by helicopter, and that fewer than 3 per cent of those who arrived alive at the base hospital later died. These were powerful therapeutic factors contributing to the mental health of the men in the field.

Still, there were breakdowns in the field, and in all of the years of fighting in Vietnam there were more emotional problems that came to the attention of the medical units than the combined total of those who had been killed or wounded by the tangible acts of war.

Cary

On his way into the field for the first time in Vietnam, Cary witnessed another marine cradling a dead buddy and sobbing beyond comfort. "I promised myself I'd never let that happen to me. I'd play the loner and not get attached to anyone who is going to get killed. It was like I lost all respect for love. So I built a wall around me." The wall crumbled one summer day below the DMZ. "Alpha and Bravo companies were wiped out and we were sent in to pick up the bodies. After three days in the hot sun the bodies stunk. I picked up one and the arms came off in my hands. All the time we were under fire. I couldn't help myself. I just went to pieces."

The history of military psychiatry dates back to World War I when "shell shock" was considered to be the physical impact of a artillery round's concussion on the brain, resulting in eccentric or hysterical behavior. By World War II, "battle fatigue" was interpreted by Freudian psychiatrists as a manifestation of deep, inner personality conflicts, and casualties were moved from the front lines to the safety of hospitals and the rear, and yet the illness persisted and even deepened.

The cumulative lessons of the two World Wars and Korea were refined into a plan of treatment and put into practice in Vietnam. Essentially, the thesis was that mental breakdowns in the field were due as much to physical exhaustion as to any other cause.

The patient was confined to bed rest as near his unit as possible, and impressed always with the fact that he was going back to duty as soon as possible. He was never evacuated to the rear, where his guilt over deserting his outfit might reinforce his fixation, unless he was a psychotic and helpless.

This treatment of "nervous exhaustion" produced impressive statistical results and perhaps prevented more serious psychic damage. Yet the long range effect on the soldier who returned home fully aware of his moment of mental collapse is not known. Ronald Glasser, a former Army medical officer who wrote the book "365 Days," which recorded the experiences of physicians in Vietnam, raised that point.

'Nervous Exhaustion'

"[The new treatment] works," he wrote. "The men are not lost to the fight and the terrifying stupidity of war is not allowed to go on crippling forever.

"At least, that's the official belief. But there is no medical or psychiatric follow-up on the boys after they've returned to duty. No one knows if they are the ones who die in the very next firefight, who miss the [boobytrap] wire stretched out across the tract, or gun down unarmed civilians. Apparently the Army doesn't seem to want to find out."

Military psychiatrists identified three major periods of stress for a G.I. in Vietnam. When he first arrives and is overcome by culture shock and his illusions about the war are shattered, when he goes off on his rest and recreation leave and the last month of duty when he has to sweat out the final days of survival so he can go home alive.

"Everybody has the date he's going home circled on his calendar and the emotion is very extreme because he's getting out and leaving his buddies in the unit," observed Eleanor Kyle, a chief social worker in the V.A.'s medical and surgical program in Washington.

"There's some guilt about leaving them, but the desire to survive is greater. What effect these strong emotions have on a person's mental health is something we don't know. Some of the guys can't handle it, but many do quite well."

Richard

"When I was on short-time calendar was when I got all messed up in my head. I had 10 days left in my tour and they ordered me to go on bunker duty with a bunch of [*new guys*]. *I said I wasn't pulling no bunker duty with new guys, they'll get me killed, but they put us out there anyway. Imagine, me with 10 days to go. I was scared. I wouldn't let any of them stand guard duty alone. They would've fallen asleep and gotten all of us shot. I sat on top of that bunker for 10 straight nights, sweating out every minute. I started smoking for the first time in my life and I still haven't broken the habit, and that was two years ago."*

The ones who make it home are flown to California with the mud and dust still on their shoes. They are in a hurry to get home and they get their wish, reaching the living rooms of America in less than two days from the war zone. They are processed to civilian status in four to six hours by an assembly line of doctors and clerks set up in an old post office building that looks like a cargo shed.

The new veterans are the lucky ones—the survivors—coming home sound in body from a struggle that has killed more than 38,000 of their number and wounded 303,000 more. But the war's casualty list does not end at the gate to the Oakland Army Terminal, where most of the processing takes place.

There are no bands there. No welcoming committees of grateful citizens. There is a black ghetto, the smell of industrial wastes, and usually a long line of traffic backed up to the ramps of the Bay Bridge to San Francisco. For the young men who pass this way, the cab ride from Building 640 to the airport is the slowest thing that has happened to them since leaving the jungles of Vietnam barely 24 hours earlier.

'The Good Old Days'

"One advantage of the good old days of World War II," remarked Dr. Jonathan Borus, of Walter Reed Army Hospital, who believes he is the only Army psychiatrist to have done extensive research on the problems of the returning Vietnam veteran, "was the troop ship that took three weeks to a month to come home. A man had more time to go through the transition of change, and he could have some of his fantasies about home knocked down by the other guys.

"And in the States he spent a few weeks in a processing center, which broke him gradually into civilization before he got home. Now events move too rapidly. My God, the Marines even bring them home in jungle fatigues."

Paul

"I'd write home and tell my parents I had been in a firefight, and when I got home I found out they actually thought I spent the year in Vietnam fighting forest fires. We'd sit around those first few days watching the war news on television and my dad would say Did you do that? And I'd say. Yeah, I did that, I had to do that to go on living. And my folks got scared, man. They thought their little boy was a killer."

A lot of the veterans were having trouble at home before they entered the Army, and any expectation that things had magically changed was dissipated a few days after their discharge.

Dr. Carl R. Stuen of the psychiatric staff at the V.A. hospital in Tacoma, Wash., studied a group of disturbed patients who had served in Vietnam and learned that more than 80 per cent had enlisted in the service and had not been drafted. Correlating this with other background data, Dr. Stuen speculated that enlistment had been an attempt to escape problems at home or with society, or was viewed as a way to "find a place to belong—to create an identity."

In another V.A. study compiled by Dr. Gayle K. Lumry and Dr. Gordon A. Braatz of the psychiatric staff at the V.A. hospital in Minneapolis, which contrasted the Vietnam veteran against his World War II counterpart, it was found that the incidence of schizophrenia was lower among the former group (Vietnam). But the proportion of personality disorders had climbed from 35 per cent (World War II) to 54 per cent (Vietnam).

In large measure because of the battlefield treatment of such cases, the incidence of a classical combat neurosis like hysterical paralysis has nearly disappeared in Vietnam, Dr. Lumry said in an interview. However, there has been a corresponding rise in suicidal acts, which she suspects is related to dramatic social changes in the society and not to the combat experience.

And because the nature of the draft from 1964 to 1969 tended to draw men from the minorities and lower economic ranges of whites, she noted, this crop of veterans is more ill-prepared than perhaps any other in the ability to gather forces, shape plans and cope with the complex society and rapid transition.

Dr. Lumry agreed that her findings, like the Stuen report in Tacoma, were based on research done with patients who for one reason or another had sought help from the Government, and no data exist on the faceless veterans who have remained silent and unidentified.

Still, the Tacoma and Minneapolis studies have formed the core of the V.A.'s response to the problem and the conclusion that the Vietnam veteran has not been greatly disturbed by his combat experience and that those who have suffered mental breakdowns or severe depressions had either a predisposition to mental illness or had encountered problems at home that could not be worked out in a satisfactory manner.

Sonny

Sonny said he had wanted to enlist in the Marine Corps at 17 to make his father proud. "I wanted to turn Vietnam into a greasespot and I dreamt about coming home a hero to ticker-tape parades. Maybe if I came back with only a single row of ribbons I'd be proud, like I had done something for my country." His Vietnam tour ended unheroically. A corporal in his outfit struck him and he lost the sight in one eye. He tried to resume high school after his medical discharge but "could not stand the looks of my classmates when they found out I had been in Vietnam." He could not find work. One night at a party he took mescaline for the first time. "The bathroom turned into fields of Vietnamese I had killed and all I could see was blood all over the walls and the floor, and the bodies of gooks grinning at me." A few nights later he swallowed 48 sleeping tablets. "I couldn't commit suicide in a violent way. It had to be in a soft, gentle way. I had my stomach full of violence." Friends found him and rushed him to a hospital.

The PVS proponents have charged that the Government's refusal to accept Vietnam as a trauma that has had a profound and lasting psychological impact on a considerable number of veterans has resulted in a policy of official neglect to the young men it had asked to serve the country.

Dr. Robert Lifton of Yale, Dr. Gerald Caplin of Harvard, Dr. Chaim Shatin of New York and Dr. Peter Bourne of Atlanta, among others, have detected disturbing elements among nonpsychotic veterans that they feel are quite unlike the disorders that developed after other wars. Significantly, these physicians have worked primarily with veterans who have been reluctant to seek help in the V.A.'s wards and clinics. Their conclusion, while they do not consistently share one another's views, points to a malaise that is directly traceable to the Vietnam experience.

Dr. Lifton referred to "psychic numbing," the inability to love, and Dr. Shatin mentions the "grief of soldiers," the compounded shame and guilt over surviving a war where so many others had perished. And there is the question of the morality of the war itself.

Michael

Michael is embittered by those veterans who express guilt over the war. He thinks they are copping out, placing the blame on Vietnam when the problem really exists deep within themselves. He sees his own troubles that way, and yet in long conversations his thoughts always seem to return to Vietnam and the agony and sweat of the war here. "I was in Vietnam three days.—I was 18 years old.—And we found this G.I. hung up by the river and he was shot in the knees and the shoulders and the VC had cut out his groin. They were like animals." He was wounded on one patrol and left for dead until his cries summoned back his unit. "But the worst for me was a chopper lift into the Horseshoe south of Danang. We were trying to land and rounds were coming through the floor. The chopper was cut up so badly we had to return to the landing zone and board another and head back into the whole goddam mess again. A friend of mine—Whitey, we called him—got killed before the chopper even landed. He got hit in the head and I held him in my arms and I swear to God I didn't even know where I was."

The tour changed his attitude about the war, which he now calls "such a stupid, wasteful thing." Back in this country he began having blackouts and unexplained attacks of anxiety. He lashed out blindly at friends. "I got to hate what I was, a sort of semimercenary. I wouldn't even wear the uniform if I could help it. It was like everyone thought you were a killer or something worse." He works now as a lineman for New York Bell Telephone Company and believes he has his problem under control with the help of 100 milligrams of Librium a day. "Just enough to knock the edge off my nerves, just like a good shot of whisky." But the Librium has not stopped the recurring nightmare that is always the same. He is wounded and covered with blood and the mud of Vietnam, and he sees the VC moving silently through the eel grass toward him. He screams for his buddies to come back and help him, but they are all dead. Overhead, in a circling helicopter, is Whitey, but he, too, is dead.

The veterans keep returning and slip back into America with no bands playing and almost without notice. They land in California, heavy with sleep, and are processed for discharge in Oakland.

"We can separate 225 bodies a day here, 24 hours a day, seven days a week—it's efficient as hell," says Capt. Barbara Parker, the base information officer. "The paper work is routed into data processing machines in one direction and the bodies go off in another direction and the two meet up at the end, all packed up and ready to go home."

The men are issued final paychecks and leave on a journey to retrace the steps that carried them one year earlier to an uncertain war. On their way off the base, they pass Warehouse 4, the mortuary, where other military travelers from Southeast Asia are also processed, awaiting final shipment home in crated wooden coffins.

When the processing is complete, the men are gathered in a briefing room where 10 color combat photographs taken in Vietnam hang on the pale green walls, and a chief warrant officer named Edward Terwilleger cautions them about excessive taxi rates to the local commercial airports.

Then Warrant Officer Terwilleger stiffens and says: "Gentlemen, on behalf of the President and the Chief of Staff, thank you very much for your service. Dismissed."

* * *

August 27, 1972

AN ACCOUNT OF THE COLLISION OF TWO SOCIETIES

By STANLEY HOFFMANN

FIRE IN THE LAKE: The Vietnamese and the Americans in Vietnam.
By Frances FitzGerald
491 pp. Boston: Atlantic-Little, Brown. $12.50.

Fire in the lake is the image for revolution in the Chinese Book of Changes, the I Ching, and it's the title of this extraordinary book by Frances FitzGerald. Miss FitzGerald, a young American freelance writer who has spent much time in Vietnam during the past six years, has written partly a history of South Vietnam, partly a study of American policy there, and partly an account of what this policy has done to a people we have destroyed in order to save from Communism. "Fire in the Lake" is all these and much more: a compassionate and penetrating account of the collision of two societies that remain untranslatable to one another, an analysis of all those features of South Vietnamese culture that doomed the American effort from the start, and an incisive explanation of the reasons why that effort could only disrupt and break down South Vietnam's society—and pave the way for the revolution that the author sees as the only salvation.

It had been a stable society based on ritual, ancestor worship and a profound sense of unanimity. Its fundamental units were the family and the village, tied to the land. Miss FitzGerald shows in a brief historical survey how French colonialism began to disturb the old order, yet affected differently the three regions into which the French had divided Vietnam: Tonkin, Annam and Cochin China. She shows how the National Liberation Front broke through the peasants' passivity with a systematic encouragement of hatred, directing the villagers' long repressed resentments against their landlords toward the bureaucrats appointed by the Diem regime. The N.L.F. was able to exploit traditional habits of discipline and cohesion, while training its members to rely not on their traditional elders but on each other. The Front thus offered both a traditional uniformity and loyalty to the state, and a modern revolution of individual self assertion. As in China, Miss FitzGerald argues, the Confucian heritage prepared the Vietnamese peasants for a Marxist-Leninist movement.

By contrast, the Diem regime turned out to represent a mixture of reaction and anarchy, of authoritarian oppression and administrative impotence: an "attenuated French colonial regime," reminiscent of the World War II Vichy Administration, that the Americans mistook for a real government. When the Buddhist revolt of 1963 opened their eyes, the United States threw its support to the South Vietnamese Army—and has not withdrawn it yet.

Perhaps the most horrifying part of Miss FitzGerald's analysis is her account of American pacification policy. Instead of working toward the development of South Vietnam, as many American social scientists have deceived themselves into believing, pacification has principally meant the pouring of huge sums into the sponge of a faction-ridden army and government bureaucracy. Miss FitzGerald documents how this sudden wealth has exaggerated traditional class differences, making South Vietnamese officials even less attentive to the peasants than ever. Elections, to a people who see in them only a way of ratifying a pre-existing choice or settlement, have in American democratic terms been meaningless—a farce and charade played out to satisfy an American myth. As Miss FitzGerald shows, the South Vietnamese Government became an American service, which in turn used the Americans to protect itself from its own people.

As a result of inflation, search-and-destroy operations and massive bombing, the traditional trilogy of state, village and family has been shattered. The country has become a nation of refugees in shanty-towns. Miss FitzGerald demonstrates how the mass production of uprooted peasants has extended to the whole population the disorganization that French colonialism brought to a small élite. The most brilliant part of her analysis goes far deeper than the rhetoric of bad puppets and blind programs to reveal a new type of colonial relationship. For this she makes good use of the scholarship of the great French sociologist of Buddhism and of Vietnam, the late Paul Mus, and she also takes advantage of the profound psychological insights of two important students of colonialism, Frantz Fanon and, above all, O. Mannoni.

She describes the deep ambivalence of the South Vietnamese. On the one hand they have regarded their American protectors as omnipotent, treating them with the same reverence as they once did the French. And on the other hand they have resented them, both for their might and for the uncertainty about their permanence; so they ignore their advice. In a society based on rilial piety and the suppression of anger, ambivalence and rage have turned either into passivity (hence the indifference of most of the South Vietnamese toward their Government as well as toward the National Liberation Front) or into self-destruction—symbolic (as, often, in the behavior of the Government) or real (as in the case of the last Buddhist revolt in 1966 and in individual acts of immolation).

As for the Americans, they have been condemned to argue that things have been better than they seemed—hence the mania for measurements, and "the only uncertainty was what was being measured." Or else, out of frustration, they succumbed to the itch to take over. American resentment at a society that showed no "gratitude" and to which they could not relate took at best (if that is the word), the revealing form of insults against the "Gooks" or metaphors comparing the adversary to termites or to Indians, or at worst the brutal form of indiscriminate bombings and killings. Miss FitzGerald briefly and clearly shows how high-level policy prepared the ground for such atrocities as Mylai.

This terrifying American "self-deception through self-interest" has not ended with Vietnamization. The Thieu regime, as the author demonstrates, is utterly dependent on American support, and consists of one-half of the population, armed by us, dominating the other. The root of the problem is the Saigon regime, so that military successes do not change the picture; they merely prolong the agony. The awful paradox is that American arms and their social effect—the displacement of the villagers—have indeed weakened the N.L.F. and made much of its appeal to the peasants irrelevant, but nothing has taken its place. However, the destruction of all the traditional connections and of all the old particularisms, the very scale of the disorder, corruption and anomie, the alienation of the people in the camps and slums mean "that the moment has arrived for the narrow flame of revolution to cleanse the lake of Vietnamese society." We can postpone this moment, but only by polluting the lake even more, and making the flame fiercer at the end.

Miss FitzGerald's analysis, written before the recent North Vietnamese offensive, should help us understand why even apparent battlefield successes of "our side" provide, in the long run, no way of saving the unsavable. It should also, by its very depth and by its admirable style—cool empathy, restrained indignation, quiet irony, devastating vignettes—help us realize the monumental scope of what went wrong and what we did wrong. Ours has not been a colonialism of acquisition and exploitation but an imperialism of overbearing and destructive benevolence. This has truly been an immoral war. The ethics of political action is an ethics of consequences. To see America in the mirror of present-day South Vietnamese society is such a shock that many of our officials and, alas, social scientists, continue to refuse to look. What is more evil—the use of disproportionate and corrupting means on behalf of an unreachable and utterly unrealistic, if idealistic, goal, as under President Johnson, or the persistent and increased use of such means on behalf of the realistic, but relatively minor goal of extrication without further disgrace, as under President Nixon? To any reader of this fine book the idea that we have some face left to save will seem a very sad joke, and one conclusion imposes itself. Our last duty now is not simply to get out leaving behind a monstrous machine still greased and geared by us, but to create the conditions for the independent, national Government of South Vietnam that could begin the cleansing of the lake.

Stanley Hoffmann, professor of government at Harvard, is the author of "Gulliver's Troubles."

* * *

October 11, 1972

M'GOVERN DETAILS PLAN TO END WAR ON INAUGURATION

Would Stop the Bombing and Halt All American Support of Regime in Saigon

RENEWS NIXON ATTACK

Would Dispatch Shriver to Hanoi to Arrange for the Return of P.O.W.'s

By CHRISTOPHER LYDON
Special to The New York Times

CHICAGO, Oct. 10—Senator George McGovern detailed tonight his plans for withdrawal from Vietnam, including a visit to Hanoi by his Vice President to speed the return of American prisoners.

Drawing the choice between himself and President Nixon as "four more years of war or four years of peace," Mr. McGovern built on two-year-old campaign pledges and told a national television audience that if elected President he would take the following steps:

Halt the bombing of North Vietnam and end all military and political support of South Vietnam's military Government next Jan. 20, Inauguration Day.

Soon afterward send Sargent Shriver, his Vice President, to Hanoi "to speed the arrangements" for the return of American prisoners.

Allow the Vietnamese to work out their own settlement, and cooperate to see that any settlement, including a coalition government, gains international recognition.

At the conclusion of the war, request Congress to adopt "an expanded program for our veterans."

Give jailed and exiled draft evaders "the opportunity to come home." He did not use the word "amnesty."

Order the closing of American bases in Thailand, but only "after all our prisoners have been returned."

Quiet Persuasion

The heart of Senator McGovern's plan was not in the few fresh particulars but was in his reaffirmation that quiet persuasion in place of the current bombing would free the prisoners within 90 days. The same three months, he said, would permit the removal of troops and "all salvageable American military equipment."

Mr. McGovern's speech, recorded last Sunday in Washington, was aimed at a prime-time audience that included more than 20 million viewers on the Columbia Broadcasting System and a number of other stations across the nation.

The setting of Mr. McGovern's speech was the office of the Senate majority leader, Mike Mansfield, in the Capitol.

Hammers at Nixon

Beyond his own peace plans, long sections of the McGovern speech hammered at President Nixon and one of the central difficulties of the troubled McGovern campaign: That many voters—a majority in some polls—credit Mr. Nixon with massive troop withdrawals from Vietnam and pick the President, not the Democratic nominee, as "the real peace candidate."

Thus, one of Mr. McGovern's principal efforts tonight was to re-identify Mr. Nixon with the war—as a supporter of involvement and escalation before he took office, and as the commander, in recent weeks, of "the heaviest aerial bombardment the world has ever known."

Vietnam, he said, constitutes "the sharpest and most important difference between Mr. Nixon and me in the 1972 Presidential campaign."

"In the last four years," he said of the Nixon record, "550 more Americans have been taken captive or listed as missing in action—more than 100 of them in the last six months."

The war has cost 20,000 American lives and $60-billion in the same period, he said, and it continues to fuel domestic inflation.

"The bombing of Indochina has doubled under the present Administration," the Presidential nominee said, and President Nixon remains committed to the South Vietnamese Government of President Nguyen Van Thieu—an even less defensible regime, in Mr. McGovern's view, than it was when Mr. Nixon inherited the war from President Johnson.

Noting the abolition of local elections in South Vietnam, the closing of newspapers and "the execution of 40,000 people without trial," Mr. McGovern charged: "This corrupt dictatorship that our precious young men and our tax dollars are supporting cannot be talked clean by official lies."

"Mr. Nixon would continue this war to preserve General Thieu's power," he said, reiterating lines from his campaign speeches. "On that he and I disagree. I say General Thieu is not worth one more American dollar, one more American prisoner, one more drop of American blood."

Dismissing old promises of "decisive military action" and the accelerating new reports of a negotiated peace, he said: "I fear continued war is what the Nixon Administration has in store if, they stay in power."

In discussing the "coming home" of draft evaders, he said: "Personally, if I were in their position, I would volunteer for two years of public service on subsistence pay, simply to demonstrate that my objection was not to serving the nation, but to participating in a war I thought was morally wrong."

In the same spirit of "reconciliation," he said he would "oppose any so-called war crimes trials to fix the blame for the past on any citizen or any group of citizens."

Mr. McGovern's televised speech text was issued in Washington and at planeside as he campaigned here this afternoon.

Complementing his return to basic campaign topics, the Senator began today also as a return to his original constituency—the antiwar young.

In what constituted a preview of the theme in his Vietnam address, he told 15,000 people, mostly students, in the field house of the Western Michigan University that it was a "tragic deception" to contend that the war had been waged to salvage democracy in Southeast Asia.

Mr. McGovern said recently in an interview that he would spend more time on campuses revitalizing the youth movement that fueled his candidacy in the primaries. His appearance at Western Michigan today was only the second campus visit since he was nominated. His schedule calls for more university stops across the country this week.

In Chicago tonight, Senator McGovern drew more than 10,000 people at $15 apiece to a "grass-roots" fund-raising affair in eight dining rooms of the Conrad Hilton Hotel and another nearby.

* * *

October 27, 1972

KISSINGER ASSERTS THAT 'PEACE IS AT HAND'

NEW TALK NEEDED

U.S. Breaks Silence on Efforts and Urges Further Session

By BERNARD GWERTZMAN
Special to The New York Times

WASHINGTON, Oct. 26—Henry A. Kissinger said today that "peace is at hand" in Indochina and that a final agreement on a cease-fire and political arrangement could be reached in one more negotiating session with the North Vietnamese "lasting not more than three or four days."

The remaining details, he said, would not halt the rapid movement toward an end to the war.

"We must remember that, having come this far, we cannot fail and we will not fail over what still remains to be accomplished," he said during an hour-long briefing for newsmen.

Inspection a Factor

These remaining problems include last-minute American desires to strengthen the machinery for international inspection, a wish to make sure that South Vietnam can sign the draft agreement along with Hanoi and Washington, and a number of questions arising from linguistic differences in the English-language and Vietnamese versions.

Some of these, although minor on the surface, could lead to some delay in reaching a final agreement, despite Mr. Kissinger's definite effort to present a hopeful picture.

Breaking the Administration's silence on the intensive secret peace efforts of the past few weeks, Mr. Kissinger confirmed North Vietnam's announcement broadcast by the Hanoi radio this morning that a breakthrough had occurred at the Paris talks on Oct. 8 and that the two sides had reached over-all agreement on a ninepoint plan to end the fighting and establish a new political order in South Vietnam.

Timing Is Disputed

But Mr. Kissinger, who has conducted the negotiations for President Nixon for nearly four years, disputed Hanoi's contention in that broadcast that the United States had consented, as a condition of the agreement, to sign the accord by Oct. 31. He acknowledged, however, that the Administration had made "a major effort" to sign by that date.

Mr. Kissinger, President Nixon's adviser on national security, sought to convey, in the jammed White House news-briefing room, a sense of optimism for the settlement of the war. He tended to minimize the differences that remained with Hanoi and the problems that had arisen last week in his talks in Saigon.

Summary by Kissinger

He seemed eager to assure the American people and the North Vietnamese Government that the Administration was seeking a settlement along the tentative lines already reached. He also seemed intent on keeping relations with Saigon steady in this stormy period.

"We will not be stampeded into an agreement until its provisions are right," he said, aiming his remarks at Hanoi; "we will not be deflected from an agreement when its provisions are right," in an allusion to Saigon's efforts to hold up an agreement.

Crucial to Mr. Kissinger's presentation was his desire to persuade Hanoi not to make a major issue over the failure to achieve an agreement by Oct 31—as seems likely—but to accept Mr. Nixon's offer to hold one more negotiating session in Paris.

He said that Hanoi had been told that Mr. Kissinger would meet with Le Duc Tho, the Hanoi Politburo representative, in Paris or elsewhere—but not in Hanoi—whenever North Vietnam wanted. At present, Mr. Tho is in Hanoi, and Mr. Kissinger refused to guess when such a meeting could take place. But it was clear that he hoped it would occur soon.

Mr. Kissinger, after asserting that Hanoi had given "a very fair account" of the draft agreement in its broadcast, offered his own summary of the accord, as it is shaping up. It was clear from his remarks that he believed, and wanted to convince the newsmen, that the agreement represented a considerable achievement for the United States.

He said that the Oct. 8 proposal by Hanoi for the first time made it possible to negotiate concretely.

"It proposed," he said, "that the United States and Hanoi, in the first instance, concentrate on bringing an end to the military aspects of the war that they agree on some very general principles within which the South Vietnamese parties could then determine the political evolution of South Vietnam, which was exactly the position which we had always taken."

Outlining the apparent concessions made by the North Vietnamese, Mr. Kissinger said that on Oct. 8. "They dropped their demand for a coalition government which would absorb all existing authority. They dropped their demand for a veto over the personalities and the structure of the existing government." The latter was an allusion to Hanoi's allowing Nguyen Van Thieu to remain as South Vietnam's President in the transitional period.

Discussing the role of South Vietnam in the negotiations. Mr. Kissinger stressed that although Saigon did not necessarily have a veto on American actions. Mr. Nixon would not deal with Hanoi without consulting South Vietnam.

Discussing his five days of talks in Saigon last week, Mr. Kissinger said:

"Saigon, as is obvious from the public record, has expressed its views with its customary forcefulness both publicly and privately. We agreed with some of their views. We didn't agree with all of them and we made clear which we accepted and which we could not join."

Mr. Kissinger said the North Vietnamese included agreement for the first time to a formula permitting a simultaneous discussion about Laos and Cambodia.

The principal provisions of the agreement, as summarized by Mr. Kissinger, called for a cease-fire in place in South Vietnam, the withdrawal of American forces within 60 days, and a total prohibition of reinforcement of troops—thus preventing North Vietnam from infiltrating more men into South Vietnam than the 145,000 reported there now.

Existing military equipment—including aircraft—would be replaced on a one-to-one basis by equipment of similar type and characteristics, under international supervision, he said.

He said that all captured military personnel and foreign civilians would be repatriated within the same time period as the withdrawal 60 days—and that North Vietnam said it would account for all prisoners and men the United States has listed as missing in action not only in Vietnam but throughout Indochina.

On a possibly controversial point, Mr. Kissinger said that South Vietnamese civilians—Vietcong agents—held prisoner in South Vietnam would be released through negotiations between Saigon and the Vietcong. This removed a potential problem because it meant that American prisoners would not be held captive until all Vietcong were released.

On the political aspects of the settlement, Mr. Kissinger noted that the Vietcong and Saigon would negotiate on the timing of elections, the nature of elections, and the offices to be set up.

An institution called the National Council of Reconciliation and Concord with representatives from the Vietcong the Saigon administration and neutrals would be set up to help promote the maintenance of the cease-fire and to supervise the elections that would be agreed upon, he said.

Mr. Kissinger stressed that this council was not a coalition government but rather "an administrative structure." The terms of the agreement would be guaranteed by joint commissions of the four sides—the United States. North Vietnam, South Vietnam, and the Vietcong, and an international commission to which disagreements could be referred.

Associated Press

Henry A. Kissinger discussing peace plans yesterday. Speaking of provisions for supervision of elections in Vietnam, he said they were so complex it seemed that only his colleague, Ambassador William H. Sullivan, left, understood them completely.

The portions dealing with supervision were so long and complex that Mr. Kissinger, a former Harvard professor, said they "will no doubt occupy graduate students for many years to come, and which, as far as I can tell, only my colleague Ambassador Sullivan understands completely." William H. Sullivan is a Deputy Assistant Secretary of State for East Asia and Pacific Affairs. He accompanied Mr. Kissinger on his trip to Saigon.

Secretary of State William P. Rogers had already begun consulting nations on belonging to an international commission that will be set up at a conference, presumably in Paris, some 30 days after the agreement is signed. France, Poland, Canada and Japan, are among the nations mentioned for the commission.

The agreement, Mr. Kissinger said, "will usher in a new period of reconciliation" between the United States and North Vietnam. The United States, by the accord, is pledged to help reconstruct the countries of Indochina. One report, earlier this year, said the administration was thinking in terms of $7.5-billion in grants in aid.

"Now, ladies and gentlemen, in the light of where we are," he said, "it is obvious that most of the most difficult problems have been dealt with. If you consider what many of you might have thought possible some months ago compared to where we are, we have to say that both sides have approached this problem with a long-term point of view, with the attitude that we want to have not an armistice but peace."

He asked these questions: "Now, what is it, then, that prevents the completion of the agreement? Why is it that we have asked for one more meeting with the North Vietnamese to work out a final text?" And he answered them by saying the chief reason was that after five years of negotiated stalemate, it was difficult to get a perfect agreement in the short period following Oct. 8.

4 Days of Negotiation

He was in Paris on Oct. 8, together with his deputy, Gen. Alexander M. Haig Jr., and instead of flying back to Washington to discuss the new Hanoi plan, he said they stayed in Paris for four days to negotiate—sometimes for 16 hours a day.

The specific problems that have arisen, he said, consisted of "six or seven very concrete issues that with anything like the goodwill that has already been shown, can easily be settled."

For example, he said, it has become obvious that there will be a temptation by both Saigon and the Vietcong to mount offensives in the first days of a cease-fire to establish political control over a given area.

"We would like to avoid the dangers of the loss of life, perhaps in some areas even of the massacre that may be inherent in this, and we, therefore, want to discuss methods by which the international supervisory body can be put in place at the same time that the cease-fire is promulgated," he said.

Because of the different situations in Laos and Cambodia, he said, the United States wanted to discuss ways of speeding the talks going on in those countries so that cease-fires there would occur at about the same time as in Vietnam.

In addition, certain "linguistic problems" have arisen between the English and Vietnamese texts, he said. This was particularly important insofar as the national council was concerned—to insure that it did not appear as a coalition government a term that is anathema to President Thieu, who refuses to share power with the Communists.

Referring to Hanoi's disappointment with the delay on final agreement, he said:

"But they know or they should know and they certainly must know now that peace is within reach in a matter of weeks or less, dependent on when the meeting takes place, and that once peace is achieved we will move from hostility to normalcy and from normalcy to cooperation with the same seriousness with which we have conducted our previous less fortunate relationships with them."

Mr. Kissinger said that the United States wanted to make it clear that the North Vietnamese allow the South Vietnamese Government to sign the peace document, which Hanoi originally conceived as a Hanoi-Washington signing, to be signed in Hanoi first, and then by foreign ministers in Paris.

He said at first it was not clear whether Saigon wanted to participate in the signing, and "it seems to us not an unreasonable proposal that a country on whose territory a war has been fought and whose population has been uprooted and has suffered so greatly, that it should have the right to sign its own peace treaty."

This is not an insuperable problem, he said, but it will require redrafting of the document, and more time.

Despite these problems, he said that "What stands in the way of an agreement now are issues that are relatively less important than those that have already been settled."

Mr. Thieu, in a speech on Tuesday, sharply attacked the idea of a coalition government. But Mr. Kissinger said that Mr. Thieu was not talking about the current peace plan in that speech. "I think we all recognize the fact that political leaders speak to many audiences at the same time," he said.

Although from his remarks, Mr. Kissinger left the impression that he thought Hanoi had made the major concessions toward an accord, he did not gloat.

He called the arrangement "a compromise settlement in which neither side achieves everything, and in which both parties have the necessity of posturing themselves for their constituency."

Asked about the problems that arose in Saigon, Mr. Kissinger said, "We are confident that we will reach agreement within the time frame that I have described to you." He would not discuss what the United States would do if Mr. Thieu refused to agree to a settlement, but he implied that the United States might sign anyway, since the cease-fire was an objective "strongly" held by Washington.

* * *

October 27, 1972

U.S. THREAT TO SAIGON

Kissinger Statements Are Telling Thieu He Can No Longer Prevent U.S. Pullout

By MAX FRANKEL
Special to The New York Times

WASHINGTON, Oct. 26—At a time of suspicions, fear and resentment on the path to truce in Vietnam, the White House today pronounced a veiled threat to Saigon and an unmistakable commitment to Hanoi that seal the bargain even before it is signed.

"Peace is at hand," Henry A. Kissinger could say—within "weeks or less"—because, as he put it, while Saigon's views deserve a respectful hearing and some arrangements with Hanoi require clarification, "we cannot fail and we will not fail over what still remains to be accomplished."

That extraordinary pledge from a White House rostrum by the President's intimate adviser, chief negotiator and emissary extraordinary amounted to nothing less than an endorsement of the terms of settlement as now publicly defined, without quarrel, by the United States and North Vietnam.

At a time when Hanoi obviously fears that it is being swindled, that pledge served to reiterate the private undertakings that Mr. Nixon and Mr. Kissinger offered in writing earlier this month.

And at a time when Saigon clearly fears that it is being abandoned, the pledge gave notice to President Nguyen Van Thieu that there was nothing he could hope to do to prevent agreement and American withdrawal.

Hanoi's Eye on U.S. Election

The fears in Hanoi obviously relate to the timing of the American Presidential election on Nov. 7. In offering President Nixon a final signing on Oct. 31, the North Vietnamese were offering a climactic week of peace headlines in the closing week of the campaign and were seeking assurances that no objections in Saigon and no second thoughts in Washington would offset that balance of interests.

When Mr. Kissinger, mired in discussions with President Thieu in Saigon last week, asked for the third delay in two weeks—one that would carry beyond Nov. 7—the men in Hanoi gave way to a decade of mistrust and suspected the worst. They published the draft agreement and the record of Washington's delays, hoping either to provoke a Presidential reaffirmation of the accord or to create two weeks of the most embarrassing possible headlines here.

Thus no matter how much the White House protests that the President never gave the election and the headlines a second thought, Hanoi never lost sight of his predicament, or of the lessons of its bargaining with another American Administration four years ago at this time.

And Hanoi succeeded in provoking both a pledge that the agreement stands and a new wave of pressure on President Thieu to acquiesce.

Solace to the South

There was no mistaking Mr. Kissinger's double purpose, once he had been forced into a public accounting. Just one more meeting with the North Vietnamese will resolve all his problems with the accord, he said; those problems "can be easily settled;" he will meet anytime, anywhere; Hanoi deserves sympathy for its "honest misunderstanding" of his delaying tactics; there will be no more.

To the South Vietnamese, he offered mostly solace. They had fought hard and deserve to be consulted on their own peace treaty, he said; they may sign it as they now seem to wish; they have raised some valid point—that pose no obstacles, and other objections with which he disagrees; it was always "clear" that he needed some time for them but "we will make our own decisions as to how long we believe a war should be continued."

In fact, he went on to explain, Hanoi can now make the decision by scheduling one more meeting of a few days.

As Mr. Kissinger identified them, the remaining difficulties seemed secondary indeed. Some dealt with the timing of a cease-fire and the emplacement of supervisors. Some dealt with translation problems. One dealt with the unofficial comments of Premier Pham Van Dong of North Vietnam.

A Delay Useful to Some

Implicitly, Mr. Kissinger acknowledged undue haste on his part in the drafting and acceptance of the proposed agreement. For instance, a subsequent round of "explanation" seems to have been needed to make sure that American prisoners of war would be released well before the Saigon Government agreed to release its political prisoners. At the final session, the Americans will want some further guarantees against last-minute fighting and grabbing of territory before the division of the country into zones of rival administration.

Moreover, President Thieu seems to be using the current delay to prepare his forces for disputed claims of sovereignty, and the Pentagon is using the delay to accelerate arms shipments that will be forbidden under the cease-fire.

There is enough going on now and enough vagueness in the agreement itself to cause endless trouble in the weeks and months to come, including long and difficult political negotiations in South Vietnam disputes over territory and populations and appointments, over the prerogatives of the rival administrations, rival recruitment for military service, rival taxes and fundamental violations of the cease-fire and the rules forbidding military reinforcement.

But all these risks, including the real risk of protracted terror and guerrilla warfare, have now been discontinued here as the impending bargain is adjudged as the fairest possible for the foreseeable future.

Political Contest Still On

The essential concession from Hanoi in this accord, both sides agree, is the agreement to begin with a concrete military standstill and to continue the political contest in South Vietnam under arrangements still to be negotiated.

As Mr. Kissinger emphasized, President Thieu will be free to marshal his forces to wage that contest and will be limited only by "some very general principles" in the basic agreement. For instance, Mr. Kissinger noted, the Saigon Government and the Vietcong are pledged to "do their utmost" to settle internal matters within three months, not that they must do so within three months.

Indeed, the expectation here is that the division of authority, the restoration of government services and the creation of a new political system inside South Vietnam may take many months longer and some questions may not be resolved for years. The situation is far more complex than that of Laos at the time of cease-fire there in 1962. The feelings run much deeper, the stakes are larger and rival forces are not nearly so neatly aligned in contiguous regions. And yet the rival Laotian princes never achieved anything better than de facto partition of their country.

Since South Vietnam cannot be logically partitioned into workable segments, and with a powerful North Vietnam so interested in the outcome of the political struggle, no one here doubts that Mr. Thieu and his supporters face a long period of challenge and uncertainty.

Nixon's Key Concession

The key concession to Hanoi in return was President Nixon's willingness, despite his uncertainty, to let 145,000 North Vietnamese troops remain in South Vietnam in clearly defined and legal enclaves to support a Vietcong political effort that has always appeared more skillful than that of its adversaries.

Without risks on each side, however, no one in Washington ever imagined a plausible settlement that could survive even for a month. Mr. Nixon's satisfaction is that he refused, for four long years, to collaborate in the outright destruction of the Thieu Government or in any other arrangement assuring a Vietcong political triumph.

His critics, including Senator George McGovern, the Democratic candidate, contend that something very similar could have been achieved long ago. It is not an argument that will be settled soon in a country that was rent by the war almost as much as the Vietnam whose division it struggled to preserve.

* * *

October 27, 1972

THE END OF THE TUNNEL

By JAMES RESTON

WASHINGTON, Oct. 26—How did it happen? And what remains to be settled before a cease-fire in Vietnam? These are the questions now being discussed here at the end of the long dark tunnel.

Four factors seem to have broken the stalemate:

- President Nixon's decision of last May 8 to break the Communist offensive by mining Haiphong harbor, and committing his aircraft carriers and B-52's to the battle.
- His compromise offer on that same day to "stop all acts of force throughout Indochina" and withdraw "all American forces from Vietnam within four months," provided all prisoners of war were released and an internationally supervised cease-fire had begun.
- The decision of the Soviet Union and China to tolerate the President's military counteroffensive and, after the successful defense of South Vietnam by Saigon's army and American air power, to urge Hanoi and the South Vietnamese Communists to accept Mr. Nixon's compromise.
- The defeat of Gen. Vo Nguyen Giap's "total victory" faction in the Hanoi Politburo, after the failure of the Communist Easter drive, by the reconstruction faction that feared continuation of the war would not capture South Vietnam but might destroy North Vietnam.

There will, of course, be endless arguments about whether peace could have come years ago, if, as the hawks believe, there had been more bombing or, as the doves insist, more willingness to compromise in the last years of the Johnson Administration or the first years of the Nixon. But so far as this last decisive phase of the long tragedy is concerned, it was undoubtedly the combination of power and compromise that broke the Communist offensive, and, with the restraint of Moscow and Peking, persuaded Hanoi that it had more to lose by continuing the battle than by compromising.

It has been a long time since Washington has heard such a candid and even brilliant explanation of an intricate political problem as Henry Kissinger gave to the press on the peace negotiations.

He was precise and generous to all parties concerned, understanding of Hanoi's eagerness to sign the truce within the next few days, sympathetic to Saigon's desire to be a party to the settlement of a war fought on its own territory, conscious of the terrible dangers of ambiguity in the language of the hurriedly drafted truce agreement, but firm in his insistence on ending the war on terms that would minimize the killing during the transition from war to peace.

"We will not be stampeded into an agreement until its provisions are right," he said in a statement that was obviously intended for Hanoi. "And," he added, aiming at Saigon, "we will not be deflected from an agreement when its provisions are right."

There is reason for saying that Kissinger meant by this that the United States will not give General Thieu in Saigon a veto over the truce agreement, but at the same time won't be hurried into signing an agreement that leaves important details unsettled.

For example, it is not clear in the draft agreement as now written where the North Vietnamese troops will go after they leave Cambodia and Laos—whether into North Vietnam or South Vietnam. This is not unimportant.

Nor is it clear that the international force to supervise the cease-fire will be in place and operating effectively at the moment of the cease-fire, for if it isn't, the temptation to scramble for territory at great loss of life may be unavoidable on both sides.

Also, there is an important ambiguity—maybe it is only a misunderstanding between the Vietnamese and English language translations—on the question of whether the proposed National Council of Reconciliation, which is to help arrange the final political settlement between the North and South, is to be merely an "administrative structure"—as it appears in the English translation—or maybe some kind of new coalition government structure, as it could be interpreted in the Vietnamese language.

Fortunately, at the end of his four-day meeting with the Communists in Paris, which broke the stalemate, Dr. Kissinger had a long philosophic talk with Le Duc Tho in which they agreed to defend the principles of their agreement and not allow technicalities to prevent the movement, not only to a cease-fire but to reconciliation and the reconstruction of Vietnam.

Accordingly, while Hanoi has known since last Sunday night that the United States wanted another meeting to clarify these important details and has not yet answered or agreed to such a meeting, Dr. Kissinger is confident that Hanoi will agree to talk again and that the differences can be settled both with Hanoi and Saigon.

He does not exclude the possibility of a troubled and even angry delay, but is confident that the truce will be signed at least before the end of November, and if this proves to be true, the efforts of Dr. Kissinger in these last few months will make one of the most intriguing chapters in the long and chequered history of American diplomacy.

* * *

November 1, 1972

THIEU CALLS DRAFT ACCORD 'SURRENDER TO COMMUNISTS'

President, in a National Day Address, Denounces the Agreement as 'Only a Cease-Fire to Sell Out Vietnam'

By CRAIG R. WHITNEY
Special to The New York Times

SAIGON, South Vietnam, Wednesday, Nov. 1—President Nguyen Van Thieu today denounced the draft peace agreement that was to have been signed yesterday as "a surrender of the South Vietnamese people to the Communists."

In a speech broadcast over the national radio this morning, Mr. Thieu referred specifically to the agreement and denounced its provisions in the strongest terms he has yet used.

"The draft agreement which would have been signed on Oct. 31 is only a cease-fire to sell out Vietnam," he said in Vietnamese in a speech marking National Day. "In South Vietnam there is not only one Nguyen Van Thieu who is an obstacle to this agreement to surrender, but there are 17.5 million South Vietnamese who are opposed to such an agreement."

The draft agreement has been acknowledged by both the North Vietnamese, who broadcast a summary of it last week, and by Henry A. Kissinger, who negotiated it in Paris at the beginning of last month.

Mr. Thieu's objections to the cease-fire were very similar to those made by his Foreign Minister, Tran Van Lam, in an interview over the weekend with The New York Times.

Mr. Thieu did not reject a cease-fire or negotiated settlement but mentioned several objections his Government has to the United States-North Vietnam draft agreement.

In his speech, Mr. Thieu continued to mix up public demands by the Communists and private agreements they have made with the Americans.

This confusion is taken by American officials here as signaling that Mr. Thieu is speaking to his domestic political audience only and does not pose as serious an obstacle to the realization of an accord as his words suggest. But they are not sure.

President Thieu outlined his objections to the draft agreement. These were, first, that it does not require the withdrawal of the North Vietnamese troops now in South Vietnam. Mr. Thieu, in his speech today, estimated the number of these as 300,000 to 400,000. American military and intelligence sources here estimate the number as less than half that many.

The North Vietnamese, the President said, "are perfidious as they ask the Americans and allies to withdraw their troops but they do not mention the withdrawal of their own troops."

Second, he said, the North Vietnamese "are perfidious because while referring to Indochina they refer to three countries, but in reality there are four—Cambodia, Laos and North as well as South Vietnam." He added, "By saying that, they reserve for themselves the right to be in South Vietnam and keep their troops here."

Third, he said, the North Vietnamese "have grandiose talk about the self-determination of the people of Vietnam while they are imposing a dictatorial three-part regime in the South from the top down to the local level in the South and wipe out our Constitution."

Such grandiose talk, Western observers here note, is not in the draft accord, which provides for a National Council of Reconciliation and Concord with three parts to encourage and preside over further discussions between the opposing sides in the South. But Mr. Thieu went on to say. "The Communists from North Vietnam are interfering in bilateral negotiations between the Government of South Vietnam and the National Liberation Front.'

Duong Van Minh, the retired general who over the last few years has represented one of the principal opposition tendencies in Saigon politics and is particularly associated with the country's Buddhists, issued a statement this morning that expressed apprehension about the nature of the peace statement being worked out and suggested without saying so that someone like himself, not Mr. Thieu, is the man to preside over a just peace.

"We worry because no one knows how the war will end, and whether a peace solution, if there is one, will fulfill or betray the deep and legitimate aspirations of our people," his statement said.

"Assuming that it is possible to agree on a just solution bringing about national conciliation, if those entrusted with the mission of implementing that solution do not sincerely wish to conciliate, then it will fail," his statement said.

Mr. Kissinger said last week that some details in the draft agreement need to be worked out with the North Vietnamese to make it acceptable to Saigon, and the North Vietnamese have stopped short of breaking off negotiations even though they had pressed for the Americans to sign the agreement as it is yesterday.

Mr. Thieu said "the Government of Vietnam and myself ask the North Vietnamese Communists to come to serious negotiations to sign a peace and cease-fire agreement."

* * *

November 14, 1972

GETTING INTO THE QUAGMIRE

By CHRISTOPHER LEHMANN-HAUPT

THE BEST AND THE BRIGHTEST
By David Halberstam
688 pages. Random House. $10.

One can praise David Halberstam's "The Best and the Brightest"—his seventh book and the sequel, in a way, to his earlier book on Vietnam, "The Making of a Quagmire"—for any number of excellent qualities: for its thoroughness and liveliness, for its clarity of detail on such hitherto confusing topics as the events leading up to the Tonkin Gulf Resolution, or for its singular accomplishment of having retold the whole painful story of the Kennedy and Johnson years, which boils down in essence to the story of America in Vietnam, and made it not only bearable to read, but even tragic in the true and exhilarating sense of that much misused word. But such manner of praise, while deserved, is superficial. What seems to me most impressive about "The Best and the Brightest" is Mr. Halberstam's unusual approach to writing contemporary history, and the unusual assets he has forced that approach to yield.

Many readers (who may remember that he first made his reputation, in the early 1960's, as a New York Times correspondent in Saigon) will already have an inkling of what this approach is from having read the author's profiles of McGeorge Bundy and Robert S. McNamara in Harper's magazine, as well as his colorful and not unadmiring sketch of Lyndon B. Johnson in Esquire. These pieces convey his ability to employ the narrative techniques of fiction without doing violence to the facts and anecdotes they contain. (Unlike certain other so-called new journalists who take liberties with the reporter's point of view, Halberstam manages to disembody his voice without provoking vertigo in the reader: this has something to do with the voice's consistency of attitude, as well as the ease with which one can imagine approximately where Halberstam's information comes from, even when he chooses not to tell us.)

But in order to see how effectively his approach works, one must read these profiles of Bundy, McNamara and LBJ—as well as the dozen or so others, of men like Chester Bowles, Walt W. Rostow Averell Harriman, Dean Rusk, William Bundy, and Gen. Maxwell Taylor: all of them the very best and the very brightest, by Halberstam's account—in the full context of his history.

Take the profile of Gen. William C. Westmoreland, for example. It appears just at the point when history is getting particularly sticky—when the complex infighting over whether or not to send United States troops to Vietnam is arousing a painful sense of deja vu in the reader (who has already read about it in several other accounts). Suddenly, onto the stage steps Westmoreland, "the most important new player. The commander." Suddenly, we are winging back in time to view scenes from the life of the man who, as the jokes had it, "could never have been anything but a general." ("Can't you see it?" a friend of his once said. "The doctor arrives with a spanking new naked baby and holds the baby out to the proud parents. 'Mr. and Mrs. Westmoreland, I'd like you to meet your son . . . General Westmoreland.' ")

Snapshots from Westmoreland's life. Westmoreland as Eagle Scout, paying his way to an international jamboree. Westy quoting Kipling's "If" to the cadets at West Point. Westmoreland the correct, the straight, the stickler for the book, "conventional" to the point of being uncomfortable with the unconventional, smart but not quite "brilliant." Westy, the leader of our forces in Vietnam, shouting at an American reporter who has just witnessed a report to the commander of how all but one ARVN trooper in a recent battle had turned tail and run: "Now you see how distorted the press image of this war is. This is a perfect example—a great-act of bravery and not a single mention of it in the *New York Times.*"

The View of History

Obviously this sort of anecdote is entertaining enough to snatch the reader's attention back into Halberstam's story just as his attention was lapsing. Yet it accomplishes much more. It enables Halberstam to make specific many of his theoretical points about American military leadership in Vietnam. It allows him to explore the background of that leadership—the traditions and institutions that shaped it. And most important, it conveys the view of history that underlies Halberstam's account—that it is the complex interaction of people and events that explains the way things are—not ideology or economics or imperialism or even someone's decision to promulgate the cold war from on high.

These same purposes are served by all of Halberstam's profiles, whether they illustrate how China specialist John Paton Davies continued to suffer from America's reaction to the "loss" of China (thus in turn explaining in part why Kennedy and Johnson were afraid to "lose" Vietnam), or the events that formed men like Robert McNamara and all the other "bright," "can do," "pragmatic" "rationalists" of the Kennedy team.

They are pearls, these profiles—pearls embedded in the flesh of Halberstam's narrative, which in turn fills the shell of our present bewilderment over recent history. And more than anything else in the book—more than Halberstam's uncanny eye for the telling detail: more than the persuasive arguments he has mounted against other versions of the period (such as Lyndon Johnson's own "The Vantage Point"); more even than the surgical skill with which he cuts to pieces the logic of American policy in Vietnam—they are what make "The Best and the Brightest" the rich, entertaining, and profound reading experience that it is.

* * *

November 25, 1972

PEACE ACTIVITY SEEN AS THROWING THIEU OFF BALANCE

By CRAIG R. WHITNEY
Special to The New York Times

SAIGON, South Vietnam, Nov. 24—The relationship between President Nguyen Van Thieu's Government and the United States has been fundamentally altered by the progress toward a peace settlement in the last six weeks, and Mr. Thieu does not seem to know quite what to make of it.

The United States Embassy is saying that the allies can accept the concessions being made by the Communists because the Vietnamization policy has succeeded in defeating the enemy on the battle-field and making him sue for peace on favorable terms.

President Thieu does not appear to believe that—though he does believe that another few years of Vietnamization and concurrent heavy American air support would accomplish it—and few diplomats outside the American Embassy believe it.

Mr. Thieu's stalling on acceptance of the terms of the cease-fire negotiated earlier by Henry A. Kissinger and the North Vietnamese stems from the fundamental difference between his appreciation of the situation and that of the Americans, according to the best-informed diplomats.

The American decision to achieve a cease-fire and lay the foundations for a political settlement appears to be irrevocable. The planning for complete troop withdrawal within 60 days of a cease-fire is going ahead, civilian concerns are being awarded secret contracts to carry on aid and support after the military leave, and Mr. Thieu is evidently resigned to having to accept the Americans' terms.

There was speculation earlier this month that Nov. 20 would be the cease-fire date. It was not—but on that day, without describing it so, the United States hastily completed the Vietnamization program by bringing in the last infusion of helicopters, fighter-bombers, transport planes, cannons and tanks.

"Vietnamization" is not even a term that American military officers here use much any more. Most seasoned military advisers have concluded that stalemate is the main achievement of Vietnamization. Many of them describe the outlines of the draft peace agreement as a sellout because they think the war is ending too soon, without the victory they believe would come—although "victory" is the word Americans are using to try to sell the cease-fire to the South Vietnamese.

The American establishment here is telling Mr. Thieu that he has won and that he has nothing to fear from the settlement. He is less than confident. In August he abolished elections at the most basic level, in the villages and hamlets, and decreed that his appointed province chiefs place men they could trust in jobs previously filled by public mandate.

Now, while the Communists talk—perhaps deceptively—of national concord, cease-fire and reconciliation. Mr. Thieu is warning of perfidy, danger and a difficult political struggle ahead. In a two-hour television speech on Oct. 24 after Mr. Kissinger, President Nixon's national security adviser, had come and irrevocably set a new course for the United States in Vietnam. Mr. Thieu said:

"If the Communists first violate a cease-fire by firing a pistol, we will reply with rifles. If they use rifles, we will reply with machine guns. If they use mortars, we will reply with cannons, and if they use cannons we will bomb them—there is no other way."

The compromise offered by the Communists on Oct. 8 leaves Mr. Thieu as head of the non-Communist Government in South Vietnam at the end of the fighting. So the Americans have the difficult task of implementing their new policy—complete disengagement and eventual accommodation—through the man who implemented the old policy—fighting the war.

"There is no other man around," a senior American official said before talk of a cease fire started. He repeated the assertion with equal conviction after Mr. Kissinger's latest visit had left some doubt about whether the United States still stood solidly behind President Thieu.

The President and his Government have been operating on a single basic premise over the last few years: that they are engaged in a life-or-death struggle with the Communists and that the only way to win is to defeat them militarily and frustrate them politically.

Mr. Thieu is the man of the "four no's"—no concession of territory to the Communists, no coalition with them, no "Communist-style neutrality," no legal status for the Communists.

"As a leader of South Vietnam, I must maintain these four no's to avoid being blamed by history and by our compatriots for letting this country fall," he said in Quinhon last August. "When I cease my presidential function and return to my status as a private citizen. I will continue to defend my four no's until death."

Now he is being asked by his American protectors to let the Communists keep the territory they won in their offensive, to let them set up a legal office in Saigon and presumably in all the other principal cities, and to trust them to help police their own cease-fire. Understandably, he has been balking—for a month now—and there has been corresponding lethargy in setting up detailed cease-fire plans.

"The Communists have never had any goodwill for peace," Mr. Thieu said a few weeks ago. "If the United States again stops bombing the North without forcing the Communists to withdraw their troops from Cambodia, Laos and South Vietnam, we will fall again into the old vicious cycle."

On Oct. 24 he said: "While the Communists are begging and exploiting the United States for a cease-fire to protect their military potential in both the North and the South, they still in fact have the intention of having a cease-fire without stopping the guns."

The President's Cabinet shares his fears. One of his ministers said recently: "For us the war is going to continue. You Americans will just withdraw and get your prisoners back, and it will be all over for you. But it's a sellout to us."

The problems of making a cease-fire work after the first 60 days and the American troop, withdrawal will be largely left to the Vietnamese under the terms of the settlement as understood so far. The North Vietnamese now appear to think that Mr. Thieu will make the agreement unworkable so that they would be justified in violating it—in effect, continuing the war under a different guise.

They hope that the Americans will decide that their man for war is not the man they need for peace. That would be a change in the United States-South Vietnamese relationship far more radical than what has happened so far; it does not yet seem likely.

* * *

November 27, 1972

U.S. TO KEEP MANY CIVILIANS IN VIETNAM

By FOX BUTTERFIELD
Special to The New York Times

SAIGON, South Vietnam, Nov. 25—Even as the United States military is packing up for its expected exit from Vietnam, American officials here are secretly planning a major postwar presence of United States civilians in Vietnam, with many of them doing jobs formerly done by the military.

About 10,000 American civilian advisers and technicians, most of them under Defense Department contract, will stay on in South Vietnam after a cease-fire, according to well-informed sources. These civilians will do everything from running the South Vietnamese military's personnel and logistics computers to teaching the Vietnamese Air Force how to fly and maintain newly provided planes and repairing the complex military communications network left behind by the United States Army.

About half of these civilian workers are already in Vietnam, with others beginning to arrive almost daily at Saigon's Tansonnhut Airport under new contracts signed confidentially in the last few weeks.

Senior American officials insist that such a continued American presence following a cease-fire period would violate "neither the letter nor the spirit of the peace settlement," as one diplomat said today. But these officials, both civilian and military, have repeatedly refused to provide any details about American planning for the postwar period.

"It might upset the Paris negotiations," a spokesman for the United States military command explained, "and it's just not in the national interest to have these things known."

A few Americans and some foreign diplomats here have expressed doubts about the wisdom of such a postwar policy.

"It's like 1961 or 1965 all over again," said one Western official who has served several tours of duty in Indochina. "The Americans are full of optimism again, and once more they are proceeding as if the Vietnamese aren't even around. They're just bringing in Americans to do the job."

Companies Were to Go

Until the events of the last month, the number of American civilian contract employes had been declining, falling from a high of more than 10,000 in 1970 to the present 5,000.

Many of the 125 American companies that held Defense Department contracts up through last month were scheduled to be phased out, knowledgeable sources say. Their contracts last month were worth just under $100-million.

Although officials have refused to divulge anything about the new contracts, two companies that are reported to have received them are Lear Siegler, Inc., and NHA, Inc.

Lear Siegler, based in Santa Monica, Calif., is a diversified manufacturer that has had a number of contracts with the Air Force for aircraft and aerospace systems maintenance. NHA, Inc., with headquarters in Dallas, was incorporated in 1968 as Norman Harwell Associates, Inc. Its name was changed to NHA soon after incorporation, and it is now engaged in land development; engineering and planning; technical data services; government contract maintenance and heavy construction.

Lear Siegler is said to have been given at least 300 new jobs servicing the 120 F-105 fighter planes that the United States rushed to South Vietnam earlier this month, and NHA is reported to have been awarded more than 200 other aircraft maintenance jobs for the South Vietnamese Air Force.

Companies Are Silent

Both companies have been advertising in The Saigon Post, an English-language newspaper, for new workers over the last two weeks. But spokesmen for the companies said they were not free to comment on their newly awarded contracts.

"The Defense Department won't let us talk about our work, so I'm not going to tell you anything," said a man who described himself as the manager at Lear Siegler. He would not give his name.

According to some critical United States officials, the contractors are being given cost-plus contracts, which fix the companies' profits as a percentage of the total cost. Thus the higher the cost of a project, the higher a company's profit. Such contracts, the opposite of the usual low-bid contract, tend to lead contractors to bring in excess personnel, since the more workers they have, the higher their profit, these officials say.

Problem of Control Seen

One problem that has apparently not been resolved is who will control these civilian contractors after the United States military command pulls out. Heretofore the United States Army Procurement Agency, under the military command, has been in charge of the contractors.

Embassy officials are known to think that the embassy, as the ranking civilian authority, should now exercise control. But there are indications that the Defense Department will try to keep its own control.

Last week, for example, a civilian dispatched by the Pentagon, Wilfred J. Curley, arrived in Saigon to take over the Army Procurement Agency from its military commander. Mr. Curley will reportedly convert the agency into a putative civilian organization.

The military command turned down all requests for an interview with Mr. Curley, on the ground that he was too busy "working out new contracts."

A.I.D. to Stay on Job

In addition to the civilian contractors, there will also be about 1,000 members of the Agency for International Development, known here as USAID, and perhaps several hundred military attaches left in Vietnam after the peace accord is signed, knowledgeable sources say.

USAID has 997 American employes in South Vietnam today, down from a high of 2,700 four years ago.

The quasi-military agency in charge of the pacification program—known as CORDS for Civil Operations and Rural Development Support—will have to be phased out in its present form, since a majority of its 1,500 members are army personnel But CORDS officials say they will probably preserve province advisory teams minus their army members.

The commissary, with its American food and liquor, will be kept open by turning it over to a civilian contractor, officials say. But the post exchange long the chief supplier of Vietnam's flourishing black market, may have to go.

* * *

December 17, 1972

KISSINGER SAYS TALKS HAVE NOT REACHED 'JUST AND FAIR' AGREEMENT; BLAMES HANOI

HE DEFENDS STAND

Also Says Washington Won't Allow Thieu to Veto a Pact

By BERNARD GWERTZMAN
Special to The New York Times

WASHINGTON, Dec. 16—Henry A. Kissinger said today that the negotiations between the United States and North Vietnam had so far failed to reach what President Nixon regarded as "a just and fair agreement" to end the Vietnam war.

Breaking the Administration's silence on his just-completed talks in Paris with Hanoi's chief negotiator, Le Duc Tho, Mr. Kissinger acknowledged that South Vietnam's objections to an agreement were serious—adding that the United States would not allow South Vietnam to veto an American decision to sign—but insisted that Hanoi must accept the largest share of blame for the failure to reach an accord.

Won't Be 'Blackmailed'

He gave no indication of when talks might be resumed. He said the two sides would remain "in contact through messages," adding: "We can then decide whether, or when, to meet again."

"We will not be blackmailed into an agreement," Mr. Kissinger said in a news conference. "We will not be stampeded into an agreement. And if I may say so, we will not be charmed into an agreement, until its conditions are right."

Mr. Kissinger seemed anxious to justify his statement on Oct. 26 that "peace is at hand," and he defended the American proposals made in the latest round of talks, which apparently brought counterproposals from Hanoi that Mr. Kissinger said had often been "frivolous."

Broke Secrecy Pledge

Mr. Kissinger said that there had been an agreement with Mr. Tho not to discuss the negotiations, but that Mr. Nixon had decided to break it because it was important not to maintain a "charade" in front of the American people.

This was an apparent reference to the mood of expectation that had been created by the Administration's oft-stated optimism of the last seven weeks.

Mr. Kissinger said the negotiations were now at "a curious point." On the one hand, he said, "we have an agreement that is 99 per cent completed," but on the other, he said, solution of the remaining 1 per cent requires a major decision by Hanoi.

Mr. Kissinger, President Nixon's chief adviser on foreign policy, said that the recent negotiations in Paris with Mr. Tho had been marked by frustration. He said that every time an agreement seemed "just within our reach, it pulled just beyond our reach when we tried to grasp it."

For example, he said, last Sunday the two sides seemed so close to an accord that Mr. Nixon summoned Gen. Alexander M. Haig Jr., Mr. Kissinger's deputy, back to Washington to prepare to go to Saigon with the proposed agreement.

Technical teams, which began work on Monday, were supposed to wrap up the agreement, Mr. Kissinger said, but instead, Hanoi brought in 17 new changes in the text. And when one problem was solved, he said, it would reappear later in a new Hanoi proposal somewhere else, either in accompanying protocols or in a list of "understandings" that would accompany the formal text of an agreement.

Mr. Kissinger provided details of some aspects of the negotiations and refrained from giving details on others.

From his discussion, he left the impression that there were two matters of substance that Mr. Nixon considered crucial to an agreement:

The first dealt with the question of an international supervisory team to check on the cease-fire.

Mr. Kissinger said Hanoi refused to discuss details of its activity until the day before he was to return to Washington. He said the United States believed the force should consist of several thousand members—5,000 has been mentioned in private—and should have freedom of movement.

But he said that Hanoi wanted to limit the force—of Canadians, Hungarians, Indonesians and Poles—to 250, of whom nearly half would be limited to headquarters. The North Vietnamese also insisted that the force should have no transport or communications of its own, and should move only with escorts, he said.

"It is our impression that the members of this [supervisory] commission will not exhaust themselves in frenzies of activity if this procedure were adopted," he said.

The second, and potentially more difficult to solve, dealt with an issue that apparently was raised by the United States in the latest round of negotiations—efforts to get the agreement to make clear that Saigon had complete sovereignty over South Vietnam.

Details of this dispute were made known to The New York Times in Paris last week, but Mr. Kissinger refused to discuss them today in more than general terms.

He said the United States wanted to insure that the agreement made it clear that "the two parts of Vietnam would live in peace with each other."

Mr. Kissinger said that this was "a fundamental point" that had been accepted two weeks ago, and then rejected by Hanoi at the talks. "We are not raising a new fundamental point. We are raising the acceptance of something that had already once been accepted," he said.

He did not explain what kind of agreement had been reached two weeks earlier, but other Administration sources said he referred to Hanoi's acceptance of the concept that the agreement would recognize the demilitarized zone between the two Vietnams. This was one of Mr. Thieu's demands. According to the sources, Hanoi apparently withdrew this agreement in the Dec. 4 round of talks. Publicly, Hanoi has consistently rejected this proposal.

"I can't consider it an extremely onerous demand to say that the parties to a peace settlement should live in peace with one another, and we cannot make a settlement which brings peace to North Vietnam and maintain the war in South Vietnam," he said.

Mr. Thieu had also been demanding the total withdrawal of all North Vietnamese forces—said by American sources to number 145,000—from South Vietnam, but the United States has rejected that demand as unreasonable, Mr. Kissinger said.

But he indicated that the United States would continue to support Saigon on the more general problem of getting a pledge from Hanoi not to intervene in South Vietnamese affairs.

He said that the United States would not allow South Vietnam to veto an American decision to sign what Mr. Nixon regarded as a good agreement.

But he said, "Today, this question is moot. We have not yet reached an agreement which the President considers just and fair."

Seems on Defensive

Mr. Kissinger's presentation was often repetitive and he seemed tired and a bit on the defensive. He left room for questions, but he failed to answer in detail queries about why North Vietnam had changed its seemingly conciliatory attitude of October.

Many published reports have charged that the impasse in the Paris negotiations was caused by the American insistence on getting Hanoi to recognize Saigon's sovereignty, in effect, giving up the idea of a united Vietnam under Hanoi's rule. Implicit in such recognition would also be the disavowal of the National Liberation Front, or Vietcong.

This interpretation has held that Mr. Nixon had to make a fundamental decision whether to continue backing Saigon or to go for the accord available with Hanoi now.

In particular, the New York Times reported from Paris in Wednesday's issue that "responsible officials" said the talks were concluding because of an impasse over the sovereignty question.

That report said that the debate over Saigon's sovereignty had gotten nowhere. It added that North Vietnam regarded the question as crucial and that Mr. Tho told Mr. Kissinger that Hanoi would insist on reopening matters already agreed upon if the United States persisted in pressing the Saigon Government's demands.

This report was not denied by the Administration in subsequent days.

As a result of the Times's dispatch, several newsmen—and some officials—had speculated that Mr. Nixon was preparing to disassociate the United States from South Vietnam's demands and to strike the best bargain it could with North Vietnam.

Mr. Kissinger, however, suggested strongly today that Mr. Nixon intended to stick by his support of Mr. Thieu's proposal and he insisted that the cause of the delay in reaching an accord lay not in Saigon but in Hanoi.

At one point, he said that sometimes the Vietnamese, who have fought for so many years, fear the risks of a peace more than they do continuing the fighting.

There is sure to be debate in coming days on whether Mr. Kissinger's analysis, blaming North Vietnam for the impasse in the talks, is justified. He said that Hanoi was sure to issue its own version of events as soon as it learned of his news conference.

Mr. Kissinger said that when the Vietnam negotiations resumed in Paris on Nov. 20, he offered three types of proposals. The first dealt with "linguistic problems," the second dealt with the international machinery for a cease-fire, to insure that the group went into action immediately, and the third with the controversial language dealing with two Vietnams.

Reports Change in Attitude

He said that for the first three days, the negotiations continued in the "spirit and attitude" of the October negotiations that led to the nine-point draft agreement.

"We presented our proposals. Some were accepted and some rejected. We had made substantial progress. All of us felt we were close to an agreement," he said.

"I do not know what decisions were made in Hanoi, but from that point on, negotiations have had the character of where a settlement was always just within our reach, but was always just beyond our reach when we attempted to grasp it," he said.

On Nov. 25, the two sides recessed in Paris, and resumed again on Dec. 4. He said that the American team thought only two or three more days of negotiations were needed to resolve the remaining issues.

But he said that on Dec. 4, Hanoi pulled back on every change agreed to two weeks earlier. Then, he said, the United States spent the rest of the week getting to where the two sides had stood when the talks resumed on Dec. 4.

"By Saturday, Dec. 9, the Americans felt they were again within reach of an agreement, and General Haig returned to Washington," Mr. Kissinger said. But beginning on Monday, Dec. 11, Hanoi seemed anxious to delay an agreement, raising one issue as soon as another one was settled, he said.

He gave no reason for the decision to suspend the talks at that point, but he suggested that Mr. Nixon believed the sessions had been unproductive.

* * *

December 19, 1972

WHITE HOUSE SAYS RAIDING IN THE NORTH WILL GO ON UNTIL THERE IS AN ACCORD

A NEW TARGET LIST

Full-Scale Attacks and Mining Revived After Lull of Two Months

By WILLIAM BEECHER
Special to The New York Times

WASHINGTON, Dec. 18—The Nixon Administration announced a resumption of full-scale bombing and mining of North Vietnam today, and the White House warned that such raids "will continue until such time as a settlement is arrived at."

Administration officials said that President Nixon, in ordering actions against military objectives in the Hanoi and Haiphong areas, had directed the Air Force and Navy to strike targets not bombed before.

[United States officials in Saigon said hundreds of planes, including B-52's, resumed attacks above the 20th Parallel in North Vietnam, carrying out the heaviest raids of the war in the Hanoi-Haiphong region. The Associated Press reported.]

Ronald L. Ziegler the White House press secretary, voiced the threat of continuing attacks north of the 20th Parallel, after a halt of nearly two months, while insisting that their renewal was consistent with the policy enunciated by Mr. Nixon on May 8 in announcing his decision to mine the ports and bomb more extensively.

He said then that the actions would cease when American prisoners were released and an internationally supervised cease-fire was in force.

Threat of New Offensive

Mr. Ziegler also linked the latest action to the threat of another North Vietnamese offensive. "The road to peace is wide open," he said. "We want a rapid settlement to this conflict." But, he added, "we are not going to allow the peace talks to be used as a cover for another offensive."

Some military analysts, puzzled, said they knew of no signs of a major offensive.

According to the Administration officials, the principal purpose of the President's action was to insure that the North Vietnamese leaders would comprehend the extent of his anger over what the officials say he regards as an 11th-hour reneging on peace terms that were believed to be settled.

Senior planners said the latest military moves were part of a concerted political, diplomatic and military campaign designed to force North Vietnam into a more conciliatory position at the bargaining table.

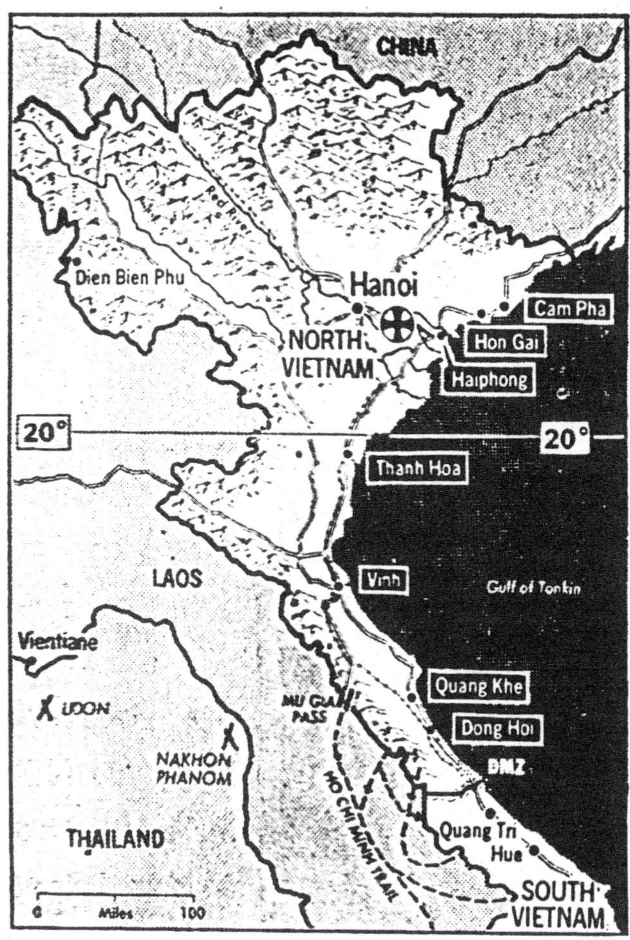

U.S. planes resumed bombing of Hanoi-Haiphong area (cross) and mining of key ports north of 20th Parallel. Sowing of mines south of line had not been halted. (Mined ports are shown with names outlined in white.)

Bids to Soviet and China

The first step came Saturday when Henry A. Kissinger, the President's national security adviser and chief Vietnam negotiator, held a news conference to deflate his optimistic projections of an early truce and to attribute much of the blame to North Vietnam.

Representations are being made with the Soviet Union, China and other nations to get them to use their influence on Hanoi, the officials said.

The broadened air campaign, including the attacks on targets never hit before, is the latest element of this effort, it was said.

The officials explained that the decision on expanded air activity was made tentatively by the President shortly before Mr. Kissinger returned Wednesday from the most recent round of private talks. They had been in frequent communication by cable.

The final decision was made after Mr. Kissinger's return, the sources said, upon discussions throughout the Government.

The decision on the mines, well-placed officials said was forced in part because there had been no mine-laying north of the 20th Parallel since Oct. 23, when air action there was halted.

The mines in such ports as Haiphong were set to deactivate late last week. If new mines had not been laid, and if no cease-fire agreement had been achieved, the officials said, North Vietnam might soon have realized that its principal port, Haiphong was clear for freighter traffic.

Also, intelligence sources said North Vietnamese officials directed an evacuation of women and children from Hanoi on Dec. 4, the day the most recent round of private talks began in Paris. The sources said they presumed that the officials realized in advance that a tougher negotiating stance might result in a renewal of the bombing.

The first official confirmation of the lifiting of the restrictions on air activity came this morning from Secretary of Defense Melvin R. Laird. He had invited photographers to his office to take pictures of him and his designated replacement, Elliot L. Richardson, who had appeared at the Pentagon for one of several transition briefings.

Hanoi Broadcasts Noted

Several reporters pressed Mr. Laird to comment on unconfirmed reports broadcast by Hanoi that bombing and mining north of the 20th Parallel had resumed.

After attempting to avoid the question. Mr. Laird said: "Air operations are being conducted throughout North Vietnam at the present time." He declined to discuss the matter further, saying it might jeopardize pilots lives.

Later Mr. Ziegler expanded somewhat on the subject, saying, "The President will continue to order any action he deems necessary by air or by sea to prevent any build-up he sees in the South."

"Neither side can gain from prolonging the war," he added, "and neither side can gain from prolonging peace talks"

As for the new targets, military officials, citing reasons of pilot safety, declined to specify what might be hit.

Since the suspension of the bombing, the Administration officials said, North Vietnam has repaired its two main rail links to China, restored 40 per cent of its destroyed electric generating capacity and repaired or built bypasses for most main bridges.

Presumably such targets will be hit again, and that, an official remarked, would come as no surprise to North Vietnam.

* * *

December 22, 1972

TERROR FROM THE SKIES

Asked whether civilian centers would not inevitably be hit during the resumed massive air assault on North Vietnam, a Pentagon spokesman replied: "No. We don't strike civilian targets." He then amended his comment to say: "We do not target civilian targets."

The difference is crucial.

The big B-52 bombers that are being used for the first time over the heavily populated Hanoi-Haiphong area are not precision weapons. Normally they operate in flights of three that lay down a pattern of bombs—twenty tons to a plane—which scatter over an area more than half a mile wide and more than a mile and a half long.

Even if the "targets" were strictly military, a great deal more than military would inevitably be caught up in such sweeping devastation, especially in a blitz that in the first two days alone is estimated to have dropped 20,000 tons of explosives—the equivalent of the Hiroshima bomb. Imagine what would happen to New York or any other American city if a comparable enemy force were unleashed to attack such targets on the Pentagon's authorized list as railyards, shipyards, command and control facilities, warehouse and transshipment areas, communications facilities, vehicle-repair facilities, power plants, railway bridges, railroad rolling stock, truck parks, air bases, air-defense radars and gun and missile sights.

It requires no horror stories from Hanoi radio to deduce that the destruction and human suffering must be very extensive indeed. And to what end?

Officials in Washington and Saigon have suggested that the raids are intended to disrupt a Communist offensive. But military men in Saigon say they have seen no indication that the North Vietnamese are preparing for such a strike.

Administration spokesmen have also reported that this brutal assault is intended to convey to North Vietnamese leaders President Nixon's displeasure over Hanoi's intransigence at the Paris peace talks. Only last week, however, a responsible American official in Paris indicated that the impasse centered on President Thieu's insistence, backed by President Nixon, that any agreement specifically recognize Saigon's authority over all of South Vietnam. This amounts to a demand that the Communists acknowledge a defeat they have not suffered on the battlefield.

No matter who is to blame for the breakdown in talks, this massive, indiscriminate use of the United States overwhelming aerial might to try to impose an American solution to Vietnam's political problems is terrorism on an unprecedented scale, a retreat from diplomacy which this nation would be the first and loudest to condemn if it were practiced by any other major power, in the name of conscience and country. Americans must now speak out for sanity in Washington and peace in Indochina.

* * *

December 24, 1972

EUROPE REACTS TO BOMBING WITH INCREASING PROTESTS

By ALVIN SHUSTER

Special to The New York Times

LONDON, Dec. 23—Western Europe is reacting to the American bombing of North Vietnam with growing protests and a mixture of sadness, disgust and anger.

Correspondents in major capitals report that almost all shades of opinion have joined in denouncing the resumption of the heavy American raids. There was talk among some left-wing groups and unions of organizing boycotts of American goods and ships.

Street demonstrations have been held in London, Rome, Copenhagen, Zurich and Amsterdam. In Rome 25,000 people heeded the call of the Italy-Vietnam Committee, a left-wing group, and turned out in a parade and rally last night. About 7,000 joined in a protest in Copenhagen today.

At official levels in the capitals, there were expressions of regret over the continued warfare and of concern that the raids might jeopardize the new relationship developed between the Soviet Union and the United States after President Nixon's visit in May. Other officials in Bonn, London and elsewhere took the view that the bombing would serve further to tarnish the image of the United States.

[At the United Nations, Secretary General Waldheim said he was greatly concerned at the continuing bombing and called for a resumption of the cease-fire negotiations.]

Despite the scattered street demonstrations, the depth of feeling among Europeans toward the bombing is difficult to gauge. The mining of Haiphong and bombing earlier this year failed to stir widespread protests. And some officials believe that, like many Americans, Europeans have grown rather numb to the events in Indochina after all the years of warfare.

The harshest official attack came today from Premier Olof Palme of Sweden, who has been a sharp critic of American policy in Vietnam. In a statement, Mr. Palme said the bombing was an outrage to be listed with Nazi massacres in World War II.

"One should call things by their proper name," he said. "What is happening today in Vietnam is a form of torture. There are no military grounds for the bombing."

The tone of newspaper editorials throughout Western Europe has been the bitterest in some time. The Daily Mirror here, a mass circulation tabloid of the left, called President Nixon a "frustrated, glib and secretive man" whose name will be blackened by the bombing.

"It is an act of insane ferocity," the Mirror said. "A crude exercise in the politics of terror. A blunder of tragic magnitude."

The Times of London said the bombing has "a particular horror because of its massive scale, its indiscriminate character and its apparent employment as an act of negotiation rather than an act of war." The Guardian joined in the protests, asking whether "Mr. Nixon wants to go down in history as one of the most murderous and bloodthirsty of American Presidents."

The President received more understanding from the conservative Daily Telegraph, which said that Mr. Nixon was clearly using power "in a just cause." It said that the kind of agreement backed by Hanoi would "in no way have squared with Mr. Nixon's requirements of a just and fair agreement."

In Paris, however, even the conservative Figaro, normally friendly to the United States, expressed disapproval over the attacks. Roger Massip, the foreign editor, asked some worried questions about the effects of the bombing.

Washington says that its honor would be saved only by a just and equitable peace, Mr. Massip wrote, but "will it not be tarnished by the destruction of a country executed by the cold determination that seems to have taken over among the leaders of the United States?"

France-Soir said that it served no purpose for "a little country, whatever the judgment that one may have about its policy, to be crushed by the greatest world power that wants to be the standard-bearer of our civilization's values."

So far, there has been only one demonstration of several thousand in France. The Government has refrained from any recent statements although it has previously deplored recourse to efforts to achieve a military solution.

In West Germany, there has been an absence of demonstrations, attributed partly to the dispersal of potential demonstrators by the holidays. Officially, the Government expressed its regrets over the continuation of the war.

The criticism in West German newspapers has been relatively muted, although the Munich Abendzeitung called the bombing "the most senseless air raids of all time."

The Norwegian Government renewed its appeal to the United States to stop the bombing and resume peace talks. In Copenhagen, even conservative newspapers denounced the raids along with Danish officials.

"It is objectionable that the United States has resumed the bombings and mining," said Premier Anker Jørgensen in a note to Washington. "It is a situation in which Denmark must express its denunciation."

The Danish dockers union said it would start action against United States ships in Danish ports, and other labor unions there proposed a boycott of American goods. The dockers union in Genoa, Italy, also said it would boycott American vessels until the end of the year as a protest.

* * *

December 31, 1972

NIXON ORDERS A HALT IN BOMBING OF NORTH ABOVE 20TH PARALLEL; PEACE TALKS WILL RESUME JAN. 8

HANOI'S REACTION

U.S. Aides Differ Sharply

ACTION IS SUDDEN

Kissinger Will Renew His Efforts With Tho, White House Says

By BERNARD GWERTZMAN
Special to The New York Times

WASHINGTON, Dec. 30—The White House announced today that President Nixon had ordered a half to the bombing of North Vietnam above the 20th Parallel and that Henry A. Kissinger would resume negotiations for a Vietnam settlement with Le Duc Tho in Paris on Jan. 8.

The announcement of the renewed efforts to seek a negotiated settlement, ending nearly two weeks of heavy bombing of Hanoi and Haiphong, also said that the technical talks of lower-level American and North Vietnamese experts would resume on Tuesday in Paris.

Gerald L. Warren, a deputy White House press secretary, said in answer to a question at a White House briefing for newsmen that "as soon as it was clear that serious negotiations could be resumed at both the technical level and between the principals, the President ordered that all bombing be discontinued above the 20th Parallel."

Cause Is Unclear

It was unclear whether the impetus for the new round of negotiations had come from Hanoi, reeling under B-52 raids, or from Washington, which was possibly looking for an excuse to suspend the latest raids because of increasing foreign and domestic pressure.

News of the renewal of the peace efforts came without much advance warning. The White House telephoned newsmen at home shortly after 9 A.M. and told them that there would be a special briefing at 9:45.

There already had been some news reports from Saigon suggesting that a halt in the bombing had been ordered, but those reports did not make clear whether it was a temporary halt—just for the New Year's holiday, similar to the 36-hour Christmas pause—or a more permanent halt. The announcement today did not specify any length of time for the halt.

After the White House briefing, the Defense Department disclosed that all bombing and all naval shelling of the North Vietnamese heartland, the area north of the 20th Parallel, had actually ceased last night, Washington time.

Mr. Warren refused to discuss how the latest development had come about. Previously, North Vietnam had said that it would not enter into further negotiations until the situation "reverted to that existing on Dec. 18"—the date when Mr. Nixon ordered the raids north of the 20th Parallel. Administration officials had said that the raids would continue until Hanoi agreed to engage in "serious" negotiations.

Panhandle Not Involved

Bombing will presumably continue in the North Vietnamese panhandle region, between the 17th and 20th Parallels.

It was not clear whether resumption of negotiations between Mr. Kissinger, who is Mr. Nixon's chief foreign policy adviser, and Mr. Tho, the Hanoi Politburo member charged with the private negotiations, presaged a successful end to their meetings.

Neither is it clear exactly what differences remain between Hanoi and Washington, and whether either side has altered its position in the last two weeks. When Mr. Kissinger and Mr. Tho broke off their negotiations on Dec. 13, they agreed not to make public the details of their talks.

The talks have had dramatic ups and downs since Oct. 26, when Hanoi disclosed that a nine-point draft agreement had been reached and Mr. Kissinger said that "peace is at hand."

On Oct. 26, Mr. Kissinger said at a news conference that additional talks were needed to wrap up final details of the agreement, which Hanoi had insisted should be signed by Oct. 31. Negotiations resumed in Paris on Nov. 20, recessed on Nov. 25 and began again on Dec. 4.

The negotiations broke down on Dec. 13 with Mr. Kissinger charging three days later that Hanoi, for unspecified reasons, had decided to procrastinate at the bargaining table, refusing to agree to the final details of an accord that he said was 99 per cent complete.

Hanoi denied that it was to blame for the delay and said that the breakdown was due to the American effort to reopen issues that went to the heart of the agreement, such as seeking language that would force Hanoi to recognize implicitly the sovereignty of the Saigon Government over all of South Vietnam.

On Dec. 18, Mr. Nixon ordered bombing raids resumed throughout North Vietnam. Such raids had been authorized last April following North Vietnam's spring offensive against South Vietnam, but on Oct. 22, in appreciation of Hanoi's "goodwill" at the negotiating table, Mr. Nixon suspended raids above the 20th parallel.

The latest raids, however, included round-the-clock flights of B-52's over the Hanoi area, the first time these strategic aircraft, which can carry up to 15 tons of explosives, had been used near populated areas. The Pentagon has announced the loss of 15 B-52's and 12 other aircraft since Dec. 18 and the loss of 93 airmen killed, captured or missing.

These raids led to charges from Hanoi that civilian targets such as homes, schools and a hospital had been destroyed. Considerable concern about the raids was expressed in other countries.

Moreover, several members of Congress, alarmed at the renewed bombing raids, had threatened to force an end of the war by withholding funds after Congress convened on Wednesday. Today's announcement would appear to ease Mr. Nixon's problems with Congress, although the Administration will be under some pressure to explain in detail what has happened in the past few weeks.

Mr. Nixon himself has not said anything about either the status of the negotiations or the bombing raids. His spokesmen have also said little, with the exception of Mr. Kissinger's news conference of Dec. 16.

But it was clear that the bombing seemed to have two primary missions: To convince Hanoi that it was not serving its interests by holding up signing of an agreement along terms suggested by Washington, and to destroy Hanoi's capacity to mount significant military attacks in case the talks proved unsuccessful.

In its statements over the past 12 days, Hanoi has insisted that it would not be coerced by the latest raids into accepting the American terms for an agreement, but it has also stressed continually that it would be willing to resume negotiations as soon as the bombing north of the 20th Parallel ceased.

Mr. Warren, at the White House, began the briefing today by announcing that Mr. Kissinger would resume talks with Mr. Tho and Xuan Thuy, the chief Hanoi negotiator in the Paris talks, on Jan. 8. He added, in response to a question that William H. Sullivan, Deputy Assistant of State for East Asian

Affairs, would return to Paris to head the technical talks on Tuesday.

The disclosure about the bombing halt came in answer to questions. "The President has ordered that all bombing be discontinued above the 20th Parallel as long as serious negotiations are under way," Mr. Warren said.

He then indicated that the raids had already stopped when he said that "as soon as it was clear that serious negotiations could be resumed at both the technical level and between the principals, the President ordered that all bombing be discontinued above the 20th Parallel."

The press secretary would not amplify on what "serious" meant. Hanoi has always insisted that it was negotiating "seriously."

Mr. Nixon was at Camp David, the Presidential retreat in the nearby Catoctin Mountains of Maryland. Mr. Kissinger was vacationing at Palm Springs, Calif., but was in daily telephone contact with the President, Mr. Warren said, and was expected to return to Washington soon to begin a concentrated series of consultations prior to the renewed talks.

Mr. Kissinger had indicated on Dec. 16 that, aside from Hanoi's dilatory tactics, some key issues remained unresolved.

These included the American desire for some wording acknowledging the sovereignty of South Vietnam and differences over the composition of the international supervisory group that would monitor the cease-fire.

The United States wanted a 5,000-man force, able to move freely, but Hanoi, according to Mr. Kissinger, wanted to limit that force to 250 men, with severe restraints on its movement.

Mr. Kissinger has said that after an agreement is reached between Washington and Hanoi, Saigon would be asked to join in the signing. Saigon has publicly demanded that any accord provide for the withdrawal of Hanoi's 145,000 men from the South: Mr. Kissinger has said that the United States would not back that demand or give Saigon a "veto" over an accord.

* * *

January 16, 1973

PRESIDENT HALTS ALL BOMBING, MINING AND SHELLING OF NORTH; POINTS TO 'PROGRESS' IN TALKS

PARIS SESSION DUE

Ziegler Says Kissinger Will Return There in 'Near Future'

By JOHN HERBERS
Special to The New York Times

KEY BISCAYNE, Fla., Jan. 15—President Nixon, citing "progress" made in the cease-fire negotiations in Paris, suspended bombing, mining, shelling and all other offensive action throughout North Vietnam today.

Ronald L. Ziegler, the White House press secretary, announced the suspension this morning after several hours of consultations between the President and his chief negotiator, Henry A. Kissinger.

This was the first time that a spokesman for Mr. Nixon has said publicly that progress had been made in the latest round of Paris negotiations. But, while acknowledging reports in a number of world capitals that an agreement had been reached between the United States and North Vietnam, Mr. Ziegler said he could not confirm the existence of an agreement for a cease-fire.

"We have made it very clear we have a mutual agreement with the North Vietnamese that we will in no way discuss the substance of the negotiations in Paris" as long as they are under way, Mr. Ziegler said.

He said Mr. Kissinger would return to Paris in the "relatively near future" as the negotiations proceed. Mr. Kissinger flew from Paris Saturday after six days of talks and conferred with President Nixon in three meetings yesterday. Last night, Mr. Nixon sent Gen. Alexander M. Haig Jr., who has been one of the chief participants in the negotiations, to Saigon to "consult" with President Nguyen Van Thieu about what Mr. Kissinger and Le Due Tho had done in Paris.

[General Haig arrived in Saigon Tuesday morning and, accompanied by Ambassador Ellsworth Bunker, went to the presidential palace to begin talks with President Thieu.]

'All Offensive Action'

Today, in announcing the halt of offensive action, Mr. Ziegler said, "Because of the progress made in the negotiations between Dr. Kissinger and special adviser Le Duc Tho, President Nixon has directed that the bombing, shelling and any further mining of North Vietnam be suspended. This order went into effect at 10 A.M. today, Jan. 15, Washington time."

"The directive which I have referred to by the President applied to action north of the 17th Parallel, the entire area of North Vietnam," Mr. Ziegler said. This includes "all offensive action" in North Vietnam, he added later, but reconnaissance action continues.

The order, Mr. Ziegler said, does not apply to military activity in South Vietnam and other countries.

Thus Mr. Nixon restricted American military activity against North Vietnamese forces to its lowest level since last spring before American offensive action in North Vietnam began on a regular basis.

President Lyndon B. Johnson, before he left office in 1969, had suspended bombing in all of North Vietnam. This policy continued generally under President Nixon, except for some raids said to have been unauthorized and some "protective reaction" strikes—in response to enemy threats or attacks—until last spring, when attacks were resumed on a regular basis.

In his television address May 8, the President said that he was stepping up the war in the North in response to military aggression by the enemy in South Vietnam and announced the mining of most North Vietnamese harbors and bombing of military targets.

Since then, bombing above the 20th Parallel has been suspended from time to time as negotiations proceeded, but air raids and other military strikes in North Vietnam below the 20th Parallel continued.

Mr. Ziegler was asked whether the North Vietnamese in return for the cessation of the bombing and mining had agreed to suspend military action in South Vietnam, especially in view of the fact that North Vietnamese aggression in the South was the reason Mr. Nixon gave in May for stepping up the bombing.

Today's action, he replied, was "unilateral." But he added: "The North Vietnamese knew and were aware that once progress in the negotiations was being made, that the United States would be prepared to take unilateral steps, make a unilateral gesture such as we have announced today in relation to the entire situation."

Mines Not Deactivated

He said the suspension of military activity did not extend to deactivation of mines laid in Haiphong and other harbors.

"The mines that are there will remain in place," he said. "The mines that are in place is a subject of negotiations and is being dealt with in the negotiations." Mr. Ziegler pointed out that the negotiations on technical matters continued in Paris today.

The President planned to spend "another day or two" at his waterfront home in Key Biscayne working on his inaugural and State of the Union addresses. But Mr. Kissinger returned to Washington tonight after several conferences with the President.

The order to suspend military action in North Vietnam was sent to military leaders last night, Mr. Ziegler said, "following a complete assessment of the negotiations, by the President, and his discussions that he had and has been having with Dr. Kissinger."

After the announcement of Mr. Nixon's military policy on May 3, talks between Mr. Kissinger and Le Duc Tho began on July 13. On Oct. 25 the White House ordered a temporary suspension of all bombing north of the 20th Parallel and on Oct. 26 Mr. Kissinger said in Washington that "peace is at hand."

But on Dec. 18, after the Administration accused North Vietnam of having failed to bargain in good faith, the bombing above the 20th Parallel was resumed, including extensive attacks on targets in Hanoi and Haiphong. The bombing above the 20th Parallel was suspended on Dec. 30, when it was announced that talks would resume. But bombing below the 20th Parallel continued until today.

Action Raises Hopes

By BERNARD GWERTZMAN
Special to The New York Times

WASHINGTON, Jan. 15—By halting the bombing, mining, and shelling of North Vietnam today, President Nixon has raised new expectations here that an end to the Vietnam war may again be near.

No details of the latest round of talks between Henry A. Kissinger and Le Duc Tho have been revealed, and some officials cautioned that it was not known whether President Nguyen Van Thieu would drop his objections to an accord.

The White House and the State Department, moreover, have said "no comment" to the spate of optimistic press reports from Saigon, Paris and elsewhere reporting that a substantial agreement had been reached.

Today's optimism, in fact, was not based on the details of the negotiations, which remain a tight secret here, but rather on external signs that the Administration's plan for a settlement was being followed.

In the past, the Administration had said that once it achieved an acceptable agreement with Hanoi, all military operations against North Vietnam would stop.

The Administration had also said that once such an accord was reached, a diplomatic effort would be undertaken to persuade South Vietnam to agree to its terms.

It has not been disclosed whether this agreement has in fact been achieved, but officials and diplomats believed that the bombing and mining would not have stopped if Hanoi and Washington were not in substantial accord.

Justification for this assessment was provided in October when Mr. Kissinger and Mr. Tho concluded their secret nine-point draft agreement and—according to accounts by Hanoi and undisputed by Washington—Mr. Nixon pledged that he would order a halt in all American military operations against North Vietnam just before initialing the agreement.

Nixon Sought Changes

That accord was not initialed because after hearing the objections of President Thieu, Mr. Nixon decided to seek changes in the original draft. But as a sign of appreciation for Hanoi's conciliatory attitude, Mr. Nixon did order a partial halt to the military operations north of the 20th Parallel.

In November and December Washington and Hanoi were unable to reach a new agreement. Hanoi resisted Washington's proposals, and made counterproposals that were equally unacceptable to Washington. This led to a breakdown of the talks on Dec. 13, and a resumption of bombing above the 20th Parallel on Dec. 18.

But on Dec. 16—two days before the renewed bombing—Mr. Kissinger made it clear that the Administration intended to keep to its plan for a settlement. He stressed that the United States was not seeking an accord that would meet all of Saigon's demands; that once Hanoi agreed to a "just and fair" settlement, the United States would not allow Saigon to veto it.

The bombing above the 20th Parallel stopped on Dec. 29. The Kissinger-Tho talks resumed on Jan. 8, and two days ago they ended with both sides noting "progress."

The developments since Saturday have fortified the feeling that an agreement was near.

First, General Haig, the Army deputy chief of staff and until this month Mr. Kissinger's chief aide, was called to Key Biscayne to consult with Mr. Nixon and Mr. Kissinger. Then he was dispatched to Saigon to consult with Mr. Thieu.

On Dec. 16 Mr. Kissinger said that when the Administration believed a settlement was imminent, Mr. Nixon had assigned General Haig the task "of presenting the agreement to our allies." Officials and diplomats concluded today that General Haig's mission to Saigon was a delayed fulfillment of that assignment.

It was assumed here that Mr. Kissinger and Mr. Tho had resolved the major questions holding up their part of the negotiations—cease-fire machinery, the establishment of a demilitarized zone, and the release of prisoners.

This assumption was fortified today when Mr. Nixon ordered the halt to all military operations in the North.

Officials and diplomats here assumed that a formal statement about the presumed agreement would not be made until General Haig had confered with Mr. Thieu. If Saigon agrees to the terms of the accord, it is presumed, simultaneous announcements would be made in Washington, Hanoi, and Saigon.

* * *

January 17, 1973

THIEU EXPECTED TO ACCEPT TRUCE PACT, OFFICIALS SAY, THOUGH PROBLEMS REMAIN

TEXT UNDER STUDY

Accord Is Reported to Contain No Provision for Hanoi Pullout

By CRAIG R. WHITNEY
Special to The New York Times

SAIGON, South Vietnam, Wednesday, Jan. 17—President Nguyen Van Thieu is expected to give his approval to the text of a cease-fire agreement brought to him yesterday by Gen. Alexander M. Haig Jr., and the Government is now going over the details of how it is to be carried out, according to Vietnamese officials close to the presidential palace.

It was reliably reported that the agreement does not contain any provisions for the withdrawal of all the North Vietnamese troops now in the South. Saigon puts the number of these troops at 300,000, but the United States estimates the total at 150,000.

However, according to Vietnamese officials close to the talks going on here, the agreement will call for re-establishment of an effective demilitarized zone centered roughly along the 17th Parallel, as was provided in the 1954 Geneva agreements, and will include a formula for Saigon's sovereignty in the area the South Vietnamese Government controls below that line.

Sizable Control Force

The accord will also provide for a sizable control and supervisory force to see that its terms are observed, the officials say.

[The Associated Press quoted South Vietnamese sources as saying that Washington and Saigon would order a cease-fire Friday to prepare for the signing of a peace agreement. The Saigon Government denied the report, according to Reuters. In Key Biscayne, the White House refused to confirm or deny such reports.]

South Vietnamese sources said that if the details of how to carry out the agreement were worked out in Saigon and in Paris to everyone's satisfaction, a cease-fire could go into effect soon. The 23,800 American servicemen here could then be withdrawn within 60 days and American prisoners of war held by the Communists could be released, they said.

General Haig, President Nixon's special envoy, who arrived here yesterday morning, brought the Vietnamese-language text of the cease-fire accord, the sources said. They of the agreement and was concerned with additional documents, called protocols, that spell out the specific details of how it will be carried out.

"There are still many details in the military protocols to be solved," one South Vietnamese official said. "But for the principles, the Government now agrees."

There was no official confirmation of this by the Government or by the United States Embassy, which is maintaining tight secrecy on all aspects of General Haig's visit here. General Haig, the Army Vice Chief of Staff, who long served as deputy to Henry A. Kissinger in the National Security Council, made no statement as he arrived at Tan Son Nhut Airport and is holding no meetings with the press during his visit.

No Truce Date Given

Soon after his arrival from the United States yesterday, General Haig and Ambassador Ellsworth Bunker went to the presidential palace for a meeting with President Thieu that lasted two hours and 35 minutes. General Haig then spent the afternoon at military command headquarters conferring with Army and Air Force commanders.

The general was accompanied on his trip here by John D. Negroponte, the Vietnam expert on the National Security Council staff, and two military assistants.

No sources here gave any date by which a cease-fire might go into effect, but there was speculation that an agreement, at least, might be announced soon, with an actual cease-fire to follow later.

Mr. Thieu is sending to Paris a delegation of military experts headed by Lieut. Gen. Vinh Loc, commandant of the National Defense College, to participate with American and North Vietnamese technical experts in drafting the military protocols. The delegation will leave this week, according to Vietnamese officials.

Mr. Thieu is now reportedly willing to accept an agreement that leaves North Vietnamese troops in the South, after having long asserted that he would fight to the end unless they were withdrawn.

The details now being worked out concern such questions as establishing the Government's membership in joint military commissions with the North Vietnamese to control the cease-fire in many parts of the country, and establishing priorities in carrying out the stages of a cease-fire and of regrouping of the troops of both sides from contested areas and battlegrounds.

The American decision to stop the bombing and shelling of North Vietnam Monday night was seen by diplomats and South Vietnamese observers here as a sign to Mr. Thieu that President Nixon was satisfied that the cease-fire agreement was acceptable and that he would not be deterred by any further objections from Saigon.

'Clever Gesture' Seen

"It is a clever gesture by President Nixon, but as long as there is no final agreement, anything like a bombing halt can only benefit the North Vietnamese," one pro-Government legislator said.

The halt in bombing was not mentioned here in the public press or on the radio until yesterday afternoon. But neither did the Government issue a public demurrer, as it did when President Lyndon B. Johnson halted the bombing of the North in November, 1968, also hoping to reach a peace agreement with the North Vietnamese.

President Thieu has made no statement to the South Vietnamese people about the imminent possibility of a cease-fire, but, according to Government sources, he and his close aides have issued orders for a new set of cease-fire contingency plans to be distributed to all Government offices in the country.

Communist officers have now begun telling their troops and agents that they may be able to spend Tet, the Lunar New Year holiday which begins Feb. 3, with their families, according to American intelligence. So far, military sources said, they are not known to have any plans for last-minute attempts to gain territory or otherwise improve their positions before a cease-fire.

General Haig is expected to visit Laos and Cambodia before going on to Bangkok, Thailand, on Friday.

* * *

January 21, 1973

WAR SCORED BY THOUSANDS IN PROTESTS IN THE CAPITAL

60,000 Join in Largest Demonstration—Objects Reported Thrown at Nixon's Car on Way to the White House

By LINDA CHARLTON
Special to The New York Times

WASHINGTON, Jan. 20—As official Washington celebrated the rites of inauguration, thousands of dissenters demonstrated with marches, speeches, placards and rallies. They were generally orderly protests marked by minor scuffles and a few arrests.

The turnout at the day's major demonstration—one of three scheduled to more or less coincide with the swearing-in ceremony at the Capitol—lived up to its organizers' predictions. The city police estimated the crowd at the Washington Monument grounds at between 25,000 and 30,000, but the National Park police said there were 60,000, and one television network put the figure at 100,000.

Among the crowd that had marched to the monument grounds from the nearby Lincoln Memorial were many of the approximately 2,500 members of Vietnam Veterans Against the War who had marched across the Memorial Bridge from Arlington National Cemetery. They joined the major demonstration, sponsored by two coalitions of antiwar groups, after staging a mock treaty signing ceremony.

On the other side of Washington, and just a few blocks from the site of Mr. Nixon's formal oath-taking, between 500 and 1,000 persons took part in a demonstration sponsored by Students for a Democratic Society and its allied Maoist Progressive Labor party, with uninvited but active contingents of "Yippies"—adherents of the so-called Youth International party.

It was this demonstration that the security forces had foreseen as a potential cause of disruption beyond its prescribed area, and it did fulfill the pledge of its leaders to march near enough to the Capitol "so that the people can hear us."

Their chants were barely audible in the inaugural stands, but the police delayed the march, evidently not by coincidence, until the ceremonies were under way. The march, which started at a playground at 8th and H Streets, Northeast, about 11:30 A.M., did not reach the rally site at Union Station until 12:40 P.M., as the departing guests at the ceremony were hurrying out of the cold.

The march was allowed, but the accompanying police insisted that the marchers stop at each intersection for traffic. "Obviously our aim was to delay the march as much as possible, and it wasn't very hard," said a sergeant who would not identify himself.

A bizarre feature of this demonstration was a 10-foot-long papier-maché rat with Mr. Nixon's face, carrying a blood-stained baby doll in its teeth. The rat was later confiscated by the police.

In addition to the three announced demonstrations, several persons along the route from the Capitol to the White House held antiwar and anti-Nixon signs—"The Emperor Has No Clothes," said one. Some spectators made obscene gestures, and on one occasion, a piece of fruit was thrown at Mr. Nixon's car, but it splattered on the roadway.

That incident took place near 14th Street and Pennsylvania Avenue, two blocks from the White House, at a point where stone-throwing demonstrators had been reported on the police radio a few minutes previously. As Mr. Nixon's limousine moved toward the area, Secret Service agents moved up to surround his car, and other security agents headed into the crowd.

Although several members of Congress were on the long list of speakers scheduled for the rally co-sponsored by the national Peace Action Coalition and the People's Coalition for Peace and Justice, a threatened boycott of the swearing-in ceremonies by Congressmen failed to materialize in strength. Only one of the 15 black Representatives was present, however. Representative Charles C. Diggs, Jr., Democrat of Michigan, said that he attended out of respect for the office of the Presidency.

The rally began shortly after 2 P.M. and continued late into the afternoon, but the cold weather and the familiarity of much of the rhetoric combined to disperse the crowd within little more than an hour. By 4 P.M., it was estimated that no more than 10,000 persons remained.

The admonitions of many of the speakers to maintain order were heeded by most of the crowd—largely but not entirely young people and almost entirely white.

There were occasional attempts at disruption. Small groups of youths lowered the American flags surrounding the Washington Monument, burned them and hoisted replacements, including Vietcong flags. At one point, an S.D.S. contingent on a flatbed truck tried to edge through the crowd. The truck was blocked by a cordon of marshals used by the sponsoring groups.

As the last of the inaugural parade passed 14th Street, an unorganized group of demonstrators fell in behind it. About 25 policemen rushed into the roadway to disperse them, pushing some into the crowd on the sidewalk.

One demonstrator, 20-year-old Philip Dill of Baltimore, was surrounded by the police and taken, his head bleeding, to a nearby special divisions truck. Several similar scuffles were reported along and near the parade route, but all were resolved without major incident.

In the early evening, the metropolitan police reported 33 arrests of demonstrators, including two juveniles.

* * *

January 24, 1973

VIETNAM ACCORD IS REACHED; CEASE-FIRE BEGINS SATURDAY; P.O.W.'S TO BE FREE IN 60 DAYS

TROOPS TO LEAVE

On TV, Nixon Asserts 'Peace With Honor' Is Aim of Pact

By BERNARD GWERTZMAN
Special to The New York Times

WASHINGTON, Jan. 23—President Nixon said tonight that Henry A. Kissinger and North Vietnam's chief negotiator, Le Duc Tho, had initialed an agreement in Paris today "to end the war and bring peace with honor in Vietnam and Southeast Asia."

In a televised report to the nation, a few hours after Mr. Kissinger returned to Washington, Mr. Nixon said a cease-fire in Vietnam would go into effect on Saturday at 7 P.M., Eastern standard time.

Simultaneous announcements were made in Hanoi and Saigon.

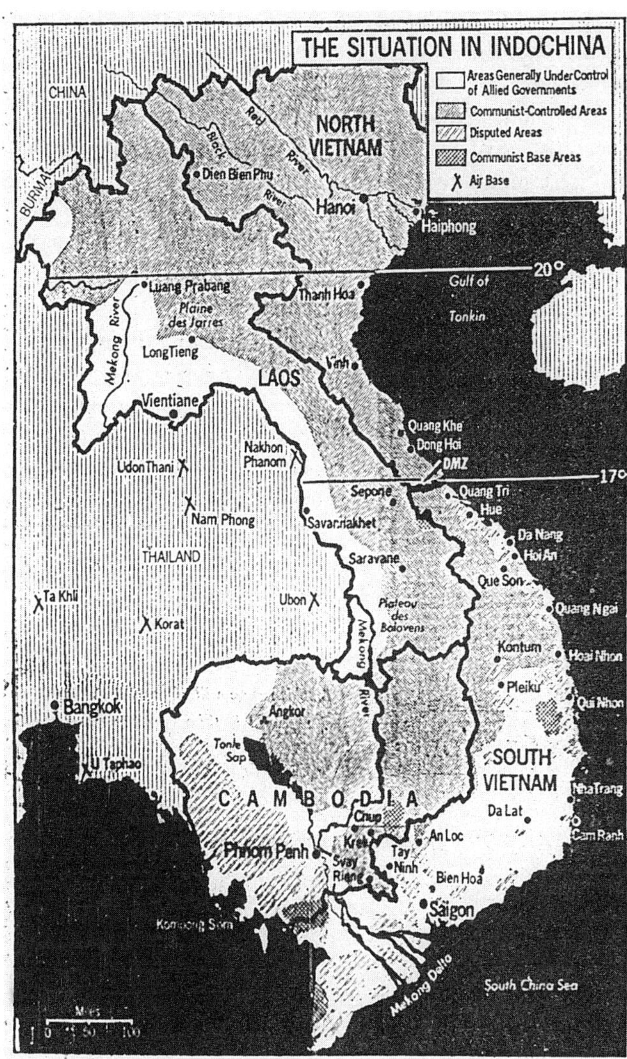

Maps shows approximate areas held by Communist and Government forces in South Vietnam, Laos and Cambodia. While Communists control large regions, population concentrations are mostly in Government dominated areas.

Mr. Nixon said that under the terms of the accord—which will be formally signed on Saturday—all American prisoners of war would be released and the remaining 23,700-man American force in South Vietnam would be withdrawn within 60 days.

Wider Peace Indicated

He referred to "peace" in Southeast Asia, suggesting that the accord extended to Laos and Cambodia, which have also been engaged in the war. But there was no direct mention of those two nations today, and it is not known if the cease-fire extends to them as well.

Obviously pleased by the long-awaited development, ending the longest war in American history, Mr. Nixon said the Hanoi-Washington agreement "meets the goals" and has the "full support" of President Nguyen Van Thieu of South Vietnam.

Earlier Mr. Thieu had expressed strong reservations about the draft agreement worked out by Mr. Kissinger and Mr. Tho in October.

Tonight Mr. Nixon sketched only the outline of the accord. The full text of the agreement and accompanying protocols will be issued tomorrow by joint agreement with Hanoi, he said.

It was not possible, for instance, to determine from Mr. Nixon's 10-minute address what changes had been made in the agreement since October.

In his brief description of the accord, Mr. Nixon said that the cease-fire would be "internationally supervised," a reference to the projected force of Canadians, Hungarians, Indonesians and Poles who will supervise the truce. But he did not say how large the force would be. The United States has wanted a highly mobile force of about 5,000 men. The North Vietnamese have suggested a substantially smaller force.

Mr. Nixon also said nothing about the controversial problem of the demilitarized zone that straddles the border between North and South Vietnam. Saigon has wanted this line reaffirmed to make sure, legally, that there are two Vietnams, and Hanoi had resisted this. All the President said on the subject was that the people of South Vietnam "have been guaranteed the right to determine their own future without outside interference."

Captive Issue Avoided

Nothing was said either about the release of the thousands of prisoners in Saigon's jails, many of whom were jailed on suspicion that they were Vietcong agents. At one point in the negotiations, Hanoi was seeking to make the release of American prisoners conditional on the release of Saigon's captives.

Some of these questions may be answered tomorrow when Mr. Kissinger holds a news conference at 11 A.M. It will be televised by the major networks.

Last fall, the President insisted that he would agree only to a "peace with honor," and tonight he insisted that the accord met "the goals that we considered essential for peace with honor."

Apparently in an effort to ease possible apprehensions in Saigon, Mr. Nixon pledged that the United States would continue to recognize Mr. Thieu's Government "as the sole legitimate Government of South Vietnam."

He also pledged—"within the terms of the agreement"— to continue to supply assistance to South Vietnam and to "support efforts for the people of South Vietnam to settle their problems peacefully among themselves."

The actual agreement is understood to provide machinery for the eventual reconciliation of the Saigon Government with the Vietcong. But officials here have expressed doubts in recent days that the two rivals for power would be able to resolve their hostility.

Calling on all involved parties to adhere to the agreement "scrupulously," Mr. Nixon also alluded to the Soviet Union and China, saying, "We shall also expect other interested nations to help insure that the agreement is carried out and peace is maintained."

It is expected that Secretary of State William P. Rogers will sign the agreement in Paris on Saturday at the former Hotel Majestic, along with the Foreign Ministers of North Vietnam, South Vietnam and the Provisional Revolutionary government, or Vietcong.

Mr. Nixon ended his speech with words to the various parties to the accord, their allies, and to the American people.

Cooperation in Future

To the South Vietnamese, who in the end listened to American entreaties and did not balk at the accord, he said, "We look forward to working with you in the future." He added that the United States and South Vietnam would be "friends in peace as we have been allies in war."

To the North Vietnamese, he said, "As we have ended the war through negotiations, let us now build a peace of reconciliation."

He said that the United States would make "a major effort" to help achieve that goal, but he stressed that Hanoi would have to reciprocate. Previously, Mr. Nixon has talked about a $7.5-billion program to rehabilitate North Vietnam and South Vietnam over a five-year period. Of that total, $2.5-billion would be earmarked for Hanoi.

Making a firm call for support from Moscow and Peking, Mr. Nixon said: "To the other major powers that have been involved, even indirectly, now is the time for mutual restraint so that the peace we have achieved can last."

U.S. Aid Believed Limited

Under the terms of the accord, it is believed, the United States is limited in the amount of military aid it can supply Saigon. But American officials have warned that if the Russians and the Chinese continue to supply Hanoi with extensive military equipment the balance of power could be upset.

Mr. Nixon said nothing about a key controversial item in the negotiations—the presence of 145,000 North Vietnamese in South Vietnam. But previously, Mr. Kissinger had said that the United States would not ask Hanoi to pull these forces back because they would be needed to protect the Vietcong enclaves permitted under the accord.

To the American people, he explained his silence of recent months about the situation in Vietnam. He said that if he had discussed the efforts to achieve an agreement, "it would have seriously harmed and possibly destroyed the chances for peace."

He ended his speech with some words about Lyndon B. Johnson, who died yesterday on the eve of the settlement. He said that no one would have welcomed this peace more than he.

Earlier, on Mr. Kissinger's return from Paris, the President set in motion a series of evening conferences before his televised report to the nation.

Mr. Nixon first met with his Cabinet officers to give them a report on the Vietnam situation, then conferred with the top Congressional leaders from both parties.

The White House said that Mr. Nixon had invited to that session the Senate majority leader, Mike Mansfield of Montana; the Senate Republican leader, Hugh Scott of Pennsylvania; the House Speaker, Carl Alpert of Oklahoma; the House Republican leader, Gerald R. Ford of Michigan, and the House Democratic leader, Thomas P. O'Neill Jr. of Massachusetts.

Throughout the day, despite the reports from Saigon and Paris about the initialing of the agreement, the White House refrained from any substantive comment.

Ronald L. Ziegler, the White House press secretary, met briefly with newsmen at about 1 P.M., after having spent much of the morning at a meeting with Mr. Nixon and White House aides.

Mr. Ziegler limited himself to announcing that Mr. Nixon would address the nation on the "status of the Vietnam negotiations," and that he would hold meeting with the Cabinet officers and Congressional leaders tonight. In addition, Mr. Ziegler said a larger session with members of Congress would be held tomorrow morning at the White House.

The substantive talks on a Vietnam settlement began in January, 1969, in the former Hotel Majestic in Paris, the same place Mr. Kissinger and Mr. Tho held their session today.

Meetings Around Paris

The negotiations that produced the actual agreement, however, took place in villas in and around Paris between Mr. Kissinger and Mr. Tho, beginning in August, 1969.

The holding of those negotiations remained a closely guarded secret until last Jan. 26 when Mr. Nixon disclosed them in a speech accusing Hanoi of delaying tactics.

After North Vietnam's offensive in South Vietnam last spring, the secret talks resumed.

A decisive breakthrough was achieved early in October when the United States and North Vietnam agreed to a nine-point draft agreement whose outline was made public by Hanoi on Oct. 26, and was confirmed by Mr. Kissinger that same day in his "peace is at hand" news conference.

Hanoi had originally insisted that the draft be signed by Oct. 31, but Mr. Nixon asked for further meetings to tighten the terms of the agreement and to meet some of South Vietnam's objections.

The talks resumed in Paris on Nov. 20 and recessed on Nov. 25. When they began again on Dec. 4, Hanoi objected to the proposals made by the United States in the previous round, and made counterproposals that Mr. Kissinger later called "frivolous." Those talks broke down on Dec. 13.

Reportedly angry over Hanoi's tactics, Mr. Nixon ordered the war's heaviest bombing of Hanoi and Haiphong—from Dec. 18 to 29. The raids, which included strikes by B-52 bombers, were called off north of the 20th Parallel on Dec. 29 with the announcement by the White House that Hanoi had agreed to resume "serious" talks.

Apparent Accord on Jan. 13

The negotiations opened on Jan. 8 and concluded with an apparent agreement on Jan. 13. Two days later all bombing, mining and shelling of North Vietnam ceased, and on Jan. 18—last Thursday—it was announced that Mr. Kissinger and Mr. Tho would meet again "for the purpose of concluding the text of an agreement."

Gen. Alexander M. Haig Jr., who until this month was Mr. Kissinger's chief deputy, returned to Washington on Sunday after a mission to Saigon to persuade President Thieu to add his agreement to the accord worked out by Hanoi and Washington.

Mr. Haig was with Mr. Nixon early this morning when first reports of the conclusion of Mr. Kissinger's Paris meeting were received here.

* * *

January 24, 1973

WAR LEAVES DEEP MARK ON U.S.

By JAMES RESTON

Special to The New York Times

WASHINGTON, Jan. 23—America is moving out of Vietnam after the longest and most devisive conflict since the War Between the States. But Vietnam is not moving out of America, for the impact of the war there is likely to influence American life for many years to come. Though it is probably too early to distinguish between the temporary and the enduring consequences, one thing is fairly clear: There has been a sharp decline in the respect for authority in the United States as a result of the war—a decline in respect not only for the civil authority of government but also for the moral authority of the schools, the universities, the press, the church and even the family.

There was no cease-fire on this front. Vietnam did not start the challenge to authority, but it weakened respect for the executives who got the nation involved in the war in the first place, for the Congress that let it go on for more than a decade and for the democratic process of debate, which failed to influence the course of battle for years and which finally declined into physical combat and sporadic anarchy.

Even after a cease-fire, there will still be considerable contention in the country over whether the challenges to authority are good or bad.

Many Americans have maintained that it was precisely the dissent and the defiance that forced social reform at home and a settlement abroad.

Others have argued that the war produced a whole new revolutionary climate in America, which encouraged the Communists to prolong the conflict and disrupt the nation's unity and the previously accepted attitudes, standards and restraints in American public and private conduct. But few Americans challenge the proposition that for good or bad, something has happened to American life—something not yet understood or agreed upon, something that is different, important and probably enduring.

Even at the moment of the Vietnam compromise, there was a rash of teacher strikes in several of the great cities of the nation; one-time members of the Central Intelligence Agency, some of them former White House consultants, were confessing in court that they had been involved in a conspiracy to spy on the Democratic party and its leaders during the 1972 Presidential election campaign, and there was a controversy at Madison Square Garden over the playing of the national anthem before major sporting events.

The direct costs of the war to the Untied States are easier to estimate than the indirect. Vietnam cost 46,000 American lives and, at a minimum, $110-billion. That does not take into account long-range obligations to veterans, which may add up to $50-billion more, nor does it include the costs of fighting in Laos and Cambodia and the continuing military establishment in Thailand.

Nor does it take into account the cost to the peoples of Indochina in dead, wounded, maimed and homeless, and in the destruction of their lands, which are almost beyond accurate calculation.

The imponderables—the changes in attitudes and assumptions, for example, and the decline in truthfulness and self-confidence—promised to be even more significant for the future than the financial strain.

Among other things, Vietnam changed the nation's way of looking at itself and the world, reduced its willingness to get involved in distant continental land wars for ambiguous reasons, and envenomed the relations between the political parties and between the President and Congress.

The American people seem less confident about many things they took for granted. They are not so sure, for example, that the United States always prevails in foreign conflicts, that big guys always lick little guys, that money and machines are decisive in war, and that small states would rather surrender than risk American military might.

Even the two World Wars of this century did not have quite the same effect on American society. They divided Western civilization, destroyed its old empires, broke its domination over world politics, and changed the lives of Britain and Germany, but they did not challenge quite so many assumptions of American life as the long struggle in Vietnam.

In 1937 Munich became a symbol of appeasement and the dangers on nonintervention, dangers that, in turn, encouraged more overseas commitments by the United States than by any other nation. In the nineteen-seventies, on the other hand, Vietnam became a symbol of the dangers of intervention and led to American withdrawal and even fears of American isolation.

The tone of President John F. Kennedy's inaugural address in 1961 at the beginning of the deep involvement in Vietnam and the tone of President Nixon's second inaugural address during the last phase of the cease-fire negotiations illustrate the change in the American mood and commitment.

Prudent Pledge by Nixon

"Let every nation know, whether it wishes us well or ill," Mr. Kennedy said in his oft-quoted promise, "that we shall pay any price, bear any burden, meet any hardship, support any friend, oppose any foe to assure the survival and the success of liberty. This much we pledge—and more."

After the disappointments and disillusions of the ensuing 12 years, President Nixon was more prudent and modest in pledging what the American people would do.

"We shall do our share in defending peace and freedom in the world," he said. "But we shall expect others to do their share. The time has passed when America will make every other nation's conflict our own, or make every other nation's future our responsibility, or presume to tell other nations how to manage their own affairs."

Moreover, the disillusionments of Vietnam not only led to a more modest estimate of what the United States could or should do to help maintain freedom and order in the world, but they also seemed to encourage a downward reappraisal of what government could do to maintain the health and welfare of the poor at home.

Yesterday, when former President Lyndon B. Johnson died, with the Vietnam peace agreement near completion in Paris, the heroic themes of his Administration—his Great Society, his war on poverty, his bills on civil rights and voting rights—were very much in the news. But by this time the emphasis if not the direction of American policy at home was undergoing a marked change.

"A person can be expected to act responsibly only if he has responsibility," President Nixon said at his second inaugural. "So let us encourage individuals at home and nations abroad to do more for themselves. Let us measure what we will do for others by what they will do for themselves."

In short, after Vietnam the emphasis is not on what government can do but on what it cannot and should not do; not on welfare but on work; not on a compassionate society but on a competitive society in which the comfortable majority will pay less in taxes and everyone will rely more on himself and less on the Federal Government.

Perhaps these are merely changes in style and rhetoric, due more to Mr. Nixon's philosophy than to the experiences of Vietnam; but particularly in the field of foreign affairs America after Vietnam is likely to regard the world as a much more complicated and diverse place than it did in the fifties and sixties.

For most of the last decade this country has been preoccupied with Vietnam on the assumption that the 2 percent of Asia's population that live there were critical to the worldwide struggle between the irreconcilable forces of darkness and light. This and many other illusions have been modified if not rejected.

It was widely believed, for example, that Communism was a monolithic force working on a vast and centrally controlled strategy to change the balance of power in the world and threaten the vital security and commercial interests of the United States.

The Communist threat to Greece and Turkey in the late forties, the invasion of South Korea by North Korea, the blare of Communist pronouncements and the expansion of Soviet and Chinese influence all encouraged the belief—which persisted even after the Chinese-Soviet split—that the United States was confronted by a vast conspiracy that could be turned back only by its power and countermeasures.

Furthermore it was widely believed in the fifties and sixties that the system of collective security alliances that had helped preserve and reconstruct the advanced industrial nations of Western Europe could be adapted to primitive societies lacking in industrial and political tradition. Part of this popular belief was that if American commitments were not met in one place—say, Vietnam—they could be regarded as worthless in other critical areas—say, Europe—and that if Vietnam fell other nations would fall—"like dominoes," as the popular saying of the day went.

Even before the cease-fire agreement drew near, President Nixon had begun to question those assumptions and shape foreign policy to the changing situation. The split between Moscow and Peking and the need in both China and the Soviet Union for surplus grain and modern technology gave him the opportunity to renew diplomatic contact with Peking and, despite Vietnam, to negotiate new agreements with Moscow on trade and arms control.

The likelihood is that the trend toward limited cooperation between the major powers will be even more marked with the final withdrawal of the United States from Vietnam.

Thus the United States, the Soviet Union and China all seem to have learned some of the lessons of the Vietnam war, limited their use of power and avoided a direct military confrontation.

Role of Public Opinion

A major question here is whether the Russians will again be tempted to assist in another "war of national liberation" in the belief that Vietnam was so painful for the United States that no President of the Vietnam generation would be tempted to intervene.

The experts in Washington are divided on the question, but the majority seem to believe that for the foreseeable future Peking and Moscow will decide that they have more to gain by cooperating with the United States than in risking another confrontation.

It is less clear that the lessons of the war have been learned in Washington. President Nixon has clearly reduced overseas commitments and tempered the cold war rhetoric, but the habit of centralizing foreign policy decisions in the White House, where so many of the Vietnam blunders were made, is persisting, as is the heavy influence of the military on foreign policy.

Charles W. Yost, one of the nation's most experienced diplomats, observes in his book "The Conduct and Misconduct of Foreign Affairs" (Random House, 1972) that in the first three years of the Vietnam war American public opinion did not exhibit either a stimulating or an inhibiting effect on United States leaders, but that Mr. Kennedy, Mr. Johnson and, at first, Mr. Nixon were so afraid of what public opinion might do if they "lost" the war that they misjudged both the problem in Vietnam and attitudes at home.

"There are many depressing examples of international conflicts," he writes, "in which leaders have first aroused their own people against a neighbor and then discovered to their chagrin that even when they judged the time had come to move toward peace, they were prisoners of the popular passions they had stimulated."

President Nixon's argument that the United States had to keep following his policy or look like "a pitiful, helpless giant" is only one of many illustrations to be found in Vietnam policy; but the chances are that this sort of thing will not be heard again for some time.

Meanwhile, Mr. Nixon does have to deal with the consequences of the war at home: with a kind of spiritual malaise; with the continuing opposition to his theme that the end of the war will not release additional funds for social reconstruction at home, with the resentment of policies reached in secret and not explained to Congress or the people; with the dangers of returning soldiers facing unemployment and exhortations to be self-reliant; and with an American conscience troubled over the bloodshed and sorrow.

The guess here is that it will take some time to restore the self-confidence of the pre-Vietnam years, but it may be that the destruction of many popular misconceptions in Vietnam will produce a more mature, if sadder, nation.

* * *

January 25, 1973

U.S. EXPECTS TRUCE IN LAOS AND CAMBODIA; P.O.W. AIRLIFT FROM HANOI TO START SOON; KISSINGER AND THO GIVE DETAILS OF ACCORD

CAPITAL BRIEFING

Goals 'Substantially Achieved,' Kissinger Says of Efforts

By BERNARD GWERTZMAN
Special to The New York Times

WASHINGTON, Jan. 24—Henry A. Kissinger said today that the United States had "a firm expectation" that the Vietnam cease-fire that goes into effect on Saturday would soon extend to both Laos and Cambodia as well.

Speaking at a 90-minute news conference, following the release of the text and the four protocols, or annexes, of the Vietnam accord he initialed in Paris yesterday, Mr. Kissinger said that the United States had "substantially achieved" the negotiating goals it had set for an "honorable agreement."

Mr. Kissinger, who was personally involved throughout the four years of what he called the "peaks and valleys" of negotiations, presented the Administration's argument that it had secured a "fair and just" settlement, one that he said could not have been achieved four years ago.

[In Saigon, President Nguyen Van Thieu's closest adviser said the South Vietnamese Government was prepared to meet with the National Liberation Front 24 hours after the cease-fire agreement was signed to discuss the political future of the country.]

Series of Key Points

Besides revealing that the United States had indications from Hanoi to expect a formal cease-fire in Laos and an informal, de facto halt to the fighting in Cambodia, Mr Kissinger made the following major points at his news conference:

- As part of the provision for the release of American prisoners within 60 days, North Vietnam has agreed to allow United States Air Force medical evacuation planes to land at Hanoi to pick up prisoners who were confined in North Vietnam and Laos. The first release of prisoners was expected no later than 15 days after the formal signing Saturday. Prisoners in South Vietnam will be released there. North Vietnam said no Americans were prisoners in Cambodia.
- The agreement makes it clear "that there is an entity called South Vietnam," and that any unification of North Vietnam and South Vietnam will be decided only by negotiations and not by military force—an issue of some importance to Saigon.
- The demilitarized zone was recognized in the accord at American insistence to enforce the provision against, the infiltration of and equipment from North Vietnam into South Vietnam.
- North Vietnam was not obliged by the accord to remove its troops—estimated at 145,000—from South Vietnam, a goal sought by Saigon, but provisions of the accord bar any replacement or reinforcement of those forces. Thus, the United States expects North Vietnam, on its own, to reduce gradually its forces in the South, even though this was not written into the agreement.
- The United States has pledged to contribute to the future rehabilitation of the Indochina area, but discussions "of any particular sum" will take place only after the other agreements are in force.
- An international conference on Vietnam will take place within 30 days, and both the Soviet Union and China are expected to attend. No site has been chosen yet.
- The United States will exercise restraint in shipping military equipment to the area and "we believe that the other countries—the Soviet Union and the People's Republic of China—can make a very major contribution to peace in Indochina by exercising similar restraint."

1,160 Men in Force

In discussing the agreement in his news conference at the Executive Office Building, next to the White House, Mr. Kissinger went through the accords in detail. He said that one of the "thorniest" issues in the negotiations had dealt with the release of prisoners.

He noted that at one point, the North Vietnamese sought to link the release of the American prisoners with that of South Vietnamese prisoners in Saigon jails.

But, as he pointed out, the final agreement returned to the original nine-point draft agreement of October and provided that civilian Vietnamese prisoners would be handled independently of the Americans.

Another crucial issue centered on the international machinery to supervise the cease-fire.

Originally, the United States had proposed a 5,000-man force made up of Canadians, Hungarians, Indonesians and Poles. The North Vietnamese, at one point, suggested that the force be limited to only 250 men.

The eventual compromise, as made public today, called for a force of 1,160 men, equally divided among the four nations. The observers, who will be based only in South Vietnam, will be assigned to regional and border areas to check on movement into the country and to report on cease-fire violations.

At the State Department today. Secretary of State William P. Rogers, who will sign the accord for the United States Saturday, called in the ambassadors from the nations participating in the international control group and explained their responsibilities.

Mr. Kissinger said that once the expected cease-fire in Laos took effect, the Ho Chi Minh Trail network, the main supply route from North Vietnam to South Vietnam, would cease to function.

The Laotian cease-fire, he said, will be a formal one, similar to the Vietnam agreement, between the Government and the Communist-led Pathet Lao.

But because of the various factions in Cambodia, it is only expected that "a de facto cease-fire will come into being over a period of time relevant to the execution of this agreement," he said.

Mr. Kissinger stressed that the agreement contained "substantially" the modifications sought by the United States in the original nine-point accord reached in October.

A key modification, he said, was the defining of the "linguistic" problem raised by the National Council of National Reconciliation and Concord, a three-part group of Saigon, Vietcong, and neutralist elements to supervise new elections.

President Thieu of South Vietnam feared that Hanoi was trying to use language to cloak a disguised coalition government, something he would not accept. Mr. Kissinger said the final language eliminated such ambiguities.

No Monopoly of Anguish

In his presentation, Mr. Kissinger sought to demonstrate in some detail that the modifications he said were needed in the accord during his Oct. 26 news conference had been essentially achieved.

He noted, in running through the chronology of the last few months, that the talks had broken down last month and he said the heavy bombing of the Hanoi area, from Dec. 18 to 29, was necessary then "to make clear that the United States could not stand for an indefinite delay in the negotiations."

He declined the invitation from a questioner, however, to attribute the success of the last round of talks, from Jan. 8 to 13, solely to the bombing attacks.

But he did say: "I can only say that we resumed the negotiations on Jan. 8 and the breakthrough occurred on Jan. 9 and I will let those facts speak for themselves."

Mr. Kissinger ended his long opening remarks with a plea for reconcilation, not only in Indochina but also in the United States.

"It should be clear by now that no one in the war has had a monopoly of anguish and that no one in these debates has had a monopoly of moral insight," he said. "And now at last we have achieved an agreement in which the United States did not prescribe the political future to its allies, an agreement which should preserve the dignity and the self-respect of all the parties. And together with healing the wounds of Indochina, we can begin to heal the wounds in America."

The actual text of the document was called "Agreement on Ending the War and Restoring Peace in Vietnam." It was accompanied by four protocols, or documents detailing how to carry out the cease-fire. One dealt with the return of captured military and civilian personnel, both foreign and Vietnamese.

Protocol on Commissions

Another dealt with an American obligation to remove and deactivate the mines that were laid in the ports and waterways of North Vietnam since Mr. Nixon's order of May 8, 1972, to step up military action against North Vietnam.

A third protocol concerned the carrying out of the cease-fire in South Vietnam and the joint military commissions made up of Americans and the three Vietnamese parties. The fourth concerned the International Commission of Control and Supervision.

The broad sweep of the documents did not seem to go much beyond the nine-point draft agreement reached by Mr. Kissinger and Le Duc Tho, the chief Hanoi negotiator, in Paris in October, but not signed then.

At that time, Mr. Kissinger said that while the United States was seeking modifications, it did not intend to reject the nine-point accord altogether.

The actual text of the October draft was not made public, only Hanoi's summary, which Mr. Kissinger did not dispute. So without that draft, it was difficult today to make a detailed comparison.

But the main provisions remained the same. The military sections called for an internationally supervised cease-fire, to be followed by the withdrawal of all American forces within 60 days, and the release of all American prisoners in the same period of time.

The new agreement also provided—as did the draft—for the South Vietnamese to decide their own future, and for the withdrawal of all foreign troops and the closing of foreign bases not only in South Vietnam but also in Cambodia and Laos.

Mr. Kissinger today listed the changes that were sought and achieved since Oct. 26.

He said the United States wanted the international control commission to be in place at the time of the cease-fire to avoid last-minute efforts by Communist forces to seize territory.

Under the current agreement, he said, the international commission, as well as the four-party group made up of Americans and the three Vietnam elements, will meet within 24 hours of the cease-fire, with some forces in place within 48 hours, and the rest within 15 to 30 days.

The second goal, he said, was the desire for a cease-fire in Laos and Cambodia at about the same time as the one in Vietnam. The United States now expects the fighting in Laos and Cambodia to stop sooner than it would have had the accord been signed in October, Mr. Kissinger said.

A Linguistic Problem

Mr. Kissinger recalled the linguistic problem over the National Council of National Reconciliation and Concord and said it had been resolved.

"I pointed out on Oct. 26," he said, "that we would seek greater precision with respect to certain obligations, particularly without spelling them out as they applied to the demilitarized zone and to the obligations with respect to Laos and Cambodia. That, too, has been achieved."

He also claimed that the American effort—made public at his Dec. 16 news conference—to find some language that would make clear that the two Vietnams should live in peace with each other proved productive.

"We did not increase our demands after Oct. 26 and we substantially achieved the clarifications which we sought," he said.

Throughout Mr. Kissinger's news conference, he returned to the need for reconciliation and for the healing of wounds.

He said it was clear that "whether this agreement brings a lasting peace or not depends not only on its provisions but also on the spirit in which it is implemented."

"It will be our challenge in the future," he said, "to move the controversies that could not be tilled by any one document from the level of military conflict to the level of positive human aspirations and to absorb the enormous talents and dedication of the people of Indochina in tasks of destruction." He added:

"We will hope in a short time the animosities and the hatred and the suffering of this period will be seen as aspects of the past."

* * *

January 25, 1973

AMONG THE LAST G.I.'S, JOY, ANGER AND DISBELIEF

By JOSEPH B. TREASTER
Special to The New York Times

SAIGON, South Vietnam, Jan. 24—The last American soldiers in South Vietnam received the news today that the war was finally ending for them with emotions that ranged from elation and relief to disappointment, anger and resentment.

For some who had grown fond of the special life-style here, there was a sense of loss. And there were some young men who had lived with the war more than half their lives, who had been crushed when their hopes for peace were shattered late last year, and simply refused to believe when they heard President Nixon announce the agreement to stop shooting at 8 A.M. Sunday, Saigon time.

"I just ain't going to believe it till Sunday and I see we don't go out anymore," said Specialist 4 John Victor Bilton, a 19-year-old radio operator from Miami, as he returned to the Bien Hoa air base this afternoon from an operation with a platoon of South Vietnamese rangers.

'Not Like World War II'

There were some parties this evening but, for the most part, they were rather subdued. "This is not like the end of World War II," said Capt. Herbert Carter, a 29-year-old helicopter pilot from Harrisonville, Mo. "We didn't win a war. There's nothing clearcut. Nobody surrendered. I think most people feel like I do: No matter what they set up here, it's going to slip back to the way it was in '61 and '62 and I don't think any of us expect the North Vietnamese to keep up their part of the bargain."

Not all of the servicemen interviewed today agreed with Captain Carter. In fact, if anything was clear, it was that there was no more consensus on the war among the men closest to it than there has been found in the United States.

Some lamented the loss of 46,000 American dead, and one or two mentioned the bloody battle for Hamburger Hill, without being quite sure where the hill was or what it is called now.

Professional Soldier's View

A professional soldier's answers followed national policy. Lieut. Col. Robley W. Davis was standing in the hallway of a huge air-conditioned office building at Tan Son Nhut air base. Colonel Davis, who is 41 and in his second tour in Vietnam, said: "We've finally arrived at the point where the President said we were going to arrive and on the terms he said we would do it."

As he spoke, commanders of helicopter units throughout South Vietnam crowded into the corridor. They were about to be briefed by a brigadier general on how they were to execute the final plans for departure.

Outside, half a dozen helicopter gunners, all 20 or 21 years old, gathered around the kind of light observation helicopter that they "ride shotgun" in.

"I didn't exactly cry," said Specialist 4 Terry Goodge of Antonito, Colo. "I just don't want to go home. I've got a year and a half left in the Army and I don't want to spend it in the States."

"I've got a decent job here," Specialist Goodge continued, "and you can have a good time here. The money's good; I get flight pay and combat pay."

A major who commands a support unit of about 500 men in Saigon said he thought that 90 per cent of his soldiers were sorry they had to go home.

"I really hate to leave myself," said the officer, who is on his third tour. "We have good working conditions. We have a set mission to do and we feel like we have a purpose in life, so everyone's fairly happy."

A pilot listing the advantages of life in Saigon, began: "Cheap women, cheap booze, cheap food—where else can you get a big ole' red lobster for $2?" An Air Force mechanic added: "An enlisted man doesn't have to pay taxes and we get free stamps, too. You just write on the envelope 'Free' and away it goes."

One Gunner Very Mad

Sgt. Ronald Heiselman of Rockland, Me., another of the gunners, said on his first tour here he initially felt it had been a good idea for Americans to help in Vietnam. "But you'd try to help these people and they'd just steal from you and try to get money out of you any way they could," he said. When he heard the news today, Sergeant Heiselman said he was "kind of mad." "I've got so recently that I want to go out there and get rid of them all."

"They're no different," Sergeant Heiselman continued in a smoldering fury. "I hate the Vietnamese on both sides. But I've still got to give credit to the North Vietnamese Army At least they're fighting."

Chief Warrant Officer 2 John Schillereff of Seattle, who is known as Onion, and Chief Warrant Officer 2 Robert Woutes Monette, who are both in their second tours and fly as a team in a Cobra helicopter gunship, said they were waiting for the weather to clear over War Zone C northwest of Saigon so they could go out on a patrol when they heard the news.

"I looked at Onion and he looked at me," Mr. Monette said, "and I had goose pimples and he had goose pimples."

Mr. Monette said the American infantry advisers at Tay Ninh brought a couple of bottles of cold duck and some paper cups out to the helicopters parked on a little airstrip near their' headquarters, and everybody drank a toast to the end of the war. Nobody seemed to talk much.

There were half a dozen American infantrymen with the South Vietnamese ranger platoon when it returned to Bien Hoa this afternoon. Most of them seemed to agree that the United States had done the right thing in sending troops to South Vietnam; some of them said this was the wrong time to quit.

Specialist Bilton, the radio operator who doubted whether there would actually be a cease-fire that would permit Americans to go home, said he thought the United States should never have gotten involved.

"But I'm glad I was here for this experience," he said. "It's something I can tell my daughter I did."

What would he tell her?

"Well, I wasn't really in the war," he said sheepishly. "We didn't do any real fighting. I was just there. That's all I'm going to say."

* * *

January 26, 1973

VIETNAM AFTERMATH

It's over. Or at least it is supposed to be tomorrow; completion and announcement of agreement between the United States and North Vietnam did not deter final, senseless acts of combat just before the cease-fire is to take effect.

The very notion of an end to the Vietnam war is hard to comprehend in the abstract, so accustomed have we all become to the outpouring of spirit, wealth and manhood which the decade past has demanded of us.

This Republic has learned much about itself, about its leaders, about the world and the meaning of power from the ordeal it suffered in mountains and rice paddies half-way around the globe. Not all the lessons are comforting—in fact few of them are.

If Vietnam is to have any meaning at all, these lessons must be defined and absorbed by a coming generation just as the problems of the war dominated the sensitivities of the generation now maturing. "No More Vietnams" has already become a sort of national battle cry. It is now the country's great task to ensure that this expression of hope will be turned into reality.

Vietnam spanned the era of American foreign policy after World War II, from the epoch when the prime objective was "containment" of international Communism, to the present day when co-existence with Communism is seen as possible, necessary and desirable—for mutual benefit and survival. The Communist world, too, has evolved. The United States might not have gone into Vietnam had the depth of schism between the Soviet Union and China been clearly perceived; it could not have come out safely if this schism had not become the dominant reality to both Moscow and Peking. Some will argue that America's firmness in Vietnam has hastened the growth of a less overtly menacing form of national Communism; it certainly did not retard this evolution, as pessimistic Americans feared it would.

When President Kennedy led the nation into what became an open-ended military commitment to a struggling small state, the United States Government was confident in its own power, and skill, and it enjoyed the confidence of the American people. As President Nixon succeeds finally in extracting the nation, poorer and wiser, from the commitment, confidence is not a sentiment in surplus across the land.

Americans today have learned to distrust the notion of a war to end wars. Yet it is possible to retain a certain faith. It may not be empty rhetoric to believe that the scars of Vietnam can bring new strength as they heal, strength gathered in a clearer definition of the priorities for the use of national power. Strength can come from a more precise evaluation of the possibilities and limitations inherent in that power. And strength can spring from understanding, from tolerance and from humility.

* * *

January 26, 1973

VOICES OF CONSCIENCE

Throughout the long years of America's ill-fated involvement in the war in Indochina, the peace symbol remained a persistent expression of determination and hope. As time went on and the yearning for an end to the bloodshed grew in intensity, that symbol's message became emblazoned in the minds and hearts of millions. It formed a nonpartisan bond for many, who agreed on little else.

Now that the official protocols at last give hope that the killing and suffering may indeed come to an end, it would be an ungrateful act of instant historical revisionism to fail to note the contribution of the peace movement. That movement gave expression to a facet of the American character which ought not be forgotten at the very moment when its prayers appear—at least temporarily—to have been answered and its goals approached. Few nations have managed in time of war to keep the voices of peace so compellingly raised. Few nations would, under similar circumstances, have allowed those voices to be so clearly heard.

Occasionally there were excesses and abuses. The sign of peace, like any symbol, was at times defiled by small bands of those who tried to exploit the protest and the anguish for their own less honorable purposes and politics. But for the most part the movement remained simply, the conscience of a coalition: young and old, religious leaders and veteran politicians, idealists and pragmatists worked and marched under its banner.

It in no way belittles the tough efforts of the skillful negotiators who eventually hammered out the agreements to give recognition now to those who doggedly kept pointing and pushing toward peace. Many—particularly the young—never faltered in their conviction that peace was too serious a matter to be left to Government. Their faith would be ill served if those often unpopular but never despairing efforts were now to be allowed to fade unrecognized from memory.

* * *

January 27, 1973

FOR THE VIETNAMESE, NO CESSATION OF PAIN

By MALCOLM W. BROWNE

Special to the New York Times

SAIGON, South Vietnam—For most of the people of South Vietnam the end of the war—if it is the end of their war—is coming far too late for rejoicing.

Few Vietnamese can even recall without a few moments' reflection when the war began. Most have spent the largest part of their lives at war.

For many Vietnamese the three decades of strife have worn away the old passions of nationalism, political hatred, revenge and even sorrow. There remains only a feeling of numb resignation to whatever the future may bring and a

VIETCONG ACTIONS AGAINST CIVILIANS IN SOUTH VIETNAM

(Civilians killed ■ , or abducted ▨ since 1966. Source: U.S Defense Department)

13,000
12,000
11,000
10,000
9,000
8,000
7,000
6,000
5,000
4,000
3,000
2,000
1,000
0

1966 1967 1968 1969 1970 1971 1972

Totals: 31,463 civilians killed, 49,000 abducted

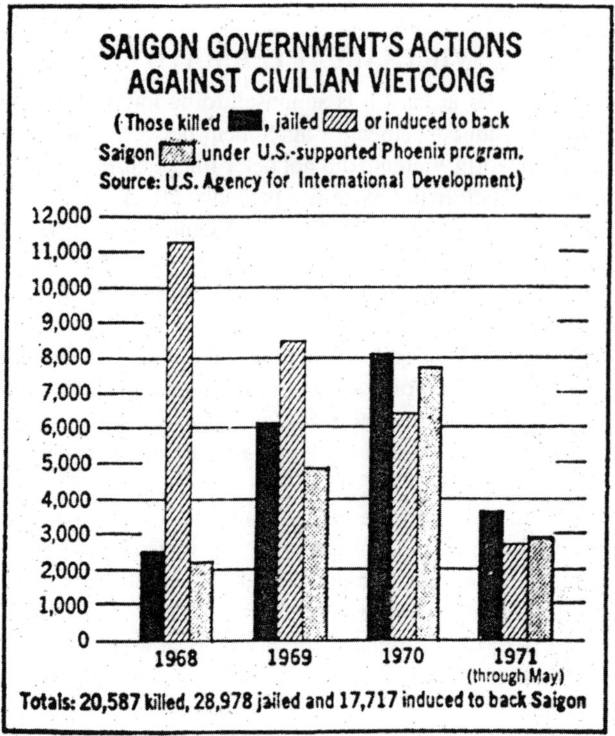

strong urge to escape into the traditional Vietnamese diversions of chess, gambling with cards and drinking baxide, a powerful rice liquor.

With probably around a million Vietnamese killed just in the time since 1959, when war began anew, there is scarcely a family that has not lost at least one member. Many more have been injured or maimed.

Nor will the killing and the maiming cease with the end of hostilities. Despite the passing of a generation, farmers are still killed on Okinawa and other battlegrounds of World War II by old mines and bombs. Vietnam has been seeded with far more of these lethal legacies than any other land.

The main victims of the war have been men, and in many ways South Vietnam now seems to be a nation dominated by hard-minded, lonely and sometimes bitter women for whom idealism and even personal feeling appear to have been largely extinguished.

Two such women, both war widows, are Mrs. T., a 64-year-old former teacher originally from the Mekong Delta province of Kien Hoa, and her 35-year-old daughter-in-law, a slightly built woman named Lang.

Abroad, people receive news reports on the ending of war in Indochina, but neither Mrs. T. nor Lang took any interest in such things. When they are not busy preparing meals on a kerosene stove for the many children living with them, they pass the time in silence, gambling with the tiny cards, marked with lacquered Chinese characters that are universally used in Vietnam.

The big occasions of the year, even the normally joyous season of Tet, the lunar New Year, are mostly associated now with rites that must be performed at the cemeteries where their men are buried.

It is the same for most of the other families in the crowded middle-class Saigon neighbor-hood of Tan Dinh, where Mrs. T. lives.

In common with many older Vietnamese, she looks back with warm nostalgia to the days of the French colony before World War II. There were political stirrings in the nineteen-thirties. But they had little impact on the lives of most Vietnamese.

The rigid patterns of traditional family life kept existence for most people unexciting but secure. Vietnam had a wealth of food and has a warm climate, so that in the old days at least it was spared the suffering that has afflicted much of the rest of Asia.

The shock of change, which has been continuing ever since, first hit Mrs. T., along with millions of other Vietnamese, when the Japanese arrived at the beginning of World War II.

"The real surprise," an old Vietnamese said, "was not so much that a foreign army was invading us but that it was systematically locking up the French authorities who many of us had taken for granted would be the masters of Vietnam forever."

In North Vietnam the Japanese occupation is remembered as harsh, although Vietnamese have never forgotten that Japan gave Ho Chi Minh his first chance to govern. In the South the Japanese yoke was comparatively mild. Mrs. T.'s children remember friendly Japanese soldiers, sharing their lunches with them.

Opening Path to Independence

The important thing about the Japanese occupation, in the eyes of many Vietnamese, was that it raised the possibility of throwing off Western colonial rule for good.

While Vietnam—though under the Japanese yoke—was free of French colonial administration for the first time in a century, the Vietminh came into being, with stirring songs of independence, a red flag with a golden star, and, incidentally, Communist ideology. Even Vietnamese officials who had spent their lives working in the French civil service were deeply stirred.

Mrs. T.'s husband was such an official, working as an administrator under a French province chief before the war. Mr. T. chose not to join the Vietminh because his suspicions had been aroused by the overbearing ways of some of the local leaders, but he strongly supported the cause of independence.

A family living in the house next door—a house smaller than that of the T. family—embraced the Vietminh completely. It happened that the head of this family, Mr. N., was an enemy of Mr. T. because of quarrels over property boundaries, an old financial dispute and a certain amount of jealousy.

Such quarrels between neighbors, taken for granted in peaceful nations, have tended to become blood feuds in Vietnam, spurred to violence by civil war.

Underground Once More

After World War II the Vietminh ruled the Mekong Delta until the French finally came back in strength to drive them underground again. Before the French returned, Mr. T.'s hostile neighbor suddenly emerged as a provincial commissar, with the power of life and death.

Among his first acts was to denounce Mr. T. before a session of the provincial people's tribunal as a French stooge and spy. Vietminh soldiers arrested Mr. T., released him some weeks later and then rearrested him. His family never saw him again and has assumed that he was among the thousands of civil servants executed by the Communists.

The family—mother, two daughters and five sons—dedicated itself to the lifelong cause of destroying Communists, although none had a clear idea then of what Communism was supposed to be.

The following years, particularly the early nineteen-fifties, were hard for both the T. family and its enemy, the N. family, which had gone underground.

Mrs. T. had received a modest pension from the French, paid in opium, which at the time was regarded as a much more stable medium of exchange than paper currency. Using the opium, she purchased a few acres of rice land in the delta and sent several of her older children to France, where they subsequently worked their way to college degrees.

A Nation Polarized

Mr. N., for his part, had taken his sons into the underground to join the growing corps of guerrillas dedicated to the destruction of "foreign imperialism."

The war for independence was on, and the nation was becoming polarized, not only by political ideologies but by blood debts and the hatred they engendered. Most Vietnamese accepted the need to gamble their lives on a struggle to throw out the French, whose army was equipped with the latest American weapons.

The first Indochina war probably cost the Vietnamese people a million lives, but it ended in victory in 1954. With peace and the division of Vietnam along the 17th Parallel, the people had to decide whether to cast their futures with the Communist-led North or the anti-Communist South.

In Saigon a new Government came to power under Ngo Dinh Diem, a Roman Catholic, who was installed through United States influence largely because of his strongly anti-Communist convictions.

His Government became predominately Catholic in an overwhelmingly Buddhist country. Because of the new influence of Catholics—an influence that often discriminated against non-Catholics in assigning contracts and jobs—there was a wave of nominal conversions to Catholicism.

The conversions deeply split the T. family. Buddhists charged their Catholic brothers with being mercenary traitors to their faith; to this day the family remains divided.

No such division affected the N. family, which had dedicated itself to the Communist-led apparatus that succeeded the Vietminh in South Vietnam. Mr. N., head of the family, died of tuberculosis, but he had extracted pledges from his sons and daughters to continue the fight. Among the children too young to participate in the pledge was Lang, who ended up on the other side.

Some North, Some South

Some of the N. family went north, to join the new Hanoi Government. Some remained in the South to join the clandestine organization called Mat Tran Giai Phong, or National Liberation Front. Later, when the Saigon Government came to realize the gravity of the threat posed by the front, it devised the supposedly insulting sobriquet Vietcong to describe it.

Under the 1954 Geneva accords ending the Indochina war—both the United States and the Diem Government refused to sign them—Vietnam was to be unified and to hold general elections within two years. After President Diem refused to participate in such elections, the second Indochina war began.

Among the first moves by the Vietcong was to carry out a sweeping land-reform program in the Mekong Delta, effectively blocking the half-hearted reform attempted later by the Diem Government. The land seized by National Liberation Front guerrillas included Mrs. T.'s plot, which she has never been able to visit since. Despite that, the Saigon Government continued collecting land taxes from her on pain of criminal prosecution.

Initially the war involved political underground work on the part of the Vietcong. Members of the T. family were constantly being stopped at roadblocks and asked to listen to lectures or to give small donations.

In the villages, the Vietcong sometimes employed terror but generally sought to ingratiate themselves by being helpful with farming chores, health and education. The guerrillas sometimes sought to protect villages against the excesses of the Saigon Government's militia, which often acted like simple bandits.

Meanwhile, the war began to become more noticeable as military cemeteries filled and terrorists' bombs exploded not only in the provincial towns but also in Saigon.

Great Flood of Americans

Then the Americans began coming, almost imperceptibly at first but later in a great flood. With them came post exchanges, the black market, television (for the Vietnamese as well as the foreigners), hundreds of thousands of jobs, more money than anyone had known existed and the demon of rising expectations.

For the most dedicated nationalists, non-Communist as well as Communist, things began to look too much like colonial times. In the cities Vietnamese could no longer persuade taxi drivers to stop since the Americans were able to pay more. There were too many "big nose" soldiers walking around with too many Vietnamese girls.

Most South Vietnamese accepted the American presence, although few of them really liked it.

In 1963 the whole nation passed through the worst crisis since independence, when the non-Communist opposition to Mr. Diem's increasingly repressive Government suddenly coalesced behind the leadership of a group of Buddhist monks, several of whom had committed suicide by immolating themselves.

In many parts of the country the Vietcong were achieving smashing victories, and it seemed that the country was dissolving. In the midst of it all, a group of generals led by Duong Van Minh united to stage a coup d'état, overthrowing and murdering Mr. Diem and his brother and close adviser, Ngo Dinh Nhu.

The unstable mix of religion and politics was in turmoil again, splitting Mrs. T.'s family into Catholic and Buddhist factions.

But the heaviest blow to Mrs. T. that year was the announcement from her favorite son that he intended to marry his childhood neighbor Lang—daughter of the man who had ordered his father's death.

Spectacular Attacks Staged

By Tet in February of 1965 it seemed apparent that the Vietcong would win in a matter of weeks. A spectacular series of Communist attacks on Feb. 7 prompted the first landing of American combat troops and the first sustained bombing campaign against North Vietnam.

The American presence rose to more than half a million men over the next four years, and North and South Vietnam were carpeted by the heaviest rain of bombs the world had ever seen.

As the Vietnamese were mobilized, all of Mrs. T.'s sons were finally drafted, most as officers because they held college degrees. The loss of the civilian jobs they had held, coupled with growing families, imposed desperately heavy financial strains on all of them.

For the first time in their recent history the Vietnamese were no longer growing enough rice to feed themselves and were dependent on American charity. The price of everything, including rice, rose rapidly while soldier pay remained small.

On the other side of the war, the late Mr. N.'s family was fighting hard. His sister had lost a leg in an American air raid, but as late as July, 1972, she was still believed to be leading a Vietcong district combat unit in action in the delta. Some of Mr. N.'s sons were also active in the Vietcong, one serving as a field doctor.

The new soldier-husband of their sister Lang was assigned by the Saigon Government in 1966 to fight in exactly that part of the Mekong Delta where his brothers-in-law were on the other side. He was killed a few weeks after Tet.

The conflict wore on President Nixon changed the U.S. stance and the Americans began to leave in large numbers. They will be remembered, among other things, for the window they provided on the world. The military forces and civilian contractors built tens of thousands of miles of roads and made it possible for many Vietnamese to see their country for the first time—at least for a while.

American and Vietnamese economists decided in the late nineteen-sixties that there was too much money floating around in the superheated war-time economy. To soak some of it up Saigon agreed to relax the import duty on motorcycles. The result was a flood of Japanese-built vehicles that have changed the social structure.

Even the peasant families of poor soldiers could often afford the new Hondas and Yamahas, and a family too poor to afford one was subjected to a certain amount of snobbery and even derision.

Those who could not afford them took to stealing them. The police attached little serious interest to the resulting crime wave, devoting most of their energies to political arrests.

The Impact of Television

Another aspect of the American impact was television, at first broadcast from airplanes that circled major cities for hours at a time. It has also given the Vietnamese a broader view of the world, in addition to strong social pressure to own television sets.

"Our Vietnamese women are among the greatest materialists in the world," a Saigon sociologist said. "Vietnam has always had a semimatriarchal society, and now, with so many men dead or economically disabled by being in the army, the women have all the real power, and when a woman demands that her husband get a television set or Honda, he is under the heaviest pressure to do so.

"In my opinion, this is one of the chief reasons for the incredible amount of corruption and theft we have in Vietnam at every level of existence. We are to blame, but you Americans certainly have not helped."

Now the city jobs are drying up, and the easy money has ceased to flow. To go on living the South Vietnamese will have to return to the rice fields. There is general agreement it will be a traumatic experience.

As for the Communists, their approach in communities occupied since their spring offensive has been to confiscate most of the new American gadgets, especially the motorcycles.

In the course of the long war, and particularly since 1965, the population has been turned upside down. Since April alone there have been roughly a million refugees. Entire provinces, Quang Tri among them, have been stripped of population.

Cities at Bursting Point

Cities have grown to the bursting point with refugees or people interested in making more money than they could as farmers. The population of Saigon, never exactly known, probably doubled to about three million.

Centuries of family tradition, often associated with the graveyards of ancestors, have been shattered. At least one of the mountain tribes of the central plateau has ceased to exist as a distinct ethnic group. The Government moved its people hundreds of miles from their homes and forced them to conform to the tribal patterns of another, larger group speaking a different language.

The dislocation of life will have such staggering effects that some political experts believe only the Communists will be able to impose order harshly enough to rebuild the nation.

Mrs. T.'s family, in common with most South Vietnamese, will stay, come what may.

"At this stage the Communists cannot hurt us," she said. "We are just small people. Besides, where else could we go?"

Mrs. T. and Lang picked up their cards. Neither has any political views about anything any more, and the blood feud between their families is no longer important. Life must go on.

* * *

January 28, 1973

VIETNAM PEACE PACTS SIGNED; AMERICA'S LONGEST WAR HALTS

CEREMONIES COOL

Two Sessions in Paris Formally Conclude the Agreement

By FLORA LEWIS
Special to The New York Times

PARIS, Jan. 27—The Vietnam cease-fire agreement was signed here today in eerie silence, without a word or a gesture to express the world's relief that the years of war were officially ending.

The accord was effective at 7 P.M. Eastern standard time.

Secretary of State William P. Rogers wrote his name 62 times on the documents providing—after 12 years—a settlement of the longest, most divisive foreign war in America's history.

The official title of the text was "Agreement on Ending the War and Restoring Peace in Vietnam." But the cold, almost gloomy atmosphere at two separate signing ceremonies reflected the uncertainties of whether peace is now assured.

The conflict, which has raged in one way or another for over a quarter of a century, had been inconclusive, without clear victory or defeat for either side.

Involvement Gradually Grew

After a gradually increasing involvement that began even before France left Indochina in 1954, the United States entered into a full-scale combat role in 1965. The United States considers Jan. 1, 1961, as the war's starting date and casualties are counted from then.

By 1968, when the build-up was stopped and then reversed, there were 529,000 Americans fighting in Vietnam. United States dead passed 45,000 by the end of the war.

The peace agreements were as ambiguous as the conflict, which many of America's friends first saw as generous aid to a weak and threatened ally, but which many came to consider an exercise of brute power against a tiny nation.

Built on Compromises

The peace agreements signed today were built of compromises that permit the two Vietnamese sides to give them contradictory meanings and, they clearly hope, to continue their unfinished struggle in the political arena without continuing the slaughter.

The signing took place in two ceremonies. In the morning, the participants were the United States, North Vietnam, South Vietnam and the Vietcong. Because the Saigon Government does not wish to imply recognition of the Vietcong's Provisional Revolutionary Government, all references to that government were confined to a second set of documents. That set was signed in the afternoon, and by only the United States and North Vietnam.

At the last moment, it was found that two copies in English of the texts, which were to have been signed by Mr. Rogers and North Vietnam's Foreign Minister, Nguyen Duy Trinh, in the afternoon ceremony, were missing.

The plan had been to give a signed copy in each language to each of the four delegations. The United States prepared the English documents and had given the two copies to the South Vietnamese to inspect. They were not returned, leaving a total of six instead of eight sets of documents to be signed by the United States and North Vietnam.

These texts began by saying that North Vietnam "with the concurrence of the Provisional Revolutionary Government of the Republic of South Vietnam" and the United States "with the concurrence of the Government of the Republic of Vietnam" had reached agreement.

South Vietnam's foreign minister, Tran Van Lam, indicated that he did not want to accept signed copies of this text, because Saigon objects to mention of the revolutionary government by that name.

Asked whether the South Vietnamese action might weaken or undermine the degree of Saigon's "concurrence," American officials said, "No, no. They have concurred."

Each of the other delegations wound up with four sets of signed agreements. Saigon took only two, the English

In the morning ceremony at the Hotel Majestic in Paris were, from the left, the Vietcong, North Vietnamese, South Vietnamese, and U.S. delegations.

and Vietnamese versions mentioning only "parties" to the conference.

In the morning ceremony, all four parties signed identical agreements, except for one protocol, or annexed document, in which the United States agreed to remove the mines it had planted in the waters of North Vietnam.

The preamble on the four-party documents mentioned no government by name and referred only to the "parties participating in the Paris conference on Vietnam."

That was the formula that had broken the final deadlock.

Almost immediately after the morning session involving four foreign ministers, military delegations of the Vietcong and the North Vietnamese flew off on their way to Saigon.

They, with American and South Vietnamese officers, will form a joint military commission that is to carry out the cease-fire. Their departure for the South Vietnamese capital gave a touch of reality to the strangely emotionless way in which the rite of peace was performed in Paris.

After the morning ceremony, which lasted 18 minutes, the four foreign ministers, their aides and guests filed wordlessly through separate doors into a curtained foyer.

Toast 'Peace and Friendship'

There, participants said, they clinked champagne glasses, toasted "peace and friendship" and shook hands all around. But such amiability was concealed from observers and above all from the cameras that might have recorded a scene of the Vietnamese enemies in social contact.

A similar 15 minutes of cordiality followed the 11-minute afternoon ceremony, attended only by the American and North Vietnamese delegations.

The agreement was signed at the gigantic round table, covered with a prairie of green baize, where the four parties to the Paris conference have been speechifying at each other, and often vilifying each other, almost weekly for four years.

The great ballroom of the former Hotel Majestic, where the table stands, is crammed with crystal and gilt chandeliers, lush tapestries and ornate gilt moldings. But the scene was as glum as the drizzly, gray Paris sky outside. The men all wore dark suits.

The touches of human color were few. Mrs. Nguyen Thi Binh, Foreign Minister of the Vietcong Provisional Revolutionary Government, wore an amber ao dai with embroidery on the bodice, an unusual ornament for her.

Mrs. Rogers wore a dress with a red top and navy skirt. In the afternoon, when there were only two delegations and thus more room for guests, all the American secretaries who had been involved were brought in and they brightened the room.

Colored-Leather Bindings

The texts of the agreements were bound in different colored leather—red for the North Vietnamese, blue for the United States, brown for South Vietnam and green for the Vietcong. French ushers solemnly passed them around on each signature. Mrs. Binh overlooked one place to sign and had to be given an album back for completion.

Mr. Rogers and Mr. Trinh used a large number of the black pens and then handed them to delegation members as souvenirs. William J. Porter, the new Deputy Under Secretary of State who had been the United States delegate to the semi-public talks until this month, flew to Paris with Mr. Rogers and sat at the table with him.

Heywood Isham, acting head of the United States delegation, Marshall Green, Assistant Secretary of State for East Asian and Pacific Affairs, and William H. Sullivan, Mr. Green's deputy, who has been leading technical talks with the North Vietnamese here, completed the American group at the table.

Two rectangular tables, carefully placed alongside the main table to symbolize the separation of the four delegations into two warring sides at the start of the conference in 1969, were reserved for the ambassadors of Canada, Hungary, Indonesia and Poland.

Their countries are contributing troops to an international commission that is to supervise the cease-fire.

Mr. Rogers and his Washington-based aides flew home immediately after the ceremony. Unexpectedly, Mr. Lam went with them.

Mr. Sullivan remained in Paris to receive the list of American prisoners from Hanoi and to hold further technical meetings on the many unsettled details of how arrangements are to be carried out.

At the airport before leaving, Mr. Rogers made his only comments on the event so long awaited with spurts of hope and bitter despair.

"It's a great day," he said.

He said President Nixon had devoted himself to building a structure of peace and continued: "The events in Paris today are a milestone in achieving that peace."

"I hope there'll be a cease-fire soon in all of Indochina," he added.

* * *

February 13, 1973

FIRST PRISONER RELEASE COMPLETED

142 Men Seem In Reasonably Good Health

By JAMES P. STERBA
Special to The New York Times

CLARK AIR BASE, the Philippines, Tuesday, Feb. 13—The first released American prisoners of the Vietnam war were greeted with cheers of welcome and tears of joy here yesterday as they stepped off military evacuation jets. They looked in better physical condition than most onlookers had expected, and the hospital commander here pronounced their general health "reasonably good."

The last of four evacuation planes touched down here at 11 P.M. (10 A.M. Monday, New York time), carrying 19 military men and seven civilians released in South Vietnam. Three other planes, carrying 116 prisoners released in Hanoi, had arrived yesterday afternoon.

The first prisoner to step onto the red carpet was Capt. Jeremiah A. Denton of the Navy, the ranking officer aboard the first plane back from Hanoi. Captain Denton, in captivity for nearly eight years, stepped to a microphone and said:

"We are honored to have the opportunity to serve our country under difficult circumstances. We are profoundly grateful to our Commander in Chief and to our nation for this day. God bless America!"

Alvarez Arrives

He was followed by Lieut. Comdr. Everett Alvarez Jr. of the Navy, a prisoner for more than eight years and the first American pilot shot down and captured in the Vietnam war.

By 11:45 P.M. all the men were in the Air Force hospital here. The earlier arrivals from Hanoi held reunions with one another in the wards and were allowed to choose their own rooms. After preliminary medical checks—which found their conditions "reasonably good," in the words of the hospital commander, Col. John W. Ord—the men were offered steak, chicken, baked potatoes, french fries, corn on the cob, cream puffs and strawberry short-cake.

Maj. Miriam W. Fortune, the hospital's head dietitian, said steak, eggs and ice cream were the most popular items.

"Many ate ice cream in the line before they got their main dishes," she said.

Because of their late arrival time, the prisoners from South Vietnam—whose release was delayed because of a dispute over an exchange of Communist prisoners—were fed a light meal before going to bed, military spokesmen said.

Many of the arrivals from Hanoi telephoned their families in the United States and met military escort officers assigned to accompany them back to Travis Air Force Base. Calif., after medical examinations and debriefings here.

From Travis, the men will fly to local military hospitals to meet their families.

[Some of the prisoners could be returning to the United States "in a matter of days," according to a Reuters dispatch from Washington that quoted the Pentagon spokesman, Jerry W. Friedheim. Reuters said that while Mr. Friedheim would not be more specific about the timing of the flights home, he did say that many of the men were well enough to leave now.]

Yesterday's arrivals here completed the first phase of the prisoner repatriation. Similar numbers of prisoners are to be released by the Communists at intervals of about 15 days. in proportion to the American withdrawal of troops from South Vietnam. The protocol on prisoners in the Paris agreement of

Jan. 27 said that all prisoners of war must be released within 60 days.

Only four of the released prisoners—three from the North and one from the South—had to be carried off the planes in litters. The rest walked out, down a ramp, and over a red carpet to waiting ambulance buses. For a few it was difficult, and the expressions of determination to do it by themselves brought tears to the eyes of many of the military officers and newsmen.

Some of the prisoners stepped briskly out of the planes, smiling and pointing their thumbs up.

Chants of "Welcome Home!" by spectators from the base greeted the prisoners as they stepped from their planes. More than 1,000 base residents—boys in baseball and Boy Scout uniforms, women sitting on lawn chairs, babies, airmen with movie cameras—looked on.

Many people wept. John Ward, a 13-year-old sixth grader, said, "I was crying and they were real tears. I just felt very emotional." He was wearing a prisoner-of-war bracelet bearing the name of Leonard C. Eastman, a Navy commander who arrived on the third plane from Hanoi.

The first plane from Hanoi carried 40 repatriated prisoners, 29 of whom the North Vietnamese had listed as sick or wounded. Some of their ailments were obvious as they walked off—stiff legs, shriveled arms, joints that did not work. One man came out on crutches he has been using for more than five years.

There was also an evident lack of muscle coordination for some. There was little color in most of their faces.

Spirits, however, were extremely high. A public affairs officer accompanied each plane from Hanoi and later described some of what went on during the flights.

"After we got onto the airplane and closed the doors, there was hugging of each other and hugging of nurses and a tremendous elation on their faces," said Richard Abel, an Air Force lieutenant colonel who accompanied the first plane back from Hanoi.

"Tears in some eyes, yes, but they were certainly tears of happiness," Colonel Abel said "Their spirits were just fantastic. They were alive, they were happy to be home, they talked and talked and talked some more."

He said the men were glad to get American cigarettes, that they avidly read Stars and Stripes, the military newspaper, and news magazines, and that they liked the rather tasteless nutrient drink they were served because it was cold.

There were prayers, Colonel Abel said, adding that one of the senior men on board told him, "You know, Dick, I couldn't have made it if it wasn't for Jesus Christ, and being able to look up and see Him in some of the trying times."

Colonel Abel said he asked Captain Denton, as senior man on board, to make a brief statement on landing at Clark but that he did not brief the captain on what to say.

Each of the three senior officers made statements when they arrived here from Hanoi.

Col. Robinson Risner of the Air Force, senior prisoner on the second plane, said: "It's almost too wonderful to express. On behalf of all the other men who have been prisoners. I would like to thank you all. I would like to thank our President and the American people for bringing us home to freedom again. Thank you ever so much."

And Capt. James A. Mulligan of the Navy, senior officer and spokesman on the third plane from Hanoi, said, "It has been our privilege to serve you Americans these many years and during this time our faith in our God, our country and in our families has never wavered. Today I'd like to thank the President of the United States and our families for maintaining their faith with us and making this wonderful day possible. Thank you."

Maj. Raymond C. Schrump of the Army, the first man off the final plane, from Saigon, said simply, "It has been a long time. I want to thank each and every one of you for such a very, very fine welcome."

While the prisoners released from South Vietnam wore Vietnamese sandals and hospital garb issued during the flight, those returning from Hanoi wore clothes that they had received from the North Vietnamese shortly before they were released—blue trousers, light blue shirts, brown belts, black shoes, and light gray-green jackets. The North Vietnamese had also given each man a black flight bag.

All but the three litter patients released by Hanoi today lived in the Hoa Lo prison camp. Officials did not say where it was, other than near Hanoi.

Describing the departure of the second plane to leave Hanoi, Lieut. Comdr. Milton S. Baker said of the men he accompanied, "They were rather solemn as they were escorted up to the aircraft. Once inside the aircraft they really became elated. The reaction on take-off—shouts, cheers, thumbs up, that sort of thing, elation generally."

Commander Baker said medical treatment on the flight was limited to two aspirins and some nosedrops. The men drank coffee, tea and the nutrient drink, smoked, read, and asked dozens of questions on subjects ranging from sports to women's liberation.

The first thing the prisoners who boarded the third plane noticed was the perfume of the flight nurses, according to a military spokesman who was on the plane.

"Wow, smell that perfume!" he quoted one of them as having said. There was also a contraband copy of Playboy magazine aboard that was thumbed through avidly, although some prisoners were said to have been taken aback by photos of totally nude women. Most of the men have been in prison since the days when the nudity was less than total.

Frank A. Sieverts, the State Department's specialist on prisoner-of-war affairs, went into Hanoi along with the advance team this morning. He said several of the prisoners asked him who had won the war. He said his answer was: "The South did not lose and the North did not win."

Roger E. Shields, the Pentagon's prisoner-of-war expert, who also went to Hanoi for the pick-up, said he was satisfied with today's operation even though it was delayed two hours by bad weather in the North and more than 12 hours by disputes in the South. He said the prisoners from Hanoi

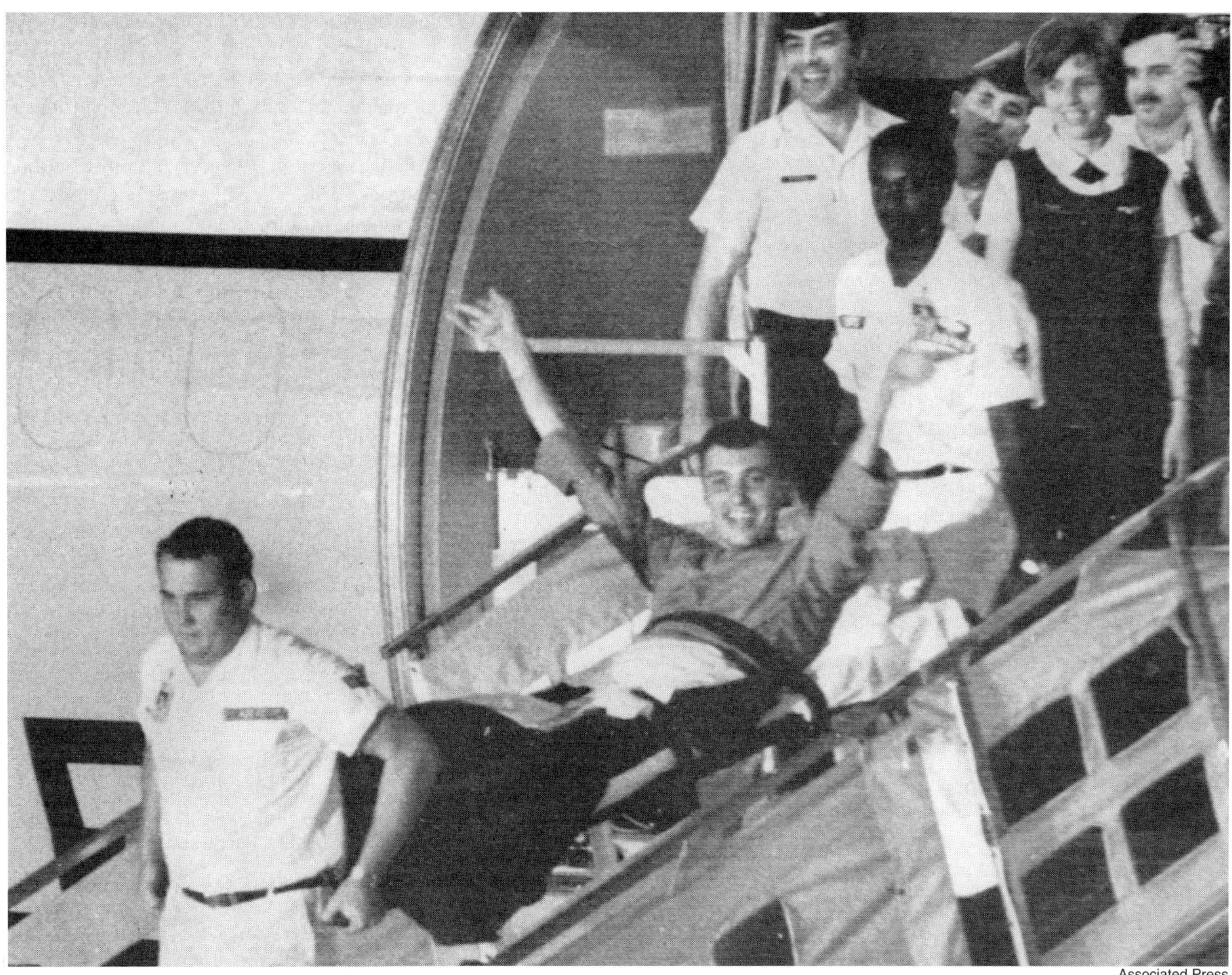

Associated Press

Air Force Capt. David E. Baker of Huntington, L.I., being carried on a stretcher from the jet plane that took him from Saigon to Clark Air Base. He was released at Loc Ninh.

"said they have some things they want to tell us and they are very concerned about giving us information on other prisoners on our lists." Some 1,300 Americans are listed as missing in action.

On the first flight to the Clark base. Captain Denton said, he told the men that on arrival he intended to salute the flag and fellow officers and to shake hands with military dignitaries there to greet them—Adm. Noel A. M. Gayler, Commander in Chief of United States forces in the Pacific, and Lieut. Gen. William G. Moore Jr., commander of the 13th Air Force. He said that he did not tell the men they also had to do so, but that each did.

When the planeload of 27 prisoners from South Vietnam landed late tonight, completing the pick-up, Col. Leonard W. Johnson Jr., commander of the evacuation mission into Saigon, turned to Roger Shields of the Pentagon and said, "Well, we got them back."

* * *

February 18, 1973

'THE MOVEMENT,' WITH THE WAR EBBING, PONDERS ITS ROLE IN A NATION AT PEACE

By ANTHONY RIPLEY

Special to The New York Times

WASHINGTON, Feb. 17—With the war officially over in South Vietnam, many of the leaders of a decade of protest in the United States are trying to define a place for themselves and their followers in a nation at peace.

There is among them a search for new issues and a determination to revive old ones, but above all there is a deeply felt need to maintain the sense of urgency that brought hundreds of thousands of Americans into the streets in demonstrations.

Few in "The Movement," as the nation's militant groups of the political left call themselves, predict that things will be the same with the central rallying point—the long war—gone.

"It's just going to split in a thousand directions," said David Mixner of Hartford, one of the leaders of the now-disbanded Vietnam Moratorium Committee.

Most are aware and perhaps somewhat proud of the impact their collective passion has had even in the most remote areas of the country, where the peace sign and antiwar folk music have become almost too familiar to notice.

Turn to Other Issues

Many hope the political energies released can be channeled into an attack on poverty, or racism, or "insults" to the environment, or social irresponsibility of corporations, or all of them together.

Some groups, especially those that are pacifist or that predate the Indochina war, see peace as an on-going cause for they believe, as Cora Weiss of the Women's Strike for Peace said, "The war is not over; the causes of war are not eliminated."

Others are simply too busy at the moment to think very far ahead. They feel the situation in Vietnam is fragile at best, and remain profoundly cynical about any total American pullout.

"No one's out of business—not yet," said Michael Segal of the Indochina Peace Campaign group in Boston. "No one's deceived or lulled or expecting too much."

When the Vietnam cease fire accords were signed in Paris, Jerry Gordon, coordinator of the National Peace Action Coalition, issued a statement saying in part, "We don't believe it," and scheduled a Feb. 23 march on the White House to demand, "out now."

But asked after a recent news conference what he might be doing in five years, he replied softly: "I don't know."

And from an independent perspective, many who are sympathetic to the antiwar movement think, nonetheless, it is finished. This view was expressed, in a matter-of-fact tone, by a fallen-away Trotskyite of the nineteen-thirties who asked that his name not be used:

"The peace movement has won so they've lost. They'll be the last to realize they changed the course of United States foreign policy. They'll be disorganized and aimless for a number of years. And precisely because they were right about the war, they're going to be hated."

Whether or not the peace groups become objects of hatred, they have always seemed disorganized. Indeed, it is difficult for their own leaders to be sure they know from week to week just what The Movement consists of or how many people take part in it.

This is because organizations have tended to form for specific purposes and then change as need, political design or argument dictated.

The Spring Mobilization Committee, for example, became the National Mobilization Committee to End the War in Vietnam. That, in turn, became the New Mobilization Committee, which later split into the National Peace Action Coalition and the People's Coalition for Peace and Justice.

Arguments over tactics, slogans, the influence of the Trotskyites, the need for civil disobedience—all caused regrouping. Some organizations, like the Congressional Clearinghouse to End the War and Project Pursestrings, sprang up for a moment and then died away.

Trying to count the membership of these shifting groups is equally difficult.

Mr. Gordon of the National Peace Action Coalition described that group as "a loose coalition of coalitions, the local level and the Student Mobilization Committee."

"We don't have members," he said. "Our strength is reflected in how many we can get out in the streets."

Mr. Mixner and Sam Brown, another of the old Vietnam Moratorium leaders, said that at its height, the organization had a list of 70,000 to 100,000 "key people" scattered throughout the nation.

There have been four major sections in the peace movement, none clearly delineated because of overlapping memberships, but identified by some knowledgeable participants this way:

- PEACE GROUPS. These tend to be on-going pacifist organizations, many of them founded well before the Vietnam war. Included would be the American Friends Service Committee, SANE, Women's Strike for Peace, Clergy and Laity Concerned about Vietnam and the Roman Catholic peace activists like the Rev. Philip Berrigan. For the most part, their members were willing to join any other movement working for peace.
- THE HARD LEFT. This includes the remnants of the old "New Left" movement, the old Students for a Democratic Society, the Socialist Workers Party and other advocates of radical change. Many took a leading role in the mobilization committees and their successors.
- THE POLITICAL LIBERAL LEFT. This includes the young people of the "dump Johnson" movement, supporters of the Presidential complaints of Eugene McCarthy and George McGovern and leaders of the Vietnam Moratorium.
- MIDDLE OF THE ROAD. This includes all those people who generally supported peace and reform in government and who took part in many demonstrations, but who never joined any group.

'Dark Night of the Soul'

David Dellinger, a pacifist since World War II and a leader of many demonstrations, expects the postwar period to be a time of national introspection.

"Nixon has done a lot of talking about peace with honor," Mr. Dellinger said. "There can't be any peace with honor until we face up to the fact that the war was without honor.

"Just as Germany was deNazified after World War II, we've got to become de-Nixified—or whatever—perhaps that's not the right way to put it because it involves the whole bipartisan structure of American policy.

"We'll have to go through some dark night of the soul to find what human values made it possible for that war to go on."

Sanford Gottleib of SANE, the Rev. Richard G. Fernandez of Clergy and Laity Concerned, and Lyle Tatum of the American Friends Service Committee all said that their organizations had been strengthened during the war and would continue to have much work to do.

Many of the hard left groups are concentrating on the problems with the truce.

In Boston, Dr. Sidney Peck, of the People's Coalition, along with Tom Hayden and his wife, Jane Fonda, held a news conference to announce the plans.

The plans included pressure to cut off American aid to the Government of South Vietnam's President Nguyen Van Thieu; pressure for private and Congressional inquiries into detention of political prisoners in the South; the setting up of watchdog committees to make sure the truce terms are followed, and support for the rebuilding of Bach Mai hospital in Hanoi, which was struck during the heavy December bombing raids.

Fred Branfman, formerly with the hard-left Project Air War and now codirector of the Indochina Resource Center in Washington, said he thought the "solid core" of the peace movement would concentrate on "the probability of continuing war."

He said they would look for signs of covert military and political warfare backed by the United States.

Mr. Branfman was particularly disturbed over recent Pentagon announcements that the search for men missing in action might go on for years. Such a search, he said, could serve as a cover for military operations.

He said that it would be very hard to predict the future of the peace movement until it was known whether the Thieu Government or the Vietcong government dominates in South Vietnam.

On the political liberal left, Mr. Brown, of the old Moratorium Committee, is now a writer in Denver. He worked on the campaign that kept the winter Olympic games out of Colorado.

Even before the truce, he said, many in the demonstration organizations were drifting away, entering politics on a local level in college towns like Berkeley, Calif., Boulder, Colo., and Ann Arbor, Mich.

"An end to the war leaves a vacuum in the lives of those who built a career out of the war," Mr. Brown said.

"Many," he said, "find themselves almost stunned with "a lot of the guideposts gone."

"Many of the young grew up in a nation that seemed constantly at war," he said.

"The war was the great unifying factor on the left," he said. "People will now step back and rethink things."

The demonstration during President Nixon's inauguration was much larger than even the planners had expected and it gave heart to many in the movement that the old militancy, the old sense of urgency, still prevailed.

Mr. Mixner saw it as a bit of "memorabilia—the last of the biggies," and said, sadly that it was the only one he missed.

Mr. Gottlieb, of SANE, says the young come in "like gang-busters and then they are gone," turning back to private personal concerns.

"I hope it's temporary but they lack staying power," he said. "That's what's needed. You can't expect the Pentagon to give up after one battle."

* * *

March 29, 1973

RICHARDSON SEES CLEAR AUTHORITY TO BOMB CAMBODIA

Says Nixon's Constitutional Right Is Not Linked to G.I. Presence in Vietnam

CRITICISM ON INCREASE

Senators Mansfield, Javits and Fulbright Question Legality of the Raids

By JOHN W. FINNEY
Special to The New York Times

WASHINGTON, March 28—Secretary of Defense Elliot L. Richardson maintained today that the President had clear constitutional authority to continue bombing in Cambodia to clean up a "lingering corner of the war."

Speaking to newsmen as criticism of the bombing increased on Capitol Hill, Mr. Richardson did not specify what the constitutional authority for continuing the bombing was, but he declared that it was not dependent upon the presence of American forces in Vietnam.

In the past the Administration has cited the President's inherent powers as Commander in Chief to protect those troops.

Final Pullout Today

Taking direct issue with Mr. Richardson's statements, Mike Mansfield, the Senate Democratic leader, said to newsmen that President Nixon would have no constitutional authority to order bombing raids in Cambodia once all American combat forces were withdrawn from South Vietnam. The withdrawals are scheduled to be completed tomorrow.

Senator Jacob K. Javits, Republican of New York, was drafting a Senate speech that he expects to deliver tomorrow questioning the propriety and legality of the continued bombing. Senator J. W. Fulbright, chairman of the Foreign Relations Committee, was preparing a letter to Secretary of State William P. Rogers demanding an explanation of the authority for the bombing.

White Paper Is Due

Meanwhile State Department officials reported that the Administration was drafting a white paper giving its position in what is developing into another confrontation between the executive branch and Congress over the President's war-making powers. The white paper may be issued tomorrow.

The White House stated yesterday that the bombing in Cambodia would continue until the Communist forces there agreed to a cease-fire.

Mr. Richardson, who made his comments before appearing before the Senate Armed Services Committee, said that the "main point" to be made on the President's constitutional authority "is simply that a cease-fire has not been achieved in Cambodia."

"So what we are doing in Cambodia is continuing to support our ally there against the continuing efforts to disrupt communications, to isolate Phnom Penh," he continued. "We are engaging in air strikes only at the request of the Cambodian Government."

Mr. Richardson's use of the word "ally" to describe the Cambodian Government seemed to go significantly further than past policy statements of the Administration, including some made by Mr. Richardson when he was Under Secretary of State in 1970 during the incursion of American forces into Cambodia.

Following a policy laid down by Prince Norodom Sihanouk, who was deposed as Cambodia's chief of state in 1970, the present Government of President Lon Nol has explicitly removed Cambodia from the protection of the 1954 treaty by which the United States and other countries established the South East Asian Treaty Organization. This action seemed to be recognized earlier by Mr. Richardson, who as Acting Secretary of State wrote the Senate Foreign Relations Committee on May 30, 1970, that "the SEATO treaty has no application to the current situation in Cambodia."

At the time of the Cambodian incursion, President Nixon and other Administration officials repeatedly emphasized that the purpose of the operation was not to help defend the Government of Cambodia but rather to help defend American and South Vietnamese troops in South Vietnam against North Vietnamese attacks staged out of Cambodia.

When the American troops were withdrawn from Cambodia in June, 1970, President Nixon said: "The only remaining American activity in Cambodia after July 1 will be air missions to interdict the movement of enemy troops and materials where I find this necessary to protect the lives and security of our forces in South Vietnam."

In his remarks to newsmen today, Mr. Richardson acknowledged that "protection of American troops was a primary function of a great many of the air activities engaged in Indochina." But he went on to argue:

"What we have now is a situation in which there is a kind of lingering corner of the war still under way, and so the United States is simply continuing to give the kind of support there that we were giving up to the point where a Vietnam cease-fire was negotiated."

Testifying today before a House Foreign Affairs subcommittee, Marshall Green, Assistant Secretary of State for East Asian and Pacific Affairs, suggested that the bombing had a political purpose of exerting pressure on North Vietnam to accept a cease-fire in Cambodia. While declining to go into the question of constitutional authority, Mr. Green offered the following explanation of the bombing:

Clenched Fist, Open Hand

"It is related to our desire to see a cease-fire brought about in Cambodia. Our experience in these very difficult negotiations shows that it takes a combination of a clenched fist with one hand and an open hand with the other to bring about negotiations with these characters in Hanoi."

At the same time Mr. Green acknowledged that the Lon Nol Government had a problem of finding a party on the other side with which to negotiate a cease-fire. The Cambodian insurgent forces, he noted, are divided into three principal factions—forces trained in North Vietnam, the Khmer Rouge and a third group with "a China orientation."

Senator Mansfield said in an interview that the United States was getting itself into a position of "keeping in power a regime in Cambodia that does not have the confidence of the people, and doing it with the power of B-52 bombers."

"If we are not careful," he said, "we have got the makings of another Vietnam."

* * *

March 30, 1973

FORMER P.O.W.'S CHARGE TORTURE BY NORTH VIETNAM

By STEVEN V. ROBERTS
Special to The New York Times

WASHINGTON, March 29—Former prisoners of war told chilling stories today of mental and physical torture at the hands of their North Vietnamese captors.

In news conferences across the country, the men said they had been beaten, tied, shackled and starved until they provided information about American war plans or signed antiwar statements and confessions of war crimes.

But to many of the men, the most devastating treatment was prolonged periods of solitary confinement. As Col. Robinson Risner put it at Andrews Air Force Base in Maryland: "Can you imagine someone putting you in a closet and closing the door and saying, 'See you in six months'?"

The former prisoners talked about their captivity hours after the last of the American prisoners of war landed at Clark Air Base in the Philippines. Until now, the men had refused to discuss details of their life in Communist prisons for fear of jeopardizing the release of comrades still behind bars.

By and large, the men kept a firm hold on their emotions and even joked occasionally. In describing life in solitary confinement, Capt. Wendell Rivers told a conference at Bethesda Naval Hospital that "you can get up at 6 in the morning and fall asleep at 8 at night and walk all day in circles around your room."

"But you have to reverse direction once in a while so you don't fall down," he added.

But occasionally their anger and bitterness spilled out and their voices quavered. As one former prisoner put it recently, the older prisoners "lived on hate" for their captors and the Communist system. And it was not really clear today how that hatred colored their tales of an experience that Colonel Risner described as "severe torture, degradation, deprivation, humiliation, you name it."

In San Francisco, Comdr. Richard A. Stratton said he thought the North Vietnamese should be tried for "war crimes" for their treatment of prisoners. Commander Stratton was the subject of a famous picture in which he was shown bowing to his captors. Today he said he had been forced to appear at a news conference and had decided to act drugged to discredit his own appearance.

Asked what purpose the stories of torture might serve, Lieut. Col. John A. Dramesi said at Andrews: "It gives you some idea what we've been up against all these years. People over here have been screaming that the North Vietnamese are humane and their cause is just. Well, this shows how humane and just they are."

Torture and other harassment declined dramatically after October, 1969, the prisoners said, and few men were forced to make statements. Food improved, they said, and prisoners were moved into larger groups. In the fall of 1970, following the unsuccessful raid on the Son Tay prison camp, most of the prisoners were moved to a central prison in Hanoi and sharply.

Officials here attributed the 1969 improvement to United States efforts begun earlier that year to muster world opinion toward improving the treatment of prisoners.

By early 1971 the men were able to organize the fourth allied prisoner-of-war wing, with Col. John P. Flynn as commander and Colonel Risner as vice commander, the prisoners explained. The wing hewed to strict military procedures and controlled many aspects of prison life.

From the earliest days, the prisoners said, they tried to communicate with each other by tapping on the walls or flashing hand signals when they had the rare chance to see each other. When the system was working, the men could transmit about six or eight words a minute, but they were frequently caught and often punished for their "comming," as the technique was called.

The men interviewed today conceded that there had been disagreements among the prisoners at times, but none of them said they had witnessed any fist fights. Nor did any of them say they would press charges against any prisoners for disobeying orders from the camp commander or cooperating with the enemy.

Two senior pilots and several dozen younger men captured in the last year had made voluntary statements against the war and had met frequently with foreign visitors to Hanoi. These acts violated the regulations set down by the camp commanders, but the men today seemed in a forgiving mood and played down the possibility of legal reprisals.

It was the question of torture that dominated the news conferences. Some details had leaked out before, but the stories released today sketched a far more complete picture of alleged mistreatment.

For example, Colonel Risner said he had been tied so tightly into a ball that his shoulders popped out of their sockets and his toes were pushed against his mouth. On other occasions, he said, an iron bar was lashed to his ankles, where it gradually bit into his flesh.

Lieut. Comdr. Everett Alvarez, the first American pilot shot down over North Vietnam, was not tortured for the first two years. But in mid-1966 he was made to sit on a stool for four or five days, with no sleep or food, he said. Several prisoners said they had been shackled to the bunks and had wallowed in their own waste for weeks at a time.

In most cases, the prisoners wound up signing statements or even making tape recordings that were later broadcast over Radio Hanoi, they said. As James A. Mulligan put it at a news conference in Portsmouth, Va., "I've been broken. I think everyone here has been broken. We went through agony over and over again."

New Insights

None of the prisoners actually saw a fellow prisoner die in captivity, but Colonel Risner said he was sure that some men had "died at the hands of the North Vietnamese," either through positive mistreatment or lack of adequate medical care.

Their experience prompted some of the men to gain new insights into themselves. Lieut. Col. John Dunn said he had been stunned to realize his own limitations. "I found myself doing things I thought I never would, like making statements against my country," he explained at Bethesda. "I was sure that I was a superman, and that I could go right down the line to my death."

But he found out, he said, that his captives were more "clever" than he imagined. Most prisoners would have found it easier to face a firing squad than the "continuous high level of pain" inflicted on them, he said.

Commander Alvarez said he had finally capitulated when he decided it "wasn't worth dying for," but later he felt remorse and wished he had died, he said.

Captain Rivers recalled spending nine days in isolation with nothing but bread and water and "crying like a baby" for 15 minutes. But after he "had a good cry," he said, he became convinced that he would survive.

Captain Rivers tempered the unrelenting criticism of the North Vietnamese by noting that while the prisoners often ate badly, they usually ate almost as well as the guards, and sometimes even better. Moreover, he said, the medical care the men received was no worse than that afforded the North Vietnamese people.

Colonel Dramesi provided the most dramatic story of the day when he described how he and another prisoner had escaped from one prison for about 24 hours. Equipped with native-looking clothes, and with their faces colored, the two men climbed a wall and even made their way through a peasant village unnoticed. But they were seized the next day in a massive manhunt.

Colonel Dramesi said he had been severely tortured when he was recaptured. His partner, Capt. Edwin Atterbury, was never repatriated. Colonel Dramesi strongly implied that Captain Atterbury had died in prison, possibly from the effects of mistreatment after the escape attempt.

One former prisoner charged that some men had been subject to homosexual attacks along with the beatings. "There are a lot of queers in that society," said Lieut. Col. Leo K. Thorsness at Scott Air Force Base in Illinois. "Many of these people enjoyed their job and did it more thoroughly than necessary."

THE WAR AFTER THE WAR

April 4, 1973

NIXON PLEDGES AID TO THIEU BUT NOT U.S. INTERVENTION

By R. W. APPLE Jr.
Special to The New York Times

SAN CLEMENTE, Calif., April 3—President Nguyen Van Thieu of South Vietnam left the Western White House today with a promise of continuing economic aid but without a specific pledge of American military action if his country is imperiled.

After two days of meetings with President Nixon, which a joint communiqué said produced a "full consensus," President Thieu visited a naval hospital in San Diego before returning to Los Angeles for a dinner given by Gov. Ronald Reagan of California.

The communiqué said the talks were held "in a very cordial atmosphere." Among other things, the two leaders promised to carry out the provisions of the Paris peace agreement "scrupulously" and to work for peace in Laos and Cambodia as well as Vietnam.

[In Saigon, a fresh effort to end the siege of a South Vietnamese ranger outpost failed when Government delegates to the military commission walked out of a meeting.]

'Purposefully Indefinite'

But the principal points were stated in language described by White House officials as "purposely indefinite."

Mr. Nixon agreed with Mr. Thieu that South Vietnam would "need greater external economic assistance in the initial years of the postwar era," and promised "adequate and substantial economic assistance" for the rest of this year.

For the future, however, President Nixon committed himself only "to seek Congressional authority for a level of funding for the next year sufficient to assure economic stability and rehabilitation."

Since the communiqué also expressed hope that "other nations as well as international institutions" would help meet the needs of the South Vietnamese, it left open the possibility that the American contribution would decline.

At a briefing after the issuance of the communiqué, Ronald L. Ziegler, the White House press secretary, said he thought the United States "would be well advised" to provide in the next few years economic aid in amounts "probably beyond" the total of about $500 million for calendar 1973. But he insisted that he could not be sure of the outcome until after detailed analysis and negotiations with the Congress.

Mr. Ziegler said the South Vietnamese had outlined their economic needs in specific terms but had not said exactly how much they wanted from the United States. He described the Saigon representatives as "satisfied" with American responses.

As was the case yesterday, no Vietnamese spokesman was available for comment. But Bui Diem, the former Ambassador to Washington, joined his thumb and forefinger in an "O.K." sign when asked by a reporter how his country had fared here.

Stress on Infiltration

In addition to foreign aid, the communiqué put great stress on North Vietnamese violations of the cease-fire. The two Presidents "viewed with great concern," the communiqué said, "infiltrations of men and weapons in sizable numbers from North Vietnam into South Vietnam."

Referring to the Paris accord, the statement said:

"Actions which would threaten the basis of the agreement would call for appropriately vigorous reactions."

This language was a bit stronger than that used in Mr. Nixon's news conference warning to the North Vietnamese last month, in which he spoke darkly of the probable "consequences" of continued infiltration. But it was not as explicit as that used this weekend by Defense Secretary Elliot L. Richardson, who spoke bluntly of a resumption of American bombing raids.

A White House official concerned with foreign policy noted privately that Mr. Nixon had not committed himself to any joint response with Saigon, and that the communiqué said nothing about who would make the "reactions," when they would come or what sort of Communist actions would trigger them.

Flexibility Retained

"We retain total flexibility," the official declared.

The communiqué made a number of other points, including these:

Mr. Nixon "expressed satisfaction with the development of political institutions" in South Vietnam and "noted the political stability that has prevailed" there recently—phraseology that will bolster Mr. Thieu's standing at home.

Mr. Nixon mentioned his "great interest in contacts between the rival South Vietnamese parties which are taking place in Paris"—a goad to Mr. Thieu to get on with the task of reconciliation with the Vietcong as called for in the accords.

Both Presidents spoke hopefully of "a normalization of relations with all countries of Southeast Asia"—presumably including North Vietnam. According to reliable sources, that phrase did not particularly please Mr. Thieu.

In all, Mr. Nixon and Mr. Thieu held almost five hours of formal meetings, with an additional four hours together at social events, including a poolside luncheon at Mr. Nixon's home, Casa Pacifica, this afternoon.

Immediately after the luncheon, Mr. Nixon and Mr. Thieu made brief farewell statements—with President Nixon telling his Asian ally that "you can be sure that we stand with you"—and then Mr. Thieu boarded a helicopter.

Thursday he will speak to the National Press Club in Washington.

* * *

May 24, 1973

AFTER SEVEN YEARS, A P.O.W. TRIES TO ADJUST TO A CHANGED WORLD

By DOUGLAS E. KNEELAND
Special to The New York Times

DAYTON, Pa.—Wendell Alcorn has been gone a long time.

But kneeling in the dusty straw on the barn floor, his fingers, remembering things his mind should have long forgotten, are firm and sure as he tinkers with the rusting motor of the old grain augur.

Some things don't change.

Lieut. (j.g.) Wendell R. Alcorn was a 26-year-old Navy pilot when his A-4 Skyhawk, roaring in over Haiphong at 100 feet, was shot down Dec. 22, 1965, just 20 days and 28 missions after his first combat flight off the carrier Enterprise. For more than seven years, until last Feb. 12, he was locked up in a series of nine different North Vietnamese prison camps.

Now a 33-year-old lieutenant commander, his youthful face and smile still much like the younger pictures that adorn the spotless white farmhouse, he is back home like all the other war prisoners, trying to weave into the present those threads of absent years.

In some ways, for Wendell Alcorn, those missing years might never have been. He looks more country boy than naval officer as he putters around in denims and scuffed boots in the red barn, remembering.

Glancing up at the cob-webbed elevator that over the years has sent thousands of bales of hay tumbling onto the loft above, he pointed at the chain and gears near the top.

"My dad cut his finger off in that thing—in that chain up there," he said, his eyes clouding at the memory.

But some things do change.

His father, John Alcorn, committed suicide in 1968, apparently overwhelmed by the ceaseless work of the 116-acre dairy farm that has been in the family for generations and perhaps by thoughts of the son who had already languished three years in the prison camps.

Picking at the rotting roof of a small shed beside the barn, that son returned, says sadly:

"If someone isn't here to fix things every day, it just all falls apart."

With his father dead and his brother, Donald, and sister Nelda, both married and living out of the state, his mother, Mrs. Ruth Alcorn, has lived alone on the once-prosperous farm at the end of a winding dirt road about seven miles west of Dayton.

A neighbor, Ray White, has rented the land to raise barley, corn and oats for his own livestock, but there has been no one to tend to the daily hammer-and-nails up-keep that it takes to stay ahead of the wind and weather.

Some things do change.

Small Changes at Home

And for Ray Alcorn (Ray is a Navy nickname that has clung incongruously since everyone misguessed his middle name, Reed, in a game back in preflight days) the changes he has noticed most after being shut off from his world for seven years have been in small things, close to home.

Politics, philosophies, national goals, styles and sexual mores may have shifted drastically across the nation, but most things come slowly to Dayton, a drowsy village of about 700 persons, set amid the disappearing farms and played-out coal mines in the greening hills of western Pennsylvania, some 60 miles northeast of Pittsburgh.

Standing in the milking shed and gazing at the empty stalls where 30 cows once stood, Ray Alcorn shook his head.

"It was quite a shock," he said, "the first time I walked down here and there were no animals around."

A Pennsylvania State University graduate in forestry, he joined the Navy in the fall of 1961 when he was unable to find a job in his chosen field. He had worked on the farm all his life, including summers while he was going to college, and had no desire to stay with it.

"You know, the first thing I noticed when I got back was that there were no fences around here," he said, appreciatively, looking off into the distance across the wooded hills and valleys. Then, he added, "I've thought about it sometimes, but I don't suppose I'll ever come back here."

So he is checking out all the equipment that has lain idle since his father's death, trying to get it into shape for sale at an auction soon.

He plans to stay in the Navy when his convalescent leave is up in July unless he can get a job as an airline pilot. Either way, his mother will once again be alone on the farm.

Climbing on the old orange Allis-Chalmers tractor to give the working parts of a hay rake a test run up across a field above the house, he mused:

"You know, even the lay of the land somehow seems different to me. This hill up here used to seem a lot steeper. But I walked up there the other day and it seemed to have flattened out."

Stopping at the top of the hill, near a row of fruit trees, he waved his arm across the landscape

"No one's hardly farming around here any more," he said. "There used to be an old guy over there and he's dead and the people over there and up the road are gone."

The New York Times/Bill Wingell

Wendell R. Alcorn, former Navy pilot and prisoner of war, on a tractor on the family farm near Dayton, Pa. He was getting things in shape for sale at an auction.

It's not that Ray Alcorn hasn't noticed other changes, besides the homely ones, since he returned to the United States. He has.

Sitting over a root beer milk shake and a cheeseburger in Dinger's restaurant, which used to be in a green shingled frame building on Dayton's unpretentious Main Street and has since moved to one next door with pink shingles, he pondered some of them.

"I suppose one of the biggest changes I've seen is the long hair on men," he said. "When I went away it was pretty well accepted that any man with long hair was a hippie type. Since I've gotten back. I've found that it doesn't mean anything—that guys with long hair are just like anybody else."

Language and Movies

"Then there are a few new expressions. The one that struck me most was 'up tight.' I'd never heard that before—and this expression 'doing your own thing.'

"I've really noticed the change in movies. I've only seen three, I guess. 'Deliverance.' 'The Godfather,' and 'Godspell,' but I wasn't very much impressed. The use of foul language, the extreme amount of violence I just never imaged they would have on the screen—those mainly were the things that turned me off."

As for the nudity in some of the popular magazines, he said that it "amazed me that they had that type of thing right out in the open."

But the change that surprised him most, as a young bachelor who has been dating heroically in an attempt to make up for seven lost years, is "all these young girls who tell they're on the pill."

Not that Dayton has been much less shocked by many of the latest trends than Ray Alcorn. In these conservative hills he has found few signs of attitudinal changes, even toward the war in Vietnam.

A strong supporter of President Nixon's Vietnam policies, like many fellow prisoners he has encountered nothing but reassurance in his reception by the home folks.

No Dissent on War

"I certainly haven't seen any dissent or apathy toward the war," he said. "As far as I can tell, everyone's been 100 per cent behind the Government."

There have, of course, been some changes in Dayton since Ray Alcorn's been gone. He had never seen the new, modern one-story elementary school that replaced the aging two-story brick one, which is now being used for storage by one of the town's two grocers. Some new buildings and black-top roads have been built at the fairgrounds where each August the Dayton Fair, the village's biggest annual event, is held.

Along Main Street, the Keyston National Bank has put up a compact brick building, knocking down the sprawling old one and leaving space for the town's first parking lot. Clark's Variety has taken over where the Faust Drug Store used to be. Reed Hoffman's Ford agency, the only car dealership in Dayton, is gone. And Preston Bittinger, the barber, was forced to move when the bank building was razed. Now, he's across the street in what was once the town's hotel, but he's getting on in years and is only open three days a week.

Still, not everything is different. Frank Bly's Funeral Home is still there. Raymond Barrett's lumber yard remains probably the biggest business in town. And Bill Hallman and his son, Jerry, are still operating the Dayton Feed Mill in a weathered store that's almost 100 years old. The Grange has torn down its sagging hall, but unlike the Odd Fellows, who have given up the ghost, they're still meeting—now in the headquarters of Dayton Memorial Post 995 of the American Legion.

Chatting over coffee at Dinger's, Mayor Clifton J. King, who had been Ray Alcorn's high school agriculture teacher, but who retired a couple of years ago after a series of heart attacks, thought for a bit about what shifts had taken place in the attitudes of Dayton residents in the last six or seven years.

"I would say probably there's been some progressing," he said. "I would say most of it's been for the good. I'd say more of them realize that communities have to get together, that what's good for Kittanning (20 miles to the southwest] is good for us and what's good for us is good for Kittanning.

"Oh, there's been some streets that's been paved that weren't paved. And we've got ourselves a borough garage—and we went down to Butler and bought a used grader I think will do us some good. And we bought a new truck to keep our street superintendent from getting killed and a new tanker for the fire department.

"We have done away with the old Board of Trade and we do have a new Chamber of Commerce. Now, if we could just get a small industry in, it would do so much."

Pausing again, he concluded:

"I can't think of anything else. We don't do anything very earth-shaking, I guess."

At the high school, "Welcome Wendell" was spelled out in large letters in the front windows of one wing, a reminder of Dayton's recent Wendell Alcorn Day. In his office, Leonard L. Holt, the principal, who had been there in the days when the former prisoner of war was on the school's basketball team and played the saxophone in the band and orchestra, also stopped to consider the question of change.

"Change comes a little bit slower in a rural area such as this," said Mr. Holt dapper in a gold jacket, gold shirt, striped tie and brown pants. "However, we have noticed some changes taking place. The high school student is becoming a little more sophisticated and a little more free in his thinking and his action.

"But we have no more problems than we did when Wendell was going to school. Wendell and the group he went to school with were not bad. They were lively, and they kept me hopping sometimes."

Then as his former student smiled, he asked:

"Do you remember, Wendell, the day you dropped your trousers when you went off the stage on Senior Day and exposed your polka-dot shorts?"

Seven years is a long time, but Wendell Alcorn is home, where the folks all greet him happily, where nobody calls him Ray—and where nothing changes a whole lot.

* * *

July 18, 1973

SECRET RAIDS ON CAMBODIA BEFORE '70 TOTALED 3,500

By SEYMOUR M. HERSH
Special to The New York Times

WASHINGTON, July 17—United States B-52 bombers made at least 3,500 secret bombing raids over Cambodia in a 14-month period beginning in March, 1969, Defense Department sources disclosed today.

In addition, a Pentagon spokesman, Jerry W. Friedheim, acknowledged at a news briefing that falsified reports were officially ordered and made after the strikes in an effort to prevent disclosure of the raids, which he said were fully authorized by President Nixon and Melvin R. Laird, who was Secretary of Defense at the time.

Mr. Friedheim also said that "hundreds of missions" were flown monthly, but refused to provide a more specific total. Other sources said, however, that as many as 400 missions were flown in some months and that the number of such flights, when officially tabulated, could exceed 4,000.

20% Go Unreported

At the time, the sources said the total number of B-52 missions in all of Southeast Asia were running at the rate of 1,500 to 1,800 monthly, meaning that as much as 20 per cent of the over-all operations were officially going unreported to the public.

The B-52 bombers usually attack in units, or "cells," of three, but statistically the missions are tabulated on a basis of one flight by one B-52. The first official announcements of the secret raids was made yesterday by Secretary of Defense James R. Schlesinger, who defended them as being necessary for the protection of the lives of American soldiers.

Hughes Charges Lying

Today, meanwhile, Senator Harold E. Hughes, Democrat of Iowa, issued previously classified Pentagon statistics that he said showed that the Defense Department deliberately lied to the Senate Armed Services Committee in 1971 and 1973 reports on the bombing operations in Cambodia.

During a committee hearing yesterday into the falsification of records in connection with the bombing, Mr. Hughes had complained that an unclassified report made available to him by the Defense Department had not listed any B-52 raids in Cambodia until the May, 1970, invasion. At the Pentagon news briefing today, however, Mr. Friedheim assorted that some members of the Armed Services Committee had been fully briefed on the Cambodian operation. Other Senators, he said, specifically mentioning Mr. Hughes by name, were not so informed.

'Deliberately Not Included'

Asked why Pentagon statistics supplied to Mr. Hughes did not list the 1969 and 1970 bombing raids in Cambodia, Mr. Friedheim said they were "deliberately not included," and said, that the decision to do so had been "determined by senior civilian and military officials here." He would not elaborate.

The subsequent release of the classified reports by Mr. Hughes was made in direct response to the Friedheim statement. Those reports, the Senator said in a statement, show that the Nixon Administration deliberately "deceived the committee," and his personal office, by not showing any B-52 bombing missions before May, 1970, in Cambodia.

Both classified responses, he said, issued in 1971 by the former Secretary of the Air Force, Robert C. Seamans Jr., and last March by the former Secretary of Defense, Elliot L. Richardson, contain zeros—"not blanks indicating information was withheld, but zeros declaring that there were no B-52 strikes inside Cambodia."

"And today," he added, "we learn that in fact there were more than 100 sorties each month for 14 months."

"If Congress and the American people have been lied to in this instance," Senator Hughes asked, "how can we have any confidence in Pentagon spokesmen when they come before the committee in classified, closed session and ask for billions of dollars?"

To Expand Inquiry

The Senator, who was instrumental in promoting last year's hearings into the unauthorized bombing of North Vietnam by former Gen. John D. Lavelle as well as the current hearings into the Cambodian air operations, also announced that the Armed Services Committee would expand its investigation to determine how and why the Pentagon submitted the false statistics.

He quoted Senator Stuart Symington, the acting chairman of the committee, as having "expressed his personal indignation" over today's Pentagon statements and said that the Missouri Democrat had agreed to summon high officials "under oath to tell us precisely what happened in these bombing operations and falsification of reports."

"Although I am the one who has requested this investigation," Senator Hughes said with obvious anger, "I am not the only member of the committee who has been kept in the dark."

In a brief telephone interview, Senator Symington confirmed Mr. Hughes's remarks. "I want to go to the bottom of this," Mr. Symington said. "I don't like people destroying evidence."

In interviews today, a number of present and former high Government officials expressed concern over the Pentagon's admissions that it had deliberately falsified official bombing reports after the strikes in an effort to disguise the raids.

No Evidence of Orders

In a statement yesterday to the Armed Services Committee, Gen. George S. Brown, the newly approved Air Force Chief of Staff who headed Southeast Asian air operations in 1969 and 1970, acknowledged the false reporting but described it as being "in accord with instructions."

Interviews today with high officials of the White House, National Security Council and the Pentagon produced no evidence that any such high-level orders were issued.

Military sources did confirm, however, that information about the Cambodian raids was directly provided to President Nixon and his top national security advisers, including Henry A. Kissinger.

The sources said that the unusual method of reporting—which bypassed the normal lines of communication—was set up to avoid public disclosure of the raids. The system was not changed, sources said, although The New York Times published a dispatch about the B-52 raids in Cambodia on May 9, 1969—about two months after they began.

Major Told Story

The current dispute arose Sunday in an interview by The Times with a former Air Force major, Hal M. Knight of Memphis, who told of falsification of reports and destruction of documents dealing with the B-52 operations.

In public testimony before the Senate Armed Services Committee yesterday, the former officer said he decided to inform the Senate about his experiences after reading newspaper accounts of the Lavelle hearings last fall.

"It became obvious to me," Mr. Knight testified, "that the committee was unaware of what had taken place while I was out there. General Lavelle apparently was disciplined for doing the same thing on a small scale that I was doing on a big scale."

Pentagon officers agreed today that General Lavelle was ousted in 1972 for doing the same thing—falsifying records—that apparently had been authorized by some responsible Government official three years earlier.

* * *

August 16, 1973

EFFECT OF BOMBING: IT HELPED, BUT PEACE IS STILL ELUSIVE

By SYDNEY H. SCHANBERG
Special to The New York Times

PHNOM PENH, Cambodia, Aug. 15—Military experts here agree that the bombing of Cambodia—half a million tons in four and a half years—was the only thing that kept the Government of President Lon Nol from falling, and that it slowed the impetus of the enemy offensive and prevented the insurgent forces from massing in large enough numbers to take Phnom Penh. In short, their view is that the bombing gave the badly disorganized Government forces some breathing time. But Western military attachés also point out that it was the sheer massiveness—not necessarily the effectiveness—of the bombing that kept the enemy's hands off the capital. Whether it crippled the enemy's ability to take the country in the near future is quite a different question.

Trying to assess whether the bombing accomplished its stated purpose is difficult not only because the documentary evidence needed is not available but also because the Nixon Administration kept changing its description of what that purpose was.

In the early years the Administration insisted that the raids were designed only to destroy the lines of supply to the North Vietnamese and Vietcong troops operating in Cambodia, primarily in the border sanctuaries next to South Vietnam. However, when the insurgents began their offensive in February with the help of the North Vietnamese, the Administration, faced with voluminous eyewitness evidence, acknowledged that the emphasis had shifted to close combat support for Cambodian troops in trouble.

A high official at the United States Embassy in Phnom Penh recently described the purpose as follows: "To bring the enemy to the negotiating table we have to convince them that military victory is not possible. The only way is to make it as costly as possible for them is to continue fighting."

How Did They Do It?

Though the bombing presumably inflicted considerable casualties, there is no sign that the insurgents have been persuaded that military victory is impossible—particularly now, when the planes are gone.

One of the key unanswered questions is this: How have the insurgents—without any planes of their own, and without the extensive artillery support the Government troops have, with only small arms and mobile weapons like mortars and recoilless cannon and rockets—been able not just to match the Government forces, which are more than twice their size, but to push the Government troops back and sustain the offensive for six months without any significant lull?

Since the insurgents are not superhuman, there must be other explanations for their success. Although American officials condemn their terrorist tactics, they have also described them as determined and capable.

An embassy official who believed in the bombing put it this way recently: "They have strong leadership, men trained in Hanoi. They believe in strong discipline. They shoot deserters. They are strongly motivated. They are less fatalistic than the Khmers on this side. They believe they can change their environment."

"Perhaps as long as the bombing doesn't create disorder and destroy their discipline, it doesn't hurt their organization too much," he continued. "They must be exhausted after six months, but they're still pushing hard."

Weakness in the Army

There is also a widely held belief in Western embassies here that the insurgents' successes are sometimes less a reflection of their strength than of the army's many weaknesses.

Numbering no more than 30,000 men when the Cambodian conflict began in 1970, the army, which had been trained by the French colonial administration to build roads and other public works rather than to fight, was hastily expanded to about 200,000 in so short a time that proper training and motivation were difficult if not impossible.

Colonels became generals overnight, living high in expensive villas in Phnom Penh while poorly paid soldiers sat in monsoon rains at lonely out-posts trying to fight off the insurgents.

Sometimes the troops were not paid because their commanders had pocketed the funds. Sometimes commanders created phantom soldiers and pocketed their pay, too.

It was a corrupt, demoralized army long before the enemy offensive began this year—and most military observers here think that little has changed since. Desertions are frequent, and many deserters end up on the other side.

As for the bombing, experts on air power have always stressed that the effectiveness of conventional bombs is limited by the quality of the troops on the ground—that bombing can only support troops and make their task easier; it cannot win wars.

One advantage for the insurgents is mobility. Using a combination of guerrilla and conventional tactics, they have been able to move and attack almost where they choose, while the Cambodian troops have been more or less pinned down, compelled to defend fixed positions. Moreover, they became dependent on the bombing, rarely trying to push forward without it.

Everyone in Phnom Penh—politicians, generals, foreign diplomats—assumes that losses from the bombing were high, but there are no accurate figures. Newsmen have appealed to the United States Embassy for evidence of casualties but it has always said that it has none.

Few bodies of insurgents are found on the bomb-pocketed battlefields. Although this can be attributed in part to the enemy's tactic of trying to carry away all dead and wounded, it raises questions about the Government's frequent claims of hundreds killed here and hundreds there.

There is little doubt that after February, when the bombing was stepped up in response to the insurgents' offensive—over 300,000 tons were dropped in the last six months alone—enemy casualties increased. How much of an increase is the question. The Government's claims add up to the elimination of the insurgent forces.

Efficacy Lower Near Cities

American Embassy analysts acknowledged that air power was less effective, because more restricted, in populated areas than in open areas—which means that as the insurgents pushed closer to Phnom Penh the efficacy of the air strikes was proportionately reduced.

Further, as the fighting moved closer to the capital and the bombing was intensified, the number of bombing errors increased. These errors had been occurring throughout the war in Cambodia, and especially during the offensive this year, but they were suddenly dramatized by the B-52 bombing of the Mekong River town of Neak Luong. Official figures now show 137 dead and 268 wounded there—mostly soldiers and their families living in the town—and some sources think the toll was somewhat higher.

The Seventh Air Force, whose more than 400 jet fighter-bombers from bases in Thailand and 150 B-52's from Thailand and Guam carried out the air war here, always described its activities as precision bombing based on careful aerial photography and reconnaissance. However, reliable sources here report that the maps used were in most instances old and that the precision of the bombing depended largely on information provided by Cambodian ground commanders, who are often fatigued, incompetent and panicky.

A few days ago the air attaché at the embassy, Col. David H. E. Opfer, acknowledged at a press briefing that Cambodian commanders often supplied erroneous information.

Some Western military attachés believe that the bombing at night, which is when the B-52's made most of their raids, was largely preventive—that is the laying down of large amounts of explosives in areas where Cambodian intelligence suspected the enemy might try to cross. As such, the attachés believe, the raids were singularly ineffective.

On the other hand they agree that when fighter-bombers caught insurgent troops in the open, away from populated areas, they apparently cut them up badly.

The embassy, in assessing the bombing, often said that it bought time for the Cambodian Government to prepare to defend itself. The crucial question, of course, is whether there has been enough time—and determination—for the Cambodian forces to fill the gap left by the United States bombers.

* * *

September 8, 1973

IN THE MEKONG DELTA, A WAR WITH 2 FACES

By FOX BUTTERFIELD
Special to The New York Times

CAN THO, South Vietnam, Sept. 1—In a muddy field beside the Bassac River here, 50 Japanese engineers are quietly erecting a large power plant that will eventually provide electricity to two-thirds of the populous Mekong Delta.

On a lonely country road in Chau Doc Province 60 miles to the west, a rickety old bus hits a Communist mine, blowing a dozen bodies into the ripening green rice fields.

These are the two faces of the war that has persisted in the delta since the cease-fire officially began last January. United States officials say it is unclear whether the South Vietnamese Government or the Communists have been more successful.

Shooting Is Persisting

On the one hand both the Government and the Vietcong have embarked on major efforts to enhance their popular appeal through economic and political development in the delta, South Vietnam's demographic heart, with almost 40 per cent of the population of 18 million. The Saigon Government, for example, is constructing $132 million worth of roads, bridges and irrigation facilities in the delta.

On the other hand, despite the withdrawal of the last American military forces, the shooting has continued unabated, Vietnamese officers say, with an average of 100 South Vietnamese soldiers killed or wounded every day this year in the delta alone. That is a rate equal to the number of casualties during the big Communist offensive last year, and higher than in many previous periods during the interminable war.

"All you can safely say so far of the situation since the cease-fire," an experienced American official remarked, "is that both sides are pushing ahead full steam with their separate programs, and they are going to continue to collide."

Contradictions Abound

One problem in analyzing the post-cease-fire situation is that for every statistic or trend there seems to be an opposite statistic or trend.

The Communists have made some local gains in Chuong Thien Province, in the lower delta, but at same time the Government has made equal gains in Dinh Tuong, in the center of the delta, long a heavily Vietcong province and a key rice-producing and communications area.

Over all, neither side appears to have won any really significant advantage, with the fighting costly but indecisive.

Another statistic whose meaning is hard to judge is the slow but gradual trickle of peasants who have begun returning to their abandoned land in Vietcong-controlled territory since of the end of United States air strikes.

American officials had long proudly insisted that the thousands of peasants who fled to Government areas under the threat of United States artillery or air power were "voting with their feet." Now that the threat is ended, some farmers are going back to their fields—60 families in one remote district of Kien Giang Province last month, local officials report.

The question is: Is this number so small as to indicate that most people do not want to live under the Vietcong or large enough to mean the opposite?

The Government's economic-development projects are part of a broad effort ordered by President Nguyen Van Thieu earlier this year to try to increase the Government's popularity now that it can no longer count on United States military support to sustain it. In purely financial terms, at least, the results are impressive.

The Can Tho power plant, being built with a $20-million long-term loan from Japan, will eventually generate 200 million watts, nearly as much as the country's present capacity. The high towers for the transmission lines, many of which have been installed across half a dozen provinces in the delta, are a visible symbol of the Government's presence and an inviting Vietcong target.

With $18.5-million in United States aid funds, the Government is totally overhauling its network of primary roads in the delta and building 450 miles of additional roads and 232 bridges. A further $93.2-million in American aid is helping to construct three major irrigation systems.

The largest single project, not scheduled to begin until 1975, is a bridge across the main channel of the Mekong near My Tho. It will cost at least $25-million to $30-million, to be provided by the United States and Japan.

The Communists' development program appears to be on a far more modest scale in their areas of the delta. According to Government count, the Vietcong clearly control only 4 per cent of the delta's seven million people, though the actual figure is believed by some officials to be closer to 10 to 15 per cent.

Whatever the size of Vietcong territory, both United States intelligence analysts and the few foreigners who have recently visited remote Vietcong villages report that the Communists are making strenuous efforts to improve their standard of living, roads and schools, which have long lagged behind those in Government areas. Apparently to help out, North Vietnamese specially trained as teachers or village administrators have begun appearing this summer as far south as the foot of the Camau Peninsula.

In an effort to compete politically with the Communists, the Government has also begun sending teams of trained people into delta villages, but with mixed results. The groups, known as province mobile-operation teams, are supposed to consist of 20 to 30 specialists, headed by a major or lieutenant colonel, who will spend a week in each village talking with people and helping them solve their problems with the Government—taxes, land titles, payments to veterans and the like.

In some of the more pacified provinces, among them Sa Dec, the teams have reportedly been useful and have actually helped settle old grievances. But in other areas only low-level teams with no authority have been sent, and they cannot accomplish much.

Occasionally, as some American officials have reported, the teams degenerate into little better than carpetbagging expeditions. "The local people view them as a group of fruit-picking, women-chasing tourists who descended on the village" for no good purpose, an American wrote in a monthly report.

* * *

November 8, 1973

HOUSE AND SENATE OVERRIDE VETO BY NIXON ON CURB OF WAR POWERS; BACKERS OF BILL WIN 3-YEAR FIGHT

TROOP USE LIMITED

Vote Asserts Control of Congress Over Combat Abroad

By RICHARD L MADDEN

Special to The New York Times

WASHINGTON, Nov. 7—The House and the Senate, dealing President Nixon what appeared to be the worst legislative setback of his five years in office, today overrode his veto of a measure aimed at limiting Presidential power to commit the armed forces to hostilities abroad without Congressional approval.

The House voted first—284 to 135, or only four votes more than the required two thirds of those present and voting—to override the veto. The Senate followed suit nearly four hours later by a vote of 75 to 18, or 13 more than the required two-thirds.

It was the first time in nine attempts this year that both houses had overridden a veto and the first time legislation has become law over the President's veto since Congress overrode a Nixon veto of a water-pollution control measure in October, 1972.

First Such Action

Supporters of the measure, who had waged a three-year effort to enact it into law, said it was the first time in history that Congress had spelled out the war-making powers of Congress and the President.

The White House said in a statement that Mr. Nixon felt the Congressional action today seriously undermines this nation's ability to act decisively and convincingly in times of international crisis." It declined, however, to say what the President planned to do as a result of the overriding of his veto.

With the veto overridden, the war-powers measure—couched in the form of a joint resolution, which in Congress has the same status as a bill immediately became law. It contains the following provisions:

The President would be required to report to Congress in writing within 48 hours after the commitment of armed forces to combat abroad.

The combat action would have to end in 60 days unless Congress authorized the commitment, but this deadline could be extended for 30 days if the President certified it was necessary for safe withdrawal of the forces.

Within that 60-day or 90-day period Congress could order an immediate removal of the forces by adopting a concurrent resolution, which is not subject to a Presidential veto.

The Nixon Administration had previously been stung by the legislative branch through such actions as the Senate's rejection of two nominees for the Supreme Court, Clement F. Haynsworth Jr. and G. Harrold Carswell, and the Congressional decision to end the program to develop a United States supersonic transport.

But the votes today were regarded as a rebuke of potentially greater significance because they dealt directly with the President's interpretation of his Constitutional authority.

Beyond reflecting the low political estate to which President Nixon has fallen, the Congressional action represented the most aggressive assertion of independence and power by the legislative branch against the executive branch in many years.

Several Republicans insisted that they were not striking at Mr. Nixon because of the Watergate scandal, but up to now he had managed to rally enough Republican strength in Congress to sustain his vetoes. Voting against him today were 86 Republicans in the House and 25 in the Senate.

Earlier this year Congress forced a halt in the United States bombing in Cambodia as of Aug. 15, but until today both houses had never been able to muster a two-thirds vote to override Mr. Nixon's vetoes of measures dealing with the nation's involvement in combat abroad.

Mr. Nixon had vetoed the war-powers bill Oct. 24 on the ground that it was "clearly unconstitutional." He said then—as the White House reiterated today—that it would "seriously undermine this nation's ability to act decisively and convincingly in times of international crisis."

Before the House overrode the veto, Representative Gerald R. Ford of Michigan, the minority leader and Vice President-designate, made a strong appeal against the bill.

'Potential for Disaster'

Mr. Ford said that the bill "has the potential for disaster" because it takes away the President's flexibility to deal with a foreign crisis.

In the Senate, Senator Thomas F. Eagleton, Democrat of Missouri, taking another tack, said that the bill was "a horrible mistake" because it gave the President "unilateral authority to commit troops any where in the world for 60 to 90 days."

He said that under it, Mr. Nixon could order the armed forces deployed in the Middle East immediately and be required only to inform the Congressional leaders. He shouted:

"How short can memories be? My God, we just got out of a nightmare."

2 Principal Authors

The principal authors of the measure, Representative Clement J. Zablocki, Democrat of Wisconsin, and Senator Jacob K. Javits, Republican of New York, argued that had the measure been law earlier, it would not have restricted Mr. Nixon's recent actions, such as the alert of the armed forces, during the Middle East war.

Immediately after the Senate vote Senator John G. Tower, Republican of Texas, said that he hoped that the constitutionality of the measure would be tested in the courts "at the very earliest opportunity." Mr. Tower, who opposed the bill, did not say how such a test might be initiated.

The vote had been expected to be close in the House, which had approved the measure on Oct. 12 by a vote of 238 to 123, just short of two-thirds.

2 Vote at Last Minute

One factor in the success of the move to override the veto was a gain of several votes from a handful of liberal Democrats who had voted against the measure previously on the grounds that it gave the President additional war powers.

Among them were Representatives Bella S. Abzug of Manhattan and Elizabeth Holtzman of Brooklyn, both Democrats, who watched the tally boards and then in the final seconds before the voting period ended inserted their cards into the electronic machine and voted to override the veto.

The Democratic side of the House broke into cheers and applause when Speaker Carl Albert, Democrat of Oklahoma, announced at 1:44 P.M. that two thirds of those present had voted in the affirmative and that the measure had been passed, "the President's objections to the contrary nothwithstanding."

In the House, 198 Democrats and 86 Republicans voted to override the veto, while 32 Democrats and 103 Republicans voted against overriding. In the Senate, 25 Republicans and 50 Democrats voted to override while three Democrats and 15 Republicans voted against.

Legislation to curb the President's war-making powers was first proposed in 1970 as a reaction to the long United States involvement in the Indochina conflict without a Congressional declaration of war.

The proposals languished until last year when, with the support of Senator John C. Stennis, Democrat of Mississippi and the influential chairman of the Senate Armed Services Committee, who became one of the sponsors, a bill was approved by the Senate. But the House approved a much milder version, and the measure died in conference.

Legislation on war powers was introduced again when the new Congress convened in January. On July 18, by a vote of 244 to 170, the House passed a measure that would have set a 120-day limit on the commitment of United States troops to combat abroad without Congressional approval. Two days later, the Senate, by a vote of 70 to 18, approved its own version making the limit 30 days.

On Oct. 4 there emerged from a Senate-House conference committee the compromise with a 60-day limit that both houses subsequently adopted, that the President vetoed and that went into effect today.

* * *

January 27, 1974

SOUTH VIETNAM, A YEAR AFTER TRUCE, IS STILL RACKED BY INDECISIVE WAR

By JAMES M. MARKHAM
Special to The New York Times

SAIGON, South Vietnam—The year that has elapsed since the signing of the Paris peace agreements on Jan. 27, 1973, has not brought peace to South Vietnam.

But the war that continued throughout 1973 and into 1974—an essentially military struggle, with sharp economic consequences—appears to have established no distinct momentum in favor of either the Communists or the Saigon Government.

"It was not as decisive a year as one might have thought it would be last February," said an American diplomat looking back over 12 months in which, according to Saigon Government figures, almost 60,000 Vietnamese, 45,000 of them Communists, have died in petty skirmishes and battles now forgotten.

Though bloodletting has been as extensive as it was before, neither side could claim stunning victories or significant territorial acquisitions. Nor, despite continual accusations, could either side demonstrate convincingly that it was more sinned against than sinning.

Saigon Keeps Up 'Harassment'

In the Mekong Delta, on the central coast and, above all, in the skies over most of the country, Saigon Government forces initiated many actions. It was a rare province where Government artillery could not be heard in "harassment and interdiction" fire into Communist held areas.

As the first anniversary of the Paris agreements approached, President Nguyen Van Thieu offered this definition of "peace" to an audience in Can Tho: "Real peace is territorial security, protection of the harvests, production increase, self-development. It consists in weakening the Communists, defeating them, annihilating their tax collectors, their assassination squads."

The President then ordered his troops to attack the Communists in their zones of control instead of waiting to be attacked.

The North Vietnamese and their Vietcong allies, whose internal declarations have urged "skillful" military actions that would arouse little public attention, kept constant pressure on the South Vietnamese, who were sometimes overextended.

Attacks on militia posts, shellings of base camps, a run of assassinations in the delta and on the central coast, bridges repeatedly blown up on the main north-south highway, a daring and professionally executed guerrilla raid on the nation's largest petroleum depot—all these kept the Government forces waiting for the next blow.

In the Central Highlands the North Vietnamese made several bold strikes at outposts near their independent road system, which they expanded rapidly.

The New York Times/Nguyen Ngoc Luong

Long after the cease-fire, a South Vietnamese woman watches the burial of her husband, a Ranger private killed in action east of Saigon. The cemetery is in Bien Hoa.

But military analysts were mystified by the Communists' inability or unwillingness to push these attacks to their logical military conclusion, and some speculated that they were experimenting, trying to coordinate armor, infantry and air support better than they did in their big offensive in 1972.

Several American intelligence-gathering agencies—not to mention the South Vietnamese, whom foreign military men consider prone to exaggeration—could not agree on the pace of North Vietnamese infiltration of men and weapons into the South.

Big-Unit Actions Stressed

There was a consensus, however, that after a year of "peace" the Communists were probably as strong as they were before the 1972 offensive and that proponents of the doctrine of big-unit warfare remained in the ascendancy in Hanoi (even though Gen. Vo Nguyen Giap, the most prominent articulator of that position, has been out of public view for four months).

In the fall—just when, as more than one non-American diplomat noted, the Vietnam aid bill was working its way through Congress—there was a wave of talk of "offensives."

South Vietnamese commanders became exceptionally nervous over what they perceived as a deterioration of their positions north and northwest of Saigon, where Communist units seemed to be inching forward.

President Thieu was more vociferous than any South Vietnamese in his predictions of a strike in the 1972 pattern: he was soon joined by American spokesmen, who voiced ominous warnings to Hanoi. The Communists replied that accusations that they were plotting an offensive were a slander.

Recently, Mr. Thieu has begun congratulating his generals for blunting a long-planned—but still possible—North Vietnamese thrust. At the same time some Americans who once foresaw an onslaught seem to be hedging their bets.

"Offensive? It's a false question," a European ambassador remarked. "The 'offensive' is already on. But a big offensive, like 1968 or 1972? That was necessary during the American war, but not now. They don't have to stage a big offensive now."

Eventual Attack Foreseen

Other analysts disagreed, saying the Communists would ultimately strike in force, but only when economic and political conditions were more propitious.

"They are conducting a form of warfare that seems designed to create economic misery," said a high-ranking non-American diplomat with considerable experience here. He suggested that Saigon's softest point might be the morale of its 1.1 million men under arms. Poorly paid, unable to help their families, weary of an endless war, many soldiers are displaying signs of indiscipline and of harsh behavior toward the people they are supposed to protect.

Though no distinct movement in favor of one side or the other has been recorded on the battlefield, South Vietnam is suffering badly on the economic front.

With no prospect of significant foreign investment or foreign aid and no likelihood of a reduction in the financial burden of the armed forces, which consume half the national budget, the economy is once again in deep trouble, according to most economists. Without United States support, the money economy would simply collapse.

Inflation is raging at 65 per cent a year, so real income has plummeted. A sharply unfavorable balance of trade—exports in 1973 were $62-million and imports $740-million—has drained away $73-million of fast dwindling reserves of hard currency, which have dropped to about $180-million.

Cost of Imports Soaring

American economic and military assistance may rise slightly in dollar terms in 1974, but a jump of 43 per cent in the prices of key imports—oil, gasoline, rice, cement, fertilizers—has effectively slashed the Saigon Government's purchasing power.

However, some thoughtful Vietnamese cautioned against automatic predictions of uprisings by angry, hungry, unemployed people.

On the one hand, they said, continued pressure from the Communists and from the Government's pervasive police apparatus tend to keep grievances in check. Most opposition political leaders say they are unwilling to send what few activists they might have to the barricades unless the United States modifies its support of the Thieu Government.

On the other hand, the predominantly agricultural economy may absorb shocks that would crack the social order of an industrialized state.

At the same time, but less visible to the outside world, North Vietnam's socialist economy reportedly had a fairly bad year, losing a large part of the rice crop to severe typhoons.

As the North was still recovering from the devastating effects of the American bombing, campaigns, Nhan Dan, the Communist party newspaper, said that "difficulties and hardships will continue for a long time." That theme, frequently repeated, encouraged some students of the North Vietnamese scene to conclude that the leadership, which is noted for caution, was not planning any abrupt change in strategy.

Divergent Assessments

In retrospect, it is evident that a year ago both President Thieu and his Communist adversaries were aware that the arduously drafted Paris agreement would not bring peace to the South. Only Americans were convinced of the power of words and moral suasion.

Months of slanging matches between Saigon and the Vietcong's Provisional Revolutionary Government, both here and at Paris, have resolved none of the many outstanding issues. The two sides were unable to agree even on a schedule for the resumption of prisoner releases, which were unilaterally halted by Saigon last July to protest purported misbehavior by Communists at one release site.

Furthermore, President Thieu has made it plain that he considers the "third force" neutralists, who are supposed to play a balancing role in the tripartite National Council of National Reconciliation and Concord, little more than fellow travelers of the Communists.

And the Communists have shown no signs—nor has Mr. Thieu, for that matter—of wanting to lay down their guns and their military option.

So the stalemate continues. The prospect, according to most observers, is that the political situation will remain frozen while the military and economic fronts are highly mobile. Real peace is nowhere at hand.

* * *

February 19, 1974

VISITOR FINDS VIETCONG AREA WAR-WEARY TOO

By JAMES M. MARKHAM
Special to The New York Times

TUONG SON, South Vietnam—The crowded minibus bumps through the devastated landscape that lines both sides of Route 1 in Binh Dinh Province, on the central coast.

"There are lots of Communists over there," says a grinning South Vietnamese private, pointing toward the low mountains that cut sharply down to the flatlands and rice fields near the sea.

"Beaucoup VC," adds another soldier, speaking the G.I. argot that has rubbed off on the whole country. We make the appropriate faintly frightened faces.

In less than an hour, after shedding these unwanted soldiers, who have hitched a ride, we cross over to the little-known "other side."

It is the beginning of a week-long journey through Vietcong territory in a society that does not look radically different from the one along Government-held Route 1. Here people go on foot, not in cars, they use kerosene lamps and do not have electricity, but, generally, they are at least as prosperous as the rural inhabitants of the parts of Binh Dinh that are under Saigon's control.

The area is one in which the Communist party members, village and hamlet officials, guerrillas, teachers, rice farmers, wives and children are as weary of the war as Vietnamese on the Saigon side. Perhaps even wearier since they are shelled daily and nightly.

But here on the other side many people display an ideological awareness and a seeming determination to "unify the fatherland" that are noteworthy—perhaps a result of conviction or intensive indoctrination or Binh Dinh's hoary revolutionary tradition, or all of these.

We are given no real opportunities to glimpse the "iron discipline" that Communists traditionally impose on their societies, but we find a social order that is distinctly more orderly than the one we left several hundred yards from the main road.

On our way in, we change from the minibus to a taxi and then after a few more miles we get down at the thinly populated junction that has been fixed as a rendezvous point by the Vietcong's military delegation in Saigon; dingy refugee shanties face the highway.

We sling our knapsacks on our backs and walk toward a reddish side road leading off Route 1. It is 10:30 A.M. and quite hot, but I am wearing the appointed blue jacket; my camera hangs as instructed from my left shoulder, a white handkerchief is tied to the camera's strap.

Charles Benoit, an American consultant and former journalist in Saigon who speaks fluent Vietnamese, ducks into a little tea shop and chats with the owner.

"If only the nationalists would stop firing artillery, we would have peace," the old man complains. "But they keep firing and the liberation troops shoot back."

Hearing the old man's anti-Government turn of phrase—"liberation troops"—Mr. Benoit says to me: "We're in the right place."

We continue toward the reddish road. No one in sight.

A Small Boy Replies

We turn onto the dirt road. A small boy dressed in blue pedals toward us. From his left hand he flashes a rolled-up mosquito net. It is supposed to be a handkerchief, but the resemblance is close enough.

"There's our friend," Mr. Benoit says.

We walk at a normal pace behind the boy, who stays 20 feet in front of us and pedals just fast enough to keep his balance. A hundred yards to our left is a sleepy South Vietnamese Army outpost girdled with barbed wire.

The road narrows to a path and makes a slight dip, putting us out of sight of the outpost. The boy—he is perhaps 8—dismounts, turns around, grins broadly and shakes our hands in a manly fashion.

Several hundred yards from Route 1 we have crossed an uncharted line that divides the area held by the Saigon Government from that held by the Vietcong's Provisional Revolutionary Government. We are in what the Vietcong call a liberated area. Fifty yards farther down the path a young man dressed in gray—a can bo, or member of a Communist cadre—is slipping on his black rubber Ho Chi Minh sandals. He comes forward and shakes hands. I say something polite in my meager Vietnamese; Mr. Benoit chats amiably.

Symbol of Authority

We walk a little farther and are joined by a confident-looking woman who has a small canvas bag looped over her shoulder—a symbol of authority, it turns out, in a society that shuns rank and insignia. Another young woman follows, holding inexplicably, a bunch of fresh white flowers.

We are told to hurry by an exposed point lest the outpost spot us. We sit in the narrow shade of a blasted building; the woman tells us that it was a school until the South Vietnamese Army began its operation to clear Route 1 shortly after the ostensible cease-fire in January, 1973.

Two guerrillas in their late teens appear out of the bushes. One is carrying an American-made M-79 grenade launcher and wearing a beltful of yellow-tipped grenades; the other has a Chinese-made AK-47 automatic rifle over his shoulder. They are dressed in pale blue uniforms and wear floppy blue Mountie hats with chin straps.

We set off Indian-file—first the AK-47, then the woman with the bag, then Mr. Benoit, then me, then the M-79, then the young women with the flowers—on a footpath that meanders across an empty stretch of undulating dry land.

Two artillery rounds land somewhere off to the right, among splintered and topless coconut trees. Close enough to be unsettling, but too far to be dangerous.

"Are you afraid they are going to land on you?" asks the woman with the bag. It is almost a challenge.

Large Bunkers Everywhere

Our little party winds down to a group of houses. The settlement looks like any on the Saigon side except that large bunkers are everywhere. Low thatch and wood structures are scattered amid a bucolic setting of coconut trees and drowned rice fields. People smile and return our Vietnamese greetings.

Soon we pass under a bamboo bower from which hangs the red, blue and orange flag of the Provisional Revolutionary

Government. With permission from the woman with the bag, we take our first pictures.

"Hey, how about a little peace?" a man stripped to the waist shouts from the courtyard of his house. "What's all this war?" He laughs but does not seem to be joking.

We arrive at a hamlet office. An official wearing a white shirt set off with a red and gold Ho Chi Minh button—given to those who have made "significant contributions to the revolution"—greets us stiffly.

We are obviously tired and thirsty. Two fresh coconuts with holes in the tops are produced, and we drink from them greedily while our host gives us a stern lecture on the Paris cease-fire agreements.

Camera Makes a Hit

The guerrilla with the AK-47 fondles my Nikkormat camera and makes it clear that he would not object at all if I gave it to him. He takes a picture of an adjacent rice paddy, out of focus.

I tell him in Vietnamese: "My work is camera, your work is AK-47." Mr. Benoit translates my Vietnamese into Vietnamese and the camera is returned.

We have walked more than a mile; another mile along we stop in a larger hamlet, which looks prosperous despite the fact that almost all its concrete buildings are destroyed. We pass several bicycle-repair shops, a soft-drink and general store and a place that advertises itself as a tape-recorder repair shop. Vietcong flags dangle from house fronts.

We are taken to a thatch-covered shelter surrounded by fresh rubble. It was destroyed two weeks ago by artillery, we are told.

Several hundred yards away, at the first tree line, Communist and Saigon Government forces appear to have made contact. From the noise it sounds as if the Government troops are spraying the coconut trees with mortar and automatic-weapons fire while the Communists answer with the precise burp-burp of AK-47's.

"There they go again," a small boy says.

In a few days we will become accustomed to Saigon's unrelieved, random shelling of rice fields, hamlets and a charred, desolate buffer zone that separates the two sides in Hoai Nhon District. The Vietcong do not invite us on any "punishment" missions against the other side.

Local people complain angrily about the shelling of civilian areas, which they assert is intended to drive them "onto the road" and under Government control. But they do not seem intimidated.

All the houses we visit have bunkers. The bunkers are often larger than the houses themselves, which several people say they have rebuilt more than once since the cease-fire.

The shelling and air strikes—we do not witness aerial attack during our week's stay—appear to be the unhappiest part of life in Hoai Nhon. "It is so fine here," an old man says, "but when the artillery starts I just cry. I lie down in the rice field and the buffalo just stand there."

The shelling is a useful pretext for dispersing crowds of small children who often gather around us. "What would happen if an artillery round landed on you?" one of our guides often asks.

"Do not play too far from the bunker" is an injunction from mothers to children that can be heard more than once.

At our temporary resting place we sit down on a sturdy Vietnamese table-bed and are served a lunch of noodle soup, beer and orange drink. All the food comes from Government-held areas—our first indication that President Nguyen Van Thieu's "economic blockade" of Vietcong zones is not working, at least not here.

The woman with the bag, who has whipped up the repast on a charcoal stove, apologizes for the lack of drinking water. "It has to be boiled," she says, displaying a consciousness of hygiene that can be observed elsewhere. We soon learn, for example, to use one end of the chopsticks to serve ourselves from the communal platter and the other to eat with.

Four rugged men wearing khaki uniforms and sporting the Victorian-era pith helmets used by Vietcong soldiers swing through the gate. They join the group on the table-bed, and the highest-ranking one—his rank is apparent only from his demeanor and large leather hip pouch—gives us a long lecture about self-restraint in the face of multiple cease-fire violations by the "Saigon administration," as it is known here.

The official, who has a knotty face and high cheek bones, says, when asked, that he is a native of Binh Dinh Province, but Mr. Benoit says he speaks with a distinct Hanoi accent.

We are waiting for two Hondas to take us to the hamlet where we will spend the evening. As we wait, I, carrying a long-lens camera, wander unaccompanied out of the compound and onto the main path.

Nurse in the Party

About 50 yards from the compound I encounter a short man in a gray uniform with a pistol on his hip; his right ear is mangled. I tell him that I am a journalist visiting the area. Wordlessly, he directs me back to the compound.

In the coming days we are accompanied almost everywhere we go—except to the toilet—typically by several cadre members as well as a male nurse carrying a first-aid kit and at least one guerrilla with an AK-47, presumably to protect us in case the sight of Americans angers someone, which does not happen.

While we have many spontaneous conversations with ordinary people as we walk around the district—covering five to eight miles a day—most of our substantial contacts are prearranged. By the same token, we are asked what we want to see and some of our requests are granted.

The stiffness of our first few hours in "liberated" Hoai Nhon soon passes and we are on an informal basis with several of the cadre men who escort us. But the "guided tour" nature of our visit never alters and we see what our hosts want us to see.

As we walk we are surprised by the appearance of general well-being. In Saigon, the Communist-held areas are often painted in drab colors as impoverished places devoid of people.

Cloth and Transistor Radios

Here in Hoai Nhon there appear to be many people. They are decently dressed—in varying colors and kinds of cloth—and they look adequately fed, or certainly not malnourished. A number have transistor radios over their shoulders, invariably tuned to the Vietcong's Liberation Radio or Radio Hanoi. Others pedal along the dirt paths on bicycles. A few motorcycles but no cars jounce past.

As we turn into the heart of Hoai Nhon, vast expanses of green rice paddies stretch ahead.

It is the eve of Tet, the Lunar New Year, the most sacred time of the year for Vietnamese, and there is an air of buoyancy about the people we chat with along the way.

We are struck by the simplicity of the forms of address. Vietnamese has a complicated, hierarchical system of pronouns, but here most people are addressed informally as "older brother" or "older sister."

In the hamlet of Tuong Son, where we will stay, there is a small thatch cottage surrounded by an extensive truck garden. We are greeted by a wiry 30-year-old official named Thao, a district-level official who says he will be our guide while we are in Hoai Nhon.

Dinner—a feast of chicken, pork, tomatoes, hand-milled rice, beer and tea—is served at our table, which abuts a traditional household altar whose centerpiece is a colored photograph of Ho Chi Minh. Tet cakes and candies wrapped in red paper are piled on the altar.

As dusk falls a kerosene lamp is lit. Our translator, a 29-year-old soldier named Thinh, says that the liberated areas do not have electricity yet but that they soon will.

Two hammocks are hung at the end of our cottage. Gratefully, we climb in, exhausted. Mr. Thinh sits at the table writing in his diary by the light of the kerosene lamp; the eve of Tet is a sentimental time for Vietnamese diarists. We fall asleep.

"Phao!" Mr. Thinh shouts. "Artillery!"

We are being shelled, closely. The shells—105-mm ones—scream high across the star-spattered sky and smash into the ground.

We grope toward the bunker, which is already crammed with people from the compound. Mr. Benoit, Mr. Thinh and I are the last in and are not really protected.

The shells keep cracking around us—the nearest one lands 30 yards away—but the young women from the kitchen are giggling and making jokes. "We have eaten their bullets and shells for a long time," one says after the barrage ends. "We are used to this."

Back in our hammocks we find it less easy to sleep. At 11 P.M. by our watches newly set on Hanoi time—Indochina time, as our hosts call it, an hour later than Saigon time—the sky is suddenly incandescent with scores of white flares. Automatic-weapons fire rolls up and down the line.

It is midnight and Saigon's soldiers are bidding farewell to the Year of the Buffalo and greeting the Year of the Tiger. The spectacular display goes on for about 10 minutes.

An hour later the Communists unleash a deafening storm that ripples through the darkness, lasting at least as long as their enemies' display. Red tracer bullets cut daring arrows across the sky.

Mr. Thinh picks up a carbine and slips out the door. A few minutes later he returns and announces sheepishly: "I shot off 30 rounds."

I try to find a comfortable position in my hammock. We get to sleep.

* * *

April 18, 1974

U.S. AID TO THE SAIGON GOVERNMENT: SHOULD THE COMMITMENT CONTINUE?

By JOHN W. FINNEY

Special to The New York Times

WASHINGTON, April 16—The bookkeeping that the Pentagon said had enabled it to discover $266-million extra in previously appropriated funds to buy arms for South Vietnam seems to have for the moment avoided a collision between Congress and the Nixon Administration over immediate aid to the Saigon Government. But it will not silence the debate over the extent of the basic American commitment to support that Government.

In some ways it is a replay, in more muted tones, of the debate that raged when the United States was involved militarily in the Vietnam war. The opposing sides are much the same, with the Administration arrayed against Congressional doves, who had been largely quiescent for the last year.

The underlying arguments are also much the same. The Administration contends that the United States has a continuing political and moral commitment to insure "self-determination" for the people of South Vietnam. The doves maintain that the United States should be disengaging from the political and military problems there, leaving the Vietnamese to reach their own political solutions.

The debate was reinforced by an Administration request for an emergency $474-million increase in military aid to South Vietnam—it will get the $266-million instead—which would have brought the total in the current fiscal year to $1.6-billion.

Reflecting a growing desire in Congress for disengagement from Vietnam, the House of Representatives unexpectedly rejected the request for $474-million by a vote of 177 to 154.

The White House, its prestige and power on Capitol Hill weakened by the Watergate affair, found itself drawn into a foreign-policy battle with Congress in which it faced probable defeat. Then it avoided a showdown by finding an accounting procedure permitting it to continue military aid while staying within the $1.126-billion ceiling imposed by Congress.

The Background

With the withdrawal of American troops after the Paris cease-fire accords in January, 1973, the principal American involvement in Vietnam—aside from planes poised in Thailand and on carriers in the South China Sea—consists of military and economic aid to the Government of President Nguyen Van Thieu. Saigon is completely dependent on the aid to provide its armed forces with everything from ammunition to oil and to finance essential imports.

The aid, after falling gradually in the wake of the withdrawal, is starting to increase again. For the fiscal year that begins July 1 the Administration has proposed $2.4 billion in military and economic aid—a 65 per cent increase over the amount approved by Congress for the current fiscal year.

The Administration originally asked that Congress authorize a $2.1-billion ceiling for this fiscal year. After the cease-fire the request was reduced to $1.6-billion, but Congress put the ceiling at $1.126-billion.

Administration Views

Expansion of the military aid is required to fulfill a political and moral commitment the Administration maintains. It is not a written commitment, nor does it flow, as previous Administrations argued, from the Southeast Asia Treaty. Rather, as Secretary of State Kissinger put it in a recent letter to Senator Edward M. Kennedy, it grows out of long involvement and out of participation in the 1973 agreements.

As a signatory, Mr. Kissinger said, "the United States committed itself to strengthening the conditions which made the cease-fire possible and to the goal of the South Vietnamese people's right to self-determination." Combined with a certain obligation from our long and deep involvement in Vietnam," he said, "we have thus committed ourselves very substantially, both politically and morally."

In line with this commitment, the United States' objective is to provide South Vietnam with the means to defend itself and to develop a viable economy so that the North Vietnamese will eventually conclude that political solutions are preferable to military ones.

Because of the introduction of troops and equipment into the South in violation of the agreements, the Administration maintains, North Vietnam still poses a military threat. South Vietnam needs continuing aid to deter attack and to keep the present rough but tenuous military balance.

In the Administration view United States support is not open-ended. The next 18 to 24 months should determine whether South Vietnam can deter a Communist military takeover, establish a viable economy and push Hanoi into political accommodation. To reduce or cut off aid now would be to waste the huge American investment in pursuit of self-determination for South Vietnam, Administration officials say.

"We have invested heavily, in lives and treasure, in Southeast Asia," the Deputy Secretary of Defense, William P. Clements Jr., argued before Congress. "The results could be tragic if we should fail to give this modest additional support, which is but a fraction—a sorely needed fraction—of our prior efforts."

"I could not sleep if I thought I was taking action that was making all the American sacrifices in vain." Representative William G. Bray of Indiana, the ranking Republican on the House Armed Services Committee, told the House. "Let us continue to give South Vietnam at least a fighting chance."

Opposition Views

In developing arguments for continued military aid, according to critics of the policy, the Administration is propounding a new rationalization for continued heavy involvement in Indochina.

As Senator Kennedy put it in commenting on the Kissinger letter: "From presumed commitments under the SEATO treaty, the Gulf of Tonkin resolution and the President's power to protect our troops, we have now moved to commitments under the Paris agreement which was not submitted to the Senate as a treaty."

The Paris agreements should have led the United States down a new road of disengagement from Indochina, the critics say: instead the Administration is continuing down the old road of overinvolvement.

Rather than promoting a political solution, the military aid, in the view of the critics, is perpetuating the fighting and encouraging President Thieu not to reach a political accommodation which, it is widely held, would lead to his downfall.

As long as the United States continues to supply more than $2-billion in military and economic aid, said Representative Robert L. Leggett, Democrat of California, "there is going to be no effort on the part of the Saigon Government to effect any compromise whatsoever with the people against whom they are fighting."

The opponents of expanded aid say that Congress moved toward disengagement last year by reducing military supplies to a level more than adequate to meet South Vietnam's needs. Now, they say, the Administration is seeking to circumvent a Congressional decision. With pressing needs and inflation on the home front, they insist, continued large investments of military and economic aid are irresponsible.

Now that "peace with honor" has been attained, Representative Otis G. Pike, Democrat of Suffolk County, said, it is time to worry about "honor in this country." Rather than spending more money in Vietnam, he added, "let's spend it on our own Vietnam veterans."

Senator Alan Cranston, Democrat of California and a leader of the opposition, commented: "We have finally stopped wasting lives in Vietnam. We must now stop wasting American dollars there too."

* * *

September 17, 1974

FORD OFFERS AMNESTY PROGRAM REQUIRING 2 YEARS PUBLIC WORK

A 'RE-ENTRY' PLAN

Goodell Named Head of Clemency Unit—Hesburgh Included

By MARJORIE HUNTER
Special to The New York Times

WASHINGTON, Sept. 16—President Ford offered conditional amnesty today to thousands of Vietnam era draft evaders and military deserters who agree to work for up to two years in public service jobs.

"My sincere hope," he said in a statement, "is that this is a constructive step toward calmer and cooler appreciation of our individual rights and responsibilities and our common purpose as a nation whose future is always more important than its past."

In announcing his "earned reentry" program, the President also established a nine-member Presidential clemency board to review the cases of those already convicted or punished for desertion or draft evasion.

Mr. Ford designated Charles E. Goodell, a former Republican Senator from New York and an early critic of United States involvement in the Vietnam war, as chairman of the clemency board.

Among others named to the clemency board was the Rev. Theodore M. Hesburgh, president of the University of Notre Dame, who has called for unconditional amnesty.

Effective Immediately

The amnesty program became effective immediately when President Ford signed a Presidential proclamation and two Executive orders just before noon in the Cabinet Room of the White House. Earlier, he explained details of the program to Congressional leaders of both parties. No Congressional action is needed.

In his proclamation, the President declared that "desertion in time of war is a major, serious offense," and that draft evasion "is also a serious offense." Such actions, he said, need not "be condoned."

"Yet," he continued, "reconciliation calls for an act of mercy to bind the nation's wounds and to heal the scars of divisiveness."

President Ford denied tonight at his news conference that the amnesty plan was in any substantial way linked to his unconditional pardon of former President Richard M. Nixon on Sept. 8—an action that has created widespread controversy throughout the nation.

Asked at his news conference tonight why he had granted only a conditional amnesty to draft evaders while granting a full pardon to Mr. Nixon, the President replied:

"Well, the only connection between those two cases is the effort that I made in the one to heal the wounds involving charges against Mr. Nixon and my honest and conscientious effort to heal the wounds for those who had deserted military service or dodged the draft."

Mr. Ford said that, in the case of Mr. Nixon, "you have a President who was forced to resign because of circumstances involving his Administration and he has been shamed and disgraced by that resignation."

Under the program, draft evaders or deserters who have not been convicted or punished have until next Jan. 31 to turn themselves in to the authorities, reaffirm their allegiance to the United States and agree to spend up to two years in public service jobs, such as hospital attendants or conservation

The United States Attorney or military service head would decide the length of alternative service to be performed by each individual. The President set no minimum period of service, but he said that the maximum two-year requirement could be "reduced" for "mitigating circumstances," such as family hardship.

Placement of persons in public service jobs would be administered by the director of the Selective Service System, Byron, V. Pepitone. He said today that applicants would be encouraged to find their own jobs, subject to approval by his agency.

For those already convicted or punished for desertion or draft evasion, the new Presidential clemency board will review cases on an individual basis. Priority will be given to those now in prison, and officials said that their confinement would be suspended as soon as possible.

Federal officials gave varying estimates of the number of deserters and evaders potentially eligible under the program. The estimates ranged from 28,000 to 50,000 or more.

Some officials said that 15,500 draft evaders would be eligible for clemency. Of these, 8,700 have already been convicted and 4,350 are under indictment, 4,060 are listed as fugitives, 3,000 of them in Canada. There are 130 persons now serving prison sentences for draft evasion.

Officials also said that 660 deserters were serving prison sentences or awaiting trial, and about 12,500 others were still at large, with about 1,500 of these now living in Canada.

Deputy Attorney General Laurence Silberman said today that those agreeing to participate in the plan should be prepared to serve the full 24 months of public service employment, although "mitigating circumstances" might lessen the term of service.

He said that those who failed to live up to the agreement would be subject to prosecution for the original charge of draft evasion or desertion.

The clemency program would cover offenses that took place between the Senate ratification of the Gulf of Tonkin resolution on Aug. 4, 1964, and the day the last United States combat soldier left Vietnam, March 28, 1973.

Officials said that clemency would not be considered for deserters or evaders who faced other, unrelated charges.

Draft evaders would be required to "execute an agreement" acknowledging allegiance to the United States and pledging to fulfill the period of alternative service. Deserters would be required to take an oath of allegiance to the United

The New York Times/Mike Lion

President Ford during his news conference at the White House last night.

States, as well as agreeing to fulfill the term of alternative service.

Officials estimated the cost of the program at about $2-million, most of this for processing and administrative details. The salaries for deserters or evaders would be paid by the employer.

President Ford disclosed that he was considering a "work re-entry" program for draft evaders and military deserters in a speech to the Veterans of Foreign Wars in Chicago on Aug. 19.

The White House had indicated that Mr. Ford would announce the program early last week, but this was postponed in the aftermath of the widespread criticism over the President's pardon of Mr. Nixon.

President Ford's choice of Mr. Goodell as chairman of the clemency board was viewed as an effort to placate critics of the Vietnam war who have pressed for unconditional amnesty.

Mr. Goodell, 48 years old, fell from favor with the Nixon Administration because of his strong stand against the Vietnam war policies. He lost his Senate seat in 1970 to James L. Buckley, Conservative-Republican, following a campaign in which Nixon forces helped engineer Mr. Goodell's defeat.

Mr. Goodell, now a Washington lawyer, is a long-time friend of President Ford's and was part of a group of young Republicans who helped install Mr. Ford as House minority leader nearly 10 years ago.

Other members of the clemency board are as follows:

Father Hesburgh, 57, former chairman of the United States Commission on Civil Rights, who was dismissed from that post by President Nixon.

Robert H. Finch, 51, Los Angeles lawyer. He was Mr. Nixon's first Secretary of Health, Education and Welfare and later served as a counselor to Mr. Nixon.

Gen. Lewis W. Walt, 61, a retired assistant commandant of the Marine Corps. He served in World War II and in the Korean and Vietnamese wars.

Vernon E. Jordan, 39, executive director of the National Urban League, an organization concerned with the advancement of minority groups. He was a lawyer-consultant to the United States Office of Economic Opportunity.

James Maye, executive director of the Paralyzed Veterans of America.

Dr. Ralph Adams, 59, president of Troy State University in Alabama and a brigadier general in the Alabama Air National Guard.

James P. Dougovita, 28, a teaching aide for minority students at Michigan Tech University. He served in the Vietnam war and is now a captain in the Michigan National Guard.

Aida Casanas O'Connor, 52, a lawyer who is now serving as assistant counsel to the New York State Division of Housing and Community Renewal in New York City.

* * *

October 6, 1974

WITHOUT NIXON, MR. THIEU'S WORLD IS NOT WHAT IT WAS

By JAMES M. MARKHAM

SAIGON—On the night Richard Nixon resigned as President of the United States, a huge rock perched atop a grotto in the Vietnamese village of Tri Thuy ominously split in two.

No one has confirmed that this supernatural event did in fact occur on the birthplace of President Nguyen Van Thieu, but the tale is being told in Saigon opposition circles. An omen.

Its point is simple. The unabating American financial and psychological disengagement from South Vietnam, capped by the fall of Mr. Thieu's most committed American patron, has weakened him in the eyes of his own people.

An Infirm Alliance

It is hardly coincidental that as American policymakers seem more and more inclined to put Vietnam behind them, opposition to Mr. Thieu in his own country has begun to build. An infirm alliance of Catholics, Buddhists and newspapermen has in the past few weeks demanded the eradication of official corruption and the establishment of press freedom and other democratic liberties.

Catholics, once pillars of the regime, have been the boldest in their attacks. Last month, the Rev. Tran Huu Thanh, a conservative priest who once ghosted texts on the opaque doctrine of "Personalism" for the late President Ngo Dinh Diem, accused Mr. Thieu and his relatives of illegally enriching themselves.

After a series of small demonstrations and after South Vietnam's ranking prelate, the Archbishop of Saigon, blessed the anticorruption front, Mr. Thieu last week went on national television to defend himself.

Falling back on old arguments; Mr. Thieu for two hours warned his audience that the Communists were infiltrating the newly invigorated opposition and that only vigilance would foil their plans for an imminent full-scale offensive—a now perennial prediction—but he also promised to relax the tough press law and to open the political process to "serious-minded" parties. His own Democracy party is now the only legal political grouping.

Mr. Thieu appears to be calculating that the new opposition's lack of leaders and its internal divisions—the Buddhists and Catholics do not really trust each other—will hamper its activities. Few doubt that he is capable of fiercely cracking down, but such a move might fail by creating the martyrs the opposition could use.

Moreover, the President is known to have closely followed United States Congressional reaction to the South Korean regime's repression of a similar Christian-led opposition. The South Vietnamese feel that Congress has already cut aid to Saigon severely; further cuts could be fatal.

Angered at Mr. Thieu's unwillingness to answer Father Thanh's six-count indictment, the opposition has decided to continue its campaign. Small but noisy demonstrations will probably continue but more worrisome to the regime is a deteriorating military situation.

The Fighting Gets Fierce

The summer months have seen the bloodiest, most sustained level of heavy fighting since the signing of the cease-fire agreements in Paris 20 months ago. Some military analysts believe that, particularly in the northern provinces and in the lower Mekong Delta, the Communists have achieved that critical, highly intangible edge in a war of attrition: momentum.

If so, the development comes at a bad moment for the Saigon forces. Congressional cuts in military appropriations have obliged them to begin evacuation of one-quarter of all outposts scattered around the country; fighter-bomber sorties have been halved; gasoline rations have been reduced to a third of their already skimpy 1973 levels.

Some analysts, including Americans, believe that the cuts will turn a profligate army into an economical one. But the short-term effect of the cuts has been disastrous to the morale of South Vietnamese commanders and troops.

In his speech, President Thieu complained about the reluctance of the United States to help South Vietnam the way it helped South Korea after its war; he also claimed that Washington had reneged on a pledge of "strong reaction" to Communist cease-fire violations.

"What we could really use now," said one ranking South Vietnamese official, "is some kind of strong reassurance from President Ford." At the moment, there is no sign that reassurance is coming.

* * *

January 13, 1975

DRIVE TO STEP UP WAR AID TO SAIGON OPENS IN CONGRESS

Administration Says Hanoi Moves Troops to South—Offensive Hinted

THIEU WARNS OF DANGER

He Terms U.S. Proposal for $300-Million 'Minimum' Needed for Forces

By JOHN W. FINNEY
Special to The New York Times

WASHINGTON, Jan. 30—The Administration opened an uphill battle in Congress today for additional military aid for the Saigon Government with a claim that North Vietnam was moving one and perhaps two other combat divisions into South Vietnam.

The suggestion by State and Defense Department officials was that North Vietnam might be getting into position for a major offensive, which South Vietnam would be unable to counter without additional military aid from the United States.

[In Saigon, President Nguyen Van Thieu termed the $300-million in additional aid requested from the United States Congress "the minimum" that his forces needed to defend themselves against stepped up Communist attacks.]

Until now it had been the generally accepted appraisal within the Administration that North Vietnam, while intensifying its military pressure, was not preparing for a large-scale, countrywide offensive like those in 1968 and 1972. In large measure, this appraisal rested on the fact that the Hanoi Government had not committed any divisions in its strategic reserve in Laos and North Vietnam.

Defense and State Department officials told a House Appropriations subcommittee that the Administration believed North Vietnam would not carry out a major offensive in the next six months. But, according to officials, the recent movement of divisions in North Vietnam's strategic reserve has thrown a new and confusing factor into Administration calculations.

Lieut Gen. Daniel O. Graham in an unusual public briefing on the military situation in Vietnam, testified that a North Vietnamese division had "moved out of Laos into South Vietnam." He said the division, identified by the Pentagon as the 968th, began the movement about 10 days ago.

General Graham said there was "tentative information" that two other divisions were moving from North Vietnam into South Vietnam.

Philip C. Habib, Assistant Secretary of State for East Asian and Pacific Affairs, told a reporter after the day-long hearing that the movement of the North Vietnamese divisions was being watched "with some concern" but that the significance remained unclear.

3 Explanations Offered

Among the possible explanations offered by Mr. Habib and General Graham were that the movement of the divisions represented a "feint" by North Vietnam, that the divisions would be used to reinforce expanded military activities in South Vietnam and, finally, that North Vietnam was preparing for a major offensive. Whatever the North Vietnamese intentions, it was apparent that the movement of the divisions would become an important element in the Administration's argument to a reluctant Congress to provide $300-million in military assistance to South Vietnam in addition to the $700-million already approved.

The Defense and State Department officials rested their case for additional military aid largely on what they described as the need to prepare South Vietnam for a major North Vietnamese attack.

At no point during the hearing did they contend that with $700-million in assistance South Vietnam would have insufficient ammunition and supplies to deal with the current or even an intensified level of fighting. Rather, their expressed concern was that if the fighting intensified over the next six months, South Vietnam's supplies would drop to a level at which Saigon would not be able to counter an all-out offensive.

"A major drawdown in stocks must be anticipated as combat intensifies," Eric F. von Marbod, a Deputy Assistant Secretary of Defense, testified. "Continuation of the strict conservation measures will further erode the capability and willingness of the South Vietnamese to defend against enemy initiatives."

The ensuing loss of territory and resources will undoubtedly encourage enemy aggression, and could encourage an attempt to launch an all-out offensive at a time when South Vietnamese stocks would be insufficient to counter such attack.

In the face of stiff Congressional opposition to the Administration request, the Defense Department went to unusual lengths in making public normally confidential intelligence information to support its case. In addition to the briefing by General Graham, Mr. von Marbod presented aerial reconnaissance photographs of North Vietnamese positions obviously taken by American planes over South Vietnam. He also described an "intercepted message" sent last November by the Communists in South Vietnam.

The message, which was described as "COSVN Resolution 75," was interpreted by Mr. von Marbod as "positive evidence" that the North Vietnamese intended to step up their offensive operations during the coming months. The message as translated by the Defense Department, read in part:

"Enemy air and artillery capability now limited as a result of reductions in U.S. aid. In short the enemy is declining militarily and has no chance of regaining the position they held in 1973.

"On the other hand, our position is improving. We are now stronger than we were during the Tet offensive in 1968 and the summer of 1972. We now have ample amounts of money, weapons and equipment which makes it possible for us to initiate a sustained attack on a wide front."

From the questioning it was obvious that the predominantly conservative subcommittee was troubled and divided over the Administration's request. Representative George H. Mahon of Texas, the subcommittee chairman, said the issue seemed to boil down to a question of whether the United States was "honor bound" to provide additional military aid to South Vietnam.

Mr. Habib, who helped negotiate the 1973 Paris peace agreements for Southeast Asia, said Congressional failure to provide additional funds would not "breach any legal or written agreement" with South Vietnam. But he argued that the United States had "a moral obligation" to provide South Vietnam with military equipment to defend itself.

* * *

January 17, 1975

VIETCONG SUDDENLY STEP UP ATTACKS CLOSE TO SAIGON

By JAMES M. MARKHAM
Special to The New York Times

BIEN HOA, South Vietnam, Jan. 16—A pastel likeness of Pope Paul VI, pinned to a wooden wall, benignly regards the twin sandbag bunkers in Mrs. Vu Van Tham's house.

For three weeks, her children have been sleeping in the bunkers at night. When Mrs. Tham and her husband hear the chilling phup-phup-phup of a 122mm rocket firing, they, too, scamper into the bunker.

Her family has thus far escaped the rockets that have been crashing almost nightly into Bien Hoa, and its nearby air base.

Her next door neighbors at 3–37 Pham Ouang Khanh Strest—a mud strip where Catholic refugees from North Vietnam live—were not so fortunate. On New Year's Eve at 6 A.M., a Chinese-made rocket pierced the tin roof of the square concrete house and hit Vu Thi Day, a 16-year-old schoolgirl.

The rocket did not explode, though it broke the sleeping girl's body in two—"like a loaf of bread" a neighbor recounted. The girl was killed instantly. Her family, terrified at the continuing attacks and frightened by the unexploded missile lodged 10 feet under their house, fled to another Catholic refugee community far from the air base.

Tension and Anxiety

The nocturnal rocketing of Bien Hoa, which lies 15 miles northeast of Saigon, is one element of a suddenly stepped-up campaign of sabotage, terrorism and assassination by Vietcong guerrillas on four sides of the capital.

Scattered guerrilla exploits, some of them on the very outskirts of Saigon, have stirred tension and anxiety, but not panic, in hamlets and villages of Gia Dinh and Bien Hoa Provinces.

A policeman in Thanh Loc village, five miles north of Saigon, pointed at a thick clump of bushes and observed.

"They may be in there watching us and you never know until they open fire. Then you know, but it is too late."

"They are like crickets," the policeman added. "They disappear when you approach, but you know very well they are near you."

The guerrilla campaign around Saigon apparently has several objectives. It makes Saigon edgy, gives the impression that the Government is not in control, ties down troops that are needed to check larger military thrusts elsewhere and, on occasion, claims an important military or economic target.

A week ago, a Communist sabotage team broke into the Thu Duc power station, five miles northeast of Saigon, and blew up a transformer. Saigon was blacked out from 4 to 5 in the morning.

Had the sabotage team been more expert, a French engineer observed, it would have placed the explosive charge on a generator a few yards from the transformer. "That would have taken at least 48 hours to repair," he said, with a jolly laugh.

Early on the morning of Jan. 6, Vietcong gunners fired a dozen rockets at the huge Phu Lam communications center on the western fringe of Saigon. The six rockets that fell on the grounds of the center did no damage; six others fell into an adjacent slum area, killing four people and wounding 13.

Another evident target is the sprawling Nha Be petroleum depot, seven miles southeast of Saigon, which was blown up a year ago, sending up almost half the country's civilian gasoline stocks in an enormous cloud of gray-black smoke that hung over the city for two days.

The Saigon military command on occasion laconically recounts aborted attempts on Nha Be in its daily communiqués, as on Jan. 4: "In Gia Dinh province, at 2045 last night, Government militiamen detected two Communist frogmen in the docking area of Esso fuel depot northeast of Nha Be district town. The militiamen killed both the frogmen and captured one mine."

To some foreigners and even some Vietnamese, it comes as a revelation that guerrillas can operate with impunity in the orchards, forests and rice fields on the edges of a city of three million people.

A Song Recalled

But the guerrillas have always been there. A hoary song, for example, celebrates the victories of the people of An Phu Dong over the French. In 1975, An Phu Dong, which nestles in a bend of the Saigon River four and a half miles north of the capital, is still "insecure."

In fact, a principal road, running from the town of Lai Thieu to the Saigon suburb of Go Vap past An Phu Dong, is now "dangerous," according to local people.

Intimately informed on the area, the guerrillas can operate with a certain precision. On the evening of Jan. 9, they reportedly entered Dan Tri hamlet, near An Phu Dong, and knocked on the doors of off-duty militiamen, demanding their weapons. Nineteen weapons were said to have been collected that night.

It is uncertain how the guerrilla campaign will unfold in the Saigon area. Much may depend on the success, or failure, of Communist main-force units in their current dry season campaign.

In Saigon there are predictions of terror or rocket attacks in the city. But some military analysts dismiss such notions, judging that the Communists want to avoid headline-grabbing undertakings in favor of actions that gradually and undramatically, undermine the Government's hold.

"I think they would be pretty stupid to rocket Saigon," said one Western military analyst who believes the Communists want to avoid giving the world the impression that they have scrapped the Paris peace agreements.

Virtually all military units in the Capital Military District have been on full alert for three months. Militia and ranger teams are sweeping the farmlands north of Go Vap and around Nhon Trach, 11 miles southeast of the capital.

* * *

January 22, 1975

HEAVY PSYCHOLOGICAL TOLL IS HALF-HIDDEN BUT SHATTERING RESULT OF THE LONG VIETNAM WAR

By JAMES M. MARKHAM
Special to The New York Times

SAIGON, South Vietnam, Jan. 21—An outsider in South Vietnam is forcefully struck by the appearance of normality almost everywhere. In the bustling cities, in the beautiful, expansive countryside, people conduct their lives in seeming obliviousness to the war.

After decades of foreign intervention and civil conflict, this may be one of the people's most precious achievements, but it appears to be extremely costly.

The mental stress of a war whose weapons have been as much psychological as military has been enormous, and since the uneasy cease-fire of January, 1973, it appears to have become even more intense.

"In the beginning there was great hope for peace," a Saigon psychiatrist said, "and now the despair is greater because there had been hope."

He said that after it became apparent that the fighting would continue, a number of women with draft-age sons came for treatment for acute depression. They had hoped that their 17-year-olds and 18-year-olds would be spared.

Agonizing Crossroads

Among teenagers reaching the agonizing crossroads of deferment or of conscription until age 43, a rise in the number of cases of schizophrenia has been noted, the psychiatrist reported. In Europe and America the onset of analogous crises usually comes much later, he added.

Dr. Tran Minh Tung, a former Minister of Health and a pioneer in mental health in South Vietnam, agreed that the sundering of the cease-fire and the continuing war had had a dispiriting effect on "the mind of the people."

"Maybe the people have become more war-weary, more pessimistic about the outcome, even though the people were very blasé about the prospect of peace," he suggested. "But still we did entertain some hope."

Dr. Cao Van Le, who runs the country's one overloaded mental institution, at Bien Hoa, north of Saigon, believes the sharp economic decline after the American disengagement added importantly to the level of stress, with the patient load tripling in a year.

Bien Hoa has slightly fewer than 2,000 resident patients, the bulk of them psychotics who became uncontrollably violent at home, Dr. Le said, and about 20 outpatients appear daily for a month's drugs.

Drug Supply Reduced

The American pullout has reduced the drug supply, so shock therapy is widely used to make up the difference. Aside from helping to train a few doctors, the United States has given no assistance to South Vietnam's fledgling mental-health program.

A. Terry Rambo, a Vietnamese-speaking American who, as a social anthropologist, has made several studies of stress, has noted "much more open display of violence—fist fights in the streets, to a small degree violent crime, and suicides." Such behavior is extremely unusual for Vietnamese, who are disciplined from infancy to smother aggressive impulses in personal relations.

Mr. Rambo and others believe that the greatest psychological pressures are on people in "contested" zones in rural areas where control passes back and forth between the Communist and Saigon sides.

In a study two years ago on the people of Ben Suc, who were uprooted from their village—believed to be sympathetic to the Vietcong—by the United States Army in 1967, it was found that the level of strain was significantly higher than ever recorded in studies of other nations and cultures.

Sixty-five per cent of those interviewed, the new study reported, "register above the point which, by the clinical standards of North America, would be considered an indicator of need for consultation and very probably for therapeutic aid."

Army operation in 1967 split up families that, for a variety of reasons, have not been reunited. Students of Vietnamese behavior believe that the enduring institution of the family—the focus of the most intense loyalties—is probably the strongest guarantee against psychic and social disintegration.

Discussing earlier problems, Dr. Tung, the former Health Minister, recounted that after he had helped the villagers from some war-torn Mekong Delta districts, he soon had a flood of patients from the area, mostly poor people who made the long trip in hope of relief.

They complained of bombing and shelling attacks, he said, and they were worried about their teenagers conscripted into militia units, about a husband abducted by the Vietcong or a brother jailed on suspicion of helping the Communists.

"They suffer," the doctor said. "They think this is fate. They do not blame the officials. They do not blame the Communists."

Gary D. Murfin, a political scientist at the University of Hawaii, is completing a study on the long-term effects of the dislocation of 10 million of South Vietnam's 19 million people from 1965 to 1974. He argues that forced relocation for political reasons generates such psychological strain that people become immune to appeals to loyalty.

Another Saigon psychiatrist said that many psychotic patients appeared to have trouble establishing a national identity.

"Some say they are French, some Americans, other nationalist—but what is it, a nationalist?" he said. "They feel the other side is perhaps more Vietnamese—that it has a stronger identity in psychological terms."

"But," the psychiatrist added, "the other side is also more fatiguing, disciplined, demanding."

"Almost all my paranoid schizophrenics believe they are being followed by the C.I.A. or the political police," he continued. "The simple, uneducated ones talk about the political police, the younger, more educated ones about the C.I.A."

He maintained that the suspiciousness bred by civil war had led the Vietnamese to develop "a total loss of confidence in one another" apart from the family.

Even a casual observer can see manifestations of this suspiciousness: a bureaucracy in which no one trusts another to do his job, a Government that sees most signs of opposition as Communist plots, the governed who rarely believe their leaders and who concoct the most fantastic, Byzantine explanations for the simplest events.

"We live very much in an atmosphere of distrust," Dr. Tung remarked. "We have become more or less paranoid in this war."

* * *

March 18, 1975

SOUTH VIETNAM REPORTED YIELDING MOST OF CENTRAL HIGHLANDS AREA; MAIN EVACUATION ROUTES CUT OFF

A MAJOR PULLOUT

Saigon Takes Action After Two Weeks of Sharp Reverses

By JAMES M. MARKHAM
Special to The New York Times

SAIGON, South Vietnam, Tuesday, March 18—The Saigon Government has decided to abandon most of the Central Highlands of South Vietnam because the area has become militarily indefensible, well-placed Western sources said today.

The decision, one of the most momentous of the long Vietnam war, was made after 14 days of sharp military reverses in the vast, rolling highlands. It was certain to have important political reverberations.

The area to be abandoned was reported to include the pivotal border provinces of Darlac, Pleiku and Kontum. South Vietnam has 44 provinces but these three are among the largest. They were the cradle of American involvement in the war and cover most—but not all—of the high, mountain-studded plains that are commonly regarded as making up the Central Highlands.

Defensibility Considered

These provinces are divided along administrative lines, however, while the Saigon military command's decision could be expected to follow lines of military defensibility, perhaps leaving parts of the three provinces still within its new line of defense and consigning parts of adjoining highlands provinces to the other side.

The Government might try to hold certain sections of the highlands either as staging areas for further withdrawal or as staging points for future actions. One informant indicated that the Government might even attempt to retake the city of Ban Me Thuot, giving itself an anchor in the southern highlands, but the sources doubted that such an attempt would be made.

It could not be learned how swiftly the movement of Government forces from the highlands—and particularly the important cities of Pleiku and Kontum—was unfolding.

According to some accounts, Government units were trekking down little used paths and provincial roads because the two main routes leading out of the region, 19 and 21, are cut.

Speedy Action Taken

"I think it can be said that the Vietnamese moved very quickly," one Western analyst said this morning, "and that once the decision was made it was carried out with considerable speed."

The well-placed Western sources said that, with the civilian populations alerted to the pullout, airports had become a difficult withdrawal route and that most of the troops—and civilians who wanted to leave—might have to fight their way out.

The decision to abandon the area was reportedly made sometimes after Friday when President Nguyen Van Thieu flew to the coastal city of Nha Trang to confer with Maj. Gen. Pham Van Phu, commander of Military Region II, which includes a stretch of the central coast as well.

Starting late last week, after the North Vietnamese seized the important highlands town of Ban Me Thuot and began rocket attacks on the corps headquarters and airfield at Pleiku, General Phu quietly began moving his staff to Nha Trang. The western defenses of Pleiku itself were threatened with tank-led attacks reported around the key district seat of Thanh An.

Reported to have weighed heavily in the decision to abandon the region were the vastness of the highlands, the enhanced North Vietnamese logistics and road systems, on which they have been feverishly working since the signing of

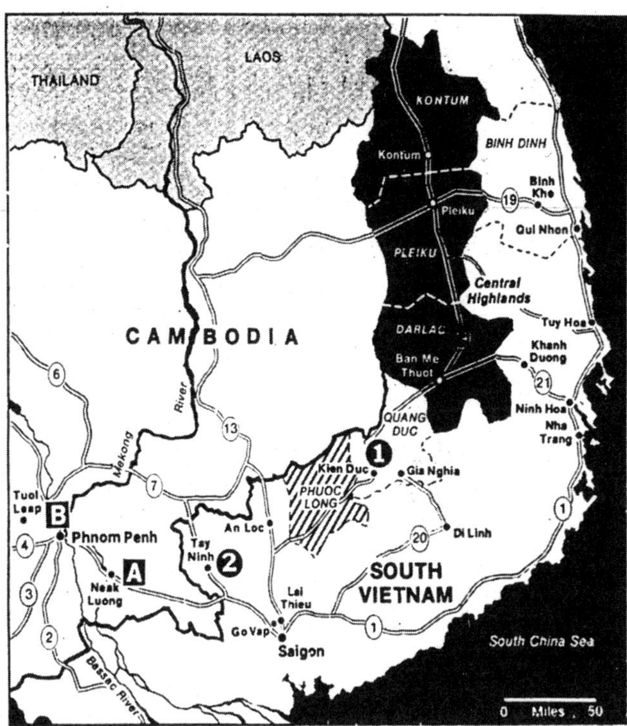

Saigon decided to abandon a roughly three-province area (shown in black). Phuoc Long Province (diagonally shaded) was previously lost. Kien Duc (1) was target of Communist drive, and heavy fighting was reported near Tay Ninh (2). In Cambodia, airstrip of Neak Luong (A) was attacked by rebels. Pressure was kept on capital (B).

the Paris peace agreements in January, 1973, and the increasing number of Communist troops in the area.

Also, with Routes 19 and 21 cut since the Communists began their highlands offensive on March 4, the South Vietnamese Air Force, already restricted by cuts in American assistance, faced the prospect of a long, costly airlift to the embattled area, with little likelihood of its paying off in the long run.

Decision Ratified

On Saturday, according to one account, the National Security Council in Saigon ratified the decision that Mr. Thieu and General Phu sketched out in Nha Trang. It could not be learned what kind of consensus Mr. Thieu had built up for the move, which is expected to be a stunning blow to the morale of the nation. But there were no visible signs of dissent.

Military analysts have long considered the withdrawal an eventual necessity. General Phu had only two regular infantry divisions, the 22d and 23d, to defend his vast corps command. The bulk of the 22d had been committed to the defense of Binh Dinh Province, which rises from the ricelands of the coast to the highlands.

The 23d Division was believed to have been battered in the fight for Ban Me Thuot, which the North Vietnamese attacked early on March 10.

In addition, the II Corps area had roughly the equivalent of a division, about 10,000 men, in rangers and perhaps another division of regional forces.

Hanoi Force Put at 45,000

The exact strength of the North Vietnamese forces in the area is a matter of guesswork, though last month one reliable Western estimate put the total at 45,000.

But since then there have been reports of heavy infiltrations of North Vietnamese into the area. The Saigon command charged last week that elements of the 316th Division, a famous one that fought at Dien Bien Phu, had been seen in the highlands.

In addition, the North Vietnamese 320th and 10th Divisions are believed to be operating in the Darlac-Quang Duc area of the southern highlands, the 968th around Pleiku and the 3d at Binh Dinh.

The Communists also have regional forces and autonomous regiments—those not attached to a division—in the highlands.

Darlac, Kontum and Pleiku Provinces represent about 16 per cent of South Vietnam's land surface and their population of a half million compares with a nationwide population of 19.5 million.

One Western military analyst said that the pullout decision was "not all black" in that it would permit the South Vietnamese forces to regroup in the more defensible coastal areas, where their lines of communication are shorter and those of their foes extended.

A measure of the success of the regrouping operation, which is unparalleled in the recent history of the war, will be the number of troops and civilians who manage to walk, ride, fly or fight their way to the coast.

One knowledgeable informant said that a possible escape route was the little used provincial route leading out of Phu Bon Province to the town of Tuy Hoa on the coast.

It seemed possible that some military or civilian refugees might manage to move down Route 21 from Ban Me Thuot to Ninh-Hoa on the coast. That highway is cut near the town of Khanh Duong, but Route 19 is cut in many places.

Also, army engineers have been improving an old French colonial road descending from the Quang Duc Province capital of Gia Nghia to Di Linh on Route 20.

One of the last correspondents known to be in Pleiku, Nguyen Tu, who works for the respected daily Chinh Luan, described the town on Sunday as a nightmarish place. He said people were running around the streets as if they were caught in a trap, clinging to their most precious possessions. He said every imaginable kind of vehicle was being used in efforts to get out of the city, but that there was no real exit.

In yesterday's fighting, North Vietnamese tanks and troops mounted heavy assaults in remote, mountainous Quang Duc Province and stepped up attacks around Saigon, the military command said.

The regional thrusts, which the command called a nation-wide Communist offensive, are now viewed with increased anxiety by Western military analysts. "It's grim and it's going to get grimmer," said one knowledgeable Western military source. "Every military region is in trouble now."

Losses Recounted

In recent weeks, the South Vietnamese have lost a vital province capital, Ban Me Thuot, retained only a tenuous grip on the key city of Tay Ninh, 65 miles northwest of Saigon, shifted the II Corps headquarters to Nha Trang, lost a half dozen district capitals in the highlands and other areas and witnessed a series of increased attacks around Saigon.

The Saigon command's spokesman, Lieut. Col Le Trung Hien, said in response to a question on Monday that the North Vietnamese attacks are "more serious" than the 1968 Tet offensive and the spring offensive of 1972. "The situation will be very critical if the enemy can cut the vital routes permanently," he said.

Although most Western military analysts would disagree with the official South Vietnamese assessment, there is a feeling among them that the momentum of the attacks is increasing and that Saigon's forces are hard-pressed.

Perhaps the command's most significant announcement was that North Vietnamese troops and tanks had mounted a series of assaults against the Kien Duc district headquarters and at the Nhon Ca airfield in Quang Duc Province. The attacks, according to military sources, are aimed at Gia Nghia, the province capital.

The district of Kien Duc, 120 miles north-east of Saigon, was the scene in December, 1973, of the first frontal assault by the Communists on a district capital since the cease-fire agreement. The North Vietnamese seized the district capital, held it for several days and were finally repulsed by heavy South Vietnamese tank and fighter bomber attacks.

At a press briefing this morning, Colonel Hien asserted that "there are movements of troops in the highlands but these movements of troops were made for tactical reasons." He added that "no such withdrawal decision has been posed for the South Vietnamese forces in the highlands yet."

The command reported heavy fighting at an important district town, Dinh Quan, 55 miles northwest of Saigon. Colonel Hien said that the attack completed the cutting of all but one of the country's principal roads leading out of the highlands to the coast. Dinh Quan lies on Route 20, which runs from the area north of Saigon to the hill resort of Dalat.

The command also reported heavy shelling and ground attacks around Binh Khe, a district town on Route 19 in the highlands.

* * *

March 19, 1975

A HIGHLANDS MOTHER ESCAPES; BUT PAYS A TERRIBLE TOLL

By BERNARD WEINRAUB
Special to The New York Times

SAIGON, South Vietnam, March 18—Her face swollen with grief, Ly Thi Van stands beside a half-open door near the Saigon docks, clutching her infant son and staring vacantly at scooters and buses speeding past.

She has lost three children in the recent surge by North Vietnamese troops across the Central Highlands—a surge that resulted in the Government's decision to abandon most of the highlands and that has stirred terror among tens of thousands of South Vietnamese.

Ly Thi Van seems in shock. "Whenever we ask her a question she starts to cry," says her sister, Ly Thi Tinh, also a refugee from the Central Highlands town of Ban Me. Thuot. "We don't talk about—" and she stopped and bit her lip and turned away.

Husbands Died In War

The sisters are widows. Ly Thi Van's husband, a 34-year-old master sergeant named Bui Duc Hoan, died last year on a patrol in the highlands.

The husband of Ly Thi Tinh, also an enlisted man, was killed in the highlands in 1966. The 33-year-old woman has a son of 10. The two women, carrying bundles of clothes, pots and photographs came to Saigon the other morning to stay briefly with an uncle.

Both women have lived for years in Ban Me Thuot, a pleasant town of Vietnamese and Chinese shopkeepers, of farmers, montagnard tribesmen, Italian and French coffee planters and American missionaries. They lived next to each other in thatch-roofed homes near the sector command post, working as rice venders and collecting widows' pensions of about $80 every three months.

Last week the North Vietnamese began their fierce rocket and tank attack on the sleepy town, an attack that was part of the Communist advance across the highlands.

"We didn't know what to do," said Ly Thi Tinh in Vietnamese. "We picked up everything in bags and ran to the neighbor's home. Everyone was crying. What to do? What to do?

"We ran to the airstrip where there were helicopters. We closed our eyes. We did not want to open them. Everywhere there were bodies, there were shells flying all over. I knew I would die."

At a crossroads leading to the airstrip the fighting was so intense that the women and their children turned back, ran through alleyways and hid on a rubber plantation with hundreds of other refugees. Their fears were compounded because many were widows and families of South Vietnamese soldiers, and others were refugees from North Vietnam who came south in 1954. "Everyone was sure we would die," she repeated.

In the confusion and panic that followed, the two sisters and their family split up. Ly Thi Van and her five children—ranging in age from 18 months to 15 years—began their flight from Ban Me Thuot with hundreds of others, dashing east along a road crammed with refugees.

Family Boards Bus

About three miles out, the family boarded a packed bus bound for Phuoc An, 30 miles east, on Route 21. Somewhere along the route—Ly Thi Van can barely speak about the incident—the bus and trucks were halted at a roadblock set up by the Vietcong.

Speaking in a murmur, she said: "We saw other buses stop, too. There were three VC on the road and many hidden in the jungle, many, many VC. All of a sudden we heard planes overhead. The VC became panicky. Everybody became panicky. One VC in the jungle yelled, 'Open fire.' Another VC near the buses said 'No, don't fire, everyone's a civilian.' "

"There was a mistake, I don't know what happened," said the 36-year-old woman. "There were explosion all around, the bus exploded. People began firing at us." Her voice trailed off.

In the moments that followed, she saw the charred body of her 8-year-old son beside the bus. Clutching her infant, Ly Thi Van saw her groaning 9-year-old son on the ground. She picked up the boy and began running.

"All the way he was crying," she said. "All the way he said that his chest was burning. Oh my God! What could I do? Then he stopped crying. I looked at him. His lips were getting darker and darker and darker, and he died."

A third child, a teen-age boy, is missing and presumed dead. The woman buried the 9-year-old with the help of montagnard tribesmen who fed her and the infant and took them to the district capital of Phuoc An. There the sisters were reunited. Ly Thi Tinh, her child and a wounded uncle spent about three days walking the 30 miles from Ban Me Thuot to Phuoc An.

'It Was a Miracle'

"It was a miracle," she said. "We stayed at the air-field in Phuoc An and we met a helicopter pilot, a friend of my husband from Ban Me Thuot. He took us to Nha Trang by helicopter."

From Nha Trang, a city on the South China Sea 200 miles northeast of Saigon, the women and their children flew to Saigon. "We asked for money, we begged for money and people helped us," said Ly Thi Tinh. "You sometimes meet good people."

The women lost their savings, their jewelry, the documents enabling them to collect war-widow pensions. "Everything went up in smoke, everything," said Ly Thi Tinh. Her sister gripping the infant, trembled and groaned and began to weep.

* * *

March 22, 1975

ROAD OUT OF HUE: LONG NIGHTMARE

As Thousands Flee South, Highway Is Vast Scene of Human Suffering

By MALCOLM W. BROWNE
Special to The New York Times

HAI VAN PASS, South Vietnam, Saturday, March 22—By the thousands, the people are abandoning Hue, the former

Associated Press

South Vietnamese refugees fleeing from Hue on civil and military vehicles. Those at right shared a trailer with earth-moving equipment. Throngs in northern area were allowed by North Vietnamese and Vietcong to move freely.

capital of Vietnam, and the road south from the city is a scene of human suffering.

The armed forces are also moving out, some by landing craft, some in military vehicles, some bundled into trucks with family members, furniture and food.

No one seemed in the slightest doubt yesterday that Hue and the rest of the north were being left to the Communists. A harried colonel stopped his jeep long enough to say, "Yes, yes, the evacuation will be finished in several days, several days."

Refugees were pouring toward the coastal city of Da Nang not only from Quang Tri and Hue to the northwest, but also from provinces farther south, in the belief that these were also finished.

Here at the Hai Van Pass—a scenic cut in a small range of jagged hills projecting into the South China Sea between Hue and Da Nang—the exodus was a nightmare.

There was no real panic, but the sheer volume of trucks, buses, army vehicles, cattle, bicycles, motorcycles and pedestrians along narrow, badly asphalted Route I, created conditions for countless accidents.

In a short period at one spot, this correspondent witnessed three serious accidents, one of them probably fatal.

Road Open All Night

Complicating the problem, the road, which is normally closed by a curfew, is open all night, unhindered by any Communist harassment despite the closeness of major North Vietnamese units. Thus, empty vehicles are flowing north in a volume nearly equal to those going south, to pick up more passengers.

The 120-mile round trip from Da Nang to Hue, normally covered in about four hours, is now taking vehicles 36 hours or more.

Most wealthy residents have left by air, paying for enormously expensive flights out.

The military is making some use of the road, but appears to be depending more on an airlift from Hue, in addition to a fleet of landing craft that has been embarking troops near Hue and taking them down the coast to Da Nang.

Their cargo has included artillery—even 175-mm guns—an indication that the Government's forces are abandoning

Hue notwithstanding a denial made by President Nguyen Van Thieu Thursday.

Few Heard of Speech

Very few of the refugees had heard that speech, in which the President said that the armed forces would fight to the end, except in two highlands provinces that were being abandoned.

"I didn't hear the speech myself," a Hue taxi driver said, "but most of us know from friends who did listen that he said the Government was abandoning Hue."

Such ignorance of Government intentions or statements appeared to be universal.

"We knew nothing of this," a housewife said, as she prepared a roadside lunch for her young children, "until I had to go to a Government office in Hue and was told that my problem would have to be handled by another office, since that one was leaving. So I went to another office, and that one was leaving too, and right away all of us realized that the whole Government and the army were leaving. So we started leaving too."

A man in another place said:

"It's so strange and terrible this time. In the other bad times, in 1968 and 1972, lots of us became refugees too. But this time there's no fighting, no reason. Hue is being shelled a bit now, but that's not why we are leaving. We are leaving because the Government is giving our home to the Communists."

American sources in the area, who asserted that Hue was not being abandoned, said, however, that American aircraft had been used to ferry all Westerners, regardless of nationality, out of Hue, and that the evacuation, except for a half dozen American officials, was complete.

This evacuation was carried out not in the conviction that Hue was lost, it was explained, but "to meet the wishes of the persons concerned, who seemed to fear for their safety."

Vietnamese military police were helping to unsnarl the worst of the traffic jams along the road, but apart from them and some ambulance service for the many accident casualties, there was no evidence of the slightest Government assistance to the refugees.

Thirty pupils from a secondary school near Da Nang, on their own initiative, cooked up a load of potatoes and carried cans of fresh water to the suffering families in stalled vehicles. Some of the travelers seemed infuriated at the young people, perhaps because of their relatively good fortune, and threw the offered potatoes and water back at them.

But a young boy dressed neatly in a threadbare suit gratefully accepted some potatoes and said in English: "Wow, these potatoes number one, man. You know, we really get hungry and thirsty on this long trip. I used to have many G.I. friends at Phu Bai where I live, but they all gone. Too bad. Now I gotta go too. Last night two VC come. Just two. But we know they all around us now."

A somewhat older boy, also traveling alone, said his father was sick and would stay in Hue.

"He just say to me, you will have a better life in Da Nang, so go now, and leave me here. So I will go to my uncle if I can find him."

In the chaos of the trip children and babies were getting lost. One man got all the way to Da Nang before realizing his baby had disappeared on a bus, and choking with sobs, he appealed for help in getting back to the Hai Van Pass.

But there are no vehicles to be had, except for people with money—lots of it.

Many Decide to Stay

Travelers said that although most of the shops and markets of Hue were closed, apparently no major looting had begun. They said they knew of many people who had decided to remain in Hue.

"It's their home, and maybe there is really no more place to run to," one said.

"There are some people in Hue," another said with embarrassment, "who maybe do not think it will be so bad when the Vietcong come. So they stay."

People were also pouring into Da Nang from cities down the coast, notably Quang Tin and Quang Ngai. They appeared to fear that both would be lost soon, although there has been relatively little fighting.

Many of the northern refugees were finding places with families and friends, having made the long trek before.

But schoolyards' side streets and the city stadium in Da Nang were rapidly filling up with families.

* * *

March 24, 1975

DEFINING A COMMITMENT

In the face of the setbacks suffered by President Thieu, the principal issues concerning the American involvement in South Vietnam's defense are being distorted as a result of the extreme positions taken both by the Ford Administration's military spokesmen and by those who respond to the crisis with demands for instant termination of American aid.

Defense Secretary Schlesinger has tried to persuade the American people that the current North Vietnamese attack was provoked by the declining rate of military assistance. At the other extreme, those who demand an end to American military aid, either at once or within a few months, would make it impossible to test South Vietnam's willingness and capacity to defend itself. Adoption of such counsel would, in the event of a collapse of Saigon's defenses, strengthen the hand of those who want to shift the ultimate and perhaps even the entire blame for such a defeat to the United States. Though without foundation in the long, tragic history of the Indochina conflict, such a distortion could have serious consequences on the political scene.

A rational and honorable response to both the critical short-term situation in Vietnam and this country's long-term policy toward Saigon calls for a clear understanding that additional aid will be forthcoming only within the continuing process of phasing out American military subsidies, in line with amply articulated previous Congressional directives.

It is crucial that the Administration provide public assurances of precisely such an understanding now in order to eliminate once and for all any subsequent misunderstanding or distortion of the American commitment. Clarity on this matter would become vital should President Thieu's forces find themselves incapable of holding even the greatly reduced defense perimeter. The line should be drawn now between this country's readiness to honor its promise of a continuing but declining aid commitment—an obligation that for better or worse we clearly have—and the unacceptable view that is increasingly suggested by leak and rhetoric from the Pentagon that the United States must save Saigon and President Thieu at whatever cost—an obligation that we clearly do not have.

It will undoubtedly be argued that to spell out such a policy may impose serious limitations on President Thieu's freedom of action, with the implication that it may thereby reduce his political and military effectiveness. Mr. Thieu's past record suggests that, quite to the contrary, such an explicit statement of American intention may be the only way to persuade him to broaden his Government's political base and thus strengthen his popular support. Such steps, resisted much too long by President Thieu, far from being political luxuries, are as essential to South Vietnam's defense as guns and ammunition.

* * *

March 27, 1975

SKEPTICISM ON DOMINO THEORY

Administration View Disputed by Aides and Diplomats

By LESLIE H. GELB
Special to The New York Times

WASHINGTON, March 26—Secretary of State Kissinger restated at his news conference today the classic domino theory, which links American security in one place to American security everywhere else.

"We must understand that peace is indivisible," he said. "The United States cannot pursue a policy of selective reliability. We cannot abandon friends in one part of the world without jeopardizing the security of friends everywhere."

In the same vein, President Ford has recently expressed the idea that foreign reactions to developments in Indochina tend to validate the domino theory. That judgment, however, is not shared by Administration foreign policy specialists, the American intelligence community or many foreign diplomats.

Interviews with Administration experts and interviews conducted by New York Times correspondents overseas show that even in those few countries where leaders feel that American credibility has been somewhat impaired by Congressional reluctance to provide more military aid to Indochina, there are no signs of a basic reassessment of policy toward the United States.

The results clearly indicate that foreign leaders gauge their relations with the United States by their own experience with Washington and their own particular alternatives to dealing with Washington, and not by events in Indochina.

President's Reliability at Issue

In the United States, the higher the Administration official being interviewed, the more likely he is to subscribe to some form of the domino theory, although not by that name.

Yet, even among these high officials, the issue is not so much the importance of Indochina and how its future relates to American security. To these officials, the real issue is the outcome of the battle between Congress and the President. To them, the real domino is the prospect of a collapse abroad of Presidential reliability and predictability as a result of Congressional unwillingness to support Mr. Ford's policies.

Many members of Congress feel that the resort to the domino image by Mr. Ford, Secretary of State Kissinger and Secretary of Defense James R. Schlesinger is merely a tactic to dramatize the issue, force Congress to support the Administration policy and pin the blame on Congress if Indochina falls into Communist hands.

Senator Edward M. Kennedy, Democrat of Massachusetts, said: "All of these theories are part of the effort being made by the Administration to intimidate Congress and the American people by covering up the failure of our national policy in Indochina. Why else would the Administration use such rhetoric and ignore our basic obligation to end the violence in a situation where its policy can only lead to failure?"

Term Used by Eisenhower

The domino theory—the notion that a Communist victory in Indochina would almost inevitably lead to Communist gains and a weakening of the American position in the world—has a long history. The term "domino" in foreign policy was first made famous by President Dwight D. Eisenhower in April, 1954.

With French forces surrounded at Dien Bien Phu in the final phase of France's Indochina war, he said: "Finally, you have broader considerations that might follow what you would call the 'falling domino' principle. You have a row of dominoes set up, you knock over the first one, and what will happen to the last one is the certainty that it will go over very quickly. So you could have a beginning of a disintegration that would have the most profound influences."

The roots of this line of thought run back to the so-called Truman doctrine of 1947, which provided a domino-like rationale for providing aid to Greece and Turkey to counter Communist threats. Its branches ran into the nineteen-sixties, highlighted in 1963 by President John F. Kennedy's saying: "I believe it. I believe it." As the decade wore on, the image faded, and was replaced with high officials' making the public case for helping South Vietnam in terms of maintaining the credibility of American commitments.

In recent weeks, Mr. Schlesinger and Mr. Kissinger have made public comments to the effect that the domino theory had been overly discredited. Last week in Indiana, President Ford took this one step further.

Asked if he believed that Cambodia was "vital" to American security, the President answered, "I think it is." He went on to refer to news reports about Thailand's asking for the withdrawal of American forces and the Philippines' reviewing its relationship with the United States.

Threat to Security Seen

Then he said: "I think these potential developments to some extent tend to validate the so-called domino theory. And if we have one country after another, allies of the United States, losing faith in our word, losing faith in our agreements with them, yes, I think the first one to go could vitally affect the national security of the United States."

Administration officials say that the intelligence community has consistently rejected this analysis. According to these officials, intelligence reports continue to say that the loss of Cambodia and South Vietnam would have adverse and negative consequences for American policy, but that even in the worst circumstances these consequences would be controllable and manageable.

In Thailand, officials who were interviewed said that the Thais were reluctant to sever their connection with Washington completely because they did not see anyone else able to provide them with protection. Charunphan Issarangkun na Ayuthaya, who was Foreign Minister until recently, said that the Government was ready to talk with any government that emerged from the conflict in Cambodia.

Administration experts said they had been aware of this Thai position for several weeks. They also said that the increasing willingness of the Thais to deal with Communists in Indochina and with China was something that Washington had been encouraging for four years.

The experts explained that this progress had been speeded up by developments in Indochina, but said that they did not see the acceleration as damaging American Interests. They said they did not expect Thailand to ask formally for a complete withdrawal of American forces from her territory in the next year or so.

With respect to the Philippines, these experts said that there were a few newspaper editorials questioning ties with the United States, but that there was no evidence from the Philippine Government that any of its leaders were contemplating a reassessment of policy.

Leaders in the Philippines were said to view events in Indochina now as the foreseeable consequence of the American troop withdrawal from Vietnam and of the detente with China and the Soviet Union that followed.

The unwillingness of Congress to vote more aid for Indochina is seen in the Philippines as an understandable reaction to the seemingly endless Indochina war. Administration experts saw no sign that the Philippine Government would ask Washington to withdraw from Clark Air Base or the Naval base at Subic Bay, the two major United States installations in that country.

Reports from South Korea and interviews with the Administration specialists indicated a more serious impact in Seoul, which has been heavily dependent on United States military and economic support. But they reported that the South Koreans, close neighbors of both China and the Soviet Union, were not likely to alter their policy of maintaining close ties with the United States.

Indonesia's Foreign Minister, Adam Malik, cited the latest developments in Indochina in expressing doubts about the reliability of the United States, but American diplomats were said to feel that strains in relations between the two Governments had already been growing before the deterioration of the situation in Vietnam and Cambodia.

Interviews with officials in Japan, Australia and leading nations of Western Europe showed no evidence of a rethinking of relations with Washington. In fact, Administration area specialists stated that most leaders in those countries applauded the prospect of the United States finally moving toward total disengagement from Indochina.

In the Middle East, the reactions are mixed, often confusing, but generally more serious. Some Israeli officials said that Congressional inaction on Indochina had to raise questions in their minds about a similar future Congressional reaction on aid to Israel. More specifically, these officials expressed concern about whether Israel could put her trust in any American-backed guarantee.

Worry About Kissinger

Other Israeli diplomats said that Indochina was not an issue for their country. What they worried about, they said, was not the reliability of Congress but the motives of Mr. Kissinger. Support for Israel in Congress still runs high.

From Cairo it was reported that a leading Egyptian official noted what he called the decline of American power around the world as a result of events in Vietnam, Cambodia and Portugal, and added that "another failure" in the Middle East would add powerfully to that tendency.

It is this sense that events in the world are going against the United States, coupled with what some call the "disarray" in Washington, that really troubles high Administration officials.

In private conversations, high Administration officials brush aside specific reactions in specific countries at this time. They look to more general and more intangible effects. One high State Department official put it this way: "Others watching the split between Congress and the President have to ask if the United States has a foreign policy, and are we calculable?"

Most of these high officials were pessimistic about the chances of keeping Indochina non-Communist. Asked why senior officials nevertheless persisted in raising the American stakes in Indochina through rhetoric about dominoes, they responded uniformly. The rhetoric, they said, is aimed at Congress, not at the world.

Asked if private messages had been sent to American ambassadors overseas to explain this, they all said no.

* * *

March 31, 1975

HANOI FORCES MOVE SOUTH AFTER OCCUPYING DA NANG; U.S. SHIPS TO AVOID COMBAT

RESISTANCE SCANT

Government's Troops Reported Fleeing—Streets Jammed

By BERNARD WEINRAUB
Special to The New York Times

SAIGON, South Vietnam, Monday, March 31—A speedy North Vietnamese force moved into chaotic Da Nang yesterday and met scant opposition from demoralized fleeing Government troops, according to Western and South Vietnamese military sources here.

Some fighting was reported in the city but South Vietnamese army and marine units were reported to have crumbled rapidly. Streets were said to be swollen with refugees and mobs of frantic families.

The loss of Da Nang—the second largest city in South Vietnam and the headquarters of United States Marines during the years of American involvement here—is considered perhaps the biggest single reverse the Saigon regime has had yet.

Thrust Down Coast

There were reports that the North Vietnamese were sweeping southward along the coast, and that such cities as Qui Nhon, the third largest in the nation, and Tuy Hoa were seriously threatened by the Communist advance. American officials and South Vietnamese were being evacuated from these port cities, Western sources said.

The Qui Nhon airfield is reported packed with soldiers and families vainly seeking to flee by plane. Virtually all flights to Qui Nhon have been stopped because of the panic at the airport.

The Saigon command said this morning that heavy fighting had flared near Binn Khe, a district town about 25 miles northwest of Qui Nhon and on the highway leading to the port. Military officials say that the threatened loss of Qui Nhon would give the North Vietnamese a substantial coastal belt that reaches into the center of the nation and would enable the Communists to pick up another major port in their offensive.

With the loss of Da Nang, the outlook for the South Vietnamese armed forces now seems grim. One Vietnamese military source said that there were about 100,000 troops in and around the Da Nang area—most of them on the run or trapped. The troops come from Government units that were considered some of South Vietnam's best: the First, Second and Third Infantry Divisions, the Marine Division and about a half-dozen ranger battalions.

At this point, South Vietnam's northernmost military zone—Military Region I—is under virtually complete Communist control after a stunning disintegration of Government and military authority. Moreover the loss of Da Nang, a city that seemed militarily invulnerable two weeks ago, was a severe blow to President Nguyen Van Thieu, whose government was in disarray.

The New York Times/Andrew H. Malcolm

A shipload of refugees from Da Nang, South Vietnam, arriving at Cam Ranh Bay.

News of the loss of Da Nang was made public here dramatically yesterday morning by South Vietnam's Deputy Premier, Phan Quang Dan, who said at a news conference: "It is lost. The Communists have taken Da Nang."

Later in the day, the Saigon command's spokesman, Lieut. Col. Le Trung Hien, said: "We have lost contact with our headquarters in Da Nang city. We know the situation in the city was in serious chaos. The order has not been restored. It is difficult for us to find out what is happening in the city."

Although North Vietnamese Army units had moved to within three miles of the city to the south and west—and had fired rockets and shells at the American-built airport and naval base in recent days—the loss of the city of 500,000 was widely attributed to a breakdown in the army ranks, the influx of as many as 1.5 million refugees and to conditions in streets that verged on anarchy.

"Law and order evaporated," said a Western source. "There was no battle of Da Nang. It was a rout."

One reliable Western source said last night that North Vietnamese soldiers were known to be moving through the streets of Da Nang, a city 370 miles northeast of Saigon. A Vietcong spokesman in Saigon, Maj. Phuong Nam, said the Communists had been in complete control of Da Nang since Saturday afternoon. "And it is true, the Vietcong flag is flying in Da Nang."

By last evening, however, there was some confusion in Saigon about developments in Da Nang and North Vietnamese movements in the city. One highly informed intelligence source said: "Certainly there are North Vietnamese Army forces in Da Nang. There's not all that much organized resistance but there are plenty of people around with guns and it's chaotic."

There were reports of looting, mass desertions among Government forces, fires in the city and chaos as refugees packed piers and bridges to board barges for ships standing offshore in the South China Sea. Heavy rains and rough waves were thwarting the feverish flight of families and soldiers seeking to flee the port by boat.

The United States Military Sea Command is operating several chartered ships for the operation. Two of the cargo vessels, the Pioneer Contender and the Pioneer Commander were near Da Nang late yesterday afternoon and boarding nearly 15,000 refugees for the 15-hour trip south to Cam Ranh Bay. A reliable Western source said that the North Vietnamese were not thwarting the evacuation and that the operation would continue.

Nearly 30,000 refugees, clinging to railings and packing the decks of freighters and ships, have arrived in Cam Ranh Bay from Da Nang in a desperate and fevered flight from the North Vietnamese. Tens of thousands of others, including army deserters, are still awaiting evacuation from Da Nang, a city that seems to have fallen into the hands of the North Vietnamese virtually by default.

Western sources here say that, President Ford's decision to send four United States amphibious ships to help evacuate refugees is not expected to have any insignificant impact on the operation. The four ships—each carries 2,000 people—will arrive in the area within the next day. But, with thousands seeking to flee, the arrival of the four transports are viewed here as insignificant, given the need and the panic of the civilian refugees.

With the loss of Da Nang, military officials said, were millions of dollars worth of equipment, including scores of airplanes, tanks and artillery pieces. Within the last few weeks, the South Vietnamese Army has lost more than $1-billion in American-made equipment in the rapid abandonment of two-thirds of the nation.

North Vietnam now controls virtually the entire upper half of South Vietnam, freeing some of its ten infantry divisions in the north to press southward along the coast to Qui Nhon, 175 miles south of Da Nang, Tuy Hoa, and possibly even Nha Trang and Cam Ranh Bay. These two enclaves, now swarming with tens of thousands of refugees, are now considered vulnerable by South Vietnamese military authorities.

A reliable Western source said last night that North Vietnamese activity had picked up sharply and abruptly along the coast in recent days. Two port cities, Qui Nhon and Tuy Hoa, 45 miles to the south, were being evacuated. And the major city of Nha Trang, about 95 miles northeast of Saigon, is now suffering a scare that has resulted in an abrupt demand for airline tickets to Saigon and rumors of an impending North Vietnamese attack.

The loss of Da Nang was viewed as the largest single reverse experienced by Government forces in Vietnam. From the time that the North Vietnamese seized Hue, the former imperial capital, 40 miles to the north, and then the provincial capital of Tam Ky, about 50 miles south of Da Nang, it was obvious to military analysts that Da Nang was in some peril.

But few Vietnamese and few Americans expected the city to be lost so rapidly.

'Collapse of Order'

"It fell without a fight," said one highly informed Western source. "One of the tragedies is that you had marine elements fighting outside the city, but inside there was simply a collapse of internal order. It swept all over the city. It was sheer panic."

Clearly, the panic that swept Da Nang was the result of President Thieu's decision to abandon the northern two-thirds of the nation, the abrupt flight of hundreds of thousands of refugees in the northern provinces and the Central Highlands, the erosion of army morale and widespread desertions, the collapse of administrative authority in the provinces and the lack of Government preparation for the flow of refugees.

What has especially shaken army morale is the fact that Lieut. Gen. Ngo Quang Truong, the commander of Military Region I, and his staff were forced to leave their headquarters on Saturday for a navy ship on the South China Sea. General Truong is considered one of the best officers in the Army, and his evacuation was the result of a North Vietnamese rocket and artillery barrage as well as the panic.

* * *

April 3, 1975

A FEAR-SWEPT SAIGON IS ON BRINK OF CHAOS

By BERNARD WEINRAUB

Special to The New York Times

SAIGON, South Vietnam, April 2—This capital is on the brink of chaos. The streets are humid and eerily silent at night as soldiers cluster on street corners or sprawl on the pavement and sleep beneath tamarind trees.

By day, fear and rumor breed among the capital's two million people. The airport is packed. Foreigners are rapidly shipping home their ceramic elephants and furniture and stereo sets. Vietnamese men stand in small groups reading the afternoon newspapers then quickly walk home.

"C'est fini, c'est fini," a Vietnamese Roman Catholic priest repeated over and over at the airport. A Vietnamese man, with tears in his eyes, said good-by to an American and whispered hoarsely: "We will survive in Vietnam. Another million people may die perhaps, but we will survive and be proud."

A Sense of Doom

There is a sense of doom now in Saigon, a sense of engulfing darkness in a capital that seems terrified. A Vietnamese woman burst into tears the other day at a restaurant. "What's going to happen to us?" she asked companions. "Will they shoot us? Will they shoot my family? What's going to happen?"

In a small apartment near downtown Saigon, the 23-year-old widow of a soldier, with two small children, trembled and bit her lip. "Where is there to go after Saigon?" she asked. "What is here to do? Wait, wait, wait."

An American in his office at the embassy shrugged and said: "I asked my wife to leave, I begged her to, and she said no, she wants to stay with me until the end." He smiled and said: "It's the end of the line, isn't it? It's going so fast I can't believe it."

President Nguyen Van Thieu's abrupt decision to abandon most of the northern two-thirds of the nation and concentrate his defenses around Saigon and the Mekong delta has resulted in what even senior Government officials term a debacle. "It is not a question of the North Vietnamese on the offensive and making this a military conquest," said one European official, whose embassy has begun burning documents. "The North Vietnamese are taking the country by default. I'm sure they're as incredulous as everyone else. The army is mad with fear and panic. It's all collapsing before our eyes."

Amidst the disintegration of the army and the loss of Government control, nearly two million refugees have sought to flee from the northern provinces and the Central Highlands, and are now pouring into Saigon. They are staying with families, and living in row after row of shacks built of straw and scraps.

"People are fleeing to Saigon because this is the only place they have faith in," said one defense analyst. "But there's a tremendous danger of all of this gathering momentum right here of it turning ugly and violent against foreigners, especially Americans, who are getting out. People are saying 'You got us into this and now you are running out.' And what in God's name is going to happen to us?"

People Are Desperate

An American official, who as spent nearly a decade here, said: "My phone hasn't stopped ringing. People keep coming over to the house. They're desperate. These are people who have worked with us. They don't know what to do. A colonel and his family just came over. His wife was crying. They're going to Vung Tau and try to get on any boat that's leaving. They're that desperate. And this Government has made no initiative to calm the people. The Communists are stepping right into the vacuum."

At Givral's, a coffee shop that is a meeting place for journalists, minor officials and soldiers and their girlfriends, a longtime Vietnamese reporter said: "How could it happen so quickly? Hue, Da Nang, Nha Trang. Sometimes I think that when the Communists take over Saigon I'll go to the Saigon River and drown myself. We don't like the Communists, you know. But sometimes I think I'm too old to care. It's all gone."

Soldiers without limbs, and some utterly dazed, beg defiantly in downtown Saigon and explode in Vietnamese curses when foreigners brush past. An American official getting a haircut the other day was the target of a tirade by several Vietnamese youths who spoke of United States "betrayal" of the Vietnamese people. Foreigners out after the 10 P.M. curfew have been roughed up by the police and the army.

Rumors Everywhere

Rumors fly. According to some, six, perhaps even eight North Vietnamese divisions are in the Saigon area and this once-gracious and unhurried capital now lives in fear. Still, the sidewalks are crammed with vendors and the prices of rice, spices and vegetables have risen as much as 50 per cent in the last few weeks.

There are rumors that Communist demolition attacks will touch off rioting, looting and violence against foreigners. There are rumors of coup plots against Mr. Thieu. Vietnamese politicians and journalists angrily charge that the Vietnamese President remains in power largely because of the support by the United States Embassy and Administration. There are rumors of deals between Mr. Thieu and the Communists, although that are vehemently denied by Government officials.

Among foreigners here, there is some feeling that the North Vietnamese may not even try to push into Saigon but merely lob shells and rockets into the city and Ton Son Nhut air base. Such a step would cut off commercial flights and, given the tensions in the capital, stir the same panic and rioting and looting that resulted in the loss of Da Nang and other cities.

"The North Vietnamese could just sit on the edge of Saigon, push up the pressure a bit and then watch all the poisons ooze out," said one angry American official.

* * *

April 11, 1975

FORD ASKS $972-MILLION IN AID FOR SAIGON AND RIGHT TO USE TROOPS FOR EVACUATION; FEARS IT IS 'TOO LATE' TO HELP CAMBODIA

EARLY VOTE URGED

A Big Sum Said to Be Needed to Rescue Up to 200,000

By BERNARD GWERTZMAN
Special to The New York Times

WASHINGTON, April 10—President Ford appealed to Congress tonight to approve "without delay" nearly a billion dollars in military and humanitarian aid for Saigon to give

South Vietnam a chance to "save itself" as a country and make possible a large-scale evacuation of Americans and South Vietnamese "should the worst come to pass."

In a nationally televised address to a joint session, Mr. Ford painted a gloomy picture of the situation in South Vietnam.

Faced with various options, Mr. Ford said, he decided to ask for $722-million in military aid—more than twice the $300-million sought earlier—and $250-million in economic and humanitarian aid for Saigon.

Purpose of Aid Stated

Mr. Ford stressed that this large request, which he asked to be acted on by April 19—a week from Saturday—was meant not only to keep Saigon from a military collapse, but to buy time for allowing the United States to try to arrange a political solution between Hanoi and Saigon.

This would also allow the orderly withdrawal, if necessary, of 6,000 Americans and of tens of thousands of Vietnamese, or a total estimated by some as high as 200,000.

The President also asked Congress for clear authority to use troops for the possible evacuation, and officials disclosed that the American embassy in Saigon, which had been resisting evacuation, had been ordered to begin a reduction of the number of United States Government employes still in the city.

A Plea on the C.I.A.

Late in the speech, the President made an impassioned plea to Congress not to allow its investigations of the intelligence community to destroy national security or harm the effectiveness of the Central Intelligence Agency.

As to Cambodia, Mr. Ford seemed to acknowledge that Phnom Penh was on the verge of collapse. Without even repeating his old aid proposal for $222-million, he asserted that aid for the Cambodians may be "too late."

His point was underscored tonight when an Administration official said the fate of Phnom Penh would probably be decided in the next few days.

The President said he planned to go to Western Europe for a meeting with allied leaders in the near future and said it was necessary for the North Atlantic community to take stock of common problems.

Although Congress greeted other remarks in the speech with applause, his proposals for aid to Saigon were met with silence, reflecting the overwhelming opposition to further military support.

Because of the possible collapse of the Saigon Government, even if it receives more aid, Mr. Ford asked Congress to "clarify immediately" his authority to use troops to assure an orderly evacuation of Americans and endangered South Vietnamese "if the very worst were to happen."

In a sense, the appeal for nearly a billion dollars could be seen as a way to insure the safe exit of those thousands of people.

But the linkage of the evacuation with the aid request could also be interpreted as an effort to obtain the money from a critical Congress by raising the issue of a safe evacuation.

In the speech, which lasted just over an hour, Mr. Ford avoided blaming Congress directly for the situation in Indochina. He often called for unity between the executive and legislative branches.

Applause was limited, and in comments by members, it was clear that while Mr. Ford's appeal for humanitarian aid had support, many seemed strongly opposed to military aid.

About half the speech was devoted to Indochina, with the other half to the rest of the world. Mr. Ford evidently wanted to give the impression that despite the setbacks in Indochina, the United States was not paralyzed.

He said events in Southeast Asia had to be kept in "proper perspective" and again affirmed ties to allies and warned adversaries not to test American will.

On the whole, Mr. Ford did not alter any of his basic policies. He did try to appear conciliatory toward Congress, urging that it "put an end to self-inflicted wounds" and restore national unity.

But he did not shrink from criticizing Congress for its actions in such contentious areas as its denial of aid to Turkey over Cyprus and its efforts to link trade benefits to the Soviet Union with relaxed emigration policies.

Mr. Ford dealt only briefly with such crucial areas as relations with the Soviet Union and China. Portugal was not mentioned.

The brunt of his remarks about areas outside Indochina was to affirm commitments to allies in Asia, Western Europe and Latin America and to seek a peace in the Middle East.

The aid request for Saigon resulted from discussions after the mission of Gen. Frederick C. Weyand, Army Chief of Staff, to South Vietnam.

Mr. Ford made it clear that the $722-million had been recommended by General Weyand to stabilize the military situation and provide "the best opportunity for a political solution."

Carl Albert, Speaker of the House of Representatives, who met with the President in the afternoon to discuss the speech, said he did not know whether Congress would approve military aid for Saigon.

"Any kind of aid for Southeast Asia today is tough," Mr. Albert said.

Although the President did not seem to believe that the chances for negotiations were good, he called on North Vietnam—and asked Congress to join in the appeal—to cease military operations immediately.

He said the United States was urging the other members of the 12-nation international conference on Vietnam to use their influence to halt the fighting. Diplomatic notes have been sent to all the Vietnam guarantors, including the Soviet Union and China, he said.

Choices Reviewed

Reviewing the background of his decision on Vietnam, Mr. Ford said "the options before us are few and time is short."

He said Americans could decide to do nothing more and "we could shut our eyes and wash our hands of the whole matter—if we can." He said he could also have asked Congress for authority to re-introduce military forces.

Evidently ruling such extreme choices out, he said there were two narrower options.

These are to keep to his request, made in January, for $300- million in military aid and additional economic and humanitarian assistance, or to increase the military aid to "enable the South Vietnamese to stem the onrushing aggression."

He said the billion-dollar package might enable Saigon to stabilize the military situation, thereby permitting the chance for a negotiated political settlement between North and South Vietnamese.

"If the very worst were to happen," he said, the additional aid would "at least allow the orderly evacuation of Americans and endangered South Vietnamese to places of safety."

Mr. Ford said that, in addition to 6,000 Americans still in South Vietnam, there were 'tens of thousands' of South Vietnamese who had worked for the United States Government or American companies and "whose lives, with their dependents, are in grave peril."

He said there were also "tens of thousands of other South Vietnamese intellectuals, professors and teachers, editors and opinion-leaders who have supported the South Vietnamese cause and the alliance with the United States, to whom we have a profound moral obligation."

Alluding to concern among American allies, the President said they "must not think for a minute that the United States is pulling out on them or intends to abandon them to aggression."

"Members of the Congress, my fellow Americans, this moment of tragedy for Indochina is a time of trial for us," Mr. Ford said.

"It is a time for national resolve. Let us put an end to self-inflicted wounds. Let us remember that our national unity is a most priceless asset. Let us deny our adversaries the satisfaction of using Vietnam to pit Americans against Americans."

He noted that some Asian allies had been disquieted by the events in Indochina and said that he would meet with the leaders of Australia, New Zealand, Singapore and Indonesia.

A special endorsement was given to the security treaty with Japan, which he called "the cornerstone of stability in the vast reaches of Asia and the Pacific." He also stressed the importance of the security relations with South Korea.

The President said that before his trip to Europe, probably in May or June, he wanted Congress to lift its ban on military aid to Turkey, imposed because of Turkey's military action on Cyprus.

He noted that the Senate Foreign Relations Committee had already adopted a bill ending the ban which went into effect Feb. 5, and said that enactment by the Congress was necessary to prevent a rupture in relations with Turkey.

In an apparent gesture to the pro-Greek forces in Congress, Mr. Ford said he would also request economic and military aid for Greece.

Because of the current reassessment of policy in the Middle East, Mr. Ford had little to say about that part of the world.

"We have agreed in principle to reconvene the Geneva conference," he said. "We are prepared as well to explore other forums."

Although the President and Mr. Kissinger had privately laid the blame on Israel for the breakdown in the Secretary's recent mediation effort, Mr. Ford said only that the issues between Israel and Egypt "are vital to them and not amenable to easy or quick solutions."

Refers to Soviet Trade

Mr. Ford asked for permission to waive the Congressional ban on trade preferences to members of the oil cartel, which includes Ecuador and Venezuela.

He also mentioned the long dispute over trade benefits to the Soviet Union asserting that remedial legislation was urgently needed. Congress has refused to grant nondiscriminatory tariffs or government-backed credits unless the Soviet Union relaxes its emigration policies.

The President also urged Congress to carry out its investigation of the Central Intelligence Agency, "with maximum discretion and dispatch" to avoid crippling a vital institution. He said he would work with Congressional leaders to devise ways of allowing effective review while protecting vital information.

It was President Ford's first major foreign policy address, and he had worked closely with Mr. Kissinger in its preparation.

He began by noting that his purpose was to review relations with the rest of the world "in the spirit of candor and consultation."

In discussing Vietnam and Cambodia, Mr. Ford accused Hanoi of having "systematically" violated the cease-fire accords.

* * *

April 16, 1975

BATTLE ON AT PHNOM PENH'S EDGE

CAMBODIA WINDUP

Defenders Shift Units in Effort to Stem Reds' Advance

By SYDNEY H. SCHANBERG
Special to The New York Times

PHNOM PENH, Cambodia, Wednesday, April 16—The insurgents, closing in on Phnom Penh from almost all sides, reached the southern edge of the city after dark yesterday, and heavy fighting was under way.

Exchanges of machine gun, mortar and small arms fire were intense and flames from houses and a factory turned the sky pink around the United Nations Bridge on the city's southern edge.

Marines guard the helipad near the U.S. Embassy as a helicopter takes off with evacuees.

People fleeing the scene said the Communist-led insurgents were firing bazooka-like B-40 rockets into Government lines and also setting fire to homes. These witnesses said the Government forces were using armored personnel carriers equipped with mortars and heavy machine guns to try to block the insurgents from breaking into the city.

Troops Are Shifted

Throughout the day, as the Government's position steadily crumbled, its forces moved to try to halt the insurgents' advances, abandoning posts all around the outer defense perimeter and bringing the troops back by helicopter to defend Phnom Penh.

On Monday, after having been poised outside the city for weeks, the insurgents began their big push. The pullout of the American Embassy on Saturday and the simultaneous halting of the American supply airlift, which had been keeping the Phnom Penh Government alive, was apparently the signal for the insurgents to move.

The initial drive came primarily from the west and northwest. Yesterday the insurgents attacked from all sides.

Refugees Swell City

For the second day, refugees by the thousands continued to stream toward the city, already swollen to more than two million people. The city, however, seemed strangely calm.

The insurgents were driving from the north along Route 5, from the northwest across a marshy plain; from the west, where the airport was virtually cut off, and from the south and southeast, where Government troops were reported abandoning their positions. South of the city, one unit tried to save itself by jumping into the Bassac River and swimming across to its west bank. Several men drowned.

As of early evening, there was growing nervousness but no panic inside the city, and the Government was still vowing to fight to the last man.

In the shifting and chaotic battlefield situation, it was difficult for newsmen to reach the actual front lines, but they could get close enough to note that the Government's defenses appeared to be falling apart.

By mid-afternoon the insurgents had driven into the southern industrial suburb of Takhmau, three miles from the city's edge, after having subjected the area to heavy shelling.

As Government troops pulled back their artillery pieces and other equipment closer to Phnom Penh, a sea of fleeing refugees from Takhmau also swept north toward the city. Military police at the entrances to the city tried to block them because the Government fears that insurgent infiltrators might be slipping in with them.

Others poured toward the city from the southeast, where the Cambodian insurgents were also advancing up Route 1. These refugees, however, were blocked from entering the capital as military policemen threw barbed-wire roadblocks across the bridge leading into the southern part of the city.

At nighttime, the rebels were reported less than a mile and a half from the crowds gathering at the bridge.

On the crucial western approach, it appeared that the capital was virtually cut off from its airport at Pochentong, which had been Phnom Penh's last supply link with the outside world.

The insurgents cut the road to the airport at a point about two miles from the city by moving into part of Pochentong town, which straddles the route.

The Government was apparently still in control of the airfield itself, and military planes—small bombers, helicopter gunships and other strike aircraft—were still flying.

But the airport, which could be observed from a distance, was being heavily shelled, and it appeared that, to escape the bombardment, some planes were using an auxiliary runway about a mile south of the airport.

Government troops were reported to have abandoned the market town of Prek Phnou, six miles northwest of Phnom Penh on Route 5. In the evening an insurgent bombardment blew up a fuel depot along that highway only about two miles from the city, setting a spectacular blaze that lighted the sky and could be clearly seen in the northern part of Phnom Penh.

On the east, Government troops gave up the village of Arey Khsat, their last position on the cast bank of the Mekong, opposite the city.

Though the river is a barrier to a large surface assault, the pullout gives the insurgents a free hand to shell the city from the cast bank.

Besides abandoning several positions on the city's outer defenses, the Government was also taking soldiers from distant isolated province capitals, such as Takeo and Svay Rieng, and flying them into Phnom Penh to try to save the city. This probably means that those towns will now fall.

Communication with the outside world was cut off from late yesterday afternoon until early this morning because the main communications transmission center at Kambol had been overrun by insurgents. Transmission was restored when an old Chinese transmitter was pressed into service.

Message by Sirik Matak

Government leaders have said they will never surrender. And last night a leading Cambodian figure, Lieut. Gen. Sisowath Sirik Matak, a former Premier who was once regarded by the Americans as the only hope for reversing Phnom Penh's fortunes, sent a telegram to President Ford saying that Cambodians would die rather than surrender and accusing the President of abandonment and betrayal.

The cablegram, alluding to the American pullout, said:

"We will struggle now alone without your support. The Khmer people have already paid a very heavy sacrifice in human lives for you Americans to enable you to disengage from South Vietnam. Your policy of abandonment of a poor country, decided brutally without warning or preparation, puts us in a position of heart-breaking betrayal."

The general said that if the insurgents break into Phnom Penh, "there will be in this capital of two million a terrible carnage. The Communists will find only ruins and desolation. We will die on our soil achieving our last desire—to die in freedom. I lay on the American conscience all Khmer deaths, present and future."

While the American airlift has ended, two drops of supplies were made yesterday on Phnomh Penh, landing shortly after 5 P.M. in the Olympic stadium.

These were the first since the airlift, the main source on which Phnom Penh depended for food, fuel and ammunition. Fuel supplies are now dwindling, and how long the Government planes can keep flying is uncertain.

The situation with ammunition may be even worse. The two main ammunition dumps sit beyond the airport, and with the road cut, the Government forces cannot reach them without running a gantlet of fire.

Yesterday the Government was trying with difficulty to build a defense line around the university, which is within city limits. Armored personnel carriers with mortars were pulled back from Pochentong town and positioned around the university complex.

A young couple sat through it all pulling up grass and throwing it at each other.

Staircases leading to the rooftops of university building were blocked by furniture barricades manned by students. This was apparently someone's idea of preventing infiltrators from getting rooftop vantage points.

As night fell, military policemen roamed the university area with loudspeakers, ordering people to stay inside their homes so that infiltrators could be easily discovered.

At the hotel Phnom, where most of the remaining foreigners are staying, officials reported that the Defense Minister, Hou Hong, had refused the request of the International Red Cross to turn the building into a protected neutral zone. The Red Cross had also sought the approval of the insurgents, and it was not known what response they had received from them, if any.

Red Cross officials staying in the hotel moved out last night and returned to their residences in the city.

While there was no panic here, worry was clear on many faces. The Staff at the cable office perused all the foreign journalists' dispatches with all the bad news and then went about their duties as normal.

One official did ask a journalist to help him get his family out of the country.

In Tuol Kork, a neighborhood in the northwestern section of Phnom Penh, the insurgents' rockets and shells set fire to a rubber sandal factory, sending billows rising skyward and also sending several hundred people fleeing.

A jeep raced by on its way to a hospital, a badly wounded child in the back. Entire families were running, and yet an investigation showed that only one part of the neighborhood had fled in terror, the part near the burning factory. The rest of the district appeared calm.

* * *

April 22, 1975

THIEU RESIGNS, CALLS U.S. UNTRUSTWORTHY; APPOINTS SUCCESSOR TO SEEK NEGOTIATIONS; EVACUATION OF ALL AMERICANS CONSIDERED

10-YEAR RULE ENDS

Vice President Huong, 71 Years Old, Takes Office in Saigon

By MALCOLM W. BROWNE
Special to The New York Times

SAIGON, South Vietnam, April 21—President Nguyen Van Thieu, denouncing the United States as untrustworthy, resigned tonight after 10 years in office.

He immediately appointed his Vice President, the 71-year-old Tran Van Huong, to replace him.

He said that President Huong would immediately press the enemy to cease all acts of war and enter into peace negotiations. The Vietcong have said repeatedly that they would not negotiate while Mr. Thieu held office.

[A spokesman for the Vietcong delegation in Saigon said Tuesday the resignation of President Thieu "decidedly cannot change the situation," Reuters reported.]

Accuses the U.S.

In an impassioned address to the nation, President Thieu defended his character and the accomplishments of his regime while chronicling its collapse. He called for peace, but also said the successor government would fight on.

Speaking before assembled members of his Government and National Assembly at the Presidential Palace, President Thieu accused the United States of breaking its promises to support an anti-Communist Government in Saigon.

Mr. Thieu said that he had objected in October, 1972, to Secretary of State Kissinger's "acceptance of the continued presence of North Vietnamese troops in South Vietnam."

Pledge by Nixon

Mr. Thieu added that South Vietnam would fight on to defend the territory left to it. The armed forces chief of staff, Gen. Cao Van Vien, also spoke briefly, to say that his troops would continue fighting to "defend the homeland against the communist aggressors."

"I resign but I do not desert," President Thieu said in concluding his one-and-a-half-hour address. "From this minute I will put myself at the disposal of the President and people. I will continue to stay close to you all in the coming task of national defense. Good-bye to you all."

His voice taut with emotion, President Thieu devoted most of his speech to a scathing criticism of the United States, saying:

"The United States has not respected its promises. It is unfair. It is inhumane. It is not trustworthy. It is irresponsible."

Mr. Thieu said that former President Richard M. Nixon had described all accords, including the Paris peace agreement, as "pieces of paper" unless they were implemented, and had therefore promised Saigon not only military and economic aid, but also "direct and strong United States military intervention" in the event the Communists broke the accord.

But then, Mr. Thieu said, Watergate undid American resolve in aiding Vietnam, and Washington deserted its ally. By the time former Vice President Spiro T. Agnew visited Saigon later, he said, Mr. Agnew spoke "coldly," referring only to "Vietnamization" of the war and continuing military and economic aid, but not of President Nixon's promise before the Paris accord to send American troops and B-52's if needed.

The State Department has said that there was no specific commitment by the United States to intervene militarily. And the White House noted earlier this month that any private assurance given by Mr. Nixon was no longer valid because of the Congressional ban on American combat activity in Indochina imposed in August, 1973.

"Let me say that we need at least $722-million, plus the B-52's" Mr. Thieu said today. "Let me say that we need immediate—I say immediate—shipment of arms and equipment to the South Vietnam battlefield."

"I would challenge the United States army to do better than the South Vietnamese army without B-52's," the President said.

President Huong was sworn into office immediately at the assembly and Government meeting tonight in the Presidential Palace.

Speech by Huong

In a brief speech, he praised the achievements of the outgoing President, noted that he was assuming a great responsibility, and called for national unity, saying: "United we live, divided we die."

President Thieu's resignation was one of two major demands the Vietcong have called prerequisites to any peace talks.

The other is that "all American military men and advisers disguised as civilians" leave Vietnam.

In a broadcast today, the Vietcong appeared to set a time limit for the latter demand as "two to three days, or in 24 hours even." The broadcast was strongly threatening in tone, and implied that if the conditions were not quickly met, a full-scale military drive would be launched on Saigon.

It was not immediately clear whether President Thieu's resignation and the current outflow of Americans would satisfy the Vietcong demands.

But it has been apparent in the last two days that the Communist side would now prefer a political finale to the war, rather than bald military victory.

President Thieu's decision tonight was clearly based on the desire of most of the people of this city to avoid the destruction and loss of life that a final battle would cause.

Presumably, the battered and demoralized Saigon troops commanded by General Vien will be ordered to fight only in a defensive way, to safeguard positions they hold until such time as peace talks of some kind end the war.

A senior Western diplomat said: "Military defeat always carries with it terrible political concomitants. We can only hope now that the physical suffering of the vanquished can be reduced as much as humanly possible under the circumstances."

Curfew in Saigon was advanced an hour tonight, to 8 P.M. But for the first time, policemen and soldiers stationed around the city seemed to be paying little attention to the many curfew violators in the streets.

The electric tension of recent weeks and days seemed a little relaxed, and soldiers were joking with each other.

One said with a laugh, "Well now how long will Papa Huong be able to look after affairs of state?"

Little Hope Offered

In his speech, President Thieu offered little hope that his resignation would bring better times.

Mr. Thieu said that it was popular now to blame him for everything "just as in 1963, everything was put on the head of the late Mr. Diem," a reference to President Ngo Dinh Diem, who was overthrown and assassinated that year.

"There now seems to be a formidable propaganda campaign, the toxicity of which is even reaching some of our soldiers," Mr. Thieu said.

President Thieu asserted that simply because he was leaving office to another man did not suggest a basic difference in their viewpoints. And he added that President Huong would press Washington for more aid.

"President Huong, like myself, is a patriot," he said.

"Both of us want to negotiate—unconditional negotiations. Let them say anything, let them even tear up the Paris accord if they want, but let us have a dialogue. Let us have immediate, unconditional negotiations."

President Thieu recapitulated at length his political battles of the last 10 years, particularly those with the United States.

He said that when confronted with a draft Vietcong peace proposal on Oct. 26, 1972, "I told the Americans that if I accepted it, I would be a traitor to my country. I would be selling out South Vietnam to the Communists. So I protested against the proposed accord for three months."

He said his objection was to three main points.

The first was a demand that a tripartite coalition government be created, extending from the central government all the way down to hamlet level.

The second was Vietcong insistence that Indochina be considered to consist of three states—Laos, Cambodia and only one Vietnam, presumably a Vietnam led form Hanoi rather than Saigon.

"I said that if one Vietnam was not possible, it would be better to leave it divided at the 17th Parallel," he said.

The third point was "Mr. Kissinger's acceptance of the continued presence of North Vietnamese troops in South Vietnam."

In the end, a compromise was agreed to.

"Afterward," Mr. Thieu said, "President Nixon told me that all accords are only pieces of paper, with no value unless they are implemented. What was important, he said, was not that he had signed the accord, but that the United States would always stand ready to help South Vietnam in case the Communists violated the accord."

Mr. Thieu said that, to discuss this matter, the President had invited him to the United States.

"I asked that the United States should be ready to come back in force to help directly, not just Vietnamization, in case the Communists renewed their aggression against South Vietnam.

"The most important question in my view, at that time, was direct United States intervention.

"So I won a solid pledge from our great ally, leader of the free world, that when and if North Vietnam renewed its aggression against South Vietnam, the United States would actively and strongly intervene."

When Mr. Thieu visited Mr. Nixon in 1973 after the accord was signed, the American President reiterated the pledge, President Thieu said. But then, matters changed.

"Unfortunately, there was Watergate," he said, "and United States politics have greatly affected the volume of aid to South Vietnam, as well as Vietnamization."

The crucial test, Mr. Thieu said, came when Communist forces attacked and overran an outpost in 1973.

"By then, the United States did not intervene, and that encouraged the Communists to move on to attack other places," he said.

Generals Criticized

President Thieu assigned the major share of blame for recent events here to the United States, but he also had criticism for some of his generals.

"Recently the time came for us to take a decision. After the fall of Ban Me Thuot, I asked the generals whether they could hold Kontum and Pleiku and they said they could not.

"So we made the political decision not to hold Kontum and Pleiku, but would use our troops to retake Ban Me Thuot. That was the practical and political decision I took after consultation with the Prime Minister and commanding generals, but unfortunately, withdrawal is the most difficult of operations.

"The withdrawal from Kontum and Pleiku did not help us retake Ben Me Thuot."

The problem of the balance of forces, overwhelmingly in favor of the Communists, led to the fall of Hue, Da Nang, Nha Trang and the other towns lost in the last few weeks, he said.

The reduction in American aid "reduced our armed forces' war potential by 60 per cent," he said, and this was complicated by some mistakes by "some bad commanders."

Despite his plea for peace, President Thieu said:

"We will have to fight with sheer determination, regardless of how many troops and how much equipment we have left. I expect harder battles ahead."

In describing American political pressures on him, President Thieu spoke of the 1971 election, in which all opponents refused to run against him on the ground that the election was rigged.

Apparently referring to the United States, Mr. Thieu went on to say: "They plotted to create a power vacuum in Vietnam to impose a solution on us. I was determined not to let that happen, so I decided to run, even after other slates had withdrawn."

* * *

April 24, 1975

FORD SAYS INDOCHINA WAR IS FINISHED FOR AMERICA

By RICHARD L. MADDEN
Special to The New York Times

NEW ORLEANS, April 25—President Ford, calling on the nation to develop an agenda for the future, declared today that the war in Indochina was finished "as far as America is concerned."

Mr. Ford urged the beginning of what he called "a great national reconciliation" and added:

"We are saddened, indeed, by events in Indochina. But these events, tragic as they are, portend neither the end of the world nor of America's leadership in the world. Some seem to feel that if we do not succeed in everything everywhere, then we have succeeded in nothing anywhere."

Mr. Ford said he rejected "such polarized thinking." He said the United States could and should help others to help themselves.

"But," he went on, "the fate of responsible men and women everywhere in the final decision rests in their own hands."

The President made his remarks in a speech to more than 4,500 members of the student body of Tulane University, who greeted his appearance and speech in the campus field house with prolonged and enthusiastic applause, particularly his comment that the war was finished as far as this nation was concerned.

The speech was clearly intended to put an end to the debate over the nation's involvement in Indochina and the recent Communist successes while urging the United States to look instead to the future.

Ron Nessen, Mr. Ford's press secretary, said the Administration was not dropping its request to Congress for nearly $1-billion in military and humanitarian aid for South Vietnam. He said the aid was still needed to stabilize the deteriorating situation there.

The speech, which made no reference to the request for aid to South Vietnam, appeared to differ from some of the past statements of Secretary of State Kissinger, who has said that events in one part of the world almost necessarily affect foreign policy elsewhere. But Mr. Nessen said that Mr. Kissinger had worked on the preparation of the speech and had approved it.

Mr. Ford, chatting with reporters on Air Force One on his way back to Washington, was asked if Secretary Kissinger had played any part in the preparation of the speech.

"No," he replied. But when an aide reminded the President that all foreign policy speeches are sent to the National Security Council for comment, Mr. Ford said: "It went through the system. The N.S.C. knew about it."

In his speech earlier, Mr. Ford noted that the United States had won a victory over the British in New Orleans in 1815, two weeks after the signing in Europe of an armistice ending the War of 1812. Thousands died, he said, because the combatants in the Battle of New Orleans had not got the word of the peace agreement.

"Today America can regain the sense of pride that existed before Vietnam," Mr. Ford said.

"But it cannot be achieved by refighting a war that is finished—as far as America is concerned," he said. "The time has come to look forward to an agenda for the future, to unity, to binding up the nation's wounds and restoring it to health and optimistic self-confidence."

In New Orleans, he said, "a great battle was fought after a war was over."

"In New Orleans tonight," he continued, "we can begin a great national reconciliation. The first engagement must be with the problems of today—and of the future."

Continuing to sound the theme of "reconciliation, not recrimination" that he had used in a speech on Saturday in Concord, Mass., Mr. Ford asked today "that we stop refighting the battles and recriminations of the past." He added:

"I ask that we look now at what is right with America, at our possibilities and our potentialities for change and growth, and achievement, and sharing. I ask that we accept the responsibilities of leadership as a good neighbor to all peoples and the enemy of none. I ask that we strive to become, in the finest American tradition, something more tomorrow than we are today."

Ground Breaking Ceremony

Mr. Ford flew to New Orleans this morning to take part in a ground-breaking ceremony for a museum to house memorabilia of Representative F. Edward Hébert, the 73-year-old Louisiana Democrat who was ousted last January as chairman of the House Armed Services Committee. A large crowd, including many schoolchildren, applauded as the President put on a white hard hat and, with Mr. Hérbert, turned a shovel of dirt at the site of the proposed library, which is adjacent to an amusement park.

Later, at a luncheon speech to the 73d annual convention of the Navy League at the Fairmont Hotel, Mr. Ford told a receptive audience that the nation could not afford any further cuts in defense spending without endangering national security.

"However good their intentions, those who claim that America is over-armed and over-spending on defense are dead wrong," he said.

Later, the President flew by helicopter to an offshore oil-drilling rig operated by the Gulf Oil Corporation 35 miles off the mouth of the Mississippi River.

* * *

April 28, 1975

SAIGON HEARS THE FIGHTING AT ITS EDGE

By FOX BUTTERFIELD
Special to The New York Times

SAIGON, South Vietnam, Monday, April 28—A heavy column of black smoke rose over the edge of Saigon today as advance Communist forces moved close to the city limits.

South Vietnamese Air Force helicopters fired rockets into the Communist positions on the Saigon River at Newport, a former United States port complex on the road to Bien Hoa. The Communists fired back with AK-47 automatic rifles, and the noise was clearly audible inside the city.

Only a few lightly armed South Vietnamese combat policemen and militiamen guarded the road on the northeastern edge of the city. They made no effort to dig in, and several Government officers simply stood around watching the helicopters firing at the Communist forces.

Seize End of Bridge

The Communist troops, who had seized the far side of the Newport Bridge over the Saigon River, were believed to be part of major North Vietnamese units moving rapidly toward Saigon from Bien Hoa, 15 miles to the northeast. Another group of Communist troops reportedly had occupied a crossroads two miles beyond the bridge on the way to the biggest South Vietnamese ammunition dump, at Cat Lai.

The Communist advance blocked all traffic at the large Hang Xanh intersection, the main gateway to Saigon from the north. Combat policemen wearing flak jackets, helmets and mottled green and brown uniforms stood behind barbed wire barricades, forcing all traffic back into the city.

It was the closest fighting to Saigon since the Communists' Tet and spring offensives of 1968.

The Communist troops this morning apparently had only small arms and no mortars or antiaircraft guns. If they had fired a few mortar shells into the city, it appeared that the few nervous Government soldiers would have instantly fled.

According to soldiers along the road, the huge column of smoke came from a gasoline storage dump operated by the United States Agency for International Development, It was unclear whether it had been set afire by the Communists or by South Vietnamese artillery after the Communists had entered the area.

United Press International

A South Vietnamese woman sifting through the rubble of her home, destroyed yesterday in first rocket attack on Saigon since 1971. Five rockets were fired into capital.

During the morning Government helicopters hovered over the edge of Saigon, firing rockets that made a heavy wooshing sound and left trails of brown smoke.

But the rockets did not seem to have any effect on the Communist troops, who kept firing back with their AK-47 rifles.

The Newport base complex that came under attack was built by the United States Navy and housed a large commissary that Americans used for their food shopping.

Several American ships had been standing by at Newport to help if needed in the evacuation of Americans and Vietnamese from Saigon.

* * *

April 30, 1975

MINH SURRENDERS, VIETCONG IN SAIGON; 1,000 AMERICANS AND 5,500 VIETNAMESE EVACUATED BY COPTER TO U.S. CARRIERS

FORD UNITY PLEA

President Says That Departure 'Closes a Chapter' for U.S.

By JOHN W. FINNEY
Special to The New York Times

WASHINGTON, April 29—The United States ended two decades of military involvement in Vietnam today with the evacuation of about 1,000 Americans from Saigon as well as more than 5,500 South Vietnamese.

The emergency helicopter evacuation was ordered last night by President Ford after the Saigon airport was closed because of Communist rocket and artillery fire. The 1,000 Americans were the last contingent of a force that once numbered more than 500,000.

They were carried by a fleet of 81 American helicopters to carriers in the South China Sea.

The helicopters removed the 5,500 South Vietnamese citizens because their lives were presumed to be in danger with a Communist take-over of South Vietnam. Over the last two weeks, a total of about 55,000 South Vietnamese have been removed. Most of them will come to the United States. The helicopter flights ended the United States evacuation of South Vietnamese.

Last Marines Evacuated

The final withdrawal of Americans was completed at 7:52 P.M., about two hours after the White House had announced the evacuation was completed, when 11 marines were taken by helicopter from the roof of the American Embassy in Saigon. Officials said that the marines, the last of a security guard sent in to protect the evacuation, were safely removed although small-arms fire had broken out around the deserted embassy.

President Ford, in a statement issued by the White House, said the evacuation "closes a chapter in the American experience." In a plea for national unity in the post-Vietnam period, the President said:

"I ask all Americans to close ranks, to avoid recrimination about the past, to look ahead to the many goals we share and to work together on the great tasks that remain to be accomplished."

Appeal by Kissinger

At a news conference, Secretary of State Kissinger appealed to North Vietnam not to storm Saigon by force because the United States believed the new South Vietnamese Government was prepared to capitulate.

Mr. Kissinger said a bloody take-over by the Communists was now "unnecessary" since the Saigon Government of Gen. Duong Van Minh was "ready to draw the conclusions from the existing situation and in fact was formed to correspond to the demands of the Communist side."

The last Americans were removed by a fleet of 81 helicopters flying from Navy ships off South Vietnam. Nearly 1,000 combat marines went ashore to protect the evacuation and air cover was provided by Navy and Air Force F-4 fighter-bombers. This same aircraft for more than eight years was the main bomber of the United States in the Vietnam war.

16-Hour Operation

The helicopter evacuation—the largest ever conducted by the armed forces—took more than 19 hours, far longer than had been expected by the Pentagon, which had been planning on an operation of less than four hours to remove the Americans still in South Vietnam.

Two marines were lost and presumed dead when their helicopter, which was flying rescue guard duty off the carriers, crashed into the South China Sea. Two other marines standing guard at the American Defense Attache's office at Tan Son Nhut airport were killed yesterday by Communist rocket fire in an attack that directly led to Mr. Ford's decision to order the evacuation of all Americans today.

The first marine helicopter to land at Tan Son Nhut airport today reportedly came under gunfire as did a later helicopter carrying evacuees back to the carriers. There were no casualties.

F-4 Fires Back

A Navy F-4 flying air cover came under antiaircraft fire and, according to the Pentagon, took "countermeasures," either bombing or strafing the anti-aircraft position. A Navy A-7 attack bomber was ditched in the ocean after it ran into mechanical problems, but the pilot was rescued.

The evacuation effort, which began at 12:45 A.M., Eastern daylight time, continued until 7:52 P.M. The White House reportedly postponed an announcement throughout this afternoon that the final American had been removed.

The operation was delayed by the weather, by the limited landing areas around the American Embassy in downtown Saigon, by an unexplained radio message that delayed the first landing of marine helicopters by about an hour and finally by

United Press International

A crewman from an American helicopter helping evacuees to the top of a building in Saigon for flight to a U.S. carrier.

pilot fatigue in the final stages of the evacuation. Another factor, as the press secretary, Ron Nessen, acknowledged to reporters, was that "a larger number of South Vietnamese were evacuated than had been anticipated."

The original Defense Department and State Department announcement early today stated that "the President has ordered the evacuation of the remaining Americans from South Vietnam."

Authority Explained

The assumption in the original Pentagon planning was that a limited number of South Vietnamese might be evacuated but that the emphasis would be upon removing some 1,000 remaining Americans. This assumption was in line with the Administration's position that the President, as Commander in Chief, had the authority to use armed forces to remove Americans but needed authority, not yet given by Congress, to permit the armed forces to evacuate South Vietnamese.

In the end, however, even in the absence of specific Congressional authority, the Administration decided to evacuate several thousand South Vietnamese who had gathered at the Defense Attaché's Office and at the embassy.

At a televised briefing that followed conclusion of the operation, Secretary of State Kissinger said he did not believe that there had been "an undue delay" in the evacuation because of the decision by Ambassador Graham A. Martin that large numbers of South Vietnamese should be removed before all Americans were finally evacuated.

Mr. Kissinger said that Mr. Martin, who more than any other official dictated the pace and timing of the evacuation, felt "a strong moral obligation" to South Vietnamese who had worked with the United States, which, the Secretary said, "is not the worst fault in a man."

Furthermore, he said, Ambassador Martin was "in a very difficult position" of having to make judgments over the last week on how quickly the American contingent could be reduced without "triggering a panic" that would have complicated the removal of Americans.

Mr. Kissinger maintained that the Administration's objectives in the phased withdrawal were achieved. "We got out with all the personnel there without panic and without the substantial casualties that could have occurred if civil order had broken down."

At the same time, he said, "We all went through a somewhat anxious 24 hours because until the last helicopter had left we couldn't really know whether an attack on any of these compounds might start or whether missiles would be used."

Mr. Martin and his closest aides were on the last helicopter to leave the embassy grounds.

Relations 'in Abeyance'

With Mr. Martin's departure, Mr. Kissinger said, American relations with the South Vietnamese Government, which has been supported by the United States ever since the French withdrew in 1954, were "in a state of abeyance."

United Press International

Vietnamese civilians climbing onto a bus carrying evacuees as it tried to make its way into the U.S. Embassy compound in Saigon yesterday during the final evacuation of Americans. Others, at left, tried to scale the walls of the complex in a desperate effort to be taken along.

Mr. Kissinger hinted that as a result of discussions through intermediaries, North Vietnam, which had been shelling the airport, permitted the evacuation of Americans and South Vietnamese from the Defense Attaché's Office.

The initial evacuation effort concentrated on Tan Son Nhut, where more than 4,000 people were removed by helicopter in the first few hours.

Flight Delayed

The first flight of helicopters, which had left the carrier Hancock at 12:45 A.M., had been scheduled to land at Tan Son Nhut at 2 A.M. But just as the helicopters were about to land, a command came across the radio telling them to delay their landing until 3 A.M.

The lead helicopter, carrying Brig. Gen. Richard Carey of the Marine Corps, proceeded to land, coming under some gunfire. But the other helicopters circled for nearly an hour as Adm. Noel A. M. Gayler, Commander in Chief Pacific, and other high-ranking officers broke in, demanding to know who had issued the order. As of tonight, the Pentagon still had not determined who gave the spurious order.

With all the people evacuated from Tan Son Nhut under the protection of some 800 marines who had been flown in, the evacuation effort shifted to the embassy. There the operation was limited to two landing places, the embassy roof and a parking lot. Only two helicopters could come in at a time.

Toward the end of the operation, an 80-minute break was called, apparently, as explained by Pentagon officials, because of "pilot fatigue," in addition, night had fallen, complicating the helicopter operations.

As dawn approached, the final flight of 19 helicopters went in to rescue 125 Americans and 475 South Vietnamese still at the embassy.

Defense Secretary James R. Schlesinger sent a message to the armed forces telling them that "in this hour of pain and reflection you may feel that your efforts and sacrifices have gone for naught."

"That is not the case," he said. "When the passions have been muted and the history is written, Americans will recall that their armed forces served them well. Under circumstances more difficult than ever before faced by our military services, you accomplished the mission assigned to you by higher authority. In combat you were victorious and you left the field with honor."

The Departments of State and Defense issued the following joint statement on the evacuation of American citizens from Saigon:

"The President has ordered the evacuation of the remaining Americans from Vietnam. The military situation around Saigon, particularly around the airport, has deteriorated to such an extent that this measure has become necessary to insure their safety.

"This operation is being carried out by U.S. military helicopters and is being protected by a security force of U. S. marines and tactical aircraft. Force will not be used unless essential to protect the lives of those involved.

"The evacuees will be taken temporarily to carriers offshore before being moved onward to the U.S.

"We do not have precise figures on the numbers of Americans involved, but it should be about 800 to 900."

* * *

May 1, 1975

COMMUNISTS TAKE OVER SAIGON; U.S. RESCUE FLEET IS PICKING UP VIETNAMESE WHO FLED IN BOATS

'HO CHI MINH CITY'

Communications Cut Soon After Raising of Victory Flag

By GEORGE ESPER
The Associated Press

SAIGON, South Vietnam, April 30—Communist troops of North Vietnam and the Provisional Revolutionary Government of South Vietnam poured into Saigon today as a century of Western influence came to an end.

Scores of North Vietnamese tanks, armored vehicles and camouflaged Chinese-built trucks rolled to the presidential palace.

The President of the former non-Communist Government of South Vietnam, Gen. Duong Van Minh, who had gone on radio and television to announce his administration's surrender, was taken to a microphone later by North Vietnamese soldiers for another announcement. He appealed to all Saigon troops to lay down their arms and was taken by the North Vietnamese soldiers to an undisclosed destination.

[Soon after, the Saigon radio fell silent, normal telephone and telegraph communications ceased and The Associated Press said its wire link to the capital was lost at 7 P.M. Wednesday, Saigon time (7 A.M. Wednesday, New York time).]

[In Paris, representatives of the Provisional Revolutionary Government announced that Saigon had been renamed Ho Chi Minh City in honor of the late President of North Vietnam. Other representatives said in a broadcast monitored in Thailand that former Government forces in eight provinces south of the capital had not yet surrendered, but no fighting was mentioned.]

The transfer of power was symbolized by the raising of the flag of the National Liberation Front over the presidential palace at 12:15 P.M. today, about two hours after General Minh's surrender broadcast.

Hundreds in Saigon Cheer

Hundreds of Saigon residents cheered and applauded as North Vietnamese military vehicles moved to the palace grounds from which the war against the Communists had been directed by President Nguyen Van Thieu, who resigned April 21, and by President Ngo Dinh Diem, who was killed in a coup in 1963.

Broadcasting today in the early hours of the Communist take-over, the Provisional Revolutionary Government's representatives said:

"We representatives of the liberation forces of Saigon formally proclaim that Saigon has been totally liberated. We accept the unconditional surrender of Gen. Duong Van Minh, President of the former Government."

Colonel Shoots Himself

Meanwhile, many former soldiers sought to lose themselves in the populace. However, one police colonel walked up to an army memorial statue, saluted and shot himself. He died later in a hospital.

Shots rang out at one point around the City Hall. A North Vietnamese infantry platoon, dressed in olive-drab uniforms and black rubber sandals, took up defense positions in the square in front of the building. They exchanged shots with a few holdouts. Some people on motorbikes looked apprehensively to see where the firing was coming from. In a short while it subsided.

Coastal Ships Jammed

Between General Minh's surrender broadcast and the entry of the Communist forces into the city, South Vietnamese soldiers and civilians jammed aboard several coastal freighters tied up along the Saigon River, hoping to escape. They dejectedly left the ships as the Communist troops drove along the waterfront in jeeps and trucks, waving National Liberation Front flags and cheering.

As the Communist troops drove past, knots of civilians stood in doorways and watched without apparent emotion. Later, as more North Vietnamese troops poured into the city, many people began cheering.

Ky Nhan, a Vietnamese who had been submitting photographs to The Associated Press for three years, came to the agency's office with a Communist friend and two North Vietnamese soldiers and said, "I guarantee the safety of everybody here."

"I have been a revolutionary for 10 years," said Mr. Nhan. "My job in the Vietcong was liaison with the international press."

This correspondent served them Coca-Cola and some leftover cake.

One of the soldiers, a 25-year-old sergeant named Binh Huan Lam, said he was from Hanoi and had been a soldier for 10 years.

"I have not married because it was not necessary during the war," he said.

Arrival Described

After smoking a cigarette, Tran Viet Ca, a 24-year-old private, told the Americans he had served seven years in the North Vietnamese Army.

"Two days ago we attacked Bien Hoa," he said. "Today we drove down the highway past the United States Army base at Long Binh. Our forces were led by a brigade of tanks. There was a little resistance, but most Saigon soldiers had already run away. Then we drove into Saigon."

Loud explosions were heard in the late afternoon in Saigon. They were said to have taken place aboard an ammunition barge burning in the Saigon River, but no damage was reported in the city except at the United States Embassy and other American buildings, which Saigonese looted. At the embassy they took virtually everything, including the kitchen sinks and a machine to shred secret documents.

A bronze plaque with the names of five American servicemen who died in a 1968 attack by Communist guerrillas was torn from the lobby wall. An Associated Press correspondent retrieved it.

Another memento from the embassy that was saved was a color portrait of former President Richard M. Nixon and his family, inscribed "To Ambassador and Mrs. Graham Martin with appreciation for their service to the nation. From Richard Nixon."

A French businessman who said he was taking refuge in the New Zealand Embassy grabbed the picture.

"I know the ambassador," he said. "I will personally deliver it to him in the United States some time in the future."

Outside the embassy, Thong Nhut Bouelvard was littered with burned cars.

* * *

May 1, 1975

'LIBERATION'

The end, when it finally came, was sudden, sharp and definitive. No negotiations, no period of transition to dampen the exhilaration of the Vietnamese Communists in Hanoi, victorious in their thirty-year war for Indochina.

Theirs now is the victory of conquest, not of conciliation. All the intricate arrangements for political transition, which the United States had helped to negotiate more than two years ago and then proceeded to forget, came to naught. The Vietcong, organized as the Provisional Revolutionary Government of South Vietnam, now rules unchallenged over Saigon.

The effects of this upheaval will not be quickly assimilated in the global power balance. Nor will the lessons of victory—and defeat—be evident in their full impact for months to come. Much will depend on what happens now: on the speed and equity with which South Vietnam's new leaders restore the normal life of their nation, and the magnanimity—or lack thereof—which they display to Vietnamese and foreigners who resisted Hanoi's designs for take-over.

Retention in political office of Duong Van Minh, South Vietnam's President in the last tumultuous days, could give some symbolic assurance to a confused and weary population; Nguyen Thi Binh, the P.R.G. Foreign Minister, has at least suggested that such gestures of continuity are under consideration. Vietnamese Communist spokesmen in Paris, moreover, are rushing to assure that foreign lives and property will be protected under a new regime of nonalignment. Certainly on the technical level, the problems of maintaining civil order and basic government services will be as great for the new government as they were for the old in its last weeks, particularly with a capital flooded by refugees.

The example of Cambodia—what little is so far known—is not encouraging. Since the fall of Phnom Penh to the Communist-led insurgents exactly two weeks ago, all normal communications from the capital have been cut off. Some 600 foreigners, including neutral diplomats, officials of international relief organizations and newsmen, were confined in isolation in the French Embassy where food and basic supplies were rapidly depleted. When finally the United Nations succeeded in arranging for their evacuation, the only means authorized was a truck convoy to the Thai border 250 miles away, despite availability of a French aircraft in nearby Vientiane.

The habits and suspicions of years of insurgency will not quickly disappear. But the new leaders in both Cambodia and South Vietnam have long asked for support from the entire world. If they wish to be recognized and treated as responsible governments, the first step is to act like responsible governments.

PART IX

THE AFTERMATH OF WAR, 1975–2000

NATIONS IN TORMENT

May 4, 1975

PRESIDENT VOWS NATION WILL KEEP PLEDGES ABROAD

U.S. Will Remain Strong, He Says at Commissioning of Nuclear Carrier Nimitz

By RICHARD L. MADDEN
Special to The New York Times

NORFOLK, Va., May 3—Four days after the evacuation of the remaining Americans from South Vietnam, President Ford pledged today that the United States would keep its commitments abroad and would remain militarily strong.

Speaking at pierside ceremonies at the scommissioning of the nuclear aircraft carrier U.S.S. Nimitz, the world's largest warship, Mr. Ford told an applauding crowd of more than 10,000 that jammed Pier 12 under sunny skies:

"We are strong, we will continue to be strong. We will keep our commitments, and we will remain a great country."

Symbol of 'Determination'

Without clearly mentioning the concerns of some allies about the recent collapse of United States-supported governments in Cambodia and South Vietnam, Mr. Ford said that the Nimitz was joining the fleet "at an auspicious moment, when our determination to strengthen our ties with allies across both great oceans and to work for peace and stability around the world requires clear demonstration."

He said that the Nimitz, the nation's second nuclear-powered carrier, along with other American forces worldwide, would make "critically important contributions" toward world peace.

With the carrier at his back, Mr. Ford said he saw the Nimitz "as a symbol of the vast power, productive skill and economic strength of America" and so would others around the world.

'Readiness and Flexibility'

He added: "To all, this great ship is visible evidence of our commitment to friends and allies and our capability to maintain those commitments."

He said the evacuation of Americans and South Vietnamese from Saigon last Tuesday demonstrated the "readiness and flexibility" of aircraft carriers "in the successful execution of national policy."

Without the five carriers that operated off South Vietnam and the Marine and Air Force helicopters that flew from their flight decks, he said, "we could not have rescued all the remaining American citizens and thousands of endangered Vietnamese from Saigon within 20 hours."

The crowd interrupted the President with applause as he congratulated the evacuation force for "the work that was done."

Mr. Ford stood at attention on an elevator of the huge carrier as the orders to "Take the first watch" and "Break the commission pennant" were given, officially marking the Nimitz as a ship of the United States Navy.

The President noted that he had served as "a lowly lieutenant" on the aircraft carrier Monterey under Admiral of the Fleet Chester W. Nimitz in the Pacific during World War II. That carrier, he noted, would probably fit on the hangar deck of the Nimitz.

U.S. Strength Emphasized

Both Secretary of Defense James R. Schlesinger, who introduced the President, and Mr. Ford used the occasion to reaffirm that the United States would remain strong.

Mr. Schlesinger said that Mr. Ford had declared with "unmistakable clarity" that the United States "will maintain a military balance around the world."

Mr. Ford said the ship was a "double symbol for today's challenges." He said the Nimitz was a symbol of the United States's resources, skill, energy "and of our massive but controlled military strength." He added:

"Whether her mission is one of defense, diplomacy or humanity, the Nimitz will command awe and admiration from some; caution and circumspection from others, and respect from all."

He praised Admiral Nimitz, who died in 1966 at the age of 80, as a man who "learned by his mistakes and was tolerant of others—but always in command."

Admiral Nimitz, he said, had "turned defeat into victory and made the broad Pacific again worthy of its name."

"It is my determination to keep it that way, the way all the oceans and continents ought to be," Mr. Ford said. "But Fleet Admiral Nimitz and this fine ship both tell us that controlled strength is the sure guarantor of peace."

Before flying back to Washington in early afternoon, Mr. Ford joined Capt. Bryan W. Compton Jr., the skipper of the Nimitz, on the hangar deck to cut an 1,800-pound commissioning cake—a white layer cake covered with chocolate frosting. The President cut a slice with a sword handed to him by Captain Compton and then ate the slice.

* * *

May 9, 1975

CAMBODIA REDS ARE UPROOTING MILLIONS AS THEY IMPOSE A 'PEASANT REVOLUTION'

Old and Sick Included; Economy Is at Standstill

By SYDNEY H. SCHANBERG
Special to The New York Times

The writer of the following dispatch remained in Cambodia after the American evacuation and was among the foreigners who arrived in Thailand last Saturday. His dispatches were withheld, under an agreement among all the confined correspondents, until the remaining foreigners were transported to safety yesterday.

BANGKOK, Thailand, May 8—The victorious Cambodian Communists, who marched into Phnom Penh on April 17 and ended five years of war in Cambodia, are carrying out a peasant revolution that has thrown the entire country into upheaval.

Perhaps as many as three or four million people, most of them on foot, have been forced out of the cities and sent on a mammoth and grueling exodus into areas deep in the countryside where, the Communists say, they will have to become peasants and till the soil.

No One Excluded

No one has been excluded—even the very old, the very young, the sick and the wounded have been forced out onto the roads—and some will clearly not be strong enough to survive.

The old economy of the cities has been abandoned, and for the moment money means nothing and cannot be spent. Barter has replaced it.

All shops have either been looted by Communist soldiers for such things as watches and transistor radios, or their goods have been taken away in an organized manner to be stored as communal property.

Even the roads that radiate out of the capital and that carried the nation's commerce have been virtually abandoned, and the population living along the roads, as well as that in all cities and towns that remained under the control of the American-backed Government, has been pushed into the interior. Apparently the areas into which the evacuees are being herded are at least 65 miles from Phnom Penh.

In sum the new rulers—before their overwhelming victory they were known as the Khmer Rouge—appear to be remaking Cambodian society in the peasant image, casting aside everything that belonged to the old system, which was generally dominated by the cities and towns and by the elite and merchants who lived there.

Foreigners and foreign aid are not wanted—at least not for now. It is even unclear how much influence the Chinese and North Vietnamese will have, despite their considerable aid to the Cambodian insurgents against the Government of Marshal Lon Nol. The new authorities seem determined to do things themselves in their own way. Despite the propaganda terminology and other trappings, such as Mao caps and Ho Chi Minh rubber-tire sandals, which remind one of Peking and Hanoi, the Communists seem fiercely independent and very Cambodian.

Isolation From World Seen

Judging from their present actions, it seems possible that they may largely isolate their country of perhaps seven million people from the rest of the world for a considerable time—at least until the period of upheaval is over, the agrarian revolution takes concrete shape and they are ready to show their accomplishments to foreigners.

Some of the party officials in Phnom Penh also talked about changing the capital to a more traditional and rural town like Siem Reap, in the northwest.

For those foreigners, including this correspondent, who stayed behind to observe the take-over, the events were an astonishing spectacle.

In Phnom Penh two million people suddenly moved out of the city en masse in stunned silence—walking, bicycling, pushing cars that had run out of fuel, covering the roads like a human carpet, bent under sacks of belongings hastily thrown together when the heavily armed peasant soldiers came and told them to leave immediately, everyone dispirited and frightened by the unknown that awaited them and many plainly terrified because they were soft city people and were sure the trip would kill them.

Hospitals jammed with wounded were emptied, right down to the last patient. They went—limping, crawling, on crutches, carried on relatives' backs, wheeled on their hospital beds.

The Communists have few doctors and meager medical supplies, so many of these patients had little chance of surviving. On April 17, the day this happened, Phnom Penh's biggest hospital had over 2,000 patients and there were several thousand more in other hospitals; many of the wounded were dying for lack of care.

Silent Streets, Eerie Lights

A once-throbbing city became an echo chamber of silent streets lined with abandoned cars and gaping, empty shops. Streetlights burned eerily for a population that was no longer there.

The end of the old and the start of the new began early in the morning of the 17th. At the cable office the line went dead for mechanical reasons at 6 A.M. On the previous day, amid heavy fighting, the Communist-led forces had taken the airport a few miles west of the city, and during the night they had pressed to the capital's edges, throwing in rockets and shells at will.

Thousands of new refugees and fleeing soldiers were filling the heart of the capital, wandering aimlessly, looking for shelter, as they awaited the city's imminent collapse.

Everyone—Cambodians and foreigners alike—thought this had to be Phnom Penh's most miserable hour after long days of fear and privation as the Communist forces drew closer. They looked ahead with hopeful relief to the collapse of the city, for they felt that when the Communists came and the war finally ended, at least the suffering would largely be over. All of us were wrong.

That view of the future of Cambodia—as a possibly flexible place even under Communism, where changes would not be extreme and ordinary folk would be left alone—turned out to be a myth.

Inadequate Descriptions

American officials had described the Communists as indecisive and often ill-coordinated, but they turned out to be firm, determined, well-trained, tough and disciplined.

The Americans had also said that the rebel army was badly riddled by casualties, forced to fill its ranks by hastily impressing young recruits from the countryside and throwing them into the front lines with only a few days' training. The thousands of troops we saw both in the countryside and in Phnom Penh, while they included women soldiers and boy militia, some of whom seemed no more than 10 years old, looked healthy, well organized, heavily armed and well trained.

Another prediction made by the Americans was that the Communists would carry out a bloodbath once they took over—massacring as many as 20,000 high officials and intellectuals. There have been unconfirmed reports of executions of senior military and civilian officials, and no one who witnessed the take-over doubts that top people of the old regime will be or have been punished and perhaps killed or that a large number of people will die of the hardships on the march into the countryside. But none of this will apparently bear any resemblance to the mass executions that had been predicted by Westerners.

[In a news conference Tuesday President Ford reiterated reports—he termed them "hard intelligence"—that 80 to 90 Cambodian officials and their wives had been executed.]

Refugees Poured In

On the first day, as the sun was rising, a short swing by automobile to the northern edge of the city showed soldiers and refugees pouring in. The northern defense line had obviously collapsed.

By the time I reached the Hotel Le Phnom and climbed the two flights of stairs to my room, the retreat could be clearly seen from my window and small-arms fire could be heard in the city. At 6:30 A.M. I wrote in my notebook: "The city is falling."

Over the next couple of hours there were periodic exchanges of fire as the Communists encountered pockets of resistance. But most Government soldiers were busy preparing to surrender and welcome the Communists, as were civilians. White flags suddenly sprouted from housetops and from armored personnel carriers, which resemble tanks.

Some soldiers were taking the clips out of their rifles; others were changing into civilian clothes. Some Government office workers were hastily donning the black pajama-like clothes worn by Indochinese Communists.

Shortly before 9 A.M. the first rebel troops approached the hotel, coming from the north down Monivong Boulevard. A crowd of soldiers and civilians, including newsmen, churned forth to greet them—cheering and applauding and embracing and linking arms to form a phalanx as they came along.

The next few hours saw quite a bit of this celebrating, though shooting continued here and there, some of it only a few hundred yards from the hotel. Civilians and Buddhist monks and troops on both sides rode around town—in jeeps, atop personnel carriers and in cars—shouting happily.

Most civilians stayed nervously indoors, however, not yet sure what was going on or who was who. What was the fighting inside the city all about, they wondered; was it between diehard Government troops and the Communists or between rival Communist factions fighting over the spoils? Or was it mostly exuberance?

Some of these questions, including the nature of the factionalism, have still not been answered satisfactorily, but on that first day such mysteries quickly became academic, for within a few hours, the mood changed.

The cheerful and pleasant troops we first encountered—we came to call them the soft troops, and we learned later that they were discredited and disarmed, with their leader declared a traitor; they may not even have been authentic—were swiftly displaced by battle-hardened soldiers.

While some of these were occasionally friendly, or at least not hostile, they were also all business. Dripping with arms like overladen fruit trees—grenades, pistols, rifles, rockets—they immediately began clearing the city of civilians.

People Driven Out

Using loudspeakers, or simply shouting and brandishing weapons, they swept through the streets, ordering people out of their houses. At first we thought the order applied only to the rich in villas, but we quickly saw that it was for everyone as the streets became clogged with a sorrowful exodus.

Cars stalled or their tires went flat, and they were abandoned. People lost their sandals in the jostling and pushing, so they lay as a reminder of the throng that had passed.

In the days to follow, during the foreign colony's confinement in the French Embassy compound, we heard reports on international news broadcasts that the Communists had evacuated the city by telling people the United States was about to bomb it. However, all the departing civilians I talked with said they had been given no reason except that the city had to be reorganized. They were told they had to go far from Phnom Penh.

In almost every situation we encountered during the more than two weeks we were under Communist control, there was a sense of split vision—whether to look at events through Western eyes or through what we thought might be Cambodian revolutionary eyes.

Brutality or Necessity?

Was this just cold brutality, a cruel and sadistic imposition of the law of the jungle, in which only the fittest will survive? Or is it possible that, seen through the eyes of the peasant soldiers and revolutionaries, the forced evacuation of the cities is a harsh necessity? Perhaps they are convinced that there is no way to build a new society for the benefit of the ordinary man, hitherto exploited, without literally starting from the beginning; in such an unbending view people who represent the old ways and those considered weak or unfit would be expendable and would be weeded out. Or was the policy both cruel and ideological?

A foreign doctor offered this explanation for the expulsion of the sick and wounded from the hospital: "They could not cope with all the patients—they do not have the doctors—so they apparently decided to throw them all out and blame any deaths on the old regime. That way they could start from scratch medically."

Some Western observers considered that the exodus approached genocide. One of them, watching from his refuge in the French Embassy compound, said: "They are crazy! This is pure and simple genocide. They will kill more people this way than if there had been hand-to-hand fighting in the city."

Another foreign doctor, who had been forced at gunpoint to abandon a seriously wounded patient in midoperation, added in a dark voice: "They have not got a humanitarian thought in their heads!"

Whatever the Communists' purpose, the exodus did not grow heavy until dusk, and even then onlookers were slow to realize that the people were being forcibly evacuated.

For my own part, I had a problem that preoccupied me that afternoon: I, with others, was held captive and threatened with execution.

After our release, we went to the Information Ministry, because we had heard about a broadcast directing high officials of the old regime to report there. When we arrived, about 50 prisoners were standing outside the building, among them Lon Non, the younger brother of President Lon Nol, who went into exile on April 1, and Brig. Gen. Chim Chhuon, who was close to the former President. Other generals and Cabinet ministers were also there—very nervous but trying to appear untroubled.

Premier Long Boret, who the day before had made an offer of surrender with certain conditions only to have it immediately rejected, arrived at the ministry an hour later. He is one of the seven "traitors" the Communists had marked for execution. The others had fled except for Lieut. Gen. Sisowath Sirik Matak, a former Premier, who some days later was removed from the French Embassy, where he had taken refuge.

Mr. Long Boret's eyes were puffy and red, almost down to slits. He had probably been up all night and perhaps he had been weeping. His wife and two children were also still in the country; later they sought refuge at the French Embassy, only to be rejected as persons who might "compromise" the rest of the refugees.

Mr. Long Boret, who had talked volubly and articulately on the telephone the night before, had difficulty speaking coherently. He could only mumble yes, no and thank you, so conversation was impossible.

There is still no hard information on what has happened to him. Most people who have talked with the Communists believe it a certainty that he will be executed, if indeed the execution has not already taken place.

Soothing General

One of the Communist leaders at the Information Ministry that day—probably a general, though his uniform bore no markings and he declined to give his name—talked soothingly to the 50 prisoners. He assured them that there were only seven traitors and that other officials of the old regime would be dealt with equitably. "There will be no reprisals," he said. Their strained faces suggested that they would like to believe him but did not.

As he talked, a squad crouched in combat-ready positions around him, almost as if it was guarding him against harm.

The officer, who appeared no more than age 35, agreed to chat with foreign newsmen. His tone was polite and sometimes he smiled, but everything he said suggested that we, as foreigners, meant nothing to him and that our interests were alien to his.

Asked about the fate of the 20 or so foreign journalists missing in Cambodia since the early days of the war, he said he had heard nothing. Asked if we would be permitted to file from the cable office, he smiled sympathetically and said, "We will resolve all problems in their proper order."

Clearly an educated man, he almost certainly speaks French, the language of the nation that ruled Cambodia for nearly a century until the nineteen-fifties, but he gave no hint of this colonial vestige, speaking only in Khmer through an interpreter.

In the middle of the conversation he volunteered quite unexpectedly: "We would like you to give our thanks to the American people who have helped us and supported us from the beginning, and to all people of the world who love peace and justice. Please give this message to the world."

Noting that Congress had halted aid to the Phnom Penh Government, he said, "The purpose was to stop the war," but he quickly added: "Our struggle would not have stopped even if they had given more aid."

Attempts to find out more about who he was and about political and military organization led only to imprecision. The officer said: "I represent the armed forces. There are many divisions. I am one of the many."

Is Asked About Factions

Asked if there were factions, he said there was only one political organization and one government. Some top political and governmental leaders are not far from the city, he added, but they let the military enter first "to organize things."

Most military units, he said are called "rumdos," which means "liberation forces." Neither this commander nor any of the soldiers we talked with ever called themselves Communists or Khmer Rouge (Red Cambodians). They always said they were liberation troops or nationalist troops and called one another brother or the Khmer equivalent of comrade.

The nomenclature at least is confusing, for Western intelligence had described the Khmer Rumdos as a faction loyal to Prince Norodom Sihanouk that was being downgraded by Hanoi-trained Cambodians and losing power.

The Communists named the Cambodian leader, who was deposed by Marshal Lon Nol in 1970 and has been living in exile in Peking, as their figurchead chief of state, but none of the soldiers we talked with brought up his name.

One over-all impression emerged from our talk with the commander at the Information Ministry: The military will be largely in charge of the early stages of the upheaval, carrying out the evacuation, organizing the new agrarian program, searching for hidden arms and resisters, repairing damaged bridges.

The politicians—or so it seemed from all the evidence during our stay—have for the moment taken a rear seat. No significant political or administrative apparatus was yet visible; it did not seem to be a government yet, but an army.

The radio announced April 28 that a special national congress attended by over 300 delegates was held in Phnom Penh from April 25 to 27. It was said to have been chaired by the Deputy Premier and military commander, Khieu Samphan, who has emerged—at least in public announcements—as the top leader. Despite that meeting the military still seemed to be running things as we emerged from Cambodia on Saturday.

One apparent reason is that politicians and bureaucrats are not equipped to do the dirty work and arduous tasks of the early phases of reorganization. Another is that the military, as indicated in conversations with Khmer-speaking foreigners they trusted somewhat, seemed worried that politicians or soft-living outsiders in their movement might steal the victory and dilute it. There could be severe power struggles ahead.

After leaving the prisoners and the military commander at the ministry, we headed for the Hotel Le Phnom, where another surprise was waiting. The day before, the Red Cross turned the hotel into a protected international zone and draped it with huge Red Cross flags. But the Communists were not interested.

Order Hotel Emptied

At 4:55 P.M. troops waving guns and rockets had forced their way into the grounds and ordered the hotel emptied within 30 minutes. By the time we arrived 25 minutes had elapsed. The fastest packing job in history ensued. I even had time to "liberate" a typewriter someone had abandoned since the troops had "liberated" mine earlier.

We were the last ones out, running. The Red Cross had abandoned several vehicles in the yard after removing the keys, so several of us threw our gear on the back of a Red Cross Honda pickup truck and started pushing it up the boulevard toward the French Embassy.

Several days before, word was passed to those foreigners who stayed behind when the Americans pulled out on April 12 that, as a last resort, one could take refuge at the embassy. France had recognized the new government, and it was thought that the new Cambodian leaders would respect the embassy compound as a sanctuary.

As we plodded up the road, big fires were burning on the city's outskirts, sending smoke clouds into the evening sky like a giant funeral wreath encircling the capital.

The embassy was only several hundred yards away, but what was happening on the road made it seem much farther. All around us people were fleeing, for there was no refuge for them. And coming into the city from the other direction was a fresh battalion marching in single file. They looked curiously at us; we looked nervously at them.

In the 13 days of confinement that followed, until our evacuation by military truck to the Thai border, we had only a peephole onto what was going on outside, but there were still many things that could be seen and many clues to the revolution that was going on.

We could hear shooting, sometimes nearby but mostly in other parts of the city. Often it sounded like shooting in the air, but at other times it seemed like small battles. As on the day of the city's fall we were never able to piece together a satisfactory explanation of the shooting, which died down after about a week.

We could see smoke from the huge fires from time to time, and there were reports from foreigners who trickled into the embassy that certain quarters were badly burned and that the water purification plant was heavily damaged.

The foreigners who for various reasons came in later carried stories, some of them eyewitness accounts, of such things as civilian bodies along the roads leading out of the city—people who had apparently died of illness or exhaustion on the march. But each witness got only a glimpse, and no reliable estimate of the toll was possible.

Reports from roads to the south and southeast of Phnom Penh said the Communists were breaking up families by dividing the refugees by sex and age. Such practices were not reported from other roads on which the refugees flooded out of the capital.

Executions Reported

Reports also told of executions, but none were eyewitness accounts. One such report said high military officers were executed at a rubber plantation a couple of miles north of the city.

In the French Embassy compound foreign doctors and relief agency officials were pessimistic about the survival chances of many of the refugees. "There's no food in the countryside at this time of year," an international official said. "What will they eat from now until the rice harvest in November?"

The new Communist officials, in conversations with United Nations and other foreign representatives during our confinement and in statements since, have rejected the idea of foreign aid, "whether it is military, political, economic, social, diplomatic, or whether it takes on a so-called humanitarian form." Some foreign observers wondered whether this included China, for they speculated that the Communists would at least need seed to plant for the next harvest.

Whether the looting we observed before we entered the French compound continued is difficult to say. In any case, it is essential to understand who the Communist soldiers are to understand the behavior of some of them in disciplinary matters, particularly looting.

They are peasant boys, pure and simple—darker skinned than their city brethren, with gold in their front teeth. To them the city is a curiosity, an oddity, a carnival, where you visit but do not live. The city means next to nothing in their scheme of things.

One Kept, the Rest Given

When they looted jewelry shops, they kept only one watch for themselves and gave the rest to their colleagues or passers-by. Transistor radios, cameras and cars held the same toy-like fascination—something to play with, as children might, but not essential.

From my airline bag on the day I was seized and threatened with execution they took only some cigarettes, a pair of boxer underwear shorts and a handkerchief. They passed up a blue shirt and $9,000 in cash in a money belt.

The looting did not really contradict the Communist image of rigid discipline, for commanders apparently gave no orders against the sacking of shops, feeling, perhaps, that this was the least due their men after five years of jungle fighting.

Often they would climb into abandoned cars and find that they would not run, so they would bang on them with their rifles like frustrated children, or they would simply toot the horns for hours on end or keep turning the headlights on and off until the batteries died.

One night at the French Embassy, I chose to sleep on the grass outside; I was suddenly awakened by what sounded like a platoon trying to smash down the front gates with a battering ram that had bright lights and a loud claxon. It was only a bunch of soldiers playing with and smashing up the cars that had been left outside the gates.

Though these country soldiers broke into villas all over the city and took the curious things they wanted—one walked past the embassy beaming proudly in a crimson-colored wool overcoat that hung down to his Ho Chi Minh sandals—they never stayed in the villas. With big, soft beds empty, they slept in the courtyards or the streets.

Almost without exception foot soldiers I talked with, when asked what they wanted to do, replied that they only wanted to go home.

* * *

May 12, 1975

END-OF-WAR RALLY BRINGS OUT 50,000

By PAUL L. MONTGOMERY

About 50,000 people, including many veterans of 10 years of antiwar marches and rallies in the city, filled the Sheep Meadow in Central Park yesterday for an afternoon's celebration of peace in Vietnam and Cambodia.

It was a joyous all-day carnival of songs and speeches in the perfect sunshine, hugging reunions of people who had last met at one demonstration or another. For some, there was an undercurrent of sadness, as if something more than the war—youth, perhaps—had ended, too.

Peter Yarrow, the singer, sang the antiwar song "If You Take My Hand, My Son" as he had at many peace rallies, and the chorus rolled in in waves from the big crowd on the meadow. Some who were in high school when they heard the song first now had children of their own to sing it to.

Mr. Yarrow recalled singing it at the Moratorium in Washington in the fall of 1969.

"I remember the feeling then—that somehow by coming together we could make a life in which people would not kill or hurt each other any more," he said. "It was in the conscience of the young that this war was stopped."

10 Days' Notice

The event was organized on 10 days' notice by a coalition of antiwar groups, many of them going back to the early nineteen-sixties when American involvement in Vietnam was hardly a major issue. Cora Weiss of Women's Strike for Peace, co-chairman of the celebration, recalled that when she first started collecting money for an ad in 1962, the frequent response was "Where's Vietnam?"

Mrs. Weiss said that even at her personal low when the bombing of North Vietnam was resumed at Christmas 1972, she always thought there would be a day of celebration like yesterday's. "You have to think that, or else you can't go on," she said.

Many of the speakers referred to what they called the unfinished business of the war—medical and other aid for the Vietnamese and Cambodian people, and the drive for total and unconditional amnesty for America's war resisters.

Representative Elizabeth Holtzman, Democrat of Brooklyn, made the briefest speech:

"It's finally happened! It's real! The only unfinished business is to bring our boys home—total and complete amnesty for all."

Amnesty the Issue

Representative Bella S. Abzug, Democrat of Manhattan, also referred to the issue. "If your government can open the treasury to Vietnamese refugees," she said, "it can welcome back our own young people."

Louise Ransom of Americans for Amnesty, whose son was killed in Vietnam seven years ago, told the crowd that there were still a half million men in exile, facing charges or with undesirable discharges because they had opposed the war. "We in the antiwar movement who encouraged them bear a special responsibility," she said.

Among the other speakers and entertainers were Barbara Dane, Ossie Davis, Tom Paxton, David Dellinger, Richie Havens, Paul Simon, Odetta, the American Indian Movement drummers, Harry Belafonte, the Deadly Nightshade, Phil Ochs, representatives of veterans' and labor groups, and Vietnamese and Cambodian residents of the United States.

Many Memories

For those who had participated in the peace movement from its early days in the city—the all-night meetings, the frequent hostility of bystanders, the first mass draft-card burning in the Sheep Meadow in 1967, the parades up Fifth Avenue, the early-morning rides to Washington—there were many memories yesterday:

Joan Baez, Pete Seeger, and the Rev. Fred Kirkpatrick looking up into the sun and singing "Carry It On"; Grace Paley, the novelist and early peace activist smiling and looking for an ice-cream vendor in the crowd; Anita Hoffman, wife of Abbie and their child. America playing in the grass; the Bread and Puppet Theater cavorting in the sea of blue jeans over the meadow.

"There's lots of lumps in lots of throats." said Pamela Chapman, one of the 50,000 at the gathering. "It's unbelievable. Today is the first day I really realize the war is over."

* * *

May 16, 1975

PRAISE FOR THE PRESIDENT

Domestic and Foreign Triumph Is Seen As U.S. Reasserts Its Presence Abroad

By JAMES M. NAUGHTON
Special to The New York Times

WASHINGTON, May 15—By nearly-every measure President Ford's military venture in the Gulf of Siam was being evaluated here today as a diplomatic and domestic political triumph. The merchant ship Mayagüez, steaming once more through Southeast Asian waters, serves as a visible symbol of United States resolve to remain an influence—and, if necessary, a military presence—abroad despite the recent debacle in Indochina.

Democrats in Congress who expect their party to elect the successor to Mr. Ford in 1976 termed his actions right and accorded him high marks for leadership. Republican conservatives who had begun questioning his capacity declared him, in the words of one, "a man who knows how to act."

The President's decision to use marines, warships and military aircraft to retrieve the crew and recover the Mayagüez from their Cambodian captors was, White House officials acknowledged, a calculated gamble with a broad purpose.

The military operation was mounted without any certainty on the whereabouts of the captive seamen and with no guarantee that the broad goal of demonstrating United States resolve for worried allies or potentially capricious opponents would be buttressed by the rescue. The real test, a White House aide said when the outcome was still in doubt yesterday, would be how many of the 39 crew members were saved.

All were. That the crew was surrendered by a small boat flying a white pennant rather than rescued by the marine landing forces did not diminish the belief here that pluck had been more responsible than luck.

'I'm Glad It Worked'

"It worked," said Senator Robert C. Byrd of West Virginia, the Senate Democratic whip. "I'm glad it worked. It's certainly a plus for the country. It will strengthen our prestige throughout the world."

Administration officials, including Secretary of State Kissinger and Secretary of Defense James R. Schlesinger, were said to have been eager to find some dramatic means of underscoring President Ford's stated intention to "maintain our leadership on a worldwide basis."

The occasion came with the capture of the vessel. While Administration officials emphasized that the first objective of the rescue operation was to save the American crew, they made it clear that they welcomed the opportunity to show that Mr. Ford had the will and the means to use American power to protect American interests.

Mr. Schlesinger described the operation as a "judicious and effective use of American force for purposes that were necessary for the well-being of this society."

Public response to the President's action, judging by the telephone calls, letters and telegrams received by the White House, continued to be strongly favorable. The count today was about 5 to 1 in support of the President.

The overwhelmingly positive initial reaction from the public and the international community suggested that, barring qualms about casualties, there was broad agreement with Mr. Ford's use of force.

The boldness and speed of the rescue venture also appeared to have enhanced the President's political standing in the wake of the collapse of American efforts in Indochina and amid persistent economic difficulties.

"He's etched a sharper profile in the minds of the people as a leader," according to Representative John B. Anderson of Illinois, the third-ranking House Republican leader.

"I am proud of him today," said Senator Jesse A. Helms, Republican of North Carolina, one of several conservatives who have been considering support for a third-party challenge to Mr. Ford.

By one Administration account the rescue operation coincided with Mr. Ford's determination to build on his image as

United Press International from the Department of Defense

U.S. marines moving out on Tang Island after landing by copter yesterday to take the Mayagüez and crew.

a decent, unaggrandizing President by showing that he could also be firm when the occasion required it.

Senator Byrd, agreeing that the operation was "a plus for the President, and it ought to be," said nonetheless that in government "those who cheer today often curse tomorrow."

He and others in Congress expressed muted concern that Mr. Ford's decisiveness might have been at the expense of an obligation under the War Powers Act of 1973 to consult with Congressional leaders before committing United States forces to combat situations. The act, according to one of its architects, Senator Thomas F. Eagleton, Democrat of Missouri, obliges the President to "at least hear out their advice" before rejecting their recommendations.

Moreover, Senator Edward W. Brooke, Republican of Massachusetts, sent to Secretary Kissinger a detailed list of questions about the seizure and recapture of the Mayagüez, asserting that the responses would facilitate judgments as to the wisdom of the operation.

For all that, Representative Anderson said that the complaints voiced on Capitol Hill were mild and that they did not diminish the psychological boost the nation had received because Mr. Ford "applied the balm of Gilead to the wounds we suffered in our ignominious departure from Indochina."

On balance the sharp reversal of fortunes seemed to be similar to that attributed 13 years ago to President John F. Kennedy because of his decisive actions in the Cuban missile crisis.

In an article written in 1962 Mr. Kissinger, then a professor at Harvard, said that Mr. Kennedy had "boldly seized an opportunity given few statesmen; to change the course of events by one dramatic move."

Mr. Kissinger reportedly counseled Mr. Ford to take bold action in the Gulf of Siam. As the Secretary wrote of the confrontation with the Russians over the missiles, "the President's stroke demonstrated that a great power leads not so much by its words as by its actions, that initiative creates its own consensus."

* * *

May 27, 1975

REFUGEES' FAMILY LIFE STRAINED BY WEEKS OF WAITING

By JON NORDHEIMER

Special to The New York Times

CAMP PENDLETON, Calif., May 26—A stillness descends on Camp 1 shortly after sunset, a time for the Vietnamese refugees to draw inside the Quonset huts and canvas field tents that have sheltered many of them for nearly a month now.

The mess hall closes, and only the clatter of pots and pans from inside the kitchen is heard, broken at times by the hydraulic groan of garbage trucks forklifting away the day's refuse.

On the bottom mattress of a bunk bed in Quonset hut 64365 sits Doan Trieu Dac, and opposite him sits his wife, Le Thi, a woman of winsome beauty whose age (35) and children (six) have failed to introduce a line of fatigue in her face.

Four weeks of camp life, following four weeks of arranging the family's escape from Saigon, have produced a strain on the couple, and it is more clearly evident in Mr. Dac's thin face.

Volley ball and pickup soccer games in the open fields on the periphery of Camp 1 finally surrender to the darkness, and many of the young players drift to an asphalt covered lot where the Marines show outdoor movies on the screen that is held 15 feet off the ground between two telephone poles.

The films shown every night are a grainy product from Hollywood's back-lot days, vintage cowboy and action movies that have even been retired from television late shows around the nation. But the audience seated around the screen in a half-circle, and huddled in the green field jackets issued every refugee by the Marines, appears to enjoy this vision of America, and it is about the only contact they have had with the world that awaits them outside the gates of this processing center.

Mr. Dac, smoking a cigarette, sits about 50 yards from the rise and fall of the movie's English-language sound track.

The children are either at the movies or have left the hut to visit with friends elsewhere in the village. Mr. Dac's 59-year-old mother rests in another bed, and soon she will drop off to sleep, a slumber that is now less troubled and fitful than her first night here when she awoke to fears about where she was.

Time in the camp has also eased the tone of the nightly conversations between Mr. Dac and his wife. In the beginning there were many disputes. At first, Mr. Dac would scold his children for leaving the hut to play, fearing they would become lost in the strange camp, or he would chastise them for failing to get an early start in the long meal lines.

Mrs. Dac would cry and complain that her husband did not care for the children or love her enough. She would break down and for the first time in their marriage she spoke harsh words against her husband.

Mr. Dac was sensitive to his wife's complaints. For years he struggled to provide a good home for his wife, whose grandmother was a descendant of the Vietnamese royal family. He suffered the silent criticism of her relatives, who were in positions of power and influence in Saigon, while he was a low-level civil servant, a refugee from Hanoi who went to South Vietnam in 1954 to begin a new life with few resources.

The New York Times/David Strick

Doan Trieu Dac with his wife, Le Thi, beside him, their six children and his mother, Nguyen Thuyet Ngan, right, assembled for a picture in the Quonset hut they occupy in Camp Pendleton, Calif. All have unpaid jobs there.

A Prized Skill

He did speak English, however, a skill that in 1954 was prized by his American rescuers, who then as now relied on the bilingualism of the Vietnamese to carry out the evacuation. Mr. Dac's fluency carried him into several jobs with American military and intelligence units before he became an assistant to a course director in the South Vietnamese Army's National Defense College.

These associations convinced Mr. Dac, who is 42, that his position would be untenable in a Communist controlled state, so once it became obvious in early April that South Vietnam was on the verge of collapse, he plotted his family's escape.

Mr. Dac had little money. The family lived in a small house in a slum area of Saigon.

Mrs. Dac had gone to work as a key-punch operator at the Ministry of Land Reform. They had once owned a car, but were forced to sell it when inflation and soaring gasoline prices pinched their income.

In mid April the Dacs both requested leaves from their jobs and the family journeyed to the seaside resort of Vung Tau, where order had been restored after remnants of an evacuated South Vietnamese Army unit had terrorized the town.

Mr. Dac's plan was to rent a junk that would carry them to an evacuation flotilla that was expected to form out at sea. But the ships failed to materialize, and the family returned to Saigon, where after several days of desperate effort Mr. Dac was able to get them aboard an American evacuation plane that departed on April 25.

After stops at the Philippines and Guam, the family arrived at Camp Pendleton on May 2, among the first groups of refugees arriving without friends or family in the United States.

"On the eve of our departure in Saigon," says Mrs. Dac, who speaks no English, "we would joke that once we got to the U.S. we would get fat eating American food. But look at him," she continues, indicating the gaunt figure of Mr. Dac seated on the next bed. "His face has become so emaciated despite all the food here."

"How can I eat," Mr. Dac tells a visitor to the hut, "when I have a million worries turning around in my head?"

His principal concern, of course, is that after four weeks in the camp the Dac family is no closer to getting an American sponsor.

Sponsor. It is one of the first words the Vietnamese learn here. Like "Coca-Cola" or "G.I.," it is not translated into Vietnamese. In the mess halls and processing center lines, wherever the refugees gather, the word pops into Vietnamese conversations, uttered almost with a sense of piety and salvation.

Spun-SORE is the way many of the Vietnamese pronounce the word. "Is there any news about a spun-SORE for you?" they ask each other daily.

Mr. Dac held his family back from the official processing because he feared in those first days of confusion following arrival that he and his family would be forced out of the camp to fend for themselves.

"Sitting here is like sitting on hot fire," Mr. Dac said back then, "but the prospect of being kicked out of camp into the streets is even more dreadful."

His wife shared his anxiety. "We will probably be booed and shoved about in the streets," she had said.

Now there is more confidence that they will not end up as beggars in a strange, hostile land. But the prospect of spending many months in Camp 1 can be spiritually debilitating.

"We don't know anything about outside life yet," said Mr. Dac. "My children ask me about American life and customs, such as should they say hello to strangers, and how do the American women get to the market to shop? I do not know many of these answers myself."

The one lesson he has tried to impress on his four sons and daughters, who range in age from 9 to 16, is that they must not be idle.

"I spent half of my lifetime working for Americans," he remarks, "and I know Americans. They work very hard. I tell my children they have to be self-supportive, even when they are young. I want to teach my children to practice working, because no American owes them a penny."

Consequently, everyone in the Dac family has a job in the camp, for which there is no pay. The children work as aides in the mess hall, helping to clear and clean tables. There is also work to be done in the Quonset hut, where 38 other refugees in addition to the Dacs are quartered.

In the first fortnight here, Mr. Dac helped organize the infrastructure of the Camp 1 command post, designed to give refugees a measure of control in camp life. Since then he has gone to work in a child-care center and school operated by a local agency that has contracted with the Government to provide "survival English" lessons for young refugee children.

Everyone's 'Very Busy'

Mr. Dac's wife and mother also teach at the school, accompanied by a 14-year-old daughter who assists them. The older son, 16, works in the nearby Y.M.C.A. tent, helping distribute recreation equipment to the refugees.

"We all keep very busy so that time goes by quickly," Mr. Dac relates with a toothy grin that seems to acknowledge that he hopes to attract the interest of Americans who appreciate his family's industry. "Some families just make line for chow and sit around all day," he said. "That is not for us."

After nightfall, however, there is time for reflection, and beyond Mrs. Dac's outward composure this is the time of day she lapses into a melancholy encouraged by thoughts of the fate of her family left behind in Vietnam.

The couple talks softly as the grandmother drifts off to sleep on another bed. A bare electric bulb burns in a ceiling socket. There are several other hushed conversations among the rows of bunk beds. Soon the children will return, wash up, and the family will sleep.

But Mr. Dac will remain awake in the darkness of the hut until after midnight, the glowing ash of a cigarette his beacon of distress. Among all his concerns, he worries that the family will still be in the camp on June 22.

That is the date of his father's death, and as the oldest son in his family, it is Mr. Dac's responsibility to perform a Confucian ritual to honor his father.

On that day he must prepare an altar of candles and lay out articles of food and clothing and paper money for the benefit of his father's spirit. He will burn incense and call on his father's ghost in an ancient address of fealty and respect:

"Father, today is your anniversary day. We are your son, Mr. Dac. Would you mind to come up and join the family and help give them good health and happiness?"

Since the money and clothing are burned at the conclusion of the ceremony, poor Confucians like Mr. Dac traditionally purchase ersatz money and paper clothing for the ritual from specialty stores. But these materials are not available in the camp, and Mr. Dac has not yet devised the manner in which he shall also succor to the ghost of his dead father.

For the moment, he is troubled that he has such a long way to go to provide for the living, and he is saddened by the weight of that knowledge.

* * *

May 27, 1975

THE VIETNAM DISEASE

By TOM WICKER

Memorial Day is supposed to honor the dead of the nation's wars but it also is a better time than most to give some thought to war's living wreckage. For example:

On the night of June 10, 1971, Donald G. Kemp, a former Army ranger who had served in Vietnam on long-range reconnaissance patrols, went to bed and fell into one of the combat nightmares about which he had complained regularly since returning from Vietnam in 1967.

Mr. Kemp customarily slept with a gun under his pillow. That night, when his wife made an effort to wake him from his nightmare, he grabbed the gun, shot and killed her. He is now serving a life sentence in Wisconsin.

That is only one example of the serious but largely unnoticed problems of "post-Vietnam syndrome," or PVS, the label by which the extraordinary psychological difficulties of hundreds of thousands of Vietnam veterans have come to be identified.

"PVS is when you get out, struggle, try to make your life seem relevant, and wig out," says Samuel Schorr, who served with the 86th Combat Engineers Battalion in Vietnam, and who now works in Chicago for Vietnam Veterans Against the War. "We've all wrecked relationships. We've all tried dope, and wrecked attempts to go to school, get a job."

It may surprise some Americans that there are about 7.4 million Vietnam-era veterans, of whom 2.5 million served in Southeast Asia. Here are some sad facts about them:

Of those who were married before they went to Vietnam, 38 per cent were separated or getting divorced six months after their return.

About 500,000 have attempted suicide since discharge.

As many as 175,000 probably have used heroin since getting out of the service; as many as 100,000 might have used it in Vietnam.

Recently, 13,167 of these men were listed as 100 per cent disabled for psychological and neurological reasons.

(The figure for heroin use overseas was reported by The New York Times two years ago. All the other statistics are from a comprehensive series of articles in Penthouse Magazine.)

Dr. Chaim Shatan, a psychoanalyst at New York University who has worked closely with 145 Vietnam veterans, believes that specific and unique psychological hardships were imposed on them by the kind of war they fought. For one thing, he thinks, the public has "no idea of the isolation, the utter isolation that these men experienced: It was different even from Korea. They were one tiny unit, a squad of five or six guys . . . surrounded by suffering and hostility, totally unsupported, on the alert, never knowing when another attack was coming."

He also believes the DEROS system—Date Estimate Return from Overseas—under which soldiers went to Vietnam with their dates of return prefixed, added to their isolation. "In World War II, you went over with your unit in most cases, and came back with your unit. In Vietnam it was 'FNG.' That was your welcome, '—new guy.' "

Dr. Charles R. Figley, a psychologist at Purdue, was 20 years old and in the Third Marine Division when he waded ashore at Da Nang in 1965, among the first American ground troops to face combat in Vietnam. He believes the sense of isolation was not relieved by discharge.

"Veterans were largely rejected by other students," he points out. "If they don't hang out together, they keep it all inside of them. They are afraid that somehow they're going to be found out, that they did something evil."

Hot, humid weather like that of Vietnam can bring on nightmares, flashbacks, depressions, Dr. Shatan says. One mental specialist, Sarah Haley of the Veterans Administration in Boston, has found that even ordinary child-rearing can bring on symptoms of PVS. When young children enter an aggressive stage, fathers who are veterans sometimes find a forgotten aggressive instinct triggered in themselves.

Dr. Shatan and others say the Veterans Administration, which provided good psychiatric services after World War II, has not been so alert to the problems of PVS. Worse, the V.A. does not treat any disorder that occurs two years or more after discharge; and in many cases PVS takes more than two years to affect a veteran obviously enough to require treatment. The result is that many Vietnam veterans are not getting the help and services they need, although they may have been as badly wounded as many of those who suffered physical injuries.

One likely reason is that many Americans would like to forget everything about Vietnam. "I wish this country could have two cognitive notions," Dr. Figley says. "One, being ashamed of this war. Two, being proud of its veterans."

(Note: This article was prepared with the active assistance of David White of The New York Times.)

* * *

August 24, 1975

PATHET LAO ANNOUNCE VIENTIANE TAKE-OVER

By DAVID A. ANDELMAN
Special to The New York Times

BANGKOK, Thailand, Aug. 23—The Communist-led Pathet Lao took over Laos today, marking the last chapter in the rise to power of Communist-led movements in Indochina.

Some 300,000 people gathered on a parade ground in the capital, Vientiane, today to "welcome the people's revolutionary administration," according to broadcasts of the Vientiane radio and the Pathet Lao news agency, monitored here and in Hong Kong.

The rally marked the end of a process that began formally in Laos three months and two days ago, a process that has, so far, been generally peaceful.

According to the Pathet Lao news agency, the crowd at the rally was addressed by Thao Moun, identified only as chairman of the "uprising committee," who said that the advent of the new administration marked a major turning point in the development and growth of Vientiane Province.

The status of Premier Souvanna Phouma and King Savang Vatthana was not clear. Both had planned visits outside the country this month that were abruptly canceled last week, apparently because of the imminence of today's ceremonies and the spreading reports that if they left they would not return.

The Pathet Lao has said it continues to respect and recognize both Prince Souvanna Phouma as the head of the Government and the King as the head of state.

Vientiane Province was the last of the country's provinces to be "liberated," a process that has meant the arrival of Pathet Lao troops in strength, backed by tanks but accompanied too by cheers from much of the population.

Tonight, the time allotted for the regular nightly broadcast in French by the Vientiane radio was pre-empted by a broadcast in the Lao language accompanied by background sounds of throngs cheering and singing as the announcement of the Pathet Lao take-over was made.

Earlier today, the Vientiane radio announced the take-over of Laos's royal capital, Luang Prabang, 130 miles northwest of Vientiane, in a similar celebration earlier this week.

In that broadcast, the radio repeatedly referred to the "liberation" as a victory over "the United States imperialists and their henchmen."

'New Period of Struggle'

"This seizure of power" by the Pathet Lao "is of great importance" the broadcast said. "It is encouraging the Lao people in the new period of their struggle. Under foreign rule, especially since the United States invaded Laos, the centuries-old royal capital has been turned into a training center for the mercenary army to carry out air and ground attacks against the liberated zone of Laos."

The take-over of Vientiane Province, which had been expected for weeks, was heralded last night when the Laotian authorities sealed the country's borders, cut all international telecommunications, and closed airports for 24 hours.

Thailand, which has a long border with Laos, went further, Kampol Klinsukol, the Governor of Nong Khai Province, ordered the entire frontier sealed for at least what was expected to be a five-day celebration in Vientiane. The Laotian capital is just across the Mekong River from Thailand.

There have been a growing number of border incidents along this frontier, most of them involving river patrol craft, and diplomats of the two countries have been expelled in recent weeks as the bitterness has grown.

There have been, however, no reports of any incidents along the border while the celebrations were going on in Vientiane.

Today's "liberation" was the last of a series of such celebrations that began May 20 when Pathet Lao troops and tanks rolled through Savannakhet, a major southern provincial capital. Student demonstrators had prepared the groundwork there by ousting the right-wing administration, which had been linked with Vientiane, in a week-long demonstration that included the house arrest of 12 American aid officials.

The pattern was repeated in province after province, spreading in May from the southern panhandle area northward into all the area originally controlled by the right-wing Vientiane side of what had been the year-old provisional Government of national union.

After the take-overs started, the Laotian Premier, Prince Souvanna Phouma, a neutralist, said he had ordered that there be no resistance to any of the Pathet Lao actions in an effort to "avoid any bloodshed."

It was at the end of a long war that the coalition Government was established in April, 1974, with the aim of sharing responsibility equally between members of the old right-wing Vientiane side, the Pathet Lao and a group of avowed neutralists.

Under those terms, each party was to administer the territory it controlled at the time of the cease-fire.

The takeover of Savannakhet and neighboring Pakse, apparently marked the end of this arrangement, although the Pathet Lao and Prince Souvanna Phouma continued, almost to the end, to preserve the fiction of a coalition arrangement.

However as so-called people's courts spread through the ministries, anti-American and pro-Communist demonstrators began to take to the streets and most of the strong figures behind the right-wing element of the coalition fled abroad.

Control Tightened

Gradually, the Pathet Lao augmented its administrative control, closing bars and nightclubs, imposing restrictions on travel and sending hundreds of government and military officials off to "re-education courses" in which they were encouraged to confess "reactionary" leanings.

* * *

July 3, 1976

2 PARTS OF VIETNAM OFFICIALLY REUNITED; LEADERSHIP CHOSEN

By The Associated Press

BANGKOK, Thailand, July 2—North and South Vietnam were officially reunited today after more than 20 years of war, and, Hanoi was declared the capital. The Hanoi radio said that leaders of the new Socialist Republic of Vietnam had been elected in the National Assembly by secret ballot.

The radio, monitored here, said that an "explosion of applause" had greeted the unification announcement in the 492-member Assembly.

The former North Vietnamese flag, anthem and emblem were approved as symbols of the country.

"A new page of Vietnamese history has been turned," the broadcast said. "At this moment, 8:30 A.M. [9:30 P.M. Thursday New York time] on July 2, 1976, the Vietnamese nation is officially considered as a unified country from Cao Lang to Cau Mau."

Cao Lang is the northernmost point of what was North Vietnam, and Cau Mau is the southernmost peninsula of the former South Vietnam.

Vietnam was divided by the 1954 Geneva Agreement that followed the French defeat at Dien Bien Phu. The last Americans were withdrawn from the South on April 30, 1975, following the Communist victory over the Saigon forces supported by the United States.

The Hanoi broadcast did not say how the decision on reunification had actually been made.

The formal reunification announcement was something of an anticlimax, since Hanoi and Saigon have during the last year described Vietnam as one country. But the two halves maintained separate government machineries and leaders until today.

As many Western observers had expected all but one high Government office went to North Vietnamese leaders rather than to those who had fought in the south.

The exception was Dr. Nguyen Huu Tho, former president of the Provisional Revolutionary Government of South Vietnam, who will be one of two Vice Presidents. The other will be Nguyen Luong Bang, North Vietnam's Vice President since 1969.

The largely ceremonial post of President went to 88-year-old Ton. Duc Thang, formerly North Vietnam's head of state. Pham Van Dong, a skilled administrator and diplomat, retained his title of Prime Minister.

Truong Chinh, a hard-liner who is said to be pro-Chinese, will be chairman of the standing committee of the Assembly.

There was no initial indication that changes would occur in the highest ranks of Vietnam's Communist Party, the Lao Dong, where all major decisions are made.

Most observers say that the top five men in the party's 11-man Politburo are First Secretary Le Duan, Mr. Chinh, Prime Minister Dong, Phan Hung, a southerner, and Deputy Prime Minister Nguyen Vo Giap, the general who defeated the French at Dien Bien Phu.

The top leadership is composed mostly of men in their late 60's. Almost all helped found the Communist Party, fought the Japanese and the French and directed the struggle against the United States and the Saigon governments it backed.

Reliable sources said that although Hanoi's leadership might have had its internal disputes over the years, it had had 30 years of continuity and none of the purges that have marked Soviet and Chinese Communism.

The following short biographies of some of the top officials elected today were compiled from authoritative sources.

Ho Chi Minh's Successor

President Thang has held that position in North Vietnam since the death of Vietnam's revolutionary leader, Ho Chi Minh, in 1969. At 88, he is not considered a significant figure and is not a member of the party Politburo.

His anti-French activities as a leader of student strikes forced him into exile. He returned to Vietnam in 1927 and enrolled in the Revolutionary Youth League. Mr. Thang later spent 15 years in jail for complicity in murder and sedition. He was one of the more extremist members of North Vietnam's Communist Party.

Prime Minister Dong has held that post in North Vietnam since 1950 and is considered the No. 3 man in the party's power structure.

In his late 60's, Mr. Dong is known as a sophisticated but uncompromising bargainer, skilled in international diplomacy. He is thought to lean closer to Moscow than to Peking.

Like his colleagues, he entered revolutionary politics early in life and was sentenced by the French to six years' hard labor in 1929. A favorite of Ho Chi Minh, he took part in a number of key international meetings, including the 1954 Geneva Conference.

Hard-Line Ideologist

Mr. Chinh, 59, has been chairman of the National Assembly's standing committee for 16 years. He is known as a hard-line, pro-Chinese Communist and is the chief ideologist of the leadership.

During the war against the French, he rose quickly but suffered a brief eclipse when he was accused of being tougher than the party line directed in 1956. He was generally thought to be responsible for mass executions that accompanied the new regime's efforts at land reform in North Vietnam.

Vice President Bang, 72, has held that post in North Vietnam since 1969 and has been on the Central Committee of the party since 1945.

Another veteran of French jails, his early specialty was labor agitation. He has held key party and government posts and was once ambassador to the Soviet Union.

Vice President Tho, the lone southerner in the group, was a Saigon lawyer and agitator against the French in the 1950's and during the early United States involvement in his country.

After periods in prison and under house arrest, he fled into the countryside in 1962 and helped found South Vietnam's National Liberation Front. He was chosen to head the front's Central Committee in 1962 and its Presidium two years later.

* * *

July 12, 1976

VIETNAM

Vietnam is united after 22 years; the old Vietminh movement rules an undivided country from its capital of Hanoi. The flag and anthem of North Vietnam are now seen and heard officially from Cao Lang in the north to Cau Mau in the south.

The formal proclamation of reunification on July 2 created barely a ripple in faraway foreign capitals that once had assigned strategic significance to every square kilometer of Vietnamese landscape. The all-consuming passion of a whole political generation, Vietnam has all but disappeared from the American consciousness, except in bitter memory that few in or out of public life want to revive.

The ultimate collapse of the United States war effort on April 30 last year has had none of the dire consequences that the war's supporters had predicted; if anything, the effect on

American life and this country's global position has been beneficial—lifting an impossible burden that drained, not enhanced, American security. In Vietnam itself, there has been no bloodbath—though the continuing detention of formerly influential South Vietnamese in "reeducation camps" smells more and more of long-term repression.

Vietnam and the United States would both benefit from an early establishment of diplomatic relations, though the threat of an election campaign may not be the ideal moment to raise any sensitive issue that can be put off.

Ever maneuvering among eager foreign influences, including the rival Communist superpowers, the Vietnamese leaders remain hopeful of United States investment and development assistance—lest they grow too dependent on the largesse flowing in from the Soviet Union. Establishment of official relations might even make it easier to obtain whatever information may still be available about missing American servicemen.

In any event, there is no longer any need for perpetuating this country's estrangement from a non-aligned national Communist force of great potential influence in Southeast Asia.

* * *

August 22, 1976

F.B.I. REPORTEDLY STOLE MAIL IN ITS DRIVE ON WAR FOES

Special to The New York Times

The following article was written by John M. Crewdson based on reporting by him and Nicholas M. Horrock.

WASHINGTON, Aug. 21—Justice Department prosecutors have found evidence that the Federal Bureau of Investigation agents stole letters and parcels from the United States mails as part of a wide range of illegal techniques directed at the militant antiwar movement over the last five years, sources familiar with the investigation said today.

The prosecutors have also found firm evidence that the agents conducted illegal wiretaps and room buggings, according to these sources.

The sources said that the new illegalities were discovered recently in the course of an examination by the department's Civil Rights Division of a number of burglaries committed during the same period by F.B.I. agents hunting fugitive terrorists in the New York City area.

Those agents, who numbered between 20 and 30, were assigned between 1970 and 1973 to an elite "Weathfug squad" in the bureau's Manhattan office. The acronym is derived from the name of the fugitive group, the Weather Underground Organization, whose members have taken credit for several bombings during that period.

In the course of their largely unproductive three-year search, members of the Weathfug group illegally entered the residences of relatives and associates of the underground terrorists in hopes of finding clues to their whereabouts.

The agents who committed those burglaries, and the F.B.I. executives, including W. Mark Felt, the bureau's former associate director, and Edward S. Miller, its retired intelligence chief, are now subjects of a criminal investigation by the Justice Department's Civil Rights Division.

But the sources said that department lawyers had discovered in the course of interviewing some of the F.B.I. agents who have been granted immunity from prosecution in return for their testimony about the Weathfug agents that members of the team had also conducted unauthorized electronic surveillance of their targets and stolen their mail.

It has previously been reported that the F.B.I. conducted a formal program of intercepting mail in this country between 1940 and 1966, in an effort to identify and locate undercover agents of hostile foreign intelligence services working in this country.

But while that effort was carried out with the assistance of the postal authorities, the mail thefts discovered by the Justice Department prosecutors involved simply stealing letters from the mail boxes of associates of the Weather fugitives.

Letters Were Taken

According to the sources, the letters were taken by the F.B.I.'s Manhattan headquarters where it was rumored among other agents that the Weathfug squad "had a teakettle going in the back room."

Once the letters had been opened and their contents examined, the sources said, they were remailed or replaced in the boxes from which they had been stolen.

Because the mail thefts occurred within the past five years, they are subject to prosecution under Federal statutes that prohibit tampering with or delaying first-class mail.

The sources also said that the Justice Department had learned that the Weathfug agents had illegally bugged many of the homes and offices they burglarized and had placed unauthorized wiretaps on telephones in those places and at other locations that had not been the targets of burglaries.

While many of the burglaries were carried out for the purpose of sifting garbage and looking for clues, such as traces of soil or out-of-town matchbooks that would indicate the recent presence of a visitor, one source said that a number of the burglaries had been carried out because of the need to "service," the bugging devices by replacing their batteries.

One of the sources said that, for all the planning that went into the burglaries, the Weathfug squad had "never turned up a decent lead" to aid their hunt for the fugitive bombers.

None of the wiretaps or bugs, the source added, had been accompanied by a court order or written approval of the Attorney General. Asked whether the surveillances were therefore illegal, the source replied, "Of course they were."

The Civil Right Division, which is headed by J. Stanley Pottinger, has officially enlarged its investigation of criminal activities by F.B.I. agents to include the mail thefts, buggings and wiretaps, one source said, adding that he expected indictments to be returned in those matters as well as the burglaries.

A Federal grand jury in New York City will begin to hear testimony presented by Mr. Pottinger's office next week, but indictments are understood to be months away.

* * *

August 29, 1976

PEACE, WITH HONOR

By ARI L. GOLDMAN

MASSAPEQUA—For the first time since he came back from Vietnam eight years ago, Ron Kovic is at peace with himself, his community and with his country. The war robbed him of his youth. A bullet in his spinal cord meant that he would never play baseball again, never wrestle, never jump over fences, never run along the beach holding a girl's hand. Paralyzed from the chest down, he would never walk again.

His return in 1968 was the beginning of a period of criss-crossing the country and the globe by hand-controlled automobile and jet airplane. He searched and ran for years, but now he has come home to Massapequa, to the block where he grew up, and he is at peace.

"I've died enough and suffered enough," he said while sitting in his wheelchair in front of his family's modest home on Toronto Avenue here. "Now I feel that I can live and have a life ahead of me. Writing the book helped me understand that."

"Born on the Fourth of July," the book that gave him this hope for the future, was written by Ron Kovic in excruciating pain and anguish. The book was published last week by McGraw-Hill to reviews that acclaimed it as one of the best books to come out of the Vietnam experience.

It is the poignantly told story of a boy who was born on the nation's birthday and grew up in the America of John Wayne, Howdy Doody, John F. Kennedy and Sputnik, who played baseball and stickball, had girlfriends, joined the Boy Scouts and enlisted in the Marine Corps.

It is the story of killing and being killed on the battlefields of Southeast Asia. The story of coming back to a town built by veterans of a prouder war who didn't understand the veterans of Vietnam. It is an account of one man and one community, but it could be the account of a whole generation and a whole country.

"It is the story of the American dream becoming the American nightmare," Ron Kovic said.

With his book, he said, he has turned that tragedy into triumph. "Since the book was published I don't feel the anguish, I don't feel the isolation.

"I exposed great personal failures in my book that would send other men into hiding. I had to keep telling myself to tell everything, everything. It had to be the American story—the complete American story. Only through pouring out that naked truth could I truly represent the young American who went to war and the society that sent him to war."

Ron Kovic was one the almost 60,000 Nassau and Suffolk youths who were sent to Vietnam. Many of them came back silent, almost afraid to articulate what had happened to them.

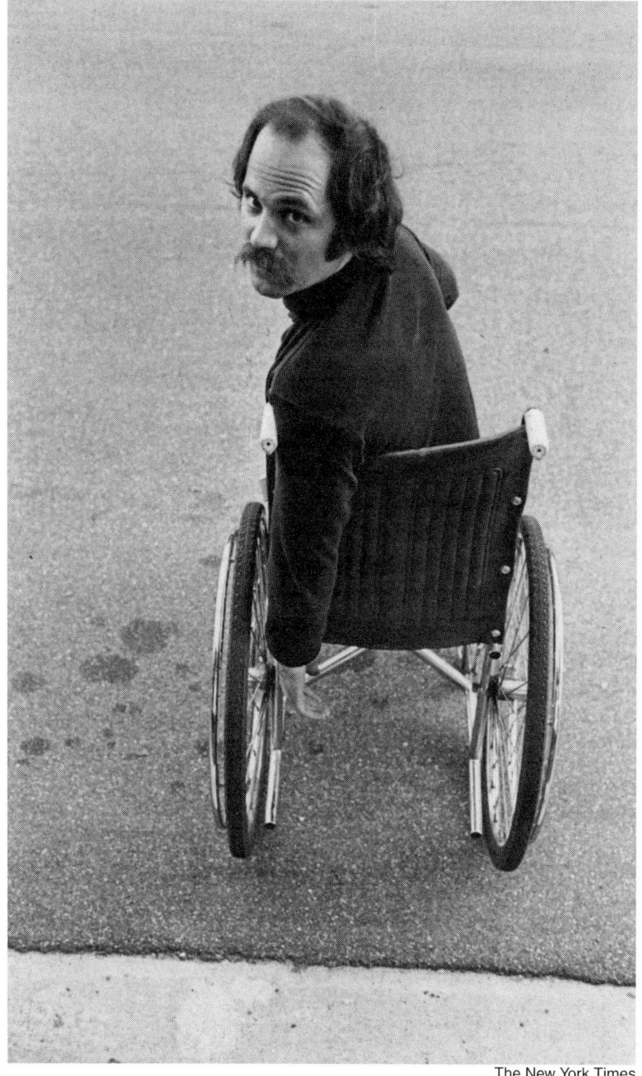

The New York Times

Ron Kovic

Many came back with deep physical and mental scars that would not heal. Mr. Kovic's anguish was so great that it cried out for expression:

"There is no real healing left anymore," he wrote, "everything that is going to heal has healed already and now I am left with the corpse, the living dead man, the Easter Seal boy, the cripple, the sexlessman, the sexlessman . . . the man who can't make children . . . the bitter man with the nightmares, the murder man, the man who cries in the shower."

"In my book," Mr. Kovic said the other day, "I told the nation the kind of things that one would only tell his most intimate lover. I shared these things with the whole country. America shares my tragedy and my triumph."

The final chapter of his story—the triumph—is not told in "Born on the Fourth of July" That triumph was played out last month on the podium of the Democratic National Convention in front of 40 million Americans and it is being played out daily on the streets of Massapequa and in the continual stream of letters and calls he receives from an admiring public.

At the convention in Madison Square Garden last month, Mr. Kovic, who turned 30 on July 4, seconded the symbolic Vice Presidential nomination of Fritz Efaw, a draft resister. In what was described by The New Yorker as one of the three best speeches of the convention (the others being those of the nominees Jimmy Carter and Walter Mondale), Ron Kovic began with the epitaph he wrote at the beginning of his book:

I am the living death
the memorial day on wheels
I am your yankee doodle dandy
your john wayne come home
your fourth of july fire-cracker
exploding in the grave

Since the convention, Mr. Kovic, who had lived in California for the last five years, has been living with his family in Massapequa, where he grew up with his five brothers and sisters. He is busy these days doing television talk shows, interviews with reporters from national magazines and book signings at major bookstores. But he spends much of his time wheeling up and down his old block in his wheelchair chatting with neighbors, visiting with old friends who drop by and returning the waves and the smiles of passers-by.

"They never did that before," he said one Sunday recently as a car slowed down and the driver shouted hello.

"The first few years when I came home there was alienation, loneliness, isolation, fear, rejection—rejection through ignorance and not knowing what was going through this boy's head who came home in a wheelchair and sat alone in the front yard patting the dog's head," Mr. Kovic said as he stopped his almost-always moving wheelchair, locked its wheels and leaned it back against his purple 1965 Mustang.

"It was hard to say hello to me then, because it was hard for them to admit their guilt and complacency in the war. Not saying hello to me in front of the house or at Arthur's Bar kept everything neat and clean. But now saying hello to me is to say: You've done it, Ron, we don't have to feel guilty about you anymore, now we love you.

"The power of 'Born on the Fourth of July' took away the feelings of guilt that had been there before. The book said to them, 'You don't have to feel guilt. I've made something proud and honorable out of this whole tragedy. And you don't have to feel guilt about this tragedy anymore, because it is now a triumph.'

"They're waving because they're applauding a hero. There was no hero who came home eight years ago in a wheelchair. Now I've become a hero. There is no more guilt, now love flourishes. There are still a lot of people to reach, and a lot more to learn, and this is the beginning . . ."

His voice trails off as a former high-school classmate drives up and her three young children pour out of the car. He hadn't seen the woman since their days together at Massapequa High School. They talk about old times and his new book. He takes her youngsters in his lap and gives them wheelchair rides.

Later, over dinner at Musicaro's, an Italian restaurant where he once stopped for pizza as a child, Mr. Kovic recalled what it was like when he first came back to Massapequa from the war.

"I would wake up in the morning with nothing to look forward to. . . . I'd drag my dead body out of bed and into a wheelchair and spend the day as a paraplegic.

"Back then, all I wanted was a girlfriend, even when I came back paralyzed. I used to feel terrible pain going to the bars, going to the discotheques.

"For a long time, for years, there was nothing. I agonized. Coming home, pushing up the ramp in front of the house, putting my hand in the holy water, making the sign of the cross and praying to God that I could survive, that I could have a girlfriend, something that could take me out of the hell of being in this goddamned room every morning. I prayed that I could make some kind of sense out of what had happened to me."

After almost three years of living in Massapequa, Mr. Kovic moved to California, where he became active in the Vietnam Veterans Against the War. "It gave me a sense of purpose, something to do beside feel sorry for myself." He led antiwar rallies, joined hunger strikes, occupied Senators' offices.

In 1972, he talked his way into the Republican National Convention in Miami and began to shout antiwar slogans as Richard M. Nixon accepted the convention's nomination for "four more years." Mr. Kovic was spat on and screamed at by the delegates around him and was whisked away by security guards.

He was arrested nine times in those years for his antiwar activities. At a rally in California, he was thrown out of his chair and kicked and beaten and arrested by undercover agents.

During those years of fighting for peace in Vietnam, his personal quest for peace seemed somehow beyond reach. "I took trips to Mexico, to Europe, to Cambodia," he said. "I ran all over the country, hundreds and thousands of miles, looking and searching like thousands of other veterans who came back. The lost generation seeking some kind of identity again, some kind of fulfillment from a life crushed and destroyed by the war. Religion lost, patriotism lost, home and family lost. We had lost faith in every ideal we had been brought up to believe in."

The most difficult of those years of searching, Mr. Kovic said, was last year, the year that he wrote his book. The idea for "Born On The Fourth Of July" began when he was recovering from his wounds in the Veterans' Administration Hospital in 1968.

"I had a great fear back then," he said. "It wasn't the fear of dying or of not being able to walk again or of not being able to have sex. My great fear was that the incredible injustice of my experience would never be recorded."

He knew that he had to write it all down, he said, but he also knew that it would be torment. The book "gushed" out of him in four months over the period of a year and a half. "When you have a thorn in you," he said, "you don't take your time pulling it out."

During the writing, he smashed his typewriter against the floor in frustration, he tore up the manuscript three times and he disappeared from his home in Santa Monica for weeks and months.

Connie Panzarino, a 28-year-old woman from Long Beach who has been in a wheel chair all her life, "stood by me like no one else," Mr. Kovic writes in the book's acknowledgments, "listening through nights and days, caring and loving, understanding and encouraging, wiping the tears from my eyes."

Writing the book meant reliving experiences that most people would want to forget. How he shot and killed another American soldier in the panic of battle. How he participated in the slaying and maiming of a group of Vietnamese children, who sat in a grass hut. How a .30-caliber machine-gun bullet entered near his shoulder, ripped through one lung and severed his spinal column. How he suffered as he lay in his excrement in a Veterans' hospital in the Bronx as rats ran about the ward. How his broken body sought love with a prostitute in Mexico.

"The book was my last gasp," he said, "I had reached a point of desperation in my life that I cannot describe. I was so upset, so distraught."

Miss Panzerino, who had gone to join him in California while he wrote the book, said she feared he would go insane. "I really didn't care about the book any more, I cared about Ron," she said. "But I knew it was something he had to do."

"After he wrote the chapter about killing the children he came into the bedroom," she recalled. "He read the chapter to me and I cried. Then he asked me if I still loved him.

"His biggest fear was that people would reject him because of what he was revealing about himself."

Since the publication of "Born On The Fourth Of July" and since excerpts from it were published in the July issue of Playboy, the critical reviews and the response from readers has been overwhelmingly positive.

"Once people began to read the book, a great relief has come to my life," Mr. Kovic said. "Relief from tension and pain has come suddenly, almost like a miracle."

The scene at Arthur's Bar in Massapequa also has changed. In the book, Mr. Kovic describes how he would sit in the corner feeling sorry for himself and getting drunk when he sought companionship there after returning from the war.

On a recent Saturday night, he rolled his wheel chair on the dance floor and friends and admirers surrounded him. Young men and women who went to school with him, and some who had never seen him before, came over, put their arms around him and hugged him.

"I'm reading the book, Ron, it's beautiful."

"Hey, I saw you on television."

"You're looking great, Ron. I never saw you smile so much."

Ron Kovic jumped up and down in his wheel chair to the music of the rock band. "I wrote it [the book] so there wouldn't be pity. I wrote it so they would understand."

The next night he is in Long Beach, visiting Miss Panzerino. They leave her apartment together and take their wheel chairs up to the Boardwalk. Mr. Kovic locks the wheels of his chair and leans it against the railing, his back to the Atlantic Ocean.

He says he believes his book will be widely read and will be a great antiwar testament, on the order of "All Quiet on the Western Front" and "Johnny Got His Gun."

Whatever happens to the book one can clearly see that it has done so much to ease the torment in one man's life. A strikingly handsome man with a floppy mustache and big, warm, friendly brown eyes, he feels more with the half of his body that is alive than most men feel with their whole being.

"The Pacific Coast is nicer," Mr. Kovic says as he turns his chair to the ocean. "But here the air, the seasons, the smell, and the sounds are more familiar. That is why I came home."

"I want to feel that sense of innocence that I knew before the war. I have undergone a renaissance. I have been born again through the writing of 'Born On The Fourth Of July.' "

After they sit on the boardwalk for a while, the couple wheels back to Miss Panzerino's apartment. There they hold hands as they sit and talk with a friend of Miss Panzerino and a reporter. Suddenly Mr. Kovic says that he would like to be alone with Miss Panzerino and asks the two visitors to wait outside.

The two visitors sit on the grass in front of the house and talk. A few minutes later, they can hear a Joan Baez record playing. It is an antiwar song that Miss Baez wrote after she met Kovic, called "Where's My Apple Pie."

I volunteered for the last-one,
And I don't want to moralize,
But somehow I believed we deserved the best
For the way we threw away our lives.
Cause we all believed in something.
Although it wasn't very clear,
But I know it wasn't rats in a hospital room
And a broken-down wheel chair.
So where's our apple pie, my friends,
Where's our apple pie?
We were walked and wheeled from the battlefield
So where's our apple pie?

* * *

December 21, 1976

ANTIWAR ACTIVISTS APPEAL TO HANOI

By BERNARD GWERTZMAN
Special to The New York Times

WASHINGTON, Dec. 20—Daniel Ellsberg, Joan Baez, Daniel and Philip Berrigan and dozens of other antiwar activists of the 1960's and 1970's have protested to the leaders of unified Vietnam about reports of repressive acts carried out since the capture of Saigon last year.

Couched in tones more of sorrow than anger, the letter noted that the signers had often criticized the actions of President Nguyen Van Thieu of South Vietnam when he "filled the American-funded prisons with thousands upon thousands of innocent people."

Citing reports that as many as 300,000 people might now be in Communist detention centers, the letter said "we cannot be silent now, even though America's intervention is ended."

Avoidance of Historical Pattern Urged

"We voice our protest in the hope that your Government can avoid repetition of the tragic historical pattern in which liberators gain power only to impose a new oppression," the letter said.

"We therefore call upon you to honor the concern for human rights which you have expressed in both informal agreements and in countless conversations with peace activists. We call for a complete public accounting of those detained or imprisoned, indicating, as well, the charges for which they are held.

"We call on the Government of Vietnam to facilitate on-the-spot inspection by the United Nations, Amnesty International or other independent international agencies in order to assure that those in the Government's charge are treated in accord with international convenants regarding human rights. We call on you to release any individuals who are held purely because or their religious or political convictions. We call for government recognition of the right to open and free communication."

Second Such Appeal Sent to Hanoi

The appeal, sponsored by James H. Forrest, editor of Fellowship, a pacifist publication of the International Fellowship of Reconciliation, was the second such document sent to Vietnam's observer at the United Nations, Dinh Ba Thi.

In October, a letter from SANE, which describes itself as a "citizens' organization for a sane world," also raised questions about the reports of detained people. No response was received, according to Sanford Gottlieb, the organization's executive director, who also signed the Forrest letter.

D. Gareth Porter, a supporter of Vietnam who has been directing a group called the Indochina Resources Center, said the SANE letter had been based on inaccurate information. Mr. Gottlieb said today that there was a paucity of confirmed information. But Washington continues to receive reports of arrests and other repressive acts that force thousands of Vietnamese to flee.

* * *

January 6, 1977

EXIT ROUTES CLOSING FOR INDOCHINA REFUGEES

By DAVID A. ANDELMAN
Special to The New York Times

SONGKHLA, Thailand, Jan. 1—One day late this month, the captains of four small Vietnamese fishing boats plan to set out from this southern Thai port with 80 to 100 refugees for a 3,000-mile voyage across the South China Sea to Australia.

These refugees from Vietnam are hazarding the trip in wooden boats 30 feet long because, they said recently, they have virtually given up hope of making their way by any other means from the crowded Vietnamese refugee camp here to a new life in a Western country. There are now 811 Vietnamese at the Songkhla camp.

They, and many of the international relief officials who have dealt with the refugee problem for the last two years, believe that such attempts will become increasingly frequent in the coming months.

Moreover, the three Communist countries of Indochina—Vietnam, Cambodia and Laos—seem on the verge of closing off the escape routes, and the countries that have been accepting them are increasingly reluctant to continue doing so.

According to the Thai Government, there are 77,151 Indochinese refugees in Thailand with the largest number, 63,766, from Laos, 10,699 from Cambodia, and 2,686 from Vietnam.

While the Vietnamese and Cambodian contingents are relatively small, they are viewed with great suspicion by Thai authorities. Laotian refugees—chiefly of the Mco and Yao hill tribes—blend far better ethnically and racially with the Thais, who understand their language and culture from centuries of close contact.

More and more, the refugees from Vietnam who arrive in Songkhla and the other principal center at Laem Sing are virtually illiterate—farmers or fishermen who have little schooling and no real trade and speak only Vietnamese.

Those who land at other points in the area—in Malaysia, Singapore or Indonesia—are generally given some food and fuel and sent on their way again with the suggestion that they head for Thailand, the only country in the region willing, for the present, to accept them.

Minefields Reported in Cambodia

But no refugee considers Thailand as a final destination. And the Thais, who see these refugees as a continuing source of friction with neighboring Indochina, are becoming increasingly reluctant hosts.

Western refugee programs, too, are drying up. The United States officially ended its program last June, although relatives of refugees now in the United States are still being accepted as immigrants if they show up in refugee camps here.

Australia is willing to accept a few hundred if they have marketable skills and, more important, if they speak English. France is willing to accept a few who speak French.

So the refugees, in desperation, have set up a small school in the camp—a tin-roofed shack with a few rows of benches. Each morning, one of their number who speaks the language serves as a tutor, with no books, only a small pad of notepaper for each pupil.

Most of the Laotian refugees are concentrated in camps along the Mekong River boundary between the two countries—from Chiang Saen in the north through Nong Khai, opposite Vientiane, and into northeastern Thailand. The Cambodians are concentrated in camps along that frontier, chiefly at Surin and Aranyaprathet. The Vietnamese, all of whom are now the so-called "boat cases," are in facilities at Laem Sing and Songkhla.

Vietnam appears to be doing the most to halt the flow of refugees, but many recent arrivals from Cambodia have reported having to elude stepped-up border patrols and make their way through extensive minefields now lining the frontier regions.

A Cambodian soldier is now reportedly assigned to each fishing boat that puts out from the country's southern ports, virtually cutting off that escape route. But at least 100 people a week still find their way across the borders, some now carrying crude maps of the minefields.

Laos has reportedly halted the release of detainees from re-education centers or begun to ship those finished with the programs to resettlement in remote jungle areas deep in the interior. The aim seems to be to stop their steady flow across the Mekong River to exile in Thailand.

Recent Vietnamese arrivals at the Songkhla camp, where most of the small boats that leave Vietnam wind up, said that officials there, in an attempt to block further defections, have begun raising taxes on private fishing vessels to the point where their owners are unable to pay, then seizing the boats and manning them with Government officials and troops. The drain of the boats is a major worry for the Vietnamese Government, which has given increased fish production economic priority.

According to the refugees, Vietnamese officials have also been establishing a network of agents provocateurs to entice would-be refugees into revealing their contacts and routes of escape. Hundreds have reportedly been jailed in recent weeks, particularly in the central coastal area around Vung Tau near Saigon and in the Mekong Delta.

Vietnam has also reportedly multiplied its armed patrols of offshore waters and fortified some of the coastal islands that had been jumping-off points for refugees. A number of boats have been fired on in recent weeks, according to some who escaped and several refugees arrived here last month either dead or wounded from gunshots.

Some refugees estimated that at least 20,000 Vietnamese were ready to flee their country.

Two days before Christmas, 28-year-old Cuong arrived at Songkhla with nothing but the pair of slacks and the shirt he wore when he left Vung Tau 10 days before. He was a teacher in Saigon when the city fell to the Communists in April 1975. He refused to give his full name since, he said, his parents, brothers and sisters were still in Cholon, the Chinese section of Saigon.

More than a year ago, he gave up his profession and became a fisherman, having bought a 25-foot trawler with what money he had been able to scrape together.

He did not, he said, have the hands of a fisherman and the first months were difficult. But, he said, he "established a pattern—out each morning, back each night."

"Then, one day, I added a few extra hands, sailed out to the fishing grounds, then that night I just kept going," he said.

He took only two days' worth of food and water, hoping, once he hit the major international shipping lanes, to be picked up by a large vessel. But in 13 days on the South China Sea, he saw only one freighter and it passed by without slowing.

The New York Times/David A. Andelman

A Vietnamese child in the refugee camp at Songkhla, Thailand.

By Dec. 20, when he sighted land about 100 miles north of Songkhla, the small boat was nearly swamped. The heavy waves more than a mile offshore finished it—the boat broke apart, dumping the eight passengers into the water. Six drowned immediately. One made it to shore, and seeing Cuong struggling in the water several hundred yards from shore, swam out and rescued him, Thai police picked them up a short time later and, on Dec. 23, they were at the refugee center in Songkhla.

It was a story repeated with variations by many of the Vietnamese refugees here at Songkhla. Others had even more elaborate plans to avoid surveillance by Vietnamese officials—taking small boats to a rendezvous with larger trawlers standing offshore or assembling in one of the myriad creeks and streams that form the Mekong Delta, waiting until nightfall to make a dash for the ocean.

It is becoming increasingly clear, international relief officials say, that no country wants them. "We are worried that a permanent Palestinian situation is developing here," said one senior United Nations refugee official. "And that is most emphatically what we do not want."

He said that the United Nations had cut the daily food ration by 25 percent, hoping that the Thai Government would pick up the difference or, even better, begin a program of resettlement for these refugees.

But Thailand has said that is only a last resort. It would prefer to send them back where they came from or, ideally, find some other countries that will accept them.

"Even that's an endless circle," admitted one United Nations official. "Every time a country announces it's taking some more, a few weeks later we see another new wave of refugees."

* * *

January 22, 1977

CARTER PARDONS DRAFT EVADERS, ORDERS A STUDY OF DESERTERS; VETERANS PROTEST, OTHERS SPLIT

10,000 AFFECTED NOW

Action Postponed on Nearly 100,000 Who Fled Armed Forces During War

By CHARLES MOHR
Special to The New York Times

WASHINGTON, Jan. 21—President Carter granted a pardon today to almost all draft evaders of the Vietnam war era, but he left unsettled the status of those who deserted the armed forces in the long Asian conflict.

In effect, the first major act of the new President offered immediate, full legal relief to a relatively small number—estimated by the Justice Department at about 10,000—of predominantly white, middle-class and upper-class young men who either fled the country or refused to enter military service.

For the nearly 100,000 men who entered but then deserted the armed forces, many of whom were black, poor or disadvantaged, Mr. Carter postponed action but said that he would "immediately" initiate a study of a process that might accelerate the review of their cases with a view toward upgrading less-than-honorable discharges.

Protests and Praise

The President's actions drew protests, some of them vehement, from some veterans organizations and from some conservative politicians. There was mild praise from some pro-amnesty groups but also complaint that his decision was too grudging.

Although he holds no official position, Mr. Carter's close friend, Charles Kirbo, played a major role in fashioning the policy announced today in the President's first full day in office and is believed to have helped resist pressures for a more generous package. On Jan. 12, David Berg, a Houston lawyer who drafted the program, spent many hours at the Atlanta law offices of Mr. Kirbo seeking his approval, and Mr. Kirbo was at the White House today.

The pardon was the most important action in a day largely occupied with hours of White House social events to mark the arrival at the mansion of Mr. Carter and his family.

Fruit juice and pastries were served at a series of large receptions for people around the country who had offered the Carters lodging in the former Georgia Governor's 20-month Presidential campaign: for the Congress and diplomatic corps, for Democratic party officials and representatives of labor and business and for the "peanut brigade" and other Georgians who helped and hoped in the long campaign.

Avoiding, as he had in his political travels, the word "amnesty," President Carter this morning signed a pardon proclamation and an Executive order instructing the Attorney General to put the action into effect.

Mr. Carter had promised such a pardon during his political campaign and had also said that deserters should have their cases handled on a "case-by-case basis." He had also said it was difficult to reach this decision because he felt admiration for those who "did not know where Sweden is" and who were too patriotic or inarticulate or ill-informed to resist or evade military service.

One effect of today's act, however, was to give relief to those who did know how to reach Sweden while delaying it for deserters who became bona fide war resisters. A Justice Department spokesman said today that most of those affected by the pardon are about 8,700 people who have been convicted of draft violations, at least five of whom are still in prison. About 1,800 others, he said, are fugitives, about 1,600 of them in foreign countries such as Canada.

The two documents granted a "full, complete and unconditional pardon" to all persons who "may have committed any offense between Aug. 4, 1964, and March 28, 1973, in violation of the Military Selective Service Act., with two exceptions: cases alleging acts of force or violence "deemed to be so serious by the Attorney General as to warrant continued prosecution" and cases involving employees of the Selective Service System.

Upgrading of Deserters

Jody Powell, the new White House press secretary, said that "a very minor portion, a handful" of cases would be excluded by the exceptions.

Deserters, some of whom acted in protest against the unpopular war and others for different reasons, were not included.

Mr. Powell said that Mr. Carter "will act immediately to initiate a study, involving the military, looking toward a possible upgrading by category of discharges [for such deserters] or an expanded and accelerated review process." Mr. Powell later said that nonmilitary persons would also be involved in the study, but he could not identify them or set any timetable for the report.

Mr. Powell said that no clemency was contemplated for deserters who received dishonorable or bad-conduct discharges. This left open the possibility of an upgrading of those who received, or may receive upon surrendering themselves, undesirable discharges.

The American Veterans Committee said in a statement that if the President "wishes to fulfill his inaugural promises of compassionate justice" his pardon should include deserters and "bring these young people back into our society."

Estimates of Those Involved

Representative Edward I. Koch, Democrat of Manhattan, also called for pardon for disadvantaged deserters who "also deserve compassion," some of whom he said did not understand legal ways to evade induction.

Just how many people will be affected by today's decision was not wholly clear, but in a practical sense it left uncovered many more than those to whom it offered succor. Some sources have estimated that a large number, perhaps several hundred thousand people, failed to register for the draft and were thus in violation of the Selective Service Act. However, they were not in any real, immediate legal jeopardy and the pardon wiped their slates clean before any derogatory record could be written on them.

In a practical sense, the pardon was for those who refused or evaded induction. A pro-amnesty organization has estimated this number at about 23,000, but Government figures show only 13,222 such persons.

In contrast, the final report of former President Ford's clemency board, released recently, said that there were 10,115 Vietnam era deserters who had not been discharged from service and 90,000 who had received less-than-honorable discharges for desertion or being absent without leave offenses. Mr. Powell said today that the Defense Department had informed him that there were 4,500 deserters "still at large."

Today's pardon will permit draft evaders in exile abroad in such nations as Canada, Sweden and France to return home. Those who retained American citizenship will be safe from threat of prosecution. Those who took foreign citizenship and who were legally decreed to be "undesirable aliens" may now apply for entry to the United States as aliens and for citizenship under the immigration procedures applying to any such immigrant.

During his campaign, Mr. Carter had said emotionally that reaching his position on pardon for war resisters was the most difficult decision he had had to make. But the documents he signed today were dry and legal in tone.

They drew, however, some heated response. Senator Barry Goldwater, Republican of Arizona, called the pardon "the most disgraceful thing that a President has ever done" and said it "will utterly destroy" the effectiveness of any attempt to reinstitute selective service inductions in a time of national crisis.

The new Republican national chairman. Bill Brock, said that the pardon should "dismay all Americans" and called it a "slap in the face to all those Americans and their families who did their duty."

Discriminatory Move Seen

In contrast, Louise Ransom of the National Council for Universal and Unconditional Amnesty, said that "since draft resisters are essentially white, middle-class and well educated, and the military resisters [deserters] are primarily disproportionately from the poor and minority groups, we feel that this is a very discriminatory pardon."

"I'm disgusted with it," Senator Jake Garn, Republican of Utah, said of the pardon. T. Cooper Holt, executive director of the Veterans of Foreign Wars, said. "This is probably one of the saddest days in the history of our country, even surpassing the Watergate days."

Mr. Powell said that the President did not expect his decision to achieve overwhelming popular acclaim, saying the White House felt the "sum total" of those who disagreed with it either because they thought it was too lenient or not lenient enough "probably exceeds 50 percent."

Mr. Carter and his advisers believe the formula announced today was a "responsible and moderate course to follow," Mr. Powell said.

* * *

April 2, 1977

HOW SCIENTISTS IDENTIFY REMAINS OF DEAD IN VIETNAM

By WALLACE TURNER
Special to The New York Times

HONOLULU, April 1—On Saturday, March 19 an Air Force transport plane landed here to deliver the remains of 12 men dead for a decade. The Vietnamese Government had turned them over to a group dispatched by President Carter to receive them and had supplied the names that the Vietnamese believed belonged to the remains.

On Tuesday, March 29, 11 coffins were shipped by military transport to Oakland, Calif., for distribution and burial by next-of-kin of the fliers who had died in bombing attacks against North Vietnam.

In the intervening 10 days, scientists in the Central Identification Laboratory, working with information gathered by the Joint Casualty Resolution Center, discovered that one set of remains were those of a 50-year-old Southeast Asian, not those of Maj. Curtis A. Eaton of the Air Force, who bailed out near Hanoi on Aug. 14, 1966. He had been reported missing in action.

The Asian's remains are being held at the laboratory awaiting instructions. Major Eaton is still listed as missing in action.

The scientists also discovered that another set of remains were not those of Capt. Lawrence H. Goldberg of Cloquet, Minn., but those of Lieut. Patrick E. Wynne of Satellite Beach, Fla., who had been in the same airplane with Capt. Goldberg.

A Separate Problem

The Joint Casualty Resolution Center was set up to help to recover and identify remains of Americans lost in the Vietnam War. The center has active case files on 2,505 military personnel and 41 civilians who are missing in action or are listed as killed in action, body not recovered.

The center was established in Vietnam in 1973, then moved to Thailand. Last May it moved to Barbers Point Naval Air Station here. When American forces left Southeast Asia, the center concentrated on compiling information about each of the missing on whom it had files.

These files contain dental records, X-rays, physical description, blood types, hair descriptions and details of the last military action in which the missing had participated.

This material is computerized, so when the Vietnamese have said that they have a body that was in a plane that was shot down in a certain location, the computer can provide records on crashes within a 200-mile radius of that place. The computer will provide similar data on other fragments of information fed into it.

The examination of the bodies is done by the Central Identification Laboratory, which operates in a pier area on the Honolulu waterfront. Scientists first test remains for blood type, which can be determined from bones or hair or even fingernails and toenails. Then X-rays are made of teeth and bones.

Teeth are compared with dental charts. A tooth cracked or a leg broken in a high school football game in 1958 might have been X-rayed last week to provide the final identification of a combat pilot who died in Vietnam in 1965.

Each set of remains is assigned a number until a final decision is made, when a recommendation on identity is forwarded to the Armed Services Graves Registration Organization. The military services are responsible for the final identification but the laboratory's recommendations have always been followed.

* * *

May 4, 1977

PERSPECTIVES OF U.S. FOREIGN POLICY SHARPLY ALTERED SINCE SAIGON'S FALL

By HEDRICK SMITH

Special to The New York Times

WASHINGTON, May 3—"You know," a ranking foreign policy official observed, "no one talks about Vietnam anymore."

It was perhaps a slight exaggeration, but his stark comment underscores how drastically the perspective of American foreign policy has altered since the collapse of the Saigon Government two years ago.

With the fires of conflict now grown cold, the Carter Administration not only has begun the process of normalization with Hanoi but is working on plans to withdraw American ground forces from Korea and has started moving gingerly toward full diplomatic relations with China and revision of American security commitments to Taiwan, while White House officials talk privately of the need for shifting some of the Pacific Fleet to the Atlantic. All these moves would have been unthinkable in the Vietnam era.

No longer is Vietnam the prism through which Washington views the world. No longer is it the touchstone by which it measures the loyalty of allies. No longer does it set the mood and tone of political life in this city.

Dissidents Reinstated

Members of the Establishment who were dissidents on Indochina policy have been reinstated in government. For example, W. Anthony Lake, who resigned from the national security staff of Henry A. Kissinger in 1970 in protest over the invasion of Cambodia, is now director of policy planning at the State Department. Paul C. Warnke, who led the fight within the Pentagon against the American bombing of North Vietnam, is the Carter Administration's chief arms negotiator. Richard Moose, who wrote many of the critical Indochina reports for the Senate Foreign Relations Committee, is now Deputy Under Secretary of State.

With the hindsight of history, Secretary of State Cyrus R. Vance, who as Deputy Secretary of Defense played a major role in the American buildup in Vietnam, has publicly said that he now feels that "it was a mistake to intervene in Vietnam." And those who know him well say that the Vietnam war is the single most important experience in shaping his current outlook, causing him, among other things, to be wary of American involvement in the bubbling conflict in Zaire.

Even the style of diplomacy has been affected. "For so many years, Vietnam was the focus of attention for the entire Asian Bureau at the State Department," one veteran diplomat said. "For a year or a year and a half after the fall of Saigon, we sort of thrashed around not knowing what to do without an hourly Vietnam-related crisis."

Career Patterns Affected

Even career patterns have been affected. At the State Department, guerrilla warfare specialists are out of favor and economists with an understanding of trade are being touted as the diplomats of the future. At the Pentagon, ambitious career men can no longer seek fast promotions in Vietnam but have to stand in line for the command assignments in Europe and Korea.

In Congress, the foreign policy subcommittees and their staffs have grown and have become increasingly involved in the nitty-gritty of diplomacy or zealous about scrutinizing any foreign commitments. Where President Carter has difficulties on Capitol Hill now, they have grown out of domestic issues and do not reflect the rancid, mistrustful bitterness that so often poisoned relations between the White House and Congress in the Vietnam era.

Most fundamentally, perhaps, with the shift away from the policy of confrontation and containment, the new American President can think once again about forging a national consensus on foreign policy and can strive for the kind of bipartisan feeling that existed during World War II and for 20 years afterward.

Quite deliberately, the Carter Administration has seen the negotiations with Vietnam in Paris as a way to settle the painful legacy of the past and to clear away the final debris of the Vietnam War.

"I felt there were festering sores that had to be dealt with—Vietnam, Cuba, the Panama Canal," Secretary Vance said in an interview, "and to that end, we decided to take action early in the Administration."

A Basically Peaceful Asia

In Asia itself, policy-makers had feared that the final disaster in Saigon, which came with such a frightening rush two years ago, might set off new expansionist pressures elsewhere in Southeast Asia or on the Korean peninsula and might frighten other Asian nations into loosening their ties to the United States.

But today, the Carter Administration looks out with equanimity on an essentially, peaceful Asia and, to its pleasant surprise, finds itself required to reassure nations like Indonesia, Japan, South Korea, Thailand or China that what it now has in mind is retrenchment but not withdrawal.

"The day when we were obsessed by security commitments is over and that strengthens us because it frees us," explains Richard Holbrooke, Assistant Secretary of State for East Asian Affairs. "We want a peaceful and stable Asia in which no external power dominates. But the old days of single-minded fight-the-Chinese-everywhere are over."

One token of the new post-Vietnam mood is the quiet burial being arranged for the Southeast Asia Treaty Organization, a cornerstone of American policy in Asia for two decades. It will quietly pass out of existence on June 30. "The big issue at Seato headquarters now," one Asia specialist quipped, "is what to do with the furniture."

More fundamentally, with China and the Soviet Union so persistently at loggerheads, their armies facing each other across a long and disputed frontier, Washington's perception of China has been almost totally reversed.

No Military Threat From China

In the Carter White House, as was the case in the Ford Administration, the Government in Peking is now seen as a moderate partner of sorts rather than as a militant menace. Not only do the new Chinese leaders share an interest in checking Soviet influence or expansionism in Asia, but, from Washington's current perspective, they are too preoccupied with internal affairs to pose a military threat—even to the island of Taiwan.

Indeed, the passing of the Vietnam era with its devotion to containment has so altered the American outlook that for the time being the Carter Administration has trouble devising a single Asian policy. It has several—for Japan, for China, for Korea, for the Philippines and for Southeast Asia—all loosely aimed at promoting regional cooperation and maintaining peace and stability without American military engagement.

In the final quarter of this century, the policy-makers expect trade and economic issues to assume increasing importance. Few Americans, they point out, realize that American trade with East Asia already outstrips the much more publicized trade with the European Common Market countries. Last year, for example, two-way American trade with Asia totaled $52.6 billion compared with $43.3 billion with the Common Market region.

But in the more immediate future, the Carter Administration is equally concerned with adjusting the American military presence in the Pacific Region to the new objectives of American policy. The Administration has no present intention of altering security commitments to such allies as Japan, South Korea, Australia, New Zealand or the Philippines but it wants to shift to what one White House official called "an offshore policy."

Specifically, this means keeping President Carter's campaign pledge to withdraw American ground forces from Korea—the last major units on the Asian mainland. But the President has promised the South Korean leaders, as well as the Japanese and Australians, who were concerned about this pullback, that it would be carried out gradually to avoid upsetting the balance of power in Asia.

Moreover, policy-makers point out, the 40,000 American troops in Korea include about 12,000 Air Force personnel, armed with nuclear weapons at present. The Administration's present thinking is that these forces will remain in Korea even after the ground pullout, thereby maintaining the protective nuclear umbrella over South Korea and continuing to provide a "trip-wire" deterrent against attack from the North.

Cutback in Philippines Is Probable

Similarly, in the Philippines, the apparent intention is to work for an ultimate reduction in the 15,000 American servicemen based at Clark Air Base and the Subic Bay Naval Base rather than abandoning these installations. Both were important staging areas in the Vietnam era.

The Philippine Government has been pressing Washington to renegotiate its rights to these bases and to compensate Manila with large amounts of military aid. The Ford Administration offered $1 billion in military and economic aid over the next five years, but President Ferdinand E. Marcos rejected that, demanding $1 billion in military aid alone.

But the Carter Administration, in its mood of retrenchment, feels it is in a stronger bargaining position. "We're going to be sellers instead of buyers now," said one high official. "We've been had over the years on these base deals. But now they want us to keep them there. That means we have a mutual interest in the bases, and if people want to have a base on their territory, maybe we should not pay so much."

On China, the most delicate issue is how to shift to full diplomatic relations under the terms of the communiqué signed by President Richard M. Nixon at Shanghai in 1972 and to relax the current American security commitments with Taiwan without inviting Peking to try to take over Taiwan by force.

Not until Secretary Vance journeys to Peking next fall does the Administration expect to make much progress with the mainland Government on this issue. But there are policy-makers who believe that a "formula for accommodation" can be worked out, on the assumption that Peking will not try to take over Taiwan by force but will adapt over the medium term to a separate Taiwan so—long as the American security commitment is withdrawn.

Similarly, most policy-makers believe that over time Americans will be prepared to adjust to normal diplomatic relations with the Vietnamese Government in Hanoi. The most ticklish issue has been the Vietnamese demand for aid as reparations for war damage and casualties.

* * *

May 5, 1977

U.S. WON'T BAR HANOI FROM U.N.; VIETNAM TO PRESS HUNT FOR MISSING

Progress Toward Normal Ties Is Made as First Round of Paris Talks Concludes

By FLORA LEWIS
Special to The New York Times

PARIS, May 4—The United States and Vietnam made progress today toward normalization of relations, with the United States pledging that it would not veto Vietnam's admission to the United Nations and that it would lift a trade embargo after diplomatic relations had been established.

In turn, the Vietnamese promised to intensity efforts to provide information about Americans listed as missing in action in the Vietnam War.

Both sides showed satisfaction with the results of two days of the talks, although it was clear that there were still important problems outstanding. The sides expressed their views with careful reserve. The two delegations said they had agreed to meet here again in about two weeks for a second round of talks.

'Cordiality and Frankness'

The two-day session was held in Vietnam's elaborate but unfinished new embassy. The next session, probably at the same level as the meeting that has just been concluded, is to be held in the United States Embassy.

Deputy Foreign Minister Phan Hien of Vietnam, and its chief negotiator, read a statement to the press in his embassy terming the talks "constructive and useful" and their atmosphere one of "cordiality and frankness." Later, in the United States Embassy, the American spokesman Morton Smith used the same words. There was no joint communiqué and no formal American statement.

Mr. Hien welcomed the American pledge not to obstruct his country's admission to the United Nations, but insisted on an "immediate" end of the trade embargo, separate from further negotiations on aid and relations. The American spokesman said his country's position remained that lifting the embargo had to be part of normalizing of relations.

However, it was learned that the leader of the United States delegation, Richard Holbrooke, the Assistant Secretary of State for Asian Affairs, told the Vietnamese today that the United States promised to end the embargo once relations and embassies were established. It is a nuance of timing, but it was an important change that the United States was now prepared to make the pledge, even though it would rather wait for an agreement.

A U.S. Promise Is Disclosed

On the issue of aid, there were similar subtle differences in public and private positions. Publicly, the Vietnamese maintained that "a contribution to healing the wounds of war and to reconstruct the country" was an American obligation that must be "linked" to establishment of relations.

Mr. Hien said, in answer to a question, that the aid pledged in a letter from President Richard M. Nixon at the time of the 1973 Paris cease-fire agreement amounted to $3.25 billion, plus another billion or billion and a half in what he called "concessional aid," and indicated that Hanoi still demanded that amount.

The Vietnamese negotiator did say, in response to other questions, that the "form" of aid was a matter to be discussed—a hint that loans, credits, private American gifts, and United States contributions through international aid agencies would all be included in calculating the total. Mr. Smith, the American spokesman, said the Vietnamese had not mentioned the Nixon letter in the talks, nor had they specified any aid figure.

The Vietnamese brought up a list of goods, conveyed to Leonard Woodcock, president of the United Automobile Workers, during his special mission to Hanoi in March, as their requirements. They asked if the Holbrooke mission was "aware of the document." The goods were said to be worth approximately $1 billion and to reflect Vietnam's expectations from all sources of Western aid, not just the United States.

'War Reparations' Shunned

Thus the private request seemed considerably lower than what appeared to be the level of aid demanded publicly. At one point, when a French reporter asked "how much reparations" Hanoi demanded, Mr. Hien went out of his way to break in and say: "We never use the words 'war reparations." He repeated, instead, the formula-word "contributions," but did not give a figure.

Mr. Smith said that when the aid issue came up, the United States explained the need for Congressional approval, listed American humanitarian gifts exempted from the embargo and mentioned American endorsement of a World Bank loan.

Even grant-aid was not ruled out by the United States delegation, though this was envisaged as a question that could only be raised after normal relations had been developed.

It was also disclosed that since the Woodcock mission, Hanoi has sent Washington the name of one more missing American serviceman. But Mr. Smith said that "verification" has not been completed, so no details could be given. He said additional information had been provided in the cases of some missing Americans already named by the Vietnamese.

These talks took place nine years to the week since the initial United States-North Vietnamese peace negotiations opened here under the leadership of W. Averell Harriman and the man was to become the present Secretary of State, Cyrus R. Vance. Since then the United States has used its United Nations veto power three times against Vietnamese membership.

United States delegation in 1968 and came to know Phan Hien quite well during informal tea-break chats. During the current meetings, they discussed their first.

Mr. Hien is considered by the Americans to be one of Hanoi's best diplomats. He smiles a great deal and uses more fluent, less rigid language than many of his official compatriots.

This morning, Mr. Holbrooke and his team had to stand in the rain outside the locked gates of the Vietnamese Embassy for several minutes because their opposite numbers had not yet arrived and the unfinished embassy is not yet in regular use. Plants and rock gardens and pictures have been supplied, however, to give it an air of warmth, though there is not much furniture.

As this round of talks neared its end, the Vietnamese Committee for Human Rights, a Paris-based organization of expatriates, distributed an open letter to President Carter today, calling on him not to establish relations with Vietnam or give it any aid until repression has been ended.

'U.S. Bears Part of Responsibility'

"Whether you accept it or not," the letter said, "the United States bears a great part of the responsibility before world history for the annexation of South Vietnam by the Communists and for the imprisonment of hundreds of thousands of their own allies."

It protested against the repression of religion, the forced movement of population, the re-education camps, and detention of political prisoners in Vietnam.

* * *

October 16, 1977

VIETNAM ERASING AMERICAN IMPRINT, BUT VESTIGES REMAIN

By HORST FAAS
By The Associated Press

This dispatch was written by a photographer and reporter who covered the war in Vietnam for 12 years. He recently revisited the country.

SAIGON, Vietnam—From the old imperial capital of Hue in the north to Saigon in the south the Communist Government of Vietnam is busily eradicating the imprint of the American era.

Indelible symbols remain, however.

A young child smiled at me in a kindergarten in Da Nang, a city where American troops spent eight years pursuing victory. She had curly brown hair and markedly Western features. It was obvious she was different from the others.

And there were stubborn holdouts from the old days.

The mother of Vietnam's last emperor, Bao Dai, lives in a small apartment in Hue, a Vietnamese official said. She is still active at 98 years of age, one of the few members of the aristocracy who has not fled from Hue or been imprisoned by the Communist rulers.

But almost everything else seen during a recent two-week visit to Vietnam with a German tourist group seemed altered or in transition.

Tan Son Nhut at Rest

A lone helicopter hovered lazily over the once-frenzied Tan Son Nhut airport outside Saigon. At the height of the war this was one of the busiest airports in the world, with a plane landing and taking off every minute.

The tarmacs were still lined with helicopters, transport planes and jets. But they were immobile and obviously unused.

The airport baggage handlers declined tips, and as we drove into town on tourist buses I noticed that the former American nerve-center in Vietnam, "Pentagon East" as it was called, had been hammered down into piles of fine rubble. Other major American installations near the city have been similarly dismembered.

From the air the former Long Binh army base looked like a huge transistor board with all the wires and components ripped out.

Jungle Is Taking Over

Already the jungle is taking over, slowly and inexorably covering this tangle of bunkers, empty roads and concrete fences where in 1965 the first American soldiers sent to Vietnam clashed with the Vietcong.

I had hoped to meet old acquaintances from the war years, but the guide who showed our tourist group around cautioned us about trying to talk to the local people. There are many "reactionaries" in Saigon, he said, who might "confuse you."

But one day I noticed a familiar face as our group walked down Tu Do Street. It was that of a former part time Associated Press employee. He was riding a bicycle. He circled warily around us several times without speaking. Then he pedaled off. But he had smiled at me.

Another time we passed by the stall of a street vendor near the old Associated Press office. Behind the stall was the mother of a boy who had worked in the AP photo darkroom. He fled to the United States when the Saigon government collapsed a little more than two years ago. For one fleeting second we looked at each other. She nodded almost imperceptibly. Again I had made contact with another time and another world.

Saigon's Center Is Clean

The center of Saigon was unaccustomedly clean, kept that way by bands of broom-wielding women who sweep the streets early each morning.

It was in the streets that the difference between then and now was greatest.

During the war years Saigon's economy was artificially pumped up with American aid, and a consumer society flourished. But now only a pathetic memory of those booming days was visible as peddlers offered G.I. winter underwear from Korean war days and battered transistor radios.

While the sound of motorcycles was heard, it is the bicycle that has become the main form of transportation in the city. Private cars seem a thing of the past because of gas rationing.

Horst Faas/Associated Press

A young girl of mixed parentage, third from right, is a reminder of the American presence in Da Nang, where U.S. troops spent eight years. She was photographed in one of the hundreds of new kindergartens in the city.

Officials conceded that hundreds of thousands of Vietnamese were unemployed. We could see them in the streets, aimlessly walking in groups or lolling in park chairs amid handicapped people and youths with nothing to do.

The old six-story United States Embassy is now used by the Vietnamese petroleum company, which hopes to exploit oil reserves found off the coast by American companies.

The Americans are officially recalled in the northern city of Da Nang, but in the worst way. In the former American headquarters beside the Da Nang River stands the Museum of American War Crimes, where teen-age girls in white silken robes show tourists a replica of a torture chamber equipped with whips and cactus thorns. They tell visitors that women prisoners were tortured here by the Americans.

Southern Involvement Ignored

Large photographs, mainly from Western newspapers, document American involvement in the war. What is noticeably missing are references to the South Vietnamese forces and their involvement, possibly as a gesture of reconciliation by the North Vietnamese rulers to their former southern opponents.

Outside the war museum signs of the American years have been erased.

Graffiti painted by United States Army and Navy engineers who built the winding road over the Hai Van Pass above Da Nang have been removed, but high up on a rock could be seen the phrase "Albert, one day short," the work of a G.I. counting the days to go home.

Tips of MIG's Seen

From the pass the Da Nang air base looks like a huge aircraft carrier with empty flight decks. But close up I noticed the red-nose tips of Soviet-built MIG-21-fighters poking from shelters built by the United States Air Force to protect its planes from Vietcong rockets.

Da Nang formerly was the booming home of nearly one and a half million people. On this journey I found the city sedate and quiet, its population down to 350,000. The only excitement we encountered came when a Russian tourist's watch was torn from his wrist by a young beggar in front of the Orient Hotel.

Before we left Da Nang our group walked along China Beach. The Vietnamese talked of building tourist hotels there, and I remembered American marines, relaxing here while on leave from the fighting front, telling me that after they had won the war they would be back to build motels on China Beach.

Tourist Hopes for Hue

Vietnam also has tourist hopes for Hue, the elegant seat of imperial power for 100 years until France colonized Vietnam. I first visited that city in the early 1960's, when it was the determinedly independent center of opposition to President Ngo Dinh Diem, who was later assassinated in a coup.

Then came the battles of the 1968 Tet offensive when thousands of inhabitants were killed in battle or slain on the beaches by the Vietcong. The gloom of those days remains.

The huge central market building erected with American aid leaked like a huge tent when we visited, and thousands of farmers and traders huddled in pools of water. A large picture of Ho Chi Minh beamed down on the sodden gathering a companion piece to the huge plaster statue of the revolutionary leader that now stands in the imperial palace grounds among the bronze images of former emperors.

* * *

November 20, 1977

THE DIFFERENT WAR

By C. D. B. BRYAN

DISPATCHES
By Michael Herr
260 pp. New York; Alfred A. Knopf. $8.95.

During the past few years I have tried to read most of the Vietnam books that have been published. I read them hoping to understand the war, to know what it was like to fight there, how it differed from all our other wars. Some, like Bernard J. Fall's devastating Dienbienphu book, "Hell in a Very Small Place," already seem distant and dated. Others, like Daniel Lang's "Casualties of War" and Jonathan Schell's "Village of Ben Suc" were chilling in their reflection of some of our servicemen's murderous detachment. I tried to finish Frances FitzGerald's "Fire in the Lake," but although I was dazzled by the brilliance with which she illuminated Vietnam's political landscape, her book never quite penetrated my tangled emotions. Gloria Emerson's "Winners and Losers: Battles, Retreats, Gains, Losses and Ruins from a Long War" intrigued me, but for the wrong reasons: I was far more moved by the obvious impact the war had had on her than I was by its impact on those she wrote about.

Certain books seemed to me to capture exactly the mood and madness of specific aspects of the war; I am thinking here of Mailer's "Armies of the Night," Mary McCarthy's "Medina," Seymour Hersh's book on My Lai, Tom Wolfe's Navy carrier-pilot piece, "The Truest Sport: Jousting With Sam and Charlie," from his collection "Mauve Gloves & Madmen, Clutter & Vine," and Robert Jay Lifton's heart-breaking study of returning veterans in "Home From the War." Ron Kovic's mortification in "Born on the Fourth of July" and Ronald J. Glasser's burn ward memories in "365 Days" haunt and hurt.

In recent months I've read Philip J. Caputo's critically acclaimed "A Rumor of War" and Larry Heinemann's "Close Quarters," already lost in the shuffle, I fear, though I thought it was the better book. Caputo had a brief moment on the best-seller list: but now there is a book that seems to be making all the right sort of incoming noises that indicate a direct hit: Michael Herr's "Dispatches."

Quite simply, "Dispatches" is the best book to have been written about the Vietnam War.

"Dispatches" must be read because, even if there already exists a surprisingly rich selection of writings on Vietnam, nothing else so far has even come close to conveying how different this war was from any we fought—or how utterly different were the methods and the men who fought for us. Here Michael Herr writes about coming under fire:

"Once it was actually going on, things were different. You were just like everyone else, you could no more blink than spit. It came back the same way every time, dreaded and welcome . . . your senses working like strobes, free-falling all the way down to the essences and then flying out again in a rush to focus, like the first strong twinge of tripping after an infusion of psilocybin, reaching in at the point of calm and springing all the joy and all the dread ever known, ever known by everyone who ever lived, unutterable in its speeding brilliance, touching all the edges and then passing, as though it had all been controlled from outside, by a god or by the moon. And every time you were so weary afterward, so empty of everything but being alive that you couldn't recall any of it, except to know it was like something else you had felt once before. If remained obscure for a long time, but after enough times the memory took shape and substance and finally revealed itself one afternoon during the breaking off of a firefight. It was the feeling you'd had when you were much, much younger and undressing a girl for the first time."

Vietnam required not only new techniques of warfare, but new techniques in writing as well. News cameramen and photographers could show us sometimes what the war looked like, but an entirely new language, imagery and style were needed so that we could understand and feel. Until Michael Herr no reporter or writer seemed to capture it. The previous books seem to have been trapped in styles left over from previous wars, and I read them feeling as dissatisfied with their attempts to explain the Vietnam experience as I have been with the astronauts' tedious responses to questions on what it was really like to orbit in space or walk on the moon. (Only Yuri Gagarin's thrilling "I am Eagle!" tells me anything at all.)

Herr's literary style derives from the era of acid rock, the Beatles films, of that druggy, Hunter Thompson once-removed-from-reality appreciation of The Great Cosmic Joke. He was covering Vietnam for Esquire—"Esquire, wow, they got a guy over here?" a Marine asks him, "What the . . . for? You tell 'em what we're wearin'?" (General Westmoreland asked Herr if he planned on doing "humoristical" pieces). Secondly, as Herr notes, he wasn't there to fight, he "was there to watch. . . . Talk about impersonating an identity, about locking into a role, about irony: I went to cover the war and the war covered me; an old story, unless of course you've never heard it." While the newspaper and news magazine correspondents were writing against daily or weekly deadlines, Herr's stories wouldn't appear in Esquire until five months after they'd been written. This lag gave him the opportunity to write thoughtful, polished, tough, compassionate pieces in which he could be careful to capture the image exactly: "Sitting in Saigon," he tells us, "was like sitting inside the petals of a poisoned flower. . . ." Or, on Saigon's motorbike riding Vietnamese "cowboys": "They could snap a Rolex off your wrist like a hawk hitting a field mouse." Or here, on how the Mission Council during the brutal Tet Offensive "joined hands and passed together through the Looking Glass. Our general's chariot was on fire, he was taking on smoke and telling us some incredible stories of triumph and victory that a few high level Americans had to ask him just to cool it and let them do the talking. A British correspondent compared the Mission posture to the captain of the Titanic announcing, 'There's no cause for alarm, we're only stopping briefly to take on ice.' "

Herr's dispatches are as formless as the war they covered. The book is divided into six chapters, the first and last of which are "Breathing In" and "Breathing Out." In between comes "Hell Sucks," about the battle for Hue, which I believe was the first of Herr's brilliant pieces to be published. Then comes "Khe Sanh," which one reads convinced of how very, very lucky we were to get out of there at all. "Illumination Rounds," a series of quick studies, and "Colleagues," which, with the altogether lovely self-deprecating humor and restraint he shows throughout this book, Herr barely resists subtitling "Those Crazy Guys Who Cover the War: A Movie Romance."

It is in this chapter that the author's ambivalence toward his assignment can best be seen. In one place he writes: "I think Vietnam was what we had instead of happy childhoods." In another: "We [war correspondents] were called thrill-freaks, death-wishers, wound-seekers, war-lovers, hero-worshipers, closet-queens, dope-addicts, low-grade alcoholics, ghouls, communists, seditionists, more nasty things than I can remember. . . . All kinds of thieves and killers managed to feel sanctimonious around us, battalion commanders, civilian businessmen, even the grunts until they realized how few of us were making any real money in it. There's no way around it, if you photographed a dead Marine with a poncho over his face and got something for it, you were some kind of parasite. But what were you if you pulled the poncho back first to make a better shot, and did that in front of his friends? Some other kind of parasite, I suppose. Then what were you if you stood there watching it, making a note to remember it later in case you might want to use it?"

To Michael Herr's everlasting credit he never ceased to feel deeply for the men with whom he served; he never became callous, always worried for them, agonized over them, on occasion even took up arms to defend them. His greatest service, I'm convinced, is this book. What more need one really say about our young who fought in Vietnam than this: ". . . along the road." Herr writes, "there is a two-dollar piece of issue. A poncho which has just been used to cover a dead Marine, a blood-puddled, mud-wet poncho going stiff in the wind. It has reared up there by the road in a horrible streaked ball. I'm walking along this road with two black grunts, and one of them gives the poncho a vicious, helpless kick. 'Go easy, man,' the other one says, 'That's the American flag you gettin' your foot into.' "

There is music in Herr's book—there is the rock music that accompanied the grunts everywhere in Vietnam, like some bizarre movie score to their alienation: Jefferson Airplane, Frank Zappa and the Mothers, the Grateful Dead, the Doors, the Beatles (whose "Magical Mystery Tour" had a grimly ironic meaning) and the Rolling Stones (whose song "Citadel" left-veterans of the battle for Hue chilled). Herr relates the following astonishing experience while crossing a rice paddy under fire: "We made it to the wall with two casualties. There was no way of stopping their fire, no room to send in a flanking party, so gunships were called and we crouched behind the wall and waited. There was a lot of fire coming from the trees, but we were all right as long as we kept down. And I was thinking, Oh man, so this is a rice paddy, yes, wow! when I suddenly heard an electric guitar shooting right up in my ear and a mean, rapturous black voice singing, coaxing 'Now c'mon baby, stop acting so crazy,' and when I got it all together I turned to see a grinning black corporal hunched over a cassette recorder. 'Might's well,' he said. 'We ain' going nowhere till them gunships come. . . .' That's the story of the first time I heard Jimi Hendrix." "Dispatches" is filled, too, with the special kind of music going on inside a generation of heads gathered to watch tracers, shells and flares lighting up the night.

Shortly after Michael Herr arrived in Vietnam he met a truly frightening member of a Long Range Reconnaissance Patrol team. "What a story he told me," Herr writes. "As one-pointed and resonant as any war story I ever heard. It took me a year to understand it:

'Patrol went up the mountain. One man came back. He died before he could tell us what happened.'

"I waited for the rest," Herr continues, "but it seemed not to be that kind of story; when I asked him what had happened he just looked like he felt sorry for me, f—d if he'd waste time telling stories to anyone dumb as I was."

I didn't really understand the story either—until I finished Michael Herr's book. Now, I'm afraid, I understand the story all too well.

C.D.B. Bryan is the author of "Friendly Fire," an account of how the death of a soldier in Vietnam affected his parents in Iowa.

* * *

April 30, 1978

FOR INDOCHINA, ENDLESS WARS

Old Enmities Revived After U.S. Departure

By HENRY KAMM
Special to The New York Times

BANGKOK, Thailand, April 27—Three years ago it was all over. The National Liberation Front's red and blue flag with a gold star flew over Saigon's Doc Lap Palace. After 30 years, the war in Indochina had ended with the surrender of Saigon on April 30, 1975. Peace brought rejoicing, even among many of the defeated and their foreign backers. The killing had gone on too long.

The victory had been complete in Vietnam, Cambodia and Laos. Whatever the victors would make of their countries, their grip was sure, and so, at last and at least, there would be peace.

New Violence in Region

Now, three years after the last round was fired, the last village bombed, the last mother killed with her child in that war, Vietnam and Cambodia are fighting each other, Vietnamese planes are firing rockets at mountain villages in Laos. And Thailand, the only country of the Indochinese peninsula spared by the war, fights skirmishes against incursions across its borders with Laos and Cambodia.

To be sure, the fighting is minor compared to the horrors that preceded peace, but peace was illusory. The wars on which the United States had grafted itself are finished, but the unresolved struggle for Indochina continues, and Southeast Asia is ill at ease.

The accusations of barbarous misdeeds that have been exchanged by Vietnam and Cambodia would be widely written off as anti-Communist propaganda if they came from another source. Those who fled Cambodia after the Communist victory related the horrors of a vast number of murders, forced evacuation of cities and regimentation of life on an inhuman scale. Skeptics who thought the accounts were malevolent inventions of the right wing may revise their judgments when the Hanoi radio broadcasts them daily.

Decolonization Is Seen

During the war, some people rejected suggestions by hardliners in the Pentagon that Vietnam's goals might extend beyond its borders after the war. Now those people may wonder what to make of Phnom Penh's ritual allegation that Hanoi is determined to create an Indochinese federation under its domination.

A notion much discussed by Indochina watchers in Asia, both Westerners and Asians, is that the process of decolonization, delayed by the continuation of direct Western intervention until 1975, is now in full swing. They view the Vietnamese-Cambodian conflict, along with the unrest on the Thai-Cambodian border, in this context.

France, in this view, arrived on the Indochinese scene late in the last century and halted regional developments by imposing its dominant presence. When France established its hold over Cambodia and Laos, it put an end to a rapid erosion of Cambodian territory by Vietnam from the east and Thailand from the north.

Now, these experts assert, these conflicts over the survival of an independent Cambodian nation have resumed. Historical enmities, frozen but not forgotten during the French and American interventions, have once more come to the surface. Cambodia, fearing both its neighbors—Vietnam perhaps with more justification now than Thailand—is struggling fiercely against what it perceives to be a threat to its national existence.

Forces Now Released

The analysts do not necessarily believe all Cambodian charges of Vietnamese subversion and barbarities nor justify Cambodia's actions. But they contend that the conflict should be seen in the light of a historical enmity submersed but not forgotten for a century. Forces restrained by colonialism and its American aftermath, they believe, have now been released to take their course in a strictly Asian context.

As for Laos, the view of most Indochina watchers is that as a viable country, it has always been a myth. There are 30,000 to 50,000 Vietnamese troops within its borders and its northern tip is under Chinese domination.

The Indochinese contestants are not, of course, acting out their policies without influence from the Communist world to which they all belong. China, with apparent reservations, supports Cambodia, while the Soviet Union has thrown its weight behind Vietnam and Laos.

Vietnam's Reaction to Raids

In this alignment, too, Indochina watchers believe that an ancient antagonism, that between China and Vietnam has played a role in drawing Vietnam much closer to Moscow than to Peking

Because of Cambodia's alignment with China, Vietnam is thought to be exercising great restraint in its military reaction to Cambodian border intrusions that have killed or maimed many civilians and ruined some towns and villages from the southern end of the border on the Gulf of Siam to Tay Ninh Province west of Saigon.

Vietnam is assumed to be unwilling to risk offending China by pushing its troops to Phnom Penh and overthrowing the regime of Prime Minister Pol Pot. But recent visitors to Hanoi, journalists and international officials, have come away with the impression that Vietnam has made the removal of the Prime Minister, who is also the head of the Cambodian Communist Party, its principal objective.

There are reports in Thailand that Vietnam appears to be organizing thousands of Cambodians, including some from the ethnic Cambodian minority in Vietnam, some of those Cambodians who fled the Pol Pot regime and some of those who were taken to Vietnam during the major military incursion at the end of last year, to form the nucleus of a pro-Vietnamese Cambodian movement.

The travelers assume that Vietnam intends to use this movement either to populate a "liberated zone" in the course of a renewed limited thrust into the neighboring country or as a "fifth column" to assist in the overthrow of the regime.

Neighbors Are Watchful

The non-Communist nations of Southeast Asia, particularly the five members of the Association of Southeast Asian Nations—Indonesia, the Philippines, Thailand, Malaysia and Singpore—watch Indochina with anxiety. While trying to maintain proper relations with Vietnam and indicating satisfaction with their progress, officials express concern, always specifying that their names not be printed, over Hanoi's long-term aims. "Thailand is our barometer," a ranking Indonesian security official said. He added that he hoped the United States would show its continuing concern for Southeast Asia by not yielding to Vietnamese demands for extensive economic assistance.

Thailand is confronted with the dilemma of suffering frequent incursions from Cambodia, mainly by combined Cambodian and Thai Communist forces based in Cambodia, while hoping that Cambodia will remain strong enough to resist Vietnam. No matter how difficult a neighbor Pol Pot's Cambodia is, in the Thai view, a Cambodia subservient to Vietnam would be even less desirable.

Thailand and the rest of the nations in the association view Vietnam as their principal potential adversary. And, while remaining concerned over what China's future intentions might hold for them, they look to Peking for the time being as their principal hope for restraining the ambitions for regional hegemony that they suspect Vietnam of harboring.

* * *

May 28, 1978

FEW SCARS FOR EX-HANOI POW'S

By ROBERT LINDSEY
Special to The New York Times

LOS ANGELES, May 27—Five years after they came home from North Vietnam, almost 300 former prisoners of war, many of them now beginning to show the paunch and gray hair of middle age, were reunited here this weekend for the first time.

For most of the former prisoners, the reunion was a time not only to reminisce about an ugly past and comrades who did not survive, but also to express wonder at how little, after five years, their lives had been scarred by their captivity.

"The thing that impresses me most about this group is how normal we all turned out," said George Day, a former Air Force colonel who won the Medal of Honor while being held prisoner in Vietnam. Mr. Day, now 53 years old and a lawyer in Fort Walton Beach, Fla., is being urged by local groups to run for political office.

"We had all these forecasts from the doctors and the headshrinkers of how bad we'd all turn out because of the deprivation, the isolation, the bad food, the malnutrition, and so forth," he said. "But it didn't happen that way."

"You can't go through an experience like that and have it not change both your lives," said Connie Collins. Her husband, Tom, an Air Force colonel who was among the first Americans captured in 1965, had just met and warmly embraced his prison roommate, Lieut. Comdr. Denver Key, whom he hadn't seen in five years.

"I had to take over some of the things that he used to do and it was hard to relinquish things," she continued. "Even now, he says I'm too tough on the children, and I say he's too lenient; but really, he's normal and we're normal and we're very happy."

"I think faith was the common thread that got a lot of us through; the thing you get from faith is hope," said Capt. Eugene McDaniel, who spent six years in captivity after his A-6 Intruder was shot down over Hanoi in 1967.

Simple Things Appreciated

Captain McDaniel, who is 46 and is the commanding officer of the aircraft carrier U.S.S. Lexington, said that many prisoners he had known in North Vietnam had developed a religious faith that remained after their release, and a deep appreciation for simple things in every day life.

"You've got to go through the valley to appreciate the mountaintop," he said. "I learned to appreciate the small things."

He acknowledged that a few of the former captives had had trouble adjusting to life after their return to the United States, but he insisted that they were very few.

Researchers at a Navy facility in San Diego that has sought to monitor the progress of the former captives said that studies of previous prisoners of war indicated that physical and mental difficulties resulting from captivity sometimes arose five to 10 years after release. But the researchers confirmed that, with relatively few exceptions, the POW's of the Vietnam War had not had serious problems.

"They're fine; they're no different than anybody else," said Comdr. William Ferris of the study center, adding that special physical examinations were administered to the men every year and that no problems had been found.

Similarly, he said, there had been no pattern of psychological ailments.

"I think there's almost zero incidence of mental disorders and not a very high incidence of physical disorders," Mr. Day said.

'We Were a Little Different'

"I think primarily it's because we were a little different than some of the prisoners before," he continued. "We were organized; we had an effective religious program; there was a high incidence of college degrees in the group—I'd say it was close to 98 percent."

For the most part, the reunion, which often had much of the atmosphere of a reunion of old college classmates, was apolitical.

At a news conference this morning, several of the former prisoners still on active duty declined to answer questions about what they thought of the Carter Administration's defense policies. But Mr. Day, noting that he was no longer in the service, called President Carter "incompetent" and characterized his cancellation of the B-1 bomber and his delay of the neutron bomb as "two of the dumbest decisions made in the history of the country."

For all the sense of camaraderie and joy at the reunion, there was at least one remnant of the past that recalled the bitterness that once divided the country over the war in Southeast Asia.

Two days ago a former prisoner, Edward Miller, a retired Marine colonel who is now a lawyer in Santa Ana, south of here, sued a former Air Force captain, John Nasmyth, who runs a successful aircraft business near here, for slander and invasion of privacy.

Mr. Miller, who said he would not attend the reunion, is seeking $10 million in the lawsuit, contending that Mr. Nasmyth had accused him falsely on a local radio show of collaborating with his captors and receiving favorable treatment.

The reunion of the prisoners at the Marriott Hotel, the first since many of them gathered on the White House lawn after their release in the spring of 1973, was largely the idea of former Gov. Ronald Reagan of California and H. Ross Perot, a Dallas computer millionaire who sought to expedite the release of the prisoners during the war. The mechanics of the reunion were handled largely by conservative political friends of the two men.

* * *

December 10, 1978

A VIETNAM VETERAN EMERGES FROM A LOST DECADE

By ROBERT REINHOLD
Special to The New York Times

RICHMOND, Va.—For six years, Douglas Schwinn relived in his dreams that terrible afternoon when North Vietnamese troops encircled his infantry company on a godforsaken hill near the Cambodian border.

Drenching sheets of rain lashed the forest, mortar rounds whistled over-head, rifles cracked, the enemy closed in and he hugged the ground in cold terror. Then ripping pains tore through his chest and his arm. As he got up and staggered, another bullet sliced into his leg. A fourth bullet hit his shoulder. A grenade burst nearby, filling his body with shrapnel.

Now the nightmares have stopped. But long after many Americans have done their best to forget Vietnam, Doug Schwinn cannot. He never will.

Ten years ago I met Doug in Vietnam, just days after he was cut down. His slender 20-year-old body lay swathed in bandages at an Army hospital. The story of his medical care and evacuation written then was a hopeful one. It told of how key advances in military medicine had saved his life and limbs and returned him home to what his Army doctors predicted would be a reasonably normal life.

Though military medicine could heal his body, it could do nothing to prevent the hell Doug Schwinn was to face back home.

It could do nothing to prevent him from slipping into drug addiction and despair. It could not save his marriage or his job, nor prevent his car wreck. It could not prevent his drug arrests and felony convictions. Nor could it prevent him from trying to end the life it had saved.

Psychologists who have studied Vietnam veterans like Doug Schwinn—300,000 were wounded—say that his experiences were very typical. For thousands of young men, the experts say, bodily wounds have healed by now, but not the psychological ones.

The Doug Schwinn story, as it happens, has a happy ending. In the last year he has managed to overcome his addiction to painkillers. Though he still has difficulty finding regular pipe-welding work close to home, he has a devoted new wife, Mariou, and a 5-year-old stepson, Chris; they live in a modest garden apartment here.

Thousands of other veterans have not been so fortunate. They are still plagued by drug addiction, sleeplessness, depression, marital discord and other adjustment problems.

Set Back 10 Years by War

And even Doug, before he pulled his life together, paid for two and a half months in Vietnam with 10 years of his life and almost everything he treasured. At age 30, he is only now starting out at a point most men reach at 20—as a newlywed looking for work.

"I lost everything," he said. "I had a good wife. I had a nice home. I lost my, son back in Ohio. I'm rebuilding it now. It's been 10 years. But I'm going to rebuild it."

They were 10 years of intense pain, sometimes physical, mostly emotional. There was the wrenching experience, after his divorce, of driving all the way from Virginia to his hometown in Ohio to see his young son, only to drive by the house, see the boy playing and leave without stopping. Ultimately he would allow his former wife's new husband to adopt the youngster, who had just about forgotten his real father.

The years have changed Doug in many ways. In the hospital, he was an innocent-looking youth with blond peach fuzz on his chin who seemed dazed by what had happened to him and who felt rather sorry for himself. Today, sitting at the dining room table of his small, immaculate apartment with his wife, he is a strapping man with a mustache and goatee. It is difficult to see that he was grievously wounded, without a close look at his malformed left hand.

Has Gained Confidence

He seems confident and at ease with himself now. He approaches life with maturity and sophistication and speaks of his unhappy past articulately, although his speech, peppered with words like "doggone" and "shoot," quickly betrays his small-town Midwestern origins.

It was out of Barberton, Ohio, in 1968 that the Selective Service plucked Doug, a 20-year-old who had never used even aspirin. Unquestioning ("I just went ahead and did what I was told to do"), he left a new bride and soon found himself a foot soldier, a grunt, in a faraway war that he has since come to view as a senseless waste.

He never joined the antiwar movement, but he saw things in Vietnam that troubled him. He says he watched in amazement when his lieutenant called in a Cobra gunship and "dusted away" a friendly village in which he reported seeing a woman with a rifle.

He saw heavy combat about 10 times before that day he was felled. Just as in the movies, his life was saved, he believes, because the bullet was slowed by the Bible in his chest pocket. He still has the bloodstained book, with a ragged hole through the middle, and the slug is still embedded in his chest.

Evacuated by Helicopter

Like thousands of other wounded, he was evacuated by a helicopter to a field hospital near Saigon, and then when his condition stabilized, to the Valley Forge Army Hospital in Phoenixville, Pa., for follow-up treatment. He spent a year and a half there, undergoing 11 operations on his arm alone.

There were many complications. The wounds healed slowly and became infected. The long, idle days were filled with pain, soothed with liberal doses of painkillers. But he finally emerged in relatively good shape in January 1970 and went home to Ohio.

It was all downhill from there.

"From being on drugs in the hospital. I got hooked on drugs, bad," he said. Codeine, Darvon, Valium and other painkillers became his daily diet. At first they came, legally, from the Veterans Administration. When it finally cut off his supply, he found clever ways to fool pharmacists. He would pretend to be a doctor and call in prescriptions by phone to dozens of different drugstores. "I went to pick it up and, you know, they had it all ready for me," he said.

Began to Experience Seizures

The pills—he popped 30 to 40 a day—slowly destroyed his life. The six-foot one-inch veteran's weight dropped to 135 pounds, and he began to have seizures, which terrified his young son. He stopped working. It was not difficult to get along, since he receives tax-free disability payments of $823 a month from the Veterans Administration.

Finally, a druggist tripped him up and a squad of narcotics agents arrived one day and took him to jail. He was tried, convicted and received a suspended one- to five-year sentence, with four years probation.

Divorce proceedings followed. Then he totaled his brand new car. But he went right on having phony prescription orders filled. "I just screwed up my whole marriage," he said.

Divorced, he moved to Virginia, where, after a brief unsuccessful stay at a religious retreat, he lived with his retired father in Lynchburg. All the while he popped pills; even when his father took him to a drug rehabilitation program in Richmond he stepped out of the waiting room and headed for the nearest drugstore with a phony Darvon prescription.

Judge Was Sympathetic

Again he was arrested. Again he was convicted. Again a sympathetic judge let him off with probation. He went right back to the drugstore for more pills.

Then, in March of last year, he attempted suicide by swallowing 80 blue Valium pills and a six pack of beer. He woke up three days later, groggy but alive.

As with so many addicts, the decision to change came only when despair was total. "My parents would not have anything to do with me anymore," he said. "They more or less disowned me. I had hurt so many people I didn't have any friends at all. My brother and sister told me never to come around again. I had just hurt and used all my friends That's when I made up my mind to get off drugs. I was just tired. I was run down."

So last year he committed himself to a strict-regimen drug program at the Maguire V.A. Medical Center in Richmond. There he met Marlou, now his wife.

Knew About Drug Problem

"He just seemed like a nice decent guy to me," she said, reaching over and touching his wounded left elbow. "I knew from the beginning about his drugs, but that didn't bother me because I knew he was serious. I helped him."

"I have not felt better in my life than right now." Doug said, gazing at Marlou. "I feel good about everything. I'm getting a new start; she's getting a new start."

Doug's apparent recovery is confirmed by his Virginia probation officer, Lynwood A. Jones, who said he was "thoroughly convinced" that Doug was free of drugs.

Unlike many other Vietnam veterans, Doug expresses little anger. "I am not bitter," he said. "I guess a lot of guys would be, but I'm not. The Government has treated me good ever since I have been back."

Indeed, he seems to take the blame himself for most of his troubles. He insisted over and over again that it was all his own weakness. The Army was *not* to blame for his addiction, his wife was *not* to blame for the divorce, his friends and family could *not* be faulted for giving up on him.

Unlike many Vietnam-era veterans, he has only praise for his treatment by the Veterans Administration, which continues to give him and his family free medical care and which paid for his reschooling as a welder.

If Doug truly harbors no deep-seated bitterness, he is unusual, according to Dr. John Wilson of Cleveland State University and Dr. Charles R. Figley of Purdue, psychologists who have studied hundreds of Vietnam-era veterans. They say that many, particularly those who saw frequent combat, continue to have severe, often delayed, psychological difficulties accompanied by intense guilt, resentment and anger.

That Doug Schwinn apparently does not harbor such feelings may help to explain his ability to change. For seven years, he concedes, "nobody could tell me nothing." But he, has since matured, developed a love for life and his work (when he has it) and evolved a healthy acceptance of what he is and is not.

'I'm Doing Right Now'

"I've done a lot of bad things, and a lot of wrong," he said. "But I'm doing right now. If I could make-up for the bad things I did to people. I'd truly try right now."

What he is now, by all appearances, is a suburban family man. He dreams of a new house. He loves his new Dodge Custom van, and dotes on his stepson, for whom he is being the father he wasn't to his natural son.

Physically, his wounds still give him bad days. He maintains that he can do most things normal people do, only a little differently. He has been denied construction jobs because employers do not believe he can handle the work. But last summer he managed to go water skiing.

Ten years ago, as I left Doug in the Army hospital, his surgeon told me he probably would lead a "fairly normal life," but that he would never be able to play tennis.

Douglas Schwinn recently began to play tennis.

* * *

December 10, 1978

NOW ASIA FRETS ABOUT 'UGLY VIETNAMESE'

By HENRY KAMM

BANGKOK—The war to determine whether the three countries of Indochina would be Communist or not was won by the Communists three years ago. The struggle over whether Indochina should be in the Soviet or the Chinese camp continues.

Vietnam has clearly thrown in its lot with the Soviet Union, having signed a friendship treaty containing a clause for possible military cooperation. In Laos, the voice and the army of Vietnam are dominant, except for remote northern regions under heavy Chinese influence.

The political temperature in the region rose last week as Vietnam proclaimed a Cambodian liberation front that evoked memories of earlier Indochina wars, and the United States cautioned Hanoi not to go too far in its conflict with Cambodia.

Cambodia is China's ally and client, and the Balkan adage, "with friends like these you don't need enemies" may well apply to this relationship. Cambodia practices Maoism in its extreme form, emptying its cities and organizing its population into labor-camp communes. It does so while China is de Maoizing, causing some embarrassment to Chinese officials and diplomats who have to defend their ally while also justifying the Peking regime's new trend.

But no matter what Peking thinks of Phnom Penh's internal policies, its realpolitik leaves it little choice but to support the regime of Prime Minister Pol Pot. It has no other client in the region, and the alternative to Mr. Pol Pot would be a pro-Vietnamese regime, giving the Soviet Union a new toehold.

China's support is being severely tested because the Cambodian Government has committed the ultimate provocation that a client state can inflict on its protector: it has got itself involved in a war it cannot win, an experience that other powers have suffered through in Indochina. For reasons that remain murky, except that they are rooted in an ancient and visceral mutual enmity, clashes between Vietnamese and Cambodian Communists that began even while they were still fighting a common enemy, erupted into warfare openly acknowledged last year.

Last summer, the Vietnamese Army carved out, without publicly acknowledging it, a strongly held salient inside Cambodia in one of the great battlegrounds of previous Indochinese wars. It is the rubber plantation region that stretches on both sides of the border, north of Ho Chi Minh city, once Saigon, and northeast of Phnom Penh.

Then came the autumn monsoon, and as they had done so efficiently in earlier wars, the Vietnamese dug in and massed troops and logistical supplies; they fought a political war while preparing for the next dry season. The political war consisted of vilifying the Pol Pot regime, comparing it to its pro-American predecessor and nonindigenous tyrants like Hitler, and creating in its propaganda the image of a Cambodian anti-Pol Pot guerrilla movement.

No doubt, observers say, there have been local risings in Cambodia, but they have seen nothing to support Vietnam's claim of a national rising that has affected 16 of Cambodia's "pre-liberation" 19 provinces. Refugee reports have told only of frequent purges, new Khmer Rouge chiefs killing the old. Observers have also noted a coincidence—places in which Hanoi Radio spoke of uprisings often were places in which Vietnamese troops were present.

Last week Vietnam stepped up its propaganda campaign significantly, serving notice that it remained determined to escalate the political war. (Militarily, Hanoi had already delivered this message by a recent intensification in fighting which some analysts, perhaps prematurely, labeled as the opening of the traditional dry-season offensive.) Hanoi Radio announced the founding in what it called the "liberated zone" of Cambodia—in April 1975, the same station had found that all of Cambodia had been liberated—of a Kampuchean (Cambodian) National United Front for National Salvation. The front was described as complete with armed forces, a central committee, a news service and a radio station, which broadcasts presumably from Vietnam.

A Vietnamese military advance toward the Mekong River town of Kratie last week suggests that Hanoi may be preparing to add to the front's attributes a countergovernment, established in an enlarged "liberated zone," and gradually sap the strength of the Phnom Penh regime. The front could also serve as a device to mask more extensive Vietnamese military designs in Cambodian colors. However Vietnam uses the front, it will certainly do its utmost to prevent a repetition of the last Cambodian opposition front established under its aegis. The front Vietnam sponsored in 1970, in whose name its troops fought for the first two years of its existence, is the present Phnom Penh Government.

Whatever Hanoi chooses to do, it is held to be beyond doubt that it could defeat Cambodia militarily and install a puppet regime in Phnom Penh as it has done in Vientiene. But the international cost of outright aggression might be judged to be too high. While it is held unlikely that China would commit its own armies to save an ally in distress, Peking could put political and military pressure on Hanoi, albeit with the same risk to its reputation as Hanoi incurs by its actions in Cambodia.

The United States last week publicly tilted away from its neutral stance in the Cambodian-Vietnamese conflict and criticized Vietnam without endorsing Cambodia and its frightful human-rights record. Hanoi has been put on notice that normalization of relations with the United States cannot be forthcoming if Vietnam openly invades a neighboring country.

The United States shares the concerns that are common to China and non-Communist Southeast Asia. The worst result of the conflict, in their view, would be Vietnamese domination of Cambodia. Not only is a Vietnam in control of all Indochina feared for its own sake, but a weak Soviet presence is preferred to a strong one in a region where the Soviet Union so far has failed to make gains.

The ironical upshot is that Washington once more feels that for overriding political reasons it must, implicitly, at least, rally to the defense of a regime that is notorious for its violations of human rights.

Henry Kamm is chief Asian diplomatic correspondent for The New York Times.

* * *

January 8, 1979

HANOI REPORTS CAMBODIAN CAPITAL CONQUERED BY 'INSURGENT' FORCES; LONG GUERRILLA CONFLICT FEARED

VIETNAM IN KEY ROLE

13 of Its Regular Divisions Are Reported Involved in Broad Offensive

---

By HENRY KAMM
Special to The New York Times

BANGKOK, Thailand, Jan. 7—The Cambodian capital, Phnom Penh, was captured today, Vietnam and the insurgent front it is backing in Cambodia announced tonight.

"The regime of dictatorial, militarist domination of the Pol Pot-Ieng Sary clique has completely collapsed," the radio announcement declared. Nothing was said about the whereabouts of Prime Minister Pol Pot and Deputy Prime Minister Ieng Sary.

The Hanoi broadcasts also reported the conquest of Kompong Som, Cambodia's only major seaport and the point of entry for almost all the war material China has sent to Cambodian forces to allow them to continue fighting. Two airports that can be used by large transport planes—in Siem Reap and Kompong Chhnang—apparently remained in Government hands.

Vietnamese Said to Play Chief Role

The broadcasts credited the "revolutionary armed forces" of the Cambodian National United Front for National Salvation with the "liberation" of Phnom Penh and other regions.

But political, diplomatic, military and intelligence analysts here and elsewhere have said that the war in Cambodia was being fought by as many as 13-regular Vietnamese divisions and supporting troops, numbering about 100,000 men.

Most of the analysts here see a strong possibility that Hanoi's announcement of the collapse of the Pol Pot regime may be premature and that Cambodia may be facing a long period of guerrilla war. Such fighting would severely test both Vietnam's ability to maintain its official position that its troops are not involved and the Pol Pot forces' capacity to continue fighting without the supplies they have up to now been receiving from China.

[The United States said that in the wake of the reports of the Cambodian capital's fall priority should be given to the withdrawal of Vietnamese forces-from Cambodia and the avoidance of direct Soviet and Chinese involvement.]

[A Soviet press commentary indicated that the "liberation" of Phnom Penh had the support of the Kremlin and was welcomed by it.]

Fighting Started in Late 1977

Analysts in Bangkok who follow developments in Indochina feel that the goal of Vietnam in the fighting, which erupted in late 1977, is to bring down the Government of Mr. Pol Pot, which came to power in 1975 after having captured Phnom Penh from the right-wing Government of President Lon Nol with the aid of the Vietnamese.

After gaining power, however, the Cambodian Government rejected Hanoi's leadership, aligned itself with China—the power that Hanoi most fears—and engaged in raids along the Vietnamese border. Cambodia contends that parts of the Mekong delta that are ruled by Vietnam rightfully belong to Cambodia.

Analysts with access to monitoring of battlefield communications have said they have seen no evidence of any significant presence of Cambodian insurgents on the principal fighting fronts, which now appear to cover almost all of Cambodia.

In addition to the capture of Phnom Penh and Kompong Som, the broadcasts also announced that the "revolutionary armed forces and people completely liberated" the provinces of Kampot, Takeo, Prey Veng, Kompong Cham and Kandal.

Vast Area in Vietnamese Hands

Together with five other provinces known to have been seized over the last 10 days, this would mean the Vietnamese had gained control of all of Cambodia east of a diagonal line reaching from the northeastern point where the Mekong River crosses from Laos into Cambodia to the country's southwesternmost corner.

Furthermore, the broadcasts stated that "revolutionary armed forces" had gained control of "vast regions" in seven other provinces. Only two of Cambodia's 19 provinces, farthest from Vietnam, went unmentioned in the reports.

In view of reports by informed sources that the Vietnamese forces have largely confined their columns to the main roads and of the near emptiness of Cambodia's cities and towns as a result of the expulsion of their populations after the Communist victory in 1975, analysis find it difficult to determine how effective Vietnamese control of the conquered areas is.

The lightning advance of the Vietnamese troops since the present offensive got fully rolling in the last days of December is assumed to have bypassed heavily populated communes and significant Government military units. Mr. Pol Pot two days ago issued a call to his troops that was interpreted here as an order to prepare for a large-scale guerrilla war against the invaders. The Cambodian Government's army is believed to number 60,000 at most.

Lon Nol Regime Fell in 1975

The "liberation" of Phnom Penh came almost 45 months after the last remnants of the American-backed Lon Nol regime surrendered to the Communist forces under control of Mr. Pol Pot. The Lon Nol Government surrendered on April 17, 1975. According to the Hanoi broadcasts, Phnom Penh was captured at 12:30 P.M. today, 12:30 A.M. in New York.

The announcement by the Cambodian insurgent radio said:

"After annihilating and disintegrating the regular force divisions of the Pol Pot long Sary army, and after destroying the external defense line, the revolutionary army, acting in coordination with the people, has entered Phnom Penh from all directions.

"The revolutionary forces occupied the vital positions of the enemy inside the city and the key organs of the reactionary Pol Pot-Ieng Sary administration. Today at 12:30 the capital of Phnom Penh was completely liberated. The regime of dictatorial, militarist domination of the Pol Pot-leng Sary clique has completely collapsed.

"The red flag, with five towers at the center, of the Kampuchean National United Front for National Salvation is fluttering on the tops of all buildings in Phnom Penh."

Kampuchea is the traditional name for Cambodia, adopted by the Communist regime after its takeover in 1975.

Government Radio Is Silent

The Cambodian Government radio broadcast its last program from 11:30 A.M. until noon, a half-hour before the city's reported fall, without mentioning the critical nature of the situation. Suspicions among observes here were first aroused when monitors noted that the stations did not come back for the scheduled 5:30 P.M. broadcast. The announcement of the fall was first broadcast by the insurgent radio at 9:37 P.M., followed 13 minutes later by the Hanoi radio.

In the absence of news of the whereabouts of Mr. Pol Pot and his associates, speculation here centered on possibilities that they may have been evacuated to China by air or have fled into the countryside, either to save their lives or to continue to lead a resistance movement. When the Communist-led forces seized the capital in 1975, the vast waves of killing that have marked their regime began with the execution without trial of all leaders of previous governments.

In a broadcast by the rebel radio less than three hours before its announcement of the conquest of Phnom Penh, Heng Samrin, the leader of the Salvation Front, called on troops of the Pol Pot army to turn their weapons against their officers. "The revolution will forgive and admire anyone who has done good for the nation," he said.

In a long statement broadcast last night, the front promised to abolish in its "liberated zone" many of the excesses of the Pol Pot regime, which organized the entire nation of perhaps seven million into communes, separated families, emptied the towns and destroyed the Buddhist religion and most of the traditional culture.

The front pledged to let families reunite freely and return to their regions of origin. Former city dwellers; however, were told that they could return "when the situation in the whole country permits." The front promised freedom of religion and the building or repair of destroyed temples.

The insurgent group said it would abolish the governmental and administrative bodies of the Pol Pot regime and replace them with elected "people's self-management committees." These committees, it said, will consist of people who suffered at the hands of the Pol Pot regime, persons of "meritorious service to the people" and respected elders.

The front promised also to provide general health care, which has been virtually nonexistent since 1975, and to build schools for all children 7 to 10 years old. Schools also virtually vanished under the Pol Pot regime.

Appeal Made to Defectors

The Salvation Front said it would welcome defectors from the Pol Pot Government and army and ruled out reprisals against prisoners of war. It said, however, that defectors would have to be examined for their past actions before being granted full rights of citizenship.

In a statement bound to infuriate China, which is believed to have thousands of advisers in Cambodia, the Salvation Front invited those people also to defect in return for good treatment. And it warned that advisers "who oppose the revolution will be duly punished." The whereabouts of the Chinese adviser and their status if they fall into Vietnamese hands is one of the most critical questions remaining unanswered.

Little is known here about the fate of members of the small diplomatic corps in Phnom Penh, though most of the Chinese Embassy staff was believed to have returned to China.

* * *

February 20, 1979

CHINA IN VIETNAM: A MATTER OF HONOR

By FOX BUTTERFIELD
Special to The New York Times

HONG KONG, Feb. 19—On the night American troops invaded Cambodia in 1970, President Nixon explained to a national television audience that he had acted because, "when the chips are down," the United States could not appear to be a "pitiful, helpless giant."

"It is not our power but our will and character that is being tested tonight," Mr. Nixon said.

Something of the same kind of concern with what nations, or their leaders, think of as honor seems to have been on Peking's mind last week when it attacked Vietnam.

The Chinese had become increasingly angry, frustrated and humiliated by Vietnam's actions—the expulsion of 180,000 ethnic Chinese from Vietnam, a nagging series of border incidents, Hanoi's signing of a friendship treaty with Moscow in November and then its overthrow last month of the Pol Pot regime in Cambodia, Peking's ally.

Particularly galling was China's belief that the Soviet Union was behind Hanoi's moves. The Chinese have, in some ways, inherited the psychology and the containment policy of John Foster Dulles, and tend to see the Russians everywhere.

With Mao Tse-tung dead, Peking is no longer accusing Moscow of revisionism—"consumer Communism"—but the deep traditional enmity between the two nations remains.

Commitment to Its Friends

China's leaders therefore came to feel that a failure to act against the Vietnamese-Russian colossus would cast doubt on Peking's commitment to its friends and to itself.

Teng Hsiao-ping, China's senior Deputy Prime Minister, hinted at this sentiment today in his first public comment since the Chinese offensive began on Saturday. The time had come, Mr. Teng said, when the Chinese people had "to take a position demonstrating that they do care."

"They cannot tolerate any aggression against them," he added, "that could be misconstrued as indifference or weakness, or just being pushed around."

Mr. Teng made his remarks in a meeting in Peking with the Secretary General of the Organization of American States, Alejandro Orfila of Argentina.

Emphasis on Limited Aims

Mr. Teng stressed Peking's limited aims: "This action will be a limited one, an action reacting to provocation that will be circumspect to take care of this particular situation, and it will not be extended or expanded in any other way."

He may have had in mind China's lightning war with India in 1962, when the Chinese inflicted an embarrassing defeat on New Delhi and then swiftly pulled back.

But as the United States discovered in Vietnam, limited wars do not always end on schedule. They tend to be harder to stop than to start. This is particularly so when the Vietnamese are involved; they see themselves as heirs of a 2,000-year tradition of repelling invaders—Chinese, Japanese, French and American.

Indeed, Vietnam today rejected Peking's call, made the day the Chinese attack began, for negotiations to settle the dispute. "What is to be negotiated when Chinese troops are still trampling our soil?" Radio Hanoi asked. "That is tantamount to a robber whetting his knife to compel the house-owner to negotiate the haul."

Second Use of Same Metaphor

Ironically, that was the same metaphor Hanoi used in the late 1960's when it demanded that the United States withdraw from South Vietnam before negotiations could start.

As the inventors of the modern "people's war," the Chinese are aware of its dangers, and analysts here believe Peking may have had two motives for its attack beyond the salving of national pride.

One was military and tactical: to relieve pressure on Mr. Pol Pot's guerrilla forces, who are resisting the estimated 150,000-man Vietnamese Army in Cambodia. Analysts here say the evidence is too fragmentary to know whether Hanoi has diverted any of its troops in Cambodia to counter the Chinese attack, which did not deter a Vietnamese delegation, headed by Prime Minister Pham Van Dong and the army chief of staff, Gen. Van Tien Dung, from signing a "treaty of peace, friendship and cooperation" yesterday in Phnom Penh with the Cambodian regime installed by Hanoi in January.

The second motive is more problematical, but some diplomats believe Peking may have hoped to use its attack to help start talks leading to the creation of a Cambodian Government that would not be controlled by Vietnam.

Cambodia's Primary Conflict

Peking's approach to Cambodia has shifted markedly in the last few weeks, with far less talk about supporting Mr. Pol Pot. Instead, China has a new policy of trying to create what the Communist Party paper, Jenmin Jih Pao, termed a "most extensive national, democratic and patriotic united front." The main "contradiction" in Cambodia, the paper said last week, is no longer between different classes or political groups but between Cambodian and Vietnamese.

The Cambodians, therefore, should "readjust" their policies and use the united-front strategy as a "magic weapon for victory," the paper explained. As part of this effort, Peking gave a hero's welcome to Prince Norodom Sihanouk last week when he returned from representing the Pol Pot Government at the United Nations. The Chinese may be hoping the Prince could be a compromise candidate to head a new regime in Phnom Penh.

Unless Peking can bring the fighting to a swift conclusion, some analysts feel the adventure carries a greater possibility of risk than gain for China.

For one thing, the Soviet Union may soon find itself drawn into supporting Vietnam by the same motive that prompted the Chinese to attack—saving face. Moscow has already declared it would "honor its obligations" under its friendship treaty with Vietnam and warned Peking to "stop before it is too late." The Russians have 44 divisions, nearly a million men, on their 5,000-mile frontier with China, and they are far better armed than the Chinese.

Stoking Fears About Taiwan

China is also risking its new relationship with the United States. Congress is debating President Carter's decision to cancel official relations with Taiwan and send an ambassador to Peking. The incursion into Vietnam may increase fears among conservative supporters of Taiwan that Peking cannot be trusted to work for peaceful reunification with the island.

Some Asian diplomats, noting that China's offensive came shortly after Mr. Teng's return from the United States, think the Chinese may have been buoyed by a belief that Washington would support them against the Vietnamese and Russians. An official on Taiwan called Peking's attack "China's playing of the American card."

American diplomats stress that such a conclusion by China would be a serious misreading of the Carter Administration's position, but the coincidence in timing is still there.

CONTESTED LEGACIES

April 15, 1979

MENTALLY WOUNDED ARE RARE, BUT NOT NEARLY RARE ENOUGH

By ROBERT REINHOLD

WASHINGTON—To judge from much of television and the movies, the Vietnam combat veteran is a ticking time bomb, apt to explode in crazed frenzy. "The Deerhunter," the movie about insanity among former prisoners of war that won several Academy Awards last week, sharpens that image, although another award-winning film, "Coming Home," softens it somewhat by presenting a sensitive portrait of a veteran's readjustment.

Much has been written about the Vietnam veteran and his putative resentment, rage, guilt, alienation, family troubles, drug abuse, alcoholism, joblessness and mental breakdown. Not long ago, a reporter looked up a former Army infantryman whose grievous wounding was the subject of a story 10 years ago and found that the soldier, Douglas Schwinn, was just emerging from an agonizing decade marked by drug addiction, nightmares, divorce, despair and suicide attempts.

How typical are such cases? Drug abuse and other signs of emotional disturbance are common. Are those who served in Vietnam really different from others?

Almost all authorities agree that a majority of the 2.8 million who went to Vietnam have made a reasonably smooth readjustment, blending, though not always easily, into a society that gives them little thanks. Most are largely indistinguishable from others of their age—now about 30—and background.

But a consensus is emerging that a substantial minority, particularly those like Doug Schwinn who saw heavy combat, continue to suffer difficulty severe enough to require medical attention five years after the last American left Vietnam. It was called shell shock in World War I, combat fatigue in World War II and Korea. Now it's "post-traumatic neurosis."

Whatever it's called, psychiatrists say the delayed reaction to stress is a painful emotional upheaval often suffered by those who survive combat, floods, fires, auto wrecks or other life-threatening experiences. Symptoms include guilt feelings, instability, sleeplessness, irritability, emotional numbing, moodiness and sometimes violent tendencies.

According to Dr. Jack Ewalt, a Veterans Administration psychiatrist, this "post-Vietnam syndrome" affects about one in five Vietnam veterans—as many as half a million people. Some specialists, like Lieut. Col. E. Robert Worthington, an Army psychologist say that veterans with adjustment problems had them even before entering service. Others, like Prof. John P. Wilson of Cleveland State University, argue that combat left many a soldier emotionally crippled.

Dr. Ewalt says that the best research shows a direct war effect. In a review of 21 studies involving 7,751 veterans in all, Dr. Charles R. Figley of Purdue University found that while Vietnam-era veterans in general were pretty normal, those who were in or near combat exhibited an unusual number of psychological ailments.

Many have gotten in trouble with the law. Last year the Justice Department estimated that there were 58,000 veterans in prison, of whom a majority served in Vietnam. According to Corrections magazine, there are indications that many Vietnam veterans behave better in prison than do other inmates and might have greater potential for rehabilitation. But, the magazine says, few are getting the Government disability benefits legally due them or the payments they could collect for completing academic courses.

The reason is that they don't know their rights and that prison officials, fearful of creating a "rich" and powerful prison elite, don't want them to know. The Veterans Administration is sometimes blamed. "We're caught in a cross-fire," says James Cox, national director of veterans assistance for the V.A., "between those who say we're not doing enough and the others who are saying, 'Why are you giving this money to criminals?' "

Hostility to the veterans is often undisguised. "The first day I came home I was called a 'baby killer' by my kid brother and the 'bunch who lost the war' by some drunk down at the

V.F.W.," said one veteran quoted by Dr. Figley in a recent book he edited, "Stress Disorders Among Vietnam Veterans."

Looking back, psychiatrists and military men trace much of the trouble to the rotation system used to assign troops in Vietnam. Soldiers were sent for fixed tours of duty in the combat zone. The makeup of companies and platoons was therefore constantly changing, depriving soldiers of the emotional support of close companionship. As a result, many a soldier entered combat feeling isolated. "The guy came in alone and left alone," said Dr. Figley.

Adding to the difficulty was the suddenness of return. Soldiers went from foxhole to fireplace in hours, with no time to decompress as World War II soldiers could do on the troopships that took them home. And it was the first war in which self-relief was readily at hand in the form of marijuana and heroin.

The Government has only recently begun to recognize the extent of post-Vietnam psychological ailments. Because many who need help do not seek out treatment. Dr. Ewalt has been trying to obtain money to start an "outreach" effort to bring psychiatric, counseling and other services to ghetto neighborhoods where combat veterans are concentrated. So far Congress has not approved the plan.

What may hamper any such effort is a deep resentment among veterans of the public image of those who served in Vietnam. According to Dr. Figley, the media, along with psychologists and psychiatrists, have made it more difficult to reach men in need of help by putting psychiatric labels on normal stress reactions. Said Dr. Figley: "People don't think flood survivors are all crazy."

* * *

May 27, 1979

FILMS AND PLAYS ABOUT VIETNAM TREAT EVERYTHING BUT THE WAR

By HANS KONING

The Academy Awards clinched it. Suddenly, we are told, the Vietnam War has become accepted as a proper subject for every form of American popular art. The war has come out into the commercial artistic mainstream, ready to take Oscars, National Book Awards for fiction and hours of prime TV playtime. Now, while entertained, we can purge our doubts and guilts and heal the suppressed divisions of the war years. Indeed, the chairman of the department of psychiatry at Northwestern University, Dr. Harold Visotsky, has gone so far as to inform us that Hollywood is thus providing "our own Nuremberg trials."

It is surely a gratifying idea that America, in this quintessentially American way—that's to say through its popular culture—would come to grips and be coping with its Vietnam past. Let us look at some of these recent dramas and melodramas in order to find out what the intentions of their producers or writers were, as far as can be judged from the finished products.

The most prominent are indeed the two Oscar-winning movies, "The Deer Hunter" and "Coming Home." On the stage, we have had Michael Herr's book of reportage, "Dispatches," made into a musical by Elizabeth Swados, and David Berry's play, "G.R. Point," which was seen on Broadway for a brief run. On television, ABC devoted three hours of a Sunday evening in April to the screening of "Friendly Fire." On the literary scene, Tim O'Brien's novel "Going After Cacciato" won the 1979 National Book Award for fiction.

All this did not come out of the blue. We have had Vietnam films before ("Green Berets," "The Boys in Company C") and we have had plays from writers such as David Rabe, whose "Sticks and Bones" was also seen on television, albeit only after much delay prompted by second thoughts on the part of the network. The difference is that in the past those works dealing with Vietnam were supposed to be controversial and difficult, outside the world of Show Business—unless, of course, they stuck to a simple and traditional Geronimo type of treatment such as a John Wayne could (maybe) get away with.

But now producers and investors no longer blanch at the word "Vietnam." Supposedly "The Deer Hunter" has done for that war what "Gentleman's Agreement" did for anti-Semitism; it made it acceptable for consideration in the popular arts.

"The Deer Hunter," the biggest of them all so far, both in terms of investment (money and professional effort) and public response, tells the stories of three American blue-collar workers, establishes their small steel mill town background and then follows them to Vietnam where they serve in the Green Berets. Made by Michael Cimino with the lead role played by Robert DeNiro, it has won its fistful of Oscars for "best film" and a row of other "bests."

In the movie, the steelworkers go off to do their duty to God and country and they return without any cynicism or disillusionment, let alone feelings of guilt. No one stands accused except the old enemy, the Vietcong, and it is a Vietcong even more darkly devilish than he was on our wartime 7 o'clock news. For example, a group of Vietnamese women and children are killed with a grenade in the film, but the grenade thrower is not an American, he's a Vietcong. So much for American Nuremberg trials. A viewer watching Mr. Cimino's camera move in on Ho Chi Minh smiling down from his picture frame upon that now well-discussed Russian roulette fantasy (where U.S. prisoners of war are forced to play Russian roulette with one another) may be justified in feeling he is being stirred up once more to go hunt for Reds.

It isn't that the people making such a film necessarily set out to be warmongers; everyone who has worked on movies knows how haphazardly even their most crucial elements may come into being. But neither Mr. Cimino nor the critics and prize-givers who applauded the film showed any particular awareness of the moral issues it raised. "The Deer Hunter" doesn't exult in the war, yet neither does it question the war's good guys/bad guys purposefulness. "Coming

Home" and most other recent dramatizations of the war fall in a different category. They *do* question. What remains to be seen, however, is *what* they question.

Hal Ashby's "Coming Home"—released early in 1978 and now getting renewed attention having won its three Academy Awards—is about a marine sergeant who returns from the war as a paraplegic. On one level it is a story of love and of a sense of human recognition between this man (played by Jon Voight) and an officer's wife (Jane Fonda) whose husband also returns a cripple, albeit a mental rather than a physical one. On another level "Coming Home" means to confront us with the wreckage war leaves in its wake, more specifically with the fate of the war's American veterans, but the film does not question the war itself so much as our attitude toward those men. A typical thematic scene shows a group of officers' wives who publish a news-letter at a California army base refusing an article about poor conditions at a veterans' hospital because it makes unpleasant reading. They, like all of us, presumably don't wish to entertain such unpleasant news, and this well-meaning film makes us face those realities. Realities about the treatment of American veterans, that is, and even about the conduct of the war, but not about its morality.

"Friendly Fire," the TV play by Fay Kanin (from the magazine report and a later book by C. D. B. Bryan), is really a tale of Pentagon bungling. It is, to a large degree, a documentary, telling us of the actual fate of an American soldier, Michael Mullen, who was killed in Vietnam by an American artillery shell. Such battle deaths were listed by the Pentagon as due to "friendly fire," and were not included in the weekly tally of war casualties; when Michael's mother wanted to find out precisely what had happened to her son, she ran into a bureaucratic wall.

The drama of "Friendly Fire" is very much the drama of the pointlessness of Michael's death. (A viewer may even feel that the Pentagon, in its only too tangible concreteness, actually helped Mrs. Mullen to bear her sorrow—it was there, a target for her bitterness and an outlet for her grief.) In real life, even before Michael had gone overseas, his mother was against the war; the TV play is not. When Michael Mullen on his last day of leave is shown pointing to the picture of an Indian chief in his room, and quotes this man as having said how, loving his people, he fought for them, we understand Mullen to mean that the Americans are "the Indians" in the Vietnam War, defending their world. "Friendly Fire" does not question Mullen's going to war; it questions army incompetence and hamhandedness.

It is surprising how, exactly as in "Friendly Fire," so many of our Vietnam plays are centered on Americans who died in Vietnam because of things other Americans did. After all, such deaths are the exception rather than the norm in war. David Berry's "G. R. Point" (the title stands for "Graves Registration Point") is a play about a snooty New England college graduate who is assigned to an Army graves registration, or body collecting, unit along with a couple of tough city blacks, a hillbilly, a Puerto Rican and an Italian. After winning an Off Broadway Obie, "G. R. Point" moved to Broadway in April of this year and ran there for one month. The playwright dedicated his work to four army friends of his who were killed in Vietnam by an American tank shell, and the play's casualties result from a similar mistake. And when we go back from Mr. Berry all the way to David Rabe, who in 1971 was the first to try and force the Vietnam experience into theatrical form with "The Basic Training of Pavlo Hummel," we will recall that Private Hummel, too, was killed by "friendly fire." Hummel, after a period in base camp where he tries against all the odds of his own personality to become one of the boys, is shipped to Vietnam where he is killed with a grenade thrown by an American sergeant he has insulted.

After "Hummel," Mr. Rabe wrote a second war play, "Sticks and Bones," first seen here in the winter of 1971–1972. In this play, a blinded veteran returns to a smug, know-nothing parental home—a "Deer Hunter" type home, one might say. Rather than trying to grasp what he has been through, his family inpresses upon the veteran that it is he who is out of tune with normal, real, life; so much so that they drive him to suicide in the end. Here we have come to the ultimate in battle death through "friendly fire" to be killed by one's parents. Finally, in Rabe's third war play, "Streamers," the action never leaves base camp, and its violence of American army barracks warfare is the unadulterated domestic brand, in all its senselessness and apple-pie familiarity.

Now it is surely no coincidence that the writers so regularly choose American compatriots of the victims as their instruments of death. Wouldn't the reason be that in this way the other side, the Vietnamese, remain as invisible as they have been during all the war years? In each case, we are shown a Vietnam which is nothing more than a handy background for what is otherwise violent American drama. Action gains starkness and contrast there; Vietnam is seen as the testing ground for relations between American young men. It is a convenient place to have them face the basic questions of life, courage, death.

"G. R. Point" illustrates in still another way the fact that these productions are set in, but are not about, Vietnam. Here is a play written by a man who was there, but the play's only contact with that country, and its people and its fate, comes in the shape of a Vietnamese camp follower who, as more than one first-night critic noted, is a caricature of such pidgin English and pidgin reactions and emotions that she would have embarrassed the makers of Charlie Chan, that Mysterious Oriental out of the innocent Hollywood 30's. As for the way the play's New England college boy (or Hummel, or Paul in the novel "Going After Cacciato") faces danger and death, nothing is said about it that wasn't said as well, or better, in "Sergeant York," or for that matter another generation earlier in "Journey's End," or in the (German) novel and famous Lewis Milestone movie, "All Quiet on the Western Front." Whether, why, or how the Vietnam War was different from any other war is simply not touched upon.

This leads to the second motif: sorrows of crippled men returning and of bereaved parents. It is a traditional theme and the central theme of most of the works mentioned here, and also of several other television shows which returned the war to our living rooms; it is the most tangible and individual expression of war's tragedy. But in order to tell us something about our Vietnam past, there must of necessity be more to the theme than the bare fact of a crippled or dead young man; otherwise, our Labor Day weekend road casualties could serve as well for a subject, if not dramatically then morally.

When we scrutinize the fates of soldiers in "Coming Home," in "Friendly Fire" and in Rabe's plays, we see such fates made more poignant by—by what? By the fact that the war sullied our honor and laid waste a nation? Or, speaking for an adversary position, that it failed to stop the Communists? No, their poignancy lies in the fact that "it was all a mess." This, if anything, seems to be the only message writers and directors either dare, or wish, to give us. Paul, the central character of "Cacciato," says it for all of them: "Why was the war fought? He didn't know . . . he didn't know where the truth lay . . . he simply didn't know." And this Paul in turn sounds very much like the hero of "All Quiet on the Western Front," played by Lew Ayres in the 1930 movie, and whose name, by the way, was also Paul.

We are shown, then, the aftermaths of war, but it is an almost abstract war familiar from many older plays, films and novels about earlier wars. If Vietnam was different—perhaps because for the first time in modern history a large part of a nation refused to let its patriotism override its sense of justice—this distinction is not accepted; or if accepted, it is not shown, let alone explained.

Mullen's death in "Friendly Fire" was pointless because he was killed by us rather than by the enemy, not because the war was pointless or even immoral. Jon Voight in his wheelchair isn't all that different from Marlon Brando in his World War II wheelchair ("The Men"). Voight lacks the consolation that he was crippled in an unavoidable conflict, but he shows no thought for the other side, no thought of a possible American guilt, and neither does any other Vietnam veteran, crippled or whole, recently portrayed for us.

This new crop of examples of popular art neither rejects nor accepts the idea of American guilt—it ignores it. One would welcome a courageous assertion of either point of view, airing the deep divisiveness which this nation in fact lived through. But all that remains buried. We are taken as far as, but not one inch beyond, the 1930's concept of war as "a mess." The theme of "it was all a mess" is a traditional one once a war is won or lost. In the latter case it may come sooner and more naturally, but the German concept of World War I, which they lost, as seen in "All Quiet," seemed to many Americans an adequate description of our part in that war, which we won.

In the meantime, no writer or director has yet dealt with "the other side," where there were no helicopters for evacuation and no telegrams to relatives, where in fact those relatives, men, women, and children, were killed together with the combatants.

And the result is that our former enemy has remained as invisible as ever; and the bottom line question, "Are we a moral nation?", has not yet been asked, much less answered. Francis Coppola's Vietnam film "Apocalypse Now" will be released Aug 15 in New York, and may change this; many who have seen an early print of the film report it does.

Until that judgment is in, however, nothing seems closer to expressing the true feeling of those tragic days, for this writer anyway, than a brief moment in the current film "Hair," made by a Czech-born director to music by three Americans whose 60's musical "Hair" was surely colored by Vietnam but never mentioned it. A line of soldiers marches into the dark, unfillable belly of a huge transport plane bound for the war as we hear the words of a song written in 1967: "We starve, look at one another short of breath . . . facing a dying nation of moving paper fantasy, listening for the new told lies . . . silence tells me secretly everything . . ."

Hans Koning's latest novel, "America Made Me," will appear next winter.

* * *

August 14, 1981

HANOI STILL HOLDS THOUSANDS IN CAMPS

By HENRY KAMM
Special to the New York Times

MAKUNG, Pescadores—More than six years after the Communist victory, countless thousands of Vietnamese who served the former Saigon Government remain imprisoned in jungle camps, uncharged, untried and unsure whether they will ever be released.

Although the Government in Hanoi announced in response to international criticism that in no case would the imprisonment for "re-education" exceed three years, the outflow of refugees continues to bring to other shores men who have only recently been released from such concentration camps.

Pham Van Phu, who was arrested in June 1975 for having been a judge in Saigon Criminal Court, arrived at this island group in the Formosa Strait on a small fishing boat in mid-June. He said he was released last January from a "re-education" camp at Xuyen Moc in Dong Nai province, about 200 miles north of the former South Vietnamese capital.

About 4,000 prisoners remained, Mr. Phu said, of which all but 200 had been junior officers, lieutenants and captains in the South Vietnamese Army. The others were low-level and medium-level civil servants like himself. The Xuyen Moc camp was particularly big, the 41-year-old former judge said, but every province in South Vietnam is known to have one or more camps.

Senior Officers Sent to the North

Like other former camp inmates, Mr. Phu emphasized that only lower-ranking officers and civil servants remained in southern camps, while those of senior level in the military and the old Government, as well as those accused of "crimes against the people," were sent to the north. A feeling has long taken root among their families that those in northern camps will never be released.

Throughout his imprisonment, during which his weight dropped from 138 to 99 pounds, Mr. Phu said he had never been confronted with any accusation or interrogated. His release, like his arrest, was accompanied by no comment or justification.

The only aspect of camp life that might justify the term "re-education," Mr. Phu said, was the occasional reading by one of the prisoners to his work gang of an editorial from one of the party newspapers, which the group was then to discuss. But the former judge said that such discussion lasted only as long as a guard was watching.

Similarly, he added, the daily review of the group's work, to be followed by mutual and self-criticism, never went on beyond the presence of the guards, all of whom were North Vietnamese. Only in the first month of his imprisonment was Mr. Phu subjected to nine political lectures and ordered to write and rewrite at least 15 times a detailed account of his life.

Hard Labor With Minimal Food

For the rest of Mr. Phu's five and a half years of imprisonment, his and his fellow inmates' lot was hard labor with minimal food, bare shelter, ragged clothes and a total absence of any medical attention. The work consisted of clearing the jungle and planting the corn and root crops that were almost their only fare.

"We couldn't live without the food that our families bring us," said the former judge, glancing at his wife, who, sitting at his side through his long narration, mirrored on her intense face the recollection of years of anguish. "We had to submit a list of the food we brought, and if, for instance, we listed only 'beans' instead of 'red beans,' they would confiscate it," said his wife, Mrs. Pham Van Phu, whose eyes look older than her 35 years.

The family visits occurred every two months and were limited to 30 minutes. "Almost every time I went I saw men carrying bodies and I was afraid," Mrs. Phu said, looking at her husband. "Many died in the beginning," he said.

Mr. Phu recalled the death of a well-known writer, Nguyen Manh Con, who demanded to be freed after the three stated years of "re-education" were up. He was told that he could be released into prison. He went on a hunger strike and died after about a month.

Problems Continue After Release

Hunger was a constant of camp life, Mr. Phu recalled, on a diet that was rarely supplemented by vegetables and only three times a year by fish or meat the judge held up two fingers to indicate the size of the ration on the Lunar New Year, Ho Chi Minh's birthday and independence day.

Consistent with accounts of others released from "re-education," Mr. Phu said that his problems did not end with his release. To be allowed to return to live with his wife in their old home required a residence permit given only to those holding permanent jobs, and no permanent jobs were available for persons without a residence permit.

The objective of this Kafkaesque procedure, according to former detainees, was to put pressure on them to return with their families to such regions as those in which they were imprisoned, to try to eke out a livelihood from jungle areas prisoners were clearing. Instead, like many other former prisoners, Mr. Phu used his temporary legal stay in Ho Chi Minh City, Saigon's new name, to arrange for his escape.

Mr. Phu, who prefers to speak only of matters that he has seen, said he could not estimate the total of political prisoners still detained. But a friend who escaped with him, Bui Huu Do, a hydraulic engineer, said, "Where there are prisons there are prisoners, and there are five or six camps in every province."

* * *

August 22, 1981

LOSS OF HOPE LEADS VIETNAMESE TO BRAVE THE SEA

By HENRY KAMM
Special to the New York Times

HONG KONG—Tran Thi Yen, her husband and their three young children fled from Vietnam because, she said, "we wanted to have a future for the children." Three other young women from southern Vietnam nodded sympathetically, as if to say that they had escaped for the same reason.

Today, three of the four are widows, and 9 of their 11 children are dead. How many people died on their boat, how many families were lost without survivors, will never be known. The 16 who made it as far as a refugee camp here know only that there were more than 70 aboard when their boat left the southern fishing port of Rach Gia on June 28.

While the debate goes on outside Vietnam over whether the thousands who continue to flee do so merely to improve their material well-being, the "boat people" who reach shore give the same reasons that those who preceded them have been giving since 1975 to explain their decision to flee.

Feelings of Hopelessness

The reasons can be summarized as a sense of hopelessness, a loss of faith that Vietnam under its present regime will become a livable country again in their lifetimes.

Some report that they never had any hope, because any connection, however slight, with the regimes that governed in Saigon from 1954 until 1975 is held against them and their families. Others say they greeted the Communist victory with hope, believing that whatever their doubts about the system, the end of the war meant peace, national reconciliation and reconstruction of the ravaged country.

However modest their education, the refugees volunteer sooner or later that a major factor was the absence of liberty.

The conversations are long because the interpreter has been cautioned not to put questions in a leading way. Mrs. Yen first cited her hopes for her children's future and then the fact that her husband, a hairdresser, could not work at his job when the electricity was cut off four days out of seven. The continual imposition of petty taxes also made work fruitless, she said.

But they would not have stayed even if life were materially easier, the 25-year-old woman said, "because we had no liberty."

Perils Were Known in Advance

She is alone now and smiling determinedly so as not to burden an outsider with her grief. Like the other boat people who have reached land, she said she and her husband had known about the perils with which nature and man confront those who set out in coastal fishing craft across the ocean, but they took the risk willingly. What the survivors universally say is presumably also true for those whose boats disappear without trace.

Hong Kong officials say that as the typhoon season advances, there is a significant increase in the number of boats reaching here and neighboring Macao on which many passengers have died from hunger, thirst and exposure, and many survivors are in a state of serious malnutrition. Mrs. Yen's boat fits that description.

About half of those aboard were from Ho Chi Minh City, the former Saigon, the others from towns and villages of the Mekong River delta. They included people without a past that was objectionable to the present Vietnamese authorities as well as junior officers and petty officials of the Saigon regime who had been released from "re-education" camps.

Objective Was Singapore

They set out in the hope of reaching Singapore or to find in the sea lanes leading to that active port a freighter that would pick them up. But on their second day at sea the waves became so high that they took a vote and decided to turn back. The next day a wave carried away most of their food and water.

For four days they drifted helplessly, seeing neither ship nor shore. "The children began to die, the littlest ones first," said Dinh Hien, a former lieutenant who after the death of the boat's owner acted as the group leader.

On the sixth day after their decision to turn back, their engine no longer working, they spotted two fishing boats and hopes rose. "We had buried five children in the sea the day before," said Mr. Hien. The boats got close enough for the refugees to shout at them, but their crews paid no heed. "That day, grown-ups began to die," Mr. Hien said.

Boat Drifts Away From Islands

Two islands came into sight, after a night of storm, and they ripped out planks from the deck to try to improvise oars. "But the force of man was not enough against the force of nature," Mr. Hien said. "The winds carried us away." Death continued to carry off passengers, and their near ones no longer kept the bodies in hope of burying them on land.

Ships and boats passed close to them but none stopped, perhaps because the crews did not see the clothes that they were waving or the fires they lit at night.

On the 15th day a freighter, the Maersk Pinto, stopped nearby and began lowering food, water and clothes by rope. But the waves, higher than a house, the survivors said, smashed their boat against the freighter and it capsized.

"They threw rings to us," Mr. Hien said, "but most didn't have the strength to reach them." Four men climbed for safety on ropes lowered from the ship, but one fell to his death when he was near the top. "I climbed with my teeth," said a teen-age boy. By the time the freighter had lowered a lifeboat, there were only 13 left to be saved, two of them young children.

* * *

February 21, 1982

VIETNAM AND SALVADOR—A BATTLE FOR HEARTS AND MINDS

By FLORA LEWIS

WASHINGTON—The words from the scene are chillingly familiar. The President said, "We are losing the fight with the guerrillas in the countryside." The visiting American general said the United States would have to rethink its policy of not allowing American advisers to accompany local troops on combat missions. The Defense Minister told visiting Congressmen that a government victory was not possible without more United States military aid. A non-American diplomat said the government "cannot win without troops from the United States, or someone."

But the country is not Vietnam and the time is not the early 1960's. It is El Salvador and the time is last week. More and more people are asking openly whether El Salvador is going to be another Vietnam. The question itself is important, reflecting popular fears and moods. That is one difference. Nobody asked at the time of the Gulf of Tonkin incident, when President Johnson got a Congressional blank check to intervene in Vietnam, whether he was getting us into another Korea. This time, there is a sense of caution and a deep distrust of what the bureaucrats call "incrementalism," asking for a little more and then a little more, so that it doesn't sound like a dangerous and dubious long-term commitment until suddenly the country finds itself in a full-scale war with no way out but giving up.

That distrust underlies the question. But the comparison means different things to different people. To some, Vietnam is a metaphor for a blind plunge into a no-win morass. Their question is whether expanded United States aid and possibly military involvement in Salvador would defeat the rebels' attempt to win government power.

Some Differences

To others, Vietnam means an immoral and pernicious intervention in another society which shouldn't be undertaken regardless of whether it might succeed or not. And to some, Vietnam means primarily a tremendous drain on resources and young men's lives which frayed America's own social fabric and left painful scars of division at home while projecting the image of the "Ugly American."

Nobody is suggesting Vietnam as a positive analogy, as an inspiring crusade or a noble mission. Ambassador Jeane J. Kirkpatrick came closest to attempting to justify it when she was asked at a conference of American Legion leaders last week whether the United States might be repeating in El Salvador a pattern that had failed in Vietnam. "I don't think we were driven out of Vietnam," she replied. "I think we left." That hardly answered the legionnaire's question, but it does raise the issue of why "we left."

In a report to the Speaker of the House on his visit to El Salvador, Representative John P. Murtha, a Pennsylvania Democrat who was a Marine officer in Vietnam, warned against "deciding these kinds of debates on the emotions of Vietnam."

There are obvious differences in the two situations. El Salvador is in Central America, not a faraway country few Americans ever heard of until they started being sent to fight there. Logistics are much easier. The United States would have fairly short supply lines.

It is a small country, though densely populated, with only five million people. And it is a country, unlike South Vietnam which was only half of a nation supposedly temporarily divided by the 1954 Geneva accords ending the French war. Those accords provided for elections which were to lead to reunification. Saigon refused to implement them and sought to turn the demilitarized zone between North and South into a state border. That added a nationalist factor to the social and political civil war, an issue which doesn't exist in El Salvador.

That difference also means that the insurgents do not have a natural base for sanctuary, resupply and recruitment adjoining, but not inside, the combat zone. At present, the neighboring Governments of Honduras and Guatemala are hostile to them, though these countries would certainly be affected by an expanded war and cannot be considered indefinitely stable.

The nearest regime friendly to the guerrillas is Nicaragua, which has no land border with El Salvador but is not far by sea across the Gulf of Fonseca. Farther away is Cuba and far away is its Soviet ally.

Senior officials insist on another important difference—the nature of the regime and the society. The Salvadoran junta has embarked on land reform and has promised other development efforts. Vietnam did not have the gross inequity in agricultural tenure and oligarchic rule that has characterized Salvador, but it was conquered by Japan in World War II and emerged from colonial rule and occupation a fragmented, fragile and sharply divided society.

In culture and religion, Salvador is homogeneous while Vietnam is a Buddhist country with a large Catholic minority, many feuding sects, and had an important Chinese minority.

But the same United States officials who point to land reform as an important, encouraging distinction between Salvador and the South Vietnam which the United States fought to "save from Communism" offer the same reason for American intervention now. Without using the words, they argue the domino theory. If the insurgents win in Salvador, that will lead to the overthrow of regimes in Guatemala and Honduras, and maybe Costa Rica. That could endanger Panama and spread insurrection in Colombia and Venezuela, and so on through the hemisphere, they say.

In this way, tiny Salvador is portrayed as a crucial bridgehead to vast American strategic interests as Vietnam was said to be the line against the peril of Communist China.

It is true that the United States has far more important strategic interests in Central America than it ever had in Indochina. There is already talk in Washington of the danger that an unfriendly regime in Salvador would mean in case of "resupply needs for Europe." That is officialese for the possibility of a war in Europe which would require huge American military reinforcements and drastically reduce troops and supplies available for continental defense.

But despite the crucial geographic difference, these scenarios advanced by the supporters for expanded military do tend to sound more like than unlike the talk of the Vietnam build-up years.

Challenging the Body Count

Other similarities are more striking. The most glaring is the regime's failure to meet urgent social needs, leaving a desperation that nourishes the call to revolution. Administration officials argue that reform has been launched and that its limited effectiveness has been due to disruption by guerrillas who want to polarize feelings to the extremes of right or left. But other observers doubt the junta's capacity to push peaceful reform.

President Jose Napoleon Duarte is probably a good deal more democratic-minded than any leader South Vietnam produced, but he has not been able to dominate authoritarian elements in the security forces and on the right. President Reagan has certified that the junta made "progress" last year in gaining control of the security forces and reducing what are euphemistically called human rights violations—that is, the murder of noncombatants.

But that view is widely challenged and charges are multiplying that statistics are being faked, as in Vietnam, to justify a political decision. Representative Stephen J. Solarz, Democrat of Brooklyn, notes that the United States Embassy in San Salvador estimates 6,000 noncombatants were killed last year, while the Salvadoran Archbishopric, Amnesty International and several other sources put the total killed at 12,000—an increase, not a decline. Further, Mr. Solarz notes that in terms of total population, 6,000 is a percentage equivalent to more than 270,000 in the United States. As in Vietnam, human devastation in El Salvador is provoking mounting moral outrage in the United States and among friendly countries. While Americans aren't doing the killing, they are increasingly being blamed for not stopping it.

European diplomats and Mr. Solarz say that President Duarte wants to start negotiations for a settlement but that Washington sides with Salvadoran security forces opposed to the idea. A senior American official says privately that while he doesn't expect a military victory over the rebels, he expects it will take another six or seven years before they become convinced they can't win by force of arms and "desirable" conditions for negotiations can emerge.

That assessment is not being made publicly by the Administration because it doubts that American opinion would accept such a long-term commitment. The effect is similar to the gradual revelation of the difficulties of America's engagement in Vietnam, though the difference is that at least some of the decision-makers now appear to know that there is no quick, easy way to achieve their policy goals in El Salvador.

And, as in Vietnam, the United States must confront harsh disputes and infighting in the regime it supports. Last week, the right-wing extremist Roberto d'Aubuisson, who was described as a "pathological killer" by the previous United States Ambassador to El Salvador, was reported as gaining strength in the election campaign. He could emerge as a dominant force in the junta, displacing Washington's favorite, Mr. Duarte. Some leftists may even vote for Mr. d'Aubuisson, the report said, on the grounds that he would drive many thousands of Salvadorans to support the guerrillas against him.

Another similarity is the role of the church. The Salvadoran hierarchy, like leading Vietnamese Buddhist officials during their war, want above all to find ways to end the killing. Therefore it urges a compromise that would inevitably give the rebels a share of government power. Washington is convinced, as it was in Vietnam, that such a compromise would lead to total Communist domination. There are members of Congress who flatly disagree and call for negotiations, but the official view is on the same line the Johnson and Nixon Administrations held toward Vietnam.

Meanwhile, foreign opinion about United States involvement is also developing much as it did during the Vietnam war and perhaps even more strongly, precisely because of the precedent. Canada and Mexico signaled disapproval by refusing the request to send observers to next month's Salvadoran elections.

Whatever the real extent of Soviet-originated aid to the guerrillas, Moscow's propaganda is drawing benefits from America's role in El Salvador. The neutralist movement in Europe is gaining support from people who ask, "What is the difference between Salvador and Poland, or Afghanistan?" and conclude that the two superpowers are equally menacing to peace and other nations' independence.

In the end, the sum of differences and similarities to Vietnam is probably that the chances of military success are higher in Salvador, but the stakes are much greater and the political cost to America would be no less and possibly more because attitudes reflect cumulative condemnations. There is also the unforeseeable risk of widening the war. Pulling out of Vietnam was costly to the United States in many ways, but it is hard to imagine any way that the United States could pull out of Central America if it fails. That is the ultimate difference.

* * *

October 7, 1982

VIETNAM MEMORIAL: QUESTIONS OF ARCHITECTURE; AN APPRAISAL

By PAUL GOLDBERGER

When a plan by Maya Yang Lin, a 21-year-old Yale architecture student, was selected last year as the winner of a nationwide competition to find a design for the Vietnam Veterans Memorial on the Mall near the Lincoln Memorial in Washington, it was hailed by the architectural press with words such as "stunning," "dignified" and "eminently right." The reaction was less enthusiastic from Vietnam veterans themselves, some of whom found the proposed memorial rather more cool and abstract than they would have liked. Nonetheless, Miss Lin's scheme, which is neither a building nor a sculpture but, rather, a pair of 200-foot-long black granite walls that join to form a V and embrace a gently sloping plot of ground between them, was approved rapidly by the Department of the Interior, the Fine Arts Commission and other public agencies that have jurisdiction over what is built in official Washington.

Construction began last March. Next week, however, the Fine Arts Commission will hold a public hearing to consider a revised design for the memorial, despite the fact that by now the granite walls—on which are carved the names of all 57,692 Americans who were killed in Vietnam from 1963 to 1973—are nearly complete. Opposition to the scheme from Vietnam veterans, which was muted when Miss Lin's design was first announced, later grew so intense as to lead to the unusual step of a proposed design change in mid-construction.

Threat to Integrity Seen

The hearing is scheduled for Oct. 13, and the battle lines have already been drawn fairly sharply. On one side, defending the changes, will be the Vietnam Veterans Memorial Fund, the organization that sponsored the architectural competition and had committed itself to building the winning scheme, as well as an advisory committee of Vietnam veterans who were among the more outspoken critics of the original design.

On the other side is not only Miss Lin, the designer, but the American Institute of Architects, which has taken a strong public position in defense of the original design and which sees the move to change the memorial as a threat to the integrity of the system of architectural competitions in general. Robert M. Lawrence, the institute's president, wrote this summer to J. Carter Brown, chairman of the Fine Arts Commission: "What we have here is nothing less than a breach of faith. The effort to compromise the design breaks faith with the designer who won the competition and all those who participated in this competition."

Associated Press

A panel being installed on the Vietnam War Memorial.

What has provoked the heated emotions, however, is less the integrity of architectural competition than the specifics of Miss Lin's design. To many of the Vietnam veterans, her scheme was too abstract to reflect the emotion that the Vietnam War symbolized to them, and too lacking in the symbols of heroism that more conventional monuments contain. They saw in the simple granite walls on which the names of the dead are inscribed not merely a means of honoring the dead, but a way of declaring that the Vietnam War was in some way different from past wars—from wars such as World War II, whose heroism could be symbolized in such a vibrant and active memorial as the Iwo Jima Monument just across the Potomac River, which contains a statue of marines struggling to raise the American flag.

A Statue Is Proposed

The changes in the Vietnam Memorial, therefore, have all been in the direction of making it less of an abstraction, and more realistic. When the Vietnam Veterans Memorial Fund decided some months ago to give in to criticism of the design from Vietnam veterans, it named an advisory committee consisting entirely of Vietnam veterans, in contrast to the jury of internationally known architects and design professionals who had selected Miss Lin's design. That committee selected Frederick Hart, a 38-year-old sculptor who had been a partner in a losing entry in the original competition, and commissioned him to create a realistic sculpture to act as the memorial's new centerpiece.

What Mr. Hart has created is an 8-foot-tall statue of three armed soldiers, one black and two white, which would be placed within the triangular piece of land between Miss Lin's granite walls. The revision of the design also includes a 50-foot-tall flagpole outside the granite walls, and thus it will change the view of the observer who is looking at the memorial in any direction.

Mr. Hart claims that his statue will "preserve and enhance" Miss Lin's design, and will "interact with the wall to form a unified totality." Miss Lin, however, disagrees and in a letter to the Memorial Fund on Sept. 20 she called the changes an "intrusion" that "destroys the meaning of the design."

A Subtle Design

Ironically, it is the very strength of the original design—its ability to be interpreted in a variety of ways—that is making for the current controversy. Miss Lin's original scheme is, in a sense, a tabula rasa, a blank slate—not a room, not a building, not a plaza, not a park, not a conventional memorial at all. It is a place of reflection, where the gradually sloping land, the thousands of carved names on somber granite and the view of the buildings of official Washington in the distance should combine to create an understated, yet powerful, presence.

It is a subtle design, like every great memorial capable of being given different meanings by each of us. The anguish of the Vietnam War is present here, but not in a way that does any dishonor to veterans. To call this memorial a "black gash of shame," as Tom Carhart, a Vietnam veteran who was another losing entrant in the competition, has said, is to miss its point entirely, and to fail to see that this design gives every indication of being a place of extreme dignity that honors the veterans who served in Vietnam with more poignancy, surely, than any ordinary monument ever could.

The Lin design is discreet and quiet, and perhaps this is what bothers its opponents the most. It is certainly what bothers Mr. Carhart, whose own design was described as "a statue of an officer offering a dead soldier heavenward." By commissioning the Hart sculpture and the flagpole, the Vietnam Veteran Memorial Fund seems intent on converting a superb design into something that speaks of heroism and of absolute moral certainty. But there can be no such literalism and no such certainty where Vietnam is concerned; to try to represent a period of anguish and complexity in our history with a simple statue of armed soldiers is to misunderstand all that has happened, and to suggest that no lessons have been learned at all from the experience of Vietnam.

Presence of the Names Speaks

The Vietnam Veterans Memorial, as it now nears completion, could be one of the most important works of contemporary architecture in official Washington—and perhaps the only one that will provide a contemplative space of the equal of any in the past. The insertion of statues and a flagpole not only destroys the abstract beauty of that mystical, inside-outside kind of space that Maya Yang Lin has created; it also tries to shift this memorial away from its focus on the dead, and toward a kind of literal interpretation of heroism and patriotism that ultimately treats the war dead in only the most simplistic of terms.

For in the original design, the dead are remembered as individuals through the moving list of their names carved against the granite. It is the presence of the names, one after the other, that speaks. But if the statues are added, they will overpower the space and change the mood altogether. A symbol of loss, which Miss Lin's design is, will become instead a symbol of war. The names of the dead and the hushed granite wall will become merely a background for something else, and the chance for a very special kind of honor—and for a very special kind of architecture—will be lost.

* * *

November 14, 1982

VIETNAM VETERANS' PARADE A BELATED WELCOME HOME

By PHILIP M. BOFFEY

Special to the New York Times

WASHINGTON, Nov. 13—Thousands of Vietnam veterans marched away from a decade of indifference today and paraded proudly past the White House to a memorial whose history recalls the divisiveness of their war.

Disabled veterans hobbled along with canes, gamely responding to cadence counts; paraplegics wheeled themselves or were pushed; blind veterans listened to reports of what was happening from their friends, and an army of marchers and walkers, dressed in everything from baggy fatigues to camouflage suits to full-dress uniforms or sport jackets, moved slowly along Constitution Avenue, waving tiny American flags and raising their fists in triumph.

It was a catharsis for openly moved spectators and for veterans who have long felt themselves a neglected, discarded army—reviled by some as "baby killers," often scorned by others for failing to win, largely ignored by a public eager to forget an unpopular war.

The camaraderie was almost palpable as veterans embraced in the streets or locked hands in ritual handshakes. After years of self doubt and resentment at public indifference, they were staging their own celebration, a coming-out party given by veterans for veterans.

But it was not the heroes' welcome, the ticker-tape parade with roaring crowds and an outpouring of gratitude, that many veterans openly long for. Long sections of the viewing stand were half empty, and some blocks along the 10-block parade route had but a single broken line of spectators on each side.

The marchers, their number estimated by the organizers at 15,000, counting Vietnam veterans, veterans of other wars, bands, military units and other supporters, were led by, among others, Gen. William C. Westmoreland of the Army, retired, the commander of American forces in Vietnam. Afterward, the general called the march "quite an emotional experience—something I never thought would take place."

The five-day "National Salute to Vietnam Veterans," which culminated in the march to the new memorial, was designed, according to its chief organizer, Jan C. Scruggs, "to stimulate the long overdue national recognition that has largely been denied to those of us who served in our nation's longest war."

But on this raw, blustery morning in the capital, with winds gusting enough to spill coffee out of cups and put goose pimples on the majorettes, there was little indication that any vast segment of the public had rallied to their cause.

The New York Times

The contingent from New York State, one of the largest in the parade, broke up into city delegations. The Rochester group appears above.

Crowd Estimated at 150,000

The National Park Police estimated that perhaps 150,000 people attended some portion of the parade or dedication ceremonies, but if that many were there, they were swallowed up in the expanses of the mall. A District of Columbia policeman commented that the crowd was far smaller than he had been led to expect. And James Weber, of West Haven, Conn., a 27-year-old spectator, lamented that "there should be millions here," not simply a crowd comparable to that at "a pro football game."

Those who did brave the gusts kept up a steady patter of clapping, punctuated by bursts of louder applause and cries of "Thank you, Indiana, thank you," or "Yeah, Iowa," or "God bless you" as the various state delegations passed by.

But every now and then a hint of the old divisions over the war broke forth. James Mahoney, a Navy veteran from Washington, D.C., was brandishing a sign urging "No More Wars, No More Lies, No More Stone Memorials" when an unidentified member of the New Jersey delegation wrenched it from his hands and smashed it. "He said he didn't agree with me," Mr. Mahoney said later.

Another protester, Peter Poccia of New York City, a former medical corpsman in the Marines, joined other antiwar groups at the end of the line of march, carrying his own hand-lettered sign: "We Killed, We Bled, We Died for Worse Than Nothing."

At the end of the parade, marchers and spectators alike continued along Constitution Avenue to dedication ceremonies at the site of the new Vietnam Veterans Memorial, about 200 yards from the Lincoln Memorial, in a corner of the Mall.

Expression of Gratitude

Here the theme was healing and long overdue recognition for a job done without thanks. Helen J. Stuber, national president of the American Gold Star Mothers, whose only son was killed in Vietnam, expressed her gratitude that "after all these years, our country is pausing to honor the Vietnam veterans."

The memorial itself remains an object of dispute. It is essentially a V-shaped wall of polished black marble on which are etched the names of all 58,000 American servicemen who died in the war, arranged chronologically by date of death.

Almost from the start, those who supported the war have complained that the memorial diminishes those it seeks to honor. The V shape, they say, is reminiscent of the peace symbol flashed by antiwar demonstrators. The black color, they say, is too negative. The situation of the marble slabs, in a depression on the Mall, is, they say, offensively inconspicuous, not like the heroic monuments associated with war memorials.

Those conflicts were partially resolved by a recent decision to add a sculpture of three servicemen as well as a flagstaff next year. The statue will be off to one side.

Dissension Among Veterans

And dissension over the memorial continues to run high, even among the veterans. "We want a statue and a flagpole, too, right at the apex of the memorial," said Donald Sherman, a paralyzed veteran who watched the parade from his wheelchair. "The flag is what we fought for, isn't it?"

But John Beam, an Army artillery veteran from Baltimore, carried a sign opposing the additional statuary as a glorification of war that "will stand in silent approval as we march by on our way to the next war."

At the memorial site, Al Keller Jr., national commander of the American Legion, which raised more than $1 million of the $7 million cost of the memorial, sought to heal the still festering wounds.

"There are those who say the war in Vietnam brought shame on America," he said. "There are those who say this memorial would bring shame on those who fought the war. But there is no shame in answering the nation's call. There is no shame in serving with honor and courage in difficult times. And there is no shame in enshrining the names of fallen comrades in immutable stone for generations to recall."

* * *

June 24, 1984

A NEW COLLEGE GENERATION DISCOVERS VIETNAM

By GENE I. MAEROFF

The Vietnam War, largely shunned on America's campuses for almost a decade, is the subject of more and more courses as a new generation of students seeks to learn about a divisive chapter in the nation's history.

Young people who had not yet been born when John F. Kennedy began sending troops to Vietnam are hearing of strange-sounding places like An Loc, Khe Sanh and Bien Hoa and straining to comprehend what happened in that Southeast Asian nation.

"There is enormous interest among the young in learning more about the Vietnam period," said Marilyn Young, who teaches a course on the war at New York University. "These kids were babies when the war was at its height, but they are profoundly curious to discover what upset their country so much."

The courses often portray America's role in the war as a phase in Vietnam's history rather than as an isolated event. Actions in Washington are frequently studied in terms of how the reality of the situation in Southeast Asia jibed with the view of American decision-makers.

New York University is one of a growing number of institutions offering new courses on the Vietnam War. At the University of Massachusetts at Amherst, which already had a course, interest is so strong that Richard Minear, the professor, had to turn away students. And faculty members around the country, eager to start courses, are exchanging information on existing courses so that they can write their own curriculums.

"At practically every regional meeting of Asian historians there is now a session on how to teach the Vietnam War," said Daniel Bays, a history professor at the University of Kansas. "We don't have a course on it yet at Kansas, and we are starting to feel guilty because we feel we should be doing it."

High school and college teachers from throughout the country met in New York City this month to explore how they could help those who wanted to create courses on Vietnam.

When the Asia Society sponsored a curriculum unit on the Vietnam War last year, the guide was distributed to the 17,000 teachers who belong to the National Council for the Social Studies. WGBH, the public television station in Boston, has widely circulated a curriculum guide that it prepared to accompany last fall's series "Vietnam: A Television History."

Interest in Vietnam among students coincides with the emergence of a new body of scholarship, based on interviews and papers that have become available only in recent years. This allows the courses to take cognizance of complexities and nuances that were not apparent in the courses taught during the war and in the highly charged period after South Vietnam's surrender in 1975.

There is no count available on how many courses on the Vietnam War are being offered, but Allan E. Goodman, an associate dean of the School of Foreign Service at Georgetown University, is about to conduct a survey. Experts say the growing interest is the result of several developments.

For one thing, enough time has passed for the topic to be treated more dispassionately. Many high school and college students regard an examination of the Vietnam War as similar to looking at World War II or the Korean War.

Movies Raise Questions

"It is remote from their personal experience and they can deal with it more neutrally than an earlier generation that felt involved in the war," said Robert A. Divine, who includes a section on the Vietnam War in a course on diplomatic history that he teaches at the University of Texas at Austin.

Moreover, young people have questions after seeing such movies as "The Deer Hunter" and "Apocalypse Now" and after watching the recent television series on the war.

Finally, criticism of United States intervention in Central America is provoking interest in comparisons with what occurred in Vietnam.

Some students at N.Y.U., for instance, returned from a demonstration against United States involvement in Central America wondering about the meaning of the slogan on a button that read: "El Salvador is Spanish for Vietnam."

"We remember seeing the Vietnam War on television as children," said Anne V. Mullen of McLean, Va., who took the university's Vietnam course, "and we heard our parents talking about the war. Now, we hear about Central America and we want to understand why people are drawing parallels with Vietnam."

Teaching Approach Varies

The approach of the courses differs from institution to institution, and the focus depends on the professor's academic discipline. Charles F. Keyes, an anthropologist at the University of Washington, includes the Vietnam War in a course on the civilization and culture of Southeast Asia.

At the University of Michigan, Ernest P. Young, a historian in the Center for Chinese Studies, traces the modern era of colonialization, noting that American involvement in Vietnam coincided with the dismantling of colonial empires. He also discusses Vietnam's experience with the French and the Japanese before delving into the era of American involvement.

"What I try to show students," said James Pinckney Harrison of Hunter College of the City University of New York, "is there was nothing wrong with the United States trying to demonstrate that the Communist technique of guerrilla warfare could be defeated, but that Vietnam was the worst possible place to try to do it." Neither the North Vietnamese regime nor

South Vietnam upheld human rights, he said, but there was greater support among the people for the Communists.

Lessons of History

Professor Divine at the University of Texas attempts to show students how the Americans misapplied the lessons of history.

"The L.B.J. generation of foreign policy makers had their view shaped by the events leading to World War II and what they learned was to stand firm and never negotiate," he said, referring to the Johnson Administration. "They learned the lesson so well that they misapplied it in Vietnam. The interesting thing is that now some Americans would misapply the lesson of Vietnam and become isolationists."

The increasing classroom exposure to Vietnam follows a period in which many institutions shied away from such courses.

"There was a time in the middle 1970's when everyone thought they knew all there was to know about the subject," said Professor Young of New York University.

Furthermore, according to some authorities, the outcome of the war left some people uneasy with the idea of teaching about it.

"We lost the war and a lot of the courses that existed were discontinued," said Jane Werner, a research associate at Columbia University who taught a course on the war at the University of Arizona. "The aftermath of the war was troubling to the nation and there was a period of silence."

Revival of Interest

Professor Harrison of Hunter College, who has been teaching about the war since 1973, said that interest dropped in the late 1970's but that now he saw "increased desire" to learn about Vietnam. Professor Harrison teaches about American involvement in the context of the long string of wars and revolutions in Asia. His work in the course contributed to his book, "The Endless War: Vietnam's Struggle for Independence," now being used on many campuses.

The war can now be taught as history rather than as a current event, lessening the potential for controversy and muting passion.

Alexander B. Woodside began teaching about the war at Harvard University in the late 1960's, while the military battles were raging in Vietnam and peace protests were spreading in the United States. Now he teaches it as history in a course at the University of British Columbia.

"At Harvard I was talking about the inevitability of the Communist victory," Professor Woodside recalled, "and now I find myself discussing the losing side and trying to pretend that the outcome of the war was not preordained."

Role of Antiwar Activists

Some of the instructors teaching the courses say their interest stems, in part, from experience as antiwar activists.

"I suppose it is a way for us older people who lived through it to work out our feelings," said Andrea McElderry of the University of Louisville. "It lets me get objective about a situation that was a moral stance to me at the time."

Professor McElderry, an Asian historian, teaches about the war with Richard Pfeiffer, an American historian. At the time of the war, she was a doctoral student at the University of Michigan, where she joined protests against the war, while he was in combat in Vietnam.

An unusual twist is that Vietnamese refugees are enrolled in the courses on some campuses. At the University of Washington, for instance, almost a dozen former "boat people" who fled South Vietnam sat side by side this year with Americans in a course on Vietnam.

After the students saw a film portraying the most egregious effects of American influence on Saigon, which was depicted as a city filled during the war with prostitutes, orphans and shoeshine boys, the immigrants complained that the film, "The Sad Song of Yellow Skin," did not show the Saigon that they knew.

More Documents Available

Another effect of the passage of time is that there is now a wealth of documents available on American involvement in Vietnam that have been made public by the Freedom of Information Act. Thus, some courses are rich in original source material, an unusual experience for students accustomed to the synthesis of the textbook approach.

For example, "Presidential Decision Making in the Vietnam War," a course offered at the University of California at Davis for the first time last year, provided students with access to the 15,000 pages of photo copies of documents that Larry Berman, the professor, has accumulated for his own writing.

What seemed to make the various courses more popular this year was the 13-part series on public television.

"It was a great leap forward for those who wanted to teach about Vietnam because it brought the war to life for many of the students," said John Israel, a professor at the University of Virginia, who incorporated what was aired on television into the readings and lectures of his course, "Vietnam's American Interlude."

However the courses are taught, it is clear that the attitudes of today's students and the atmosphere in the classrooms are different from what prevailed when young people felt more personally involved.

Among those enrolled in the course this year at the University of Michigan, a center of protest during the war, were several cadets in the Reserve Officers Training Corps, who sometimes wore their uniforms to class. Fifteen years ago, activists regarded R.O.T.C. units as symbols of American involvement in Vietnam and were trying to drive them off campuses.

* * *

September 12, 1984

MORE VIETNAMESE TO GET PERMISSION TO ENTER THE U.S.

By BERNARD GWERTZMAN
Special to the New York Times

WASHINGTON, Sept. 11—Secretary of State George P. Shultz announced today that the United States was ready to admit the thousands of Vietnamese children fathered by Americans as well as 10,000 former and current Vietnamese political prisoners from "re-education" camps.

He appealed to Hanoi to live up to a promise to let them go.

Vietnam's Prime Minister, Pham Van Dong, said in May that Hanoi would be willing to send all the so-called Amerasian children as well as the inmates of the "re-education" camps to the United States. He said there were 15,000 such children. Many of them are ostracized in Vietnamese society because of their skin color. Vietnamese officials have said there were about 10,000 prisoners in the "re-education" camps.

'Two New Initiatives'

State Department officials said they believed the total number of children fathered by Americans before 1975, when South Vietnam was captured by the Communists, was closer to 8,000. Most of them live with their Vietnamese mothers and Vietnamese siblings. The State Department says it believes the number of current prisoners may be anywhere from 6,000 to 15,000. Mr. Shultz made the announcement in separate testimony to Senate and House judiciary subcommittees on refugees. He said he wanted to announce "two new initiatives" approved by President Reagan.

The first, he said, is that "the United States will accept for admission all Asian-American children and their qualifying family members now in Vietnam." He said he hoped they could be brought into the United States over a three-year period.

'Undisputed Ties to Our Country'

"Because of their undisputed ties to our country," he said, "these children and family members are of particular humanitarian concern to the United States."

The second initiative, Mr. Shultz said, is "for the resettlement of political prisoners currently and previously confined in the 're-education camp' prisons in Vietnam and their qualifying family members." He said he hoped that 10,000 such prisoners and their families could be resettled in the United States over a two-year period.

Because many of those prisoners were former South Vietnamese military and civilian officials with close ties to the United States they "are of particular humanitarian concern to the United States," he said.

"Success in both of these initiatives will require the good will and cooperation of the Vietnamese Government," Mr. Shultz said. "We hope the Vietnamese will now respond to these new appeals."

A delegation headed by Robert L. Funseth, the senior deputy assistant secretary for refugees in the State Department, will go to Geneva early next month for a meeting with Vietnamese officials in connection with an annual executive board session of the United Nations High Commissioner for Refugees. Mr. Shultz said the matter would be raised with the Vietnamese there.

The Administration had been pressed by many members of Congress and by voluntary agencies to be more outspoken in support of allowing Amerasian children and political prisoners into this country. The initial reaction to Mr. Shultz's presentation today was positive.

Roger P. Winter, director of the United States Committee for Refugees, said, "We are very pleased that the Administration at the highest levels has made this commitment."

Some Concerns Are Raised

He added, however, that it was "critical" that there be "vigorous discussions" with the Vietnamese soon, and that bureaucratic obstacles not be put in the way. The judiciary subcommittees also praised the program.

There was concern, however, voiced by some groups. Albert P. Blaustein, chairman of the Human Rights Advocates International, which has been arguing that the Amerasian children are American citizens and should be allowed immediate entry to the United States, said, "We do not approve of the position taken by the State Department because the department position is to treat the children as if they were refugees and to handle them through refugee procedures."

He also was critical of Mr. Shultz's plan to bring them into this country over a three-year period, which he said was too long, and "would rob them of the chance to be children."

Since 1975, 700,000 Vietnamese have been resettled in the United States, about half of the worldwide total of 1.3 million. Most of those had escaped by boat to other countries, such as Thailand, and were later admitted to the United States.

In recent years, Vietnam has agreed to a United Nations-sponsored system known as the Orderly Departure Program, by which some 10,000 Vietnamese a year have been coming to the United States legally. Of that number, about 3,000 Amerasian children and their families have been admitted to this country.

Mr. Shultz said the United States hoped to use the departure program for securing the release of the rest of the children and the political prisoners.

70,000 Refugees a Year

Over all, he said, the United States would admit 70,000 refugees worldwide in the fiscal year beginning Oct. 1, of which 50,000 would be from East Asia. This was approximately the number admitted in the current fiscal year. Of the 50,000 total, 10,000 a year are reserved for those in the Orderly Departure Program, but Mr. Shultz indicated that number could be increased if the Vietnamese allow large numbers of children and prisoners to depart.

Some voluntary agency officials expressed concern that Mr. Shultz had not been more forthcoming in saying there was no limit on admission if the Vietnamese would open their doors to let the children and prisoners out.

* * *

December 3, 1984

ARGUMENTS OF WESTMORELAND TRIAL RESEMBLE SOME KEY DISPUTES IN 1960'S

By CHARLES MOHR

The key, and disputed, arguments in Gen. William C. Westmoreland's libel suit against CBS, in which the general may finish testifying today, bear a strong resemblance to some of the key disputes among American officials in the 1960's about how the Vietnam War could best be prosecuted. While those arguments are not easy to summarize briefly, one school of thought seemed to believe the war could be won by killing people and another school believed it would be more useful to influence people—as well as killing some of the most intractable enemy.

The evidence in the general's $120 million suit against the network, arising from a 1982 documentary titled "The Uncounted Enemy: A Vietnam Deception," is in less dispute than the arguments. General Westmoreland and witnesses friendly to him do not deny that when information came to light in 1967 that the numbers of Communist homeguard, hamlet militia had been seriously underestimated, these groups were excluded from a military accounting system of enemy strength that had previously included them.

The CBS documentary called this a "deception," of President Johnson and other superiors, and the retired general says such language defamed him.

Counting Enemy Strength

General Westmoreland has contended during a week of testimony that he had little choice but to change the method of counting enemy strength. He argues that excluding the "self-defense and secret self-defense" Communist units from the order of battle, which the military accounting system is officially called, made it more meaningful and honest. He also says that to permit a raw addition of the new numbers to the order of battle would mislead and alarm the American press and public with an impression that enemy strength was increasing after he had indicated it was slowly beginning to level off and decrease.

The CBS broadcast and the mountain of declassified documents obtained by attorneys show that some of General Westmoreland's professional intelligence officers, as well as some Central Intelligence Agency analysts, believed that the self-defense forces and local Communist political structure were an "integral" part of the enemy strength and should be counted and included in the order of battle.

There is a parallel between all this and debates two decades ago about the conduct of the war.

Back then General Westmoreland preferred to employ United States troops mainly in a battle of attrition against "main force" North Vietnamese Army units and high quality Vietcong guerrillas, leaving so-called pacification of the population and countryside primarily to South Vietnamese units and American officials passionately interested in the inexact art of counterinsurgency warfare.

Control of the Hamlets

Such officials, exemplified by John Paul Vann, perhaps the most admired of the counterinsurgency thinkers, believed that to dry up the sea in which the hardcore guerrillas swam it was necessary to regain control of South Vietnam's hamlets, and that to do so the local Vietcong organization had to be converted, eliminated or rendered harmless. Maj. Gen. Nguyen Duc Thang, the Vietnamese pacification chief, strongly agreed.

General Westmoreland has testified that he paid no attention to intelligence about the self-defense forces as long as the estimated total was a "static" number, but decided to purge them from the order of battle when the estimates sharply increased.

"We are not fighting those people; they are basically civilians," the general testified, adding they were "very inconsequential," poorly armed and had "practically no military capability of consequence."

The general's experience of four-and-one-half years in the war makes him a powerful witness. However, not everyone agreed with his analysis then.

In a then secret message in 1967, Mr. Westmoreland's military chief of staff, Maj. Gen. Walter T. Kerwin Jr., told troop commanders: "Mines and booby traps continue to cause a significant portion of our friendly casualties. In 1966 approximately one-third of friendly casualties were caused by this means and it appears that this casualty level will continue for 1967." The main body of General Kerwin's message instructed units on procedures to reduce the number of "dud" American artillery shells and bombs. Various kinds of Vietcong units showed great ingenuity in converting such duds, and captured hand grenades, into booby traps.

Casualties Laid to Civilians

No one in the 1960's would have contended that all such booby traps were prepared and laid by hamlet irregulars. However, many American officials and soldiers believed that many were.

Frustration about the difficulty of distinguishing between harmless and hostile civilians played a major role in the war. The March 1968 massacre of civilians by a unit of the Americal Division at the hamlet of My Lai was attributed, in part, by some participants to anger that casualties from booby traps and sniping mounted for months while American soldiers seldom saw an actual enemy soldier.

That the political and irregular militia units were deemed by some officials to have some value was shown by the devotion of substantial assets in manpower and money to the

"Phoenix" program meant to neutralize them by covert actions in contested or Vietcong hamlets.

On the other hand, it is equally true that some officers and officials in the 1960's tended to agree with the view expressed this month in court by witnesses for the plaintiff. The United States Marines, who predominated militarily in the northernmost portion of South Vietnam, initiated a program of "combined action platoons," in which small combined units of Marines and Vietnamese troops sought to pacify rural hamlets, with as little violence as possible.

In general, United States Army officers did not regard the Marine approach as useful or sound, and the Marines were eventually discouraged from pursuing the course.

Mr. Vann and General Thang tried to encourage government hamlet chiefs to sleep in their own hamlets because many preferred the security of small military outposts. To those who occasionally accompanied the officials on such hamlet sleepouts, the experience could be mentally and physically harrowing. Vietcong militia sometimes had to share guns, but they had guns.

Restraints on Westmoreland

Another interesting aspect of the nine-week libel trial—which may continue into February—is that it recalls and, in some cases, illuminates historical features of the war.

One of these is what officials, who operated behind a somewhat opaque and rosy screen, themselves believed they were accomplishing or could reasonably expect to accomplish. Another is the restraints under which General Westmoreland had to operate, but which in some cases he seems to have willingly accepted.

The general testified that in April 1967 he told President Johnson and other high civil officials that he wanted more troops on the principle of "reinforcing success." He took to Washington with him two proposals. One called the "optimum" force augmentation called for 200,000 more troops. The second, described as a "minimum essential force," called for 100,000 reinforcements.

General Westmoreland's testimony is that he told the policy makers that with the larger force he could bring the war to "some kind of conclusion"—defined as forcing Hanoi to negotiate peace—in three years, and the smaller one would prolong the war for five years. Whether much of Congress or the public contemplated that much prolongation of combat as likely is open to debate.

'Essential Minimum Force'

Later in Saigon, the general said, he suggested to Secretary of Defense Robert S. McNamara a more politically palatable "modified, essential minimum force," which would provide 80,000 more troops. General Westmoreland said he believed that by hiring Vietnamese civilians to do logistic chores and adding combat units to existing formations he could get the same fighting power with "less overhead."

Mr. McNamara accepted the proposal, apparently with great relief.

"Mr. McNamara came from American business," the general testified, "and he was very statistically oriented. He was very anxious to fight this war as efficiently as possible. I have heard him say he wanted to end the war without having great stockpiles of material as we had in World War II."

But, having testified frequently about the progress he believed had been made by 1967 and that he anticipated in future years, General Westmoreland told the jury that the North Vietnamese "always" had the capability of reinforcing their forces in the South, "and the President certainly knew that."

Such lengthy testimony has, therefore, left at least some ambiguity as to when, if ever, officials believed the war could be ended successfully and how best to reach that goal. The present trial will decide the libel question, but is no more likely to settle these questions than did the spirited arguments of the 1960's.

* * *

February 19, 1985

A JOINT STATEMENT ENDS LIBEL ACTION BY WESTMORELAND

By M. A. FARBER

Gen. William C. Westmoreland and CBS ended their libel suit yesterday with a joint statement that expressed the network's respect for the general's "long and faithful service to his country" and the general's esteem for CBS's "distinguished journalistic tradition."

In the two-page statement, the network said it "never intended to assert, and does not believe, that General Westmoreland was unpatriotic or disloyal in performing his duties as he saw them" as commander of United States forces in Vietnam from 1964 to 1968.

In its own separate statement, CBS said it stood by the fairness and accuracy of the 1982 documentary that prompted the general's $120 million libel action.

CBS officials said the program had not accused the general of being disloyal or unpatriotic. Rather, it said, the broadcast presented "charges that General Westmoreland and his command misled the public, the Congress and the President about enemy troop strength to advance the political argument that the war was being won."

General Claims Victory

The general immediately claimed victory in the three-year-old legal battle over the CBS Reports documentary that accused his command of engaging in a "conspiracy" to understate enemy capability in 1967.

"I got all I wanted," he declared at a news conference, saying the statement amounted to an "apology" by CBS. The 70-year-old retired general said he had brought the suit "to defend my honor" and could now go home to South Carolina and "try to fade away."

Minutes later, at their own news conference, CBS officials denied that the statement constituted an apology.

No Monetary Award

"Our purpose here," said Van Gordon Sauter, the executive vice president of the CBS broadcast group, "is not to calibrate who won and who lost."

What was important, he said, was that General Westmoreland had dropped his libel action "without any monetary award or retraction" and that CBS retained complete faith in the broadcast. "I personally do not view that statement as an apology," Mr. Sauter said.

Mr. Sauter said the documentary—"The Uncounted Enemy: A Vietnam Deception"—had been "subjected to perhaps the most intensive scrutiny ever brought to bear on a journalistic effort" and had been "vindicated." He called the suit the most serious of its kind in the history of television.

The suit brought by General Westmoreland attracted national attention by raising questions about the ethics and practices of television journalism, by casting doubt on the integrity and credibility of military intelligence in wartime, and by challenging the First Amendment rights of the press.

The accord that signaled a conclusion to the suit after 18 weeks of testimony in Federal District Court in Manhattan was announced late Sunday. It was filed yesterday with Judge Pierre N. Leval, who was expected to ratify it this morning and dismiss the jury.

Richard Benveniste, the foreman of the jury, said yesterday he was "still stunned" by the settlement. "We went so long to come to an end like this. I'd have liked to have gone the whole route."

Jurors Told Not to Discuss Case

Mr. Benveniste, a 34-year-old commercial casualty underwriter, said, "A lot of people will think we spent five months for nothing. But I don't look at it that way. The two sides decided what was best, and our decisions at this moment are really insignificant."

Mr. Benveniste declined to discuss his opinions of the case, saying Judge Leval's office had told jurors to withhold comment until tomorrow.

But one juror, who asked not to be identified, said his "gut opinion"—formed on the basis of "little comments I heard around the jury room"—was that the jury was "leaning toward CBS more than 50 percent."

"Not everyone in there was sold on either side," he said. "It would have been a long deliberation. We would have had to really dig into it."

The juror's remarks indicated that, in a case where the outlines of much of the testimony had been known for months if not years, the aplomb of the lawyers and the manner of their witnesses—the "chemistry" in the courtroom—were important determinants of jury reaction.

CBS Lawyer Impressed Juror

David Boies, the chief lawyer for CBS, "was an excellent lawyer," the juror said. "You could see the difference between him and the plaintiff's side. He had more professionalism, more experience. That might have had an effect on some of the jurors. Boies's charm was a selling point."

But the juror said that several of the witnesses for General Westmoreland were "too cocky."

In this regard, he particularly singled out Robert W. Komer, the former chief of the pacification program in Vietnam, whom both Dan M. Burt, General Westmoreland's principal lawyer, and Mr. Boies had considered one of the strongest witnesses for General Westmoreland.

Particularly impressive, the juror said, was Robert S. McNamara, the former Secretary of Defense, who testified for General Westmoreland.

The juror said that Maj. Gen. Joseph A. McChristian and Col. Gains Hawkins, both of whom were key witnesses for CBS in recent weeks, were "maybe more convincingly believable" than many others who took the stand.

Positions 'Placed Before Public'

In their joint statement, CBS and General Westmoreland said they believed their positions had "been effectively placed before the public for its consideration and that continuing the legal process at this stage would serve no further purpose."

Historians, they said, "will long consider this and other matters related to the war in Vietnam. Both parties trust their actions have broadened the public record."

The documentary charged that, for political and public relations reasons, General Westmoreland's command had deliberately distorted the true size and nature of the North Vietnamese and Vietcong forces in South Vietnam in the months before the Tet offensive of January 1968. As a result of this "conscious effort," it said, President Johnson and American troops, as well as the public, were left "totally unprepared" for the offensive.

The broadcast specifically accused General Westmoreland of imposing an "arbitrary ceiling" of 300,000 troops on reports of enemy strength, and said his senior aides had "systematically blocked" reports by junior officers of a substantially greater North Vietnamese infiltration than was made known.

A Claim of Libel

General Westmoreland denied that he had acted improperly, and claimed that the program libeled him by saying he had deceived the President.

The defendants, in addition to CBS, were George Crile, the producer of the documentary; Mike Wallace, its narrator; and Samuel A. Adams, a former C.I.A. analyst who served as a paid consultant for the program.

Mr. Sauter, who said that CBS could not allow itself to be "intimidated by those seeking to constrain free inquiry," said the network regretted that General Westmoreland "and his supporters felt compelled to bring this suit. We feel now, as we did three years ago, that this issue should never have been brought to court."

In reply to questions, Mr. Sauter said CBS felt "no chilling effect" from the suit and that the public had "an unnecessary apprehension of the media."

At General Westmoreland's news conference at the Harley Hotel, the general and Mr. Burt read aloud three times the passage of the joint statement about the general's loyalty.

Foundation Financed Lawsuit

"If that statement had been made after the CBS program was aired," the general said, "it would have satisfied me." Indeed, he said, had that statement been issued at any time since the broadcast on January 23, 1982, "it would have ended the episode."

Mr. Burt—whose conservative Capital Legal Foundation has financed the suit at a cost of more than $3 million—said that General Westmoreland brought the action only "to clear his name and that, in my heart, is what I believe has been done.

"Many said the dispute didn't belong in court," Mr. Burt added. "But there was no alternative. And now this case has ended, as it began, in an unexpected fashion."

Mr. Burt said that he had discussed possible settlements with CBS lawyers ever since the suit was filed in September 1982. Some of the approaches—such as those last week—were made by him, he said; others by lawyers for the network. But only now, he said, was CBS prepared to join in a statement affirming the patriotism of his client.

Prior Settlement Bid Failed

"All I can tell you," he said, "is that what I never could get, I got. It was the equivalent of an apology. That's how I see it; others may see it differently."

Until last week, the only confirmed efforts to settle the dispute had occurred in 1982, nearly a half-year after the 90-minute broadcast.

In July 1982, soon after a CBS internal investigation of the documentary, Mr. Sauter, then president of CBS News, proposed a 45-minute follow-up program, with another 15 minutes for the general to state his views.

General Westmoreland, however, demanded a published apology, a "full retraction" on the air that met his approval and "was not less than 45 minutes in duration," and some payment. The general also sought access to the CBS internal investigation.

The talks collapsed, and four days later General Westmoreland filed suit.

No Loss of Confidence

Yesterday, Mr. Burt denied that his recent overtures to CBS were based on the continued high costs of the litigation, pressures from financial backers, a loss of confidence by General Westmoreland or a belief that he was losing the case.

"We felt just as good as in the beginning and all along," he said. "We felt our cross-examinations were going nicely. But you have to keep an eye on what you came for. Many civil suits are settled out of court."

General Westmoreland said he had "not lost faith" in Mr. Burt over the course of the trial, which was scheduled to go the jury next week.

At the CBS news conference, Mr. Boies insisted that until last week Mr. Burt had demanded "money or an apology or both" and that was what had blocked a settlement.

"When a plaintiff wants to drop a lawsuit without any money or apology," he said with a smile, "I think you ought to let him."

'I'll Let It Speak for Itself'

Just as Mr. Burt had declined to speculate on CBS's willingness to settle at this time, Mr. Boies refused to speak for Mr. Burt. "You'll have to ask him," he said.

Mr. Boies refused to accept a characterization of the accord as a "total victory" for CBS. "I'll let it speak for itself," he said.

Mr. Boies said that CBS had never questioned General Westmoreland's good motives for the actions portrayed on the broadcast.

"That's something I've been saying for a long time, and it is undoubtedly true," he said. "I said it in my opening statement to the jury, so if that's all Mr. Burt wanted, he had it then."

In his opening statement last October, Mr. Boies said, "One can conceive of a situation in which one genuinely believes we ought to be in that war, we ought to continue to escalate and continue to add more troops and the only way to do this is to convince people we are winning, convince people there is light at the end of the tunnel."

* * *

March 31, 1985

WHAT AMERICANS THINK NOW

By ADAM CLYMER

Ten years after the end of the Vietnam War, the lessons it once seemed to teach about placing restraints on the use of power are losing effect. Americans are increasingly prepared to use troops, whether in El Salvador or in Europe, and are about equally divided on employing the Central Intelligence Agency to overthrow unfriendly governments, a New York Times Poll shows.

The war itself is even less popular today than when Saigon fell, but the poll of 1,533 adults last month showed that its legacy of distrust of government and the military is wearing away. The unquestioning faith of the early 1960's has not returned, but there is a trend of steadily growing trust—highest among college-age youths, 59 percent of whom said Washington could be trusted to do the right thing all or most of the time. Among everyone else, only 45 percent thought so.

Those same 18- to 22-year-olds were also among the most likely to share President Reagan's endorsement of the Vietnam War as a "noble cause," and to believe it "taught us that military leaders should be able to fight wars without civilian leaders tying their hands."

Taken together, these findings strongly suggest that restraints on the use of power will grow even weaker as the confident post-Vietnam generation gains political importance. That growing trust is critical: a general faith in government helps overcome doubt on specifics, especially in foreign affairs.

Still, there is no blank check for adventurism, in general or in specific situations, such as the invasion of Grenada. The 47 percent who trusted Washington all or most of the time is notably more than the 35 percent found by the Institute for Social Research at the University of Michigan in 1974, when the war, racial troubles and Watergate had combined to flatten traditional faith, but it is much less than the 76 percent in 1964. Grenada is more intriguing. When those interviewed, by telephone from Feb. 23 through 27, were asked to rate Washington's handling of recent foreign-policy situations on a scale of 1 to 10, Grenada got an average rating of 5.66. But another kind of activism, the Camp David Middle East negotiations of the Carter years, did even better, at 6.45.

However far this trend ultimately goes, the mood now clearly differs from that of the mid-1970's. To test changes in attitude, last month's Times Poll repeated many of the questions employed in a national poll the Chicago Council on Foreign Relations conducted in November 1974.

When asked if United States troops should be used in a list of crises, support was higher in 1985 in every case. The biggest change occurred when respondents were asked about an invasion of Western Europe. In 1974, 40 percent favored using troops and 40 percent did not; this time, 54 percent were in favor and 32 percent opposed. The 18-to-29 group, presumably the fighters, now divide 55 to 37 percent in favor. In 1974, they split evenly. (Past Times polling, however, suggests that draft-age youth may become less enthusiastic if war seems less hypothetical.)

Support for using United States troops in El Salvador, if all else failed to stop Communism, was not an issue in 1974. So when last month's poll found 47 percent supporting their use and 43 percent opposed, the best measuring point was a June 1983 Times/CBS News Poll that showed 32 percent in favor and 57 percent opposed.

One step short of committing troops is deploying the C.I.A., and last month's poll found that 44 percent approved the C.I.A.'s working "secretly inside other countries to try to weaken or overthrow governments unfriendly to the United States." Although 46 percent disapproved, the difference is statistically insignificant, within the poll's margin of sampling error of plus or minus 3 percentage points.

As for the Vietnam generation itself, those now aged 30 through 38, the sense of alienation remains strong. Where 55 percent of the public, and just 48 percent of those 18 to 29, say "the government is pretty much run by a few big interests," and not for the benefit of all, 61 percent of the Vietnam generation say that. On many questions, the theme seemed to be, "Don't trust anyone, if you're over 30."

This 30-to-38 group, despite its dovish reputation, is also the most hawkish. More than anyone younger or older, they support using troops in Western Europe and are convinced that the Soviet Union is a real and constantly growing threat to the United States. They are also quite favorable to using the C.I.A. to undermine unfriendly governments.

But the Vietnam generation did not get there through any revisionist views of the war itself. Only 20 percent of its members now feel the United States "did the right thing in getting into the fighting in Vietnam," while 73 percent say it should have stayed out. As a whole, the public responded almost identically, with 19 percent saying the United States' role was right and 73 percent disagreeing. In 1972, as both war and protest wound down, the Michigan poll found 29 percent agreeing and 57 percent disagreeing.

The Vietnam experience is deeply contradictory. For example, many people say the war was immoral but still believe it taught us that we must sometimes back unwholesome governments because Communist regimes are worse. One indisputable lesson is how little many in the United States know, or are willing to remember, of the searing Vietnam War. In the latest poll, just three Americans in five could say the United States sided with South Vietnam.

Adam Clymer, an assistant to the executive editor, is in charge of polling at The Times.

* * *

March 31, 1985

THE WAR AND THE ARTS

By SAMUEL G. FREEDMAN

Early in the film "Uncommon Valor," the father of an American soldier who is missing in action, years after the Vietnam War, goes in search of his son's Marine buddies. One by one, the father enlists them to join him on a mission to Indochina to find and free his son. "There's a lot of unfinished business," he tells them. "Over there." That brief moment reveals a great deal about the way the Vietnam War is affecting the popular culture and fine art of America today. "Uncommon Valor" represents the vanguard of art that declares America was right in Vietnam, that replaces recrimination with congratulation. And the film's image of returning to the Vietnam War attests to a national obsession that goes beyond history and politics: a need to complete the "unfinished business" of Vietnam, to make individual sense of it.

That compulsion, coming after years of avoidance, has taken the form of an outpouring of paintings, poems, songs, plays, films, novels, sculptures and television shows about the war. Much of the recent work has been created by veterans, and virtually all of it concerns them. Americans devour it all, hungry in part for a genuine reconciliation and in part for a feel-good to dispel the self-doubt of the 1960's.

The depictions of the war and its domestic aftermath range from the imposing Vietnam Veterans Memorial to the intimate poetry of Michael Casey, from the high art of Lanford Wilson's play "Fifth of July" to the mass appeal of television's "The A-Team." Vietnam literature now numbers several hundred volumes. An exhibit of art by Vietnam War veterans, titled "Vietnam: Reflexes and Reflections," has been touring the country since 1981. "Tracers," a drama about the war written and performed by a troupe of veterans, has played to sold-out houses and critical acclaim in Los Angeles, Chicago and New York. In the guise of Tom Selleck on television's "Magnum, P.I." and Chuck Norris in two "Missing in Action" films, the Vietnam veteran is a hero, a hunk.

For creative artists as well as purveyors of pulp, war has always provided the essential ingredients of human drama—life and death, bravery and cowardice, loyalty and betrayal. "War is the best subject of all," Ernest Hemingway once wrote. "It groups the maximum of material and speeds up the action and brings out all sorts of stuff that normally you have to wait a lifetime to get."

To the usual chemistry of combat, the Vietnam War added even more volatile elements. Vietnam was America's ideological civil war, pitting hawk against dove, hard hat against peacenik. Patriotism gave way to revulsion, to a questioning of the national character. And most important for the men who fought the war—as it seems to be for the country—Vietnam had no clear ending, neither victory nor surrender. Their art is a search for that final, missing piece.

"For anyone who's been through an extremely traumatic experience," says W. D. Ehrhart, a Vietnam veteran and a poet, "there's a driving need to explore it, to understand it. There is a turmoil inside. Those of us who could, articulated it with writing, painting, whatever. The veterans who had trouble with drugs, who had bad marriages, who couldn't cope, were part of the same thing. People like me were lucky to have a constructive way to channel that energy. My own experience is no longer inconclusive. The national experience is still unresolved, but, personally, I've closed the circle."

From the veterans has come a view of the war dramatically different from the one propounded by the antiwar artists of the 1960's and early 70's. The new vision can be measured in the distance from "M*A*S*H" to "Magnum, P.I." on television, from "Who'll Stop the Rain?" to "The Deer Hunter" on film, from "Alice's Restaurant" to "Still in Saigon" in song, from Leon Golub to Roger Brown in art.

Some of the art and popular culture that subscribe to a conservative view of the war—"Uncommon Valor," for instance—argue outright that American intervention in Vietnam was moral and justified. John M. Del Vecchio's novel, "The 13th Valley," recalls World War II literature in its description of American valor and victory on the battlefield. Although Brown's paintings do not directly address the Vietnam War, they mock the kind of left-wing national-liberation movement that the United States fought there. The title of one piece accuses Latin American intellectuals of directing "their Marxist terrorist movements from safe quarters in Mexico City and Columbia (sic) while their Indian peasant recruits do the fighting and dying. . . ." The visual images in many of the latest Vietnam War films recall television newscasts during the war—tortured captives, crippled children, weeping widows. But now these people are shown as the victims of Communist despots, not American imperialists. This is true even of a politically liberal film like "The Killing Fields." While implying that American bombing contributed to the ferocity of the Khmer Rouge, the film is unsparing in showing the Khmer Rouge's genocide in Cambodia.

More common than a political or polemical outlook, however, is the calculatedly apolitical one. Rather than raise the still-divisive issue of American intervention in Vietnam—was it right or wrong—much of the current art and popular culture concentrate on the experience of the American soldier, both in the field and back at home. The war criminal of the 1960's is the hero of the 1980's. At the most extreme (the karate-chopping movie star Chuck Norris, for instance), he is the gung-ho hero Vietnam has lacked since "The Green Berets" and Sergeant Fury comic books.

The veterans on the television shows "Magnum, P.I." and "The A-Team," who use the teamwork and guile they acquired in Vietnam to fight crime in America, typify a second, more moderate approach. The most frequent image of all is the survivor-as-hero, the soldier who fought under insane conditions in Vietnam and then rebuilt his life in an ungrateful America. The simplicity of that stereotype accounts, no doubt, for much of its appeal. The survivor-hero may be a far cry from Audie Murphy or Sergeant York, but he is far more palatable to the public than the heroin-shooting, shotgun-slinging, suicidal veteran of the first wave of post-Vietnam War culture—which itself followed the "war criminal" caricature of soldiers during the antiwar movement. If anything, the current image of the Vietnam veteran facing a ferocious enemy on behalf of a Government he distrusts adds to his fictive stature. "It strengthens the hero image," says Alan Brinkley, an associate professor of history at Harvard who specializes in 20th-century American history. "He's someone who's been through the fire and come out stronger, someone who's been tested by failure, someone who's been betrayed—either by his leaders for not being allowed to fight without restraints or, more moderately, by his country for being sent at all. That's a theme in a lot of the literature." Veneration of the veteran is the lowest common denominator in the cultural equation; it has become the point of consensus for Americans—and artists—who widely disagree on almost anything else concerning the Vietnam War. This helps explain the phenomenon of Bruce Springsteen's song "Born in the U.S.A." The song tells a story that was inspired in part, Springsteen has said, by the death in Vietnam of the drummer in his first band. A small-town boy goes to fight in Vietnam. His brother, who had fallen in love with a Vietnamese woman, is killed at Khe Sanh. The surviving brother returns to the United States and cannot find a job. He turns to the Veterans Administration for help and gets excuses. "Nowhere to run," Springsteen concludes, "ain't got nowhere to go." Yet when he breaks into the song in concert, his audiences break out American flags.

Ron Kovic, the disabled Vietnam veteran who wrote the autobiography "Born on the Fourth of July," may have explained that seeming contradiction when he recently told Rolling Stone magazine: "One thing that Bruce's music teaches us is that even with all the things that happened in that war, with all the suffering, we can still love America. We can love it for the good things, not the bad."

Consider another paradox. A 1980 Veterans Administration poll asked Vietnam veterans which feature films portrayed them most favorably. The highest ratings went to John Wayne's "The Green Berets" and to "Coming Home"—which starred Jane Fonda, an actress who personified American sympathy for North Vietnam during the war. But the popularity of these two apparently incompatible films makes sense; both celebrate heroism. "The Green Berets" offers victory in combat. "Coming Home" offers victory at home, as a paraplegic veteran overcomes his handicap to build an independent life and win the love of a beautiful woman. For all the political differences in the two films, the veteran in "Coming Home" could well have been a soldier in "The Green Berets."

"At first, Vietnam frustrated America because we had no Iwo Jima, no Patton, no MacArthur," says John Milius, who co-wrote "Apocalypse Now" and produced "Uncommon Valor," but never served in Vietnam because of a medical deferment. "There were acts of heroism every day, but there was no hero. But now the country wants to embrace the character of the Vietnam veteran. I predict that the Vietnam veteran—because he lost the most, because he did it seemingly for nothing—will become the most romanticized war hero in American history." If Milius is right, it will complete a remarkable turnabout in American culture. During most of the Vietnam War, the artistic response to American soldiers ranged from ambivalence to outrage. Popular culture showed a curious oblivion to the war. Or perhaps it was deliberate escapism. In the second week of May 1968—the week with the most American deaths during the war—the No. 1 song was Bobby Goldsboro's lachrymose "Honey" and the most popular television show was "Rowan & Martin's Laugh-In."

But Vietnam politicized American fine artists to a degree unknown since the Depression. Those who had left behind the social realism of the 1930's for art-for-art's-sake, those too young to remember anything but existential prose and Abstract Expressionist painting, suddenly made relevance their credo. This political consciousness informed all the major art forms—Yvonne Rainer's "War" in dance; "MacBird!" "Viet Rock," the Living Theater's "Antigone" in theater; Leonard Bernstein's "Mass," Richard Wernick's "Kaddish Requiem" in classical music—but it was most apparent in visual art, perhaps because Vietnam was the first war fought on television.

Most of the politicized artists urged American withdrawal from the war and their recurrent images included domestic protest and Vietnamese pain. The plight of American soldiers in Vietnam was not equally evident, and it was also obscured by the class divisions the war created in American society. With college deferments from the draft, it was largely the children of poor and working-class parents, not of the intelligentsia, who fought in Vietnam. But the intelligentsia made the art.

Such artists as Jane Fonda, the singer Joan Baez and the author Susan Sontag visited Hanoi during the war and saw firsthand the destruction by American bombs. Clemens Starck's 1965 poem "On a Clear Day" likened the American intervention in Vietnam to Egyptians pursuing the fleeing Moses. "The Vietnam Songbook," a 1969 collection of protest songs, bore the dedication: "To the people of Vietnam, whose struggle for liberation embodies the hopes of all humanity." Draft resistance became a favorite theme in songs, from Arlo Guthrie's deadpan "Alice's Restaurant" to Phil Ochs's anthemic "I Ain't Marchin' Anymore."

The nightly footage of parents heaving with grief and children charred by napalm provided striking images for visual artists. The response grew as extreme as the "body art" of Chris Burden, Vito Acconci and others, who had themselves bound, shot and tortured to illustrate human suffering. Much more common, however, were evocations of Vietnamese anguish. Peter Saul's 1967 painting "Saigon," one of the major pieces of antiwar art, showed the American soldiers symbolically raping Vietnamese women with their weapons. Leon Golub, Nancy Spero and Rudolf Baranik produced numerous works portraying the Vietnamese victims of American arms.

"I felt as bad for our soldiers as I did for the Vietnamese," says Baranik, a World War II veteran. "They suffered. They were miserable. But the way we felt about American soldiers did not translate itself into art. There was clearly greater suffering by the Vietnamese. They were being napalmed. They were having their culture destroyed."

It seemed easier, and more politically acceptable, for artists to identify with American soldiers by distancing them from Vietnam. The major antiwar films of the Vietnam years—adaptations of the novels "Catch-22" and "M*A*S*H"—were set in World War II and the Korean War. Both films sympathized with individual soldiers while criticizing the war itself. A 1973 episode of the television series "M*A*S*H" showed the doctors tending to Korean civilians whose village had been mistakenly shelled by American troops. "Look," a demoralized Hawkeye Pierce told a general during the episode, "we've been fighting here for two years. Can't we quit? Surely the Government's made a profit by now." It was heady stuff for prime-time television.

The Vietnam War also affected culture in subliminal ways. Along with student activism, drug use, sexual freedom and other factors, it catalyzed and unified the counterculture.

"Take the play 'Hair,' one of the icons of the counterculture," says Alan Brinkley of Harvard. "There's almost nothing in there about the war, and yet it's hard to imagine that show taking the same form without the war." Joan Baez suggests that the most important artist in the antiwar movement was Bob Dylan, even though he "never took a stand, never was on a march." "The important thing was not the content of the songs," she says, "but the context of the times."

Vietnam was not only the first war fought on television, but the first one fought to a rock-and-roll soundtrack. Much of the music crackled with its own kind of violence, and Jimi Hendrix's songs, in particular, directly echoed the sounds of sirens, gunfire and bombs. At the same time, for an army of teen-agers in an alien land, rock-and-roll was a touchstone to home. "Despite what some may choose to think, rock & roll was never fundamentally antiwar," Lee Ballinger, a Vietnam veteran who is an associate editor of the newsletter Rock & Roll Confidential, has written. "It was a soundtrack for the entire process, of which opposition was only a part."

Some of the most arresting moments in Vietnam-related art fuse images of war and music. A soldier in "Tracers" plays his M-16 like an electric guitar. Napalm ignites a jungle as The Doors sing "The End" in "Apocalypse Now." As early as 1972, pop musicians like Marvin Gaye and Curtis Mayfield began singing about the painful readjustment of Vietnam veterans, and the subject re-emerged a decade later in the songs of Dan Daley ("Still in Saigon"), Huey Lewis ("Walking on a Thin Line") and Billy Joel ("Goodnight Saigon").

When Saigon fell in 1975, it was as if those last helicopters left behind not only Vietnam but memory itself. A collective amnesia set in. Novels written by veterans and war correspondents had started appearing in the late 1960's and early 70's, but many of the best—Ward Just's "Stringer," James Park Sloan's "War Games," Robert Roth's "Sand in the Wind"—quickly slid out of print. John Clark Pratt, a veteran, never found an agent willing to handle "Vietnam Voices," his anthology of fiction and nonfiction writing about the war. Eighty-five publishers rejected W.D. Ehrhart's Vietnam poetry before he paid a vanity press $1,500 to print it. Only years later did small commercial publishers pick up his work.

The post-Vietnam art that did sustain itself commercially was notable for its harrowing view of the war. "Apocalypse Now" abounded with images of cruelty and madness—soldiers surfing amid an air strike, helicopters attacking to the strains of Wagner, a Green Beret colonel playing God to Montagnard tribesmen. David Rabe's Vietnam trilogy, which appeared between 1969 and 1977, showed the war turning soldiers against themselves and their friends. In "Sticks and Bones," a blind veteran slit his wrists, while "Streamers" and "The Basic Training of Pavlo Hummel" both ended with the murder of soldiers by their comrades. Robert Stone's novel "Dog Soldiers"—and its film treatment, "Who'll Stop The Rain?"—made heroin the metaphor for the war's poisonous effect on America.

Such art was impassioned and original, but before long the Vietnam veteran as junkie, emotional cripple or ticking time bomb became a stock character in American culture. The stereotype made many veterans angry enough to finally tell their own stories, stories they had held inside for years. John M. Del Vecchio has said that his disgust with "Apocalypse Now" spurred him to write "The 13th Valley." "Taxi Driver" was the turning point for Thomas Bird, the artistic director of the Vietnam Veterans Ensemble Theatre Company, which was founded in 1978 and which produced "Tracers." "That movie didn't explain anything about Travis Bickle," he says. "It was enough that he had served in Vietnam for him to be a psychopath."

The flood of literature by and about veterans was a key factor in altering how American culture appraised the war, but it was not the only factor. By the late 1970's, it was apparent that even with the Americans gone from Vietnam, war and atrocities continued. Joan Baez published an open letter in 1979 denouncing political repression by the Communist regime in Vietnam, and it was signed by such antiwar artists as the poet Allen Ginsburg and the novelist William Styron.

America, meanwhile, began to turn to the right. Neil Young, whose 1970 song "Ohio" eulogized the students slain at Kent State, last year endorsed Ronald Reagan for President. High-school walls that had carried peace signs a generation earlier bore the message "Nuke Iran." It is difficult to say which came first—the conservative upsurge or the rehabilitation of the Vietnam veteran—but each trend nourished the other.

"There's a need to show we have the will and the character we had before Vietnam," says William Alexander, a professor of English at the University of Michigan who teaches a course on "Vietnam and the Artist." "A need to rethink ourselves to the basic American good guy."

The volte-face came in the late 1970'S. Two of the finest books about the war—"Dispatches," a memoir of the war by the journalist Michael Herr, and "Going After Cacciato," a novel by the Vietnam veteran Tim O'Brien—appeared respectively in 1977 and 1978. Without endorsing the war, both wrote movingly about the men who fought in it. "I think that those people who used to say that they only wept for the Vietnamese never really wept for anyone at all," Herr wrote, "if they couldn't squeeze out at least one for these men and boys when they died or had their lives cracked open for them."

In 1979, "The Deer Hunter" won the Academy Award as best picture and Jon Voight and Jane Fonda took the Oscars as best actor and actress for "Coming Home." Suddenly, Vietnam was not only a safe subject but a trendy one. Both films sent out particularly strong messages. Although "Coming Home" included an antiwar speech by Voight's character and the political awakening of Fonda's, it simultaneously seemed a mea culpa for the excesses of the movement. Here was "Hanoi Jane," after all, playing the wife of an American soldier.

"The Deer Hunter," the epic of three young steelworkers who go to war together, represented a return to a World War II type of cinema. The only atrocities in the film are committed by Vietnamese Communists, who resemble the evil "Japs" of 1940's B-movies.

They throw a hand grenade into a bunker of women and children; they make their American captives play Russian roulette. And while one of the Americans perishes and another loses his legs, the film ends not in sorrow but in affirmation, their friends singing "God Bless America."

Several movies and television shows have gone even further. "Uncommon Valor" is a ritualized re-enactment of the war, with a draft, boot camp and combat in the Asian jungle. Only this time the Americans win, and this time they are fighting the good fight. "No one can dispute the rightness of what you're doing," their leader says on the eve of the rescue mission. In a recent two-part episode of "Magnum, P.I.," the three veterans return to Indochina to liberate a leader of the anti-Communist resistance.

Interestingly, such films and shows have inherited from the antiwar movement a distrust of the American Government. The C.I.A. tries to stop the veterans from undertaking their mission in "Uncommon Valor." Chuck Norris in "Missing in Action" rescues M.I.A.'s even as American senators are holding feckless negotiations with the Vietnamese for their release.

The antiwar movement has come in for skeptical treatment. The Sixties survivors in "The Big Chill" are all disenchanted with their liberal values. A ghetto teacher has become a writer for People magazine. A legal-aid lawyer has gone corporate. The inference is given that a friend who committed suicide started his downhill slide by turning down a fellowship for political reasons. The central character in David Rabe's "Hurlyburly"—the most incisive examination yet of America's post-Vietnam malaise—is Eddie, an embittered idealist trying to numb his political conscience under drink, drugs and women. Writers who dodged the draft or received medical deferments have created a genre of breast-beating magazine essays, notably Christopher Buckley's "Viet Guilt" and James Fallows's "What Did You Do in the Class War, Daddy?"

The literature and visual art created by veterans, however, is more personal than polemical. "When you think about novels about the war, they're rarely political," says Tim O'Brien. "Because the issues you confront are personal, not political. Staying alive, burning a village, watching the bombs fall. The primary things one cares about in battle aren't the political issues. It's being scared, being brave. Those are things that go back to Homer. Those are the ancient things."

The absence of a common political cause largely defines Vietnam literature and separates it from a lot of American war fiction. Much Vietnam literature makes a conscious connection to the disillusioned writing that emerged after World War I from the British and from the American expatriate Ernest Hemingway. O'Brien opens "Cacciato" with a quotation from Siegfried Sassoon. Ehrhart cites the poet Wilfred Owen as a major influence. Allusions to Hemingway's "A Farewell to Arms" appear in several novels. Even in the film "Apocalypse Now," the character Kurtz recites T. S. Eliot's "The Hollow Men," a poem of post-World War I sorrow.

Why the affinity between these writers of World War I and Americans of Vietnam? "An absence of clear purpose is the easiest answer," O'Brien suggests. "A loss of naïveté." Ehrhart says: "There is a sense of being in a war without moral purpose or physical gain. In World War I, you were in the same trenches every day. In Vietnam, you patrolled the same villages every day."

If the best Vietnam literature took its tone from post-World War I writers, it shared its style with such modernists as Alain Robbe-Grillet. The action in the Vietnam novels is usually fragmented, the dialogue riddled with military jargon, pidgin Vietnamese and American black patois. The theater of war is drawn so realistically and in such detail—fog, swamps, snipers; pizza parlors and Dairy Queens airlifted in to create a semblance of home—that it becomes absurd, surreal. In that context, gallantry seems besides the point. Survival is all. (There are exceptions, of course; Del Vecchio's "The 13th Valley" and James Webb's "Fields of Fire" both portrayed traditional valor.)

Of all the cultural forms, visual art most closely parallels fiction in its depiction of the soldier's Vietnam. The exhibit "Vietnam: Reflexes and Reflections," which includes 120 paintings, photographs and sculptures by 63 veterans, is distinctive for its uniform anguish. The images in the exhibit—which has earned the praise of art critics in Chicago, Washington and New York—include the skull of a G.I. impaled on a stake, a rural mother receiving the news her son is dead, a soldier cradling a dead Vietnamese child.

Not only does this art stand apart from the triumphal evocations of World War II, it also departs from the fairly traditional fare in the official armed services Vietnam archives. "I see an awful lot of agony in the art," says Sondra Varco, the executive director of the Vietnam Veterans Arts Group, which, founded in 1981, organized the exhibit. "There is no feeling of victory. These people don't feel like heroes."

The question remains whether the totality of individual artistic responses to the war amounts to a national response. Certainly, a period of healing is under way. But the healing is partly self-deception, for it does not acknowledge the fissures that remain from the war. "The phase now," says the playwright David Rabe, "is to make up a tolerable explanation for Vietnam. Our appetite is for a substitute answer, not the real answer. We'll salve ourselves."

This is a nation, after all, that could not agree on a single memorial to the Vietnam War in Washington. It needed both the somber wall, engraved with the names of the fallen, and a statue of three soldiers, innocents who look one year out of the backfield of a high-school football team.

"Those monuments are the closest thing we have to a common text," says Gordon O. Taylor, a University of Tulsa English professor who has studied Vietnam literature on a Guggenheim Fellowship. "I think of them as a kind of narrative that we as a nation are still learning how to read."

Samuel G. Freedman is a New York Times culture reporter.

* * *

April 17, 1985

FOR MANY FROM VIETNAM, LIFE IN U.S. IS STILL HARD

By FOX BUTTERFIELD
Special to the New York Times

WESTMINSTER, Calif.—When Dr. Pham Van Triet fled Saigon by boat on April 29, 1975, as the city fell to the Communists, he felt he had lost everything: his home, his medical practice and the land of his ancestors.

United Press International

Vietnamese refugees bargaining over the price of fish at a market in the Michoud section of New Orleans.

In the United States, where his Vietnamese medical degree was not recognized, Dr. Triet was so poor at first that his family had to split up, living in trailers with Americans willing to take them and existing on food stamps.

Eventually, Dr. Triet taught himself English, on an old television set donated by a church, and he got his American medical license. Now he heads the anesthesia department of a hospital near here, runs his own clinic in this Orange County community and drives a Mercedes.

Nguyen Viet Hung fled Vietnam by boat in 1981 when he was 17 years old, after being conscripted by the Communist government to fight in Cambodia. In the United States he found himself unable to learn English or get a job.

Troubled by nightmares of the killing he had seen in Cambodia and without parents to supervise him, he drifted into a Vietnamese youth gang in San Diego. Last fall he was arrested after a shooting outside a roller rink.

Those two stories represent the widely divergent experiences of the 467,000 Vietnamese refugees who have fled to the United States in the decade since the collapse of South Vietnam.

Some have emerged successfully from their hegira, like Dr. Triet. But they are the exceptions, according to leaders in the Vietnamese community and Americans who have worked most closely with the refugees. For many Vietnamese, life in the United States has proved much harder than they imagined. "To say the Vietnamese have been successful in America is a myth," said Do Yen, editor of a Vietnamese-language newspaper here in Westminster, which has the heaviest concentration of Vietnamese in the country.

"It is a fairy tale created by Americans to prove that America is still the land of opportunity," he said. "In Vietnam we lost everything, then the boat people drowned or were raped by Thai pirates, and when we got to America many people couldn't speak English and only got jobs as janitors. So we can't really enjoy the United States. Even the affluence and the California weather seem so strange.

"Maybe in time the children will be successful."

Indeed, several young Vietnamese have founded their own electronics concerns in the high-technology area south of San Francisco.

Two Vietnamese, including the daughter of a former South Vietnamese Army colonel, are to graduate this spring from the United States Military Academy at West Point, the first Indochinese to do so. An uncounted number of Vietnamese will be high school valedictorians this June.

On the other hand, Ruben G. Rumbaut, a professor of sociology at the University of California at San Diego who is conducting continuing research on Vietnamese in that area, found that the average income was $11,550 for a family of four and that 55 percent of them were living below the Federal Government's poverty line in 1983. He said that was the largest percentage of any ethnic group.

'Sense of Insecurity'

Pham Cao Duong, once a distinguished professor of Vietnamese history at the University of Saigon, who now teaches French at a Huntington Beach high school, says he thinks the refugees feel "a constant sense of insecurity."

In Vietnam they had their families to fall back on, Mr. Duong observed. "But here," he said, "everything is work, work, work. Everything depends on your job, and if you get sick or have a bad relationship with your supervisor you may lose your job and the bank will take your house.

"In America we gained political freedom but lost economic freedom."

To some extent, all immigrants to the United States have experienced these troubles, said Jeanne F. Nidorf, a psychologist who is a professor at the University of California at San Diego and has specialized in working with Indochinese.

Strong Family Culture

But the Vietnamese family culture was so strong, she said, that the refugees seem to suffer more from being cut off from the homeland than do other recent refugees.

"The ancestors provided the constraints on them, and they can't conceive of a new life in America away from their ancestors' tombs," she said.

Mr. Duong says it is important to note that never before in Vietnam's long, tortured history, under rule by the Chinese and the French and then the years of war, did Vietnamese flee their country.

"It is a unique event for us," he said. "In the past we said it was already a big misfortune if you had to leave your native village."

Symptoms of Depression

One manifestation of the troubles the Vietnamese refugees face, according to Miss Nidorf and others who have studied them, is that an unusually large number suffer from depression. "So many people come in with the symptoms," Miss Nidorf said, "that the Vietnamese interpreters now say, 'There's nothing wrong with her—we've all got that.' "

In one case, she said, a Vietnamese woman in her early 40's came in complaining of constant headaches, lack of appetite and insomnia. She was so depressed she could not remember words in her English class or hold a job.

The woman believed there was something physically wrong with her, as do most Vietnamese, Miss Nidorf said, since they grew up in a culture where there is no word for mental health and psychiatry is largely unknown.

But Miss Nidorf learned from the woman that her husband had been killed in the war and that she had watched as her daughters died of thirst and exposure on the South China Sea while trying to flee Vietnam. The woman had exhausted her three years of Federal refugee aid and was out of work, living in a tiny one-room apartment.

'Fantasies of Omnipotence'

Another of Miss Nidorf's patients felt so guilty about being unable to stop Thai pirates from raping his sister that he had become psychotic. "He has fantasies of omnipotence, saying he talks with the President of the United States," Miss Nidorf said.

Professor Rumbaut, in his San Diego survey, used a test developed by the National Center for Health Statistics to measure psychological well-being. He found that while 74 percent of Americans showed good mental health, only 23 percent of the refugees did. Conversely, while only 9.7 percent of Americans displayed clinically significant distress, 45 percent of the refugees did. And while 16 percent of Americans showed some minor depression, 32 percent of the refugees did.

Even more important in analyzing the refugees' situation, Mr. Rumbaut said, is the little-known fact that more Vietnamese have actually arrived in this country since 1980 than in the first five years after the war.

Vietnamese Still Arriving

From 1975 through 1979, 185,700 Vietnamese were admitted, according to the Office of Refugee Resettlement in the Department of Health and Human Services. From 1980 to January of this year, 281,300 arrived. And they are still coming, with about 25,000 projected this year.

To Mr. Yen, the journalist, that is a sign that "the war is not really over."

All studies of Vietnamese as well as Cambodian and Laotian refugees show that the longer they live in America the better they do. Robert L. Bach of the State University of New York at Binghamton, in a report last year for the Office of Refugee Resettlement, estimated that the number of Indochinese immigrants with jobs rises by 10 percent for each year they are here.

Mr. Rumbaut's San Diego survey supports that conclusion. He found that 64 percent of the Vietnamese here less than three years had not found jobs and 67 percent still depended on welfare, but that for those here three to five years the figure dropped to 42 percent without jobs and 46 percent on welfare.

And only 15 percent of those here more than five years had not found jobs and only 11 percent were still on welfare.

Schooling Improves Prospects

Another critical factor is education. Almost two-thirds of the refugees with less than six years of schooling have not held jobs in the United States and are dependent on welfare, according to Professor Rumbaut's research. But less than half of those with six to 12 years of education lack jobs and are on welfare, and among those who have been to college less than a quarter do not have jobs.

The importance of education in how refugees fare tends to heighten the contrast between the earlier and the later refugees because most of those who fled in 1975 were better educated, more urban and already spoke some English. Many of the more recent refugees have been poorer, less educated people from the countryside.

Problems of New Immigrants

For new arrivals in America, the immediate problems are those of survival: finding a job, mastering English and finding housing, which for people without any savings can be prohibitively expensive, especially in California, where 40 percent of the Vietnamese have settled.

Then, for many, there is a psychological problem, the realization that they must accept a severe drop in status.

Mr. Duong is relatively well off, having fallen only from the esteemed rank of professor at South Vietnam's leading university to high school teacher.

But he knows a former army general who is now a waiter in a restaurant. "To Americans, such stories are not unusual," Mr. Duong said, "but to Vietnamese, they are shocking," for Vietnamese believe in the Confucian precept that those who work with the mind govern those who work with their hands and that manual labor is degrading.

According to the Office of Refugee Resettlement, over half the adult refugees from Indochina held white-collar jobs at home but less than a third have found similar occupations here. The proportion holding blue-collar jobs has almost tripled.

The single largest occupation for the Vietnamese is as assemblers in electronics factories, the Federal refugee agency reports. But the electronics jobs they hold are usually low-paying with little chance of advancement.

Surprises in America

Life in America is full of surprises for the Vietnamese.

"Many Vietnamese say the Americans are like the Communists," said Mr. Yen, the journalist, because "they work so hard, they have so many taxes and they organize everything with Social Security numbers and computers.'

Many Vietnamese, accustomed to fearing the brutal police in their homeland, find it hard to deal with the American police system. The results can be tragic.

Miss Nidorf related the case of a former peasant and soldier who fled to the United States after escaping from a Communist re-education camp where he labored clearing the jungle. He settled in San Diego, worked hard as a baker, went to school at night and helped pay for an apartment for his wife's sister and young son.

One day he dropped by his sister-in-law's apartment, found the child alone and took the boy to his own home. But when the man walked back to tell his sister-in-law that the boy was taking a nap, he saw police officers outside the building and panicked. He picked up the boy and drove to Mexico before turning himself in. He has now been charged with kidnapping.

The Vietnamese who have prospered in the face of these obstacles trace much of their success to the old Vietnamese values of family solidarity, thrift and reverance for education.

In Fremont, Calif., Bui Le, a 33-year-old electronics engineer with a Ph.D. from Stanford, founded his own computer company in 1982 after tinkering in his parents' garage along with two other refugees. The enhancement board they invented for the I.B.M. PC computer has enabled the sales of their concern, Orchid Technology, to grow 200 percent a year, and it now employs 100 people.

Success With a Twist

Mr. Le is proud to be an American citizen and sees his rise as a typical success story, though with a Vietnamese twist. Because he was a refugee, he could not get backing from venture capitalists and got all his financing from Vietnamese friends and relatives. His father and mother still work as technicians in other electronics plants.

Do Quang Binh, a slight, modest 17-year-old whose father was a police officer in Nhatrang before the family escaped 10 years ago, has a straight-A average at Helix High School in San Diego and is a candidate for valedictorian.

Like boys his age in Vietnam, Binh does not date or participate in school sports, and he lives with his parents and four older brothers and sisters. One brother, now a computer programmer, recently bought the family a large new house. An older sister, a mathematician with a naval electronics concern, bought a new car for the family's use. Like many Vietnamese, the family members share their income.

'Highest Value on Education'

"I think my good grades in school come from the encouragement my parents have given me," Binh said. "In Vietnam, we place the highest value on education, where some Americans think school must be fun."

"There is a reciprocal arrangement," added one of Binh's sisters, a 24-year-old social worker. "In Vietnam the parents provide everything for the children. Then when they grow old, they expect the children to support them."

Mr. Duong, the former history professor, suggested that being young helps in the adjustment to America, saying: "The younger you are, the faster you can enter the new life. For the elderly, being Vietnamese can be too much of an obstacle to overcome."

At the same time, Mr. Duong, who has a daughter majoring in biology at U.C.L.A., contends it is a fable that all Vietnamese do well academically. Both truancy and incidents of juvenile crime are increasing among Vietnamese students, he notes.

Conflict of Americanization

Moreover, young Vietnamese face a cruel paradox, he said. To do well in America they must become more Americanized; that is, assertive, independent and questioning in school. Yet their parents, who want them to get high grades, are afraid that the children will lose their cultural heritage of deference to authority.

As Vietnamese gradually overcome the initial problems of survival in America, Mr. Duong voices fear that a new trouble is brewing: conflict between the generations.

In some ways the greatest hardship is faced by the young people who have come to the United States by themselves in the past few years, those whom refugee officials call "unaccompanied minors" and fellow Vietnamese term "the dust of life." Often their fathers have been kept in re-education camps and their mothers have arranged their escape, hoping they will eventually be able to bring the whole family to America.

The Path to a Youth Gang

Mr. Hung, the gang member in San Diego, is one of these. His father, a former employee of the Central Intelligence Agency in the Mekong Delta, was arrested after the Communist takeover and his mother was required to divorce him. The new Government stopped Mr. Hung's schooling when he was 11 years old, and in 1979 he was drafted and sent into Cambodia with the first wave of Vietnamese invaders.

A thin, nervous man, Mr. Hung said he was haunted by the sight of heads of the slain lying in the fields and took to smoking marijuana. Only two of the 12 members of his squad survived the fighting. A sister whom he loved very much and two nieces disappeared at sea trying to leave Vietnam.

In San Diego, although an older brother was already there, Mr. Hung says he felt very lonely, and he was frustrated at his inability to learn English or find a job. Members of the Black Jackets gang, who drove fast cars and occasionally smuggled drugs from Mexico, provided a new family. The charges stemming from his arrest last fall were dropped.

The Guilt of Surviving

A more subtle problem that troubles many refugees is the guilt they feel as survivors, said Mr. Yen, the journalist. "As Buddhists," he said, "we fear that if we are comfortable now, we will be punished later."

It is not just an emotional urge, he said, that "many Vietnamese are working so hard, holding two jobs, either to pay back their families for arranging their escape or help keep them from hunger in Vietnam now."

Like many Vietnamese, Mr. Yen regularly sends money back to his relatives in Vietnam, over $1,000 a year, a large sum for him. Because the American embargo on trade with Vietnam limits what the refugees can send home, Mr. Yen, like others, uses an underground channel, a friend with the right contacts in Vietnam.

Last year a report by the Senate Banking, Housing and Urban Affairs Committee estimated that the refugees remitted more than $200 million a year to Vietnam, an enormous boon in an impoverished country whose official foreign reserves are only $16 million.

Although the refugees face many problems in the United States, almost all feel they were right move here.

At St. Anselm's Episcopal Church's refugee center in Garden Grove, Calif., 17 newly arrived Vietnamese were taking an English class. Pham Van Kinh, the oldest at 56, a former military policeman who escaped from a re-education camp last year, spoke a common sentiment when he said, in accented but earnest English, "I lost my country, but I gained my life."

* * *

April 18, 1985

U.S. POWER IN ASIA HAS GROWN SINCE VIETNAM

By LESLIE H. GELB

Special to the New York Times

WASHINGTON, April 17—Ten years after the defeat of South Vietnam, there is widespread agreement among policy analysts that the position of the United States in Asia is stronger now than at any time since the end of World War II. In April 1975, it was in shambles.

A decade ago, in victory, North Vietnam looked invincible. Now the economy of united Vietnam is stagnating and Hanoi is mired down in its own "Vietnam" in Cambodia.

In the span of 10 years, policy analysts say, Vietnam, the Soviet Union and most Communist movements in Asia tumbled from victory or ascendancy to decline, while the United States moved from defeat to a position of strength.

The turnaround was due largely to a change in the politics of American policy-making toward Asia. For 40 years, no foreign-policy issue was more divisive than Asia from what to do about China right after World War II, through the Korean War to Vietnam. But in the last 10 years, after the opening to China and the end of the Vietnam War, few policy issues have garnered more bipartisan support.

Yet the question of who lost Vietnam is still hotly disputed by the people who once struggled over policy and fought the war.

Among the issues raised are these:

- Why did the defeat not lead Asian countries other than Cambodia and Laos to fall under Communist control like "a row of dominoes," as President Eisenhower and his successors predicted? Did America's stand in Vietnam delay or make possible America's current position of strength in Asia?
- Why have Hanoi and Moscow been unable to capitalize on their victory? Has the war irretrievably turned hawks and doves on Vietnam into policy adversaries? And what parallels are to be drawn for Central America?

The questions and answers about the Vietnam experience slice deeply into virtually every central foreign-policy issue in the Reagan Administration, from Central America to Grenada, Lebanon and terrorism.

Defense Secretary Caspar W. Weinberger has argued for any military intervention around the world only as "a last resort," with full public backing, and "with the clear intention of winning."

Secretary of State George P. Shultz has maintained that "there is no such thing as guaranteed public support in advance," and that a great power must be prepared to use doses of force to buttress diplomacy.

Asia Today

The belief that the United States position in Asia has never been stronger in 40 years is shared by Vietnam doves like Richard C. Holbrooke, Assistant Secretary of State for East Asia in the Carter Administration, and Vietnam hawks like Paul D. Wolfowitz.

"It is clear that the whole condition of East Asia is today far better than the most optimistic would have predicted 10 years ago," Mr. Wolfowitz said.

"Even compared to the end of World War II, it is far better because the countries of Asia are far more self-reliant, don't look to us as much as they did before; but when they do, we are there."

These two men and other Asian experts—Robert A. Scalapino of the University of California at Berkeley, Donald S. Zagoria of Hunter College, and Winston Lord, president of the Council on Foreign Relations—produce an almost identical litany of examples to back up this optimistic picture.

China as U.S. Ally

China, instead of being the principal adversary, has become a strategic ally in many ways. It restrains North Korea, aids guerrillas in checking Vietnam in Cambodia, has called off support for Communist insurgents in Thailand and elsewhere, and ties down a third of the Soviet armed forces on its border.

With the notable exception of the Philippines, most Asian countries are enjoying political stability almost unprecedented for this century. The stability rests on a blend of authoritarianism, democracy and substantial economic growth.

According to State Department figures, the economies of the members of the Association of Southeast Asia Nations, or Asian—which include Thailand, Indonesia, Malaysia, Singapore, the Philippines and Brunei—have each grown on the average of 7 percent a year over the last 10 years. This is about twice the global average growth after discounting for inflation. American trade with the Pacific Basin area now exceeds its trade with Europe.

Relations with Japan are generally deemed to be good, though marred by continuing friction over America's lopsided trade deficit with its most important Asian ally.

'A Pacific Destiny'

Soviet military power in the region has grown considerably over the decade. This includes substantial use by Russian ships, including submarines, and reconaissance aircraft of the former major American base at Cam Ranh Bay in Vietnam.

Nonetheless, Pentagon experts generally subscribe to the assessment of Robert O'Neill, an Asian scholar and director of the London-based International Institute for Strategic Studies. Given American military and naval power in the region and deployments under way, he said in a recent article, "there is little prospect that the United States will be outclassed in power projection and other strategic capabilities in the Pacific" provided there are no major crises elsewhere.

"Americans do have a Pacific destiny," said Michael H. Armacost, the Under Secretary of State for Political Affairs. "All these factors tended to guarantee that the fatigue and frustration with Southeast Asia bred by the bitter outcome of the war was a transitory phenomenon."

Vietnam's Troubles

Alone among those interviewed, former Secretary of State Dean Rusk sounded a note of caution. "I don't think we know yet the full consequences of the war," he said. "North Vietnam still has a lot of digesting to do in South Vietnam, Laos and Cambodia."

Vietnam is now a country of 60 million people with an army of 1.2 million—the fourth largest in the world after China, the Soviet Union and the United States. Per capita income is estimated by the State Department to be about $125 a year, only about one-fourth that of its Asian neighbors.

The State Department also estimates that the Soviet Union supplies Vietnam with about $2 billion annually. This constitutes about one-seventh of Vietnam's gross national product. While the economies of every Asian country have more than doubled in the last decade, Vietnam's shows almost no growth.

Vietnam's real drain and quagmire is Cambodia. An estimated 160,000 Vietnamese troops are trying to hold the cities against and searching the jungles for several different guerrilla forces numbering, according to various estimates, anywhere from 40,000 to 80,000. "There is no end of this war in sight," noted Mr. Holbrooke and others.

'Clumsy' Soviet Diplomacy

Spurred by Congress, the Reagan Administration last week made known its willingness to aid the guerrillas as well.

The Soviet Union has tied its fortunes in Southeast Asia to Vietnam and Vietnam's war in Cambodia. This has set Moscow against the Asian countries, and left both Vietnam and the Soviet Union almost totally isolated on Cambodia, even in the United Nations.

In addition, as Mr. Lord pointed out, "Soviet diplomacy in the area has been particularly clumsy, especially with Japan," thus further strengthening American standing. This includes Soviet threats to Japan about closer relations with Washington and the absence of any important diplomatic role on the Korean Peninsula.

The Domino Theory

In 1954, President Eisenhower evoked an image of American stakes in Vietnam that was in one form or another used by all of his successors through Richard M. Nixon.

"You have a row of dominoes set up," Mr. Eisenhower said. "You knock over the first one, and what will happen to the last one is the certainty that it will go over very quickly." To Eisenhower, this meant Laos, Cambodia, Thailand, Burma, the Malay peninsula, Indonesia and perhaps the rest of Asia as well.

Mr. Nixon globalized this domino theory during his Presidency, saying that the loss of Vietnam would reduce the United States to "a pitiful, helpless giant" and destroy United States credibility worldwide. Few dispute that credibility was lost, if not because of the loss of Vietnam then because the United States seemed deeply divided and turning inward.

'The Opening to China'

However, while Laos and Cambodia fell, as almost all predicted, the other Asian dominoes stood.

Mr. Lord argued that in this result "the most crucial factor was the opening to China" in 1971, two years before the Paris cease-fire agreement ending American participation in the Vietnam War and four years before the final debacle in Saigon. "This helped to put Indochina in perspective and ease the pain of our exit, and restrain Hanoi," he said.

Professor Scalapino stressed that the loss of Vietnam "raised questions about American credibility, but it also raised the quotient of Asian self-reliance."

That element of self-reliance is central to Professor Zagoria's analysis. "Revolutions," he said, "though influenced by external factors, are largely determined by indigenous factors." Thailand and Indonesia, he argued, were able to get themselves together politically, economically and militarily to beat down Communist insurgencies.

A Crucial Question

"The Philippines proves the point," he continued. "Unlike the rest of Southeast Asia, they didn't have the economic dynamism, commitment to equity and leadership," and so their insurgency has gotten out of hand "with no noticeable external support."

But, and here is the nub of the debate, did American involvement in Vietnam delay the flowering of American-Chinese ties and Asian self-reliance and growth, or did it make those developments possible?

Did, for example, the war blind American leaders to the historical tensions and conflicts between China and the Soviet Union and China and Vietnam?

William P. Bundy, Assistant Secretary of State for East Asian Affairs in the Kennedy and Johnson Administrations, said in an interview: "No, I was aware of the splits." But the record shows that few other officials were.

Asian Nations Strengthened

In any event, Mr. Bundy maintained that the Asian countries "were much stronger by the time the war ended, and all of that had some relationship to our being in Vietnam." They were "not as jittery as they were in 1964." In other words, the war gave them time to get their houses in order.

Mr. Holbrooke countered that "2,000 years of Chinese-Vietnamese enmity and hundreds of years of Chinese and Russian mutual suspicions were suspended when they united against us in Vietnam."

"We could not improve relations with Japan, develop our relations with China or give impetus to Asian self-reliance until we ended our involvement in Vietnam," he added.

Those who made American policy, he said, "put American prestige on the line in that place in the world where we had the least chance of success and in the name of strengthening America, they weakened it—the Vietnam boil had to be lanced before the rest was possible."

Who Lost Vietnam?

All of this ties into the matter of responsibility for the defeat of South Vietnam and to the lessons learned, lessons that are applied variously to the current situation in Central America and elsewhere.

Most pronounced today are the accusations by Mr. Nixon and his former chief adviser, Henry A. Kissinger. They put the blame on Congress for "irresponsibility," the press for "misreporting" and liberals, intellectuals, and antiwar activists for being virtually anti-American.

In his recent book, "No More Vietnams," Mr. Nixon asserts that the war was won in 1974, until these groups pulled the rug out from under the victory by limiting American aid to Saigon and forbidding American military retaliation against Hanoi for breaches of the 1973 Paris accords.

Mr. Rusk, too, said he believed that the war was lost here, but not because of conspiracies of the left. "A lot of people at the grass roots came to the conclusion that we couldn't tell them when the war would end. So they said chuck it. War weariness was the cause of defeat. Just plain impatience, not misinformation. We could not honestly tell them when it was going to be over," said the former Secretary, who is now teaching at the University of Georgia.

'Ultimate Responsibility'

Other thoughts came through the Rusk retrospective. "After all, we did go half way around the world to meet our treaty commitments," he said. He added, "I told President Kennedy he had to think about what there was in South Vietnam to support."

Mr. Holbrooke placed "the ultimate responsibility" with the South Vietnamese.

"We aided them for 20 years, fought alongside them for 10, lost almost 60,000 Americans in combat, mortgaged our economy for the war," he said. "It is a travesty to say that after all this, we and not they lost the war."

Was the American effort worth it? William Bundy, one of the main architects of the war, offered this conclusion: "When I say the war bought time for Asia to become stronger, I'm not saying in retrospect that this proves the war was wise. The price was too high even for that. Taking all the elements into account—the internal divisions, the human loss of life—it was a national tragedy."

* * *

April 22, 1985

ISSUE OF MISSING IN VIETNAM HAS NOT FADED AFTER DECADE

By ANDREW H. MALCOLM
Special to the New York Times

LINTHICUM, Md.—Donald Shay's father is retired now. Donald's little sister has two young children of her own. His fiancée finally married someone else. And Donald's mother doesn't bake his favorite apple pie much anymore; the good smell brings back too many bad memories.

Mr. Shay doesn't know any of this. And he may never know. In fact, his family may never know where he is, or where he was when he died, if he died. For Mr. Shay is one of 2,477 Americans still missing in action from the Vietnam War.

Ten years after the fall of Saigon and 15 years after that smiling, 24-year-old lacrosse player flew off a radar screen into his family's memory somewhere over Indochina, no one knows for sure what happened to any of the missing Americans.

More Than Mere Statistics

But in one of the more mysterious legacies of that painful era in American history, these men who went off to war as individuals have now become, as a group, much more than simply a sad statistic. They are the subject of movies, books and songs, the object of angry demonstrations, earnest petitions and solemn vigils, the focus of intense Presidential interest, microscopic analysis and secret satellite photography and the heart of some delicate diplomatic exchanges trying to bridge broad cultural chasms.

The alleged remains of some missing men, reduced to bones and fragments after years in the jungle, have even become the currency of a ghoulish, clandestine commerce that preys on the hopes and fears of families and refugees.

"Somehow," said one United States Government official, "the mystery of their disappearance and their deaths have taken on a peculiar life of their own."

For military records, all but one of the missing are officially presumed dead, ending the pay, automatic promotion and service benefits accruing for years. Only the case of a single missing flier remains active for symbolic reasons. But for diplomatic records, the missing remain a live issue, a major obstacle to the normalization of relations between Vietnam and the United States and a lever for some Southeast Asian lands to keep the United States in the region as a political counterbalance.

For some family members, the missing relative is dead, a sad part of a slowly fading past that might somehow still miraculously reappear and complicate a brand new life. Other relatives still wait, in hope that their loved one might walk back through the door some day, perhaps tomorrow.

For the children of the missing, many of them not so childish anymore, the absent father is often but a dim memory, kept alive on den walls or treasured tape cassettes by sisters, brothers, mothers, fathers or wives, some of them remarried, some of them happy now, some of them troubled, all of them scarred.

"It's been such a long time to be uncertain," said Ann Mills Griffiths, whose brother vanished in Vietnam nearly two decades ago. "You want to be realistic. But you're afraid to give up hope."

By the standards of war, America's 2,477 Vietnam missing are few, thanks to modern recovery methods, the nature of land fighting and new forensic technology that enables investigators to identify even partial remains by, for instance, electronically reconstructing a skull from a fragment.

Tallies of the Missing

The Center for Military History still lists 3,350 missing in action from World War I, 8,177 in Korea, where M.I.A. teams still mount occasional search excavations, and 78,777 from World War II, when many were lost at sea.

Of the Vietnam missing, 706 were in the Army, 937 in the Air Force, 500 in the Navy, 291 in the Marine Corps and 1 in the Coast Guard. The other 42 were civilians. Of the missing, 1,101 disappeared in or over South Vietnam, 719 in North Vietnam, 569 in Laos, 82 in Cambodia and 6 over China.

Privately, American officials and relatives admit there is little hope of accounting for many of the missing, perhaps even a majority, and most likely for all those who disappeared in Cambodia, the scene of almost continuous fighting since.

In addition, 1,186 of the total missing are really listed as Killed in Action—Body Not Recovered. These are, for instance, pilots whose planes were seen to crash with no parachutes or soldiers who were killed on patrol under circumstances in which comrades could not retrieve the body.

An unknown number will never be found because there are no remains to find. Last year when members of Congress pressured Lieut. Gen. James A. Williams, director of the Defense Intelligence Agency, to tell them how many realistically might be found, he testified: "Some of these people have disappeared by being completely obliterated. If you have ever watched an explosion disintegrate somebody, you would understand that that happens."

A Lower Priority

A full accounting of both prisoners of war and missing was part of the 1973 Paris accords that arranged United States disengagement from the Vietnam conflict, where 58,022 Americans died. North Vietnam returned 591 prisoners in 1973, and another 134 returned or escaped at other times. But with the American withdrawal and the fall of Saigon 10 years ago this month, the missing got a lower priority by a Government and public eager to put the divisive war behind. Few remains were returned; 102 since 1973, including two non-Americans.

Two commissions reported to President Carter that there were no live American prisoners remaining in Indochina. And each military service moved administratively to declare all the missing dead.

What happened in 1980 was the election as President of Ronald Reagan, who as Governor of California spoke out often and emotionally for the need of a full accounting. He was photographed wearing one of the M.I.A. bracelets engraved with the name of a missing man and sold in the war to show symbolic support. The President still keeps five M.I.A. bracelets hanging in his study next to the Oval Office.

"The way our system of government works," said one aide, "if the President is personally interested in something, then the Government is interested in it. And Mr. and Mrs. Reagan are personally very interested in M.I.A.'s."

New Place on Agenda

In the past four years this interest, displayed through numerous speeches and public references, through many private telephone calls and letters to M.I.A. families and through countless Reagan Administration meetings and a still-secret 10-point National Security Council strategy, has raised the subject to what the President calls "the highest national priority."

It has also left few Government officials willing to question the campaign or to be quoted by name. "Few people in the Vatican," said one, "would tell the Pope they question the faith."

The broad public and private strategy has involved efforts to mobilize the Government's bureaucracy, the intelligence community and bipartisan political support to transmit a convincing signal to Hanoi that an accounting is necessary before any aid or normalizing of relations.

The President got an unusual security clearance for Mrs. Griffiths, the executive director of the National League of M.I.A.-P.O.W. Families. She now routinely attends relevant meetings of the National Security Council as well as diplomatic negotiations in New York and Hanoi. One result has been to dissipate the harsh criticism the league has aimed at previous "do-nothing" Administrations. "For a while," said Mrs. Griffiths, a Californian whose organization says it has 3,000 M.I.A. family members and 15,000 concerned people as supporters, "our families felt they were fighting their own Government as well as the Vietnamese."

But another result, tied in with a growing public willingness to address the emotional legacies of the war, has been the eager involvement of a variety of groups and individuals who profess patriotism but have at times complicated diplomatic efforts. "It's a very thin line," said one Administration strategist.

Veterans Groups' Actions

Veterans groups have helped gather millions of petition signatures demanding accountings of the missing from the Vietnamese, and they recently provided the Hanoi Government with details on some unmarked burial sites of its missing. One small group has staged a round-the-clock vigil at the Vietnam Memorial since Dec. 24, 1982.

Others, however, have burned Vietnamese flags before that country's mission to the United Nations, while some groups raise money from Americans to mount "rescue raids," which produced no verifiable results and complicated official talks.

What seems to capture the public imagination on the missing is the lingering uncertainty about their fate and, in the view of some, a wishful willingness to believe any scrap of information and to distrust any Vietnamese denials about remaining prisoners of war.

"We have returned everyone," Le Kim Chung, Vietnam's deputy permanent representative to the United Nations, said in an interview. "Also, why would we want to keep them? We have enough troubles without keeping Americans."

Mr. Le also denounced as fabrications refugee reports of caches of American remains. One Vietnamese undertaker who fled to the United States told Congress he saw 400 such remains in a Hanoi warehouse, which many in Washington believe.

Sightings of Whites

What has proven most tantalizing to M.I.A. families and the 18 Defense Intelligence Agency analysts assigned full time to sifting data about the missing are reports of "live sightings," usually from refugees, of a white in Indochina in a particular place on a particular date. According to Col. Gerald S. Venanzi, a former prisoner of war who is the Pentagon's senior authority on the missing, there have been more than 750 reported sightings since 1973, some of prisoners and some of men free of visible restraints.

All refugee camps have multilingual posters seeking information about the missing. Those responding are interviewed by special teams, sometimes using polygraphs, or lie detectors. "We have him describe his village, his house, where he saw the Caucasian," said one intelligence official who sought anonymity. "With computers we can cross-check his identity with other refugees from the same village. And with satellites we can photograph the place right down to the fence in his yard."

Analysts believe some stories are fabrications planted by Vietnamese to discredit refugee reports and consume valuable tracking resources. Other reports turn out to be Europeans or stem from refugees seeking favorable immigration treatment. There is no pattern to the sightings, but 175 such reports remain unresolved, prompting officials to say they cannot rule out the possibility some prisoners remain.

Should live Americans be found, officials said, the President has authorized any means necessary to extricate them. "This could range from diplomacy to black helicopters in the night," said one official.

'Maybe He's Better Dead'

Edna Hicks clings to such reports as proof that her son Terrin, a 31-year-old pilot when his plane was downed over North Vietnam in 1968, could be alive. "It'd be a miracle, a long shot, I know," said Mrs. Hicks, now 70 years old, who sometimes still speaks of her son in the present tense. "Some days you feel he's alive. Some days not. And then you think, what would he be like after 17 years of imprisonment and torture? Maybe he's better dead."

To some, the inability of such vast intelligence capabilities to confirm the existence of a live American prisoner is proof that none exist and suggests the Administration is using rhetoric to fuel false hopes.

The Administration's known interest is also fueling a brisk border business in bones, as refugees, resistance forces and others appear, usually in Thailand, with plastic bags purportedly containing American remains, some of which are really animal bones. Various forms of military identification have also been offered, some belonging to American soldiers long since safely home.

That is how Nicholas Brooks of Newburgh, N.Y., finally came home 12 years after parachuting from his stricken plane over Laos. His remains were delivered to Bangkok by a Lao resistance member and identified at a special military laboratory in a concrete-block warehouse in Honolulu. Technicians there can determine age, sex, race, blood type and basic stature even from partial remains. Physical characteristics such as height, weight, broken bones and dental records for all the missing have been computerized.

Using other Asian governments and the United Nations for pressure, the Reagan Administration continues negotiations for the return of M.I.A.'s from Laos, where a joint excavation team recovered remains from an American crash site in February, and from Vietnam, which turned over the remains of six others in March.

Outlook Seems to Improve

Detailed files for each man, concentrating on cases believed most physically accessible, are turned over to Vietnamese at meetings in a sparsely furnished Foreign Ministry room in Hanoi. The Vietnamese, citing humanitarian reasons and saying families of the missing are victims of the war like themselves, recently agreed to increase these sessions to a minimum of six a year. Both sides say they detect increasing cooperation. One United Nations official called it "a definite defrosting" of the M.I.A. issue with a "mounting momentum" that also affords Vietnam a window from its diplomatic isolation.

In regular visits to Hanoi and quiet dinners in New York, American officials seek to quicken the pace of returns, calling it "good-will money in the bank" for future Vietnamese-American relations.

Mr. Le says the process will take time, that Vietnam has 300,000 missing of its own, that it lacks recovery resources and that a proper American attitude would speed things. He cites as "unhelpful" and Reagan aides describe as "unnecessary" a recent House rider to provide $5 million in arms for Cambodian rebels fighting Vietnamese forces. Mr. Le said diplomatic relations, as the United States has with Laos, would be necessary for joint excavations.

The United States is known to have suggested instead that American experts survey crash and burial sites for an excavation estimate, which the Administration will pay.

"The war is over," said Mr. Le. "We want to look straight ahead to the future and a new chapter in relations between our two countries."

Donald Shay's mother here, Sara Frances, does not like to talk about the Vietnamese authorities. For a while she wrote many foreign governments, even Laotian royalty, about her missing son, and she went to Thailand. She also immersed herself in M.I.A. league work.

Donald was home on leave in the summer of 1970 when he proposed to Jane Morris, a stewardess. They had met in college. They agreed to marry in December at the end of his photo-reconnaissance tour in Thailand.

In a conversation the next day in the Shay family's backyard on Hilltop Road under the big maple tree that had grown up with the Shay youngsters, Donald Shay's sister, now Mary Louisa Rutledge, suggested that the couple marry immediately during the leave.

Prospects of Widowhood

"As if he could see into the future," Lieutenant Shay's sister recalled the other day, "he said: 'No, we'll wait till I get back. I'd never want to make her a widow.' "

Four months later, one month before his combat tour was to end, Donald Shay disappeared. The engagement ring arrived in the mail a few days later. Eighteen months ago Janet Morris married someone else. "I have my own son now," she said, "and I know how a mother feels."

For several years Dr. and Mrs. Shay held out strong hopes for their only son's return. The optimism has faded. "I no longer think I'm going to hear from him tomorrow," said Mrs. Shay, who still wears her son's M.I.A. bracelet. "But I won't accept that he's dead until I hear something definitive."

Mrs. Shay's daughter, an opponent of the war, gave up hope for her brother sooner. "The uncertainty was like ripping off a big bandage every day," she said. And so the other day when her 6-year-old son, Donald, pointed at his uncle's photo in the den and asked who it was, Mrs. Rutledge didn't say anything about M.I.A.'s or P.O.W.'s or Government negotiations or radar screens. "That's Mommy's brother," she said. "He's not living anymore."

* * *

May 1, 1985

SOLDIERS, TANKS AND ROCK 'N' ROLL IN PARADE MARKING FALL OF SAIGON

By BARBARA CROSSETTE
Special to the New York Times

HO CHI MINH CITY, Vietnam, April 30—The sun had just risen behind the twin-spired city cathedral today when high-stepping troops and rumbling Soviet tanks began their parade down the Street of April 30 to mark a decade of Communism in what was once known as the Republic of South Vietnam.

The procession started almost exactly at 7:52 A.M., the hour 10 years ago when a helicopter carrying the last American and South Vietnamese evacuees rose from the roof of the United States Embassy when this city was called Saigon.

Today, as jets flew overhead and the ranks of soldiers, sailors, militiawomen, militiamen, factory workers and students passed

Associated Press

Vietnamese troops marching past painting of Ho Chi Minh during celebration in city renamed for the leader.

by, the scene at first suggested a strictly Kremlin-inspired occasion. Nine members of the ruling Politburo, including Prime Minister Pham Van Dong and Le Duan, the Communist Party leader, sat on the reviewing stand among military officers and foreign Communist or fraternal delegations.

But then a local band on the sidelines broke into Vietnamese rock and down the street came roller skaters and a motorcycle club, strutting children and a small sea of women in the brightly colored traditional tunics called ao dais.

"We don't have this kind of parade in Hanoi," a Government official here for the occasion remarked. "This is South Vietnamese."

For Ho Chi Minh City, as it is now known, the 10th anniversary of its fall to North Vietnam has also provided an occasion to celebrate itself. Floats bore the industrial and agricultural products of the South as well as reminders of its culture. A few Buddhist monks and Roman Catholic priests sat in the reviewing stand as honored guests.

The anniversary has also given the city the chance to outline the future of its metropolitan area of 3.5 million people, where the spirit of free enterprise, encouraged during the "American" years has not been subdued.

Finally, the event has allowed outsiders in this very secretive country glimpses into the security measures taken in the sometimes recalcitrant South, where dozens of people have recently been tried, and several executed, for subversion.

Crowds Large but Quiet

Crowds were large but quiet today around the reviewing stands near the former presidential palace. City officials said the audience included 50,000 "organized watchers" brought in by local party committees.

They said they had no reliable estimate of how many others had come on their own. The ranks were swelled by hundreds of street urchins looking for something exciting to watch while doing a little panhandling on the side.

It was difficult to judge reactions. There were no cheers or applause except from the invited guests. A man in the crowd who talked with a Western reporter was hauled off by the police. Contact with foreigners is against the law.

Few Americans accepted Hanoi's invitation to attend the celebrations this week as friends of the country. David Dellinger, one of the Chicago Seven who demonstrated outside the 1968 Democratic National Convention, is here. So is John McAuliff, the head of the Indochina Reconciliation Project, a program of the American Friends Service Committee that campaigns for improved ties between Hanoi and Washington.

Antiwar Activists Absent

Jane Fonda, the actress, Cora Weiss, a peace activist, and the Rev. William Sloane Coffin, pastor of the Riverside Church in Manhattan, who were all prominent antiwar activists, were reported to have turned down invitations.

The more than 150 Western reporters, most of them American, here attract great interest but no apparent hostility from residents. The journalists' reasons for coming baffle some residents. "Why would you want to come for the anniversary of an occupation?" an elderly shopowner asked a reporter.

Conversations with Government officials and city residents who were willing to talk indicate that the unfinished business of absorbing the private businesses of Ho Chi Minh City into the Socialist state will dominate local efforts for some time to come.

Mai Chi Tho, who as chairman of the Ho Chi Minh City Peoples Committee functions as the Mayor, said in a news conference Sunday that the local government's main objective was to turn the city from a consumer society spoiled by the false economy of the past to a producer society contributing in very large part to the development of the country. Vietnam is one of the world's poorest nations.

Very Gradual Change

Within that context, he said, family businesses remain important, at least during the transition period, which he said would likely go on until the year 2000. After that, Mr. Tho said collectivization of production, technology and culture, would be completed.

Local shopkeepers say they are under great pressure to turn over their businesses to the state. One shopowner said a new round of takeovers was coming next month and that his family had only a few weeks to decide what to do. Refusing a partnership with Government means unemployment, the shopkeeper said. He said his family would leave the country if it did not have members still in prison camps.

Reporters here heard frequent complaints that it seems economically unsound to continue to squeeze local private enterprise, which has given this city considerably more vitality than Hanoi appears to have. Asked about this concern, a Government official gave the often-heard reply: "Transforming the South into a Socialist society will always be our first objective."

"Socialism cannot work unless everyone participates," Mr. Tho said.

Corruption Remains a Problem

Corruption is said to be worse than ever here, a situation related to economic hardship and common even in more prosperous Asian cities. Two Government employees were executed recently for siphoning and reselling Government gasoline. Such sentences do not seem to deter others, residents say.

Educated professionals, denied the right to work or practice because of their middle-class backgrounds and suspected or real connections to the previous regime, talk about having "right-" and "left-" hand professions, the one they were trained for, and the one they have to engage in to survive in a city where a cup of coffee can cost two days' pay. The relative abundance of consumer goods indicates the money is found somewhere.

Mr. Tho, 62 years old, a brother of Le Duc Tho and a man often mentioned as a candidate for the next generation of leadership, was candid about the city's problems. Ho Chi Minh City, he said, is short of electricity. There is high unemployment coupled with a population growth rate of 2 percent a year, which will mean five million people in the city by the end of the century.

On the other hand, a paper released by Mr. Tho to coincide with the anniversary listed as achievements by the city the promotion of a climate of "innovative working methods," the "promotion of small industries," particularly traditional handicrafts, and a growth in foreign trade. He says the city is a leader in Vietnam in industry, technology, international communications and culture.

Proud of the Police

Mr. Tho, an internal security expert, is also proud of the city's police. He told reporters Sunday, "Here we have no demonstrations like you do in the West, and no guerrilla groups like they have in the Philippines, Malaysia or Thailand."

While Vietnamese officials and Western diplomats in Hanoi say there is no serious resistance movement operating in the South, surveillance here is said to be intense. A resident said he recently saw 16 longhaired plainclothesmen materialize within seconds to seize a man who was shouting on the street. There are occasional Government admissions and trial records that suggest some dissidence does exist.

On Monday when officials took reporters to meet several "re-education camp" inmates north of the city, one of the prisoners said he had been arrested in 1982 for joining a "counterrevolutionary militia." He said he had been forced to join by former officers of the South Vietnamese Army.

A former professional now unemployed in Ho Chi Minh City for refusing to accept "political direction," said that something more widespread than open dissent was "passive noncooperation" with Government policies.

"In this cause of national reconciliation" an army officer at the city's military command said, "we know many people are happy, but there are others who are not."

U.S. to Press Efforts on Missing

WASHINGTON, April 30 (UPI)—President Reagan promised stepped-up efforts today to press the countries of Southeast Asia to account for all Americans killed in the Vietnam War.

"The key to resolution of this issue lies in obtaining the full cooperation of the Governments of Vietnam and Laos," Mr. Reagan said in a report to Congress on the 2,477 Americans still missing or unaccounted for in Southeast Asia.

While progress has been made in obtaining fuller cooperation from both countries, Mr. Reagan said, the United States "should not be regarded in any way as satisfied with the current situation or the progress we have made."

"Cooperation has been much too slow," he said, "and we must continue to pursue every possible avenue to reach a level which offers maximum potential for results."

Mr. Reagan said his Administration had "vigorously pursued" a full accounting through high-level visits by American officials to Vietnam and Laos, upgraded intelligence efforts, a campaign to focus public attention on missing soldiers and close coordination with the National League of Families of American Prisoners and Missing in Southeast Asia.

Among the positive diplomatic steps cited by Mr. Reagan were agreements by Vietnam to increase bilateral meetings on the issue to six from four and to consider the missing Americans separately from other matters.

Vietnam turned over the remains of eight Americans in 1984 and six on March 20 of this year, including—for the first time—two men said by the Vietnamese to have died while being held as prisoners of war.

* * *

June 17, 1985

DESERTERS IN SWEDEN: AN ODD LITTLE 'V.F.W. POST'

By BARNABY J. FEDER
Special to the New York Times

STOCKHOLM—One day a few years ago, as David Smith was driving the No. 52 bus here, a Swedish passenger and a Yugoslav immigrant got into an argument. The driver stopped the bus and tried to break it up.

Then the Yugoslav started shouting at him. "You Swedes all stick together!" he screamed. Mr. Smith, annoyed at the insult to his fairness, threw him off the bus.

He recalled the anecdote with an ironic smile. A 39-year-old with dark, curly hair, brown eyes and a gold earring in his right ear, he could hardly look less Swedish.

Mr. Smith, now a Stockholm bus dispatcher, deserted his unit at Fort Ord in California rather than be sent to Vietnam. Like many of the hundreds of young Americans who made their way to Sweden during the Vietnam War era as deserters or draft resisters, he remembers well the days when he felt what a fellow American called "the intense desire to be a super Swede."

Numbers Have Dwindled

Those days are gone. Nearly 1,000 Americans came here during the Vietnam years; the 50 to 75 believed to remain are all-but-invisible members of Swedish society. Few of them see other Americans regularly, and they say they rarely think about how Swedish or American they are.

Some have become Swedish citizens. Bruce Mayor, who came here from the San Francisco area in 1968, just before reaching draft age, has served in the Swedish Army and has run for a seat in Parliament.

Those who fled to Sweden were a small part of the 27 million draft-age Americans who faced decisions about their future during the Vietnam era. Almost 9 million did military service during those years, including 3.4 million who actually spent time in Southeast Asia. Tens of thousands are estimated to have gone to Canada to escape the draft.

Unlike the Americans who went to Canada, more than two-thirds of those in Sweden were deserters rather than draft evaders. Most of the deserters say their action was spontaneous.

Steven Kinneman, who grew up in a what he describes as "a typical working-class family in Indianapolis," deserted from the Army in Thailand in 1967 and wandered in Laos for five years before making his way here.

Having overcome years of anger and bitterness, Mr. Kinneman says he now feels "the process of growing into our new lives is finished."

He and his companion, Bitte, have three children and have scraped together enough money from their jobs at a day care center to make that most Swedish of all investments—the purchase of a summer cabin in the Baltic archipelago.

To endure in Sweden, Americans like Mr. Kinneman had to learn a new language, adapt to a different culture and eventually establish themselves as functioning adults, in nearly every case without having previously lived on their own.

Relationships Didn't Survive

In many cases they were isolated from relatives and friends who could not afford to travel to Sweden. Although some had wives or companions who joined them here, interviews and published studies indicate that none of the relationships survived the move to Scandinavia.

Although the exiles, as they initially called themselves, were denied political refugee status, they were welcomed far more than in Canada. Indeed, they were lionized in some intellectual and cultural circles.

"The United States is no longer the country to which rebels and revolutionaries flee," wrote Vilhelm Moberg, the author of "The Immigrants," an epic novel about the journey of 19th-century Swedish peasants to the United States. "Just this category of people are instead now leaving the U.S.A. and going in exile to Canada and Europe. For me, these Americans fulfill the great heritage of their country; in reality they are faithful to this heritage."

'Such a Long Time Ago'

"It all seems like such a long time ago," said Richard Bailey, a 37-year-old inventory control manager for a small electronic components company in suburban Stockholm. He deserted from Southeast Asia in November 1967 with three other Americans and came to Sweden from Japan. Once here, the four came to prominence as activists against American policy and encouraged other American soldiers to desert. Only one of the other three, Michael Lindner, is still in Sweden; he works nearby as a carpenter.

Most of the Americans who came here soon found that survival in a new land was too demanding to leave much energy for political activism. The Americans also got bad publicity because of crime and drug use among some of them. By 1977, even the large Stockholm group had been reduced to what Mr. Kinneman called "an odd type of V.F.W. post."

The more than 100 blacks who came to Sweden, many of whom were reacting to racial problems in the military as much as the threat of going to Vietnam, had a particularly tough time. The southern port of Malmö, where most of the blacks arrived and settled, turned out to be the city least receptive to the deserters.

"We didn't come here intending to make a new life," said Michael Deberry, who deserted in West Germany in 1971 and now works as a lathe operator. "We came here to get away. For three years, I lived with a packed suitcase ready to go."

'Would Never Have Seen Sweden'

"Let's face it," said Herbert Washington, a black American who also deserted in West Germany. "Except for Vietnam, I would never have seen Sweden in my life, not even as a tourist."

Today, he said, probably fewer than 5 of the 75 blacks who went to Malmö remain.

Nearly all the Americans who remain here have visited home, but the question of returning permanently is not an easy one.

"I still get calls from my parents in Pawtucket, Rhode Island, trying to get us to move back," said Mr. Washington, who married a Dane and has two children. "But they aren't living any better there than we are here."

A social worker who handles young adults with drinking, drug and crime problems, Mr. Washington said employment prospects in Rhode Island in his field looked grim when he visited his family. "I'm 44, with a wife and two kids to think about," he said.

Trying to Fit In

One of those who did go home from Sweden, Irving Rubin, said he felt torn between the two countries. "We were brought up in ways that don't fit there, but we learned adult values that don't fit here," he said by telephone from his home in Rockland, Mass., where he returned in 1978 after two earlier visits. He is now considering moving back to Sweden or moving to Israel.

Many of the Americans here said they felt that the next generation of young men in the United States may well face the kind of choice they did.

"Here we go again," said one of them, Jim Walch, when asked about United States policy in Central America.

Mr. Walch, who was notified that he had been given conscientious objector status after he moved here from Wisconsin in 1969, is a teacher with a research interest in preschool education. He is married with three children and has a suburban home, an interest in Swedish folk music and a quiet, eminently Swedish manner. He cast an absentee ballot for the Rev. Jesse Jackson in last year's Democratic Presidential primary in Wisconsin.

"There are lots of different ways of leaving," said Mr. Walch, who suggested that some men who never emigrated dropped further out of American life than those who did.

Views of Vietnam War

Most of the Americans in Sweden said they still considered the Vietnam War a brutal, immoral error. Many would like to see reparations paid to the Vietnamese. Nonetheless, a common theme among them is sympathy for those who went to Vietnam.

"Everyone I was in the Army with was a nice guy," Mr. Males said, "and I hope they get better treatment."

Despite that attitude, the welcome that Vietnam veterans are finally being accorded in the United States has reopened old wounds. Many of the deserters are bitter that President Carter's 1977 amnesty program offered them less-than-honorable discharges.

"I still feel I didn't do anything wrong," said Mr. Smith, the bus dispatcher. "Just because you left America doesn't mean you don't love it."

* * *

December 20, 1986

KEEP AN EYE ON HANOI

So far only the faces are different in Vietnam, but policy changes could be next. If these bring relaxation of control at home and in Cambodia, they could be of enormous importance to the people of Indochina and open some interesting opportunities in the Soviet-Chinese-American triangle.

Economic reformers dominate the new leadership lineup announced at this week's Communist Party Congress. Vietnam has been mired in deep poverty, the price of doctrinaire

Communism and aggression in Cambodia. The Vietnamese people need relief.

As for foreign relations, the new team might be ready to rethink policy toward Cambodia. Vietnam's military occupation of that country has been long and frightful, and fuels a deadly civil war. Hanoi's insistence on retaining control of Cambodia is the main reason the world has isolated Vietnam.

If the new leaders would shift the focus to development, they could reassess their present dependence on the Soviet Union. The Russians provide them, as an anti-Chinese ally, about $1 billion yearly. For Vietnam to leave Cambodia would allow repositioning between Moscow and Peking and help to open the door with Washington as well.

The party congress, the first since the death last summer of the veteran Communist leader Le Duan, designated Nguyen Van Linh as party chief, and replaced 5 of the 13 politburo members. Mr. Linh, the new party leader, was Hanoi's top official in South Vietnam before and after unification. His familiarity with the South's more open economic style made him an advocate of economic decentralization and raising production through material incentives rather than ideological exhortations. These views were resisted in the past and only the announcement of a new economic program will show how far Hanoi is prepared to go now. Nevertheless, the promotion of other leading economic reformers is a positive sign.

A hint of a possible change on Cambodia comes from the retirement of both Le Duc Tho and Gen. Van Tien Dung, two leaders closely linked to present policies. Economic revival virtually depends on reversing those policies, which have drained resources and provoked a cutoff of Western and Japanese assistance.

Vietnam's revolutionary cadres endured years of sacrifice, sustained by dreams of development and nationalist glory. Instead, they have reaped underdevelopment and dependence on support from Hanoi's only ally, the Soviet Union. If Vietnam's new leaders seek a constructive way out of the mess and provide more information about Americans missing in action and related issues, Washington should be ready to pay heed and encourage a welcome trend. Policy made in Vietnam can still reverberate in the largest capitals.

* * *

August 3, 1987

DESPITE GAINS, MANY VIETNAMESE REFUGEES ARE REFUSING TO LET WAR END

By KATHERINE BISHOP
Special to the New York Times

SAN JOSE, Calif., July 29—Despite their pride in noteworthy social and economic gains and the reality of rapidly growing political influence, the war has not ended for many Vietnamese refugees here.

"I have a responsibility and a duty as an American," said Ho Quang Nhut, a San Jose insurance agent who was a philosophy teacher in Saigon before he became one of the first "boat people" to escape to Malaysia with his wife and children in 1976. "But in my heart, my family and friends are still there. How can I forget?"

Support of resistance movements against the Communist Government of Vietnam remains a top priority for many of those who fled the country after the "Day of Shame," April 30, 1975, when Saigon fell to the forces of North Vietnam. Some express concern, however, about the growth of intolerance among refugees for anything short of outspoken anti-Communism and support of covert United States military aid to guerilla forces.

80,000 Registered Voters

The role that the Vietnamese refugees should play in United States politics is a pervasive subject of debate in "Little Saigon," where the opening of more than 300 businesses over the last five years has transformed a downtown neighborhood once dotted with vacant storefronts. The number of Vietnamese in the city is now approaching 10 percent of the population.

Mr. Nhut, now 48 years old, is one of three co-chairmen nationwide of the League of Vietnamese Voters in the United States. Of the more than 500,000 Vietnamese living in this country, approximately 80,000 are registered to vote, most of them as Republicans because that party is perceived as more staunchly anti-Communist, Mr. Nhut said. The organization expects to add another 60,000 to that total in the next four years.

Mr. Nhut said that his group recently lobbied some Republican members of Congress for military aid to the "freedom fighters" they believed were poised to attempt an overthrow of the Vietnamese Government from within the country with the assistance of troops training along the border regions with Laos and Cambodia. It was their "bad luck" to have raised the issue at the time of controversy over aid to the Nicaraguan contras, he said.

Scooped Local News Media

In recent years a number of incidents in recent years have galvanized the anti-Communist sentiments of the refugee community. In 1985, a group of militants attacked a San Jose bookstore run by the Socialist Workers Party.

The most recent occurred in June, when a news program on Vietnam Liberty Television, which had begun broadcasting the first privately produced half-hour nightly news program in Vietnamese from a small office in nearby Santa Clara, scooped the local news media.

The story involved Tom Hayden, a State Assemblyman and former anti-war protester who had traveled to North Vietnam in the war, who had been asked to give the commencement address at San Jose City College, a two-year community college with a large number of Vietnamese-American students. As chairman of the subcommittee on higher education, Mr. Hayden was scheduled to speak on the topic of the future of the community college system.

The speech was canceled after Vietnamese-language newspapers editorialized against it, saying that Mr. Hayden and his wife, Jane Fonda, were partly responsible for the Communist victory. Some militant leaders threatened a demonstration, saying they would not guarantee it would be nonviolent.

Hayden Is Assailed

Nguyen Tiep, a San Jose attorney who is considered a moderate and whose name is frequently mentioned as a possible candidate for political office from the community, was one of the leaders in the protest. Mr. Tiep, a 41-year-old former captain in the legal research department of the Saigon police, was the first Vietnamese-American on the Santa Clara County Republican Central Committee.

"This is not a freedom of speech issue," he said. "He is a traitor."

Mr. Tiep also led a group advocating a total boycott of the college by Vietnamese students who he said made up more than 20 percent of the students, a formidable prospect in a time of declining enrollment in this state's community colleges.

While the threatened boycott was called off after college administration apologised, Mr. Tiep said that Vietnamese students would still boycott classes taught by faculty members who assisted Mr. Hayden in making a brief surprise appearance at the ceremony.

Mr. Hayden, who said he believed his right to free speech was violated in the college incident, has also expressed concern in interviews about reports of resistance activities by former generals of the South Vietnamese military. "I think that they have a clandestine network that is not monitored and for all anyone knows is operating outside the law," he said.

Often Meet at Restaurant

About 30 former generals living in the area form an association known as the Dien Hong, which meets regularly for activities that its members say are strictly social. The Dien Hong includes such members as Do Kien Nhieu, a former brigadier general and the last mayor of Saigon, and Bui Dinh Dam, a former major general in Vietnam and now a social worker in San Jose.

They often meet at a Vietnamese restaurant in nearby Mountain View, which is owned by Dr. Nguyen Ton Hoan, who was vice premier of the Republic of Vietnam in 1964 under Gen. Nguyen Khanh and a leader in the Dai Viet or "Greater Vietnam" party. He is not a member of the Dien Hong.

"We are organizing an international movement to support the idea of a free Vietnam," Dr. Hoan, 70, said. "But it is too early to talk about the resistance. It's not the right time."

Lai Duc Hung, a former captain in the South Vietnamese Army who now lives in San Jose and serves as the general secretary of the Coalition of Nationalist Vietnamese Organizations of Northern California, a group representing 52 organizations, said the Dien Hong was part of the coalition.

"Some of the organizations are secret," Mr. Hung said. "There are a lot of things we cannot talk about."

Representatives of three of the four resistance groups in Vietnam are part of the coalition, Mr. Hung said. "We try to create a chain for people to contact them," he said, "but we don't collect money. They have an account to send money to."

While acknowledging that there are some "radical views" within the community, most leaders appear to regard them as inevitable.

"The wounds are so deep they cannot forget and cannot forgive," said Nguyen Manh. "It will remain with them a long time."

* * *

August 10, 1987

VIETNAMESE EASE LIMITS ON ARTISTS AND WRITERS

By BARBARA CROSSETTE
Special to the New York Times

HANOI, Vietnam, Aug. 6—At the 11th-century Temple of Literature in a quiet Hanoi park, there are three gates leading to the inner courtyard. The ornate one in the middle is for kings. Two modest ones flank it. One is for soldiers and the other for writers and scholars.

"In ancient times, there were literary mandarins and military mandarins," Nguyen Du Chi, an art historian, said. "But it was the literary mandarins who entered the court first, to advise the king."

While writers, artists and dramatists interviewed this week about contemporary Vietnam avoided the use of what they call "feudal" terms, their message was the same. As the country struggles after decades of war to build a peacetime society, the literary mandarins are again advising the king.

"We Vietnamese can live without breakfast before going to work," said Pham Thi Thanh, founder and director of the Youth Drama Group. "But our hearts are dependent on the arts."

Intellectual Ferment

Vietnam, and Hanoi most of all, is in intellectual ferment. Artists are turning to Expressionism, playwrights to self-indulgent, personal themes of relationships gone wrong. The youth group has gone on stage to pillory teachers who sell exam papers.

"I have been a journalist for 35 years, and this is the most interesting period of all," said Huu Tho, an editor of Nhan Dan, the Communist Party daily newspaper. "In wartime, we couldn't speak our minds."

"During wartime, we can say that leaders and writers had to unite ideologically in the cause of national defense," Ly Hai Chau, director of a literary publishing house, said.

"But in peace, the writer can return to a reflection of ordinary life—offering new ideas and being in the forefront of public opinion."

Little Is Sacred

The change has come in the last year or two, in the company of economic liberalization and a self-criticism campaign before which little is sacred, not even the Communist Party's leadership over the last half-century.

There are limits to expression in Hanoi—except in a small, clandestine publishing world that an outsider cannot measure. And there is a fear among some that the door to expression can be closed as easily as it was opened.

There can be no movement to challenge the Communist principles of the country's founders. Nor would anyone start a campaign against the nine-year-old war in Cambodia that drains already slender resources and asks a new generation of men to risk their lives.

But in a recent book, "Time Gone Away," Le Luu tells the story of an ordinary man defeated by life who describes in flashbacks the failures of his society and his own passivity in the face of those failures. The success of the book is described as sensational.

Change From Within

Vu Tu Nam, director of the Vietnam Writers' Association publishing house, said the book, which appeared last year, could not have been published three or four years ago. At the literary publishing house, Mr. Chau said he was reviewing manuscripts that had been rejected in previous years.

Vietnamese who are sensitive to suggestions they are under Soviet influence say the wave of introspective criticism is not a development that has been forced on the country by Moscow, Hanoi's patron.

Rather, they say, it is something that comes from within Vietnam itself, just as economic changes in the city grew out of five years of experience with "contract" private-enterprise farming, or from a reluctant admission that some of the methods that had been used by the south could be applied without damaging the Communist orthodoxy of the north.

In Hanoi, private businesses, which are beginning to expand under liberalized city laws, are drawing families back together into ancestral homes and neighborhoods from scattered cooperatives.

New Currents

Old habits return, even in rough economic times. This year, for example, Hanoi got a gardening club.

The new currents, thus, move in two directions: inward toward a revival of ancient Vietnamese cultural traditions—not only in the arts—and outward for broader links with the world.

Vietnam's poverty, intellectuals say, is creating a stagnating isolationism. A European ambassador here said this disturbs many Vietnamese who remember that this was once one of the most cosmopolitan societies in Asia.

While shelves in Hanoi bookstores groan under the weight of unsold heavy Soviet technical volumes, readers, translators and publishers press on a visitor lists of books by American authors they would like to have—Kurt Vonnegut, William Styron, Eric Segal—or they simply ask for "anything new." They want to go beyond Mark Twain, Jack London and John Reed. Alex Haley's "Roots" was a recent success.

Novels in Limited Supply

Contemporary Vietnamese novels and short-story collections are printed in limited quantities because of a shortage of paper, and they sell out almost before they reach the stores. Mr. Chau remarked that Vietnam must be unique in the world in having a black market in its own literature.

At night, the Vietnamese flock to theaters through repeated power failures to see exquisitely costumed actors recreate old plays in auditoriums that are little better than stifling barns.

"We can be nationalistic, modern, realistic and romantic," said Mrs. Thanh, who studied theater in the Soviet Union, as she guided a visitor around the Youth Drama Group's rehearsal rooms. Her aims, she said, were "to praise love and life" and to link a new generation of wartime children with their rich, but forgotten past.

"The best things of Vietnam have been abandoned everywhere—not only in the theater," she said.

* * *

August 23, 1987

PRAGMATISM AND DOGMA VIE AS VIETNAM'S REGIONAL RIVALS

By BARBARA CROSSETTE
Special to the New York Times

HO CHI MINH CITY, Vietnam, Aug. 20—For more than a decade, a power struggle has been going on in Vietnam that many Vietnamese seem to regard as the final stage of an unfinished revolution.

The picture of this struggle that emerges from several weeks of interviews with officials, journalists and business people in both state and private sectors is partly one of a test of wills between Hanoi's orthodox Marxists—whose ideas of development are rooted in the Soviet Union's Stalinist era or the most radical period of Chinese Communism—and a group of more pragmatic and flexible leaders.

Communism is not being challenged here. But Vietnamese say openly that the party has lost the public's confidence. If it fails to regain this, "who knows what will happen," an editor said.

Inevitably, this clash has involved a broader confrontation between the isolated, undeveloped, agrarian culture of northern Vietnam and the cosmopolitan, entrepreneurial south. Those differences predated the introduction of Communism to Vietnam by Ho Chi Minh half a century ago.

Process Began in 1975

As described candidly by many Vietnamese, the process of unifying the nation seems in retrospect to have begun rather than ended in 1975 with the fall of this city, formerly Saigon. In the end, much that is southern may prevail. But the battle is not over.

In a new atmosphere of outspokenness in Vietnam today, details are emerging of the machinations behind leadership struggles that led in December 1986 to the naming of Nguyen Van Linh, a northerner who spent much of his career in the south, as general secretary of the Communist Party.

Those who have observed the power struggle at close range over the last 12 years tell Orwellian stories of armed economic police sent to ferret out people who were suspected of encouraging free enterprise or otherwise undermining the official policy of total state control of goods and services.

"We lived in terrible times from 1975 to the early 1980's," the owner of a small bakery said. "We were afraid of everything."

Editors recount tales of unwritten pacts among journalists to protect vulnerable new political thinkers from entrenched hard-liners.

Old Jobs, New Masters

"In the first few years after unification, we had certain duties," said Tuat Viet, an editor of Saigon Giai Phong, the local Communist Party newspaper. Mr. Viet, a southerner educated in Hanoi who was sent back to the south after 1975, said those duties involved promoting North Vietnamese policies and persuading people here to go on working for new masters with no managerial skills.

Mr. Viet said, "But by 1978, we began to see the contradictions between improving production and the backward system of management we had. Journalists in this city began to recognize that we needed some changes.

"In 1975, Ho Chi Minh City was the most developed economy in Vietnam," he said. "But can you imagine that a few years later this city, in the middle of the fertile Mekong Delta, had to rely on grain imported from abroad? People could not accept that."

Crusading politicians and journalists focused their attacks on a system of state subsidies that was stifling or even reversing economic growth, while leading to large-scale corruption and the abuse of political power.

'Oppressed by Officials'

"To be frank, we were being oppressed by party and state officials—only they had the power to oppress," said Huu Tho, deputy editor in chief of Nhan Dan, the Communist Party daily paper.

The critics also zeroed in on the Ho Chi Minh generation's enthusiasm for large-scale, Soviet-supported industrial and energy projects, which ran counter to Vietnamese traditional economic patterns—and in any case have delivered almost no results.

Vietnam now ranks 161st among 164 nations measured by the United Nations in per capita gross national product, a provincial official in Phu Khanh said in an interview, repeating the figure several times.

In discussing the degree to which Vietnam has swung along behind successive Soviet policies, Vietnamese journalists and others say that the struggle between orthodox Marxists and pragmatists was well under way by the late 1970's, before the Gorbachev era in the Soviet Union.

'Vietnamese Are Very Clever'

"Economic renovation must be in line with our country's traditional practices," Mr. Tho said. "History tells us if you just imitate others, you fail."

But Vietnamese add that the example set by the Soviet party leader has been a prop of tremendous value to like-minded people here.

"The Vietnamese are very clever," a Government official said. "We make use of these Russian ideas for our own purposes."

For the moment, most Vietnamese say confidently, the pragmatists led by Mr. Linh are not only in control, but also very popular.

Mr. Linh, whom southerners now credit with quietly supporting heretical economic practices—small private enterprises, in particular—while head of the Communist Party here in the late 1970's, was apparently purged from the Politburo by hard-liners in 1982. His return in 1985 marked the beginning of two years of steady change.

Orthodox Marxists Powerful

But followers of the orthodox Marxists, symbolized in most Vietnamese minds by the late party leader, Le Duan, and his immediate successor, Truong Chinh, remain powerful.

Diplomats say Mr. Chinh—the architect in the 1950's of a disastrous attempt at forced collectivization—fought up to the eve of the Sixth Party Congress last year to block Mr. Linh's ascent.

Foreign visitors still encounter old-style party cadres in Government offices—or don't meet known hard-liners because they refuse to be interviewed by journalists from democratic countries.

"The resistance to change is still large," an editorial board member at Saigon Giai Phong said in a conversation at the newspaper office. "The obstacles are many." Among these he listed the entrenched bureaucrats whose jobs may now be threatened.

'Struggle Is Still Complex'

"The struggle is still complex," Mr. Viet said. "A zigzag route may be unavoidable. But the present trend is clear. This is a demand of 60 million people, 60 million people who refuse to continue living with a stagnant bureaucracy."

The story of Ngyuen Thi Thi, who is 65, gives life to the political abstractions now being discussed in Vietnam.

Mrs. Thi, who runs a successful food processing network based on smallscale family businesses, is no capitalist. Her Communist credentials are impeccable: a guerrilla at 18, she ran as a courier between the North Vietnamese and their southern operatives.

Her husband was beheaded under the regime of President Ngo Dinh Diem in 1959, she said. On her office wall are pictures of her meeting in 1968 with Ho Chi Minh. She is a Socialist Hero with seven medals to her credit.

In Charge of Rice Distribution

But she is also a southerner.

After 1975, when Hanoi moved its team into the south, Mrs. Thi was put in charge of rice distribution for Ho Chi Minh City.

As she visited small outlets around the city, she quickly discovered that many shopkeepers had other skills. She turned over 1,000 of her 7,000 distribution points into small factories that made noodles, cookies, cakes, starch and other cereal.

"In 1980 and 1981, the Economic Police decided that I was making a mistake by establishing this network," she said. "I was told this was contrary to socialist economic management.

"One day, about 60 armed police surrounded my office," she said. "But luckily, I did not go to jail. Nguyen Van Linh and Vo Van Kiet were in Ho Chi Minh City then. And they gave me the green light to go ahead."

Mr. Linh was in disgrace within a year, the victim of hard-liners. But by 1985 he and Mr. Kiet, now head of national economic planning, had re-emerged in major roles, their policies vindicated.

"The hard-liners are still strong," she said, "but they are unlikely to be able to reverse the present trend.

"We believe in these new leaders," she said, "because they once shared our difficulties."

* * *

April 8, 1988

ECHOES OF VIETNAM

A Superpower Is Desperate to Leave, But in Afghanistan It Is the Russians

By CRAIG R. WHITNEY
Special to the New York Times

WASHINGTON, April 7—Only a few weeks ago, the Reagan Administration seemed to be risking failure in the Afghan peace talks—insisting, because its conservative supporters in the Senate insisted, on the right to keep supplying the insurgents with weapons after a Soviet withdrawal began, despite an earlier pledge to cut them off.

In fact the risk may have been blown out of proportion, exaggerated by distorted memories of how the Vietnam War was lost to the Communists after a "sellout" cease-fire 15 years ago. There are parallels—in Afghanistan this year, as in Vietnam in 1973, a superpower tired of entanglement in an unwinnable war is determined to get itself out. But this time it is the Soviet Union.

Most doubts here about the seriousness of the Soviet intention to leave vanished in early February, when the Soviet leader, Mikhail S. Gorbachev, made a speech on Soviet television saying he was ready to begin a pullout of the 115,000 Soviet troops from Afghanistan by May 15 if agreement could be reached in the negotiations in Geneva sponsored by the United Nations. A political settlement of the civil war in Afghanistan, he said, was up to the Afghans afterward.

Since Moscow was no longer insisting on leaving a Communist-dominated government in power after it left, the main political question for the Reagan Administration was how easy the United States should make it for the Russians to get out.

An Embarrassing Hitch

"They invaded that country, and they have to get out," a senior Administration official said at the time.

But there was an embarrassing hitch: Two years ago, American negotiators had pledged in the United Nations talks to guarantee that all "outside interference"—including supplies to the insurgents—would stop once a Soviet withdrawal began.

President Reagan, who according to his advisers was aware of the pledge to stop supplying the guerrillas, nevertheless said, "You can't suddenly disarm them and leave them prey to the other Government." The Russians, for their part, had made no promise to stop aiding the Government in Kabul.

So conservatives in Washington, inside and outside the Administration, began pressuring the President to insist that the Russians also stop sending supplies to Kabul. Without such a provision, Senator Gordon J. Humphrey, Republican of New Hampshire, said in Geneva yesterday, President Reagan should reject the agreement.

Supplies for Both Sides

But Administration officials discovered a face-saving way out of the quandary: if the Russians were determined to get out, and apparently resigned to leaving their Afghan allies to an uncertain fate, the United States could insist on the right to keep supplying the insurgents as long as the Soviet Union kept supplying Kabul.

When the Soviet Foreign Minister, Eduard A. Shevardnadze, was in Washington last month, he apparently agreed to this idea.

The Afghan Communist leader, Najibullah, is believed to have objected, which is why American diplomats believe Mr. Gorbachev and Mr. Shevardnadze took him to Tashkent, the largest Soviet city near Afghanistan, for some serious talk yesterday and today.

Since they got him to agree that the "last obstacles to signing the agreements have now been removed," as a joint Soviet-Afghan statement put it today, the Russians can now free themselves for foreign-policy initiatives elsewhere unencumbered by the heavy mortgage of foreign military intervention in an Islamic third-world country.

A Question of Survival

What happens to their ally is not so clear. Even if the Soviet Union keeps supplying it, how can Mr. Najibullah's regime, which controls little more than the area around Kabul and has hundreds of thousands of well-armed insurgents sworn to bring it down, survive without the Soviet Army's help?

The circumstances seemed strongly reminiscent of the arm-twisting that President Nixon and Secretary of State Henry A. Kissinger had to do on on their nervous ally in Saigon, Nguyen Van Thieu, when the United States finally decided to get out of Vietnam.

Then, after an offensive by the Communist forces of North Vietnam in 1972, the United States reached agreement with Hanoi on a cease-fire and a withdrawal of American forces—only to be thwarted by Mr. Thieu, who correctly feared that his Government could not survive on its own. "I see that those whom I regard as friends have failed me," he said.

He stalled until January 1973, when Mr. Nixon had to threaten the South Vietnamese leader with "inevitable and immediate termination of U.S. economic and military assistance which cannot be forestalled by a change of personnel in your Government," before Mr. Thieu bowed to the cease-fire terms.

Conservative Support

As in Afghanistan, the cease-fire in Vietnam did not come with a finished political settlement. During the next two years, the Soviet Union and China continued to supply the North Vietnamese with military aid, while Congress cut back aid to the South Vietnamese. Mr. Thieu lost his nerve, and when Hanoi staged a new offensive in 1975, Saigon was quickly overrun.

So in Afghanistan in 1988, conservatives in Congress—who saw to it that the Afghan guerrillas were supplied covertly with arms, ammunition and Stinger anti-aircraft missiles to fight Soviet helicopters—were determined not to leave them in the lurch.

In fact, both the insurgents and the Kabul regime have reportedly been oversupplied in recent weeks by their superpower patrons as a hedge against a negotiated arms cutoff.

In Congress and in the Administration, the view is that Mr. Najibullah will probably not survive in power very long after the Russians leave, no matter now much aid they give him. But if the Communist regime does fall, what will succeed it is not so clear.

The guerrillas are divided, but a victory by them could lead to an Islamic fundamentalist regime in Afghanistan, linked to Iran, which has also supplied them. In that case, all the sophisticated Stinger missiles now being rushed to the insurgents could become a threat to United States interests.

But in their eagerness to speed a Soviet withdrawal, few officials here seem to be much concerned with such long-term questions.

* * *

August 23, 1988

REOPENING AN OLD WOUND

Quayle's Guard Duty in Vietnam War Era Puts the Focus Again on National Trauma

By E. J. DIONNE Jr.
Special to the New York Times

WASHINGTON, Aug. 22—This was supposed to be the election in which the postwar baby boom came into its own in American politics. It's been a rough coming-out party. Last year, Democratic candidates struggled with personal issues that arose out of the counterculture of the 1960's—sexual behavior and drugs.

Now, the most traumatic issue of all, the Vietnam War, has come back to haunt Senator Dan Quayle of Indiana, the 41-year-old conservative whom Vice President Bush chose as a running mate in the hopes of winning an edge with the voters of the baby boom.

Will America ever get over the 1960's? Will the Vietnam generation, and the nation, ever get over the Vietnam War?

The reaction to Mr. Quayle's decision of 19 years ago to join the National Guard, which vastly decreased the odds of his serving in Vietnam—a perfectly legal decision, as Mr. Bush's campaign has noted repeatedly—suggests that the war, in a phrase popular in the 1960's, has come home to stay. The traumas of that war are not easily repressed and the moral debates it set off will not go away.

Among President Reagan's goals was to overcome "the Vietnam syndrome," a malaise discerned by conservatives. The phrase referred to the nation's new, post-Vietnam preoccupation with avoiding direct military intervention anywhere, in order to prevent the United States from getting bogged down in "another Vietnam."

Toward that end, the Administration encouraged a more positive evaluation of the war. More important, it tried to push forward a trend that was already well under way: granting Vietnam veterans the respect they deserved for serving their country in an unpopular war, a respect that was denied many of them when they first returned home.

Some on the political right have tried to put this trend to the service of their cause, and films such as "Rambo" served as a symbol for a newly assertive America that had shaken off the guilt and anxiety of Vietnam.

But the movement to honor veterans of Vietnam was much broader than that. Even intense and unreconstructed opponents of the war, like Jane Fonda, have spoken of their admiration for those who fought the war and the terrible way middle-class foes of the war treated those too poor, too patriotic or too unconnected to get out of fighting it.

Those who had avoided service in the war, especially through such painless means as student or medical deferments or a lucky draft number, began to speak of "Viet

Guilt," as the writer Christopher Buckley put it in the title of a September 1983 article in Esquire.

From very different viewpoints, Mr. Buckley, who used to write speeches for Mr. Bush, and Jim Fallows, who had written speeches for former President Jimmy Carter, both wrote about how badly they felt that Vietnam, their generation's war, had been someone else's battle.

Mr. Fallows called his essay, which appeared in the Washington Monthly in October 1975: "What did you do in the Class War, Daddy?" He spoke of the sense that as members of the upper middle class, he and his friends had avoided fighting in a conflict that had taken or ruined the lives of their less privileged countrymen.

Mr. Fallows said he was referring to "the mainly white, mainly well-educated children of mainly comfortable parents who are now mainly embarked on promising careers in law, medicine, business, academics."

"Vietnam," Mr. Fallows wrote in a passage that might be seen now as prefiguring Mr. Quayle's troubles, "has left us with a heritage rich in possibilities for class warfare."

Eight years later Mr. Buckley wrote that "by not putting on uniforms, we forfeited what might have been the ultimate opportunity, in increasingly self-obsessed times, of making the ultimate commitment to something greater than ourselves: the survival of comrades."

'Trauma Caused by the War'

Morris Dickstein, a professor at Queens College in New York City who is the author of a highly acclaimed book, "Gates of Eden: American Culture in the Sixties," said that most of the rich collection of Vietnam films and novels did not appear until the 1980's. "The extent of the trauma caused by the war came through in the fact that it took popular culture, which usually moves very quickly, so long to deal with it," he observed.

Professor Dickstein said that the trauma could be traced not only to the personal struggles of individuals, but also to politics. "It was traumatic for conservatives because they couldn't face the fact that the war had been a mistake," he said. "And it was traumatic for radicals because they couldn't face the fact that victory for the other side did not lead to a bright future but to dictatorship and a bloodbath."

Senator Quayle burst into this slow healing process, clearly unprepared for the consequences. And his initial, clumsy response suggested that he had not thought too much about the matter.

"If only he had said that he felt some guilt for not having fought in the war," lamented a Republican consultant, who asked not to be identified. "That wouldn't have solved his problem, but it would have helped a lot."

Mr. Quayle's experience with the war did not fall neatly onto either side of the 1960's barricades. On the one hand, he was for the war, not against it. But Mr. Quayle did not rebel against the anti-war movement to such an extent that he was willing, as were many young, midwestern conservatives, to go fight the war.

Bush's Defense of Quayle

In his running mate's defense today, Mr. Bush invoked the fact that Mr. Quayle was not a draft resister, but instead joined the National Guard. "It's true, he didn't go to Vietnam because he wasn't called," Mr. Bush told the Veterans of Foreign Wars convention. "But here's another truth: He didn't go to Canada and he didn't burn his draft card."

But Professor Dickstein said this line of argument may beg the more troublesome question raised by Mr. Quayle's experience: Some young men risked their lives in the war itself. "Other people risked their lives in other ways—by going to Canada, by burning their draft cards, by going to jail," he said.

By doing none of these, Mr. Quayle occupied a morally ambiguous world whose answer to the war was neither a clear yes not a clear no. This is the moral world inhabited by most in Vietnam generation, including many who joined the National Guard, as Mr. Quayle did.

But few of those who live in this world feel heroic about it, as Mr. Buckley and Mr. Fallows say. Few of them would say that their choice was anything equivalent to that of the Vietnam veterans. But Mr. Quayle seemed to be doing something very much like this on Saturday when he told a news conference: "Serving in the Indiana National Guard is a patriotic thing to do. I served my country."

It is a sign of just what a quagmire Vietnam generation politics can be that Vice President Bush was making two arguments in defense of his running mate that seemed almost contradictory. This weekend, the Republican Presidential candidate asked Americans to be understanding of Mr. Quayle as a young man who grew up in traumatic times. But Mr. Bush also tried to rekindle the very feelings that so divided Americans in that period when he addressed the veterans today.

"He did not burn his draft card," Mr. Bush said, "and he damned sure didn't burn the American flag." Mr. Bush's words were the surest indication that whatever the popular verdict on Mr. Quayle, the choices and the language of the Vietnam Era remain very much a part of American politics in 1988.

* * *

October 18, 1988

ONE MAN AS AN AMERICAN METAPHOR IN VIETNAM

By DAVID K. SHIPLER

A BRIGHT SHINING LIE: John Paul Vann and America in Vietnam
By Neil Sheehan
Illustrated. 861 pages. Random House. $24.95

Well into Neil Sheehan's masterly study of American involvement in Vietnam, his hero, John Paul Vann, is skillfully revealed as a character of tragic flaws. One gradually begins to realize that Lieutenant Colonel Vann, the American military adviser who in 1962–63 is idolized by reporters as a compulsive truth teller, is something of a compulsive liar in his private life; that his stubborn morality and humaneness in warfare mask a remarkable capacity for personal cruelty as he uses and discards women; that his genuine acts of selfless courage are accompanied by a bizarre need to fabricate tales of other acts of bravery and defiance that never took place. As the flaws multiply and accumulate, practically every noble attribute of the man turns out to have its shadowy antithesis, like a towering statue's inverted reflection in a dark pool beneath.

Colonel Vann thus becomes a metaphor for America—the righteous, naïve, can-do America that divided the world neatly into good and evil, struggling to impose its notion of right on a broad scale while creating or ignoring more particular wrongs. So, to protect the South Vietnamese from the imagined spread of Chinese Communism, South Vietnamese peasants had to be bombed and shelled, their villages burned, their families uprooted and resettled. To fortify a non-Communist, pro-Western Government in South Vietnam, the corruption and authoritarianism of its leaders had to be tolerated, the incompetence and cowardice of its army covered up, the social injustices of the society promoted and subsidized.

Colonel Vann railed against these self-delusions in his early years as an Army officer assigned to advise the South Vietnamese Seventh Infantry Division in the Mekong Delta, where the Vietcong—the heirs of the anticolonialist Vietminh—were just taking shape as a fighting force. Focusing at first on the pure military problem, he urged in vain that isolated South Vietnamese militia outposts be closed to deny the Vietcong a steady source of American weapons, captured when the posts were easily overrun. He cajoled and flattered and ranted in a futile effort to push reluctant South Vietnamese commanders into decisive combat. The commanders, under orders from President Ngo Dinh Diem to keep their units intact for defending the regime against any possible coup, staged elaborate raids in areas mostly devoid of Vietcong, intentionally let guerrilla forces escape and fabricated huge body counts.

All this, supplemented by fancy maps purporting to show spreading areas of Government control, convinced wishful-thinking American generals and political leaders that the war was being won. Colonel Vann, increasingly conscious of the need for a social revolution as well as military reform, opened a futile campaign of memos and briefings to bring the truth to the American generals, who did not want to hear.

Colonel Vann left Vietnam and the Army in 1963, but the war had worked its way into his system like a malaria parasite. He could not free himself, and he returned to South Vietnam as a senior civilian adviser with the Agency for International Development in 1965, there to command troops, in effect, and gradually infect himself with his own deluded optimism—which he sold to President Nixon and Henry A. Kissinger—that the South Vietnamese could take over the war themselves and win it. He died in a helicopter accident in 1972, "believing he had won his war," Mr. Sheehan writes.

It was in the delta in the early 1960's that Colonel Vann first met Neil Sheehan, a young reporter for United Press International; David Halberstam of The New York Times and others who were impressed by his candor and readiness to risk his Army career—or so Colonel Vann made it appear—to puncture the myths being made in Saigon and Washington. "The American reporters shared the advisors' sense of commitment to this war," writes Mr. Sheehan, who was a correspondent in Vietnam for The New York Times from August 1965 to August 1966. "Our ideological prism and cultural biases were in no way different. We regarded the conflict as our war too."

And so this work seems to have something of an autobiographical aura for Mr. Sheehan, an act of discovery and cleansing. It is the fruit of a 16-year search through the ruins of Mr. Sheehan's own disillusionment for the essence of the man who embodied America's vision and blindness, its principles and its immorality. The result is a profoundly infuriating chronicle of personal and national failure.

Oddly, the book's only real lapse was one of Colonel Vann's flaws, too. The Vietnamese are not real people but merely props in the book's scheme, cardboard characters, as they were in Colonel Vann's scheme, in America's scheme. Rarely does a figure in the South Vietnamese military and political establishment appear who is not venal, corrupt, cowardly, brutal.

Even the characters who emerge in some detail are caricatures, faceless, with no perspective on Colonel Vann or the American involvement that Mr. Sheehan thinks worth recording. Colonel Vann uses them to fight his war and to satisfy his sexual appetite. He promises at least two Vietnamese women simultaneously that he will marry them when he already has an American wife and children. He fathers a daughter by one of them, and strangely, Mr. Sheehan never tells us what happens to the woman or the child. Did they get out in 1975? Were they left behind? Does he simply not know? They are left to fade into the sea of anonymous, pitiful Vietnamese, as if the readers should not need to care. This is an American book about America, full of symbols of callousness.

On one level, it is a compelling, graphic and deeply sensitive biography, ranging back historically into Colonel Vann's ancestors and intimately into his troubled youth as an illegitimate child of an alcoholic prostitute. But it is much more than biography. Mr. Sheehan's long efforts have also produced one of the few brilliant histories of the American entanglement in Vietnam, reaching into the antecedents of the conflict (including Ho Chi Minh's 1945 appeals, ignored by Washington, for Vietnam to be made an American protectorate) and probing intimately into the struggles on the battlefields of Vietnam and in the offices of Washington.

Mr. Sheehan's battle reporting is thrilling and fast-paced, as thorough as that of Bernard Fall, the political scientist who was killed in Vietnam, and more readable. His clear-eyed skepticism is as devastating as David Halberstam's, and better informed with the passage of years in which immense detail has come to light. Mr. Sheehan's skillful weaving of anecdote and history, of personal memoir and psychological profile give the book the sense of having been written by a novelist, journalist and scholar all rolled into one. It would be comforting if all Presidential candidates, members of Congress, Government officials and military officers read it.

David K. Shipler, a correspondent in Vietnam for The New York Times from 1973 to 1975, is a senior associate of the Carnegie Endowment for International Peace in Washington.

* * *

May 8, 1989

FIVE YEARS AFTER SETTLEMENT, AGENT ORANGE WAR LIVES ON

By STEPHEN LABATON

Five years after the $180 million settlement in the case brought by thousands of Vietnam veterans and their survivors against the makers of the herbicide Agent Orange, the outcome of the complex civil case is still being criticized by veterans and undergoing scrutiny by the legal community.

Since the landmark settlement was reached five years ago yesterday, about $3 million—less than 2 percent of the fund—has gone to veterans and their families, and many of those payments have been made in recent weeks, delayed because of legal wrangling, administrative snags and procedural matters. At most, veterans injured by the herbicide can expect to receive $12,600 each, spread over the next five years.

By contrast, more than $20 million has already gone to plaintiffs' lawyers, court-appointed officials, retained experts and the company that administers the veterans' claims, court records show.

Many veterans, who have attributed birth defects, cancers and other illnesses to exposure to the defoliant Agent Orange, view the litigation as a symbol of their mistreatment by society and the Government.

"You can't in all honesty say that the legal system worked—it hasn't," said Frank McCarthy, a veteran in Orlando, Fla., who has been involved in organizing veterans since the outset of the case. "It has destroyed my belief in the judicial system forever, and the majority of the vets in this litigation feel this way."

The legal community is also re-examining the case, which has been closely watched for more than a decade because of its enormous size, the novel legal questions involved, its potential impact on the chemical and insurance industries and its treatment of the veterans' complaints of health disorders.

In assessing the broader effect of the suit on United States law, lawyers and judges say that although the case is used as a model for complex cases, it also shows shortcomings in the ability of the courts to resolve difficult cases.

Some legal experts have focused on the fact that the settlement, by barring other lawsuits and punitive damages, insulated the chemical makers and insurance carriers from a potentially ruinous onslaught of additional litigation.

Defense lawyers have received a total of $75 million to $100 million from the seven chemical companies that were defendants in the suit—Dow Chemical, Monsanto, Diamond Shamrock, Uniroyal, T. H. Agriculture and Nutrition, Thompson Chemical and Hercules.

Prof. Peter H. Schuck of Yale Law School, whose extensive writings on the case include the book "Agent Orange: Mass Toxic Disasters in the Courts," said: "The disparity between the costs of processing this case and the return to the plaintiffs is unusually stark. There is no question that the major beneficiaries in this case have been the litigators rather than their clients, a phenomenon no means unique to this case."

Judge's View in Retrospect

Even Judge Jack B. Weinstein of the Federal District Court in Brooklyn, who forged the settlement and has overseen it, acknowledges that the settlement was little more than a "stopgap measure" that was necessary at the time because the legislative and executive branches had failed to deal with the health and other problems facing veterans.

Professor Schuck, however, contends that the outcome shows that tort law, the centuries-old legal field intended to compensate victims for civil wrongs, is lacking.

"This case demonstrates the bankruptcy of tort law as a mechanism for rationally allocating the burden of risk in cases of this kind," he said. "Judge Weinstein did the best with a bad thing. Some vets will see a modest recovery."

Professor Schuck advocates a system closer to no-fault recovery, so that plaintiffs would not have to show that the defendants caused their injuries. In exchange, any awards would be limited to out-of-pocket losses, not awards for pain and suffering or emotional distress. He also proposes more regulation to deter companies from marketing dangerous products.

The cost of carrying out the Agent Orange settlement, which, given the size of the case, Judge Weinstein sees as reasonable, is the latest aspect of the long case to be criticized by veterans, who have also challenged the selection of a unit of Aetna Life and Casualty to process claims. Court records show that the Aetna unit, Axia Services Inc., has billed the settlement fund more than $2.9 million to process some $3 million in claims. Franklin R. Ericson Jr., a vice president of Axia, said the processing bill appeared high because it represented start-up costs.

Many veterans say they cannot understand the delay in payments.

"I feel extreme outrage because people who really need it aren't benefiting but are coming up with an empty sack," said Charles Pace, who was a soldier in Vietnam from 1966 to 1968 and now lives in Houston. He said he suffers the aftereffects of exposure to Agent Orange, including chloracne—a skin condition—and problems with his immune system.

In a recent interview, Judge Weinstein said that when the settlement was reached, he thought payments would be made to veterans and survivors within a year.

"It turned out to be more complex than I thought," said the 67-year-old judge, who has written influential books on civil procedure and evidence. "The great social problems are not solved by the courts. They focus attention on them and try to have some impact."

Congressional Action This Year

Earlier this year, Congress gave what the veterans consider a belated recognition of the problem when it decided that payments from the settlement fund could not be used to reduce Social Security payments. But the Internal Revenue Service has threatened to tax the interest on the fund, which has reached $60 million.

As a legal matter, the case presented the thorny question of how to compensate victims. In Judge Weinstein's view, there was no showing that Agent Orange had actually caused their maladies, although statistically, as a group, the veterans have suffered more from illnesses and deformed children than the rest of the population.

The seeds for the Agent Orange litigation were sown in 1965, when the United States began a six-year program of spraying some 10 million gallons of the herbicide over as much as 10 percent of Vietnam to clear foliage and make it difficult for the Vietcong to hide.

Tens of thousands of servicemen were exposed to Agent Orange and a byproduct, a dioxin called TCDD, which has been linked to various illnesses, cancers and genetic disorders in children. The chemical companies and other scientists have disputed the causes of the disorders.

The lawsuit was filed in 1978 by Paul Reutershan, who had served on a helicopter crew in Vietnam. Mr. Reutershan died of stomach cancer shortly after his lawyer filed the action, but the case grew to represent an enormous group of veterans and their families.

Using a novel approach for the case, Judge Weinstein proclaimed that the chemical companies could be liable to the veterans as a class on a theory of "general causation," while, simultaneously, he threw out veterans' individual claims.

The consolidation of the veterans' claims was later used in the Dalkon Shield case, where close to 200,000 people are said to have been injured by the A. H. Robins Company's intrauterine device. And the method is now viewed by mainstream theorists as the traditional way to resolve mass toxic disasters.

The Agent Orange settlement was reached shortly before a trial was to begin. Since then, the fund has been divided into three categories: $170 million to compensate victims; $52 million for special education and counseling programs, and more than $13 million for lawyers' fees and expenses.

Since June, when the Supreme Court declined to intervene in the case, more than 1,500 payments have been made, many of them in the last few weeks. So far, more than 31,000 applications have been filed by veterans and their families.

Judge Weinstein said the two cases were not comparable because Agent Orange plaintiffs could not prove the defoliant caused their maladies.

The veterans have also been critical of the more than $13 million that has gone to the plaintiffs' lawyers and of the fact that one of the lawyers has been disciplined for improprieties and two are under investigation.

Kenneth R. Feinberg, the special master appointed by Judge Weinstein to oversee the case, and other members of his firm have received more than $3 million in fees and expenses from the litigation. Mr. Feinberg has come under criticism for appointing the Aetna unit, since the carrier was also a major insurer of the chemical companies that settled the lawsuit.

* * *

September 26, 1989

VIETNAMESE QUIT CAMBODIA TODAY BUT FACE HEAVY BURDENS AT HOME

By STEVEN ERLANGER
Special to The New York Times

HO CHI MINH CITY, Vietnam, Sept. 25—For a country about to enjoy what could be its first prolonged period of peace in many decades, Vietnam today displays little sense of celebration.

The long Cambodian military adventure, nearly 11 years requiring much sacrifice from the common soldier and citizen, officially ends Tuesday when the last Vietnamese infantryman is scheduled to cross the border at Moc Bai in Tay Ninh Province.

But the experience in Cambodia is ending in ambivalence, with no ringing victory. Vietnam's client regime in Cambodia is established, but not quite secure. While at least 25,300 Vietnamese soldiers have died and 55,000 have been seriously wounded, the Khmer Rouge still threaten the Cambodian Government that Hanoi installed after it invaded on Dec. 25, 1978, quickly overthrowing the Khmer Rouge regime of Pol Pot.

No Diplomatic Payoff

Diplomatically, too, there is no evident payoff for Vietnam for having finally heeded Western and Asian calls for a withdrawal. The United States remains standoffish, insisting on a comprehensive diplomatic settlement in Cambodia—which now seems far away—before normalizing relations with Vietnam or, it seems, lifting an embargo on aid and trade with Hanoi.

Rather than national joy, there is increased weariness as the Vietnamese, more than a million of whom died in the Vietnam War, concentrate on the many problems this tattered and still isolated nation continues to face. Among them is overpopulation, unemployment, increasing crime, intermittent hunger, party corruption, an aged leadership and even a Communist world that is no longer familiar, with cracks in Poland, Hungary and the Soviet Union seeming to sunder the bloc.

About Cambodia, a noted Vietnamese writer said: "There is individual relief, that our fighting is over, and collective resignation. We have borne a great sacrifice, and we could bear no more." The Cambodians, he said, "will just have to do the best they can."

For most individuals here, even the leadership question is scarcely worth discussing. "It's them and us," said a young man in a cafe. "It seems that they don't often think of us, and we don't think of them."

'A Chance to Rebuild'

A Vietnamese official said: "Withdrawing from Cambodia doesn't mean we have a sigh of relaxation. But it is very important, for now we have a chance to rebuild our own society in an easier atmosphere."

The central issue for Vietnam today is the economy. Despite improvements since recent moves away from central management and state subsidies, the economy still lags considerably behind the aspirations of the people, whose numbers are growing rapidly. Many of these economic concerns tend to be expressed as a determination to try to give decent jobs, or at least job training, to returning soldiers.

This city has already experienced difficulties caused by some demobilized soldiers no longer content with the farm who come here but find little work, and with city-born veterans who join criminal gangs.

"Spiritually," a senior editor said, "all they get is a medal."

The Government's policy is to give returning soldiers some priority in schools, hospitals and job placement, and in chances to work abroad, a program intended to ease the job pressure here and to help pay Vietnam's external debts. Officially, veterans also have the right to return to their former employers.

In Conflict With Reality

"The problem is the reality and capacity of the society," the editor said. "That very factory doesn't have material with which to work, so what can they do? The policy and the reality are very different."

Another senior journalist said: "They think they have contributed to the country, and they want society to be grateful. But in this economic situation, there are many difficulties. We cannot afford what each one of them wants. That's our most difficult problem."

There has also been some friction between those who fought in brutal surroundings, with rampant malaria and often inadequate food and shelter, and those who remained at home.

"There are people in the same generation who did not have to participate in the Cambodian war, who just stayed here and did smuggling and had a happy life," another writer said, "I worry about the consequences."

Crime Is on the Rise

These feelings mix with another source of national shame—the flight of Vietnamese in flimsy boats to whatever country might possibly take them. People joke bitterly, "If the lamppost could walk, it would go, too."

Associated Press

Vietnam is displaying little sense of celebration as its troops return home from nearly 11 years of occupation in Cambodia. In Phnom Penh yesterday, smiling Vietnamese troops waved goodbye to cheering Cambodians as convoy moved past the royal palace.

At the same time, the press is full of articles about increasing crime, of housebreaking and acts of violence.

Responsible people speak with some despair of the growing "chaos" of life.

Despite the domestic problems, the Vietnamese feel much pride in having rid Cambodia of Pol Pot, under whose rule more than a million Cambodians died.

Nguyen Duy, a much-admired poet who entered Cambodia with the Vietnamese Army as a correspondent, remembers the color black—"the black of the pajamas, the black of the skin of those who were dying or very ill."

"The long queues of the orphans have haunted me for 10 years," he said. "The people had become animals. They ate anything they could find along the road—grass, leaves, frogs, insects. They were like the black ants of Africa that move through a field and leave it devastated. and it was Vietnamese soldiers who gave them their first grain of rice."

* * *

February 11, 1990

HANOI REMAINS TRUE TO COMMUNISM, BUT PARTY IS MAKING MORE CHANGES

By STEVEN ERLANGER

Special to The New York Times

HANOI, Vietnam, Feb. 10—Moscow may have embraced the changes sweeping Eastern Europe, but Vietnam's leaders are mostly sticking to the old-time religion, at least for now.

There is no question that the Soviet party's decision to abandon its absolute political dominance, at least in principle, has come as a shock to Vietnam's leaders, Eastern European diplomats and some Vietnamese officials say.

"They didn't expect it," an Eastern European diplomat said of the Vietnamese. "In fact, I think they thought it was impossible. They must respond. But for now, I don't think it will do more than accelerate the changes already under way."

The Politburo and high-ranking party and Government officials, including senior editors, have gathered this week in Ho Chi Minh City, formerly Saigon, to hammer out plans for a meeting, now postponed until March. They will also discuss an important party congress, likely to be held toward the end of this year, that will set out the first new party program since 1960 and endorse a new party leader to replace General Secretary Nguyen Van Linh, 74 years old and in uncertain health, who has decided to retire.

Official press organizations here reported the Soviet decision simply and without delay. But there have been no official reactions, comments or editorials, and officials and newspaper editors interviewed have responded with caution.

In a typical comment, Bui Tin, deputy editor of the party newspaper, People's Daily, stressed the right of each Communist country to make its own decisions based on its own realities and stage of development.

"I think the situation can be changed here in the longer-term future," Mr. Tin said. "but not now."

When pressed about the possibility of a multiparty system, Nguyen Van Dang, deputy editor of The Communist Review, the party's theoretical journal, finally said: "It's very difficult to give an answer. The party leaders are meeting now."

'Don't Be Surprised'

A younger editor, taking notes in the interview, at one point asked to say something. "Don't be surprised if we change our policy," he said passionately. "The only people who continue with the same policy forever are either stupid or dead."

While there are strong opinions about the pace and substance of changes within the party, it has historically maintained a collective front and discouraged factionalism. But it was not slow to begin its own renewal.

Mr. Linh, a pragmatist with political roots in southern Vietnam, came to office at the last party congress in December 1986 with a program of "doi moi," or renovation, which in many ways resembled the program of political and economic restructuring that the Soviet President, Mikhail S. Gorbachev, calls perestroika.

Urging party self-criticism and apologizing for some disastrous errors of ideology-driven policy that have marred Vietnam's recovery from nearly a half-century of warfare, Mr. Linh sanctioned private enterprise and market prices to try to revive an isolated, declining economy.

Collectivization was largely dismantled, state subsidies to state-owned enterprises have disappeared, the inflation rate has been cut to 25 or 30 percent, down from 600 to nearly 1,000 percent in 1988, and there has been an explosion of private shops, restaurants and new houses.

Attacks on Bureaucracy

He has also moved to dilute the Stalinist nature of the party, attacking bureaucracy and favoritism, purging corrupt and lazy officials, loosening controls on the press and cultural life and preaching more democracy in the party and equality under the law.

There are also moves under way to strengthen the role and authority of the national assembly and separate the party from the day-to-day running of the state.

But these themes have become much more pronounced since the collapse of Communist government after Communist government in Eastern Europe, Even the party leadership, which lived comparatively simply, is giving up most of its resort villas and special privileges, including the party shops.

In August, Mr. Linh assailed the new Solidarity-led Government in Poland, saying it had resulted from capitalist subversion, and People's Daily called for an uprising against an "reactionary coup d'état." But by autumn the tone had changed.

Mr. Tin, deputy editor of People's Daily, said a new assessment of Eastern European upheaval emerged from a sharp debate within the Politburo; it held that the crisis stemmed from internal causes, in particular from the deformation and corruption of the various Communist parties. People's Daily apologized to the Poles.

Leading Role of the Party

But Mr. Linh, who has a powerful conservative wing to mollify, has been explicit about maintaining the leading role of the Communist Party and excluding any idea of multiparty democracy in Vietnam.

As recently as Feb. 2, in a major speech commemorating the 60th anniversary of the founding of the Vietnamese party, he said the party had been selected to lead the nation by the people and as a result of Vietnam's difficult history.

"Apart from the Communist Party, in Vietnam there is no other party of any class and section of the population capable of shouldering that role," he said. "It was so in the past, it is so now and it will be so in the future."

Senior diplomats here, whether from Western countries or Eastern ones, believe that his comments will prove to be right for some years to come.

"Further change is not only inevitable but acknowledged," a Western diplomat said. "But change will continue to come through the party, and in all likelihood it will continue to come, as the Vietnamese say, 'cautiously and step by step.' "

Vietnam's leadership seems to think it can balance economic and political development, another diplomat said. "Thus far, they've pulled it off, which has been a pretty neat trick."

So far, there have been few signs of domestic pressure for the party to change. Vietnam not only lacks severe ethnic and nationalist pressures like the ones Moscow faces, but despite large unemployment, ordinary life for most people in Vietnam has become noticeably better as a result of Mr. Linh's policy of renovation, not worse as they are perceived to have become in the Soviet Union.

Few Vietnamese are likely to think that instability will do anything more than undermine whatever economic progress is already under way.

Even in southern Vietnam, an economic and trading boom has reduced potential political discontent, somewhat diffused in any event by Mr. Linh's relaxation of central economic controls. The party has also moved to resolve land disputes deriving from a more liberal agricultural policy that brought some farmers to demonstrate in Ho Chi Minh City last year.

Other Political Strengths

The party also has other, considerable political and historical strengths, diplomats say. It is identified with decolonization, liberation and unification in a country with no real prior experience with functioning parliamentary democracy, even in the south.

Perhaps most important, after such a long period of deprivation in Vietnam's many wars, the populace sees some real improvements coming from the leadership of a self-critical and renovating party, even if the pace of change is disappointing to some.

"The party is changing," a Western diplomat said. "and I think people are now beginning to believe that it means to do what it says."

BEYOND THE COLD WAR

March 11, 1990

TOO EMBARRASSED NOT TO KILL

By ROBERT R. HARRIS

THE THINGS THEY CARRIED
By Tim O'Brien.
273 pp. Boston: Seymour Lawrence/Houghton Mifflin Company.
$19.95.

Only a handful of novels and short stories have managed to clarify, in any lasting way, the meaning of the war in Vietnam for America and for the soldiers who served there. With "The Things They Carried," Tim O'Brien adds his second title to the short list of essential fiction about Vietnam. As he did in his novel "Going After Cacciato" (1978), which won a National Book Award, he captures the war's pulsating rhythms and nerve-racking dangers. But he goes much further. By moving beyond the horror of the fighting to examine with sensitivity and insight the nature of courage and fear, by questioning the role that imagination plays in helping to form our memories and our own versions of truth, he places "The Things They Carried" high up on the list of best fiction about any war.

"The Things They Carried" is a collection of interrelated stories. A few are unremittingly brutal; a couple are flawed two-page sketches. The publisher calls the book "a work of fiction," but in no real sense can it be considered a novel. No matter. The stories cohere. All deal with a single platoon, one of whose members is a character named Tim O'Brien. Some stories are about the wartime experiences of this small group of grunts. Others are about a 43-year-old writer—again, the fictional character Tim O'Brien—remembering his platoon's experiences and writing war stories (and remembering writing stories) about them. This is the kind of writing about writing that makes Tom Wolfe grumble. It should not stop you from savoring a stunning performance. The overall effect of these original tales is devastating.

As might be expected, there is a lot of gore in "The Things They Carried"—like the account of the soldier who ties a friend's puppy to a Claymore antipersonnel mine and squeezes the firing device. And much of the powerful language cannot be quoted in a family newspaper. But let Mr. O'Brien explain why he could not spare squeamish sensibilities: "If you don't care for obscenity, you don't care for the truth; if you don't care for the truth, watch how you vote. Send guys to war, they come home talking dirty."

In the title story, Mr. O'Brien juxtaposes the mundane and the deadly items that soldiers carry into battle. Can openers, pocketknives, wristwatches, mosquito repellent, chewing gum, candy, cigarettes, salt tablets, packets of Kool-Aid, matches, sewing kits, C rations are "humped" by the G.I.'s along with M-16 assault rifles, M-60 machine guns, M-79 grenade launchers. But the story is really about the other things the soldiers "carry": "grief, terror, love, longing . . . shameful memories" and, what unifies all the stories, "the common secret of cowardice." These young men, Mr. O'Brien tells us, "carried the soldier's greatest fear, which was the fear of blushing. Men killed, and died, because they were embarrassed not to."

Embarrassment, the author reveals in "On the Rainy River," is why he, or rather the fictional version of himself, went to Vietnam. He almost went to Canada instead. What stopped him, ironically, was fear. "All those eyes on me," he writes, "and I couldn't risk the embarrassment. . . . I couldn't endure the mockery, or the disgrace, or the patriotic ridicule. . . . I was a coward. I went to the war."

So just what is courage? What is cowardice? Mr. O'Brien spends much of the book carefully dissecting every nuance of the two qualities. In several stories, he writes movingly of the death of Kiowa, the best-loved member of the platoon. In "Speaking of Courage," Mr. O'Brien tells us about Norman Bowker, the platoon member who blames his own failure of nerve for Kiowa's death. Bowker "had been braver than he ever thought possible, but . . . he had not been so brave as he wanted to be." In the following story, "Notes" (literally notes on the writing of "Speaking of Courage"), Mr. O'Brien's fictional alter ego informs the reader that Bowker committed suicide after coming home from the war. This author also admits that he made up the part about the failure of nerve that haunted Bowker. But it's all made up, of course. And in "The Man I Killed," Mr. O'Brien imagines the life of an enemy soldier at whom the character Tim O'Brien tossed a grenade, only to confess later that it wasn't "Tim O'Brien" who killed the Vietnamese.

Are these simply tricks in the service of making good stories? Hardly. Mr. O'Brien strives to get beyond literal descriptions of what these men went through and what they felt. He makes sense of the unreality of the war—makes sense of why he has distorted that unreality even further in his fiction—by turning back to explore the workings of the imagination, by probing his memory of the terror and fearlessly confronting the way he has dealt with it as both soldier and fiction writer. In doing all this, he not only crystallizes the Vietnam experience for us, he exposes the nature of all war stories.

The character Tim O'Brien's daughter asks him why he continues to be obsessed by the Vietnam War and with writing about it. "By telling stories," he says, "you objectify your own experience. You separate it from yourself. You pin down certain truths." In "Good Form," he writes: "I can look at things I never looked at. I can attach faces to grief and love and pity and God. I can be brave. I can make myself feel again." You come away from this book understanding why there have been so many novels about the Vietnam War, why so many of Mr. O'Brien's fellow soldiers have turned to narrative—real and imagined—to purge their memories, to appease the ghosts.

Is it fair to readers for Mr. O'Brien to have blurred his own identity as storyteller-soldier in these stories? "A true war story is never moral," he writes in "How to Tell a True War Story." "It does not instruct, nor encourage virtue, nor suggest models of proper human behavior, nor restrain men from doing the things men have always done. If a story seems moral, do not believe it. If at the end of a war story you feel uplifted, or if you feel that some small bit of rectitude has been salvaged from the larger waste, then you have been made the victim of a very old and terrible lie. There is no rectitude whatsoever. There is no virtue. As a first rule of thumb, therefore, you can tell a true war story by its absolute and uncompromising allegiance to obscenity and evil." Mr. O'Brien cuts to the heart of writing about war. And by subjecting his memory and imagination to such harsh scrutiny, he seems to have reached a reconciliation, to have made his peace—or to have made up his peace.

Flashes From the Foliage

Almost all the dramatic furnishings of "The Things They Carried"—characters, scenery, incidents—are embedded in the Vietnam War. But the book is not about Vietnam and not about war, Tim O'Brien said in a telephone interview from his home in Boxford, Mass. There are almost no Vietnamese in the book, none with names anyway, a reflection of ignorance among the soldiers, the 43-year-old writer said. Mr. O'Brien draws on his year in Vietnam, but the character named Tim O'Brien is "just a 21-year-old kid at war. I did not know the culture or the language. I was afraid of dealing with stereotypes. I did try once, with the Tim character, to imagine the life of the man I killed, and that was the nearest I could come."

Nor is there much war in "The Things They Carried," and that too was typical. "It was like trying to pin the tail on the Asian donkey," Mr. O'Brien said, "but there was no tail and no donkey. In a year I only saw the living enemy once. All I saw were flashes from the foliage and the results, the bodies. In books or films it is desirable to have a climactic battle scene, but the world does not operate in those gross dramatic terms. In Vietnam there was a general aimlessness, not just in the physical sense, but beyond that in the moral and ethical sense."

So what's the book about? "It is a writer's book on the effects of time on the imagination. It is definitely an antiwar book; I hated the war from the beginning. [The book] is meant to be about man's yearning for peace. At least I hope it is taken that way."

Robert R. Harris is an editor of The Book Review.

* * *

January 27, 1991

DEVIL OF A WAR

It May Not Be Vietnam, but Parallels Are Inescapable

By R. W. APPLE Jr.

DHAHRAN , Saudi Arabia—For all of President Bush's passionate insistence to the contrary, the war in the Persian Gulf has more than a few similarities to the war in Vietnam, in the sort of problems that it poses if not in the probable outcome.

To begin with, the United States is trying, as ever, to substitute firepower for manpower. Outnumbered by an enemy who sees himself battling for his life, and who is therefore willing to fight to the last 16-year-old, the United States is not even considering national mobilization. Nor are its allies. So warplanes and ships and bombs and missiles will have to even out the equation here, as Lyndon B. Johnson meant them to do in Vietnam.

"We shall cut the limbs and the branches from the Iraqi war machine so that it no longer casts its shadow over Kuwait," said Air Marshal Sir David Craig, chief of the British defense staff, promising there would be no ground assault by the allies "until a successful land battle is assured."

But assuring that is not easy, which is why Mr. Bush, Secretary of Defense Dick Cheney and others in Washington talked of the struggle that lies ahead in such sober terms as they reviewed the first week's action.

History is littered with the bones of the overconfident, not least in this region. No less a strategist than Winston Churchill was very nearly ruined by the British defeat at Gallipoli in 1915, when a supposedly backward power, the Ottoman Empire, overcame a dominant one, the British Empire, on the beaches of the Dardanelles.

Put in its simplest terms, the allied strategy is to bomb Baghdad and the rest of Iraq into military impotence, or something approaching it. As in Southeast Asia, the notion is to so thoroughly disrupt the enemy's capacity to communicate, to resupply, to maneuver and to fight that he either gives up or comes unglued in battle.

But as in Vietnam, the enemy is not without resources to combat this strategy. If Saddam Hussein lacks the protective cover of the jungle, the active support of a patron nation like the Soviet Union and the ability to bring in supplies through neighboring countries—things that helped to sustain Ho Chi Minh through the long years of battle—he has some others: what he himself called this week "the superior willpower and patience" of a country that sees itself menaced by a huge, alien force; years of preparation for the kind of pounding Iraq is now taking, in the form of back-up communications networks, subterranean command posts and steel-and-concrete bunkers for its planes; and the ability to patch up, adapt, make do.

Already, American intelligence officers say, the Iraqis are managing to repair roads and railroads and runways and even some radars, just as the Vietnamese repaired the Paul Doumer Bridge in Hanoi again and again. Their facilities are being "degraded"—Pentagonese for worn down—but not eliminated, but then facilities matter less to Baghdad than manpower.

Vietnam taught the lesson that if there are no shoes, bits of old tires will do, and Iraq could manage better than expected by husbanding its resources and maintaining its morale in the face of adversity. There is something about living under persistent, prolonged air attack, as the people of London and Hanoi demonstrated, that brings out human grit.

Not enough, say the allies, and they are surely right, although measuring these things is difficult, especially given the paucity of information from Iraq or from the Pentagon.

The American-led coalition, with sophisticated weapons and a more sophisticated approach to this war than the last, scored significant early victories by knocking out nuclear-weapons plants, blasting power stations and battering the elite Republican Guard on whom Mr. Hussein counts heavily.

Then, too, Saddam Hussein is fighting a conventional war, not a guerrilla war, and he is fighting it on a desert plain, not in jungles, rice paddies and mountains. All the better for the foreigners, always at a disadvantage in rough and unfamiliar terrain.

But he is fighting a conventional war with unconventional means. As the bombs rained down on Iraq last week, and allied commanders searched in the aerial photographs for evidence of how badly they had bloodied Mr. Hussein, he sought to hurt them, and to demonstrate his own capacity to strike back, by indirect means. If the allies would not oblige by charging directly into his dug-in defense, if he could not bomb them as they bombed him, he could try to weaken their coalition, sow perplexity and savage their emotions.

Hence the Scud surface-to-surface missile barrages on Israel and Saudi Arabia, barrages purposely directed at civilian targets, to try to bring the Israelis into the war and to drive at least some Arabs out of the anti-Iraq coalition. Hence the propaganda interviews with allied prisoners of war, designed to weaken resolve in the West. Hence the appalling oil discharge into the Persian Gulf, designed to complicate any amphibious assault, to disrupt military and civil water supplies and to discombobulate allied thinking.

President Bush, a Marquess of Queensbury man all the way, said that the Iraqi dictator had a sick mind. American generals huffed and puffed and said none of his actions had military significance. But each of the things that Westerners considered dirty tricks or low blows make life harder, in one way or another, for Mr. Bush and his commanders, and they all make Saddam Hussein look like a dukes-up guy, unafraid of the American bully. That's what he looks like to many ordinary hero-starved Arabs, if not to their governments.

"By God, tell me whether you are not pleased to have brothers who enjoy such strength and such determination," Baghdad Radio said in a broadcast on Saturday. "Do you not feel proud to see us stand up against all the Arabs' enemies, not scared or frightened? Then why do you not join us? We now represent the Arabs' awakening from the ocean to the gulf."

An overstatement, at best.

But what was evident at week's end was that Mr. Hussein is not going to go quietly, and that almost certainly means a much longer war than many in Washington had been hoping for, punctuated by more unpleasant surprises like the spreading oil slick.

If, as Mr. Cheney said, the Iraqis are powerless to change the ultimate outcome of the war, they seem to retain ample scope for altering its shape and timetable and, most of all, its aftermath.

* * *

April 26, 1991

U.S. TO GIVE VIETNAM $1 MILLION; ASSISTANCE IS FIRST SINCE THE WAR

By CLIFFORD KRAUSS
Special to The New York Times

WASHINGTON, April 25—The Bush Administration said today that it would provide financial assistance to Hanoi for the first time since the Vietnam War, approving a small but symbolically significant aid package for Vietnamese disabled during the fighting.

The announcement that $1 million would be made available for artificial limbs comes less than a week after the two nations agreed to open an office in Vietnam to resolve the cases of American soldiers missing since the war. It represents one more cautious step in a slow warming of relations that began two years ago.

Ties Hinge on Cooperation

Administration officials reiterated that an initiation of full diplomatic relations or the lifting of a 15-year trade embargo would hinge on Hanoi's cooperation in accounting for all missing American soldiers and in reaching a diplomatic settlement to the civil war in Cambodia.

But in the statement announcing the aid, Richard H. Solomon, Assistant Secretary of State for East Asian and Pacific Affairs, also pointedly expressed appreciation for Vietnam's program of economic reforms.

State Department officials said the Agency for International Development would funnel the $1 million in aid through private American humanitarian groups, which will produce the artificial limbs in Vietnam.

The limbs will go to people who suffered their wounds during the Vietnam War, including soldiers from the North and South Vietnamese armies, members of the Vietcong and civilians.

Officials said the program would be similar to efforts for the disabled in Afghanistan, Uganda and Mozambique. They said they could not estimate how many people would be treated.

"It's a sign of new cooperation," said a State Department official who monitors Vietnam. "But it is not a step toward resuming diplomatic relations." No Government officials will be sent to Vietnam to work on the aid program, he added.

Mr. Solomon told the Senate subcommittee on East Asian and Pacific affairs that the United States had conditionally pledged aid involving artificial limbs and child care in 1987, when Vietnamese and American officials first agreed to work together on accounting for the missing soldiers.

"We have found some improvements in cooperation, but limited results," Mr. Solomon said, "and Vietnam really needs to accelerate unilateral and joint efforts to achieve the results we are seeking."

Role of Office in Hanoi

Referring to the temporary office on M.I.A.'s that will be opened in Hanoi, he said: "It will have no diplomatic or political responsibilities, and should not be seen as a first step in the normalization process. It can, however, help to accelerate normalization once a Cambodia settlement is signed."

The United States still lists some 2,276 Americans as missing or unaccounted for in the Vietnam War. Since August 1987, Vietnam has turned over more than 288 sets of remains, but only 117 have been identified as those of Americans. Most of the others were judged not to be the remains of Americans or could not be identified.

Ann Mills Griffiths, executive secretary of the National League of Families of American Prisoners and Missing in Southeast Asia, said the aid program was "a very positive move," adding: "We are hopeful the temporary office may facilitate greater results. But that is up to the Vietnamese."

Gen. John Vessey, the special envoy to Hanoi on prisoners of war and the missing, has focused on 119 "discrepancy cases" in which the United States believes that soldiers were seen alive after their planes were shot down or they were otherwise separated from their units.

Progress in 13 Cases

Kenneth C. Quinn, a Deputy Assistant Secretary of State who is working with General Vessey, told the Senate subcommittee that American-Vietnamese technical teams had made progress in 13 of those cases by digging up remains and retrieving other evidence.

Economic aid to Vietnam has long been a center of controversy. During negotiations with the Carter Administration in 1977, Vietnam insisted that the United States had an obligation to contribute billions of dollars toward the country's postwar recovery.

The Vietnamese based their claim on two documents. One was the Paris cease-fire agreement of 1973, which pledged American support for Vietnam's reconstruction. The second was a letter sent by President Nixon to Prime Minister Pham Van Dong after the cease-fire that reportedly pledged more than $4 billion in food and reconstruction aid.

Neither the Ford nor the Carter Administration accepted Hanoi's argument, maintaining that its invasion of South Vietnam in 1975 broke the cease-fire agreement.

The prospect of diplomatic ties vanished in December 1978, when Vietnam invaded Cambodia to overthrow the Khmer Rouge regime of Pol Pot. But relations slowly began to improve in 1989, when Hanoi removed the last of 140,000 Vietnamese combat troops from Cambodia.

Although Vietnam still provides a considerable number of military advisers to Phnom Penh, the Bush Administration moved to increase cooperation last July by opening talks with Hanoi on ways to make peace in Cambodia.

U.S. Licenses Aid Groups

Secretary of State James A. Baker 3d went a step further that month when he said the Administration would encourage private American groups to offer humanitarian aid to Vietnam. The Administration has since licensed 36 organizations or individuals to provide $4.3 million in relief.

Administration policy drew a good deal of criticism today from both Republican and Democratic senators.

Senator John Kerry of Massachusetts, a Vietnam veteran and a Democratic critic of the Administration's Vietnam policy, welcomed the announcement. But the senator, who will travel to Hanoi next week, suggested that the Administration was "holding the people of Vietnam and our own relationship and our own benefits that we gain from it a prisoner—not just to our feelings about the Vietnam War, but prisoner also to the Cambodian conflict."

He said the missing soldiers could be more rapidly accounted for if the Administration expanded its trade and communications with Hanoi.

Senator Robert C. Smith, Republican of New Hampshire, asserted in testimony before the subcommittee that United States intelligence agencies had not been aggressive enough in following up "live sighting reports" of American servicemen who could still be alive in Vietnam.

Talk of Sighting P.O.W.'s

Mr. Smith complained that the agencies had "repeatedly denied" Congressional requests to review "first-hand accounts from refugees who say they have seen American P.O.W.'s in captivity in Southeast Asia, some as recently as January 1991."

Senator Jesse Helms, Republican of North Carolina, said he agreed with Mr. Smith. "I'm not criticizing Vietnam as much as I am our own Government," Mr. Helms said, referring to information on the missing servicemen. "I've never heard as much double-talk as I have gotten each time when you try to reason or learn something from our Government."

* * *

July 28, 1991

FOR FAMILIES OF M.I.A.'S, NEW HOPE, OLD DESPAIR

By SETH MYDANS

Special to The New York Times

LOS ANGELES, July 27—Last year, 17 years after her husband, an Air Force pilot, disappeared without a trace over Hanoi, Barbara Cleary O'Connor received from Vietnam a rubbing of his dog tag, complete with his serial number and blood type.

"It was a shock," said Mrs. O'Connor, who lives in Wayland, Mass. "It meant there was some information about him. I truly thought he had not survived. I never would have remarried if I had thought there was the slightest glimmer of hope."

Nothing further came of that brief glimmer. But now again, as a photograph that is said to show three other missing American servicemen in Vietnam is drawing public attention, Mrs. O'Connor said, "You can't help but think: 'Oh, my gosh. What if?' "

Old Wounds Reopened

For the parents, wives, siblings and children of the 2,273 American servicemen still unaccounted for in the Vietnam War, every new report of a sighting, every new promise by the Government in Hanoi, every new delivery of boxes of bone fragments—some of them human, some animal—stirs old pains and fresh disappointments.

These feelings are also kept alive by cottage industries in both the United States and Southeast Asia that collect or manufacture photographs, packets of remains and reports of sightings of servicemen missing in action.

The most recent center of attention is the photograph of three middle-aged men who appear to be holding a placard with a date and cryptic lettering. Three families have come forward to assert that these men are their missing relatives. But the Pentagon says that while analysis of the photograph was inconclusive the biographical data that accompanied it were false and that the picture itself had passed through the hands of known fakers.

On Friday, Brent Scowcroft, the President's national security adviser, said there was no credible evidence that Vietnam still held any American servicemen.

This weekend a Deputy Assistant Secretary of State, Kenneth Quinn, is meeting with officials in Vietnam and Laos to seek information about missing fliers; the State Department would not give any other information about his mission.

The source of the photograph is uncertain, but it apparently passed through the hands of one of several American groups that have played on the emotions of missing servicemen's families with urgent fund-raising appeals.

"If I cannot raise $13,671.71 by October 31," reads an appeal, this one in 1986 by Operation Rescue, a group headed by a retired Air Force lieutenant colonel, Jack Bailey, "vital intelligence gathering cannot continue. And an American serviceman will die in the jungles of Vietnam."

Another appeal, by the Skyhook II Project, says: "We're close to making contact with an American P.O.W. who has been alone since his fellow prisoner died of natural causes less than a year ago. That effort could fail for lack of funds. Please be as generous as you can." The head of that project is John LeBoutillier, a Republican Congressman from Long Island from 1981 to 1983.

Both appeals were quoted, among many others, in a 1987 analysis by the Federal Defense Intelligence Agency, which concluded, "For all their 'proof' and the untold millions of dollars raised, none of these groups or individuals have yet to furnish even the slightest shred of evidence of P.W.'s, much less secure the return of a living American captive."

Seeking the Mafia's Help

Victimized by groups like these, Maureen Dunn of Randolph, Mass., said she was once persuaded to travel to New York for a fruitless meeting with members of the Mafia in search of information about her husband, a Navy pilot who was shot down in 1968. There is no evidence the Mafia has been extensively involved in schemes involving missing servicemen.

Another time, Mrs. Dunn said, she traveled in great secrecy to Canada, where she waited in vain in the back pew of an empty church for a promised meeting with a man who had said he had information for her.

Now, as an active member of the National League of Families of American Prisoners and Missing in Southeast Asia, she said, "I must receive 5 to 10 dog-tag stories a week. It's a cottage industry, let me tell you, and it's a terrible emotional roller coaster for the families."

The league, a lobbying group, works with the American Government to seek the return of any remaining live prisoners or their remains and to obtain a full accounting of the missing.

Hopes continue to be fueled by the sheer number of Americans believed to have been captured, by continuing reports of live sightings and by the fact that the Vietnamese Government has concealed evidence of missing Americans.

For Mrs. O'Connor, the unsettling stirring of hope came when a Vietnamese refugee presented the rubbing of her husband's dog tag to American officials with the notion of trading it for resettlement in the United States. Since then, she said, half a dozen other refugees have come forward with similar rubbings, but with no evidence that her husband, Major Peter Cleary, is alive.

One of the most colorful rescue schemes was launched in 1983 by James (Bo) Gritz, a retired Army lieutenant colonel who led a band of mercenaries into Laos, where they were promptly ambushed and fled.

George Brooks of New Windsor, N.Y., the father of a missing Navy pilot, remembers that mission well. He said he contributed about $30,000, including his son's insurance money, to Mr. Gritz, whom he called "a very persuasive speaker."

In part, he said, he acted out of a frustration that is shared by many families with what they see as the Government's slow pace, political swings and occasional confusion or misinformation in individual cases.

Kate Rothacker of Mission Viejo, Calif., said that perhaps because her brother had been shot down during a secret mission for the Air Force the Government told her family that he was dead. The family later discovered that Pentagon records showed a clear possibility that he had parachuted to safety.

A Political Tool

"It's real hard to describe the low that you feel at the deception that they pulled," Ms. Rothacker said.

At one point President Richard M. Nixon tried to use the families of missing servicemen as a political counterweight to antiwar protests. For example, he invited them to the White House, where they were serenaded with "The Impossible Dream" and praised for their patriotism.

President Jimmy Carter, emphasizing normalization of relations with Vietnam, declared the missing-in-action cases closed and transferred all but one symbolic name to the status of killed in action.

Since President Ronald Reagan took office, the Government has taken a more active approach to the issue, and more than 100 Government officials are now assigned to the search for answers. But the Government has had to deal with shifts of policy on the Vietnamese side, which has parceled out remains over the years as one of its few bargaining tools in the slow movement toward re-establishing diplomatic relations.

The last live American to emerge from captivity in Vietnam since the release of American prisoners in 1973 was Robert Garwood, a Marine private who had deserted and who asked to return home in 1979, four years after the end of the war.

He was court-martialed, convicted for collaborating with the enemy and for assaulting another American prisoner, and received a dishonorable discharge.

Since the war ended in 1975, the Pentagon has received 1,483 firsthand reports of live sightings of possible Americans in Indochina, said Comdr. Edward Lundquist, a spokesman for the Defense Department. Only about a quarter of these have been determined to be fakes; 1,008 have been definitely identified as Americans, including missionaries and jailed civilians but not any of the missing servicemen. Three hundred of the sightings were of Private Garwood.

Tired of Waiting

As of now, 103 first-hand reports of sightings remain unresolved, Comander Lundquist said, including 45 involving an American in captivity and 58 involving an American said to be living freely somewhere in Vietnam, Laos or Cambodia.

Two of the live sighting reports, in 1984 and 1986, seemed to involve Clarence N. Driver, a retired Air Force major who was flying for Air America when he was shot down over Laos on March 7, 1973. But his wife, Allene, who is now 66 years old and has never remarried, has grown tired of hoping.

"I feel that unless they are going to do something about it, I'd rather they don't tell us anything any more," she said. "It gets your hopes up and then nothing happens."

But as in a growing number of families, the younger generation is beginning now to take over the struggle because, as Mrs. Driver's 34-year-old daughter, Sharon, said, "We realize that our moms are tired and it's our turn to try to keep that spark alive."

Miss Driver said news coverage of the recent air war in the Persian Gulf revived their memories and sharpened their feelings of loss.

"Every time a plane was shot down, wow, it just brought back memories of the day when I was 16 and my father's plane was shot down," she said. "It's like this. Just pretend you're talking to someone you love very much on the telephone and that person says, 'Hold on a second; I'll be right back,' and they never come back."

* * *

October 9, 1992

CAMPAIGN FOCUS ON VIETNAM REVIVING DEBATES OF THE 60'S

By MICHAEL KELLY with DAVID JOHNSTON
Special to The New York Times

WASHINGTON, Oct. 8—In the fall and winter of 1969, several important things happened in the life of a bright, ambitious young man named Bill Clinton.

After months of elaborate effort, he finally beat the draft for the Vietnam War, drawing a number high enough in the new national lottery that he would never be inducted. He became, in a small way, a figure within the antiwar movement, helping to organize one of the largest marches on Washington the movement ever produced and serving as a chief organizer of two small demonstrations in London. He took a trip through the Scandinavian countries, Russia and Czechoslovakia.

In later years, as Mr. Clinton charted the political course toward his childhood dream of the Presidency, he did not often publicly speak of the events of that year, and when he did, it was in vague and passive terms, as if he had been a sort of accidental tourist of his times.

'Just a Fluke'

To hear Mr. Clinton bear reluctant witness to his past, it had been "just a fluke" that he was never drafted. Of peace demonstrations, he remembered only that he had "attended two or three, to hear the speeches."

Now, in the fall of 1992, with Mr. Clinton close to his goal, those who would stop him have turned their increasingly frightened attention to events 23 years ago, hoping to find in them something that will convince voters that a change from George Bush is not worth the risk of Bill Clinton.

The Bush campaign's effort to use episodes from Mr. Clinton's past to embarrass him began with accusations from surrogates and finally, this week, from the President himself.

What the Story Shows

The story, as far as it is clear, of Mr. Clinton's antiwar activities in 1969 and what he and the Republicans alike are saying about that in 1992 is illustrative of several points about that time and this one.

It shows, as Democrats are saying publicly and even some Republicans are saying privately, how desperate the Republicans have become. It shows, as Republicans like to say, how Mr. Clinton has tended to shade the edges of his life.

But above all, it shows how sharp the difference remains between Mr. Bush's world and Mr. Clinton's, between the clear moral absolutes of the generation of World War II and the muddied gropings of those who came of age during the Vietnam War.

The exact nature of Mr. Clinton's antiwar activities has been confused by both Republican exaggeration and Democratic obfuscation. But a basic outline seems clear.

Although Mr. Clinton has described his participation in peace demonstrations as limited to that almost of a curious passer-by, the candidate's previous statements and those of several friends and of antiwar protesters indicate a more substantial involvement. Mr. Clinton was a chief organizer of two London rallies in the fall of 1969 and also helped, to an apparently much lesser degree, organize the huge march on Washington on Oct. 15, 1969.

Yet, if Mr. Clinton appears to have minimized his activities, it also appears true that the Republicans are wrong to depict him, as they have in an escalating campaign that critics have called red-baiting, as a major antiwar organizer or Communist sympathizer.

No evidence has surfaced indicating that the young Mr. Clinton ever took part in any violent political actions or was an important antiwar organizer, or was ever radicalized in the process. And despite many Republican insinuations to the contrary, neither has evidence been produced to indicate that Mr. Clinton's 1969 trip to the Soviet Union and Czechoslovakia was financed or controlled by the Soviet Government.

Indeed, many of those involved with Mr. Clinton at the time recall him as something of a milquetoast by the fire-breathing standards of late 1960's radicalism, a young man driven by a desire to remake his country, not to reject it.

It is also clear that the actions of the 23-year-old Mr. Clinton—in avoiding military induction, in demonstrating against the foreign policy of the United States, even in traveling to the Soviet Union—were not unusual in the context of his generation. Indeed, they were almost prototypical of those who, like Mr. Clinton, were part of the intellectual elite of that generation.

A Generation Apart

But if Mr. Clinton was typical of his class and time, the actions of that class and the tenor of that time was not at all typical of American history; no other generation has ever acted in quite the fashion as Mr. Clinton's did, nor stirred more unresolved passions. Now, in the person of Mr. Clinton, American voters face for the first time the possibility that a generation that once took to the streets to publicly denounce America will lead it.

What is unknown—but will be known on Nov. 3—is whether it matters much anymore.

As Mr. Clinton pointed out today, "Mr. Bush in his Inaugural Address had a wonderful phrase about how the Vietnam War cleaves us still and it was time to put it behind us." He added, "And now, because he's behind, he's tried to raise all the challenges of that time."

The Republican campaign to paint Mr. Clinton as a man with a secretly militant history began on Sept. 18, the first night of eight in which a quartet of conservative Congressmen took to the deserted floor of the House of Representatives to denounce Mr. Clinton for the benefit of C-Span cameras.

The speeches of Representatives Robert K. Dornan, Randy (Duke) Cunningham and Duncan Hunter, all Republicans from California, and Sam Johnson, Republican of Texas, were extraordinary for a level of violent, hyperbolic accusations that echoed the red-baiting rhetoric of 40 years ago.

In nightly tirades, the speakers described Mr. Clinton as a "useful idiot" to the Soviet Government, as a man who, in other countries would have been "tried as a traitor or even shot," as a "full-time organizer for demonstrations against his country in a foreign country," as a man "directly responsible" for the deaths of American military men in Vietnam. They compared the Democratic Presidential nominee to Tokyo Rose, the anti-American radio propagandist of World War II, and to Ho Chi Minh, the Communist leader of North Vietnam.

On Wednesday, Mr. Bush himself picked up the brush.

"I cannot for the life of me understand mobilizing demonstrations and demonstrating against your own country, no matter how strongly you feel, when you are in a foreign land," Mr. Bush said, in an interview on the CNN program "Larry King Live." "Maybe I'm old-fashioned, but to go to a foreign country and demonstrate against your own country when your sons and daughters are dying halfway around the world, I am sorry but I think that is wrong."

Clinton Forced to Respond

Mr. Clinton was forced to respond, and did so today, calling Mr. Bush "desperate" and saying he felt "really sad" for him.

Mr. Clinton said, as he has always said, that he had been an outspoken opponent of the war, but defended his activities in 1969 as innocent and minor. He said he "helped put together a teach-in at the University of London" and that had been "the only thing I ever helped put together." He acknowledged that he had "participated" in a demonstration at the American embassy.

Mr. Clinton's own words, included in a letter he wrote on Dec. 3, 1969, appear to belie the claim that he organized, or helped to organize, only one event, the teach-in.

"I have written and spoken and marched against the war," he wrote in a letter to the director of the Reserve Officers Training Corps at the University of Arkansas, explaining why he had reneged on a commitment to join the program. "After I left Arkansas last summer, I went to Washington to work in the national headquarters of the Moratorium, then to England to organize the Americans here for demonstrations Oct. 15 and Nov. 16."

The "Moratorium" Mr. Clinton referred to was one of two enormous international antiwar protests of 1969, culminating in a huge protest march in Washington on "Vietnam Moratorium Day," Oct. 15.

David Mixner, a national co-chairman of the Moratorium, recalls Mr. Clinton as "not at all a major player in the antiwar movement" but as someone who helped, in a small way, in the summer of 1969 to organize the fall protests.

"He did some weeks of volunteer work that summer," said Mr. Mixner, who now runs a political consulting business in Los Angeles. "But he was not a full-time employee nor a full-time volunteer. He assisted, I remember that, but if you asked me how, I couldn't tell you. He might have been stuffing envelopes."

In the fall, Mr. Clinton returned to England for his second year in the Rhodes scholar program at Oxford. On Moratorium Day, about 300 people, mostly American students, demonstrated peacefully outside the American Embassy in London. The rally featured two well-known figures, the actor Paul Newman and his wife, Joanne Woodward. It is apparently this rally that Mr. Clinton claims in his December 1969 letter to have organized.

Ira Magaziner, who was a fellow student at Oxford in 1969 and is now a senior economics adviser to the Clinton campaign, said he remembered the October rally but did not recall Mr. Clinton as an organizer. Like several of Mr. Clinton's friends of that time who were interviewed this week, he remembers the student from Arkansas as intensely interested in issues like the war and racism, but not as a radical.

'Very Conventional Group'

"This was a very conventional group of people, not people who were burning flags or shouting 'pig' at the police," he said. "This was a group of people who had succeeded at school and were in the mainstream in their campuses and believed very much in solutions within the system."

On Nov. 15, in conjunction with the second major wave of protests in America, another demonstration was held in front of the American Embassy at Grosvenor Square. This rally, known as "the March of Death," was larger than the October rally, drawing about 1,500 people, who filed silently in front of the embassy. The marchers bore a coffin and, according to a contemporary account, carried cards with the names of servicemen who died in Vietnam. They walked to a megaphone in front of the embassy, called out the name and then dropped the card into a makeshift coffin.

Republicans have said Mr. Clinton took part in this demonstration and even helped negotiate with American Embassy officials to take the coffin inside. It is not clear if this is true.

What is clear, both by his own account and those of others present, is that Mr. Clinton played a role in organizing a related, but separate, demonstration on Nov. 16, which also took place at the American Embassy and across the square at St. Mark's Church.

That rally was peaceful, according to both witnesses and news accounts, but pointed in its message of disapproval of American conduct in the war. "We marched past the steps of the American Embassy," said Richard Stearns, a Rhodes scholar who is now a circuit court judge in Massachusetts. "I remember we all laid little white crosses on the steps, in silence, one by one, and then marched across the square to the church."

These same accounts—and all verifiable accounts to date—also argue strongly against Republican claims and insinuations that Mr. Clinton was either a major organizer of antiwar protests or a radical one.

In the case of the Nov. 16 rally, for instance, Mr. Clinton's friends recall that he wished to hold the rally a day later than the "March of Death" affair precisely because he thought the larger demonstration would be too radical.

Mr. Stearns said that while there were many radical and Communist-influenced groups involved in the antiwar protests in London at that time, Mr. Clinton shunned them. "They were pretty much over the edge of what Bill considered respectable," he said.

A second aspect of Mr. Clinton's activities that has come under heavy Republican assault is a 40-day trip in late 1969 and early 1970 to several Northern European and Eastern bloc countries, including the Soviet Union. Mr. Clinton has been vague about the details of the trip, and his New Year's Eve visit to Moscow in 1969 has been the subject of the most searing attacks by Republicans.

Mr. Bush elevated the attack on the issue on Wednesday evening. During an appearance on "Larry King Live" he asked about the trip. "I don't want to tell you what I really think," Mr. Bush said, adding, "To go to Moscow, one year after Russia crushed Czechoslovakia, not remember what you saw there."

* * *

November 15, 1992

U.S. TEAM IN HANOI STUDIES RELICS OF THE MISSING

By PHILIP SHENON
Special to The New York Times

HANOI, Vietnam, Nov. 14—Up a musty stairwell in a museum commemorating the triumphs of the People's Army of Vietnam, a team of American investigators sit hunched over laptop computers and a camera tripod, trying to end what for many American families is the continuing torment of the Vietnam War.

Every half hour or so, a group of Vietnamese museum workers slowly make their way up the steps, lugging another assortment of relics collected from the enemy, the United States, in that long-ago war.

The relics examined by the Pentagon investigators one morning this week included an American-issue military parachute, a pocket flare gun, an airman's helmet with the wearer's name on it, a blue-felt Air Force captain's cap, a plastic flap from the fuel tank of an American military jet, a single pink cotton handkerchief and a pair of red-and-white socks—all of it hidden away for years in unlit storerooms in the Museum of the People's Army, the national war museum in Hanoi.

2,265 Still Missing

This, the American investigators say, is what they have been waiting for.

If they are correct, these bits and pieces of metal, rubber and cloth—along with thousands of black-and-white photographs stored elsewhere in the museum—will allow the United States to determine the fate of many of the 2,265 Americans who are still officially listed as unaccounted for from the Vietnam War.

It was only last month, after an American researcher alerted the Pentagon to the treasure trove in the museum, that the Hanoi Government agreed to allow a Defense Department team to come in to study the full collection.

Reuters

An American investigator, Eric Frandsen, photographing a pair of boots in Hanoi, Vietnam, that belonged to an American pilot.

Breakthrough Is Seen

The commander of the American investigators now working in Vietnam, Lieut. Col. Jack Donovan, described Vietnam's new open-access decree as a breakthrough.

"I've heard this described as the central biggest development since 1973 in terms of accounting for missing Americans," he said. It was in 1973 that United States ground forces pulled out of Vietnam.

Until last week, Americans investigators had only guessed at what might be found in the war museum, three blocks from Ho Chi Minh's mausoleum in the heart of the Vietnamese capital. Only a small fraction of the articles were actually on public display in the museum, which draws a steady stream of visitors. Now they know it contains personal items and military gear taken from scores, and perhaps hundreds, of American soldiers, pilots and sailors who were captured or killed in North Vietnamese territory.

"My gut feeling is that our work is going to be very valuable," said James Minihan, a 26-year-old Navy petty officer from Jacksonville, N.C., who spends his days at the museum tapping away on the keyboard of a laptop computer, cataloging the relics as they are placed on the floor on a white sheet of paper and photographed. "The Vietnamese have kept very complete records on this material."

Vietnam is eager for normal diplomatic relations with the United States and is desperate for Washington to lift the economic embargo it has imposed since the end of the war. Since 1988, it has allowed Pentagon investigators into the country to search for the remains of Americans missing from the war. The Defense Department opened an office in Hanoi last year.

No Single Depository

There is no single repository in Vietnam for wartime army records and artifacts gathered from American soldiers. Instead, records and relics are scattered throughout the country in dozens of war museums and archives, some built by individual provinces and cities to commemorate their local contribution to the war against the Americans and, earlier, against the French.

The Americans, who until last month had been granted access to only a few museums and archives in Vietnam, are now discovering how meticulous the Vietnamese record-keeping was.

In the Army Museum in Hanoi, the well-preserved relics range from military penknives and wristwatches to bicycle-sized chunks of jagged metal from the wings of B-52 bombers shot down over North Vietnamese territory. Virtually all of the items inspected so far have been carefully tagged to show where and when they were found.

The artifacts may help the Pentagon determine exactly where individual soldiers died and how, or where American planes went down and whether their pilots survived. That in turn will help American search teams decide which areas of the Vietnamese countryside should be combed for human remains.

'Pieces of the Puzzle'

"The end result of work does not take place here in Hanoi," said Chief Warrant Officer Gary Fulton of West Des Moines, another of the investigators working at the museum. "We're getting pieces of the puzzle that will take us back out into the field."

As he spoke, a Vietnamese museum worker carefully laid an American aviator's helmet on the paper-covered floor so it could be photographed from several different angles.

"That could be valuable," said Chief Fulton, motioning to a small, worn name tag that had been affixed to the outside of the helmet, apparently by the airmen who had once worn it. Mr. Fulton showed the helmet to a reporter on condition that the name not be used.

Some of the relics inspected by the investigators will be of no use in determining the fate of missing Americans. They were taken from prisoners of war who were freed by the Vietnamese years ago, or they are so innocuous that it will be impossible to link them to any one person.

"We were given a brown leather wallet—empty, no identification, no pictures inside," said Petty Officer Eric Frandsen, 28, of Lansing, Mich., the team's photographer. "I photographed it. I don't know how valuable something like that would be."

Many Bear Identification

But many other artifacts turned over so far by the Vietnamese do bear a name, a serial number or some other notation that could help American investigators tie them to a missing soldier or pilot, or to a particular battle, crash or ambush.

The Pentagon team has inspected American-issue military parachutes and life vests in recent days that, while they have no name tags, are stamped with a series of inspection dates, which should make it possible to determine with some accuracy when the survival equipment was used by a serviceman.

The names and other details can be checked against information stored in the laptop computers carried by the American investigators. The computers hold a detailed electronic dossier on each of the 2,265 Americans—2,262 men, 3 women—who remain missing in Vietnam, Laos and Cambodia. Of these the vast majority are assumed to have been killed in combat, and are listed as missing because circumstantial evidence of death has yet to be backed up with physical proof.

The Pentagon investigators are still in the very early stages of their work, and they are reluctant to guess how long the inspections in Hanoi and elsewhere in the country will take.

Wary of Raising Hopes

They are even more reluctant to estimate how many of the 2,265 cases of missing Americans might be solved by their work. They say their optimism, which is palpable here, might raise false hopes among the families of the missing,

"This work is going to help us answer questions concerning the fate of a number of missing Americans," said Robert J. Destatte, a Defense Intelligence Agency analyst whose career has been dedicated since 1979 to the search for missing Americans. "I'm confident we're moving in the right direction. But it's going to be a long process."

Some of his colleagues say the search for missing Americans is likely to continue for years.

The Vietnamese Government has already provided the Bush Administration with the thousands of photographs of dead Americans taken by Vietnamese military photographers during the war and stored in the People's Army Museum.

Librarian Was the Key

The exact sequence of events that led Hanoi to turn over the photographs and to announce last month that it would grant the Pentagon full access to the war archives remains a mystery, although it is one clearly linked to the unusual relationship between the Vietnamese Government and an American researcher, Ted Schweitzer, who was given access to photographic archives at the Army Museum earlier this year.

According to the Vietnamese, Mr. Schweitzer, a 50-year-old librarian, was allowed to rummage through the museum's collection after he told museum directors that he was writing a book about the war. Vietnamese officials say they were later surprised and irritated when he turned over the results of his research to the Pentagon.

During a search of the archives, Mr. Schweitzer found thousands of photos of American servicemen who had been captured or killed by the Vietnamese. Last summer, after telling associates that he had failed to interest New York publishers in a book, Mr. Schweitzer turned the photographs over to the Defense Department.

Mr. Schweitzer is now back in Hanoi, this time as a Pentagon consultant. But the other American investigators here say they rarely see him and know almost nothing about him. He did not respond to repeated requests for an interview.

Hiding Material Denied

Mr. Schweitzer's disclosure of the photos raised new questions about whether Hanoi has been hiding information that might have resolved the fate of missing Americans years ago.

Le Van Bang, director of American affairs at the Vietnamese Foreign Ministry, said that material in the museums had always been available to the United States, but that Pentagon investigators had chosen to conduct their investigation on a case-by-case basis—requesting information about a specific soldiers instead of requesting access to everything in the museum archives. "We were not hiding anything," he said.

But Pentagon investigators working in Vietnam say the recent disclosures prove that they have been misled for years by the Vietnamese. They add, however, that the new Vietnamese pledge of cooperation is so important that there is nothing to be gained by attacking the Vietnamese publicly.

"If there was a misunderstanding with the Vietnamese, it is not so important now as the fact that we have an agreement that pleases everybody," Mr. Destatte said. "Certainly it pleases everybody on our side."

* * *

March 27, 1993

WITH AID GONE, A ONCE-BUSTLING PORT TURNS QUIET

By HENRY KAMM

Special to The New York Times

HAIPHONG, Vietnam, March 24—Vietnam's largest port, until a few years ago backed up with ships waiting to be unloaded and masters and shipping agents angry over costly delays, stands nearly idle. Only three or four in the long row of berths are occupied; stacks of empty containers await cargoes that do not come or go.

"The port is a victim of the end of the Soviet Union and the other socialist states," Nguyen Van Nha, the deputy harbor master, said. He was interviewed in the stillness of what was once a bustling flight of offices at dockside.

Haiphong was the main point of entry for everything that the Soviet Union and its allies sent to Vietnam. In its poverty and near-isolation from the non-Communist world, it was their ward. Much of what Vietnam ate, the fertilizer and pesticides that made its rice grow, raw materials for its industries and the arms, ammunition and equipment to keep its large army girded in war and peace arrived here.

The aid has vanished since its donors have themselves become recipients of foreign assistance.

Good Rice Harvests

Moreover, Mr. Nha said, northern Vietnam has been experiencing excellent rice harvests in recent years, so the one million or so tons that sometimes had to be brought from the south have not been needed. Haiphong port is operating at half or less of its yearly handling capacity of five million tons, the harbor master said.

At best, Mr. Nha said, the port handled 3.2 million tons a year in the crisis years of 1978–80, when Vietnam invaded and occupied Cambodia. Bureaucratic central control once made the port notorious for delays in loading and unloading, but since the Vietnamese program of economic liberalization and decentralization, cargo-handling has been greatly speeded. This makes the emptiness of the port even greater.

The loss of port activity poses a grave problem of social conscience for a country that remains Communist and cannot admit having unemployment.

"We employ more than 5,000 people, but at the moment we require limited numbers of workers," Mr. Nha said. It was an understatement that fell far short of describing the virtual absence of anybody on the dock at 2 in the afternoon, except for a cleaning crew of cheerful women and a fierce-looking North Korean guarding his freighter.

"We try to divide the work among them," the deputy harbor master continued. Shifts are shortened, he said, and the night shift was eliminated. He said workers were sent for training to increase efficiency for the future and given language courses. Most of Vietnam seems to believe that English is the key to prosperity.

Truong Van Thai, a Polish- and Belgian-trained port-management specialist who is secretary of the harbor administration, said workers were being laid off if no work or training could be found for them at 75 percent of their pay. Base pay is about $30 a month, high for this country, where teachers earn $20.

"We know we will need them again, so we don't want to lose anybody," he said.

Pointing to the extensive warehouses, rebuilt after the end of the devastating years of American bombing in 1973, Mr. Thai said that 10 years ago the port was fining shippers for not removing their cargoes promptly. "Now we give them 10 days' storage for free for imports and 20 for exports," he said. "And our warehouses are still empty."

No Ill Feeling Toward U.S.

The bombs have not been forgotten. "They were horrible days," said Vu Thi Ngoc, a flower vendor opposite the Opera. "Every few minutes the sirens sounded. We haven't gotten over it."

But Mrs. Ngoc, echoing a theme heard throughout Vietnam, said she "really" harbored no ill feelings toward any American and wished the United States would end its boycott. "You can't keep that sentiment of bitterness forever," she said. "If the Americans come back in peace, it will be good for both of us."

The deputy harbor master said Haiphong's main hope was becoming a transit port for China's southern inland provinces like Yunan. He said the Governor of Yunan had said on a visit that he could provide more than two million tons of cargo a year to a port that is only about 600 miles from Kunming, Yunan's capital.

Looking More Prosperous

Despite the plight of its chief employer, this bustling city of half a million people looks far more prosperous than it did before liberalization. The main reason is that an extensive new private sector is providing second and third jobs in a "gray" economy. "Nobody can survive on Government pay," said a geographer selling trinkets on a Hanoi street.

Small shops offering a great variety of bottom-of-the-line clothes and consumer goods give the old port city's main streets a scent of its pre-Communist past. Fine old French-colonial buildings—the Opera House, Government palaces and hotels—have received long-overdue coats of paint. A new hotel, Haiphong's only high-rise, is being built with Hong Kong money.

It dwarfs the lovely 100-year-old refurbished hotel next to it, which has restored its name, l'Hôtel du Commerce. After the Communist victory in 1954 it had been renamed, Soviet-style, as Friendship Hotel.

But the street on which it stands has kept its name. It is still called Dien Bien Phu Street, after the battle that ended French colonialism in Indochina.

* * *

November 12, 1993

A BELATED SALUTE TO THE WOMEN WHO SERVED

By ERIC SCHMITT
Special to The New York Times

WASHINGTON, Nov. 11—Marion Birkhimer had been waiting 25 years for this day, ever since she returned from a two-year tour as head surgical nurse on the hospital ship Repose off the Vietnam coast.

In 1968, Americans did not want to hear about the pains soldiers were suffering in an unpopular war, Ms. Birkhimer said. And they especially did not want to hear from the women who served in Vietnam and later became a forgotten part of the conflict's forgotten corps.

But today, Veterans Day, those women finally heard from the nation. In civilian dress or combat fatigues, wearing their medals and ribbons, female veterans gathered by the thousands on the Mall for a dedication of a new memorial to honor women who served during the Vietnam War.

'We Never Listened'

"It's long overdue," said Ms. Birkhimer, a 26-year Navy veteran from Ocala, Fla., daubing tears from her eyes during an interview. "We were supposed to be the brave ones and not have emotions. Military nurses have repressed so much."

Nearly 20 years after the war ended, Vice President Al Gore dedicated the bronze sculpture of three women helping a wounded male G.I., a symbol of healing set in a grove of trees 300 feet from the low black wall that is the Vietnam Veterans Memorial.

"In the tense, sometimes confusing peace that followed, we never listened to their story," Mr. Gore said of the women. "And we never properly thanked them. Dedicating this memorial gives us occasion to do both."

Mr. Gore, who was an Army journalist in Vietnam, was the White House's natural choice to speak at today's ceremony. President Clinton, who has had a strained relationship with the military partly because he avoided the draft during the Vietnam War, was heckled during a Memorial Day speech at the Vietnam memorial. Mr. Clinton today attended a wreath-laying at the Tomb of the Unknowns and spoke at Arlington National Cemetery.

Feeling of Vindication

After years of neglect, the women said they felt vindicated by the belated recognition. "There are just no words for what I'm feeling," said Mae Jones of Baltimore, a 20-year Army veteran who served in Vietnam as a communications specialist for two years. "It's just wonderful."

The statue honors 11,500 women who served in Vietnam—as nurses, intelligence analysts, air traffic controllers and many other roles—as well as 265,000 other women who served in the military during the Vietnam era.

Three-quarters of the women in Vietnam were exposed to hostile fire. Eight of them died in the fighting, and many others were wounded. About 58,000 of the nearly three million men who served in Vietnam were killed.

The Vietnam Veterans Memorial includes the names of the eight military women who were killed there. Ten years ago, Diane Carlson Evans, a former Army nurse in Vietnam, began what turned out to be a $4 million project to commemorate the surviving women.

The sculpture itself, designed by Glenna Goodacre of Santa Fe, N.M., has drawn flak from some architects, who protest that another statue will detract from the emotional power and artistic integrity of the Vietnam Veterans Memorial. A third memorial in the vicinity, a sculpture of three servicemen, honors combat troops.

Associated Press

Washington: Veterans embracing near the memorial to women who served during the Vietnam War.

Today, though, it was hard to find any dissenters. Female veterans said their country only now was recognizing their contribution. "Welcome home, ladies, welcome home!" bellowed one bearded male veteran in combat fatigues, as thousands of female veterans marched down to the new memorial this morning. "Stand tall! Stand tall!"

Old friends and comrades embraced in tearful reunions on the Mall and at gatherings Wednesday night.

Too Painful to Forget

Doris I. Allen, a former Army intelligence analyst from Oakland, Calif., and Kathy Poole, a former Army personnel clerk from Dallas, last saw each other in 1970 in Vietnam. They reminisced about huddling in bunkers while Vietcong rockets exploded overhead.

"I don't think most people want to remember the bad times," said Ms. Allen, a retired psychologist who served three tours in Saigon and Long Binh.

But some of those memories were too painful to forget. Ms. Birkhimer recalled: "I remember one patient who was brought in with a head injury. His brains were oozing out onto the gurney, and I tried to wrap his head with Ace bandages. He kept asking me: 'Am I going to be all right? Am I going to be all right?' I knew he was going to die. It was all so pitiful."

The women also recalled the slights of a male-dominated military. Ms. Allen said her commanding officer had recommended she receive the Legion of Merit medal, but that higher superiors denied her the award "because I was a woman."

Priscilla Miller, a 72-year-old former Navy anesthetist from Williamsburg, Va., who served in World War II and in Korea as well as Vietnam, said it took the Persian Gulf war, and its popular support, to force Americans to re-examine the conflict in Southeast Asia, and how the country had treated its veterans.

"The gulf war was brought home to Americans every night on television, just as we lived it every day in Vietnam," said Ms. Miller, who attended today's ceremony with two old friends who also served as Navy anesthetists at the first American hospital in Saigon, Owedia Searcy, 70, of Annapolis, Md., and Charlotte Clark, 70, of Chincoteague, Va.

While the memorial served to salute the deeds of Vietnam-era veterans, it also served as an inspiration to the hundreds of active-duty troops and reservists who turned out today.

"Each and every one of these women deserve this statue," said Sgt. First Class Joanne Frazier, 38, who has served in a Virginia National Guard infantry unit for 11 years. "It's about time."

* * *

February 4, 1994

CLINTON DROPS 19-YEAR BAN ON U.S. TRADE WITH VIETNAM; CITES HANOI'S HELP ON M.I.A.'S

By DOUGLAS JEHL
Special to The New York Times

WASHINGTON, Feb. 3—President Clinton today ordered an end to the trade embargo on Vietnam, casting away a central remnant of one of America's most divisive wars and opening a potentially lucrative market to American goods.

After nearly two decades of a bitter peace, Mr. Clinton said it was now time to acknowledge the cooperation Vietnam has shown in the search for evidence of the 2,238 Americans still officially listed as missing from that conflict, which ended in 1975. He said opening the door to trade would benefit that still-unfinished search.

At a White House ceremony this afternoon, Mr. Clinton said he was lifting the trade embargo "because I am absolutely convinced it offers us the best way to resolve the fate of those who remain missing and about whom we are not sure."

Allowing Liaison Offices

The step taken by Mr. Clinton stops short of restoring diplomatic relations with Vietnam. But it will allow the United States and Vietnam each to open a liaison office in the other's capital, the highest level of ties between them since the long and painful war that left more than 58,000 Americans dead before the United States withdrew from the conflict in 1973.

The United States informed Vietnam of the decision this afternoon, and the White House said trade between the two countries would resume as soon as the Commerce Department could draft the necessary regulations, probably within the next several weeks.

The idea of reaching out to Vietnam had been vigorously opposed by the American Legion and others among the nation's leading veterans' groups, making the decision a sensitive one for Mr. Clinton. He had to overcome criticism from them during his presidential campaign for having avoided the military draft during the Vietnam War.

Bid to Avoid Political Attacks

In an effort to avoid a new round of damaging attacks, Mr. Clinton announced his decision this afternoon only after meeting privately with representatives of veterans' organizations. The White House also released a sheaf of endorsements from distinguished Vietnam-era commanders, including Gen. William C. Westmoreland, the former commander of United States forces in Vietnam, and Adm. Elmo Zumwalt, the Navy's top officer in the final years of the war.

But Mr. Clinton appeared determined to show no great pleasure in his decision, which he announced by reading a passionless statement in the Roosevelt Room of the White House.

To Mr. Clinton's immediate right was Gen. John Shalikashvili, Chairman of the Joint Chiefs of Staff. Others positioned next to the President were Secretary of State Warren Christopher, Defense Secretary Les Aspin, who served in Vietnam as a civilian assistant to Defense Secretary Robert McNamara, and Anthony Lake, the President's national security adviser, who volunteered for service in Vietnam as a young diplomat. In the audience were Democratic Senators John F. Kerry of Massachusetts, a veteran who had called for an end to the embargo, and Bob Kerrey of Nebraska, who lost a leg and won the Medal of Honor for his heroism in Vietnam.

While Mr. Clinton has spoken repeatedly of the importance that expanded trade holds for the United States economy, he insisted today that the potential for American economic gains played no part in his decision. But it was greeted with delight and relief by American businessmen who had complained that an anachronistic policy was denying them a share of the Vietnamese market that advocates say could be worth up to $6 billion a year in trade involving American companies.

The plan to lift the embargo had been unanimously recommended several weeks ago by Mr. Clinton's top Cabinet officers and by the Joint Chiefs of Staff. But aides said the President calculated that his position would be strongest if he waited for the endorsement that the Senate provided in a vote last week before making his decision public.

'Get It Over With'

As late as this morning, White House officials had said that Mr. Clinton had not made up his mind about the embargo and that he would not announce his decision before Saturday. But Administration officials had long since made clear that his commitment was irrevocable, and aides said he had wanted to "get it over with" once he finally initialed his approval.

Officials said Mr. Clinton had not made his decision until he reviewed a final packet of information about the search for American prisoners of war and those missing in action, but they would not be more specific.

In explaining their decision to go ahead now, Mr. Clinton and his top deputies praised Vietnam today for having been more cooperative last year than in any year since the end of the war in the effort to resolve the mystery about those who are still listed as missing.

Some Remains Returned

Since July alone, Vietnam has returned to the United States the remains of 39 individuals believed to have been American personnel, bringing to 67 the number of sets of remains handed over in 1993. Only three of those sets have so far been conclusively identified as the remains of United States servicemen. Vietnam has also provided new help in investigating claims of live sightings of missing Americans, and in sharing wartime documents.

Mr. Clinton, who eased some sanctions against Vietnam on two occasions last year but refused to lift the embargo, said today that the progress met the conditions he had set for a restoration of trade. Without fully explaining his reasoning, he said he had also concluded that an end to the embargo represented "the best way to continue getting information" about those Americans who are still missing.

But that argument has found little resonance among the nation's largest veterans' groups, including the American Legion, whose national commander warned Mr. Clinton in advance of the decision that it would be regarded as "a betrayal" of veterans, the missing and their families.

Meeting With Veterans

In a sign of how important the White House regarded their reaction, the veterans' representatives invited on short notice to the White House this afternoon were briefed not just by Mr. Clinton, but also by Mr. Christopher, Mr. Lake, General Shalikashvili and Mr. Aspin. Both sides described the discussion as cordial, but the veterans said later that it had done nothing to change their minds.

Larry Rivers, executive director of the Veterans of Foreign Wars, said he and others had told Mr. Clinton that they intended "to keep him at his word to keep Vietnam accountable." Ann Mills Griffiths, who heads the National League of Families of American Prisoners and Missing in Southeast Asia, chose not to attend the meeting and said she believed Mr. Clinton had "clearly broken his promise" to maintain pressure on Hanoi.

But relations between the White House and veterans remain so delicate that even John Wheeler, who led fundraising efforts for the Vietnam Memorial and helped Mr. Clinton during his presidential campaign to deflect criticism from Vietnam veterans, combined his statement of support with one chiding the President for "an embargo on vets" within the Administration. White House officials said they could not dispute Mr. Wheeler's assertion that only 8 percent of the men among Mr. Clinton's senior appointees are military veterans.

With the directive he issued today to the Departments of State, Treasury and Commerce, Mr. Clinton set aside the embargo the United States imposed against North Vietnam in 1964 and extended to cover all of Vietnam after the fall of the South Vietnamese Government on April 30, 1975.

Other Restrictions Remain

Administration officials emphasized tonight that the lifting of the embargo would not spell an end to other restrictions imposed by Congress against Vietnam, which will continue to prohibit sales of weapons and some high-technology goods. In an odd twist, they also said the Trading with the Enemy Act would be left in place, although only to insure that Vietnamese assets frozen by the United States remain in American control until the two countries can agree on their disposition.

The officials also strongly rejected characterizations that the step represented a reward for Vietnamese cooperation, and spoke with some lingering bitterness at a briefing today of the years in which Vietnam had confounded rather than helped the American search for the missing.

Mr. Clinton, who took extraordinary steps to avoid military service in Vietnam, was in the odd position today as Commander in Chief of marking an end of sorts to a war in which he, unlike many of his contemporaries, did not take part. But he insisted today that his decision had not been complicated by that fact.

"Everybody my age, whether they were in Vietnam or not, knew someone who died there, knew someone who was wounded there," the 47-year-old President said. "And I think people in our generation are perhaps more insistent on trying to get a full accounting, more obsessed with it, than perhaps people who are younger and people who are older, except those who had children."

* * *

February 4, 1994

A PASSION SPENT, FINALLY

By R. W. APPLE, Jr.
Special to The New York Times

WASHINGTON, Feb. 3—It was Lyndon B. Johnson's war, though the initial commitments were made by John F. Kennedy. The peace, such as it was, was the handiwork of Richard M. Nixon, but that was tainted by the stench of defeat.

Now, irony of ironies, fate has chosen Bill Clinton to lead the nation in consigning the whole sad, ugly ordeal to the dim recesses of memory—the same Bill Clinton who, like Dan Quayle and many other privileged members of his generation, managed to avoid service in the rice paddies of the Mekong Delta or the jungles of the Central Highlands, on the carriers in the Gulf of Tonkin or the choppers of the First Cavalry Division.

Some organizations that represent veterans of the war protested bitterly even before President Clinton announced the lifting of the 19-year embargo this afternoon. No doubt a spirited scrap will ensue. But many voters, if the polls are to be believed, agree with Mr. Clinton and with the Senate, which voted overwhelmingly last week to end the embargo.

Tragedy to Opportunity

Trade follows the flag, it is said, and mutual diplomatic recognition between Hanoi and Washington is not likely to be delayed many years more, though the President specified that it would have to wait upon "a full and final accounting" of America's losses.

Slowly, almost imperceptibly, Vietnam has turned from a tragedy into an opportunity. Having watched their German and British counterparts making large investments there, having pondered the prospects of turning the one-time enemy into the next Thai- or Malay-style success story, American businessmen have pushed relentlessly for today's change.

But it took more than that; it took a political strategy. That was cobbled together largely by Winston Lord, the Assistant Secretary of State for East Asian and Pacific Affairs, who persuaded Hanoi to provide enough answers to the vexed question of prisoners of war and servicemen still missing to enable Mr. Clinton to win the support of important public figures who had the credibility on Vietnam that he did not.

Among those, by far the most important were a pair of Senators—John Kerry, a Massachusetts Democrat who won the Silver Star as a patrol-boat commander in the Delta, and John McCain, an Arizona Republican, the son and grandson of admirals, who bailed out of his naval attack plane after it was hit over North Vietnam and spent five and a half years in an enemy prison camp.

"I feel we are finally putting this war behind us, as we have put every war behind us," Senator McCain said by telephone from his home in Phoenix. "A nation must do that, and I am grateful to have survived to see it, when so many of my friends did not. I feel it is in our interest to have a strong counterweight to China, the growing military and economic power in the region, and I feel this will help us a lot economically."

Another who served in Vietnam emphasized the geopolitical aspect.

"We really need to have a relationship with these people, not for the past but for the future," said Frank Wisner, a career diplomat, now a senior Defense Department official, who served as a provincial adviser in the Highlands. "Vietnam is a key actor along the Pacific Rim as we, they, the Chinese and others in the area head into the next century."

A Cultural Benefit

A scholar who studied American troops during the war and has studied them since foresaw another benefit.

"Not many people realize it yet," said Charles Moskos of Northwestern University, one of the country's leading military sociologists, "but this will do what the peace treaty never did. More Americans will go to Vietnam. They will see how much the Vietnamese people like Americans, and how many supported the American intervention. That will redound to the credit of the Vietnam veterans and of the serving military today."

If so, the President's action will truly represent the closing of a chapter in American history.

The war and its aftermath helped to shape American public life for three decades. Even when the shooting stopped, the United States found it agonizingly difficult to follow Lincoln's injunction to "bind up the nation's wounds, to care for him who shall have borne the battle and for his widow and for his orphan." The anguish of the families of the P.O.W.'s and the M.I.A.'s, the travail of the boat people and the devastation wrought by defoliants on the landscape of Indochina all kept the pain alive in peoples' minds.

Political Waves and Ripples

The war forced President Johnson into retirement, almost certainly cost Hubert H. Humphrey the Presidency, planted the seeds of doubt and discouragement about government in the minds of the electorate and the news media and helped keep the Democrats out of the White House for most of the 1970's and 1980's. The image of the last CH-46 helicopter lifting off the roof of the United States Embassy in Saigon on April 30, 1975, burned a hole in the national psyche.

"After that," said the novelist Ward Just, who worked as a war correspondent in Vietnam, "I thought we'd be better off without each other for a while. Vietnam had a bad effect on us, and, God knows, we had a terrible effect on Vietnam. Now I think it's time to see whether we can't all behave like grown-ups. I think most people feel that way, actually."

Like the Vietnam War memorial, like the end of the war itself, today's decision has been a long time coming.

A Decade of Agony

Thirty-one years ago, in January 1963, the weakness of the American-advised South Vietnamese troops was revealed to an American officer named John Paul Vann and, through him, to many others, in the debacle at the hamlet of Ap Bac.

Twenty-six years ago, on Jan. 31, 1968, the North Vietnamese and the Vietcong launched the Tet offensive, attacking on many fronts at once, capturing the old capital of Hue and penetrating Saigon itself.

Twenty-one years ago, on Jan. 27, 1973, a peace treaty was signed in Paris by the United States, the South Vietnamese, the North Vietnamese and the Vietcong. The next day, a cease-fire took effect.

Those events are almost as distant from today as the battles of World War I were from those of World War II. Many who took part in them or witnessed them have retired or died, and new generations have grown up for whom names like Ia Drang and Parrot's Beak seem as remote as Belleau Wood or Iwo Jima.

In a sense, time was Bill Clinton's ally. Fewer and fewer people cling to the past. And even for many of those who do, as Leo Thorsness, a former Air Force P.O.W., said this week, one day "the passion is gone."

* * *

February 5, 1994

VIETNAM WELCOMES U.S. DECISION ON EMBARGO

By PHILIP SHENON

Special to The New York Times

HO CHI MINH CITY, Vietnam, Feb. 4—In the crowded streets of a city still better known to the world as Saigon, there was a sense today that the war was finally over, the last battle concluded half a world away in the corridors of the White House.

The news that President Clinton had decided to lift the American trade embargo against Vietnam reached here today shortly before dawn, and by breakfast it was the only topic of conversation to be found in much of Ho Chi Minh City, the city that the Americans had to flee in humiliation a generation ago.

Reuters

Free Pepsi-Cola was served on the streets of Ho Chi Minh City yesterday as American companies tested a market opened by President Clinton's lifting of the United States embargo on trade with Vietnam.

"A heavy burden has been lifted," said Lam Thanh Sy, a 38-year-old high school mathematics teacher who recalls the boyhood terror of rushing into a bomb shelter with his parents. "We in Vietnam have felt that we were not allowed to participate in the world as full citizens because of the embargo. Now at last we are allowed to forget the war."

A Matter of Perspective

He was standing in the shadow of a large statue of Ho Chi Minh, the Vietnamese revolutionary leader, in a small, well-tended public park near city hall. A few feet away, a photographer, Hoang Hon Thanh, was snapping pictures of happy families posed beneath the statue.

"Me? I'm happy too," he said. "And I'm happy for a simple reason. Five years ago, I bought a Polaroid. Now that the embargo is lifted, I can finally buy some film for it."

The Vietnamese Government said in a statement released in Hanoi today that it was thankful to President Clinton for his decision to lift the embargo. The statement by Deputy Foreign Minister Le Mai pledged Vietnam's continued cooperation in determining the fate of 2,200 Americans still missing from the Vietnam War, the issue most often cited by the United States in keeping the trade embargo in place for so long.

"This decision meets the desire of the American and the Vietnamese peoples," Mr. Mai said, praising the President for having opened "a new page in U.S.-Vietnam relations." He called on Washington to consider establishing full diplomatic relations with Vietnam.

Fast-Growing Market

American corporations have been planning for years for the moment when they would be allowed back into Vietnam, a market of nearly 71 million consumers that even with the American embargo in place has emerged as one of the fastest-growing and most dynamic in Asia.

And so only hours after they heard the announcement from Washington, Americans began marching back onto the streets of Ho Chi Minh City, this time armed with checkbooks and marketing plans and wearing suits and ties.

Vietnam remains one of the world's poorest countries, with a per capita annual income of less than $500, but economists agree that with its diligent, well-educated work force and untapped natural resources, Vietnam has the potential to catch up with its booming Southeast Asian neighbors.

In a country where smuggled Coca-Cola is the most popular drink, Pepsi was the first to act. This morning, Pepsi began legitimate distribution for the first time since the

1970's, handing out bottles free to passers-by. This weekend, Pepsi says, television viewers here will see a new commercial featuring Miss Vietnam, 18-year-old Ha Kieu Anh, one of Vietnam's most popular celebrities.

Other American companies were not far behind in the battle to make their presence felt here. Coca-Cola announced that it would spend $45 million in Vietnam over the next five years. American Express said that Vietnam's foreign trade bank had agreed to accept the American Express charge card, making it the first American card to return to Vietnam since 1975. United Airlines reported here that it would soon begin service to Ho Chi Minh City from Los Angeles under a route authority it purchased in 1986 but, because of the embargo, had not been able to use.

In the streets of Ho Chi Minh City, many Vietnamese reacted to the lifting of the embargo with a sort of giddy excitement. There was for some the thought of renewing ties to an old, prosperous friend, the United States.

"My mother told me that when the American soldiers were here, there was lots of candy and many television sets and nice cars," said Tran, the 8-year-old son of a factory worker. "I think it will be fun to have the Americans here."

The end of the American embargo only made worse the usual crush today at the international airport in Ho Chi Minh City, once the American-run Tan Son Nhut Air Base.

Anxious to Return

Nineteen years after they joined the panicked evacuation out of what was then Saigon, large American corporations were struggling today to get their salesmen and marketing executives on the first flights heading back into the city.

John R. Guy, director of international sales at Briggs & Stratton Corporation, a Milwaukee-based manufacturer of gasoline engines, arrived in Ho Chi Minh City on a flight from Bangkok, Thailand, and went immediately to work. He is here to search for a Vietnamese partner.

His enthusiasm about his first trip to Vietnam was tempered by worries about his competitors, Asian and European manufacturers that were not hobbled by the American embargo. Some have been at work in Vietnam for years. "All of my major competitors are Japanese," he said. "And they are already in Vietnam."

Can Briggs & Stratton hope to catch up with the Japanese? "It's my job to make sure that we can," Mr. Guy said with some confidence. "This isn't impossible." Briggs & Stratton, he said, thinks that Vietnam could become the company's major Asian market within four years.

* * *

May 13, 1994

BATTLEFIELDS OF KHE SANH: STILL ONE CASUALTY A DAY

By MALCOLM W. BROWNE
Special to The New York Times

KHE SANH, Vietnam—A quarter century has passed since one of the most costly battles of the Vietnam War raged across the desolate Khe Sanh plateau, but this old battlefield near the former border between North and South Vietnam is still filling hospital beds with fresh victims.

The bare brown earth for miles around remains seeded with unexploded shells and bombs—a legacy of the 77-day siege in 1968, when some 40,000 North Vietnamese troops tried in vain to overrun the 5,000 United States marines holding the Khe Sanh bastion.

In the battle American forces rained 100,000 tons of bombs (equivalent in destructive force to five Hiroshima-size atomic bombs) and 158,000 large-caliber shells on the hills surrounding the base, killing an estimated 15,000 Communist soldiers.

Some of these projectiles, along with a considerable number of Vietnamese shells, were duds. But they remained alive and they are still killing unwary farmers bringing new land under cultivation. Dr. Pham Sy Dan, director of the Quang Tri Province Hospital at Dong Ha, said that people newly wounded at Khe Sanh and other battlefields in the province are admitted at the rate of one a day. Victims killed outright are not counted in this total.

The land around Khe Sanh is poor and ill suited to most crops, but it has nevertheless become valuable as a result of population pressure. Since the end of the war, Vietnam's population has grown by more than 60 percent—it now exceeds 72 million—and crowding has become particularly acute for farmers in the Red River Delta of northern Vietnam. Growing numbers of them leave home to seek land in the south, and many have settled in previously underpopulated regions.

The plow has come even to the dangerous fields of Khe Sanh. Men, women and children are dying here whenever their draft buffaloes plow up old bombs and shells. But an even greater hazard to life and limb is the thriving scrap metal business.

Residents of the region, including Van Kieu tribesmen as well as ethnic Vietnamese, are attracted by the easy money that can be made by finding and selling scrap metal to the steel plant at Thai Nguyen in northern Vietnam.

Dealers pay about seven cents a pound for military scrap, and with the help of $50 metal detectors imported from Thailand, scavengers can easily find enough metal around Khe Sanh to make a living. Common scrap includes big chunks of steel shrapnel, spent artillery cartridges, rockets, and intact shells and bombs.

Paying With Their Lives

For miles around, the ground of Khe Sanh is pitted and furrowed by the shovels of these scrap diggers—men, women and children who can earn up to $2 a day, a relatively good income. But some of them pay dearly for their booty, or their crops.

During a visit to the Quang Tri Province hospital, an ambulance delivered Tran Van Nam, a 22-year-old scrap metal hunter whose face and arms were horribly injured by an explosion that also killed his 30-year-old brother. The two men had been plowing a field.

Artificial Limbs Scarce

On one of the nearby wooden pallets that serve as beds in Vietnamese hospitals lay Ho Dung, a 13-year-old girl who was wounded five days earlier by a bomb explosion that blew out both her eyes and amputated a leg and an arm. In agony, she rolled blindly from one side to another on her wretched pallet.

Another victim, Nguyen Van Bon, was digging up sweet potatoes near his home in Vinh Linh village when a shell exploded and crippled him. Mr. Bon has five children.

Artificial limbs are scarce and expensive in Vietnam, and many victims of munition explosions take to the streets of nearby towns to beg. The Belgian-based relief organization Handicap International is building a simple workshop at the Quang Tri hospital with a lathe and a curing oven for manufacturing prosthetic arms and legs.

"But it would be far better if these terrible injuries could be stopped in the first place," said Mulpas Thy, a Belgian expert supervising the workshop.

Le Xuan Thong, chairman of the Huong Hoa District People's Committee, says that army experts occasionally survey old battle areas for unexploded munitions, but that so much territory is affected that it would be impossible to clear all of it.

No Warning Signs

Metal detectors can only locate munitions buried less than one foot deep, he said, and many dangerous projectiles escape detection even when search teams sweep battlefields. The best the experts can do is erect signs warning against dangerous areas, officials say.

In any case, no warning signs are visible at Khe Sanh.

Very few of the scrap collectors who scavenge here had even been born at the time of the battle of Khe Sanh, which lasted from Jan. 21 to April 7, 1968. Many of these boys and girls are illiterate, there being no schools in many rural hamlets, and none show interest in the fading inscription on a small stone monument that proclaims Khe Sanh as "America's Dien Bien Phu"—an allusion to the French bastion in northwestern Vietnam that fell to the Communists 40 years ago.

In fact, Khe Sanh was not an American defeat; though the American forces suffered 205 killed and 852 wounded in the siege, they held on.

Abandoned by Marines

But two months after the siege was broken, American commanders decided that Khe Sanh was not needed for the war effort after all. They ordered the Marines to abandon the base and destroy everything that had stood upon it—fortifications, bunkers, buildings, supply depots, an airport. Only the metal scrap and the dud projectiles remained.

Some American servicemen wondered later why so many had had to give their lives for territory deemed expendable so soon after the battle.

Ghosts of the past haunt Khe Sanh. At a bridge across the Ben Hai River near here stands a Communist monument marking the official northern terminus of the Ho Chi Minh Trail, and not far away is a national cemetery containing the graves of 10,360 North Vietnamese and Vietcong soldiers who died along the trail in the war. The cemetery is one of 72 graveyards for Communist troops dotting Quang Tri Province alone.

An official of a local People's Committee looked out across a vast field of white grave markers, shook his head, and said, "We paid dearly for this land."

* * *

March 16, 1995

'BOAT PEOPLE' PREFER DEATH TO HOMELAND

By PHILIP SHENON

MORONG, Philippines—Tran Ba is so desperate to avoid being forced back home to Vietnam that in a protest this month he doused himself with kerosene in front of horrified Philippine guards and threatened to set himself afire.

"Next time I will light the match," said Mr. Ba, who left Vietnam four years ago believing that he had been promised a new life in the United States.

Ta Thi Ngoan, a 53-year-old tailor who has been detained here since 1988, has told the guards that she is prepared to kill herself and her 10 children if they are returned to Vietnam. "If I go back to Vietnam, I will go straight to prison," she said. Her neighbor, Kim Thi Ng, said several families in the detention camp here had stored rat poison. "People are very serious about suicide," Mrs. Ng said.

Two decades after the first boatloads of Vietnamese pushed off the shores of their homeland into the treacherous waters of the South China Sea, the final chapter of their exodus is being written in detention camps like the one here along the mountainous western coast of the Philippines.

For many of these Vietnamese, who have spent years in these camps only to face a forced return to Vietnam, the final chapter will in many ways be tragic. The question is whether it will be violent as well.

In February, Southeast Asian governments announced final plans to close the camps, which have housed the more than 800,000 Vietnamese who fled their homeland after 1975. The closings mean that the 46,306 Vietnamese left in the camps today—those who have been unable to find third countries willing to accept them—will soon be compelled to return to Vietnam.

Forcing them home will be an ugly, possibly dangerous business, as tens of thousands of people are pushed or

The New York Times

Twenty years after they began fleeing their homeland, thousands of Vietnamese remain in detention in Southeast Asia. Many at this Philippine camp say they would rather die then be forced to return home.

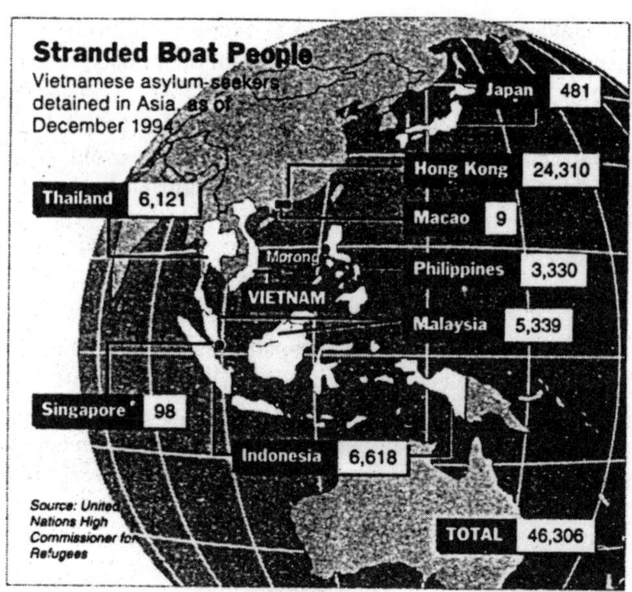

dragged onto planes headed for Vietnam, which many of them had hoped never to see again.

As the clock ticks down, violent outbursts are becoming common in the detention camps.

In Indonesia last June, two Vietnamese boat people set themselves on fire and died in a protest over plans for their forced return to Vietnam.

Hundreds of Vietnamese in camps in Hong Kong have announced suicide pacts, and more than 200 were injured last April in a clash with the police after refusing to move to another camp in preparation for their forced return. There have been scores of cases of self-mutilation by Vietnamese who have insisted that they would rather die than return home.

"Many of these incidents were carried out more with a view toward attracting attention than causing real harm," said Jahanshah Assadi, director of the Hong Kong mission of the United Nations High Commissioner for Refugees. "But we've had attempts at hanging, attempts at self-immolation, people taking a knife or sharp-edged instrument and puncturing their arms, legs, stomachs."

A New Vietnam Can't Allay Old Fears

If they are forced back, many of the Vietnamese will return to a country different from the one they left years ago. Vietnam has abandoned Marxist economics and embraced the free market. The economy is booming, with job opportunities unimaginable in the 1980's.

Vietnam remains an authoritarian country that imprisons political dissidents. But United Nations investigators who visited there say they found no credible evidence that any of the 68,000 asylum-seekers who have already returned have faced harassment from the Government. The Hanoi Government has vowed to treat the returning Vietnamese humanely.

While Vietnam's economic boom and the assurances of the United Nations should give comfort to those Vietnamese still in the camps, many are clearly still terrified about what they will confront if they are forced to go back home.

Hiram A. Ruiz, an analyst of the U.S. Committee for Refugees, a private group based in Washington, has visited the detention camps and said the threats of suicide and other violence were not surprising. "They have lost years of their lives, risked everything, given up everything in hopes of living in a different country," he said.

Of the Vietnamese left in camps in Southeast Asia, more than half—about 24,300—are in Hong Kong, held in overcrowded barbed-wire compounds that have long been an expensive embarrassment to the Hong Kong Government. The others are scattered throughout Southeast Asia, with about 3,300 still held in the Philippines.

Western Sympathy Finally Runs Dry

When the boat people began pouring out of Vietnam after Communist forces toppled the American-backed Government of South Vietnam in 1975, they were met with sympathy, especially from the United States, which took in more than a million Vietnamese over the last 20 years.

But the West's sympathy has run out. Virtually all of the Vietnamese who made it to Hong Kong and other Southeast Asian way stations in the 1990's have been labeled economic migrants—not refugees, a label that requires substantiated proof of fear of persecution in Vietnam—and were refused entrance to the United States and other countries.

In 1989 Vietnam and its neighbors reached agreement on a plan that was supposed to have all of the remaining asylum-seekers back in Vietnam by the end of this year.

The December 1995 deadline is almost certain to pass with tens of thousands of Vietnamese still held in the camps, but governments in the region vow to complete the returns within a few months of the original schedule, probably by the middle of next year. Vietnam has agreed to take back 3,600 boat people each month.

Refugee groups and human rights campaigners have long praised the Philippines for having run some of the most humane detention camps. But the Manila Government is eager to see the last of the Vietnamese go home and to close its last two camps—one here on the central Philippine island of Luzon and the other on the remote southern island of Palawan.

"This has already dragged on so long," said Rodolfo Severino, under secretary of the Department of Foreign Affairs. "But we're caught in a real dilemma. We're not the kind of people who would deliberately harm other people. We're trying to persuade the Vietnamese to go home voluntarily. That would be best."

For most of the Vietnamese still in the Philippines, persuasion has not worked, particularly for the 270 left behind here in the Philippine Refugee Processing Center, about 50 miles west of Manila, in the coastal province of Bataan.

If Nothing to Lose, It's a 'Paradise' Lost

The center was opened in 1980 with money from the United States and the United Nations to house Vietnamese who had been approved for asylum and were waiting to move to the United States and other countries.

Once, the camp's airy wooden barracks along a pleasant stretch of the coast—a paradise compared with the camps in Hong Kong—held as many as 18,000 refugees at a time.

Today it is empty except for the 270, who have been threatening since late last year to join in mass suicide if the Government tries to remove them. The camp is covered with handwritten signs that state the threat bluntly: "We'd Rather Die" and "We Are Prepared to Die Here, Even Under Force."

The administrator of the camp, Jose Busco, has worked here periodically since 1986 and said he regarded many of the Vietnamese as friends. "Basically everybody is peaceful," he said.

But the concern about violence is evident in a map of the camp posted at one end of Mr. Busco's conference room. The map's legend marks out the individual bunkers in the camp and notes the threat posed by people living in each of them.

A Vietnamese-American priest who ministers to the Vietnamese here, the Rev. Joseph Trong, says many are serious about killing themselves. "These people have nothing to lose," he said.

No Asylum in U.S., So Where to Go?

The Vietnamese here arrived not by boat but by plane, after they had been approved by the United States Government for a program known as Orderly Departure. The program was set up under the Carter Administration to offer asylum to Vietnamese affiliated with the former South Vietnamese Government and to Amerasian children and their families.

But after arriving in the Philippines, the 270 Vietnamese remaining here were thrown out of the program, most after American officials determined that they had falsified their immigration papers.

In many cases, the Americans asserted that the Amerasians, most of them children of American soldiers, were traveling with Vietnamese who were only pretending to be family members in hopes of getting to the United States.

"There have been a very small number of people who were found to be ineligible," said James Nealon, the spokesman for the United States Embassy in Manila. "The United States is acknowledging our level of responsibility in this issue. We're working very closely with the Vietnamese Government to repatriate those concerned."

Repatriation is what the people here say they fear.

Mrs. Ng, an English-language interpreter from Ho Chi Minh City, the southern capital formerly known as Saigon, has a 25-year-old Amerasian daughter whose father, Mrs. Ng said, was an American soldier.

After leaving Vietnam in 1992 under the Orderly Departure Program, they arrived in the Philippines to be told that their application to continue to the United States had been denied, and that they would have to find some other country to accept them, or return to Vietnam.

"They said that we falsified the documents," she said. "But nobody told us in detail what we had done wrong. I still do not know."

Mrs. Ng, who insisted that she did not falsify her documents, said she feared that she and her daughter would be labeled spies if they returned to Vietnam.

"We know the mentality of the Vietnamese Communists," she said. "They would think that we have stayed in the Philippines all these years to be trained by the Americans, by the C.I.A., and we would be put in prison as soon as we go back. This is why people would rather die here than go home to Vietnam."

* * *

April 16, 1995

McNAMARA'S RETREAT

By MAX FRANKEL

IN RETROSPECT: The Tragedy and Lessons of Vietnam
By Robert S. McNamara with Brian VanDeMark
Illustrated. 414 pp. New York: Times Books/Random House. $27.50.

In his 79th year, Robert S. McNamara at long last offers the public a glimpse of his aching conscience. The most willful Vietnam warrior in the Kennedy and Johnson Administrations, he was also the first at the top to admit defeat, in private. He then stood silent on the war for a quarter-century and drowned his sorrow in good works at the World Bank. Mr. McNamara personified the slow maturing of America's foreign policy from cocky interventionism to cost-conscious realism, yet for a generation he refused to explain his conversion, explore his mistakes, judge his colleagues or instruct posterity. The pain, or the guilt, was simply too great. As he states in the preface to "In Retrospect": "This is the book I planned never to write."

Until now, he contends, the story of how "the best and the brightest" got it wrong in Vietnam has not been told. But David Halberstam, who applied that ironic phrase to his rendering of the tale 23 years ago, told it better in many ways than Mr. McNamara does now. So, too, did the Pentagon Papers, that huge trove of documents assembled at Mr. McNamara's behest when he first recognized a debt to history. The contemporary analyses in the papers, which were leaked to The Times in 1971, stand up so well that they now serve their patron as a major source.

What Mr. McNamara adds to the public record are some White House documents and tape transcripts revealing, most notably, his own agonized attempts in 1967 to persuade President Lyndon B. Johnson to stop sending more men to the slaughter: the Secretary of Defense who had come to tame the Pentagon with managerial wizardry ended up desperately begging for a fig leaf for withdrawal, in the form of a coalition that would inevitably give the Vietcong dominance in Saigon. Mr. McNamara says he does not know to this day whether he thus quit or was fired. "Maybe it was both."

But he left with a whimper, not a bang. So why speak out now? The main reason, he says, is that he has "grown sick at heart witnessing the cynicism and even contempt" with which so many Americans view their institutions and leaders. He knows how much Vietnam contributed to that disaffection; he would never deny the war's terrible damage. But he hopes to prove that the mistakes were "mostly honest," even if traceable to a ghastly ignorance of the Vietnamese people, culture and terrain, and the historical forces of that time.

Why should the rest of us relive his agony? Mr. McNamara, characteristically statistical, points to "11 major causes for our disaster in Vietnam" in a chapter called "The Lessons of Vietnam." But implicitly his book screams another lesson: Though cynicism and contempt for power are destructive of government, a respectful skepticism is essential, and rarely wrong.

By delaying his war memoir so long, Mr. McNamara has greatly compounded the difficulty of his mission. Now that the Soviet Union lies in ruins and American corporations beg for business in China and Vietnam, no one under the age of 50 can be expected to fathom the fears and phobias of the 1960's to which he rightly ascribes the Indochina disaster. President Dwight D. Eisenhower, the most venerated American of the time, had taught—and the Kennedy and Johnson teams never dared to doubt in time—that if South Vietnam was "lost" to Communism, Laos, Cambodia, Thailand and Malaysia would fall like dominoes, imperiling India, Burma, Indonesia and the Philippines, if not also Japan, and emboldening the Russians and Chinese to extend Communist conquests by military force or subversion in ways that would sooner or later provoke a nuclear World War III, the very destruction of civilization.

Yes, that is how America's leaders spoke to each other and, all too persuasively, to the public. Mr. McNamara's book reminds us that they even repeated the litany in memos to their Presidents, to inoculate them against any temptation to retreat from Vietnam. And if all those dominoes were not cause enough, there were promises to be kept in order to preserve the value of America's other diplomatic threats and commitments.

Mr. McNamara and his generation came to power convinced that the "appeasement" of Nazi Germany—the failure to block its early grasp for Europe's dominoes—had led inevitably to a catastrophic World War II. Averting another such disaster, they were sure, required punishing anything resembling Communist aggression in its earliest stages, when the cost would be tolerable. That was their creed as they rebuilt Western Europe and stood toe to toe with the Soviet armies across Germany, fought to a bloody stalemate against China in Korea, threatened war over Berlin and risked war to force Soviet missiles out of Cuba. Thus "contained," the Soviets and Chinese took to endorsing "wars of liberation," thereby qualifying even distant uprisings as threats to American security. Mr. McNamara's first assignment from President John F. Kennedy was to augment America's nuclear power, whose use was unimaginable, with the forces and weapons they were sure would be needed to fight "conventional" wars.

From this bed of doctrine grew what Mr. McNamara considers his team's most fateful error: mistaking Ho Chi Minh's nationalist drive to unite Vietnam as the challenge of a monolithic Communist world. That misjudgment foreclosed any discussion of how an American withdrawal from Indochina could be made strategically tolerable. It even prevented analysis, before the plunge, of how high a price the commitment was worth. Mr. McNamara's dry rendering of those fateful tenets of containment fails to convey the passion with which they were embraced. And he mostly ignores their powerful resonance in domestic politics.

Kennedy, no less than Johnson, subscribed to these simplistic doctrines and the misjudgments they inspired, even though Mr. McNamara, without persuasive evidence, deems it "highly probable" that Kennedy would have pulled back from massive intervention in a second term. This presumes that had Kennedy lived, the same cast of senior officials would have avoided what Mr. McNamara describes as a second tier of error: the failure to live by the mantra that the battle in Vietnam was political, a fight for the "hearts and minds" of an abused peasantry, and that Americans could assist but never supplant the South Vietnamese.

In this pew, Mr. McNamara himself was a prominent sinner. His can-do spirit found no mission impossible, even as Saigon's governments and armies crumbled. His domineering intellect and predilection for systems analysis made him a pathetic victim of erroneous and deceptive military audits of bodies counted, weapons captured, sorties flown, supply lines ruptured. Soon enough, as the press decided, it became "McNamara's war," and certainly America's.

Mr. McNamara deplores the absence of political advice from old Asia hands who had been driven from Government service in the McCarthy purges. But as he proves again in this memoir, he did not easily integrate political wisdom and intuition into his analyses. Even in retrospect, he does not associate the drift into war in Vietnam with the Republican taunts that Democrats had "lost" China to Communism. (Kennedy was afraid to recognize not only China but even Outer Mongolia!) Mr. McNamara cannot bring himself to believe that the election calendar affected Johnson's willingness to escalate the war in 1965 but not in 1964 or, as Johnson eventually confessed to Doris Kearns, that he stayed the course in Asia because he feared losing effectiveness at home—like Truman after the "loss" of China—much as he feared the repercussions of defeat abroad.

Finally, Mr. McNamara recounts a third tier of error—escalating pattern of military misjudgment. He is hard on the Joint Chiefs of Staff for their misplaced optimism in the early years, their always excessive faith in high-tech weapons and their later expectations that massive bombing and frontal battles could wear down the Vietnamese enemy. He is remiss in not fully rebutting the postwar claims that timid civilians had tied the military's hands with unreasonable limits on troop commitments and bombing targets. Mr. McNamara emphasizes how little was accomplished by bombings heavier even than those in World War II. And he explains Johnson's caution in target selection by recalling the fear that a more rapid escalation could provoke Chinese intervention. But Americans who cannot accept David's triumph over Goliath draw more belligerent "lessons" from this history, which Mr. McNamara should have engaged more directly.

Even more disappointing is Mr. McNamara's unwillingness to explore the human tragedies and political legacies of this longest American war. What was it like to send tens of thousands to their deaths in an increasingly dubious cause? How did the strain affect the men in charge? We get a glimpse of Jacqueline Kennedy beating him on the chest in protest against the war, and of angry insults hurled on the ski slopes, but no real introspection. Mr. McNamara says the war tore deeply at his own family, but quickly adds: "I am not comfortable speaking in such terms."

What then of the political legacy? How, without growing cynical, can citizens protect themselves against the stubborn ignorance and misplaced zeal of their leaders? In the darkest days, Mr. McNamara remembers, he watched the demonstrators from his Pentagon window and insisted that his subordinates show respect for the freedoms of speech and assembly. But he took refuge—and takes it even now—in opinion polls that recorded support from the majority of Americans who, as he well knew, had been misinformed and denied vital information at every major turn.

"Looking back," he writes, "I clearly erred by not forcing . . . a knock-down, drag-out debate over the loose assumptions, unasked questions and thin analyses underlying our military strategy in Vietnam. I had spent 20 years as a manager identifying problems and forcing organizations—often against their will—to think deeply and realistically about alternative courses of action and their consequences. I doubt I will ever fully understand why I did not do so here."

Yet even now Mr. McNamara means he should have stirred debate only inside the small circle of Presidential counselors led by himself, Secretary of State Dean Rusk and McGeorge Bundy, the national security adviser (later succeeded by Walt Rostow). Mr. McNamara blames Johnson for going to war furtively, with no regard for the rights of Congress and the public, but he rejects any obligation to resign in protest or, once out of office, to share his policy disagreements with the country. Cabinet officers, he contends, should have a constituency of one: the President—from whom they derive all authority and through whom alone they can be held accountable.

That is surely the right ethic for normal times. Unelected officials should not steal their President's mandate to pursue an independent course. But a thousand dead Americans a month create their own constituency. Even military discipline admits a higher duty than hierarchical loyalty when power is badly used and puts lives at risk.

Mr. McNamara relieved his private turmoil by reading poetry, and shared his misgivings with Robert F. Kennedy and a few other intimates. But he refused to abandon or attack the President whom he had helped to guide into quicksand. He and Johnson "loved and respected" each other, in a bond that even now, in retrospect, keeps the public at a distance looking on, with skepticism, I hope.

Max Frankel, a columnist for The New York Times Magazine and a former executive editor of The Times, was a Washington correspondent covering diplomacy and the White House in the 1960's.

* * *

July 12, 1995

U.S. GRANTS VIETNAM FULL TIES; TIME FOR HEALING, CLINTON SAYS

By ALISON MITCHELL

WASHINGTON, July 11—Saying the time was at hand to "bind up our own wounds," President Clinton today extended full diplomatic recognition to Vietnam 22 years after the American withdrawal from a bitterly divisive war that still scars the national psyche.

Mr. Clinton, the one-time student protester who avoided serving in a war he once said he "opposed and despised," announced the normalization of relations in a brief ceremony in the East Room attended by military figures, the families of those still missing in action and members of Congress who were veterans of the war and prisoners of the Vietnamese.

"This moment offers us the opportunity to bind up our own wounds," the President said, evoking words used by Lincoln at the end of the Civil War. "They have resisted time for too long. We can now move onto common ground."

"Let this moment," he said, "in the words of the Scripture, be a time to heal and a time to build."

But the decision drew criticism as well as support from legislators, veterans' groups and families of missing servicemen.

Mr. Clinton said the United States would continue to press Vietnam for a full accounting for the 2,202 United States service personnel officially listed as missing in Southeast Asia. He said that in the months since he lifted the United States trade embargo on Vietnam in February 1994, the remains of 29 more missing Americans had been identified and Hanoi had turned over hundreds of pages of documents.

"We will keep working until we get all the answers we can," Mr. Clinton said. "Our strategy is working."

Vietnam's Prime Minister, Vo Van Kiet, responded positively to Mr. Clinton's decision in a statement broadcast Wednesday morning, Hanoi time. He pledged to continue Vietnam's cooperation in helping to account for missing Americans.

Mr. Clinton's announcement of full diplomatic relations completed a process begun by the Bush Administration in 1991 when Washington and Hanoi agreed on a detailed series of steps that would lead to recognition. Recognition was sought as eagerly by American business groups as it was bitterly opposed by the American Legion and some relatives of Americans missing in the war.

But the move was particularly risky for a President whose efforts as a young man to avoid military service in Vietnam became a campaign issue in 1992, and who faces an electorate still sharply divided over the unpopular war that took 58,000 American lives.

The often loquacious Mr. Clinton spoke somberly for just under 10 minutes, ending with "God bless America." Several Congressional veterans of the war stood by his side as he made his announcement; Senator John McCain, the Arizona Republican who spent more than five years as a Vietnamese prisoner of war, was closest. Afterward, Mr. McCain praised Mr. Clinton for an "act that required some courage."

Yet 20 years after the last helicopter rising from the roof of the United States Embassy in Saigon became an indelible image of American defeat, Congress was as bitterly divided over Mr. Clinton's move as it once was over the war itself.

Senator Bob Dole, a veteran of World War II whose right arm remains withered from his wounds, denounced Mr. Clinton's decision from the Senate floor, saying the President had not addressed the "central question" of whether Vietnam is continuing to withhold information and remains that could be easily provided.

"The President ignored this question in announcing his decision for the very good reason that all signs point to Vietnam willfully withholding information which could resolve the fate of many Americans lost in the war," said Mr. Dole, the Senate majority leader and the leading contender for the Republican Presidential nomination.

Mr. Dole said the lawmakers would monitor the progress of relations with Vietnam, and he warned that Congress must approve funds for any diplomatic operations in Vietnam and that the Senate must confirm any ambassador.

Senator Trent Lott, the majority whip from Mississippi, said he would support efforts to amend appropriations legislation to stop the opening of a United States Embassy in Vietnam. "What's the reason for doing this?" he asked. "How do you justify recognizing Vietnam and not recognizing Taiwan?"

But Senator Bob Kerrey, a Nebraska Democrat who attended the White House ceremony, vowed to fight efforts to block embassy funding. "It's a total mistake," he said. "It's wallowing in the past." Mr. Kerrey, who lost part of one leg and won the Medal of Honor in Vietnam, added that if Mr. Dole or others tried to make political gain by blocking embassy funding, they would "face people like me who say, 'Shame on you.' "

Veterans were also divided. John Sommer, the executive director of the more than 3 million member American Legion—the nation's largest veterans group—condemned the move, saying that normalization of relations left the Administration with little leverage to extract more information about the missing. But a group calling itself the Vietnam Veterans for Reconciliation handed out leaflets supporting the President on the White House lawn after the ceremony.

Mr. Clinton's decision to recognize Vietnam had been endorsed by all of his senior advisers, according to Anthony Lake, the national security adviser. Mr. Lake said Gen. John Shalikashvili had polled the Joint Chiefs of Staff over the weekend and had found unanimous support.

Aides said the President's decision stemmed, in part, from a desire to act now, before the 1996 campaign moves into full gear. It was also partly dictated by Secretary of State Warren M. Christopher's trip to Asia at the end of this month to meet with foreign ministers of the Association of Southeast Asian nations.

The President announced that Mr. Christopher will now visit Vietnam early next month, which will make him the first Secretary of State to visit the country since the American-backed Government in Saigon fell to Communist forces in 1975.

While in Hanoi, Mr. Christopher will negotiate the details of the restoration of diplomatic relations.

Resumed ties to Vietnam could give the Administration an important Asian ally at a time when relations with China have become more tense, although officials denied today that the policy change was in any way related to China.

In Beijing, a Chinese Government spokesman welcomed the news. "The Chinese Government has always stood for improvement of relations between the United States and Vietnam," said a Foreign Ministry spokesman, Shen Guofang.

In his broadcast statement, Mr. Kiet said Vietnam would negotiate with the United States "to set up a new framework for the relationship between the two countries on the basis of respect, independence, and mutual benefit of the two countries in harmony with the rule of international law."

The Administration was silent today on who would become the ambassador to Vietnam, an appointment that could be fraught with symbolism. Officials said the Administration wanted a distinguished appointee, perhaps a veteran, who would face no trouble in a confirmation hearing. Among names under discussion are Under Secretary of State Peter Tarnoff; Frank G. Wisner, the Ambassador to India, or Mr. Lake himself. All three made their names in Vietnam.

Administration officials said they had now set up interagency groups to examine such questions as trade, investment and tax treaties, all of which are of interest to American companies that were allowed to begin doing business in Vietnam in February 1994, when the President lifted the trade embargo.

By some estimates, Vietnam will spend $7 billion during the next seven years on roads, ports and a modern telecommunications system.

Willard A. Workman, vice president of the international division of the United States Chamber of Commerce, said businesses hoped that the announcement would clear the way for crucial United States agencies, including the Export-Import Bank and the Overseas Private Investment Corporation, to help American companies in Vietnam.

* * *

November 10, 1995

IN HANOI, A LOOK BACK AT A VIETNAM WAR FLASH POINT

By TIM LARIMER

HANOI, Vietnam, Nov. 9—Two old adversaries came face to face here today, and Robert S. McNamara, the former Defense Secretary, asked his Vietnamese counterpart a question that he said had plagued him for years: What really happened in the Gulf of Tonkin in 1964?

In a meeting in a military guest house here, the former North Vietnamese commander, Gen. Vo Nguyen Giap, confirmed that the North Vietnamese attacked American ships once during a tense week in August 1964, but he reiterated that a second supposed attack, which led to the first American bombing of North Vietnam, never happened.

President Johnson used the reports of two attacks on American ships in the Gulf of Tonkin on Aug. 2 and 4 to ram a war resolution through Congress.

Whether the second attack actually occurred has been widely disputed and ultimately doubted, and the suspicion that the Administration had misled Congress about the attack became one of the most divisive issues of the war.

Mr. McNamara, for his part, said in his recent book on the war that the second attack was "probable but not certain."

Today he told General Giap, "To this day I don't know what happened on Aug. 2 and Aug. 4, 1964, in the Tonkin Gulf." General Giap responded that on Aug. 4, "there was absolutely nothing."

But more than 30 years ago, Mr. McNamara was called upon by the Johnson Administration to verify that the Aug. 4 attack did occur, to insure that the American retaliation was justified. He testified later in the Senate that he had "unimpeachable" proof of the second attack.

On Friday Mr. McNamara told reporters just before his departure: "General Giap made it absolutely clear it hadn't occurred. If we had known that at the time, we wouldn't have carried out the military attack. We wouldn't at that time have sent up to Congress the resolution that ultimately was used as the authority for the escalation of the war."

The incident was a milestone in the war.

On Aug. 2, 1964, the American destroyer Maddox was patrolling the waters of the gulf, monitoring North Vietnamese communications, when it was surrounded by North Vietnamese junks. The ship's commander said he thought the junks were preparing to attack, and ordered his crew to fire if they came within 10,000 yards. When they did, the Maddox fired, and the junks began pursuing it, firing torpedoes.

General Giap said a "local coast guard unit launched the attack" on Aug. 2. He did not elaborate on whether the local unit was acting on its own or on orders from superiors, something Mr. McNamara later said he had been hoping to find out.

What happened on Aug. 4 has continued to puzzle war historians. That night, in stormy weather, the Maddox reported it was under attack again, but the weather interfered with its radar, its sonar was not functioning properly and there were no sightings of attacking boats by American planes in the area.

But based on early reports, President Johnson ordered retaliatory air strikes. And on Aug. 7, Congress passed the Gulf of Tonkin Resolution, which the Johnson and Nixon Administrations both used as the authority to escalate the war. The House voted 416-0 in favor of the resolution; the Senate approved it 88-2.

Today Mr. McNamara said, "This was such a red-hot issue, I was determined I was going to put the question to Giap today."

Inquiries in the years to come, including Mr. McNamara's testimony before the Senate Foreign Relations Committee, made it appear increasingly unlikely that there was any hard evidence that an attack had occurred.

The committee chairman, Senator J. William Fulbright, Democrat of Arkansas, voted in favor of the resolution but later became one of the strongest opponents of the war, saying he regretted his earlier support for broad legislation that allowed the United States to take "all necessary measures" in Southeast Asia.

The exchange today between the two former war strategists was part of a visit by a delegation from the Council on Foreign Relations to invite Vietnamese leaders to a proposed conference that would investigate the "missed opportunities" that could have ended the war sooner—or avoided it altogether.

Karen Sughrue, the council's vice president for programs, said the Vietnamese authorities they met appeared ready to hold the conference, which would bring together Government officials and military leaders from that era next year in Hanoi. No final agreement has been reached.

In an interview today, Mr. McNamara said that one thing he found remarkable about his meeting today was "the lack of hostility and the willingness to meet and discuss what was in a very real sense a tragedy for both nations."

"There's really no difference between him and me," he added.

Both he and General Giap, he said, want to explore the misunderstandings that worsened the conflict. But in their conversation, they did not agree on every aspect. General Giap told Mr. McNamara that he believed the patrols of the gulf undertaken by the Maddox were a deliberate ploy to draw the United States into the war.

"The Johnson Administration had devised a plan of sabotage activities on the sea and in the air in order to seek the approval of Congress," he said.

Later, Mr. McNamara said General Giap's analysis "is absolutely without foundation."

The contrasts between the two Vietnam War figures was evident today.

General Giap, 84, who led the early military campaigns against French colonialists before the Vietnam War, wore his olive-green military uniform. Mr. McNamara, 79, a Ford Motor Company executive before he took the reins of the military in 1961, and president of the World Bank later in his career, wore a blue suit.

The Vietnamese general sat comfortably, smiling and talkative. He posed for pictures with the journalists gathered nearby. He looked like a grandfather holding court in the family room.

Mr. McNamara appeared more the eager and slightly nervous technocrat, scribbling notes on a yellow legal pad as General Giap spoke.

Behind them hung an ornate wooden carving with two elephant tusks, a war souvenir taken from the palace of Nguyen Van Thieu, South Vietnam's last President.

"The fact that McNamara came here to see me shows that the situation has changed," General Giap said after the meeting. When he received guests during the war, he noted wryly, referring to the bombing raids that were part of Mr. McNamara's war strategy, "I had to do it underground, in a shelter."

Many Vietnamese, aware of Mr. McNamara's acknowledgment in his recent book, "In Retrospect: The Tragedy and Lessons of Vietnam," that the American war effort was a mistake, expected him to apologize to the Vietnamese victors. He did not. Nor did General Giap or any other official ask for such an apology, according to observers who sat in on the meetings.

"Normalization has been re-established," said General Giap. "There is nothing to reconcile."

* * *

November 12, 1996

A PAINFUL ROAD FROM VIETNAM TO FORGIVENESS

By ELAINE SCIOLINO

WASHINGTON, Nov. 11—It is one of the most enduring and painful images of the Vietnam War: 9-year-old Phan Thi Kim Phuc running naked toward the lens of a camera, holding her arms outstretched and screaming in agony and terror as napalm seared her small body.

Kirsten Elstner for The New York Times

Nick Ut/Associated Press

At 9, Phan Thi Kim Phuc became a horrific image of the Vietnam War; yesterday, she laid a wreath at the Vietnam Veterans' Memorial.

Thrust into fame as a symbol of the horror of war, she endured a score of surgical operations, was used as a propaganda tool by her government, became a college student in Cuba and sought political asylum in Canada. Now 33, Ms. Kim Phuc lives what she calls a "normal, happy life" in a one-room apartment in an Asian neighborhood in Toronto with her husband and 2-year-old son.

And in an act of reconciliation and forgiveness nearly a quarter of a century after her ordeal, she came to Washington for the first time to lay a wreath today at the Vietnam Veterans Memorial.

"I have suffered a lot from both physical and emotional pain," she told the audience of several thousand people, who greeted her with two standing ovations. "Sometimes I could not breathe. But God saved my life and gave me faith and hope. Even if I could talk face to face with the pilot who dropped the bombs, I would tell him, 'We cannot change history, but we should try to do good things for the present and for the future to promote peace.' "

In events across the country, veterans marked the day of remembrance for their fallen comrades. In New York, spectators were few at the annual march of war heroes, but the parade held a poignancy for those who did attend.

But perhaps the most moving memorial service today was the one in Washington where Ms. Kim Phuc confronted the country that had caused her so much personal pain. It was "a most historic moment," said Jan C. Scruggs, president of the Vietnam Veterans Memorial Fund, in introducing her.

She tightly embraced Col. Norm McDaniel, a retired Air Force colonel held as a prisoner of war in Vietnam, who guided her through the crowd so they could jointly lay a wreath of carnations, iris and amaryllis at the wall. She pressed her hand to her stomach and clenched her jaw over and over to keep from crying as taps was played.

She held the hand of a park policeman who led her through the crowd away from a tangle of television cameras. And she stopped briefly to shake hands with members of the First Battalion, 44th Artillery, as they reached out to thank her.

"It's important to us that she's here, part of the healing process," said John Huelsenbeck, who was part of a group laying a wreath on behalf of its unit. "We were just kids doing our job. For her to forgive us personally means something."

Joe Bellardo, who was a sergeant with the unit, added, "When we realized who she was, we all started bawling."

It was in June 1972, during a fight between troops from North and South Vietnam in the Central Highlands of the South, that an American commander ordered South Vietnamese planes to drop napalm near a pagoda where villagers had taken refuge. Two of Ms. Kim Phuc's younger brothers were killed instantly; she and a third brother were badly burned.

Nick Ut, the Associated Press photographer who took the photograph of Ms. Kim Phuc screaming in horror, put her into his van and rushed her to a South Vietnamese hospital, where she spent 14 months recovering from the third-degree burns that covered more than half her body. The photograph won a Pulitzer Prize.

It was so painful to have her wounds washed and dressed that she lost consciousness whenever she was touched. Later, American plastic surgeons working in Vietnam spent months grafting her skin and rebuilding her body.

For several years, the world seemed to forget about the little girl in the photograph. She was discovered by the Vietnamese Government only when a Dutch film crew sought her out in Vietnam in 1984. She resented the endless interviews and photographs the Government subjected her to, and when the opportunity to study in Cuba came along in 1986, she seized it.

There, however, she suffered from asthma and developed diabetes, which blurred her vision. She was forced to abandon her studies, first in Vietnam, where she studied medicine, then in Cuba, where she studied pharmacology.

Married to Bui Huy Toan, a fellow Vietnamese student in Cuba, two years ago, the newlyweds spent their honeymoon in Moscow. On the long flight back to Cuba, she told her husband that she was going to get off the plane when it refueled in Gander, Newfoundland, and not get on again. During the stopover, they stayed behind.

"In front of me I had nothing, but I felt so happy I got free, I got freedom," she said in an interview in her hotel on Sunday evening. "No clothes, no money, no family, no friends, no knowledge—nothing at all. But God helped me. Somehow, some way, he prepared the people to help me."

With the help of some Quakers, she and her husband received political asylum in Canada. The family was on welfare until last year, when her husband, a computer specialist, was able to get paying employment. He now holds down two jobs as a nurse's aide with the disabled.

Ms. Kim Phuc decided to come to Washington after groups of Vietnam veterans invited her to participate in today's event. She traveled with Shelley Saywell, the prize-winning independent Canadian filmmaker, who is finishing a one-hour documentary on her life that will be broadcast on Canadian television early next year.

"I wanted to share my experience with people so that they feel better," Ms. Kim Phuc said. "Behind that picture of me, thousands and thousands of people, they suffered—more than me. They died. They lost parts of their bodies. Their whole lives were destroyed, and nobody took that picture."

During an initial visit to the Vietnam Veterans Memorial wall on Sunday, Ms. Kim Phuc said, she was terrified at first to see so many veterans in American soldiers' uniforms because it brought back too many memories of the war.

"I was scared, and I remember my nightmare," she said. "Then I said to myself, 'The uniforms, that is normal. Oh, Kim, be strong. Try not to think so much.' "

Much harder was to see the names of the tens of thousands of American war dead chiseled into the polished black granite walls. "How many people died for a stupid war—it was just something, how can I say, a very stupid thing to do," she said. "It was very hard. A lot of memories came in."

Ms. Kim Phuc's wide, round, open face is perfectly smooth, and it is only when she pulls up her left sleeve that an outsider gets a glimpse of the devastating, mottled scars that extend to her chest and back like some strange, ridged relief map.

In addition to diabetes, asthma and migraine headaches, she still suffers from severe pain from the burns, which left her without sweat or oil glands.

"When the weather changes, the pain comes—like I am cut, cut," she said. "I try to keep down my pain, thinking, thinking to control my pain. I ask my husband, Tell me stories, funny stories, or ask me something, so I have to answer him. And that is the way I can live day by day. And I never think something sad."

As a child, Ms. Kim Phuc cried because she could not wear short-sleeved dresses like the other girls in her village; now, as a wife and mother, she considers herself blessed.

She sends money every month to her parents, who still live in Vietnam, but she has not seen them since she left. She delights in telling how her son, Thomas, can count up to 50 in three languages: Vietnamese, English and Spanish.

A Baptist, she studies English at night and hopes to attend a Bible college someday. She will become eligible for Canadian citizenship in January.

"I built my life very normal with everything I do," said Ms. Kim Phuc, whose name means "Golden Happiness" in Vietnamese. "My character is not sad, not angry. In my house, I'm always laughing, smiling, smiling."

* * *

August 10, 1997

ROBERT McNAMARA AND THE GHOSTS OF VIETNAM

By DAVID K. SHIPLER

Not long after dawn, Robert S. McNamara set out on a rapid walk through the half-light of Hanoi. A steamy drizzle soon soaked his dark blue jogging shorts and shirt. He stared intently ahead, barely glancing at the Vietnamese along the way as he marched in a loping stride through the city he ordered bombed some 30 years ago. He walked too quickly for the beggars or the barefoot children selling postcards to keep up with him. He did not seem to notice a boy hawking copies of "The Quiet American." He raced across currents of whizzing motorbikes and bicycles laden with impossibly huge bundles of fruit and shoes and large tin boxes, balanced as ingeniously as weapons had once been on the Ho Chi Minh Trail.

Peasant women in conical hats crisscrossed in front of him, moving gracefully beneath shoulder poles slung heavily with round baskets of bananas and litchi nuts. One woman squatting at the curb made an enticing gesture toward her pile of reddish litchis but got no reaction. He did not look into the faces of the people. He did not linger to gaze at their colorful wares. He was driven by another agenda, a mission he talked about incessantly as he walked.

In a few hours on this Friday in June, one of the more unusual efforts in the history of warfare was to begin. McNamara, three other former American officials, two retired generals and six historians would sit down with former North Vietnamese officials, diplomats, generals and scholars led by Nguyen Co Thach, a courtly former Foreign Minister, for a four-day discussion of what Americans call the Vietnam War and Vietnamese call the American War. Their main focus would be defined by McNamara's growing conviction that "each of us could have achieved our geopolitical objectives without that terrible loss of life," that both sides missed concrete chances to end the fighting during his tenure as Secretary of Defense from 1961 to 1968.

The thesis amounted to a confession of profound error, and this return to Vietnam—McNamara's second since the war—seemed likely to be a lonely journey into a regretful past. Despite his coterie of aging officials and younger historians, it was he above all who bore the burden. The others in the delegation had not conceived the war; they had worked at its margins, had followed orders or had tried to negotiate its end. With most of the war's key architects dead or declining to attend, McNamara stood as the only senior policy maker of the era to visit Hanoi and admit that the war should not have been fought and could not have been won. He wanted it studied as a cautionary tale for the next century. "Human beings have to examine their failures," he declared. "We've got to acquaint people with how dangerous it is for political leaders to behave the way we did."

If penance drove him to Hanoi, it was carefully concealed. The way McNamara examined his failure in Vietnam was to intellectualize it, diagnose it, pinpoint the variables that might have been revised. He was hoping that the Vietnamese would do the same, but they would frustrate him again, as they had 30 years before.

Robert McNamara believes that American leaders acted out of honorable principles, as he argued in his 1995 book, "In Retrospect: The Tragedy and Lessons of Vietnam." "Yet we were wrong, terribly wrong," he wrote. "We owe it to future generations to explain why." This admission, which generated a mixture of admiration and vilification among Americans, earned him an enthusiastic welcome when he first visited Hanoi in November 1995. The quotation and his book are displayed in a museum in Ho Chi Minh City that features photographs of Americans torturing Vietnamese.

Now he had returned to Vietnam, not so much to test his thesis as to prove it. The title of the conference was a question: "Missed Opportunities?" But there was no question mark for McNamara. He was eager for Thach and the other Vietnamese to confirm what he believed he knew. The war had resulted in the reunified, Communist Vietnam that Hanoi had desired. But Vietnam had not become the agent of Soviet and Chinese Communism that Washington had feared; Communism in Indochina had not toppled the dominoes of Thailand, Malaysia, Indonesia and other Asian countries, as Dwight D. Eisenhower had wrongly predicted when he relinquished the Oval Office to John F. Kennedy in 1961. At that early stage, before the arrival of American combat troops in 1965, could the same ends have been realized at the bargaining table as, later, on the battlefield? Why did Hanoi repeatedly rebuff secret American attempts to open peace talks from 1965 to 1968? Why did the bombing of North Vietnam fail to force capitulation? And a key issue for McNamara: "If the United States had invaded North Vietnam, would the Chinese have intervened?" he asked. He had opposed the military chiefs' recommendations of an invasion because he feared China would enter the war; from the Vietnamese he would now seek vindication for that assessment.

McNamara talked as he walked briskly around the Lake of the Restored Sword at the heart of Hanoi. Had he known the legend of this lake in the 1960's, he would have understood the anti-Chinese thrust of Vietnam's historical devotion to independence. The story goes that in the 15th century, when the Ming Dynasty ruled Vietnam, a fisherman named Le Loi found in his net a magical sword that empowered him to lead his people in a 10-year struggle that drove the Chinese out in 1428. Le Loi became Emperor. As he then offered gratitude to the spirit of the lake, a giant golden tortoise snatched the sword and restored it to the depths.

Much of what the Vietnamese would try to explain to the Americans in the coming days touched on this mystical passion to be rid of foreign domination, whether by the Chinese for a thousand years, the French colonialists for more than a century, the Japanese during World War II or the Americans after the French defeat in 1954. It was the necessity of resisting the United States, the generals and diplomats in Hanoi would say, that drove North Vietnam into a temporary, pragmatic reliance on Chinese and Soviet aid.

"The basic lesson is: understand your opponent," McNamara concluded sorrowfully as he strode along the lake. The lesson worried him. "We don't understand the Bosnians, we don't understand the Chinese and we don't really understand the Iranians."

It was more than intellectual interest that brought some of McNamara's colleagues to Hanoi. Unfinished business drew Chester L. Cooper, a veteran C.I.A. analyst, White House aide and State Department adviser who had been present at practically every fork in this rough road since the French war in Indochina in the early 1950's. He had been the point man in the Johnson Administration's secret, failed diplomacy of the mid-60's, running all over the world to send offers to the North Vietnamese. "Many of the names we will be confronting are names that I remember being these elusive, gray, unfriendly, unfathomable people whose attention I had been trying to get for several years," Cooper said before leaving for Hanoi. And he also sought something more personal. "How do these people feel about me walking around, going back to a place after you've destroyed it? How will they feel? How will I feel?"

Feelings were not on McNamara's agenda. "That's not what I'm focusing on," he declared before the trip. "I may not tell you how I'm feeling." And he never did, even when questioned about the thoughts that were running through his head as he walked around this city, among these people. "I try to separate human emotions from the larger issues of human welfare," he replied. "Human welfare requires that we avoid conflict. I try not to let my human emotions interfere with efforts to resolve conflict." It seemed an odd dichotomy, one that recalled McNamara's inability to invest his policy making with the compassion he may have felt.

Self-revelation was not the style of these aging men, now in their 70's and 80's. The Vietnamese, meanwhile, had been ordered in writing not to give interviews. "Stone statues" was how one American described the Vietnamese after the first day's discussions—an image that mercifully broke down somewhat as time passed.

The Americans were less guarded. Cooper told the Vietnamese that he had resigned from the White House in quiet protest in 1966 and then agreed to work "on negotiations only" at the State Department until he concluded in December 1967 that the diplomatic feelers were "a charade." Nicholas deB. Katzenbach, who was Under Secretary of State from 1966 to 1969, had "some responsibility for negotiations," he said, "but there was always somebody around to sabotage them." Francis M. Bator, deputy national security adviser from 1965 to 1967, specialized in European affairs and only listened to Lyndon Johnson's anguished monologues about Vietnam. Gen. William Y. Smith, now retired from the Air Force, never served in Vietnam; as a major, he was an aide in the White House and for the Joint Chiefs of Staff.

The delegation's single combat veteran of the war was from the Army, Lieut. Gen. Dale Vesser, who is now retired, a sturdy man with a laconic style. From 1966 to 1971, he did two tours and several special missions in Vietnam. How did he feel being in Hanoi? "I have never had anything but respect for the people we fought," General Vesser said. "They were very good, and they were fighting for what they believed in. So being in Hanoi, other than feeling an obligation to those Americans who didn't come back, doesn't excite strong emotions."

Deciding to attend this conference brought Vesser considerable flak from colleagues in the Army, the service most badly wounded by the war and most bitter about McNamara and his book. At least half a dozen generals declined invitations. One of them, John H. Cushman, came close to going but then pulled out. A former brigade commander, he remembered the pain of returning to old battlefields a few years ago and meeting officers from the other side. "I'm just not comfortable being seated opposite these people exploring the missed opportunities," he said. "My constituency is my brigade. I think my constituency would not quite understand why I linked up with this effort to find out what we did wrong."

Something of the same concern made the trip to Hanoi unattractive to Gen. William Westmoreland, who commanded U.S. forces in Vietnam and who, at age 83, sounds as if he were frozen in time. "We did not lose a single battle against those people," he insisted. "They defeated us psychologically. I must say, I can just imagine the attitude of my troops when they read in the paper that the old man goes to Hanoi." To do so "would suggest that we're submitting to them, because we never lost a battle," he repeated. "It would be totally inappropriate for me as having led our troops to go and make homage to the enemy."

Walt W. Rostow, President Johnson's hawkish national security adviser, did not go because he anticipated that most of the information would come from American documents and memoirs. "I don't think that Hanoi's in a mood to give us anything equivalent, like the access to American policy in this period," he predicted. "After all, they are Communists. I don't want to join in an exercise that will be 90 percent American and 10 percent Hanoi." Furthermore, he added, "we were awfully well informed about them. I know all the answers to those questions."

The skepticism also infected foundations, 13 of which turned down requests for financial support, according to James G. Blight of Brown University's Thomas J. Watson Jr. Institute for International Studies, the American organizer of the meeting. Only the Rockefeller Foundation came through.

The doubts raised the stakes for the Hanoi meeting. The Americans, especially McNamara, were keen to prove the skeptics wrong by making sure the conference would succeed in opening up the secretive North Vietnamese decision-making process. The aim was to persuade the Vietnamese to break with their closed tradition and provide official documents from the period as well as personal recollections. The conference organizers provided voluminous background material from newly opened archives in Moscow, Washington, Eastern Europe and even Beijing, which included, for example, Chinese minutes of conversations in the 1960's between Mao Zedong and the North Vietnamese Prime Minister, Pham Van Dong.

Only Vietnamese documents were missing, and the Vietnamese organizer—the Foreign Ministry's Institute for International Relations—pledged early on to provide archival material. When a deadline passed in April without the promised papers having appeared, McNamara pounded the table at a Washington meeting of the American team and threatened not to go to Hanoi. "They have not met this condition!" he said. "I'm very skeptical that we can add to history unless we have documentary evidence. If we can't achieve that, I don't know if the conference should go forward." But he was bluffing, and in the end, no Vietnamese papers materialized.

That failure turned out to be a telling sign that the American skepticism about the conference was being echoed in Vietnam's corridors of power. Two weeks before the sessions, Hanoi rejected a proposal to hold daily, American-Vietnamese news briefings for fear that hard-liners in the Communist Party press would use them to attack the moderates who had organized the meeting. Then, hours after the American delegation arrived in Hanoi, the Vietnamese hosts at Hanoi's Institute for International Relations reneged on a longstanding agreement to allow CNN to tape the conference.

The development soured the atmosphere at first. McNamara fretted that the mood would be too guarded for candid discussion. The American team met alone to consider canceling the conference—an empty threat with the entire delegation already in Hanoi. The Vietnamese then made a small compromise: CNN could get one of the four days on tape. And so went the negotiations about discussing 30-year-old attempts to start negotiations.

The nervousness about the TV camera reflected the uncertain boundaries of Vietnamese political discourse. Open debate on foreign or military policy is still taboo, especially on so sacred a topic as the war.

But acerbic complaints about the economy, which is increasingly geared to private enterprise and foreign investment, are now acceptable, and the police apparatus that once conducted block-by-block monitoring of ordinary residents in the former South Vietnam has been considerably relaxed. Political jokes are popular, and real life is often funnier. An irreverent young man who spent a year in prison after trying to escape by boat in the early 1980's recently received a surprise invitation: to join the Communist Party. He was amused, and he declined.

Vietnamese in political life, adrift in crosscurrents of ambiguous guidelines, must swim skillfully. Though the former Foreign Minister, Nguyen Co Thach, championed this conference, he sought to rein in his delegation. He often answered probing questions smilingly but with enigmatic single sentences. Sometimes he bluntly put subjects off-limits. When pushed to reveal what disagreements had existed among policy makers about negotiating with Washington, he said quietly, "There were discussions, but we are not permitted to publicize them." Because of Vietnam's long history of foreign domination, "our habit is to keep secrets in order to defend ourselves," he explained. "Sometimes we cannot even get access to our own secrets, so how can we share that with others?" Thus were McNamara's principal objectives foiled. But he soldiered on without evidence of despair, obsessed by the task of flushing information out of every hiding place.

It is a tricky time, as Vietnam casts one eye warily on China and the other expectantly on the United States and its powers of investment. The museum in Ho Chi Minh City that was once called the Museum of American War Crimes became the Museum of War Crimes and is now simply the Museum of War Remnants. Inside, however, the condemnation of America remains searing. On the one hand, the victory over the United States stands as a landmark of national heroism. On the other, with half its population having been born since the end of the war, Vietnam seems poised to move on. It has warmly welcomed Pete Peterson, the first American Ambassador to Hanoi and a former prisoner of war. In what seems apt symbolism, the prison where he was held, the "Hanoi Hilton," is being partly demolished for a luxury high-rise, with some outer walls of the prison to be retained as a monument. Peterson drives by two or three times a day, "and it doesn't bother me," he said, "which is good. It means I have healed."

Healing is usually easier for the victors than the vanquished, and the Vietnamese at the table displayed none of the Americans' anguish. As winners, they also seemed less impelled toward self-criticism. McNamara and the other Americans came to Hanoi eager to get the Vietnamese to admit that they, too, had made mistakes in failing to pursue policies that might have avoided or curtailed the war. But that would have amounted to an unimaginable confession that Vietnamese reunification and independence could have been won with less sacrifice. No national myth is shattered lightly.

The Hanoi conferees met in a bright, cool room at the French-renovated Hotel Metropole, removed from the sultry streets. Reference books and papers were stacked and strewn before the participants, who wore earphones to hear the interpreters in windowed booths. The shape of the table was not an issue: it was a square, created from many long tables.

But there had been differences over the scope of the discussions. McNamara wanted to cover his term, 1961–68. The Vietnamese insisted on beginning in 1945, following the defeat of the Japanese in World War II. In the ensuing vacuum, they noted, Ho Chi Minh staked his claim for Vietnamese autonomy by including a passage from the American Declaration of

Independence in his own declaration. They recalled his letter to President Truman—unanswered—seeking support for independence. Vietnam's most serious mistake, sardonically noted by Tran Quang Co, a former First Deputy Foreign Minister, came before 1945, when "we considered the U.S. a leading democratic country, which was opposed to colonialism," he said. "Therefore, we thought the U.S. would support our desire for independence. But we were wrong."

A quite different image of America had been fixed in the minds of the men around the table when the United States facilitated the return of French troops to re-establish France's colonies in Indochina, then provided financial and logistical support for the French in their unsuccessful war against the Viet Minh and then refused to sign the 1954 Geneva accords that called for Vietnamese elections. This was the picture of a colonialist power with "ambitions to become master of the world," said Thach, who from 1960 to 1975 was the North Vietnamese Foreign Ministry's chief specialist on the United States.

Woven into the harsh language was an instructive analysis of how misperceptions became reality. Co identified four mistaken images that shaped American behavior. First, when the 1954 accords divided Vietnam along a "provisional" line, Washington saw something more permanent, underestimating the drive for reunification. "We never had two Vietnams," Co declared. "We had only one Vietnam. But the U.S. assessed it as two Vietnams."

Second, the Americans "misjudged the nationalist character of the revolution," he said. McNamara had already made the same point, admitting that Washington "underestimated the nationalist aspect of Ho Chi Minh's movement. We saw him first as a Communist and only second as a Vietnamese nationalist."

Third, "the nature of the struggle was not to undermine neighboring countries," Co continued. "The U.S. failed to understand the objective of our war. It was only for our own national liberation and reunification." This negated the domino theory.

And finally, Washington "misjudged the relations between Vietnam on the one hand and China and the Soviet Union on the other." Co pointed out what has become especially obvious since the demise of the Soviet Union: Vietnam was not a tool of world Communism. The theme resounded passionately throughout the conference. It meant that the central premise of the American motivation to defend South Vietnam was false. If these concepts seemed like echoes from the past, they were. Much of what the Americans were being told, and were now accepting, the antiwar movement had argued 30 years before.

In his opening statement on Friday morning, McNamara conceded that American behavior after World War II had caused the Vietnamese to form misimpressions "that the United States' principal goal in Southeast Asia was to destroy the Hanoi Government and its southern ally, the N.L.F."—the National Liberation Front, or Vietcong. But "we in the Kennedy Administration had no such view and no such aims in Vietnam," he insisted. "On the contrary, we believed our interests were being attacked all over the world by a highly organized, unified Communist movement, led by Moscow and Beijing, of which we believed—I think incorrectly—that the Hanoi Government of Ho Chi Minh was a pawn." He acknowledged having underestimated the Sino-Soviet rift.

The Vietnamese listened closely, but they seemed truly puzzled by the American obsession with the spread of Communism and sought more explanation. "If the reason was to fight Communism," they asked in a list of questions submitted beforehand, "why did the U.S. not help China in 1949, or why did the U.S. not help the Batista regime in Cuba in 1959?" They never got an answer, only a litany of conflicts, including two that nearly took the superpowers to war: the Berlin and Cuban missile crises of 1961 and 1962.

"We felt beset and at risk," McNamara said. "This fear underlay the Kennedy Administration's involvement in Vietnam." (A symmetrical domino theory gripped Moscow and Beijing, the American team had been told in Washington by Chen Jian, a Chinese scholar teaching in the United States. Newly obtained Soviet and Chinese documents reflected a fear that if North Korea or North Vietnam were lost, the Communist revolution could be reversed in Manchuria and perhaps all of China as well.)

Politely but pointedly, the Americans asked the Vietnamese to take some responsibility for their image. "If you believe that another country has a misperception about what you are trying to do," asked Katzenbach, the former Under Secretary of State, "my question is, What should you do to cure that misperception?" And later, adding that the domino theory was wrong but not irrational, he said: "I put myself in your place. The problem was, how would I, how would Vietnam, convince the United States that there was no domino theory?" Laughter but no answers came from the Vietnamese. Robert Brigham, an historian from Vassar, went on to point out that Chinese rhetoric in 1962 portrayed the N.L.F. as the first of many united fronts, "and nothing we saw coming out of Hanoi dissuaded us of that."

Once, Cooper turned the question around: "I would like to ask you if any mind-sets of Vietnam about the U.S. were wrong." A long silence followed. In private conversations later, the Vietnamese explained that the Foreign Ministry's sources of information on the United States had been limited to news summaries and issues of Time and Newsweek. They did not get any daily American newspapers, they said: a subscription to The New York Times was too expensive.

A couple of new facts emerged, not enough to revise the history books but sufficient for a lesson on how one side can read elaborate meaning into a coincidence and then react to the meaning rather than to the event itself. On Feb. 7, 1965, an American advisers' compound and airfield at Pleiku, South Vietnam, came under attack; eight Americans were killed and many more wounded. As Cooper explained to the Vietnamese generals across the table, Americans saw great significance in the timing. On that day, Cooper was in Saigon with McGeorge Bundy, the national security adviser at the time; they had been sent by President Johnson to assess the deteriorating military situation. Furthermore, on the same day the Soviet Premier, Aleksei Kosygin, was visiting Hanoi.

The choice of such a decisive moment to conduct the first specific attack on Americans was seen by Washington as a calculated policy move by Hanoi. In retaliation, the United States began its bombing raids on North Vietnam, which continued until the fall of 1968. Now Cooper wanted to know why Hanoi did it.

The answer came from Lieut. Gen. Dang Vu Hiep, a rotund, jolly-looking former deputy of the army's political department who was then stationed near Pleiku. "This was a spontaneous attack by the local commander" who acted under general orders to treat the South Vietnamese Army and its American advisers as equal enemies—"no discrimination," he remarked with a smile. The assault, by 30 commandos, had been planned long in advance, he explained, but the timing was coincidental. No specific instructions for the attack came from Hanoi, and "we did not know Bundy was in Saigon," he insisted. "We were just attacking, so we had no reason to criticize our people for attacking. They got first-class medals." Since the Russians were trying to restrain Hanoi from fighting in the south, Kosygin "was not pleased, but he couldn't say anything," General Hiep added during a break.

Had the role of the local commander been known at the time, Washington would have seen the incident differently, both Cooper and McNamara conceded. "I think we'd have put less weight on it and put less interpretation on it as indicative of North Vietnam's aggressiveness," McNamara said. The same held for the Aug. 2, 1964, assault by North Vietnamese patrol boats on the American destroyer Maddox in the Tonkin Gulf, McNamara added. That, too, was the initiative of a local commander, according to Gen. Nguyen Dinh Uoc, who heads the Institute of Military History. The alleged second Tonkin Gulf attack, on Aug. 4, never occurred, McNamara had been told by Gen. Vo Nguyen Giap, the military commander of North Vietnam during the war, in November 1995. At the time, the supposed attack had been used by President Johnson to secure a Congressional resolution providing broad authority for military action. Such details were mere footnotes, however, since the Vietnamese and American historians agreed that Washington would have found another pretext to bolster the decaying position of the Saigon Government.

Luu Doan Huynh, a Vietnamese scholar, came as close as anyone to giving McNamara what he wanted on China's probable response to an American invasion of North Vietnam. But the answer came in the form of analysis, not documentary evidence, and so it remained inconclusive. The Vietnamese were asked to supplement what had been learned from Chinese documents about a secret 1965 meeting in which Ho Chi Minh won from Mao Zedong a commitment to send Chinese troops in case of an American invasion. Nguyen Co Thach replied curtly: "I have no evidence. Thank you."

Huynh went on to explain that China regarded north Vietnam as part of a buffer zone within its sphere of influence. "So China made adequate preparations," he said. "There was an agreement" under which thousands of Chinese engineering troops were stationed in North Vietnam to help with road construction. "They displayed their equipment for you to see from the air," he remarked. "The Chinese factor was a deterrent, but that did not mean we were very eager to use it. We wanted to fight you alone."

The answer resolved nothing. "Hanoi's top leadership asked for and received commitments," Brigham said later. "It is not clear that China intended to follow through on those commitments."

Robert McNamara is still something of the systems analyst he was as a statistical control officer during World War II, as president of the Ford Motor Company, as Secretary of Defense and then as president of the World Bank. On his morning walks he calibrates his pace to four miles an hour and was pleased one rainy day to discover, on a hotel treadmill, how many calories he could burn. During the war he was so impressed by the logic of statistics that he tried to calculate how many deaths it would take to bring North Vietnam to the bargaining table. Now he wanted to know why his reckoning had been wrong, why the huge casualties that he had helped inflict had failed to break the will of the men in Hanoi. He came and left with the most durable stereotype between enemies: that the other side is a people not sufficiently swayed by loss of life.

His ruminations about this began at the Americans' April meeting in Washington, where he, Cooper and General Vesser agreed that casualties did not seem to weigh heavily with North Vietnam, either in diplomacy or military planning. "Was there any consideration of the human cost in Hanoi as they made these decisions?" McNamara asked. "Is the loss of life ever a factor?" He noted that while 58,000 Americans had been killed, the most authoritative estimate—in a September 1995 article by General Uoc—put the number of Vietnamese deaths at 3.6 million. "It's equivalent to 27 million Americans!" McNamara exclaimed.

To explain this to himself, he remembered seeing, during World War II in China, a worker fall and get crushed by a huge roller flattening earth for an airfield. The Chinese laborers laughed. There were some people to whom life was not the same as to us, he reasoned as he stood one evening in the hotel lobby. "We'd better understand that and write it down."

"Were you influenced by that loss of life?" he asked in the conference. "Did it move you to probe the negotiations?" Considering that a man responsible for so many casualties was accusing his enemies of caring less, the Vietnamese responded with exceeding courtesy. At first, when McNamara asked Thach the question over lunch, "the answer was, They paid no attention whatever to the casualties," McNamara reported triumphantly. "What I thought was—and I was wrong—that a very high rate of casualties would lead them to be interested in trying to find a less costly way of achieving their objectives—i.e., negotiations." But all he had got was the standard line that the cause was worth any sacrifice, based on the often-quoted mantra of Ho Chi Minh: "There is nothing more precious than freedom and independence."

If a second question was asked—did you do anything to minimize casualties?—the conversation suddenly opened onto a different level, beneath the propaganda. A colonel at the Army Museum in Hanoi, for example, explained to me how he had lived for months in narrow tunnels underground, how units would attack where the enemy was weak, fall back where it was strong, use the fewest men and weapons possible for the task and "hold you by the belt," which meant staying so close to American troops that they could not call in air strikes or artillery without risking self-inflicted casualties.

McNamara did not travel more than a few blocks from the Hotel Metropole, or he would have seen that virtually every village has a monument to the fallen; indeed, one junior Government official, pointing to a new monument under construction, complained that the money could be better spent supporting survivors of the slain. And a major topic of press coverage and conversation is the belief that Agent Orange caused birth defects in children of soldiers.

When the Vietnamese officials across the table tuned in to what McNamara was trying to say, they parried firmly. "If McNamara thought that the leaders of Vietnam did not pay attention to the losses and suffering of the Vietnamese people while continuing the war," Co said, "this is a mistake, a misunderstanding by the United States, which is terribly wrong. The war did happen on Vietnamese soil. We suffered a thousand times more than the U.S. did." Then he delivered a final thrust: "I thank you, McNamara, for giving us more understanding of your country."

McNamara remained baffled by Hanoi's failure to respond to Washington's negotiating probes, which included at least seven feelers put out by the Johnson Administration from 1965 to 1968 through Norwegian, Canadian, Polish, Soviet and other intermediaries, and at direct American-North Vietnamese meetings in Paris, Moscow and Rangoon. Usually these were accompanied by halts in the bombing of North Vietnam, during which the White House made known its expectation that Hanoi would curtail the flow of troops and weapons to the south. But the flow, not easy to control precisely, seemed to continue or to increase. And on the American side the bombing was sometimes resumed at inopportune moments—either because the weather cleared and permitted previously approved targets to be hit (as McNamara reports in his book) or because the White House refused to postpone a strike (as Cooper complained).

The Americans were intensely curious to know why Hanoi had not taken up the negotiating offers. In one instance it seemed as mundane as a misunderstanding over an appointment in Warsaw. The American version has been widely published: on Dec. 6, 1966, the American Ambassador to Poland, John Gronouski, was scheduled to meet with the North Vietnamese Ambassador to receive a reply to a proposal for talks. Gronouski waited in the office of the Polish Foreign Minister, Adam Rapacki, but the Vietnamese envoy did not show up. For 30 years this has been interpreted as a rebuff.

But at the conference, a retired Vietnamese diplomat, Nguyen Dinh Phuong, gave another version. He had been dispatched from Hanoi to Warsaw for the meeting, he said. He had arrived on Dec. 3 (a day that bombing was resumed) and waited with his ambassador at the North Vietnamese Embassy on Dec. 6. "We waited the whole day," he said, "but the U.S. Ambassador did not show up. On the 7th, the U.S. bombed more forcefully in downtown Hanoi. We concluded that the U.S. did not want to have negotiations."

Other answers were much less specific than the historians had hoped for but vividly illuminated the clash of perceptions. The Vietnamese doubted the sincerity of the negotiating offers, which they saw as propaganda ploys to mollify domestic and international criticism, to picture the Johnson Administration as peacemaker and Hanoi as warmonger. McNamara pounded the table and insisted that "many, I would say most" overtures were not "primarily" for propaganda. But how was anyone at the time to know? The men in Hanoi had been as ignorant as the American public of McNamara's growing doubts in 1966 and 1967 that the war could be won. They interpreted the use of intermediaries, as opposed to direct contacts, as part of the public-relations campaign to convince other countries of Washington's supposedly peaceful intentions. "We used intermediaries because we couldn't get to you," Cooper countered. But the suspicion was heightened by the Administration's failure to take up Vietnamese initiatives, including a four-point negotiating plan from Prime Minister Pham Van Dong.

Alert to what Washington did rather than what it said, the North Vietnamese interpreted each bombing halt as a "smoke screen" hiding further escalation. "For these peace initiatives to be convincing," Co remarked, they "should not have been conducted in the context of escalating war, in the context of increasing bombing against the north, in the context of the massive introduction of U.S. troops in the south. We interpreted those peace initiatives as war efforts, not genuine peace efforts." When President Johnson proposed aid for reconstruction as part of a peace plan, the North Vietnamese felt he was trying to "buy our surrender" by giving sweets, Luu Doan Huynh said. "If you don't like these sweets, you'll be eaten!"

McNamara pressed the Vietnamese on why they showed no interest in a 1967 offer of a cease-fire, an American withdrawal and reunification. "Was anything better than that obtained in 1973, six years later, after hundreds of thousands additional killed?" he asked. "I think not."

"We could not enter into negotiations under the pressure of bombing," Thach replied.

The North Vietnamese felt bludgeoned and blackmailed and dishonored by the bombing, but rather than weakening their will, the officials and generals at the table said, it had actually forged resilience. Yet they demanded a permanent bombing halt as a precondition for negotiations, and once they got it in the fall of 1968, they opened the Paris talks in 1969 with the Nixon Administration, which led to the 1973 agreement on American withdrawal. Negotiations result when "either party realizes it cannot win on the battlefield," commented Nguyen Khac Huynh, a former Deputy Foreign Minister.

That was why two of the American historians, George C. Herring of the University of Kentucky and Charles E. Neu of Brown, were skeptical that negotiations could have succeeded in the mid-1960's. Outside the conference room, Neu noted that anyone who pushed negotiations then was marginalized by the Johnson White House and that McNamara became the ultimate example. Herring agreed. "We need Walt Rostow here," he said, "because he would correct McNamara's view about where negotiations could go, which is way too optimistic."

Could negotiations have been successful when the United States had not yet resigned itself to a reunified Vietnam under Hanoi's control? "No," Cooper said. "I think they would have been long, heart-rending, ulcer-producing, frustrating." As for McNamara, "I don't know if he's revising history, but he's asking a lot of history."

But McNamara stuck to his conviction that had he known what he now knew, and had President Johnson grabbed the issue of Vietnam as insistently as he had the civil-rights issue, a negotiated solution could have been found.

Lyndon Johnson stayed in Vietnam largely because he feared the reaction from the right if he lost the war, his aide Francis Bator explained. The "central mission of his Presidency," Bator said, was getting the Civil Rights Act, the Voting Rights Act, Medicare and other Great Society programs through a dubious Congress, and he did not think he could risk being seen as irresolute on Communism. "He was deeply gloomy about the war throughout," Bator told the Vietnamese on the final day. "I believe that during 1966–68 he would have happily accepted a negotiating process." Bator was struck by the symmetry of error. "Our mistakes and your mistakes caused both of us to suffer dearly."

At the end, the Americans were taken to a frustrating meeting with General Giap, the short, gray-haired master military strategist, who gave a propaganda lecture lasting more than an hour, ignoring McNamara's pleas for answers to substantive historical questions submitted beforehand. "You're certainly winning the war of words," McNamara said through a brave smile. The same thing happened three days earlier with Foreign Minister Nguyen Manh Cam, who had stonewalled questions in favor of a polemic about American misdeeds. This so annoyed Cooper that he scribbled a note: "This gives me déjà vu: 1954, 1961, 1970. Enough already!" But on balance, Cooper said later, "I'm awfully glad I came. It closes the loop for me. I admire their guts."

By the end of the conference, McNamara pronounced the meetings a successful first step in examining the war. It was hard not to admire his relentless spirit of inquiry. But his attractive trait of self-criticism and his faith in the power of knowledge weigh against the memory of what he did, the criticism he screened out at the time, the facts he refused to consider in his policy making. Now he was willing to accept blame, but he also sought to spread the guilt around, to extend the circle of error to the North Vietnamese. They were not ready to play that game. "Of course," Co countered at the closing news conference, "the opportunities were missed by the U.S. side, not by the Vietnamese side." McNamara came back: "I don't think they were all missed by the U.S."

On that discordant note, and immediately after the unsatisfying session with General Giap, McNamara rushed to catch a plane. He was flying to New York for a meeting to discuss anticorruption efforts in Africa. "I'm tilting at windmills all over the world," he chuckled. Then he planned to go mountain climbing in Colorado.

"I think McNamara is a delicate personality, despite his mountain climbing," Cooper said. "He's running fast so the ghosts don't catch him," said another American, paraphrasing an observation made by others who have watched him.

In the streets of Hanoi, McNamara's lean frame, slightly bent, looked sinewy or fragile. One could not be certain. He is 81, and he is hurrying through the twilight.

* * *

April 23, 1999

VIETNAM EXPERIENCE UNITES SENATORS ON EVERYTHING EXCEPT KOSOVO

By ALISON MITCHELL

WASHINGTON, April 22—A generation ago, John Kerry, a decorated Navy lieutenant, came home to lead protests against the Vietnam War that he had served in. Max Cleland, a young Army captain, lost his legs and an arm when he reached for a loose grenade that exploded. Chuck Hagel, an Army sergeant, was wounded alongside his brother. John McCain, a Navy pilot, was shot down, imprisoned and tortured in Hanoi.

Now as Congress grapples with Kosovo, and Vietnam-era words and phrases like "quagmire" and "fighting with one hand tied behind the back" resonate once again, these Vietnam combat veterans in the Senate and two more—Bob Kerrey of Nebraska and Charles S. Robb of Virginia—speak with the special authority of experience. But the vexing questions of this war have pulled them in different directions.

Mr. McCain, the Arizona Republican who is seeking his party's Presidential nomination, has been perhaps the most vocal and influential Congressional hawk, urging the Administration to fight to win in Kosovo. He said he thought Vietnam had taught the nation the danger of waging war with too many constraints.

But Mr. Cleland said it was time for a cease-fire and an exit strategy. "I don't think there is a military solution in Kosovo," he said.

Trying to force a debate that the Congressional leadership has sought to avoid, Mr. McCain has introduced a resolution that would pave the way for ground troops by authorizing President Clinton to employ "all necessary force" against Yugoslavia. Three of Mr. McCain's fellow Vietnam veterans stand with him.

"One of the lessons of Vietnam is: if you are going to send American forces into harm's way, you don't do it in a limited way," Mr. Kerry, a Massachusetts Democrat, said. "You don't do it tying hands behind your back ahead of time. You don't ask people to give their lives for something less than the prospect of success."

But Mr. Kerrey of Nebraska, a Medal of Honor winner who lost his leg in Vietnam, and Mr. Cleland think unbridled escalation of the Yugoslav conflict without public support could turn it into another Vietnam. Mr. Cleland, a Georgia Democrat, compares Mr. McCain's measure with the Tonkin Gulf resolution of 1964 that gave the President authority to take "all necessary steps" in Southeast Asia.

The war quickly escalated: some 550,000 American troops were there by 1969.

"I am not," Mr. Cleland said, "going to vote as a U.S. Senator for my generation's version of a Gulf of Tonkin resolution, which has come to mean an open-ended, ill-defined conflict in which you commit Americans, particularly on the ground, and get a bunch of people killed and argue about why they were there later."

Mr. McCain complained of "this kind of optimistic rosy scenario that is so harmful in the long run to the credibility of the Government." He compared the daily pronouncements from NATO of bridges destroyed and targets hit in Belgrade with the optimistic—and discredited—Pentagon briefings in Saigon that came to be known derisively as the "five o'clock follies."

Mr. Cleland bristles at what he sees as "mission creep, war by increments, war by committee." That, he says, leads to "open-ended ill-defined conflict where you have a strategy for neither victory nor exit."

The Senators who want to open the door to ground troops still say air power, diplomacy and the threat of a ground war might yet force the Yugoslav President, Slobodan Milosevic, to negotiate. But Mr. McCain also bluntly says that should the air campaign fail, 60,000 to 70,000 troops could be needed to drive the Serbs from Kosovo and return the ethnic Albanians refugees home under NATO protection. "The bulk of it would have to be the United States," he said quietly.

Mr. Kerrey of Nebraska, by contrast, said a ground war for Kosovo "raises the price tag beyond what I think this operation is worth" and beyond what the American people would support.

"Americans care deeply about the humanitarian crisis and are willing to spend the time and money necessary to help the refugees," he said, "but to fight and retake the land called Kosovo and drive the Serbs out? I doubt that one."

Perhaps it is not surprising that these six men cannot take the same side. But the division is poignant because the six say they have developed an unusual bond and sometimes quite consciously try to stand together on matters related to southeast Asia.

Mr. Hagel said that the six keep an eye on one another's positions, even though they range from liberal to conservative. "If one of us is too far out and maybe somewhere where the others aren't, you kind of wonder why," Mr. Hagel said.

Mr. Robb remembers when, as Governor of Virginia, he was the only Vietnam combat veteran who was a governor. Then he learned of another combat veteran and Democrat—Mr. Kerrey—running for Governor of Nebraska. He sought him out to campaign for him. "We have been close for a long period of time," Mr. Robb said.

Mr. Kerry and Mr. McCain in particular have had to overcome the divisions of Vietnam to become close friends. As an anti-war protester in 1971, Mr. Kerry led veterans in a demonstration at the Capitol where they threw away their medals. Mr. McCain heard about the protest while still locked away in the notorious Hoa Lo prison.

Even years later, Mr. McCain said, Mr. Kerry's action still "offended me." He said, "it didn't mean there was an adversarial relationship. There was a certain distance between us."

But in 1991, they sat across from each other on a military transport plane flying a Congressional delegation to Kuwait after the gulf war. They talked about Vietnam through the night.

That conversation never stopped. Together they investigated whether there were still missing prisoners of war in Vietnam. In 1993, their mission took them to the Hanoi prison where Mr. McCain had spent most of his nearly six years in captivity. The senators visited Mr. McCain's cell.

Mr. Kerry describes that moment as "this eerie remarkable experience of standing in this place where he wondered whether he would ever come out alive." Mr. McCain this week struggled to control his emotions as he tried to give his account of that visit to the prison. "Now they've torn it down," he finally said.

* * *

May 16, 1999

VIETNAM SEES WAR'S LEGACY IN ITS YOUNG

By SETH MYDANS

HO CHI MINH CITY, Vietnam, May 15—In what amounted to a chance second-generation reunion from the war years, five teen-age girls laughed and chattered at a lunch table the other day, all of them patients in a hospital for severely deformed or mentally retarded children.

Their fathers had been soldiers from different parts of North Vietnam who fought in the same area of Tay Ninh Province in the south and dispersed to their homes when the war ended in 1975. Then they had children. The area where they fought had been heavily sprayed with the herbicide Agent Orange in a wide-ranging, decadelong campaign by the United States to deprive its enemy of forest cover and food crops.

Officials here are convinced that the five teen-agers—along with tens of thousands of other deformed children of war veterans and exposed civilians—are the victims of the herbicide and its poisonous residue, dioxin. Reunions like the one in the hospital here are not uncommon, the officials say.

But Vietnam's scientific studies have been sketchy and its evidence is often anecdotal. Until there is firm proof that chemical herbicides are to blame, the United States says it cannot take responsibility.

Vietnam has raised the issue only glancingly in talks with the United States, said Ambassador Douglas Peterson. But it arises repeatedly among people here who say it is one of the most painful remnants of a war that ended 24 years ago.

In a country where Americans are generally welcomed with friendship, the absence of aid from the United States for deformed children is one issue that still rankles.

It is a subject that the Government-controlled press keeps alive with occasional reports and that is sometimes placed on the agendas of foreign delegations, who are shown shelves full of glass bottles with labels like "Deformed baby with two heads, one body."

"You talk so much about human rights and humanity," said Dr. Le Cao Dai, who runs the Agent Orange program of the Vietnamese Red Cross. "No human rights in China. No human rights in Vietnam. So why, these children, are they not eligible for human rights?"

American officials and many independent researchers caution that there is no certainty that Agent Orange is responsible for the illnesses and birth defects, which can have other causes and can be found in other countries in the region.

The Veterans Association in Washington now offers compensation for 10 diseases as well as for the birth defect spina bifida that have been determined to be linked, or possibly linked, to the spraying in Vietnam.

The United States says more accurate tests are needed to confirm the Vietnamese assertion that there are victims here as well.

"The Agent Orange issue in this country is driven by propaganda," said a diplomat. "They would have you believe that every deformed baby is a result of Agent Orange. And the same with American G.I.'s."

From 1962 to 1971, the United States sprayed 12 million gallons of defoliant over more than 10 percent of what was then South Vietnam. Some 14 percent of the area's forests were destroyed, according to United States figures, and broad stretches of the landscape are still bare of trees.

The strongest evidence so far that some areas are still contaminated was published last October by a Canadian environmental research group, Hatfield Consultants.

In a five-year study of the Aluoi Valley in central Quang Tri Province, the researchers found high levels of dioxin in the soil, in fish and animal tissue, and in the blood of people born after the war.

"If such data were collected in most Western jurisdictions, based on similar sampling levels, major environmental cleanup and more extensive studies would be implemented," the report said. "As Western-based scientists, we can hardly recommend less be done in Vietnam."

The study was careful not to draw conclusions about the contentious question of human victims of the chemical spraying. But David Levy, vice president and senior scientist of Hatfield, said in an interview that logic would suggest that there were victims.

Over the years, tests conducted by Vietnamese and foreign researchers in certain localities here have documented high levels of contamination of breast milk and blood. Though the methodology may not be as rigorous as that in more-developed nations, the findings are often striking.

Dr. Dai said sharp contrasts are evident between the south, which was sprayed, and the north, which was not, and between northern residents who fought in the south and those who did not.

"Of course, to be very accurate, we need to have more medical study to confirm the causes," said Dr. Nguyen Thi My Hien, the director of the hospital here, the Thanh Xuan Peace Village, that cares for deformed children. But she said she believed that about 80 of her 100 patients were victims of chemical spraying.

One of these is Nguyen Cong Nang, 11, the severely retarded son of a former soldier who is himself disabled, with metal shrapnel lodged behind his right eye. Now the father, Nguyen Van Hien, 45, spends his days at the hospital, feeding and bathing his son and rocking him to sleep at nap times.

He said that all three of his sons had birth defects and that friends from the war also had children who were born deformed.

"For us it was O.K.," he said of his fellow soldiers. "We were happy to sacrifice on behalf of the next generation. But these children are innocent of the war. They are a generation of victims who are the children of victims."

The chance reunion of the children of battlefield comrades included Nguyen Thi Thoa, 15, whose body is covered with black blotches and whose younger brother died of heart disease. Dr. Hien described the blotches simply as a melanin disorder and said: "It is a very serious case. We are confused about how to treat it."

Sitting by her were two sisters, Nguyen Thi Thuong, 15, and Nguyen Thi Khuyen, 13, both of whom have mild mental retardation and whose growth has been severely stunted.

Dr. Hien said the sisters' father had been unable to bear their ailments and had fled their home. After their mother brought them to live at the hospital, the doctor said, the parents reunited and had another baby, who was also born deformed.

That story is not unusual, said Dr. Dai of the Red Cross. Parents often consider such births to be punishments for their sins and keep trying for healthy children, only to produce more sick ones.

In some cases, the parents are ostracized by fellow villagers for these presumed sins and exiled to live at the edges of rice fields.

In a final humiliation for these unlucky veterans, he said, "People sometimes say, 'This is happening to you because you killed too many people when you fought in the war.' "

* * *

July 7, 1999

CU CHI JOURNAL; VISIT THE VIETCONG'S WORLD: AMERICANS WELCOME

By SETH MYDANS

CU CHI, Vietnam—The rattle and pop of automatic weapons greet a visitor. Young women in the black pajamas of the Vietcong flit through the woods. A man in green fatigues picks his way down a narrow trail, leading a small platoon of foreign tourists.

This is the site of the Cu Chi tunnels, one of the most famous battlegrounds of the Vietnam War. Today it is one of the country's prime tourist attractions, part of a new industry of war tourism. Sometimes, these spots seem to be memorials to wartime propaganda as much to the war itself.

Following the man in green fatigues, the tourists arrive at an open-sided hut, where the women in black show them to their seats. There, on a big-screen television set, the Vietnam War plays on: B-52's drop strings of bombs, villagers run for cover, Communist guerrillas fight back.

For those who still don't get the message, a narrator says:

"Cu Chi, the land of many gardens, peaceful all year round under shady trees . . . Then mercilessly American bombers have ruthlessly decided to kill this gentle piece of countryside . . . Like a crazy bunch of devils they fired into women and children . . . The Americans wanted to turn Chu Chi into a dead land, but Cu Chi will never die."

Knitting past and present jarringly together, the gunfire in the film mingles with that of the nearby firing range, where visitors can pay $1 a bullet to shoot an AK-47 rifle.

Since the war ended in 1975 with a Communist victory, Vietnam has rebuilt and moved on. It is almost impossible to find anyone who still talks like the soundtrack of the Cu Chi film. Even the young women in black, who work as guides and ground keepers, dismiss the hard language, repeating instead today's Government line: we're all friends.

But in their new struggle for foreign currency, the Vietnamese are exploiting their harsh history, offering visits to long-forgotten places that were once considered vital to America's national interests. Most of the visitors here are foreigners; the Vietnamese who come are mostly schoolchildren with their teachers.

The Cu Chi tunnels, a 75-mile-long underground maze where thousands of fighters and villagers could hide, are at the top of the list of tourist spots for Ho Chi Minh City, 45 miles to the southeast. Another is the city's Museum of War Remnants, with its displays of captured weapons and its catalogue of horrors, which only recently amended its name, with changing times, from the Museum of American War Crimes.

Hue, the ancient capital, familiar to many Americans as the scene of heavy fighting in the Tet offensive in 1968, is the hub of a network of war tours. Streetside kiosks offer lists of attractions: "Khe Sanh, Dong Ha, Marble Mountain, China Beach, bombed-out church, DMZ with statue of Ho Chi Minh."

Even the site of the American massacre at My Lai has been turned into something of a theme park, with a cemetery, museum, storytellers and a memorial reading, "Forever hate the American invaders."

There are plans to develop the DMZ—the wartime demilitarized zone separating the north and the south—as well as parts of the Ho Chi Minh Trail.

Many visitors to these sites, like most of their guides, are too young to remember the war. Relatively few tourists come from the United States. For most people who come here, the war is a distant curiosity.

But for the last few years, since travel to Vietnam became more open, groups of American veterans have come in search of remembered battlefields. A small number of American tour companies specialize in guiding them and gaining permission to visit remote areas.

"They get a feeling of closure; that's the big benefit of going back as a veteran," said Richard Schonberger, director of veterans programs at a travel agency in Washington called Global Spectrum.

"We left suddenly," he said. "Now you know how the story ended. All the Vietnamese are very friendly. It's a different country now."

That can be disorienting, said Chuck Searcy, the Hanoi representative of Vietnam Veterans of America, which now runs prosthetics and rehabilitation programs.

"Everything has changed," Mr. Searcy said. "Almost every time, the vets are disappointed. They can't figure out where anything was: was it here or was it that hill over there? That piece of rusted metal was the gate to a big army base. You go to Long Binh: it's an export-processing zone now."

One American tour company uses a global positioning satellite to pinpoint battle locations for its clients, said Paulette Curtis, a graduate student in social anthropology at Harvard who is studying returning veterans.

"I've been to Hill 10, Hill 37, Hill 55 and Hill 65," she said, naming old battlegrounds. There isn't much to see. "You go to Khe Sanh and it's just coffee plantations and black pepper trees. The world of the vets' tour is completely different from the rest of Vietnam."

The sites that have been restored for tourists are almost as unrecognizable with their soft drink stands, hawkers and eager guides.

At Cu Chi, the visitor is greeted by a sign reading: "Please try to be a Cu Chi guerrilla. Wear these uniforms before entering tunnel." Black pajamas, pith helmets, rubber sandals and old rifles are available.

Here and there, holes in the ground are labeled: "B-52 crater."

The woods are dotted with souvenir kiosks. These items are available: a lighter made from a bullet, a pen made from bullets, a bullet on a chain, rubber sandals, an "I've Been to the Cu Chi Tunnel" T-shirt.

Also abundantly available, as they are wherever tourists are awaited in southern Vietnam, are Zippo lighters engraved with reproductions of the swashbuckling mottos that were popular among American G.I.'s:

"Death is my business and business has been good."

"I know I'm going to heaven because I've already been to hell: Vietnam."

"I am not scared just lonesome. Vietnam 68-69."

The tunnels themselves are undeniably impressive. Throughout the war, the South Vietnamese Communists, or Vietcong, continually expanded the three-level network, which included mess halls, meeting rooms, an operating theater and even a tiny cinema.

When the war was over, the people of Cu Chi went to work on the tunnels once again, widening parts of them and adding steps and lighting so that foreign tourists could wriggle in.

"I got claustrophobia big time," said Lawrence W. Goichman, a recent visitor from Stamford, Conn. "I crawled about 30 yards and then I took the first emergency exit."

But he added: "It's very clean down there. The guide said they have someone dusting every day."

He said he enjoyed his visit to Cu Chi. But he said the Vietnamese still have some work to do in developing their tourist sites. "Let's put it this way," Mr. Goichman said. "It wasn't as good as Disneyland."

* * *

April 13, 2000

VIETNAM FINDS AN OLD FOE HAS NEW ALLURE

By SETH MYDANS

HO CHI MINH CITY, Vietnam—For months, a giant portrait of Vietnam's revolutionary leader, Ho Chi Minh, stared out across a central square at a billboard showing the American fashion model Cindy Crawford.

"The glorious victory of Communism will last 1,000 years," the portrait of Ho proclaimed. Miss Crawford's portrait, offering for sale an expensive watch to count the hours, smiled enticingly and said nothing.

The portrait of Miss Crawford is gone now as this raucous, bustling city—still known to almost everybody as Saigon—smartened itself up to celebrate the high point of Vietnamese Communism: What Hanoi calls the liberation of the nation, after 30 years of war, from foreign domination by the French and then by the Americans.

It was 25 years ago, on April 30, 1975, that the last fleeing helicopter lifted off the roof of the American Embassy and the first tanks of the North Vietnamese smashed through the gates of the presidential palace a few blocks away.

Some 58,000 American soldiers were dead, along with an estimated 3 million Vietnamese, military and civilian, both in the north and south. The ruinous decade-long conflict known to Americans as the Vietnam War, and to Vietnamese as the American War, was over.

But in its way, a quarter of a century later, the war is still being waged here, even though more than half the population of 78 million was born after 1975.

Ho Chi Minh and the alluring faces of Western capitalism still confront each other, emblems of Communist Vietnam's celebrated past and of a more complicated future it has not yet decided to embrace. In the capital, Hanoi, a cumbersome, suspicious leadership still hesitates between them, fearing to lose in the global marketplace what it won, at such cost, on the battlefield.

"Now the war is all over and they have the liberty and independence and freedom they made such sacrifices for," said the United States ambassador, Pete Peterson, himself a war veteran who spent six years in a North Vietnamese prison.

"But the world has redefined those things," Mr. Peterson said. "What is independence in the global economy? Now a country is more appropriately graded on interdependence. And liberty from what? Happiness today is defined by the individual. They couldn't have assumed in their wildest imagination a situation like this."

The old fighters whose ingenuity and perseverance defeated a superpower seem to have been overwhelmed by the challenges that confronted them in building a new, independent nation.

By fits and starts over the years they have let in some fresh air, opening the economy somewhat and cautiously allowing more religious and social freedoms. But now they seem to have paused at a crossroads, divided and stuck, gripping the reins of political and economic control for dear life, almost frenetic in their stasis.

"Fighting a war was easy," said a retired North Vietnamese Army lieutenant who now works for a private company in Hanoi and wholeheartedly supports his government. "I tell you, to fight is easier than to manage. You cannot go too quickly. If you go too quickly something can go wrong. Every official in a high position says, in a very big voice, we have to do something. But when he reaches that point he realizes how difficult it is."

Following their victory, the Communist leadership, struggling to unify a nation that had torn itself apart in war, tried disastrously to implement a socialist economy throughout the country even as the defeated superpower worked actively to lock them out of the world economy.

Carlyle S. Thayer, an Australian expert on Vietnam, calls that first decade "winning the war and losing the peace." Then in 1986 Vietnam embarked on an experiment in openness called "doi moi"—fundamental renovation—and the world rushed in briefly, in the early 1990's, with more investment and aid than the country could manage or absorb. And through the late 1970's and the 1980's, Vietnam was also engaged in more warfare, as it occupied Cambodia and fought off a punitive attack by China.

Before that second decade had run out, Vietnam had lost its chief patron and aid donor with the collapse of the Soviet Union; foreign investors had begun to flee in frustration over

Christopher Brown/Saba

Vietnam's leaders appear caught between the Communism of the celebrated past and the draw of capitalism. In Hanoi, the capital, vendors on a bustling downtown street.

the bureaucracy, corruption and slippery legal system that crippled their work; and conservative forces had raised a hue and cry about the corrupting influence of "social evils" imported from the free-thinking West.

In a speech in February, Vietnam's top Communist leader, Le Kha Phieu, warned once again that the battle with the West is still on, though the arena is now the economy. "They continue to seek ways to completely wipe out the remaining socialist countries and attack the movements for independence, democracy and social progress," he said. "We should never relax our vigilance for a minute."

Under this watchful leadership, Vietnam today seems like a nation of bees buzzing inside a bottle, thrumming with repressed energy. Many of the same difficulties that drove away foreign investors—along with stifling limits on local business practices—are crippling the efforts of Vietnamese entrepreneurs. And an insistence on government control of major industries serves as a sea anchor slowing economic growth.

"If the government ever got out of the way here, this country would put the rest of Asia to shame," said a Western economic analyst who represents an international aid agency in Hanoi. "Go to the villages. Vietnam defines industriousness."

What he was talking about would amount to a revolutionary step for the Communist leadership, a redefinition of their victory 25 years ago. While they wait and consider, said Ambassador Peterson, "there is probably no developing country with such a vast void between potential and realization."

View of America: Fascination and Distrust

The next difficult step for Vietnam in its reintegration into the larger world is the signing of a trade agreement with the United States that embodies the free-market prescriptions of the International Monetary Fund. It would open Vietnamese markets to perhaps $800 million a year in new investment and send a signal that Hanoi is ready once again to do business with the world.

The pact was initialed by trade negotiators last November but then came to a dead stop as Hanoi began having second thoughts. Its economic prescriptions challenged too many vested interests and raised too many fears of a loss of central government control. And it roused a deeply held distrust of the United States.

"They have a kind of vague fear that there is something between the lines," said a Vietnamese economics professor,

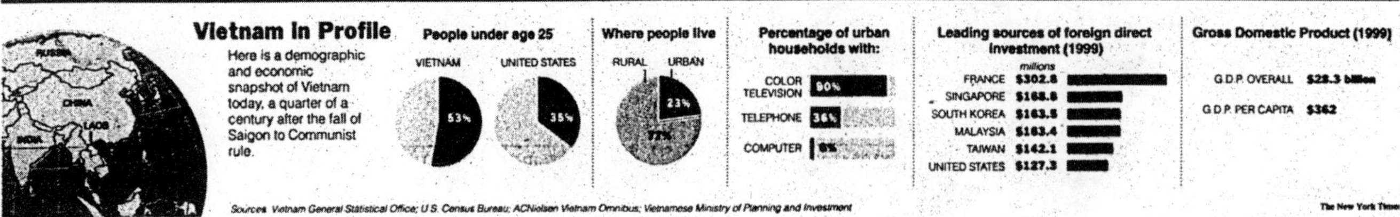

speaking of his government on condition of anonymity. "It's still a wartime generation that is governing this country and they do not completely trust American intentions."

Americans are received with real warmth today, both in the north and in the south. But that warmth does not for the most part extend to their government.

Although Hanoi now allows as many as 1,300 students to study in the United States each year, it remains leery of their views when they return, the economist said. "They say, 'You are coming back from America so perhaps you have been duped.' "

After so many years of war, and so many years of postwar hostility, said Tom Vallely, director of the Vietnam program at the Harvard Institute of International Development, "I think it's difficult and maybe impossible for them to believe you can have a win-win situation with the United States."

For nearly two decades after the war ended, the United States maintained a trade embargo, arguing that Hanoi was slow to provide information on missing American soldiers and that Vietnam was acting aggressively by occupying its neighbor, Cambodia, from 1979 to 1989.

President Clinton lifted the embargo in 1994 and established full diplomatic relations the following year. American investors, many motivated by postwar sentiment, flooded in with what Ambassador Peterson called "visions of grandeur" that ended in disappointment.

Today, trade between the two countries remains small, with Vietnam shipping $650 million worth of goods to the United States each year and American companies selling $350 million in exports to Vietnam.

There are other reminders of the costs of the American war: continuing generations of babies born deformed because of the effects of the chemical defoliant Agent Orange and continuing generations of farmers and children who are killed and maimed by unexploded bombs and mines.

These explosives, ranging from mortar rounds to antipersonnel mines to buried 500-pound bombs, shift and rise to the surface with the annual floods that torment the central provinces, frustrating efforts to clear new farmland.

But when the United States offered a $750,000 program of mine-clearing and training several years ago, the Vietnamese refused because it would once again cause uniformed American soldiers to be based on Vietnamese soil.

Despite these legacies of war, Vietnamese appear fascinated by the United States. It sometimes seems the entire nation is studying English, the language of commerce.

And after two decades of postwar refugees, nearly a million of whom are now in the United States, there is now a waiting list of thousands who have applied to immigrate to join their relatives.

And in a curious twist, the dollars sent home by these refugees, now well over $1 billion a year, are one of the country's largest sources of foreign currency—a much larger contribution than if these same people had remained in Vietnam.

Even in a museum here that still displays the "war crimes" of Americans, a woman selling souvenirs made out of bullets took an American visitor aside recently to ask how she could emigrate to the United States.

Throughout its history, Vietnam has been the victim of its geography, fighting off periodic invasions by its northern neighbor, China—most recently in 1979. During the American war, the Communists of North Vietnam found themselves leaning on China, as well as on the Soviet Union, for support. Now, Hanoi may see the United States as its necessary buffer against its big and powerful northern neighbor.

"America now is an alternative to China," the Vietnamese economist said. "To counter the Chinese threat we must lean towards the West—not because we like the West, but because the Chinese Army is 2.5 million strong."

Recently, a young Foreign Ministry official enumerated Vietnam's official grievances against the United States, then went on to describe with relish a recent trip he had taken through several American states.

He recalled that in the 1940's, Ho Chi Minh had made overtures of friendship to the United States that were rebuffed. "That is the tragedy and the drama of Vietnam," he said. "It never wanted to be enemies with America."

Political Control Vs. a Free Market

Apart from China, only Vietnam is attempting the acrobatic feat of creating a capitalist economy under the control of a Communist government. Clearly, though, it is suffering from a greater fear of heights.

Though Vietnamese leaders insist that they follow no outside models, they thrive on cautionary tales: the Soviet Union that collapsed when it loosened its government's grip, Indonesia that dissolved into disorder with the ouster of a strong leader, Asian economies that imploded because of their dependence on the global marketplace.

Dennis de Tray, the International Monetary Fund's senior resident representative in Vietnam, says the country has its own successful model to emulate in opening its economy—the decision a decade ago to end collectivized agriculture.

"They went from near starvation to the world's second largest rice exporter overnight," Mr. de Tray said. "And they did it with one simple change, by letting farmers keep their own rice. If you lived through this, why not just go ahead, guys, go for it. This is as good an example as I've seen in the world."

Indeed, he said, despite Vietnam's current stagnation, it has covered a good deal of ground in the last decade. "Ten years ago this was a country that did not even have the vocabulary of trade, the vocabulary of a legal system, the vocabulary of economics, the vocabulary of a central banking system," he said. "So why are they hesitating now to take the next step?"

With a per capita income of just $360 a year, Vietnam is one of the poorest nations in the world, with nearly 80 percent of its population in the countryside, most of them on the edge of poverty. The government, whatever its political agenda, is clearly committed to raising living standards, according to political analysts.

But with agriculture making up only a small part of national income, the next liberalizations must come in a growth of private enterprise in other sectors, foreign experts agree. At the moment, medium or large-scale private companies make up less than 2 percent of the economy.

"Vietnam needs to open up the domestic private sector to get things going beyond photocopy stands and noodle shops, to get people investing in small manufacturing businesses instead of just providing a service to their neighbors," said Robert Templer, the author of "Shadows and Wind: A View of Modern Vietnam" (Little, Brown 1998).

And, said one Vietnamese who owns a small business in Hanoi, local bureaucrats who enforce scores of often ambiguous regulations must undergo a fundamental shift in attitude. "It has to be 'do whatever is not forbidden,' " he said, "rather than 'do only what is permitted.' "

But under Vietnam's political system, none of this is so simple.

First, both Vietnamese and foreign experts say, the government is hobbled by a decision-making process that demands consensus—some say unanimity—in a leadership with increasingly diverse economic interests. A veto, it seems, can come from just about anywhere.

Second, the government is not yet convinced it can carry out its acrobatic balancing act, fearing that an open marketplace will lead to political pluralism.

Thus, every time the economy opens up a bit, it seems, restrictions on free speech and political activity grow tighter and political rhetoric grows harsher.

At this moment of uncertainty, for example, almost no nonofficial Vietnamese would allow their names to be printed in this article. As one businessman in Ho Chi Minh City put it, with a touch of bitterness, "We have freedom here, but it is under control."

The American War Is Ancient History

In a cozy refuge from the rain, six teenage boys sat in a tiny arcade in Hanoi jittering and shouting in their seats as they played war games on a row of computers.

To the sounds of synthetic gunfire, the computers charted their progress with exclamation points:

"Long was blown away by Ken's super rocket!"

"Nam caught Ken's hand grenade!"

Exactly 25 years ago, boys their age were firing real rockets and throwing hand grenades in North Vietnam's final assault on the South.

What did these postwar youngsters think of that? The question was greeted with blank stares.

"Twenty-five years ago?" said one boy. "Is that right?"

For the large majority of Vietnamese who were born after the war, or who were only children when it ended, much of it apparently seems, literally, ancient history.

"It is just one of a whole series of events that they are supposed to revere in school, but for many of them it doesn't have any more specific meaning than the Vietnamese victories over the Chinese in the 10th century," said Peter Zinoman, a professor of Vietnamese history at the University of California at Berkeley.

"Another reason for their disengagement," he added, "is this whole new culture of consumption that does sort of preoccupy them."

Vietnam has seen little of the kind of political debate, national soul-searching or artistic reconsideration of the war that has helped the United States to try to draw lessons since the fall of Saigon.

In part this is because an unqualifiedly heroic version of the war is essential to the legitimacy of the Communist Party. There is no disputing official propaganda.

A result is that art, journalism and policy discussions remain constricted by political boundaries as well as by a genuine respect for the elderly heroes of the Communist victory. "Making compromises is something we have to do now," said a Hanoi-based official in his late 30's. "We cannot make our fathers feel so unhappy. They are our fathers. What can we do? We must accommodate their thinking."

For younger Vietnamese eager to get onto the world's fast track, he conceded, this delicacy can be maddening.

"As my father often says, 'You didn't live under the French. You didn't see how people were starving.'

"I say, 'Other countries in the region are moving ahead now and they are prosperous.'

"He says, 'They're in crisis.'

"I say, 'Now they are emerging and they are moving faster than we are. We should have taken advantage but we didn't take advantage.' "

The young official seemed ready to burst with frustration.

"What Vietnam is doing now is toddling, like a child," he said. "So I say to them, 'Why not try the adult method: firm, but faster!' "

As some Vietnamese like to say, 25 years is a long time in a human life but a short time in history. Most people here agree that change will come in its own good time.

But without America's openness in discussing and digesting its history, the future, when it does arrive, may indeed be the alien visitor the country's leaders fear.

There are already signs that they may be losing control of their own history. Tu Anh, for example, a company project manager who was born in 1975, talked in surprising detail the other day about the long-ago war.

But her information did not come from textbooks or her elders. The source she cited was a pirated copy of the movie "Forrest Gump."

* * *

November 11, 2000

MAKING ECONOMIC LIFELINE OF A WARTIME TRAIL

By SETH MYDANS

SON TRACH, Vietnam—Sometimes when the road builders set off their blasting caps here along the old Ho Chi Minh Trail, one of the bulldozer operators gives an involuntary, comical little duck of the head, as if someone were dropping bombs nearby.

"Then I realize I don't need to be afraid," said the operator, Nguyen The Du, 53. "I tell myself: 'Don't worry. The war is over.' "

Sometimes when monsoon rains wash out the newly carved road here in Vietnam's remote western mountains and the workers huddle under tarpaulins, Mr. Du is overcome by a sudden wave of loneliness.

"I remember how we sat around talking, just the way we're sitting now, and it was always in our minds that at any moment, one of us could be dead," he said. "Somebody's face comes back to me suddenly as if he had just disappeared, the way he disappeared back then."

Mr. Du is one of Vietnam's heroes, a survivor of six years as a youth volunteer on the Ho Chi Minh Trail, one of the most dangerous places to be for a Communist fighter during the Vietnam War.

He is back here again today, near what used to be the demilitarized zone between the North and the South, part of a hugely ambitious new effort to carve a real 1,000-mile highway through the mountains along the route of the former trail.

When he worked here before, filling bomb craters as fast as they were made, the trail was a shifting network of jungle paths along both sides of the Laotian border. The workers here like to say it was that trail that defeated the American military, transporting men and equipment from North to South despite some of the heaviest nonstop bombing of the war.

The new project is perhaps as characteristic of today's Vietnam—as President Clinton prepares to visit the country next week—as that stubborn, ingenious effort was of the Communists' spectacular wartime success. It is cumbersome, expensive, controversial and, say its critics, wrongheaded.

It diverts scarce resources into a monumental project that is more in tune with the past than the future, the opponents say, benefiting entrenched interests and offering questionable benefits. Vietnam already has a north-south highway and a parallel rail line, though both are in bad repair.

In this way, the project represents a continuing tug of war among Vietnam's leaders—over how much and how fast to open up to the world's new global economy, and how much to preserve of the centralized, steel-mill and cement-plant approach that characterized its Communist models, Russia and China.

"The Ho Chi Minh Highway is a symbol of not understanding how to invest in the modern world," said Tom Vallely, a Harvard-based expert on Vietnam's economy and a persistent critic of the project.

"You could use the same resources to improve the educational system, the telecommunications system, the Internet system, which are essential to the modernization of Vietnam," he said. "This highway represents the old economy. The Internet is the real road. I think the big question for them is, do they want to go for the old-economy road or the new-economy road."

Mr. Vallely suggested that with a five-year Communist Party Congress due early next year, the project amounted to a political giveaway to some of the cumbersome state-owned enterprises—like the overpriced cement monopoly—that stand to lose if market reformers gain the upper hand.

He said he doubted that international donors would put money into the highway.

The World Bank and the Asian Development Bank, two of Vietnam's leading donors, say they have not been asked to help although they have assisted other road projects, for instance repairing the current north-south route, Highway 1.

Vietnamese leaders say the four-year, $680 million project will give a badly needed lift to its transportation system and will help develop the Central Highlands. And they are using it as a propaganda rallying point, evoking heroic wartime images as they call for a mass mobilization of labor.

But the project has also become the focus of unusual opposition within the country. Its cost and its threat to nature preserves and endangered wildlife are causing concern, as is its potential disruption of the traditional way of life of the hill-tribe minorities that populate the mountains.

In a rare sign of opposition, The Saigon Times reported in 1997: "Most deputies of Ho Chi Minh City, Haiphong and Quang Ninh expressed their concern over the feasibility. Some even voiced their doubts about the economic efficiency of this proposed artery route." They reportedly suggested that the existing highway and railroad be upgraded.

Planners say the project will involve 60 million working days, and one proposed way to find workers, apparently modified this month in the face of bad publicity, has been particularly controversial: mobilizing unpaid labor on a grand Communist scale reminiscent of Soviet and Chinese projects.

Vietnam itself has a history of mass labor projects for irrigation, flood control and national defense. Some 300,000 volunteers like Mr. Du worked on the original Ho Chi Minh Trail.

This time, according to the official press, as many as a million people living along the route would be drafted to contribute 10 days each of free labor, or would pay a fee to be exempted.

"A far-reaching movement must be begun to carry on the great mettle of the nation with which we will march toward a new peak," said Prime Minister Vo Van Kiet three years ago, employing the grandiose language of Communist exhortation. "This will be a great construction site with the work of millions of people."

But he was apparently aware of the darker images he might be invoking, and asserted that no intellectuals or professionals would be drafted to wield picks and shovels.

Still, Vietnam is changing. Private enterprise is growing; there is no longer a war to unify the people, and the idea of volunteer labor is highly unpopular. With the project just getting under way this fall, the government appeared to back off the plan, saying workers would be paid a minimum of about $1 a day.

"There is no forced labor involved in this project," said Bui Viet Bao, an official of the Ministry of Labor. "They are all people who want to find work."

That is not implausible, in one of the poorest nations in the world, where per-capita income averages $370 a year—even less in these remote mountain areas—and where rural unemployment can reach 30 percent.

So the project is proceeding, with plans for more than 300 bridges and six high-speed lanes at some points. And despite proposed alternatives, it has not been diverted away from national parks.

Opponents say it will cut through or pass close to 10 environmentally protected areas, including Vietnam's first national park, in the north, and the Phong Nha nature preserve here in Quang Binh Province. Environmentalists say logging and plantation-building have cost Vietnam one-third of its forest cover in just the past 15 years.

The government deflects the criticism, arguing that the current north-south road is narrow, prone to flooding and inadequate, and that the new highway will link isolated communities in the highlands.

And with foreign goods and ways of life invading Vietnam as it opens to the outside world, the project evokes some of the Communist Party's strongest images of past heroism. "The new road is at the heart of the Vietnamese people," said Duong Tuan Minh, the project's deputy general director.

Past and present overlapped the other day as Mr. Du, the bulldozer operator, sat over a bowl of pungent noodle soup in a tin-roofed shack by the side of the construction site.

Unexpectedly, a small television set behind him began broadcasting black-and-white documentary film of wartime youth volunteers like himself, rushing to fill bomb craters on the trail.

Mr. Du looked at the screen and seemed a little distracted.

"Things are quite different now," he said. "Back then, we were part of a huge thing, a national duty. We worked beyond our capacity. Nothing could stop us. Back then we didn't care about dying. We just worked as hard as we could. Now it's different, but I still do the best I can."

* * *

November 18, 2000

HUGE CROWD IN HANOI FOR CLINTON, WHO SPEAKS OF 'SHARED SUFFERING'

By DAVID E. SANGER

HANOI, Vietnam, Nov. 17—Tens of thousands of Vietnamese, many of them former soldiers who once battled the United States, poured into the streets of Hanoi today to welcome President Clinton, waving to his motorcade and watching on television as he told the nation that "shared suffering has given our countries a relationship unlike any other."

Speaking at the Vietnam National University, a bust of Ho Chi Minh just behind him, Mr. Clinton repeatedly went out of his way to honor soldiers on both sides of "the conflict we call the Vietnam War and you call the American War," equating their sacrifices, but never delving into the causes they represented.

Instead, he gave his Vietnamese audience—no one knows how many of the country's 78 million people were watching—a description of the Vietnam memorial on the Mall in Washington, where the names of the American dead are etched in black stone. "Some American veterans also refer to the 'other side of the wall,' the staggering sacrifice of the Vietnamese people on both sides of that conflict—more than three million brave soldiers and civilians," Mr. Clinton said.

The president and his huge entourage of officials, members of Congress and business executives were clearly taken by surprise at the warmth of the reception he got on this city's chaotic streets. The size and enthusiasm of the crowds was particularly striking because Vietnam's leaders treated the president with polite but distant formality, as if they were still unsure about how far they wanted to take this new opening with a former enemy.

One senior administration official here said tonight that he sensed that the Vietnamese leaders "were a little bit nervous about what they were seeing on the streets."

But if Vietnam's president and prime minister were cautious about their visitor, Mr. Clinton was equally careful about how he spoke of the war's legacy and Vietnam's record of repressing dissidents. His comments equating the struggles of American and Vietnamese forces made for the kind of speech that it would be hard to imagine any president giving if he had to face re-election—especially a president who opposed the war and actively maneuvered to avoid the draft. But he seemed ebullient about his reception today, and liberated by the fact that he is leaving office in eight weeks and three days.

Asked why the president had made no moral judgments about America's failed effort to save South Vietnam or about the North's ultimately successful drive to unify the country under Communist leadership, Mr. Clinton's national security

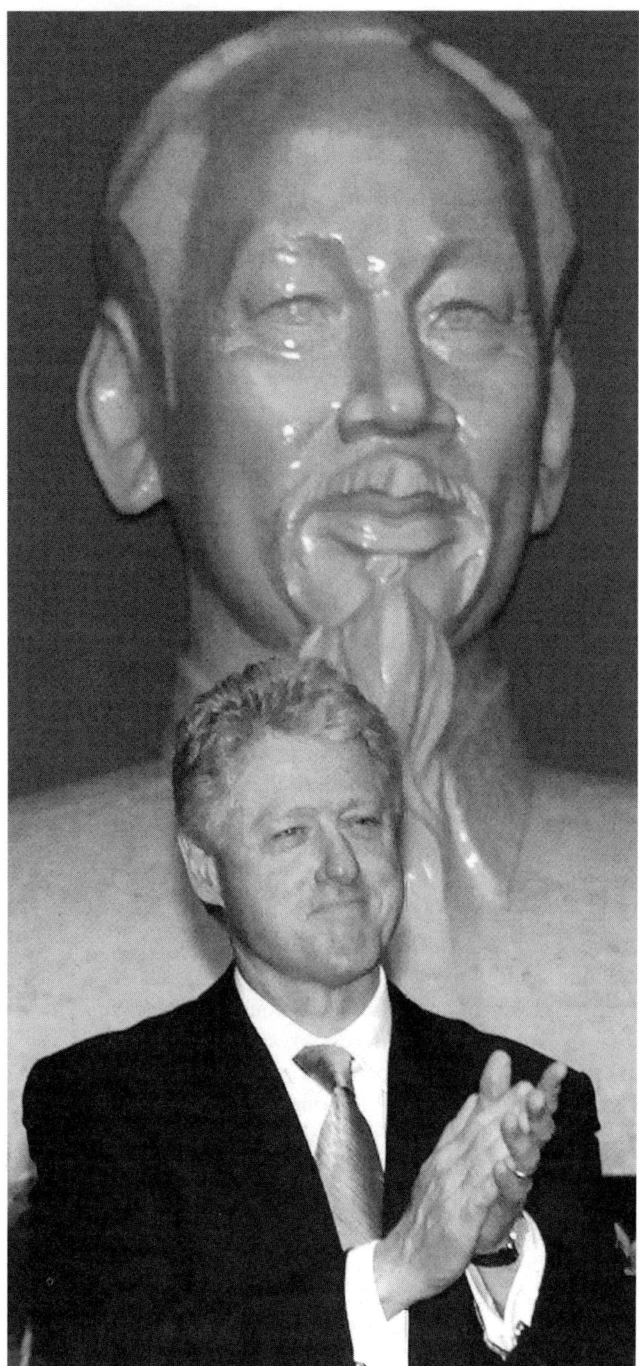

Associated Press

With a bust of Ho Chi Minh behind him, President Clinton took part in welcoming ceremonies yesterday at the Presidential Palace in Hanoi.

adviser, Samuel R. Berger, said the president wanted to focus on the future.

"The national interest now is not served by re-arguing the debates surrounding the war," he said.

At a toast at a state dinner tonight, Mr. Clinton said: "The history we leave behind is painful and hard. We must not forget it but we must not be controlled by it."

The president similarly stepped extremely carefully when he raised Vietnam's suppression of dissent and its limits on emigration. While clearly calling for more openness, Mr. Clinton said in his speech that "we do not seek to impose these ideals, nor could we." That was a far cry from his challenge to Jiang Zemin, China's president, that Beijing was "on the wrong side of history," or his repeated harsh critiques of Fidel Castro.

Even though Mr. Clinton scaled back his human rights message, President Tran Duc Luong and the government's chief economic reformer, Prime Minister Phan Van Khai, stiffened today when he brought up the subject in private meetings. Both men, according to American officials, said "we may have different definitions of human rights," and said they had to worry about the rights of Vietnamese to eat and get an education before they moved toward America's agenda.

But the diplomatic wordplay was overwhelmed by the surreal images, starting with the sight of the Presidential limousine winding through Hanoi's streets with a Vietnamese flag on one fender, the Stars and Stripes on the other.

For a few moments today there was concern when the crowds grew overenthusiastic. Mr. Clinton plunged into a crowd on a busy shopping street and to the brief alarm of the Secret Service was mobbed by a crowd eager to touch any piece of his clothing. After a few minutes, security agents pulled Mr. Clinton out of the crowd and into his car.

But within minutes he was out of his car again, along a street of small shops selling everything from dishwashers to pirated music on cassette tapes and CD's. He popped into a cooperative that sells fabrics and purses and other goods made in the countryside, buying Christmas presents for his family.

Then he took his staff to lunch at a small cafe called Know One, Teach One that is well known in the city for giving jobs to the capital's young homeless. A bit shocked, the young waiters fumbled with soups and sandwiches as they ran up and down a narrow stairway to serve the meal.

The whole city seemed equally surprised. Mr. Clinton's visit was not a secret, of course, but the government had done nothing to promote a large turnout to greet him. The articles that ran in Vietnam's obedient newspapers about the president's imminent arrival were small and understated. A hard-fought soccer match pitting Vietnam against Indonesia won far larger billing on television, along with details of government plans to build new roads.

There was only one banner celebrating the arrival of "President William Jefferson Clinton and Spouse" visible to those entering the city. Today was an ordinary workday.

But people came anyway. The crowds lined Mr. Clinton's route, never cheering but constantly waving, children and grandchildren held aloft to catch a glimpse of the largest motorcade this city has ever seen.

Just before 4 p.m., people gathered in front of television sets in storefronts to catch Mr. Clinton's half-hour speech, an oddity in a country where the leadership feels no need to explain itself. The White House had provided the government with a translation of the speech into Vietnamese because, as one administration official put it, "we've learned the hard way what happens when you let your host do its own translation."

It was unclear if any of Mr. Clinton's phrases were altered to fit the Communist Party's liking when the translation was read by a Vietnamese as the president spoke.

Mr. Clinton said he arrived here "conscious that the histories of our two nations are deeply intertwined in ways that are both a source of pain for generations that came before, and a source of promise for generations yet to come." He cited phrases about life, liberty and the pursuit of happiness that Ho Chi Minh had lifted from Jefferson in writing Vietnam's own version of a declaration of independence.

But he quickly moved to his now-familiar arguments about the new age of mutual dependence, telling his audience that globalization "is the economic equivalent of a force of nature" and that it "is not going away." Vietnam, he said, must learn to harness it "like wind or water." And he told the student elite of the country that "your next job may well depend on foreign trade and investment."

"Come to think of it," he said, "since I have to leave office in about eight weeks, my next job may depend on foreign trade and investment."

He delicately argued that Vietnam's people should support the reformers in the government who are pressing for a loosening of the state controls that have choked the economy here and sent foreign investors fleeing.

"Only you can decide if you will continue to open your markets, open your society and strengthen the rule of law," he said. "Only you can decide how to weave individual liberties and human rights into the rich and strong fabric of Vietnamese national identity."

It is not clear how the argument will play out in the behind-the-scenes power struggle that appears under way here in Hanoi between conservatives who fear that economic opening will undermine their power and economic reformers who say that the only other choice is an economic spiral downward. Right now, the conservatives appear to have the upper hand.

"That's for the moment," a senior administration official said tonight. "You look at all those young people" who came out to greet the president today, he said. "It's going to be hard to tell them what to think."

GENERAL INDEX

Abbas, Ferhat, 8
Abrams, Creighton W.: and bombing halt, 486, 488–89; effectiveness of, 493; on Laos incursion, 597; on pacification programs, in 1971, 615; on U.S. tactics, 477; on U.S. withdrawals, 518–19
Abzug, Bella S., 778
Acheson, Dean: on Ho Chi Minh, 16; on military aid to French, 20, 21–22, 24, 30; on recognition of Asian states, 15
advisers, U.S.: evacuation of, in fall of Quangtri (1972), 657, 658; frustrations of, 134, 137; introduction of combat role, 217–18, 222–26; post-Paris peace agreement plans for, 696–97; problems of, 538; role of, in 1971, 642–43
Afghanistan, Soviet Union in, 849–950
African Americans: in anti-war movement, 299–300, 348–49, 351, 354, 376, 510, 551; in armed forces, 311, 348, 354, 442–47, 443, 445, 447, 642; on assassination of King, Jr., 439; on assassination of R. F. Kennedy, 452–53; at Democratic Convention of 1968, 470; deserters in Sweden, 844
Agency for International Development (USAID), 696–97
Agent Orange, 853–54, 890–91
See also defoliation
Agnew, Spiro T.: anti-war protests and, 499, 550; on press, 547–48
agriculture in South Vietnam: inadequate government support for, 120 *See also* land reform
agrovilles, 90–91 *See also* relocation of peasants
aircraft, North Vietnamese MIGs, 206–7; U.S. efforts to strike, 309; use in 1972, 655
aircraft, U.S.: in 1964, 181–82; C-47 planes, 305; effectiveness of, 360; F-104 Starfighters, 310; jet fighters, introduction of, 182, 193; in jungle warfare, 220; in Laos incursion, 599; North Vietnamese downing of, 337; SR-71 planes, 484; surveillance flights over North Vietnam, 484; types and roles of, 309–10; U-2 planes, 182, 197, 484; Viet Cong destruction of, 197, 209–10, 393, 397, 411, 426, 506 *See also* B-26 bombers; B-52 bombers; helicopters
aircraft carriers, U.S., routine aboard, 275–76
air defenses: North Vietnamese, Chinese bolstering of, 206–7 *See also* anti-aircraft fire
air strikes. *See* bombing
air support, U.S.: in 1965, 260, 261; in 1972, 679; in Easter Offensive (1972), 651–52, 654, 659; efficacy of, 305–6, 659; at Iadrang River valley battle (1965), 279; power of, 305; South Vietnamese dependence on, 653, 676
Alcorn, Wendell, 729–31
Algeria, independence movement in, 7–8
American Civil Liberties Union, Pentagon Papers and, 624–25
amnesty for Viet Cong, U.S. plan for, 128
Annam: France's inept response to, 32; independence movement in, 1–2, 4, 5, 8–9, 12; Indo-Chinese fear of, 21
anti-aircraft fire, North Vietnamese and Viet Cong, 390, 425–26; in 1965, 276; in 1966, 308; in 1972, 655–56, 668; in Easter Offensive (1972), 651–52, 653; at Hamrong Bridge, 336; in Laos, 598–99, 602, 616; U.S. countermeasures, 226, 305, 670
anti-draft movement, U.S.: in 1964, 180–81; in 1967, 351; in 1968, 457–58
anti-infiltration devices, 484
anti-U.S. sentiment: among Binh Xuyen, 77; among French nationals in South Vietnam, 76, 77–78; in Britain, 343; of Buddhists, 201, 208, 295, 299; causes of, 88–89; in China, 43, 110, 214; intervention and, 173–74; in Laos, 784; in North-Vietnamese propaganda, 79; in South Vietnam, 151, 164, 238, 360, 388, 486, 647–48; in South Vietnamese army, 206–7
anti-war movement, international: in 1967, 357–58; in 1972, 700–701
anti-war movement, U.S.: in 1964, 180–81; in 1965, 230–32, 258, 267–74; in 1966, 312; in 1967, 349–52, 371–73, 374–77; in 1969, 499–501, 507–8, 519–21, 540–42, 547, 549–51; in 1972, 663–65; in 1973, 706–7; among academics, 245; on campuses, 572–76; civil rights movement and, 299–300; Clinton's role in, 863–65; communist influence in, 376; in Congress, 676–77, 677–78; counterdemonstrations, 351, 352, 542, 547, 551, 576–78, 580–81; by drafted soldiers, 509–11; F.B.I. surveillance of, 786–87; impact on U.S. culture, 709–11, 715; Johnson on, 258–59, 273, 300–301; King Jr. and, 299–300, 348–49, 351, 354; and Laos incursions, 590–91; and Mylai massacre, 554; Nixon on, 545, 571–72, 578–80, 618; and North Vietnamese repression, 789–90; numbers involved, 724; postwar demands, 778; postwar role of, 723–25; recommended reading for, 602–4; soldiers' view of, 271, 379; structure of, 724; television's incitement of, 358–59; veterans in, 617–20, 619, 620, 788–89, 819; victory celebration (1975), 778–79; war crime accusations against U.S., 602–11
Ap Bac, battle of, 136–37, 146; impact of, 139, 141, 158
Apbia Peak, battle of, 515–16
appeasement, U.S. presidents' view of, 633
Armed Forces Radio Service, bombing of, 204
Armistice (1954), 55–57
Army Field Manual, on conduct in war, 604, 607–8, 609
Army of the Republic of (South) Vietnam (ARVN)
- avoidance of battle by, 139, 141, 168, 172, 173, 175, 329, 362, 381, 382
- branches and related services: Civil Guard, 89, 108, 126, 133; militias, 543, 659; Popular forces, 535, 537, 543; Ranger units, 108, 123, 330; Regional forces, 535, 537–38, 543; Special Forces, 163
- and Buddhist crisis (1963), 147, 148–49
- campaigns and engagements: in 1962, 112, 123; in 1963, 136–37; in 1968, 437; in Laos incursion, 601–2
- command problems in, 109, 112, 126–27, 159, 330, 362
- interrogations: of prisoners, 401, 410, 462, 494–95; of villagers, 119–20, 120, 128
- leadership of, 539–40, 660–61
- living conditions, pay and benefits, 330, 536–37, 615
- looting by, in 1968, 417
- military position: in 1960, 91; in 1961, 101, 108; in 1962, 124–25, 126–27, 130, 134; in 1963, 145–47, 159–60; in 1964, 186; in 1969, 492–94; in 1974, 737–38, 745; in 1975, 745, 748–50, 756, 764
- military role of: in 1965, 252; in 1966, 322, 327

mobilization, in 1968, 440
morale: in 1960, 91; in 1962, 113; in 1963, 144; in 1965, 209, 233, 251; in 1966, 329, 330, 331; in 1967, 354, 362, 388; in 1969, 536–37; in 1971, 601–2; in 1974, 738; in 1975, 757, 758; desertions, 330, 331, 535, 658, 659; post-armistice, 70; and resentment of U.S. troops, 538
in Ngo Dinh Diem regime, misapplication of, 172, 175
peasant's hatred of, 329
political role of: anti-government demonstrations, in 1966, 296; corruption in, 330, 362, 536, 537, 539; government's fear of, 141, 143; loyalties of, post-armistice, 76; opposition to Ngo Dinh Diem in, 143; overthrow of Ngo Dinh Diem, 160–62, 166; overthrow of Tran Van Huong, 207
resistance to U.S. advice, 175, 207
size and strength: in 1954, 85; in 1960, 93; in 1962, 126; in 1964, 186, 199, 201; in 1965, 232, 251, 252; in 1966, 330; in 1967, 359; in 1969, 535; as percent of population, 329; post-armistice, 71
tactics and results, 110, 129, 130–32, 134, 318
in Tet Offensive (1968), 393, 402–3, 410–11, 411
training, 70–71, 101, 108, 110, 111, 112, 115, 327–31, 535–36, 538
U.S. commitment to, 193, 292–94, 597, 742, 754–55, 763
U.S. equipping of, in 1968, 439, 440, 460
U.S. evaluation of: in 1962, 134; in 1963, 137, 139; in 1965, 223, 250; in 1966, 327–31; in 1967, 355, 362; in 1969, 493, 534–40; in 1970, 557–59; in 1971, 597; in 1972, 653
U.S. soldiers' opinion of, 380
weaponry upgrades in 1969, 535
artillery: North Vietnamese, in Easter Offensive (1972), 653; South Vietnamese, efficacy of, 740–41; U.S. policy on, as war crime, 606; Vietnamese, at Dienbienphu (1954), 38, 41
ARVN. *See* Army of the Republic of (South) Vietnam
Asia, political situation in 1980s, 835–37
A-Team (TV show), 828
Atlantic Charter, and Colonialism, 3–4
atomic energy, international control efforts, 44
atrocities: Mylai massacre, 551–54, 556–57, 595–96, 608–9, 611–15; by South Vietnamese army, 128; U.S., veterans' reporting of, 618; by Viet Cong, 401, 409
Australian army in Vietnam, 248
Au Truong Thanh, 363

B-26 bombers, advantages of, 310
B-52 bombers: bombing in Laos, 283; in Cambodia, 731–32; at Iadrang River valley battle (1965), 279; number in theatre (1972), 676; uses and effect of, 305, 306, 344, 356, 512–13, 601, 602, 652, 655–56, 657, 665–66, 667–68, 700, 702, 731–32
Baez, Joan, 789–90
Baker, James A. III, 860
Ban Me Thuot, fall of (1975), 750–51
Bao Dai, 16; and Binh Xuyen, 76, 77; character and background, 18–19, 22, 67, 86; as cold war puppet, 16; French support for, 78; at Geneva Conference, 46; leadership of, 18, 22, 23, 24, 32, 73; military forces of, 15, 22; political defeat (1955), 79, 80; popular opinion of, 67; and post-armistice South Vietnam, 66, 67; reinstallation of, 12, 13, 14–15, 19
Bao Dai regime: in 1954, 62; defections from, 51; diplomatic recognition of, 15, 16; legitimacy of, 17; local government in, 19; military situation, 15, 19; military strength and competence of, 15, 22, 37; territory controlled by, 17, 19; U.S. aid to, 20–21
Basic Training of Pavlo Hummel (Rabe), 811, 812
Belafonte, Harry, 349, 352, 779
Bentre, in Tet Offensive (1968), 406
Berger, Samuel, 489–90
Bernstein, Leonard, 551
Berrigan, Daniel, 789–90
Berrigan, Philip, 789–90
Berry, David, 810, 811
Best and the Brightest (Halberstam), 693–94
Bevel, James, 352
Bickel, Alexander M., 624, 630
Bidault, George, 32, 46, 48–49, 49, 53, 57
Bienhoa, Viet Cong attack at, 197
Binhson hamlet, pacification program in, 584–85
Binh Xuyen, 66, 67, 71, 75, 76–77, 80, 85, 89
Black, Hugo L., 630
Blackmun, Harry A., 628–30, 631
blockade of North Vietnam. *See* mining of ports in North Vietnam
Blum, Léon, 5, 6, 7
boat people, 790–91, 813–14, 831–35, 875–77
Bollaret, Emile, 12, 13
bombers, U.S.: number in theatre, in 1972, 676
See also B-26 bombers; B-52 bombers
bombing (U.S.): cluster bombs, 305, 357; of demilitarized zone, in 1968, 483; laser-guided and precision bombs, 668; volume of, 309, 718; as war crime, 604–11
bombing (U.S.) in Cambodia: in 1969, 512–13; in 1973, 725–26; pre-1970, 731–32; purpose and efficacy of, 733–34
bombing (U.S.) in Laos: in 1966, 309–10; in 1968, 481, 482–85; of supply lines, 202–3, 207, 280, 283
bombing (U.S.) in North Vietnam: in 1964, 188–89; in 1965, 210–13, 220–21, 225, 227–28, 232, 233, 235–36, 275–76, 279, 281, 283; in 1966, 286–87, 295, 306–8; in 1967, 332–33, 355, 364–65, 385; in 1972, 655–56, 656, 665–66, 666, 667–68, 675–76, 676, 701–3; British opinion of, 343, 344; Chinese reaction to, 214–15, 221; of civilian targets, 233; debate over, 180, 198, 200, 205, 210, 213, 220–21, 308; decision to begin, 636; efficacy of, 567, 623; goals of, 220–21, 224, 225, 354; halting of, 393, 431–33, 433–34, 453–54, 460, 481–82, 482–85, 486–90, 504, 637, 703–5; impact of, 481, 484–85, 679, 692, 700, 738, 867–68; as issue in Paris negotiations, 448–49, 450, 451; Johnson on, 188–89, 198, 211, 229, 233; McNamara on, 365–67; of missile sites, 309; napalm in, 226–27; Nguyen Van Thieu on, 679; Nixon on, 594; North Vietnamese reaction to, 651, 889–90; political risks of, 307, 365, 366; restrictions on, 607; resumptions of, 644–46, 699–700; soldiers' opinion of, 466; South Vietnamese training for, 184–85; Soviet reaction to, 214–15, 221; U.S. casualties in, 481; vulnerability of Northern economy to, 195
bombing (U.S.) in South Vietnam: in 1972, 676; at Iadrang River valley battle (1965), 279; peasant's opinion of, 672–73
Bond, Julian, 469
Bongson plain, battle of, in 1968, 389
booby traps, Viet Cong, 132
Born on the Fourth of July (Kovic), 787–89, 828–29
Boun Oum, 94, 99, 121
Bourguiba, Habib, 7
Bowen, Thomas W., 657, 658
Bowles, Chester, 388–89
Boyles, John, 374, 473
Bradley, Omar N., 27, 28
Brant, Joseph, 152
Brennan, William J., Jr., 630
Bright Shining Lie: John Paul Vann and America in Vietnam (Sheehan), 851–53
Brinkley, David, 154
Brinks billet, bombing of, 203–4
Britain: anti-U.S. sentiment in, in 1967, 343; on Chinese communist revolution, 14; on Chinese invasion of Indo-China, 29, 31; colonial revolts post-WW II, 3; and Geneva Conference, 51; importance of Indo-China to, 40; in post-WW II Vietnam, 1, 2; on solution in Southeast Asia, 206; Soviet post-WW II offensive against, 4
Bronze Stars, 554, 617
Bruce, David K. E., 588, 593
Buddha's Birthday truce (1977), 355
Buddhist Institute for Religious Affairs, 208
Buddhists in South Vietnam: activism of, 208; activism against Ngo Dinh Diem regime, 141–42, 143, 144–45, 147–49, 150–51, 160, 161, 163, 165, 174; activism against

Nguyen Cao Ky regime, 295–97, 297–99, 300, 302–3, 363; activism against Nguyen Van Thieu regime, 744–45; activism against Tran Van Huong regime, 201, 210; anti-Americanism of, 201, 208, 295, 299; as communist tool, 149, 154, 295
Bui Van Lim, 537
Bundy, McGeorge, 210, 262, 347
Bundy, William P., 196, 388, 836–37
Bunker, Ellsworth: appointment as ambassador, 347; and bombing halt, 486; efforts to spur South Vietnamese reforms, 388; and Paris peace negotiations, 488, 489; on prospects for victory, 385, 408
Burdick, Eugene, 88–89
Burger, Warren E., 629–30, 631
Burma: communist insurgency in, 136; impact of Geneva settlement (1954) on, 62; as target of Chinese aggression, 30
Bush, George H. W., 662, 851
business: in North Vietnam, post-armistice, 79; in South Vietnam, French-owned, 77
  See also entries under economy

C-47 aircraft, 305
Cahill, William T., 575
Calley, William Laws, Jr., 551–57, 554, 595–96, 608–9, 610–15
Cambodia: anti-communist rioting in, 562, 564; army size and strength, 733, 807; army training, 74; cease-fire expectations (1973), 711, 712, 713; Chinese support for (1970s), 805, 807, 808–9; as communist staging area, 183, 282–83, 302, 385, 388–89, 418, 477–78, 483, 512–13; communist tactics in, 733; communist takeover in, 759, 760–62, 771, 773, 774–78; conflict with South Vietnam (1958–59), 87, 89; conflict with Vietnam (1970s), 806; diplomatic recognition of, 15, 16; French peace proposals for, 48; as French protectorate, 13; and Geneva peace agreement, 49, 55, 56, 57, 63; neutrality of, 183; North Vietnamese in, 61, 565, 566–67; overthrow of Sihanouk, 562; political situation in 1954, 51; refugees from (1977), 790–91; relations with North Vietnam, 563; relations with United States, 563–64; in Sino-French peace agreement, 53, 54; Socialist Republic of Vietnam aggression in, 801–2, 805–6, 806–7, 835, 836, 845, 854–55; U.S. aid to, 20–21; U.S. bombing in, 512–13, 725–26, 731–32, 733–34; U.S. intervention in, 282–83, 302, 566–67, 567–71, 583–84
Cambodian National United Front for National Salvation, 806, 807
Camp Hollaway, attack on (1965), 210
Camranh Bay: Johnson visit to, 324–27; in Tet Offensive (1968), 397
Canbos, 73
Can Lao party, 92
Cao Dai, 66, 67, 71, 75, 89
Cao Van Vien, 178, 327
Carmichael, Stokely, 352, 358
Carpenter, William S., 306
Carpentier, Marcel, 23
Carswell, G. Harrold, 565
Carter, Jimmy: foreign policy under, 794–95; and normalization of relations with Hanoi, 794, 795–96; on pardon of deserters, 792–93; pardon of draft evaders, 792–93; policy on missing soldiers, 862; withdrawal from Korea, 795
casualties
  civilian: in 1968, 477; efforts to reduce, 266–67; at Mylai massacre, 551–57; U.S. tactics and, 132, 266, 567
  French, 24, 27, 28, 30, 31, 36–37
  from friendly fire, 288, 666–67
  identification of remains, 793–94, 840
  Laotian, in 1971, 610
  North Vietnamese: in 1965, 277; to 1966, 304; in 1967, 356; to 1967, 360; in 1968, 475–76; to 1969, 504, 517; in 1970, 570, 589; to 1970, 589; to 1972, 679; North Vietnamese reaction to, 889; reporting of, 516
  reliability of statistics on, 128, 134, 140, 158–59, 199, 304–5, 386–87, 412, 516–17, 534
  South Vietnamese, 175; in 1962, 128, 132, 133; in 1963, 136, 146; in 1964, 204–5; in 1965, 250, 281; to 1965, 234; in 1966, 297, 330; in 1968, 395, 397, 398, 399, 400, 403, 406, 411, 416; in 1969, 534; to 1969, 504; in 1970, 589; to 1970, 589; in 1971, 593; to 1971, 604, 606; to 1972, 679; in 1973, 734, 737–38; Popular Forces, 537; in Tet Offensive (1968), 395, 397, 398, 399, 400, 403, 406, 411, 416; U.S. treatment of, 608
  TV coverage of, 358
  U.S.: in 1961–1964, 180, 185, 208; in 1962, 24, 124, 125, 127, 132; in 1963, 138; in 1964, 197, 202, 203–4; in 1965, 206, 207, 209–10, 215, 224, 248, 249, 250, 275, 277, 281; to 1965, 234; in 1966, 288, 297, 306, 321, 330; to 1966, 301; in 1967, 356, 357, 415; to 1967, 360; in 1968, 390, 394, 395, 397, 398, 399, 403, 407, 413, 416, 458–59, 475; to 1968, 436; in 1969, 504, 505, 506, 515, 525, 534; to 1969, 503–4; in 1970, 565, 570, 584, 589; to 1970, 589; to 1972, 679; in bombing of North Vietnam, 481; Johnson on, 249; Nixon's efforts to reduce, 524; public reaction to, 311; reporting of, 277–79; in Tet Offensive (1968), 394, 395, 397, 398, 399, 403, 407, 413, 416
  Viet Cong, 239; in 1962, 128, 132, 133; in 1963, 136, 146; in 1964, 236; in 1965, 224, 248, 249, 250, 260–61; to 1965, 234; in 1966, 297, 309; to 1966, 304; in 1967, 415; to 1967, 360; in 1968, 389, 390, 397, 398, 399, 400, 403, 407, 411–12, 437; in 1969, 515; to 1969, 504, 516, 517; in 1970, 589; to 1970, 589; to 1972, 679; reporting of, 516; in Tet Offensive (1968), 397, 398, 399, 400, 403, 407, 411–12; as U.S. goal, 356–57
  Viet Cong treatment of, 239
  Viet Minh, at Yencuba (1951), 24
  Vietnamese, in War, 716
  See also medical care
Catholic(s) in South Vietnam: anti-communist feeling of, 120; anti-Nguyen Van Thieu activism, 744–45; civil unrest in 1966, 300; flight from North Vietnam, 69, 70; impact on Vietnamese culture, 717, 718; Ngo Dinh Diem as, 76, 86, 127, 141, 145, 163; Ngo Dinh Diem regime as, 129, 142, 143, 144, 156, 717; South Vietnamese opinion of, 174
CBS network, Westmoreland libel suit against, 823–26
central coastal region, military and poliical situation in 1963, 174
central highlands: military and political situation in 1963, 174; South Vietnamese abandonment of (1975), 748–51; U.S. efforts to control, 281
Central Intelligence Agency (C.I.A.): in Laos, 591; and Laotian peace settlement, 123; in South Vietnamese politics, 154, 162; weather manipulation experiments, 670–72
Central Office for South Vietnam (COSVN), U.S. efforts to destroy, 570–71
Cheng Heng, 562
Chen Yi, 122
Chiang Kai-shek, 11, 64
Chicago Eight, 542
children of mixed race, Vietnam's rejection of, 822
China: agenda in Southeast Asia, 135; aggression against Formosa and Hong Kong, 29; aggression in Southeast Asia, 896; agreement with France on Indo-China, 53–54; anti-U.S. propaganda, 43, 110; communist revolution in, 11–12, 13, 68; conflict with Vietnam, in 1970s, 808–9; demeanor of diplomats from, 341; French recognition of, 178, 179; and Geneva Conference, 46, 49; importance of Vietnam War to, 167; and neutralized Vietnam, 182; Nixon visit to, 648–49; policy on guerilla wars, 144, 183, 184; policy on peace negotiations, 227, 235, 262; recognition of Viet Minh regime, 15, 18; relations with North Vietnam, 341; relations with U.S., in 1980s, 836; response to bombing of North Vietnam, 214–15, 221, 224–25; rift with Soviet Union, 339–41; secret U.S. negotiations with, 205; struggle for Indo-China, in

1970s, 805–6; subversive activities by, 93; United Nations admission, 53; U.S. perception of, in 1977, 795; U.S. warnings to, in 1964, 188; as U.S. adversary, 217; Vietnamese fear of, 18, 29 *See also* economic aid, Chinese; military aid, Chinese; *entries under* Chinese
Chinese army: capabilities in 1952, 29; in Korean War, 28; reputation of, 27–28; size in 1952, 30; in Vietnam, 41
Chinese invasion threat in Indo-China, 14–15, 27–28, 28–30, 31; in 1964, 202; in 1965, 234–35, 242, 255, 280, 281, 282; in 1967, 365; in 1971, 593; U.S. response to, 41–45
Chinese Nationalists, in Burma, 30
Chinese support for North Vietnam: in 1954, 72; in 1960, 91; in 1964, 184; in 1965, 214–15, 234, 238, 242, 279–80; in 1967, 333, 339–41
Chinese support for Viet Minh regime, 23, 28, 29, 32, 34, 38, 41, 63, 68
Chomsky, Noam, 609
Chou En-lai, 46, 49, 53, 57
Christmas bombing (1972), 699–703
Christopher, Warren, 880
Chuong Thien, battle of (1963), 158
C.I.A. *See* Central Intelligence Agency
Civil Guard, 108; anti-subversion activities, 89; recruitment for, 133; size, in 1962, 126
civilians, Vietnamese
casualties: in 1968, 477; efforts to reduce, 266–67; at Mylai massacre, 551–57; and U.S. tactics, 132, 266, 567
daily life of, impact of war on, 259–60, 264
identity cards, 382
See also peasants in South Vietnam
Civil Operations and Rural Development Support (CORDS) program, 615, 616, 642–43, 697
civil unrest in South Vietnam
in 1960, 92
by Buddhists, 208; against Ngo Dinh Diem regime, 141–42, 143, 144–45, 147–49, 150–51, 151–52, 160, 161, 163, 165, 174; against Nguyen Cao Ky regime, 295–97, 297–99, 300, 302–3, 363; against Nguyen Van Thieu regime, 744–45; against Tran Van Huong regime, 201, 210
in central coastal region, 174
in Hue, in 1966, 296
against neutralization of Vietnam, 171
See also rioting
civil unrest in United States. *See* anti-war movement
Clark, Mark W., 34, 63
Clay, Frank B., 129
Cleveland, Harlan, 109
Clifford, Clark M., 439–40
Clinton, Bill: avoidance of Vietnam service, 863–65; diplomatic recognition of Vietnam, 879–81; restoration of trade with Vietnam, 870–71; visit to Hanoi, 899–901
cloud seeding, U.S. military uses of, 670–72
cluster bombs, 305, 357
Cochin China: Provisional Government in, 9; Vietnamese independence movement in, 5, 8–9
Coffin, William Sloane, Jr., 458
Cogny, René, 52
Colby, William E., 543
cold war: in Carter administration, 795; communist aggression in, 104; cost of, 20–22; Geneva settlement and, 58; in Laos, 99–101, 107; Vietnam as focal point of, 16–19, 25, 140, 144, 166–68, 217, 227, 258, 292–94, 315, 711 *See also* Chinese invasion threat in Indo-China; neutralized Vietnam
college courses on Vietnam War, in 1980s, 820–21
Collins, J. Lawton, 71, 72, 75, 129
colonialism: British, 3; Dutch, 3–4; French, 1–8, 14; post-WW II collapse of, 1–8, 10–12; strategies of, 10; U.S. opinion of, 14, 15 *See also* independence; nationalism
combat troops, U.S.: in 1965, 235, 240–41; advisor status dropped, 217–18; arrival of, 222–24, 225–26; debate over, 241–42; final withdrawal of, 679–80; offensive actions, in 1965, 248–49; rules of engagement, 1965, 266–67; tactics, and civilian casualties, 132, 266, 551–57, 567; television broadcasts of, 358–59; uses of, 242–43, 250–52; Viet Cong reaction to, 267
Coming Home (film), 810–11, 812, 829, 830
command problems: in Army of the Republic of (South) Vietnam, 109, 112, 126–27, 159, 330, 362
command structure: of joint U.S.-Vietnamese forces, 252, 254; of Viet Cong, 133, 240, 344–45, 379, 462–63, 493–94
communication(s): and illiteracy, 11; Vietnamese disruption of, 9, 12, 19, 23; Vietnamese proficiency in, 23
communist aggression, 104; awakening international community to, 108–9; and escalation debate, 195–96; neutralized Vietnam and, 182–83; and North Vietnam, 86–87, 93–94, 233–35; strategy in Southeast Asia, 122–23, 135; strategy in Vietnam, 140; U.S. acceptance of, 104; Vietnam as testing ground for, 167
See also cold war; terrorism
communist infiltration of South Vietnam: in 1954, 51; in 1958, 88; in 1959, 89; in 1963, 173; in 1964, 196, 200–201; in 1965, 233–35, 251; in 1966, 296, 308, 320–21; in 1967, 343, 356–57; in 1968, 484; in 1972, 654, 658; Johnson's response to, 215; from Laos, 124; post-armistice, 64, 67, 69, 73; in Tet Offensive (1968), 401–2, 406–7; U.S./South Vietnamese countermeasures, 90–91, 200–201, 224, 233, 280, 320–21, 356–57 (*See also* relocation of peasants)
communists: Chinese revolution, 11–12, 13, 68; in Europe, 323; fomenting of post-WW II colonial unrest, 5, 6, 7–8, 10–11, 14; in post-WW II France, 6, 14; resistance to, effective, 135–36; rise of in Vietnam, 7; uncompromising goals of, 35; U.S. opinion of, 14; in U.S., 180–81, 270, 376; and Vietnamese independence, 5, 12
Community Defense and Local Development Plan, 615–16
Composite Intervention Forces, 180
Conco Island, battle of, 336
Conduct and Misconduct of Foreign Affairs (Yost), 711
Cong An, 174
Congress, U.S.: administration secrecy and, 113–15; aid-reduction threats, in 1963, 156; and aid to South Vietnam, 741–42, 745, 759; criticism of Defense Department, 731–32; and Ford policies, 754–55, 759; on Geneva settlement (1954), 57, 58; hearings on Vietnam War, 180, 292–94; and Johnson policies, 188, 189–91, 212, 218, 244–45, 245–46, 250, 254, 259, 314, 352–53, 354, 364, 366, 372–73, 373–74, 377, 419, 422–25; and Nixon policies, 506–7, 557–59, 568–69, 575, 581–83, 587–88, 676–77, 677–78, 741–42; and Nixon Supreme Court nominees, 735–36; reaction to Tet Offensive, 402–3; U.S. presidents' view of, 633; veterans in, 890–91; War Powers Act (1973) enactment, 735–36
conscientious objectors, 312, 313; King Jr. call for, 348–49; to Vietnam War only, 600–601
constitution of South Vietnam (1956), 83–84
containment: British policy on, 14–15; Geneva settlement (1954) and, 40–41, 61–63; Kennedy on, 168; as psychologically damaging policy, 633–34; SEATO and, 65; strategies for, 59, 75; U.S. policy on, 13, 14–15, 28, 29, 30–31, 32, 44
Cooper-Church amendment, 582–84
CORDS. *See* Civil Operations and Rural Development Support program
corruption: in Socialist Republic of Vietnam, 842; in South Vietnam government, 92, 108, 113, 117, 120, 362–63, 388, 457, 539, 633 (*See also* reform in South Vietnam); in South Vietnam hospitals, 416–17; in South Vietnam military, 330, 362, 536, 537, 539
cost of Vietnam War
to French, 20–22, 24, 28, 31, 36–37
to North Vietnam, 192
to U.S., 709–11; 1954–1964, 186; in 1964, 180; in 1965, 235, 255; in 1967, 348, 359, 361, 371; in 1971, 616; political and diplomatic costs, 313–15; Senate objections to, 138–39
See also economic aid; military aid
Cronkite, Walter, 154, 155
Cuba, offers of assistance to North Vietnam, 335

Cu Chi tunnels, tourist reenactments at, 893–94
culture
of North Vietnam, social control via canbo system, 73
of South Vietnam: impact of U.S. on, 454–57; impact of War on, 715–19; South Vietnamese intellectuals on, 673–75
of U.S., impact of War on, 709–11, 715, 729–31, 878
Cushman Robert E., Jr., 415

Dalat, in Tet Offensive (1968), 401
Daley, Richard J., 469
Danang: under communist rule, 798; fall of (1975), 755–57; Nguyen Cao Ky occupation of, 300; pacification efforts around, 361; in Tet Offensive, 393, 397
Dang Van Quang, 539
Dang Vu Hiep, 887
Dang Xuan Khu, 22
d'Aubuisson, Roberto, 816
Dautieng, Viet Cong attacks on (1969), 505–6
de Castries, Christian, 38, 47, 48
Deer Hunter (film), 810, 830
Defense Department, congressional criticism of, 731–32
defensive fortifications, construction of, 118
defoliation: chemicals used for, 561; efficacy of, 567; extent of defoliation, 561; health and environmental impact of, 559–62, 853–54, 890–91; as South Vietnamese strategy, 112; in Viet Cong propaganda, 238
de Gaulle, Charles: Kennedy on, 155; neutralist vision for Vietnam, 152–53, 178–79; peace plan for Vietnam, in 1966, 323
de Lattre, Bernard, 27, 49
de Lattre de Tassigny, Jean-Marie, 25–27, 32
Dellinger, David, 374, 376, 542
Del Vecchio, John M., 828
Demilitarized Zone: North Vietnamese assault across, in 1972, 651–52; in Paris peace agreement, 705, 708, 712; in Paris peace talks, 501
democracy, Ngo Dinh Diem on, 80
Democratic Party (U.S.): Convention of 1968, 466–68, 469–71, 471–74; Convention of 1976, 787–88
Democratic Republic of Vietnam. *See* North Vietnam
Denton, Jeremiah A., 721
dependents of U.S. personnel, evacuation of (1965), 210
DEROS (Date of Estimate Return from Overseas), 465
deserters
South Vietnamese, 330, 331, 535, 658, 659
U.S.: debate on pardon of, 792–93; life in Sweden, in 1980s, 843–44; number of, 793
Viet Cong, 235–40, 240, 295, 297, 355, 363, 387, 495, 544
Dewey, A. Peter, 1–2
Dienbienphu, seige of (1954), 38–41, 46–49; lessons of, 49–50; Vietnamese artillery at, 38, 41
Dirksen, Everett McKinley, on Vietnam policy, 506
Dispatches (Herr), 799–800, 810, 830
Distinguished Service Crosses, 325, 524
Dobrynin, Anatoly F., 221, 222, 663
Do Cao Tri, 174, 539
dogs, U.S. military, 112, 129, 136
Dole, Robert J., 581–82, 880
Dominican revolution, U.S. intervention in, 245, 246–47
domino theory: critique of, 711, 754–55, 785–86, 835, 836–37, 887; Eisenhower on, 42–44; Kissinger on, 754; in Pentagon Papers, 633
Donghoi, as Viet Cong staging area, 212–13
Don That Trinh, 561
Douglas, William O., 630
Doung Van Minh, 161
Do Van Cung, 84
draft, military: African Americans and, 311; in France, 32; increase of, in 1965, 254–55; under Nixon, 668–70; U.S. reaction to, in 1966, 311
draft evasion, 269–70, 272, 273; Ford amnesty program, 743–44; pardon of, 778–79, 792–93; U.S. investigation of, 270–71
draft exemptions, for objection to single war, 600–601
Drinan, Robert F., 618
drug abuse: by U.S. soldiers, 532–34, 620–22, 640–41; by veterans, 783, 803–5
Duarte, Jose Napoleon, 815–16
Du Bridge, Lee A., 561
Duc Lap, 315–20
Dulles, John Foster: on Chinese aggression, 41–42; on defense of Taiwan, 64; domino theory and, 129; evaluation of, 50; and Geneva conference, 45–46, 52, 54, 57–58; on Philippine defense, 135; and U.S.-led coalition in Indo-China, 42–43, 44, 45; on U.S. intervention, 51, 52, 74; on Vietnamese leadership, 129
Duncanson, Dennis J., 457
Duong Dinh Thao, 589
Duong Van Minh: after Ngo Dinh Diem overthrow, 168; and elections of 1967, 363; and fall of Saigon, 767; fate of, 771; as military junta leader, military situation faced by, 175; ousting of, 177–78; and overthrow of Ngo Dinh Diem, 164, 718; on Paris peace agreement, 693; surrender to North Vietnamese, 770; U.S. opinion of, 176; and U.S. support, 170
Du Quoc Dong, 248

eagle flights, 130–31, 379
Easter Offensive (1972), 651–55; fall of Quangtri, 656–59; impact of, in North Vietnam, 692; South Vietnamese army performance in, 659–62; U.S. air support in, 676; U.S. reaction to, 655–56, 662–63
economic aid, Chinese, to North Vietnam, 184
economic aid, Soviet: to North Vietnam, 184; to Socialist Republic of Vietnam, 836, 845
economic aid, U.S.
to Laos, 106
to North Vietnam: as peace negotiation incentive, 228–29
to Socialist Republic of Vietnam, 796, 860–61, 896
to Southeast Asia, 135
to South Vietnam: in 1957, 86; in 1958, 87; in 1962, 133; to 1962, 129; to 1963, 155; in 1964, 181–82; in 1965, 235; in 1968, 455; in 1973, 728–29; in 1974, 738, 741–42; in 1975, 745–46, 758–60; administration of, 642–43; direct aid to peasants, 127; Eisenhower on, 69–70, 86–87; under Johnson, 170; misdirection of, 120; necessity of, 83; Nixon on, 521; South Vietnamese dependence on, 742; for Special Forces, 163; Vietnamese control of, 127–28
economy of North Vietnam: in 1964, 183–84, 195; in 1965, 227–28; in 1967, 332–33; post-armistice, 68–69, 79; and U.S. bombing, 332–33, 651
economy of Socialist Republic of Vietnam, 844–45, 894–98, 896–97; in 1977, 797–98; in 1980s, 836, 845, 848–49, 855; in 1985, 842; in 1990s, 867–68, 873–74, 876; in 2000, 898–99
economy of Southeast Asia: in 1980s, 836; Nixon on, 522; post-WW II industrialization plans for, 12
economy of South Vietnam: in 1956, 83; in 1958, 87–88; in 1961, 107–8; in 1965, 263–64; in 1974, 738; contingency planning for peace, 322; efforts to bolster, 113; post-armistice, 69; post-Paris peace agreement, 734–35; U.S. efforts to improve, 170; U.S. impact on, 455–56
Eden, Anthony, 28–29, 44, 46, 49, 53, 57, 61
education in South Vietnam: in 1966, 294; in 1968, 457
Efaw, Fritz, 788
Eisenhower, Dwight D.: on aid to South Vietnam, 69–70, 86–87; anti-communist coalition-building efforts, 42–43, 44; on communist aggression, 57; critiques of, 52; on domino theory, 42–44; on Geneva settlement (1954), 57–58; on Philippine defense, 135; psychology of, 633, 634; response to Laos invasion, 95–96, 97; on U.S. involvement in Vietnam, 43, 52; on Vietnam War, 271
elections
in Geneva settlement (1954), 58, 65, 75, 78, 81, 84
in Laos, 122
Nixon proposal for (1969), 514

in South Vietnam: in 1967, 363–64, 367–69; Buddhist agitation for, 295–301; government suppression of, 127; impossibility of, 113; local, 361, 544, 615; Nixon on, 565
elephants, as victims of Vietnam War, 474–75
Ellsberg, Daniel, 627–29, 789–90
El Salvador, U.S. policy in, 814–16
Ely, Paul, 71, 74
embargo of Socialist Republic of Vietnam, 796, 860, 866, 870–74, 896
Emergency Civil Liberties Committee, 181, 624–25
entertainment for U.S. troops, in 1968, 458–59
environment, as victim of Vietnam War, 474–75
See also defoliation
escalation, U.S.: in 1964, 185–86, 186, 188–89, 195–96, 198; in 1965, 215–17, 242–44, 244–45, 250–52, 252, 254–55; in 1966, 308–9; in 1967, 359–60, 360–61, 365, 369, 371, 377; in 1968, 418–21, 422–25, 428–29, 432; advisor status of U.S. troops dropped, 217–18; combat troops' arrival, 222–24; debate over, 191–92, 196–97, 198–200, 215–17; European allies on, 205–6; under Kennedy, 186; overview of, in Pentagon Papers, 623; U.S. combat role asserted, 217–18 *See also* bombing (U.S.) in North Vietnam; combat troops, U.S.
Etherington-Smith, Gordon, 210
European Defense Community, 59

F-104 Starfighters, 310
Fall, Bernard B., 330
family law, in South Vietnam, under Ngo Dinh Diem, 150
fear, as Viet Cong weapon, 118–20, 159, 239, 319, 494, 557, 717, 746
Federal Bureau of Investigation (F.B.I.), surveillance of anti-war movement, 786–87
Felt, Harry D., 92–93
fifth column. *See* communist infiltration of South Vietnam
films about Vietnam War, 810–12, 827–31
fine arts, Vietnam in, 829
fire: Buddhist suicide by, 141–42, 273, 303; U.S. Quaker's suicide by, 273–74
Fire in the Lake (FitzGerald), 685–86
First Amendment, and Pentagon Papers, 629–31
Fishel, Wesley R., 86
Fisher, Adrian S., 614
FitzGerald, Frances, 685–86
flame throwers, in search and destroy missions, 136
floods, in South Vietnam, U.S. aid for, 109, 110
flower power, 351
Fontainebleau conference (1946), 5, 6, 17
food, war-induced shortages in, 18
Foot, Michael, 344
Ford, Gerald: amnesty program, 743–44; congressional opposition to, 754–55; on domino theory, 754, 755; on fall of Cambodia, 759; and fall of South Vietnam, 757, 758–60, 767–70; and Mayagüez incident, 779–80; on U.S. commitments, 765, 773
foreign policy, U.S.: under Carter, 794–95; on Chinese intervention in Vietnam, 41–42, 42–44; on colonialism, 15; on communist aggression, 57, 58; on containment in Asia, 13, 14–15, 28, 29, 30–31, 32, 41, 44; critique of (1954), 50; on Geneva settlement (1954), 57; impact of Vietnam War on, 835–36; importance of Indo-China to, 6, 39–40; in Indo-China, in 1978, 806; on Indo-Chinese self-rule, 20–21, 43; under Johnson, 169–70, 178–79, 195–96, 205, 215–17, 245–48, 253–54, 634, 635–37, 890; under Kennedy, 634–35; in Laos, 121; lessons of Dienbienphu (1954), 49–50; under Nixon, 521–22, 710–11; overthrow of Ngo Dinh Diem, 162–63; overview of, 623, 631–37; and Pentagon Papers, 623, 625–26; on post-WW II Asia, 4–5, 5, 14, 15; in Vietnam, 185 *See also* escalation; intervention, U.S.
Formosa: impact of Geneva settlement (1954) on, 62; as target of communist aggression, 29
Formosa resolution, 244
Forrest, James H., 790
Fort Jackson Eight, 510
Four Points, 285, 333–34, 436, 503
foxholes and tunnels, Viet Cong, 306, 382, 384, 893–94
fragging, 642
France
agreement with China on Indo-China, 53–54
cost of Vietnam war, 20–22, 24, 28, 31, 36–37
domestic politics: and commitment to Southeast Asian defense, 31–33; Constitution of 1946, 6; and draft, 32; post-WW II conflicts in, 6; and Viet Nam policy, 14–15
foreign policy: agreements of 1946, 17; Asian *vs.* European priorities in, 30–32, 33; importance of Indo-China to, 6, 39–40; on international intervention in Indo-China, 45; Paris Agreements of March 8, 1949, 15, 22; political undermining of Viet Nam Republic, 12, 13, 15; poor quality of, 32; on self-rule in Indo-China, 21, 28, 33, 35, 36
at Geneva Conference, 48–49
post-armistice: in Cambodia, 74; relations with North Vietnam, 68, 73; in South Vietnam, 71, 74; Vietnamese hatred of, 11; Vietnamese request for withdrawal, 65; withdrawal strategies, 35–36, 40
public attitudes about Vietnam involvement, 27, 32, 36
recognition of communist China, 178, 179
solutions for Vietnam: forced negotiations theory, 205; neutralist solution, 152–53, 178, 182, 205–6
See also colonialism, French; *entries under* French
Free Democratic Party, 92
free-fire zones, 567
French army in Vietnam
critique of, 50
at Dienbeinphu, 38, 40, 47–48
leadership, 25–27
military position: in 1946–1947, 7, 8–9, 12; in 1949, 15; in early 1950s, 19, 23–24, 26, 28, 32, 33–35; in 1954, 40, 51, 62
morale, 26–27, 33–34, 37, 50
strategy, 36–37
troop strengths and readiness, 31–32, 34–35, 35–36, 37
French community in South Vietnam: decline of, 80; dislike of America, 76, 77–78; opposition to Ngo Dinh Diem, 76, 78; Vietnamese dislike of, 77
French Union, 13, 15; efforts to preserve, 35; U.S. policy on, 20–21
Friendly Fire (TV play), 810, 811, 812
Fulbright, J. W.: on bombing of Cambodia, in 1973, 725; on cost of War, 138; on Nixon peace overtures, 588; on nuclear arms, 412–13; Pentagon Papers and, 628; on Tonkin Gulf resolution, 582, 583, 881; on U.S. in Vietnam, 292–94, 373; on Vietnamization of War, 558

Galard-Terraube, Genevieve de, 47
Galbraith, John Kenneth, 575
Gardner, Fred, 510
Garwin, Richard L., 412–13
General Mobilization Law (South Vietnam, 1968), 494
Geneva Accords (1954), 55–57; and bombing of North Vietnam, 214; as cause of Vietnam War, 717; compliance in 1970, 566; Eisenhower on, 43; elections in, 58, 65, 75, 78, 81, 84; enforcement of, 63–64, 71, 93–94; implementation of, 66, 67; on jet aircraft, 182; and Laos, 202, 203; in North Vietnamese negotiations, 285; North Vietnam manipulation of, 111, 174; political complications of, 45; as restriction on U.S. in Vietnam, 110–11, 113; settlement options, 40–41, 44–45, 46, 48–49, 51, 53–54; significance and impact of, 61–63; South-Vietnamese rejection of, 81; U.S. reaction to, 57–59; Viet Minh reaction to, 61
Geneva Conference on Far Eastern affairs (1954), 38, 40, 45–46
Geneva conference on Laos (1961–62), 124, 125–26
Geneva Convention, and U.S. conduct in Vietnam, 607, 608

geopolitical power, post-WW II, 4–5
Gillespie, Francis J., 23–24
Gillette, Guy Porter, 600–601
Going After Cacciato (O'Brien), 810
Goldberg, Arthur J., 283, 286, 377
Goldwater, Barry: international opinion of, 245; on pardon of deserters, 793; on U.S. escalation, 188, 191–92; Vietnam policies, 196–97
Gorbachev, Mikhail, 849
Gottlieb, Sanford, 790
government of North Vietnam, 194–95; diplomatic contact with, history of, 435; at Paris peace talks, 449, 453–54, 464, 502–3 (*See also* negotiations); policy on negotiations, 227, 235–36, 258, 262, 283, 284, 285, 331, 333–34, 341, 343–44, 365, 371, 432–33, 434–36, 436, 448–49, 451, 464, 481–82, 484, 485–86, 487–90, 492, 503, 508, 526, 545, 564–65, 588–89, 677, 691; post-armistice, 73; on U.S.-Chinese talks, in 1972, 648–49
government of South Vietnam: alternatives to Ngo Dinh Diem, 129; corruption and inefficiency of, 92, 108, 113, 117, 120, 362–63, 388, 457, 539, 633; effectiveness of as key to victory, 135–36; impact of Tet Offensive on, 401; on internationally-supervised elections, 514; leadership vacuum in, 674–75; at local level, 318; on Nixon *vs.* Johnson policies, 485, 487; peasant's dislike of, 362–63; policy on negotiations, 289, 322–23, 434, 436, 486–90, 490–91, 491–92, 509; power centers in, 143; power *vs.* Viet Cong, 118–19; territory controlled by, 361, 386, 408, 442, 542–44; Tet Offensive and, 416, 442; traditional Tet shutdown, 388; U.S. power over, 166–67, 456–57, 642–43; U.S. support for, in 1972, 663; and Vietnamization of War, 509; weakness of, 198, 199, 205, 360 *See also* reform in South Vietnam
G.R. Point (Berry), 810, 811
Gracey, Douglas D., 1, 2
Greene, Graham, 81–83
Gregory, Dick, 473–74
Griswold, Erwin N., 630
Gromyko, Andrei A.: and Laotian peace, 124, 125, 126; on peace negotiations, 321, 323
Guam conference (1967), 346–47
guerilla warfare: effectiveness of bombing against, 220; Mao Tse Tung on, 180; against North Vietnam, 112, 180, 184–85; South Vietnamese army training and, 330; strategies against, 112 (*See also* defoliation); U.S. efforts against, 101, 109–10, 130, 134, 305, 493; U.S. studies of, 108–9 *See also* terrorism
Gurfein, Murray I., 623–25, 627, 631
Guthrie, Arlo, 550
Hagerty, James C., 96
Haig, Alexander M., Jr., 703, 704, 705
Haiphong: in 1993, 868; bombing of, 306–8, 364, 655–56
Haiphong harbor: in 1993, 867–68; blockade of, 289; mining of, political risks in, 309; strategic importance of, 308, 309, 340
Hair (play), 829
Hajj, Messali, 8
Halberstam, David, 693–94
Hamburger Hill, 515–16
Hanoi: bombing of, 306–8, 364, 655–56; daily life in, 54, 79, 194, 339; diplomatic community in, 341; in Geneva peace agreement (1954), 56, 66; Viet Minh takeover of, 67–68
Hanoi Conference (1997), 884–90
Harkins, Paul D., 113, 176
Harlan, John M., 628–30, 631
Harriman, W. Averell: on Agnew, 549; and election of Nixon, 485; and Laotian peace, 124, 125; negotiations with Soviets, 257; on Nixon policies, 548, 549; and peace negotiations, 283, 284–85, 435, 449, 450, 451, 452, 453, 463–64, 487, 488, 495, 496–97, 505; as POW liaison, 310
Hart, Frederick, 817–18
Ha Van Lau, 452, 487
Hawaii meeting (1968), 436
Hayden Tom, 845–46
Heath, Donald, 67
helicopters: flushing out Viet Cong with (eagle flights), 130–31, 379; in Laos incursion, types and roles, 599; losses, in 1965, 207; in medical evacuation, 478–81; in Operation Junction City (1967), 344–45; tactical uses of, 112, 129, 260, 305; vulnerability of, 112, 146; and weather, 130
Henderson, Oran K., 612, 614
Herr, Michael, 799–800, 830
Herter, Christian A., 93
Hietduc Valley, military operations in, 525
Hill 861, battle of (1968), 391
Hill 881, battle of (1967), 355–57, 414–15
history of Vietnam, 716–17, 886–90; in North Vietnamese propaganda, 336
Hoa Hao, 66, 67, 71, 75, 89
Hoang Xuan Lam, 651
Ho Chi Minh: character and background, 7, 10, 11, 12, 19, 35, 194, 528–32; as cold war puppet, 16, 17–18, 22; communist support for, 13–14, 18; death of, 527–28; French accord with (1946), 17; French resistance to, 12; on liberation of South Vietnam, 63; and militancy of North Vietnam, 183, 227; and Ngo Dinh Diem, 86; and North Vietnamese peace conditions, 283, 284; in North Vietnamese propaganda, 79; and Paris peace negotiations (1968), 449; on peace with France, 48; popularity of, 9, 18, 68, 84, 527–28; ties to Soviets and Chinese, 340, 341; U.S. opinion of, 16; and Vietnamese independence, 5–6, 7, 8, 13, 32; on War casualties, 517
Ho Chi Minh City: in 2000, 894–95; Saigon renamed as, 770
Ho Chi Minh Trail: in 2000, 898–99; efforts to interdict, 200–201, 202–3, 280, 356–57, 482–85, 589–90, 592–93, 671; as engineer marvel, 617; volume of traffic, 108, 130, 202, 280, 483, 616–17, 650–51
Hoffman, Abbie, 542
Hoian, in Tet Offensive (1968), 393
Holbrooke, Richard, 795, 796, 836
Hong Kong, as target of communist aggression, 29
Hong Samrin, 807
Honolulu conference: of 1963, 169–70; of 1966, 289–91, 295
Hoopes, Townsend, 609
Hoppenot, Henri, 79
Ho Tan Quyen, 165
Hue: anti-U.S. sentiment in, 648; civil unrest in, 296, 299; in Easter Offensive, 657–58, 660; in Geneva peace agreement, 56; in Tet Offensive, 399–400, 405–6, 409, 416–17
Humphrey, Hubert H.: and Democratic platform of 1968, 466–68; and election of 1968, 429, 486; inspection tour of Vietnam (1966), 291–92; and negotiation offers to North Vietnam, 1965, 283; presidential nomination 1968, 469–71; on prospects for peace, 435; on riots at 1968 Chicago Democratic Convention, 474
Huntley, Chet, 154
Hunynh Van Cau, 133
Huu Xuan, ousting of, 177
Huynh Van Cao, timidity of, 168

Iadrang River valley battle, 1965, 276–79, 283
identity cards, 382
independence: Annamese independence movement, 1–2, 4, 5, 8–9, 12; Asian choice of paths to, 12; from French rule, 5–6, 7, 8–9; for South Vietnam, 65, 76, 83 *See also* colonialism; nationalism
India: and Geneva settlement, 40; neutralism of, 183; SEATO and, 65
Indo-China: economic and strategic importance of, 18, 21, 39–40, 43, 52, 633, 765; in French foreign policy, 6; Soviet-Chinese struggle over, in 1970s, 805–6; symbolic value for French and U.S., 39–40; United States foreign policy on, 20–22; U.S. power in, in 1980s, 835–37 *See also* Chinese invasion threat in Indo-China; Southeast Asia
Indonesia: impact of Geneva settlement on, 62; independence movement in, 12
infiltration. *See* communist infiltration of South Vietnam
infrared search equipment, U.S., 305

infrastructure in South Vietnam: as anti-communist measure, 91; construction post-Paris peace agreement, 734; U.S. construction of, 718; Viet Cong impact on, 263–64 *See also* sabotage
In Retrospect: The Tragedy and Lessons of Vietnam (McNamara), 877–79
Institute of Secular Affairs of the Unified Buddhist Church, 297, 303
intellectuals, South Vietnamese, on future of South Vietnam, 673–75
intelligence, military: of communist offensives in 1962, 124–25; faulty, at Dienbienphu (1954), 49–50; Operation Phoenix, 462–63, 494–95, 615, 823–24; peasants as key to, 117, 118, 119, 127; Pentagon Papers' description of, 632–33; South Vietnamese, 126–27, 158, 462–63, 477; South Vietnamese failure to act on, 139, 141; surveillance flights over North Vietnam, 483, 484; U.S., 109–10, 477
International Control Commission for Cambodia, 389
International Control Commission for Laos, 125
International Control Commission for Vietnam: efforts to revive, 99; Hanoi offices, 341; and U.S. involvement in South Vietnam, 110–11
International War Crimes Tribunal of Earl Russell, 357–58
interrogation of prisoners: by South Vietnamese, 401, 410, 462, 494–95
interrogation of villagers: by South Vietnamese army, 119–20, 120, 128; by U.S. Marines, 321
intervention, U.S.: debate over, 51–52, 111, 113, 134, 173–74, 209; depth of commitment, in 1962, 133; Dulles on, 51, 52; factors in, 167; France and, 45–46, 110; goals of, under Johnson, 195–96; history of, 129; Kennedy on, 109–10, 115; and public opinion in Vietnam, 134 *See also* escalation, U.S.
Iron Triangle, pacification efforts in, 338–39
Istiqlal movement (Morocco), 8

Jacobson, George, 398
Japan: impact of Geneva settlement (1954) on, 62; occupation of Vietnam, 716–17; post-WW II incitement of nationalism by, 2, 4, 10, 11
Javits, Jacob K., 725, 736
jet fighters, introduction of, 182, 193
Johnson, Lyndon B.: accession to presidency, 170; on air strikes in North Vietnam, 188–89, 198, 211, 222, 229, 233, 287, 364–65; on anti-war movement, 258–59, 273, 300–301, 353; appointment of South Vietnamese ambassador, 250; on atomic weapons in Vietnam, 412–13; congressional support for, 188, 189–91, 212, 218, 244–45, 245–46, 250, 254, 259, 314, 352–53, 354, 364, 366, 372–73, 373–74, 377, 419, 422–25; and Democratic platform of 1968, 466–67; on deployments to Vietnam, 254–55; domestic programs, and cost of War, 347–48; and election of 1964, 199; on election of 1968, 481–82; on escalation of war, in 1964, 196; evaluation of presidency, 710; evasive stance on war, 243–44; on foreign policy progress, 178–79; foreign policy under, 169–70, 178–79, 195–96, 205, 215–17, 245–48, 253–54, 604–11, 634, 635–37, 890; Guam conference (1967), 346–47; Hawaii conference (1968), 436; on importance of Vietnam War, 258, 371, 373; Kennedy (R. F.) on, 426–28; negotiation offers to North Vietnamese, 228–29, 232, 233, 235–36, 243, 255, 257–58, 262–63, 273, 283–85, 321–23, 365, 370–71, 428, 431–33, 433–34, 434–36; on negotiations with National Liberation Front, 342; on neutralized Vietnam plan, 178–79; on North Vietnam aggression, 210, 211–12, 215; in North Vietnamese propaganda, 337; Pacific tour (1966), 322–27; on Paris negotiations, 448–49, 481–82; peace pressures on, in 1966, 331; on peace process, 331, 418, 459–61; press's hostility toward, 245, 246; on progress of war, 249–50, 634; psychology of, 633; reelection bid, 331, 387–88, 429–31, 433–34; on reforms in South Vietnam, in 1966, 290–91; request for U.N. peace conference, 286–87; summit with Nguyen Cao Ky, 289–91; support for South Vietnam, 170–71, 346–47, 359, 459–61; on Tet Offensive, 403–5; on U.S. strategy, 257–58; as vice-president, 107–8, 128; Vietnam policy under, 169–70, 178–79, 195–96, 196–97, 205, 215–17, 245–48, 253–54, 504; Vietnam visit (1966), 324–27; war aims, 169–70, 255
Joint Casualty Resolution Center, 793–94
Jorden, William J., 450, 451, 464, 487, 496, 502
Juin, Alphonse-Pierre, 23, 24, 27–28, 29

Kanin, Fay, 811
Kaplan, Harold, and Paris peace talks, 511
Katzenbach, Nicholas de B., 270–71
Kennedy, Edward M.: and Democratic Convention of 1968, 469, 470; on military strategy, 515; on U.S. aid commitment to South Vietnam, 742; on Vietnam policy, 754
Kennedy, John F.: on aid to South Vietnam, 110–11, 112, 156; approach to Soviets, 99–100; assassination of, 170; on Buddhist crisis, 144, 147–48, 154, 156–57; on containment, 168; and defense of Laos, 102–4, 114–15; on extent of U.S. involvement, 1962, 113; foreign policy, critique of, 634–35; on importance of Vietnam War, 155; meeting with Khruschchev (1962), 122; on price of liberty, 710; psychology of, 633, 634; and secrecy about Vietnam, 113–15; support for Ngo Dinh Diem, 143–44, 161, 162; and U.S. troops in Thailand, 121; on U.S. troops to South Vietnam, 109–10, 115; on Vietnam War progress, 130
Kennedy, Robert F.: assassination of, 452–53; diplomatic efforts by, 435; presidential bid, 426–28; on prospects for victory, 407–8, 408–9, 426–28
Kent State University shootings, 572–74, 578
Kerry, John Forbes, 617–18, 860, 872, 890–91
Khesanh: strategic importance of, 413–14; unexploded ordinance in 1990s, 874–75; U.S. defense of, 355–57, 389–91, 393, 401, 403, 410, 412, 413–16, 417–18, 425–26, 437
Khmer Rouge, takeover in Cambodia, 774–78
Kienhoa Province, pacification efforts in, 294
Killing Fields (film), 828
King, Coretta Scott, 551
King, Martin Luther, Jr.: assassination of, 438–39; on Vietnam involvement, 299–300, 348–49, 351, 354
Kirkpatrick, Jeane J., 815
Kissinger, Henry M.: on fall of South Vietnam, 767; as foreign policy adviser, 597; on Mayagüez incident, 779, 780; and Paris peace talks, 485, 676–77, 687–92, 697–99, 701–3, 702–3, 703–5, 709, 711–13; and U.S. warnings to Soviet Union, 663; on U.S. aid commitment to South Vietnam, 742; on War, 597
Koch, Edward I., 792
Komer, Robert W., 347, 442, 462
Kong Le, 95, 98, 121
Kontum, in Tet Offensive, 397
Korea, U.S. withdrawal under Carter, 795
Koster, Samuel W., 609–10
Kosygin, Aleksei N.: on defense of North Vietnam, 210, 211, 212, 214; and peace negotiations, 343
Kotouc, Eugene M., 612, 614
Kovic, Ron, 787–89, 828–29
Krushchev, Nikita, 122, 125, 126
Kuomintang (Chinese Government party): post-revolution, 13; support for Viet Minh party, 7
Kwangtung, anti-communist resistance in, 29

La Chambre, Guy, 65
Ladejinsky, Wolf, 86
Laichan, French defense of, 34
Lai Hou Tai, 77
Laird, Melvin R.: on bombing in South Vietnam, 508, 699; on economic aid to South Vietnam, 642; and troop withdrawals, 565; on U.S. withdrawal, 670
Lake, W. Anthony, 794
Lalande, André, 47

Lamoreaux, Lewis S., 275–76
land reform in South Vietnam: communist subversion of, 89; government efforts, 120; by Viet Cong, 119
language, English supplanting of French, 78, 80
Laniel, Joseph, 47, 48, 57
Lansdale, Edward G., 129
Lao Dong, 785
Laos: air attacks on communist supply lines, 202–3, 207, 280, 283; air defenses, Chinese bolstering of, 206–7; allied incursions in, 282, 589–94, 596–99, 601–2, 616–17; cease-fire expectations in, in 1973, 711, 712, 713; Chinese post-WW II occupation of, 2; civil war in, 94, 99–104, 114–15, 122–26; communist aggression in, 94–98, 104, 136, 193; communist propaganda in, 106, 107; as communist staging area, 123, 124, 200, 201, 202–3, 414, 418, 634; communist strategy in, 121–22; communist takeover of, 783–84; communist terrorism in, 91; culture and people of, 104–6; diplomatic recognition of, 15, 16; French peace proposals for, 48; as French protectorate, 13; and Geneva peace agreement, 49, 55, 56, 57, 63; geography of, as hurdle for conventional forces, 96–97; government of, 99–100; Kennedy on defense of, 102–4; North Vietnamese in, 93, 94–95, 97, 98, 100, 238, 565, 566–67; popular discontent in, 106–7; refugees from (1977), 790–91; royal family of, 106; in Sino-French peace agreement, 53, 54; Soviet aid to rebels in, 99–101; U.S. support for, 20–21, 99–101, 102–4, 122; Viet Minh attacks in, 34, 47, 61; Vietnamese aggression in 1978, 801–2, 805
See also bombing (U.S.) in Laos
La Thanh Nghe, 363
Lavelle, John D., 732
laws of war, and U.S. conduct, 604
Layton, John B., 374
Lebanon, independence from France, 5, 6
Lederer, William J., 88–89
Le Duan, 195, 527, 845
Le Duc Tho, 464, 487, 697, 704, 705, 709, 845
Lee Quang Tang, 163
Le Guang Chanh, 342
Le Minh Dao, 176–77
Le Quang Tung, 152, 161, 164, 165
Letourneau, Jean, 23, 24
Le Van Hao, 658
Le Van Kim, 176, 177
Le Van Vien, 75, 76, 78
Liberation Radio, 296–97, 741
Li Mi, 30
Lin, Maya Yang, 816–18
Liu Kwei-po, 68
Locninh, attack on (1968), 476
Lodge, Henry Cabot: as ambassador, 143, 148, 155, 250–51, 347; and Buddhist crisis of 1963, 154; consultation with Johnson, 169–70; and Humphrey tour of 1966, 291; Long An inspection tour, 176–77; on Ngo Dinh Diem regime, 162–63; on Ngo Dinh Nhu, 155–56; and Paris peace talks, 501–3, 511; and U.S. support for military regime, 171; on Viet Cong attacks on Saigon, 504
Long Boret, 776
Lon Nol: critique of, 566–67; request for U.S. aid, 568, 570; and SEATO, 726; seizure of power by, 562–64; status of government, July 1970, 584; surrender of power, 807; U.S. support of, 733
Lord, Winston, 871–72
loss of Vietnam War, cause of, 837
Lo Van Vien, 66, 67
Luce, Philip A., 181
Lynd, Staughton, 230
Ly Thi Van, 750–51
Ly Van Sau, 650

MacDonald, Malcolm, 124
U.S.S. *Maddox,* 187, 188–89, 881, 882
Maddox, Lester G., 470, 547
Magnum, P.I. (TV show), 828
Mai Chi Tho, 842
mail, between North and South Vietnam, 193
Mailer, Norman, 374, 473
Malaya, impact of Geneva settlement (1954) on, 62
Malik, Yakov A., 565
Manila conference (1966), 321–23, 327, 373
Manila declaration, 64, 65
Mansfield, Mike: on aid to South Vietnam, 69; on bombing of Cambodia, in 1973, 725; on congressional support in 1968, 424; on cost of War, 138; on Johnson style, 246; on negotiations, 232; on progress of War, 254; on South Vietnamese police, 144; support for Johnson policies, 188; on U.S. commitment, 233; on Vietnam policy, 506
Mao Tse Tung, on guerilla warfare, 180
Marshall, George C., 24, 634
Marshall, Thurgood, 600–601, 630
martial law in South Vietnam: in Buddhist crisis of 1963, 147, 148, 151, 152; during overthrow of Ngo Dinh Diem, 161; in Tet Offensive (1968), 401
Martin, Graham A., 767
Marty, Andre, 7
*M*A*S*H* (TV show), 829
Mayagüez incident, 779–80
McCain, John, 872, 890
McCarthy, Eugene J.: and anti-war movement, 550–51, 551; on Democratic platform of 1968, 466–67; and election of 1968, 469, 472; presidential bid (1968), 426–28
McCormack, John W., 52
McGarr, Lionel C., 101
McGovern, George: and anti-war movement, 551, 575, 618; and election of 1968, 469, 470–71; Hanoi's backing of, 677; on Nixon Vietnam policy, 506–7, 691–92; on repeal of Tonkin Gulf resolution, 582; Vietnam platform, 686–87
McKissick, Floyd, 352
McNamara, Robert S.: on air strikes in North Vietnam, 211, 309, 365–67, 656; attempt on life of, (Saigon, 1964), 334–35; on lessons of Vietnam, 877–79, 884–90; on military buildup, in 1965, 232; on needed deployments, in 1967, 359; on North Vietnam aggression, 233–35; in North Vietnamese propaganda, 334–35, 337; Pentagon Papers and, 623, 632; pledge of U.S. support, 170–71; on population under South Vietnamese control, 408; on prospects for U.S. victory, 130, 157, 386; on resettlement of peasants, 116; in Tet Offensive, 402; on Tonkin Gulf incident, 881–82; on U.S. aid, 181–82, 186; on U.S. role in South Vietnam, 1962, 115; on Viet Cong tactics, 182; visits to Vietnam in 1990s, 881–82, 884–90; visit to Ngo Dinh Diem, 128; visit to South Vietnam (1963), 171
McNamara Line, 415
McNaughton, John T., 635
Meadlo, Paul, 613
Medals of Honor, 306
medical care
  by South Vietnamese doctors, 416–17
  U.S., 417–18, 803, 804; amputation rate, 479; field hospitals, 417–18; quality of, 478–81
  for villagers, 120, 316
Medina, Ernest L., 612–14
Mekong delta: overview of, 146; in Tet Offensive (1968), 399; U.S. patrols in, 377–84; Viet Cong activity in 1963–64, 145–47, 168, 171, 174–75, 176; Viet Cong activity in 1971, 615, 616; Viet Cong activity in 1973, 734–35
Melby, John, 24
Mendés-France, Pierre, 53, 55–56, 57, 58
MIAs. *See* Missing in Action (MIA) soldiers
military aid, British, to French, 15
military aid, Chinese: to Laos, 206–7; to North Vietnam, 114, 206–7, 279–80; to Viet Minh regime, 23, 28, 29, 32, 34, 37, 38, 41
military aid, North Vietnamese, to Pathet Lao, 100
military aid, Soviet: to North Vietnam, 280, 335, 653; to Pathet Lao, 99–101
military aid, U.S.
  to Cambodia, training, 74
  to French Indo-China: direct, 45–46; evaluation of, 49–50; financial, 15, 20–21, 21–22, 23–24, 30, 33, 35–36, 41, 42; withdrawal of, 71
  to Laos, 99–101, 102–4
  Johnson on, 108

to South Vietnam: in 1958, 87; in 1961, 109–10, 110–11, 111–12; in 1962, 114, 115, 133; to 1963, 155; in 1964, 181–82, 186, 200–201; in 1965, 232–33, 235; in 1969, 535; in 1973, 712; in 1975, 753–54, 758–60; air defenses, 210; combat support, 111–12; corrupting aspects of, 135, 175; Eisenhower's offer of, 69–70; post-Paris peace agreement plans for, 696–97, 708; reconnaissance, 111; threats to cut (1963), 153–54, 155–56; training, 70–71, 101, 108, 110, 111, 112, 115, 327–31, 535–36, 538

Military Assistance Advisory Group, assassination attempts against, 89–90

military junta in South Vietnam (1963–64): leadership, U.S. opinion of, 176; ousting of, 177–78; overthrow of Ngo Dinh Diem, 160–68

militia, South Vietnamese, 543, 659

mining of ports in North Vietnam, 662–63, 699–700, 704; debate over, 180; political risks of, 309, 662–63; removal of mines, 713

Missed Opportunities Conference (Hanoi, 1997), 884–90

missiles: North Vietnamese SAMs, 335, 653, 670; U.S. Zunis, 187, 276

missile sites, North Vietnamese, U.S. bombing of, 309

Missing in Action (MIA) soldiers: efforts to recover, 310, 796, 838–40, 843, 860, 861–62, 865–67, 870, 871–72, 879–80; and identification of remains, 793–94; number in past wars, 838; number in Vietnam War, 436, 838, 866

Mitchell, David, 551, 553

Mitchell, John N., 624

Mobilization Committee to End the War in Vietnam, 472, 473

Moch, Jules, 24

Molotov, Vyacheslav M., 46, 49, 57, 61

Mondale, Walter F., 618

Montagnards: flight from Viet Cong, 130; political sympathies, 174; training program for, 141

Mooney, Harley F., Jr., 315

Moore, Joseph H., 185, 227–28

Moore, Robin, 370

Moose, Richard, 794

Morrison, Mrs. Norman R., 542

Morrison, Norman R., 273–74, 335

Moyers, Bill D., 253, 254, 273, 290–91

Mullen, Michael, 811

Muskie, Edmund S., 469, 644

Mutual Defense Assistance Act, 20

Mutual Security Program, 41

Mylai massacre, 551–54; international reaction, 551–54; and moral dilemma of war, 556–57; trial, 595–96, 611–15; as war crime, 608–9

Mytho, Viet Cong attacks on (1969), 506

Nam Il, 49

napalm: in bombing of North Vietnam, 226–27; friendly-fire casualties from, 666–67; uses and effects of, 226–27, 305

Nasser, Gamal Abdel, 257

National Governors Conference (1967), opinion of War at, 371–72, 377

National Guard: Kent State shootings, 572–74, 578; mobilization of, 419

National Guardian, 180

nationalism in Asia: communist fomenting of, 5, 6, 7–8, 10–11, 14; Japanese fomenting of, 2, 4, 10, 11; leadership of, 12, 18; origins of, 10; post-WW II surge in, 1–8, 10–12; in South Vietnam, 77–78 *See also* independence

National League of M.I.A.-P.O.W. Families, 839, 860, 862, 871

National Liberation Front: Chinese opinion of, 341; history of, 717; North Vietnamese support for, 333, 334; and Paris peace negotiations, 481–82, 489, 492, 494–95, 501–3; on peace prospects, in 1966, 287; and South Vietnam elections, 293; U.S. negotiations with, in 1967, 341–42; U.S. willingness to negotiation with, 228

National Mobilization Committee to End the War in Vietnam, 374–77, 499–500

National Revolutionary Movement, 92

natural resources of Southeast Asia, as incentive for conquest, 12, 18

Navarre, Henri-Eugène, 36, 37, 49, 52

Navarre Plan, 49–50

negotiations
- in 1967, 343–44
- in 1972, 701–3
- with China, secret (1964), 205
- Johnson offers of: in 1964, 193; in 1965, 228–29, 232, 233, 235–36, 243, 255, 257–58, 262–63, 273, 283–85; in 1966, 321–23; in 1967, 365, 370–71, 433–34; in 1968, 428, 431–33, 434–36
- Johnson on, 418; in 1968, 459–61
- mediation efforts, in 1965, 217–18, 257
- Nixon offers of: in 1970, 586–89; in 1972, 662, 669
- Nixon on, 265–66
- North Vietnamese policy on, 227, 235–36, 258, 262, 283, 284, 285, 331, 333–34, 341, 343–44, 365, 371, 432–33, 434–36, 436, 448–49, 451, 464, 481–82, 484, 485–86, 487–90, 492, 503, 508, 526, 545, 564–65, 588–89, 677, 691, 889–90; Four Points, 285, 333–34, 436, 503; sources of, 341
- Paris peace talks, 1968, 450–52, 463–64, 481–82; agreement to halt bombing, 486–90; debate leading to, 448–49; election of Nixon and, 485–86; North Vietnam exploitation of, 449, 453–54, 464; procedural issues in, 489, 491–92; soldiers' opinions of, 465–66; U.S.-South Vietnamese quarrels over, 486–87, 489–90; and U.S. elections, 486; Viet Cong in, 289, 492
- Paris peace talks, 1969: Nixon's approach to, 526; opening of, 495–97; procedural issues in, 495–97; U.S. criticisms of, 503–4; U.S. proposals, 501–3; Viet Cong proposals, 511–12, 514
- Paris peace talks, 1970–1972, 586–89, 593–94, 595, 649–50
- Paris peace talks agreement (1972), 687–95, 705–6, 711–13; breakdown in negotiations, 697–99, 702; efficacy of, 737–38, 746–47; Kissinger on, 711, 713; Nguyen Van Thieu on, 763, 764; Nixon on, 707–9; promise of aid to North Vietnam in, 796; resumption of negotiations, 702–3, 703–5; signing of, 719–21; soldiers' reaction to, 713–14; South Vietnamese and, 690, 691, 693, 694–95, 703; South Vietnam in, 697–98; U.S. commitment to, 694–95
- with Socialist Republic of Vietnam, in 1977, 794, 796–97
- South Vietnamese in, in 1968, 481–82
- South Vietnamese policy on: in 1966, 289, 322–23; in 1968, 434, 436, 486–87, 490–91
- South Vietnamese public opinion on, in 1968, 437
- U.S. conditions for, 218–19, 224–25, 258
- and U.S. election of 1968, 331
- with Viet Cong, 228–29, 285, 289, 341–42, 492, 497
- Viet Cong policy on, 503, 588–89, 763
- *See also* Geneva Conference on Far Eastern affairs (1954)

Negre, Louis A., 600–601

Nehru, Jawaharial, 183

Neo-Destour party (Tunisia), 7

Neo Lao Hak Sat party, 95

Netherlands: colonial revolts post-WW II, 3–4; and Indonesian independence, 12

neutralized Vietnam: Chinese policy on, 205; as communist victory, 173, 174; coup of 1964 and, 178; debate over, 182–83, 198, 200, 205–6, 217; de Gaulle plan for, 152–53, 178–79; French version of, 182; South Vietnamese objections to, 165, 166, 170–71; U.S. policy on, 636; Viet Cong plans for, 209

New-Life village program, 291, 292 *See also* relocation of peasants

New Mobilization Committee to End the War in Vietnam, 550

New York Times, and Pentagon Papers: debate over publication, 625–26; halting of publication, 623–25; Supreme Court decision on, 626–27, 629–31

Ngo Dinh Can, 92, 127, 141, 164, 174

Ngo Dinh Diem: accession to Presidency, 79, 84; advisers and confidants, 86, 92, 147;

assassination attempt on, 84; and Buddhist crisis (1963), 141–42, 143, 147, 148–49, 150; character and background, 66, 76, 84–86; and command of South Vietnamese army, 112, 126–27; on communist threat, 87–88; on Geneva pact elections, 81, 84; leadership of, 74–75, 86, 88, 126, 127–28, 129, 141; meeting with Johnson (1961), 107–8; military strategy of, 175; North Vietnam terrorism and, 90; overthrow and death of, 160–62, 162–63, 163–65, 166–68, 634, 718; policies and programs, 76, 77, 79–80, 85, 87–88, 90–91; political pressures on, 66–67, 68, 69–70, 71, 73, 75–76, 78, 92, 141; popularity of, 84–85, 92, 126, 127, 141, 154, 156, 161, 165, 168; on South Vietnamese army, 71; U.S. support for, 74, 113, 117, 129, 143–44, 145, 148, 150, 154–55, 155–56, 161, 162–63; and U.S. aid, 127–28; and U.S. reform plans, objections to, 127–28; as U.S. puppet, 717

Ngo Dinh Luyen, 92

Ngo Dinh Nhu: and Buddhist crisis (1963), 147, 151, 152, 154; character and background, 92; controversy surrounding, 166; influence of, 126, 127; Kennedy on, 154–55; neutralist Vietnam and, 165, 166; overthrow and death of, 160, 163–65; and pacification program, 127, 174; U.S. requests for removal of, 155–56; on U.S. military advice, 175

Ngo Dinh Nhu, Madame: and Buddhist crisis (1963), 148, 149–50, 151, 152, 154, 336; controversy surrounding, 92, 166; influence of, 127

Ngo Dinh Thuc, 127, 155, 164, 174

Ngo Trong Hieu, and overthrow of Ngo Dinh Diem, 164

Nguyen Cao Ky: on covert operations in North Vietnam, 184; and elections of 1967, 363, 367–69; Hawaii meeting with Johnson, 436; and Johnson visit to Vietnam, 324; leadership of, 363, 457; on negotiations, 289, 342; and Paris peace negotiations, 489, 503; on peace prospects, in 1968, 460; political challenges faced by, 251, 295–97, 297–99, 300–301, 302–3; on progress of war, in 1967, 346; on South Vietnam reforms, 289–91; summit with Johnson, 322

Nguyen Chanh Thi, 178, 300

Nguyen Co Thach, 886, 887

Nguyen Dinh Thuan, 93

Nguyen Duc Thang, 457, 539, 823, 824

Nguyen Hai Tan, 2

Nguyen Huu Tho, 362, 785

Nguyen Khanh: anti-Americanism of, 208–9, 267; on attacks on North, 185, 189; character and background, 205; Johnson and, 179; leadership of, 193; and neutralist Vietnam, 209; overthrow of, 198, 296; overthrow of military junta, 177–78; overthrow of Tran Van Huong, 207

Nguyen Lan, 178

Nguyen Luong Bang, 785

Nguyen Manh Cam, 890

Nguyen Ngoc Loan, 399

Nguyen Ngoc Tho, 83, 90, 160, 163

Nguyen Phu Duc, 503

Nguyen Thanh Le: and Paris peace negotiations, 450, 451, 452, 464, 486, 487, 593

Nguyen Thi Binh, Mrs.: and Paris peace negotiations, 588–89, 720, 721; on U.S. aggression, 593

Nguyen Trieu Dan, 512, 589

Nguyen Van Hinh, 66–67, 73

Nguyen Van Linh, 845, 848–49, 856

Nguyen Van Loc, 401

Nguyen Van Thieu: on bombing of North Vietnam, 679; and corruption, 539; criticisms of, 754; on defense of Hue (1975), 753; definition of secure areas, 543; definition of victory, 737; and elections of 1967, 367–69; at Guam conference, 346, 347; Hawaii meeting with Johnson, 436; Kennedy (R. F.) on, 407; on Laos incursions, 589, 590; leadership of, 363, 457, 494; on negotiations, in 1968, 482, 485, 491; and Nixon, 324, 325, 522, 744–45, 763; on North Vietnam perfidy, 693; on Paris peace agreement, 690, 693, 694–95, 705–6, 707–8; and peace negotiations, 486, 487, 488, 489–90; political opposition, in 1974, 744–45; popularity of, 539; resignation, 763–65; U.S. support for, 459–61, 728–29, 753–54; on U.S. perfidy, 763, 764; on U.S. withdrawals, 517–19; on Vietnamization of War, 439–40, 522, 534, 558

Nguyen Van Tran, 72

Nguyen Van Troi, 334–35

Nguyen Van Vinh, 453

Nguyhen Thanh Le, 501

Nhatrang, in Tet Offensive (1968), 393, 397, 398

night vision equipment, U.S., 305, 309

U.S.S. *Nimitz,* commissioning of, 773–74

Nixon, Richard M.: on anti-war movement, 545, 571–72, 578–80, 618; and Cambodian intervention, 567–71, 584; China visit, 648–49; congressional criticism of, 506–7, 557–59, 568–69, 575, 581–83, 587–88, 676–77, 677–78, 741–42; and election of 1968, 421–22, 470, 485–86; and election of 1972, 690–91; foreign policy, 521–22, 710–11; on international role of U.S., in 1973, 710; on Kent State University shootings, 572; on Laos incursion, 597–98; on loss of Vietnam War, 837; mining of ports in North Vietnam, 662–63; negotiations offers, 586–89, 662, 669; in North Vietnamese propaganda, 648–49; and Paris peace agreement, 707–8; and peace negotiations, 497, 503, 508–9, 513–14, 522–23, 546, 565, 568, 595, 677; pledge to end War, 421–22; policy on missing soldiers, 862; on prisoners of war, 598; on progress of War, in 1971, 594–95; resignation, 744–45; South Vietnamese government on, 485; support for Nguyen Van Thieu, 522, 744–45, 763; support for South Vietnam, 728–29; Supreme Court nominees, 735–36; on U.S. escalation, 188; on Viet Cong attacks on Saigon, 504; and Vietnamization of War, 508–9, 513–14, 517–19, 545–46, 557–59; Vietnam policy, 265–66, 503–5, 506–7, 507–9, 524, 526, 546, 547, 568–69, 571, 594, 602–11, 610, 656, 663; visit to South Vietnam, 522–25; and War Powers Act (1973), 735–36; withdrawal of U.S. forces under, 517–19, 544–46, 564–66, 597, 668–70

Nolting, Frederick E., Jr.: and Buddhist protests, 145; leverage with South Vietnamese government, 128; on Ngo Dinh Diem government, 143–44; on prospects for South Vietnam, 113; removal of, 143; on U.S.-Vietnamese cooperation, 137

No More Vietnams (Nixon), 836–37

normalization of relations with Hanoi, 879–81; benefits of, 872; Carter and, 794, 795–96; MIA soldiers and, 866; and Vietnamese aggression in Cambodia, 854

Norodom Sihanouk: and Cambodian alignment, 51, 74, 183; character and background, 563; Chinese support for, in 1970s, 808; overthrow of, 562–64; on relations with U.S., 513; U.S. relations with, 282; on U.S. pursuits into Cambodia, 388, 389; on Viet Cong in Cambodia, 385

Norodom Suramarit, 563

North Africa, French colonial revolts in, 7

North Vietnam: air defenses, 206–7, 233, 276, 308, 336, 598–99, 602, 616, 651–52, 653, 655–56, 668; characteristics of populace, 538; Chinese support for, 72, 91, 110, 184, 214–15, 234, 238, 242, 279–80, 333, 339–41; as communist puppet, 335; daily life in, 332, 337, 650–51; as exporter of revolution, 183, 193–95, 200; fierce independence of, 335–36; free Vietnamese flight from (1954), 54, 69, 70, 74; geography and people of, 194; militancy of, 183, 184; morale, in 1967, 333–37; population, 195; relations with China, in 1967, 341; relations with France, post-armistice, 68, 73; Soviet support for, 184, 210, 211, 212, 214–15, 242–43, 333, 339–41, 663; support for Viet Cong, 130, 159, 174, 183–84, 200, 211–12, 213, 226, 242; territory controlled in South Vietnam, 361, 386,

408, 442, 542–44, 679; U.S. debate over attacks on, 180, 183–84, 184–85, 185, 189, 196 *See also* bombing (U.S.) in North Vietnam; government of North Vietnam; People's Army of (North) Vietnam (PAVN); *and specific topics*
North Vietnamese army. *See* People's Army of (North) Vietnam (PAVN)
nuclear weapons, proposed use in Vietnam, 50, 51–52, 234, 369, 412–13; in 1971, 593
Nunn, Louie B., 575
Nuttle, David, 129

O'Brien, Tim, 810, 857–58
O'Daniel, John W. "Iron Mike," 70–71, 72, 86
Office of Civil Operations, 338
Ogilvy, Richard, 575
O'Gorman, John P., 653
Operation Cedar Falls, 338, 361
Operation Dewey Canyon Three, 618
Operation Junction City, 344–45, 361
Operation Manhattan, 361
Operation Pegasus, 437
Operation Phoenix, 462–63, 494–95, 615, 823–24
Operation Rang Dong, 361
Operation Sunrise, 116–17

pacification programs, 294–95, 823; in 1960–1962, 90–91, 112, 116–17, 120, 127, 130; in 1965–1966, 267, 281, 322–23, 327, 329; in 1967–1969, 347, 361, 386, 419, 525, 542–44; in 1970–1973, 559, 584–85, 615–16, 735; and bombing campaigns, 605; and Easter Offensive (1972), 659–60; impact of Tet Offensive on, 411, 442; by U.S. Marines, 824 *See also* relocation of peasants in South Vietnam
Pacific Charter (1954), 65
Paris Agreements of March 8, 1949, 15, 22
Paris (Fontainebleau) Conference (1946), 5, 6, 17
Paris peace agreement (1972), 687–95, 705–6, 711–13; breakdown in negotiations, 697–99, 702; efficacy of, 737–38, 746–47; Kissinger on, 711, 713; Nguyen Van Thieu on, 763, 764; Nixon on, 707–9; promise of aid to North Vietnam in, 796; resumption of negotiations, 702–3, 703–5; signing of, 719–21; soldiers' reaction to, 713–14; South Vietnamese and, 690, 691, 693, 694–95, 697–98, 703; U.S. commitment to, 694–95 *See also* Paris peace talks *under* negotiations
partitioning of Vietnam, 55–57; implementation of, 66, 67
Pathet Lao movement: army size, 121; North Vietnamese support for, 183, 184; regional communist support for, 95; Soviet aid to, 99–101; strategy, 121–22; takeover of Laos, 783–84; and U.S. in Laos, 202
PAVN. *See* People's Army of (North) Vietnam
peace symbol, meaning of, 715
peasants in South Vietnam: attitude toward War, 141; characteristics of, 329; displacement of, 718–19; efforts to rally after Diem overthrow, 168; impact of Tet Offensive on, 411; impact of War on, 117–18, 315–20; as inadvertent casualties, 132, 266, 567; as key to victory, 117–21, 176–77; life of, 117; opinion of South Vietnamese army, 329; opinion of U.S. soldiers, 379; political sympathies of, 318–20; reforms desired by, 120; suffering at U.S. hands, 604–11; support for Viet Cong, 291; U.S. soldiers' opinion of, 382; Viet Cong control of, 173 *See also* civilians; pacification programs; public opinion in South Vietnam
Peck, Sidney, 472
Pen Nouth, 564
Pentagon, storming by anti-war protesters, 374–77
Pentagon Papers, 623, 631–37
  Ellsberg arrest and indictment, 627–29
  halting of publication, 623–25
  publication of: debate over, 625–26; Supreme Court on, 626–27, 629–31
People's Army of (North) Vietnam (PAVN)
  in Cambodia (1970), 562, 567–71
  defections from, 304
  in Laos, 121, 202, 601, 602
  military position: in 1968, 476–77; in 1969, 505–6, 534; in 1970, 565
  in Quangtri, in 1972, 672–73
  size and strength: in 1964, 186, 195; in 1967, 334, 360; in 1968, 421
  in South Vietnam, 234, 251, 262–63; in 1965, 279–80, 280, 281–82; in 1966, 297; in 1968, 401, 419, 476, 484; in 1969, 493; in 1972, 691; in 1975, 745–46, 750; Iadrang River valley battle (1965), 276–79; under Paris peace agreement, 691, 693, 703, 712; in Tet Offensive (1968), 394, 410
  strategy and tactics, 205; in 1967, 377; in 1968, 453–54, 475–77, 476–77; in 1969, 493; in 1971, 602; in 1972, 672–73; in Easter Offensive (1972), 654–55; in Tet Offensive (1968), 401, 403, 411
  tensions with Viet Cong, in 1966, 297
"people sniffer," 464–65
People's Revolution party, 239
People's Self-Defense Force (South Vietnam), 535, 616; in 1971, 615
Persian Gulf War, parallels with Vietnam War, 858–59
Pham Bieu Tam, 151
Pham Dang Lam, 489, 501–2, 593–94, 650
Pham Van Dong: and Death of Ho Chi Minh, 527; on determination of North Vietnam, 333–37, 597; diplomacy by, 339, 341; and Geneva settlement, 49, 55, 57, 61; on peace negotiations, 333–34; on release of prisoners, 822; on unification of Vietnam, 78
Pham Van Lieu, 291
Pham Van Phu, 749, 812–13
Phan Hien, 796–97
Phan Huy Quat, 163, 241–42
Phan Khac Suu, 201, 367
Phan Quang Dan, 92
Phan Thi Kim Phuc, 882–84
Phan Van Dong, 195
Philippines: impact of Geneva settlement (1954) on, 62–63; U.S. relations with under Carter, 795
Phnom Penh, communist takeover in, 774–75
Phoumi Nosavan, 94, 95, 121
Pignon, Leon, 13
Piper, David W., 181
plays about Vietnam War, 810–12
Pleiku: in Tet Offensive (1968), 393, 397; Viet Cong attack on (1965), 210, 211, 212, 213
Pleven, René, 24
Podgorny, Nikolai V., 283
police in South Vietnam, 330, 535; fear of, 239; press and, 144; treatment of protesters, 303; use of force, 596; violent suppression of Buddhist protesters, 144–45, 147
Pol Pot, 806, 807
Popular forces (South Vietnam), 535, 537, 543
Popular Republican Movement (France), 6
Porter, William J., 649
ports, North Vietnamese, mining of, 662–63, 699–700, 704; debate over, 180; political risks of, 309, 662–63; removal of mines, 713
Post-Vietnam Syndrome (PVS), 680–85, 781–82, 809
Pottinger, J. Stanley, 786
Powell, Jody, 792
press: access to U.S. bases, in 1972, 679; Agnew on, 547–48; and allied incursion into Laos, 591–92; casualty reports and, 277–79; hostility toward Johnson, 245, 246; in North Vietnam, 73; reporting on combat operations, in 1965, 248; in rioting, at Democratic Party Convention of 1968, 472–73; in South Vietnam, harassment of, 144, 152, 303; and television broadcasts of combat, 358–59
Princi, Peter W., 627
prisoners of war
  in Geneva peace agreement (1954), 57
  Nixon on, 598
  North Vietnamese: exchanges with South, 738; extended imprisonment of, 812–13; number of, 310; psychological scars of, 802–3; readjustment after return, 729–31; release under Paris peace accords, 721–23; treatment of, 310, 323, 726–28; U.S. efforts to recover, 649–50, 662, 688, 707, 712
  South Vietnamese: exchanges with North, 738; Tet Offensive freeing of, 393; treatment of, 128
  in Tet Offensive, 401, 410

U.S.: in 1965, 260–61; in 1968, 466; interrogation of, 261, 321; shooting of, 279; in Tet Offensive (1968), 411
Viet Cong: treatment of, 239; U.S. soldiers as, 236
See also interrogation of prisoners
propaganda
Chinese: on Chinese intervention, 280; against U.S., 43
North Vietnamese: in 1967, 335–36, 337; in 1968, 434; in 1972, 648–49; in Cambodia, 563; canbo system of, 73; in Hanoi, 79; in Laos, 94, 106, 107; against South Vietnam, 89, 91; against U.S., 70, 73, 227
of Socialist Republic of Vietnam, 798; in 1978, 805; in 1990s, 892, 893–94
South Vietnamese, 92, 238–39; in 1967, 387; weakness of, 177
Soviet, anti-Western, 59
U.S., ineffectiveness of, 312
of Viet Cong: in 1962, 119; in 1965, 238, 267; in 1966, 295, 296–97; in 1972, 648; success of, 159, 177; Tet Offensive as, 401, 402; in villages, 133
Provisional National Assembly (South Vietnam), 75
psychological problems: of POWs, 802–3; of relocated peasants, 748; of veterans, 680–85, 782–83, 803–5, 809–10; of Vietnamese refugees, 833
psychological stress, among South Vietnamese, in 1975, 747–48
psychological warfare, U.S., 387
public, U.S.: and evasive administration rhetoric, 241–42, 243–44; ignorance about Vietnam War, 113, 216, 254–55, 271, 273, 369; Johnson's attempt to mobilize, 169; North Vietnamese on, 337; reaction to War, in 1966, 311–13; will to defend freedom, 58
public opinion
in Europe: about U.S., 440–41; on Vietnam War, 205–6
in France: about Indo-China War, 27, 32, 36; about U.S., in 1968, 441
in French Indo-China, 58–59; efforts to sway, 14, 15, 18, 19, 22, 23, 24, 32, 50, 65
global: on U.S. in Laos, 202; on U.S. in Vietnam, 408
in Laos, communist efforts to sway, 121–22
in Socialist Republic of Vietnam: on lifting of U.S. embargo, 873–74; on War, 897–98
in South Vietnam: in 1962, 127, 130; about Catholics, 174; on Americans, 454, 457; apathy in, 362; in Buddhist crisis of 1963, 152; efforts to sway, 109–10, 117–21, 120–21, 177, 266–67, 289–91, 322–23, 346, 387; of government, 362–64; on outcome of War, 378; on peace negotiations, 438; peasant relocations and, 116; on resistance to communists, 113; on South Vietnamese government, 659–60; U.S. intervention and, 134; on U.S. bombing, 672–73; on Viet Cong, 493, 494–95, 659–60; on War, 315–20
in U.S.: on anti-war movement, 351; on government, in 1985, 826–27; importance of, 50; as key to victory, 304–5; on Nixon policies, 568–69, 571; and pressure for progress, 387–88; on South Vietnamese apathy, 388; of veterans, 680–85, 783, 788, 809–10, 818, 850–51; on War, 371–73, 826–27, 827–31
U.S.S. *Pueblo* incident, 411
"Puff, the Magic Dragon," 309
Pushkin, Georgi M., 124

Quangkhe, U.S. bombing of, 220, 226, 227
Quangngai, Viet Cong attacks on, in 1969, 506
Quangtri: fall of (1972), 651, 656–59, 660, 672–73; in Tet Offensive (1968), 401
Quangtrung basic training center, 535–36
Quayle, Dan, 850–51
Quiet American (Greene), 81–83
Quinhon, Viet Cong attack on, 215
Quinim Pholsena, 94–95, 126

race relations, U.S.: in 1968, 433; in armed forces, 641; rioting after King, Jr. assassination, 438–39; rioting in 1967, 359–60
See also African Americans
Radford, Arthur W., 43–44, 46, 51–52, 52, 72
Radio Hanoi, 741, 805
Ramsey, Lloyd B., 525
Raskin, Marcus, 609
Reagan, Ronald Wilson: aid to Cambodian guerillas, 836; and closing of California university system, 575; and El Salvador, 815; on MIAs, 838, 843, 862; support for Afghan insurgents, 849–950; on U.S. strategy, 369, 372
Red Cross, and North Vietnamese prisoners of war, 310, 323
Red River delta: French defense of, 34; in French-Viet Minh settlement, 53–54; in Geneva peace agreement (1954), 56
reeducation of prisoners, by South Vietnam, 128
Reedy, George, 189, 218, 222
reform in South Vietnam: efforts to encourage, in 1967, 388; government program in 1966, 322; government resistance to, in 1967, 388; as key to victory, 289–91, 291–92, 294–95, 540; land reform, 89, 120; needed reforms, 294–95; resistance to U.S. recommendations, 127–28, 137, 175
See also corruption, in South Vietnam government
refugees
in Cambodia, 761, 774–78
from North Vietnam (1954), 54, 69, 70, 74
from Socialist Republic of Vietnam, 790–91, 813–14, 855, 875–77, 882–84; anti-communist activism by, 845–46; forced repatriation of, 875–77; U.S. acceptance of, 822–23, 876; in U.S., 781–82, 790, 831–35
in South Vietnam (1975): in fall of central highlands, 750–51; in fall of Da Nang, 756, 757; in fall of Hue, 751–53; in fall of Saigon, 767–70, 770–71
South Vietnamese treatment of, 295
Regional Forces (South Vietnam), 535, 537–38, 543
Reinhardt, Frederick G., 79
religion in U.S.: anti-war movement in, 313; in armed forces, 378, 384
religion in Vietnam: sectarian political activity, 66, 67, 71, 75–76; Tran Van Huong on, 198; U.S. impact on, 454–55; U.S. refugees and, 782 *See also* Buddhists; Catholic(s)
relocation of peasants in South Vietnam (Strategic and New Life hamlets), 90–91, 112, 116–17, 127, 130, 140–41, 144, 172; bitterness engendered by, 177, 338–39; efficacy of, 174, 318–19; in Mekong delta, 174–75; military impact of, 146–47; psychological impact of, 748
reparations, Vietnamese demands for, 796–97, 860
Republican Party, U.S.: anti-Clinton activism, 863–65; opposition to Kennedy policies, 113–14
reserve forces, U.S., call to active duty, 255, 280, 281, 419, 428, 432, 439–40
Revolutionary Development Program, 559
rhinoceroses, as victims of Vietnam War, 474–75
Rhodes, James A., 572
Richardson, Elliot L., 570, 725–26
Riesman, David, 312
rioting
anti-French, post-WW II, 1, 7
in Cambodia, anti-communist, 562, 564
in South Vietnam: in 1964, 199; after overthrow of Ngo Dinh Diem, 163, 164; against Nguyen Cao Ky regime, 296, 297, 303
in U.S.: by anti-war demonstrators, 374–77, 550, 590–91, 663–65; on college campuses, 572–74, 575; by counterdemonstrators, 576–78; at Democratic Party Convention 1968, 469, 471–74; at Kent State University, 572–74, 578; after King, Jr. assassination, 438–39; race-related (1967), 359–60
See also civil unrest
Rogers, William P., 597, 624, 719, 721
Rostow, Walt W., 108, 109, 418
Rowe, James, 427
Ruff Puffs. *See* Popular forces; Regional forces
Rusk, Dean: briefing of allies by, 110; critique of, 246; on future of Southeast Asia, 836; at Geneva conference on Laos, 124, 125; on importance of Vietnam War, 373–74;

Johnson on, 326; on loss of Vietnam War, 837; on U.S.S. *Maddox* attack, 187; on negotiations, 342; and negotiations with North Vietnam, 218–19, 425, 434; in Pentagon Papers, 632; on prospects for peace, 285, 286, 287, 354; on prospects for victory, 360, 418; on stakes of Vietnam War, 292–94; transition briefings, 96; on U.S. commitment to South Vietnam, 193; on U.S. policy, in 1968, 422–25; on U.S. strategy, 262; on Viet Cong terrorism, in 1965, 257

Russell, Earl, 357–5

sabotage

in North Vietnam: in 1964, 184–85; in 1967, 356–57

in South Vietnam: in 1959, 89; in 1960, 91; in 1961, 101; in 1963, 173; in 1964, 199; in 1966, 294; in 1975, 747; government countermeasures, 90–91, 112, 116–17; of transportation lines, 263–64, 294, 356–57

Saigon

daily life in: in 1955, 80–81; in 1962, 118; under communist rule, 797–98

fall of, 766–71; communists' anniversary celebration of, 840–43; guerilla activity preceding, 746–47; panic during, 757–58

port facilities, 297

post-WW II riots in, 1, 2

renaming of, 770

Viet Cong attacks on: in 1969, 504; in Tet Offensive (1968), 394–98, 394–99, 400–401

Viet Cong attempts to isolate, 174

Sainteny, 68

Salan, Raoul, 34–35

Salinger, Pierre, 157–58, 169

Sanchez, Manolo, 579

SANE, 790

Savang Vathana, 94, 106, 783–84

Saywell, Shelley, 883

Schlesinger, James R., 753, 769, 779

Schuck, Peter H., 853

Schweitzer, Ted, 866–67

Schwinn, Douglas, 478–81, 803–5, 809

SDS. *See* Students for a Democratic Society

Seaman, Jonathan O., 344

SEATO. *See* Southeast Asian Treaty Organization

secrecy, U.S.: in Cambodian bombing, 731; and Pentagon Papers, 625–26; validity of, 113–15

Seeger, Pete, 352

Self-Defense Corps (South Vietnam), 126, 133

Sharp, U. S. Grant, Jr., 187, 364

Sheehan, Neil, 851–53

Shelepin, Aleksandr N., 283–84

Sherburne, Philip, 272

Shultz, George P., 822, 836

Shuman, Robert, 20

Sianouk, Norodom, 13

Silver Stars, 617

Sisavang Vong, 106

Sisowath Sirik Matak, 562, 564

Smith, Walter Bedell, 49, 53, 54, 56, 57

Socialist party, in France, 14

Socialist Republic of Vietnam: aggression in Indo-China, 801–2, 805–7, 835, 836, 845, 854–55; alliance with Soviet Union, 805; anniversary celebration of fall of Saigon, 840–43; art and literature in, 846–47; conflict with China, 808–9; daily life in, 797–99, 886; flight from, 790–91, 813–14, 822–23, 831–35, 845–46, 855, 875–77, 876, 882–84; government of, 784–85, 844–45; ideology in, 847–49, 856–57; normalization of relations with, 794, 795–96, 854, 866, 872, 879–81; police and security in, 842; prison camps in, 812–13; reparation demands, 796–97, 860; repressive measures and U.S. peace activists, 790–91; Soviet aid to, 836, 845; U.S. aid to, 796, 860–61; U.S. embargo of, 796, 860, 866, 870–74, 896; and U.S. MIA soldiers, 796, 840, 856–57, 870, 871–72, 873, 879–80; view of U.S., in 2000, 895–96

Soerkarno, Achmed, 10, 11

soldiers, Khmer Rouge, characteristics of, 778

soldiers, South Vietnamese: living conditions for, 330; opinion of Viet Cong, 537; opinion of War, 537 *See also* Army of the Republic of (South) Vietnam

soldiers, U.S.: anti-war activism by, 509–11; on anti-war movement, 271, 379; armaments, 305; arrival and processing in South Vietnam, 461–62; on assassination of R. F. Kennedy, 452–53; daily life of, 311, 377–84, 525, 593; drug abuse by, 532–34, 620–22, 640–41; on King Jr. assassination, 438–39; marriage to Vietnamese, 584–85; mistresses of, 259–60; and moral dilemma of war, 556–57; morale, 381, 382–83, 461; opinion of bombing of North, 466; opinion of Laos incursion, 598–99; opinion of Paris talks, 465–66; opinion of peasants, 382; opinion of South Vietnamese, 457; opinion of South Vietnamese army, 380, 592; opinion of Viet Cong, 379; opinion of War, 378–79, 381, 383, 384, 480, 492–93, 646–47; reaction to Paris peace agreement, 713–14; refusal to fight, 381–82, 525; rotation system for, 810; supplies for, 264; vocabulary of, 274–75

Songbe, Viet Cong attacks on, in 1969, 505

Songgram, Pibul, 11

Songmy massacre, 551–54; international reaction to, 554–56; and moral dilemma of war, 556–57

Son Ngoc Thanh, 51

Souphannouvong, Prince, 95, 121

Southeast Asia: anti-communist efforts in, 135–36; Chinese agenda in, 135; Chinese aggression in, 896; communist agenda in, 135; communist strategy in, 122–23; economic and strategic importance of, 135–36, 140; economy of, 522, 836; natural resources as incentive for conquest, 12, 18; Rusk on, 836; U.S. economic aid to, 135; U.S. involvement in, 135–36 *See also* Indo-China

Southeast Asian Treaty Organization (SEATO): Cambodia and, 726; and defense of Vietnam, 292, 293; demise of, 795; establishment of, 64–65; and Laos, 96, 102, 103–4, 121, 123, 124; South Vietnam and, 87, 93; U.S. commitments in, 135; U.S.-led efforts to establish, 42–43, 44, 45, 50

Southern Christian Leadership Conference, 299

South Vietnam: ambassador to U.S., 150; characteristics of people, 538; Constitution of 1956, 83–84; daily life in, in 1975, 747; fall of (1975), 770–71, 773–74, 797; geography and people of, 194; and invasion of North Vietnam, 597; morale, 416–17, 543, 673–75; North's intentions toward, 63; population, 195; post-armistice political situation, 64, 66–67, 68, 69, 71, 73, 74–75, 75–76; status as republic, 79–80 *See also* Army of the Republic of (South) Vietnam; government of South Vietnam; *and specific topics*

South Vietnamese Air Force: in 1969, 535; capabilities of, 180, 181; training, 184–85

South Vietnamese army. *See* Army of the Republic of (South) Vietnam (ARVN)

South Vietnamese Marines, in Easter Offensive (1972), 660, 661

South Vietnamese Navy, in 1969, 535

South Vietnam Liberation Front, 239

Souvanna Phouma: on bombing in Laos, 482, 485; on bombing of North Vietnam, 485; and communist takeover, 783–84; and Laotian peace settlement, 124; overthrow of, 94; reinstatement of, 121; Soviet support for, 95, 99; and U.S. bombing in Laos, 202, 204, 309

Soviet Union: in Afghanistan, 849–950; foreign policy success of, 88; at Geneva Conference (1954), 46, 49; on Johnson style, 247; Kennedy administration approach to, 99–100; in Laos, 1960–61, 94–95, 97; military power in Asia, in 1980s, 836; military prestige of, and Vietnam conflict, 40; and neutralized Vietnam, 182–83; North Vietnamese independence from, 335; policy on colonial empire, 8, 10; policy on guerilla wars, 144, 183, 184; policy on peace negotiations, 227, 257, 283–84, 321; post-WW II atomic espionage by, 4, 5; post-WW II offensive against British

Empire, 4; as power behind Vietnamese communists, 22; propaganda, anti-Western, 59; recognition of Viet Minh regime, 15, 16, 18; response to bombing of North Vietnam, 214–15, 221, 224; retreat from communist doctrine, 856; rift with China, 339–41; and Southeast Asian conflict, 28; struggle for Indo-China, 805–6, 806; support for North Vietnam, 210, 211, 212, 214–15, 242–43, 333, 339–41, 663; support for Socialist Republic of Vietnam, 809; support for Viet Minh regime, 63, 68; and U.S. withdrawal as precedent, 711; on Viet Cong in Cambodia, 388, 389
Spock, Benjamin, 349, 376, 457–58
Spring Mobilization Committee to End the War in Vietnam, 351, 352
SR-71 planes, surveillance flights over North Vietnam, 484
"starlight," 309
statistics on War: body counts as U.S. goal, 356–57; reliability of, 128, 134, 140, 158–59, 199, 304–5, 386–87, 412, 516–17, 534
Stennis, John, 582
Stephenson, Hugh, 79
Stewart, Potter, 630
Sticks and Bones (Rabe), 811, 812
Stone, I. F., 230
Strategic Hamlet program. *See* relocation of peasants
strategy and tactics
North Vietnam, 205; in 1967, 377; in 1968, 453–54, 475–77, 476–77; in 1969, 493; in 1971, 602; in 1972, 672–73; in Easter Offensive (1972), 654–55; in Tet Offensive (1968), 401, 403, 411
South Vietnam, 101, 108–9, 110, 112, 116–17, 119–20, 127, 129, 130–32, 134, 140–41, 318
United States: in 1965, 241, 252, 257–58, 262–63; in 1966, 288; in 1967, 344, 356–57, 360, 383; in 1968, 418; critiques of, 281–82, 596–97; Johnson on, 257–58; McNamara on, 365–67
Viet Cong, 130, 174; in 1964, 205; in 1965, 209; in 1966, 295, 305–6; in 1968, 401, 403; in 1971, 593, 616; in 1973, 737–38; in Mekong delta, 1963, 146; post-Paris peace agreement, 735; in Tet Offensive (1968), 401, 403, 410, 411
Student Nonviolent Coordinating Committee, 299, 376
student rebellions in South Vietnam, 1963, 151
Students for a Democratic Society (SDS), 270, 271, 272
Sullivan, William H., 702–3
Sulzberger, Arthur Ochs, 630
Sun Yatsen, 10
supply lines, North Vietnamese: efficacy of, 616–17; efforts to interdict, 200–201, 201, 202–3, 207, 226, 234, 287, 296, 332–33, 414, 415, 418, 504–5, 594–95, 646; volume of traffic, 483, 650–51
See also Ho Chi Minh Trail
Supreme Court, U.S.: on draft exemptions, 600–601; on publication of Pentagon Papers, 626–27, 629–31
Symington, Stuart, 731–32
Syria, independence from France, 5, 6

Ta Quang Buu, 56
Taylor, Maxwell D.: briefing of South Vietnamese, 201; on halt to bombing, in 1968, 432; on prospects for peace, 257, 285; on prospects for victory, 157–58, 175, 180, 192–93, 195, 258, 386; resignation of, 250–51; on South Vietnamese government, 207; South Vietnamese opinions of, 208–9; strategy recommendations, 109–10, 127, 198, 199; testimony before Congress, 293
Tayninh, attack on (1968), 476
television: combat shown on, 358–59; introduction to Vietnam, 718–19
Teng Hsiao-ping, 808
terrorism against South Vietnam, 717–18; in 1961, 104; in 1962, 113; in 1964, 180, 182, 203–4; in 1965, 257; in 1968, 476; in 1971, 616; in 1972, 679; in 1975, 746; assassinations, 89–90, 91, 101, 108, 506; bombings, 90, 203–4; government countermeasures, 90–91, 91, 119–20 (*See also* relocation of peasants); methods and results, 89, 90–91, 92; number of terrorists, 1960, 91; as Viet Cong weapon, 118–20, 159, 239, 319, 494, 557, 717, 746 *See also* sabotage
Tet Offensive (1968), 393–402, 406–7
communist strategy in, 401, 403, 410, 411
impact of, 409–12; on civilians, 477; on daily life in South Vietnam, 438; Johnson on, 403–5; on morale, 399, 416–17, 418; on North Vietnam leadership, 528; on pacification programs, 543; on South Vietnamese control, 442; on U.S. politics, 402–3, 407–9, 418–21, 422–25, 637; on U.S. public opinion, 411; on Viet Cong, 411–12, 492–93, 493–94
military situation following, 475–77
number of troops in, 410
preparations for, 389–91, 401, 410
Thailand: communist designs on, 122; communist insurgency in, 136; raids into Laos, 107; refugees from communism in, 790–91; as target of Chinese aggression, 30; U.S. bases in, in 1972, 679; U.S. military in, 121, 282; U.S. relations with, 755; Vietnamese aggression in, 801–2
Thai troops, in South Vietnam, pacification program and, 584
Than Chanh Thanh, 491
Than Van Don, and Buddhist crisis (1963), 152
Thao Moun, 783
Thich Huyen Quang, 303
Thich Tam Chau, 201, 297–98
Thich Tri Quang: anti-Americanism of, 208–9; and neutralist Vietnam, 209; protests against Nguyen Cao Ky regime, 296, 297, 298
Things They Carried (O'Brien), 857–58
13th Valley (Del Vecchio), 828
Timmes, Charles J., 126
Ton Duc Thang, 785
Tonkin delta: military situation in, 1954, 51; Vietnamese assaults, in 1954, 38–39
Tonkin Gulf incident, 187–89, 196, 881–82
Tonkin Gulf resolution, 189–91, 218, 244; attempted repeal of (1970), 581–82; and U.S. commitment to South Vietnam, 292–94
Ton That Dinh: and Buddhist crisis (1963), 152; in junta leadership, 176; ousting of, 177; and overthrow of Ngo Dinh Diem, 164
Ton That Khien, 551, 552
Tourane, in Geneva peace agreement (1954), 56
tourism in Socialist Republic of Vietnam, 893–94
trade: Asian raw materials and, 12; in North Vietnam, 339–41; in South Vietnam, 77, 87–88; U.S.-Vietnamese in 1999–2000, 895–96, 896
Tran Buu Kiem, 497, 501–2, 503; at Paris peace talks, 512
Trangbang, fighting (1972), 666–67
Tran Hoai Nam, 501
Tran Le Xuan. *See* Ngo Dinh Nhu, Madame
transportation: South Vietnamese economy and, 264; Viet Cong effect on, 263–64, 294, 356–57
Tran Thien Khiem, 462, 539
Tran Tu Oai, and Buddhist crisis (1963), 152
Tran Van Chuong, 150
Tran Van Don: and Buddhist crisis, 147, 152; in junta leadership, 176; ousting of, 177
Tran Van Huong: appointment as president, 763; Buddhist protests against, 201; character and background, 198, 764; and elections of 1967, 363, 367, 368, 539; overthrow of, 207; policies, 197–98; U.S. support for, 201
Tran Van Huu, 24
Tran Van Lam, on Paris peace agreement, 693
Tri Quang, 152
troop carriers, amphibious, tactical importance of, 129
truces, North Vietnamese exploitation of, 355
True-heart, William C., 148
Truman, Harry S: on Asian nationalism, 15; psychology of, 633; on Southeast Asian threats, 28
Truman doctrine, 754
Trung sisters, 336
Truong Chinh, 195, 527–28, 785
Truong Dinh Dzu: and elections of 1967, 367, 368; imprisonment of, 539

Tunisia: and French Union, 13; independence movements in, 7
tunnels and foxholes, Viet Cong, 306, 382, 384, 893–94

U-2 planes, 182, 197, 484
U Aung San, 11
Ugly American (Lederer and Burdick), review of, 88–89
Uncommon Valor (film), 827, 828
Uncounted Enemy: A Vietnam Deception (TV documentary), 823, 825
United Nations: Atlantic Charter, 3–4; Chinese admission to, 53; mediation efforts, 217–18; post-WW II role of, 4; and U.S. Vietnam involvement, 114; on U.S. intervention, 51; Vietnam in, 795–96
United States: commitment to South Vietnam, 193, 292–94, 742; French dislike for, 76; and Geneva pact, 49, 51, 110–11; power in South Vietnam, 166–67, 456–57, 642–43; prestige of, and Vietnam conflict, 40, 74, 207 *See also specific topics*
United States Agency for International Development, 642
United States Military Assistance Advisory Group, 101
Unlawful orders, duty to obey, 557
U.S. Air Force: on bombing of North Vietnam, in 1972, 675; introduction of jet fighters, 182, 193; planes deployed, 1964, 181–82 *See also* aircraft, U.S.
U.S. Army: morale, in 1971, 637–42; Rangers, 132; Special Forces, 112, 185, 186 *See also* combat troops, U.S.; U.S. military forces
U.S. embassy in Saigon: in fall of Saigon, 767–68; in Tet Offensive, 394–98, 398–99
U.S. Marines: arrival in Vietnam, 222–24; in defense of Khesanh, 413–16, 417–18, 437; at Hill 881 (1967), 355–57; morale, in 1968, 391; pacification programs, 607, 824; patrol by, in 1966, 320–21
U.S. military forces
- accommodation of South Vietnamese by, 140
- civilian noncombat support for, 359
- early military action, 111, 115
- evaluation of South Vietnamese army: in 1962, 134; in 1963, 137, 139; in 1965, 223, 250; in 1966, 327–31; in 1967, 355, 362; in 1969, 493, 534–40; in 1971, 597; in 1972, 653
- and guerilla warfare, 130
- impact on South Vietnamese culture, 718–19
- military situation: in 1965, 281–82; in 1966, 296–97, 304–5; in 1967, 359, 360–64; in 1969, 492–94, 505–6; in 1972, 646–47
- morale: in 1965, 252; in 1969, 509–11, 525; in 1971, 641–42; racial tensions, 641; retention rates in 1971, 641–42
- Mylai massacre, 551–54; international reaction, 551–54; and moral dilemma of war, 556–57; trial, 595–96, 611–15; as war crime, 608–9
- offensives, in 1967, 338, 344–45
- preparations for defense of Laos, 1961, 95–96, 97
- role, 1954–1964, 185–86
- in Southeast Asia, 1962, 121
- South Vietnamese army reform attempts, 137
- tactics, 613, 614; in 1968, 477; in 1969, 493, 515, 535
- in Thailand: 1962, 121; in 1972, 669
- troop strength: 1954–1964, 186; 1961–1965, 237; in 1962, 125, 130, 134; in 1963, 137, 148, 157, 169; in 1964, 185, 199; in 1965, 209, 225, 235, 241, 249, 253, 254–55, 280–81; in 1966, 297; in 1967, 371; in 1968, 418, 439–40, 440, 454–57; in 1970, 565; in 1972, 646, 652, 654, 668, 669, 679
- *See also* combat troops, U.S.; U.S. Air Force; U.S. Army; U.S. Marines; U.S. Navy

U.S. Navy: patrols off North Vietnam, 187–88, 189; strength off Vietnam, in 1972, 669, 679
USAID. *See* Agency for International Development
U.S.O. entertainment, 458–59
Ut, Nick, 883
U Thant, mediation efforts, 217–18, 224–25, 283, 284–85, 314, 342

Vance, Cyrus R., 485, 487, 496, 497, 794
Vann, John Paul, 823, 824
Van Thanh Cao, 116
Van Tien Dung, 845
Vesser, Dale, 885
veterans: in anti-war movement, 617–20, 619, 620, 788–89, 819; bitterness of, 804–5, 853–54; in Congress, 890–91; drug abuse by, 803–5; number of, 783; opinion of embargo of Vietnam, 870, 871; opinion of pardon for draft evaders, 792, 793; Parade to Vietnam Memorial (1982), 818–20; postwar experiences of, 787–89; psychological problems of, 680–85, 782–83, 803–5, 809–10; public opinion of, 680–85, 783, 788, 809–10, 818, 850–51; return to Vietnam as tourists, 893–94
Veterans Administration, performance of, 783
victory for South Vietnam, U.S. assessment of prospects for: in 1962, 112–13, 126–30, 130, 134; in 1963, 140–41, 156–60, 171–76; in 1964, 180, 192–93, 193, 199; in 1965, 216, 249–50, 267, 281–82; in 1966, 331; in 1967, 352–55, 360–61, 385; in 1968, 407–8; in 1969, 534; in 1972, 679; after Ngo Dinh Diem overthrow, 168; pressure for positive reports, 387–88; reliability of, 134, 140, 158–59, 199; in Tet Offensive (1968), 399
Vientiane, Laos, 104
Viet Cong
- amnesty for, 128
- atrocities committed by, 401, 409
- campaigns and engagements: in 1962, 125; in 1963, 141, 145–47, 173, 174–75, 176; in 1964, 197, 236; in 1965, 209–10, 210–11, 215, 216, 260–61, 279; in 1966, 287–88; in 1967, 355–57; in 1968, 389–91; in 1975, 746–47, 748–51, 756–57
- defectors from, 235–40, 240, 295, 297, 355, 363, 387, 495, 544
- difficulty of identifying, 128
- economic impact of, 263–64
- impact of Tet Offensive on, 411–12, 492–93, 493–94
- inside view of, 235–40, 738–41
- international view of, 290
- land redistribution by, 717
- military position: 1962–1963, 175–76; in 1963, 171–72; in 1965, 251; in 1968, 476–77; in 1969, 492–94, 505–6, 534; in 1974, 737–38, 745; in 1975, 745
- morale, 240; in 1965, 233, 262; in 1966, 296–97; in 1968, 404; in 1974, 739
- and negotiations: at Paris, 492, 497; policy on, 503, 588–89, 763; U.S. willingness to negotiate with, 228–29, 285, 289, 492; with U.S., in 1967, 341–42
- North Vietnamese control of, 239
- North Vietnamese support for, 174, 183–84, 200, 211–12, 213, 226; in 1965, 242
- origin of term, 717
- political arm of. *See* National Liberation Front
- propaganda, 119, 133
- reaction to U.S. buildup (1965), 267
- recruitment by, 133, 237–38, 318, 387, 494
- reeducation of, 128
- size and strength: in 1962, 125, 126, 130, 132–33; in 1963, 139; in 1964, 186, 199; in 1965, 226, 251; in 1966, 297, 304; in 1967, 355, 386; in 1968, 401, 461, 462
- South Vietnamese public opinion of, in 1969, 493, 494–95
- South Vietnamese strategies against, 101, 108–9, 112, 116–17, 119–20, 127, 140–41
- strategy, 130, 174; in 1964, 205; in 1965, 209; in 1966, 295, 305–6; in 1968, 401, 403; in 1971, 593, 616; in 1973, 737–38; in Mekong delta, 1963, 146; post-Paris peace agreement, 735; in Tet Offensive (1968), 401, 403, 410, 411
- structure and leadership, 133, 240, 379, 493–94; efforts to uproot, 462–63; U.S. search for command center, 344–45
- support for, 111, 119, 159, 180
- tactics and results, 101, 108–9, 118–20, 127, 130–32, 133, 134, 136–37, 140, 173, 174–75, 199, 213, 239, 266, 361, 717–18, 746–47, 823; 1963, 158–60; 1964, 182;

in 1964, 236; in 1965, 261, 319; in 1966, 305–6; in 1969, 493
tenacity of, 159, 329, 360
tensions with North Vietnamese army, in 1966, 297
territory controlled by: in 1967, 361, 386; in 1968, 408; in 1969, 543; post-Tet Offensive, 442
treatment of dead, 239
tunnels and holes, 306, 382, 384, 893–94
U.S. soldiers' opinion of, 379
U.S. supporters of, 180–81
See also National Liberation Front; terrorism against South Vietnam
Viet Minh (Nationalist) party: anti-French military operations, 8–9; communist ties of, 7; goals of, 9, 35; origins of, 716–17; U.S. post-WW II support for, 5
Viet Minh regime: armament types and quantities, 25; communist block recognition of, 15, 16, 18; communist support for, 16, 18, 20, 21, 23, 28–29, 32, 34, 38, 63, 68; daily life under, 717; establishment in Hanoi, 67–69, 73, 79; French efforts to undermine, 12, 13, 15; Geneva armistice, reaction to, 61; independence, 5; intentions toward Laos and Cambodia, 61; military position, 7, 8–9, 12, 15, 19, 23–24, 29–30, 34–35, 40; military strategy and competence, 15, 23, 24, 25, 32, 34, 37, 48; peace demands at Geneva, 53–54; popular support for, 68; post-WW II constitution, 5; relentlessness of, 15, 37; support for, 22; territory controlled by, 14, 15 *See also* North Vietnam
Vietnam: constituent regions, 21; history of, 336, 716–17, 886–90; reunification of, 784–85; strategic importance of, 166–68, 785–86, 794
Vietnamese Committee for Human Rights, 796
Vietnamization of War: critiques of, 540, 557–59, 610; and Easter Offensive (1972), 659–62; introduction of policy, 439–40; and mobilization in South Vietnam, 440; Nixon plans for: in 1969, 508–9, 513–14, 517–19, 545–46; and North Vietnamese offensive, in 1972, 644–46; success of, 439–40, 460, 669, 694–95
Vietnam Memorial: debate over, 816–18, 819–20; veterans' parade to (1982), 818–20; for women, 868–69
Vietnam Moratorium, 540–42; Clinton involvement in, 864
Vietnam Veterans Against the War, 618, 788
Vietnam War: costs and benefits of, in 1966, 313–15; impact on Asian future, 836–37; impact on U.S., 709–11, 715; impact on U.S. culture, 872, 878; impact on U.S. foreign policy, 794–95, 814–16, 835–36; Kennedy on importance of, 155; overview of, 716–19; as undeclared war, 215–17, 241–42, 243–44, 244–45
villages: construction of defensive fortifications, 118; Viet Cong control of, 361 *See also* peasants in South Vietnam; relocation of peasants in South Vietnam
Vinh Loc, 539; and Paris peace agreement, 705
Vishinsky, Andrei Y., 4, 28, 30
Voice of the Armed Forces, 160
Vong, Sisavang, 13
Vo Nguyen Giap: and Death of Ho Chi Minh, 527, 528; Dienbienphu assault (1954), 38, 39; on liberation of South Vietnam, 63; meetings with McNamara in 1990s, 881–82, 890; North Vietnamese diplomacy and, 341; in North Vietnam politics, 195; on relations with Soviet Union, 227; strategy of, 34, 205, 654–55; on Tonkin Gulf incident, 881–82; Westmoreland on, 354
Vu Van Giai, 660
Vu Van Mau, 151–52, 160

Walt, Lewis W., 357, 414–15
warfare in Vietnam, ambiguity and complexity of, 130–35
Warnke, Paul C., 794
War Powers Act (1973), enactment of, 735–36
Washington Post, and Pentagon Papers, 626, 627, 629, 630
Watergate scandal, political impact of, 736, 741, 763
Wayne, John, 370, 461
weaponry
modern, limitations of, 133, 134
North Vietnamese: in 1968, 476; AK-47 rifle, 479; antiaircraft guns, 207; capture of, 477; in Easter Offensive (1972), 653; infiltration into South Vietnam, 483
"Puff, the Magic Dragon," 309
South Vietnamese, in 1969, 535
U.S.: of foot soldiers, 305; M-16 rifle, 479; sophistication of, 305–6; Viet Cong capture of, 146, 159, 160, 175–76, 200, 213, 236; Viet Cong response to, 146, 175
Viet Cong: in 1963, 146, 173; in 1964, 197; in 1965, 209, 213; in 1967, 360; in 1969, 535; U.S. capture of, 297, 412
weather manipulation experiments, U.S., 670–72
Wehrle, Leroy S., 264
Weinberger, Caspar, 835
Weinstein, Jack B., 853–54
Westmoreland, William C.: on African Americans in armed forces, 354, 447; on bombing of North Vietnam, 467; on civilian casualties, 266–67; as commander of forces in Vietnam, 176; effectiveness of, 493; on ending embargo, 870; inspection of terrorist damage, 205; Johnson on, 325, 326; on Khesanh, 414; libel suit against CBS, 823–26; manpower requests, 255, 359, 418–21, 419, 428; and McNamara Line, 415; in North Vietnamese propaganda, 337; in Parade to Vietnam Memorial (1982), 818; and Paris peace negotiations, 488; and press, 248; on prospects for victory, 352–55, 360, 385, 408, 633; reassignment out of Vietnam, 436; on return to Vietnam, 885; on Tet Offensive, 399, 401; on training of South Vietnamese army, 329; on U.S. embassy attack, 395; on Vietnamization of War, 440
Weyand, Frederick C., 401, 651
Wheeler, Earle G., 402, 415, 524
Whetmore, Edward, 541
White, Byron R., 630
White, Robert I., 572
wildlife, as victims of Vietnam War, 474–75
Williamson, Ellis W., 248
Wilson, John, 376
Wilson, Mrs. Dagmar, 374
withdrawal of U.S. forces: in 1972, redeployment within theatre, 669–70; in fall of Saigon, 767–70; final combat troops, 679–80; homecoming celebrations, in 1969, 519–21; under Johnson, 169, 171, 180, 185; as negotiating point, in 1969, 504; under Nixon, 508–9, 517–19, 544–46, 564–66, 597, 642–43, 668–70; offer of, in 1966, 321–23; plans for (1965–1969), 209, 460, 493
women: in South Vietnamese solidarity movement, 150, 164; U.S. memorial to, 868–69; in Vietnamese independence movement, 9
World Council of Churches, on Vietnam conflict, 225
World War II: anti-colonial nationalism following, 1–8; impact on Asia, 10

Xuan Thuy: on Nixon peace proposal, 588; and Paris peace negotiations, 450, 451, 464, 502, 503, 650; on U.S. aggression, 593

Yarrow, Peter, 778
Yencuha, battle of, 24–25
Yippies, at Democratic Party Convention of 1968, 472
York, Don J., 125
Yost, Charles W., 711
Young, Andrew, 299
Young, Kenneth T., 449

Ziegler, Ronald L., 566, 570, 618, 669–70, 676, 699, 703
Zuckert, Eugene M., 180

BYLINE INDEX

Alden, Robert, 74, 80–81, 83
Andelman, David A., 783–784, 790–791
Apple, R. W., Jr., 274–276, 282–283, 287–288, 309–310, 327–331, 356–357, 360–364, 367–369, 387–388, 728–729, 858–859, 871–872
Arnold, Martin, 590–591
Ayres, B. Drummond, Jr., 494–495, 515–516, 532–534, 639–642

Baldwin, Hanson W., 36–37, 39–41, 49–50, 61–63, 100–101, 179–180, 198–200, 410–412
Beecher, William, 308–309, 359–360, 439–440, 462–463, 482–485, 512–513, 556–557, 699–700
Belair, Felix, Jr., 138–139
Bigart, Homer, 116–117, 126–130, 576–578, 595–596, 611–614
Bishop, Katherine, 845–846
Blumenthal, Ralph, 559–562
Boffey, Philip M., 818–820
Borders, William, 547
Browne, Malcolm W., 673–675, 715–719, 751–753, 763–765, 874–875
Bryan, C. D. B., 799–800
Buckley, Tom, 338–339, 344–345, 377–384, 393–398, 534–540
Butterfield, Fox, 666–667, 696–697, 734–735, 766–767, 808–809, 831–835

Callender, Harold, 4–5, 13–15, 20–21
Campbell, Kenneth, 13
Charlton, Linda, 706–707
Clines, Francis X., 580–581
Clymer, Adam, 826–827
Crewdson, John M., 786–787
Crossette, Barbara, 840–843, 846–849

Dale, Edwin L., Jr., 185–186, 418–420
Dallos, Robert E., 358–359
Darnton, John, 663–665
Davis, Robert Gorham, 81–83
Dionne, E. J., Jr., 850–851
Durdin, Peggy, 104–107
Durdin, Tillman, 19, 23–24, 28–30, 38–39, 61, 66–70, 75–76, 77–78, 79, 87–88, 89, 90–92, 135–136, 591–592

Eder, Richard, 253–254
Emerson, Gloria, 584–586, 592–593, 601–602, 646–647
Erlanger, Steven, 854–857
Esper, George, 770–771

Faas, Horst, 797–799
Farber, M. A., 824–826
Feder, Barnaby J., 843–844
Fenton, John H., 457–458
Finney, John W., 240–241, 302, 373–374, 412–413, 422–425, 466–468, 506–507, 557–559, 581–583, 677–678, 725–726, 741–742, 745–746, 767–770
Fitzgerald, Frances, 315–320
Frankel, Max, 112–113, 114–115, 162–163, 166–168, 178–179, 217–219, 220–221, 224–225, 242–243, 249–250, 262–263, 310, 313–315, 321–323, 324–327, 346–347, 370–371, 403–405, 418–420, 431–433, 434–436, 448–449, 508–509, 544–546, 594–595, 631–637, 690–692, 877–879
Franklin, Ben A., 499–501, 509–511
Freedman, Samuel G., 827–831

Gelb, Leslie H., 754–755, 835–837
Giniger, Henry, 588–589
Goldberger, Paul, 816–818
Goldman, Ari L., 787–789
Graham, Fred P., 600–601, 614–615, 623–625, 626–627, 629–631
Grose, Peter, 152–153, 184–185, 193–195, 200–201, 203–204, 385, 388–389
Gruson, Sydney, 125–126, 205–206
Gwertzman, Bernard, 486–490, 687–690, 697–699, 701–703, 707–709, 711–713, 758–760, 789–790, 822–823

Hailey, Foster, 10–12, 16–19, 84–86
Halberstam, David, 132–135, 136–137, 139, 140–142, 143, 144–147, 151–152, 158–160, 163–165, 168, 171–176, 596–597
Halloran, Richard, 527–528
Hamilton, Thomas J., 48–49, 53–54, 55–57
Harris, Robert R., 857–858
Herbers, John, 540–542, 549–551, 703–705
Hersh, Seymour M., 650–651, 670–672, 731–732
Hess, John L., 649–650
Hoffmann, Stanley, 685–686
Hofmann, Paul, 491–492, 495–497, 503
Horrock, Nicholas M., 786–787
Hunter, Marjorie, 743–744

James, Michael, 25–27
Jehl, Douglas, 870–871
Johnson, Thomas A., 409, 442–447
Johnston, David, 863–865
Jorden, William J., 97–98, 99–100

Kalb, Bernard, 83–84
Kamm, Henry, 551–553, 562–564, 616–617, 801–802, 805–807, 812–814, 867–868
Kelly, Michael, 863–865
Kenworthy, E. W., 108–111, 154–155, 169–170, 189–191, 292–294, 548–549
Kerry, John Forbes, 617–618
Kifner, John, 572–574
Kneeland, Douglas E., 729–731
Koning, Hans, 810–812
Krauss, Clifford, 860–861
Krock, Arthur, 243–244

Labaton, Stephen, 853–854
Langguth, Jack, 197–198, 202–224, 259–260
Larimer, Tim, 881–882
Lawrence, W. H., 102–104
Lehmann-Haupt, Christopher, 693–694
Leviero, Anthony, 42–44
Lewis, Anthony, 343–344, 450–452, 566–567, 665–666
Lewis, Flora, 719–721, 796–797, 814–816
Lieberman, Henry R., 33–35, 54, 70–71, 72, 78, 79–80
Lindsey, Robert, 802–803
Loftus, Joseph A., 311–313, 374–377
Lubasch, Arnold H., 187–188
Lukas, J. Anthony, 471–474
Lydon, Christopher, 686–687

Madden, Richard L., 735–736, 765, 773–774
Maeroff, Gene I., 820–821
Malcolm, Andrew H., 838–840
Markham, James M., 737–741, 744–745, 746–750
Middleton, Drew, 44–45, 511–512
Mitchell, Alison, 879–881, 890–891
Mohr, Charles, 191–192, 213, 228–229, 266–267, 280–281, 294–295, 300–301, 304–308, 320–321, 389–391, 398–402, 492–494, 505–506, 792–793, 823–824
Montgomery, Paul L., 778–779
Mydans, Seth, 861–862, 891–899

Naughton, James M., 779–780
Nevard, Jacques, 93–95, 121–122, 130–131

Nordheimer, Jon, 680–685, 781–782
O'Kane, Lawrence, 180–181
Onis, Juan de, 571–572

Peterson, Iver, 598–599, 642–643
Phelps, Robert H., 428–429'
Pomfret, John D., 254–255, 301–302
Prial, Frank J., 574–576

Randal, Jonathan, 355–356
Raymond, Jack, 92–93, 96–97, 111–112, 181–182, 220, 222–223, 225–227, 233–235, 250–252
Reed, Roy, 299–300
Reinhold, Robert, 478–481, 627–629, 803–805, 809–810
Reston, James, 27–28, 50–51, 113–114, 195–196, 205, 215–217, 263–264, 281–282, 503–504, 654–655, 692, 709–711
Ripley, Anthony, 723–725
Roberts, Gene, 405–406, 442, 459–461, 464–466, 477–478, 486–490
Roberts, Steven V., 519–521, 726–728
Robinson, Douglas, 267–270, 348–352, 458–459, 474–475, 553–554
Rose, Jerry A., 117–121
Rosenthal, A. M., 76–77

Salisbury, Harrison E., 332–337, 339–341
Sanger, David E., 899–901
Schanberg, Sydney H., 656–659, 660–662, 672–673, 733–734, 760–762, 774–778
Schmidt, Dana Adams, 65, 95–96, 357–358
Schmitt, Eric, 868–869
Sciolino, Elaine, 882–884
Semple, Robert B., Jr., 257–258, 421–422, 513–515, 521–525, 564–566, 567–570, 578–580, 586–588, 597–598, 662–663, 668–670, 676–677
Shabad, Theodore, 214–215
Sheehan, Neil, 260–261, 265–266, 276–279, 297–299, 302–303, 413–416, 418–420, 481–482, 602–611, 623
Shenon, Philip, 865–867, 872–874, 875–877
Shipler, David K., 851–853, 884–890
Shuster, Alvin, 589–590, 620–622, 700–701
Smith, Hedrick, 143–144, 160–162, 170–171, 176–178, 341–342, 364–367, 386, 418–420, 453–454, 463–464, 485–486, 486–490, 490–491, 517–519, 794–795
Smith, Terence, 542–544, 570–571
Sterba, James P., 525, 721–723
Sulzberger, C. L., 5–8, 22, 45, 74–75, 122–123
Szulc, Tad, 147–149, 155–158, 192–193, 615–616

Tanner, Henry, 501–503, 554–556
Topping, Seymour, 182–184, 206–210, 227–228, 236–240, 267, 279–280, 295–297
Treaster, Joseph B., 425–426, 437, 647–648, 667–668, 675–676, 679–680, 713–714
Trumbull, Robert, 8–9, 63–64, 88–89, 101, 107–108, 112, 123, 124–125, 153–154
Turner, Wallace, 793–794

Waggoner, Walter H., 52
Walz, Jay, 35–36, 86–87
Wehrwein, Austin C., 270–271
Weinraub, Bernard, 384, 387, 406–407, 416–418, 438–439, 452–453, 454–457, 461–462, 475–477, 750–751, 756–758
White, Theodore H., 30–33
White, William S., 41–42, 57–58
Whitman, Alden, 528–532
Whitney, Craig R., 651–654, 655–656, 659–660, 693, 694–695, 705–706, 849–850
Wicker, Tom, 188–189, 210–213, 215, 232–233, 235–236, 244–248, 283–285, 286–287, 289–292, 331, 352–355, 402–403, 407–409, 426–428, 429–431, 469–471, 507–508, 782–783
Windeler, Robert, 370